THE DISASTROUS PONTIFICATE
Pope Francis' Rupture from the Magisterium

PRAISE FOR THIS BOOK

"The catastrophic turmoil the Catholic Church experienced from 2013 to 2025 is directly attributable to things Pope Francis said and did. This important book sets forth in careful detail Pope Francis' specific statements and decisions that contradict Catholic doctrine and conflict with the perennial practice of the Church, such as the admission of some divorced and civilly remarried Catholics to Holy Communion and the blessing of homosexual couples. The reader will be able to judge for himself the differences between Pope Francis's words and deeds and what the Church has always taught and required in practice."

—THE REV. GERALD E. MURRAY, J.C.D., Pastor, St. Joseph Church, New York, NY; author of *Calming the Storm: Navigating the Crises Facing the Catholic Church and Society*

"It is possible for popes to teach in a misleading or even erroneous way when not speaking *ex cathedra*. Although this is extremely rare in Church history, it has happened in a handful of cases, the examples of Honorius and John XXII being the best known. As this book demonstrates, Pope Francis clearly outdid them in the number and gravity of his problematic statements and actions. One does not have to agree with everything in the book (and I don't) in order to see the force of its cumulative case. It took the Church over forty years formally to condemn the error of Honorius. Theologians and churchmen will in coming years and decades have to grapple with Francis's dubious doctrinal legacy. As they do, they will find this book an invaluable resource."

—EDWARD FESER, Professor of Philosophy, Pasadena City College

"This comprehensive study clearly shows that the pontificate (2013–2025) of the late Pope Francis generated a great deal of confusion throughout various areas of Church teaching. The significance of this study is that it presents Pope Leo XIV with the challenges he must answer in order to put the Catholic Church back on the right path of the Magisterium. I heartily recommend this work for its clarity and the strength of its arguments."

—EDUARDO ECHEVERRIA, former Professor of Philosophy and Systematic Theology at Sacred Heart Major Seminary, Detroit; author of *Pope Francis: The Legacy of Vatican II*

"Not a few Catholics viewed the many troubling pronouncements of Pope Francis as merely ambiguous, imprecise, or poorly translated. Grave though such deficiencies would be, readers of this book will discover—sorrowfully—that the reality is far more serious. The author provides an unflinching catalogue of the manifold errors that have marred Francis's teaching, with scarcely any domain of faith or morals escaping the reach of what must, unavoidably, be called a 'disastrous pontificate.' At the same time, this book serves as a true *enchiridion* of authoritative sources drawn from Sacred Scripture, Sacred Tradition, and the Church's Magisterium, each deployed with precision to expose and refute those errors. This volume will prove indispensable to the future pontiff and council tasked, as the book's dedication foresees, with restoring what has been compromised in Francis's pontificate. The author confronts, with unflinching clarity, questions that many prefer to evade, above all this: If subjection to the Roman Pontiff is necessary for salvation, how are the faithful to respond when a pope, in non-definitive teaching, appears to impose error or even heresy upon them? Every page of *The Disastrous Pontificate* reveals an author of manifest fidelity, animated by profound love for Christ and His Church, and endowed with theological erudition."

—MICHAEL SIRILLA, Professor of Systematic and Dogmatic Theology, Franciscan University of Steubenville; author of *The Ideal Bishop: Aquinas's Commentaries on the Pastoral Epistles*

"*The Disastrous Pontificate*—the adjective derives from Cardinal Pell—is the work of a one-time papalist, brought up to show huge respect for the See of Peter and its bishops, but with the election of Jorge Bergoglio as Pope Francis, coming to realize his naivete. Now sadly disillusioned and unblinkingly facing the changed reality, 'Dominic J. Grigio' has written a full-scale, dispassionately clinical analysis of Bergoglio's rule, identifying through the entire pontificate countless divergences from Catholic truth. These range from 'correcting' traditional Christology while exhibiting indifference to the unique nature of the Christian revelation in order to curry favour with secularists, Muslims, and other enemies of Christ, to condoning the abuse of minors by clergy, encouraging homosexual ascendancy, and playing down the wickedness of abortionists. In 680, Pope Honorius was posthumously condemned by the Sixth Ecumenical Council—a condemnation endorsed by the succeeding pope—for far lesser deviations from Christian dogma and doctrine that those achieved by Bergoglio. Hence Grigio's book is not only a vital historical record but in effect a clarion call for a similar *damnatio memoriae* to be handed out to a more recent heresiarch, in the hope that at least some of the damage he has inflicted on the Catholic Church can, over time, be repaired. That this book has had to be published anonymously—for fear of reprisals—is a further blot on the Catholic escutcheon."

—**JOHN RIST**, Professor Emeritus of Classics and Philosophy at the University of Toronto; former Father Kurt Pritzl Chair in Philosophy at the Catholic University of America; author of *Infallibility, Integrity and Obedience: The Papacy and the Roman Catholic Church, 1848–2023*

"This remarkable book is both exhaustive and exhausting. Exhaustive, in that it records, explains, and provides refutation for every misstep and misstatement made by Pope Francis. Exhausting, because there is so very much material to cover. Here in one massive volume is a thorough catalogue of the ways in which the late Pontiff confused the faithful, along with a defense of the truths he undermined."

—**PHILIP F. LAWLER**, author of *Lost Shepherd: How Pope Francis Is Misleading His Flock*

"Meticulous, dispassionate, and charitable, this book bears invaluable witness to what has certainly been the most disastrous pontificate, from the doctrinal point of view, in the entire history of the Catholic Church. It covers virtually all aspects of the doctrinal errors that have been spread by words, deeds, and omissions during Francis's reign, and contrasts it with an equally complete background of theological sources. It is certainly the fruit of suffering, prayer, and study during an unprecedented crisis; it is no less certainly a very useful tool for the ongoing struggle."

—**CLAUDIO PIERANTONI**, former Professor of Medieval Philosophy, University of Chile; co-editor of *Defending the Faith Against Present Heresies*

"Written by an author immensely learned in theology, filled with an intense love for the Church and for immortal souls, and devastated by the sight of the immense harm done to the Church by Francis, this book demonstrates without a shadow of a doubt the sharp contradiction between Francis's teachings and those of the Gospels, the authentic Magisterium of the Church, and the greatest Popes and theologians of the past."

—**JOSEF SEIFERT**, Founding Rector of the International Academy of Philosophy in Liechtenstein and President Emeritus of the John Paul II Academy for Human Life and the Family

THE DISASTROUS PONTIFICATE

Pope Francis' Rupture from the Magisterium

Dominic J. Grigio

Os Justi Press

Os Justi Press
P.O. Box 21814
Lincoln, NE 68542
www.osjustipress.com

Send inquiries to
info@osjustipress.com

ISBN 978-1-965303-59-7 (paperback)
ISBN 978-1-965303-60-3 (hardcover)
ISBN 978-1-965303-61-0 (ebook)

Layout by Jitendra Thakur
Cover by Michael Schrauzer

*Dedicated to the future pope and ecumenical council
who will address these errors*

Acknowledgements

Of necessity, I cannot publicly acknowledge those who have offered me advice and criticism that has greatly improved the contents and structure of this book. However, thank you to those who have helped me for your insights, patience, and generosity.

I would also like to thank the creators of a number of invaluable online resources that greatly helped me and to recommend in particular to readers:

- the priests who compiled, and translated, the Denzinger-Bergoglio, available at: en-denzingerbergoglio.com, and,
- two laymen with a deep love for the Church Fathers, one who provides online the writings of the Church Fathers at newadvent.org and the other who has created the Church Fathers Scripture search engine, available at: catholiccrossreference.online/fathers.

Two works in particular have been the inspiration of this book — Fr. Ludwig Ott's *Fundamentals of Catholic Dogma* and Fr. Heinrich Denzinger's *Enchiridion Symbolorum et Definitionum*. The faithful owe Fr. Ott and Fr. Denzinger our undying gratitude for helping us stand our ground, 'no more children tossed to and fro, and carried about with every wind of doctrine by the wickedness of men, by cunning craftiness, by which they lie in wait to deceive' (Eph 4:14).

Contents

Introduction

One of the profound joys of being a Catholic is our deep affection for the pope, which inspires millions to go on pilgrimage to the Holy See in Rome for a chance to see the Successor of St. Peter. I remember as a young boy standing between my parents on the Solemnity of SS. Peter & Paul singing Cardinal Wiseman's stirring hymn '*God Bless Our Pope*' (1862) that gave me a palpable sense of belonging to the Catholic Church:

> Full in the panting heart of Rome,
> Beneath the apostle`s crowning dome,
> From pilgrim`s lips that kiss the ground,
> Breathes in all tongues one only sound:

> God bless our Pope,
> God bless our Pope,
> God bless our Pope,
> The great, the good.

During my pilgrimages to Rome, I have walked in the footsteps of St. Peter to feel close to the Rock, the Prince of the Apostles, the Keeper of the Keys of Heaven, the First Pope. I've prayed in the Titulus Pudentiana, built over the home of Senator Pudens where St. Peter resided for several years as Bishop of Rome. I've walked to the Church of Domine Quo Vadis on the Via Appia Antica, where St. Peter, after meeting Christ, turned back to face martyrdom in Rome. I've meditated in the Mamertine prison beneath San Pietro in Carcere, where St. Peter was held before his crucifixion. I've venerated the heavy iron chains that once bound St. Peter at San Pietro in Vincoli. I've knelt by the Obelisk in St. Peter's Square, marking the site where St. Peter was crucified, and finally, I've prayed at St. Peter's tomb beneath the majestic dome of St. Peter's Basilica.

For many, the highlight of any pilgrimage to Rome is to see and hear the pope, either during the Wednesday audience or the Sunday Angelus. To realise, that through the apostolic succession, he is the living embodiment of the Petrine charism stretching back two thousand years to the first pope appointed by Our Lord Jesus Christ. The ancient papal title, the *Vicar of Christ on earth*, isn't an empty honorific, but an awe-inspiring reality that elicits reverence and filial obedience to the pope who represents the authority of Our Lord Jesus Christ over the one, holy, catholic and apostolic Church.

It is almost beyond comprehension to understand how one man can bear to be entrusted by God with such a heavy responsibility as that of protecting, teaching and correcting more than one and a half billion souls. To add to this responsibility, the pope is the preeminent witness of the Gospel to six billion souls around the world. From the moment of accepting election by the Sacred Conclave of Cardinals, to be worthy of the trust placed in him, the pope must measure every word he speaks and writes and consider his every act of commission and omission. To fail to do so, especially due to the global amplification of the mass media, he risks misleading countless souls to commit mortal sin and the grave danger of hell.

Something of the enormity of this responsibility is conveyed by accounts of the reaction of Cardinal Sarto during the 1903 Conclave that elected him Pope Pius X. The historian Yves Chiron recounts that after the fourth vote, that saw the number of cardinals voting for Cardinal Sarto substantially increase, he declared, 'that he was not made for the Papacy, and that people had been using his name without consulting him'. Cardinal Merry del Val recounted finding Cardinal Sarto late at night during the Conclave praying in the Paolina chapel:

> It was close to midnight when I entered the silent, shadowy chapel…I noticed a cardinal kneeling on the marble floor near the altar, lost in prayer, his head in his hands and his elbows resting on a little bench. It was Cardinal Sarto. I knelt beside him and, in a low voice, gave him the message with which I had been entrusted. His Eminence, as soon as he had understood me, raised his eyes and slowly turned his head towards me, with tears pouring from his eyes…The only words I had the strength to utter, which came to my lips spontaneously, were: 'Eminence, have courage, the Lord will help you.'[1]

Two months later, Pope St. Pius X wrote of his anguish on being elected pope in his first encyclical, 'From the supreme apostolic throne, to which we have been elevated by the inscrutable counsel of God, it is not necessary to mention to you first how, with great tears and prayers, we tried to remove from ourselves this formidable burden of the pontificate.' He went on to explain that the cause of his anguish was twofold: accepting the 'most serious charge of feeding the flock of Christ' and assuming responsibility for finding 'a remedy' for the 'great evil' afflicting society — 'apostasy from God'. He admitted that the latter responsibility was the hardest to bear, 'We were terrified beyond all else by the disastrous state of human society today.'[2]

Pope St. Pius X went on to explain that the reason why he accepted the 'formidable burden of the Pontificate', despite his misgivings and distress, was total reliance on 'divine assistance', 'We take courage in Him who strengthens Us…relying on the power of God'.[3]

Our instinctive veneration of the pope is elicited by the tradition that the Successors of St. Peter have a special relationship with this divine assistance — the Holy Spirit. After the descent of the Holy Spirit on the Apostles and the Blessed Virgin Mary at Pentecost it was St. Peter who was the first to proclaim the apostolic kerygma — the resurrection of Our Lord and his Gospel of the coming of the Kingdom and his call to conversion. (Acts 2:1-36).

This recognition of the special relationship between the Holy Spirit and the pope is the basis of our trust in the indefectibility and infallibility of the Petrine office and the indefectibility of the Holy See. Having said this, our trust isn't blind or slavish but rests on rational criteria explicitly formalised at the First Vatican Council and Second Vatican Council:

- The Holy Spirit is not promised to the Successors of St. Peter that they might claim a new revelation so as to teach an innovative doctrine.[4]
- The Holy Spirit is promised to the Successors of St. Peter 'so that with His assistance, they might faithfully guard and expound the revelation handed down through the Apostles, that is, the Deposit of Faith.'[5]
- In particular, the Successors of St. Peter receive, through the Holy Spirit, the charism of 'truth and never-failing faith' so that through them the 'entire flock of Christ' 'might be kept away from the poisonous food of error and be nourished with the sustenance of heavenly doctrine'.[6]

[1]Chiron, Y [2002] *Saint Pius X: Restorer of the Church.* Kansas City: Angelus Press, p. 126
[2]Pope St. Pius X [1903] *Encyclical E Supremi*, para 1,3 [Online] Available at: www.vatican.va [Accessed on: 22 January 2025]
[3]*Op cit*, para 4.
[4]First Vatican Council [1870] *Dogmatic Constitution Pastor Aeternus*, chap 4 [Online] Available at: www.vatican.va; cf. Second Vatican Council [1964] *Dogmatic Constitution Lumen Gentium*, para 25 [Accessed on: 8 February 2025]
[5]Op cit.
[6]Ibid.

- Our Lord Jesus Christ and the Holy Spirit hand on the word of God, entrusted to the Successors of the Apostles, through sacred tradition 'in its full purity, so that led by the light of the Spirit of truth, they may in proclaiming it preserve this word of God faithfully, explain it, and make it more widely known.'[7]
- The teaching office of the Successors of the Apostles is 'not above the word of God, but serves it, teaching only what has been handed on, listening to it devoutly, guarding it scrupulously and explaining it faithfully in accord with a divine commission and with the help of the Holy Spirit, it draws from this one deposit of faith everything which it presents for belief as divinely revealed.'[8]
- 'In accord with God's most wise design', the Magisterium of the Church 'cannot stand' without being 'connected and associated with' Sacred Tradition and Sacred Scripture'.[9]

The presence of these dispositions and actions in the exercise of the Petrine office forms the rational foundation for our trust in the special relationship between the Holy Spirit and the Pope. The possibility that this relationship could break down has been deemed so unlikely that it has only been considered in the theoretical speculations of a select few theologians, including Cardinal Thomas de Vio Cajetan (1469–1534) and St. Robert Bellarmine, S.J. (1542–1621).

However, this book lays out evidence — through the juxtaposition of Pope Francis' words and actions with the perennial Magisterium of the Church — that we face an unprecedented crisis in the Church's history. It presents a Pope who:

- Introduces innovative doctrines.
- Fails to guard and expound the Deposit of Faith.
- Does not protect Christ's flock from the poisonous fruit of error.
- Distorts the word of God to promote an ideological agenda.
- Detaches his teaching office from both Sacred Tradition and Sacred Scripture, in opposition to God's most wise design.

Such a breakdown in the relationship of a pope with the Holy Spirit is so distressing to contemplate that it is understandable that many will be tempted to reject it out of hand without considering the evidence, while others may refuse to examine it out of a sense of loyalty to the Successor of St. Peter. However, such avoidance is not an option if we take seriously the responsibilities that we assumed when we received the sacraments of baptism and confirmation.

During his often-turbulent pontificate, Pope St. John Paul II emphasised the Church's crucial mission to safeguard the Deposit of Faith amidst both internal heresy and external erroneous ideologies. With the support of Cardinal Joseph Ratzinger, then Prefect for the Congregation for the Doctrine of the Faith, he directly confronted significant theological errors propagated by several prominent priests, including Fr. Hans Küng, Fr. Edward Schillebeeckx, Fr. Leonardo Boff, Fr. Gustavo Gutiérrez, Fr. Charles Curran, Fr. Tissa Balasuriya, and Fr. Anthony de Mello. These cases became causes célèbres, highlighting the challenges of widespread erroneous teachings disseminated through liberal seminaries, Catholic universities, and media outlets. Despite some controversial decisions,[10] safeguarding and elucidating the deposit of faith remained a consistent priority for Pope St. John Paul II.

To further this crucial mission to safeguard the Deposit of Faith in the Church, the Congregation for the Doctrine of the Faith [1989] required that all who taught Catholic

---

[7]Second Vatican Council [1965] *Dogmatic Constitution Dei Verbum*, para 9 [Online] Available at: www.vatican.va [Accessed on: 8 February 2025]
[8]Op cit.
[9]Ibid, para 10.
[10]For example, the 1986 World Day of Prayer for Peace in Assisi

theology, whether clergy and laity, must make a profession of faith that included these affirmations:

> With firm faith, I also believe everything contained in the word of God, whether written or handed down in Tradition, which the Church, either by a solemn judgment or by the ordinary and universal Magisterium, sets forth to be believed as divinely revealed.[11]

> I also firmly accept and hold each and everything definitively proposed by the Church regarding teaching on faith and morals.

Furthermore, in his apostolic constitution *Fidei Depositum* [1992] — addressed to the hierarchy and 'all the People of God' — Pope St. John Paul II underscored the importance of the entire Church, including the laity, in safeguarding the doctrines of the Church, 'Guarding the Deposit of Faith is the mission which the Lord has entrusted to his Church and which she fulfils in every age.' Pope St. John Paul II[12] canonically addressed the threat posed by clergy and lay theologians promoting erroneous teaching in his apostolic constitution, *Ad Tuendam Fidem* [1998], emphasising the importance of protecting the Faith:

> To protect the Faith of the Catholic Church against errors arising from certain members of the Christian faithful, especially from among those dedicated to the various disciplines of sacred theology we, whose principal duty is to confirm the brethren in the faith (Lk 22:32), consider it absolutely necessary to add to the existing texts of the Code of Canon Law and the Code of Canons of the Eastern Churches, new norms which expressly impose the obligation of upholding truths proposed in a definitive way by the Magisterium of the Church, and which also establish related canonical sanctions.[13]

It's crucial to recognise that Pope St. John Paul II aimed to protect and reinforce a fundamental responsibility shared by every member of the Church, not solely by clergy, theologians, and catechists — the duty to safeguard the Deposit of Faith. This responsibility isn't an ability conferred by ecclesial authority external to our Christian discipleship; rather, it's an intrinsic capacity granted through the grace of the theological virtue of Faith by the Holy Spirit.

This prudential dimension of faith is formally acknowledged by the Church as the *sensus fidei*, the intuitive understanding of faith by individual believers, and the *sensus fidelium*, where this sense is collectively manifested in the whole Church, guided by the Holy Spirit. During my first year of undergraduate studies in Divinity one of my lecturers told the class that the more we studied the Faith, and the more that we prayed, the more we would develop a 'Catholic nose' so that we would be able to distinguish between genuine Catholic doctrine and false teaching. The International Theological Commission described the *sensus fidei* as an '*instinct of faith*':

> The sensus fidei fidelis is a sort of spiritual instinct that enables the believer to judge spontaneously whether a particular teaching or practice is or is not in conformity with the Gospel and with apostolic faith. It is intrinsically linked to the virtue of faith itself; it flows from, and is a property of, faith. It is compared to an instinct because it is not primarily the result of rational deliberation, but is rather a form of spontaneous and natural knowledge, a sort of perception (aisthesis).[14]

The Second Vatican Council outlined several criteria to ensure that our exercise of the *sensus fidei* genuinely expresses the theological virtue of faith:

---

[11]Congregation for the Doctrine of the Faith [1989] *Profession of Faith and Oath of Fidelity* [Online] Available at: www.vatican.va [Accessed on: 10 February 2025]

[12]Pope St. John Paul II [1992] *Apostolic Constitution Fidei Depositum* [Online] Available at: www.vatican.va [Accessed on: 10 February 2025]

[13]Pope St. John Paul II [1992] *Apostolic Constitution Ad Tuendam Fidem* [Online] Available at: www.vatican.va [Accessed on: 10 February 2025]

[14]International Theological Commission [2014] *Sensus Fidei in the Life of the Church*, para 49 [Online] Available at: www.vatican.va [Accessed on: 11 February 2025]

1. *Guided by the Magisterium*: It must be practiced under the guidance of the Church's perennial teaching authority, the Magisterium, which serves as the authentic interpreter of the Word of God.
2. *Obedient to Sacred Tradition and Scripture*: There should be faithful and respectful adherence to the Word of God as it is found in Sacred Tradition and Sacred Scripture, acknowledging both as sources of divine revelation.
3. *Unwavering Commitment*: It involves an unwavering commitment to the faith that has been handed down 'once for all to the saints' (Jude 1:3), maintaining the integrity of the Deposit of Faith without alteration.
4. *Fruits of Deepening and Living Faith*: The exercise of *sensus fidei* should bear fruit in the form of a deeper understanding of the faith through correct doctrine, and its application in daily life, leading to a more profound and lived Christian witness.

These principles help safeguard the authenticity of the *sensus fidei*, ensuring it aligns with the Church's teaching and contributes to the spiritual growth of the faithful.[15]

This book is intended to assist those Catholics who feel that some of Pope Francis's teachings and actions may not align with Sacred Tradition, Sacred Scripture, and the Magisterium of the Church. It aims to affirm that your intuitive sense of faith, or *sensus fidei*, is a true manifestation of the virtue of faith, guided by the Holy Spirit.

This affirmation does not suggest that we assume the role of judges over Pope Francis or challenge the legitimacy of his office. We adhere to the ancient principle of the Church, 'The First See is judged by no one,' (Can. 1404) which is reflected in the understanding of papal authority (Can. 331). However, as part of our duty to protect the Deposit of Faith and in exercising our *sensus fidei*, we have both the right and the obligation to respectfully critique the Pope's statements when they appear to deviate from the doctrines of the Church. This right and duty are recognised within the framework of the Code of Canon Law:

> According to the knowledge, competence, and prestige which they possess, they have the right and even at times the duty to manifest to the sacred pastors their opinion on matters which pertain to the good of the Church and to make their opinion known to the rest of the Christian faithful, without prejudice to the integrity of faith and morals, with reverence toward their pastors, and attentive to common advantage and the dignity of persons. (Can. 212 §3).

This book has been written out of a sense of duty to our common responsibility to safeguard the Deposit of Faith, sensitive to the imperative handed down from the apostles to all the faithful to maintain 'the integrity of faith and morals'. (I Cor 11:2; II Thess 2:15; I Tim 6:20; II Tim1:13-14; Tit 1:9). To this end, across a wide range of doctrinal disciplines — from Anthropology to Soteriology — this book meticulously compares and contrasts the teachings of Pope Francis with Sacred Tradition, Sacred Scripture, and the perennial Magisterium. The analytical section, *The Errors of Pope Francis*, alongside an extensive collection of source texts titled *Sources: The Errors in the Light of Scripture, Tradition, and the Magisterium*, collectively argue that Pope Francis has committed significant errors in the exercise of his teaching office. Additionally, *The Questionable Words and Deeds of Pope Francis and His Appointees* chronicles his papacy, revealing the breadth of his erroneous teachings, their impact within the Church, and their practical ramifica-tions. The immediate challenge facing all the faithful is to vigilantly guard against these errors in the certain hope that, in God's appointed time, they will be reconsidered and rectified by a future Successor of St. Peter.

The title of this book, '*The Disastrous Pontificate: Pope Francis' Rupture from the Magisterium*' was inspired by Cardinal Pell's succinct summation of Pope Francis' pontificate contained in his famous Demos Memorandum. (*The full texts of the Demos Memoranda are included as an appendix.*) It was distributed anonymously among his

---

[15]Second Vatican Council [1964] *Dogmatic Constitution Lumen Gentium*, para 12 [Online] Available at: www.vatican.va [Accessed on: 11 February 2025]

fellow cardinals during Lent 2022 in preparation for a future conclave. Cardinal Pell was in a position to observe the full extent of the disaster rocking the Church due to his role as the Vatican's Prefect of the Secretariat for the Economy and a member of Pope Francis' Council of Cardinal Advisers.

Cardinal Pell introduced his highly critical assessment of Pope Francis' pontificate with the following observation:

> Commentators of every school, if for different reasons, with the possible exception of Father Spadaro, SJ, agree that this pontificate is a disaster in many or most respects; a catastrophe. The Successor of St. Peter is the rock on which the Church is built, a major source and cause of worldwide unity. Historically (St. Irenaeus), the Pope and the Church of Rome have a unique role in preserving the apostolic tradition, the rule of faith, in ensuring that the Churches continue to teach what Christ and the apostles taught. Previously it was: *'Roma locuta. Causa finita est.'* [Rome has spoken. The matter is settled]. Today it is: *'Roma loquitur. Confusio augetur.'* [Rome speaks. Confusion increases].[16]

Cardinal Pell's outline of the extent of the disaster created during Pope Francis' pontificate just in the sphere of Faith and morals alone presented an assessment of the Church that was nothing short of catastrophic:

i)   The Christo-centricity of teaching is being weakened; Christ is being moved from the centre. Sometimes Rome even seems to be confused about the importance of a strict monotheism, hinting at some wider concept of divinity; not quite pantheism, but like a Hindu panentheism variant.

ii) The Christo-centric legacy of St. John Paul II in faith and morals is under systematic attack. Many of the staff of the Roman Institute for the Family have been dismissed; most students have left. The Academy for Life is gravely damaged, e.g., some members recently supported assisted suicide. The Pontifical Academies have members and visiting speakers who support abortion.

iii) Cardinal Hollerich rejects the Christian teaching on sexuality. The Papacy is silent. This is doubly significant because the Cardinal is explicitly heretical; he does not use code or hints. If the Cardinal were to continue without Roman correction, this would represent another deeper breakdown of discipline, with few (any?) precedents in history. The Congregation for the Doctrine of the Faith must act and speak.[17]

Cardinal George Pell wrote these criticisms of the papacy under Pope Francis out of his deep, heartfelt love for the Petrine office. In 2002, as the Archbishop of Sydney, Cardinal Pell spoke of his admiration for the papacy during his homily for the Feast of Ss Peter and Paul:

> The bishops of Rome, successors of Peter, came to embody this supreme tradition of orthodoxy, this guarantee of the faithful transmission of Christ's teaching, which Peter and Paul had handed over to the Christians in Rome…we should pray in thanks for the institution of the papacy. Conquerors and tyrants have often understood the importance of the office of pope much better than we do. Napoleon imprisoned two popes, Pius VI and Pius VII. Hitler boasted at table that when he won the War he would set up a pope in each country; and every nation the Communists took over they tried to set up a national Catholic Church and separate bishops, priests and people from the pope. Despite the bad popes, despite the Great Schism of popes and anti-popes around 1400, the papacy is a miracle of grace.[18]

---

[16]Demos [2022] *The Cardinal Pell memo in full* [Online] www.cal-catholic.com [Accessed on: 25 March 2025]

[17]Op cit.

[18]Pell, George [2004] *Be Not Afraid: Collected Writing.* Sydney: Duffey & Snellgrove, p.97

It is with this sure hope in the papacy as a miracle of grace that we look forward to a new pope who will restore the Church. As Cardinal Pell concluded,

> The new pope must understand that the secret of Christian and Catholic vitality comes from fidelity to the teachings of Christ and Catholic practices. It does not come from adapting to the world or from money. The first tasks of the new pope will be to restore normality, restore doctrinal clarity in faith and morals, restore a proper respect for the law and ensure that the first criterion for the nomination of bishops is acceptance of the apostolic tradition. Theological expertise and learning are an advantage, not a hinderance for all bishops and especially archbishops. These are necessary foundations for living and preaching the Gospel.[19]

---

[19]Ibid.

Safeguarding God's Truth During a Time of Error

God's Truth and Man's Inclination to Falsehood

Truth is intrinsic to the Being of the Most Holy Trinity. Truth is manifested in the Only Begotten Son of God, the Word of God made flesh 'full of grace and truth' (Jn 1:14). As the consummation of God's revelation in Salvation History, our Lord Jesus Christ is Truth Incarnate. It is only through the truth of the Son that we can come to the Father. (Jn 14:6). To accomplish this, the Father and the Son send the Holy Ghost to lead us into the Truth. (Jn 16:13).

As adopted children of the Father, and brothers of our Lord Jesus Christ, adhering to divine truth and speaking truthfully are essential to being Christian. Our Lord commands us to be straight-forward and truthful, 'But let your speech be yea, yea: no, no: and that which is over and above these, is of evil.' (Mt 5:37). Lying and deceit are absolutely alien to God, 'it is impossible for God to lie.' (Heb 6:18; cf. Tit 1:2). As the First Vatican Council declared, God can 'neither deceive nor be deceived'. (*Dz* 1789); a reality lyrically conveyed in Fr. Gerard Manley Hopkins' translation of St. Thomas Aquinas' hymn *Adoro Te Devote* in the sentence, 'Truth Himself speaks truly, or there's nothing true.'

Therefore, it follows that lying and deception, including intentionally spreading confusion and ambiguity about God's revelation, are inimical to the life of grace, 'He who saith that he knoweth him, and keepeth not his commandments, is a liar, and the truth is not in him. But he that keepeth his word, in him in very deed the charity of God is perfected; and by this we know that we are in him.' (I Jn 2:4-5).

The devil — the Original False Prophet

Our Lord names the devil, the ultimate enemy of God's Truth, the 'father of lies',

> He was a murderer from the beginning, and he stood not in the truth; because truth is not in him. When he speaketh a lie, he speaketh of his own: for he is a liar, and the father thereof. (Jn 8:44).

The devil deceived our first parents into the primordial sin of disobedience by lying about the word of God, 'And the serpent said to the woman: No, you shall not die the death.' (Gen 3:4). By saying so, the devil is the original false prophet who brazenly contradicts God's actual commandment to Adam, 'And he commanded him, saying: Of every tree of paradise thou shalt eat: But of the tree of knowledge of good and evil, thou shalt not eat. For in what day soever thou shalt eat of it, thou shalt die the death.' (Gen 2: 16-17).

Since our fallen nature was formed by the devil's lies about God's primeval commandment, lying — and especially lying about the word of God — is a concupiscent inclination in man. Without the waters of baptism, we are the children of the father of lies,

> Why do you not know my speech? Because you cannot hear my word. You are of your father the devil, and the desires of your father you will do...He that is of God, heareth

1

the words of God. Therefore you hear them not, because you are not of God. (Jn 8:43-44;47).

This sinful orientation in man to reject the truth of God was behind the mysterious hostility our Lord Jesus Christ faced when He came to His own, the people of Israel who had been chosen, and formed, to receive the Word of God, 'He was in the world, and the world was made by him, and the world knew him not. He came unto his own, and his own received him not.' (Jn 1:10-11).

Though freed from subjugation to the devil by the waters of Baptism, we remain damaged by original sin, and tempted by a preference for epistemological and moral darkness,

> the light is come into the world, and men loved darkness rather than the light: for their works were evil. For every one that doth evil hateth the light, and cometh not to the light, that his works may not be reproved. (Jn 3:19-20).

God Helps Us See through the Deceptions of False Prophets

Throughout Salvation History we see false prophets, as agents of the devil, seeking to exploit this wound in human nature among the people of the Old Covenant and the New Covenant.

False Prophets in the Old Testament

The Lord warned, through the prophet Jeremiah, that false prophets deceived the people by speaking their own words and not the Word of God: 'Thus saith the Lord of hosts: Hearken not to the words of the prophets that prophesy to you and deceive you: they speak a vision of their own heart, and not out of the mouth of the Lord.' (Jer 23:16). False prophets can be identified by the consequences of their deceptions — they foment disobedience against the Lord's commands, and instead of calling sinners to repentance they encourage the immoral in their evil:

> And I have seen the likeness of adulterers, and the way of lying in the prophets of Jerusalem: and they strengthened the hands of the wicked, that no man should return from his evil doings: they are all become unto me as Sodom, and the inhabitants thereof as Gomorrha. (Jer 23: 14).

The prophet Ezekiel described false prophets as those who commit the worst possible deceit by presenting their own 'spirit' as God's Holy Spirit:

> Son of man, prophesy thou against the prophets of Israel that prophesy: and thou shalt say to them that prophesy out of their own heart: Hear ye the word of the Lord: Thus saith the Lord God: Woe to the foolish prophets that follow their own spirit, and see nothing […] Have you not seen a vain vision and spoken a lying divination: and you say: The Lord saith: whereas I have not spoken. (Ezek 13: 2-3;7).

The errors taught by false prophets, proceeding from a 'disobedience that blinds',[1] lead those who follow them far from the ways of God into a steep descent into irrationality and immorality:

> And it was not enough for them to err about the knowledge of God, but whereas they lived in a great war of ignorance, they call so many and so great evils peace […] And all things are mingled together, blood, murder, theft and dissimulation, corruption and unfaithfulness, tumults and perjury, disquieting of the good, forgetfulness of God, defiling of souls, changing of nature, disorder in marriage, and the irregularity of adultery and uncleanness. For the worship of abominable idols is the cause, and the beginning and end of all evil. For either they are mad when they are merry: or they prophesy lies, or they live unjustly, or easily forswear themselves. (Wis 14: 22;25-28).

---

[1] Léon-Dufour, L [1988] *Dictionary of Biblical Theology.* Ijamsville: The Word Among Us Press, p.144

The error of false prophets inevitably leads those deceived by them to the ultimate act of apostasy — replacing the true worship of God with the veneration of demonic idols:

> For they went astray for a long time in the ways of error, holding those things for gods which are the most worthless among beasts, living after the manner of children without understanding. (Wis 12:24).

False Prophets in the New Testament

Our Lord Jesus Christ warned the faithful to be on their guard against those who assume office in the Church but who teach and act contrary to the truths of the Catholic Faith: 'Beware of false prophets, who come to you in the clothing of sheep, but inwardly they are ravening wolves.' (Mt 7:15). As deception is the hallmark of such false teachers, our Lord gave a rule of thumb by which to see through their disguise, 'By their fruits you shall know them. Do men gather grapes of thorns, or figs of thistles? … Wherefore by their fruits you shall know them.' (Mt 7:16;20). Instead of being good to harvest and eat like ripe grapes and figs, the teachings of false prophets can only pierce and hurt those who touch them like sharp thorns and thistles.

The grapes that our Lord wants us to harvest, instead of the thorns and thistles of false prophets are His commandments:

> Abide in me, and I in you. As the branch cannot bear fruit of itself, unless it abide in the vine, so neither can you, unless you abide in me. I am the vine; you the branches: he that abideth in me, and I in him, the same beareth much fruit: for without me you can do nothing. (Jn 15:4-5).

Our Lord explains that in order to enjoy the fruit of the divine vine His 'words must abide in you' (Jn 15:7) and we must keep His commandments, 'If you keep my commandments, you shall abide in my love; as I also have kept my Father's commandments, and do abide in his love.' (Jn 15:10). The teachings of false prophets are thorns and thistles because they seek to cut off Christians from the living vine — the words and commandments of our Lord Jesus Christ.

Our Lord goes on to warn that false prophets are so dangerous because they assume the appearance of being appointed by God. These deceivers can even appear to be apostles, performing some of the signature acts of apostolic ministry — they prophesy, cast out demons, perform miracles, and invoke the Name of the Lord (Mt 7:22); but our Lord warns that those who claim to be apostles are false if they do not do the Will of the Father and do not base their actions on the words of His Son. (Mt 7:24-27).

Commenting on Matthew 7:15-20, the Church Father St. Vincent of Lerins takes up our Lord's warning about the deception of false prophets, pointing out that they can be detected by the dissonance between their use of sacred Scripture — when they 'wrap themselves in the language of the Divine Law' — and their 'fruits' — their rage against the Faith and destruction of the Church:

> What are the ravening wolves? What but the savage and rabid glosses of heretics, who continually infest the Church's folds, and tear in pieces the flock of Christ wherever they are able? But that they may with more successful guile steal upon the unsuspecting sheep, retaining the ferocity of the wolf, they put off his appearance, and wrap themselves, so to say, in the language of the Divine Law, as in a fleece, so that one, having felt the softness of wool, may have no dread of the wolf's fangs. But what says the Saviour? 'By their fruits you shall know them;' that is, when they have begun not only to quote those divine words, but also to expound them, not as yet only to make a boast of them as on their side, but also to interpret them, then will that bitterness, that acerbity, that rage, be understood; then will the ill-savour of that novel poison be perceived, then will those profane novelties be disclosed, then may you see first the hedge broken through, then the landmarks of the Fathers removed, then the Catholic faith assailed, then the doctrine of the Church torn in pieces.[2]

---

[2] St. Vincent of Lerins. *Commonitorium*, Chap. 25, para 66 [Online] Available at: www.newadvent. org [Accessed on: 22 September 2022]

In the epistles of the apostles, false teachers are synonymous with false prophets, because like the latter they lead people away from the teachings of our Lord. St. Peter identifies false teachers as those who revile the 'way of truth' out of a sinful desire to indulge in sexual immorality, especially sexual perversion:

> And especially them who walk after the flesh in the lust of uncleanness, and despise government, audacious, self willed, they fear not to bring in sects, blaspheming… But these men, as irrational beasts, naturally tending to the snare and to destruction, blaspheming those things which they know not, shall perish in their corruption […] Having eyes full of adultery and of sin that ceaseth not: alluring unstable souls, having their heart exercised with covetousness, children of malediction. (II Pet 2: 10;12;14).

Similarly, St. Paul describes false teachers as those who do not serve Jesus Christ, but their own 'appetites'. They can be identified by the dissension and difficulties they create in opposition to the doctrines of the Church:

> Now I beseech you, brethren, to mark them who make dissensions and offences contrary to the doctrine which you have learned, and avoid them. For they that are such, serve not Christ our Lord, but their own belly. (Rom 16:17-18).

St. Paul further identifies pride and self-seeking as motivating false teachers to openly contradict the teachings of our Lord Jesus Christ:

> If any man teach otherwise, and consent not to the sound words of our Lord Jesus Christ, and to that doctrine which is according to godliness, he is proud, knowing nothing…supposing gain to be godliness. (I Tim 6:3-5).

St. John goes so far as to describe false teachers as 'antichrists' due to their erroneous teachings about the Incarnation. Such false teachers not only oppose the teachings of our Lord but go so far as to attack the mystery of the union of the divine and human natures in the one person of the Son of God:

> Dearly beloved, believe not every spirit, but try the spirits if they be of God: because many false prophets are gone out into the world. By this is the spirit of God known. Every spirit which confesseth that Jesus Christ is come in the flesh, is of God: And every spirit that dissolveth Jesus, is not of God: and this is Antichrist, of whom you have heard that he cometh, and he is now already in the world. (I Jn 4:1-3).

Teaching Christological errors about the Incarnation is the ultimate sign of the activity of a false prophet and false teacher, because they signify the rejection of the divine truth embodied by our Lord Jesus Christ, one divine person, two natures, true God and true man.

The demonic origin and inspiration of false prophets is fully revealed in the Apocalypse of St. John the Apostle. Though he is describing the eschatological False Prophet who proceeds the Antichrist, the sacred text exposes the demonic servitude of false prophets throughout Salvation History. The purpose of every false prophet, whether he consciously knows it or not, is to deceive people away from worshipping God, so that they worship Satan:

> And the beast was taken, and with him the false prophet, who wrought signs before him, wherewith he seduced them who received the character of the beast, and who adored his image. These two were cast alive into the pool of fire, burning with brimstone. (Rev 19:20).

The Apocalypse reveals the supernatural reality that the false prophets of every age are agents in the war against God that has its origin in the rebellion of Satan and the fallen angels. On the human front of this war, the goal of Satan has always been the apostasy of the faithful:

> And he opened his mouth unto blasphemies against God, to blaspheme his name, and his tabernacle, and them that dwell in heaven. And it was given unto him to make war with the saints, and to overcome them. (Rev 13:6-7; cf. Lk 18:8, Mt 24:12).

The Apocalypse also reveals how the goal of Satan, through his servants the false prophets, will be defeated, through 'the sword of him that sitteth upon the horse, which proceedeth out of his mouth'. (Rev 19:21) — that is, through the Word of our Lord Jesus Christ:

> For the word of God is living and effectual, and more piercing than any two edged sword; and reaching unto the division of the soul and the spirit, of the joints also and the marrow, and is a discerner of the thoughts and intents of the heart. (Heb 4:12).

Safeguarding the Truth

Having experienced first-hand the betrayal of the Lord — the apostasy of Judas, the denial of St. Peter, the desertion of the apostles and the murderous persecution of Saul — the faithful transmission of our Lord's teaching and commandments were of paramount importance to the apostles. They knew from personal experience the ruination that came from building on the shifting sand of human thinking and not on the rock of Christ's divine Wisdom.

The apostles also knew that the faithful transmission of Christ's words and deeds was the Lord's expressed priority for their mission and that He promised to send them the Holy Spirit to assist them stay true to His teaching:

> But the Paraclete, the Holy Ghost, whom the Father will send in my name, he will teach you all things, and bring all things to your mind, whatsoever I shall have said to you. (Jn 14:26)

During the forty days after His Resurrection, He continued to teach the apostles and disciples about Himself and the Kingdom of God (Lk 24:27; Acts 1:3) and our Lord gave the apostles the commission to authentically proclaim and teach His Gospel to the whole world, 'Teaching them to observe all things whatsoever I have commanded you.' (Mt 28:20).

For all these reasons, safeguarding the teaching and commandments of our Lord and handing them on whole and intact to the next generation, with the imperative to do the very same, was a priority for the apostles. They expressed this priority in two ways — through the *Parathēkē* [the Deposit of Faith] and through *Paradosis* [Tradition].

Preserving the Deposit of Faith

St. Paul adapted a legal term to refer to revealed truths entrusted into the care of the Church, and all Christians. The Greek word *Parathēkē* [*depositum*] was originally a Roman legal term referring to a 'deposit', either money or property, that was entrusted into the care of another with the obligation to protect it and, eventually, return it in the original, pristine condition.[3]

The safeguarding of the Deposit of Faith was highlighted as a particular concern of bishops. In his first letter to Timothy, the Bishop of Ephesus, St. Paul wrote:

> O Timothy, keep that which is committed to thy trust, avoiding the profane novelties of words, and oppositions of knowledge falsely so called. (I Tim 6:20).

An imperative St. Paul again emphasised in his second letter to Bishop Timothy:

> Hold the form of sound words, which thou hast heard of me in faith, and in the love which is in Christ Jesus. Keep the good thing committed to thy trust by the Holy Ghost, who dwelleth in us. (II Tim 1:13-14).

Writing in the 5th century, commenting on St. Paul's Letters to St. Timothy, the Church Father St. Vincent of Lerins makes clear what is required from those entrusted with the Deposit of Faith:

---

[3]The Navarre Bible [2005] *Saint Paul's Letters to the Thessalonians and Pastoral Letters*. Dublin: Four Courts Press, p.102

Who is the Timothy of today, but either generally the Universal Church, or in particular, the whole body of The Prelacy, whom it behooves either themselves to possess or to communicate to others a complete knowledge of religion? What is 'Keep the deposit'? 'Keep it,' because of thieves, because of adversaries, lest, while men sleep, they sow tares over that good wheat which the Son of Man had sown in his field. 'Keep the deposit.' What is 'The deposit'? That which has been entrusted to you, not that which you have yourself devised: a matter not of wit, but of learning; not of private adoption, but of public tradition; a matter brought to you, not put forth by you, wherein you are bound to be not an author but a keeper, not a teacher but a disciple, not a leader but a follower. 'Keep the deposit.' Preserve the talent of Catholic Faith inviolate, unadulterate. That which has been entrusted to you, let it continue in your possession, let it be handed on by you. You have received gold; give gold in turn. Do not substitute one thing for another. Do not for gold impudently substitute lead or brass. Give real gold, not counterfeit.[4]

Without using the phrase, St. Vincent of Lerins is describing false prophets, those who substitute the gold of God's Truth with a 'lead' counterfeit of their own devising. In contrast, St. Vincent of Lerins describes the right attitude towards the Deposit of Faith — those who entrusted with Divine Truth should receive it with humility and obedience, seeing themselves as disciples, not masters, as students, not teachers, as guardians not innovators. Only in this way, can the apostolic faith be handed on 'inviolate' and 'unadulterated.'

St. Paul warned about those who posed the greatest threat to the Deposit of Faith — the false prophets and those Christians who were inclined to accept their counterfeit gospel. He warned that, like the devil, false prophets would present themselves as 'angels of light':

But though we, or an angel from heaven, preach a gospel to you besides that which we have preached to you, let him be anathema. (Gal 1:8); For such false apostles are deceitful workmen, transforming themselves into the apostles of Christ. And no wonder: for Satan himself transformeth himself into an angel of light. (II Cor 11:14).

St. Augustine — and other Church Fathers following The Book of the Apocalypse, (2:1-29:3:1-22) — referred to the bishop of a diocese as an angel entrusted with the care of his people.[5] Those bishops who reject the Deposit of Faith by proclaiming a false gospel are like Satan, pretending to be 'angels of light' so as to deceive, when in reality they are rebels against God and enemies of the Church.

Such false prophets would have no impact on the transmission of the Deposit of Faith if they did not have an audience susceptible to their deceptions and lies. St. Paul describes these Christians as being inclined to reject sound doctrine:

For there shall be a time, when they will not endure sound doctrine; but, according to their own desires, they will heap to themselves teachers, having itching ears: And will indeed turn away their hearing from the truth, but will be turned unto fables. (II Tim 4:3-4).

The pressure to conform to worldly, anti-Catholic ideologies, creates the milieu in which some of the baptised, with their inherent concupiscent inclination to reject Divine Truth, are susceptible, even eager, to embrace a false gospel. This temptation is all the greater if the false bishop is lauded by the fallen world as an 'angel of light' — a progressive leader, the epitome of 'compassion' because he throws off the shackles of 'rigid' doctrine.

Handing on the Apostolic Tradition

Faced with the responsibility of safely transmitting the Deposit of Faith, St. Paul used the Greek word *Paradosis* to convey what was required. *Paradosis* means the giving of

---

[4] St. Vincent of Lerins. *Op. cit.*, Chap. 22, para 53 [Online] Available at: www.newadvent.org [Accessed on: 22 September 2022]
[5] The Works of Saint Augustine: A Translation for the 21st Century. *Letters 1-99. Vol.II/1.* New York: New City Press [2001]. Letter 43, Para 23

a gift into the hands of another. It also contains the sense of being able to hand over the gift because the recipient is trusted to do the right thing with it.[6] The experience of paradosis in the early Church is the origin of the Catholic understanding of Tradition.

St. Paul saw the giving of the gift of the Deposit of Faith to others as involving a deeply personal relationship between giver and recipients. We see the importance of this relationship in the following passages:

> Now I praise you, brethren, that in all things you are mindful of me: and keep my ordinances as I have delivered them to you. (I Cor 11:2); The things which you have both learned, and received, and heard, and seen in me, these do ye, and the God of peace shall be with you. (Phil 4:9)

This special personal bond between apostles and disciples was intended as a guarantee of preserving the authenticity of the Deposit of Faith, exemplified by the transmission between bishops known as the Apostolic Succession. The Apostolic Succession is a relationship of trust stretching back across time to the Twelve Apostles personally chosen by our Lord.

The other guarantee of authenticity of transmission is a spirit of reverence and obedience to the Deposit of Faith among the recipients that arises from the recognition that it is God's Word, not man's. Though given as a gift by men to men, the gift is a divine mystery, not an invention of human beings:

> For I give you to understand, brethren, that the gospel which was preached by me is not according to man. For neither did I receive it of man, nor did I learn it; but by the revelation of Jesus Christ. (Gal 1: 11-12); Therefore, we also give thanks to God without ceasing: because, that when you had received of us the word of the hearing of God, you received it not as the word of men, but (as it is indeed) the word of God, who worketh in you that have believed. (I Thess 2:13)

This authentic transmission of the Faith would be beyond the capacity of man, with our inclination to heresy and apostasy, without the assistance and inspiration of the Holy Ghost. As St. Irenaeus expressed it:

> [Our faith] which, having been received from the Church, we do preserve, and which always, by the Spirit of God, renewing its youth, as if it were some precious deposit in an excellent vessel, causes the vessel itself containing it to renew its youth also. For this gift of God has been entrusted to the Church, as breath was to the first created man, for this purpose, that all the members receiving it may be vivified; and the [means of] communion with Christ has been distributed throughout it, that is, the Holy Spirit, the earnest of incorruption, the means of confirming our faith, and the ladder of ascent to God. 'For in the Church,' it is said, 'God has set apostles, prophets, teachers,' (I Corinthians 12:28) and all the other means through which the Spirit works; of which all those are not partakers who do not join themselves to the Church, but defraud themselves of life through their perverse opinions and infamous behaviour. For where the Church is, there is the Spirit of God; and where the Spirit of God is, there is the Church, and every kind of grace; but the Spirit is truth.[7]

The Holy Spirit inspired the Evangelists to commit sacred Tradition to writing as the Four Gospels, the most important act in the apostolic Church of preserving, and handing on, the Deposit of Faith. Having 'God as their author',[8] Sacred Scripture, interpreted in the light of sacred Tradition, became the ultimate standard by which the words and deeds of all Christians were measured:

---

[6] Dillon, M [1995] *Paradosis* in Journal of the British Society of Phenomenology. Vol.26, No 3, October [Online] Available at: www.tandfonline.com [Accessed on: 21 July 2022]

[7] St. Irenaeus. *Against Heresies*, Bk. III, Chap. 24, para 1 [Online] Available at: www.newadvent.org [Accessed on: 22 September 2022]

[8] First Vatican Council [1870] *Dei Filius*, Chap. 2, para 7 [Online] Available at: www.ewtn.com [Accessed on: 22 September 2022]

All scripture, inspired of God, is profitable to teach, to reprove, to correct, to instruct in justice, that the man of God may be perfect, furnished to every good work. (II Tim 3:16-17)

For this reason, Sacred Scripture, and sacred Tradition are known as the 'supreme rule of faith':

[The Church] has always maintained them [sacred Scripture] and continues to do so, together with sacred tradition, as the supreme rule of faith, since, as inspired by God and committed once and for all to writing, they impart the word of God Himself without change, and make the voice of the Holy Spirit resound in the words of the prophets and Apostles.[9]

The Supreme Rule of Faith

The apostolic imperative of *paradosis* and *paratheke* was expressed by the Church Fathers as the *Regula fidei*, the Rule of Faith, sometimes also known as the *Regula veritatis*, the Rule of Truth. The *Regula fidei* is the body of sacred Scripture and apostolic Tradition safeguarded by the perennial Magisterium, by which the truth of a contemporary teaching or action could be measured and assessed. The term 'rule', also known as 'canon', derives from the Greek word *kanón*, referring to a 'level' or 'measuring rod' used by builders to assess if something was true and correct.

Using the metaphors of measurement and demarcation, Sacred Scripture reveals that during times of crisis and tribulation God requires that his faithful people carefully distinguish the divine from the profane. This is necessary when the faithless and false intentionally seek to confuse their errors and apostasy with divine Truth and the Faith.

Almighty God commanded the Prophet Ezekiel to witness the measurement, in spirit, of the new Temple of the Lord so as to establish its demarcation from the idolatry and abominations introduced into the former Temple by its faithless kings, priests and people:

And he brought me in thither, and behold a man, whose appearance was like the appearance of brass, with a line of flax in his hand, and a measuring reed in his hand, and he stood in the gate [...] [The Lord told Ezekiel] They who have set their threshold by my threshold, and their posts by my posts: and there was but a wall between me and them: and they profaned my holy name by the abominations which they committed: for which reason I consumed them in my wrath. [...] And be ashamed of all that they have done. Shew them the form of the house, and of the fashion thereof, the goings out and the comings in, and the whole plan thereof, and all its ordinances, and all its order, and all its laws, and thou shalt write it in their sight: that they may keep the whole form thereof, and its ordinances, and do them (Ezek 40:3; 43:8;11).

The prophet Zechariah was also given a vision of a young man measuring Jerusalem, signifying God's promise to dwell in the city and protect those who remained faithful. (Zech 2:1-5). God Himself would be the demarcating wall of protection, 'And I will be to it, saith the Lord, a wall of fire round about: and I will be in glory in the midst thereof.' (Zech 2:5).

In the Book of the Apocalypse, during the vision of the eschatological final battle, God commands St. John to measure the Inner Temple and faithful worshippers so as to distinguish them from the outer court of the Temple — the Court of the Gentiles — which will be handed over to destruction by the enemies of God:

And there was given me a reed like unto a rod: and it was said to me: Arise, and measure the temple of God, and the altar and them that adore therein. But the court, which is without the temple, cast out, and measure it not: because it is given unto the Gentiles, and the holy city they shall tread under foot two and forty months (Rev 11:1-2).

[9] Second Vatican Council [1965] *Dei Verbum*, para 21 [Online] Available at: www.vatican.va [Accessed on: 22 September 2022]

Commentators interpret this passage from the Apocalypse as revealing that what is measured and demarcated as true, holy, and faithful is under the 'special protection of God'.[10] This is reassuring to know during times of destruction wrought by the false prophet and the antichrist. God has given us a tool to distinguish true teaching from false teaching, the true teacher from the false teacher, so as to remain under the protection of God — the *Regula Fidei*, the Rule of Truth. Living by the *Regula Fidei* enables us to know that we remain within the protective power of God:

> The Church, 'like a stranger in a foreign land, presses forward amid the persecutions of the world and the consolations of God', announcing the cross and death of the Lord until He comes. By the power of the risen Lord it is given strength that it might, in patience and in love, overcome its sorrows and its challenges, both within itself and from without, and that it might reveal to the world, faithfully though darkly, the mystery of its Lord until, in the end, it will be manifested in full light (*Lumen Gentium* 8).

What We Can Learn from Church Fathers about the Regula Fidei

Those Church Fathers who emphasised the necessity of upholding, and living by, the *Regula Fidei*, did so in response to various types of disobedience, including moral and doctrinal heresy being disseminated within the Church.

Pope St. Clement of Rome (c. 88 to 99)

Though Pope St. Clement I — the immediate successor of St. Peter — doesn't use the exact phrase *Regula Fidei* in his Letter to the Corinthians, he does refer to its necessary role in the Christian life. Pope St. Clement wrote, 'Therefore let us abandon empty and futile thoughts, and let us conform to the glorious and holy rule of our tradition'. (I Clement 7:2).[11] Pope St. Clement explains that conforming to the 'glorious and holy rule of our tradition' means being orientated to the past, 'Let us turn to every age that has passed, and learn that, from generation to generation'. He contrasts the 'holy rule of our tradition' with those who engage in 'empty and futile thoughts', which St. Paul described as indicative of rejection of divine Truth in favour of false teaching (II Tim 4:3-4).

It follows that a warning sign that someone is a false teacher is the dismissal of this orientation to the past, such as claiming it turns the Church into a museum or mummifies the Church or suggesting Christians shouldn't look to the past, but only look forward to the future. Upholding the *Regula Fidei* means living lives informed by the past, to the actions of God in Salvation History. Instead of doing as Pope St. Clement exhorts, false teachers focus on the future as if it were a tabula rasa on which they are free to impose their own words and deeds. The mistake that such false teachers make is in thinking of Salvation History as being mere human actions made remote, and inaccessible, by the passage of time. They forget that the events of Salvation History are divine actions that exist in the eternal 'now' of God, that we can access through the Holy Ghost, especially through His action in divine liturgy. As Sergei Bulgakov writes about the liturgical year:

> It is not merely a commemoration of the events of the Gospel or other events in the Church's life, in an artistic form. It is also an actualisation of these facts, their renewal upon earth. The Christmas service does not merely commemorate the birth of Christ. In it Christ is truly born in a mystery, as at Easter He rises again. So with the Transfiguration, the entry into Jerusalem, the mystery of the Last Supper, the passion, burial and ascension of Christ....The life of the Church in her liturgy, discloses to our senses the continuing mystery of the Incarnation. The Lord still lives in the Church, under that

---

[10] The Navarre Bible [2005] *The Revelation of John* [The Apocalypse]: Dublin: Four Courts Press, p. 73-74; Harrington, WJ [1993] *Revelation. Sacra Pagina*. Collegeville: The Liturgical Press, 1993. p. 119.
[11] Holmes, MW [1999] *The Apostolic Fathers: Greek Texts and English Translations*. Grand Rapids: Baker Books, p.37

same form in which He was once manifest on earth, and which exists eternally; and it is the function of that Church to make those sacred memories living, so that we again witness and take part in them.[12]

Through the activity of the Holy Ghost in sacred Scripture and the sacraments — and our adherence to the *Regula Fidei* — we enter into the eternal drama of Salvation History. In this way we 'conform to the glorious and holy rule of our tradition'.

St. Irenaeus of Lyons (130 to c. 202)

The phrase *Regula Fidei* was coined by St. Irenaeus, the Bishop of Lyons, a disciple of St. Polycarp, who in turn was a disciple of St. John the Apostle, the Beloved Disciple of our Lord Jesus Christ.

St. Irenaeus first used the term in his work *The Demonstration of the Apostolic Teaching*, a catechetical work for converts. He also referred to it as the 'rule of the truth' (*Against Heresies*, Bk. I, Chap. 9, 4). St. Irenaeus tells the converts that they must rigidly adhere to the Rule of Faith if they are not to suffer the 'pestilence' of heretics, 'those who by wicked and perverse doctrines corrupt not themselves only, but others also.' In order to be protected from heresy, the Rule of Faith must be held without any 'deviation':

> Now, that we may not suffer ought of this kind [the venom of heresy], we must needs hold the rule of the faith without deviation, and do the commandments of God, believing in God and fearing Him as Lord and loving Him as Father. [...] This then is the order of the rule of our faith, and the foundation of the building, and the stability of our conversation.[13]

If the Christian retains unchanged in his heart, the *Regula Fidei*, or *Regula Veritatis*, received at baptism, he will be able to distinguish the 'gems' of Faith from the 'figments' of heresy (*Against Heresies*. Bk. I, Chap. 9, 4).

St. Irenaeus also understood the *Regula Fidei* as being universally binding, irrespective of nationality or language:

> As I have already observed, the Church, having received this preaching and this faith, although scattered throughout the whole world, yet, as if occupying but one house, carefully preserves it. She also believes these points [of doctrine] just as if she had but one soul, and one and the same heart, and she proclaims them, and teaches them, and hands them down, with perfect harmony, as if she possessed only one mouth. For, although the languages of the world are dissimilar, yet the import of the tradition is one and the same. For the Churches which have been planted in Germany do not believe or hand down anything different, nor do those in Spain, nor those in Gaul, nor those in the East, nor those in Egypt, nor those in Libya, nor those which have been established in the central regions of the world. But as the sun, that creature of God, is one and the same throughout the whole world, so also the preaching of the truth shines everywhere, and enlightens all men that are willing to come to a knowledge of the truth.[14]

The universally binding nature of the *Regula Fidei* must be insisted on during a time when false teachers propose an erroneous relativistic understanding of 'inculturation', asserting that doctrines can be adapted to the culture or social norms of a country or region. This fragmentation of the Church's catholicity into so called 'national churches' denies the *Regula Fidei*'s universal claim to truth.

St. Irenaeus insisted that no one in authority in the Church — either through eloquence or incompetence — had the power to teach doctrines that diverged from the

---

[12] Bulgakov, S [1932] *L' Orthodoxie*, p.180 quoted in Underhill, E [1937] *Worship*. London: Nisbet & Co, p.76

[13] St. Irenaeus. *The Demonstration of the Apostolic Teaching*, para 3 [Online] Available at: ccel.org [Accessed on: 22 September 2022]

[14] St. Irenaeus. *Against Heresies*, Bk. I, Chap. 10, para 2 [Online] Available at: www.newadvent.org [Accessed on: 22 September 2022]

Regula Fidei, because 'no one is greater than the Master' who entrusted the Deposit of Faith to the Church:

> Nor will any one of the rulers in the Churches, however highly gifted he may be in point of eloquence, teach doctrines different from these (for no one is greater than the Master); nor, on the other hand, will he who is deficient in power of expression inflict injury on the tradition. For the faith being ever one and the same, neither does one who is able at great length to discourse regarding it, make any addition to it, nor does one, who can say but little diminish it.[15]

St. Irenaeus pointed out the absurdity of those who claim to have the authority or superior knowledge that enables them to ignore or change the *Regula Fidei*. There are those false teachers who mistakenly claim that sacred Scripture is ambiguous, and they have the correct interpretation, or those who make the impossible claim that they have access to a truth greater than that expressed by God:

> When, however, they are confuted from the Scriptures, they turn round and accuse these same Scriptures, as if they were not correct, nor of authority, and [assert] that they are ambiguous, and that the truth cannot be extracted from them by those who are ignorant of tradition....For every one of these men, being altogether of a perverse disposition, depraving the system of truth, is not ashamed to preach himself. But, again, when we refer them to that tradition which originates from the apostles, [and] which is preserved by means of the succession of presbyters in the Churches, they object to tradition, saying that they themselves are wiser not merely than the presbyters, but even than the apostles, because they have discovered the unadulterated truth. (*Against Heresies*, Bk. III, Chap. 2, 1-2)

During these times of hubristic scientism and moral relativism there are false teachers within the Church that assert, for example, God's revelation on sexual morality expressed in doctrine must be revised due to recent developments in psychology, sociology and biblical exegesis. A true understanding of the *Regula Fidei* exposes this as nonsensical.

Tertullian (c. 160 to c. 225)

An advocate in the law courts of Carthage, Tertullian was an adult convert from paganism who was ordained as a priest. With his professional training in legal argument, Tertullian engaged in apologetics and polemics against heresy.

Tertullian argued for the authority of the *Regula Fidei* by tracing it back to its origin in the divine identity and teaching of our Lord Jesus Christ. The origin of the *Regula Fidei* in the divine identity of our Lord has profound implications about how we relate to it. Tertullian wrote:

> But our Lord Christ has surnamed Himself Truth, not Custom. If Christ is always, and prior to all, equally truth is a thing sempiternal and ancient. [For this reason,] The rule of faith, indeed, is altogether one, alone immoveable and irreformable (*On the Veiling of Virgins*, Chap. 1).

Just as our Lord is eternal and unchanging, His revelation contained in sacred Scripture and Holy Tradition is eternal and unchanging.

The origin of the *Regula Fidei* in our Lord's teaching also means that it cannot be questioned in the way that purely human knowledge can be questioned with a view to developing or changing it. Tertullian wrote: 'This rule, as it will be proved, was taught by Christ, and raises among ourselves no other questions than those which heresies introduce, and which make men heretics'.[16]

---

[15] *Ibid.*

[16] Tertullian. *Prescription against Heretics*, Chap. 13 [Online] Available at: www.newadvent.org [Accessed on: 22 September 2022]

Tertullian wrote that any inquiry into matters of Faith must be conducted within the proper limits established by God's revelation, and must never proceed from sources that are destructive or evil:

> No man gets instruction from that which tends to destruction. No man receives illumination from a quarter where all is darkness. Let our 'seeking,' therefore be in that which is our own, and from those who are our own: and concerning that which is our own — that, and only that, which can become an object of inquiry without impairing the rule of faith.[17]

This 'immoveable', 'irreformable' and 'unquestionable' nature of the *Regula Fidei* is why the 'development of doctrine' can never mean a deepening understanding of doctrine that contradicts or replaces the original truths revealed by God. The development of doctrine can only mean a deepening understanding within the limits established by revelation. As the First Vatican Council declared:

> For the doctrine of faith that God has revealed has not been proposed like a philosophical system to be perfected by human ingenuity; rather it has been committed to the spouse of Christ as a divine trust to be faithfully kept and infallibly declared. Hence, also that meaning of the sacred dogmas is perpetually to be retained which Holy Mother Church has once declared, and there must never be a deviation from that meaning on the specious ground and title of a more profound understanding [can. 3] 'Therefore, let there be growth and abundant progress in the understanding, the knowledge, and wisdom, in each and all, in individuals and in the whole Church, at all times and in the progress of ages, but only within the proper limits, i.e., within the same dogma, the same meaning, the same judgment.' [Vincent of Lerins, *Commonitorium*, 23, 3] (Dogmatic Constitution, *Dei Filius*, On the Catholic Faith, Chap. 4).[18]

With this understanding of the nature and authority of the *Regula Fidei*, Tertullian warns against that those who use the status of their position in the Church to assert that their erroneous teaching is true, arguing that the truth of faith isn't proved by personal status, but that personal status is proved by upholding the Rule of Faith:

> But what if a bishop, if a deacon, if a widow, if a virgin, if a doctor, if even a martyr, have fallen from the rule (of faith), will heresies on that account appear to possess the truth? Do we prove the faith by the persons, or the persons by the faith? No one is wise, no one is faithful, no one excels in dignity, but the Christian; and no one is a Christian but he who perseveres even to the end.[19]

Tertullian argues that only those who uphold the *Regula Fidei* can be trusted to possess true sacred Scriptures, holy Traditions, and authentic teaching:

> With whom lies that very faith to which the Scriptures belong. From what and through whom, and when, and to whom, has been handed down that rule, by which men become Christians? For wherever it shall be manifest that the true Christian rule and faith shall be, there will likewise be the true Scriptures and expositions thereof, and all the Christian traditions.[20]

Grades of Certainty in the Regula Fidei

Since the time of the apostles, it was recognised that the Deposit of Faith consisted of different types of truth. St. Paul distinguished between teaching that he 'received from the Lord' and his own personal teaching which he delivered with the authority of an apostle.

---

[17] *Ibid.*, Chap. 12
[18] Denzinger, H [2010] *Compendium of Creeds, Definitions, and Declarations on matters of Faith and Morals.* San Francisco: Ignatius Press, p. 606, Dz 3020
[19] Tertullian. *Prescription against Heretics*, Chap. 3 [Online] Available at: www.newadvent.org [Accessed on: 22 September 2022]
[20] *Ibid.*, Chap 19

When St. Paul uses the phrase, 'I received from the Lord', he is signalling to the reader that he is handing on truths that he received from Tradition going back to Jesus Christ. For example:

> For I have received of the Lord that which also I delivered unto you, that the Lord Jesus, the same night in which he was betrayed, took bread…(I Cor 11:23); But to them that are married, not I but the Lord commandeth, that the wife depart not from her husband (I Cor 7:10).

Sometimes St. Paul explicitly distinguished teaching which he gave with his apostolic authority from teaching he had received from the Lord: 'For to the rest I speak, not the Lord. If any brother hath a wife that believeth not, and she consent to dwell with him, let him not put her away.' (I Cor 7:12). In this type of teaching St. Paul is addressing a marital situation not addressed by our Lord's teaching by applying divine truth about the indissolubility of the marriage bond.

Over the centuries the Church deepened her understanding of the different types of truth contained in the Deposit of Faith, resulting in a classification of grades of certainty pertaining to doctrines which determine how we relate to them. The following is based on Dr. Ludwig Ott's summary of the theological grades of certainty:[21]

Divine Faith [**fides divina**]. The highest degree of certainty belongs to truths directly revealed by God. If the Church pronounces that such a truth is contained in Revelation, then the high degree of certainty is confirmed by the infallible teaching authority of the Church (*fides catholica*). If the divine truth is confirmed by a solemn declaration of a pope or an ecumenical council, then it has the certainty of '*de fide definita.*' Example: The Dogma of the Most Holy Trinity.

Faith of the Church [**fides ecclesiastica**]. These are doctrines that the infallible teaching office of the Church has definitively decided are to be accepted with faith in the sole authority of the Church. Example: The Dogmas of the Immaculate Conception and the Bodily Assumption of Our Lady.

Teaching with the Closest Connection to the Faith [**sententia fidei proxima**]. These are doctrines regarded by the Church as a truth of Revelation, but which have not been definitively promulgated. Example: The various doctrines of the Atonement.

Teaching Pertaining to the Faith [**sententia ad fidem pertinens**]. These are doctrines on which the Magisterium has not definitively pronounced but has clearly decided are necessary corollaries of Revelation. Example: Mary as co-redemptrix.

Common Teaching [**Sententia communis**]. These are popular doctrines about which it is, at present, permissible to have free opinions. Example: The possibility that children who die without sacramental baptism receive vicarious baptism through the desire of the parents (Cajetan). Ott states that this is possible but cannot be proved from Revelation.

Theological Opinions [**Sententia probabilis**]. These are teachings that are recognised as being in agreement with the 'consciousness of the Church', such as pious opinions. Examples: Devotion to Victim Souls. Venerating the Holy Shroud of Turin as the burial cloth of Jesus.

The least degree of certainty is given to tolerated opinions [*opinio tolerata*] which are weakly founded but are tolerated by the Church. Example: Jesus was crucified above the tomb of Adam at Calvary.

Inerrancy, Indefectibility, and Infallibility

The Holy Ghost helped the Church deepen her understanding of the nature of the *Fidei Depositum* and the *Regula Fidei*, by crystallising three doctrines — the inerrancy of

---

[21] Ott, L [1957] *Fundamentals of Catholic Dogma.* Cork: The Mercier Press, Ltd, p.9-10

sacred Scripture, the indefectibility of the Church, and the infallibility of the Church. The divine origin of the truths expressed by the *Fidei Depositum* and the *Regula Fidei*, and the assistance of the Holy Ghost in their transmission down the generations, give a uniqueness to this knowledge that is not found in human-derived knowledge:

> …God in his infinite goodness has ordained man to a supernatural end, viz., to share in the good things of God that utterly exceed the intelligence of the human mind, for 'no eye has seen nor ear heard, nor the heart of man conceived, what God has prepared for those who love him' (I Cor 2:9) (First Vatican Council, Dogmatic Constitution, *Dei Filius*, On the Catholic Faith, Chap. 2).[22]

The Inerrancy of Sacred Scripture

Though Biblical inerrancy had been a belief regarding the *Regula Fidei* since the Church Fathers, it wasn't expressed in a magisterial document until the 19th century in response to attacks on its veracity from science and historical studies. The a priori dismissal of the divine authorship of sacred Scripture by 19th century secularists, reduced the Bible to the category of fallible man-made literature.

In reaction to these attacks, the First Vatican Council underlined the divine authorship of sacred Scriptures, denying that they were the product of 'unaided human skill':

> These books the church holds to be sacred and canonical not because she subsequently approved them by her authority after they had been composed by unaided human skill, nor simply because they contain revelation without error, but because, being written under the inspiration of the holy Spirit, they have God as their author, and were as such committed to the church (Dogmatic Constitution, *Dei Filius*, on the Catholic Faith, Chap. 2, 7).

Pope Leo XIII (1878 to 1903) deepened the Church's understanding of the connection between divine authorship and the 'unlimited inerrancy' of sacred Scripture:

> For all the books which the Church receives as sacred and canonical, are written wholly and entirely, with all their parts, at the dictation of the Holy Ghost; and so far is it from being possible that any error can co-exist with inspiration, that inspiration not only is essentially incompatible with error, but excludes and rejects it as absolutely and necessarily as it is impossible that God Himself, the supreme Truth, can utter that which is not true.[23]

If Truth is intrinsic to the Being of the Most Holy Trinity, and deception and error are alien to the actions of God, then as God is the author of sacred Scripture, through the inspiration of the Holy Ghost, then sacred Scripture must be inerrant, for 'the Bible is a reflection of the mind of God, who is the perfection of Truth.'[24]

It is important to bear in mind that this magisterial understanding of the unlimited inerrancy of the Bible doesn't impose the obligation of a fundamentalist, literal interpretation of sacred Scripture. Since the time of the Church Fathers there was the awareness that the Bible contained different types of Truth, expressed in the four senses of Scripture — literal, allegorical, moral, and anagogical. (*Catechism of the Catholic Church*, 117-118). This understanding of the Bible's different types of Truth deepened with the Historical-Critical study of the various literary genres that comprise sacred Scripture and the literary intentions of the human agents God chose to express His Truth.

The Second Vatican Council's Dogmatic Constitution on Divine Revelation, *Dei Verbum*, further deepened the Church's understanding of Biblical inerrancy, especially the role of those who were inspired by the Holy Ghost to transmit divine Truth through the written word:

---

[22] Denzinger, H [2010] *Op. cit.*, p. 602, Dz 3006
[23] Pope Leo XIII [1893] *Providentissimus Deus*, para 2 [Online] Available at: www.vatican.va [Accessed on: 22 September 2022]
[24] Hahn, S [2009] *Catholic Bible Dictionary*. New York: Doubleday, p.389

In composing the sacred books, God chose men and while employed by Him they made use of their powers and abilities, so that with Him acting in them and through them, they, as true authors, consigned to writing everything and only those things which He wanted.[25]

The Council Fathers of Vatican II even went so far as to explain God's purpose in making sacred Scripture inerrant, 'God wished truth to be recorded in the Bible, namely, to facilitate our salvation. The purpose of inerrancy is our salvation':[26]

Therefore, since everything asserted by the inspired authors or sacred writers must be held to be asserted by the Holy Spirit, it follows that the books of Scripture must be acknowledged as teaching solidly, faithfully and without error that truth which God wanted put into sacred writings for the sake of salvation. (*DV* 11)

With our concupiscent inclination to reject God's Truth, and the endless series of false prophets and false teachers emerging in the Church exciting this inclination, God has made sacred Scripture the bedrock of Truth for the sake of our salvation. Those who contradict God's absolute condemnation of sodomy (Gen 19:1-29; Rom 1:24-27; I Cor 6:10; I Tim1:10) or use weasel words to contradict our Lord's absolute prohibition of divorce and 're-marriage' (Mk 10:2-12, Lk 16:18) not only reject doctrine but also dismiss the inerrancy of sacred Scripture. Those who seek to undermine trust in the truthfulness of the Bible make themselves enemies of salvation.

The Indefectibility of the Church

In order to understand the doctrine of the indefectibility of the Church it is necessary to always keep in mind that the Catholic Church is not merely a human institution with a human history. Instead, the Catholic Church originates from the mysterious initiative and plan of the Most Holy Trinity, fulfilled in the Incarnation and Paschal Mystery of our Lord Jesus Christ, true God and true man, and the sending of the Holy Ghost, the Spirit of Truth.

The doctrine of the indefectibility of the Church makes explicit the imperishable and indestructible covenant between God and His Church expressed by Christ's two-fold promise — that 'the gates of hell shall not prevail against it' (Mt 16:18), and 'behold I am with you all days, even to the consummation of the world' (Mt 28:20).[27]

There is a paradox at the heart of the Church — the paradox of the holiness of Christ that radiates from the midst of the Church made up of concupiscent, sinful men. The fundamental principle here is that it is Christ who is One, Christ who is Holy, Christ who is Catholic, and Christ who is Apostolic. And it is the eternal, immutable Christ who makes the Church indefectible, not inconstant man who is prone to error and heresy. Human beings are 'the Church' when, through grace and the supernatural virtues, they co-operate and participate in these personal attributes of Christ.

It is only from this Christocentric perspective that we can begin to understand the mystery of the indefectibility of the Church — 'her imperishableness, that is, her constant duration to the end of the world, and the essential immutability of her teaching, her constitution and her liturgy.'[28]

The Church Fathers employed the symbol of the moon to convey the paradox that underpins the mystery of indefectibility — the Church as the union between the eternal, immutable Christ and mortal, mutable man. The Church, like the moon, does not produce her own light, but can only reflect the light of Christ. Furthermore, the waxing and waning of the moon that never fails, symbolises the changing fortunes, and inherent constancy, of the Church moving through history. St. Ambrose wrote:

---

[25] Second Vatican Council [1965] *Dei Verbum*, para 11 [Online] Available at: www.vatican.va [Accessed on: 22 September 2022]

[26] Hahn, S [2009] *Op. cit.*, p.389

[27] Ott, L [1957] *Op. cit.*, p. 297

[28] *Ibid.*, p. 296

The Church, like the moon, seems to lose light, but she does not. She can be cast in shadow, but she cannot lose her light. For example, the Church is weakened by the desertion of some in time of persecution, but is replenished by the witness of her martyrs. Wherefore, glorified by the victories of blood shed for Christ, she may pour forth all the more abundantly over the entire world the light of her devotedness and her faith.[29]

St. Augustine also saw the moon as an allegory of the Church, seeing the bright side of the moon and her dark side as the contrast between the spiritual, holy members of the Church and carnal, sinful members of the Church. The bright side is illuminated by Christ, while the darkened moon is caused either by the 'obscuring clouds' of 'blasphemous attacks and slanders' against Christianity, or an 'eclipse' of persecution and bloodshed that results in 'the weak being frightened off the name of Christian' or under the cover of such darkness Christians committed sins and crimes instead of remaining steadfast. [30]

This recognition that the Church was the union of indefectibility and defectibility resulted in the understanding that individual 'churches' within the universal Church could be subject to decay and 'accidental changes':[31]

> The gift of indefectibility plainly does not guarantee each several part of the Church against heresy or apostasy. The promise is made to the corporate body. Individual Churches may become corrupt in morals, may fall into heresy, may even apostatise. Thus at the time of the Mohammedan conquests, whole populations renounced their faith; and the Church suffered similar losses in the sixteenth century. But the defection of isolated branches does not alter the character of the main stem.[32]

The Vatican II Dogmatic Constitution on the Church, *Lumen Gentium*, spells out the conditions necessary for all the faithful — 'from the Bishops down to the last of the lay faithful' to remain in the light of the indefectibility of Christ and not sink into the darkness of heresy and sin. *Lumen Gentium* 12 affirms that the Church 'cannot err in matters of belief' if the following conditions are met:

1. 'That discernment in matters of faith is aroused and sustained by the Spirit of truth.' In other words, the Church is preserved from error when she acts in conformity to the Spirit of truth who has inspired sacred Scripture, assisted in the handing on of Tradition and guided the Magisterium down the ages. Any discernment of the Faith that is aroused and sustained by any other spirit, such as the spirit of the world, will not meet the conditions necessary for indefectibility.
2. The sacred teaching office must inculcate 'faithful and respectful obedience' to the word of God, fully recognised as God's Truth, not man's truths.
3. The entire Church — from the bishops down to the last of the lay faithful — must adhere 'unwaveringly to the faith given once and for all to the saints'.
4. The entire Church can only authentically understand God's Truth if she 'penetrates it more deeply with right thinking and applies it more fully in its life.' Members of the Church will fall into error if they abandon the 'right thinking' that the Church has encouraged down the centuries for the popular fads and fashions of the world.

These conditions, necessary for remaining within the indefectibility of the Church, apply equally to every member, including the pope, the Sacred College of Cardinals, the Orders of Bishops, Priests, Deacons, and all the faithful.

---

[29] St. Ambrose. *Hexameron, Paradise*. Chap. 2, para 7 [Online] Available at: archive.org [Accessed on: 23 September 2022]

[30] The Works of Saint Augustine: A Translation for the 21st Century [2001] *Expositions of the Psalms, 1-32 (III/15)*. New York: New City Press. Psalm 10, p.161-162, Para 3-4.

[31] Ott, L. *Op. cit.*, p.296

[32] *Catholic Encyclopedia* [1913] The Church [Online] Available at: www.newadvent.org [Accessed on: 23 September 2022]

The Infallibility of the Church

The doctrine of the infallibility of the Church declares that it is impossible for the Church to fall into error. It expresses divine truths about the Church revealed by our Lord concerning His role, and the role of the Holy Spirit, in the Church.

The infallibility of the Church expresses in doctrinal form Christ's promises to the Church — that He would assist the Church until the end of time (Mt 28:18-20) and that the Holy Spirit will assist the apostles and their successors in understanding and teaching revelation, 'he will teach you all truth' (Jn 16:12-15; cf. Jn 14:25-26).

Like inerrancy and indefectibility, infallibility is a supernatural attribute that is 'the specific effect of the Holy Ghost who fills, animates, and guides'[33] the Church. Infallibility belongs to the Holy Ghost, who has 'responsibility for what the Apostles and their successors may define to be part of Christ's teaching…insofar as the Holy Ghost is responsible for Church teaching, that teaching is necessarily infallible: what the Spirit of truth guarantees cannot be false.'[34]

It follows, that Infallibility is not an *intrinsic* attribute belonging to an individual or office holder in the Church but is a grace bestowed by the Holy Spirit. Dr. Matthias Scheeben explains:

> In the teaching body accordingly, infallibility is not its *very own attribute*, inasmuch as it is neither rooted in the special intrinsic completeness of its members, nor is it given in the first place and directly for such an internal completeness of its members, or as a component of their *gratia gratum faciens* [grace that makes a soul pleasing to God = sanctifying grace] and therefore is proper to it neither *radicaliter* [radically] nor *finaliter* [as an end], but rather belongs to it only as a ministerial, instrumental attribute or as a gratia gratis data [grace freely given = grace of office] or as a simple charism.[35]

The grace, or charism, of supernatural infallibility, is bestowed on the Church by the Holy Spirit in two ways — infallibility is given to the Magisterium in the active sense of an 'inability to lead astray by its teaching', and to the body of believers in the passive sense of 'an inability to be misled by following the teaching' of the Magisterium.[36] Of course, sinful human beings, can block the fruition of the grace of infallibility through their concupiscent inclination to reject God's truth and replace it with their own erroneous interpretations.

The Active Infallibility of the Magisterium

The two modern ecumenical councils — Vatican I and Vatican II — set out the conditions necessary for the fruitful reception of the grace of active infallibility in the Church by the pope and bishops in union with him.

The First Vatican Council narrowly restricted the exercise of the charism of infallibility to being an explicit, formal act when the pope makes a declaration *ex cathedra* 'defining doctrine regarding Faith or Morals'.[37]

The First Vatican Council also defined exactly what was meant by doctrine in the context of the exercise of infallibility — it was not something that could be improved upon by the application of human sciences or thinking. The grace of infallibility could only be exercised to protect and promulgate the divine deposit of faith entrusted to the Church:

> …the doctrine of the faith which God has revealed is put forward not as some philosophical discovery capable of being perfected by human intelligence, but as a

---

[33] Scheeben, M [2019] *Handbook of Catholic Dogmatics*. Book One. Part One. Steubenville: Emmaus Academic, p.139

[34] *Catholic Encyclopedia* [1913] Infallibility [Online] Available at: www.newadvent.org [Accessed on: 23 September 2022]

[35] Scheeben, M [2019]. *Op. Cit.,* p. 140

[36] *Ibid.,* p. 139

[37] First Vatican Council [1870] Dogmatic Constitution on the Church of Christ, *Pastor Aeternus,* [Online] Available at: www.ewtn.com [Accessed on: 24 September 2022]

divine deposit committed to the spouse of Christ to be faithfully protected and infallibly promulgated.[38]

The First Vatican Council went on to state that the infallibility of the Holy Spirit was not granted to the successor of St. Peter to misuse divine revelation to introduce 'new doctrine' but to guard and faithfully proclaim the deposit of faith received from the apostles:

> For, the Holy Spirit was not promised to the successors of Peter that by His revelation they might disclose new doctrine, but that by His help they might guard sacredly the revelation transmitted through the apostles and the deposit of faith, and might faithfully set it forth.[39]

The Second Vatican Council further elaborated the conditions necessary for the exercise of active infallibility by the pope and bishops in union with him. When the pope and bishops define a judgement regarding doctrine and morals they are obliged to abide by, and conform to the deposit of faith, as expressed by sacred Scripture and sacred Tradition:

> …they pronounce it in accordance with Revelation itself, which all are obliged to abide by and be in conformity with, that is, the Revelation which as written or orally handed down is transmitted in its entirety through the legitimate succession of bishops and especially in care of the Roman Pontiff himself, and which under the guiding light of the Spirit of truth is religiously preserved and faithfully expounded in the Church.[40]

The pope and bishops must also be diligent to inquire properly into revelation, making sure that they do not introduce a 'new revelation' into the deposit of faith:

> The Roman Pontiff and the bishops, in view of their office and the importance of the matter, by fitting means diligently strive to inquire properly into that revelation and to give apt expression to its contents; but a new public revelation they do not accept as pertaining to the divine deposit of faith. (*LG* 25)

Vatican II's Dogmatic Constitution on Divine Revelation, *Dei Verbum*, makes it clear that the teaching body — the magisterium of the pope and bishops — does not have carte blanche but is subservient to the Deposit of Faith:

> This teaching office is not above the word of God, but serves it, teaching only what has been handed on, listening to it devoutly, guarding it scrupulously and explaining it faithfully in accord with a divine commission and with the help of the Holy Spirit, it draws from this one deposit of faith everything which it presents for belief as divinely revealed. (*DV* 10).

The charism of infallibility can only be legitimately exercised to listen devoutly, guard scrupulously and explain faithfully the Deposit of Faith. Any teaching that exceeds this mandate is not an authentic expression of the Magisterium.

The Passive Infallibility of the Faithful

The Holy Spirit grants to those faithful who do not block the grace of infallibility with sins against the faith — such as schism, heresy and apostasy — the charism of an 'inability to be misled by following the teaching' of the Magisterium. The Holy Spirit promises to protect the faithful from being misled into error by false prophets and false teachers.

This understanding of the working of passive infallibility is a necessary corrective to those who assume that the 'obedience of faith' means blind obedience to the teaching

---

[38] First Vatican Council [1870] *Dei Filius,* Chap. 4, para 13 [Online] Available at: www.ewtn.com [Accessed on: 22 September 2022]

[39] *Op. cit.*

[40] Second Vatican Council [1964] The Dogmatic Constitution on the Church, *Lumen Gentium*, Chap. III, para 25 [Online] Available at: www.vatican.va [Accessed on: 24 September 2022]

body, even when they misuse magisterial authority to teach error. A historical example of the exercise of passive infallibility was the role of the laity in rejecting the imposition of the Arian heresy on the Church by the majority of eastern bishops. St. John Henry Newman wrote:

> … in that time of immense confusion the divine dogma of our Lord's divinity was proclaimed, enforced, maintained, and (humanly speaking) preserved, far more by the '*Ecclesia docta*' [laity] than by the '*Ecclesia docens*;' [clergy] that the body of the episcopate was unfaithful to its commission, while the body of the laity was faithful to its baptism; that at one time the Pope, at other times the patriarchal, metropolitan, and other great sees, at other times general councils, said what they should not have said, or did what obscured and compromised revealed truth; while, on the other hand, it was the Christian people who, under Providence, were the ecclesiastical strength of Athanasius, Hilary, Eusebius of Vercellæ, and other great solitary confessors, who would have failed without them.[41]

Here we see the passive infallibility of the laity counteracting the misuse of active infallibility by the bishops, thereby upholding Christ's promises to protect the Church from error. The Arian crisis saw the 'obscure, the unlearned, and the weak constitute her [the Church's] real strength'[42] because of their steadfast obedience of faith.

The Obedience of Faith

While God bestows on the Church the graces of inerrancy, indefectibility and infallibility to safeguard and hand on the deposit of faith, he expects members of the Church to play their part through the obedience of faith — yet another unmerited grace to help sinful man respond to, and understand, divine Truth. The Second Vatican Council's Dogmatic Constitution on Divine Revelation, *Dei Verbum*, defined the obedience of faith as follows:

> 'The obedience of faith' (Rom 16:26; see 1:5; II Cor 10:5-6) 'is to be given to God who reveals, an obedience by which man commits his whole self freely to God, offering the full submission of intellect and will to God who reveals,' and freely assenting to the truth revealed by Him. To make this act of faith, the grace of God and the interior help of the Holy Spirit must precede and assist, moving the heart and turning it to God, opening the eyes of the mind and giving 'joy and ease to everyone in assenting to the truth and believing it.' To bring about an ever deeper understanding of revelation the same Holy Spirit constantly brings faith to completion by His gifts. (*DV* 5).

There is a complex inter-play between man's natural freedom and the supernatural capacities bestowed by divine grace that enable the obedience of faith.

St. Paul describes faith as 'bringing into captivity every understanding unto the obedience of Christ' (II Cor 10:5). Commenting on this passage, St. Thomas Aquinas writes, 'The believer's mind is said to be made captive in the sense that it is governed by forces foreign to itself, and not according to its natural powers'. (*De Veritate*, 14). We must freely assent to our minds being governed by Divine Truth — expressed in the dogmas and doctrine of the Church — and the Theological Virtues of Faith, Hope and Charity; and to be capable of that free assent we need to be moved by grace, 'Faith is the act of the intellect when it assents to divine truth under the influence of the will moved by God through grace'. (*ST* II.II. q2.a9).

Our Lord bestowed power and authority on the apostles, and their successors, to uphold the 'obedience of faith' in the Church, and to elicit the 'obedience of faith' from individual believers. As St. Paul expresses it, referring to Jesus as the source of this com-

---

[41] St. John Henry Newman [1859] *On Consulting the Faithful in Matters of Doctrine* [Online] Available at: www.newmanreader.org [Accessed on: 24 September 2022]

[42] St. John Henry Newman [1833] *Arians of the Fourth Century*, Note 5. The Orthodoxy of the Body of the Faithful during the Supremacy of Arianism. [Online] Available at: www.newmanreader. org [Accessed on: 24 September]

mission, 'By whom we have received grace and apostleship for obedience to the faith, in all nations, for his name.' (Rom 1:5). It is through the sacrament of Baptism — administered by the apostolic ministry — that we commit ourselves to the obedience of faith:

> Know you not that all we, who are baptized in Christ Jesus, are baptized in his death? […] But thanks be to God, that you were the servants of sin, but have obeyed from the heart, unto that form of doctrine, into which you have been delivered (Rom 6: 3;17).

We receive the faith from the Church. 'It is the Church that believes first, and so bears, nourishes and sustains my faith' (CCC 168). The disposition necessary to receive this faith is obedience to the Church, our Mother. St. John Chrysostom wrote that Christ gives us the grace necessary for the obedience of faith:

> To obedience, he says, not to questioning and parade (κατασκευὴν) of argument but to obedience. For we were not sent, he means, to argue, but to give those things which we had trusted to our hands. For when the Master declares anything, they that hear should not be nice and curious handlers of what is told them, but receivers only; for this is why the Apostles were sent, to speak what they had heard, not to add anything from their own stock, and that we for our part should believe concerning His Name.[43]

The apostles demanded — and the Church continues to demand — obedient faith as the necessary response to the word of God. And the successors of the apostles have the power to impose the sanction imposed by Christ for disobedience to the faith, 'He that believeth in him is not judged. But he that doth not believe, is already judged: because he believeth not in the name of the only begotten Son of God' (Jn 3:18).[44]

From the beginning it was understood that the obedience of faith was a matter of salvation, as the necessary response of man to God. Obedience is intrinsic to the relationship of the Incarnate God the Son to God the Father: 'And whereas indeed he was the Son of God, he learned obedience by the things which he suffered'; 'He humbled himself, becoming obedient unto death, even to the death of the cross.' (Heb 5:8; Phil 2:8). The obedience of the incarnate Son of God is the cause of our salvation, as St. Paul expresses it, Christ 'became, to all that obey him, the cause of eternal salvation.' (Heb 5:9).

As the Son is obedient to the Father, the Christian must be obedient to Christ if he is to share in his salvific life, 'He that hath my commandments, and keepeth them; he it is that loveth me. And he that loveth me, shall be loved of my Father: and I will love him, and will manifest myself to him'(Jn 14:21; cf. Jn 15:10-15).

Our Lord's last earthly act before his ascension to heaven was to commission the apostles to teach obedience to his commands:

> And Jesus coming, spoke to them, saying: All power is given to me in heaven and in earth. Going therefore, teach ye all nations; baptizing them in the name of the Father, and of the Son, and of the Holy Ghost. Teaching them to observe [obey] all things whatsoever I have commanded you (Mt 28: 18-20).

What does Jesus mean by obedience? It is not the servile, slavish obedience of an autocratic dictatorship:

> You know that the princes of the Gentiles lord it over them; and they that are the greater, exercise power upon them. It shall not be so among you (Mt 20: 26-27).

Rather, it is the obedience that come from being trusted by a superior to share in his plans and purposes:

> I will not now call you servants: for the servant knoweth not what his lord doth. But I have called you friends: because all things whatsoever I have heard of my Father, I have made known to you (Jn 15:15).

---

[43] St. John Chrysostom. *Commentary on Romans* 1:5 [Online] Available at: catenabible.com [Accessed on: 24 September 2022]
[44] Scheeben, M [2019] *Op. cit.*, p. 259-260

Jesus expects from us the virtue of obedience — only possible through grace and the assistance of the Holy Spirit — that he gave as the Son to the Father. Jesus' obedience of the Father was a deeply personal and intimate union of wills, 'the only begotten Son who is in the bosom of the Father'. (Jn 1:18). This is the same obedience that we profess every time we pray the Lord's Prayer, 'Our Father who art in heaven, hallowed be thy name. Thy kingdom come. Thy will be done on earth as it is in heaven' (Mt 6:10).

It is through this Holy Obedience — as a manifestation of sanctifying grace — that we enter into the life of the Most Holy Trinity. At the conclusion of the trinitarian theophany during the Transfiguration of Our Lord, the Father commands, 'And a voice came out of the cloud, saying: This is my beloved Son; hear him.' (Lk 9:35). Obedience derives from the Latin word *ob-audire*, to 'hear or listen to'. The Father commands us to 'listen' to Jesus, as His definitive and final revelation entrusted to the Church. Therefore, Holy Obedience is only expected towards that which is in conformity with the deposit of faith and the rule of faith. Obedience cannot be demanded to any doctrine or disciple that contradicts the apostolic faith.

Obedience in the Church

Recognising that Holy Obedience is constitutive of the Church, and essential to salvation, the Church has deepened her understanding of the types of authority exercised by the Magisterium and the various degrees of obedience required from the faithful. Pope St. John Paul II (1978 to 2005) writes that obedience to Christ's truth is essential to salvation, because we are made holy by 'obedience to the truth' (I Pet 1:22). Only obedience to Christ is protection against the 'darkness of error' and sin':

> This obedience is not always easy. As a result of that mysterious original sin, committed at the prompting of Satan, the one who is 'a liar and the father of lies' (Jn 8:44), man is constantly tempted to turn his gaze away from the living and true God in order to direct it towards idols (cf. I Thes 1:9), exchanging 'the truth about God for a lie' (Rom 1:25). Man's capacity to know the truth is also darkened, and his will to submit to it is weakened. Thus, giving himself over to relativism and scepticism (cf. Jn 18:38), he goes off in search of an illusory freedom apart from truth itself.[45]

The Church defines three different types of obedience, determined by the source of doctrine and the nature of the doctrine, that are required by all members of the Church, from the pope down to the last of the lay faithful:

The Assent of Divine and Catholic Faith

This type of obedience requires that personal assent is based 'directly on faith in the authority of the word of God (*doctrines de ide credenda*)'.[46] This assent of faith is an expression of the theological virtue of faith, received as a supernatural grace from God. Basically, 'divine and Catholic faith' is required when the Magisterium makes a solemn infallible declaration that a doctrine is found in Revelation contained in sacred Scripture and holy Tradition. A truth that is contained in the word of God, but is not defined by the Church, is to be believed by 'divine faith', and a truth contained in the word of God and has been solemnly and infallibly declared by the Church must be held with 'divine and Catholic faith.'[47]

The sources of these infallible declarations can be the pope when he speaks '*ex cathedra*,' [Extraordinary Magisterium] or by an Ecumenical Council in union with the pope [Extraordinary Magisterium] or proposed for belief by the perennial and universal Magisterium of the Church [Ordinary Magisterium]. Due to their source, these

---

[45] Pope St. John Paul II [1993] Encyclical *Veritatis Splendor*, para 1 [Online] Available at: www.vatican.va [Accessed on: 24 September 2022]
[46] Congregation for the Doctrine of the Faith [1998] *Doctrinal Commentary on Concluding Formula of 'Professio Fidei'* [Online] Available at: www.ewtn.com [Accessed on: 24 September 2022]
[47] The Canon Law Society of Great Britain and Ireland [1999] *The Canon Law: Letter & Spirit*. London: Geoffrey Chapman, p.417

truths are considered 'irreformable'. (First Vatican Council, Dogmatic Constitution on the Church of Christ, *Pastor Aeternus*, Chap. 4. Dz 3074).

The First Vatican Council defined this type of obedience as the 'full submission of intellect and will by faith' when 'created reason is completely subject to uncreated truth':

> Since human beings are totally dependent on God as their Creator and Lord, and created reason is completely subject to uncreated truth, we are obliged to yield to God the Revealer full submission of intellect and will by faith.[48]

This type of obedience is so fundamental to the Church that it has been defined by the *Code of Canon Law*:

> Those things are to be believed by divine and catholic faith which are contained in the word of God as it has been written or handed down by tradition, that is, in the single deposit of faith entrusted to the Church, and which are at the same time proposed as divinely revealed either by the solemn Magisterium of the Church, or by its ordinary and universal Magisterium, which in fact is manifested by the common adherence of Christ's faithful under the guidance of the sacred Magisterium. All are therefore bound to avoid any contrary doctrines (Can. 750 § 1).[49]

Cardinal Joseph Ratzinger, as Prefect for the Congregation for the Doctrine of the Faith, provided examples of the range of doctrines that require the assent of faith:

- Christological dogmas.
- Marian dogmas.
- The doctrine of the institution of the sacraments by Christ and their efficacy with regard to grace.
- The doctrine of the real and substantial presence of Christ in the Eucharist and the sacrificial nature of the eucharistic celebration.
- The doctrine of the foundation of the Church by the will of Christ.
- The doctrine on the primacy and infallibility of the Roman Pontiff.
- The doctrine on the existence of original sin.
- The doctrine on the immortality of the spiritual soul and on the immediate recompense after death.
- The absence of error in the inspired sacred texts.
- The doctrine on the grave immorality of direct and voluntary killing of an innocent human being.[50]

Religious Assent

This type of obedience is based on faith in the 'Holy Spirit's assistance to the Magisterium and on the Catholic doctrine of the infallibility of the Magisterium (*doctrines de fide tenenda*).'[51] Religious assent — derived from one's affirmation of membership of the Catholic Church — requires that doctrines concerning faith and morals must be 'firmly accepted and held' when the Magisterium proposes them 'in a definitive way', because they are 'strictly and intimately connected with Revelation', even if not divinely revealed in sacred Scripture and holy Tradition.[52] These doctrines are called Catholic

---

[48] First Vatican Council [1870] *Dogmatic Constitution on the Catholic Faith, Dei Fidei*, Chap. 3, para 1 [Online] Available at: www.papalencyclicals.net/ [Accessed on: 24 September 2022]
[49] *Code of Canon Law* [1983] [Online] Available at: www.vatican.va [Accessed on: 24 September 2022]
[50] Congregation for the Doctrine of the Faith [1998] *Doctrinal Commentary on Concluding Formula of 'Professio Fidei'* [Online] Available at: www.ewtn.com [Accessed on: 24 September 2022]
[51] *Ibid.*
[52] Congregation for the Doctrine of the Faith [1990] *Instruction on the Ecclesial Vocation of the theologian, Donum Veritatis*, 22 [Online] Available at: www.vatican.va [Accessed on: 24 September 2022]

Truths (*veritates catholicae*) to distinguish them from the Divine Truths of Revelation.[53] These doctrines are necessary for faithfully keeping and expounding the deposit of faith.[54] They are so intrinsically connected with Revelation that to deny them would undermine Divine Truths.

In response to the widespread promulgation of errors in the Church, especially by theologians, in 1998 Pope St. John Paul II added text to canon 750 to make explicit the obediential obligation of religious assent to all doctrines concerning faith and morals proposed by the Magisterium 'in a definitive way', even if they have not been solemnly proposed by the Magisterium as formerly revealed:

> Furthermore, each and everything set forth definitively by the Magisterium of the Church regarding teaching on faith and morals must be firmly accepted and held; namely, those things required for the holy keeping and faithful exposition of the deposit of faith; therefore, anyone who rejects propositions which are to be held definitively sets himself against the teaching of the Catholic Church (Can. 750 § 2).[55]

The Congregation for the Doctrine of the Faith also provided examples of the range of doctrines 'connected with revelation by a logical necessity' that require religious assent:[56]

In his apostolic letter *Ordinatio Sacerdotalis*,[57] Pope St. John Paul II reaffirmed that priestly ordination was reserved to men only must be held definitively because it was 'founded' on the word of God contained in sacred Scripture and holy Tradition, and set forth infallibly in the perennial ordinary and universal Magisterium:

> Wherefore, in order that all doubt may be removed regarding a matter of great importance, a matter which pertains to the Church's divine constitution itself, in virtue of my ministry of confirming the brethren (cf. Lk 22:32) I declare that the Church has no authority whatsoever to confer priestly ordination on women and that this judgment is to be definitively held by all the Church's faithful. (*Ordinatio Sacerdotalis*, 4).

Cardinal Ratzinger points out that though at the time Pope John Paul II did not wish to proceed to a dogmatic definition, this does not prohibit the Church at a future date solemnly declaring it as a doctrine that must be believed with the assent of faith as divinely revealed.

Pope St. John Paul II reaffirmed that the doctrine on the illicitness of euthanasia must be held definitively as 'a grave violation of the law of God':

> I confirm that euthanasia is a grave violation of the law of God, since it is the deliberate and morally unacceptable killing of a human person. This doctrine is based upon the natural law and upon the written word of God, is transmitted by the Church's Tradition and taught by the ordinary and universal Magisterium.[58]

Cardinal Ratzinger observed that the doctrine of the illicitness of euthanasia was logically connected to Revelation, though not explicitly found in the word of God 'since Scripture does not seem to be aware of the concept.' However, sacred Scripture does contain the divine truth that God is the sole author and arbiter of life and death.

There is also a category of truths known as 'dogmatic facts' that must be firmly accepted and held with religious assent. Ott defines them as 'historical facts, which not

---

[53] Ott, L *Op. cit.*, p.8.
[54] Congregation for the Doctrine of the Faith [1998] *Op cit*.
[55] Pope St. John Paul II [1998] Apostolic Letter Motu Proprio *Ad Tuendam Fidem* [Online] Available at: www.vatican.va [Accessed on: 24 September 2022]
[56] Congregation for the Doctrine of the Faith [1998] *Op. cit*.
[57] Pope St. John Paul II [1994] *Ordinatio Sacerdotalis* [Online] Available at: www.vatican.va [Accessed on: 24 September 2022]
[58] Pope St. John Paul II [1995] Encyclical *Evangelium Vitae*, para 65 [Online] Available at: www. vatican.va [Accessed on: 24 September 2022]

revealed, but which are intrinsically connected with revealed truth.'[59] For example, the legitimacy of the election of the pope, the celebration of an ecumenical council, the canonisation of saints, the declaration of Pope Leo XIII in the Apostolic Letter *Apostolicae Curae* on the invalidity of Anglican ordinations.[60]

The final category of truths requiring the religious assent of firm acceptance and adherence are *Truths of Reason*. These are philosophical definitions, which have not been revealed, but are intrinsically associated with revealed truths in two ways; either as presuppositions — the possibility of supernatural knowledge, proofs of God's existence, the existence of the soul, freedom of will — or employed in the promulgation of dogma — philosophical truths such as person, substance, consubstantial, transubstantiation.[61]

The faithful must reject any school of philosophy or philosophical term that undermines the Truths of Reason that are intrinsically associated with revealed truths:

> ...the Church, which along with the apostolic office of teaching, received the charge of guarding the deposit of faith, has also from God the right and the duty to proscribe what is falsely called knowledge (cf. I Tim 6:20), lest anyone be decided by philosophy and vain fallacy (cf. Col 2:8). Hence all believing Christians are not only forbidden to defend as legitimate conclusions of science such opinions that they realise to be contrary to the doctrine of faith, but they are seriously bound to account them as errors that put on the fallacious appearance of truth (First Vatican Council. Dogmatic Constitution on the Catholic Faith, *Dei Filius*, Chap. 4.).[62]

The Submission of Will and Intellect

This type of obedience calls for the religious submission of will and intellect to doctrines that the Magisterium does not intend to proclaim 'definitively'.[63] These include all doctrines that have not been solemnly declared or proposed as definitive but are an 'authentic' expression of the perennial and universal ordinary Magisterium of the Roman Pontiff or the College of Bishops.

As well as including solid principles of the Faith, they contain 'contingent and conjectural elements' that are reformable. 'It often only becomes possible with the passage of time to distinguish between what is necessary and what is contingent.'[64] The Magisterium issues such doctrines for three reasons: 1) As a warning against ideas and opinions that could lead to error; 2) To arrive at a deeper understanding of revelation; 3) To recall the conformity of a teaching with the truths of faith.[65] Erroneous or dangerous opinions and ideas contrary to such reformable doctrines can be designated '*tuto doceri non potest*' [not able to be safely taught].[66]

The Code of Canon Law defines the religious submission of will and intellect as follows:

> While the assent of faith is not required, a religious submission of intellect and will is to be given to any doctrine which either the Supreme Pontiff or the College of Bishops, exercising their authentic Magisterium, declare upon a matter of faith and morals, even though they do not intend to proclaim that doctrine by definitive act. Christ's faithful are therefore to ensure that they avoid whatever does not accord with that doctrine (Canon 752).

Canon Law makes the distinction between the 'authentic' magisterium of the pope and college of bishops and their 'infallible' magisterium.[67] The 'authentic magisterium'

---

[59] Ott, L *Op. cit.*, p.8
[60] Congregation for the Doctrine of the Faith [1990] *Op. cit.*
[61] Ott, L *Op. cit.*, p.9
[62] Denzinger, H [2010] *Op. cit.*, p.606, Dz 3018-3018
[63] Congregation for the Doctrine of the Faith [1990] *Op. cit.*, para 23
[64] *Ibid.*, para 24
[65] Congregation for the Doctrine of the Faith [1998] *Op. cit.*, para 10
[66] *Ibid.*
[67] The Canon Law Society of Great Britain and Ireland [1999] *The Canon Law: Letter & Spirit*. London: Geoffrey Chapman, p.419

does not have the highest authority because it is non-infallible, non-definitive, and non *ex cathedra*.[68]

The faithful are expected — out of loyalty to the Church — to seek to understand these doctrines 'within the logic of faith and under the impulse of obedience to the faith…The willingness to submit loyally to the teaching of the Magisterium on matters *per se* not irreformable must be the rule'. (*Donum Veritatis*, 23). However, the Church allows for questions to be raised concerning the 'timeliness, the form, or even the contents of magisterial interventions' (*Donum Veritatis*, 24).

Furthermore, in light of the fact that these doctrines are reformable, it is recognised that various degrees of adherence of mind and intellect are permissible, determined by discerning the ideas and intent of the pope or bishop. *Lumen Gentium* 25 proposes a number of indicators that must be taken into account when judging the degree of submission of mind and intellect required by a pope: 'His mind and will in the matter may be known either from the character of the documents, from his frequent repetition of the same doctrine, or from his manner of speaking.'

Therefore, judging the degree of submission of will and intellect required by papal teaching depends on ascertaining the 'mind and will' of the pope in the matter. For example, Pope Francis clearly indicated his 'mind and will' in the introduction to his Post Synodal Exhortation *Amoris Laetitia* when he wrote:

> Since 'time is greater than space', I would make it clear that not all discussions of doctrinal, moral or pastoral issues need to be settled by interventions of the magisterium. Unity of teaching and practice is certainly necessary in the Church, but this does not preclude various ways of interpreting some aspects of that teaching or drawing certain consequences from it.[69]

Cardinal Raymond Burke, former prefect of the Supreme Tribunal of the Apostolic Signatura, concluded from this declaration in *Amoris Laetitia* that Pope Francis intended to indicate that his post synodal apostolic exhortation was not magisterial teaching but his own personal thoughts:

> The only key to the correct interpretation of *Amoris Laetitia* is the constant teaching of the Church and her discipline that safeguards and fosters this teaching. Pope Francis makes clear, from the beginning, that the post-synodal apostolic exhortation is not an act of the magisterium (3). The very form of the document confirms the same. It is written as a reflection of the Holy Father on the work of the last two sessions of the Synod of Bishops. For instance, in Chapter Eight, which some wish to interpret as the proposal of a new discipline with obvious implications for the Church's doctrine, Pope Francis, citing his post-synodal apostolic exhortation *Evangelii Gaudium*, declares:

> I understand those who prefer a more rigorous pastoral care which leaves no room for confusion. But I sincerely believe that Jesus wants a Church attentive to the goodness which the Holy Spirit sows in the midst of human weakness, a Mother who, while clearly expressing her objective teaching, 'always does what good she can, even if in the process her shoes get soiled by the mud of the street' (308).

> In other words, the Holy Father is proposing what he personally believes is the will of Christ for his Church, but he does not intend to impose his point of view, nor to condemn those who insist on what he calls 'a more rigorous pastoral care. The personal, that is, non-magisterial, nature of the document is also evident in the fact that the references cited are principally the final report of the 2015 session of the Synod of Bishops and the addresses and homilies of Pope Francis himself. There is no consistent effort to relate the text, in general, or these citations to the magisterium, the Fathers of the Church and other proven authors.

---

[68] Miras, J, et al [2004] *The Exegetical Commentary on Canon Law.* Vol.3. Downers Grove: Midwest Theological Forum, p.3269-70

[69] Pope Francis [2016] Post-Synodal Apostolic Exhortation *Amoris Laetitia*, para 3 [Online] Available at: www.vatican.va [Accessed on: 24 September 2022]

What is more, as noted above, a document which is the fruit of the Synod of Bishops must always be read in the light of the purpose of the synod itself, namely, to safeguard and foster what the Church has always taught and practiced in accord with her teaching.

In other words, a post-synodal apostolic exhortation, by its very nature, does not propose new doctrine and discipline, but applies the perennial doctrine and discipline to the situation of the world at the time.[70]

There are other indications that the faithful are justified in approaching Pope Francis' documents as expressions of his personal opinion.

Many of Pope Francis' documents are self-referential. Prior to Pope Francis, pontifical documents – papal encyclicals, apostolic letters, and apostolic exhortations – claimed magisterial authority by citing the *Fidei Depositum* expressed in the work of previous popes, councils, liturgy and saints. This tradition situated the pontifical document within the ordinary magisterium of the Church. However, an examination of non-scriptural citations shows that Pope Francis quotes himself as a major source. For example, his encyclical *Fratelli Tutti* contains 288 non-scriptural citations, of which nearly 180 citations are from the documents, homilies and speeches of Pope Francis.[71]

Another indication that some of Pope Francis' documents – or at least parts of his documents – should be considered his personal opinion and not an expression of the ordinary magisterium – is his use of non-Catholic sources. While other popes quoted non-Catholic sources as examples of error,[72] Pope Francis presents non-Catholic sources as authoritative statements. For example, his encyclical *Laudato Si* marks a radi-cal – and untenable – departure from magisterial teaching by presenting the religious writings of a Muslim mystic as an authoritative source in the section 'Sacramental Signs and the Celebration of Rest'[73] (*Laudato Si* 232, footnote 159).

The Canonical Profession of Faith

The Code of Canon Law stipulates that those assuming certain offices, or positions, in the Church make a personal profession of faith (Can. 833). In 1989 the Congregation for the Doctrine of the Faith issued the formula of this profession of faith, which includes the explicit obligation to uphold the three types of holy obedience – the Assent of Divine and Catholic Faith, Religious Assent and The Submission of Will and Intellect:

With firm faith, I also believe everything contained in the word of God, whether written or handed down in Tradition, which the Church, either by a solemn judgment or by the ordinary and universal Magisterium, sets forth to be believed as divinely revealed.

I also firmly accept and hold each and everything definitively proposed by the Church regarding teaching on faith and morals.

Moreover, I adhere with religious submission of will and intellect to the teachings which either the Roman Pontiff or the College of Bishops enunciate when they exercise their authentic Magisterium, even if they do not intend to proclaim these teachings by a definitive act.[74]

[70] Burke, R [2016] *'Amoris Laetitia' and the Constant Teaching and Practice of the Church* [Online] Available at: www.ncregister.com [Accessed on: 25 September 2022]

[71] Kabel, S [2020] *Citation Sources in Papal Documents* [Online] Available at: sharonkabel.com [Accessed on: 25 September 2022]

[72] For example, Pope Benedict XVI's encyclical *Deus Caritas Est* contains quotations from the atheist philosopher Friedrich Wilhelm Nietzsche to illustrate a misconception about the Christian approach to love. Pope Benedict [2005] *Deus Caritas Est*, para 3 [Online] Available at: www.vatican.va [Accessed on: 25 September 2022]

[73] Pope Francis [2016] Encyclical *Laudato Si'*, para 232, footnote 159 [Online] Available at: www.vatican.va [Accessed on: 25 September 2022]

[74] Congregation for the Doctrine of the Faith [1988] *Profession of Faith* [Online] Available at: www.vatican.va [Accessed on: 25 September 2022]

Those obliged to explicitly state their adherence to this threefold holy obedience include all who have received the sacrament of Holy Orders since 1989 — bishops, priests and deacons — and every archbishop elevated to the sacred College of Cardinals. All things being equal, Archbishop Jorge Mario Bergoglio of Buenos Aires will have publicly professed his adherence to threefold holy obedience when he was elevated to the sacred College of Cardinals by Pope St. John Paul II in 21 February 2001.

In his 1998 Apostolic Letter Motu Proprio *Ad Tuendam Fidem* [To Protect the Faith] Pope St. John Paul II stated that making this explicit profession of adherence to holy obedience was necessary not just for those who undertook theological investigations but also those 'united to a particular power in the governance of the Church'. Pope St. John Paul II saw this solemn commitment to holy obedience as necessary because the Church was threatened by errors promulgated by members of the faithful:

> TO PROTECT THE FAITH of the Catholic Church against errors arising from certain members of the Christian faithful, especially from among those dedicated to the various disciplines of sacred theology, we, whose principal duty is to confirm the brethren in the faith (Lk 22:32), consider it absolutely necessary to add to the existing texts of the *Code of Canon Law* and the Code of Canons of the Eastern Churches, new norms which expressly impose the obligation of upholding truths proposed in a definitive way by the Magisterium of the Church, and which also establish related canonical sanctions.[75]

The Role of the Pope in Safeguarding the *Fidei Depositum*

Though all the baptised have the responsibility of safeguarding the Deposit of Faith through living by the Rule of Faith, no one has greater responsibility than the Bishop of Rome, the successor of St. Peter. Each contemporary pope is the supreme teacher of the Faith and guardian of doctrine.

The primacy of St. Peter over doctrine and discipline was recognised from the beginning of the Church. After his conversion St. Paul went to Jerusalem to learn from St. Peter, 'Then, after three years, I went to Jerusalem, to see Peter, and I tarried with him fifteen days' (Gal 1:18). Later St. Paul, accompanied by St. Barnabas, went to Jerusalem to consult on disputed issues which were resolved at the Apostolic Council led by St. Peter.

The role of the pope as supreme teacher of the faith was solemnly declared by various councils. The Second Council of Lyons (1274) stated that the Bishop of Rome has 'the duty to defend the truth of the faith, and it is his responsibility to resolve all disputed matters in the area of faith' (*Dz* 861). While the Council of Florence (1439) acknowledged him as 'the father and teacher of all Christians' (*Dz* 1307).

The Rock of Petrine Faith

The primacy of St. Peter, and his successors, as the supreme teacher and guardian of doctrine was instituted by our Lord Jesus Christ and is to be sustained by him until the end of the world. The Petrine Faith is the foundation stone on which Christ builds his Church, 'And I say to thee: That thou art Peter; and upon this rock I will build my church, and the gates of hell shall not prevail against it.' (Mt 16:18).

It is St. Peter's faith — expressed in the aboriginal credal formula, 'Thou art Christ, the Son of the living God.' (Mt 16:16) — that is the holy rock on which the Church is built. It is a faith that is not of his own making, but is rather an explicit grace of God, 'Blessed art thou, Simon Bar-Jona: because flesh and blood hath not revealed it to thee, but my Father who is in heaven.' (Mt 16:17).

What is the significance of the Petrine Faith being called a 'rock' by our Lord? In the Old Testament 'rock' represents the solidity and safety that God provides to those that seek refuge in him:

---

[75] Pope St. John Paul II [1998] Apostolic Letter Motu Proprio *Ad Tuendam Fidem* [Online] Available at: www.vatican.va [Accessed on: 25 September 2022]

> Our God is our refuge and strength: a helper in troubles, which have found us exceedingly. Therefore we will not fear, when the earth shall be troubled; and the mountains shall be removed into the heart of the sea. Their waters roared and were troubled: the mountains were troubled with his strength (Ps 45:2-4).

In the Old Testament God's rock-like shelter of the faithful is also conveyed by the metaphors of *citadel, rampart, strong tower* and *harbour*. God shares this rock-like stability and solidity with Abraham through the grace of faith. Abraham, the father of the faith, is described in terms of rock, 'look unto the rock whence you are hewn' (Isa 51:1). A rabbinical text describes Abraham's faith in terms of solidity and safety that holds 'back chaos, the onrushing primordial flood of destruction, and thus sustains creation':

> YHWH spoke: 'How can I create the world, when these godless men will arise to vex me?' But when God looked upon Abraham, who was also to be born, he spoke: 'Behold, I have found a rock upon which I can build and found the world.'[76]

Our Lord describes obedience to his teaching as building on a foundation of rock that will protect us during destructive storms:

> Everyone therefore that heareth these my words, and doth them, shall be likened to a wise man that built his house upon a rock, And the rain fell, and the floods came, and the winds blew, and they beat upon that house, and it fell not, for it was founded on a rock. (Mt 7: 24-25).

When Jesus designates St. Peter as the rock on which he builds his Church, he is saying that the Petrine Faith will protect the faithful by sharing in his security and stability as God. It is important to understand that this Petrine quality does not derive from the original Peter merely as a man, but is a grace from God, 'flesh and blood hath not revealed it to thee, but my Father who is in heaven.' St. Peter, and successive popes, are rocks when they themselves are obedient to the revelation of God's Truth. Consequently, the Petrine Faith is stable, dependable, unchangeable and consistent through time.

The Power of the Keys

St. Peter's role as supreme teacher and guardian of the Faith is also conveyed by our Lord bestowing on him, and his successors, the power of the Keys:

> And I will give to thee the keys of the kingdom of heaven. And whatsoever thou shalt bind upon earth, it shall be bound also in heaven: and whatsoever thou shalt loose on earth, it shall be loosed also in heaven. (Mt 16:19).

In the Ancient Near East, the bestowal of 'keys' was a symbol of authority and control over a household, for keys had the power to lock or unlock doors to grant entry; such as the authority vested in a vizier or chamberlain over the royal household. It was a position of trust bestowed by the king who remained the ultimate authority over the household. The Book of Isaiah recounts Eliakim receiving the power of the keys from God over the House of David:

> And I will lay the key of the house of David upon his shoulder: and he shall open, and none shall shut: and he shall shut, and none shall open. (Isa 22:22).

The key handed to Eliakim does not belong to Eliakim, it is not his personal possession, but belongs to God and is the property of the House of David.

The symbolism of our Lord handing St. Peter the 'keys of the kingdom of heaven' conveys that the Son of God has entrusted Peter, and his successors, with the role of doorkeeper to the door of Faith that gives access to the Kingdom of God (Acts 14:27).

Pope Clement VI (1342-1352) explained that the power of the keys gave the successor of St. Peter doctrinal authority over the Church:

---

[76] Ratzinger, J [1996] *Called to Communion: Understanding the Church Today.* San Francisco: Ignatius Press, p. 56

> …when doubts arise concerning the Catholic faith, the Roman pontiff alone is able to put an end (to them) by an authentic decision that must be adhered to inviolably; and what he himself determines to be true, by virtue of the authority of the keys handed over to him by Christ, is true and catholic, and what he determines to be false and heretical must be considered as such.[77]

The important thing to bear in mind in this regard, is that though Christ has handed over the powers of the key to St. Peter, the keys remain Christ's, representing his absolute sovereignty over the Church, 'These things saith the Holy One and the true one, he that hath the key of David; he that openeth, and no man shutteth; shutteth, and no man openeth' (Rev 3:7). What the pope does with the power of the keys must, therefore, be in conformity with the will of Christ, expressed in the Deposit of Faith and the Rule of Faith.

Our Lord emphasised the authority of the Petrine Office to safeguard doctrine by linking the power of the keys with the duty of 'binding and loosing'. This is a rabbinical expression referring to the authority of the rabbi to prohibit or permit questions submitted to him for consideration.[78] Ratzinger commented that as well as standing for the authority to make doctrinal decisions it also denoted a further disciplinary power to impose or lift a ban.[79]

There is a direct connection between the exercise of these Petrine doctrinal and juridical powers on earth and these acts being mirrored in heaven, 'And whatsoever thou shalt bind upon earth, it shall be bound also in heaven: and whatsoever thou shalt loose on earth, it shall be loosed also in heaven.' (Mt 16: 19). Some commentators interpret this as meaning that heaven ratifies the decisions taken by a pope. But this needs further examination and explanation. It can't mean that every doctrinal judgment and decision made by a pope is automatically ratified by heaven even if it contradicts God's revelation. This would absurdly make man the master of God's truth, when in reality man is mastered by God. What it must mean is that a pope could never make a doctrinal judgment that contradicts God's revelation. Our Lord's promise of heaven's ratification of the power of binding and loosing is an implicit declaration of the indefectibility of the Petrine office.

This brings us to an antinomy at the heart of the Church's teaching about the doctrinal authority of the Petrine office — on the one hand, tradition acknowledges the indefectibility of the Bishop of Rome, while on the other, tradition has considered the implications of a heretical pope on the throne of St. Peter.

The Indefectibility of the Bishop of Rome

The origin of the doctrine of the indefectibility of the Supreme Pontiff can be traced back to the Lucan account of the primacy of St. Peter:

> And the Lord said: Simon, Simon, behold Satan hath desired to have you, that he may sift you as wheat: But I have prayed for thee, that thy faith fail not: and thou, being once converted, confirm thy brethren (Lk 22:32).

The key point here is that the Son of God personally prayed that St. Peter's faith would not 'fail'. The Greek word translated as 'fail' is *ekleipó* which has a range of meanings, from fail and cease to come to an end, expire and die.[80] This could cover various sins against the faith, from a temporary loss of faith to apostasy. St. John Chrysostom interpreted ekleipó in this context as meaning 'that thou be not finally lost.'[81]

[77] Denzinger, H [2010] *Op. cit.*, p.311 1064
[78] Wilhelm, J etc. [1899] *A Manual of Catholic Theology Based on Scheeben's 'Dogmatik'*. Vol II. Chicago: Benziger Brother, p. 308
[79] Ratzinger, J [1991] *Op. cit.*, p. 63
[80] *Strong's Concordance* [1890] [Online] Available at: biblehub.com [Accessed on: 25 September 2022]
[81] St. John Chrysostom *Commentary on John* 13.36 [Online] Available at: www.newadvent.org [Accessed on: 25 September 2022]

Understanding that there can be nothing more efficacious than the prayer of the Son of God, the Church has come to understand this divine prayer as meaning that Jesus gave St. Peter a 'privilege which is both personal and transferable. Peter's faith, despite his fall, cannot fail because it is supported by the efficacious prayer of our Lord himself.'[82] St. Augustine commented that our Lord's prayer 'procured' God's preservation of St. Peter's faith, 'that it should not fail by giving way to temptation.'[83]

Commenting on Luke 22:32, Tertullian describes Christ's prayer as a shield protecting St. Peter's faith from the devil:

> 'Behold, Satan asked that he might sift you as grain; but I have prayed for you that your faith fail not;' that is, that the devil should not have power granted him sufficient to endanger his faith. Whence it is manifest that both things belong to God, the shaking of faith as well as the shielding of it, when both are sought from Him — the shaking by the devil, the shielding by the Son. And certainly, when the Son of God has faith's protection absolutely committed to Him, beseeching it of the Father, from whom He receives all power in heaven and on earth, how entirely out of the question is it that the devil should have the assailing of it in his own power!'[84]

Our Lord's prayer does not mean that St. Peter's faith was automatically preserved from failing, as if he had no free will in the matter. As always, the relationship between grace and nature is complex. St. Augustine, the Doctor gratiae [Doctor of Grace], examined the relationship between our Lord's prayer and St. Peter's faith. He asks the question, in the light of Christ praying that Peter's faith would not fail, could Peter's faith have failed if he had willed it? St. Augustine answers that St. Peter's faith could not fail because our Lord had prepared his will, 'But because "the will is prepared by the Lord" therefore Christ's petition on his behalf could not be a vain petition.' According to St. Augustine, our Lord's prayer gave Peter 'a most free, strong, invincible, persevering will!' with which he could make the response of faith after his loss of faith represented by his threefold denial of our Lord (Jn 18:15–27; cf. Mt 26:33–35; Mk 14:29–31; Lk 22:33–34). St. Augustine concludes:

> Behold to what an extent the freedom of the will is defended in accordance with the grace of God, not in opposition to it; because the human will does not attain grace by freedom, but rather attains freedom by grace, and a delightful constancy, and an insuperable fortitude that it may persevere.[85]

St. Augustine goes on to say that St. Peter's faith did not fail because he 'gloried in the Lord':

> Therefore when Christ says, 'I have prayed for thee that thy faith fail not,' we may understand that it was said to him who is built upon the rock. And thus the man of God, not only because he has obtained mercy to be faithful, but also because faith itself does not fail, if he glories, must glory in the Lord.[86]

This is clearly a reference to Peter's Christological profession of faith, the Church's foundational act of glorying in the Lord, 'Thou art Christ, the Son of the living God.' (Mt 16:16).

What does this mean for our understanding of the indefectibility of the successors of St. Peter? There are a number of possible implications arising from these patristic insights into the significance of Christ's prayer for Peter's faith. Our Lord's prayer

---

[82] The Navarre Bible [2003] *Saint Luke's Gospel* Dublin: Four Courts Press, p.180.
[83] St. Augustine. *On the Proceedings of Pelagius*, Chap. 35 [Online] Available at: www.newadvent. org [Accessed on: 25 September 2022]
[84] Tertullian. *On Running Away from Persecution*, part 4 [Online] Available at: www.newadvent.org [Accessed on: 25 September 2022]
[85] St. Augustine. *On Rebuke and Grace*, Chap. 17 [Online] Available at: www.newadvent.org [Accessed on: 26 September 2022]
[86] *Ibid.*, Chap. 38

doesn't guarantee that every doctrinal judgement and declaration of the pope is automatically indefectible, but rather that our Lord gives the necessary grace to enable the pope's will to be free, strong, invincible and persevering in the face of temptations against the Faith. But like all graces, the extent of the recipient's co-operation depends on whether or not he places obstacles in the way of grace or through disposition and virtue has placed himself in a position to receive this grace of indefectibility. The pope will be in such a position if he leads a life that 'glories in the Lord', that is, that he remains true to divine revelation, just as St. Peter did with his Christological profession of faith which he received from God, not from human thinking. A pope who glories in the world, or humanity, or himself, rather than our Lord Jesus Christ, will not be shielded by Christ from sins against Faith.

The Preservation of the See of Rome from Error

Multiple sources can be cited to support the understanding that the See of Rome, the See of Peter, will be preserved from error. The traditional belief that the See of St. Peter will be preserved free of error brings together the doctrinal primacy and indefectibility of St. Peter with St. Paul's praise of the faith of Roman Christians, 'your faith is spoken of in the whole world.' (Rom 1:8). As the location of the martyrdom of St. Peter and St. Paul, Rome held a unique reputation for her preservation of the apostolic Faith from error.

Dr. Ludwig Ott observed that it was an apostolic doctrine that 'the See of St. Peter always remains unimpaired by any error, according to the divine promise of our Lord the Saviour made to the chief of His disciples'. (Lk 22:32).

In his letter to the Romans, St. Ignatius of Antioch (c. 50 to c. 98/117) referred to the purity of the Roman Christians' faith, 'filled inseparably with the grace of God, and are purified from every strange taint.'[87] After listing the early popes, St. Irenaeus of Lyons (c. 130 to c. 202) explains that their witness as bishops of Rome provides 'abundant proof that there is one and the same vivifying faith, which has been preserved in the Church from the apostles until now, and handed down in truth.'[88] Furthermore, St. Cyprian, referring to St. Paul's praise of the Romans' faith (Rom 1:8), wrote about the absurdity of heretical and schismatic bishops seeking union with the See of St. Peter:

> …they still dare — a false bishop having been appointed for them by, heretics— to set sail and to bear letters from schismatic and profane persons to the throne of Peter, and to the chief church whence priestly unity takes its source; and not to consider that these were the Romans whose faith was praised in the preaching of the apostle, to whom faithlessness could have no access.[89]

Famously, the Formula of Pope St. Hormisdas (514 to 523) expressed the indefectibility of the See of Rome, incorporated into decree of the First Vatican Council (1869 to 1870) (*Dz* 3066).[90] Pope St. Hormisdas declared:

> The beginning of salvation is to guard the rule of the right faith and to deviate in no way from the determinations of the Fathers. And because one cannot ignore the words of our Lord Jesus Christ when he said, 'You are Peter, and on this rock I will build my Church' [Mt 16:18], what was said has been borne out by actual results, for in the Apostolic See that Catholic faith has always been preserved immaculate.[91]

It is important to note that Pope St. Hormisdas emphasises that guarding the Rule of Faith and not deviating from the Tradition of the Fathers are intrinsic to preserving the

---

[87] St. Ignatius of Antioch. *The Epistle of Ignatius to the Romans* [Online] Available at: www.newadvent.org [Accessed on: 26 September 2022]

[88] St. Irenaeus. *Against Heresies*, Bk. III, Chap. 3, para 3 [Online] Available at: www.newadvent.org [Accessed on: 26 September 2022]

[89] St. Cyprian of Carthage. *Epistle 54, To Cornelius, Concerning Fortunatus and Felicissimus, or Against the Heretics*, para 14 [Online] Available at: www.newadvent.org [Accessed on: 26 September 2022]

[90] Denzinger, H [2010] *Op. cit.*, p.614, *Dz* 3066

[91] Denzinger, H [2010] *Ibid.*, p. 131, *Dz* 363

Faith immaculate in the See of Rome. History shows that not all popes have done this.

The Problem of Pope Honorius I

The doctrine of the preservation of the See of Rome from error was also declared at the earlier Third Council of Constantinople (680 to 681) by Pope St. Agatho's letter to the Emperor and Council Fathers. Pope St. Agatho wrote the following about the faith of Rome:

> ...this Apostolic Church of his has never turned away from the path of truth in any direction of error, whose authority, as that of the Prince of all the Apostles, the whole Catholic Church, and the Ecumenical Synods have faithfully embraced, and followed in all things; and all the venerable Fathers have embraced its Apostolic doctrine, through which they as the most approved luminaries of the Church of Christ have shone; and the holy orthodox doctors have venerated and followed it, while the heretics have pursued it with false criminations and with derogatory hatred.[92]

However, although this ecumenical council affirmed this explicit declaration of the purity of the faith in Rome — and proclaimed that St. Peter had spoken through Pope St. Agatho — the Council Fathers went on to declare by solemn dogmatic decree that one of Pope St. Agatho's predecessors — Pope Honorius I (625 to 638) — was anathema for not defending the Apostolic Faith and for confirming 'impious doctrines':

> And with these we define that there shall be expelled from the holy Church of God and anathematised Honorius who was some time Pope of Old Rome, because of what we found written by him to Sergius, that in all respects he followed his view and confirmed his impious doctrines.[93]

Furthermore, the council's decree of anathematisation against Pope Honorius I was ratified by Pope St. Leo II (682 to 683), and his successors and by further ecumenical councils, declaring that Pope Honorius had committed treachery by polluting the purity of the Apostolic Faith of the See of Rome:

> We anathematise the inventors of the new error, that is, Theodore, Sergius, . . . and also Honorius, who did not attempt to sanctify this Apostolic Church with the teaching of Apostolic tradition, but by profane treachery permitted its purity to be polluted.[94]

Pope St. Leo II wrote a number of letters explaining that Pope Honorius I had not succeeded in permanently polluting the Apostolic Faith of Rome. In the letters Pope Leo II wrote:

> And with them Honorius, who allowed the unspotted rule of Apostolic tradition, which he received from his predecessors, to be tarnished; With Honorius, who did not, as became the Apostolic authority, extinguish the flame of heretical teaching in its first beginning, but fostered it by his negligence.[95]

The notoriety surrounding Pope Honorius is indicated in how he was addressed in the decrees of the Third Council of Constantinople. It baldly refers to Honorius I as 'Honorius who was some time Pope of Old Rome.' This is dismissive compared to its descriptions of other popes: Pope St. Agatho is referred to as 'the most holy and thrice-blessed pope of elder Rome'; and Pope St. Leo I as 'the all-holy and most blessed Leo, pope of the same elder Rome.'

It's important to note that Pope St. Leo II does not accuse Pope Honorius of being an active proponent of heresy, but of negligence in permitting the Apostolic faith to be pol-

---

[92] Third Council of Constantinople. *The Letter of Pope Agatho* [Online] Available at: www. newadvent.org [Accessed on: 26 September 2022]
[93] *Ibid.*
[94] *Catholic Encyclopedia* vol. VIII. Gregory — Infallibility [1913] New York: The Encyclopedia Press, Inc, p. 455
[95] *Ibid.*

luted by heretical teaching. As Ludwig Ott concluded, '[Pope Leo II] did not reproach him with heresy, but with negligence in the suppression of error.'[96] Pope Honorius I did not solemnly declare heresy *ex cathedra* but was negligent in the exercise of his ordinary magisterium. Concerning Pope Honorius I Prof. Roberto de Mattei wrote:

> Pope Honorius's letters…are undoubtedly magisterial acts, but in the non-infallible ordinary Magisterium there may be errors and even, in exceptional cases, heretical formulations. The pope can fall into heresy, but cannot ever pronounce a heresy *ex cathedra*. In Honorius's case, as the Benedictine patrologist Dom John Chapman observes, it cannot be affirmed that he intended to formulate a sentence ex cathedra, defining and binding: 'Honorius was fallible, was wrong, was a heretic, precisely because he did not, as he should have done, declare authoritatively the Petrine tradition of the Roman Church.'[97]

The condemnation and anathematisation of Pope Honorius I has been a cause célèbre down the centuries. Putting aside the rights and wrongs of the Council of Constantinople's condemnation of Pope Honorius, the fact remains that three ecumenical councils and a succession of popes were prepared to accept that a successor of St. Peter had either been a heretic or had been negligent in his solemn duty of safeguarding the Deposit of Faith from heresy. This controversy highlights the antinomy between the indefectibility of the Bishop of Rome and tradition's consideration of the implications of a heretical pope on the throne of St. Peter.

How Can a Heretical Pope be Possible?

Despite Pope Honorius I being condemned by three ecumenical councils for teaching heresy, or allowing heresy to be taught, (Third Council of Constantinople, Second Council of Nicaea and the Fourth Council of Constantinople) and this condemnation being confirmed by a succession of popes −, the possibility of a pope teaching heresy remains a matter of debate. Despite the facts, some even argue that it is impossible for a pope to formally teach heresy.[98] The whole issue is complicated by two apostolic doctrines that derive from the grace of Petrine primacy: that the pope is not subject to anyone's judgment and that subjection to the pope is necessary for salvation. These doctrines must weigh heavily on the mind, heart and conscience of anyone who examines the question of a pope teaching error and heresy.

The Pope is Not Subject to Anyone's Judgment

As Ott expresses it, the pope is the supreme judge of the Church 'He himself is judged by nobody…because there is no higher judge on earth than he [*prima Sedes a nemine iudicatur* − The first See is judged by none]'.[99]

This doctrine was canonically codified in the 1917 *Code of Canon Law* and remained unchanged in the 1983 *Code of Canon Law* − 'The First See is judged by no one' (Can. 1556; cf Can. 1404). This means that the Supreme Pontiff of the See of Rome, 'cannot be judged by any human power, ecclesiastical or civil. This is a prerogative which, being the supreme judge in the Church, even the Pope himself cannot renounce.' This means that 'there is neither appeal nor recourse against a judgement or a decree of the Roman Pontiff.' (Can. 333 §3). However, this doesn't prohibit an appeal to the pope to reconsider his judgement or decree in a 'particularly difficult or sensitive situation'.[100]

Pope St. Nicholas I (858 to 867) expressed this doctrine in his letter to the Emperor Michael III in the 9th century, 'Neither by the emperor nor by all the clergy nor by the

---

[96] Ott, L [1957] *Op. cit.*, p.150
[97] De Mattei, R [2019] *Love for the Papacy and Filial Resistance to the Pope in the History of the Church.* Tacoma: Angelico Press
[98] O'Regan, E [5 July 2019] *The Heretical Pope Fallacy* [Online] Available at: www.lastampa.it [Accessed on: 26 September 2022]
[99] Ott, L [1957] *Op. cit.*, p.286
[100] The Canon Law Society of Great Britain and Ireland [1999] *Op. cit.*, p.813

people will the judge be judged… "The first See will not be judged by anyone."'[101] Pope Clement VI (1342 to 1352) was even more emphatic that the pope can be judged by nobody:

> We who are so, and those who will be so in the future have been, are, and will be such that they and We were not, are not, and in the future will not be able to be judged by anyone; but that they and We have been, are, and will be reserved to the judgment by God alone; and that it was not possible, is not possible, and will not be possible for Our decisions and judgments to be appealed to any other judge.[102]

Some have interpreted this as meaning that the pope rules the Church as an absolute monarch whose doctrinal statements and judgements cannot be questioned or challenged. A number of popes have gone out of their way to dispel this misunderstanding.

Following Vatican I's declaration of the dogma of papal infallibility Pope Pius IX responded to the criticism the pope had been elevated to absolute monarch, clearly setting out the limits to papal authority:

> …the application of the term 'absolute monarch' to the pope in reference to ecclesiastical affairs is not correct because he is subject to divine laws and is bound by the directives given by Christ for his Church. The pope cannot change the constitution given to the Church by her divine Founder, as an earthly ruler can change the constitution of a State. In all essential points the constitution of the Church is based on divine directives, and therefore it is not subject to human arbitrariness…it is certainly not the Catholic Church that has embraced the immoral and despotic principle that the command of a superior frees one unconditionally from all personal responsibility.[103]

As Pope Clement VI expressed it, every pope is judged by God alone, that is by his divine laws and his divine directives communicated by Revelation.

More recently, Pope Benedict XVI emphasised that the pope is not an absolute monarch who can impose his personal opinions and whims on the Church:

> The Pope is not an absolute monarch whose thoughts and desires are law. On the contrary: the Pope's ministry is a guarantee of obedience to Christ and to his Word. He must not proclaim his own ideas, but rather constantly bind himself and the Church to obedience to God's Word, in the face of every attempt to adapt it or water it down, and every form of opportunism. […] The Pope knows that in his important decisions, he is bound to the great community of faith of all times, to the binding interpretations that have developed throughout the Church's pilgrimage. Thus, his power is not being above, but at the service of, the Word of God. It is incumbent upon him to ensure that this Word continues to be present in its greatness and to resound in its purity, so that it is not torn to pieces by continuous changes in usage.[104]

Pope Pius IX and Pope Benedict XVI have outlined warning signs when God's judgement of a pope is operative:

1. When a pope does not consider himself subject to divine laws or bound by the directives given by Christ for his Church but seeks to proclaim as laws his own ideas and desires.
2. When a pope doesn't consider himself bound by the Church's binding interpretations developed over time.
3. When a pope attempts to change the constitution given to the Church by her divine Founder.
4. When a pope seeks to issue a command that frees one unconditionally from all personal responsibility.
5. When a pope introduces continuous changes in usage.

---

[101] Denzinger, H [2010] *Op. cit.*, p. 219, *Dz* 638

[102] *Ibid.*, p.310, *Dz* 1056

[103] *Ibid.*, p.619, *Dz* 3114

[104] Pope Benedict XVI [2005] *Homily at Mass for the Possession of the Chair of the Bishop of Rome* [Online] Available at: www.vatican.va [Accessed on: 26 September 2022]

Subjection to the Pope is Necessary for Salvation

It is a doctrine of the Church that subjection to the pope is necessary for salvation. As Pope Boniface VIII (1294 to 1303) solemnly declared in *Unam Sanctam*, 'Furthermore, we declare, we proclaim, we define that it is absolutely necessary for salvation that every human creature be subject to the Roman Pontiff.' A doctrine re-iterated by the Fifth Lateran Council:

> Moreover, since subjection to the Roman pontiff is necessary for salvation for all Christ's faithful, as we are taught by the testimony of both sacred scripture and the holy fathers, and as is declared by the constitution of pope Boniface VIII of happy memory…

How are we to understand this unambiguous doctrine of the Church? As we have seen, sacred Scripture testifies to our Lord appointing St. Peter, and his successors, as the supreme teachers and guardians of the Faith. This is exemplified by the Petrine faith being the foundation of the Church and the bestowal of the power of the keys symbolising Peter's 'complete control and jurisdiction over the Church.'[105]

Tradition uses other phrases to convey the primacy and universal authority of St. Peter and his successors, that of 'shepherd of all shepherds', 'supreme pastor' and the 'supreme and universal shepherd'. These descriptors of the pope's pastoral responsibilities and authority originate from our Lord appointing St. Peter to share in his divine authority as the Good Shepherd (Jn 21:15-17; cf. Jn 10:11-15):

> And when they had eaten, Jesus said to Simon Peter, Simon, son of John, dost thou care for me more than these others? Yes, Lord, he told him, thou knowest well that I love thee. And he said to him, Feed my lambs. And again, a second time, he asked him, Simon, son of John, dost thou care for me? Yes, Lord, he told him, thou knowest well that I love thee. He said to him, Tend my shearlings. Then he asked him a third question, Simon, son of John, dost thou love me? Peter was deeply moved when he was asked a third time, Dost thou love me? and said to him, Lord, thou knowest all things; thou canst tell that I love thee. Jesus said to him, Feed my sheep (Jn 21:15-17).

Knowledge of Ancient Near East cultures helps us understand the divine and ecclesial significance of our Lord using the imagery of shepherding. Kingship and rule was described in terms of shepherding.[106] God's relationship with Israel is described in pastoral terms, '…he came forth a pastor' (Gen 49:24); '…now will the Lord feed them, as a lamb in a spacious place' (Hos 4:16); 'He shall feed his flock like a shepherd: he shall gather together the lambs with his arm, and shall take them up in his bosom, and he himself shall carry them that are with young.'(Isa 40:11).

In the light of this, John 21:15-17 describes our Lord delegating his divine authority over his flock to St. Peter. This is emphasised by the threefold nature of his command to Peter — 'Feed my lambs' (Jn 21:15), 'Tend my shearlings' (Jn 21:16), 'Feed my sheep' (Jn 21:17). In Ancient Near East cultures, a threefold command before witnesses signified the solemnisation of a contract that conferred legal rights. Therefore, 'the threefold character of Jesus' command lends a special authoritativeness and emphasis to Peter's role as shepherd'.[107]

However, though Jesus solemnly bestows authority over the flock to St. Peter, he emphasises that the flock remains his by his threefold repetition of the possessive adjective — 'my lambs', 'my shearlings', 'my sheep'. As St. Augustine commented, Jesus commands St. Peter, 'Tend my sheep as mine, not as yours':

> If you love me, think not of feeding yourself, but feed my sheep as mine, and not as your own; seek my glory in them, and not your own; my dominion, and not yours; my gain, and not yours; lest you be found in the fellowship of those who belong to the perilous

---

[105] Ott, L [1957] *Op. cit.*, p. 307
[106] Brown, R [1966] *The Gospel According to John.* Vol. II. London: Geoffrey Chapman, p. 1114
[107] *Ibid.*, p.1112

times, lovers of their own selves, and all else that is joined on to this beginning of evils? […] Let us, then, love not ourselves, but Him; and in feeding His sheep, let us be seeking the things which are His, not the things which are our own.[108]

While it is true that our Lord has delegated divine authority over his Church to St. Peter, and his successors, this authority is not absolute but is conditional on those holding the Petrine office giving primacy to Christ's teaching safeguarded by the Deposit of Faith and lived by the Rule of Faith. It is from this perspective of the conditional nature of Petrine authority that we can fully understand what is meant by subjection to the pope as necessary for salvation.

Why is obedience to the pope necessary for salvation? Through his threefold solemn delegation of authority and jurisdiction, Christ established a permanent mandate and capacity for St. Peter, and his successors, to feed and tend his sheep. The Greek word for 'feed' — *boskō* — refers to pasture, land set aside for grazing animals.[109] Shepherds lead sheep to pasture. While the Greek word of 'tend' — *poimainó* — has the meaning of a shepherd who has the responsibility for guiding, guarding and feeding the flock.[110] Without shepherds, the flock cannot find the pasture it needs, it becomes dispersed and lost, and the sheep die.

Our Lord gave this vital sustaining and protective role to St. Peter and his successors. As expressed by Vatican I:

> And it was to Peter alone that Jesus, after his resurrection, confided the jurisdiction of Supreme Pastor and ruler of his whole fold, saying: 'Feed my lambs, feed my sheep'. That which our Lord Jesus Christ, the prince of shepherds and great shepherd of the sheep, established in the blessed apostle Peter, for the continual salvation and permanent benefit of the Church, must of necessity remain for ever, by Christ's authority, in the Church which, founded as it is upon a rock, will stand firm until the end of time.[111]

This Petrine principle communicated through the apostolic succession of the popes is essential to guard and protect the Church as 'the universal sacrament of salvation' (*Lumen Gentium* 48). What is communicated through those popes who remain faithful to their mandate is the strength and faith of St. Peter:

> In order that the episcopate itself might be one and undivided and that the whole multitude of believers might be persevered in unity of faith and communion by means of a closely united priesthood, he placed St. Peter as the head of the other apostles and established in him a perpetual principal and visible foundation of this twofold unity, in order that on his strength an everlasting temple might be erected and on the firmness of his faith a Church might arise whose pinnacle was to reach into heaven.[112]

Having said this, how can we discern if a successor of St. Peter is obeying the divine mandate that makes subjection to him necessary for salvation? It is important to note that while Vatican I declares that our Lord confided this role of Supreme Pastor to Peter alone, and his successors alone, it also made clear that this is a conditional, not an absolute authority — Jesus remains the 'the prince of shepherds and great shepherd of the sheep.'

The Johannine Parable of the Good Shepherd (Jn 10:1-16) gives us the criteria to judge if a pope is obeying Jesus' mandate to feed and guard his flock.

The context given by our Lord to identify a true shepherd is how he enters the sheepfold, 'But he that entereth in by the door is the shepherd of the sheep.' (Jn 10:2). Christ describes himself as the 'indispensable door' to the Church (*Lumen Gentium* 6), 'I

---

[108] St. Augustine. *Tractates on the Gospel of John*, Tractate 123, para 5 [Online] Available at: www.newadvent.org [Accessed on: 26 September 2022]

[109] *Strong's Concordance* [Online] Available at: biblehub.com [Accessed on: 25 September 2022]

[110] *Ibid.*

[111] First Vatican Council [1870] Vatican I's Dogmatic Constitution, *Pastor Aeternus, on the Church of Christ* [Online] Available at: www.ewtn.com [Accessed on: 26 September 2022]

[112] Denzinger, H [2010] *Pastor Aeternus, op. cit.,* p.610, Dz 3051

am the door of the sheep. By me, if any man enter in, he shall be saved: and he shall go in, and go out, and shall find pastures.' (10:9). The true pope is one whose sole focus is to safeguard and expound the divine truths of Christ preserved in the Deposit of Faith.

We can also discern if a pope is leading us through the door of Christ because we can recognise the 'voice' of Christ speaking through him:

> '…and the sheep hear his voice: and he calleth his own sheep by name, and leadeth them out. And when he hath let out his own sheep, he goeth before them: and the sheep follow him, because they know his voice; I am the good shepherd; and I know mine, and mine know me' (Jn 10: 3-4;14).

In the Johannine Parable of the Good Shepherd our Lord wants us to be able to discern the difference between a good shepherd who solely focuses on Jesus, and faithfully represents him, and false shepherds who lead the flock to destruction. Our Lord distinguishes two types of false shepherds — 'thieves and robbers' and 'hirelings'.

The Greek word for 'thief' — *kleptés* — refers to a thief who steals by stealth, such as an embezzler. Among the early Christians it came to refer to false teachers who abused their authority for personal gain.[113] While the word 'robber' — *léstés* — refers to 'an unscrupulous malefactor exploiting the vulnerable without hesitating to use violence.'[114] Our Lord warns that we can distinguish the thief and robber from the true shepherd by the fact that they don't solely focus on Christ — the gate — but instead they go out of their way to avoid Christ, by using devious, illegitimate ways in the Church, 'He that entereth not by the door into the sheepfold, but climbeth up another way, the same is a thief and a robber.' (Jn 10:1). Where we see a pope not focusing on Christ, but proposing others means of salvation, such as non-Christian religions or secular messianism, we see a thief and a robber.

The hireling or hired servant — *misthótos* — proves himself not to be a shepherd when the flock is threatened. His relationship with the flock is egotistical, solely for his own benefit. Unlike the true shepherd, the hired servant does not have an intimate knowledge of the flock and is not prepared to put the safety of the flock before his own interests. The hired servant betrays the flock to its enemy, the wolf, because 'he hath no care for the sheep' (10:13). Our Lord warns that we can distinguish the hireling from the true shepherd by the fact that he leaves them prey to the wolf, the devil. Where we see a pope who leaves people in their sins by failing to stress the imperative of repentance, we see a hireling who refuses to protect them from the devil.

Clearly, while subjection to a true successor of St. Peter is necessary for salvation because such obedience sustains and protects the faithful, subjection to false shepherds cannot be required because on the contrary it would imperil salvation.

What if a Pope Teaches Heresy?

During the history of the Church, even popes have considered the consequences of a successor of St. Peter teaching heresy. Pope Hadrian II (867 to 872) told a Roman synod, referring to Pope Honorius I, that a pope teaching heresy was the only licit occasion for inferiors to resist the authority of the Roman Pontiff, [Heresy is] 'the only cause for which it is licit to inferiors to resist their superiors and to repel their perverse sentiments.'[115]

Pope Innocent III (1198 to 1216) went further, declaring that the 'Roman church' could dismiss a pope for teaching heresy:

> The Roman church can dismiss the Roman pontiff only because of fornication — I mean not carnal, but spiritual fornication, for the marriage is not carnal but spiritual — and this fornication is the sin of heresy. For 'Whoever does not believe is already condemned.' (Jn 3:18) In that sentence you can understand what is written in the Gospel you have

---

[113] *Strong's Concordance* [Online] Available at: biblehub.com [Accessed on: 25 September 2022]
[114] *Ibid.*
[115] De Mattei, R [2019] *Op. cit.*

heard, 'You are the salt of the earth, if the salt loses its savour, how shall it be salted?' (Mt 5:13).[116]

A number of implications follow from these two papal statements on a pope teaching heresy: both Hadrian II and Innocent III accepted that it was possible that a pope could teach heresy. They also implicitly accepted that papal heresy abrogated the doctrine, 'The first See is judged by none.' And they both accepted that in such a situation the pope's inferiors could disobey or act against the heretical pope. However, these corollaries arising from Pope Hadrian II and Pope Innocent III's declarations still raise a number of problems concerning the doctrines on the pope's juridical primacy and indefectibility. Since as these doctrines derive from Christ's divine words and action, they must be true despite a pope teaching heresy.

The Petrine Dichotomy of Rock and satan

The Church Fathers' exegesis of our Lord's rebuke of St. Peter, immediately following his institution of the Petrine primacy (Mt 16:22-23), suggests a way of understanding this paradox:

> 'And Peter taking him, began to rebuke him, saying: Lord, be it far from thee, this shall not be unto thee. Who turning, said to Peter: Go behind me, Satan, thou art a scandal [skandalon] unto me: because thou savourest not the things that are of God, but the things that are of men. (Mt 16:22-23)

The Church Fathers examined this 'duality' within St. Peter, wanting to understand how he could be both the 'Rock' and 'Satan' and the 'stumbling stone' [skandalon]. The gravity of the duality within St. Peter is expressed by the contrast between the words addressed to him by our Lord. In response to his Christological profession of faith Jesus says, 'Blessed art thou, Simon Bar-Jona'. Shortly after which Jesus condemns Peter for his lack of faith, 'Go behind me, Satan, thou art a scandal [skandalon] unto me'.

St. Augustine explained this Petrine dichotomy in terms of the contrast between St. Peter following God's divine revelation and St. Peter following man's sinful thoughts. St. Peter is the rock when he expresses God's truth, 'flesh and blood hath not revealed it to thee, but my Father who is in heaven' (16:17), and he is the stumbling block when he opposes God's truth with human thinking, 'thou savourest not the things that are of God, but the things that are of men.' (16:23). St. Augustine wrote:

> How could he [Jesus] now call Peter 'Satan', when a moment earlier he called him 'blessed', and 'rock'? You have no taste for the things of God, but only for human things (Mt 16:16-19, 22-23), said the Lord, yet only moments before it had indeed been to things of God that Peter's spiritual taste was sensitive, for *it is not flesh and blood that revealed this to you, but my Father, who is in heaven.* As long as Peter was seeking praise for his words in God, he was no Satan but Peter, the rock-like Peter; but when he spoke for himself, out of human weakness and merely natural love for a human being, he was addressed as 'Satan', because his attitude would have been an obstacle to his own salvation and that of everyone else. Why? Because he was trying to run ahead of the Lord, and to give earthly counsel to his heavenly leader. *Far be it from you, Lord; this will not happen.* Listen to what you are saying, Peter: *Far be it,* and *Lord.* If he is the Lord, he is acting in power; if he is the teacher, he knows what he must do, and knows what to teach. But you are trying to lead the leader, teach the teacher, give orders to the Lord, and make choices for God. You are getting much too far in front, so *get behind.*[117]

The scandal is that Peter stops being a follower behind Jesus, stops being a disciple of the Master, and instead has the presumption to try to assume the position of leadership

---

[116] Pope Innocent III [2004] *Between God and Man: Six Sermons on the Priestly Office, Sermon Three.* Washington: Catholic University of America Press, p. 3
[117] The Works of Saint Augustine [2001] A Translation for the 21st Century. *Exposition of the Psalms,* 51-72. III/17, Psalm 55 para 15. New York: New City Press

by 'going ahead of the Lord'. By presuming to impose his own fallible, erroneous thinking on God, Peter, and those like him, become 'Satan' — the adversary of God.

Joseph Cardinal Ratzinger saw the dichotomy between the Petrine Rock and the Petrine Satan and stumbling block as playing out in the history of the papacy:

> The tension between the gift coming from the Lord and man's own capacity is rousingly portrayed in this scene, which in some senses anticipates the entire drama of papal history. In this history we repeatedly encounter two situations. On the one hand, the papacy remains the foundation of the Church in virtue of a power that does not derive from herself. At the same time, individual popes have again and again become a scandal because of what they themselves are as men, because they want to precede, not follow, Christ, because they believe that they must determine by their own logic the path that only Christ himself can decide: 'You do not think God's thoughts, but man's' (Mt 16:23).[118]

What are the implications for the Church when a pope persists in no longer following Christ and becomes a 'Satan' by following their own fallible, erroneous thoughts?

Aware of the possibility of this dichotomy in the exercise of the Petrine office, when assessing a teaching of a pope it is sometimes necessary to discern if he is expressing divine revelation expressed by the Church's dogma and doctrines or instead is expressing merely human thinking through his personal opinion.

The Two Bodies of the Pope

This understanding of an intrinsic dichotomy contained within the Petrine Office was expressed in the Middle Ages as the Two Bodies of the Pope. Cardinal Burke — one of the Church's leading canon lawyers— has re-introduced this understanding in response to the erroneous teachings of Pope Francis. In these circumstances — Cardinal Burke argues — it is imperative that we distinguish between 'the words of the man who is Pope and the words of the Pope as Vicar of Christ on earth':

> In the Middle Ages, the Church spoke of the two bodies of the Pope: the body of the man and the body of the Vicar of Christ. In fact, the traditional Papal vesture, especially the red mozzetta with the stole depicting the Apostles Saint Peter and Paul, visibly represents the true body of the Pope when he is setting forth the teaching of the Church.[119]

Therefore, the first body is that of 'the body of the man who is Pope', and the second body is the 'body of the Vicar of Christ.' Cardinal Burke concludes that Pope Francis often chooses to give his private opinion, speaking in his first body:

> Pope Francis has chosen to speak often in his first body, the body of the man who is Pope. In fact, even in documents which, in the past, have represented more solemn teaching, he states clearly that he is not offering magisterial teaching but his own thinking.[120]

For example, confronted with Pope Francis' erroneous teachings on homosexual civil unions or his praise of Sr. Jeannine Gramick's affirmation of individuals engaged in homosexual sex acts, Cardinal Burke employed the distinction between the two bodies of the pope. He has variously concluded about Pope Francis' statements on such matters that they are the private opinions of the first body, 'the body of the man who is Pope':

> They are rightly interpreted as simple private opinions of the person who made them. These declarations do not bind, in any manner, the consciences of the faithful who are rather obliged to adhere with religious submission to what Sacred Scripture and Sacred Tradition, and the ordinary Magisterium of the Church teach on the matter in

[118] Ratzinger, J [1996] *Called to Communion*, op. cit., p. 61
[119] Burke, R [2017] *The Two Bodies of the Pope: Developing Lives of Peace after the Heart of Mary – Remedies for these troubled times of confusion, division and error* [Online] Available at: www.mariancatechist. com [Accessed on 26 September 2022]
[120] *Ibid.*

question.[121]...These are simply the opinions of a man, but they have nothing to do with the Magisterium of the Church.[122]

Tertullian on the Distinction between Petrine Conversation and Preaching

This distinction between the two types of communication of the pope — fallible, non-binding personal opinion, and, infallible, binding preaching of the Vicar of Christ — can be traced back to as early as the 2nd century in the teaching to the Church Father, Tertullian (c. 155 to c. 220). The occasion for Tertullian making this distinction was his exegesis of St. Paul rebuking St. Peter:

> But when Cephas was come to Antioch, I withstood him to the face, because he was to be blamed. For before that some came from James, he did eat with the Gentiles: but when they were come, he withdrew and separated himself, fearing them who were of the circumcision. And to his dissimulation the rest of the Jews consented, so that Barnabas also was led by them into that dissimulation. But when I saw that they walked not uprightly unto the truth of the gospel, I said to Cephas before them all: If thou, being a Jew, livest after the manner of the Gentiles, and not as the Jews do, how dost thou compel the Gentiles to live as do the Jews? (Gal 2:11-14).

Tertullian made the distinction between the 'conversation' and the 'preaching' of Peter, seeing the former as a less serious matter than the latter:

> Forasmuch, then, as Peter was rebuked because, after he had lived with the Gentiles, he proceeded to separate himself from their company out of respect for persons, the fault surely was one of conversation, not of preaching. For it does not appear from this, that any other God than the Creator, or any other Christ than (the son) of Mary, or any other hope than the resurrection, was (by him) announced.[123]

Tertullian went on to comment that St. Peter had been negligent in upholding the Gospel, but that he was not guilty of preaching a 'false' or 'depraved gospel' which was a much more serious matter:

> No doubt he blames him; but it was solely because of his inconsistency in the matter of 'eating,' which he varied according to the sort of persons (whom he associated with) 'fearing them which were of the circumcision,' (Gal 2:12) but not on account of any perverse opinion touching another god. For if such a question had arisen, others also would have been 'resisted face to face' by the man who had not even spared Peter on the comparatively small matter of his doubtful conversation.[124]

Underlying Tertullian's distinction between conversation and preaching is the understanding of the importance of preaching. Kerygma — the formal proclamation of the gospel — was sanctified by our Lord as his preferred way of teaching divine truth. Kerygma means to proclaim as a herald the coming of the Kingdom and the call to repentance. The Twelve appointed by Jesus were designated *apostollos* [apostles] because their primary responsibility, authority and power was to be messengers of the Gospel. Therefore, introducing errors into the Deposit of Faith through preaching is a grave betrayal of the Petrine office.

St. Thomas Aquinas on the Duty to Criticise a Pope

Though St. Thomas Aquinas didn't employ the distinction between conversation and preaching in his exegesis of Galatians 2:11-14, he concluded from St. Paul rebuking St.

---

[121] Burke, R [2020] *Statement on the Declarations of Pope Francis Regarding Civil Unions* [Online] Available at: www.cardinalburke.com [Accessed on: 26 September 2022]

[122] McLoone, D [2022] *'Opinions of a man,' not the Church: Cardinal Burke criticizes Pope Francis' praise for LGBT group leader* [Online] Available at: www.lifesitenews.com [Accessed on: 26 September 2022]

[123] Tertullian. *Prescription against Heretics*, Chap. 23 [Online] Available at: www.newadvent.org [Accessed on: 26 September 2022]

[124] Tertullian. *Against Marcion*, Chap. 3 [Online] Available at: www.newadvent.org [Accessed on: 26 September 2022]

Peter that subjects have a duty to publicly rebuke their superiors if they endangered the Faith:

> It must be observed, however, that if the faith were endangered, a subject ought to rebuke his prelate even publicly. Hence Paul, who was Peter's subject, rebuked him in public, on account of the imminent danger of scandal concerning faith, and, as the gloss of Augustine says on Galatians 2:11, 'Peter gave an example to superiors, that if at any time they should happen to stray from the straight path, they should not disdain to be reproved by their subjects.'

> To presume oneself to be simply better than one's prelate, would seem to savour of presumptuous pride; but there is no presumption in thinking oneself better in some respect, because, in this life, no man is without some fault. We must also remember that when a man reproves his prelate charitably, it does not follow that he thinks himself any better, but merely that he offers his help to one who, 'being in the higher position among you, is therefore in greater danger,' as Augustine observes in his Rule quoted above. (*Summa Theologiae* II-II.33.4).[125]

In his commentary on Galatians St. Thomas Aquinas emphasises that subjects must not fear to publicly correct prelates if their acts are a 'danger to the Gospel teaching', and 'if their crime is public and verges upon danger to the multitude.' In these circumstances 'the truth must be preached openly, and the opposite never condoned through fear of scandalising others.'[126]

The Catholic philosopher Edward Feser draws the following conclusions from St. Thomas Aquinas' reflections on St. Paul rebuking St. Peter:

1. A Catholic can correct someone with ecclesiastical authority, such as a pope or bishop. Though they lack the authority to punish a superior, they have the duty in justice to correct a prelate who is truly guilty of wrongdoing. Criticism must be expressed respectfully, and be an act of charity, not a pretence of authority over the superior.
2. The fact that Aquinas cites Paul rebuking Peter indicates that the pope is among those who can be corrected in this way.
3. The public criticism of a pope is called for 'if the faith were endangered' or if his 'crime is public and verges upon danger to the multitude.'
4. Catholics have a duty to correct a pope committing errors for the sake of the pope himself. As Feser puts it, 'If a pope is guilty of serious error and of leading others into error, one does not show greater piety or loyalty to him by pretending otherwise. On the contrary, one contributes to endangering his soul.'
5. It is not presumptuous to correct a pope, because if done as an act of charity, it is meant to help him not punish him. It is possible for one of the pope's inferiors to be better than him in some respect because, as Aquinas writes, 'there is no presumption in thinking oneself better in some respect, because, in this life, no man is without some fault.'
6. According to St. Thomas Aquinas criticism of a pope must be carried out 'with gentleness and respect' and not with 'impudence' or 'insolence'. As Canon 212§3 expresses it, we have a duty to make our concerns 'with reverence toward their pastors, and attentive to common advantage and the dignity of persons.'[127]

Furthermore, St. Thomas Aquinas — drawing out the implications of 'We ought to obey God rather than men' (Acts 5:29) — concluded 'sometimes the things commanded

---

[125] St. Thomas Aquinas. *Summa Theologiae* II-II. Question 33. Fraternal correction, 4 [Online] Available at: www.newadvent.org [Accessed on: 26 September 2022]
[126] St. Thomas Aquinas. *Commentary on Galatians*, Chap. 2 Lecture 3 [Online] Available at: isidore. co/ aquinas/english/SSGalatians.htm [Accessed on: 26 September 2022]
[127] Feser, E [2018] *The Church Permits Criticism of Popes under Certain Circumstances* [Online] Available at: edwardfeser.blogspot.com [Accessed on: 26 September 2022]

by a superior are against God. Therefore superiors are not to be obeyed in all things' (*ST* II-II, Q. 104, art. 5, sed contra). Dr. Peter Kwasniewski concludes:

> If we are convinced that something essential, something decisive in the Faith is under attack from the pope or any other hierarch, we are not only permitted to refuse to do what is being asked or commanded, not only permitted to refuse to give up what is being unjustly taken away or forbidden; we are obliged to refuse, out of the love we bear to Our Lord Himself, our love for His Mystical Body, and our proper love for our own souls.'[128]

What Happens when a Pope Teaches a False Gospel?

Until the promulgation of the 1917 Pio-Benedictine *Code of Canon Law*, the canonical tradition of the Church included a significant qualification to the doctrine, 'the first See is judged by none' [*prima Sedes a nemine iudicatur*]. Prior to 1917 the Church's authoritative compendium of canon law, the *Corpus Iuris Canonici*, included the canon, 'the pope cannot be judged by anyone, unless he has been found deviating from the faith' [*Papa a nemine est iudicandus, nisi deprehendatur a fide devius*]. (*Decretum Gratiani*, Prima Pars, dist. 40, c. 6, 3. pars).[129]

Even though this qualification was omitted from the 1917 *Code of Canon Law*, and the subsequent 1983 *Revised Code of Canon Law*,[130] this canonical tradition informs expert canonical commentary up until the present day. In the Canon Law Society of America's *New Commentary on the Code of Canon Law* (2000) Fr. Lawrence G. Wrenn, a consultor for the Pontifical Commission for the Authentic Interpretation of Legislative Texts, wrote:

> Canon 1404 [The First See is judged by no one] is not a statement about the personal impeccability or inerrancy of the Holy Father. Should, indeed, the pope fall into heresy, it is understood that he would lose his office. To fall from Peter's faith is to fall from his chair.'[131]

Natural law and divine law have been cited to justify acting against a pope for teaching heresy. John of St. Thomas OP (1589 to 1644) appealed to the natural law of self-defence against mortal danger:

> …as the heretic is an enemy of the Church, natural law provides protection against such a Pope according to the rules of self-defence, because she can defend herself against an enemy as is a heretical Pope; therefore, she can act (in justice) against him. So, in any case, it is necessary that such a Pope must be deposed.[132]

The German dogmatic theologian Fr. Matthias Joseph Scheeben (1835 to 1888) combined natural law with an implicit *two bodies of the pope* approach to explain the need to act against a heretical pope:

> Those theologians considered the most important or rather the sole [hypothetical] case of obvious and absolute temerity the one in which the pope would attempt to define a notorious heresy, or, what amounts to the same thing, to reject a notorious dogma that is held without doubt by the entire Church and thus to require the whole Church to

---

[128] Kwasniewski, P [2021] *True Obedience: A Key Consideration for Our Time* [Online] Available at: onepeterfive.com [Accessed on: 27 October 2022] cf. Kwasniewski, P [2022] *True Obedience in the Church: A Guide to Discernment in Challenging Times.* Bedford: Sophia Institute Press

[129] Schneider, A [2019] *On the Question of a Heretical Pope* [Online] Available at: onepeterfive.com [Accessed on: 26 September 2022]

[130] Bishop Athanasius Schneider explains the omission of this qualification from the Pio-Benedictine *Code of Canon Law* as due to the judgement that it was based on a spurious decree erroneously attributed to St. Boniface and incorporated into the 12th century *Decretum Gratiani*. Schneider, A [2020] *Bishop Schneider Releases Essay 'On the Question of the True Pope'* [Online] Available at: www.lifesitenews.com [Accessed on 26 September 2022]

[131] Canon Law Society of America' [2000] *New Commentary on the Code of Canon Law.* New York: Paulist Press, p. 1618

[132] John of St. Thomas OP [2014] *On the Deposition of a Pope* [Online] Available at: dominicansavrille.us [Accessed on: 26 September 2022]

abandon her faith; for in this case, they said, the pope would behave not as a shepherd but as a wolf, not as a teacher but as a madman, while on the other hand the Church or the episcopate could and would have to rise up immediately as one against the pope, although we could not say that she was rising up over or even merely against papal authority; rather she would rise up only against the arbitrariness of the person who hitherto had possessed the papal authority, but plainly through the questionable act renounced it and relieved himself of it.[133]

Though he doesn't use the terminology, Scheeben emphasises that in the circumstances of a heretical pope, the episcopacy and wider Church act against the first body of the man who is pope, and emphatically do not act against the body of the Vicar of Christ; by declaring a heresy or by rejecting a doctrine of the Deposit of Faith, the man who was pope — who had possessed papal authority — had 'renounced it and relieved himself of it'.

Having said this, the fact is that the heretical pope renounces and relieves himself of papal authority; no person or body has the power to depose a pope. As Fr. Lawrence G. Wrenn expresses it, after stating that 'to fall from Peter's faith is to fall from his chair':

> The question, however, of who or what body (probably a general council) would determine whether, in fact, the pope had fallen into heresy is unclear historically and is obviously not settled by this canon [Can. 1404]. While not a statement about impeccability or inerrancy, canon 1404 is a statement about the judicial immunity of the First See. It says that the Holy Father cannot be tried by a secular or religious court and, perhaps particularly, given the history of the question, by a general council. The Constitution on the Church of Christ of the First Vatican Council, for example, said, We also teach and declare that he [the Roman Pontiff] is the supreme judge of all the faithful to whose judgment appeal can be made in all matters which come under ecclesiastical examination. But the verdict of the Apostolic See may be rejected by no one, since there is no higher authority, and no one may pass judgment on its judgment. Hence, they stray from the right path of truth who affirm that it is permissible to appeal to a General Council against the judgments of the Roman Pontiffs, as if the General Council were a higher authority than the Roman Pontiff.[134]

One of the unresolved dilemmas posed by a heretical pope is that though his heresy must be publicly challenged and resisted, and that it is probable that he has relieved himself of papal authority, no person or body has the juridical competence or power to depose the Vicar of Christ.

Reflecting on the examination of this matter by Cardinal Thomas Cajetan (1469 to 1534), St. Robert Bellarmine SJ (1542 to 1621) and Fr. Francisco Suárez SJ (1548 to 1617), the canonists Francisco Xaver Wernz and Petri Vidal concluded:

> So, a publicly heretical pope, who by the mandate of Christ and of the Apostle should be avoided because of danger to the Church, must be deprived of his power, as nearly everyone admits. But he cannot be deprived of his power by a merely declaratory sentence.
>
> For every judicial sentence of privation supposes a superior jurisdiction over him against whom the sentence is laid. But a general council, in the opinion of adversaries, does not have a higher jurisdiction than does a heretical pope. For he, by their supposition, before the declaratory sentence of a general council, retains his papal jurisdiction; therefore, a general council cannot pass a declaratory sentence by which a Roman Pontiff is actually deprived of his power; for that would be a sentence laid by an inferior against the true Roman Pontiff.[135]

---

[133] Scheeben, M [2019] *Handbook of Catholic Dogmatics. Book One: Theological Epistemology. Part One: The Objective Principles of Theological Knowledge.* Steubenville: Emma's Academic, p. 310
[134] Canon Law Society of America [2000]. *Op. cit.*, p. 1618
[135] Wernz, F &Vidal, P [1928] *Ius Canonicum II*, n. 453 cited by Peters, E [2016] 'A canonical primer on popes and heresy' [Online] Available at: www.catholicworldreport.com [Accessed: 26 September 2022]

The grave difficulty presented by a heretical pope is illustrated by the fact that the Third Council of Constantinople declared Honorius I a heretic 42 years after his death, when he had neither a first body nor a second body.

A contemporary expression of this difficulty can be found in an essay written by Fr. Thomas G. Weinandy OFM, Cap., former chief of staff for the U.S. Bishops' Committee on Doctrine and a member of the Vatican's International Theological Commission. Weinandy proposed that Pope Francis could be, at the same time, pope of the Catholic Church and leader of a schismatic church:

> …we perceive a situation, ever-growing in intensity, in which on the one hand, a majority of the world's faithful – clergy and laity alike – are loyal and faithful to the pope, for he is their pontiff, while critical of his pontificate, and, on the other hand, a large contingent of the world's faithful – clergy and laity alike – enthusiastically support Francis precisely because he allows and fosters their ambiguous teaching and ecclesial practice.

> What the Church will end up with, then, is a pope who is the pope of the Catholic Church and, simultaneously, the de facto leader, for all practical purposes, of a schismatic church. Because he is the head of both, the appearance of one church remains, while in fact there are two.

> The only phrase that I can find to describe this situation is 'internal papal schism,' for the pope, even as pope, will effectively be the leader of a segment of the Church that through its doctrine, moral teaching, and ecclesial structure, is for all practical purposes schismatic. This is the real schism that is in our midst and must be faced, but I do not believe Pope Francis is in any way afraid of this schism. As long as he is in control, he will, I fear, welcome it, for he sees the schismatic element as the new 'paradigm' for the future Church.[136]

Weinandy presents a modern variant of the *two bodies of the pope* approach pushed to absurdity – an absurdity which doesn't lie with the author, but with the situation created by Pope Francis and his supporters.

It is unsurprising, that faced with this untenable absurdity, that there are calls to change canon law to protect the Church from papal errors. In response to Pope Francis' controversial apostolic exhortation, *Amoris Laetitia*, Rev. Dr. Aidan Nichols OP delivered a lecture in 2017 calling for the revision of canon law. Fr. Nichols proposed that the Church needed 'a procedure for calling to order a pope who teaches error'. Such a judicial process would 'dissuade popes from any tendency to doctrinal waywardness or simple negligence.' Reflecting on the doctrine that 'The First See is judged by no one', Fr. Nichols reflected that 'it is not the position of the Roman Catholic Church that a pope is incapable of leading people astray by false teaching as a public doctor':

> He may be the supreme appeal judge of Christendom…but that does not make him immune to perpetrating doctrinal howlers. Surprisingly, or perhaps not so surprisingly given the piety that has surrounded the figures of the popes since the pontificate of Pius IX, this fact appears to be unknown to many who ought to know better.[137]

Fr Nichols expressed the hope that 'given the limits on papal infallibility, canon law might be able to accommodate a formal procedure for inquiring into whether a pope had taught error.[138]

---

[136] Weinandy, T [2019] *Pope Francis and Schism* [Online] Available at: www.thecatholicthing.org [Accessed on: 26 September 2022]
[137] Hitchens, D [2017] *Leading Theologian: Change Canon Law to Correct Papal Errors* [Online] Available at: catholicherald.co.uk [Accessed on: 26 September 2022]
[138] *Ibid.*

Pope Francis and Eugenio Scalfari

Between 2013 and 2020 the Italian newspaper, *La Repubblica*, published twelve 'engagements' between Pope Francis and Eugenio Scalfari, journalist and co-founder of the left-wing, anti-Catholic newspaper. The first engagement occurred during the first six months of Pope Francis' pontificate with the Supreme Pontiff publishing an open letter on the 4th September 2013 in answer to Scalfari's questions addressed to him via the pages of *La Repubblica* (7th July & 7th August). Scalfari's account of their last conversation was published on the 30th July 2020. Over the period of eight years Pope Francis granted Scalfari privileged access not enjoyed by other journalists.

A number of Eugenio Scalfari's reports of his conversations with Pope Francis attribute to the Supreme Teacher some of the gravest errors that contravene the *De Fidei* doctrines of the Faith — that Pope Francis denied the immortality of souls and the existence of Hell (14th March 2015; 23rd March 2018); that the Son of God abandoned his divinity at the Incarnation and was only a man up to the Resurrection (or his death on the cross) when he became God again (7th July 2017; 8th October 2019), and that the resurrection of Jesus was not bodily but spiritual (5th November 2019).

What weight can be placed on Scalfari's account of Pope Francis expressing these grave errors that contravene *De Fidei* doctrines? The Vatican Press Office's responses to Scalfari's reports, even those that attributed grave doctrinal errors to Pope Francis, never flatly denied them as untruthful. Following Scalfari publishing his first face-to-face exchange with Pope Francis (1st October 2013), Fr. Federico Lombardi SJ, the director of the Holy See Press Office, was asked during a press briefing whether Scalfari's interview 'accurately captured the "sense" of what the pope had said'. To which Fr. Lombardi responded that if Pope Francis felt his thought had been 'gravely misrepresented', he would have said so'.[139] Over the seven years during which *La Repubblica* published ten more reports of Scalfari's conversations with Pope Francis, the Supreme Pontiff never once issued a personal statement warning that he had been 'gravely misrepresented'. As 'the shepherd and teacher of all Christians'[140] one would have expected Pope Francis to issue a personal statement correcting Scalfari when he published that the Holy Father denied the immortality of souls and the existence of Hell, that the Son of God abandoned his divinity at the Incarnation and that he denied our Lord's bodily Resurrection. But Pope Francis issued no such correction.

Instead, the Vatican Press Office issued various press releases and responses that did not unequivocally state that Scalfari's reports were untruthful. Following the publication of the 28th October 2014 report, Fr. Lombardi said, 'Scalfari pursues his own discourse' and, 'if there are no words published by the Holy See press office and not officially confirmed, the writer takes full responsibility for what he has written'.[141] In response to Scalfari publishing for the first time that Pope Francis denied the immortality of souls and the existence of Hell, Fr. Thomas Rosica, the English-language assistant to the Holy See Press Office, did not deny its veracity but instead replied, 'All official,

[139] Allen, JL [5 October 2013] *Dolan Confirms Error in Scalfari Interview* [Online] Available at: www.ncronline.org [Accessed on: 19 September 2022]

[140] First Vatican Council [1870] *First Dogmatic Constitution on the Church of Christ*, chap. 3 [Online] Available at: www.ewtn.com [Accessed on: 19 September 2022]

[141] *Are an Atheist Journalist's Papal Interviews Reliable?* [Online] Available at: www.catholicnewsagency.com [Accessed on: 17 September 2022]

final texts of the Holy Father are found on the Vatican website,' and since they were never published by the Holy See Press Office they 'should not be considered official texts.' 'They were', said Fr. Rosica, 'private discussions that took place and were never recorded by the journalist'.[142]

When Scalfari published for the second time (23rd March 2018) that Pope Francis denied the immorality of the soul and the existence of Hell, the Vatican issued the following response:

> The Holy Father recently received the founder of the newspaper *La Repubblica* in a private meeting on the occasion of Easter, without, however, granting him an interview. What is reported by the author in today's article is the fruit of his reconstruction, in which the precise words uttered by the Pope are not cited. No quotations in the aforementioned article, then, should be considered as a faithful transcription of the words of the Holy Father.[143]

What is noteworthy, is that the Vatican press release was couched in generalities and did not explicitly repudiate or contradict Scalfari's claim that Pope Francis denied the immorality of the soul and the existence of Hell. Considering the gravity of the allegation, such a specific response was necessary. As Raymond Arroyo, EWTN journalist and Fox News Contributor, responded on twitter about the Vatican statement, 'Not an outright denial, but a clear indication that Scalfari did not accurately quote the Holy Father. Better would have been: This story is a fabrication and of course, Francis affirms the Church's belief in hell. (Mar 30, 2018)'.

When Scalfari alleged for the second time that Pope Francis believed that the Son of God abandoned his divinity at the Incarnation (8th October 2019), Matteo Bruni, the director of the Holy See's press office released a statement:

> As already stated on other occasions, the words that Dr. Eugenio Scalfari attributes in quotation marks to the Holy Father during talks with him cannot be considered a faithful account of what was actually said but represent a personal and free interpretation of what he heard, as appears completely evident from what is written today regarding the divinity of Jesus Christ.[144]

In reaction to criticism that Bruni's statement was too vague, Paolo Ruffini, Prefect for the Vatican's Dicastery for Communication responded:

> The Holy Father never said what Scalfari wrote. Both the quoted remarks and the free reconstruction and interpretation by Dr. Scalfari of the conversations, which go back to more than two years ago, cannot be considered a faithful account of what was said by the pope. That will be found rather throughout the Church's magisterium and Pope Francis' own, on Jesus: true God and true man.[145]

The problem with both Bruni's statement and Ruffini's spoken response is that neither explicitly refute Scalfari's account of Pope Francis' very specific Christological error — that the Son of God abandoned his divinity at the Incarnation which he reassumed at death or at the Resurrection. This allegation of Christological error is so serious that it required a point-by-point doctrinal repudiation from the pope, not Ruffini's vague throw away clause, 'Jesus: true God and true man'. According to Pope Francis'

---

[142] Westen, JH [2015] *About that Pope Francis 'Interview' where He Denied the Existence of Hell* [Online] Available at: www.lifesitenews.com [Accessed on: 19 September 2022]

[143] *Statement of the Vatican Press Office on Pope's Remarks to Scalfari* [30 March 2018] [Online] Available at: www.vaticannews.va [Accessed on; 19 September 2022]

[144] Flynn, JD [9 October 2019] *Did Pope Francis Say that Jesus Isn't God? Don't Believe the Report, Vatican says* [Online] Available at: www.catholicnewsagency.com [Accessed on: 20 September 2022]

[145] Montagna, D [10 October 2019] *Abp Viganò Urges Pope to Personally Answer Claims He Doesn't Believe in Divinity of Christ* [Online] Available at: www.lifesitenews.com [Accessed on: 20 September 2022]

erroneous kenotic Christology, as recounted by Scalfari, Jesus resumed his divine nature either at his death or at his resurrection.

Archbishop Viganò pointed out that Scalfari's allegations concerning Pope Francis' Christological error were so serious, it required the Supreme Teacher to correct the confusion himself:

> Christians expect a clear answer from the Pope himself. The thing is too important; it is essential: Yes, I believe that Christ is the Son of God made Man, the only Saviour and Lord. All Christians await this clarification from him, not from others, and by virtue of their baptism have the right to have this response.[146]

What is Pope Francis' Attitude towards Scalfari's Accounts of their Conversations?

In October 2013, the US Catholic newspaper the *National Catholic Register* published a letter of clarification about Eugenio Scalfari's interview with Pope Francis from Fr. Thomas Rosica, the English-language Vatican spokesman. Fr Rosica explained that 'Scalfari has stated that he showed the text to Francis for his approval, but it's not clear how closely the pope read it'.[147]

During a conference at the Foreign Press Club in Rome on November 21, 2013, Scal-fari gave details of his conversations with Pope Francis. He admitted that all his con-versations were

> conducted without a recording device, nor taking notes while the person is speaking. 'I try to understand the person I am interviewing, and after that I write his answers with my own words... [it is therefore possible that] some of the Pope's words I reported, were not shared by Pope Francis.' [However, Scalfari also recounted that at the end of their first 80-minute conversation,] he asked Pope Francis permission to report the conversation. The Pope agreed, and Scalfari offered to send him the text before its publication. According to Scalfari, the Pope told him not to 'waste time' in sending him the text, saying, 'I trust you.' Scalfari said he nevertheless sent his text of the conversation to the Vatican on Sept. 29, together with an accompanying letter, in which he wrote, 'I must explain that I wrote up our conversation in order to let everybody understand our dialogue. Keep in mind that I did not report some things you told me, and that I report some things you did not tell me, which I wanted to insert to let the reader understand who you are.' According to Scalfari, Monsignor Xuereb, a papal secretary, called him, saying that Pope Francis had permitted its publication, and the text was subsequently published.[148]

The question is, did Scalfari follow the same procedure of conferring with Pope Francis before the publication of every account of their conversations, especially the ones containing grave doctrinal errors?

Pope Francis has given clues about his attitude towards Scalfari's controversial accounts of their conversations.

On the 25th May 2015 Pope Francis admitted in an interview that the only daily newspaper that he read was Scalfari's *La Repubblica*.[149] The Supreme teacher made this admission two months after *La Repubblica* had published Scalfari's report that Pope Francis denied the immortality of souls and the existence of Hell (14th March 2015). He gave no clarification or repudiation of Scalfari's account.

Following Eugenio Scalfari's death on 14th July 2022 *La Repubblica* published Pope Francis' eulogy for his friend, in which he referred to their conversations, making no reference to the scandal they had caused among the faithful:

---

[146] *Ibid.*

[147] Pentin, E [5 October 2013] *Vatican: Scalfari Interview Misses Details, Conflates Facts* [Online] Available at: www.ncregister.com [Accessed on: 20th September 2022]

[148] Gagliarducci, A [21 November 2013] *Pope's Words in Interview May Not Have Been His Own, Scalfari Says* [Online] Available: www.catholicnewsagency.com [Accessed on: 20 September 2022]

[149] Rodari, PL [25 May2015] *The Pope: I Don't Watch TV, I Read Only La Repubblica*

I remember how in our meetings at Casa Santa Marta, he would tell me how he was trying to grasp, by investigating the everyday and the future through meditation on experiences and great literature, the meaning of existence and life. He professed to be a non-believer, although in the years I knew him he also reflected deeply on the meaning of faith. He always wondered about the presence of God, about the last things, and about life after this life.

Our conversations were pleasant and intense, the minutes with him flew by quickly and were punctuated by the peaceful confrontation of each other's opinions and the sharing of our thoughts and ideas, and also by moments of cheerfulness.

We talked about faith and secularism, about everyday life and the great horizons of humanity present and future, about the darkness that can envelop man and the divine light that can illumine his path. I remember him as a man of extraordinary intelligence and an ability to listen, perpetually in search of the ultimate meaning of events, always eager for knowledge, and for testimonies that could enrich the understanding of modernity.... And he was enthusiastic and in love with his craft as a journalist... At the beginning of our exchanges of letters and phone calls, and during our first conversations, he had expressed his amazement at my choice to be called Francis, and he had wanted to understand well the reasons for my decision. And then, he was very curious about my work as pastor of the universal Church, and, in this sense, he reasoned out loud and in his articles about the Church's commitment to interreligious and ecumenical dialogue, about the mystery of the Lord, about God the fount of peace and source of paths of concrete fraternity among people, nations and peoples [...] From today on I will cherish even more in my heart the amiable and precious memory of the conversations I had with Eugenio that took place during these years of my pontificate.[150] [Translated by Diane Montagna]

Pope Francis' eulogy corroborates a number of facts contained in Scalfari's accounts of their conversations:

a) They discussed 'the last things, and about life after this life', which corroborates Scalfari's reports that they discussed eschatology (14th March 2015; 23rd March 2018).
b) They discussed 'the mystery of the Lord', which corroborates Scalfari's reports that they discussed Christology (7th July 2017; 8th October 2019; 5th November 2019).
c) Pope Francis expressed pleasure at the memory of their conversations, 'Our conversations were pleasant and intense', 'From today on I will cherish even more in my heart the amiable and precious memory of the conversations I had with Eugenio that took place during these years of my pontificate.'
d) Pope Francis praised Eugenio Scalfari's professionalism as a journalist, 'I remember him as a man of extraordinary intelligence and an ability to listen', 'And he was enthusiastic and in love with his craft as a journalist'.

Instead of correcting or distancing himself from Scalfari's reports of his eschatological and Christological error, Pope Francis lends support to their accuracy, by praising the professionalism of his journalism and his ability to listen. This tends to make more likely the conclusion drawn by Italian journalist, and Vaticanista, Sandro Magister:

> In this state of affairs, it is in any case highly credible that Francis truly said such things to Scalfari, seeing that he reported not once but four times in a row without the pope feeling the need to clarify anything, in each subsequent meeting with his friend.[151]

Faced with the evidence that it is highly credible that Pope Francis allowed Scalfari to publish such grave doctrinal errors, the enormity of the scandal is, frankly, overwhelming.

---

[150] Pope Francis [14 July 2022] *Il ricordo del Papa: 'Eugenio, amico laico, mi mancherà parlare con te'* [Online] Available at: www.repubblica.it [Accessed on: 20 September 2022]
[151] Magister, S [5 April 2018] *The Pope and Scalfari: Which Francis Are We Supposed to Believe?* [Online] Available at: www.lifesitenews.com [Accessed on: 20 September 2022]

The Errors of Pope Francis

Anthropology

A. *Individuals possess an inviolable ontological dignity that can never be annulled by any circumstance in which the person may find themselves or by any evil that they commit, no matter how wicked.*

Cardinal Victor Fernández's promulgation of the Dicastery for the Doctrine of the Faith's declaration *Dignitas Infinita* — signed by Pope Francis — marked the culmination of Pope Francis' teaching of the erroneous anthropological doctrine that man possess an inviolable 'infinite dignity'. Since the publication of the apostolic exhortation *Evangelii Gaudium*, Pope Francis has erroneously taught that man possesses an 'infinite dignity' unaffected by sinful acts due to being the recipient of the infinite love of God and created in His image and likeness (Gen 1:27). (*EG* 178).

In *Evangelii Gaudium* and in three other subsequent documents — the encyclicals *Laudato si'*, paragraph 65, *Fratelli Tutti*, paragraph 85, and the introduction to the Declaration *Dignitas Infinita* — Pope Francis, and laterly Cardinal Victor Fernández, selectively referenced a 1980 angelus address by Pope St. John Paul II to justify the erroneous idea that man has an inviolable 'infinite dignity'.

During his 1980 apostolic journey to the Federal Republic of Germany Pope St. John Paul II delivered an angelus address to disabled people at Osnabrück cathedral in which he taught the novel idea that man possess an 'infinite dignity':

> Diese Liebe ist der Grund eurer Hoffnung und eures Lebensmutes. Gott hat uns in Jesus Christus auf unüberbietbare Weise gezeigt, wie er jeden einzelnen Menschen liebt und ihm dadurch unendliche Würde verleiht. [This love is the reason for your hope and your courage to live. In Jesus Christ, God has shown us in an unsurpassable way how he loves every single person and thereby gives them infinite dignity.][152]

Pope St. John Paul II went on to categorically state during his Angelus address that an individual could choose to lose their 'infinite dignity' through their sins:

> Für uns Christen zählt weniger, ob jemand krank oder gesund ist; was letztlich zählt, ist dies: Bist du bereit, deine dir von Gott geschenkte Würde bewußt und gläubig in all deinen Lebenslagen und in deinem Verhalten als wahrer Christ zu verwirklichen — oder willst du diese Würde in einem oberflächlichen, verantwortungslosen Leben, in Sünde und Schuld vor Gott verspielen? [For us Christians, it matters less whether someone is sick or healthy; what ultimately counts is this: Are you prepared to consciously and faithfully realise your God-given dignity in all your life situations and in your behaviour as a true Christian — or do you want to gamble away this dignity in a superficial, irresponsible life, in sin and guilt before God?]

It is clear that Pope St. John Paul II did not understand 'infinite dignity' as transcending the individual's sinful actions, but instead that its possession depended on acting as a 'true Christian' by not losing one's dignity through an unrepented, sinful life. There is no precedent in the magisterium that supports Pope Francis' erroneous teaching that

---

[152] Pope St. John Paul II [1980] *Angelus* [Online] Available at: www.vatican.va [Accessed on: 25 April 2024]

man possesses an inviolable ontological dignity that transcends circumstances or evil actions.

Pope Francis' erroneous anthropology can be summarised under the following headings:

a) 'Every human person possesses an infinite dignity, inalienably grounded in his or her very being, which prevails in and beyond every circumstance, state, or situation the person may ever encounter.'[153]

b) Ignoring the doctrine of original sin and fallen man's concupiscent nature, Pope Francis proposed that man possesses an inviolable, infinite dignity that transcends moral circumstances and actions for two reasons: 1) Man possesses infinite dignity because he is the recipient of God's infinite love;[154] 2) God created man in His image and likeness.[155]

c) Pope Francis employed the erroneous idea that man possesses an 'infinite dignity' to propose an inviolable ontological dignity separate and distinct from three other types of violable, contingent dignities — moral dignity, social dignity, and existential dignity.[156]

d) 'The most important among these is the ontological dignity that belongs to the person as such simply because he or she exists and is willed, created, and loved by God. Ontological dignity is indelible and remains valid beyond any circumstances in which the person may find themselves'.[157] Pope Francis explicated his understanding of this inviolable, ontological dignity in his response to a homosexual comedian, 'We are all human beings and have dignity. It does not matter who you are, or how you live your life — you do not lose your dignity.'[158]

e) Pope Francis conceived of moral dignity as independent from, and separate to, ontological dignity. 'When we speak of moral dignity, we refer to how people exercise their freedom…. Individuals — when exercising their freedom against the law of love revealed by the Gospel — can commit inestimably profound acts of evil against others. Those who act this way seem to have lost any trace of humanity and dignity'.[159] On the moral level, 'sin can wound and obscure human dignity, as it is an act contrary to that dignity; yet, sin can never cancel the fact that the human being is created in the image and likeness of God.'[160]

f) Social dignity is correlated to an individual's economic living conditions, with extreme poverty forcing people to live in ways that contradict 'their inalienable dignity.'[161]

g) Existential dignity refers to medical, psychological and sociological pathologies, such as 'serious illnesses, violent family environments, pathological addictions', that 'drive people to experience their life conditions as 'undignified.'[162]

h) Cardinal Fernández, and Pope Francis, propose this fourfold differentiated possession of dignity as justifying their erroneous proposal of an inviolable,

---

[153] Dicastery for the Doctrine of the Faith [2024] Declaration *Dignitas Infinita*, para 1 [Online] Available at: www.press.vatican.va [Accessed on: 16 April 2024]

[154] Pope Francis [2013] Apostolic Exhortation *Evangelii Gaudium*, para 178; *Encyclical Fratelli Tutti*, para 85; [Online] Available at: www.vatican.va [Accessed on: 16 April 2024]

[155] Pope Francis [2015] Encyclical *Laudato si'*, para 65; Declaration *Dignitas Infinita*, para1, para 11 [Online] Available at: www.vatican.va [Accessed on: 22 April 2024]

[156] Dicastery for the Doctrine of the Faith [2024] Declaration *Dignitas Infinita*, para 11 [Online] Available at: www.press.vatican.va [Accessed on: 16 April 2024]

[157] *Op cit.*, para 7

[158] Dodd, L [2019] Pope condemns 'heartless' discrimination against gay people [Online] Available at: www.thetablet.co.uk [Accessed on: 22 April 2024]

[159] *Op cit.*, para 7

[160] *Ibid.*, para 22

[161] *Ibid.*, para 8

[162] *Ibid*

ontological dignity, 'These distinctions remind us of the inalienable value of the ontological dignity that is rooted in the very being of the human person in all circumstances.'[163]

i) Throughout *Dignitas Infinita* Cardinal Fernández, on behalf of Pope Francis, insisted that man's ontological dignity was inviolable and inalienable: ontological dignity could 'never be annulled' no matter the loss of moral dignity due to 'inestimably profound acts of evil',[164] nor the fact that 'hardships may drive people to experience their life conditions as "undignified" vis-à-vis their perception of that ontological dignity that can never be obscured.'[165]

The absence of any reference in *Dignitas Infinita* to the doctrine of original sin — and the catastrophic consequences of man's fall from the supernatural order on human nature — is an astounding omission. Pope Francis' erroneous teaching that man possesses an inviolable, pristine ontological dignity is reminiscent of the neo-Pelagian denial of original sin associated with Liberal Protestant Theology and modernism. Such an antipathy towards the doctrine of original sin, and its impact on human nature, can be found in the work of the prominent modernist Fr. Hans Küng:

> Through this interpretation of the biblical teaching on the Fall, Augustine, who had a brilliant capacity for analytical self-reflection far exceeding that of any other author of antiquity, effectively poisoned the entire Western Church with his doctrine on original sin, which is rejected down to this day by the Eastern churches.[166]

The Teaching of the Church

God is actually infinite in every perfection. (De Fide)[167]

Through sin our First Parents lost sanctifying grace and provoked the anger and the indignation of God. (De Fide)[168]

Our First Parents became subject to death and to the dominion of the devil. (De Fide)[169]

In the state of original sin man is deprived of sanctifying grace and all that this implies, as well as of the preternatural gifts of integrity. (De Fide)[170]

Pope Francis' erroneous notion that man possesses an ontological dignity that is 'infinite' in nature mistakenly bestows a divine attribute on man; according to the teaching of the Church 'infinity' is an attribute possessed solely by God. Pope Francis forgets the great dissimilarity between the creature and the Creator, 'namely the dissimilarity between the finite and the infinite.'[171] As the First Vatican Council expressed it:

> The holy, catholic, apostolic Roman Church believes and confesses there is one God, true and living, Creator and Lord of heaven and earth, almighty, eternal, immense, incomprehensible, infinite in his intellect and will and in all perfection. As he is one, unique, and spiritual substance, entirely simple and unchangeable, we must proclaim him distinct from the world in existence and essence, all blissful in himself and from himself, ineffably exalted above all things that exist or can be conceived besides him.[172]

Furthermore, to erroneously assert that man possesses an 'infinite dignity' also contradicts one of the Church's doctrines on the atonement — that man is incapable

---

[163] *ibid*

[164] *Ibid.*, para 7

[165] *Ibid.*, para 8

[166] Küng, Hans [2013] *Can We Save the Catholic Church?* London: William Collins

[167] Ott, L [1957] *Op cit.*, p.31

[168] *Ibid.*, p.107

[169] *Ibid.*

[170] *Ibid.*, p.112

[171] Ott, L [1957] *Op cit.*, p.19.

[172] Denzinger, H [2010] *Op. cit.*, p. 601 *Dz* 3001

of saving himself because he is by nature finite, contingent and sinful, devoid of any 'infinite' attributes. The Redemption is only possible due to our Lord Jesus Christ possessing 'an Infinite Divine Nature with all its Infinite Perfections by virtue of His eternal generation from God the Father.'[173] If His Passion had been the work of a mere man, finite and contingent, it 'would be deprived of its infinite value, and this infinite value is a necessary presupposition of the Redemption'.[174] The Passion had to be of infinite value due to the fact that Adam's original sin, and mankind's actual sins, are a grievous insult offered to God — an insult that is infinite because God's holiness and justice are infinite. It therefore 'demands an infinite expiation. Such expiation, however, can be achieved by a Divine Person only. To be capable of thus representing mankind, this person must be, at the same time, man and God.'[175]

Cardinal Fernández's presentation of man being constituted of a pristine ontological dignity due to being 'made in the image and likeness of God' (Gen 1:27) is also totally contrary to the Church's doctrine on the ontologically disfigured nature of fallen man. The 15th century Council of Florence described man as having lost 'entrance to the heavenly kingdom' due to the sin of the first man and consequently falling under the 'devil's dominion'.[176] In the 16th Century, the Council of Trent explicitly stated that 'the whole Adam, body and soul, was changed for the worse through the offence of his sin'. This disfigurement of the total nature of fallen man, and subjugation to demonic captivity, is the penal expression of God's 'wrath and indignation'.[177] Through original sin man exchanged sanctifying grace — 'the holiness and justice in which he had been constituted'[178] — and 'became unclean' [Is 64:6] and…'by nature children of wrath' [Eph 2:3].[179] There is no acknowledgement in *Dignitas Infinita* that man's whole nature, body and soul, was changed for the worse as a consequence of our first parent's original sin.

The Second Vatican Council even went so far as to reiterate the Church Fathers' understanding that man's 'likeness to God' has been 'disfigured' by our First Parents' original sin, 'To the sons of Adam He [Jesus] restores the divine likeness which had been disfigured from the first sin onward.'[180] The Council Fathers' understood that man is damaged on an ontological level by concupiscence:

> Although he was made by God in a state of holiness, from the very onset of his history man abused his liberty, at the urging of the Evil One. Man set himself against God and sought to attain his goal apart from God. Although they knew God, they did not glorify Him as God, but their senseless minds were darkened and they served the creature rather than the Creator. What divine revelation makes known to us agrees with experience. Examining his heart, man finds that he has inclinations toward evil too, and is engulfed by manifold ills which cannot come from his good Creator. Often refusing to acknowledge God as his beginning, man has disrupted also his proper relationship to his own ultimate goal as well as his whole relationship toward himself and others and all created things. Therefore man is split within himself.[181]

Pope Francis' erroneous contention that man possesses an inviolable, pristine ontological dignity ignores the distinctions made by Catholic anthropological doctrine concerning the two fundamental states of human nature vis-à-vis original sin, and the loss of sanctifying grace, and redemption, and the restoration of sanctifying grace

---

[173] Ott, L [1957] *Op cit.*, p. 127

[174] *Ibid.*, p. 146

[175] *Ibid.*, p. 187

[176] Denzinger, H [2010] *Op. cit.*, p.346-347 *Dz* 1347

[177] *Ibid.*, p.372 *Dz* 1511

[178] *Ibid*

[179] *Ibid.*, p. 374-375 *Dz* 1521

[180] Second Vatican Council [1965] Pastoral Constitution, *Gaudium et Spes*, para 22 [Online] Available at: www.vatican.va [Accessed on: 24 April 2024]

[181] Ibid., paras 13 [Online] Available at: www.vatican.va [Accessed on: 24 April 2024

through faith and baptism. Neither fallen man nor redeemed man is constituted with infinite dignity, because fallen man is ontologically disfigured by original sin by the loss of sanctifying grace and redeemed man, though possessing sanctifying grace, is ontologically wounded by concupiscence — a predisposition to sin.

Proof from the Sources of Faith

a) Teaching from Holy Scripture

Sacred Scripture is clear that the uncreated, eternal God possesses divine attributes that are exclusive to Him, one of which is the attribute of 'infinity'. Only God is boundless, 'Great is the Lord, and greatly to be praised: and of his greatness there is no end.' (Ps 144:3). Only God possesses limitless wisdom, 'Great is our Lord, and great is his power: and of his wisdom there is no number'. (Ps 146:5). Only God's existence is timeless, 'from eternity and to eternity thou art God'; 'I am Alpha and Omega, the beginning and the end, saith the Lord God, who is, and who was, and who is to come, the Almighty'. (Is 40:28 & Rev 1:8).

Dignitas Infinita makes the grave mistake of identifying the divine attribute of infinity with man's ontological nature due to the Old Testament account of man being created in the image [*Tselem*] and likeness [*Demuth*] of God (Gen 1:26-27). The Hebrew word *Tselem*[182] [image] is associated with idols, meaning Adam is a created, material representative of God in creation — nothing created and material has 'infinite' individuated, ontological attributes. To falsely bestow an exclusively divine attribute, such as infinity, on a *Tselem* would be to make it the pagan idol condemned throughout sacred Scripture (e.g., Ex 20:3-6; Ps 115; I Cor 10:14). The Old Testament presents man as representing God as His *Tselem* in two specific creaturely ways — as image of divine paternity through procreation and image of divine lordship through dominion over creation (Gen 1:28).

Nowhere in sacred Scripture does it say that man is an image of infinite dignity. Instead divine revelation exposes the contrary tragic reality that due to the catastrophe of our First Parent's primal sin, fallen, unredeemed man bears the disfigured, mutilated image of the sinner,[183] who is the focus of God's indignation and wrath.

Instead of possessing an inviolable, pristine ontological dignity, fallen man possesses a corrupted, stained ontological disfigurement — the absence of sanctifying grace. Man is conceived in sin, and prone to evil:

> 'For behold I was conceived in iniquities; and in sins did my mother conceive me'. (Ps 50:7); '…for the imagination and thought of man's heart are prone to evil from his youth'. (Gen 8:21). 'But every man is tempted by his own concupiscence, being drawn away and allured. Then when concupiscence hath conceived, it bringeth forth sin. But sin, when it is completed, begetteth death.' (Jm 1:14-15); 'Now then it is no more I that do it, but sin that dwelleth in me. For I know that there dwelleth not in me, that is to say, in my flesh, that which is good.' (Rm 7:17-18).

The pauline phrase describing the nature of fallen humanity conveys the biblical warning about God's indignation and wrath towards man's intrinsic sinful condition — fallen human beings are 'by nature children of wrath' (Eph 2:3). The Greek word for 'wrath', *orgé*, has the meaning of indignation, vengeance, wrath as punishment and justifiable abhorrence.[184] Simply put, unrepentant, fallen man merits God's wrath. Tertullian explained the phrase 'by nature' as referring to the 'irrational irascibility' of man 'such as proceeds not from that nature which is the production of God, but from that which the devil brought in'.[185] St. Thomas Aquinas reiterated Tertullian's interpretation that fallen man's nature has its origin with the devil, and as such deserves God's wrath:

---

[182] *Strong's Concordance* [Online] available at: www.biblehub.com [Accessed on: 10 May 2024]

[183] Léon-Dufour, X [1988] *Dictionary of Biblical Theology*. Ijamsville: The Word Among Us Press, p.330

[184] *Strong's Concordance* [Online] available at: www.biblehub.com [Accessed on: 13 May 2024]

[185] Tertullian. *A Treatise on the Soul*, Chap. 16 [Online] Available at: www.newadvent.org [Accessed on: 9 July 2022]

Thus he says we were by nature, that is, from the earliest beginning of nature — not of nature as nature since this is good and from God, but of nature as vitiated — children of an avenging wrath, aimed at punishment and hell.[186]

Divine revelation testifies that the wickedness of fallen man provokes God's wrath to the extent that God 'repented' of our creation and decided on the destruction of humanity:

And God seeing that the wickedness of men was great on the earth, and that all the thought of their heart was bent upon evil at all times, It repented him that he had made man on the earth. And being touched inwardly with sorrow of heart, He said: I will destroy man, whom I have created, from the face of the earth. (Gen 6:5-7).

Our Lord Jesus Christ, true God and true man — free of original sin — is the true 'image of the invisible God' (Col 1:15). He is the New Adam who makes possible man's restoration to sanctifying grace, 'For as by the disobedience of one man, many were made sinners; so also by the obedience of one, many shall be made just' (Rm 5:19). However, though restored through faith and baptism to the creaturely image of God in Jesus (Rm 8:29; I Cor 15:49; Col 3:9-10) man's nature remains wounded by concupiscence (Rm 7:17-18; Jm 1:14-15). Our Lord Jesus Christ, true God and true man, and by association his Mother, is the only human being who possesses an inviolable, pristine ontological dignity that is infinite. (*ST* I q. 25, a. 6)

b) The Testimony of Tradition

St. Irenaeus described the first Adam as being a 'vessel in Satan's possession' and man, made in the image and likeness of God, as 'being injured by the serpent that had corrupted him'.[187] As a consequence, salvation history is about the recovery in man of being made in the image and likeness of God, 'what we had lost in Adam — namely, to be according to the image and likeness of God — that we might recover in Christ Jesus.'[188] Irenaeus characterised the disfigurement of fallen man as being reduced to the level of the beasts:

Wherefore also he shall be justly condemned, because, having been created a rational being, he lost the true rationality, and living irrationally, opposed the righteousness of God, giving himself over to every earthly spirit, and serving all lusts; as says the prophet, 'Man, being in honour, did not understand: he was assimilated to senseless beasts, and made like to them.'[189]

According to Irenaeus, if man does not possess the Spirit [sanctifying grace] he will remain created in the image of God but will not receive the 'similitude' [likeness] because without the Spirit man is left carnal, dominated by his animal nature. It was only through the incarnation of the Son of God that redeemed human nature was restored as the image and likeness of God:

When, however, the Word of God became flesh, He confirmed both these: for He both showed forth the image truly, since He became Himself what was His image; and He re-established the similitude after a sure manner, by assimilating man to the invisible Father through means of the visible Word.[190]

Origin explained that as a creature uniquely made in the image and likeness of God man immediately 'received the dignity of God's image' but not his 'likeness'. Our realisation

---

[186] St. Thomas Aquinas [1966] *Commentary on Saint Paul's Epistle to the Ephesians: Translation and Introduction by Matthew L. Lamb, O.C.S.O.* [Online] Available at: www.isidore.co [Accessed on: 13 May 2024]

[187] St. Irenaeus. *Against Heresies.* Bk. III, Chap. 23 [Online] Available at: www.newadvent.org [Accessed on: 13 April 2024]

[188] *Op cit.,* Bk. III, Chap. 18

[189] *Ibid.,* Bk. IV, Chap. 4

[190] *Ibid.,* Bk. V, Chaps. 6 & 16

of the 'likeness' of God can only be achieved at the eschatological consummation, and 'will be conferred in proportion to the completeness of our deserts' and through the intercession of our Lord. Origen went on to raise questions as to the nature of this 'likeness' due to the ontological differences between creature and Creator:

> …it is made a question by some whether the nature of bodily matter, although cleansed and purified, and rendered altogether spiritual, does not seem either to offer an obstruction towards attaining the dignity of the (divine) likeness, or to the property of unity, because neither can a corporeal nature appear capable of any resemblance to a divine nature which is certainly incorporeal; nor can it be truly and deservedly designated one with it, especially since we are taught by the truths of our religion that that which alone is one, viz., the Son with the Father, must be referred to a peculiarity of the (divine) nature.[191]

St. Augustine explored the differences between man and God in his explication of the biblical account of man being 'made in the image and likeness of God':

1) 'that image of God was not made altogether equal to Him, as being not born of Him, but created by Him'.
2) '…he is not made equal by parity, but approaches to Him by a sort of likeness.'
3) '…man is said to be "after the image," on account, as we have said, of the inequality of the likeness.'
4) '…man might be the image of the Trinity; not equal to the Trinity as the Son is equal to the Father, but approaching to it, as has been said, by a certain likeness; just as nearness may in a sense be signified in things distant from each other, not in respect of place, but of a sort of imitation.'[192]

Having underlined the ways in which man is a creaturely image and likeness of God that is not identical with God, Augustine described how man deformed that creaturely image and likeness. He described the consequence of Adam and Eve's desire for divine knowledge of good and evil as 'a distorted appetite for being like God' that led to disgrace, reducing man to being like beasts:

> …beginning from a distorted appetite for being like God they end up by becoming like beasts…since his honor consists in being like God and his disgrace in being like an animal, *man established in honor did not understand; he was matched with senseless cattle and became like them* (Ps 49:12).[193]

St. Augustine described the original sin as 'deforming' and 'staining' the image of God in man, 'it lost righteousness and true holiness by sinning, through which that image became defaced and tarnished'.[194] In order to understand how the First Sin catastrophically deformed man's nature made in the image and likeness of God, Augustine enunciated the heinousness of the sin,

> …a number of distinct sins may be observed, if it be analysed as it were into its separate elements. For there is in it pride, because man chose to be under his own dominion, rather than under the dominion of God; and blasphemy, because he did not believe God; and murder, for he brought death upon himself; and spiritual fornication, for the purity of the human soul was corrupted by the seducing blandishments of the serpent; and theft, for man turned to his own use the food he had been forbidden to touch; and avarice, for he had a craving for more than should have been sufficient for him.[195]

---

[191] Origen. *De Principiis*, Bk. III, Chap. 6 [Online] Available at: www.newadvent.org [Accessed on: 19 April 2024]

[192] The Works of Saint Augustine: A Translation for the 21st Century: *The Trinity*. New York: New City Press, 1990 p. 383

[193] *Op cit.*, p. 331

[194] St. Augustine. *On the Trinity* [Online] Available at: www.newadvent.org [Accessed on: 20 April 2024]

[195] St. Augustine. *The Enchiridion on Faith, Hope and Love*, Chap. 45 [Online] Available at: www. newadvent.org [Accessed on: 14 May 2024]

According to St. Augustine, though conformity to Christ through baptism removes the guilt attaching to original sin, it cannot remove the wound it inflicts on man's nature which must be countered, with the assistance of grace, through chastity, virtue and asceticism:

> Carnal concupiscence is remitted, indeed, in baptism; not so that it is put out of existence, but so that it is not to be imputed for sin. Although its guilt is now taken away, it still remains until our entire infirmity be healed by the advancing renewal of our inner man, day by day, when at last our outward man shall be clothed with incorruption.[196]

Obviously, according to St. Augustine's anthropology, founded on sacred Scripture, it is incomprehensible to claim that man possesses an inviolable, pristine ontological dignity or to ascribe it infinite dignity.

St. Thomas Aquinas stated categorically that man does not possess an 'infinite dignity' in the context of the requirements needed to atone for the infinite offence of original sin, and actual sin, against God's holiness and justice:

> But no mere man has the infinite dignity required to satisfy justly an offence against God. Therefore there had to be a man of infinite dignity who would undergo the penalty for all so as to satisfy fully for the sins of the whole world. Therefore the only-begotten Word of God, true God and Son of God, assumed a human nature and willed to suffer death in it so as to purify the whole human race indebted by sin.[197]

Furthermore, Aquinas emphasised that man does not possess an equality with God through being created in his image and likeness because God 'infinitely excels its copy'. 'Infinity' is an attribute of God, not man. Man is an 'imperfect' image of God.[198]

The idea that man possesses an infinite dignity deriving from an inviolable ontological nature unaffected by sin is contradicted by Aquinas, who – like Irenaeus and Augustine – stated that sin reduces man to the level of the beast:

> By sinning man departs from the order of reason, and consequently falls away from the dignity of his manhood, in so far as he is naturally free, and exists for himself, and he falls into the slavish state of the beasts.[199]

Pope Francis and Cardinal Fernández's proposition that man's dignity can be divided into four parts, in order to preserve the inviolability of his ontological dignity, is also contrary to Aquinas' anthropology, when he states that, 'the whole of human nature has been corrupted by sin'. St. Thomas even goes so far as to say that only man's sin has 'a kind of infinity' because of the infinite offence it causes to God, 'a sin committed against God has a kind of infinity from the infinity of the Divine majesty, because the greater the person we offend, the more grievous the offence.'[200]

In conclusion, the anthropology underpinning Pope Francis and Cardinal Fernández's *Dignitas Infinita* is fundamentally irreconcilable with sacred Scripture and sacred Tradition's understanding of the nature of God and human nature. By claiming that man possesses an inviolable ontological dignity, in contradiction to doctrine on original sin, *Dignitas Infinita's* anthropology descends to the level of gnosis.

[196] St. Augustine. *On Marriage and Concupiscence*, Bk. I, Chap. 28 [Online] [Online] Available at: www.newadvent.org [Accessed on: 14 May 2024]
[197] St. Thomas Aquinas. *De Rationibus Fidei*, Chap. 7 [Online] Available at: www.isidore.co [Accessed on: 22 April 2024]
[198] St. Thomas Aquinas. *Summa Theologiae. Prima Pars.* Q 93 Art. 1 [Online] Available at: www.newadvent.org [Accessed on: 22 April 2024]
[199] St. Thomas Aquinas. *Summa theologiae, Secunda Secundæ Pars.* Q 64. Art. 2 [Online] Available at: www.newadvent.org [Accessed on: 22 April 2024]
[200] St. Thomas Aquinas. *Summa Theologiae, Tertia Pars.* Q 1. Art. 2 [Online] Available at: www.newadvent.org [Accessed on: 22 April 2024]

c) The Defence by the Magisterium

Since the 5th century the Church has declared that man was ontologically changed for the worse by Adam's transgression. In response to the soteriological and anthropological heresies of Pelagius, including the denial of the physical transmission of original sin, Pope Celestine I stated that due to the transgression of Adam 'all men lost their natural capacity and their innocence'. The impact of original sin was described in terms of an ontological 'collapse' that vitiated the faculty of free-will.[201]

The 6th century Second Synod of Orange upheld the truth against Pelagianism that as a consequence of Adam's transgression 'the whole person, body and soul…was "changed for the worse"'; emphasising that free will was 'wounded' and 'weakened'. In his summary of the synod's conclusions, Bishop Caesarius of Arles wrote:

> Thus, according to the texts of Holy Scripture and the explanations of the early Fathers quoted above, we must with God's help preach and believe the following: free will has been so distorted and weakened by the sin of the first man that thereafter no one could love God as was required or believe in God or perform for the sake of God what is good, unless the grace of the divine mercy first attained him.[202]

Pope Boniface II warned against those who ignored the revealed truth that Adam's sin perverted human nature, and instead see human nature as 'good' unaided by grace.[203]

Over time magisterial teaching used starker terms in order to convey the evil of the state of unredeemed, fallen man. The 9th century Synod of Quiercy referred to humanity being reduced to a 'mass of perdition', 'Man, using his free will badly, sinned and fell and became the 'mass of perdition' of the entire human race.'[204]

In the 19th century, Pope Gregory XVI described the nature of fallen man in apocalyptic terms drawn from the Book of Revelation:

> When all restraints are removed by which men are kept on the narrow path of truth, their nature, which is already inclined to evil, propels them to ruin. Then truly 'the bottomless pit' is open from which John saw smoke ascending which obscured the sun, and out of which locusts flew forth to devastate the earth.[205]

Pope Leo XIII employed the Pauline phrase 'by nature the children of wrath' (Eph 2: 3) to describe the ontological state of unredeemed, fallen man. The Holy Father explicated this to mean that the human race had become the 'enemies to God' because our 'whole nature had fallen into such guilt and dishonour' leaving mankind in 'ruin and eternal destruction'.[206] He also wrote that 'human nature was stained by original sin, and is therefore more disposed to vice than to virtue'. Pope Leo XIII condemned those who rejected the divine revelation concerning original sin:

> But the naturalists and Freemasons, having no faith in those things which we have learned by the revelation of God, deny that our first parents sinned, and consequently think that free will is not at all weakened and inclined to evil. On the contrary, exaggerating rather the power and the excellence of nature, and placing therein alone the principle and rule of justice, they cannot even imagine that there is any need at all of a constant struggle and a perfect steadfastness to overcome the violence and rule of our passions.[207]

Pope Pius XI also used the Pauline phrase 'by nature the children of wrath' (Eph 2: 3), which he explained as referring to unredeemed, fallen man as being 'infected by

[201] Denzinger, H [2010] *Op. cit.*, p.88-89 *Dz* 239
[202] *Op cit.*, p. 139 *Dz* 396
[203] *Ibid.*, p.141-142 *Dz* 400
[204] *Ibid.*, p. 213 *Dz* 621
[205] Pope Gregory XVI [1832] Encyclical *Mirari Vos*, para 14 [Online] Available at: www.papalencyclicals [Accessed on: 1 May 2024]
[206] Pope Leo XIII [1897] Encyclical *Divinum illud Munus*, paras 8-9 [Online] Available at: www.vatican.va [Accessed on: 30 April 2024]
[207] Pope Leo XIII [1884] Encyclical *Humanum Genus*, paras 1, 20 [Online] Available at: www.vatican.va [Accessed on: 30 April 2024]

hereditary stain, subject to concupiscences and most wretchedly depraved', deserving to be 'thrust down into eternal destruction'. The Holy Father also warned against those who ignored the doctrine of original sin:

> This indeed is denied by the wise men of this age of ours, who following the ancient error of Pelagius, ascribe to human nature a certain native virtue by which of its own force it can go onward to higher things.[208]

Pope Ven. Pius XII followed his predecessors in employing the Pauline phrase 'the children of wrath' to describe the state of fallen man, 'infected by the hereditary stain, lost their participation in the divine nature, and we were all "children of wrath."'[209]

Post-Vatican II popes referred to original sin in terms of 'disfiguring' and 'deforming' man's nature, preferring milder language to that used in the 19th and early 20th centuries.

Pope St. Paul VI referred to the 'the ruinous consequences of original sin'[210] and 'human nature so fallen, stripped of the grace that clothed it, injured in its own natural powers'.[211] Interestingly, Pope St. Paul VI emphasised the influence of the devil on man's nature:

> That fall of Adam gave the devil a certain dominion over man, from which only Christ's Redemption can free us.... He undermines man's moral equilibrium with his sophistry. He is the malign, clever seducer who knows how to make his way into us through the senses, the imagination and the libido, through utopian logic, or through disordered social contacts in the give and take of our activities, so that he can bring about in us deviations that are all the more harmful because they seem to conform to our physical or mental makeup, or to our profound, instinctive aspirations.[212]

Pope St. John Paul II, during his famous catechesis on the Theology of the Body, examined the impact of original sin on man's nature:

i)   John Paul II described man's state in terms of 'A fundamental disquiet in all human existence.'

ii) Reflecting on Genesis 3:10 the Holy Father characterised man's total situation after original sin as one of 'cosmic shame' which he identified as 'caused by the deep disorder in man made in God's image'.

iii) As a consequence of original sin 'a certain constitutive break within the human person is revealed, which is almost a rupture of man's original spiritual and somatic unity.'

iv) Fallen man feels 'cosmic shame' because he 'realises for the first time that his body has ceased drawing upon the power of the spirit, which raised him to the level of the image of God.'

v)   St. Paul expressed the realisation of this ontological rupture, 'For I delight in the law of God, in my inmost self, but I see in my members another law at war with the law of my mind' (Rm 7:22-23).

vi) 'The body is not subordinated to the spirit as in the state of original innocence. It bears within it a constant centre of resistance to the spirit. It threatens, in a way, the unity of the person, that is, of the moral nature, which is firmly rooted in the constitution of the person.'

---

[208] Pope Pius XI [1928] Encyclical *Miserentissimus Redemptor*, para 8 [Online] Available at: www. vatican.va [Accessed on: 30 April 2024]

[209] Pope Ven. Pius XII [1943] Encyclical *Mystici Corporis*, para 12 [Available at: www. papalencyclicals.net [Accessed on: 29 April 2024]

[210] Pope St. Paul VI [1964] Encyclical *Ecclesiam Suam*, paras 39 &41 [Online] Available at: www. vatican.va [Accessed on: 29 April 2024]

[211] Pope St. Paul VI [1968] Apostolic Letter *Solemni Hac Liturgia*, paras 16-18 [Online] Available at: www.vatican.va [Accessed on: 29 April 2024]

[212] Pope St. Paul VI [1972] *Confronting The Devil's Power* [Available at: www.papalencyclicals.net [Accessed on: 29 April 2024]

vii) This realisation of shame 'contains such a cognitive acuteness as to create a fundamental disquiet in all human existence.'[213]

Unlike Pope Francis and Cardinal Fernández, Pope St. John Paul II does not see a strict demarcation between the ontological nature of man, and his moral, social and existential dimensions. Pope St. John Paul II understands that the unity of the person comprises man's moral nature, 'firmly rooted in the constitution of the person':

> Original Sin causes a fundamental change in mankind.... the fact that really matters is of a moral nature and is imprinted in the very roots of the human spirit. It gives rise to a fundamental change in the human condition. Man is driven forth from the state of original justice and finds himself in a state of sinfulness (*status naturae lapsae*). Sin exists in this state, which is also marked by an inclination to sin.[214]

Pope Benedict XVI described original sin as a primal event that 'tarnishes and wounds human nature'.[215] The Holy Father also reflected on original sin in terms of its ontological impact on human existence:

> There exists an empirical aspect, that is, a reality that is concrete, visible, I would say tangible to all. And an aspect of mystery concerning the ontological foundation of this event. The empirical fact is that a contradiction exists in our being. On the one hand every person knows that he must do good and intimately wants to do it. Yet at the same time he also feels the other impulse to do the contrary, to follow the path of selfishness and violence, to do only what pleases him, while also knowing that in this way he is acting against the good, against God and against his neighbour.[216]

In order to understand this ontological contradiction in man Pope Benedict XVI referred to the work of the 17th century Catholic philosopher Blaise Pascal and his insight that man possess a 'second nature' imposed on the original nature created by God:

> This 'second nature' makes evil appear normal to man. Hence even the common expression 'he's human' has a double meaning. 'He's human', can mean: this man is good, he really acts as one should act. But 'he's human', can also imply falsity: evil is normal, it is human. Evil seems to have become our second nature.[217]

Pope Benedict XVI also addressed the question of 'infinity' in relation to Christian anthropology, in terms of man possessing a 'desire for the infinite'. He was clear that 'infinity' was a divine attribute that man did not possess, 'To say: "By nature, man is relation to the infinite" thus means saying that every person has been created so that he or she may enter into dialogue with God, with the Infinite.'[218]

Regarding redeemed man, the Church has consistently taught that even when liberated from the dominion of the devil by faith and baptism — restored by Jesus Christ, the true image of God — man bears the ontological wound of concupiscence, that leaves him attracted to sin and evil.

In the 5th century the Synod of Arles warned that man's will was so 'weakened and enfeebled' by original sin that 'he who is saved is [still] in danger'.[219] In the 9th century,

[213] Pope St. John Paul II [2005] *The Redemption of the Body and Sacramentality of Marriage* (*Theology of the Body*): *From the Weekly Audiences of His Holiness, September 5, 1979 – November 28, 1984*) [Online] Available at: www.stmarys-waco.org [Accessed on: 29 April 2024]
[214] Pope St. John Paul II [1986] *General Audience – Original Sin Causes a Fundamental Change in Mankind* [Online] Available at: www.web.archive.org [Accessed on: 25th April 2024]
[215] Pope Benedict XVI [2013] *General Audience Address* [Online] Available at: www.vatican.va [Accessed on: 25 April 2024]
[216] Pope Benedict XVI [2008] *General Audience Address* [Online] Available at: www.vatican.va [Accessed on: 25 April 2024]
[217] *Ibid.*
[218] Pope Benedict XVI [2012] *Message for the 33rd Meeting for Friendship Among Peoples* [Online] Available at: www.vatican.va [Accessed on: 25 April 2024]
[219] Denzinger, [2010] *Op. cit.,* p.119 *Dz* 339

the Synod of Quiercy declared that man's free will is only restored if he remains in a state of grace, otherwise, 'we have free will for evil, abandoned by grace.'[220] In the 19th century, Pope Gregory XVI warned, 'When all restraints are removed by which men are kept on the narrow path of truth, their nature, which is already inclined to evil, propels them to ruin.'[221]

Later popes took up Gregory XVI's understanding that virtuous, redeemed man's nature remains 'inclined to evil'. In his catechism Pope St. Pius X listed 'inclination to evil' as one of the abiding consequences of original sin.[222] Pope Pius XI wrote in his encyclical warning against the dangers of Nazism that man has a 'propensity to evil' which can only be 'repressed and conquered' 'with the assistance of grace, penance, resistance and moral effort'.[223] In an earlier encyclical he exhorted Christian educators to remember that 'There remain therefore, in human nature the effects of original sin, the chief of which are weakness of will and disorderly inclinations'.[224]

Post Vatican II popes also emphasised the doctrine that original sin leaves baptised man with an inclination to evil. Pope St. John Paul II's *Catechism of the Catholic Church* explains:

> Although it is proper to each individual, original sin does not have the character of a personal fault in any of Adam's descendants. It is a deprivation of original holiness and justice, but human nature has not been totally corrupted: it is wounded in the natural powers proper to it, subject to ignorance, suffering and the dominion of death, and inclined to sin — an inclination to evil that is called 'concupiscence'. Baptism, by imparting the life of Christ's grace, erases original sin and turns a man back towards God, but the consequences for nature, weakened and inclined to evil, persist in man and summon him to spiritual battle. (CCC 405)

In his *Compendium of the Catechism of the Catholic Church* Pope Benedict XVI also highlighted the ontological fact that as a consequence of original sin human nature is 'wounded in its natural powers' and remains 'inclined toward sin. This inclination is called concupiscence.'[225]

In the light of the Church's consistent teaching that redeemed man possesses an 'inclination to sin', Pope Francis' teaching that concupiscent man possesses an ontological 'infinite dignity' is clearly gravely erroneous — 'infinite dignity' is totally incompatible with an ontological inclination to sin and ever pressing attraction to evil.

---

[220] *Ibid.*, p. 213 *Dz 621, Dz 622*
[221] Pope Gregory XVI [1832] Encyclical *Mirari Vos*, para 14 [Online] Available at: www.papalencyclicals [Accessed on:1 May 2024]
[222] *Catechism of St. Pius X* [1908] [Online] Available at: www.ewtn.com [Accessed on: 30 April 2024]
[223] Pope Pius XI [1937] Encyclical *Mit Brennender Sorge*, para 25 [Online] Available at: www.vatican.va [Accessed on: 29 April 2024]
[224] Pope Pius XI [1929] Encyclical *Divini Illius Magistri*, paras 58, 60 [Online] Available at: www.vatican.va [Accessed on: 30 April 2024]
[225] *Compendium of the Catechism of the Catholic Church* [2005] [Online] Available at: www.vatican.va [Accessed on: 25 April 2024]

Christology

B. *When the Son of God assumed a human nature at the Incarnation, he ceased to be divine until his death on the cross. Jesus of Nazareth was a man, not God incarnate.*

The Italian journalist Eugenio Scalfari published two accounts of his conversations with Pope Francis (7th July 2017[226] and 8th October 2019,[227] *La Repubblica*) that reported the Supreme Pontiff's thoughts on the Incarnation, that expressed an erroneous kenotic Christology. Following the 2019 report, Dr. Paolo Ruffini, Prefect of the Vatican's Dicastery for Communication, stated that Scalfari's quotations of Pope Francis could not be considered a faithful account.[228] However, Scalfari did not issue an apology or correct his report, and — despite the gravity of the reported error — Pope Francis, as 'the supreme teacher of the universal Church' (LG 25), did not repudiate, contradict, or demand a retraction. Instead, Pope Francis continued to show Eugenio Scalfari signs of special favour by granting him frequent interviews.

Pope Francis' erroneous kenotic Christology can be summarised under the following headings:

a) 'Pope Francis conceives of Christ as Jesus of Nazareth, man, not God incarnate.'[229]
b) At the Incarnation, the Son of God ceased to be 'a god' and became a man until his death on the cross;[230] 'The Pope knows that Jesus really became incarnate, he became a man until he was crucified. The "Resurrectio" is in fact the proof that a God who became man only after his death becomes God again.'[231]
c) 'Jesus of Nazareth, once he became a man, though a man of exceptional virtues, was not a God at all'.[232]
d) Two events related in sacred Scripture are the 'proof-of-proofs', according to Pope Francis, that Jesus of Nazareth was not 'a god at all' but a 'man of exceptional virtue':[233] Jesus' prayer to the Father in the Garden of Gethsemane, 'Lord — said Jesus — if you can remove this bitter chalice from me, please do it, but if you can't or you don't want to, I will drink it all the way'(Scalfari's paraphrase of Mt 26:39; Mk 14:36 & Lk 22:42) and Jesus' cry from the cross, 'Lord, you have forsaken me' (Scalfari's paraphrase of Mt 27:46 & Mk 15:34).

This erroneous Kenotic Christology is similar to the ideas promulgated by the Protestant kenotic theologians of the 19th century who proposed that 'Somehow He [the Son of God] laid aside His Divine mode of existence in order to become man'.[234] Pope Ven. Pius XII condemned Protestant kenotic Christology as an 'enemy of the faith of Chalcedon' because 'they imagine that the divinity was taken away from the Word in Christ.' (Sempiternus Rex Christus, 29).[235]

[226] Scalfari, E [7 July 2017] *Scalfari intervista Francesco: "Il mio grido al G20 sui migranti"* [Online] 1 Available at: www.repubblica.it [Accessed on: 17 September 2022]

[227] White, H. [24 October 2019] *How Francis Might Deny Christ's Divinity…Sort Of* [Online] Available at: https://onepeterfive.com/ [Accessed 20 June 2022]; New Catholic [9 October 2019] *Francis to Favorite Journalist: 'Jesus was not at all a God.'* [Online] Available at: https://rorate-caeli.blogspot.com [Accessed 20 June 2022]

[228] Roberts, J. [10 October 2019] *Scalfari Claims Pope Does Not Believe Jesus 'The Man' Was Divine* [Online] Available at: www.thetablet.co.uk [Accessed 20 June 2022]

[229] *Francis to Favorite Journalist: "Jesus was not at all a God."* [Online] Available from: https://rorate-4 caeli.blogspot.com [Accessed on: 21 September 2022]

[230] White, H [24 October 2019] *Op. cit.*   [231] Scalfari, E [07 July 2017] *Op. cit.*

[232] Skojek, S [9 October 2019] *Scalfari, Friend of Francis, Claims Pope Believes Jesus Was "Not a God At All"* [Online] Available at: onepeterfive.wpengine.com [Accessed on: 17 September 2022]

[233] White, H 24 October 2019] *Op. cit.*

[234] Thompson, T.R. *Nineteenth-Century Kenotic Christology: The Waxing, Waning and Weighing of a Quest for a Coherent Orthodoxy* in Evans, C.S. [2006] *Exploring Kenotic Christology: The Self-Emptying of God*. Oxford: Oxford University Press, p.90.

[235] Pius XII [1951] Encyclical *Sempiternus Rex Christus* [Online] Available at: www.vatican.va [Accessed 21 June 2022]

The Teaching of the Church
The Divine and the human natures are united hypostatically in Christ, that is, joined to each other in one Person. **(De fide.)**[236]

Contrary to Pope Francis' erroneous kenotic Christology, dogma asserts that the Son of God remained a Divine Person at the Incarnation. The sufferings of Jesus of Nazareth do not 'prove the Kenotic error' that he ceased to be God, or only resumed his divine nature when his human nature died.

Dogma asserts that in Jesus Christ there is the Divine Person of the Son of God, and two natures which belong to the One Divine Person. 'The human nature is assumed into the unity and dominion of the Divine Person, so that the Divine Person operates in the human nature and through the human nature, as its organ.'[237] The Divine Person suffered and died in his human nature, hypostatically united — with 'no confusion, no change, no division, no separation' — to his divine nature.

The Council of Nicaea (325) promulgated its famous profession of faith that implicitly affirmed, but did not define, an unbroken continuity between the pre-existence of the Only Begotten Son of God and his Incarnate existence, including his suffering and death (*Dz* 125).

The Council of Ephesus (431) confirmed the Twelve Anathemas proposed by St. Cyril of Alexandria. Its assertion of the continuity of divine pre-existence and incarnate existence — without rupture — and the union of divine and human natures can be summarised as follows:

a) The Word from God the Father has been hypostatically united with the flesh, meaning that Christ is therefore God and man together. (*Dz* 253).
b) It is anathema to divide the divine from the human after the hypostatic union at the Incarnation. (*Dz* 254)
c) When undertaking an exegesis of sacred Scripture, it is anathema to divide the words and deeds of Christ by ascribing some of them to him as man and some of them to him as God. They must be attributed to the one Christ, the Son of God become flesh. (*Dz* 255)
d) It is anathema to deny that the Son of God suffered crucifixion and death in the flesh, though as God he is life and life-giving. (*Dz* 263).

The Council of Chalcedon (451) defined the fundamental Christological dogma of the Incarnation that exposes the error at the heart of Pope Francis' kenotic speculations. Chalcedon affirms the continuity between the pre-existence of the Son of God and his incarnational existence by defining the origin and characteristics of his divine nature from God the Father and his human nature from 'Mary, the virgin God-bearer'. Then Chalcedon affirms the unity of the two natures of Christ in one Divine Person that dispels any idea of a kenotic separation of the divine and the human:

> ...the same Christ, Son, Lord, only-begotten, acknowledged in two natures which undergo no confusion, no change, no division, no separation; at no point was the difference between the natures taken away through the union, but rather the property of both natures is preserved and comes together into a single person and a single subsistent being; he is not parted or divided into two persons, but is one and the same only-begotten Son, God, Word, Lord Jesus Christ[238] (*Dz* 302).

The Third Council of Constantinople (680 to 681) further explicated the relationship between the divine nature and human nature united in the one Divine Person, declaring that Jesus Christ is 'one of the holy Trinity'. The council's teaching can be summarised as follows:

---

[236] Ott, L [1957] *Fundamentals of Catholic Dogma.* Cork: The Mercier Press. p.144
[237] *Ibid.*
[238] Tanner, N [1990] *Decrees of the Ecumenical Councils*: Vol 1 [Online] Available at: www. papalencyclicals.net [Accessed: 21 June 2022]

a) 'Our lord Jesus Christ, even after his incarnation' is 'one of the holy Trinity and our true God'.
b) Jesus has two natures — divine and human — in which he demonstrated in one person the miracles and the sufferings.
c) Each nature — divine and human — wills and performs the things that are proper to it in a communion with the other. (*Dz* 558)[239]

The Council of Vienne (1311-1312) defined that the eternal, Only Begotten Son of the Father, true God, entered into 'time' through assuming human nature in the womb of the Blessed Virgin Mary. Contrary to Pope Francis' kenotic Christology, the incarnation into time and space did not separate the divine nature and human nature of Jesus, requiring that they be re-united at death. Rather, God's assumption of a 'human, passible body and the intellectual or rational soul' was necessary for him to gain our salvation by being 'nailed to the cross and to die on it' (*Dz* 900-901).[240]

Proof from the Sources of Faith
a) Teaching from Holy Scripture
Sacred Scripture refutes Pope Francis' assertion that Jesus was only a man, attesting to the fact that our Lord Jesus Christ is true God and true man. According to Scripture, divine and human attributes are predicates of the one Christ — Divine nature {omnipotence, eternity, divine filiation} human nature {nascence, emotions, suffering, crucifixion, death}.[241]

The Gospels and epistles contain a high Christology about Jesus — Son of God, at the right hand of God, same nature as God, pre-existence — that derive from our Lord testifying to his own divinity and the recognition of his divinity by others.

Sacred Scripture attests to our Lord's divine self-identification and assertion of divine authority and power:

i) Jesus exercises the divine prerogative of forgiving sins (Mt 9:1-18; Mk 2: 4-10).
ii) Jesus exercises divine authority over the *Torah* (Mt 5: 21-48; Mk 10:2-12; Lk 16:18) and Sabbath (Mt 12:1-8; Mk 2:23-28 & 3:1-6; Lk 6:1-5; Jn 5:1-19).
iii) Jesus claims divine authority for his teachings. The gospels record Jesus repeatedly using a phrase that is unique in Jewish literature – the 'Amen I say to you' sayings, of which there are over 31 in St. Matthew, 13 in St. Mark and 25 in St. John.[242] Jesus' use of 'Amen I say to you' suggests his consciousness of his divine authority as the Word of God.
iv) Jesus claims a unique relationship with God the Father, expressing the familiarity of the Son with the Father (Mt 11:25-26; Mk 14:36; Jn 3:35;5:19-20;8:28-29). This special relationship between Father and Son is particularly revealed in Jesus' Baptism (Matthew 3:13-17; Mark 1:10-11; Luke 3:21-22; John 1:32-34).
v) Jesus explicitly claims complete unity with God the Father (Jn 10:28-31) which is also expressed in the seven 'I AM' [*ego eimi*] declarations in John — I AM the Bread of life (6:35, 41, 48, 51); I AM the Light of the world (8:12); 'I AM the Door of the sheep' (10:7, 9); I AM the Good Shepherd'(10:11, 14); 'I AM the Resurrection and the Life' (11:25); 'I AM the Way, the Truth, the Life' (14:6) and 'I AM the true Vine' (15:1, 5).
vi) Jesus reveals his divine pre-existence (Mt 10:34; Jn 12:46).
vii) Jesus' miracles, including the Resurrection, confirm his divine nature and unity with the Father (Jn 5:16-18)

---

[239] *Third Council of Constantinople: 680-681 A. D.* [Online] Available at: www.papalencyclicals.net [Accessed: 21 June 2022]
[240] *Council of Vienne 1311-1312 A.D.* [Online] Available at: www.papalencyclicals.net [Accessed: 21 June 2022]
[241] Ott, L [1957] *Op. cit.,* p.145
[242] Just, Felix *'Amen, Amen' Sayings in the Fourth Gospel.* [Online] Available at: www.catholic-resources.org [Accessed on: 22 June 2022]

St. Paul's epistle to the Philippians contains an early Christian creed testifying to the divine nature of Jesus (Phil 2:6-7). It contains a reference to *kenosis*, 'But emptied himself [*kenosis*] taking the form of a servant.' (Phil 2:7). Ott comments on St. Paul's use of *Kenosis*:

> This Kenosis, on account of the absolute immutability of God, cannot be understood as a renunciation of the Divine Nature, but only as a renunciation (in His human nature) of the Divine Glory (δόξα). To the Divine Nature which He retained, He added the human nature.[243]

b) The Testimony of Tradition

The ante-Nicene Fathers testified that due to the Incarnation, Jesus Christ is both God and man, indivisibly united, exemplified by St. Ignatius of Antioch writing, 'For our God, Jesus Christ, was, according to the appointment of God, conceived in the womb by Mary, of the seed of David, but by the Holy Ghost.'[244] St. Irenaeus of Lyons emphasised the same, '[the] only-begotten Word, who is always present with the human race, united to and mingled with His own creation, according to the Father's pleasure, and who became flesh, is Himself Jesus Christ our Lord.'[245]

Following the Council of Nicaea and confronted by the persistence of Neoplatonic Arianism, Church Fathers emphasised that God truly 'descended' to assume a human nature, giving many proofs of his Godhead. St. Athanasius listed the miracles of Christ as proofs of his divine nature, concluding, 'Now these things showed that Christ on the Cross was God, while all creation was His slave, and was witnessing by its fear to its Master's presence. Thus, then, God the Word showed Himself to men by His works.'[246] Commenting on Philippians' Kenotic text, St. Hilary of Poitiers wrote that there was no division between the divine nature and human nature of Christ:

> Being, then, Man with this body, Jesus Christ is both the Son of God and Son of Man, Who emptied Himself of the form of God, and received the form of a servant. There is not one Son of Man and another Son of God [...] He was born also not to be at one time two separate beings, but that it might be made plain, that He Who was God before He was Man, now that He has taken humanity, is God and Man.[247]

Later Church Fathers refuted any misunderstanding that *Kenosis* meant that the Son of God renounced his Divinity at the Incarnation. St. John Chrysostom insisted that *Kenosis* did not mean a change, degeneracy or loss to the Son of God, 'while He remained what He was, He took that which He was not, and being made flesh He remained God, in that He was the Word.'[248] St. Augustine also wrote, 'He became man who was God, by receiving what He was not, not by losing what He was: so God became man.'[249]

St. Thomas Aquinas wrote that those who argued that the Son of God ceased to be divine at the Incarnation were at fault because they were 'unable to see anything but corporeal things'. Aquinas summarised Christian doctrine on the correct meaning of *Kenosis*, quoting St. Augustine, 'The Christian doctrine nowhere holds that God was so joined to human flesh as either to desert or lose, or to transfer and as it were, contract within this frail body.'[250]

---

[243] Ott, L [1957] *Op. cit.*, p.145

[244] St. Ignatius of Antioch, *Epistle to the Ephesians*. Chap. 18 [Online] Available at: www.newadvent. org [Accessed on: 22 June 2022]

[245] St. Irenaeus of Lyons. *Against Heresies*, Bk III, Chap. 16 [Online] Available at: www.newadvent. org [Accessed on: 22 June 2022]

[246] St. Athanasius. *On the Incarnation of the Word*, Chap. 19 [Online] Available at: www.newadvent. org [Accessed on: 22 June 2022]

[247] St. Hilary of Poitiers. *On the Trinity*, Bk X, Chap. 19 [Online] Available at: www.newadvent.org [Accessed on: 22 June 2022]

[248] St. John Chrysostom. *Homily* 7 on Philippians. [Online] Available at: www.newadvent.org [Accessed on: 22 June 2022]

[249] St. Augustine. *Tractate* 23 (John 5:19-40). [Online] Available at: www.newadvent.org [Accessed on: 22 June 2022]

[250] St. Thomas Aquinas. *Summa Theologiae*. Tertia Pars. q1, a1 [Online] Available at: www. newadvent.org [Accessed on: 22 June 2022]

c) The Defence by the Magisterium

Pope St. Leo the Great set out magisterial teaching on Christology through his letter to Archbishop Flavian of Constantinople. Its acceptance and acclamation at the Council of Chalcedon was instrumental in defining the foundational Christological dogma of the inextricable unity of the two natures of Christ in one Divine Person. In his letter to Bishop Julianus of Cos Pope Leo wrote two years before Chalcedon:

> …for the flesh did not lessen what belongs to His Godhead, nor the Godhead destroy what belongs to His flesh. For He is at once both eternal from His Father and temporal from His mother, inviolable in His strength, passible in our weakness […] Therefore neither was the Word changed into flesh nor flesh into the Word: but both remains in one and one is in both, not divided by the diversity and not confounded by intermixture: He is not one by His Father and another by His mother, but the same, in one way by His Father before every beginning, and in another by His mother at the end of the ages.[251]

Since the time of Pope St. Leo the Great, a succession of popes have been steadfast exponents and defenders of Chalcedon's Christological dogma of the Divine and the human natures being united hypostatically in one Divine Person, Jesus Christ.

Pope Hormisdas beautifully conveyed the interplay between the divine and human natures in the incarnate person of Jesus Christ:

> …the Son of God is himself God and man, the same (Person) is strength and weakness, lowliness and majesty, the one who redeems and the one sold, hung on the Cross and besting the kingdom of heaven, so much in our weakness that he could be killed and so much in his innate power that he could not be destroyed by death.[252]

Pope John II wrote of the inextricable union between the divine and human natures of Jesus Christ, who as one of the Most Holy Trinity, is to be understood 'as (composed) of two natures, perfect in divinity and humanity, not in the sense that the flesh existed first and was afterwards united to the Word, but that it received the origins of its being in God the Word himself.' Pope John II went on to state explicitly that once this inextricable union of divine and human natures occurred at the incarnation, 'the Son of God, our Lord, Jesus Christ… (it) ruled out any subsequent change or confusion (of his natures)'.[253]

Pope Pelagius I further elucidated the origin of the inextricable union between the divine and human natures of our Lord in the womb of the Blessed Virgin:

> …it was not that first there was created the flesh and then the Son of God came (into her), but, as it is written, 'Wisdom building a house for herself' (Prov 9:1), immediately the flesh in the womb of the Virgin (was made) the flesh of the Word of God; and accordingly the Word and the Son of God became man without any change or transformation of the nature of the Word and the nature of the flesh, one in both natures, namely, divine and human, and (thus) Christ Jesus came forth as true God and true man…[254]

Pope Benedict II explicated the inextricable union of divine and human natures through reflection on the generation of the Son from the Father and his birth from the flesh of the Blessed Virgin Mary, 'though he was born differently from the Father and the Mother; nevertheless, he is not divided in the twofold forms of nature, but he is one and the same Son of God and Son of man; he himself lives although he dies and dies although he lives; he is himself incapable of suffering although he suffers; he does not yield to suffering'.[255]

The *Catechism of the Council of Trent*, promulgated during the reign of Pope St. Pius V, drew on scholastic definitions to expound the mysterious, inextricable union between our Lord's divine and human natures. The *Catechism* describes the Incarna-

---

[251] Pope St. Leo the Great. *Letter* 35 to Julian, Bishop of Cos [Online] Available at: www.newadvent.org [Accessed on: 22 June 2022]

[252] Denzinger, H [2010] *Compendium of Creeds, Definitions, and Declarations on Matters of Faith and Morals.* Forty-Third Edition. San Francisco: Ignatius Press, p. 133 *Dz* 369

[253] *Ibid.,* p.143, *Dz* 402

[254] *Ibid.,* p.154, *Dz* 441

[255] *Ibid.,* p.196-197, *Dz* 564

tions in terms of the interplay of the natural order and the supernatural order. At the level of the natural order, 'the body of Christ was formed from the most pure blood of His Virgin Mother we acknowledge the operation of human nature'. And at the level of the supernatural order:

> But what surpasses the order of nature and human comprehension is, that as soon as the Blessed Virgin assented to the announcement of the Angel... the most sacred body of Christ was immediately formed, and to it was united a rational soul enjoying the use of reason; and thus in the same instant of time He was perfect God and perfect man.[256]

Pope Leo XIII, informed by St. Anselm's understanding of atonement, explained the necessity of the union of divine and human natures at the moment of death on the cross:

> the only-begotten Son of God became man, and on behalf of mankind made most abundant satisfaction in His Blood to the outraged majesty of His Father and by this infinite price He redeemed man for His own.[257]

Coinciding with the spread of kenotic Christology in the early 20th century, a number of popes challenged the error that the Son of God ceased to be divine at the Incarnation. Pope St. Pius X condemned Modernists within the Church for, among other things, 'not sparing even the person of the Divine Redeemer, whom, with sacrilegious daring, they reduce to a simple, mere man.'[258] Furthermore, in his Catechism of 1908 Pope St. Pius X dealt with the error directly, without naming its origin, 'Q. In becoming man did the Son of God cease to be God? A. No, the Son of God became man without ceasing to be God.'[259]

As examined earlier, Pope Ven. Pius XII directly challenged the erroneous kenotic Christology in his encyclical *Sempiternus Rex Christus* (1951) quoting Pope St. Leo the Great in his defence of true Christology, 'With the entire and perfect nature of man' - thus grandly St. Leo the Great wrote - 'He Who was true God was born, complete in his own nature, complete in ours'.[260]

Pope St. John Paul II's exegesis of Philippians 2: 6-11 expounded the correct Catholic doctrine of *Kenosis*, which is, the Son of God 'emptied' himself of glory, but not divinity, 'He plummets into the *kenosis*, the "emptying" of his divine glory, pushed to the point of death on the Cross';[261] 'It is on this path of "emptying" himself, or as it were, stripping himself of that glory to take on the *morphé*, in other words, the reality and condition of a servant';[262] 'the incarnation is truly a *kenosis* — a "self-emptying" — on the part of the Son of God of that glory which is his from all eternity'.[263]

Pope Benedict XVI also presented the genuine Catholic doctrine on *kenosis* through his exegesis of Philippians 2: 6-11. He rejects the proposition that the Son of God abandoned his divinity at the Incarnation, 'He certainly possesses the divine nature with all its prerogatives. But this transcendent reality is not interpreted or lived out under the

[256] *The Roman Catechism: The Catechism of the Council of Trent* [1556] [Online] Available at: www.saintsbooks.net [Accessed on: 29 September 2022]
[257] Pope Leo XIII [1900] Encyclical *Tametsi Futura Prospicientibus*, para 3 [Online] Available at: www.vatican.va [Accessed on: 28 September 2022]
[258] Pope St. Pius X [1907] *Pascendi Dominici Gregis*, para 2 [Online] Available at: www.vatican.va [Accessed on: 22 June 2022]
[259] Pope St. Pius X [1908] *Catechism of St. Pius X* [Online] Available at: www.ewtn.com [Accessed on: 22 June 2022]
[260] Pope Ven. Pius XII, *op. cit.*, para 29
[261] Pope St. John Paul II [19th November 2003] *General Audience Address* [Online] Available at: www.vatican.va [Accessed on: 28 September 2022]
[262] Pope St. John Paul II [4th August 2004] *General Audience Address* [Online] Available at: www.vatican.va [Accessed on: 28 September 2022]
[263] Pope St. John Paul II [2001] Apostolic letter *Novo Millennio Ineunte*, para 22 [Online] Available at: www.vatican.va [Accessed on: 28 September 2022]

banner of power, greatness and dominion',[264] and quoting St. Gregory of Nazianzus, he wrote, 'Jesus Christ "does not empty himself of any part that makes up his divine nature"'[265]

Pope St. John Paul II's *Catechism of the Catholic Church* [1997] contains a brief review of the Church's deepening understanding of Christology in response to various heresies. This included a clear exposition of the Divine nature of Christ, which Pope Francis' erroneous kenotic speculations clearly contradict. The Catechism states:

> In parallel fashion, she [the Church] had to recall on each occasion that Christ's human nature belongs, as his own, to the divine person of the Son of God, who assumed it. Everything that Christ is and does in this nature derives from 'one of the Trinity'. The Son of God therefore communicates to his humanity his own personal mode of existence in the Trinity. In his soul as in his body, Christ thus expresses humanly the divine ways of the Trinity… (*CCC* 470).

---

[264] Pope Benedict XVI [1 June 2005] *General Audience Address* [Online] Available at: www.vatican.va [Accessed on: 28 September 2022]

[265] Pope Benedict XVI [26 October 2005] *General Audience Address* [Online] Available at: www.vatican.va [Accessed on: 28 September 2022]

Ecclesiology

C. *It is contrary to the Gospel to prioritise guarding and transmitting the body of doctrine because it shows an obsession with the past.*

Pope Francis has undermined the apostolic nature of the Church by expressing errors concerning the *apostolicitas doctrinae* [the apostolicity of teaching].[266] In particular, on numerous occasions the Supreme Pontiff has expressed erroneous teachings regarding safeguarding the Deposit of Faith and the transmission of the Faith.

Erroneous notions regarding the Fidei depositum

Pope Francis suggests a false antithesis between 'the authentic Gospel of Jesus Christ'[267] and the Deposit of Faith. He, by derogatorily introducing the phrase 'monolithic body of doctrine', imputes a desire for strict rigidity to those who would uphold doctrine:

> For those who long for a monolithic body of doctrine guarded by all and leaving no room for nuance, this might appear as undesirable and leading to confusion. But in fact such variety serves to bring out and develop different facets of the inexhaustible riches of the Gospel.[268]

Pope Francis employed this false antithesis between Gospel and doctrine in his Protestant-like criticism of the Church's philosophical tradition. In his first apostolic exhortation, he warned of not reducing 'preaching to a few doctrines which are at times more philosophical than evangelical.'[269] Despite the apparent reasonableness of this, since most would agree that only preaching a few philosophical doctrines is inadequate, what it does is seek by implication to claim that any use of philosophical doctrines should be warned against. By so doing, he ignores the use of philosophical ideas to define doctrine which be traced back to the original *kerygma* of the apostles. For example, St. John the Evangelist used the Stoic concept of *Logos* (Jn 1:1) to convey the pre-existence of Jesus, and the Church Fathers employed Platonic and Aristotelian philosophy to define trinitarian and Christological dogmas.

Dismissing a concern for upholding doctrine as being closed minded, Pope Francis, by way of contrast, proposed being open to undefined changes using the metaphor of the 'God of Surprises'.[270]

Erroneous notions regarding the transmission of the Faith

Pope Francis taught a number of errors regarding the transmission of the Faith, summarised as follows:

a) Pope Francis erroneously dismissed the fact that apostolic faith necessarily involves a continuity with the past. He described it as 'a temptation to close oneself up in some of the certainties acquired in past traditions.'[271] He variously described this orientation to the past as turning the Faith into a museum[272] and Christians into mummies due to 'a tomb psychology'.[273]

---

[266] Ott, Ludwig. [1957] Op. cit., p.308

[267] Pope Francis [2013] Apostolic Exhortation *Evangelii Gaudium*, para 41 [Online] Available at: www.vatican.va [Accessed on: 23 June 2022]

[268] *Ibid.,* para 40

[269] *Ibid.,* para 165

[270] Pope Francis. [2013] *Homily at Holy Mass with the Ecclesial Movements on Pentecost Sunday*, para 1; [13 October 2014] *Morning Meditation in the Chapel of the Domus Sanctae Marthae*; [8 May 2017] *Morning Meditation in the Chapel of the Domus Sanctae Marthae* [Online] Available at: www.vatican. va [Accessed on: 23 June 2022]

[271] Pope Francis [2021] *General audience address* [Online] Available at: www.vatican.va. [Accessed on: 23 June 2022]

[272] Pope Francis [2016] *Homily during Apostolic Journey to Armenia. Gyumri, Vartanants Square* [Online] Available at: www.vatican.va [Accessed on: 23 June 2022]

[273] Pope Francis [2013] Apostolic Exhortation *Evangelii Gaudium*, para 83 [Online] Available at: www.vatican.va [Accessed on: 23 June 2022]

b) Pope Francis claimed that the use of 'completely orthodox language' and doctrinal 'formulations' fails to convey the truth of the Gospel because it is not expressed in the language and ideas of the present time.[274] Instead, the Supreme Pontiff proposed being open to 'differing currents of thought in philosophy, theology and pastoral practice'.[275] Pope Pius XII rejected such dogmatic relativism, writing, 'this is supreme imprudence and something that would make dogma itself a reed shaken by the wind.'[276]

c) Pope Francis negatively described the transmission of doctrine as an 'imposition' – '[waging] a war of words aimed at imposing doctrines'[277] – and 'dead stones to be hurled at others.'[278]

d) Pope Francis proposed a false antithesis between teaching doctrine and grace. For example, in *Amoris Laetitia* he wrote, 'Marital love is not defended primarily by presenting indissolubility as a duty, or by repeating doctrine, but by helping it to grow ever stronger under the impulse of grace.'[279] He also proposed a false antithesis between doctrine and experience, writing, 'Rather than being too concerned with communicating a great deal of doctrine, let us first try to awaken and consolidate the great experiences that sustain the Christian life.'[280] Again, note the setting up of a false opponent, which he then knocks down. There is a false assertion of extremism, subtly invoked by the descriptions employed, 'primarily presenting', 'great deal of doctrine', which then undermines their being of any value at all.

e) Those who are committed to the faithful transmission of doctrine are, according to Pope Francis, 'obsessed', 'self-absorbed promethean neopelagianists', 'narcissistic and authoritarian elitists'.[281] They succumb to 'a temptation to hostile inflexibility, that is, wanting to close oneself within the written word, (the letter).'[282] Pope Francis repeatedly chastised those upholding doctrine as displaying a 'rigidity' that derived from some secret personal or moral imbalance.[283] The term 'rigid' became his shorthand way of referring to those who upheld the importance of safeguarding and teaching the doctrines of the Faith. Pope Francis even went so far as to describe such faithfulness to doctrine as a 'sin', 'Rigidity is another perversion that is a sin against God's patience; it's a sin against the sovereignty of God.'[284]

The Teaching of the Church
The Church founded by Christ is apostolic. (De fide)[285]
Contrary to Pope Francis' undermining of the apostolic nature of the Church by dismissing her intrinsic orientation to the past, dogma testifies that our Lord founded

---

[274] *Ibid.*, para 41

[275] *Ibid.*, para 40

[276] Pope Pius XII [1950] Encyclical *Humani Generis*, para 17 [Online] Available at: www.vatican.va [Accessed on: 23 June 2022]

[277] Pope Francis [2013] Apostolic Exhortation *Evangelii Gaudium*, para 35; Encyclical *Fratelli Tutti*, 4 [Online] Available at: www.vatican.va [Accessed on: 23 June 2022]

[278] Pope Francis [2015] *Conclusion to the Synod of Bishops* [Online] Available at: www.vatican.va [Accessed on: 23 June 2022]

[279] Pope Francis [2016] Apostolic Exhortation *Amoris Laetitia*, para 134 [Online] Available at: www.vatican.va [Accessed on: 23 June 2022]

[280] Pope Francis [2019] Apostolic Exhortation *Christus Vivit*, para 212 [Online] Available at: www.vatican.va [Accessed on: 23 June 2022]

[281] PPope Francis [2013] Apostolic Exhortation *Evangelii Gaudium*, para 35, 94 [Online] Available at: www.vatican.va [Accessed on: 23 June 2022]

[282] Pope Francis [2014] *Address for the conclusion of the Third Extraordinary General Assembly of the Synod of Bishops* [Online] Available at : www.vatican.va [Accessed on: 23 June 2022]

[283] Pope Francis [2019] *Christmas Address to the Curia* [Online] Available at: www.vatican.va [Accessed on: 23 June 2022]

[284] Pope Francis [2021] *Address to the faithful of Rome* [Online] Available at: www.exaudi.org [Accessed on: 23 June 2022]

[285] Ott, Ludwig [1957] *Op. cit.*, p.308

the teaching of doctrine handed down from the apostles. As the Nicene-Constantinople Creed confesses: *'Credo in…apostolicam Ecclesiam'* [I believe in… apostolic Church]. Ott writes:

> In its origins the Church goes back to the Apostles. She has always adhered to the teaching which she received from the Apostles…The apostolicity of the succession guarantees the unfalsified transmission of doctrine and make manifest the organic connection between the Church of the present day and the Church of the Apostles.[286]

The Second Council of Nicaea (787) warned against those pastors who oppose the tradition of the Catholic Church and thereby 'faltered in their grasp of the truth'. The Church insists that upholding Tradition and the knowledge of truth are inextricably joined together. If this link is severed, all types of error follow:

> To this gracious offer some people paid no attention, being hoodwinked by the treacherous foe they abandoned the true line of reasoning, and, setting themselves against the tradition of the catholic church they faltered in their grasp of the truth.[287]

The Fourth Council of Constantinople (870) declared it imperative to uphold the traditional canons of the Church, describing them as 'so many lamps which are always alight and illuminating our steps which are directed towards God.' In particular, it described the 'exhortations and warnings of the divine canons' as lights that help distinguish the better from the worse, and the advantageous and useful from the unhelpful and harmful. The council fathers paraphrased St. Paul to emphasise the importance of upholding the Deposit of Faith, 'For Paul, the great apostle, openly urges us to preserve the traditions which we have received, either by word or by letter, of the saints who were famous in times past.'[288]

Pope Francis' rejection of Tradition's necessary orientation to the past, and his proposal of an open-minded orientation to the future abandons the safety of these doctrinal and canonical lamps that direct our feet towards God.

A thousand years later, the First Vatican Council (1870) re-iterated the indispensable role of the Deposit of Faith. Furthermore, it emphasised the importance of maintaining the original meaning of dogmas, condemning those who proposed the modernist error of the 'variability of Dogma'[289] — that there can be a change to the meaning of dogmas due to historical changes:

> …that meaning of the sacred dogmas is ever to be maintained which has once been declared by holy mother church, and there must never be any abandonment of this sense under the pretext or in the name of a more profound understanding.[290]

This makes the historical definition of dogmas binding on the faithful, and not something from which we can be dispensed due to 'differing currents of thought in philosophy, theology and pastoral practice'.

The First Vatican Council also emphasised the duty of the successors of Peter not to chase after novelty, but instead 'to religiously guard and faithfully expound the revelation or deposit of faith transmitted by the apostles.'[291]

The Second Vatican Council (1965) emphasised the apostolicity of the Church by referring to the past being intrinsic to the present and the future, 'Now what was handed on by the Apostles…the Church, in her teaching, life and worship, perpetuates

---

[286] *Ibid.*
[287] Tanner, N [1990] *Decrees of the Ecumenical Councils*: Vol 1 [Online] Available at: www.papalencyclicals.net [Accessed: 24 June 2022]
[288] *Ibid.*
[289] Lemius, J [1908] *A Catechism of Modernism*. Rockford: TAN Books, p. 37
[290] *Decrees of the First Vatican Council. Dogmatic Constitution, Dei Filius*, Chap. 4 [Online] Available at: www.papalencyclicals.net [Accessed: 24 June 2022]
[291] Vatican I's Dogmatic Constitution, *Pastor Aeternus, on the Church of Christ*, Chap. 4, para 6. [Online] Available at: www.ewtn.com [Accessed: 24 June 2022]

and hands on to all generations all that she herself is, all that she believes.' This apostolicity is so intrinsic to the nature of the Church, the council fathers used words such as 'warn' and 'fight' to underline the point:

> Therefore the Apostles, handing on what they themselves had received, warn the faithful to hold fast to the traditions which they have learned either by word of mouth or by letter (see II Thess. 2:15), and to fight in defence of the faith handed on once and for all (see Jude 1:3).[292]

The successors of the apostles have a duty to cherish the Deposit of Faith as 'the treasury of Revelation' — and by implication not to dismiss it as a museum or a mummy — and use it in 'vigilantly warding off any errors that threaten their flock (II Tim. 4:1-4).'[293]

Proof from the Sources of Faith
a) Teaching from Holy Scripture
Sacred Scripture refutes Pope Francis' error that it is contrary to the Gospel to prioritise guarding and transmitting the body of doctrine. Scripture attests that our Lord instituted the apostolic nature of the Church in order to preserve and transmit his teachings through time. The Greek word *apostolos* means not just a messenger who is sent, but a delegate sent forth with orders.[294] This apostolic nature of the Church is conveyed in Jesus' missionary mandate to the Twelve (Mt 28:18-20):

a) Jesus' mandate to the apostle gives priority to teaching his commands [*apostolicitas doctrinae*]: 'Going therefore, teach ye all nations... Teaching them to observe all things whatsoever I have commanded you'.
b) Jesus not only sends the apostles throughout the world, but also through time [*apostolicitas successionis*]: 'and behold I am with you all days, even to the consummation of the world.'

Our Lord founded the apostolic Church to transmit his teaching and commands through time. This moment in time is the origin of the apostolic Church [*apostolicitas originis*]. Therefore, this dimension of time always had an orientation to the past, to the apostolic age which began with our Lord's act of founding the Church on the Apostles. The Marcan account of the founding of the apostolic college attests that our Lord gave order of priority to teaching [*apostolicitas doctrinae*], hence the permanent importance of the apostolic *kerygma* to the life of the Church, 'And he made that twelve should be with him, and that he might send them to preach' (Mk 3:14).

It was at this historical moment that our Lord transferred to the apostles his three-fold office — the *Munus docendi* [Christ's power to teach with authority], the *Munus sanctificandi* [Christ's power to sanctify and offer sacrifice] and the *Munus regendi* [Christ's power as pastor and ruler]. (Mt 10:1-4; Mk 3:13-15; Lk 6:12-16).

The apostolic succession of the bishops [*apostolicitas successionis*] is the sacramental sign and instrument instituted by our Lord to connect all generations of Christians with the divine origin of the Church [*apostolicitas originis*], which in turn authenticates the divine authority of doctrine [*apostolicitas doctrinae*]. The essential purpose of the apostolic succession is to orientate Christians to the divine origin of the Church and her doctrine, which is in the past.

This orientation to the Church's divine origins is communicated through the sacramental sign of the laying on of hands at the ordination of bishops, and their assistants, priests and deacons. As Cardinal Ratzinger put it, it is impossible to think of the Church of Christ not being closely linked to his incarnation and his whole historical activity.

---

[292] Second Vatican Council [1965] Dogmatic Constitution on Divine Revelation, *Dei Verbum*, Chap. II, para 8 [Online] Available at: www.vatican.va. [Accessed: 24 June 2022]
[293] Second Vatican Council [1964] Dogmatic Constitution on the Church, *Lumen Gentium*, Chap. III, para 25 [Online] Available at: www.vatican.va [Accessed: 24 June 2022]
[294] *Strong's Concordance* [Online] Available at: biblehub.com [Accessed: 25 June 2022]

The laying on of hands is the physical sign of the Church's close connection with the historical event of the Incarnation.[295]

The Pauline epistles insist on the importance of safeguarding this orientation to divine origins. St. Paul's emphasises the importance of upholding sound doctrine and the irrevocable interplay between Tradition and sound doctrine. His teaching on Tradition and sound doctrine is summarised as follows:

i) Doctrine by its nature is traditional, 'hold the traditions which you have learned, whether by word, or by our epistle.' (II Thess 2:15)
ii) Christians have a duty to safeguard traditional doctrines (I Tim 6:20; II Tim 1:13-14)
iii) Sound doctrine is necessary for salvation (I Tim 4:16)
iv) Upholding sound doctrine is essential to the Christian life (Tit 1:9; 2:1; I Tim 4:6; 4:16; II Tim 4:3; II Thess 2:15)
v) Upholding sound doctrine is necessary in order to identify and reject erroneous doctrine (Rom 16:17; II Cor 11:3-4)
vi) Beware those who seek to introduce novelties into doctrine (II Tim 4:3; Eph 4:14; Heb 13:8-9)
vii) Christians must reject those who teach erroneous doctrine (Gal 1:8; Col 2:7-8; I Tim 6:3-5)

b) The Testimony of Tradition

The ante-Nicene Church Fathers had a clear understanding of the apostolic orientation towards the past and sound doctrine. St. Irenaeus emphasised that the preservation and transmission of the truth was guaranteed by a succession of bishops that could be traced back to the apostles. The apostolic origin of doctrine also guarantees that the same truth is preached throughout the world, irrespective of the language in which it is spoken. This apostolic universality protects doctrine from being corrupted by bishops teaching error:

> Nor will any one of the rulers in the Churches, however highly gifted he may be in point of eloquence, teach doctrines different from these (for no one is greater than the Master); nor, on the other hand, will he who is deficient in power of expression inflict injury on the tradition. For the faith being ever one and the same, neither does one who is able at great length to discourse regarding it, make any addition to it, nor does one, who can say but little diminish it.[296]

Tertullian also wrote that an orientation towards apostolic origins guaranteed the transmission of true doctrine, 'those moulds and original sources of the faith must be reckoned for truth, as undoubtedly containing that which the (said) churches received from the apostles, the apostles from Christ, Christ from God.' Furthermore, the truth of doctrine can only be proved by showing they originate from the apostles, 'It remains, then, that we demonstrate whether this doctrine of ours […] has its origin in the tradition of the apostles, and whether all other doctrines do not ipso facto proceed from falsehood.'[297]

With the emergence of widespread heresies, the post-Nicene Church Fathers emphasised the importance of apostolic origins and apostolic doctrine. Eusebius of Caesarea wrote that holding 'fast to the tradition of the apostles' was the main way of 'guarding against heresies'.[298] St. Augustine wrote of the necessity of defending the 'many articles

---

[295] Ratzinger, J [1996] *Called to Communion: Understanding the Church Today*. San Francisco: Ignatius Press

[296] St. Irenaeus. *Against the Heresies*, Bk 1 Chap. 10; Bk 3, Chap. 3 [Online] Available at: www. newadvent.org [Accessed on: 27 June 2022]

[297] Tertullian. *Prescription against Heretics*, Chap. 21 [Online] Available at: www.newadvent.org [Accessed on: 27 June 2022]

[298] Eusebius of Caesarea. *Ecclesiastical History*, Bk 3, Chap. 36 [Online] Available at: www. newadvent.org [Accessed on: 27 June 2022]

of the Catholic faith'[299] from the hot restlessness of heretics' and maintaining a 'pious and careful watchfulness' to protect the faith from the 'cunning fraud of the heretics'.[300] St. John Chrysostom preached that the devil's strategy is to sow division in the Church by those who spread 'opinions contrary to the teaching of the Apostles.'[301]

The Church Fathers encouraged respect for traditional doctrines as an 'ancestral inheritance' that enables us to identify 'enemies of the truth':[302]

> Therefore, as soon as the corruption of each mischievous error begins to break forth, and to defend itself by filching certain passages of Scripture, and expounding them fraudulently and deceitfully, immediately, the opinions of the ancients in the interpretation of the Canon are to be collected, whereby the novelty, and consequently the profaneness, whatever it may be, that arises, may both without any doubt be exposed, and without any tergiversation [being deliberately ambiguous] be condemned.[303]

c) The Defence by the Magisterium

In response to the emergence of the many heresies of Protestantism, Pope Leo X — in his condemnation of Martin Luther — traced their errors to 'their proud curiosity' yearning 'for the world's glory', leading them to reject the apostle's teaching. In reality those who reject apostolic doctrine are absurdly claiming, even if they don't say it explicitly, 'that the Church which is guided by the Holy Spirit is in error and has always erred.'[304]

Pope Clement XIII exhorted the world's bishops to guard the Deposit of Faith, using the image of 'foundations' to communicate the necessity of apostolic origins to the preservation of the Faith, 'It is principally your duty to stand as a wall so that no foundation can be laid other than the one that is already laid.'[305]

Pope Pius VII wrote that it was the preeminent duty of the pope, and his fellow bishops, to guard the Deposit of Faith, omitting 'no watchfulness, diligence, care, and effort'. To fail to do so would be a grave sin, 'If ever anything deters, prevents, or delays any one of us from performing this task, what a disgraceful sin he will commit!' He warned such vigilance on the part of the pope was necessary because there was 'a great conspiracy' for the 'destruction' of Christ's teaching.[306]

Popes in the 19th century were very conscious of the importance of sound doctrine for the salvation of souls, which they saw threatened by the widespread dissemination of secular errors. Pope Bl. Pius IX praised the vigilance of his predecessors for never ceasing to sedulously 'nourish the Lord's whole flock with words of faith and with salutary doctrine, and to guard it from poisoned pastures.'[307] None were more sensitive to the necessity of sound doctrine to salvation than Pope Leo XIII. His defence of the 'monolithic body of doctrine', as Pope Francis so dismissively put it, is summarised as follows:

---

[299] St. Augustine. *The City of God*, Bk 16, Chap. 2 [Online] Available at: www.newadvent.org [Accessed on: 27 June 2022]

[300] St. Augustine. *Of Faith and the Creed*, Chap. 1 [Online] Available at: www.newadvent.org [Accessed on: 27 June 2022]

[301] St. John Chrysostom. *Homily* XXXII on St. Paul's Epistle to the Romans, 16:17-18 [Online] Available at: www.newadvent.org [Accessed on: 27 June 2022]

[302] Theodoret of Cyrus. *Letter to Florentius the Patrician*, para 89 [Online] Available at: www.newadvent.org [Accessed on: 27 June 2022]

[303] St. Vincent of Lerins. *Commonitory*, Chap. 28 [Online] Available at: www.newadvent.org [Accessed on: 27 June 2022]

[304] Pope Leo X [1520] Encyclical *Exsurge Domine, condemning the Errors of Martin Luther* [Online] Available at: www.papalencyclicals [Accessed on: 28th June 2022]

[305] Pope Clement XIII [1766] *Encyclical Christianae Reipublicae, on the Dangers of Anti-Christian Writings*, para 2 [Online] Available at: www.papalencyclicals [Accessed on: 28th June 2022]

[306] Pope Pius VII [1800] Encyclical *Diu Satis*, para 11 [Online] Available at: www.papalencyclicals [Accessed on: 28th June 2022]

[307] Pope Bl. Pius IX [1864] Encyclical *Quanta Cura*, para 1 [Online] Available at: www.papalencyclicals [Accessed on: 28th June 2022]

i) It is the duty of the Church to guard and propagate Christian doctrine in its integrity and purity.[308]

ii) Bishops must diligently ensure that the heavenly doctrines of the Catholic Faith are taught early to every member of the Church, to protect them from 'the ruinous blight of error.'[309]

iii) 'Every revealed truth, without exception, must be accepted.'[310] There can be no reason to suppress any doctrine that has been handed down.[311] To do so would separate the proponent of such an action from the Catholic Church, 'whoever would recede in the least degree from any point of doctrine proposed by her authoritative Magisterium' is 'outside Catholic communion, and alien to the Church'.[312]

iv) Every doctrine must be true because if any was false the following contradiction follows, 'for then God Himself would be the author of error in man. "Lord, if we be in error, we are being deceived by Thee".[313]

v) Therefore, if a person rejected one of the Church's doctrines, he would be 'repudiating in one sweeping act the whole of Christian teaching...For such is the nature of faith that nothing can be more absurd than to accept some things and reject others. But he who dissents even in one point from divinely revealed truth absolutely rejects all faith, since he thereby refuses to honour God as the supreme truth and the formal motive of faith'.[314]

vi) By doing so, instead of 'bringing into captivity every understanding unto the obedience of Christ' (II Cor 10: 5), such a person leans 'on their own judgments, not on faith', and 'more truly obey themselves than God.'[315]

vii) The most dangerous heretics are those who 'who admit nearly the whole cycle of doctrine, and yet by one word, as with a drop of poison, infect the real and simple faith taught by our Lord and handed down by Apostolic tradition.'[316]

Pope St. Pius X warned against modernists who 'exercise all their ingenuity in diminishing the force and falsifying the character of tradition, so as to rob it of all its weight.' Pope Francis' frequent characterisation of tradition, and a corresponding concern for doctrine, as a 'tomb psychology' that reduced the Faith to being a 'museum' and Christians to being 'mummies', comes under this warning. Pope Pius X exhorts the faithful to 'condemn those who dare, after the impious fashion of heretics, to deride the ecclesiastical traditions, to invent novelties of some kind . . . or endeavour by malice or craft to overthrow any one of the legitimate traditions of the Catholic Church.'[317]

Furthermore, Pope St. Pius X criticised those who accused the Church of 'clinging tenaciously and vainly to meaningless formulas' of being 'blind':

> ...with that new system of theirs they are seen to be under the sway of a blind and unchecked passion for novelty, thinking not at all of finding some solid foundation of truth, but despising the holy and apostolic traditions, they embrace other vain, futile,

---

[308] Pope Leo XIII [1896] Encyclical *Satis Cognitum*, para 9 [Online] Available at: www.vatican.va [Accessed on: 28th June 2022]

[309] Pope Leo XIII [1878] Encyclical *Inscrutabili Dei Consilio*, para 13 [Online] Available at: www.vatican.va [Accessed on: 28th June 2022]

[310] Pope Leo XIII [1896] Encyclical *Satis Cognitum*, para 9 [Online] Available at: www.vatican.va [Accessed on: 28th June 2022]

[311] Pope Leo XIII [1899] *Testem Benevolentiae Nostrae, letter written to Cardinal James Gibbons,* Archbishop of Baltimore [Online] Available at: www.papalencyclicals [Accessed on: 28th June 2022]

[312] Pope Leo XIII [1896] Encyclical *Satis Cognitum, ibid.*

[313] *Ibid.*

[314] *Ibid.*

[315] *Ibid.*

[316] *Ibid.*

[317] Pope St. Pius X [1907] Encyclical *Pascendi Dominici Gregis*, para 42 [Online] Available at: www.vatican.va [Accessed on: 28th June 2022]

uncertain doctrines, condemned by the Church, on which, in the height of their vanity, they think they can rest and maintain truth itself.[318]

Pope Pius XI's rebuke of those who portray the deposit of truth as 'laborious trouble' can equally apply to Pope Francis' depiction. For example, when Pope Francis depicted those dedicated to transmitting doctrine in all its integrity and purity as 'waging a war of words aimed at imposing doctrines' and hurling 'dead stones' at others in need. Such a dismissive approach denies that God had revealed 'a doctrine of faith and morals, by which man should be guided through the whole course of his moral life.[319]

Pope Ven. Pius XII called out the 'mirage of glittering phrases' that people use to trick themselves and others to abandon the 'the unifying and elevating doctrines of Christ's love':

> …they were resigning themselves to the whim of a poor, fickle human wisdom; they spoke of progress, when they were going back; of being raised, when they grovelled; of arriving at man's estate, when they stooped to servility. They did not perceive the inability of all human effort to replace the law of Christ by anything equal to it; 'they became vain in their thoughts' (Rom 1:21).[320]

The post-Vatican II popes, preceding Pope Francis, all expressed the urgent need to defend the Deposit of Faith from an upsurge of the errors in the Church. Even Pope St. Paul VI warned of a resurgence of Modernism in the Church, which he described as 'secular philosophies and secular trends' seeking to 'vitiate the true teaching and discipline of the Church of Christ.' To counter this drive among 'many people to adopt the most outlandish views', Pope Paul VI exhorted the Church to return to 'Sacred Scripture' and 'Apostolic Tradition…interpreted and explained by the tradition of the Church under the inspiration and guidance of the Holy Spirit.'[321]

The imperative to defend the Deposit of Faith intensified during the pontificate of Pope St. John Paul II. He was very aware of the importance of the apostolic nature of the Church and its orientation to the past:

> …the Holy Spirit implanted in the Church an apostolic charism, in order to keep this revelation intact. Through his words Jesus was to live on in his Church: I am with you always. And so the whole ecclesial community became conscious of the need for fidelity to the instructions of Jesus, to the deposit of faith. This solicitude was to pass from generation to generation – down to our own day.[322]

Recognising the danger posed by those within the Church attacking the Deposit of Faith, Pope St. John Paul II took canonical steps in an attempt to constrain their influence. *The Revised Code of Canon Law* (1983) stated that 'A person must believe with divine and Catholic faith all those things contained in the word of God, written or handed on, that is, in the one deposit of faith entrusted to the Church… All are therefore bound to avoid any contrary doctrines. (Can. 750 §1).

Fifteen years later, in reaction to persistent disobedience and the defiant dissemination of error, Pope John Paul II issued the Motu Proprio, *Ad Tuendam Fidem*, to include new norms into canon law, 'which expressly impose the obligation of upholding truths proposed in a definitive way by the Magisterium of the Church, and which also establish related canonical sanctions.' The new canon clearly stated that a person who rejects any doctrine that has been proposed definitively by the Magisterium is opposed to the

---

[318] *Ibid.*, para 13

[319] Pope Pius XI [1928] Encyclical *Mortalium Animos*, para 8 [Online] Available at: www.vatican.va [Accessed on: 28th June 2022]

[320] Pope Pius XII [1939] Encyclical *Summi Pontificatus*, para 31 [Online] Available at: www.vatican.va [Accessed on: 28th June 2022]

[321] Pope St. Paul VI [1964] Encyclical *Ecclesiam Suam*, para 26 [Online] Available at: www.vatican.va [Accessed on: 28th June 2022]

[322] Pope St. John Paul II [1979] *Homily for the Solemnity of the Ascension of Our Lord* [Online] Available at: www.vatican.va [Accessed on: 28th June 2022]

'doctrine of the Catholic Church.' (Can. 750 §2). This takes up, and canonically codifies, Pope Leo XIII's understanding that if a person rejects a single doctrine they reject all Catholic doctrine. The Motu Proprio also introduced an obligatory *Profession of Faith* and *Oath of Fidelity* to be taken by all newly ordained clergy and persons assuming office in the Church.

The Congregation for the Doctrine of the Faith's *Doctrinal Commentary on the Profession of Faith* emphasised a point made by Pope Pius XII that progress in time could not be a justification to change doctrine, 'No content is abrogated with the passage of time; instead, all of it becomes an irreplaceable inheritance.'[323]

Pope Benedict XVI, quoting St. Jerome, succinctly summed up the Catholic understanding of the irrevocable union between apostolic origins, apostolic doctrine and apostolic succession:

> Saint Jerome recalls that we can never read Scripture simply on our own. We come up against too many closed doors and we slip too easily into error… An authentic interpretation of the Bible must always be in harmony with the faith of the Catholic Church. He thus wrote to a priest: 'Remain firmly attached to the traditional doctrine that you have been taught, so that you may exhort according to sound doctrine and confound those who contradict it'.[324]

---

[323] Congregation for the Doctrine of the Faith [1998] *Doctrinal Commentary on concluding Formula of 'Professio Fidei'*, para 12 [Online] Available at: www.vatican.va [Accessed on: 28th June 2022]
[324] Pope Benedict XVI [2010] Apostolic Exhortation *Verbum Domini*, para 30 [Online] Available at: www.vatican.va [Accessed on: 28th June 2022]

Eschatology (1) — Denial of the Necessity of Faith

D. *The soul of an atheist who does natural good will enter into Heaven.*
During his conversation with Eugenio Scalfari, reported in *La Repubblica* (15th March 2015),[325] and, on the occasion of his pastoral visit to a parish in Rome in 2018,[326] Pope Francis gave his thoughts about the eternal destiny of atheists. At both times, the Supreme Pontiff expressed an erroneous eschatology, summarised under the following headings:

a) If an atheist does natural good, such as loving others or being a caring parent, they will be 'welcomed by the Father' into heaven, 'what about those with no faith? The answer is that if one has loved others at least as much as himself, (possibly a little more than self) the Father will welcome him.'[327]
b) At the individual judgement immediately following death, God does not take into account the possession of faith, but only how one has lived one's life, 'Faith is of help but that is not the element of the one who judges — it's life itself.'[328]
c) Therefore, doing good is more important than possessing the grace of faith.[329]
d) We can pray to our atheist family and friends who have died

The Teaching of the Church
The justification of an adult is not possible without Faith. **(De fide)**[330]
The souls of the just which in the moment of death are free from all guilt of sin and punishment for sin, enter into Heaven. **(De fide)**[331]
The souls of those who die in the condition of personal grievous sin enter Hell. **(De fide)**[332]
Contrary to Pope Francis' erroneous teaching on eschatology, the grace of faith is essential for justification, without which it is impossible for a soul to be in a state of sanctifying grace; which is absolutely necessary in order to enter into Heaven. Without these graces, the souls of unrepentant atheists, dying in grievous sin, enter Hell.

The Council of Trent (1547) explicitly declared that the 'unbelieving' are excluded from the Kingdom of God due to the lack of the graces of faith and justification:

> In opposition also to the subtle wits of certain men, who, by pleasing speeches and good words, seduce the hearts of the innocent, it is to be maintained, that the received grace of Justification is lost, not only by infidelity whereby even faith itself is lost, but also by any other mortal sin whatever, though faith be not lost; thus defending the doctrine of the divine law, which excludes from the kingdom of God not only the unbelieving...[333]

In response to the emergence of systematic atheism, combined with scientism, in the 19th century, the First Vatican Council warned that fundamental principles of unbelief placed adherents in danger of Hell — the denial of God (*Dz* 3021), radical materialism that excludes the supernatural (*Dz* 3022), and denial of the creation of the world by God out of nothing (*Dz* 3025).[334]

Faced with the materialist atheism of the Soviet Empire, and the secular atheism of the West, the Second Vatican Council declared that atheists are not 'free of blame'

---

[325] Scalfari, E [15th March 2015] *What Pope Francis May Say to Europe's Nonbelievers* [Online] Available at: rorate-caeli.blogspot.com [Accessed on: 29 June 2022]
[326] Pope Francis [2018] *Pastoral Visit to the Roman Parish of San Paolo della Croce in Corviale.* [Online] Available at: press.vatican.va [Accessed on: 29 June 2022]
[327] Scalfari, E [15th March 2015] *Op. cit.*
[328] *Ibid.*
[329] Pope Francis [2018] *Op. cit.*
[330] Ott, L [1957] *Op. cit.*, p.252
[331] *Ibid.*, p.476
[332] *Ibid.*, p.479
[333] Council of Trent [1547] *Decree on Justification*, Chap. 15 [Online] Available at: www.thecounciloftrent.com [Accessed on: 29 June 2022]
[334] Denzinger, H (2010) *Op. cit.*, p. 607

for wilfully shutting out God from their hearts, 'Undeniably, those who wilfully shut out God from their hearts and try to dodge religious questions are not following the dictates of their consciences, and hence are not free of blame.' The council fathers called on the whole Church to repudiate atheism's 'poisonous doctrines and actions', rejecting atheism 'root and branch'.[335]

Proof from the Sources of Faith
a) Teaching from Holy Scripture
Contrary to Pope Francis' judgement about the good acts of atheists deserving Heaven, the Old Testament is clear that unbelievers do not have the capacity to do good because their rejection of God corrupts everything, 'The fool hath said in his heart: There is no God. They are corrupt, and are become abominable in their ways: there is none that doth good, no not one.' (Ps 13:1). Commenting on this psalm, St. Augustine wrote, 'no human beings can act rightly until they know the one God.'[336] The Book of Ezra warns atheists that they face the wrath of God, 'The hand of our God is upon all them that seek him in goodness: and his power and strength, and wrath upon all them that forsake him.' (Ezra 8:22).

The New Testament also explicitly condemns those who embrace atheism, and especially atheist apostates. Our Lord himself makes clear the fate of those who deny him, 'But he that shall deny me before men, I will also deny him before my Father who is in heaven.' (Mt 10:32-33). There is no hope for those who do not believe in the Son of God, they 'shall not see life; but the wrath of God abideth on him.' (Jn 3:36). Commenting on this passage, St. John Chrysostom points out that our Lord does not say that unbelievers will experience the wrath of the Son, but that they will experience the wrath of the Father, 'he refers the account of punishment to the Father, for he says not "the wrath of the Son," (yet He is the Judge,) but sets over them the Father, desiring so the more to terrify them.'[337] This severity is in marked contrast to Pope Francis' erroneous eschatology that describes the Father 'welcoming' those who have rejected his Son.

St. Paul wrote that there was no excuse for unbelief because signs of God's existence and glory exist in visible nature (Rom 1:20-21). Unbelief is inexcusable because those who refuse to believe in God are 'vain in their thoughts, and their foolish heart was darkened.' Unbelief is the consequence of listening to 'spirits of error, and doctrines of devils' (I Tim 4:1; cf. Col 2:8).

The eternal destiny of atheists is not heaven, as Pope Francis erroneously taught, but the second death of Hell:

> But the fearful, and unbelieving, and the abominable, and murderers, and whoremongers, and sorcerers, and idolaters, and all liars, they shall have their portion in the pool burning with fire and brimstone, which is the second death. (Rev 21:8).

b) The Testimony of Tradition
St. Irenaeus contrasted the unbelief of Eve with the belief of the virgin Mary to show the catastrophe of the former compared to the blessing of the latter, 'And thus also it was that the knot of Eve's disobedience was loosed by the obedience of Mary. For what the virgin Eve had bound fast through unbelief, this did the virgin Mary set free through faith.'[338]

Atheism was completely alien to the Hellenistic culture of St. Augustine, which explains why he writes that 'not even profane and abominable philosophers, who hold perverse and false opinions about [God]' would have dared to say in public, 'There is

[335] Second Vatican Council [1965] Pastoral Constitution *Gaudium et Spes*, paras 19; 21 [Online] Available at: www.vatican.va [Accessed on: 29 June 2022]
[336] The Works of Saint Augustine: A Translation for the 21st Century. *III/15 Expositions of the Psalms*, 1-32. New York: New City Press, 2000, p.176
[337] St. John Chrysostom. *Homily* 31 on the Gospel of John, John 3:35-36, para 1 [Online] Available at: www.newadvent.org [Accessed on; 30 June 2022]
[338] St. Irenaeus. *Against Heresies*, Bk. III, Chap. 22, para 4 [Online] Available at: www.newadvent.org [Accessed on; 30 June 2022]

no God.'[339] St. Augustine traced such 'contempt of God' to 'the earthly by the love of self' that glories in itself.[340] He further explained that only belief in Christ protects souls from the wrath of God:

> Believe on Christ, for you made mortal, that you may receive Him, the immortal; and when you shall have received His immortality, you shall no longer be mortal. He lived, you were dead; He died that you should live. He has brought us the grace of God, and has taken away the wrath of God. God has conquered death, lest death should conquer man.[341]

Consequently, those who die in unbelief will experience the wrath of God, not his welcome into Heaven.

St. Thomas Aquinas OP argued that unbelief was the greatest sin that 'occurs in the perversion of morals', summarised as follows:

i) Unbelief is the greatest of sins because it expresses the ultimate aversion to God that severs a soul from God.
ii) Every sin consists in aversion to God, to a lesser or greater extent, depending on its nature and gravity.
iii) The more a sin severs a soul from God, the graver it is.
iv) Therefore, unbelief is the greatest sin because 'man is more than ever separated from God by unbelief, because he has not even true knowledge of God.'[342]

Commenting on the parable of the sower of seed (Mt 13: 1–9, 18–23), St. John Henry Cardinal Newman wrote that our Lord condemned unbelievers because they 'had let the divine seed lie by the roadside, or in the rocky soil, or among the thorns which choked it.' Newman judged atheists to be morally culpable, putting their hardness of unbelief down to an inexcusable refusal to be open to our Lord's teaching, and life:

> …to be hard of belief is nothing else but to have been loth and reluctant to inquire. Those whose faith He praised had no stronger evidence than those whose unbelief He condemned; but they had used their eyes, used their reason, exerted their minds, and persevered in inquiry till they found.[343]

c) The Defence by the Magisterium
Popes only began to address atheism in the 19th century with its emergence as a social movement. Pope Gregory XVI warned that 'immoderate freedom of opinion, license of free speech, and desire for novelty' was leading individuals to a 'contempt of sacred things and holy laws.'[344] This atheistic movement was openly antagonist towards God and his Church, 'They harass religion with ridicule, the Church with insults, and Catholics with arrogance and calumny.'[345] Such atheism led to the 'bottomless pit' (Rev 9:1-2), not to Heaven.

Pope Bl. Pius IX took up his predecessor's prophetic warning concerning the dangers of atheism when he wrote about the 'present-day contempt of religion and of the

[339] The Works of Saint Augustine: A Translation for the 21st Century. [2000] *III/15 Expositions of the Psalms*, 1-32. *Op. cit.*, p.175.
[340] St. Augustine. *City of God.* Bk. XIV, Chap. 28 [Online] Available at: www.newadvent.org [Accessed on: 30 June 2022]
[341] St. Augustine. *Tractate* 14, John 3:29-36, para 6 [Online] Available at: www.newadvent.org [Accessed on: 30 June 2022]
[342] St. Thomas Aquinas. *Summa Theologiae.* Secunda Secundæ Pars. Q 10. Art 3 [Online] Available at: www.newadvent.org [Accessed on: 30 June 2022]
[343] St. John Henry Newman [1857] *Sermons Preached on Various Occasions.* Sermon 5 [Online] Available at: www.newmanreader.org [Accessed on: 30 June 2022]
[344] Pope Gregory XVI [1832] Encyclical *Mirari Vos*, para 14 [Online] Available at: www.papalencyclicals.net/ [Accessed on: 1 July 2022]
[345] Pope Gregory XVI [1840] Encyclical *Probe Nostis*, para 1 [Online] Available at: www.papalencyclicals.net/ [Accessed on: 1 July 2022]

spirit of unbelief rising from the darkness under the fallacious appearance of social progress.'[346] Eternal punishment awaits those who 'oppose the authority and statements of the same Church and are stubbornly separated from the unity of the Church and also from the successor of Peter, the Roman Pontiff.'[347]

Pope Leo XIII deepened St. Augustine's understanding that 'contempt of God' arose from 'the earthly by the love of self'. More explicitly, he wrote that those who had such an atheistic contempt of God were in the Kingdom of Satan, not the Kingdom of God, because they 'follow the fatal example of their leader and of our first parents', refusing 'to obey the divine and eternal law, and who have many aims of their own in contempt of God, and many aims also against God.'[348] Pope Leo XIII wrote that such atheism is a grave sin because it is the 'greatest perversion of liberty,' 'to deny the existence of this authority in God, or to refuse to submit to it, means to act, not as a free man, but as one who treasonably abuses his liberty'.[349]

Contrary to Pope Francis' contention that atheists can perform good acts worthy of Heaven, Pope St. Pius X upheld the tradition of the Church when he wrote that 'the will cannot be upright nor the conduct good when the mind is shrouded in the darkness of crass ignorance...if lack of faith is added to depraved morality because of ignorance, the evil hardly admits of remedy, and the road to ruin lies open.'[350]

The brutal evil of atheistic materialism became apparent during the pontificate of Pope Pius XI with the ascendancy of Soviet Communism and Nazi fascism. His teaching on the matter can be summarised under the following headings:

i)   Those who show such 'great contempt of the Divine Majesty', and trample 'under foot …the most holy institutions', outrage the 'rights of God' and 'the holy desires of the human soul in its absolute need of God.'[351]
ii) By so doing, atheists also show contempt for the human nature that God has made.[352]
iii) Furthermore, as 'belief in God is the unshakable foundation of all social order and of all responsibility on earth', atheists threaten society with 'anarchy and terrorism.'[353]
iv) As such, atheists are 'sons of darkness' in league with the 'powers of darkness against the very idea of Divinity'.[354]
v)   Therefore, those who hold such contempt of God will join the demons in eternally expiating for their crimes.[355]

Pope St. Paul VI described atheism as a growing evil, because it 'seeks to quench the light of the living God.' Its futile dogmatism strikes 'at the genuine and effective foundation for man's acceptance of a rational order in the universe'.[356] Pope Paul VI

---

[346] Pope Bl. Pius IX [1864] Encyclical *Maximae Quidem*, para 2 [Online] Available at: www.papalencyclicals.net/ [Accessed on: 1 July 2022]
[347] Pope Bl. Pius IX [1863] Encyclical *Quanto Conficiamur Moerore*, para 7-8 [Online] Available at: www.papalencyclicals.net/ [Accessed on: 1 July 2022]
[348] Pope Leo XIII [1884] Encyclical *Humanum Genus*, para 1-2 [Online] Available at: www.vatican.va [Accessed on: 1 July 2022]
[349] Pope Leo XIII [1888] Encyclical *Libertas*, para 36-37 [Online] Available at: www.papalencyclicals.net/ [Accessed on: 1 July 2022]
[350] Pope St. Pius X [1905] Encyclical *Acerbo Nimis*, para 5 [Online] Available at: www.vatican.va [Accessed on: 30 June 2022]
[351] Pope Pius XI [1932] Encyclical *Caritate Christi Compulsi*, para10 [Online] Available at: www.vatican.va [Accessed on: 30 June 2022]
[352] *Ibid.*
[353] Pope Pius XI [1937] Encyclical *Divini Redemptoris*, para 72 [Online] Available at: www.vatican.va [Accessed on: 30 June 2022]
[354] *Ibid.*, para 72
[355] Pope Pius XI [1930] Encyclical *Ad Salutem*, para 27 [Online] Available at: www.papalencyclicals.net/ [Accessed on: 1 July 2022]
[356] Pope St. Paul VI [1964] Encyclical *Ecclesiam Suam*, para 99 -100 [Online] Available at: www.vatican.va [Accessed on: 30 June 2022]

identified three types of atheism — 'the anti-God movement' that violently aims to destroy religion and all that is holy from society; philosophical atheism that denies God's existence, and hedonistic atheism, that 'rejects all religious worship or honour, reckoning it superstitious, profitless and irksome to reverence and serve the Creator of us all or to obey His law.' Living without Christ, all adherents of atheism have no hope of his promises.[357]

Pope St. John Paul II, with his experiences of living under both Nazism and Soviet Communism, saw the tragedy of atheism, like Pope Leo XIII, in terms of the St. Augustine's 'Love of self to the point of contempt for God.' And like Pope Leo XIII he saw Satan as the inspiration of atheism:

> For in spite of all the witness of creation and of the salvific economy inherent in it, the spirit of darkness is capable of showing God as an enemy of his own creature, and in the first place as an enemy of man, as a source of danger and threat to man. In this way Satan manages to sow in man's soul the seed of opposition to the one who 'from the beginning' would be considered as man's enemy — and not as Father. Man is challenged to become the adversary of God![358]

Pope John Paul II stressed that the demonic was at the heart of atheism with its *'contemptus Dei*, the rejection of God, contempt of God, hatred of everything connected with God or that comes from God.'[359] Those who reject God's love and forgiveness, separate themselves 'for ever from joyful communion with him. It is precisely this tragic situation that Christian doctrine explains when it speaks of eternal damnation or hell.'[360]

---

[357] Pope St. Paul VI [1965] *Address to the 31st General Congregation of the Society of Jesus*. [Online] Available at: whosoeverdesires.wordpress.com [Accessed on: 30 June 2022]

[358] Pope St. John Paul II [1986] Encyclical *Dominum et Vivificantem*, para 38 [Online] Available at: www.vatican.va [Accessed on: 30 June 2022]

[359] Pope St. John Paul II [1986] *Summary of Catechesis on Original Sin. General Audiences*. [Online] Available at: www.ewtn.com [Accessed on: 1 July 2022]

[360] Pope St. John Paul II [28 July 1999] *General Audience Address* [Online] Available at: www. vatican.va [Accessed on: 30 June 2022]

Eschatology (2) — Annihilationism

E. *Unrepentant souls do not go to Hell but are annihilated.*

Eugenio Scalfari published two accounts of his conversations with Pope Francis (*La Repubblica*, 15th March 2015 and 29th March 2018), reporting the Supreme Pontiff's thoughts on eschatology, which expressed an erroneous belief in Annihilationism, also known as conditional immortality.

The Vatican issued no denial following Scalfari's 2015 account, but it did issue a statement in 2018, in response to his claim that Pope Francis said that there was no Hell. According to the Vatican's press release, 'No quotes of the aforementioned article should therefore be considered as a faithful transcription of the Holy Father's words.' As it stands, this is neither a confirmation nor a denial. The fact remains, the 2018 account repeats the Annihilationism of the 2015 account, about which the Vatican remained silent.

Following the Vatican's 2018 statement, Scalfari issued no apology and did not correct his report. More seriously, despite the gravity of the reported error, Pope Francis, as 'the supreme teacher of the universal Church' (*LG* 25), did not repudiate, contradict or demand a retraction of Scalfari's account of his belief in Annihilationism. Instead, Pope Francis continued to single out Scalfari to allow him privileged access to himself.

Pope Francis' erroneous belief in Annihilationism can be summarised under the following headings:

a) A soul that has darkened the divine spark within through an egoism that suffocates love for other is self-condemned.[361]
b) Those who do not repent cannot be forgiven and therefore do not 'participate in the bliss of living in the presence of the Father.'[362]
c) 'There is no punishment, but the annihilation of that soul.'[363]
d) 'The annihilated souls will not be part of that [divine] banquet; with the death of the body their journey is ended.'[364]
e) 'There is no hell, there is the disappearance of sinful souls.'[365]

This annihilationist eschatology is similar to the erroneous ideas promulgated by some Protestant theologians in the 19th and 20th century. Edward White, a Free Church minister, held that the soul was not naturally immortal but rather, 'Immortality is the peculiar privilege of the regenerate.'[366] Such conditional immortality found acceptance among a number of Anglican clergy and theologians during the first half of the 20th century. It even found expression in the Church of England's Archbishops' Commission on Evangelism report, *Towards the Conversion of England* [1945], 'Judgment is the ultimate separation of the evil from the good, with the consequent destruction of all that opposes itself to God's will.'[367]

The Teaching of the Church
The souls of those who die in the condition of personal grievous sin enter Hell. (**De fide.**)[368]

---

[361] Scalfari, E [15 March 2015] *What Pope Francis May Say to Europe's Nonbelievers* [Online] rorate-caeli.blogspot.com [Accessed on: 2 July 2022]

[362] *Ibid.*

[363] New Catholic [29th March 2018] *'There is no Hell' — New Francis Revelation to Atheist Journalist Just in Time for Good Friday* [Online] rorate-caeli.blogspot.com [Accessed on: 2 July 2022]

[364] Scalfari, E [15 March 2015] *Op. cit.*

[365] New Catholic [29th March 2018] *Op. cit.*

[366] Cross, F (ed) [1974] *The Oxford Dictionary of the Christian Church.* Oxford: Oxford University Press, p. 328

[367] Church of England. Archbishops' Commission on Evangelism. [1945] *Towards the Conversion of England.* Westminster: Press and Publications Board of the Church Assembly, p. 23

[368] Ott, L [1957] *Op. cit.*, p.479

The punishment of Hell lasts for all eternity. (De fide.)[369]

The Athanasian Creed, also known as the *Quicumque Vult*, upholds the doctrine of the universal immorality of the soul and the eternal punishment of those who have done evil:

> …at his coming all men have to arise again with their bodies and will render an account of their own deeds: and those who have done good, will go into life everlasting, but those who have done evil, into eternal fire.[370]

A number of Ecumenical Councils in the 13th Century and 14th Century emphasised the existence of Hell and the eternal nature of the punishments of the damned. The Fourth Lateran Council declared that at the Final Judgement all the dead would participate in the resurrection of the body, 'so as to receive according to their deserts, whether these be good or bad; for the latter perpetual punishment with the devil, for the former eternal glory with Christ.' (*Dz* 801).[371]

The Second Council of Lyons addressed the destiny of the individual judgement of those who die in mortal sin or with original sin only, 'they go down immediately to hell, to be punished, with different punishments.' (*Dz* 858; cf. *Dz* 1306).[372]

In response to the heresy of Averroism, that raised doubts about the immorality of the soul, the Fifth Lateran Council dealt explicitly with the error that the soul was mortal, paraphrasing our Lord's teaching to prove the immortality of the soul and eternal punishment in Hell:

> This is clearly established from the gospel when the Lord says, They cannot kill the soul; and in another place, Whoever hates his life in this world, will keep it for eternal life and when he promises eternal rewards and eternal punishments to those who will be judged according to the merits of their life…[373]

The Second Vatican Council emphasised the importance of the resurrection of the body in understanding the eschatological destiny of souls, '…at the end of the world "they who have done good shall come forth unto resurrection of life; but those who have done evil unto resurrection of judgment" (Jn 5:29; Mt 25:46).'[374]

Proof from the Sources of Faith
a) Teaching from Holy Scripture

Through denying the immortality of all souls and eternal punishment in Hell Pope Francis is explicitly contradicting divine revelation contained in both the Old Testament and New Testament.

The Book of Judith and the Book of Isaiah use the metaphors of everlasting fire and the undying worm eating the flesh to convey the eternal punishment of the wicked, '… for the Lord almighty will take revenge on them, in the day of judgment he will visit them. For he will give fire, and worms into their flesh, that they may burn, and may feel for ever.' (Jdt 16:20-21; cf. Isa 66:24). Both the immortality of the wicked soul and the resurrection of the wicked body are implicit in Old Testament eschatology.

The eternal punishment of the wicked in Hell was an important element in the teaching of our Lord Jesus Christ, summarised as follows:

---

[369] *Ibid.*, p. 481

[370] Denzinger, H. *Enchiridion symbolorum, definitionum et declarationum de rebus fidei et morum.* [Online] Available at: http://patristica.net/ [Accessed on: 2 July 2022]

[371] *Fourth Lateran Council:* 1215 [Online] Available at: www.papalencyclicals.net[Accessed on: 2 July 2022]

[372] Denzinger, H. [2010] *Op. cit.,* p. 283

[373] Fifth Lateran Council [1513] *Condemnation of Every Proposition Contrary to the Truth of the Enlightened Christian Faith: Eighth Session* [Online] Available at: www.papalencyclicals.net/ [Accessed on: 2 July 2022]

[374] Second Vatican Council [1964] Dogmatic Constitution, *Lumen Gentium,* para 48 [Online] Available at: www.vatican.va [Accessed on: 2 July 2022]

i) The parable of the Rich Man and Lazarus (Lk 16:19-31) testifies to the immorality of all souls, good and wicked, and the torment of the wicked in Hell.

ii) Our Lord graphically warned about the punishments of Hell, saying that amputation of the sinful parts of the body was better than entering Hell. (Mt 5: 29-30).

iii) Our Lord used the Old Testament metaphors of eternal fire and the everlasting worm three times in one passage to convey the reality of punishment in Hell. (Mk 9:46-47). St. Augustine comments about our Lord's repetition of these metaphors, 'And who is not terrified by this repetition, and by the threat of that punishment uttered so vehemently by the lips of the Lord Himself?'.[375]

iv) At the general judgement, our Lord will condemn the wicked to eternal punishment, 'Depart from me, you cursed, into everlasting fire which was prepared for the devil and his angels […] And these shall go into everlasting punishment: but the just, into life everlasting.' (Mt 25:41;46).

v) At the general judgement, the wicked will be separated from the just, and the angels '…shall cast them into the furnace of fire: there shall be weeping and gnashing of teeth. (Mt 13:49-50)

St. Paul further testifies to the immorality of wicked souls and their eternal punishment, 'And they that resist, purchase to themselves damnation' (Rom 13:2), 'Tribulation and anguish upon every soul of man that worketh evil' (Rom 2:9).

Contrary to Pope Francis' Annihilationism, the Book of Apocalypse testifies that at the resurrection of the body, the wicked will be 'cast into the pool of fire' (Rev 20:15):

> But the fearful, and unbelieving, and the abominable, and murderers, and whoremongers, and sorcerers, and idolaters, and all liars, they shall have their portion in the pool burning with fire and brimstone… (Rev 21:8).

b) The Testimony of Tradition

Contrary to Pope Francis' threefold denial of the immortality of the wicked soul, eternal punishment and the existence of Hell, the Church Fathers affirm the reality of all three.

The ante-Nicene Fathers St. Justin Martyr and Tertullian[376] testified to the immortality of the soul, with the former specifically referring to the wicked:

> But I do not say, indeed, that all souls die; for that would truly be a piece of good fortune to the evil. What then? The souls of the pious remain in a better place, while those of the unjust and the wicked are in a worse, waiting for the time of judgement.[377]

The ante-Nicene Fathers also testify that the eternal punishment of the damned was a certain doctrine from the earliest days of the Church.

Pope St. Clement, the fourth in succession to St. Peter, wrote, 'nothing shall deliver us from eternal punishment, if we disobey His commandments'.[378] St. Polycarp, a disciple of St. John the Apostle, declared before his martyrdom by burning, 'Thou threatenest me with fire which burneth for an hour, and after a little is extinguished, but art ignorant of the fire of the coming judgment and of eternal punishment, reserved for the ungodly.'[379]

St. Cyprian of Carthage emphasised that the punishment of the damned would be for eternity and of infinite nature, 'Souls with their bodies will be reserved in infinite tortures for suffering.'[380]

---

[375] St. Augustine. *City of God*, Bk. XXI, Chap. 9 [Online] Available at: www.newadvent.org [Accessed on: 4 July 2022]

[376] Tertullian. *A Treatise on the Soul*, Chap. 22 [Online] Available at: www.newadvent.org [Accessed on: 4 July 2022]

[377] Willis, J [2002] *The Teachings of the Church Fathers*. San Francisco: Ignatius Press, p. 222.

[378] Pope St. Clement. *The Second Epistle of Clement*, Chap. 6 [Online] Available at: http://www.earlychristianwritings.com [Accessed on: 4 July 2022]

[379] St. Polycarp. *Martyrdoms of the Church Fathers — Saint Polycarp*, Chap. 11 [Online] Available at: www.logoslibrary.org [Accessed on: 4 July 2022]

[380] St. Cyprian. *To Demetrian*, Chap. 24 [Online] Available at: www.ewtn.com [Accessed on: 4 July 2022]

The post-Nicene Fathers also testified to the immortality of all souls, with St. Athanasius attesting that proof that God made the soul immortal is its capacity to conceive of the immortal and eternal.[381] St. Cyril of Jerusalem's testimony that the soul was the noblest work of God because it is made in the image of its creator exposes the poverty of Pope Francis' Annihilationism, that reduces the soul to a disposable thing. Rather, the soul is 'immortal because of God that gives it immortality'.[382]

St. Augustine rebutted those, like Pope Francis, who denied the eternal punishment of wicked souls by insisting that the 'unquenchable fire' and 'everlasting flame' were physical realities, not merely metaphors for spiritual suffering.[383] He rebuked those who denied the reality of eternal punishment of engaging in the futility of arguing with God. '…they who desire to be rid of eternal punishment ought to abstain from arguing against God, and rather, while yet there is opportunity, obey the divine commands.'[384]

c) The Defence by the Magisterium

By speculating about Annihilationism on two occasions with a journalist, Pope Francis ran the risk of denying individuals committing habitual mortal sins the salutary experience of the fear of Hell. As St. Augustine observed, our Lord intended to frighten people through his threefold warning about the eternal fire and the ever-lasting worm; no doubt, to motivate us to repent of our sins and commit to a firm amendment of life.

Previous popes understood the moral necessity of fear of eternal punishment in Hell for the salvation of souls. Pope Leo XII explicitly expressed this pastoral motivation when he wrote, 'Implant in the minds of the people a salutary fear; dwell on the severity of the impending divine judgment and the agony of the punishments prepared for those who die in sin.'[385] Pope Bl. Pius IX also emphasised the importance of fear of Hell for the moral life:

> They should explain precisely the particular duties of individuals, frighten them from vice, and inspire them with a love of piety. In this way the faithful will avoid all vices and pursue virtues, and so, will be able to escape eternal punishment and gain heavenly glory.[386]

Earlier popes understood the pastoral imperative to instil in sinners a salutary fear of the eternal punishments of Hell through the use of graphic language. Pope Pelagius I in his letter to the Frankish monarch, King Childebert I wrote, '…the wicked, however, remaining by their own choice as "vessels of wrath fit for destruction" (Rom 9:22) … he will hand over by a most just judgement to the punishment of the eternal and inextinguishable fire, so that they may burn without end.' (Dz 626).[387]

Pope St. Pius V's *Council of Trent's Catechism for Parish Priests*, was meant to improve the quality of homilies. Its graphic depiction of Hell was intended to instil fear:

> …that most loathsome and dark prison in which the souls of the damned are tormented with the unclean spirits in eternal and inextinguishable fire. This place is called Gehenna, the bottomless pit, and is hell strictly so called.[388]

---

[381] St. Athanasius. *Against the Heathen*, Part 2 [Online] Available at: www.newadvent.org [Accessed on: 4 July 2022]

[382] St. Cyril of Jerusalem. *Catechetical Lecture* 4, para 18 [Online] Available at: www.newadvent.org [Accessed on: 4 July 2022]

[383] St. Augustine. *City of God*, Bk 21, Chap. 9 [Online] Available at: www.newadvent.org [Accessed on: 4 July 2022]

[384] *Ibid.*, Bk 21, Chap. 21

[385] Pope Leo XII [1825] Encyclical *Charitate Christi*, para 3 [Online] Available at: www.papalencyclicals.net [Accessed on: 4 July 2022]

[386] Pope Bl. Pius IX [1846] Encyclical *Qui Pluribus*, para 26 [Online] Available at: www.papalencyclicals.net [Accessed on: 4 July 2022]

[387] Denzinger, H [2010] *Op. cit.,* p.215

[388] *The Catechism of Trent*, Article V: 'He descended into Hell, the third day He rose again from the dead.' [Online] Available at: www.clerus.org [Accessed on: 4 July 2022]

While later popes avoided such graphic imagery, they also sought to convey revealed truths concerning the immortality of the soul, eternal punishment, and the existence of Hell. The teachings of Pope St. John Paul II's pontificate are the most explicit of modern popes, summarised as follows:

i)   God's own image and likeness is transmitted to each person through the creation of the immortal soul.[389]

ii)   A human being is a unity of body and soul, with the spiritual and immortal soul being the principle of unity of the person.[390]

iii)   The soul does not perish when it separates from the body at death, and it will be reunited with the body at the final Resurrection. (*CCC* 366)[391]

iv)   Immediately after death the souls of those who die in a state of mortal sin descend into hell, where they suffer the punishments of hell, 'eternal fire.' The chief punishment of hell is eternal separation from God. (*CCC* 1035)[392]

v)   Eternal damnation or hell is not a punishment imposed externally by God but is freely chosen by those who reject his love and forgiveness once and for all, thus separating themselves forever from joyful communion with him.[393]

vi)   Hell is the ultimate consequence of sin itself, which turns against the person who committed it.[394]

vii)   The Church 'believes that there will be eternal punishment for the sinner, who will be deprived of the sight of God, and that this punishment will have repercussion on the whole being of the sinner.' (*Dz* 4657)[395]

viii)   Hell is a place of eternal suffering, with no possibility of return, nor of the alleviation of pain.[396]

---

[389] Pope St. John Paul II [1995] Encyclical *Evangelium Vitae*, para 43 [Online] Available at: www. clerus.org [Accessed on: 4 July 2022]

[390] Pope St. John Paul II [1993] Encyclical *Veritatis Splendor*, para 48 [Online] Available at: www. vatican.va [Accessed on: 4 July 2022]

[391] *Catechism of the Catholic Church* [1992] [Online] Available at: www.scborromeo.org [Accessed on 4 July 2022]

[392] *Ibid.*

[393] Pope St. John Paul II [1999] *General Audience Address*, para 1 [Online] Available at: www.vatican. va [Accessed on: 4 July 2022]

[394] *Ibid.*, para 2

[395] Denzinger, H [2010] *Op. cit.*, p. 1027-1028

[396] *Op. cit.*, para 3

Evangelisation

F. *It is wrong to seek to convert others to the Catholic Faith, especially members of other religions, such as Jews, Muslims and Hindus.*

A major erroneous teaching of Pope Francis, which he has repeated on numerous occasions, is his insistence that it is wrong to seek to convince others, especially non-Catholic Christians, to convert to the Catholic Faith. He condemns proclaiming the Gospel in order to bring about conversion as proselytism. His erroneous teaching about evangelisation is summarised as follows:

a) Seeking to convert others to the Faith is waging 'a war of words aimed at imposing doctrines.'[397]
b) Avoid all forms of argument and disputes about the Faith, but instead show a humble and fraternal 'subjection' to those who do not share the faith.[398]
c) Trying to convert people to one's own belief 'always leads to an impasse'.[399]
d) Seeking to convince others about the Catholic Faith 'is all about membership and takes your freedom away'.[400]
e) 'Proselytism is incapable of creating a religious path in freedom. It always sees people being subjugated in one way or another. In evangelization the protagonist is God, in proselytism it is the I.'[401]
f) Evangelisation is about helping people to become ever more fully themselves, rather than drawing them into your life as a Christian.[402]
g) Instead of proclaiming the Gospel with words, 'simply spread the love of God.'[403]
h) It is wrong to seek to convince non-Christians to convert to the Catholic Faith, 'In front of an unbeliever the last thing I have to do is try to convince him. Never. The last thing I have to do is speak.'[404]
i) Seeking to convert a non-Catholic Christian to the Catholic Faith is a 'very grave sin against ecumenism: proselytism. We should never proselytise the Orthodox!'[405]

Pope Francis' account of his encounter with an African catechist and her two converts to the Faith illustrates his erroneous approach to evangelisation:

> Today I felt a certain bitterness after a meeting with young people. A woman approached me with a young man and a young woman. I was told they were part of a slightly fundamentalist movement. She said to me in perfect Spanish: 'Your Holiness, I am from South Africa. This boy was a Hindu and converted to Catholicism. This girl was Anglican and converted to Catholicism.' But she told me in a triumphant way, as though she was showing off a hunting trophy. I felt uncomfortable and said to her, 'Madam, evangelization yes, proselytism no.'[406]

[397] Pope Francis [2020] Encyclical *Fratelli Tutti*, para 3-4 [Online] Available at: www.vatican.va [Accessed on: 5 July 2022]
[398] *Ibid.*
[399] Agence France-Presse [2019] *Pope Francis Urges Moroccan Christians against Converting Others* [Online] Available at: www.telegraph.co.uk [Accessed on: 5 July 2022]
[400] Spadaro, A [2019] *'The Sovereignty of the People of God': The Pontiff Mmeets the Jesuits of Mozambique and Madagascar* [Online] Available at www.laciviltacattolica.com [Accessed on: 5 July 2022]
[401] *Ibid.*
[402] Pope Francis [2020] Encyclical *Fratelli Tutti*, para 3-4. Op. cit.
[403] *Ibid.*
[404] Prestigiacomo, A [2019] *Pope Francis Tells Students How Not To Convert Unbelievers* [Online] Available at: www.dailywire.com [Accessed on: 5 July 2022]
[405] Pope Francis [2016] *Address at Meeting with Priests, Religious, Seminarians and Pastoral Workers During Apostolic Visitation to Georgia and Azerbaijan* [Online] Available at: www.vatican.va [Accessed on: 5 July 2022]
[406] Spadaro, A [2019] *Op. cit.*

The Teaching of the Church

Christ founded the Church in order to continue His work of redemption for all time. **(De fide).**[407]

Membership of the Church is necessary for all men for salvation. **(De fide.)**[408]

Since membership of the Church is necessary for all men for salvation, seeking the conversion of all men is a solemn obligation for the Church. Our Lord Jesus Christ founded the Church to continue his proclamation of the Kingdom and his call to conversion. As Ott expressed it:

> Christ ordained affiliation to the Church by founding the Church as an institution unto the salvation for all men. He endowed the Apostles with His authority, gave them a universal mandate to teach and baptise and made eternal salvation dependent on the acceptance of His teaching and the reception of Baptism.[409]

The Fourth Lateran Council declared the necessity of membership of the Church for salvation, 'There is indeed one universal church of the faithful, outside of which nobody at all is saved.'[410] The Council of Florence was explicit that pagans and Jews will suffer eternal damnation unless they are joined to the Church because 'none of those who are outside of the Catholic Church... can become sharers of eternal life.'[411]

The Second Vatican Council also taught that the Church is necessary for salvation, explaining that this is because Christ is present in his Church, 'the one Mediator and the unique way of salvation':

> In explicit terms He Himself affirmed the necessity of faith and baptism and thereby affirmed also the necessity of the Church, for through baptism as through a door men enter the Church. Whosoever, therefore, knowing that the Catholic Church was made necessary by Christ, would refuse to enter or to remain in it, could not be saved.[412]

Having explained why the Church is necessary for salvation, the Council Fathers then emphasised the missionary imperative to 'preach the Gospel to every creature' (Mk 16:16). In particular, they stressed the importance of the Church's mission to those 'deceived by the Evil One' and those exposed to final despair because they are 'living and dying in this world without God'.[413]

Accordingly, the missionary imperative of the Church to proclaim the Gospel and to call all men to conversion was a major theme of the Second Vatican Council, across many of its constitutions and decrees, summarised as follows:

a) God has constituted Christ as the source of salvation for the whole world.[414]

b) All men are called to union with Christ.[415] [Men] must be called to faith and to conversion (Rom 10:14-15)[416] so that they belong to the new people of God. The Church is destined to extend to all races and regions of the earth.[417]

---

[407] Ott, L [1957] *Op. cit.*, p. 274

[408] Ott, L [1957] *Op. cit.*, p. 312

[409] *Ibid.*, p. 312

[410] Fourth Lateran Council [1215] *Confession of Faith* [Online] Available at: www.papalencyclicals. net [Accessed on: 5 July 2022]

[411] Denzinger, H [2010] *Op. cit.*, p.1442

[412] Second Vatican Council [1964] Dogmatic Constitution, *Lumen Gentium*, para 14 [Online] Available at: www.vatican.va [Accessed on: 5 July 2022]

[413] *Ibid., para 16*

[414] *Ibid., para 17*

[415] *Ibid., para 3*

[416] Second Vatican Council [1963] Constitution on the Sacred Liturgy, *Sacrosanctum Concilium*, para 9 [Online] Available at: www.vatican.va [Accessed on: 5 July 2022]

[417] Second Vatican Council [1964] Dogmatic Constitution, *Lumen Gentium*, Op. cit., para 13, 9 [Online] Available at: www.vatican.va [Accessed on: 5 July 2022]

c) Therefore, just as Christ was sent by the Father, so also He sent the apostles… that, by preaching the gospel to every creature (Mk 16:15) they might proclaim the Paschal Mystery of the Son of God.[418]

d) The Church has received the solemn missionary mandate of Christ (Mt 28:19-20) to proclaim the saving truth from the apostles and must carry it out to the very ends of the earth. (Acts 1:8).[419]

e) The obligation of spreading the faith is imposed on every disciple of Christ, according to his state.[420]

f) By so doing, the Church announces the good tidings of salvation to those who do not believe, so that all men may know the true God and Jesus Christ whom He has sent, and may be converted from their ways, doing penance.'[421]

g) Thereby, snatching men from the slavery of error and of idols and incorporating them in Christ.

h) Therefore, the Faith must be proclaimed with confidence and constancy in order that non-Christians may believe and be freely converted to the Lord by word and example.[422]

i) The true state of the world makes clear the necessity of an intense evangelization of non-Christians.[423]

j) Contrary to Pope Francis' assertion that converting other Christians is a 'very grave sin against ecumenism', Vatican II insisted that there is no opposition between the conversion of other Christians and ecumenism, 'since both proceed from the marvellous ways of God.'[424]

Proof from the Sources of Faith
a) Teaching from Holy Scripture

Pope Francis' attempts to justify his rejection of the traditional understanding of evangelisation – proclamation and conversion – by asserting that it somehow infringes people's freedom. By teaching that non-Christians are justified in remaining Jews, Muslims and Hindus, Pope Francis is implying that rejecting our Lord Jesus Christ is a valid exercise of freedom that is morally neutral.

This is not our Lord's understanding of the authentic exercise of freedom, as he explained, 'He that is not with me, is against me: and he that gathereth not with me, scattereth.' (Mt 12:30; cf. Lk 11:23). Commenting on this passage, St. Augustine writes that, according to the Lord, those separated from the Church, even if they seem to be good, 'their separation from the Church itself renders them bad'.[425] Pope Francis ignores this fundamental reality of humanity since the Incarnation – acceptance or rejection of Christ is determinative of the moral status of every human being. This is why the missionary proclamation of the Gospel and the call to conversion to non-believers is so important. Since the Apostolic times the Church has obeyed our Lord's missionary mandate:

> But Jesus came near and spoke to them; All authority in heaven and on earth, he said, has been given to me, you, therefore, must go out, making disciples of all nations,

---

[418] Second Vatican Council [1963] Constitution on the Sacred Liturgy, *Sacrosanctum Concilium*, para 6 [Online] Available at: www.vatican.va [Accessed on: 5 July 2022]

[419] Second Vatican Council [1964] Dogmatic Constitution, *Lumen Gentium, Op. cit.*, para 17 [Online] Available at: www.vatican.va [Accessed on: 5 July 2022]

[420]*Ibid.*

[421] Second Vatican Council [1963] Constitution on the Sacred Liturgy, *Sacrosanctum Concilium*, para 9 [Online] Available at: www.vatican.va [Accessed on: 5 July 2022]

[422] Second Vatican Council [1965] Decree, *Ad Gentes*, 13, 30 [Online] Available at: www.vatican.va [Accessed on: 5 July 2022]

[423] *Ibid.*, 39

[424] Second Vatican Council [1964] Decree, *Unitatis Redintegratio*, para 4 [Online] Available at: www.vatican.va [Accessed on: 5 July 2022]

[425] St. Augustine [423] *Letter to Lady Felicia*, letter 208 [Online] Available at: www.newadvent.org [Accessed on: 6 July 2022]

and baptizing them in the name of the Father, and of the Son, and of the Holy Ghost, teaching them to observe all the commandments which I have given you. (Mt 28:18-20).

Pope Francis' repudiation of seeking to convince non-believers and other Christians of the truth of the Catholic faith so that they convert is also contrary to the teaching of Christ. The parable of the invited guests conveys this missionary imperative of apologetics: 'And the Lord said to the servant: Go out into the highways and hedges, and compel them to come in, that my house may be filled.' (Lk 14:23). The word 'compel' is the translation of the Greek word *anagkazó*, which has a number of meanings, including urgent persuasion, to make something necessary by explaining the consequences.[426] In the case of the proclamation of the kingdom, this means urgently persuading non-believers that there is no salvation outside of the Church by explaining the consequences of unbelief.

Accordingly, Pope Francis is wrong to condemn such urgent persuasion to belief and conversion as proselytism. By so doing, he is condemning the evangelisation undertaken by the Apostles, as described in the Acts of the Apostles. In his address to the crowds in Jerusalem, St. Peter sought to convince them to convert to Christianity, 'And with very many other words did he testify and exhort them, saying: Save yourselves from this perverse generation.' (Acts 2:40). St. Paul 'reasoned with them out of the scriptures' (Acts 17:2); 'And he reasoned in the synagogue every sabbath, bringing in the name of the Lord Jesus; and he persuaded the Jews and the Greeks.' (Acts 18:4). St. Paul even disputed with the Jews for three months concerning the kingdom of God (Acts 19:8).

Having encountered the Risen Lord on the road to Damascus, St. Paul felt compelled to undertake evangelisation, 'Knowing therefore the fear of the Lord, we use persuasion to men.' (II Cor 5:11), He explained that the purpose of evangelisation is to deliberately seek to elicit faith, conversion, and the reception of the sacrament of Baptism:

> How then shall they call on him, in whom they have not believed? Or how shall they believe him, of whom they have not heard? And how shall they hear, without a preacher? And how shall they preach unless they be sent as it is written: How beautiful are the feet of them that preach the gospel of peace, of them that bring glad tidings of good things! But all do not obey the gospel. For Isaias saith: Lord, who hath believed our report? Faith then cometh by hearing; and hearing by the word of Christ (Rom 10:14-17).

Sacred Scripture testifies that Pope Francis commits a grave error when he reduces evangelisation to being little more than setting a good example.

b) The Testimony of Tradition
St. Augustine conveys something of the passion that drove evangelisation during the time of the Church Fathers. Commenting on the parable of the invited guests (Lk 14:23), St. Augustine reflected on the conversion of St. Paul to explain what our Lord meant when he talked of 'compelling' people to enter the Kingdom of God'. Pointing out that our Lord knocked St. Paul to the ground and blinded him, St. Augustine wrote:

> You also read how he who was at first Saul, and afterwards Paul, was compelled, by the great violence with which Christ coerced him, to know and to embrace the truth… This light, lost suddenly by him when he was cast to the ground by the heavenly voice, he did not recover until he became a member of the Holy Church. You are also of opinion that no coercion is to be used with any man in order to his deliverance from the fatal consequences of error; and yet you see that, in examples which cannot be disputed, this is done by God, who loves us with more real regard for our profit than any other can.[427]

---

[426]*Strong's Concordance* [Online] Available at: biblehub.com [Accessed on; 6 July 2022]
[427]St. Augustine [408] *Letter to Vincentius, letter 93, para 5* [Online] Available at: www.newadvent. org [Accessed on: 6 July 2022]

He went on to describe his own conversion in terms of being compelled to enter into the Church by the 'scourges' of our Lord' that took away his 'timid hesitation'. Augustine admits that if he hadn't been compelled to enter the Church he wouldn't have realised the absurdity of the lies that had prevented his conversion up to that point:

> We were prevented from entering the Church by false reports, which we could not know to be false unless we entered it; and we would not enter unless we were compelled: thanks be to the Lord, who by His scourge took away our timid hesitation, and taught us to find out for ourselves how vain and absurd were the lies which rumour had spread abroad against His Church: by this we are persuaded that there is no truth in the accusations made by the authors of this heresy, since the more serious charges which their followers have invented are without foundation.[428]

St. Augustine's commentary on St. Peter's address to the crowds in Jerusalem at Pentecost attests to the same vitality and conviction that inspired Apostolic evangelisation. He writes that those who had hated Christ were 'pricked in their hearts and converted' 'when they perceived in Peter's address so great and divine a testimony borne in behalf of Christ'.[429] Also, in a sermon St. Augustine explained that the Jews were 'cut to the heart', by St. Peter, 'urging on them the meaning of the passion, resurrection and divinity of Christ.'[430]

St. John Chrysostom presents evangelisation as combat against opponents. He describes the apostles 'beating' the 'philosophers, the masters of oratory, the skilful debaters' and prevailing 'against them in a short space of time', 'all these were confuted and gave way when the fisherman spoke…How did the weak overcome the strong; the twelve, the world? Not by using the same armour, but in nakedness contending with men in arms.'[431]

Pope St. Gregory the Great writes that in order to effectively evangelise people it is first necessary to 'throw down' their wrong ideas and wrong things before they can be in a position to 'hear holy preaching', '…words of building up they would surely have despised, had they not first wholesomely become aware of the ruin of their throwing down.'[432]

Pope Francis' conception of evangelisation appears anaemic and ineffectual compared to the Church Father's testimony to the passion and effectiveness of authentic evangelisation.

c) The Defence by the Magisterium
During the colonial expansion of the West into the Americas, Asia and Africa, various popes expressed the understanding of evangelisation as a battle against ignorance of God and enslavement to the devil. Pope Gregory XV used such militant imagery to describe the work of missionaries:

> They fearlessly fight the Lord's battles against heresy and unbelief by private and public speech and writings… They search out those who sit in darkness and the shadow of death to summon them to the light and life of the Catholic Religion. So, fearless in the face of every danger, they bravely enter the woods and caves of savages, gradually pacify them by Christian kindness. and prepare them for true faith and real virtue. At length they snatch them from the devil's rule, by the bath of regeneration and promote them to the freedom of God's adopted sons.[433]

---

[428] *Ibid.,* para 18

[429] St. Augustine. *Tractate* 92 (John 15:26-27), para 1 [Online] Available at: www.newadvent.org [Accessed on: 6 July 2022]

[430] *The Works of Saint Augustine [1991] Sermons, III,* Sermon 77, para 4. New York: New City Press, p. 319

[431] St. John Chrysostom. *Homily 3 on First Corinthians,* para 8 [Online] Available at: www. newadvent.org [Accessed on: 6 July 2022]

[432] Pope St. Gregory the Great [590] *Pastoral Rule,* Bk. III, Chap. 34 [Online] Available at: www. newadvent.org [Accessed on: 6 July 2022]

[433] Pope Gregory XV [1840] Encyclical *Probe Nostis,* para 6 [Online] Available at: www. papalencyclicals.net [Accessed on: 7July 2022]

Pope Leo XIII saw the Church as constituted by Christ for the purpose of evangelisation for the salvation of souls, 'it is so constituted as to open wide its arms to all mankind, unhampered by any limit of either time or place. "Preach ye the Gospel to every creature." (Mk 16:15)'.[434] He also saw evangelisation as freeing peoples from being 'miserably imprisoned in the darkness of superstition!'. Referring to St. Francis Xavier 'preaching the Gospel to the Hindus', Pope Leo XIII wrote, 'he converted hundreds of thousands of Hindus from the myths and vile superstitions of the Brahmans to the true religion.'[435] He also saw evangelisation bringing an end to human slavery in Africa, 'those who have received this light have also shaken off the yoke of human slavery'. Evangelisation not only saved individual souls but also transformed cultures:

> Wherever Christian customs and laws are in force, wherever religion establishes that men serve justice and honour human dignity, wherever the spirit of brotherly love taught by Christ spreads itself, there neither slavery nor savage barbarism can exist. Rather, mildness of character and civilised Christian liberty flourish there.[436]

Previously, popes had a clear understanding about their responsibility to evangelise 'infidels', a word derived from the Latin, *infidelis*, meaning non-faithful, including all non-Christians and the unbelieving. Pope St. Pius X defined infidels as follows:

> Infidels are those who have not been baptised and do not believe in Jesus Christ, because they either believe in and worship false gods as idolaters do, or though admitting one true God, they do not believe in the Messiah, neither as already come in the Person of Jesus Christ, nor as to come; for instance, Mohammedans and the like.[437]

Unlike Pope Francis — who criticised the imposition of doctrine as a 'war of words' — Pope Benedict XV viewed the transmission of doctrine as an essential task of evangelists calling them, 'couriers of the doctrine'. Instead of condemning evangelists who sought to convert unbelievers to Christianity as Pope Francis publicly did, Pope Benedict XV saw them as 'ministers of the eternal salvation'. The thought of the multitudes dwelling in the darkness of ignorance of Christ played on Pope Benedict XV's mind:

> According to a recent estimate, the number of non-believers in the world approximates one billion souls. The misfortune of this vast number of souls is for Us a source of great sorrow. From the days when We first took up the responsibilities of this apostolic office We have yearned to share with them the divine blessings of the Redemption.[438]

Pope Ven. Pius XII was also anguished about the number of souls trapped in the darkness of unbelief, likewise referring to the one billion souls 'who sat in darkness and shadow' (Ps 106:10).[439] He also referred to the urgent need to bring 'the message of saving truth' 'to what is called "darkest" Africa, where some 85,000,000 people still sit in the darkness of idolatry.'[440] Pope Pius XII's appeal to bishops throughout the world to assist with evangelisation led to many sending *Donum Fidei* priests to the mission fields, especially in Africa.

---

[434] Pope Leo XIII [1885] Encyclical *Immortale Dei*, para 8 [Online] Available at: www.vatican.va [Accessed on: 7 July 2022]

[435] Pope Leo XIII [1893] Encyclical *Ad Extremas*, para 1 [Online] Available at: www.vatican.va [Accessed on: 7 July 2022]

[436] Pope Leo XIII [1890] Encyclical *Catholicae Ecclesiae*, para 3 [Online] Available at: www.vatican. va [Accessed on: 7 July 2022]

[437] Pope St. Pius X [1908] *Catechism of Pope St. Pius X*. Those Outside the Communion of Saints 12 Q. Who are infidels? [Online] Available at: www.ewtn.com [Accessed on: 7 July 2022]

[438] Pope Benedict XV [1919] Apostolic Letter *Maximum Illud*, paras 1,6-7 [Online] Available at: www.vatican.va [Accessed on: 7 July 2022]

[439] Pope Pius XII [1951] Encyclical *Evangelii Praecones*, para 16 [Online] Available at: www.vatican. va [Accessed on: 7 July 2022]

[440] Pope XII [1957] Encyclical *Fidei Donum*, para 20 [Online] Available at: www.vatican.va [Accessed on: 7 July 2022]

Unlike Pope Francis, Pope Pius XI viewed the evangelisation of non-Catholics as a salvific priority because they are imprisoned in error, '... it is most important that our separated brethren be led back to the unity of the Church and that non-Catholics be convinced of and delivered from their errors.'[441]

Pope St. Paul VI addressed the erroneous argument — repeated by Pope Francis — that proclaiming the Gospel and explicitly calling people to conversion infringed on they freedom. He wrote in his encyclical dedicated to evangelisation:

> It would certainly be an error to impose something on the consciences of our brethren. But to propose to their consciences the truth of the Gospel and salvation in Jesus Christ, with complete clarity and with a total respect for the free options which it presents — 'without coercion, or dishonourable or unworthy pressure' — far from being an attack on religious liberty is fully to respect that liberty, which is offered the choice of a way that even non-believers consider noble and uplifting. Is it then a crime against others' freedom to proclaim with joy a Good News which one has come to know through the Lord's mercy? [...]The respectful presentation of Christ and His kingdom is more than the evangeliser's right; it is his duty. It is likewise the right of his fellow men to receive from him the proclamation of the Good News of salvation.[442]

Pope St. John Paul II criticised those who sought to reduce evangelisation to dialogue with non-Christian religions, 'The Lord clearly exhorts his followers to make disciples of all nations, to baptize and to teach the observance of the commandments (Mt 28, 19-20).'[443] He also directly challenged those, like Pope Francis, who sought to stigmatise the conversion of non-Christians as 'proselytizing':

> Nowadays the call to conversion which missionaries address to non-Christians is put into question or passed over in silence. It is seen as an act of 'proselytizing'; it is claimed that it is enough to help people to become more human or more faithful to their own religion, that it is enough to build communities capable of working for justice, freedom, peace and solidarity. What is overlooked is that every person has the right to hear the 'Good News' of the God who reveals and gives himself in Christ, so that each one can live out in its fullness his or her proper calling. This lofty reality is expressed in the words of Jesus to the Samaritan woman: 'If you knew the gift of God,' and in the unconscious but ardent desire of the woman: 'Sir, give me this water, that I may not thirst' (Jn 4:10, 15).[444]

During the pontificate of Pope Benedict XVI, the Congregation for the Doctrine of the Faith promulgated a *Doctrinal Note on Some Aspects of Evangelisation* that challenged certain errors about evangelisation, summarised under the following headings:

i) It is erroneous to maintain 'that any attempt to convince others on religious matters is a limitation of their freedom.'[445]

ii) 'Respect for religious freedom and its promotion "must not in any way make us indifferent towards truth and goodness. Indeed, love impels the followers of Christ to proclaim to all the truth which saves"'.[446]

iii) It is erroneous to argue that as it is only legitimate to 'help people to become more human or more faithful to their own religion', it is wrong to seek their conversion.[447]

---

[441] Pope Pius XI [1926] Encyclical *Rerum Ecclesiae*, para 23 [Online] Available at: www.vatican.va [Accessed on: 7 July 2022]

[442] Pope St. Paul VI [1975] Encyclical *Evangelii Nuntiandi*, para 88 [Online] Available at: www. vatican.va [Accessed on: 7 July 2022]

[443] Pope St. John Paul II [1987] *Address to the Bishops of Ethiopia on the occasion of their 'Ad Limina' visit, para 4* [Online] Available at: www.vatican.va [Accessed on: 7 July 2022]

[444] Pope St. John Paul II [1990] Encyclical *Redemptoris Missio*, para 46 [Online] Available at: www. vatican.va [Accessed on: 7 July 2022]

[445] Congregation for the Doctrine of the Faith [2007] *Doctrinal Note on Some Aspects of Evangelisation*, para 3 [Online] Available at: www.vatican.va [Accessed on: 7 July 2022]

[446] *Ibid.*, para 10

[447] *Ibid.*, para 3

iv)   It is erroneous to maintain that Christ should not be proclaimed nor should joining the Church be promoted because people can be saved outside the Church.[448]

v)   Rather, 'the revelation of the fundamental truths about God, about the human person and the world, is a great good for every human person…living in darkness without the truths about ultimate questions is an evil and is often at the root of suffering and slavery which can at times be grievous.'[449]

vi)   Therefore, 'fully belonging to Christ, who is the Truth, and entering the Church do not lessen human freedom, but rather exalt it and direct it towards its fulfilment, in a love that is freely given and which overflows with care for the good of all people.'[450]

vii)   This 'missionary proclamation is endangered today by relativistic theories which seek to justify religious pluralism', that claim that the proclamation of the Gospel and the call to conversion is intolerant and aggressive.[451]

viii) Regarding non-Catholic Christians, to prepare and reconcile those individuals who desire full Catholic communion is not proselytism that contradicts ecumenism.[452]

ix)   'The work of ecumenism does not remove the right or take away the responsibility of proclaiming in fullness the Catholic faith to other Christians, who freely wish to receive it.'[453]

It is remarkable that the Congregation for the Doctrine of the Faith promulgated this authoritative doctrinal note in 2007, only for Pope Francis to repeat many of the same hackneyed errors nine years later.

---

[448] *Ibid.*

[450] *Ibid.*

[452] *Ibid.*, para 12

[453] *Ibid.*

[449] *Ibid.*, para 7

[451] *Ibid.*, para 10

Hamartiology (1) — 'Boasting about One's Sins'

G. *Our sins are the privileged place of encounter with Christ, and as such we can 'boast of our sins' (misquoting II Corinthians 12:9).*

Pope Francis has given meditations at Mass and public addresses that present an erroneous hamartiology, downplaying the grievous effects of sin on the life of grace. In his determination to present sin in a positive way, the Supreme Pontiff even misquotes sacred scripture. Pope Francis' erroneous hamartiology can be summarised as follows:

a) Life consists of grace and sin. 'He who does not sin is not human. We all make mistakes and we need to recognise our weakness.'[454]

b) 'The privileged place for the encounter with Christ is our sins.' Pope Francis explained that to the untrained ear this 'would almost seem heresy.'[455]

c) Pope Francis attempted to justify this statement by misrepresenting St. Paul as writing in the Second Letter to the Corinthians (12:9), he 'affirmed boasting of "only two things: of his sins and of the Risen Christ who saved him"'.[456]

d) On other occasions, Pope Francis misrepresented St. Paul as saying of himself, '"I boast only of my sins". These were scandalous words.'[457] Even in an address to the Catholic Biblical Federation, the Supreme Pontiff misquoted this passage from St. Paul to justify boasting of one's sins, telling them, 'In another passage — you biblicists know it — he says: "I will boast of my sins"' (cf. II Cor 12:9).[458]

e) Pope Francis concludes, St. Paul can boast of his sins because this is 'precisely the place where the Word of God can come and be strong.'[459]

Pope Francis' hamartiological error originated in his *eisegesis* of II Corinthians 12:9 when he mistakenly interpreted St. Paul's reference to his infirmities, or physical weaknesses, as being about his personal sins. St. Paul actually wrote, 'And he [Jesus] said to me: My grace is sufficient for thee: for power is made perfect in infirmity. Gladly therefore will I glory in my infirmities, that the power of Christ may dwell in me.'

St. Paul uses the Greek word *astheneia* which has the meaning of 'want of strength, weakness, illness, suffering, calamity, frailty.'[460] It does not have the meaning of sin, as Pope Francis wrongly asserts on numerous occasions. It is untrue to says that St. Paul boasted of his sins.

Pope Francis' downplaying of the seriousness of sin to the life of grace suggests the influence of a Protestant hamartiology that erroneously assumes the absolute or near impossibility of losing the state of grace.[461] The Supreme Pontiff's talk of 'boasting about one's sins' is reminiscent of the erroneous hamartiology of the heresiarch Martin Luther, who wrote:

> God does not save those who are only imaginary sinners. Be a sinner, and let your sins be strong, but let your trust in Christ be stronger, and rejoice in Christ who is the victor over sin, death, and the world. We will commit sins while we are here, for this life is not a place where justice resides. [...] No sin can separate us from Him, even if we were to kill or commit adultery thousands of times each day.[462]

---

[454] *Francis Calls on Religious Men to 'wake up the world'* [3 January 2014] [Online] Available at: www.lastampa.it [Accessed on: 7 July 2022]

[455] Pope Francis [18 September 2014] *Morning Meditation in the Chapel of the Domus* [Online] Available at: www.vatican.va [Accessed on: 7 July 2022]

[456] *Ibid.*

[457] Pope Francis [4th September 2014] *Morning Meditation in the Chapel of the Domus Sanctae Marthae* [Online] Available at: www.vatican.va [Accessed on: 7 July 2022]

[458] Pope Francis [2015] *Address to Participants in the Plenary Assembly of the Catholic Biblical Federation* [Online] Available at: www.vatican.va [Accessed on: 7 July 2022]

[459] Pope Francis [4th September 2014] *Op. cit.*

[460] *Strong's Concordance* [Online] Available at: biblehub.com [Accessed on: 7 July 2022]

[461] Ott, L [1957] Op. cit., p. 263

[462] Luther, M [1521] *Let Your Sins Be Strong: A Letter From Luther to Melanchthon*, Letter no. 99. [Online] Available at: www.projectwittenberg.org [Accessed on: 7 July 2022]

Only someone who discounts the possibility of losing the state of grace through mortal sin — of grievous sin separating us from Christ — could make the mistake of thinking one could boast of one's sins.

The Teaching of the Church
The grace by which we are justi ied may be lost, and is lost, by every grievous sin. **(De fide)**[463]

Before the emergence of the Protestant heretical hamartiology, it was the unquestioned understanding of Christians that sins made us enemies of God. Fr. Gerard Manley Hopkins SJ expressed this perennial understanding in his reflection on St. Ignatius of Loyola's Spiritual Exercises:

> For if you are in sin you are God's enemy, you cannot love or praise him. You may say you are far from hating God; but if you live in sin you are among God's enemies, you are under Satan's standard and enlisted there; you may not like it, no wonder; you may wish to be elsewhere; but there you are, an enemy to God.[464]

In response to the Protestant heresy, the Council of Trent defined the doctrine regarding the loss of sanctifying grace due to grievous or mortal sin, based on I Corinthians 6:9-10:

> In opposition also to the subtle wits of certain men, who, by pleasing speeches and good words, seduce the hearts of the innocent, it is to be maintained, that the received grace of Justification is lost, not only by infidelity whereby even faith itself is lost, but also by any other mortal sin whatever, though faith be not lost.[465]

Instead of viewing sin — as Pope Francis does — as the 'privileged place for the encounter with Christ' the Council of Trent described mortal sin as making sinners 'enemies of God' and 'children of wrath' (Eph 2:3).[466] Furthermore, the council fathers warned against the danger of considering sins trivial due to God's clemency, 'thinking sins less grievous, we, offering as it were an insult and an outrage to the Holy Ghost, (Heb 10:29) should fall into more grievous sins, treasuring up wrath against the day of wrath. (cf. Rom 2:5; Jas 5:3).[467]

The hamartiology of the Second Vatican Council also emphasised the serious gravity of sin to human beings:

a) Contrary to Pope Francis' assertion, 'He who does not sin is not human', Vatican II presents sin as an unnatural intrusion to human existence that 'disrupts' an individual's 'whole relationship toward himself and others and all created things.' 'Man is split within himself,' 'For sin has diminished man, blocking his path to fulfilment.'[468]

b) b) Sin is an encounter with the devil, 'But often men, deceived by the Evil One, have become vain in their reasonings and have exchanged the truth of God for a lie' (Rom 1:21,25),[469] 'Although he was made by God in a state of holiness, from the very onset of his history man abused his liberty, at the urging of the Evil One.'[470]

---

[463] Ott, L [1957] *Op. cit.*

[464] Hopkins, G. Excerpt from *An Address Based on the Opening of The Spiritual Exercises of St. Ignatius of Loyola* [Online] Available at: http://jonahs411.blogspot.com [Accessed on: 9 July 2022]

[465] Council of Trent [1547] *Decree on Justification*, Chap. 15 [Online] Available at: www.thecounciloftrent.com [Accessed on: 9 July 2022]

[466] Council of Trent [1551] *Decree on the Most Holy Sacraments of Penance and Extreme Unction*, Chap. 5 [Online] Available at: www.thecounciloftrent.com [Accessed on: 9 July 2022]

[467] *Ibid.,* Chap. 8

[468] Second Vatican Council [1965] Pastoral Constitution *Gaudium et Spes*, Part 1, Chap. 1, para 13 [Online] Available at: www.vatican.va [Accessed on: 9 July 2022]

[469] Second Vatican Council [1964] Dogmatic Constitution, *Lumen Gentium*, para 16 [Online] Available at: www.vatican.va [Accessed on: 5 July 2022]

[470] Second Vatican Council [1965] Pastoral Constitution *Gaudium et Spes*, Part 1, Chap. 1, para 13. *Op. cit.*

c) Instead of being a source of boasting, sins can lead to 'final despair'[471] and those who care little for truth and goodness, their conscience by 'degrees grows practically sightless as a result of habitual sin.'[472]

Proof from the Sources of Faith
a) Teaching from Holy Scripture

The Old Testament warns that God, in his holiness and justice, hates sins (Prov 6:16-19) and hates the wicked — God announces, 'I abhor the wicked' (Ex 23:7), He 'hatest all the workers of iniquity, thou wilt destroy all that speak a lie'; 'The bloody and the deceitful man the Lord will abhor' (Ps 5: 6-7). Sinners are the enemies of God (Mic 2:8) and they hate God (Ex 20:5; Deut 5:9; Ps 138:11).

The enemies of God are the focus of his wrath, 'The Lord is a jealous God, and a revenger: the Lord is a revenger, and hath wrath: the Lord taketh vengeance on his adversaries, and he is angry with his enemies' (Nah 1:2). And the just man who turns to sin, becomes an enemy of God:

> But if the just man turn himself away from his justice, and do iniquity according to all the abominations which the wicked man useth to work, shall he live? All his justices which he hath done, shall not be remembered: in the prevarication, by which he hath prevaricated, and in his sin, which he hath committed, in them he shall die (Ezek 18:24).

God's utter hatred of sin is expressed in prophecies of the Day of the Lord, the Day of Judgement, 'And I will distress men, and they shall walk like blind men, because they have sinned against the Lord: and their blood shall be poured out as earth, and their bodies as dung' (Zeph 1:15-17).

Far from sins being something to boast about, the Old Testament warns of the danger of sins because God can allow them, as a punishment, to lead to a moral blindness that inhibits conversion:

> Blind the heart of this people, and make their ears heavy, and shut their eyes: lest they see with their eyes, and hear with their ears, and understand with their heart, and be converted and I heal them (Isa 6:10).

Contrary to Pope Francis' assertion that he can boast of his sins because this is 'precisely the place where the Word of God can come and be strong', sacred Scripture teaches that certain sins can become the occasion of God's word transforming into the divine punishment of spiritual and moral blindness that inhibits conversion. Our Lord Jesus Christ refers to Isaiah 6:10 to explain the punishment that those who commit the sin of unbelief in him will receive, even to the extent that what little grace they have will be lost due to their sin, 'For he that hath, to him shall be given, and he shall abound: but he that hath not, from him shall be taken away that also which he hath' (Mt 13:12; cf. Luke 8:18). In this sinful situation, Jesus' word will become the occasion of them sinking into the punishment of spiritual blindness, 'because seeing they see not, and hearing they hear not, neither do they understand.' (Mt 13:13).

Following Jesus' teaching, St. John also referred to Isaiah 6:10 to explain the consequences of the Jewish people's sin of unbelief (Jn 12:40).

Tertullian referred to the punishment of Adam to explain the meaning of Jesus' warning about the punishment of sinners, '"even that which he seems to have has been taken from him" — such as the grace of paradise and the friendship of God, by means of which he might have known all things of God, if he had continued in his obedience.'[473]

The Second Letter of St. Peter highlights the danger to the justified of returning to previous sins because it also leads to the grave sin of apostasy. St. Peter warns the faith-

---

[471] Second Vatican Council [1964] Dogmatic Constitution, *Lumen Gentium*, para 16. *Op. cit.*

[472] Second Vatican Council [1965] Pastoral Constitution *Gaudium et Spes*, Part 1, Chap. 1, para 16. *Op. cit.*

[473] Tertullian. *Against Marcion*, Bk. II, Chap. 2 [Online] Available at: www.newadvent.org [Accessed on: 9 July 2022]

ful to beware those who 'speaking proud words of vanity,' about sin, who 'allure by the desires of fleshly riotousness, those who for a little while escape':

> For if, flying from the pollutions of the world, through the knowledge of our Lord and Saviour Jesus Christ, they be again entangled in them and overcome: their latter state is become unto them worse than the former. For it had been better for them not to have known the way of justice, than after they have known it, to turn back from that holy commandment which was delivered to them. For, that of the true proverb has happened to them: The dog is returned to his vomit: and, the sow that was washed, to her wallowing in the mire. (II Pet 2: 18-22).

St. Paul took up our Lord's teaching about the punishment of moral and spiritual blindness for habitual sin, summarised as follows:

i)   The wrath of God is revealed from heaven against sinners, who by their sins suppress divine truth. (Rom 1:18)
ii) Sinners are 'children of wrath' (Eph 2:3). Tertullian explains this phrase as referring to the 'irrational irascibility' that derives from the devil's mastery of sinners.'[474] Original sin and personal sins put us under the wrath of God.
iii) Sinners have 'their understanding darkened, being alienated from the life of God through the ignorance that is in them, because of the blindness of their hearts.' (Eph 4:18).
iv) St. Paul warns that those who are seduced into iniquity by Satan 'because they receive not the love of the truth, that they might be saved' will be punished by God: 'Therefore God shall send them the operation of error, to believe lying: That all may be judged who have not believed the truth, but have consented to iniquity.' (II Thess 2:10-11).
v)   God hardens some sinners just as he hardened the heart of Pharaoh. (Rom 9:17-18). St. Paul is referring to the mystery of God's permissive will allowing sinners to resist God's grace and sink deeper into sin and the punishment he inflicts as a result. As St. Thomas Aquinas explains:

> Now although the sun, so far as it is concerned, enlightens all bodies, yet if it be encountered by an obstacle in a body, it leaves it in darkness, as happens to a house whose window-shutters are closed, although the sun is in no way the cause of the house being darkened, since it does not act of its own accord in failing to light up the interior of the house; and the cause of this is the person who closed the shutters. On the other hand, God, of His own accord, withholds His grace from those in whom He finds an obstacle: so that the cause of grace being withheld is not only the man who raises an obstacle to grace; but God, Who, of His own accord, withholds His grace. In this way, God is the cause of spiritual blindness, deafness of ear, and hardness of heart.[475]

b) The Testimony of Tradition
The ante-Nicene Church Fathers had a strong sense of the harm inflicted by sin on the sinner and that sin rightly deserves the wrath of God. Lactantius sought to convey the gravity of God's anger against sinners, writing that 'because God is eternal, His anger also remains to eternity… divine anger remains for ever against those who ever sin.' In order for God's anger to be satisfied, the sinner needs a 'reformation of morals', because only by ceasing to sin can God's anger be rendered 'mortal'.[476]

Commenting on II Thess 2:10-11, St. Cyprian warns of the danger of sins that lead to the loss of sanctifying grace and the grace of repentance. He criticises those who

---

[474] Tertullian. *A Treatise on the Soul*, Chap. 16 [Online] Available at: www.newadvent.org [Accessed on: 9 July 2022]
[475] St. Thomas Aquinas. *Summa Theologiae*. First Part of the Second Part. Q. 79, A. 3 [Online] Available at: www.newadvent.org [Accessed on: 9 July 2022]
[476] Lactantius. *On the Anger of God*, Chap. 21 [Online] Available at: www.newadvent.org [Accessed on: 12 July 2022]

take such sins lightly, who make the mistake of assuming that their sins are 'small and moderate.'[477] St. Cyprian identifies prideful self-satisfaction as the sin that stops sinners repenting, driven 'mad with the alienation of a hardened mind':

> Thoughtless before their sin was acknowledged, after their sin they are obstinate; neither steadfast before, nor suppliant afterwards: when they ought to have stood fast, they fell; when they ought to fall and prostrate themselves to God, they think they stand fast. They have taken peace for themselves of their own accord when nobody granted it; seduced by false promises…'[478]

St. Augustine didn't see sins as anything to boast about, viewing sin, like St. Paul (Rom 6:20), as a form of slavery, 'If, therefore, they are the slaves of sin, why do they boast of free will? For by what a man is overcome, to the same is he delivered as a slave.'[479] The following headlines summarise St. Augustine's teaching on the gravity of sin:

i)   'By sinning, of course, you make an enemy of God.'[480]
ii) God hates our sins.[481]
iii) God's wrath at some sins is so great that he will not search out the sinner, but leave them to perish in their sin. This should make us realise his great mercy when he 'scourges us' for our sins, because he hasn't left us to perish in our sins.[482]
iv) St. Augustine warned that 'If you sin, your adversary is God's word.' He explains that the word of God says 'Don't' to every sin we are tempted to commit, 'In whatever kinds of sin you want to do by your own will, it says to you, "Don't." It's the adversary of your will, until it can become the author of your salvation.'[483]

c) The Defence by the Magisterium

A number of popes highlighted God's horror of sin, our sins deserving the wrath of God and the necessity of sorrow for our sins. No pope supports Pope Francis' bizarre call to boast of our sins.

Pope Bl. Pius IX wrote that due to the sins of men God afflicts the world with his punishments.[484] Pope St. Pius X emphasised 'horror of sin' — God's horror at our sins and the need for us to feel a sense of horror. God has such a horror of sin in themselves and because they express man's 'vicious and depraved habits and…passions which incite him to evil.'[485] And the sufferings of our Lord Jesus Christ on the cross due to our sins should evoke sorrow for sin and 'inspire us with the deepest horror of sin.'[486] Pope Pius XI also emphasised the need for horror at our sin and sorrow for sin, 'it cannot be but he will shrink with horror from all sin as from the greatest evil.'[487]

Pope Ven. Pius XII famously warned against the greatest sin besetting the world being 'men have begun to lose the sense of sin'. Pope Francis' misreading of II Corin-

---

[477] St. Cyprian. *Epistle* 54, para 13 [Online] Available at: www.newadvent.org [Accessed on: 12 July 2022]
[478] St. Cyprian. *On the Lapsed*, para 33 [Online] Available at: www.newadvent.org [Accessed on: 12 July 2022]
[479] St. Augustine. *On the Spirit and the Letter*, Chap. 52 [Online] Available at: www.newadvent.org [Accessed on: 12 July 2022]
[480] The Works of Saint Augustine: A Translation for the 21st Century. [1990] *Sermons II (20-50) on the Old Testament*. New York: New City Press, p.303
[481] The Works of Saint Augustine: A Translation for the 21st Century. [1990] *Sermons III/4 (94A-147A) on the New Testament*. New York: New City Press, p.415.
[482] *Ibid.*, p.181-182
[483] *Ibid.*, p.133-134
[484] Pope Bl. Pius IX [1849] Encyclical *Ubi Primum*, para 5 [Online] Available at: www.papalencyclicals.net [Accessed on: 12 July 2022]
[485] Pope St. Pius X [1904] Encyclical *Ad Diem Illum Laetissimum*, para 19 [Online] Available at: www.papalencyclicals.net [Accessed on: 12 July 2022]
[486] *Catechism of St. Pius X* [1908] [Online] Available at: www.ewtn.com [Accessed on: 12 July 2022]
[487] Pope Pius XI [1928] Encyclical *Miserentissimus Redemptor*, para 18. [Online] Available at: www.vatican.va [Accessed on: 12 July 2022]

thians 12:9 to justify boasting of one's sins is an example of this loss of the sense of sin, of the offence and horror that it causes God. Encouraging such an absurdly positive attitude to sin does exactly what Pope Pius XII warned about the modern attack on Catholic hamartiology deadening the sense of sin.[488]

Pope Pius XII composed a prayer to our Lady that expressed the proper horror of sin, 'O Conqueress of Evil and Death, inspire in us a deep horror of sin, which makes the soul detestable to God and a slave of hell!'[489] He reflected that sin intends to offend God:

> When a man says 'yes' to the forbidden fruit, he says 'no' to God who forbids it. When he prefers himself and his own will to the divine law, he estranges himself from God and the divine will. In this consists aversion from God and the inner nature of grave sin.[490]

Pope St. John Paul II re-emphasised aspects of the magisterium's authentic hamartiology, summarised under the following headings:

i) Sin is disobedience and revolt against God. In this proud self-exaltation, sin is diametrically opposed to the obedience of Jesus.[491]
ii) Sin is an offence against God.[492]
iii) The sinner offends God and harms himself. The sinner also becomes responsible for the bad example and negative influences linked to his behaviour. Even when the sin is interior, it still causes a worsening of the human condition...'[493]
iv) It is not possible to grasp the evil of sin in all its sad reality without 'searching the depths of God.' Sacred Scripture reveals that sin so offends God that he regretted creating man, 'The Lord saw that the wickedness of man was great in the earth.... And the Lord was sorry that he had made man on the earth.... The Lord said: "I am sorry that I have made them."' (Gen 6:5-7).[494]
v) The sinner feels God's hand weighing upon him, aware that God is not indifferent to the evil committed since he is the guardian of justice and truth.[495]

---

[488] Pope Pius XII [1946] *Radio Message to Participants in the National Catechetical Congress of the United States in Boston.* [Online] Available at: www.vatican.va [Accessed on: 12 July 2022]
[489] Pope Pius XII. *Bend Tenderly Over Our Wounds* [Online] Available at: udayton.edu [Accessed on: 12 July 2022]
[490] Letter SJ, Fr. de [1947] *Horror of Sin (Horror Peccati)* [Online] Available at: fsspx.asia [Accessed on: 12 July 2022]
[491] *Catechism of the Catholic Church,* para 1850 [1992] [Online] Available at: scborromeo2.org [Accessed on: 12 July 2022]
[492] *Ibid.,* para 1440
[493] Pope St. John Paul II [1999] *General Audience Address,* para 3. [Online] Available at: www.vatican.va [Accessed on: 12 July 2022]
[494] Pope St. John Paul II [1986] Encyclical *Dominum et Vivificantem,* para 39. [Online] Available at: www.vatican.va [Accessed on: 12 July 2022]
[495] Pope St. John Paul II [2004] *General Audience Address,* para 2. [Online] Available at: www.vatican.va [Accessed on: 12 July 2022]

Hamartiology (2) — Situation Ethics

H. *If a person commits a sexual act, knowing it is ordinarily a mortal sin, they can remain in a state of sanctifying grace due to circumstances.*

Another dimension of Pope Francis' erroneous hamartiology is his advocacy of situational ethics, irrespective of its impact on Catholic doctrine on sexual morality and the life of grace. The Supreme Pontiff's erroneous teaching on sexual morality can be summarised under the following headings:

e) 'Sins of the flesh are the lightest sins. Because the flesh is weak.'[496] The least serious sins are 'those that are less angelical, such as greed and lust.'[497]

f) It can no longer be said that 'all those in any 'irregular' situation are living in a state of mortal sin and are deprived of sanctifying grace.'[498]

g) A person committing irregular sexual acts 'may know full well the rule, yet have great difficulty in understanding its inherent values…and decide otherwise without further sin.'[499] 'It is wrong to have an 'exclusive moral fixation on the sixth commandment.'[500]

h) A person committing irregular sexual acts 'could be in a concrete situation which does not allow him or her to act differently'.[501]

i) 'Under certain circumstances people find it very difficult to act differently. Therefore, while upholding a general rule, it is necessary to recognize that responsibility with respect to certain actions or decisions is not the same in all cases.'[502]

j) 'Priests must not focus on morality below the belt… more serious sins are elsewhere.' Priests need a psychiatrist if they who seek to understand the nature of the sexual sin, 'How did you do it, and when did you do it, and how many times?'[503]

k) 'Great shepherds give people a lot of freedom. The good shepherd knows how to lead his flock without enslaving it to rules that deaden people.'[504]

Pope Francis' erroneous teaching that sexual acts ordinarily considered mortal sins are not sins depending on an individual's situation — either due to personal incomprehension or personal circumstances — is a form of situation ethics that was popular among certain liberal Protestants and liberal Catholics in the first half of the 20th century. Father Charles Curran's situation ethics typified this erroneous approach. He wrote:

> …[of the] need for a life-centred and not a confession-oriented moral theology…God has called each person by his own name. In one sense, every individual is unique; every concrete situation is unique. Frequently there are no easy solutions. After prayerful consideration of all values involved, the Christian chooses what he believes to be the demands of love in the present situation.[505]

Pope Francis' promotion of an out-dated situation ethics in a major teaching document on the morality of marriage and the family is gravely contrary to the magisterial condemnation of situation ethics upheld since the pontificate of venerable Pope Pius XII.

---

[496] Magister, S [21 January 2019] *Memo For the Summit On Abuse. For Francis, the Sins 'Below the Belt' Are 'the Lightest'*. [Online] Available at: magister.blogautore.espresso.repubblica.it [Accessed on: 13 July 2022]

[497] Spadaro, A [September 2019] *Pope's Meeting with Jesuits in Mozambique and Madagascar*. [Online] Available at: www.vaticannews.va/ [Accessed on: 13 July 2022]

[498] Pope Francis [2016] Post Synodal Apostolic Exhortation *Amoris Laetitia*, para 301 [Online] Available at: www.vatican.va [Accessed on: 13 July 2022]

[499] *Ibid.*

[500] Spadaro, A [September 2019] *Op. cit.*

[501] Pope Francis [2016] *Op. cit.*, para 301.

[502] *Ibid.*, para 302.

[503] Magister, S [21 January 2019] *Op. cit.*

[504] Spadaro, A [September 2019] *Op. cit.*

[505] Fletcher, JF [1966] *Situation Ethics: The New Morality*. Louisville: Westminster John Knox Press, p.55

The Teaching of the Church

The grace by which we are justified may be lost, and is lost by every grievous sin. **(De fide.)**[506]

Even in the fallen state, man can, by his natural intellectual power, know religious and moral truths. **(De fide.)**[507]

Contrary to Pope Francis teaching that some sexual acts in 'irregular situations' are not mortal sins, depending on the circumstances, the Church has consistently insisted that some immoral sexual acts are mortal sins, deserving of Hell if unrepented. For example, the First Council of Lyons declared regarding fornication between unmarried men and women, 'there must not be any doubt at all that it is a mortal sin, since the apostle declares that fornicators like adulterers are cast out from the kingdom of God (cf. I Cor 6:9).' And that, 'if anyone dies in mortal sin without repentance, beyond any doubt, he will be tortured forever by the flames of everlasting hell.'[508] Successive ecumenical councils — the Second Council of Lyons and the Council of Florence — re-iterated the doctrine that souls who die in mortal sin without repentance go straightway down to hell to be punished.

Re-iterating St. Paul's list of mortal sins — placing sexual sins at the top — that exclude one from the Kingdom of God, the Council of Trent stated that such sins lead to the loss of sanctifying grace, 'and all others who commit deadly sins; from which, with the help of divine grace, they can refrain, and on account of which they are separated from the grace of Christ.'[509]

Contrary to Pope Francis teaching that an individual can know God's commands about sexual sin, 'yet have great difficulty in understanding its inherent values', the Church teaches these commands are comprehensible to everyone. The First Vatican Council declared the Church's perennial understanding in this regard that God 'may be known with certainty from the things that were created through the natural light of human reason', and that:

> It is to be ascribed to this Divine Revelation, that such truths among things Divine as of themselves are not beyond human reason, can, even in the present condition of mankind, be known by everyone with facility, with firm assurance, and with no admixture of error.[510]

The Second Vatican Council declared that man has been made by God to participate in 'the divine law —eternal, objective and universal'. Therefore, through divine Providence, every individual can 'come to perceive ever more fully the truth that is unchanging'. Each person has the duty to form their conscience in this divine law so that they can make 'right and true judgments.'[511]

The council fathers also taught that conscience is the 'most secret core and sanctuary of a man' in which he finds a divine law 'written by God; to obey it is the very dignity of man; according to it he will be judged':

> In the depths of his conscience, man detects a law which he does not impose upon himself, but which holds him to obedience. Always summoning him to love good and avoid evil, the voice of conscience when necessary speaks to his heart: do this, shun that.[512]

[506] FOtt, L [1957] *Op. cit.*, p. 263.

[507] *Ibid.*, p.233.

[508] Heinrich Denzinger (2010). *Op. cit.*, p. 277-278.

[509] Council of Trent [1547] *Decree on Justification*, Chap.15. [Online] www.thecounciloftrent.com [Accessed on: 18 July 2022]

[510] *Ibid.*, p.1870

[511] Second Vatican Council [1965] Declaration *Dignitatis Humanae*, para 3. [Online] Available at: www.vatican.va [Accessed on: 14 July 2022]

[512] Second Vatican Council [1965] Pastoral Constitution *Gaudium et Spes*, para 16. [Online] Available at: www.vatican.va [Accessed on: 14 July 2022]

Though wounded by sin — which man experiences as 'rebellious stirrings in his body' — the natural dignity of man created in the image and likeness of God and called to be a Temple of the Holy Spirit, 'postulates that man glorify God in his body and forbid it to serve the evil inclinations of his heart.'[513]

Proof from the Sources of Faith
a) Teaching from Holy Scripture
From the creation of man as male and female God's commands established universal natural law for marriage and sexual morality (Gen 2:23-24; 9:7). These natural laws were re-emphasised by the divine revelation establishing the Mosaic Covenant, such as the severe condemnation of adultery (Ex 20:13; cf. Lev 20:10; Prov 6:32) and homosexual sex acts (Lev 18:22; 20:13). There was also the expectation that God would deepen man's appropriation of his divine law through a unique act of grace, that was fulfilled by our Lord Jesus Christ, '…I will give my law in their bowels, and I will write it in their heart.' (Jer 31:33). Pope Francis' promotion of a situation ethics that encourages individuals to contravene natural law and divinely revealed law is totally contrary to the testimony of the Old Testament.

Our Lord emphasised the gravity of disobeying divine law regarding sexual morality, even going so far as to extend the prohibition to include intention, as well as act. Our Lord warns that not just immoral genital sexual acts, but also immoral acts of the eyes and immoral sexual acts of the hand warrant condemnation to the punishments of Hell:

> You have heard that it was said to them of old: Thou shalt not commit adultery. But I say to you, that whosoever shall look on a woman to lust after her, hath already committed adultery with her in his heart. And if thy right eye scandalise thee, pluck it out and cast it from thee. For it is expedient for thee that one of thy members should perish, rather than that thy whole body be cast into hell. And if thy right hand scandalise thee, cut it off, and cast it from thee: for it is expedient for thee that one of thy members should perish, rather than that thy whole body go into hell (Mt 5:27-30).

By so teaching, our Lord made it clear that by rebuking lust his law concerning sexual morality extended to thoughts, because — as Tertullian commented — 'even the thought, without operation and without effect, is an act of the flesh'.[514]

Our Lord also strengthened, by re-iteration, divine law prohibiting adultery and divorce, 'Therefore now they are not two, but one flesh. What therefore God hath joined together, let no man put asunder' (Mk 10: 6-9). Nowhere does our Lord teach that there are certain situations where divine law regarding sexual morality does not apply.

Proclaiming the Gospel to pagan peoples who had not benefitted — as the Jewish people had — from the revelation of divine law, St. Paul deepened understanding of the universality of the divine law taught by Nature (Rom 1:20-21). He taught that as everyone knows God's natural law, there is no excuse to commit sexual sins, such as homosexual sex acts (Rom 1: 26-32) fornication (Col 3:5-6) and adultery (I Cor 6:9-10). St. Paul expressed incredulity that people claimed not to know that those committing sexual sin have nothing to do with the Kingdom of God, 'Know you not that the unjust shall not possess the kingdom of God? Do not err: neither fornicators, nor idolaters, nor adulterers, nor the effeminate' (I Cor 6:9-10).

Finally, St. Paul warns that sexual sins, such as fornication, desecrate the sanctity of a person's body, which through the sacraments has become a 'temple of the Holy Ghost:

> Fly fornication. Every sin that a man doth, is without the body; but he that committeth fornication, sinneth against his own body. Or know you not, that your members are the

[513] *Ibid.*, para 14.
[514] Tertullian. *On the Resurrection of the Flesh*, Chap. 15. [Online] Available at: www.newadvent.org [Accessed on: 16 July 2022]

temple of the Holy Ghost, who is in you, whom you have from God; and you are not your own? (I Cor 6:16-19).

Accordingly, Pope Francis' contention that those committing sex acts that are mortal sins — in certain circumstances — remain in a state of sanctifying grace is irreconcilable with the hamartiology of our Lord and St. Paul.

b) The Testimony of Tradition

The ante-Nicene Fathers had a strong sense of the God-given law that Nature teaches, and the consequences for those who disobey that law. Athenagoras wrote that the law contained in the organs of the human body must not be contravened. Natural laws are unlike man-made laws because a bad man can evade the latter but not the former:

> Those, then, who are forbidden to look at anything more than that for which God formed the eyes, which were intended to be a light to us, and to whom a wanton look is adultery, the eyes being made for other purposes, and who are to be called to account for their very thoughts, how can anyone doubt that such persons practice self-control? For our account lies not with human laws, which a bad man can evade....[515]

Tertullian, commenting on Romans 1:20-32, wrote about 'natural law and a law-revealing nature', warning that the act of committing unnatural sexual acts is, in itself, 'penal retribution for their error' of abandoning natural law.[516]

Church Fathers attested to the grave immorality of the sins of adultery and fornication — St. Justin Martyr insisted that not only those who commit adultery, but those who desire to commit adultery, are rejected by God,[517] while St. Irenaeus wrote that fornicators perished, 'sent into eternal fire'.[518]

To those like Pope Francis who erroneously teach others that 'Sins of the flesh are the lightest sins' St. Augustine wrote from personal experience:

> Let no one say in his heart, 'God cares not for sins of the flesh.' 'Do you not know,' says the Apostle, 'that you are the temple of God, and the Spirit of God dwells in you? If any man defile the temple of God, him will God destroy.' 'Let no man deceive himself.' [...] Take heed then what you do, take heed that you offend not the Indweller of the temple, lest He forsake you, and you fall into ruins.[519]

In his writing St. Thomas Aquinas set out the principles of natural law and the consequences of disobedience, summarised as follows:

i) The eternal law imprints on all things their 'respective inclinations to their proper acts and ends.'[520]
ii) Man, as a rational creature, has a share in Eternal Reason, which imprints the natural inclination to their proper act and end — participation as a rational being in the eternal law, which is called natural law.[521]
iii) The law of nature 'is nothing other than the light of the intellect planted in us by God, by which we know what should be done and what should be avoided. God gave this light and this law in creation.'[522]

---

[515] Athenagoras. *A Plea for the Christians*, Chap. 32. [Online] www.newadvent.org [Accessed on: 16 July 2022]
[516] Tertullian. *De Corona*, Chap. 6. [Online] Available at: www.newadvent.org [Accessed on: 16 July 2022]
[517] St. Justin Martyr. *The First Apology*, Chap. 15. [Online] Available at: www.newadvent.org [Accessed on: 16 July 2022]
[518] St. Irenaeus. *Against Heresies*, Bk. IV, Chap. 27. [Online] Available at: www.newadvent.org [Accessed on: 16 July 2022]
[519] St. Augustine. *Sermon 32 on the New Testament*, para 13. [Online] Available at: www.newadvent.org [Accessed on: 16 July 2022]
[520] St. Thomas Aquinas. *Summa Theologiae*. Prima Secundæ Partis. Q 91. Art 2. Online] Available at: www.newadvent.org [Accessed on: 16 July 2022]
[521] *Ibid.*
[522] St. Thomas Aquinas. *Collationes in Decem Praeceptis*, prologue, para 1. [Online] Available at: https://isidore.co [Accessed on: 16 July 2022]

iv) It is an error to argue that those who do not observe the law are excused by ignorance.[523]

v) Everyone bears the light of the intellect, through which we know what should be done.

vi) The devil has sown in man another law on top of natural law, that of concupiscence, making man's flesh 'disobedient to reason.'

vii) 'The result is that, although man may wish good according to reason, nevertheless by concupiscence he tends to the contrary.'[524]

viii) When anyone proceeds from passion to a sinful act through deliberate consent this does not so suddenly happen that deliberating reason cannot come to the rescue. The purpose of deliberating reason is to direct us to our last end, which is God. Deliberating reason can drive the passion away, or at least prevent it from having its effect.[525]

ix) Mortal sin occurs when a person chooses not to allow deliberating reason to come to the rescue, 'and it is thus, as we see, that many murders and adulteries are committed through passion.'[526]

It follows, that Pope Francis is gravely mistaken when he writes that it is not a mortal sin for someone to 'decide otherwise' when they 'know full well the rule' of natural law about sexual morality (*Amoris Laetitia*, 301). In fact, what he describes is the commission of a mortal sin.

c) The Defence by the Magisterium

Contrary to Pope Francis downplaying the grievous nature of mortal sin, particularly in matters of sexual mortality, the Magisterium of the Church has consistently emphasised the horror of the evil that it manifests and the enormity of the punishment it deserves. Pope Benedict XII wrote that it is God's 'general disposition' that those who die in a state of mortal sin 'go down into hell immediately after death and there suffer the pain of hell.'[527] About mortal sin, Pope St. Pius X wrote in his catechism, 'Mortal sin is a transgression of the divine Law', making it clear that mortal sin and sanctifying grace are entirely incompatible, 'It is called mortal because it brings death on the soul by making it lose sanctifying grace which is the life of the soul, just as the soul itself is the life of the body.'[528] Contrary to Pope Francis' implying there are situations in which it is not possible to commit mortal sin due to incomprehension and circumstances, Pope St. Pius X makes it clear that committing mortal sin is not a complicated matter, 'To constitute a mortal sin, besides grave matter there is also required full consciousness of the gravity of the matter, along with the deliberate will to commit the sin.' Simply put, it doesn't require 'understanding' of the 'inherent values' of the prohibition of immoral sexual acts, but only 'full consciousness of the gravity of the matter.'[529]

During the pontificate of Pope St. Paul VI, the Sacred Congregation for the Doctrine of the Faith directly addressed the question of mortal sin in the context of sexual ethics. The Declaration *Persona Humana* addressed the erroneous view that 'Sins of the flesh are the lightest sins' through an analysis of mortal sin in the context of sexual ethics, which can be summarised as follows:

---

[523] St. Thomas Aquinas. *Summa Theologiae*. Prima Secundæ Partis. Q 77. Art 8. Available at: www.newadvent.org [Accessed on: 16 July 2022]

[524] St. Thomas Aquinas. *Collationes in Decem Præceptis, op. cit.*

[525] St. Thomas Aquinas. *Summa Theologiae*. Prima Secundæ Partis. Q 77. Art 8, *op. cit.*

[526] *Ibid.*

[527] Denzinger, H. (2010). *Op. cit.*, p.303, Dz 1002

[528] Pope St. Pius X [1908] *Catechism of St. Pius X* [Online] Available at: www.ewtn.com [Accessed on: 18 July 2022]

[529] *Ibid.*

i)   'According to Christian tradition and the Church's teaching, and as right reason also recognises, the moral order of sexuality involves such high values of human life that every direct violation of this order is objectively serious.'

ii) Mortal sin is formal and direct resistance of God's commandments. Therefore, a person commits mortal sin when his action comes from direct contempt for love of God and neighbour.

iii) Mortal sin is equally found in opposition to 'authentic love' included 'in every deliberate transgression, in serious matter, of each of the moral laws. A person commits mortal sin when 'he consciously and freely, for whatever reason, chooses something which is seriously disordered.' By so choosing, the act also includes contempt of God, because it signifies rejection of God.

iv) While accepting that 'it more easily happens that free consent is not fully given' regarding 'sins of the sexual order', the CDF concluded 'it in no way follows that one can hold the view that in the sexual field mortal sins are not committed.'[530]

Contrary to Pope Francis teaching that sexual acts ordinarily viewed as mortal sins can be compatible with sanctifying grace depending on the situation, Pope St. John Paul II emphasised that sins of the flesh resulted in the '"death" of the spirit' in the life of the person. He wrote, 'So the term "death" does not mean only the death of the body, but also sin, which moral theology will call "mortal."' Commenting on St. Paul's list in Ephesians (5:3-7) of mortal sins that exclude the sinner from the Kingdom of God, Pope St. John Paul notes that St. Paul places 'sins against purity' at the top.[531]

Furthermore, Pope John Paul II rejected the argument that a situation can be so psychologically complex that it threw into question the traditional concept of mortal sin:

> For mortal sin exists also when a person knowingly and willingly, for whatever reason, chooses something gravely disordered. In fact, such a choice already includes contempt for the divine law, a rejection of God's love for humanity and the whole of creation; the person turns away from God and loses charity. Thus the fundamental orientation can be radically changed by individual acts. Clearly there can occur situations which are very complex and obscure from a psychological viewpoint and which have an influence on the sinner's subjective culpability. But from a consideration of the psychological sphere one cannot proceed to the construction of a theological category, which is what the "fundamental option" precisely is, understanding it in such a way that it objectively changes or casts doubt upon the traditional concept of mortal sin.[532]

Contrary to Pope Francis' grave error of proposing situation ethics to decide the moral nature of sexual acts, the Magisterium has defended natural law and divinely revealed law against the proponents of situation ethics since its emergence in the mid-20th century.

Pope Ven. Pius XII, in his radio message on the occasion of 'Family Day' (23rd March 1952) warned against those advocating the abandonment of divine law, natural and revealed, in favour of the 'the intelligence and determination of the individual conscience':

> In leaving every ethical criterion to the individual conscience, it jealously closes in on itself and, having been made the absolute arbiter of its own determinations, far from making the way easier for it [conscience], the way, it would divert it from the highroad, which is Christ.[533]

---

[530] Sacred Congregation for the Doctrine of the Faith [1975] *Persona Humana*, para 10. [Online] Available at: www.vatican.va [Accessed on: 18 July 2022]

[531] Pope St. John Paul II [7th January 1981] *Opposition Between the Flesh and the Spirit*. [Online] Available at: www.ewtn.com/ [Accessed on: 18 July 2022]

[532] Pope St. John Paul II [1984] Post Synodal Apostolic Exhortation *Reconciliatio et Paenitentia*, para 17. [Online] Available at: www.vatican.va [Accessed on: 18 July 2022]

[533] Pope Pius XII [1952] *Radio Message on the Occasion of 'Family Day'*, para 6-8. [Online] Available at: www.catholicculture.org [Accessed on 18 July 2022]

Four years later, the Sacred Congregation of the Holy Office promulgated the Instruction *Contra doctrinam* [Contrary to doctrine] explicitly condemning situation ethics for abandoning the objectivity of natural law:

> …they assert and teach that men are preserved or easily liberated from many otherwise insoluble ethical conflicts when each one judges in his own conscience, not primarily according to objective laws, but by means of that internal, individual light based on personal intuition, what he must do in a concrete situation.[534]

Pope St. John Paul II warned against those who proposed that the exercise of individual conscience could be freed from natural law because it 'dissociates the moral act from the bodily dimensions of its exercise'. This is contrary to the teaching of Scripture and Tradition because it 'misunderstands the moral meaning of the body and of kinds of behaviour involving it':

> Saint Paul declares that 'the immoral, idolaters, adulterers, sexual perverts, thieves, the greedy, drunkards, revilers, robbers' are excluded from the Kingdom of God (cf. I Cor 6:9). This condemnation — repeated by the Council of Trent — lists as 'mortal sins' or 'immoral practices' certain specific kinds of behaviour the wilful acceptance of which prevents believers from sharing in the inheritance promised to them. In fact, body and soul are inseparable: in the person, in the willing agent and in the deliberate act, they stand or fall together.[535]

It is contrary to the Magisterium to teach, as Pope Francis does, the exercise of freedom detached from God's natural and divinely revealed laws by downplaying the seriousness of sexual sins and privileging personal circumstances.

---

[534] Sacred Congregation of the Holy Office. [1956] Instruction *Contra Doctrinam*. [Online] Available at: www.catholicculture.org [Accessed on 18 July 2022]

[535] Pope St. John Paul II [1993] Encyclical *Veritatis Splendor*, para 49. [Online] Available at: www. vatican.va [Accessed on: 18 July 2022]

Liturgy

I. *The post-Vatican II vernacular liturgical books are the 'unique expression of the lex orandi.' Pope St. Pius V's Latin Roman Missal, revised by Pope St. John XXIII, is harming the communion of the Church.*

Pope Francis has undermined the apostolic nature of the Church, and her unity of communion, by taking actions that rupture the Tradition of the celebration of the Most Holy Sacrifice of the Mass and other sacraments, honoured for their 'venerable and ancient usage.'[536] His erroneous teachings and actions regarding liturgy are summarised under the following headings:

a) The liturgical books promulgated by St. Paul VI and St. John Paul II 'are the unique expression of the *lex orandi* of the Roman Rite.'[537] This enacts a major break with the Church's tradition, expressed in Pope Benedict XVI's Summorum Pontificum, which holds that both Paul VI's *Roman Missal* and Pius V's *Roman Missal* as 'two expressions of the Church's *lex orandi'*.[538]

b) The abrogation of all 'previous norms, instructions, permissions, and customs that do not conform to the provisions' of Pope Francis's Motu Proprio, *Traditionis Custodes*.[539] Pope Francis' claim of abrogation contradicts Pope St. Pius V's Bull *Quo Primum Tempore* (14 July 1570), that established every priest's right in 'perpetuity' to celebrate the Mass according to St. Pius V's Latin *Roman Missal*.[540]

c) Pope Francis' claim that the use of Pope St. Pius V's *Roman Missal*, was harming the unity of the Church, 'the instrumental use of *Missale Romanum* of 1962 is often characterised by a rejection not only of the liturgical reform, but of the Vatican Council II itself, claiming, with unfounded and unsustainable assertions, that it betrayed the Tradition and the "true Church".'[541]

d) The Congregation for Divine Worship and the Discipline of the Sacraments' *Responsa ad dubia* banned all bishops using the *Pontificale Romanum* that pre-dates Vatican II reforms, thereby forbidding without exception the traditional rites of confirmation and ordination.[542]

e) The expressed intention to impose the post-Vatican II vernacular liturgical books on the whole Latin-rite, 'This unity I intend to re-establish throughout the Church of the Roman Rite [...] So that the Church may lift up, in the variety of so many languages, one and the same prayer capable of expressing her unity',[543] 'I intend that this unity be re-established in the whole Church of the Roman Rite',[544] 'The Motu Proprio *Traditionis Custodes* intends to re-establish in the whole Church of the Roman Rite a single and identical prayer expressing its unity.'[545]

---

[536] Pope Benedict XVI [2007] Motu Proprio *Summorum Pontificum*, art.1. [Online] Available at: www.vatican.va [Accessed on: 19 July 2022]

[537] Pope Francis [2021] Motu Proprio *Traditionis Custodes*, art.1. Online] Available at: www.vatican. va [Accessed on: 19 July 2022]

[538] Pope Benedict XVI [2007] *Summorum Pontificum*, art, 1. [Online] Available at: www.vatican.va [Accessed on: 19 July 2022]

[539] Pope Francis [2021] *Op. cit.*, art. 8.

[540] Pope St. Pius V [1570] The Bull *Quo Primum Tempore*. [Online] Available at: lms.org.uk [Accessed on: 19 July 2022]

[541] Pope Francis [2021] *Letter to the Bishops of the Whole World, that Accompanies the Apostolic Letter Motu Proprio Data Traditionis Custodes.* [Online] Available at: www.vatican.va [Accessed on: 19 July 2022]

[542] Congregation for Divine Worship and the Discipline of the Sacraments [2021] *Responsa ad Dubia on Certain Provisions of the Apostolic Letter Traditionis Custodes.* [Online] Available at: www.vatican. va [Accessed on: 19 July 2022]

[543] Pope Francis [2021] *Letter to the Bishops of the Whole World, that Accompanies the Apostolic Letter Motu Proprio Data Traditionis Custodes.* [Online] Available at: www.vatican.va [Accessed on: 19 July 2022]

[544] Pope Francis [2022] Apostolic Letter, *Desiderio Desideravi*, para 61. [Online] Available at: www. vatican.va [Accessed on: 19 July 2022]

[545] Congregation for Divine Worship and the Discipline of the Sacraments [2021] Op. cit.

f) Denying the importance of the Latin language to the Roman Rite, exemplified by banning the use of Latin readings of sacred Scripture, 'the readings are proclaimed in the vernacular language',[546] 'the proclamation of the Word be in a language that everyone understands; otherwise it would be like laughing at the Word of God.'[547]

g) Condemning those who wish to attend the Mass of Pope St. Pius V as 'new fundamentalists'.[548]

Pope Francis' actions to restrict, and suppress, the traditional Latin Mass, are part of his wider agenda against upholding Tradition in the Church. In his address to the Pontifical Liturgical Institute of Sant'Anselmo, the Supreme Pontiff's criticism of those who attend, and participate, in the Latin Mass manifested his animus against preserving the Tradition of the Church:

> I would like to underline the danger, the temptation of liturgical formalism: going after forms, formalities rather than reality, as we see today in those movements that try to go backwards and deny Vatican Council II itself. In this way, the celebration is recitation, it is something without life, without joy. [...]
>
> When liturgical life becomes something of a banner of division, there is the odour of the devil, the deceiver, in there. It is not possible to worship God and at the same time turn liturgy into a battlefield for issues that are not essential, or indeed for outdated questions and to take sides, starting from the liturgy, on ideologies that divide the Church. [...]
>
> Indeed, these closed mindsets use liturgical matters to defend their own point of view. Using the liturgy: this is the drama we are experiencing in ecclesial groups that are distancing themselves from the Church, questioning the Council, the authority of the bishops... in order to preserve tradition. And the liturgy is used for this.[549]

The Second Vatican Council taught that 'the apostolic tradition is manifested and preserved' (Lumen Gentium 20) through the apostolic succession of bishops. Therefore, it is unaccountable that Pope Francis castigates those who seek to 'preserve tradition' through the Latin Mass.

The Teaching of the Church
The Church founded by Christ is unique and one. (**De fide.**)[550]
The Church founded by Christ is apostolic. (**De fide.**)[551]
The Roman Rite is the fundamental expression of the nature of the Church, particularly the unicity and apostolicity of her nature, as instituted by our Lord and perpetuated through time by the Holy Spirit. In the Nicene creed this is declared, 'Et *unam*, sanctam, catholicam et *apostolicam* Ecclesiam.' (Emphasis added).

Regarding the unity of the Latin rite Church, Dr. Ludwig Ott wrote that the oneness of the Church is 'above all the inner unity or unicity in the sense of being undivided', manifested, among other things, by 'unity of cult or liturgical unity',[552] *Sicut erat in principio, et nunc, et semper, et in sæcula sæculorum* (As it was in the beginning, is now, and ever shall be, world without end). This oneness of the Church must be visible and

---

[546] Pope Francis [2021] Motu Proprio *Traditionis Custodes*, art. 3 § 3. [Online] Available at: www.vatican.va [Accessed on: 19 July 2022]

[547] Pope Francis [2021] *Interview with Carlos Herrera on Radio COPE.* [Online] Available at: www.vaticannews.va [Accessed on: 19 July 2022]

[548] Pope Francis [7th October 2021] General Audience Address. [Online] Available at: www.vatican.va [Accessed on: 19 July 2022]

[549] Pope Francis [2022] *Address to the Teacher & Students of the Pontifical Liturgical Institute.* [Online] Available at: www.vatican.va [Accessed on: 19 July 2022]

[550] *Ibid.*, p. 302-303.

[551] Ott, L *Op. cit.*, p. 308

[552] *Ibid.*

perennial, manifesting one single Church − through time − one in communion, one in faith and one in worship:

> A religious society having one faith must necessarily also have unity of worship, which is the outward expression of the faith and social union of members. Hence the Catholic Church throughout the world has the one same sacrifice of the Mass, and all her members participate in the same sacraments (cf. I Cor 10:17).[553]

This unity of worship throughout the world − as an expression of the unity of the Latin rite Church − is only possible through the Roman Rite, manifested through its ordinary expression promulgated by Pope St. Paul VI and its extraordinary expression, promulgated by Saint Pius V and revised by Bl. John XXIII, 'These two expressions of the Church's *lex orandi* will in no way lead to a division in the Church's *lex credendi* [rule of faith]; for they are two usages of the one Roman rite'.[554]

During the Protestant rupture from the liturgical tradition of the Church, the Council of Trent defended 'the ancient rite of each Church' as essential to the familial unity and apostolic origins of the Church. The Council fathers condemned those proposing the vernacular celebration of the Mass as going against the ancient rites of the Church 'approved by the holy Roman Church, the mother and mistress of all churches'.[555] (The approval of the 'mother and mistress of all churches' regarding divine worship was the guarantee of the visible, familial unity of the Church.) Furthermore, the Council of Trent also emphasised the apostolic origins (*apostolicitas originis*) of the ancient rite of the Church:

> She has likewise, in accordance with apostolic discipline and tradition, made use of ceremonies, such as mystical blessings, lights, incense, vestments, and many other things of this kind, whereby both the majesty of so great a sacrifice might be emphasised and the minds of the faithful excited by those visible signs of religion and piety to the contemplation of those most sublime things which are hidden in this sacrifice.[556]

Regarding the Holy Canon of the Mass, the council fathers argued against those who sought to change it by falsely claiming that it contained errors, stating:

> And since it is becoming that holy things be administered in a holy manner, and of all things this sacrifice is the most holy, the Catholic Church, to the end that it might be worthily and reverently offered and received, instituted many centuries ago the holy canon, which is so free from error that it contains nothing that does not in the highest degree savour of a certain holiness and piety and raise up to God the minds of those who offer. For it consists partly of the very words of the Lord, partly of the traditions of the Apostles, and also of pious regulations of holy pontiffs.[557]

Regarding the use of the Latin Vulgate, both the Council of Trent and the First Vatican Council declared its authenticity and mandated its use. The Council of Trent formally ordained and declared:

> …that the old Latin Vulgate Edition, which, in use for so many hundred years, has been approved by the Church, be in public lectures, disputations, sermons and expositions held as authentic, and that no one dare or presume under any pretext whatsoever to reject it.[558]

---

[553] Wilhelm, J et al. [1898] *A Manual of Catholic Theology Based on Scheeben's "Dogmatik"*. Vol. 2. CreateSpace Independent Publishing Platform, p. 348.
[554] Pope Benedict XVI [2007] Apostolic Letter *Summorum Pontificum*, art.1 [Online] Available at: www.vatican.va [Accessed on: 5 October 2022]
[555] Council of Trent [1562] *Doctrine Concerning the Sacrifice of the Mass*, Chap. 8. [Online] Available at: www.ewtn.com [Accessed on: 20 July 2022]
[556] *Ibid.*, Chap. 5.
[557] *Ibid.*, Chap. 4.
[558] Council of Trent [1546] *Decree Concerning The Edition And Use Of The Sacred Books*. [Online] Available at: www.ewtn.com [Accessed on: 20 July 2022]

While the First Vatican Council declared that the 'old Latin Vulgate edition, are to be received as sacred and canonical.'[559] Fr. Thomas Crean OP observed that due to the Council of Trent recognising the authenticity of the Vulgate, the Church does not, in his opinion, 'have the power to "de-authenticate" the Vulgate.' The council fathers declaration of its authenticity is recognition that 'the prevalence of the Vulgate from the patristic era onwards sufficiently shows, the Church being governed by the Spirit of truth, that it is a reliable expression of the written word of God. The Council of Trent, in declaring it authentic, was thus not simply establishing a fact but recognising one.'[560]

Consequently, Pope Francis' ban on the Vulgate during the Most Holy Sacrifice of the Mass does not respect the solemn ordination and declaration of the Nineteenth Ecumenical Council, endorsed by Pope Paul III. It is questionable whether Pope Francis has the authority to de-authenticate the Latin Vulgate by prohibiting its liturgical use.

The Second Vatican Council continued the previous two ecumenical council's endorsement of the importance of Latin to the *lex orandi* of the Church, summarised as follows:

i)   'Particular law remaining in force, the use of the Latin language is to be preserved in the Latin rites.'[561]
ii) Though *Sacrosanctum Concilium, the Constitution on the Sacred Liturgy*, introduced the possibility of vernacular parts of the Mass, such as readings from sacred Scripture, it insisted that steps be taken that 'the faithful may also be able to say or to sing together in Latin those parts of the Ordinary of the Mass which pertain to them.'[562]
iii) 'The Church acknowledges Gregorian chant as specially suited to the Roman liturgy: therefore, other things being equal, it should be given pride of place in liturgical services.'[563]
iv) Though Vatican II allowed vernacular translations of the Divine Office in special circumstances, the council fathers declared, 'In accordance with the centuries-old tradition of the Latin rite, the Latin language is to be retained by clerics in the divine office.'[564]
v)   Vatican II also stipulated that seminarians 'acquire a knowledge of Latin' to assist in their studies of the Church's documents and that 'the study of the liturgical language proper to each rite should be considered necessary'. Therefore, the study of Latin liturgy should be considered necessary for Latin-rite seminarians.[565]

The Second Vatican Council's insistence on the importance of Latin to Latin-rite Catholics is in stark contrast to Pope Francis' ridicule of seminarians seeking to deepen their knowledge of Latin for the celebration of the Mass. He related the following to fellow Jesuits in 2021:

> A cardinal told me that two newly ordained priests came to him asking him for permission to study Latin so as to celebrate well. With a sense of humour he replied: 'But there are many Hispanics in the diocese! Study Spanish to be able to preach. Then, when you have studied Spanish, come back to me and I'll tell you how many Vietnamese there are in the diocese, and I'll ask you to study Vietnamese. Then, when you have learned Vietnamese, I will give you permission to study Latin.' So, he made them 'land,' he made them return to earth.[566]

[559] First Vatican Council [1870] Dogmatic Constitution, Dei Filius, Chap. 2, para 6. [Online] Available at: www.ewtn.com [Accessed on: 20 July 2022]
[560] Crean, T. [2021] St. Luke's Gospel: A Commentary for Believers. Waterloo: Arouca Press, p.xiii.
[561] Second Vatican Council [1963] Constitution on the Sacred Liturgy, *Sacrosanctum Concilium*, para 36 §1. [Online] Available at: www.vatican.va [Accessed on: 19 July 2022]
[562] *Ibid.*, para 54.
[563] *Ibid.*, para 116.
[564] *Ibid.*, para 101§1.
[565] Second Vatican Council [1965] Decree on Priestly Training, *Optatam Totius*, para 13. [Online] Available at: www.vatican.va [Accessed on: 19 July 2022]
[566] Spadaro, A. [20 October 2021] *'Freedom Scares Us': Pope Francis' Conversation with Slovak Jesuits.* [Online] Available at: www.laciviltacattolica.com [Accessed on: 20 July 2022]

Proof from the Sources of Faith
a) Teaching from Holy Scripture

The Catholic sense about the importance of preserving the Apostolic Mass — so decried by Pope Francis — can be traced back to the Lord's command to Israel, the observance of which would make them a 'priestly kingdom, and a holy nation' (Ex 19:5-6). The Lord makes preserving divinely instituted Tradition an imperative of worship, crystallised by the Jewish liturgical prayer, the *Shema Yisrael*, 'And these words which I command thee this day, shall be in thy heart: And thou shalt tell them to thy children', 'Forget not the words that thy eyes have seen, and let them not go out of thy heart all the days of thy life. Thou shalt teach them to thy sons and to thy grandsons' (Deut 6:4-9; 4:9-10).

The apostolic origin of the Church witnesses to the same divine imperative to preserve Tradition by means of the liturgy. St. Paul used the word *paradosis* to convey the sense of handing over a cherished gift to a recipient trusted to do the right thing with it.[567] This understanding was expressed in one of the fundamental sources for the Most Holy Sacrifice of the Mass, 'For I have received of the Lord that which also I delivered [*paredōka*] unto you, that the Lord Jesus, the same night in which he was betrayed, took bread' (I Cor 11:23).

This Pauline understanding of the liturgical imperative to preserve Tradition in the context of the Mass can be traced directly to the most sacred words of our Lord at his institution of the Eucharist, 'Do this for a commemoration of me.' (Lk 22:19; cf. I Cor 11:24). The Lucan and Pauline accounts of our Lord's institution of the Eucharist use the Greek word *anamnésis* meaning 'a recalling, remembrance, memory'.[568] This ritual of remembering is not merely recalling an event in the past but is also to enter into and relive the past event. It is to recall it so as to make it present.

Abbot Vonier explained that remembrance of the past was essential to the sacramental re-presentation of the Sacrifice of the Mass, paraphrasing St. Thomas Aquinas, 'The Eucharistic sacrament is performed, not through a divine imperative, but through a divine symbolism, or, if you prefer it, through a divine remembrance of the past.'[569] Dr. Matthias Scheeben wrote that our Lord instituted the Eucharist to prolong and extend his Incarnation over and over again in space and time, 'we may say with profound truth that the Eucharist is a real and universal prolongation and extension of the mystery of the Incarnation'.[570] Therefore, it follows that by obeying the divine command to preserve Tradition we participate in the 'divine remembrance of the past' that is essential to the nature of the Eucharistic presence of Christ.

Preserving Tradition is so fundamental to Christian identity that St. Paul emphasised the importance of 'standing firm' regarding Tradition, using the Greek words *stékó* which has the meaning of 'preserve'[571] and *krateó*, meaning to 'grip strongly', 'Therefore, brethren, stand fast [*stēkete*]; and hold [*krateite*] the traditions which you have learned, whether by word, or by our epistle' (II Thess 2:14); 'But prove all things; hold fast [*katechete*] that which is good' (I Thess 5:21). Furthermore, St. Paul warns us to avoid those who do not preserve Tradition:

> And we charge you, brethren, in the name of our Lord Jesus Christ, that you withdraw yourselves from every brother walking disorderly [*ataktōs*], and not according to the tradition which they have received of us. (II Thess 3:6)

The word that St. Paul used to describe those who abandoned tradition, *ataktōs*, has the meaning of breaking rank in the sense of being insubordinate to God's word.[572] It is not

---

[567] Dillon, M [October 1995] *Paradosis*. Journal of the British Society of Phenomenology. Vol.26, No 3. p.229 [Online] Available at: www.tandfonline.com [Accessed on: 21 July 2022]

[568] *Strong's Concordance* [Online] Available at: biblehub.com [Accessed on: 22 July 2022]

[569] Vonier, A. [1925] *A Key to the Doctrine of the Eucharist*. Bethesda: Bacchus Press, p. 65

[570] Scheeben, M. [1946] *The Mysteries of Christianity*. New York: The Crossroad Publishing Company, p. 485-486

[571] *Strong's Concordance* [Online] Available at: biblehub.com [Accessed on: 22 July 2022]

[572] *Ibid.*

those who preserve and hold firm to Tradition that are insubordinate to God's word, but those who condemn those who do so as being 'rigid.'

b) The Testimony of Tradition

St. Irenaeus, a disciple of St. Polycarp, who in turn was a direct disciple of St. John the Apostle, insisted on the importance of the apostolic Tradition being observed throughout the world, even referring to the necessity of its preservation, 'True knowledge is [that which consists in] the doctrine of the apostles, and the ancient constitution of the Church throughout all the world... and has come even unto us, being guarded and preserved.'[573] Also, Tertullian wrote that the presence of 'all the Christian traditions' was necessary for the manifestation of 'the true Christian rule and faith'.[574]

A number of post Nicene Church Fathers highlighted the importance of the apostolic tradition to the unicity of the Church's worship of God. St. Athanasius wrote that 'keeping to the apostolic traditions' informed their communion in prayer, '...again keeping to the apostolic traditions, we remind each other when we come together for prayer; and keeping the feast in common, with one mouth we truly give thanks to the Lord.'[575]

St. Basil of Caesarea described in detail the importance of apostolic Tradition as the origin of the Most Holy Sacrifice of the Mass, summarised as follows:

i) We have received liturgical practices 'delivered to us "in a mystery" by the tradition of the apostles'.

ii) We have received a variety of liturgical and sacramental practices 'from that unpublished and secret teaching which our fathers guarded in a silence out of the reach of curious meddling and inquisitive investigation.'

iii) The Apostles and Church Fathers 'learned the lesson that the awful dignity of the mysteries is best preserved by silence. What the uninitiated are not even allowed to look at was hardly likely to be publicly paraded about in written documents [...]... the Apostles and Fathers who laid down laws for the Church from the beginning thus guarded the awful dignity of the mysteries in secrecy and silence.'

iv) St. Basil argued that no one, 'even moderately versed in the institutions of the Church' would deny or contradict the apostolic Tradition regarding the Mass and sacraments.

v) Any attempt to reject 'such customs as have no written authority' would 'unintentionally injure the Gospel in its very vitals'.

vi) Regarding the apostolic Tradition of the Mass, St. Basil wrote: 'who has taught us in writing to sign with the sign of the cross those who have trusted in the name of our Lord Jesus Christ? What writing has taught us to turn to the East at the prayer? Which of the saints has left us in writing the words of the invocation at the displaying of the bread of the Eucharist and the cup of blessing? For we are not, as is well known, content with what the apostle or the Gospel has recorded, but both in preface and conclusion we add other words as being of great importance to the validity of the ministry, and these we derive from unwritten teaching.'[576]

St. Vincent of Lerins identified preserving 'antiquity' as one of the essential rules of the Catholic Faith, 'This rule we shall observe...if we follow antiquity, if we in no wise depart from those interpretations which it is manifest were notoriously held by our

---

[573] St. Irenaeus. *Against Heresies*. Book IV, Chapter 33. [Online] Available at: www.newadvent.org [Accessed on: 22 July 2022]

[574] Tertullian. *The Prescription Against Heretics*, Chapter 19. [Online] Available at: www.newadvent.org [Accessed on: 22 July 2022]

[575] St. Athanasius. *Festal Letters* 2, para 6. [Online] Available at: www.newadvent.org [Accessed on: 22 July 2022]

[576] St. Basil of Caesarea. *On the Holy Spirit*, Chap. 27. [Online] Available at: www.newadvent.org [Accessed on: 22 July 2022]

holy ancestors and fathers; consent, in like manner, if in antiquity itself we adhere to the consentient definitions and determinations of all, or at the least of almost all priests and doctors.'[577]

Regarding the importance of observing the rule of preserving antiquity, St. Vincent of Lerins recommended that if the contagion of innovation infected the whole Church, it was our duty to 'cleave to antiquity':

> What then will a Catholic Christian do, if a small portion of the Church have cut itself off from the communion of the universal faith? What, surely, but prefer the soundness of the whole body to the unsoundness of a pestilent and corrupt member? What, if some novel contagion seek to infect not merely an insignificant portion of the Church, but the whole? Then it will be his care to cleave to antiquity, which at this day cannot possibly be seduced by any fraud of novelty.[578]

c) The Defence by the Magisterium

In the midst of the Protestant schism, when liturgy became one of the fracture points due to heresy, Pope St. Pius V drew on the apostolic imperative to preserve Tradition, writing in his famous Bull *Quo Primum Tempore*:

> From the very first, upon Our elevation to the chief Apostleship, We gladly turned our mind and energies and directed all our thoughts to those matters which concerned the preservation of a pure liturgy, and We strove with God's help, by every means in our power, to accomplish this purpose.[579]

As the Supreme Pontiff, Pope St. Pius V rightly saw that his duty was the preservation of the Apostolic liturgy. Seeing the danger of liturgical innovation to the worship and faith of the Church, he took canonical measures to ensure the 'preservation of a pure liturgy' down the ages by granting priests the right in perpetuity to celebrate the Apostolic Mass and sacraments:

> Furthermore, by these presents [this law], in virtue of Our Apostolic authority, We grant and concede in perpetuity that, for the chanting or reading of the Mass in any church whatsoever, this Missal is hereafter to be followed absolutely, without any scruple of conscience or fear of incurring any penalty, judgment, or censure, and may freely and lawfully be used. Nor are superiors, administrators, canons, chaplains, and other secular priests, or religious, of whatever title designated, obliged to celebrate the Mass otherwise than as enjoined by Us.[580]

Like St. Vincent of Lerins, Pope St. Pius V was also aware of the constant threat posed by liturgical innovators to the Apostolic Mass, so he included canonical protection against those claiming the power to change the 'pure liturgy' or to abrogate the steps he had taken to preserve Tradition:

> We likewise declare and ordain that no one whosoever is forced or coerced to alter this Missal, and that this present document cannot be revoked or modified, but remain always valid and retain its full force.[581]

Though he wasn't writing about liturgy, Pope Leo XIII wrote about the importance of preserving Latin in education, which was under threat from secularism, describing it in terms of 'saving the sacred fire of the temple from the barbarian invader.' (II Macc 1.19-22). He appealed to his fellow bishops to '"Guard the deposit" (I Tim 6:20) with jealous care' by tasking their seminaries and schools with the duty of preserving Latin.[582]

---

[577] St. Vincent of Lerins. *Commonitory*, Chap. 2, para 6. [Online] Available at: www.newadvent.org [Accessed on: 22 July 2022]

[578] St. Vincent of Lerins. *Ibid.*, para 7

[579] Pope St. Pius V [1570] The Bull *Quo Primum Tempore*. [Online] Available at: lms.org.uk [Accessed on: 19 July 2022]

[580] *Ibid.*

[581] *Ibid.*

[582] Pope Leo XIII [1899] Encyclical *Depuis le Jour*, para 12. [Online] Available at: www.vatican.va [Accessed on: 23 July 2022]

Pope Leo XIII's successor, Pope St. Pius X, was concerned about the intrusion of the vernacular into liturgy, in particular sacred music, which he sought to counter by mandating Gregorian chant. Regarding Latin Pope St. Pius X wrote:

> The language proper to the Roman Church is Latin. Hence it is forbidden to sing anything whatever in the vernacular in solemn liturgical functions — much more to sing in the vernacular the variable or common parts of the Mass and Office.[583]

Pope Pius XI observed that attacks against the Latin language — 'the "catholic" language' — was a characteristic of Protestantism, 'it was attacked by the adversaries of catholic wisdom who in the 16th century shattered the accord Europe had in the single doctrine of the Faith.'[584] Pope Pius XI also expressed the traditional understanding of the role of the successors of St. Peter's in preserving traditional liturgy:

> …Roman Pontiffs have been so solicitous to safeguard and protect the Liturgy. They have used the same care in making laws for the regulation of the Liturgy, in preserving it from adulteration, as they have in giving accurate expression to the dogmas of the faith. This is the reason why the Fathers made both spoken and written commentary upon the Liturgy or 'the law of worship'; for this reason the Council of Trent ordained that the Liturgy should be expounded and explained to the faithful.[585]

Pope Ven. Pius XII was also clear about the importance of Latin to the Catholic Church, especially defending its use in the celebration of the Mass. He wrote that Latin is 'effective antidote for any corruption of doctrinal truth.'[586] Unlike Pope Francis, who saw Latin as less important than any number of vernacular languages, under Pope Pius XII the *Sacred Congregation of Seminaries and Universities* insisted that Latin had a special, unique place in the life of the Church, 'Latin is not merely another foreign language to be equated as a required subject or as an elective on the same level with French, German, Spanish, or Russian. Latin has been a great unifying element in Western civilisation and has been, since the fourth century AD, the official and liturgical language of the Western Church.'[587] Regarding the celebration of the Most Holy Sacrifice of the Mass, Pope Pius XII wrote of the 'absolute obligation' to use Latin:

> Yet it would be superfluous to call once more to mind that the Church has grave motives for firmly insisting that in the Latin rite the priest celebrating Mass has an absolute obligation to use Latin, and also, when Gregorian chant accompanies the Holy Sacrifice, that this be done in the Church's tongue.[588]

Eight months before the opening to the Second Vatican Council Pope St. John XXIII issued an Apostolic Constitution defending the irreplaceable importance of Latin in the life of the Catholic Church summarised as follows:

i) Latin is the rightful language of the Apostolic See through 'God's special Providence'.

ii) 'It gives rise to no jealousies. It does not favour any one nation.'

iii) The 'knowledge and use of [Latin], so intimately bound up with the Church's life, is 'important... for religious reasons.'

iv) Due to the fact that the Church is embraced by all nations and will endure until the end of time, Latin provides her with a language which is 'universal, immutable, and non-vernacular.'

---

[583] Pope St. Pius X [1903] Motu Proprio *Tra Le Sollecitudini*, para 7. [Online] Available at: adoremus. org [Accessed on: 23 July 2022]

[584] Pope Pius XI [1922] Apostolic Letter *Officiorum Omnium*. [Online] Available at: lms.org.uk [Accessed on: 22 July 2022]

[585] Pope Pius XI [1928] *Divini Cultus*. [Online] Available at: adoremus.org [Accessed on: 23 July 2022]

[586] Pope Pius XII [1947] Encyclical *Mediator Dei*, para 60. [Online] Available at: www.vatican.va [Accessed on: 23 July 2022]

[587] The Sacred Congregation of Seminaries and Universities [1958] Letter *The Proper Study of Latin*. [Online] Available at: greek-latin.catholic.edu [Accessed on: 23 July 2022]

[588] Pope Pius XII [1956] *Address to the International Congress on Pastoral Liturgy*. [Online] Available at: archive.ccwatershed.org [Accessed on: 23 July 2022]

v) Latin is the ideal language because the Church's language must be not only universal but also immutable.

vi) It is altogether fitting Latin should be used because it is 'noble, majestic, and non-vernacular.'

vii) The Latin language can be called truly catholic because it has been consecrated through constant use by the Apostolic See, the mother and teacher of all Churches, and must be esteemed 'a treasure of incomparable worth.'

Pope St. John XXIII warned the world's bishops to be on their guard against those 'eager for revolutionary changes' who wrote against the use of Latin, especially in the liturgy:

> In the exercise of their paternal care they shall be on their guard lest anyone under their jurisdiction, eager for revolutionary changes, writes against the use of Latin in the teaching of the higher sacred studies or in the Liturgy, or through prejudice makes light of the Holy See's will in this regard or interprets it falsely.[589]

Even Pope St. Paul VI expressed high esteem for the liturgical use of Latin, especially in the choral recitation of the divine office. He described Latin as 'an abundant well-spring of Christian civilisation and a very rich treasure-trove of devotion.' He exhorted priests of religious institutes to preserve Tradition, writing, 'The traditions of the elders, your glory throughout long ages, must not be belittled.' Distressed at the prospect of the abandonment of Latin, especially Gregorian Chant, by these religious institutes Paul VI wrote the following moving appeal:

> On the other hand, that choir from which is removed this language of wondrous spiritual power, transcending the boundaries of the nations, and from which is removed this melody proceeding from the inmost sanctuary of the soul, where faith dwells and charity burns — We speak of Gregorian chant — such a choir will be like to a snuffed candle, which gives light no more, no more attracts the eyes and minds of men.[590]

Pope St. John Paul II took a number of steps to support those priests and faithful who sought to preserve the tradition of the Apostolic Mass. Through his Motu Proprio *Ecclesia Dei* (1988), he established canonical measures to 'guarantee respect' for the 'rightful aspirations' of 'all those Catholic faithful who feel attached to some previous liturgical and disciplinary forms of the Latin tradition.' Pope St. John Paul also instructed the world's bishops to show respect 'for the feelings of all those who are attached to the Latin liturgical tradition' by 'a wide and generous application of the directives... by the Apostolic See for the use of the Roman Missal according to the typical edition of 1962.'[591] Furthermore, the Sacred Congregation for Divine Worship and the Discipline of the Sacraments issued the instruction *Redemptionis Sacramentum* (2004) confirming that 'Priests are always and everywhere permitted to celebrate Mass in Latin.'[592]

Pope Benedict XVI continued Pope St. John Paul II's solicitude towards the faithful preserving Tradition through the Apostolic Mass through his *Motu Proprio Summorum Pontificum* (2007), summarised as follows:

i) From time immoral 'usages universally received from apostolic and unbroken tradition' have been preserved by particular Churches.[593]

[589] Pope St. John XIII [1962] Encyclical *Veterum Sapientia*. [Online] Available at: www.papalencyclicals.net [Accessed on: 23 July 2022]

[590] Pope St. Paul VI [1966] Apostolic Letter *Sacrificium Laudis*. [Online] Available at: lms.org.uk [Accessed on: 23 July 2022]

[591] Pope St. John Paul II [1988] Motu Proprio *Ecclesia Dei*. [Online] Available at: www.vatican.va [Accessed on: 23 July 2022]

[592] Sacred Congregation for Divine Worship and the Discipline of the Sacraments [2004] *Redemptionis Sacramentum*, para 112. [Online] Available at: www.vatican.va [Accessed on: 23 July 2022]

[593] Pope Benedict XVI [2007] *Summorum Pontificum*, art.1. [Online] Available at: www.vatican.va [Accessed on: 19 July 2022]

ii) This preservation of Tradition through liturgy is essential 'so that errors may be avoided, but also that the faith may be handed on in its integrity, since the Church's rule of prayer (*lex orandi*) corresponds to her rule of faith (*lex credendi*).'[594]

iii) Eminent among popes who showed 'such proper concern' for the preservation of Tradition through liturgy was Pope St. Gregory the Great, 'He ordered that the form of the sacred liturgy, both of the sacrifice of the Mass and the Divine Office, as celebrated in Rome, should be defined and preserved.'[595]

iv) 'In every century of the Christian era the Church's Latin liturgy in its various forms has inspired countless saints in their spiritual life, confirmed many peoples in the virtue of religion and enriched their devotion.'[596]

v) Among the liturgical books of the Roman rite, a particular place belongs to the *Roman Missal*.[597]

vi) *The Roman Missal* promulgated by Pope St. Paul VI and *The Roman Missal* promulgated by St. Pius V and revised by St. John XXIII are 'two expressions of the Church's *lex orandi* [and] will in no way lead to a division in the Church's *lex credendi* (rule of faith); for they are two usages of the one Roman rite.'[598]

Against those who wrongly claimed that the Latin mass caused harm to the Church Pope Benedict XVI rejected it as an excuse to entirely forbid its celebration:

> What earlier generations held as sacred, remains sacred and great for us too, and it cannot be all of a sudden entirely forbidden or even considered harmful. It behoves all of us to preserve the riches which have developed in the Church's faith and prayer, and to give them their proper place.[599]

Unlike Pope Francis, Pope Benedict XVI possessed a sensitivity towards, and appreciation of, the importance of preserving Tradition to the nature of the Catholic Church. He expressed this in his address to members of St. Peter's Basilica Chapter, saying, 'I appreciated, Your Excellency, the fact that as Archpriest you referred to the uninterrupted presence of clergy praying in the Vatican Basilica since the time of St. Gregory the Great.'[600]

Pope Francis' criticism of the preservation of Tradition through the liturgy, and the steps he has taken to suppress it, is totally contrary to the teaching of the Church according to the sources of Faith.

---

[594] *Ibid.*

[595] *Ibid.*

[596] *Ibid.*

[597] *Ibid.*

[598] *Ibid.*, art.1

[599] Pope Benedict XVI [2007] *Letter to the Bishops on the Occasion of the Publication of the Apostolic Letter Motu Proprio Data Summorum Pontificum.* [Online] Available at: www.vatican.va [Accessed on: 23 July 2022]

[600] Pope Benedict XVI [2007] *Address to Members of the Vatican Chapter.* [Online] Available at: www.vatican.va [Accessed on: 23 July 2022]

Mariology (1) — The Blessed Virgin Mary Lost Faith in God's Promises

J. *At the foot of the Cross, witnessing the sufferings of her Son, Mary lost faith in God's promises at the Annunciation, accusing the Archangel Gabriel of being a liar and a deceiver.*

On two occasions Pope Francis taught the Mariological error that our Lady could have entertained what amount to sinful thoughts at the foot of the cross. The first was during his morning meditation in the Chapel of the Domus Sanctae Marthae (20th December 2013) the Supreme Pontiff said:

> The Gospel tells us nothing: whether She said a word or not....She was silent, but in Her heart, how many things did she tell the Lord! 'You, that day – this is what we read – told me that He would be great; You told me that you would give Him the Throne of David, His father, that He would reign forever and now I see him there!' Our Lady was human! And perhaps she had the urge to say: 'Lies! I was deceived!' John Paul II said this, speaking about Our Lady in that moment. But She, with silence, covered the mystery that She did not understand and with this silence she left this mystery so that it could grow and flourish in hope.[601]

Pope Francis did not specify which words of Pope St. John Paul II he was referencing. It may be these from his encyclical *Redemptoris Mater*, 18 'And now, standing at the foot of the Cross, Mary is the witness, humanly speaking, of the complete negation of these words.'[602] Pope St. John Paul II did not use the words or sentiment concerning Mary's thoughts at the foot of the cross that Pope Francis ascribed to him, 'Lies! I was deceived!'

The second occasion was two years later, when Pope Francis gave an address to a group of gravely ill children and their families in which he repeated the same erroneous Mariological speculation:

> I often think of Our Lady, when they handed down to her the dead body of her Son, covered with wounds, spat on, bloodied and soiled. And what did Our Lady do? 'Did she carry him away?' No, she embraced him, she caressed him. Our Lady, too, did not understand. Because she, in that moment, remembered what the Angel had said to her: 'He will be King, he will be great, he will be a prophet...'; and inside, surely, with that wounded body lying in her arms, that body that suffered so before dying, inside surely she wanted to say to the Angel: 'Liar! I was deceived.' She, too, had no answers.[603]

Pope Francis' speculation about Mary's thoughts at the foot of the cross is reminiscent of a passage from St. Cyril of Alexandra's commentary on the Gospel of St. John:

> For, doubtless, some such train of thought as this passed through her mind: 'I conceived Him That is mocked upon the Cross. He said, indeed, that He was the true Son of Almighty God, but it may be that He was deceived; He may have erred when He said: I am the Life. How did His crucifixion come to pass? and how was He entangled in the snares of His murderers? How was it that He did not prevail over the conspiracy of His persecutors against Him? And why does He not come down from the Cross, though He bade Lazarus return to life, and struck all Judaea with amazement by His miracles?' The woman, as is likely, not exactly understanding the mystery, wandered astray into some such train of thought; for we shall do well to remember, that the character of these events was such as to awe and subdue the most sober mind. And no marvel if a woman fell into such an error...What wonder, then, if a woman's frail mind was also plunged into thoughts which betrayed weakness?[604]

---

[601] Pope Francis Pope Francis [21 December 2013] *Silence Reveals the Mystery of God's Plan.* [Online] Available at: aleteia.org [Accessed on: 24 July 2022]

[602] Pope St. John Paul II [1987] *Redemptoris Mater,* para 18. [Online] Available at: www.vatican.va [Accessed on: 24 July 2022]

[603] Pope Francis [2015] *Meeting with a Group of Gravely ill Children and their Families. Chapel of the Domus Sanctae Marthae.* [Online] Available at: www.vatican.va [Accessed on: 24 July 2022]

[604] St. Cyril of Alexandria. *On the Gospel According to John,* Bk. XII. [Online] Available at: www. tertullian.org [Accessed on: 24 July 2022]

St. Cyril's speculations about Mary experiencing a lack of faith at the foot of the cross are seen as belonging to a minority of Church Fathers who thought Mary capable of committing venial sins. Contrary to this erroneous position, the majority of Church Fathers testified to Mary's sinlessness which was defined as the doctrine of the Church. Having said this, though St. Cyril speculated that Mary may have experienced a lack of faith at the foot of the Cross, he did not speculate that Mary expressed anger against God's messenger, the Archangel Gabriel, accusing him, and by inference God, of lies and deception. While St. Cyril speculated about Mary experiencing confusion and doubt, Pope Francis went further by speculating that Mary committed what amounted to venial sins. Such speculation that Mary committed sins is totally contrary to the Church's doctrine of the sinlessness of Mary.

The Teaching of the Church
In consequence of a Special Privilege of Grace from God, Mary was free from every personal sin during her whole life. (**sententia fidei proxima.**)
From her conception Mary was free from all motions of concupiscence. (**sententia communis.**)
One of the main descriptive titles of Mary declared by the Church through history is 'Immaculate', with its meaning of free from moral stain and preserved spotless from sin. For example, the Council of Lateran referred to Mary as 'the holy Mother of God and ever Virgin and immaculate'.[605] The Council of Toledo referred to our Lady as 'the holy and immaculate Virgin Mary.'[606]

For the majority of the Church's history Mary's sinlessness was not questioned. It was only in response to Protestantism's erroneous soteriology concerning the doctrine of Justification that the Council of Trent defined the Church's perennial understanding when it stated that no man 'can during his whole life avoid all sins, even those that are venial, 'except by a special privilege from God, as the Church holds in regard to the Blessed Virgin.'[607]

Contrary to Pope Francis' speculation that Mary rebelled against God at the foot of the cross, the Second Vatican Council emphasised that Mary, as the mother of Jesus, cooperated in a singular way in his redemptive death 'by her obedience, faith, hope and burning charity':

> [Mary] faithfully persevered in her union with her Son unto the cross, where she stood, in keeping with the divine plan (cf. Jn. 19:25), grieving exceedingly with her only begotten Son, uniting herself with a maternal heart with His sacrifice, and lovingly consenting to the immolation of this Victim which she herself had brought forth.[608]

Proof from the Sources of Faith
a) Teaching from Holy Scripture
Pope Francis' speculation that Mary rebelled against God at the foot of the Cross, committing the venial sin of lack of faith, is contrary to the teaching of divine revelation contained in sacred Scripture. As Dr. Ludwig Ott observed, 'Mary's sinlessness may be deduced from the text: Luke 1, 28: "Hail, full of grace!", since personal moral defects are irreconcilable with fullness of grace.'[609] St. Thomas Aquinas exegesis explains the significance of this phrase regarding Mary's perpetual sinlessness:

---

[605] The Council of Lateran [649] *Against the Monothelites*, Can. 3. [Online] Available at: http://patristica.net [Accessed on: 25 July 2022]
[606] Council of Toledo [675] *Exposition of faith against the Priscillianists*. [Online] Available at: http://patristica.net [Accessed on: 25 July 2022]
[607] Council of Trent [1547] *Decree on Justification*, Canon 23. [Online] Available at: www.ewtn.com [Accessed on: 25 July 2022]
[608] Second Vatican Council [1964] Dogmatic Constitution, *Lumen Gentium*, para 58; 61. [Online] Available at: www.vatican.va [Accessed on: 25 July 2022]
[609] Ott, L. *Op. cit.*, p.203.

The Blessed Virgin is said to be full of grace in three ways. First, as regards to her soul, she possessed all the fullness of grace. The grace of God is given for two purposes: namely, to do good, and to avoid evil; and for these, the Blessed Virgin had the most perfect grace since she avoided every sin more than any saint, except Christ. Sin is either original, and from this she was cleansed in the womb; or mortal or venial, and from these she was free.[610]

Summing up the understanding of the Church Fathers of the significance of 'Hail, full of grace', Fr. Scheeben wrote, 'Mary's wealth of grace surpassed the grace of each individual angel and saint, and also that of all taken collectively.'[611] With this understanding, the speculation that Mary committed venial sin at the foot of the Cross is unthinkable.

Mary's sinlessness is also a manifestation of her enmity towards the devil, as prophesied in the *Protoevangelium*, 'I will put enmities between thee and the woman, and thy seed and her seed: she shall crush thy head, and thou shalt lie in wait for her heel' (Gen 3:15). Consequently, Our Lady's enmity towards Satan is so total, sin is entirely antithetical to her nature, hence her Immaculate Conception that frees her from the stain of original sin. In the light of this, to speculate that Mary committed venial sins at the moment of the fulfilment of salvation history — the Son of God's redemptive sacrifice on the cross — is abhorrent.

Finally, sacred Scripture teaches us that Mary is the epitome of unreserved obedience to the will of God, when she replied, 'Behold the handmaid of the Lord; be it done to me according to thy word' (Lk 1:38). Mary's obedience loosened the knot of Eve's disobedience, 'For what the virgin Eve bound by her incredulity, the Virgin Mary loosened by her faith' (St. Irenaeus).[612] This is yet another reason why Pope Francis' speculation that Mary expressed such violent incredulity at the foot of the cross — 'surely she wanted to say to the Angel: "Liar! I was deceived"' — is so repugnant.

b) The Testimony of Tradition

The majority of the Church Fathers reverenced the Blessed Virgin Mary for being immaculate, free from the stain of all sin. St. Ephraem, famous for his hymns in honour of Mary and her role in the Incarnation, wrote, 'Thou, Lord, and thy mother, you alone are perfect holy; for in thee, Lord, there is no stain, nor is there any blemish in thy mother.'[613] St. Ambrose wrote, '[Mary] is a virgin not only uncorrupted, but a virgin untouched by all stain of sin.'[614] St. Augustine found the question of Mary committing sin not worthy of consideration:

> We must except the holy Virgin Mary, concerning whom I wish to raise no question when it touches the subject of sins, out of honour to the Lord; for from Him we know what abundance of grace for overcoming sin in every particular was conferred upon her who had the merit to conceive and bear Him who undoubtedly had no sin.[615]

Likewise, St. Bernard of Clairvaux held that Mary was preserved immune from sin throughout her life because she was the mother of Jesus, 'the destroyer of sin and death', so that 'by a privilege of singular holiness, the Queen of virgins should have led a life without sin.'[616]

Regarding Mary's role at the foot of the cross, Tradition testifies that rather than rebelling against God due to the sufferings of her Son, our Lady deliberately and

---

[610] Every, L. *St. Thomas' Explanation of the Hail Mary*. [Online] www.dominicanajournal.org [Accessed on 25 July 2022]

[611] Scheeben, MJ [1946] *Mariology*. Jackson: Ex Fontibus Company LLC, p.10-11.

[612] Ibid, *Op. cit.*, p.204.

[613] Scheeben, MJ [1946] *Mariology*. Vol.2. Jackson: Ex Fontibus Company LLC, p. 64.

[614] *Ibid.*, p.64.

[615] St. Augustine. *On Nature and Grace*, Chap. 36. [Online] Available at: www.newadvent.org [Accessed on: 26 July 2022]

[616] Scheeben, MJ [1946] Mariology. *Op. cit.*, p.128

willingly offered him as a sacrificial victim in atonement for sin. From the moment of Mary's fiat our Lady willingly obeyed God's plan of salvation even to the sacrifice of her Son. St. Ambrose wrote:

> With eyes full of pity, she looked upon her Son's wounds, by which, as she knew, would come the redemption of the world. She, who did not fear her Son's killers, assisted at his generous martyrdom…Well did she know the mystery, that she had given birth to One who was to rise; moreover, she knew that her Son's death would happen for the good of all.[617]

St. Louis de Montfort conveyed Mary's maternal participation in Jesus' suffering succinctly, 'It was Mary who nursed him, fed him, cared for him, reared him, and sacrificed him for us.'[618] He compared Mary's willingness to sacrifice her Son for God to that of Abraham's intention to sacrifice his son, Isaac. This comparison is fitting because both are the singular exemplars of faith, Abraham in the Old Testament and Mary in the New Testament. St. Alphonsus Liguori also made this comparison to explain our Lady's attitude at the foot of the cross, 'If Abraham showed a similar courage in his willingness to sacrifice his son with his own hands, we must believe that Mary would have fulfilled God's will with even greater courage, since she is more holy and more obedient than Abraham.'[619]

Tradition's testimony to our Lady's sinlessness, steadfast faith, and obedient participation in her Son's suffering is in marked contrast to Pope Francis' speculations about faithlessness and rebellion, that dishonour both the Blessed Virgin Mary and her Son.

c) The Defence by the Magisterium

The advent of the Marian age[620] — with the Church approving more Marian apparitions since 1830 than the whole previous period — has witnessed a deepening understanding of Mary's sinlessness and redemptive role at the foot of the cross. This doctrinal focus resulted in two dogmatic definitions; Pope Bl. Pius IX defined the Immaculate Conception in 1854 and venerable Pope Pius XII defined Mary's Assumption in 1950. By contrast, Pope Francis' erroneous Mariological speculation stands out as aberrational.

In his definition of our Lady's Immaculate Conception, Pope Bl. Pius IX referenced the *Protoevangelium* to explain how Mary's personal conquest of sin culminated in her role at the foot of the cross:

> Hence, just as Christ, the Mediator between God and man, assumed human nature, blotted the handwriting of the decree that stood against us, and fastened it triumphantly to the cross, so the most holy Virgin, united with him by a most intimate and indissoluble bond, was, with him and through him, eternally at enmity with the evil serpent, and most completely triumphed over him, and thus crushed his head with her immaculate foot.[621]

A succession of modern popes had a profound understanding of the importance to redemption of Mary's maternal oblation of her Son on Calvary. Pope Leo XIII wrote of Mary's full knowledge of, and consent for, our Lord's sufferings and sacrificial death, 'it was before the eyes of Mary that was to be finished the Divine Sacrifice for which she had borne and brought up the Victim.'[622] Instead of describing Mary as railing against God, Pope St. Pius X wrote that our Lady rejoiced 'that her Only Son was offered for the

---

[617] Luigi Gambero, *Mary and the Fathers of the Church*. San Francisco: Ignatius Press, 1999, p.202-203.
[618] St. Louis Marie de Montfort [1843] *True Devotion to the Blessed Virgin*, para 18. [Online] Available at: www.montfort.org.uk [Accessed on: 27 July 2022]
[619] St. Alphonsus Liguori [1750] *The Glories of Mary*. Liguori: Liguori Publications, p.17
[620] Miravalle, M. *The Age of Mary*. [Online] www.marian.org [Accessed on: 27 July 2022]
[621] Pope Bl. Pius IX [1854] Apostolic Constitution *Ineffabilis Deus*. [Online] www.papalencyclicals. net [Accessed on: 27 July 2022]
[622] Pope Leo XIII [1884] Encyclical *Iucunda Semper Expectatione*, para 3. [Online] Available at: www. vatican.va [Accessed on: 27 July 2022]

salvation of mankind.'[623] Pope Benedict XV wrote that Mary surrendered 'her mother's rights over her Son for the salvation of human beings, and to appease the justice of God, so far as pertained to her, she immolated her Son.'[624]

Pope Ven. Pius XII re-iterated St. Irenaeus' comparison of Mary's obedience with Eve's disobedience to explain the Mother of God's redemptive role:

> It was she, the second Eve, who, free from all sin, original or personal, and always more intimately united with her Son, offered Him on Golgotha to the Eternal Father for all the children of Adam, sin-stained by his unhappy fall, and her mother's rights and her mother's love were included in the holocaust.[625]

Pope St. Paul VI deepened the Church's understanding of Mary's interiority at the foot of the cross by reflecting on the role of the Holy Spirit in strengthening our Lady at the Annunciation and at the Crucifixion, enabling her 'to consent to the will of the heavenly Father who wanted her to be associated as a mother with the sacrifice her Son was offering for mankind's redemption.'[626]

Pope St. John Paul II often highlighted Mary's willing co-operation in the sacrificial suffering of her Son on the Cross, summarised as follows:

i) Mary's obediential faith enabled her to suffer in her Son's sacrifice, 'How obedient she was at the moment of the Annunciation, and then — at the foot of the cross — obedient even to the point of assenting to the death of her Son, who became obedient "unto death"!';[627] 'Mary gave her consent in faith at the Annunciation and maintained it without hesitation at the foot of the Cross';[628] 'Through this faith Mary is perfectly united with Christ in his self-emptying... At the foot of the Cross Mary shares through faith in the shocking mystery of this self-emptying.'[629]

ii) Mary was able to share in the sacrifice of her Son because she was sinless, 'without a single sin to restrain her, she gave herself entirely to the person and to the work of her Son; she did so in order to serve the mystery of redemption with him and dependent on him, by God's grace.'[630]

iii) Mary shows the depth of her obedience at the foot of the cross, in reference to Luke 1:32-33, 'And now, standing at the foot of the Cross, Mary is the witness, humanly speaking, of the complete negation of these words... How great, how heroic then is the obedience of faith shown by Mary in the face of God's "unsearchable judgments"!'[631]

iv) Maternal consent to the immolation of her Son, 'lovingly consenting to the immolation of the victim to whom she had given birth';[632] 'consenting to the immolation of this victim which she herself had brought forth'.[633]

---

[623] Pope St. Pius X [1904] Encyclical *Ad Diem Illum Laetissimum*, para 12. [Online] Available at: www.vatican.va [Accessed on: 27 July 2022]
[624] Pope Benedict XV [1917] *Admodum Probatur*. [Online] www.ewtn.com [Accessed on: 27 July 2022]
[625] Pope Pius XII [1943] Encyclical *Mystici Corporis Christi*, para 110. [Online] Available at: www.vatican.va [Accessed on: 27 July 2022]
[626] Pope St. Paul VI [1975] *Letter of Pope Paul VI to Cardinal Léon Josef Suenens on the Occasion of the International Marian Congress.* [Online] Available at: www.piercedhearts.org [Accessed on: 27 July 2022]
[627] Pope St. John Paul [1984] Apostolic Exhortation *Redemptionis Donum*, para 17. [Online] Available at: www.vatican.va [Accessed on: 27 July 2022]
[628] *Catechism of the Catholic Church* [1997], para 2674.
[629] Pope St. John Paul II [1987] Encyclical *Redemptoris Mater*, para 18. [Online] Available at: www.vatican.va [Accessed on: 27 July 2022]
[630] *Catechism of the Catholic Church* [1997] para 494
[631] *Ibid.*
[632] Pope St. John Paul II [1987] *Ibid.*, para 17
[633] Pope St. John Paul II [1988] *Letter to Priests for Holy Thursday*, para 2. [Online] Available at: www.vatican.va [Accessed on: 27 July 2022]

v) Mary willingly offers her Son as an expiatory sacrifice, 'she offers Jesus, gives him over, and begets him to the end for our sake. The "yes" spoken on the day of the Annunciation reaches full maturity on the day of the Cross.'[634]

vi) Mary offered herself in sacrifice with her Son at the foot of the cross, 'Mary's offering in the sacrifice of Calvary [through] "two altars: one in Mary's heart, the other in Christ's body. Christ sacrificed his flesh, Mary her soul". Mary sacrificed herself spiritually in deep communion with Christ.'[635]

Contrary to Pope Francis' nihilistic Mariological speculation, Pope Benedict XVI speculated that Mary experienced the sufferings of her Son on the cross with the faith of the Annunciation:

> The sword of sorrow pierced your heart. Did hope die? Did the world remain definitively without light, and life without purpose? At that moment, deep down, you probably listened again to the word spoken by the angel in answer to your fear at the time of the Annunciation: 'Do not be afraid, Mary!' (Lk 1:30). How many times had the Lord, your Son, said the same thing to his disciples: do not be afraid! In your heart, you heard this word again during the night of Golgotha...at the foot of the Cross, on the strength of Jesus's own word, you became the mother of believers. In this faith, which even in the darkness of Holy Saturday bore the certitude of hope, you made your way towards Easter morning. The joy of the Resurrection touched your heart and united you in a new way to the disciples, destined to become the family of Jesus through faith.[636]

As we've seen, the Magisterium's Mariology concerning Mary's sinlessness and sacrificial role at the foot of the cross exposes the poverty of Pope Francis' erroneous speculation.

---

[634] Pope St. John Paul II [1995] Encyclical *Evangelium Vitae*, para 103. [Online] Available at: www.vatican.va [Accessed on: 27 July 2022]

[635] Pope St. John Paul II [1995] *Mary Was United to Jesus on the Cross*. [Online] Available at: www.ewtn.com [Accessed on: 27 July 2022]

[636] Pope Benedict XVI [2007] Encyclical *Spe Salvi*, para 50. [Online] Available at: www.vatican.va [Accessed on: 27 July 2022]

Mariology (2) — Denial of Mary as Coredemptrix & Other Marian Titles

K. *It is wrong to venerate Mary as Coredemptrix because Jesus is the sole redeemer of mankind. Mary requires no other title apart from that of mother, woman and disciple.*

Over three successive years — 2019 to 2021 — Pope Francis publicly criticised venerating the Blessed Virgin Mary as Coredemptrix, even going so far as criticising other Marian titles. His expressed preference for reducing Mary's titles to mother, woman and disciple, reveals an erroneous *sola Scriptura* approach to Mariology.

In 2019 Pope Francis criticised those appealing to the Church to define the dogma of Mary's coredemptive role as 'foolish', 'She never presented herself as a Coredemptrix. No. disciple…When they come to us with the story according to which we should declare this, or that other dogma, let's not get lost in foolishness.'[637] The Supreme Pontiff's remarks were viewed as a response to an appeal made to him in August 2019 from one cardinal and five bishops to 'specifically and dogmatically honour her coredemp-tive role with Jesus'.[638]

In 2020 Pope Francis rejected what he referred to as all 'functional titles' from being applied to Mary, arguing that we should only call her 'Mother' as this was the only title she received from Jesus, 'He did not make her prime minister or give her "functional" titles. Only "Mother"… She did not ask for herself to be a quasi-redeemer or a coredeemer: no. There is only one Redeemer and this title cannot be duplicated. She is merely disciple and Mother.'[639]

In 2021 Pope Francis explained in more detail the erroneous assumptions behind his rejection of Mary as Coredemptrix, '…the Madonna who 'covers', like a Mother, to whom Jesus entrusted us, all of us; but as a Mother, not as a goddess, not as coredeemer: as Mother,' 'He is the only Redeemer: there are no coredeemers with Christ. He is the only one. He is the Mediator par excellence. He is the Mediator.' The Supreme Pontiff repeated his rejection of traditional titles of Mary, dismissing them as childish exaggerations:

> It is true that Christian piety has always given her beautiful titles, as a child gives his or her mamma: how many beautiful things children say about their mamma whom they love so much! How many beautiful things. But we need to be careful: the things the Church, the Saints, say about her, beautiful things, about Mary, subtract nothing from Christ's sole Redemption. He is the only Redeemer. They are expressions of love like a child for his or her mamma – some are exaggerated. But love, as we know, always makes us exaggerate things, but out of love.[640]

Pope Francis' rejection of the Church's traditional titles for Mary, in favour of a *sola Scriptura* approach to Mariology is reminiscent of the Protestant heresiarch John Calvin's criticisms, to the point of even using similar words. In his commentary on John 2:4, Calvin wrote the following about Jesus' saying, 'Woman, what is that to me':

> This saying of Christ openly and manifestly warns men to beware lest, by too superstitiously elevating the honour of the name of mother in the Virgin Mary, they transfer to her what belongs exclusively to God. Christ, therefore, addresses his mother in this manner, in order to lay down a perpetual and general instruction to all ages, that his divine glory must not be obscured by excessive honour paid to his mother.
>
> How necessary this warning became, in consequence of the gross and disgraceful superstitions which followed afterwards, is too well known. For Mary has been constituted the Queen of Heaven, the Hope, the Life, and the Salvation of the world;

---

[637] Miravalle, M [2019] *Pope Francis' Guadalupe Homily and Mary 'Co-Redemptrix'.* [Online] Available at: www.ncregister.com [Accessed on: 28 July 2022]

[638] Sandoval, J et al. [2019] *Open Letter to Pope Francis for Mary.* [Online] Available at: openletterformary.com [Accessed on 28 July 2022]

[639] Pope Francis [3rd April 2020] *Morning Meditation in the Chapel of the Domus Sanctae Marthae.* [Online] Available at: www.vatican.va [Accessed on: 28 July 2022]

[640] Pope Francis [24th March 2021] *General Audience Address.* [Online] Available at: www.vatican. va [Accessed on: 28 July 2022]

and, in short, their fury and madness proceeded so far that they stripped Christ of his spoils, and left him almost naked [...] As if she had not all the honour that is due to her, unless she were made a Goddess; or as if it were treating her with respect, to adorn her with blasphemous titles, and to substitute her in the room of Christ.[641]

The Teaching of the Church

Mary gave the Redeemer, the Source of all graces, to the world, and in this way she is the channel of all graces. **(Sententia certa)**[642]

Since Mary's Assumption into Heaven no grace is conferred on man without her actual intercessory co-operation. **(Sententia pia et probabilis)**[643]

Mary is the Mediatrix of all graces by her co-operation in the Incarnation. **(Mediatio in universali)**[644]

Mary is the Mediatrix of all graces by her intercession in Heaven. **(Mediatio in speciali)**[645]

Though the Marian title Coredemptrix only appeared in the 15th century, the understanding that it expresses about Mary's unique cooperation in her Son's redemption of mankind can be traced back to Church Fathers' reflection on sacred Scripture. Fr. Ott summarises the Church's understanding of Mary as Coredemptrix as follows:

> The title Coredemptrix = Coredemptress...must not be conceived in the sense of an equation of efficacy of Mary with the redemptive activity of Christ, the sole Redeemer of humanity (I Tim 2:5) As she herself required redemption... Her co-operation in the objective redemption is an indirect, remote co-operation, and derives from this that she voluntarily devoted her whole life to the service of the Redeemer, and, under the Cross, suffered and sacrificed with Him.[646]

The Church's tradition of venerating our Lady with 'functional' titles — as Pope Francis put it — expressing her role in salvation history can be traced back to the Council of Ephesus safeguarding her dignity and role against Christological heresies with the title Mother of God, *Theotokos*. A Marian title not found in sacred Scripture, but expressed by sacred Tradition, such as the earliest prayer addressed to Mary, the *Sub tuum praesidium*. Over time the title Mother of God inspired the addition of other devotional titles: 'the Holy Virgin is the Mother of God' (Council of Ephesus);[647] 'the holy and glorious Mother of God and ever Virgin Mary' (Second Council of Constantinople);[648] '...our undefiled lady, or holy Mother of God...'[649] (Second Council of Nicaea) ; '...the blessed and immaculate Virgin Mary mother of God...' (Council of Trent).[650]

The Second Vatican Council recognised the importance of Mary's functional titles as expressing her eternal and heavenly role, 'she did not lay aside this salvific duty, but by her constant intercession continued to bring us the gifts of eternal salvation':

> Therefore the Blessed Virgin is invoked by the Church under the titles of Advocate, Auxiliatrix, Adjutrix, and Mediatrix. This, however, is to be so understood that it

---

[641] Calvin, J. *Commentary on John* — Volume 1, Jn 2:1-11. [Online] Available at: www.ccel.org [Accessed on: 28 July 2022]

[642] Ott, L [1957] *Op. cit.*, p. 212

[643] *Ibid.*

[644] *Ibid.*

[645] *Ibid.*, p.213

[646] *Ibid.*, p. 212-213.

[647] The Council of Ephesus [431] *The Anathemas of the Chapter of Cyril*, can.1. [Online] Available at: http://patristica.net [Accessed on: 28 July 2022]

[648] Second Council of Constantinople [551] *Anathemas Concerning the Three Chapters*, can. 2. [Online] Available at: http://patristica.net [Accessed on: 28 July 2022]

[649] Second Council of Nicaea [787] *Definition of the Sacred Images and Tradition.* [Online] Available at: http://patristica.net [Accessed on: 28 July 2022]

[650] Council of Trent. [1546] *Decree on Original Sin.* [Online] Available at: http://patristica.net [Accessed on: 28 July 2022]

neither takes away from nor adds anything to the dignity and efficaciousness of Christ the one Mediator.[651]

The Second Vatican Council's defence of traditional Marian titles is contrary to Pope Francis' erroneous, Calvinistic Mariology.

Proof from the Sources of Faith
a) Teaching from Holy Scripture

Mgr. Brunero Gherardini, Dean emeritus of the faculty of theology of the Pontifical Lateran University, wrote that though the word 'Coredemption' is not found in sacred Scripture, 'it is, however, quite implicit.' Scripture makes clear that 'there is something more than a simple association between the Mother and the Son'. Though 'Coredemption does not enjoy a direct and explicit revelation in sacred Scripture [...] a typology of allusions, signs and images' enlighten the mystery of Mary:

> What is brought to light, therefore, is a woman most real and most exceptional, more unique than singular, individuated by her maternal relation to Christ, by her participation in, function and service on behalf of His redemptive mission.[652]

A collection of passages from the Old Testament, taken together, clearly prophesy that Mary as the Mother of Jesus would uniquely cooperate in His redemptive mission. The fundamental Old Testament scripture passage that testifies to Mary's coredemptive role is the Protoevangelium of Genesis, 'I will put enmities between thee and the woman, and thy seed and her seed: she shall crush thy head, and thou shalt lie in wait for her heel.' (Gen 3:15). In his exegesis of the original Hebrew, Dr. Matthias Scheeben writes that the word 'enmity' [אֵיבָה][653] in this context refers to 'an invincible enmity on the part of the woman and of the woman's seed…the invincible enmity against the serpent appears to be their concerted action, so too the victory must in some way be common to both'.[654] Simply put, the *Protoevangelium* prophesies that Mary will have a coredemptive role because it describes a woman being instrumental in Satan's defeat through her seed.

The Christological prophesies contained in Micah (5:1-2), Zephaniah (3:14-17), and Ecclesiasticus (24:3-4;12-13) describe a woman playing an essential role in the redemption of Israel: a woman in Bethlehem will give birth to Israel's true ruler, 'his going forth is from the beginning, from the days of eternity'; The 'daughter of Sion' will receive the good news that God will dwell in the midst of Israel and will bless them with redemption, 'The Lord hath taken away thy judgment, he hath turned away thy enemies'; and a woman will be praised because 'among the blessed she shall be blessed…' and 'he that made me, rested in my tabernacle' confirming Israel as God's elect.

St. Augustine's exegetical insight that 'the New Testament lies hidden in the Old and the Old Testament is unveiled in the New',[655] is exemplified in the Marian prophesies of the Old Testament being fulfilled in the words and deeds of the New Testament. The *Protoevangelium* finds its counterpart in the prophesy of Simeon (Lk 2:34-35):

> And Simeon blessed them and said to Mary his mother: Behold this child is set for the fall, and for the resurrection of many in Israel, and for a sign which shall be contradicted; And thy own soul a sword shall pierce, that, out of many hearts, thoughts may be revealed (Lk 2:34-35).

The Church Fathers and saints understood this prophesy as signifying God's decree that Mary would intimately cooperate in the redemptive suffering and death of her

---

[651] Second Vatican Council [1964] Dogmatic Constitution, *Lumen Gentium*, para 62. [Online] Available at: www.vatican.va [Accessed on: 28 July 2022]
[652] Gherardini, B [2002] *The Coredemption of Mary: Doctrine of the Church in Mary at the Foot of the Cross*, Vol. II. New Bedford: Franciscans of the Immaculate, p.44-45
[653] *Strong's Concordance*. [Online] Available at: biblehub.com [Accessed on: 30 July 2022]
[654] Scheeben, M [2020] *Handbook of Catholic Dogmatics*: Bk 5: Soteriology, Part 1: The Person of Christ the Redeemer. Steubenville: Emma's Academic, p. 30.
[655] *Catechism of the Catholic Church*, para 129.

Son. St. John Henry Newman described the different ways Jesus and Mary shared in his redemptive passion:

> But He, Who bore the sinner's shame for sinners, spared His Mother, who was sinless, this supreme indignity. Not in the body, but in the soul, she suffered a fellow-passion: she was crucified with Him; the spear that pierced His breast pierced through her soul.[656]

b) The Testimony of Tradition

Though the Church Fathers did not use the term Coredemptrix, they testify to Mary playing a unique role in her Son's redemption of sinful mankind. In light of the prophecy contained in the *protoevangelium*, Church Fathers emphasised her role in Christ defeating Satan — St. Ignatius of Antioch wrote, 'Now the virginity of Mary was hidden from the prince of this world, as was also her offspring, and the death of the Lord; three mysteries of renown, which were wrought in silence by God',[657] and St. Modestus of Jerusalem wrote: 'Through Mary, we "are redeemed from the tyranny of the devil"'.[658]

Other Church Fathers emphasised the redemptive significance of Mary's act of obedience at the Annunciation, exemplified by St. Irenaeus, who wrote, Mary 'by yielding obedience, became the cause of salvation, both to herself and the whole human race.'[659]

Early in the tradition, Church Fathers began to use the 'functional' titles — that Pope Francis disparages — to convey Mary's unique role in salvation history and the economy of grace. One of the most popular ones was referring to Mary as 'Mediatrix' — 'After the Mediator, you [Mary] are the Mediatrix of the whole world (St. Ephrem the Syrian);[660] 'And as you are gracious, compassionate, and tender-hearted, be ever present with me in this life as my Mediatrix and helper, to repel the assaults of my adversaries and to guide me to salvation' (St. Andrew of Crete);[661] 'For our sake she became Mediatrix of all blessings; in her God became man, and man became God' (St. John Damascene).[662]

Throughout the history of the Church, saints have also been keenly aware of Mary's unique redemptive role and have shown her due honour through bestowing on her unique titles: 'It is necessary that whosoever desires to obtain favours with God, should approach this mediatrix, approach her with a most devout heart because, since she is the Queen of Mercy' (St. Thomas Aquinas);[663] 'Mary, Germinatrix of the fruit, Mary, Redemptrix of the human race because, by providing your flesh in the Word you redeemed the world' (St. Catherine of Siena).[664]

St. John Eudes summarised Tradition's judgment concerning Mary's unique redemptive role and the expressions of the honour due her, which stands in marked contrast with Pope Francis' erroneous Mariology:

> Why did He confer upon her so much wisdom, goodness, meekness and such great power in heaven, in hell and on earth? It was simply that she might be worthy to

---

[656] Gregoris, N [2003] *The Daughter of Eve Unfallen: Mary in the Theology and Spirituality of John Henry Newman*. Mount Pocono: Newman House Press, p. 338.

[657] St. Ignatius of Antioch. *Epistle to the Ephesians*, Chap. 19. [Online] Available at: www.newadvent.org [Accessed on: 4 August 2022]

[658] Miraville, M. [2002] *Mary Coredemptrix: A Response to 7 Common Objections in Mary at the Foot of the Cross*, Vol. II. New Bedford: Franciscans of the Immaculate, p.154

[659] St. Irenaeus. *Against Heresies*, Bk 3, Chap. 22, para 4. [Online] Available at: www.newadvent.org [Accessed on: 4 August 2022]

[660] Miravalle, M [2017] *Introduction to Mary: The Heart of Marian Doctrine and Devotion*. CreateSpace Independent Publishing Platform p.104

[661] St. Andrew of Crete. *The Great Canon of Repentance*. [Online] Available at: smg.org.au [Accessed on: 4 August 2022]

[662] St. John Damascene. *A Little Treatise on Mary*. [Online] Available at: http://catholictradition.org [Accessed on: 4 August 2022]

[663] Mezard, P [1940] *Saint Thomas Aquinas Meditations, For Every Day*. Columbus. Ohio: College Book Co. p. 416

[664] *Ibid.*, p.100

cooperate with her Divine Son in man's redemption. All the Fathers of the Church say clearly that she is coredemptrix with Christ in the work of our salvation.[665]

c) The Defence by the Magisterium

Magisterial teaching until the 19th century was content to honour our Lady with the titles 'Mother of God', 'Blessed Virgin Mary' and 'immaculate.' But coinciding with the advent of the Marian Age, with its the series of exceptional Marian apparitions in Europe, papal teaching began to reflect more explicitly on Mary's cooperation with the Redemption and also introduce a rich variety of 'functional titles' under the inspiration of the Holy Spirit.

In his Apostolic Constitution *Ineffabilis Deus* (1854), Pope Bl. Pius IX — defining the dogma of the Immaculate Conception — reflected on Mary's redemptive role, writing, 'for to her more grace was given than was necessary to conquer sin completely.' Referring to the *Protoevangelium* Pope Pius IX was the first to use the title 'Reparatrix' to explain how Mary, as the New Eve, undid the sin of our First Parents. He also used the titles 'Mediatrix and Conciliatrix' to describe her cooperation with her Son in saving mankind from our sins:

> All our hope do we repose in the most Blessed Virgin — in the all fair and immaculate one who has crushed the poisonous head of the most cruel serpent and brought salvation to the world: in her who is the glory of the prophets and apostles, the honour of the martyrs, the crown and joy of all the saints; in her who is the safest refuge and the most trustworthy helper of all who are in danger; in her who, with her only-begotten Son, is the most powerful Mediatrix and Conciliatrix in the whole world.[666]

Pope Leo XIII, known as the Pope of the Rosary, wrote twelve encyclicals and five apostolic letters on the Most Holy Rosary, between 1883 and 1898.[667] One of the Marian themes that Pope Leo XIII returned to in his magisterial writings was that of Mary's role in the economy of grace, describing her as chosen by God to act as an 'intermediary' and 'minister' of her Son's mercies and graces, 'Mary is the intermediary through whom is distributed unto us this immense treasure of mercies gathered by God, for mercy and truth were created by Jesus Christ. (Jn 1:17). Thus as no man goeth to the Father but by the Son, so no man goeth to Christ but by His Mother';[668] 'obtain the favour of the great Virgin Mary, the Mother of God, the guardian of our peace and the minister [*administra*] to us of heavenly grace…'[669]

Pope Leo XIII venerated the Blessed Virgin Mary's redemptive role with a number of 'functional titles', including: '"our Lady, our Mediatrix," "the Reparatrix of the whole world," "the Dispenser of all heavenly gifts"';[670] 'She it is from whom is born Jesus; she is therefore truly His mother, and for this reason a worthy and acceptable "Mediatrix to the Mediator"'.[671]

During the pontificate of Pope St. Pius X, two Vatican dicasteries used the title 'Coredemptrix' in official documents: The Congregation for Rites (1908) issued a decree which concluded, 'Through this decree…may devotion to the merciful Coredemp-

---

[665] St. John Eudes [1947] *The Priest: His Dignity and Obligation*. New York: PJ Kennedy & Son, p. 135

[666] Pope Pius IX (1854) *Apostolic Constitution Ineffabilis Deus*. [Online] Available at: www.papalencyclicals.net [Accessed on: 10 August 2022]

[667] Thompson, T. *Rosary Encyclicals by Pope Leo XIII*. [Online] Available at: udayton.edu [Accessed on: 10 August 2022]

[668] Pope Leo XIII [1891] Encyclical *Octobri Mense Adventante*, 4. [Online] Available at: www.vatican.va [Accessed on: 10 August 2022]

[669] Pope Leo XIII [1883] Encyclical *Supremi Apostolatus Officio*, 1. [Online] Available at: www.vatican.va [Accessed on: 10 August 2022]

[670] Pope Leo XIII [1895] Encyclical *Adiutricem Populi*, 8. [Online] Available at: www.vatican.va [Accessed on: 10 August 2022]

[671] Pope Leo XIII [1896] Encyclical *Fidentem Piumque Animum* [Online] Available at: www.vatican.va [Accessed on: 10 August 2022]

trix increase';[672] The Holy Office (1914) issued an indulgenced prayer for reparation addressed to the Blessed Virgin Mary, which included, 'I praised thine exalted privilege of being truly Mother of God, Ever Virgin, conceived without stain of sin, Coredemptrix of the human race'.[673]

Though Pope St. Pius X did not use the title 'Coredemptrix' he wrote of the 'community of will and suffering between Christ and Mary' and the 'companionship in sorrow and suffering' shared between Mother and Son. The Supreme Pontiff employed a number of titles to venerate this coredemptive relationship, 'she merited to become most worthily the Reparatrix of the lost world and Dispensatrix of all the gifts that Our Saviour purchased for us by His Death and by His Blood', 'it has been allowed to the august Virgin to be the most powerful mediatrix and advocate [conciliatrix] of the whole world with her Divine Son'.[674]

Pius XI was the first pope to use the title 'Coredemptrix' in two allocutions to pilgrims (1933 & 1934) and a radio message (1935):

> By necessity, the Redeemer could not but associate his Mother in his work. For this reason we invoke her under the title of Coredemptrix. She gave us the Saviour, she accompanied Him in the work of Redemption as far as the Cross itself, sharing with Him the sorrows of the agony and of the death in which Jesus consummated the Redemption of mankind.[675]

But of all the popes, Pope St. John Paul II was the greatest advocate of venerating Mary with 'functional titles', including 'Coredemptrix':

i)   Mary 'participated in a marvellous way in the sufferings of her divine Son, in order to be Coredemptrix of humanity'.[676]
ii) 'Our Lady — the Coredemptrix…You will see him brutally crucified between thieves; you will see his holy side pierced by the cruel thrust of a lance; finally, you will see the blood that you gave him spilling. And nevertheless you will not be able to die!'[677]
iii) 'Mary's role as Coredemptrix did not cease with the glorification of her Son.'[678]
iv) 'May, Mary our Protectress, the Coredemptrix, to whom we offer our prayer with great outpouring, make our desire generously correspond to the desire of the Redeemer'.[679]
v)   [St. Bridget] 'invoked her as the Immaculate Conception, Our Lady of Sorrows, and Coredemptrix, exalting Mary's singular role in the history of salvation and the life of the Christian people'.[680]
vi) 'The hesitation of some Fathers regarding the title of Mediatrix did not prevent the Council from using this title once, and from stating in other terms Mary's mediating role from her consent to the Angel's message to her motherhood in the order of grace (cf. *Lumen Gentium* 62).'[681]

---

[672] *Acta Apostolicae Sedis*, 41 [1908] cited by Jones, J [2000] *The Assumption of the Blessed Virgin Mary in Her Role as the Coredemptrix* in *Mary at the Foot of the Cross: Acts of the International Symposium on Marian Coredemption*. New Bedford: Franciscans of the Immaculate, p.43.
[673] Holy Office [1914] Sacred Penitentiary Apostolic [1934] cited in *ibid.*, p.43
[674] Pope St. Pius X [1904] Encyclical *Ad Diem Illum Laetissimum*, 12-13. [Online] Available at: www.vatican.va [Accessed on: 10 August 2022]
[675] Schug, J & Miravalle, M [1995] *Mary, Coredemptrix: The Significance of Her Title in the Magisterium of the Church*. [Online] http://www.christendom-awake.org [Accessed on: 10 August 2022
[676] Kellehere, J [2001] Our Lady Coredemptrix, Pope John II, and the Conversion of Russia Today in *Mary at the Foot of the Cross: Acts of the International Symposium on Marian Coredemption*. New Bedford, Franciscans of the Immaculate, p.158.
[677] *Ibid.*
[678] *Ibid.*, p.159.
[679] *Ibid.*, p.160.
[680] *Ibid.*, p.160.
[681] Burton Calkins, A [1995] *Pope John Paul II's Teaching on Marian Coredemption* [Online] http://www.christendom-awake.org [Accessed on: 10 August 2022

vii) 'With regard to the objections made by some of the Council Fathers concerning the term "Mediatrix", the Council itself provided an answer by saying that Mary is "a mother to us in the order of grace" (*Lumen Gentium* 61).'[682]

By so dismissively rejecting the Marian title of Coredemptrix and other titles, and, by imposing an erroneous *sola Scriptura* Mariology, Pope Francis can be viewed as acting contrary to the promptings of the Holy Ghost indicated by the Magisterium.

---

[682] Pope St. John Paul II [1 October 1997] *General Audience Address* [Online] Available at: www. vatican.va [Accessed on: 10 August 2022]

Morality (1) — Antinomianism

L. *The Ten Commandments are not absolutes. Sometimes it is impossible to obey God's commandments. It can be wrong to strictly obey these commandments, laws and rules when the Holy Spirit is prompting an individual to risk stepping outside them.*

Pope Francis' frequent criticism of Christian morality founded on strict obedience of moral absolutes, such as those expressed by Ten Commandments, leaves him open to the accusation of promoting the grave error of Antinomianism (Gk. against the law). Such antinomianism would be consistent with Pope Francis' erroneous hamartiology derived from a type of situation ethics (*Hamartiology*, 2). The Supreme Pastor's erroneous criticisms of morality based on commandments, laws and rules is summarised as follows:

a) Our relationship to God's commandments, expressed in the Old Testament Law, has changed due to the justification achieved by Jesus, 'It will do us good to ask ourselves whether we still live in the period in which we need the Law, or if instead we are fully aware of having received the grace of becoming children of God so as to live in love.'[683]

b) 'The Lord Jesus did not come to abolish the law but to fulfil it, to develop it.' Here Pope Francis is partially referencing Matthew 5:17-18, when he writes, 'The Lord Jesus did not come to abolish the law but to fulfil it,' omitting 'For amen I say unto you, till heaven and earth pass, one jot, or one tittle shall not pass of the law, till all be fulfilled.' The Supreme Pontiff's reference to Jesus 'developing' the law is his own addition.[684]

c) Jesus 'develops' the Law from being the 'law of flesh' to the 'law of life'. By this Pope Francis means that the Law is no longer 'a series of prescriptions and prohibitions... instead because it is no longer a rule but the very flesh of Christ, who loves us, seeks us, forgives us, consoles us'.[685] The primary purpose of the commandments is now not to prescribe behaviour, but to encounter Christ, 'So what do we do with the Commandments? We must observe them, but as an aid to the encounter with Jesus Christ.'[686]

d) Consequently, we have left behind a morality made up of slavishly observing moral precepts to one characterised by freedom, 'Reborn in Christ, we have passed from a religiosity made up of precepts — we have moved on from a religiosity made up of precepts — to a living faith... We have passed from the slavery of fear and sin to the freedom of God's children. Here, again, is the word freedom.'[687]

e) Therefore, the Ten Commandments are no longer absolutes, because justification by faith in Jesus Christ is the determinant of moral life, '...do I scorn the Commandments? No. I observe them, but not as absolutes, because I know that it is Jesus Christ who justifies me.'[688]

f) This transformation of the Ten Commandments by Jesus' justification means that they are no longer exceptionless, negative moral norms: 'And thus, the literal negative, the negative expression used in the Commandments — "you shall not steal", "you shall not insult", "you shall not kill" — that "not" is transformed into a positive approach: to love, to make room in my heart for others, all desires that sow positivity. And this is the fullness of the law that Jesus came to bring us.'[689]

[683] Pope Francis [18 August 2021] *General Audience Address.* [Online] Available at: www.vatican.va [Accessed on: 12 August 2022]

[684] Pope Francis [28 November 2018] *General Audience Address.* [Online] Available at: www.vatican.va [Accessed on: 12 August 2022]

[685] *Ibid.*

[686] Pope Francis [18 August 2021] *General Audience Address.* [Online] Available at: www.vatican.va [Accessed on: 12 August 2022]

[687] Pope Francis [20th October 2021] *General Audience Address.* [Online] Available at: www.vatican.va [Accessed on: 12 August 2022]

[688] Pope Francis [18 August 2021] *General Audience Address.* [Online] Available at: www.vatican.va [Accessed on: 12 August 2022]

[689] Pope Francis [28 November 2018] *General Audience Address.* [Online] Available at: www.vatican.va [Accessed on: 12 August 2022]

g) Pope Francis selectively quoted St. Augustine to give the impression that he supports the erroneous position that God's commandments are not exceptionless absolutes. Seeking to explain that 'not everyone can do everything', Pope Francis wrote, 'They fail to realise that "not everyone can do everything",[690] and that in this life human weaknesses are not healed completely and once for all by grace. In every case, as Saint Augustine taught, "God commands you to do what you can and to ask for what you cannot" (*De Natura et Gratia*, 50)'.[691] Pope Francis omitted the key part of the quote from St. Augustine, '*God therefore does not command impossibilities; but in His command He counsels you both to do what you can for yourself, and to ask His aid in what you cannot do.*'[692] [Emphasis added].

h) Pope Francis argued that there are no absolute laws in the Church for a number of reasons: they are historically conditioned, 'The Church has rules or precepts which may have been quite effective in their time, but no longer have the same usefulness for directing and shaping people's lives',[693] 'It is not a matter of applying rules or repeating what was done in the past, since the same solutions are not valid in all circumstances and what was useful in one context may not prove so in another';[694] or because personal circumstances or understanding lead the individual to reject the 'rule' as impossible to observe or inappropriate, 'A subject may know full well the rule, yet have great difficulty in understanding "its inherent values", or be in a concrete situation which does not allow him or her to act differently and decide otherwise.'[695]

i) Pope Francis also teaches a version of Karl Rahner's erroneous Fundamental Option, when he writes that faced with the 'concrete life of a human being' it is 'reductive' to consider whether or not their actions correspond to a 'general rule or norm', 'because that is not enough to discern and ensure full fidelity to God'.[696] This 'Fundamental Option' approach is another way of erroneously seeking to relativise the absolute demands of God's commands. Pope St. John Paul II criticised the 'Fundamental Option' approach because it misleads an individual to assume that they 'remain faithful to God independently of whether or not certain of his choices and his acts are in conformity with specific moral norms or rules'.[697]

j) From this erroneous position, that morality does not consist of moral absolutes, Pope Francis castigates those who insist on living by exceptionless commandments, 'Their hearts, closed to God's truth, clutch only at the truth of the Law, taking it by "the letter". The path that Jesus teaches us [is] totally opposite to that of the doctors of law';[698] the 'self-absorbed promethean neopelagianism of those who ultimately trust only in their own powers and feel superior to others because they observe certain rules';[699] it is 'contrary to the promptings of the Spirit' to 'give excessive importance to certain rules, customs or ways of acting'.[700]

[690] *Catechism of the Catholic Church*, 1735

[691] Pope Francis [2018] Apostolic *Exhortation Gaudete et Exsultate*, 49. [Online] Available at: www.vatican.va [Accessed on: 12 August 2022]

[692] St. Augustine. *On Nature and Grace*, Chap. 50. [Online] Available at: www.newadvent.org [Accessed on: 12 August 2022]

[693] Pope Francis [2013] Apostolic *Exhortation Evangelii Gaudium*, para 43. [Online] Available at: www.vatican.va [Accessed on: 12 August 2022]

[694] Pope Francis [2018] Apostolic *Exhortation Gaudete et Exsultate*, 173. [Online] Available at: www.vatican.va [Accessed on: 12 August 2022]

[695] Pope Francis [2016] Apostolic *Exhortation Amoris Laetitia*, para 301. [Online] Available at: www.vatican.va [Accessed on: 12 August 2022]

[696] *Ibid.*, para 304.

[697] Pope St. John Paul II [1993] Encyclical *Veritatis Splendor*, para 68.[Online] Available at: www.vatican.va [Accessed on: 12 August 2022]

[698] Echeverria, E [2015] *Is the Gospel Opposed to the Law?* [Online] Available at: www.thecatholicthing.org [Accessed on: 12 August 2022]

[699] Pope Francis [2013] Apostolic *Exhortation Evangelii Gaudium*, para 94. [Online] Available at: www.vatican.va [Accessed on: 12 August 2022]

[700] Pope Francis [2018] Apostolic Exhortation *Gaudete et Exsultate*, 58. [Online] Available at: www.vatican.va [Accessed on: 12 August 2022]

It is a further example of Pope Francis setting up a false proposition and ascribing it to others who he then denounces, in this case the assertion that God's truth is not the truth of the law. It is also aligned to the error of Antinomianism which has bedevilled Protestantism since the beginning because it is a corollary of its fundamental error — *justificatio sola fide* [justification by faith alone] and its corresponding antipathy towards any acts of the individual having a salvific significance.

A characteristic of Antinomianism is the misrepresentation of St. Paul's theology of the Law and grace. Pope Francis selectively quotes from St. Paul to support the error that God's commandments are no longer exceptionless absolutes. For example, to support his erroneous argument that obedience to 'a series of prescriptions and prohibitions' is no longer required, he references Ephesians 2:15, 'Making void the law of commandments contained in decrees; that he might make the two in himself into one new man, making peace'. St. Paul was writing about one specific law — the law of circumcision as no longer required for membership of the people of God — and not the exceptionless, negative moral norms of the Ten Commandments, as Pope Francis concludes.

St. Paul did view salvation history as divided into two periods regarding divine Law — the old dispensation when the Law served as a teacher and tutor (Gal 3:23f; 4:1ff) and the new dispensation when the Law is interiorised and fulfilled by Jesus' commandment of love (Rom 13:8; Gal 6:2).[701] But nowhere did St. Paul teach that God's Commandments were no longer 'absolutes'. It appears that Pope Francis erroneously extends the relativisation of Israel's juridical and ritual regulations by justification in Jesus Christ to all commandments, including the Ten Commandments. This is contrary to St. Paul's understanding of the Law, who taught that observance of God's commands is absolutely necessary for 'carnal man', 'Because the wisdom of the flesh is an enemy to God; for it is not subject to the law of God, neither can it be. And they who are in the flesh, cannot please God.' (Rom 8:7-8).

The Teaching of the Church
***God gives all the just sufficient grace* (gratia proxime vel remote sufficiens)** *for the* ***observation of the Divine Commandments.* (De Fide)**[702]
The heresy of Antinomianism has appeared during various periods of the Church's history, especially among those who claimed special illumination by the Holy Spirit. As Fr. Gerald O'Collins SJ commented, Antinomianism is to be found among those who claim 'a special guidance of the Holy Spirit that delivers them from ordinary moral obligations'.[703]

In the 14th century, the Council of Vienne condemned an antinomian error promulgated by the lay movement known as the Beguines and Beghards. The Council Fathers condemned the following:

> Thirdly, that those who have reached the said degree of perfection and spirit of liberty, are not subject to human obedience nor obliged to any commandments of the Church, for, as they say, where the spirit of the Lord is, there is freedom.[704]

This claim to a freedom from the commandments of the Church inspired by the Holy Spirit can be found in the writing of Pope Francis. He has condemned those Christians who act 'contrary to the promptings of the Spirit' by 'giving excessive importance to certain rules, customs or ways of acting'. Elsewhere, he condemned 'Those measured Christians who never step outside the rules, never, because they are afraid of risk.'[705]

[701] Léon-Dufour, X [1988] *Dictionary of Biblical Theology*. Maryland: The Word Among Us Press, p. 306-307.
[702] Ott, L [1957] *Op. cit.*, p.240
[703] O'Collins, G & Farrugia, E [2000] *A Concise Dictionary of Theology*. Edinburgh: T&T Clark, p.13.
[704] Council of Vienne 1311-1312 A.D [Online] Available at: www.papalencyclicals.net [Accessed on: 13 August 2022]
[705] Pope Francis [2020] *Homily for World Day of the Poor*. [Online] Available at: www.vatican.va [Accessed on: 13 August 2022]

The Supreme Pontiff also talked of a freedom granted by being 'reborn in Christ' that gives Christians a 'freedom' that enables them to move 'on from a religiosity made up of precepts to a living faith, which has its centre in communion with God and with our brothers and sisters, that is, in love.'[706]

The Council of Trent addressed the Protestant version of Antinomianism in its *Decree on Justification* (1547). Quoting St. Augustine's 'God therefore does not command impossibilities', the Council of Trent emphasised the clause omitted by Pope Francis:

> But no one, however much justified, should consider himself exempt from the observance of the commandments; no one should use that rash statement, once forbidden by the Fathers under anathema, that the observance of the commandments of God is impossible for one that is justified. For God does not command impossibilities, but by commanding admonishes thee to do what thou canst and to pray for what thou canst not, and aids thee that thou mayest be able (St. Augustine). His commandments are not heavy (I Jn 5:3), and his yoke is sweet and burden light (Mt 11:30). For they who are the sons of God love Christ, but they who love Him, keep His commandments, as He Himself testifies (Jn 14:23); which, indeed, with the divine help they can do.[707]

To avoid any taint of Pelagianism, the Council Fathers declared that God's commandments are not impossible because God aids and assists the just in obeying them, 'For God does not forsake those who have been once justified by His grace, unless He be first forsaken by them.'

The Council of Trent also anathematised those who contend that there are circumstances in which it is impossible to obey God's commandments (Canon 18) or that an individual can attain such a degree of freedom that God's commandments no longer apply (Canon 20). The Council Fathers also condemned those who emphasised Jesus as saviour to the point of excluding his role as legislator, 'If anyone says that Christ Jesus was given by God to men as a redeemer in whom to trust, and not also as a legislator whom to obey, let him be anathema' (Canon 21).

Proof from the Sources of Faith
a) Teaching from Holy Scripture
Sacred Scripture makes it clear that God's commandments and God's covenants are inextricably linked together. The Ten Commandments [the Decalogue] were understood in the Old Testament as the 'charter of the Covenant' (Fr. Albert Gelin), to the extent that the terms 'covenant' and 'commandment' are interchangeable, 'And he shewed you his covenant, which he commanded you to do, and the ten words that he wrote in two tables of stone' (Deut 4:13).

The purpose of Law as the revealed will of God was to enable Israel to obey and imitate God's moral nature. The LORD expected Israel to adopt His ways and model her behaviour on the divine attributes of justice [*sedeq*], kindness [*hesed*] and faithfulness [*emet*]. The Commandments are the way of imitating the life and truth of God. Just as goodness and truth are eternal attributes of God, his Commandments are intended by him as exceptionless absolutes.

Obedience to the Commandments is so essential to the covenantal relationship with God that it was expressed in the quintessential prayer of the Old Testament, the *Shema Yisrael*, 'And these words which I command thee this day, shall be in thy heart: And thou shalt tell them to thy children, and thou shalt meditate upon them sitting in thy house, and walking on thy journey, sleeping and rising' (Deut 6:4-9.)

As obedience to the Commandments is so intrinsic to man's relationship with God, it should come as no surprise that the Old Testament also expresses the truth that 'God therefore does not command impossibilities':

---

[706] Pope Francis [20th October 2021] *General Audience Address.* [Online] Available at: www.vatican.va [Accessed on: 12 August 2022]

[707] Council of Trent [1547] *Decree Concerning Justification*, Chap. 11. [Online] Available at: www.ewtn.com [Accessed on: 13 August 2022]

> This commandment, that I command thee this day is not above thee, nor far off from thee: Nor is it in heaven, that thou shouldst say: Which of us can go up to heaven to bring it unto us, and we may hear and fulfil it in work? Nor is it beyond the sea: that thou mayst excuse thyself, and say: Which of us can cross the sea, and bring it unto us: that we may hear, and do that which is commanded? But the word is very nigh unto thee, in thy mouth and in thy heart, that thou mayst do it (Deut 30:11-14).

Pope Francis' erroneous contention that there are circumstances when it is not a mortal sin to disobey the commandments is totally alien to the Old Testament, 'He hath commanded no man to do wickedly, and he hath given no man license to sin: For he desireth not a multitude of faithless and unprofitable children' (Sir 15:21-22).

Pope Francis speaks as if the Law came to an end with Jesus and was replaced by grace and the Holy Spirit. But as St. Ambrose observed when commenting on St. Paul, 'For the end of the law is Christ' (Rom 10:4), Jesus is the 'end not in the sense of a deficiency, but in the sense of the fullness of the Law: a fullness which is achieved in Christ since he came not to abolish the Law but to bring it to fulfilment.' Jesus is the living, personal and perfect expression of the Law who we are called to imitate.[708] The New Testament reveals our Lord Jesus Christ as the embodiment of the Law, understood as the will of God, 'I am the way, and the truth, and the life. No man cometh to the Father, but by me' (Jn 14:6).

Jesus understands Himself as the only authentic interpreter of the God's Commandments (Mt 5:20-48). Consequently, our Lord rejects the 'precepts of men' (Mk 7:7) that adopted a legalistic and minimalist — 'what can we get away with' — approach to morality. Jesus establishes the permanent value of the Ten Commandments, while at the same time going beyond mere external observance to interior disposition:

> Do not think that I am come to destroy the law, or the prophets. I am not come to destroy, but to fulfil. For amen I say unto you, till heaven and earth pass, one jot, or one tittle shall not pass of the law, till all be fulfilled (Mt 5:17-18).

Our Lord taught that obedience to the Commandments was essential to any authentic relationship with him: 'But if thou wilt enter into life, keep the commandments' (Mt 19:17); 'If you love me, keep my commandments' (Jn 14:15); 'If you keep my commandments, you shall abide in my love' (Jn 15:10).

The New Testament also teaches that 'God therefore does not command impossibilities': 'Take up my yoke upon you, and learn of me, because I am meek, and humble of heart: and you shall find rest to your souls. For my yoke is sweet and my burden light' (Mt 11:29-30); 'For this is the charity of God, that we keep his commandments: and his commandments are not heavy' (I Jn 5:3).

b) The Testimony of Tradition
Faced with the antinomianism of the Gnostic heretics, such as the Manichaeans, who claimed special enlightenment that freed them from conventional moral norms, a number of Church Fathers testified to the importance of obedience to the Commandments to the Christian life. St. Cyprian of Carthage exhorted Christians to observe the Commandments to protect them from the 'spirit of error' that threatens their salvation:

> But how can a man say that he believes in Christ, who does not do what Christ commanded him to do? Or whence shall he attain to the reward of faith, who will not keep the faith of the commandment? He must of necessity waver and wander, and, caught away by a spirit of error, like dust which is shaken by the wind, be blown about; and he will make no advance in his walk towards salvation, because he does not keep the truth of the way of salvation.[709]

---

[708] Pope St. John Paul II [1993] Encyclical *Veritatis Splendor,* para 15. [Online] Available at: www.vatican.va [Accessed on: 16 August 2022]

[709] St. Cyprian of Carthage. *Treatise* 1, On the Unity of the Church, para 2. [Online] Available at: www.newadvent.org [Accessed on: 16 August 2022]

St. Cyprian criticised those who claimed to be Christian but did not want to 'observe the divine and heavenly commands' as being rebels who 'wish to confess Christ, and to deny Christ's Gospel'.[710] Likewise, St. Jerome rebuked those who called themselves Christians while not obeying the commandments, calling such an attitude sinful, 'In vain do we make our boast in him whose commandments we keep not. To him that knows what is good, and does it not, it is sin.'[711]

St. Augustine explained that the Commandments are not impossible because God gives his help and aid, 'I cannot doubt that God has laid no impossible command on man; and that, by God's aid and help, nothing is impossible, by which is wrought what He commands. In this way may a man, if he pleases, be without sin by the assistance of God.'[712] Elsewhere, St. Augustine stated regarding the help God gives to the just to help them keep the Commandments, 'God does not abandon the just unless they first abandon him.'[713]

St. Thomas Aquinas concluded that human goodness depended on obedience to God's Law, especially when human reason fails, because it gives us access to God's eternal Reason, 'It is therefore evident that the goodness of the human will depends on the eternal law much more than on human reason: and when human reason fails we must have recourse to the Eternal Reason'.[714] Therefore, the scenario proposed by Pope Francis that a person can know God's commandments and decide in their circumstances that they don't apply is absurd because it sets fallible human reason against the infallibility of God's Eternal Reason.

c) The Defence by the Magisterium

Following the Council of Trent upholding the truth against Protestant antinomianism — that God does not command the impossible — popes of the 18th and 19th centuries defended the Commandments from the errors of Jansenism. Bishop Cornelius Jansen's erroneous contention about the depravity of human nature and enslavement to concupiscence led to him arguing that it was impossible to obey the Commandments.[715] Pope Innocent X condemned Cornelius Jansen's error which stated that, 'Some of God's commandments cannot be observed by just men with the strength they have in the present state, even if they wish and strive to observe them; nor do they have the grace that would make their observance possible'.[716] Pope Clement XI also condemned the errors of the Jansenist Pasquier Quesnel (reminiscent of the error contained in Pope Francis' *Amoris Laetitia*, 301) which stated, 'For the preservation of himself man can dispense himself from the law which God established for his use.'[717]

In response to the spread of secularism and the corresponding decline in public morality, a succession of popes since the 19th century have defended the importance of divine Commandments and precepts as the foundation to morality. Pope Bl. Pius IX exhorted his fellow bishops to daily teach the faithful 'the most holy precepts of the Christian law'[718] so that they would turn from evil to good, 'Thus moral decency,

---

[710] St. Cyprian of Carthage. *Epistle* 24, To Moyses and Maximus and the Rest of the Confessors, para 2. [Online] Available at: www.newadvent.org [Accessed on: 16 August 2022]

[711] St. Jerome. *Against Jovinianus*, Book II, Chap. 2. [Online] Available at: www.newadvent.org [Accessed on: 16 August 2022]

[712] St. Augustine. *On Merit and the Forgiveness of Sins, and the Baptism of Infants*. Book II, Chap. 7. [Online] Available at: www.newadvent.org [Accessed on: 16 August 2022]

[713] St. Augustine. *On Nature and Grace*, Chap. 29. [Online] Available at: www.newadvent.org [Accessed on: 16 August 2022]

[714] St. Thomas Aquinas. *Summa Theologiae*. Ia-IIae, q. 19, a.4 [Online] Available at: www.newadvent.org [Accessed on: 16 August 2022]

[715] Catholic Encyclopedia [1919] *Jansenius and Jansenism* [Online] Available at: www.newadvent.org [Accessed on: 17 August 2022]

[716] Denzinger, H [2010] *Op. cit.*, p.455-456, *Dz* 2001

[717] Denzinger, H [2010] *Op. cit.*, p.503, *Dz* 2471

[718] Pope Bl. Pius IX [1846] Encyclical *Qui Pluribus*, para 21 [Online] Available at: www.papalencyclicals.net [Accessed on: 17 August 2022]

integrity of life and virtue, religion, and piety will grow each day, flourishing and dominating in the souls of all'.[719]

Pope Leo XIII, the father of the 19th century Thomist revival, taught the Angelic Doctor's insight into the indispensability of God's Law — natural and apodictic — because it gives man access to Eternal Reason:

> It follows, therefore, that the law of nature is the same thing as the eternal law, implanted in rational creatures, and inclining them to their right action and end; and can be nothing else but the eternal reason of God, the Creator and Ruler of all the world. To this rule of action and restraint of evil God has vouchsafed to give special and most suitable aids for strengthening and ordering the human will.[720]

Pope St. Pius X also taught that natural law and apodictic law are one and the same, and as such are not impossible to obey, 'without doubt we are able to observe God's Commandments, because God never commands anything that is impossible, and because He gives grace to observe them to those who ask it as they should'.[721] Quoting St. Anselm, Pope Pius X warned that disobedience to the commandments overthrows faith and reason.[722]

Pope Pius XI emphasised a truth defined at the Council of Trent, that it is a dogma of faith that our Lord is the supreme law-giver as well as Redeemer, 'it is a dogma of faith that Jesus Christ was given to man, not only as our Redeemer, but also as a law-giver, to whom obedience is due…all must obey his commands; none may escape them, nor the sanctions he has imposed'.[723] Pope Pius XI also insisted that on the exceptionless, absolute nature of the Commandments in the face of the moral anarchy unleashed by National Socialism:

> This God, this Sovereign Master, has issued commandments whose value is independent of time and space, country and race. As God's sun shines on every human face so His law knows neither privilege nor exception. Rulers and subjects, crowned and uncrowned, rich and poor are equally subject to His word. From the fullness of the Creators' right there naturally arises the fullness of His right to be obeyed by individuals and communities, whoever they are. This obedience permeates all branches of activity in which moral values claim harmony with the law of God, and pervades all integration of the ever-changing laws of man into the immutable laws of God.[724]

Pope Pius XI exhorted bishops to fulfil their sacred obligation to do everything in their power 'to enforce respect for, and obedience to, the commandments of God, as these are the necessary foundation of all private life and public morality'.[725] Furthermore, he argued that to give priority to subjective opinion over God's commandments was destructive of the individual and society, 'To hand over the moral law to man's subjective opinion, which changes with the times, instead of anchoring it in the holy will of the eternal God and His commandments, is to open wide every door to the forces of destruction.'[726]

In his famous address to the Italian Association of Catholic Midwives Pope Pius XII defended the Council of Trent's declaration that God does not command what is

---

[719] Pope Bl. Pius IX [1854] Encyclical *Neminem Vestrum*, para 7. [Online] Available at: www.papalencyclicals.net [Accessed on: 17 August 2022]

[720] Pope Leo XIII [1888] Encyclical *Libertas*, para 8. [Online] Available at: www.vatican.va [Accessed on: 16 August 2022]

[721] Pope St. Pius X [1908] *Catechism*, On the Commandments of God and of the Church. [Online] Available at: www.ewtn.com [Accessed on: 17 August 2022]

[722] Pope St. Pius X [1909] Encyclical *Communium Rerum*, para 56. [Online] Available at: www.vatican.va [Accessed on: 17 August 2022]

[723] Pope Pius XI [1925] Encyclical *Quas Primas*, para 14. [Online] Available at: www.vatican.va [Accessed on: 16 August 2022]

[724] Pope Pius XI [1937] Encyclical *Mit Brennender Sorge*, para 10. [Online] Available at: www.vatican.va [Accessed on: 16 August 2022]

[725] *Ibid.*, para 12.

[726] *Ibid.*, para 29.

impossible. He described the living out of this divine truth in terms of Christian heroism, 'To judge men and women of today incapable of continuous heroism is to do them
wrong'. Pope Pius XII has a moral realism one does not find in the teaching of Pope
Francis. He instead states that reliance on God provides you with the ability to obey
God's commandments, it is when you rely on yourself that you cannot do this:

> It is obvious that he who does not want to master himself, will not be able to do so;
> and he who thinks he can master himself, relying solely on his own powers and not
> sincerely and perseveringly seeking divine aid, will be miserably deceived.[727]

In his condemnation of the errors of Situation Ethics, Pope Pius XII defended the
universality and absoluteness of natural and apodictic divine law by arguing that the
'fundamental obligations of the moral law are based on the essence and the nature of
man, and on his essential relationships, and thus they have force wherever we find
man…No matter what the situation of the individual may be, there is no other course
open to him but to obey'.[728]

Pope St. John Paul II and Pope Benedict XVI defended morality founded on natural
and apodictic divine law against the tsunami of immorality unleashed by the so-called
Sexual Revolution of the 1960's. The encyclical *Veritatis Splendor* — the greatest defence
of Bible-based morality in modern times — was the work of both Pope John Paul II and
Cardinal Ratzinger, as prefect of the CDF.[729] It categorically rejects the moral 'creativity'
that Pope Francis would later promulgate:

> The negative moral precepts, those prohibiting certain concrete actions or kinds of
> behaviour as intrinsically evil, do not allow for any legitimate exception. They do
> not leave room, in any morally acceptable way, for the 'creativity' of any contrary
> determination whatsoever. Once the moral species of an action prohibited by a universal
> rule is concretely recognized, the only morally good act is that of obeying the moral law
> and of refraining from the action which it forbids.[730]

During his pilgrimage to Mount Sinai in 2000 Pope John Paul II defended the truth
that 'The Ten Commandments are not an arbitrary imposition of a tyrannical Lord' but
universal moral law written on the human heart 'valid in every time and place'.[731]

Pope Benedict XVI also addressed those who proposed a selective obedience to the
Ten Commandments or who questioned the possibility of obeying them, 'To break one
commandment, therefore, is to violate the entire law […] Christ without whom we can
do nothing enables us to keep it [Decalogue] with the gift of his Spirit and his grace.'[732]

To conclude, Pope Francis' antagonism towards the Law and precepts of the Church
as the foundation of moral life, reveals an antinomian approach to morality which is
totally contrary to sacred Scripture, Holy Tradition, and the Magisterium.

---

[727] Pope Pius XII [1951] *Vegliare con Sollecitudine — Address to the Italian Association of Catholic
Midwives.* [Online] Available at: rorate-caeli.blogspot.com [Accessed on: 17 August 2022]
[728] Pope Pius XII [1952] *Soyez les bienvenues — Discourse to the World Federation of Catholic Young
Women,* para 9-10. [Online] Available at: www.catholicculture.org [Accessed on: 17 August 2022]
[729] Russell Hittinger, F [27 Sept 2014] *Natural Law and Public Discourse: The Legacies of Joseph
Ratzinger* [Online] Available at: law.loyno.edu [Accessed on: 17 August 2022]
[730] Pope St. John Paul II [1993] Encyclical *Veritatis Splendor,* para 67. [Online] Available at: www.
vatican.va [Accessed on: 18 August 2022]
[731] Pope St. John Paul II [2000] *Homily at Celebration of the Word at Mount Sinai,* para 3. [Online]
Available at: www.vatican.va [Accessed on: 18 August 2022]
[732] Pope Benedict XVI [2005] *Compendium of the Catechism of the Catholic Church.* [Online] Available
at: www.vatican.va [Accessed on: 18 August 2022]

Morality (2) — Death Penalty

M. *The death penalty is a sin and is always inadmissible because it is an offence against the inviolability of life and the dignity of the person. Criminals have an inviolable, God-given right to life and not even a murderer loses this personal dignity. The death penalty is contrary to the Gospel because human life never ceases to be sacred in the eyes of its Creator, who is the only true judge.*

From the early days of his pontificate Pope Francis campaigned for the abolition of the death penalty, repeating the false claim a number of times that capital punishment 'contradicts God's plan for man and for society and his merciful justice'.[733] (cf. Video Message to the 6th World Congress Against the Death Penalty, 21st-23rd June 2016). Developing this theme of the death penalty contradicting God's will, Pope Francis stated that it is

> …contrary to the Gospel because it entails the wilful suppression of a human life that never ceases to be sacred in the eyes of its Creator and of which – ultimately – only God is the true judge and guarantor.[734]

In total contradiction of Sacred Scripture and Sacred Tradition the Supreme Pontiff even went so far as to condemn the death penalty as a 'sin':

> Let us get to specifics. Today it is a sin to possess atomic bombs; the death penalty is a sin. You cannot employ it.…[735]

In 2018 the Congregation for the Doctrine of the Faith issued a revision of paragraph 2267 of the *Catechism of the Catholic Church* on the death penalty expressing Pope Francis' erroneous teaching:

> Consequently, the Church teaches, in the light of the Gospel, that 'the death penalty is inadmissible because it is an attack on the inviolability and dignity of the person'.[736]

Subsequently, Pope Francis employed the phrase 'in the light of the Gospel' to falsely claim that the death penalty is contrary to sacred Scripture. His *eisegesis* of Scripture includes the erroneous teaching that the Fifth Commandment — Thou shalt not kill — applies to 'both the innocent and the guilty'.[737] He also reverses the meaning of Genesis 9:5-6, that mandates the death penalty for murder, to falsely teach that it prohibits the death penalty for murder:

> Let us keep in mind that 'not even a murderer loses his personal dignity, and God himself pledges to guarantee this'.… I ask Christians who remain hesitant on this point, and those tempted to yield to violence in any form, to keep in mind the words of the book of Isaiah: 'They shall beat their swords into plowshares' (2:4). For us, this prophecy took flesh in Christ Jesus who, seeing a disciple tempted to violence, said firmly: 'Put your sword back into its place; for all who take the sword will perish by the sword' (Mt 26:52). These words echoed the ancient warning: 'I will require a reckoning for human life. Whoever sheds the blood of a man, by man shall his blood be shed' (Gen 9:5-6). Jesus' reaction, which sprang from his heart, bridges the gap of the centuries and reaches the present as an enduring appeal.[738]

[733] Pope Francis [2015] *Letter to the President of the International Commission against the Death Penalty* [Online] Available at: www.vatican.va [Accessed on: 21 May 2024]

[734] Pope Francis [2017] *Address to Participants in the Meeting Promoted by the Pontifical Council for Promoting the New Evangelisation* [Online] Available at: www.vatican.va [Accessed on: 21 May 2024]

[735] Spadaro, A [2023] 'The Water Has Been Agitated' [Online] Available at: www.laciviltacattolica.com [Accessed on: 21 May 2024]

[736] *Congregation for the Doctrine of the Faith* [2018] New revision of number 2267 of the *Catechism of the Catholic Church* on the death penalty – *Rescriptum 'ex Audentia SS.mi'* [Online] www.press.vatican.va [Accessed on: 16 May 2024]

[737] Pope Francis [2022] *For the abolition of the death penalty* — September 2022 [Available at: www.youtube.com [Accessed on: 21 May 2024]

[738] Pope Francis [2017] *Encyclical Fratelli Tutti*, paras 263, 265-270 [Online] Available at: www.vatican.va [Accessed on: 21 May 2024]

Pope Francis even went so far as to imply that previous popes had been immoral to implement the death penalty for crimes in the papal states, accusing them of being unchristian:

> Sadly, even in the Papal States recourse was had to this extreme and inhumane remedy that ignored the primacy of mercy over justice. Let us take responsibility for the past and recognise that the imposition of the death penalty was dictated by a mentality more legalistic than Christian. Concern for preserving power and material wealth led to an over-estimation of the value of the law and prevented a deeper understanding of the Gospel. Nowadays, however, were we to remain neutral before the new demands of upholding personal dignity, we would be even more guilty.[739]

Pope Francis made the unsustainable claim that his prohibition of the death penalty, based on the false premise that it contradicts divine revelation, is 'not in any way contradicting past teaching'.[740] He attempted to justify his claim to continuity with magisterial teaching by selectively quoting from St. Vincent of Lérins:

> Some may say: Shall there be no progress of religion in Christ's Church? Certainly; all possible progress. For who is there, so envious of men, so full of hatred to God, who would seek to forbid it?' (*Commonitorium*, 23.1; PL 50).[741]

However, Pope Francis' absolute, unequivocal reversal of the Church's doctrine on the death penalty is not, according to St. Vincent of Lérins, a valid development because he changes and distorts sacred doctrine:

> Therefore, whatever has been sown by the fidelity of the Fathers in this husbandry of God's Church, the same ought to be cultivated and taken care of by the industry of their children, the same ought to flourish and ripen, the same ought to advance and go forward to perfection. For it is right that those ancient doctrines of heavenly philosophy should, as time goes on, be cared for, smoothed, polished; but not that they should be changed, not that they should be maimed, not that they should be mutilated. They may receive proof, illustration, definiteness; but they must retain withal their completeness, their integrity, their characteristic properties.[742]

Pope Francis' erroneous teaching on the death penalty is the latest iteration of Cardinal Joseph Bernardin of Chicago's (1928-1996) 'Seamless Garment' doctrine that seeks to foster the false presupposition that to be pro-life Catholics must equally oppose abortion and the death penalty. The Seamless Garment doctrine proposes a false equivalence between the innocent lives of the pre-born babies and the guilty lives of murderers. By misusing the doctrine of the sanctity of life, Cardinal Bernardin said:

> While the state has the obligation to defend its people against attacks on their lives … we believe the exercise of the right to capital punishment does not foster the kind of reverence for life that is needed to deal creatively and effectively with the whole range of life questions we face in our society today.[743]

The problem with Cardinal Bernardin's and Pope Francis' so called consistent-life-ethic is that they cannot claim that their ethical systems uphold Catholic doctrine as they contradict divine revelation concerning the morality of the death penalty.

The Teaching of the Church
In the state of fallen nature it is morally impossible for man without Supernatural

---

[739] Pope Francis [2017] *op. cit.*

[740] *Ibid.*

[741] *Ibid.*

[742] St. Vincent of Lérins. *Commonitory*, Chap. 23, para 57 [Available at: www.newadvent.org] [Accessed on: 29 May 2024]

[743] Millies, S [2019] *Cardinal Joseph L. Bernardin's consistent ethic of life* [Available at: www. catholicsun.org] [Accessed on: 29 May 2024]

Revelation, to know easily, with absolute certainty and without admixture of error, all religious and moral truths of the natural order. **(De Fide)**[744]

According to Fr. Ludwig Ott the reason why it is impossible for man to achieve perfect knowledge of the natural moral law without supernatural Revelation is due to the 'wound of ignorance' (*vulnus ignorantiae*) 'caused by the Fall, that is in the weakening of man's power of cognition'.[745]

The First and Second Vatican Councils state that divine revelation transmitted by sacred Scripture and sacred Tradition is necessary for man to know moral truths. These moral truths, such as the permissibility of the death penalty for murder, can be known by human reason, but as Ott re-iterates man's power of knowing moral truths has been weakened by original sin. Therefore, God has revealed his will through revelation so that man may know the moral truths 'with facility, with firm certitude, and with no admixture of error';[746] 'with ease, with solid certitude and with no trace of error, even in this present state of the human race.'[747]

In particular, the Second Vatican Council emphasised that sacred Scripture and sacred Tradition are 'the supreme rule of faith' by which man measures Truth, including moral truth, because they 'inspired by God and committed once and for all to writing'. (*Dei Verbum* 21).

However, Pope Francis' iteration of Cardinal Bernardin's inherently flawed Seamless Garment doctrine cannot be relied upon to lead one to the truth about the morality of the death penalty due to his eisegesis of sacred Scripture and his distortion of sacred Tradition. If accepted, Pope Francis' false doctrine on the death penalty can only lead to confusion, doubt and error.

Proof from the Sources of Faith
a) Teaching from Holy Scripture
The Old Testament contains divine revelation that makes clear that God imposes vindicative, retributive punishment (*poenae vindicativae*) on sinful human beings that expiates for the offences that outrage his holiness and sovereignty as Creator and Lord (Gen 6:5-7; cf. 19:20, 24-25). Contrary to Pope Francis' claim that the death penalty is contrary to God's mercy,[748] the Bible reveals God does not show mercy to unrepentant, habitual sinners, but instead imposes vindicative, retributive punishment, including the destruction of physical life:

> And God seeing that the wickedness of men was great on the earth, and that all the thought of their heart was bent upon evil at all times [....] He said: I will destroy man, whom I have created, from the face of the earth (Gen 6:5-7); And the Lord said: The cry of Sodom and Gomorrha is multiplied, and their sin is become exceedingly grievous [....] And the Lord rained upon Sodom and Gomorrha brimstone and fire from the Lord out of heaven. And he destroyed these cities, and all the country about, all the inhabitants of the cities, and all things that spring from the earth. (Gen 19: 20, 24-25)

God insistently commands that vindicative, retributive punishment is imposed by Israel on those who transgress his commands regarding the moral and ecclesial life (e.g. Ex 21:12; 14-17; Dt 17: 2-7; 21:18-23; Lev 20: 7-16, 26; 24:11-17). The detailed

---

[744] Ott, L [1957] *op. cit.*, p. 235.
[745] *Ibid.*
[746] Denzinger, H [2010] *op. cit.*, p. 602 3005
[747] Second Vatican Council [1965] Dogmatic Constitution, *Dei Verbum*, Chap. 1, para 6 [Available at: www.vatican.va [Accessed on: 29 May 2024]
[748] Pope Francis [2015] *Letter to the President of the International Commission against the Death Penalty*; [2017] *Address to Participants in the Meeting Promoted by the Pontifical Council for Promoting the New Evangelisation*; [2018] *Letter to the Bishops regarding the new revision of number 2267 of the Catechism of the Catholic Church on the death penalty*; [2018] *Audience with the Delegation of the International Commission against the Death Penalty* [Online] Available at: www.press.vatican.va [Accessed on: 21 May 2024]

series of commands stipulating the imposition of the death penalty arise from Israel's vocation to be a holy, priestly people (Ex 19:6) so as to participate in the holiness and goodness of God. Those who transgress God's commandments not only repudiate their God-given vocation to be a holy, priestly people, but also rebel against God's holiness and sovereignty. The Old Testament imposes the death penalty on those who transgress God's commandments — blasphemers (Lev 24:11-17), idolators (Dt 17: 2-7), disobedient (Ex 21:15,17; Dt 21:18-23; Lev 20:9), adulterers (Lev 20:10), sodomites (Lev 20:13) murderers (Gen 9:6; Ex 21:12) — because by their sins they offend God's holiness and sovereignty and harm the community called to be a holy, priestly people.

The Old Testament discloses that God considers murder to be a particularly heinous crime, because it is the most extreme expression of the sinner's rebellion against God:

> Whosoever shall shed man's blood, his blood shall be shed: for man was made to the image of God. (Gen 9:6)

Murder is condemned in the context of man created in the image and likeness of God (Gen 1:27). As the image [*Tselem*] of God, Adam is the created, material representative of God in creation imaging divine paternity through procreation and imaging divine lordship through dominion over creation (Gen 1:28). Murder not only destroys the physical man, but rebelliously attacks the creaturely imaging of God's sovereignty. Contrary to Pope Francis' eisegesis which bizarrely implies God condemns the bloodshed of capital punishment[749] — Genesis 9:6 demands the death penalty for murderers because according to God's command they have forfeited the right to life. As Pope Pius XII expressed it, 'by his crime, he has already disposed himself of his right to live.'[750]

The New Testament shows that our Lord Jesus Christ accepted God's commandments regarding the death penalty as a matter of course (Mt 15:3-4), while also challenging its imposition in particular circumstances, such as the stoning of the unnamed adulterous woman (Jn 8:1-11). Our Lord definitely did not reject the death penalty as sinful and inadmissible, as Pope Francis argues, seeing it as a legitimate power of rightful authority:

> But when the king had heard of it, he was angry, and sending his armies, he destroyed those murderers, and burnt their city. (Mt 22:7); But as for those my enemies, who would not have me reign over them, bring them hither, and kill them before me. (Lk 19:27)

Our Lord Jesus Christ also taught that God will impose vindicative, retributive punishment on unrepentant sinners at the eschatological judgement (Mt 25:41; Mk 9:48; Jn 3:36). St. John described this in terms of the imposition of the death penalty:

> But the fearful, and unbelieving, and the abominable, and murderers, and whoremongers, and sorcerers, and idolaters, and all liars, they shall have their portion in the pool burning with fire and brimstone, which is the second death. (Rev 21:8).

Our Lord accepted that Pilate had the authority to exercise the power of capital punishment, explaining that it was an authority given him by God, His Father (Jn 19:10-11). The Greek word for authority, *exousia*, has the sense of delegated authority and the power of judicial decision.[751] This delegated power of vindicative, retributive punishment could be cruelly misused — as it was in the case of the crucifixion of our Lord even though it was proven that he was innocent of any crime — but this misuse doesn't negate the fact that God delegates capital punishment to legitimate authority.

This understanding of God delegating vindicative, retributive punishment to legitimate authority was expressed by St. Paul in Romans 13:3-5, which became foundational to magisterial teaching on the death penalty:

---

[749] Pope Francis [2017] Encyclical *Fratelli Tutti*, para 270 [Online] Available at: www.vatican.va [Accessed on: 21 May 2024]

[750] Guernsey, A [2017] *Addresses of Pius XII on the Law, Purposes of Punishment, and the Death Penalty* [Available at: www.aguernz.medium.com [Accessed on: 28 May 2024]

[751] *Strong's Concordance* [Available at: www.biblehub.com] [Accessed on: 30 May 2024]

For princes are not a terror to the good work, but to the evil. Wilt thou then not be afraid of the power? Do that which is good: and thou shalt have praise from the same. For he is God's minister to thee, for good. But if thou do that which is evil, fear: for he beareth not the sword in vain. For he is God's minister: an avenger to execute wrath upon him that doth evil. Wherefore be subject of necessity, not only for wrath, but also for conscience' sake.

The Greek word for sword used by St. Paul, *Machaira*, apart from being the name of a short sword, symbolised the power of a judge over life and death. St. Paul explains that this judicial power is a delegated power from God to execute his wrath upon those that do evil. Pope Francis is mistaken when he seeks to invalidate this God-given civil power by emphasising its misuse by totalitarian and dictatorial regimes or through 'extrajudicial or extralegal executions'.[752]

b) The Testimony of Tradition
The Church Fathers recognised that our Lord Jesus Christ reiterated divine law's imposition of the death penalty on those who transgressed God's commandments. St. Irenaeus of Lyons referred to God as 'the most righteous Retributor', in the context of Our Lord saying, 'But when the king had heard of it, he was angry, and sending his armies, he destroyed those murderers, and burnt their city.' (Mt 22:7)[753]

Both Origen and St. Cyprian of Carthage, referring to Matthew 15:3-4, highlighted that our Lord upheld the 'imperative commandments of God' that those who transgress divine Commandments, particular the Fourth Commandment, warrant the death penalty.[754] Commenting on the same Matthean passage, St. Augustine emphasised that our Lord reiterated the death penalty as the punishment for cursing one's parents in order to show that the commandment was of divine origin, and not a manmade law, 'that it was God Himself who gave these commandments by Moses.'[755]

The pauline metaphor of the 'sword' as the symbol of God's delegated juridical power of life and death (Rm 13:3-5) was central to some of the Church Fathers' teaching on the death penalty. St. Irenaeus refers to Romans 13:3-5 to explicate his understanding that the death penalty is an expression of God's providence:

> This is the Father of our Lord, by whose providence all things consist, and all are administered by His command; and He confers His free gifts upon those who should [receive them]; but the most righteous Retributor metes out [punishment] according to their deserts, most deservedly, to the ungrateful and to those that are insensible of His kindness.[756]

Commenting on Romans 13:4-7 St. John Chrysostom also writes that the exercise of the juridical power of the 'sword' comes under God's providence in those who are carrying out God's law because 'it is God that has so shaped things'.[757]

In his encyclical *Fratelli Tutti* Pope Francis placed St. Augustine among those early Christians who 'were clearly opposed to capital punishment'.[758] But such an assertion

---

[752] Pope Francis [2017] Encyclical *Fratelli Tutti*, para 267 [Online] Available at: www.vatican.va [Accessed on: 21 May 2024]

[753] St. Irenaeus. *Against Heresies*, Bk. IV, Chap. 36, Para 6 [Online] Available at: www.newadvent. org [Accessed on: 23 May 2024]

[754] Origen. *Commentary on the Gospel of Matthew*, Bk. XI, Chap. 9; St. Cyprian of Carthage. *Epistle* 72, To Jubaianus, Concerning the Baptism of Heretics, para 19 [Online] Available at: www. newadvent.org [Accessed on: 23 May 2024]

[755] St. Augustine. *Contra Faustum*, Bk. XVI, Chap. 24; Bk. XXII, Chap. 14 [Online] Available at: www.newadvent.org [Accessed on: 23 May 2024]

[756] St. Irenaeus. *Op. cit.*

[757] St. John Chrysostom. *Homily 23 on Romans* 13:4-7 [Online] www.newadvent.org [Accessed on: 28 August 2028]

[758] Pope Francis [2017] Encyclical *Fratelli Tutti*, para 265 [Online] Available at: www.vatican.va [Accessed on: 21 May 2024]

misrepresents St. Augustine's position on capital punishment. Though he did personally appeal for clemency in some circumstances, he accepted that divine authority granted exceptions to the Fifth Commandment not to kill:

> …there are some exceptions made by the divine authority to its own law, that men may not be put to death. These exceptions are of two kinds, being justified either by a general law, or by a special commission granted for a time to some individual. And in this latter case, he to whom authority is delegated, and who is but the sword in the hand of him who uses it, is not himself responsible for the death he deals. And, accordingly, they who have waged war in obedience to the divine command, or in conformity with His laws, have represented in their persons the public justice or the wisdom of government, and in this capacity have put to death wicked men; such persons have by no means violated the commandment, 'You shall not kill.' […] With the exception, then, of these two classes of cases, which are justified either by a just law that applies generally, or by a special intimation from God Himself, the fountain of all justice, whoever kills a man, either himself or another, is implicated in the guilt of murder.[759]

St. Augustine held that divine authority empowered certain individuals with the 'power of judging' including the punishment of death which could be imposed for the 'the good of humanity'. He gave the example of the prophet Elijah killing, and ordering the killing of, the prophets of Baal (III Kings 18:40):

> Hence it is that Elijah inflicted death on many, both with his own hand and by calling down fire from heaven; as was done also without rashness by many other great and godlike men, in the same spirit of concern for the good of humanity.[760]

St. Thomas Aquinas interpreted St. Paul's justification of the delegated power of capital punishment expressed in Romans 13:3-5 in the context of the good of the community. In both *Summa Contra Gentiles*[761] and *Summa Theologiae*[762] Aquinas used the metaphor of the surgeon cutting 'off the unhealthy member if it threatens the health of the body' as applying to legitimate authorities executing criminals:

> Now every individual person is compared to the whole community, as part to whole. Therefore if a man be dangerous and infectious to the community, on account of some sin, it is praiseworthy and advantageous that he be killed in order to safeguard the common good.[763]

Furthermore, St. Thomas Aquinas refuted a number of the abolitionist arguments misinterpreting sacred Scripture that were later repeated by Pope Francis:

Pope Francis argued that the Fifth Commandment, *Thou shalt not kill*, prohibits the death penalty in all circumstances.[764] To which St. Thomas Aquinas argued that the Fifth Commandment prohibited the unjust killing of a person, not the lawful execution of the criminal:

> Hereby we refute the error of those who say that capital punishment is unlawful. They base their error on the words of Exodus 20:13, You shall not kill, which are quoted in Matthew 5:21 […]. But these arguments are of no account. For the same law that says:

---

[759] St. Augustine. *The City of God*, Bk. I, Chap. 21 [Online] Available at: www.newadvent.org [Accessed on: 23 May 2024]
[760] St. Augustine. *On the Sermon on the Mount*, Bk. I, Chap. 20 [Online] Available at: www.newadvent.org [Accessed on: 23 May 2024]
[761] St. Thomas Aquinas. *Summa Contra Gentiles*, Bk. III, Chaps. 144 & 146 [Available at: www.aquinas.cc [Accessed on: 23 May 2024]
[762] St. Thomas Aquinas. *Summa Theologiae, Secunda Secundæ Partis*, Q 64, a. 2, a.3 [Available at: www.newadvent.org [Accessed on: 27 May 2024]
[763] *Op cit.*
[764] Pope Francis [2015] Angelus Address, 21st February 2016; [2016] Video Message to the 6th World Congress Against the Death Penalty [Online] Available at: www.vatican.va [Accessed on: 21 May 2024]; [2022] For the abolition of the death penalty — September 2022 [Available at: www.youtube.com [Accessed on: 21 May 2024]

> You shall not kill, afterwards adds: You shall not permit wizards to live (Ex 22:18). Hence we are to understand that the prohibition is against the unjust slaying of a man.[765]

Pope Francis argued that the death penalty was inadmissible because it denies the individual the opportunity of healing, conversion, repentance and making amends.[766] To which St. Thomas Aquinas made a number of arguments against banning the death penalty in the hope of amendment:

> The fact that the wicked are able to amend while alive does not prevent their being justly slain, for the peril that threatens through their remaining alive is greater and more certain than the good to be expected from their amendment. Moreover, in the very hour of death they are able to repent and be converted to God. And if they be so obstinate that even in the hour of death their heart does not abandon its wickedness, it may be reckoned with sufficient probability that they will never recover from their evil ways.[767]

Pope Francis' declaration that the death penalty is a sin and totally inadmissible contradicts the Tradition of the Church that the Lord delegates vindicative, retributive punishment to legitimate authorities and that the execution of those who transgress divine commandments is the working out of God's providential care for the good of humanity.

c) The Defence by the Magisterium

The Pauline understanding of the State's divinely delegated, and mandated, imposition of the death penalty against evil-doers is central to magisterial doctrine on capital punishment (Rm 13:4-7). In the 5th century Pope St. Innocent I described those commissioned by the State to impose the death penalty as 'a minister of God, an avenger'. The Holy Father went on to describe those who criticised the death penalty as going 'against the authority of the Lord'.[768] In the 12th century Pope Innocent III explicitly taught — contrary to Pope Francis' erroneous teaching — that the death penalty does not involve mortal sin if it is conducted in a lawful, judicious manner.[769]

In the 16th century Pope St. Pius V also reiterated the pauline understanding of 'the civil authority' as the 'legitimate avenger of crime'. Instead of viewing the death penalty as contrary to the Fifth Commandment, Pius V taught that it was a necessary expression of obedience to the commandment, *Thou shalt not kill*,

> The just use of this power, far from involving the crime of murder, is an act of paramount obedience to this Commandment which prohibits murder. The end of the Commandment is the preservation and security of human life.[770]

In the 20th century Pope Ven. Pius XII sought to uphold magisterial teaching on the divinely delegated power of vindicative, retributive punishment expressed in Romans 13:4-7. This was in response to jurists rejecting the death penalty as the just punishment of the wicked. Pope Ven. Pius XII taught that:

---

[765] St. Thomas Aquinas. *Summa Contra Gentiles*, Bk. III, Chaps. 144 & 146 [Available at: www.aquinas.cc [Accessed on: 23 May 2024]

[766] Pope Francis [2015] *Address to the Joint Session of the United States Congress*; [2017] Encyclical *Fratelli Tutti*, para 265 [Online] Available at: www.vatican.va [Accessed on: 21 May 2024] [Online] Available at: www.vatican.va [Accessed on: 21 May 2024]

[767] St. Thomas Aquinas. *Summa Contra Gentiles*, Bk. III, Chap. 146 [Available at: www.aquinas.cc [Accessed on: 23 May 2024]

[768] Brugger, E [2003] *Capital Punishment and Roman Catholic Moral Tradition*. Notre Dame, Indiana: University of Notre Dame Press, p.89

[769] Denzinger, H [2010] *op. cit.*, p. 264 795

[770] Pope St. Pius V [1556] The Roman Catechism: *The Catechism of the Council of Trent*, The Sacraments: The Sacrament of Baptism; The Fifth Commandment: Execution Of Criminals [Online] Available at: http://www.clerus.org [Accessed on: 28 May 2024]

a) The State does not dispose of the individual's right to life because 'by his crime, he has already disposed himself of his right to live.'[771]
b) In light of divine revelation it is necessary to emphasise the punitive nature of the death penalty which is required as retribution and expiation for the crimes committed against God's Commandments. The protection of society is of secondary concern.[772]
c) The medicinal and vindictive aspects of the death penalty are 'more in agreement with what the sources of revelation and traditional doctrine teach regarding the coercive power of legitimate human authority.'[773]
d) It is illegitimate to dispense with the death penalty using the argument that references to its use as punishment in sacred Scripture 'correspond to the historic circumstances and to the culture of the time, and that a general and abiding validity cannot therefore be attributed to them.'[774]

Pope St. John Paul II originally taught that the 'traditional teaching of the Church' acknowledged that the death penalty was a 'well-founded…right and duty of legitimate public authority to punish malefactors'. And that the purpose of the death penalty was 'to redress the disorder caused by the offence.' (CCC 2266) (*Catechism of the Catholic Church*, 1st edition, 1992). Also, the second edition of Pope St. John Paul's *Catechism of the Catholic Church* accepted that 'the traditional teaching of the Church does not exclude recourse to the death penalty'. However, Pope St. John Paul II diverged from magisterial teaching on capital punishment when he added the proviso 'cases in which the execution of the offender is an absolute necessity "are very rare, if not practically non-existent."' (CCC 2266) (*Catechism of the Catholic Church*, 2nd edition, 1994)

In response to this expression of Pope St. John Paul II's personal opinion Cardinal Joseph Ratzinger, as prefect of the Congregation for the Doctrine of the Faith, issued a letter that emphasised Catholics could disagree with the pope's opinion on the death penalty:

> Not all moral issues have the same moral weight as abortion and euthanasia. For example, if a Catholic were to be at odds with the Holy Father on the application of capital punishment or on the decision to wage war, he would not for that reason be considered unworthy to present himself to receive Holy Communion. While the Church exhorts civil authorities to seek peace, not war, and to exercise discretion and mercy in imposing punishment on criminals, it may still be permissible to take up arms to repel an aggressor or to have recourse to capital punishment. There may be a legitimate diversity of opinion even among Catholics about waging war and applying the death penalty, but not however with regard to abortion and euthanasia.[775]

However, in 2018 Pope Francis amended the *Catechism of the Catholic Church* to reiterate his erroneous teaching that the death penalty was absolutely forbidden, 'Consequently, the Church teaches, in the light of the Gospel, that "the death penalty is inadmissible because it is an attack on the inviolability and dignity of the person"' (CCC 2267). By expressing it in such categorical terms, the Supreme Pontiff was illegitimately seeking to override the faithful's right to disagree with him on this matter.

Despite Pope Francis' attempts to suppress the faithful's right to disagree with him, the consistent testimony of sacred Scripture, sacred Tradition and the Magisterium concerning God delegating his power to the State to punish the wicked with the death penalty makes such disagreement a necessity.

---

[771] Pope Ven. Pius XII [1952] quoted in Guernsey, A [2017] *Addresses of Pius XII on the Law, Purposes of Punishment, and the Death Penalty* [Available at: www.aguernz.medium.com [Accessed on: 28 May 2024]

[772] Pope Ven. Pius XII [1952] *op. cit.*

[773] Pope Ven. Pius XII [1955] *ibid.*

[774] *Ibid.*

[775] Ratzinger, J [2004] *Worthiness to Receive Holy Communion: General Principles* [Available at: wwww.EWTN.com [Accessed on: 28 May 2024]

Morality (3) — Homosexuality

N. *The tendency to homosexuality is not a problem. God created individuals to be homosexuals and God loves them as homosexuals. The Old Testament account of the sin of Sodom is not about homosexual sex acts but concerns the sin of being inhospitable and hostile towards the stranger.*

Pope Francis' teaching on homosexuality marks a radical rupture from the doctrine of the Church. His appointments of pro-LGBT cardinals and bishops, and his public praise of priests and religious who campaign for the repudiation of divine revelation on homosexuality, indicates the depth of his commitment to this erroneous position.

Pope Francis' gravely erroneous teaching on homosexuality is summarised under the following headings:

a) Regarding the question of active, homosexual clergy, Pope Francis' infamously said, 'If someone is gay and he searches for the Lord and has good will, who am I to judge'.[776]

b) In comments to a man who is actively homosexual, Pope Francis is reported to have said affirmatively, 'Juan Carlos, that you are gay doesn't matter. God made you like this and loves you like this and it doesn't matter to me'.[777]

c) The tendency [to homosexuality] is not the problem.[778]

d) God loves homosexual persons 'as they are'.[779]

e) In comments to a man who admitted he was homosexual, Pope Francis responded, 'We are all human beings and have dignity. It does not matter who you are or how you live your life, you do not lose your dignity'.[780]

f) The State should 'support a homosexual couple in life together',[781] 'Homosexual people have a right to be in a family'.

g) According to a 2019 report commissioned by Pope Francis, and approved for publication by the CDF, the 'narrative tradition' of the Bible is neither against nor for homosexual practices. The report presented a revisionist *eisegesis*, popular among LGBT activists, about the destruction of Sodom (Gen 19:1-5) — the Old Testament account of the sin of Sodom is not about homosexual sex acts but concerns the sin of being inhospitable and hostile towards the stranger. It went on to recommend that the 'intelligent interpretation' of Biblical legislative texts (Lev 18:22; 20:13) against sodomy should avoid 'repetition to the letter that which carries with it cultural traits of that time.'[782]

h) During an interview in 2022, Cardinal Hollerich SJ — appointed by Pope Francis as the Relator General of the 2023 synod — claimed that his views on homosexuality were 'in full agreement with Pope Francis'. In response to the statement, 'The Bible has taught and the Church has taught for 2,000 years that sodomy is a sin, an abomination that cries out to heaven', Cardinal Hollerich replied that the Bible's

---

[776] John Allen [2013] *Pope on homosexuals: 'Who am I to judge?'* [Online] Available at: www.ncronline. org [Accessed on: 19 August 2022]

[777] Inés San Martín [2018] *Abuse victim says Pope Francis told him 'being gay doesn't matter'.* [Online] Available at: cruxnow.com [Accessed on: 19 August 2022]

[778] John Allen [2013] *Pope on homosexuals: 'Who am I to judge?'* [Online] Available at: www.ncronline. org [Accessed on: 19 August 2022]

[779] Christopher Lamb [2020] *Gay Children Are 'Children of God', Pope Tells Parents.* [Online] Available: www.thetablet.co.uk [Accessed on: 19 August]

[780] Charles Collins [2019] *Pope Francis Tells Gay Man 'You Do Not Lose Your dignity' on BBC show.* [Online] Available at: cruxnow.com [Accessed on: 19 August 2022]

[781] Pope Francis [2021] *In-flight press conference on return from Apostolic Visit to Slovakia.* [Online] Available at: www.catholicnewsagency.com [Accessed on: 19 August 2022]

[782] Edward Pentin [19 December 2019] *Pontifical Biblical Commission Asks, 'What Is Man?'* [Online] Available at: www.ncregister.com [Accessed on: 19 August 2022]; Diane Montagna [19 December 2019] *Vatican Publishes New Book Reducing 'Sin of Sodom' to 'Lack of Hospitality'* [Online] Available at: www.lifesitenews.com [Accessed on: 19 August 2022]

approach to homosexuality was outdated, 'But the Bible also said we should stone the woman who is adulterous. The Bible has said that the sun turns around the earth. So, ... [we] have to give an interpretation to the Bible.' When challenged, 'So the fundamental scriptural teaching on sin is being changed? Cardinal Hollerich replied, 'I know that I am in full agreement with Pope Francis'.[783] The Supreme Teacher did not repudiate, contradict or demand a retraction of Cardinal Jean-Claude Hollerich's claims about his personal views on homosexuality.

Pope Francis' erroneous teaching on homosexuality represents a school of thought among Jesuits, previously expressed by the prominent 'progressive' Cardinal Carlo Maria Martini SJ, the former Archbishop of Milan. Pope Francis praised Cardinal Martini as a prophet and as 'a father for the whole Church' who had influenced him through his writings.[784] In his book length interview *Night Conversations with Cardinal Martini* [2010], Cardinal Martini expressed his revisionist views on homosexuality, including an apologetic *eisegesis* of Scripture contrary to Tradition that accepts 'homosexual couples':

> I know there are homosexual couples, people who are highly regarded and public-minded. I have never been asked, and it would never occur to me, to judge them. The Bible judges homosexuality with strong words. The background to this problematic practice in the ancient world, when men would have boys and male lovers alongside their families. Alexander the Great is a famous example. The Bible wants to protect the family, the wife, and the children's space.
>
> In the Orthodox Church it is considered an abomination. In the Protestant Church it is treated more liberally; there are even homosexual couples in the ministry; they are allowed to minister, providing they don't promote homosexuality. We are aware of the crucial tests in this matter within the Anglican Church. In Judaism, the Orthodox strongly forbid homosexuality; in the Reform Judaism again there are particular synagogues for homosexuality. We are seeking our way through this diversity. The deepest concerns of the Holy Scriptures, however, is the protection of the family and a healthy space for children – something now seen in homosexual couples.[785]

The Teaching of the Church
The primary purpose of Marriage is the generation and bringing-up of offspring. The secondary purpose is mutual help and the morally regulated satisfaction of the sex urge. (**Sententia certa**)[786]
Marriage was not instituted by Man, but by God. (**Sententia certa**)[787]
The souls of those who die in the condition of personal grievous sin enter Hell. (**De Fide**)[788]
The Church has always taught that the only licit relationship for the 'morally regulated satisfaction of the sex urge' (I Cor 7:2) is the institution of marriage between a male and a female. Marriage was instituted by God for the procreation of children (Gen 1:28) and the mutual love and help provided by the integral complementarity of maleness and femaleness (Gen 2:18). All sexual activity outside God's institution of marriage is illicit, and in the case of homosexuality, so totally contrary to God's purpose for sexuality as to be unnatural and mortally sinful.

During the 13th century, the Third Lateran Council condemned homosexual sex acts in terms of the destruction of Sodom and Gomorrah, 'that unnatural vice for which

[783] McLoone, D [2022] *EXCLUSIVE: Pro-LGBT cardinal claims Pope Francis is in 'full agreement' with his stance* [Online] Available at: www.lifesitenews.com [Accessed on: 19 August 2022]
[784] Glatz, C [2013] *Pope Francis Hails Cardinal Martini as 'A Father for the Whole Church'* [Online] Available at: catholicherald.co.uk [Accessed on: 19 August 2022]
[785] Martini, C [2013] *Night Conversations with Cardinal Martini: The Relevance of the Church for Tomorrow.* New York: Paulist Press, p.98.
[786] Ott, L [1957] *Op. cit.,* p. 462
[787] Ott, L [1957] *Ibid.,* p. 460
[788] Ott, L [1957] *Ibid.,* p. 479

the wrath of God came down upon the sons of disobedience and destroyed the five cities with fire'. It mandated that clerics guilty of sodomy should be 'expelled from the clergy or confined in monasteries to do penance' and laymen should 'incur excommunication and be completely separated from the society of the faithful'.[789]

Thirty-six years later, the Fourth Lateran Council warned clerics against vices arising from lust, singling out homosexual sex acts, again describing sodomy in terms of the Biblical account of the destruction of Sodom and Gomorrah 'especially that on account of which the wrath of God came down from heaven upon the sons of disobedience'.[790] The Council of Vienne described homosexual sex acts as 'the deadly crime of the Sodomites'.[791]

The Fifth Lateran Council re-iterated the previous councils' condemnation of sodomy committed by clerics and laymen, again describing it in terms of the destruction of Sodom 'the wrath of God comes upon the sons of disobedience'. It stipulated that they were to be 'punished by the penalties respectively imposed by the sacred canons or by civil law'.[792]

Though the Second Vatican Council did not mention homosexuality, the Council Fathers did teach that sexual acts must be 'proper to conjugal love' and the duty of reverencing the dignity of the conjugal act:

> The sexual characteristics of man and the human faculty of reproduction wonderfully exceed the dispositions of lower forms of life. Hence the acts themselves which are proper to conjugal love and which are exercised in accord with genuine human dignity must be honoured with great reverence.[793]

The Second Vatican Council taught the truth contained in scripture and tradition that marriage between a man and a woman was 'established by the Creator and qualified by His laws'. And that sexual acts are only licit as expressions of 'conjugal love…ordained for the procreation of children':

> Thus a man and a woman, who by their compact of conjugal love 'are no longer two, but one flesh' (Matt.19:ff), render mutual help and service to each other through an intimate union of their persons and of their actions.[794]

Proof from the Sources of Faith
a) Teaching from Holy Scripture

To understand sacred Scripture's presentation of 'homosexual acts as acts of grave depravity' (CCC 2357) it is necessary to begin with God's purpose for human sexuality. God created human beings in his image as male and female for the purpose of being co-creators through the procreation and parenting of children (Gen 1:27-28). God created maleness and femaleness as an integral complementarity expressed through the conjugal act, 'Wherefore a man shall leave father and mother, and shall cleave to his wife: and they shall be two in one flesh' (Gen 2:24).

The Old Testament condemns sodomy as morally corrupt and wicked primarily because it contravenes the inherent natural purpose of complementary sex organs — the union of maleness and femaleness. As the Book of Leviticus puts it, 'Thou shalt not lie with mankind as with womankind, because it is an abomination [*toebah*]'; 'If any one

---

[789] Tanner, N [1990] *Third Lateran Council – 1179 A.D.* Canon 11. [Online] Available at: www.papalencyclicals.net [Accessed on: 19 August 2022]

[790] Tanner, N [1990] *Fourth Lateran Council: 1215.* Constitution 14. [Online] Available at: www.papalencyclicals.net [Accessed on: 19 August 2022]

[791] *Council of Vienne 1311-1312 A.D* [Online] Available at: www.papalencyclicals.net [Accessed on: 20 August 2022]

[792] Tanner, N [1990] *Fifth Lateran Council 1512-17 A.D. Reform of the Curia.* [Online] Available at: www.papalencyclicals.net [Accessed on: 19 August 2022]

[793] Second Vatican Council [1965] Pastoral Constitution *Gaudium et Spes*, para 51. [Online] Available at: www.papalencyclicals.net [Accessed on: 20 August 2022]

[794] *Ibid.*, para 48.

lie with a man as with a woman, both have committed an abomination [*toebah*], let them be put to death: their blood be upon them.' (Lev 18:22; 20:13). The Hebrew word תּוֹעֵבָה [*toebah*] has the meaning of an act that is abhorrent, disgusting, loathsome, detestable.

The Hebrew word for sexual intercourse between a husband and wife is יָדַע [*yada*]: 'And Adam knew [*yada*] Eve his wife: who conceived and brought forth Cain;'And Cain knew [*yada*] his wife, and she conceived, and brought forth Henoch' (Gen 4:1;4:17). The Book of Genesis conveys the grave depravity of the sin of the men of Sodom through the use of the word *yada*, 'And they called Lot, and said to him: Where are the men that came into thee at night? bring them out hither that we may know [*yada*] them' (Gen 19:5).

Sacred Scripture is emphatic that this misuse of sex is an abomination to God to the extent that Sodomite and abomination were synonymous. In the Old Testament it was a crime that rightfully deserved divine punishment, including exclusion from the Kingdom of God:

> And there were also sodomites in the land: and they did according to all the abominations of the nations which the LORD cast out before the children of Israel.... And Asa did that which was right in the eyes of the LORD, as did David his father. And he took away the sodomites out of the land, and removed all the idols that his fathers had made. (I Kings 14:24; 15:11-12).

The reason why the men of Sodom are condemned as exceedingly wicked sinners is due to their intent to commit an unnatural sex act that God views as abhorrent, and not because of any sin against hospitality, 'And the men of Sodom were very wicked, and sinners before the face of the Lord, beyond measure' (Gen 13:13). This unnatural rebellion against God the Creator and his institution of the conjugal union between man and woman is the epitome of sinful disobedience deserving of God's punishment.

Our Lord referred to the destruction of Sodom and Gomorrah as a reference point to the punishment that awaits the sinfully disobedient:

> Likewise as it came to pass, in the days of Lot: they did eat and drink, they bought and sold, they planted and built. And in the day that Lot went out of Sodom, it rained fire and brimstone from heaven, and destroyed them all. (Lk 17:28-30; cf. Mt 10:14-15.)

Our Lord refers to Sodom as a warning that there are sinful ways of living that are so disobedient that they are judged by God an abomination deserving total annihilation. In the light of Leviticus' condemnation of homosexual sex acts as deserving death, our Lord's reference to the total destruction of Sodom indicates his own judgment regarding the sinfulness of sodomy.

This use of the destruction of Sodom and Gomorrah as illustrative of God's judgement on the sinfulness of homosexual sex acts can also be found in the Apostles' epistles. St. Peter does so when warning about those who 'walk after the flesh in the lust of uncleanness':

> And reducing the cities of the Sodomites, and of the Gomorrhites, into ashes, condemned them to be overthrown, making them an example to those that should after act wickedly...And especially them who walk after the flesh in the lust of uncleanness and despise government, audacious, self-willed, they fear not to bring in sects, blaspheming (II Pet 2:6,10).

The early Christian text, *The Apocalypse of Peter* (written between 100 and 150 AD), interpreted II Peter 2:10 as referring to the sin of homosexual and lesbian sex acts, '... and these were they who defiled their bodies acting as women; and the women who were with them were those who lay with one another as a man with a woman'.[795] It should be noted that as well as being sinful acts in themselves, II Peter 2:10 warns that sodomy displays a contempt towards the 'government' − authority − of God.

---

[795] *The Apocalypse of Peter* [Online] Available at: www.newadvent.org [Accessed on: 24 August 2022]

St. Jude warns that the destruction of Sodom and Gomorrah teaches that those who engage in unnatural lust deserve the punishment of eternal fire (Jude 1:7).

Though St. Paul does not refer to the destruction of Sodom and Gomorrah, of all the New Testament authors, his teaching on God's condemnation of homosexual sex acts as 'acts of grave depravity' is the most explicit:

> For this cause God delivered them up to shameful affections. For their women have changed the natural use into that use which is against nature. And, in like manner, the men also, leaving the natural use of the women, have burned in their lusts one towards another, men with men working that which is filthy, and receiving in themselves the recompense which was due to their error (Rom 1:26-27).

Those campaigning to change doctrine on homosexuality argue that this passage of Romans refers to heterosexuals engaging in homosexual sex acts and claim it is not a condemnation of homosexual persons engaging in sodomy. The problem with this *eisegesis* is twofold: sacred Scripture makes it clear that 1) God created the conjugal act as the unique expression of the integral complementarity of maleness and femaleness; 2) The misuse of sex organs in ways that violate God's design and purpose for integral complementarity are a detestable, loathsome abomination that deserve the most severe divine punishment, as exemplified by the destruction of Sodom and Gomorrah.

b) The Testimony of Tradition

The Church Fathers testify to the importance of maintaining the divine Law — apparent in natural law and divine revelation — that sodomy is an act of grave depravity that warrants God's severe punishment. Tertullian emphasised the moral sense of abomination associated with the sin:

> But all the other frenzies of passions — impious both toward the bodies and toward the sexes — beyond the laws of nature, we banish not only from the threshold, but from all shelter of the Church, because they are not sins, but monstrosities.[796]

Commenting on Romans 1: 26-27, St. John Chrysostom also referred to sodomy as a 'monstrous insanity' which he concluded indicated a form of demonic possession. Being contrary to nature, St. John Chrysostom observed that sodomy must be 'irksome and displeasing' because 'genuine pleasure is that which is according to nature'. About those who exchanged the truth of God for the lie of sodomy, he observed, 'not only was their doctrine Satanical, but their life too was diabolical'.[797] Furthermore, commenting on St. Jude teaching that sodomy led to Sodom and Gomorrah 'suffering the punishment of eternal fire' (Jude 1:7), St. John Chrysostom reflected, 'Consider how great is that sin, to have forced hell to appear even before its time!' By contrasting the rain of destruction that God visited upon Sodom and Gomorrah with natural rain St. John Chrysostom sought to highlight the unnaturalness of sodomy — natural rain stirs 'up the womb of the earth to the production of fruits' and 'the reception of seed', while the 'rain of destruction' caused by their sodomy 'not only did it fail to stir up the womb of the earth to the production of fruits, but made it even useless for the reception of seed. For such was also the intercourse of the men, making a body of this sort more worthless than the very land of Sodom'.[798]

St. Augustine did not consider the sin of the men of Sodom to be a lack of hospitality but the commission of the unnatural sex acts of homosexuals. He described them as offences which 'contrary to nature are everywhere and at all times to be held in detestation and punished'.[799] St. Augustine described the nature of homosexual sex

---

[796] Tertullian. *On Modesty*, chap 4. [Online] www.newadvent.org [Accessed on: 24 August 2022]
[797] St. John Chrysostom. *Homily* 4 on Romans 1: 26-27 [Online] www.newadvent.org [Accessed on: 24 August 2022]
[798] *Ibid.*
[799] St. Augustine. *The Confessions*, Bk. III, Chap. 8 [Online] www.newadvent.org [Accessed on: 25 August 2022]

acts in a way that conveys the visceral disgust behind the original Hebrew meaning of abomination [*toebah*]:

> Such people, weighed down by malignant habit, are as it were not only dead but buried. But what must I say, brothers and sisters? Not only buried, but as it was said about Lazarus, *He's already stinking*. That massive stone placed against the tomb, that is the hard force of habit which weighs on the soul and doesn't allow it either to rise or even breathe.[800]

Pope St. Gregory the Great also described the sin of the Sodomites with the same sense of visceral disgust. He saw God's choice of foul-smelling Brimstone to destroy Sodom as being the appropriate punishment for 'the sodomites, burning with perverse desires that originated from the foul odour of flesh'.[801]

St. Thomas Aquinas categorised sodomy as 'a special kind of deformity' that rendered the sexual act 'unbecoming' to human beings for a number of reasons:

i)   Like all lustful vices, 'it is contrary to right reason'.
ii) It is called an 'unnatural vice' because it is 'contrary to the natural order of the venereal act as becoming to the human race'.
iii) This unnatural vice includes the various types of masturbation and 'copulation with an undue sex, male with male, or female with female, as the Apostle states (Rom 1:27): and this is called the "vice of sodomy"'.[802]

c) The Defence by the Magisterium

The earliest recorded magisterial defence of divine revelation's condemnation of homosexual sex acts occurred during the 4th century. The Spanish Synod of Elvira promulgated a canon imposing the most severe of penalties against men who perpetrated the homosexual abuse of boys — the denial of Holy Communion, 'even at the approach of death'.[803] St. Basil of Caesarea in Cappadocia issued a series of canons including one imposing thirty years excommunication on those who engaged in 'sodomy with men or brutes'. They were to be readmitted after 30 years if they had committed the sin through 'ignorance' and had displayed signs of genuine repentance. St. Basil included sodomites in the same category as 'murderers, wizards, adulterers, and idolaters'.[804]

The 11th century was significant for the Church deepening her moral understanding of the grave depravity of sodomy. St. Peter Damian, Doctor of the Church, wrote the *Liber Gomorrhianus* addressed to Pope Leo IX about the practice of sodomy among the Roman clergy. Like St. John Chrysostom, Peter Damian considered sodomy to be diabolical in inspiration because it is so contrary to human reason, natural law and the natural sexual desires inherent to the integral complementarity of maleness and femaleness:

> And it certainly is proper enough that those who trade their flesh to demons through such foul commerce against the law of nature, against the order of human reason, should receive a common place of prayer with the demonically possessed. For as human nature itself deeply resists these evils, and the lack of sexual difference is abhorrent, it is clearer than light that they never would have dared to engage in such perversities

---

[800] St. Augustine. The Works of Saint Augustine: A Translation for the 21st Century [1992] *Sermons on the New Testament, III/4 (94A-146A)*. New York: New City Press, p.46

[801] Pope St. Gregory the Great. *Commentary on Moralia in Job*, XIV, 23. [Online] Available at: http://www.awrsipe.com [Accessed on: 25 August 2022]

[802] St. Thomas Aquinas. *Summa Theologiae*, Secunda Secundæ Partis. Q 154. a11 [Online] www.newadvent.org [Accessed on: 25 August 2022]

[803] Synod of Elvira. 81 *Canons of the Synod of Elvira*, Canon 71. [Online] Available at: strannikjournal.wordpress.com [Accessed on: 26 August 2022]

[804] Peters, E N [2001] *The 1917 or Pio-Benedictine Code of Canon Law in English Translation with Extensive Scholarly Apparatus*. San Francisco: Ignatius Press

unless evil spirits had fully possessed them as 'vessels of wrath, fitted for destruction.' (Rom.9:22).[805]

In his canonical letter responding to St. Peter Damian, Pope St. Leo IX set out various penalties according to the nature of the sodomitical act, all of which involved expulsion from 'all grades of the immaculate Church'. Those who engaged in lesser homosexual acts, after showing signs of restraining 'their desire' and washing 'away their shameful deeds by worthy repentance' were to be readmitted to their order. But those who engaged in copulation, including the most vile sin, anal sex, were permanently excluded from their order in the Church.[806]

Pope St. Pius V promulgated a constitution in the 16th century condemning sodomy with the title, '*Horrendum illud scelus*' [That horrible crime]. He described sodomy as being so great a sin for the perpetrators that it resulted in the 'death of their souls'. Pope Pius V was explicit that homosexual sex acts caused the destruction of Sodom — not sins against hospitality:

> That horrible crime, on account of which corrupt and obscene cities were destroyed by fire through divine condemnation, causes us most bitter sorrow and shocks our mind, impelling us to repress such a crime with the greatest possible zeal.[807]

Pope St. Pius X's catechism included a section on those 'sins that are said to cry to God for vengeance', including 'The sin of sodomy' placed second after 'Wilful murder'. His catechism explained, 'These sins are said to cry to God for vengeance because the Holy Ghost says so, and because their iniquity is so great and so manifest that it provokes God to punish them with the severest chastisements'.[808]

During the pontificate of Pope St. Paul VI, the CDF issued a declaration on sexual ethics [1975] that included a section on homosexuality. It addressed those persons suffering homosexual attraction due to an 'innate instinct or a pathological constitution judged to be incurable'. It concluded that due to the objective moral order and sacred Scripture condemning sodomy as gravely depraved 'no pastoral method can be employed which would give moral justification to these acts on the grounds that they would be consonant with the condition of such people'.[809]

Early on in his pontificate, Pope St. John Paul II congratulated the US bishops for not holding out 'false hope' to homosexual persons when they upheld God's law that homosexual activity is 'morally wrong'. By so doing, they 'effectively manifested fraternal love, upholding the true dignity, the true human dignity, of those who look to Christ's Church for the guidance which comes from the light of God's word'.[810]

During his pontificate, the CDF promulgated the *Letter to the Bishops of Catholic Church on the Pastoral Care of Homosexual Persons* [1986]. Cardinal Ratzinger, the prefect of the CDF, highlighted as a concern 'an overly benign interpretation was given to the homosexual condition itself, some going so far as to call it neutral, or even good'. He concluded:

> Although the particular inclination of the homosexual person is not a sin, it is a more or less strong tendency ordered toward an intrinsic moral evil; and thus the inclination itself must be seen as an objective disorder [...] A person engaging in homosexual behaviour therefore acts immorally. To choose someone of the same sex for one's sexual

[805] St. Peter Damian. *Liber Gomorrhianus*, Chap. 14. [Online] Available at: ia802308.us.archive.org [Accessed on: 26 August 2022]

[806] Denzinger, H [1990] *Op. cit.*, p. 233-234, Dz 687-688

[807] Pope St. Pius V [1568] *Horrendum Illud Scelus* [Online] Available at: www.traditioninaction.org [Accessed on: 26 August 2022]

[808] *Catechism of St. Pius X* [1908] [Online] Available at: www.ewtn.com [Accessed on: 28 August 2022]

[809] Sacred Congregation for the Doctrine of the Faith [1975] *Persona Humana*, VIII. [Online] Available at: www.vatican.va [Accessed on: 28 August 2022]

[810] Pope St. John Paul II [1979] *Address to the Bishops of the United States of America*, para 6. [Online] Available at: www.vatican.va [Accessed on: 28 August 2022]

activity is to annul the rich symbolism and meaning, not to mention the goals, of the Creator's sexual design. Homosexual activity is not a complementary union, able to transmit life; and so it thwarts the call to a life of that form of self-giving which the Gospel says is the essence of Christian living.[811]

Furthermore, the *Catechism of the Catholic Church* (1992), issued by Pope St. John Paul II, identified 'the sin of the Sodomites (Gen 18:20; 19:13)' as one of the 'sins that cry to heaven' (*CCC* 1867). Elsewhere, the Catechism referred to sacred Scripture to condemn 'homosexual acts as acts of grave depravity, (Gen 191-29; Rom 124-27; I Cor 6:10; I Tim 1:10)'. It also drew on natural law when it concluded that homosexual sex acts 'close the sexual act to the gift of life. They do not proceed from a genuine affective and sexual complementarity. Under no circumstances can they be approved.' (*CCC* 2357).

During the Holy Year celebrations to mark the Third Millennium, Pope St. John Paul II reiterated during an angelus address that 'The Church cannot be silent about the truth, because she would fail in her fidelity to God the Creator and would not help to distinguish good from evil.' He went on to declare, 'that homosexual acts are contrary to the natural law'.[812]

Commenting on the destruction of Sodom and Gomorrah, Pope Benedict XVI defended the Church's perennial understanding that depravity, not inhospitality, was the cause of God's punishment, 'It is recounted that the evil of the inhabitants of Sodom and Gomorrah had reached the height of depravity so as to require an intervention of God...'[813]

Pope Francis, and his pontificate's, presentation of homosexuality as God's will, and the efforts taken to mitigate the immorality of sodomy, represent a reprehensible attempt to misrepresent and distort God's revelation.

---

[811] Congregation for the Doctrine of the Faith. *Letter to the Bishops of Catholic Church on the Pastoral Care of Homosexual Persons*, para 3, 7 [Online] Available at: www.vatican.va [Accessed on: 28 August 2022]

[812] Pope St. John Paul II [9 July 2000] *Angelus Address.* [Online] Available at: www.vatican.va [Accessed on: 28 August 2022]

[813] Pope Benedict XVI [18th May 2011] *General Audience Address.* [Online] Available at: www.vatican.va [Accessed on: 28 August 2022]

Sacraments — Divorce and the Sacraments

O. *Those who have a valid sacramental marriage but have divorced and entered a civil union involving sexual relations, can receive the sacraments of confession and the Eucharist following a period of 'accompaniment' with a priest.*

Pope Francis' error regarding the Sacrament of Confession:

> Diminishing the gravity of sexual sins by saying priests should not focus on sexual sins because they are the lightest sins due to the weakness of the flesh. (Cf. Hamartiology (2) *If a person commits a sexual act, knowing it is ordinarily a mortal sin, they can remain in a state of sanctifying grace due to circumstances*)

Pope Francis' error regarding the Sacrament of the Eucharist:

> Discounting the necessity of sanctifying grace for Holy Communion by insisting that the Eucharist is not a prize for the perfect but a powerful medicine and nourishment for the weak.

From the beginning of his pontificate, Pope Francis indicated his support for changing the doctrine and discipline of the Church that absolutely prohibits divorced and re-married Catholics — who engage in sexual relations — receiving the sacraments. The Supreme Pontiff began his campaign to impose his erroneous sacramental innovations when he invited Cardinal Kasper to deliver the opening speech to the 2014 Consistory on the Family, explaining his so called 'penitential path' to admit divorced and remarried Catholics to Communion. Pope Francis went on to convene two synods — the 2014 Extraordinary Synod and the 2015 Ordinary Synod on the Family — which he and his collaborators engineered to accept Kasper's sacramental innovations. The resulting post-synodal apostolic exhortation, *Amoris Laetitia* (2016), contained a form of words that some bishops' conferences claimed gave them authority to illegitimately abandon the Church's absolute prohibition on those committing adultery to receive sacramental absolution and Holy Communion.

Pope Francis' illegitimate innovation allowing divorced and civilly re-married to receive sacramental absolution and Holy Communion derives from his erroneous understanding of the sacraments of confession, the eucharist and marriage. These can be summarised under the following headings:

a) 'Sins of the flesh are not the gravest sins',[814] 'Sins of the flesh are the lightest sins. Because the flesh is weak'.[815]

b) Therefore, priests should not focus 'on the sins of sexuality, what I call morality below the belt. But the more serious sins are elsewhere.' Priests who focus on the nature and cause of sexual sins need a psychiatrist.[816] 'The confessional must not be a torture chamber but rather an encounter with the Lord's mercy which spurs us on to do our best.'[817]

c) 'The Eucharist, although it is the fullness of sacramental life, is not a prize for the perfect but a powerful medicine and nourishment for the weak',[818] '[Jesus] knows

---

[814] Pope Francis [2021] *Press Conference on Return from Apostolic Journey to Cyprus and Greece* [Online] Available at: www.vatican.va [Accessed on: 31 August 2022]

[815] Magister, S [21 January 2019] *Memo for the Summit on Abuse. For Francis, the Sins 'Below the Belt' Are 'the Lightest'.* [Online] Available at: magister.blogautore.espresso.repubblica.it [Accessed on: 30 August 2022]

[816] *Ibid.*

[817] Pope Francis [2013] Post Synodal Apostolic Exhortation *Evangelii Gaudium,* para 47. [Online] Available at: www.vatican.va [Accessed on: 31 August 2022

[818] *Ibid.*

we make many mistakes, but he does not give up on joining his life to ours. He knows that we need it, because the Eucharist is not the reward of saints, but the bread of sinners. This is why he exhorts us: "Do not be afraid! Take and eat"'.[819]

d) Jesus gives Holy Communion to those who betray him, like he did with Judas, 'he knows we are sinners; and he knows we make many mistakes, but he does not give up on joining his life to ours'.[820]

e) Pope Francis makes no mention of the requirement to repent of mortal sins and being in a state of sanctifying grace to receive Holy Communion. According to him, all that is necessary is 'the wedding garment of faith which comes from the hearing of his Word'.[821]

f) Pope Francis' erroneous hamartiology about sexual sins and his discounting the requirement of sanctifying grace in his theology of the Eucharist inform his laxism regarding those committing adultery receiving sacramental absolution and the Blessed Sacrament in some circumstances.

g) 'By thinking that everything is black and white, we sometimes close off the way of grace and of growth';[822] 'Alas, we priests are accustomed to fixed norms. At fixed standards.... [And it is difficult for us, this] 'accompanying on the way, integrating, discerning, good.'[823]

h) The divorced who have entered a new union must not be 'pigeonholed or fit into overly rigid classifications leaving no room for a suitable personal and pastoral discernment'.[824] It is necessary to 'undertake a responsible personal and pastoral discernment of particular cases, one which would recognize that, since "the degree of responsibility is not equal in all cases" the consequences or effects of a rule need not necessarily always be the same.'[825]

i) Such pastoral 'discernment can recognize that in a particular situation no grave fault exists', which has implications for 'sacramental discipline'.[826]

j) In these circumstances, persons can receive the help of the Church, including 'the help of the sacraments': Hence, 'I want to remind priests that the confessional must not be a torture chamber, but rather an encounter with the Lord's mercy' (Apostolic Exhortation *Evangelii Gaudium* [24 November 2013], 44: AAS 105 [2013], 1038). I would also point out that the Eucharist "is not a prize for the perfect, but a powerful medicine and nourishment for the weak"' (*ibid.*, 47: 1039).[827]

k) 'In complex cases, and when a declaration of nullity has not been obtained… *Amoris Laetitia* offers the possibility of having access to the sacraments of Reconciliation and Eucharist (cf. footnotes 336 and 351)'.[828]

l) Pope Francis proposed that such complex cases include couples in adulterous relationships who, he argued, cannot be expected to live together as brother and sister but instead have a duty to engage in sexual activity for the sake of family harmony and the good of their children.[829]

---

[819] Pope Francis [6th June 2021] *Angelus Address*. [Online] Available at: www.vatican.va [Accessed on: 31 August 2022]

[820] *Ibid.*

[821] Pope Francis [2022] *Apostolic Letter Desiderio Desideravi*, 5. [Online] Available at: www.vatican. va [Accessed on: 2nd September 2022]

[822] Pope Francis [2016] Post Synodal Apostolic Exhortation *Amoris Laetitia*, para 305 [Online] Available at: www.vatican.va [Accessed on: 31 August 2022]

[823] Pope Francis [1st September 2017] *Les confidences du pape François à Dominique Wolton* [Online] Available at: www.cath.ch [Accessed on: 31 August 2022] Trans. Andrew Guernsey

[824] *Amoris Laetitia*, para 298.

[825] *Ibid.*, para 300.

[826] *Ibid.*, footnote 336.

[827] *Amoris Laetitia*, footnote 351.

[828] *Pope Francis Promulgates Buenos Aires Guidelines Allowing Communion for Some Adulterers in AAS as his 'Authentic Magisterium'* [October 2016] [Online] Available at: rorate-caeli.blogspot.com [Accessed on: 31 August 2022]

[829] *Amoris Laetitia*, para 298; *Acta Apostolicae Sedis*. [2016] section 6.

m) Pope Francis misrepresented *Gaudium et Spes* 51, to justify his erroneous proposal that adulterous couples engage in sexual relations, writing 'In such situations, many people, knowing and accepting the possibility of living "as brothers and sisters" which the Church offers them, point out that if certain expressions of intimacy are lacking, "it often happens that faithfulness is endangered and the good of the children suffers" (Second Vatican Ecumenical Council, Pastoral Constitution on the Church in the Modern World *Gaudium et Spes*, 51)'.[830] But the fact is, *Gaudium et Spes* 51 only referred to validly married couples, 'But where the intimacy of married life is broken off, its faithfulness can sometimes be imperilled and its quality of fruitfulness ruined, for then the upbringing of the children and the courage to accept new ones are both endangered'.[831]

Pope Francis sought to overturn the sacramental doctrine and discipline of the Church based on erroneous moral assumptions reminiscent of Laxism, a 17th century heresy associated with the Jesuits, condemned by Pope Alexander VIII and Pope Innocent XI. Laxism excused Christians from their obligations to natural and positive law on 'slight and insufficient grounds'.[832] Laxism was 'satisfied with even a slightly probable opinion as a rule of conduct' even if it contradicted natural and positive law.[833] An example of Pope Francis proposing a Laxist position is his argument that divorcees in a second union — 'not living together as brother and sister' — can receive absolution and the Eucharist because they have a duty to engage in sexual relations for the harmony of the family and the sake of the children. In this, Pope Francis is going beyond the Laxism of the 17th century because he erroneously proposes grounds for couples to ignore their obligations to Divine Law — the Sixth Commandment, *Thou shalt not commit adultery*, and *De Fidei* doctrine regarding the Most Holy Eucharist.

Blaise Pascal's description of Jesuitical moral laxity in the 17th century seems an even more appropriate criticism of Pope Francis:

> Go and see some of these worthy fathers, I beseech you, and I am confident that you will soon discover, in the laxity of their moral system, the explanation of their doctrine about grace. You will then see the Christian virtues exhibited in such a strange aspect, so completely stripped of the charity which is the life and soul of them, you will see so many crimes palliated and irregularities tolerated that you will no longer be surprised at their maintaining that 'all men have always enough of grace' to lead a pious life, in the sense of which they understand piety. Their morality being entirely Pagan, nature is quite competent to its observance.[834]

The Teaching of the Church
From the sacramental contract of marriage emerges the Bond of Marriage, which binds both marriage partners to a lifelong indivisible community of life. **(De Fide)**[835]
The essential properties of Marriage are unity (monogamy) and indissolubility. (Sent. certa) **CIC 1013, Par. 2.**[836]
By virtue of Divine ordinance all grievous sins (mortal, serious) according to kind and number, as well as those circumstances which alter their nature, are subject to the obligation of confession. **(De Fide)**[837]

---

[830] *Ibid.*, footnote 329.
[831] Second Vatican Council [1965] Pastoral Constitution on the Church in the Modern World *Gaudium et Spes*, para 51 [Online] Available at: www.vatican.va [Accessed on: 31 August 2022]
[832] O'Collins, G & Farrugia, E [2000] *A Concise Dictionary of Theology*. Edinburgh: T&T Clark, p.137.
[833] Slater, T [1909] *A Short History of Moral Theology* [Online] Available at: maritain.nd.edu [Accessed on: 1 September 2022]
[834] Pascal, B [1657] *Lettres Provinciales*, Letter V [Online] Available at: en.wikisource.org [Accessed on: 1 September 2022]
[835] Ott, L [1957] *Op. cit.*, p. 467.
[836] *Ibid.*, p. 462
[837] *Ibid.*, p. 432

For the worthy reception of the Eucharist the state of grace as well as the proper and pious disposition are necessary. **(De Fide** *as regards the state of grace.)*[838]

In the 16th century, Protestant heresiarchs attacked the sacramental and indissoluble nature of marriage, with Luther and Calvin allowing divorce on the grounds of adultery and separation. In response, the Council of Trent defended God's institution of the indissolubility of marriage. The *Doctrine on the Sacrament of Marriage* stated:

> The first parent of the human race, under the influence of the divine Spirit, pronounced the bond of matrimony perpetual and indissoluble, when he said; This now is bone of my bones, and flesh of my flesh. Wherefore a man shall leave father and mother, and shall cleave to his wife, and they shall be two in one flesh. But, that by this bond two only are united and joined together, our Lord taught more plainly, when rehearsing those last words as having been uttered by God, He said, therefore now they are not two, but one flesh; and straightway confirmed the firmness of that tie, proclaimed so long before by Adam, by these words; What therefore God hath joined together, let no man put asunder. But, the grace which might perfect that natural love, and confirm that indissoluble union, and sanctify the married, Christ Himself, the institutor and perfecter of the venerable sacraments, merited for us by His passion.[839]

The council fathers further anathematised those who proposed that 'the bond of matrimony' could be dissolved due to 'heresy, or irksome cohabitation, or the affected absence of one of the parties'. (Canon V). The Council of Trent was absolutely categorical that those who contract a second union when the original marriage bond remains, commit the grave sin of adultery, meaning that 'both, or even the innocent one who gave not occasion to the adultery, cannot contract another marriage, during the life-time of the other' (Canon VII).

The Second Vatican Council defended the indissolubility of marriage in terms of 'an unbreakable oneness between' the spouses, that could 'never be profaned by adultery or divorce' because it is 'hallowed above all by Christ's sacrament'.[840]

Regarding the sacrament of confession, Pope Francis' contention that priests should not focus on sexual sins, and his disparagement of priests who explore the nature and cause of sexual sins as needing 'a psychiatrist' are contrary to the declarations of the Council of Trent:

> For it is manifest, that priests could not have exercised this judgment without knowledge of the cause; neither indeed could they have observed equity in enjoining punishments, if the said faithful should have declared their sins in general only, and not rather specifically, and one by one. Whence it is gathered that all the mortal sins, of which, after a diligent examination of themselves, they are conscious, must needs be by penitents enumerated in confession, even though those sins be most hidden, and committed only against the two last precepts of the decalogue, – sins which sometimes wound the soul more grievously, and are more dangerous, than those which are committed outwardly.[841]

Regarding the sacrament of the Eucharist, Pope Francis' erroneous teachings that faith alone is necessary to receive Holy Communion and his strange silence over the requirement to be in a state of grace, are also contrary to the Council of Trent, and *Code of Canon Law* (1983), Canon 916. When Pope Francis writes that all that is necessary to receive Holy Communion, is 'the wedding garment of faith which comes from the hearing of his Word'[842] he is repeating the teaching of the Protestant heresiarchs 'that

[838] *Ibid.,* p. 399
[839] Council of Trent [1563] *Doctrine on the Sacrament of Marriage* [Online] Available at: http://www.thecounciloftrent.com [Accessed on: 1 September 2022]
[840] Second Vatican Council [1965] Pastoral Constitution *Gaudium et Spes*, para 48, 49 [Online] Available at: www.vatican.va [Accessed on: 2 September 2022]
[841] Council of Trent [1551] *On the Most Holy Sacraments of Penance and Extreme Unction*, Chap. V [Online] Available at: http://www.thecounciloftrent.com [Accessed on: 2 September 2022]
[842] Pope Francis [2022] Apostolic Letter *Desiderio Desideravi*, 5. [Online] Available at: www.vatican.va [Accessed on: 2nd September 2022]

faith alone [*fides informis*] is sufficient preparation for the reception of the Eucharist'.[843] The Council of Trent taught, 'no one, conscious to himself of mortal sin, how contrite soever he may seem to himself, ought to approach to the sacred Eucharist without previous sacramental confession'.[844] The council fathers also declared, 'If any one saith, that faith alone is a sufficient preparation for receiving the sacrament of the most holy Eucharist; let him be anathema' (Canon XI).

Regarding his unprecedented sacramental innovation of allowing those engaging in habitual adultery, in certain unspecified circumstances, to receive sacramental absolution and Holy Communion, Pope Francis contravenes the solemnly defined doctrines of the Church regarding the sacrament of penance, the sacrament of the Eucharist and the sacrament of marriage.

Proof from the Sources of Faith
a) Teaching from Holy Scripture
The foundational revelation about the indissolubility of marriage is appropriately contained in the Book of Genesis's account of God's creation of man. Human beings are constituted as the integral complementarity of maleness and femaleness, the union of which requires an indissoluble bond, 'Wherefore a man shall leave father and mother, and shall cleave to his wife: and they shall be two in one [*echad*] flesh' (Gen 2:24). The Hebrew word signifying the oneness of the union between husband and wife — אֶחָד [*echad*] — is the same word that expresses the oneness of God, 'Hear, O Israel, the Lord our God is one Lord' (Deut 6:4). Created in the image and likeness of God (Gen 1:27), the marriage bond unites husband and wife in a holy 'oneness'.

The Old Testament teaches that God judges adultery as a great evil, that must be condemned with the most severe punishment, 'Thou shalt not commit adultery' (Ex 2014); 'If a man lie with another man's wife, they shall both die, that is to say, the adulterer and the adulteress: and thou shalt take away the evil out of Israel' (Deut 5:18;cf. Lv 20:10); 'And I will come to you in judgment, and will be a speedy witness against sorcerers, and adulterers' (Ml 3:5).

The Lord's covenant with Israel is presented as an indissoluble marriage, expressed through the nuptial formula, '"I take you as my people, and I will be your God"' (Ex 6:7; Lev 26:12). In the Ancient Near East culture, the covenant established a blood relationship between the contracting parties, expressed by the word, *hesed*, which conveys loyalty and affection.

Adultery is such an abhorrent evil it is employed by the prophets to convey the abomination of Israel breaking the covenant through infidelity by worshipping idols, 'I fed them to the full, and they committed adultery, and rioted in the harlot's house' (Jer 5:7) 'And I said to her that was worn out in her adulteries: Now will this woman still continue in her fornication' (Ezek 23:43).

In his defence of the indissolubility of marriage against divorce, our Lord Jesus Christ pointed to its origins in God's creation of man:

> Have ye not read, that he who made man from the beginning, made them male and female? And he said: For this cause shall a man leave father and mother, and shall cleave to his wife, and they two shall be in one flesh. Therefore now they are not two, but one flesh. What therefore God hath joined together, let no man put asunder (Mt 19: 4-6).

Our Lord reveals that indissolubility is intrinsically constitutional to those joined together by God as husband and wife. St. Augustine compared the indissolubility marriage with the indelible sacramental character imprinted on the soul by Baptism — the marriage bond cannot be 'cancelled neither by separation nor by union with

---

[843] Ott, L [1957] *Op. cit.*, p.399
[844] Council of Trent [1551] *Concerning the Most Holy Sacrament of the Eucharist*, Chap. VII. [Online] Available at: http://www.thecounciloftrent.com [Accessed on: 2 September 2022]

another'.[845] Ott comments, 'But Matrimony is not like Baptism, absolutely unrepeatable; it is however, relatively unrepeatable, that is, during the lifetime of the other marriage partner'.[846]

St. Paul made it clear that the indissolubility of marriage was a divine law, and not a man made one, that remained in force until the death of a spouse, and that if the couple separate, that they must remain single (I Cor 7:10;39).

Regarding the confession of sins, the Old Testament teaches the need to be totally open and honest about every sin, 'He that hideth his sins, shall not prosper: but he that shall confess, and forsake them, shall obtain mercy' (Prov 28:13); 'I have acknowledged my sin to thee, and my injustice I have not concealed. I said I will confess against myself my injustice to the Lord: and thou hast forgiven the wickedness of my sin' (Ps 31:5).

Our Lord's bestowal on the apostles of the power to forgive sins, implicitly commands the confession of all sin otherwise the confessor cannot judge which sins can be absolved, and which need further examination, 'Receive ye the Holy Ghost. Whose sins you shall forgive, they are forgiven them; and whose sins you shall retain, they are retained' (Jn 20:22-23). The confession of all sin is necessary to be cleansed of that which violates God's commands, 'If we confess our sins, he is faithful and just, to forgive us our sins, and to cleanse us from all iniquity'(I Jn 1:9).

Regarding the necessity of being in a state of sanctifying grace for the worthy reception of Holy Communion, St. Paul is explicit:

> Therefore, whosoever shall eat this bread, or drink the chalice of the Lord unworthily, shall be guilty of the body and of the blood of the Lord. But let a man prove himself: and so let him eat of that bread, and drink of the chalice. For he that eateth and drinketh unworthily, eateth and drinketh judgment [*krima*] to himself, not discerning the body of the Lord (I Cor 11:27-29).

When St. Paul writes that those who receive Holy Communion unworthily bring 'judgment' on themselves he uses the Greek word *krima*, which has connotations of an adverse verdict resulting in eternal condemnation.[847]

Pope Francis' erroneous sacramental theology, founded on an equally erroneous moral theology, gravely contravenes sacred Scripture about the nature of marital indissolubility, and the corresponding divine abhorrence of adultery, the grave sinfulness of which he compounds by downplaying sexual sin and his dismissal of the necessity of being in a state of grace to worthily receive Holy Communion.

b) The Testimony of Tradition

Inspired by sacred Scripture, the Church Fathers expressed a horror of adultery, both as an act and as a desire. Addressing the question of divorce and second unions, St. Justin Martyr wrote that our Lord would consider those involved guilty of the sin of adultery, 'So that all who, by human law, are twice married, are in the eye of our Master sinners'. The punishment for adultery, in deed and desire, being rejection by God, 'For not only he who in act commits adultery is rejected by Him, but also he who desires to commit adultery'.[848]

Commenting on our Lord's prohibition of divorce and re-marriage (Lk 16:18), Tertullian emphasised that the man who marries a woman divorced by her husband for the purpose of marrying another, commits adultery, as great a sin as that committed by the original husband, 'For he who marries a woman who is unlawfully put away is as much of an adulterer as the man who marries one who is undivorced'.[849]

[845] St. Augustine. *On Marriage and Concupiscence*, Bk. I, Chap. 11. [Online] Available at: www. newadvent.org [Accessed on: 3 September 2022]

[846] Ott, L [1957] *Op. cit.*, p.467

[847] *Strong's Concordance* [Online] Available at: biblehub.com [Accessed: 3 September 2022]

[848] St. Justin Martyr. *The First Apology*, Chap. 15 [Online] Available at: www.newadvent.org [Accessed on: 4 September 2022]

[849] Tertullian. *Against Marcion*, Bk. IV, Chap. 34 [Online] Available at: www.newadvent.org [Accessed on: 4 September 2022]

St. Ambrose warned Christians of the danger when civil law on divorce contradicts divine law:

> You dismiss your wife, therefore, as if by right and without being charged with wrongdoing; and you suppose it is proper for you to do so because no human law forbids it; but divine law forbids it. Anyone who obeys men ought to stand in awe of God. Hear the law of the Lord, which even they who propose our laws must obey: 'What God has joined together let no man put asunder'.[850]

Defending the indissolubility of marriage, St. Jerome wrote that no matter how arduous and immoral the circumstances, a spouse cannot remarry if the other spouse remains alive, 'A husband may be an adulterer or a sodomite, he may be stained with every crime and may have been left by his wife because of his sins; yet he is still her husband and, so long as he lives, she may not marry another'.[851]

St. Augustine testified that due to the 'sacramental character' of marriage, the union cannot be dissolved 'but by the death of one of them'. He argues that there can be no reason that justifies divorce and remarriage, not even if the marriage proves infertile and the couple desire children, 'if they shall so do, they commit adultery with those unto whom they join themselves, but themselves remain husbands and wives'.[852]

Regarding the sacrament of confession, the Church Fathers taught the imperative of confessing all sins. Pope St. Clement emphasised the importance of confessing 'sins of the flesh', drawing on St. Paul's description of the body as a 'temple to the Holy Ghost' (I Cor 6:19) in the context of fleeing 'fornication'. Pope Clement exhorted the Corinthians – known throughout the Hellenistic world for their sexual immorality[853] – to confess all their sins, 'while we are in this world, repent with our whole heart of the evil deeds we have done in the flesh, that we may be saved by the Lord, while we have yet an opportunity of repentance. For after we have gone out of the world, no further power of confessing or repenting will there belong to us'.[854]

Faced with an outbreak of sexual immorality due to Gnosticism, St. Irenaeus wrote of the importance of confession, warning of the dangers of not confessing such sins, 'but others of them are ashamed to do this, and in a tacit kind of way, despairing of [attaining to] the life of God, have, some of them, apostatised altogether'.[855]

In his book *On Repentance*, Tertullian reflected on the Prodigal Son's confession, 'I have sinned against heaven, and before thee, I am not now worthy to be called thy son' (Lk 15:21). He exhorted his readers to confess all their sins, because concealment of sins indicated defiant disobedience of God's Law, 'Confession of sins lightens, as much as dissimulation aggravates them; for confession is counselled by (a desire to make) satisfaction, dissimulation by contumacy'.[856]

Regarding the unworthy reception of the Blessed Sacrament, the Church Fathers emphatically warned against committing such a grave sin. St. Cyprian warned against those, like Pope Francis, who encourage individuals in a state of grave sin, such as habitual adultery, to receive Holy Communion:

---

[850] St. Ambrose. *Commentary on Luke 8:5* [Online] Available at: www.churchfathers.org [Accessed on: 4 September 2022]

[851] St. Jerome. *To Amandus*, Letter 55 [Online] Available at: www.newadvent.org [Accessed on: 4 September 2022]

[852] St. Augustine. *Of the Good of Marriage*, para 17 [Online] Available at: www.newadvent.org [Accessed on: 4 September 2022]

[853] The city of Corinth was so synonymous with licentiousness and debauchery in Hellenistic culture that it was the origin of the verb 'to Corinthianise' meaning 'to live a promiscuous life.' (Collins English Dictionary)

[854] Pope St. Clement. *Second Letter to the Corinthians*, Chap. 8 [Online] Available at: www. newadvent.org [Accessed on: 5 September 2022]

[855] St. Irenaeus. *Against Heresies*, Bk. I, Chap. 13, para 7 [Online] Available at: www.newadvent.org [Accessed on: 5 September 2022]

[856] Tertullian. *On Repentance*, Chap. 8 [Online] Available at: www.newadvent.org [Accessed on: 5 September 2022]

All these warnings being scorned and contemned — before their sin is expiated, before confession has been made of their crime, before their conscience has been purged by sacrifice and by the hand of the priest, before the offence of an angry and threatening Lord has been appeased, violence is done to His body and blood; and they sin now against their Lord more with their hand and mouth than when they denied their Lord. They think that that is peace which some with deceiving words are blazoning forth: that is not peace, but war; and he is not joined to the Church who is separated from the Gospel. Why do they call an injury a kindness? Why do they call impiety by the name of piety?[857]

St. John Chrysostom exhorted his people to be vigilant about receiving the Eucharist in a state of sin. Reminding them how rightfully indignant they were against those who tortured and killed Jesus, he told them they should have the same repugnance against receiving Holy Communion unworthily, 'Look therefore, lest you also yourself become guilty of the body and blood of Christ. They slaughtered the all-holy body, but you receive it in a filthy soul after such great benefits'. Instead of being lax about being in a state of sin, as Pope Francis advocates, we should seek to 'exceed in purity', recalling that the angels 'tremble, and dare not so much as look up at it without awe on account of the brightness that comes thence, with this we are fed, with this we are commingled, and we are made one body and one flesh with Christ'.[858]

St. Thomas Aquinas could not be more unequivocal about the consequences of receiving Holy Communion unworthily, 'if anyone, while in mortal sin, receives this sacrament, he purchases damnation, by sinning mortally'. He sees receiving Holy Communion while being in a state of mortal sin as a type of lying. Holy Communion sacramentally signifies being made one with the mystical body of Christ, which is only possible if the communicant has 'living faith'. Therefore, as those who are in a state of mortal sin do not have 'living faith' their Eucharistic communion is a lie because it does not signify being a member of Christ's body. St. Thomas Aquinas spells out the consequences of lying to the Blessed Sacrament:

…it is manifest that whoever receives this sacrament while in mortal sin, is guilty of lying to this sacrament, and consequently of sacrilege, because he profanes the sacrament: and therefore he sins mortally.[859]

When Pope Francis misleads individuals committing habitual adultery — due to being divorced and civilly re-married — to receive Holy Communion, he is not giving poor sinners 'medicine' but putting them in the situation where they compound the mortal sin of adultery with the mortal sin of sacrilege.

c) The Defence by the Magisterium

From the first centuries of Christianity, the Church has defended the indissolubility of the marriage bond. In the 4th century, the Synod of Elvira promulgated a canon banning divorce and re-marriage, and denying Holy Communion to those entering into illicit second marriages:

Likewise, if a believing woman has left her believing, adulterous husband and wishes to marry another, let her be forbidden to marry; if she does marry, she may not receive communion unless the husband she abandoned has previously departed this world, unless, perhaps, the exigency of illness urges the giving of it to her.[860]

In the 12th century, referencing I Corinthians 7, Pope Innocent III insisted that properly contracted marriages could not be broken, 'we strictly forbid that those rightly

[857] St. Cyprian of Carthage. *Treatise 3, On the Lapsed,* Chap. 16. [Online] Available at: www.newadvent.org [Accessed on: 5 September 2022]
[858] St. John Chrysostom. *Homily 82 on Matthew* [Online] Available at: www.newadvent.org [Accessed on: 5 September 2022]
[859] St. Thomas Aquinas. *Summa Theologiae.* Tertia Pars. Q 80. Art 4 [Online] Available at: www.newadvent.org [Accessed on: 5 September 2022]
[860] Denzinger, H. *Op. cit.,* p.49, Dz 117

contracted be broken'.[861] And in the 18th century, Pope Benedict XIV promulgated a constitution professing that 'the bond of the sacrament of matrimony is indissoluble'. He went on to stipulate that though 'separation of bed and board' was possible in cases of 'adultery, heresy, and some other causes', 'it is not lawful for them to contract another marriage'.[862]

In the early 19th century, Pope Pius VII responded to a pastoral crisis in Germany caused by certain Catholic priests giving the nuptial blessing to Catholics seeking to enter into a second marriage, having been granted a divorce by secular authorities. Pope Pius VII made the following points in his response to the Archbishop of Mainz:

i) Attempts by secular authorities to dissolve marriages by decrees of nullity have 'no value or effect in the eyes of the Church'.

ii) Due to the fact that the indissoluble bond of the first marriage cannot be dissolved, or even annulled by the sentence of a non-Catholic tribunal, any subsequent union cannot be called a 'marriage' but must be called an 'adulterous union'. 'Every union between the man and woman is adulterous.'

iii) 'Priests commit a very grave crime and betray the sacred ministry, if they approve of such marriages by their presence and ratify them with their blessing!'

iv) 'Instead of sweet and persuasive words' parish priests must 'seriously exhort the person not to commit such a grave crime and sin against the law of God', established at the creation of man (Mt 19:6).[863]

Later in the 19th century, Pope Bl. Pius IX formally condemned secularist presumptions to dissolve the marriage bond in his famous *Syllabus of Errors* [1864]. The error to be rejected by Catholics, he defined as follows, 'By the law of nature, the marriage tie is not indissoluble, and in many cases divorce properly so called may be decreed by the civil authority'.[864]

Popes of the early 20th century continued the magisterial defence of the divine law of the indissolubility of marriage against secular government's introducing civil divorce laws. Pope St. Pius X emphatically declared, 'the bond of Christian marriage cannot be dissolved by the civil authority, because the civil authority cannot interfere with the matter of the sacrament nor can it put asunder what God has joined together'.[865] In his famous encyclical defending marriage, *Casti Connubii*, Pope Pius XI wrote about the clash between human laws and Divine Law:

> Opposed to all these reckless opinions, Venerable Brethren, stands the unalterable law of God, fully confirmed by Christ, a law that can never be deprived of its force by the decrees of men, the ideas of a people or the will of any legislator: 'What God hath joined together, let no man put asunder.' And if any man, acting contrary to this law, shall have put asunder, his action is null and void, and the consequence remains (Lk 16:18).[866]

In an audience with newly married couples, Pope Ven. Pius XII warned against those who sought in every way to throw off the 'yoke' of indissolubility because they want 'the free satisfaction of its inordinate appetites'.[867]

With the wide acceptance in the 20th century of divorce and civil re-marriage, even among many Catholics, there was a corresponding campaign to pressure the Church

---

[861] *Ibid.*, p.513, Dz 2536

[862] *Ibid.*

[863] Pope Pius VII [1803] Brief *Etsi Fraternitatis* to the Archbishop of Mainz (Trans. Andrew Guernsey) [Online] Available at: aguernz.medium.com [Accessed on 6 September 2022].

[864] Pope Bl. Pius IX [1864] *The Syllabus of Errors*, error 67 [Online] www.papalencyclicals.net [Accessed on: 6 September 2022]

[865] Pope St. Pius X [1908] *Catechism of Pope St. Pius X* [Online] Available at: www.ewtn.com [Accessed on: 6 September 2022]

[866] Pope Pius XI [1930] Encyclical *Casti Connubii*, para 87 [Online] Available at: www.vatican.va [Accessed on: 6 September 2022]

[867] Pope Pius XII [1942] *Audience with Newlywed Couples.* [Online] Available at: www. marriageuniqueforareason.org [Accessed on: 6 September 2022]

to change her doctrine regarding allowing couples in adulterous unions to receive the sacraments. Throughout his pontificate Pope St. John Paul II sought to defend the prohibition of individuals in adulterous unions receiving the sacraments of confession and the Eucharist. His defence can be summarised as follows:

i)   Pope St. John Paul II took a Christological approach in defending the indissolubility of marriage, which, he wrote, is 'a fruit, a sign and a requirement of the absolutely faithful love that God has for man and that the Lord Jesus has for the Church'; 'Christian couples are called to participate truly in the irrevocable indissolubility that binds Christ to the Church His bride, loved by Him to the end';[868] 'To treat indissolubility not as a natural juridical norm but as a mere ideal empties of meaning the unequivocal declaration of Jesus Christ, who absolutely refused divorce because "from the beginning it was not so" (Mt 19,8)';[869] '[Marriage is] the image of the spousal relationship between Christ and his Church'.[870]

ii) The divorced and civilly remarried cannot be admitted to Holy Communion because their state of life 'objectively contradict that union of love between Christ and the Church which is signified and effected by the Eucharist';[871] '[They are] in a situation that objectively contravenes God's law. Consequently, they cannot receive Eucharistic communion as long as this situation persists'.[872]

iii) 'A person who is conscious of grave sin is not to celebrate Mass or receive the body of the Lord without previous sacramental confession';[873] 'Anyone who desires to receive Christ in Eucharistic communion must be in the state of grace. Anyone aware of having sinned mortally must not receive communion without having received absolution in the sacrament of penance';[874] 'in order to receive the Eucharist in a worthy manner, "one must first confess one's sins, when one is aware of mortal sin"';[875] 'The Code of Canon Law refers to this situation of a manifest lack of proper moral disposition when it states that those who 'obstinately persist in manifest grave sin' are not to be admitted to Eucharistic communion. (CIC 915).'[876]

iv) In order to receive sacramental absolution and Holy Communion, the divorced and re-married couple must repent of 'having broken the sign of the Covenant and of fidelity to Christ'. Therefore, they must be 'sincerely ready to undertake a way of life that is no longer in contradiction to the indissolubility of marriage.' If, for serious reasons such as the upbringing of children, they cannot separate, then they must 'take on themselves the duty to live in complete continence, that is, by abstinence from the acts proper to married couples'.[877]

---

[868] Pope St. John Paul II [1981] Apostolic Exhortation *Familiaris Consortio*, para 20 [Online] Available at: www.vatican.va [Accessed on: 6 September 2022]
[869] Pope St. John Paul II [2002] *Address to the members of the Tribunal of the Roman Rota*, 4. [Online] Available at: www.vatican.va [Accessed on: 6 September 2022]
[870] Congregation for the Doctrine of the Faith. [1994] *Letter to the Bishops of the Catholic Church Concerning the Reception of Holy Communion by the Divorced and Remarried Members of the Faithful*, 7. [Online] Available at: www.vatican.va [Accessed on: 6 September 2022]
[871] Pope St. John Paul II [1981] Apostolic Exhortation *Familiaris Consortio*, para 84 [Online] Available at: www.vatican.va [Accessed on: 6 September 2022]
[872] Pope St. John Paul II [1992] *The Catechism of the Catholic Church*, para 1650 [Online] Available at: www.vatican.va [Accessed on: 6 September 2022]
[873] Pope St. John Paul II. [1983] *Revised Code of Canon Law*, Can. 916 [Online] Available at: www.vatican.va [Accessed on: 6 September 2022]
[874] Pope St. John Paul II [1992] *The Catechism of the Catholic Church*, para 1415 [Online] Available at: www.vatican.va [Accessed on: 6 September 2022]
[875] Pope St. John Paul II [2003] Encyclical *Ecclesia de Eucharistia*, para 36 [Online] Available at: www.vatican.va [Accessed on: 6 September 2022]
[876] *Ibid.*, para 37
[877] Congregation for the Doctrine of the Faith. [1994] *Letter to the Bishops of the Catholic Church Concerning the Reception of Holy Communion by the Divorced and Remarried Members of the Faithful*, para 4 [Online] Available at: www.vatican.va [Accessed on: 6 September 2022]

v) It is totally inadmissible for a divorced and 'remarried' couple to decide that they can receive Holy Communion based on an appeal to personal conscience or by coming 'to a decision about the existence or absence of a previous marriage and the value of the new union.' (*Code of Canon Law*, 1085 § 2).[878]

vi) Given the gravity of the matter and the spiritual good of these persons, as well as the common good of the Church, pastors have a serious duty to admonish them that such a judgment of conscience openly contradicts the Church's teaching (*Code of Canon Law*, 978 §2).[879]

Pope Benedict XVI also categorically upheld the prohibition of sacramental absolution and Holy Communion to the divorced and remarried 'as long as their situation, which objectively contravenes God's law, persists'.[880] He continued Pope St. John Paul II's Christological defence of the sacramental prohibition, writing that the divorced and remarried cannot be admitted to the sacraments, 'since their state and their condition of life objectively contradict the loving union of Christ and the Church signified and made present in the Eucharist'.[881]

Pope Benedict XVI criticised a pastoral approach to adulterous unions that exhibited laxism, which he described as a 'complacent attitude towards the parties' that did 'not correspond with the good of the parties and of the Ecclesial Community itself'. By 'avoiding confrontation with the truth that saves,' such laxity 'can even turn out to be counterproductive with regard to each person's saving encounter with Christ... [because] it reinforces in them, if only implicitly, the tendency to forget the indissolubility of their union'. He saw such pastoral laxism as obscuring the 'integrity of the Christian mystery' through deceiving couples in difficulty.[882]

Furthermore, Pope Benedict XVI criticised those 'in certain ecclesiastical milieus' who sought the 'canonical regulation' of adulterous unions, 'independently of the validity or nullity of his/her' existing first marriage. (A similar course taken nine years later by Pope Francis with *Amoris Laetitia* and his elevation to the status of *Acta Apostolicae Sedis* of the Argentinian *Basic Criteria for the Implementation of Chapter VIII of Amoris Laetitia*.) Pope Benedict XVI's critique of this erroneous pastoral approach is as follows:

i) It is erroneous to declare matrimonial nullity through a process that formalises 'subjective claims' because there are a 'whole set of principles of the divine law which establish' the 'true and permanent anthropological meaning' of indissolubility.

ii) Pope Benedict XVI described our Lord's teaching 'What therefore God has joined together, let no man put asunder' (Mt 19: 4-6) as the 'anthropological and saving truth of marriage' that also expresses the juridical dimension of indissolubility.

iii) The matrimonial principle of indissolubility instituted by God at man's creation (Gen 1: 27; 2: 24) attains in full manifestation in Christ's union with the Church (Eph 5: 30-31).

iv) This matrimonial principle of indissolubility revealed in creation and redemption establishes 'the authentic juridical anthropology of marriage'.

v) Though 'every marriage is of course the result of the free consent of the man and the woman', 'their freedom expresses the natural capacity inherent in their

---

[878] Congregation for the Doctrine of the Faith. [1994] *Letter to the Bishops of the Catholic Church Concerning the Reception of Holy Communion by the Divorced and Remarried Members of the Faithful*, para 7 [Online] Available at: www.vatican.va [Accessed on: 6 September 2022]

[879] *Ibid.*, para 6

[880] Pope Benedict XVI [2005] *Compendium of the Catechism of the Catholic Church*, Q. 349. [Online] Available at: www.vatican.va [Accessed on: 7 September 2022]

[881] Pope Benedict XVI [2007] Post Synodal Apostolic Exhortation *Sacramentum Caritatis*, para 20. [Online] Available at: www.vatican.va [Accessed on: 7 September 2022]

[882] Pope Benedict XVI [2006] *Address to the Members of the Tribunal of the Roman Rota* [Online] Available at: www.vatican.va [Accessed on: 7 September 2022]

masculinity and femininity'. This integral complementarity objectively expresses the juridical principle, 'What therefore God has joined together, let no man put asunder'.

vi) 'The union takes place by virtue of the very plan of God who created them male and female and gives them the power to unite for ever those natural and complementary dimensions of their persons.'

vii) Pope Benedict XVI defined the fundamental juridical anthropological principle as follows: 'The indissolubility of marriage does not derive from the definitive commitment of those who contract it but is intrinsic in the nature of the "powerful bond established by the Creator"'.

viii) 'The essential juridical character of marriage is inherent precisely in the bond which represents for the man and for the woman a requirement of justice and love from which, for their good and for the good of all, they may not withdraw without contradicting what God himself has wrought within them'.[883]

Since the early days of Christianity, the Church has proclaimed, and defended, the indissolubility of marriage, and the imperative of the worthy reception of Holy Communion. Over two thousand years, Church Fathers and popes have steadfastly defended these sacraments from the erroneous ideas of Gnostics, Protestants, and Secularists, but in 2016 with the promulgation of *Amoris Laetitia* Pope Francis overturned the prohibition on those in adulterous union from receiving sacramental absolution and Holy Communion. Thereby, the Supreme Pontiff allowed sacrilege against three sacraments — confession, the Eucharist and matrimony.

---

[883] Pope Benedict XVI [2007] *Address to the members of the Tribunal of the Roman Rota*. [Online] Available at: www.vatican.va [Accessed on: 7 September 2022]

Sacraments (2) — Sacramentals: Blessings

P. *Those engaged in 'irregular relationships' that are 'morally unacceptable from an objective point of view', including those involving sodomy, can receive a blessing from a priest or deacon as a couple. Though the couple present themselves for a blessing together, the blessing does not represent acceptance or affirmation of their union or civil status as a couple. The moral requirements necessary to receive a sacrament are not required to receive such blessings of irregular relationships. There is a distinction between a ritual blessing and an informal, spontaneous blessing due to the lack of a liturgical setting, liturgical vestments and liturgical rubric.*

Pope Francis' determination to permit the 'blessing' of couples 'living in sin' — divorced and civilly remarried, those cohabiting and same-sex 'unions' — constellates a number of grave errors. He contradicts sacred Scripture, Tradition and the Magisterium concerning the holiness and justice of God, manifested through His withholding of blessing, His cursing and punishment of unrepentant sinners, the moral requirements for the reception of divine grace, and the inextricable connection between sacraments and sacramentals.

Pope Francis' decision to allow the 'blessing' of homosexual bondings and other sinful sexual relationships is an expression of other grave errors in morality and hamartiology that he holds — his antinomianism (Morality, 1), his acceptance of homosexuality as created by God (Morality, 3) and his teaching that 'sins below the belt' are ordinarily not serious due to mitigating circumstances (Hamartiology, 2).

Though the Congregation for the Doctrine of the Faith's Declaration, *Fiducia Supplicans*, permitting the 'blessing' of couples 'living in sin', was promulgated in the name of its prefect Cardinal Victor Fernández, Pope Francis was intimately involved in its composition, 'the document was discussed with the Holy Father. Finally, the text of the Declaration was submitted to the Holy Father for his review, and he approved it with his signature.'[884]

Pope Francis' and Cardinal Victor Fernández's gravely erroneous justification for the 'blessing' of couples engaging in unrepented, habitual grave sin is summarised as follows:

a) Pope Francis erroneously assumes that God practices unconditional, radical inclusion towards unrepentant sinners, such as those 'living in sin', 'The Lord blesses everyone'.[885] The Supreme Pontiff considers that God's desire to bless everyone is an expression of his unconditional love, 'the unconditional power of God's love ... forms the basis for the gesture of blessing.' (*Fiducia Supplicans*, 12).

b) According to Pope Francis, God's disposition of unconditional, radical inclusion means that he will overlook and dismiss our sins, even without the need for contrition and repentance, 'So we are more important to God than all the sins we can commit because he is father, he is mother, he is pure love, he has blessed us forever. And he will never stop blessing us.' (FS 27).

c) Pope Francis makes no mention of the requirement of contrition and repentance by sinners to benefit from the redemptive blessing of our Lord Jesus Christ, 'The great blessing of God is Jesus Christ. He is the great gift of God, his own Son. He is a blessing for all humanity, a blessing that has saved us all'. (FS 1).

d) Pope Francis erroneously assumes that, as a matter of course, due to these blessings, couples engaging in adultery, fornication or sodomy will receive actual graces that will be efficacious in their unrepentant, gravely sinful relationships, 'These forms of

[884] Dicastery for the Doctrine of the Faith [2023] *Declaration Fiducia Supplicans: On the Pastoral Meaning of Blessings* [Online] Available at: www.vatican.va [Accessed on: 14 February 2024]
[885] Pullella, P [2024] *Pope defends same-sex blessings declaration, says it is misunderstood* [Online] Available at: www.reuters.com [Accessed on: 14 February 2024]

blessing express a supplication that God may grant those aids that come from the impulses of his Spirit—what classical theology calls "actual grace"' so that 'all that is true, good, and humanly valid in their lives and their relationships be enriched, healed, and elevated by the presence of the Holy Spirit.'(FS 31).

e) The Church must emulate God's unconditional, radical inclusion and bless everyone, 'God communicates to his Church the power to bless. Granted by God to human beings and bestowed by them on their neighbours, the blessing is transformed into inclusion, solidarity, and peacemaking. It is a positive message of comfort, care, and encouragement.' (FS 19); 'Such blessings are meant for everyone; no one is to be excluded from them.' (FS 28).[886]

f) Pope Francis' erroneous assumption that God is radically inclusive towards unrepentant sinners informs his understanding of a permissive, amoral 'pastoral charity', 'in our dealings with people, we must not lose pastoral charity, which should permeate all our decisions and attitudes. The defense of objective truth is not the only expression of this charity; it also includes kindness, patience, understanding, tenderness, and encouragement. Therefore, we cannot become judges who only deny, reject, and exclude;' (FS 13) '...pastoral charity requires us not to treat simply as "sinners" those 'in situations that are morally unacceptable from an objective point of view.' (FS 26).[887]

g) Ignoring the conditions that establish if an immoral act is mortal sin, such permissive, amoral pastoral charity requires assuming that those couples 'in situations that are morally unacceptable from an objective point of view' are not guilty or responsible, 'the same pastoral charity requires us not to treat simply as "sinners" those whose guilt or responsibility may be attenuated by various factors affecting subjective imputability (cf. St. John Paul II, *Reconciliatio et Paenitentia*, 17).

h) Therefore, Pope Francis concludes that if a couple engaging in adultery, fornication or sodomy present themselves for a blessing the priest or deacon must not engage 'an exhaustive moral analysis' because 'those seeking a blessing should not be required to have prior moral perfection.' (FS 25).

i) Instead, couples whose situations are 'morally unacceptable from an objective point of view' are eligible to receive God's blessing on their relationship, despite engaging in adultery, fornication or sodomy, so that 'all that is true, good, and humanly valid in their lives and their relationships be enriched, healed, and elevated by the presence of the Holy Spirit.' (FS 31). The focus of such blessings is explicitly relational, not individualistic, that they 'have peace, health, a spirit of patience, dialogue, and mutual assistance'. (FS 38).

j) When dispensing God's blessing, Pope Francis gives priority to the fact that the couple 'love each other', excluding the immoral nature and acts of those couples who engage in adultery, fornication or sodomy, 'I do not bless a "homosexual marriage," I bless two people who love each other.'[888]

k) Pope Francis directs that priests and deacons must avoid insisting that couples presenting for a blessing must live according to God's commandments, which he characterises as 'resting its pastoral praxis on the fixed nature of certain doctrinal or disciplinary schemes.' To Pope Francis' bizarre way of thinking, to challenge the couple with God's commandments expressed through doctrine or discipline would be to indulge in 'a narcissistic and authoritarian elitism, whereby instead of evangelising, one analyses and classifies others, and instead of opening the door to grace, one exhausts his or her energies in inspecting and verifying.' (FS 25).

l) Pope Francis proposes a novel, bogus distinction between ritual and liturgical blessings' and 'non-ritualised blessings' (FS 36), as if the priest or deacon making

---

[886] Dicastery for the Doctrine of the Faith [2023] Op cit

[887] Pope Francis [2023] *Respuestas to the Dubia of two Cardinals* [Online] Available at: www.vatican.va [Accessed on: 14 February 2024]

[888] Santucci, M [2024] *Pope Francis: To be 'scandalized' by gay couple blessings is 'hypocrisy'* [Online] Available at: www.catholicnewsagency.com [Accessed on 14 February 2024]

the sign of the cross and offering a prayer of blessing isn't a 'ritual', no matter how simple and spontaneous.

m) By creating this false distinction between liturgical blessings and 'non-ritualised blessings' Pope Francis is seeking to separate blessing as a sacramental from the sacraments, 'From the point of view of pastoral care, blessings should be evaluated as acts of devotion that "are external to the celebration of the Holy Eucharist and of the other sacraments." (FS 24).

n) By so doing, Pope Francis is attempting to free his novel 'non-ritualised blessings' from any moral requirement for reception by couples engaging in adultery, fornication or sodomy. Such moral requirements are necessary for the reception of the sacraments, 'One must also avoid the risk of reducing the meaning of blessings to this point of view alone, for it would lead us to expect the same moral conditions for a simple blessing that are called for in the reception of the sacraments.' (FS 12). As we will see below such a rupture between a sacramental and the sacraments is totally contrary to the doctrine of the Church.

Pope Francis and Cardinal Victor Fernández's determination to affirm the positive aspects of the relationships of those engaging in grave sexual sins through blessing the 'couple' represents a school of thought among Jesuits. This gravely erroneous point-of-view was previously expressed by the prominent 'progressive' Cardinal Carlo Maria Martini S.J., the former Archbishop of Milan. Cardinal Martini criticised the Church for not affirming the 'positive' aspects of adulterous and sodomitical relationships, while making no mention of the presence of grievous personal sin:

> But it's not bad, if instead of casual homosexual sex, two persons should have a degree of stability and therefore in this sense the State could also favour them. I do not agree with the positions of those in the Church, who take issue with civil unions [...] The Catholic Church, for its part, promotes partnerships that are beneficial for the continuation of the human species and its stability, and yet it is not right to express any discrimination for other types of unions.[889]

The Teaching of the Church
In the case of adult recipients moral worthiness is necessary for the worthy or fruitful reception of the Sacraments. (**De Fide.**)
There is a grace which is truly sufficient and yet remains inefficacious (gratia vere et mere sufficiens). (**De Fide.**)
Not only those members who are holy but the sinners also belong to the Church. (**Sent. certa.**)
The souls of those who die in the condition of personal grievous sin enter Hell. (**De Fide.**)

There is an inextricable union between the sacraments and sacramentals, such as blessings (*benedictiones*). Though unlike sacraments, sacramentals cannot confer sanctifying grace, their purpose is to 'dispose to its reception'.[890] As the 1917 Code of Canon Law stated, 'Sacramentals are objects or actions which resemble the sacraments in some ways, and which the church uses to obtain, through her intercession, various effects, usually of a spiritual kind.' (CIC 1144).[891] This understanding of the similarity between sacraments and sacramentals was again emphasised by the 1983 Code of Canon Law, 'Sacramentals are sacred signs by which effects, especially spiritual effects, are signified in some imitation of the sacraments and are obtained through the intercession of the Church.' (CIC 1166).[892] Therefore, Pope Francis' assertion that the 'non-ritualised bless-

---

[889] Marino, I & Martini, C [2012] *Cardinal Martini: The Gays and I* [Online] Available at: www.emmaus2rome.wordpress.com [Accessed on: 15 February 2024]
[890] Ott, L [1957] *Op cit.*, p.349
[891] Leeming, P [1960] *Principles of Sacramental Theology*. London: Longmans, Green and Co Ltd, 614
[892] Pope St. John Paul II. [1983] *Revised Code of Canon Law*, Can. 916 [Online] Available at: www.vatican.va [Accessed on: 16 February 2024]

ings' of couples 'living in sin' must be separated from the moral requirements for the reception of sacraments makes no sense.

Dr. Ludwig Ott writes that sacramentals, such as blessings, are principally efficacious due to the 'intercessory prayer of the Church' because 'she is the holy and immaculate bride of Christ' (Eph 5:25-28)'.[893] The Church's competence to sanctify through blessing is a manifestation of the nuptial relationship between our Lord Jesus Christ and His bride, the Church,

> Husbands, love your wives, as Christ also loved the church, and delivered himself up for it: That he might sanctify it, cleansing it by the laver of water in the word of life: That he might present it to himself a glorious church, not having spot or wrinkle, or any such thing; but that it should be holy, and without blemish. (Eph 5:25-28).

Consequently, considering the Christic nuptial origins of the Church's power to sanctify, it is particularly abhorrent of Pope Francis to propose the 'blessing' of couples engaging in grave sexual sins, such as adultery, fornication or sodomy, that are intrinsically anti-nuptial. Furthermore, if the purpose of sacramentals is to sanctify members of the Church, so that she is without 'spot or wrinkle', 'holy and without blemish' Pope Francis' decision to 'bless' unrepentant couples engaging in sodomy — one of the four sins that cry out to heaven for vengeance — is incomprehensible.

In light of the inextricable relationship between sacraments and sacramentals the question of the moral worthiness of the recipients arises. The Council of Trent declared that '…it is unbeseeming for any one to approach to any of the sacred functions, unless he approach holily'.[894] Apart from showing worthy reverence, the moral and spiritual disposition of the recipients determines the fruitful reception of the blessing and the efficaciousness of grace bestowed by the blessing.

Pope Francis explains that the purpose of blessing those in 'irregular relationships' is that the couple receive the 'impulses of the Holy Spirit', which he also refers to as 'actual grace' 'so that 'all that is true, good, and humanly valid in their lives and their relationships be enriched, healed, and elevated by the presence of the Holy Spirit.'(FS 31). However, in order to efficaciously receive actual grace the recipients must be morally worthy by removing 'any obstacles to grace' such as 'consciousness of grievous sin' and by being in a state of grace.[895] But the one thing that is necessary for couples 'living in sin' to do in order to receive the grace of the blessing Pope Francis explicitly forbids — a moral examination leading to contrition and repentance. *Fiducia Supplicans* repeatedly instructs the ministers of the blessing not to assist the couple with moral discernment , they 'must not engage 'an exhaustive moral analysis' because 'those seeking a blessing should not be required to have prior moral perfection.' (FS 25). Thus by entrenching the obstacles to grace — unrepented grievous sins of adultery, fornication or sodomy — Pope Francis blocks the possibility of fostering a good disposition and the worthy reception of actual grace. Thereby, tragically frustrating one of the purposes inherent in the blessing — inclining the recipient to repentance and genuine devotion.[896]

The permissive, amoral 'pastoral charity' promoted by Pope Francis (FS13; 26) also encourages the couple engaging in adultery, fornication or sodomy, to render the grace inefficacious — though it is truly sufficient to inspire their repentance — through the couple's 'resistance of will'.[897] As the Council of Trent stated, man 'is also able to reject it [grace]'.[898] Such resistance to the Church's doctrine on sexual morality is a particular problem for homosexual persons due to their ideology of 'gay pride', which *Fiducia Supplicans* does nothing to address, but rather exacerbates.

---

[893] Ott, L [1957] *Op cit.*, p.349

[894] General Council of Trent: Thirteenth Session [1551] *Decree Concerning the Most Holy Sacrament of the Eucharist* [Online] Available at: www.papalencyclicals.net [Accessed on:16 February 2024]

[895] Ott, L [1957] *ibid*

[896] Leeming, P [1960] *Op cit.*, p. 616

[897] Ott, L [1957] *Op cit.*, p. 247

[898] General Council of Trent: Sixth Session [1547] *Decree on Justification* [Online] Available at: www. papalencyclicals.net [Accessed on:16 February 2024]

The radical inclusion expressed in *Fiducia Supplicans*, summed up in Pope Francis' mantra 'tutti, tutti, tutti' [Everyone, everyone, everyone],[899] forgets one thing — that outward membership of the Catholic Church doesn't guarantee salvation. As the Second Vatican Council stated,

> He is not saved, however, who, though part of the body of the Church, does not persevere in charity. He remains indeed in the bosom of the Church, but, as it were, only in a 'bodily' manner and not 'in his heart'…If they fail moreover to respond to that grace in thought, word and deed, not only shall they not be saved but they will be the more severely judged. (LG 14).[900]

Without the interior disposition of contrition and repentance leading to confession, penance and absolution through the sacrament of reconciliation, those members of the Church who remain in a state of grievous sin — who have refused God's mercy — could bring upon themselves God's justice, expressed through his punishments, including withholding his blessings, receiving his curses and the ultimate punishment, Hell.

Proof from the Sources of Faith
a) Teaching from Holy Scripture
Pope Francis' caricature of the relationship between God and man to being one in which God is only capable of bestowing blessings, including on couples engaged in objectively morally unacceptable acts, contradicts the testimony of both the Old Testament and New Testament.

The Old Testament is clear that God bestows blessings on those who keep his covenant, including the prohibition on adultery and other sexual sins, and God inflicts curses on those who transgress his covenant:

> Behold I set forth in your sight this day a blessing and a curse: A blessing, if you obey the commandments of the Lord your God, which I command you this day: A curse, if you obey not the commandments of the Lord your God, but revolt from the way which now I shew you, and walk after strange gods which you know not. (Dt 11:26-28).

Unrepentant sinners cannot hide their hard hearts from the searching judgement of God through the pretence of external religious acts, such as 'non-ritualised blessings',

> Forasmuch as this people draw near me with their mouth, and with their lips glorify me, but their heart is far from me […] Woe to you that are deep of heart, to hide your counsel from the Lord: and their works are in the dark, and they say: Who seeth us, and who knoweth us? This thought of yours is perverse…(Isa 29:13;15-16).

The warning from Salvation History is that those who defiantly break God's commandments with stubborn and rebellious hearts incur God's punishment, not his blessings,

> But the heart of this people is become hard of belief and provoking, they are revolted and gone away. And they have not said in their heart: let us fear the Lord our God, who giveth us the early and the latter rain in due season: who preserveth for us the fulness of the yearly harvest. Your iniquities have turned these things away, and your sins have withholden good things from you. (Jer 5:23-25).

God allows this blindness of heart among defiant, unrepentant sinners as a punishment that sinks them ever deeper into the tribulations of sin, 'Blind the heart of this people, and make their ears heavy, and shut their eyes: lest they see with their eyes, and hear with their ears, and understand with their heart, and be converted and I heal them.' (Isa 6:10).

---

[899] Pope Francis [2023] *Full text: Pope Francis' homily opening the Synod on Synodality* [Online] Available at: www.americamagazine.org [Accessed on: 16 February 2024]

[900] Second Vatican Council [1965] Dogmatic Constitution on the Church, *Lumen Gentium*, para 14 [Online] Available at: www.vatican.va [Accessed on: 16 February 2024]

One of the most famous blessings of the Old Testament is the blessing giving by God to Aaron the priest, and to his sons, to bestow on the people of Israel, which includes, 'The Lord shew his face to thee'. (Num 6: 24-25). To those who defiantly break the commandments, God does not 'shew his face', instead he 'hides his face', and hears not their 'prayers' for blessing,

> 'But your iniquities have divided between you and your God, and your sins have hid his face from you that he should not hear'; 'Then shall they cry to the Lord, and he will not hear them: and he will hide his face from them at that time, as they have behaved wickedly in their devices.' (Isa 59:2; Micah 3:4).

The psalms condemn the blessing of defiant, unrepentant sinners, described as those who have become blind through their apostasy, 'For the sinner is praised in the desires of his soul: and the unjust man is blessed [...] God is not before his eyes: his ways are filthy at all times. Thy judgments are removed from his sight.' (Ps 9: 102-105).

It is sinful in itself to express approval of sinners, absurdly assuming that God would do likewise 'If thou didst see a thief thou didst run with him: and with adulterers thou hast been a partaker [...] These things hast thou done, and I was silent. Thou thoughtest unjustly that I should be like to thee: but I will reprove thee, and set before thy face.' (Ps 49: 18;21).

The Old Testament testimony to God's punishment of unrepentant sinners through allowing them to reap the consequence of their sin through the hardening their hearts and increasing spiritually blindness is re-iterated in the New Testament. Though our Lord on the cross removes God's primeval punishment of the curse of original sin (Gal 3:13) refusal to repent and believe in Jesus Christ and live a life obedient to God's commandments brings down his punishment on defiant sinners. The New Testament makes clear that those in 'irregular relationships', that involve committing adultery, fornication and sodomy, are punished through exclusion from the Kingdom of God and the fellowship of the Church (1 Cor 5: 10-11; 6: 9-10; Gal 5:19; Jam 4:4; Rev 21:8).

The gospels testify that our Lord Jesus Christ explained that refusal to repent and believe in him is punished by him allowing sinners to suffer the consequences of their sin, including hardness of heart and spiritual blindness, explicitly fulfilling the prophecy of Isaiah (6:10):

> He hath blinded their eyes, and hardened their heart, that they should not see with their eyes, nor understand with their heart, and be converted, and I should heal them. (Jn 12:40; Mt 13: 13-15).

St. Paul explicates the nature of this 'blindness' as punishment from God on unrepentant sinners, using the Greek word *plánē*, derived from the noun *planaó*, meaning to wander into deviant behaviour, to wander from God's truth into delusion and sin,[901]

> And in all seduction of iniquity to them that perish; because they receive not the love of the truth, that they might be saved. Therefore God shall send them the operation of error [*plánē*] to believe lying: That all may be judged who have not believed the truth, but have consented to iniquity. (1 Thess 2:10-11).

St. Paul makes clear that the deviant behaviour of unrepentant sinners, epitomised by sodomitic relationships, is the manifestation of divine punishment — God allows defiant sinners to sink deeper and deeper into the delusion of their sin,

> Wherefore God gave them up to the desires of their heart, unto uncleanness, to dishonour their own bodies among themselves. Who changed the truth of God into a lie [...] For this cause God delivered them up to shameful affections. For their women have changed the natural use into that use which is against nature. And, in like manner, the men also, leaving the natural use of the women, have burned in their lusts one towards another, men with men working that which is filthy, and receiving in themselves the

---

901 *Strong's Concordance* [Online] Available at: biblehub.com [Accessed on: 26 February 2024]

recompense which was due to their error [*planēs*] And as they liked not to have God in their knowledge, God delivered them up to a reprobate sense… (Rom 1:24-32).

Therefore, in light of the fact that homosexuality is the manifestation of God's punishment of defiant sinners, it is incoherent to the point of absurdity to bestow God's 'blessing' on those 'couples' whom God is allowing to damn themselves. Such an act of blessing is sacrilege, colluding with such couples wandering deeper into the delusion of deviant behaviour.

b) The Testimony of Tradition

St. Irenaeus understood that there is a fundamental dichotomy in God's interaction with human beings — his bestowal of blessing, and its opposite, his infliction of blindness. God blesses those 'who believe in Him and follow Him' with 'fuller and greater illumination of mind'. And to those who 'do not believe' and 'set Him at naught', God blinds,

> God, knowing the number of those who will not believe, since He foreknows all things, has given them over to unbelief, and turned away His face from men of this stamp, leaving them in the darkness which they have themselves chosen for themselves.[902]

Reflecting on John 9:39 — 'For judgment am I come into this world, that they which see not, might see, and that they which see might be made blind' — St. Augustine concluded that according to God's judgement there are two distinct groups among human beings that must not be confused,

> For among the secret things, which contain the righteous principles of God's judgment, there is a secret which determines that the minds of some shall be blinded, and the minds of some enlightened.[903]

St. Augustine explored St. Paul's understanding of 'blindness' as punishment from God on unrepentant sinners:

1) Those unrepentant sinners who God inflicts with blindness don't know they are being punished by God, which is part of the blindness, '*The sinner has provoked the Lord, but the Lord is too angry to demand an account.* He is seething with anger all the time he does not conduct his search and seems to forget and not give heed to sins'.[904]
2) To be inflicted with spiritual and moral blindness by God means to 'be abandoned by the light of truth.'[905]
3) Those punished by spiritual and moral blindness mistakenly think that God does not judge, 'in this way God's judgements have been removed from before their face, and though they imagine that they are suffering no punishment whatsoever, this itself is the greatest condemnation.'[906]
4) Through being abandoned by the light of truth, unrepentant sinners are punished by God allowing them to reap the consequences of their deviant desires, 'Observe how God punished them more severely in handing them over to the desires of their heart, to impurity.'[907]
5) The sexual sins, in particular homosexual sex acts, are penalties for sins, 'the penalty of wickedness, though it is itself wickedness'.[908]

---

[902] St. Irenaeus of Lyons. *Against the Heresies, Bk 4,* Chap 29 [Online] Available at: www.newadvent. org [Accessed on: 26 February 204]

[903] St. Augustine. *Contra Faustum,* Bk XXI, para 2 [Online] Available at: www.newadvent.org [Accessed on: 22 February 2024]

[904] The Works of Saint Augustine: A Translation for the 21st Century. *Expositions of the Psalms.* 1-32, psalm 9. New York: New City Press,1990 p. 152-153

[905] *Op cit*

[906] *Ibid*

[907] The Works of Saint Augustine: A Translation for the 21st Century. *Answer to the Pelagians,* I/23 New York: New City Press,1990 p. 236-237

[908] *Op cit*

Commenting on Romans 1: 26-27 St. John Chrysostom described homosexuality as such a vile sin that it brought on the punishments of hell before death and particular judgement,

> But that which is contrary to nature has in it an irksomeness and displeasingness, so that they could not fairly allege even pleasure. For genuine pleasure is that which is according to nature. But when God has left one, then all things are turned upside down. And thus not only was their doctrine Satanical, but their life too was diabolical […] Consider how great is that sin, to have forced hell to appear even before its time![909]

St. Cyprian wrote that the highest degree of happiness is not to sin, and the degree of happiness next to that is to acknowledge sins. By banning moral discernment, *Fiducia Supplicans* denies both degrees of happiness to couples engaged in sexual acts that are 'morally unacceptable from an objective point of view'. Instead *Fiducia Supplicans* advocates a permissive, amoral acquiescence to the sin of the couple that condemns the minister to share in the punishment of their sinfulness,

> …those who consent unto those who do such things — who, while they are mingled in unlawful communion with the evil and sinners, and the unrepenting, are polluted by the contact of the guilty, and, being joined in the fault, are thus not separated in its penalty.[910]

Likewise, St. Augustine warned against blessing evildoers, because even though the minister of the blessing does not actually commit the sin of adultery, fornication or sodomy, he throws his lot in with the adulterer by commending what is done and by supporting the deed, 'The sinner is praised for the longings of his soul, and whoever does evil is blessed.'

Furthermore, ministers who bless couple engaged in sexual immorality not only harm themselves, they further entrench the blindness of the couple, trapping them in self-perpetuating punishment,

> …*the sinner is praised in the longings of his own soul.* The tongues of sycophants tie souls up in sins, for it is delightful to do those things in which not only is there no need to fear rebuke from anyone, but one may even hear oneself praised. *And whoever does evil deeds is blessed.* This is how they are caught in the thoughts they think.[911]

One can conclude, that as *Fiducia Supplicans* fails to call to repentance those punished by God for their wickedness, but instead blesses those who do evil and encourages them to sink deeper into the darkness of sexual deviancy, its authors have likewise been abandoned by the light of truth.

c) The Defence by the Magisterium

The divine revelation concerning God's punishment of homosexuality was explicitly safeguarded and expounded by three ecumenical councils — the Third Lateran Council, the Fourth Lateran Council and the Fifth Lateran Council. All three councils used the Pauline phrases 'sons of disobedience' deserving the 'wrath of God' to describe individuals engaging in sodomy,

> 'Let all who are found guilty of that unnatural vice for which the wrath of God came down upon the sons of disobedience and destroyed the five cities with fire…';[912] 'Let them beware of every vice involving lust, especially that on account of which the wrath

---

[909] St. John Chrysostom. *Homily* 4 on Romans 1: 26-27 [Online] www.newadvent.org [Accessed on: 27 February 2024]

[910] St. Cyprian. *Epistle 67*, para 9 [Online] Available at: www.newadvent.org [Accessed on: 26 February 2024]

[911] The Works of Saint Augustine: A Translation for the 21st Century. *Expositions of the Psalms.* 1-32, psalm 9. New York: New City Press,1990 p. 152-153

[912] Tanner, N [1990] *Third Lateran Council – 1179 A.D. Canon 11.* [Online] Available at: www. papalencyclicals.net [Accessed on: 27 February 2024]

of God came down from heaven upon the sons of disobedience';[913] 'If anyone, lay or cleric, has been found guilty of a charge on account of which the wrath of God comes upon the sons of disobedience, let him be punished by the penalties'.[914]

The Greek word St. Paul uses for 'disobedience' is *'apeitheia'* meaning obstinate rejection of God's revelation, wilful unbelief and disobedience.[915] By using 'sons of disobedience' to describe the moral state of individuals engaging in sodomy magisterial doctrine judges homosexual sex acts to be an expression of defiant rejection of God deserving not blessing but the very opposite — the punishment of divine wrath.

Furthermore, the Ecumenical Council of Vienne judged 'the deadly crime of the Sodomites' to be a grave sin against the Lord Jesus Christ himself placing it in the cate-gory of apostasy alongside idolatry and various heresies.[916]

The magisterium's judgement of sodomy as a defiant act of disobedience and apos-tasy, combined with the Council of Trent's stipulation that 'sacred functions' must be approached 'holily',[917] exposes the nonsensical incoherence of blessing sodomitic cou-ples.

Likewise, it is nonsensically incoherent to bless couples engaging in fornication and adultery. The First Council of Lyons, following I Corinthians 6:9, judged fornication and adultery a mortal sin which, if unrepented, would result in the eternal punishment of Hell, 'since the apostle declares that fornicators like adulterers are cast out from the kingdom of God.'[918]

Finally, the Second Vatican Council's warning concerning those who are members of the Church only in a 'bodily' manner and not 'in his heart' applies to those unrepen-tant couples engaged in sexual immorality, particularly sodomitic couples. When seen as an expression of defiant apostasy, such couples can be seen as failing 'to respond' to the special grace of Christ 'in thought, word and deed'. As such, they have placed themselves in grave danger, because 'not only shall they not be saved but they will be the more severely judged':

> …[at the end of the world] they who have done good shall come forth unto resurrection of life; but those who have done evil unto resurrection of judgment (Jn 5:29; Mt 25:46).[919]

One of the earliest canonical declarations regarding the magisterial approach to those engaged in sodomy or adultery was made by St. Basil, Archbishop of Caesarea in Cappadocia, during the reign of the 4th century pope St. Damasus I. St. Basil listed sodomites and adulterers among those committing heinous crimes, including bestiality, murder, witchcraft, and idolatry. Contrary to receiving a blessing, St. Basil insisted that sodomites and adulterers should receive the same punishment as murderers. He recommended that those who committed the crime of sodomy or adultery through ignorance could be received back into communion with the Church on a number of conditions: 1. Thirty years of repentance 'for the uncleanness which they committed through ignorance'; 2. Willingness to confess the sin of sodomy or adultery; 3. Leading a life over the thirty years of penance as to deserve compassion:

> They who have committed sodomy with men or brutes, murderers, wizards, adulterers, and idolaters, have been thought worthy of the same punishment; therefore observe

---

[913] Tanner, N [1990] *Fourth Lateran Council : 1215. Constitution 14.* [Online] Available at: www. papalencyclicals.net [Accessed on: 27 February 2024]

[914] Tanner, N [1990] *Fifth Lateran Council 1512-17 A.D. Reform of the Curia.* [Online] Available at: www.papalencyclicals.net [Accessed on: 19 August 2022]

[915] *Strong's Concordance* [Online] Available at: biblehub.com [Accessed on: 26 February 2024]

[916] Council of Vienne 1311-1312 A.D [Online] Available at: www.papalencyclicals.net [Accessed on: 27 February 2024]

[917] General Council of Trent: Thirteenth Session [1551] *Decree Concerning the Most Holy Sacrament of the Eucharist* [Online] Available at: www.papalencyclicals.net [Accessed on:26 February 2024]

[918] Denzinger, H [2010] *Op. cit.,* p. 277, 835; p.278, 839

[919] Second Vatican Council [1965] Dogmatic Constitution on the Church, *Lumen Gentium,* para 14, 48 [Online] Available at: www.vatican.va [Accessed on: 26 February 2024]

the same method with these which you do with others. We ought not to make any doubt of receiving those who have repented thirty years for the uncleanness which they committed through ignorance; for their ignorance pleads their pardon, and their willingness in confessing it; therefore command them to be forthwith received, especially if they have tears to prevail on your tenderness, and have [since their lapse] led such a life as to deserve your compassion.[920]

In reaction to sodomy becoming a vice among the clergy in 11th century Rome, the pontificate of Pope St. Leo IX emphasised the punishment of those committing this grievous sin. Cardinal St Peter Damian wrote a letter to Pope St. Leo IX, also known as the *Book of Gomorrah*, that emphasised the divine imperative to punish those who engaged in sodomy. Drawing on the Pauline insights into God's punishment of sodomites with moral blindness and abandonment to increasing depravity St. Peter Damian wrote,

> While they are slaves to sin he does not permit them to see what they need to do. Since the sun, that is, he who rises over death, has set for them, and after losing the sight furnished by their conscience, they are unable to judge the malice of the filthy acts that they perform [...] Accordingly, as is usually the case according to God's decrees, they who defile themselves with this corrupting vice are smitten with a due judgement of punishment and incur a benighting blindness [...] Surely, they are struck with blindness, because by the just decree of God they fall into interior darkness. They are thus unable to find the door because in their separation from God by sin they do not know how to return to him. One who tries to reach God by the tortuous road of arrogance and conceit, rather than by the path of humility, will certainly fail to recognise the entrance that is obviously right before him, or even that the door is Christ, as he himself says: 'I am the door.'[921] Those who lose Christ because of their addiction to sin, never find the gate that leads to the heavenly dwelling of the saints.[922]

In response to Cardinal St. Peter Damian's letter Pope St. Leo IX issued the letter *Ad splendidum nitentis* in which he set out punishments of various degrees of 'apostolic severity' depending on the nature of the sodomitic sex act. Those who only engaged in homosexual sex acts for a short period, and not with many others, could regain their order in the Church 'if they restrain their desire and wash away their shameful deeds by worthy repentance'. However, those who engaged in homosexual sex acts for a long period, or with many others, or who engaged in anal sex, were punished by losing forever their order in the Church,

> We withdraw any hope of recovering their order from those others who have been stained either of the two sorts of impurity that you have described, whether during a long period alone or with others, or even for a short period with many people, or who, horrible to say or hear, have sinned in the back [of others].[923]

In the 16th century, Pope St Pius V issued the Constitution *Horrendum illud scelus* that referred to sodomy as 'that horrible crime' that leads to the death of the sodomite's soul. Wanting to 'repress such a crime with the greatest possible zeal' Pope St. Pius V determined that sodomite clergy would 'be handed over to the severity of the secular authority, which enforces civil law.' He also judged that failing to punish sodomites would lead to the spread of the 'nefarious crime',

> So that the contagion of such a grave offence may not advance with greater audacity by taking advantage of impunity, which is the greatest incitement to sin, and so as to more severely punish the clerics who are guilty of this nefarious crime and who are not

---

[920] Peters, E N [2001] *The 1917 or Pio-Benedictine Code of Canon Law in English Translation with Extensive Scholarly Apparatus*. San Francisco: Ignatius Press

[921] John 10.9.

[922] St. Peter Damian [1049] *The Book of Gomorrah: St. Peter Damian's Letter 31* (1049) [Online] Available at: www.stpeterdamian.com [Accessed on: 4 March 2024]

[923] Denzinger, H [1990] *Op. cit.*, p. 233-234 687-688

frightened by the death of their souls, we determine that they should be handed over to the severity of the secular authority, which enforces civil law.[924]

The Pio-Benedictine Code of Canon Law, issued in 1917, listed sodomy in the same category of delects against the sixth commandment as adultery, debauchery, bestiality, pandering and incest. Both laity and clergy were declared 'infamous' if found guilty of sodomy or adultery, which in this sense meant, 'loss of a good name' that 'required repentance':

> Infamy of fact is the result of a widespread opinion, by which the community attributes some unusually serious delinquency, such as adultery or the like, to a person. This is more of an unfitness than an irregularity properly so called, unless sentence in court has been pronounced. It ceases therefore when one has shown by a change of life extending over a period of two or probably three years that his repentance is sincere.[925]

The proposal of blessing a 'couple' engaged in adultery, fornication or sodomy is incomprehensible from the perspective of such acts being seen as 'infamous'.

During the reign of Pope St. Paul VI, the Congregation for the Doctrine of the Faith promulgated the 1975 declaration *Persona Humana* at the height of the so called 'sexual revolution'. It reiterated the Pauline understanding that homosexual sex acts resulted from apostasy, 'In Sacred Scripture they [homosexual sex acts] are condemned as a serious depravity and even presented as the sad consequence of rejecting God.'

Unlike Pope Francis who frequently dismissed the seriousness of sexual sins (cf. Hamartiology (2)), *Persona Humana* upheld the magisterium's consistent position that 'the moral order of sexuality involves such high values of human life that every direct violation of this order is objectively serious' and that though 'prudence is recommended in judging the subjective seriousness of a particular sinful act, it in no way follows that one can hold the view that in the sexual field mortal sins are not committed.'[926]

Furthermore, in his 1967 apostolic constitution, *Indulgentiarum doctrine*, Pope St. Paul VI also upheld magisterial doctrine that sin contains its own punishment, inflicted by God's sanctity and justice, 'Therefore it has always been the conviction of the faithful that the paths of evil are fraught with many stumbling blocks and bring adversities, bitterness and harm to those who follow them.'[927]

During the reign of Pope St. John Paul II, the Congregation for the Doctrine of the Faith promulgated in 1986 a *Letter to the Bishops of Catholic Church on the Pastoral Care of Homosexual Persons*. It emphasised the Pauline understanding of homosexual sex acts exemplifying the disharmony between God and man caused by sexual sins leading to their own punishment,

> Paul uses homosexual behaviour as an example of the blindness which has overcome humankind. Instead of the original harmony between Creator and creatures, the acute distortion of idolatry has led to all kinds of moral excess. Paul is at a loss to find a clearer example of this disharmony than homosexual relations.[928]

Pope St. John Paul II further explicated this traditional understanding of grave sins containing their own inherent punishment in his post synodal apostolic exhortation, *Reconciliatio et Paenitentia*,

---

[924] Pope St. Pius V [1568] *Horrendum Illud Scelus* [Online] Available at: www.traditioninaction.org [Accessed on: 26 August 2022]
[925] Catholic Encyclopedia [1913] *Infamy* [Online] Available at: www.newadvent.org [Accessed on: 4 March 2024]
[926] Sacred Congregation for the Doctrine of the Faith [1975] *Persona Humana, para, 8,10* [Online] Available at: www.vatican.va [Accessed on: 4 March 2024]
[927] Pope St. Paul VI [1968] Apostolic Constitution, *Indulgentiarum Doctrine*, Chap1-2 [Online] Available at: www.vatican.va [Accessed on: 4 March 2024]
[928] Congregation for the Doctrine of the Faith. *Letter to the Bishops of Catholic Church on the Pastoral Care of Homosexual Persons, para 3, 7* [Online] Available at: www.vatican.va [Accessed on: 28 February 2024]

> This can occur in a direct and formal way in the sins of idolatry, apostasy and atheism; or in an equivalent way as in every act of disobedience to God's commandments in a grave matter. Man perceives that this disobedience to God destroys the bond that unites him with his life principle: It is a mortal sin, that is, an act which gravely offends God and ends in turning against man himself with a dark and powerful force of destruction.[929]

This understanding of sin containing its own inherent punishment was also reiterated in the *Catechism of the Catholic Church*, 'Grave sin deprives us of communion with God and therefore makes us incapable of eternal life, the privation of which is called the 'eternal punishment' of sin.' (1472). The *Catechism* also presents homosexual sex acts as such grave sins,

> Basing itself on Sacred Scripture, which presents homosexual acts as acts of grave depravity, (Gen 191-29; Rom 1:24-27; 1 Cor 6:10; 1 Tim 1:10), tradition has always declared that 'homosexual acts are intrinsically disordered.' (CDF, *Persona Humana*, 8). They are contrary to the natural law. They close the sexual act to the gift of life. They do not proceed from a genuine affective and sexual complementarity. Under no circumstances can they be approved. (2357)

Reflecting on the 18th chapter of Genesis, Pope Benedict XVI described the evil of the inhabitants of Sodom and Gomorrah in the Pauline sense of a depravity that locked them into a 'totalising and paralysing evil'. Such a grievous sin manifests a 'rejection of God and of love which already bears the punishment in itself.'[930] Pope Benedict XVI warned that those who 'locked' themselves into mortal sin were in danger of experiencing the 'second death' — the death of the soul,

> The authentic death, which one must fear, is that of the soul, called by the Book of Revelation 'second death' (cf. 20:14-15; 21:8). In fact, he who dies in mortal sin, without repentance, locked in prideful rejection of God's love, excludes himself from the Kingdom of life.[931]

Pope Francis, and Cardinal Victor Fernández's, proposal in *Fiducia Supplicans* of a permissive, amoral pastoral charity that encourages the 'blessing' of couples engaged in adultery, fornication or sodomy, creates the grave danger of 'locking' individuals into the inherent punishment of a 'totalising and paralysing evil'.

---

[929] Pope St. John Paul II [1984] Post Synodal Apostolic Exhortation *Reconciliatio et Paenitentia*, para 17 [Online] Available at: www.vatican.va [Accessed on: 29 February 2024]

[930] Pope Benedict XVI [18th May 2011] *General Audience Address*. [Online] Available at: www.vatican.va [Accessed on: 28 February 2024]

[931] Pope Benedict XVI [2006] *Angelus Address* [Online] Available at: www.catholic.org [Accessed on: 28 February 2024]

Soteriology

Q. *Non-Christians can live justified by the grace of God. The sacramental dimension of sanctifying grace works through non-Christian signs, rites, sacred expressions which are channels of the Holy Spirit. God wills the pluralism and diversity of religions. The Gospel of Jesus is just one source among other independent, non-Christian sources.*

Pope Francis proposed two soteriologies that erroneously presented our Lord Jesus Christ as having two different roles in relation to non-Christian religions — first, *the Anonymous Christian* model and later in his pontificate, *God wills a pluralism and diversity of religions.*

The Anonymous Christian model. Though Pope Francis doesn't use this term, his soteriology bears hallmarks of the heterodox Jesuit theologian Fr. Karl Rahner's erroneous soteriology that assumes salvific grace is not limited to the Church but is 'coterminous with human experience'.[932]

In his 2013 apostolic exhortation *Evangelii Gaudium*, Pope Francis presents a Rahnerian account of the working of grace in non-Christian religions without individuals hearing the kerygma or possessing sacramental membership of the Church. Pope Francis writes:

> Non-Christians, by God's gracious initiative, when they are faithful to their own consciences, can live 'justified by the grace of God', and thus be 'associated to the paschal mystery of Jesus Christ'. But due to the sacramental dimension of sanctifying grace, God's working in them tends to produce signs and rites, sacred expressions which in turn bring others to a communitarian experience of journeying towards God. While these lack the meaning and efficacy of the sacraments instituted by Christ, they can be channels which the Holy Spirit raises up in order to liberate non-Christians from atheistic immanentism or from purely individual religious experiences.

In *Evangelii Gaudium* Pope Francis goes much further than Vatican II's *Nostra Aetate 2, Ad Gentes 9* and *Gaudium et Spes 22* when he writes that conscientious non-Christians are 'justified by the grace of God' by 'God's gracious initiative' and 'thus "associated to the paschal mystery of Jesus Christ"'. Pope Francis is quoting from the International Theological Commission's 1997 report *Christianity & the World Religions* which takes a dubious Rahnerian approach to non-Christians. Though *Ad Gentes 9* and *Gaudium et Spes 22* refer in general terms to grace at work among non-Christians in an unknown way, none of them refer to non-Christians being 'justified by the grace of God'. The *De Fidei* doctrine of the Church is that only the sacrament of Baptism confers the grace of justification.

Also, *Gaudium et Spes 22* states that 'in a manner known only to God offers to every man the possibility of being associated with this paschal mystery'. Pope Francis misrepresents both *Gaudium et Spes* and the ITC report as making the categorical statement that conscientious non-Christians are 'associated to the paschal mystery of Jesus Christ'.

Furthermore, in *Evangelii Gaudium* 254, Pope Francis makes the unprecedented statement that the 'signs and rites, sacred expressions' of non-Christian religions are associated with sanctifying grace:

> But due to the sacramental dimension of sanctifying grace, God's working in them tends to produce signs and rites, sacred expressions which in turn bring others to a communitarian experience of journeying towards God.

Pope Francis is implying that the rites of non-Christians are somehow associated with Christian sacraments that bestow sanctifying grace. This is gravely contrary to *De Fidei* doctrine that sanctifying grace is only conferred by the sacraments of the New Covenant.

God wills a pluralism and diversity of religions model. Following exchanges with Muslims, culminating in the 2019 Abu Dhabi Agreement, Pope Francis began outlining a

---

[932] Dulles, A [4 Feb 2002] *Christ among the Nations* in America Magazine. No 3.

second erroneous soteriology that bears the hallmarks of the pluralist inter-faith the-ology exemplified by the work of another Jesuit, Fr Jacques Dupuis. (In 2001 the CDF issued a Notification about the work of Fr Jacques Dupuis SJ in order to 'safeguard the doctrine of the Catholic faith from errors, ambiguities or harmful interpretations').[933] This pluralist inter-faith soteriology reduces Jesus to being the Saviour only of Chris-tians, with the different religions recognised as ways of salvation complementary to Christianity. The salvific role of the Spirit is presented as more universal than that of Jesus Christ, inspiring the other religious ways to salvation independent of Christ. Consequently, the Church is not regarded as the universal sacrament of salvation and membership is not necessary for salvation.[934]

Pope Francis' joint declaration with the Sheikh Ahmed el-Tayeb, Grand Imam of Al-Azhar, that 'God wills the pluralism and diversity of religions', inherently denies that our Lord Jesus Christ is the one and only saviour of mankind. Pope Francis, in a convoluted way, proposed that the world's religions are other salvific journeys to God. On a number of occasions, he wrote, or said, that God wants a diversity of religions and that it is His will that they exist: 'God in His wisdom wills the pluralism and diversity of religion. This divine wisdom is the source from which the right to freedom of belief and the freedom to be different derives';[935] 'why does God allow many religions? God wanted to allow this: Scolastica (sic) theologians used to refer to God's voluntas per-missiva. He wanted to allow this reality: there are many religions… We must not fear differences. God allowed this'.[936]

In his encyclical Fratelli Tutti Pope Francis presented a pluralist explanation of other religions and Christianity's place among them, 'Others drink from other sources. For us the wellspring of human dignity and fraternity is in the Gospel of Jesus Christ'.[937] In his introduction to the video of his prayer intentions for January 2021 Pope Francis said:

> When we pray to God following Jesus, we come together as brothers and sisters with those who pray according to other cultures, other traditions and other beliefs. We are brothers and sisters who pray…The Church values God's action in other religions, without forgetting that for us Christians, the wellspring of human dignity and fraternity, is in the Gospel of Jesus Christ.[938]

Also Pope Francis does not have a problem with the divergent and contradictory ways that religions approach God, instead he focuses on his assumption of one commonality — 'we are all children of God':

> Many think differently, feel differently, seeking God or meeting God in different ways. In this crowd, in this range of religions, there is only one certainty that we have for all: we are all children of God.[939]

Pope Francis' pluralist soteriology reduces the Gospel of Jesus Christ to being the 'source' for Christians, just one 'source' among many 'sources' that are also expressions of 'God's action in other religions'. The Supreme Pontiff even went so far as to tell a group of young people during his Apostolic Journey to Singapore in 2024 that all religions led to the same God, and none were more important than other world religions:

[933] Congregation for the Doctrine of the Faith. Notification on the book Toward a Christian Theology of Religious Pluralism (Orbis Books: Maryknoll, New York 1997) by Fr Jacques Dupuis, SJ. [Online] Available at: www.vatican.va [Accessed on: 10 September 2022]

[934] Clark, F [2000] Godfaring. London: St. Paul, p.88, 91-92

[935] Pope Francis & Ahmad Al-Tayyeb [2019] Document on Human Fraternity for World Peace and Living Together. [Online] Available at: www.vatican.va [Accessed on: 9 September 2022]

[936] Pope Francis [2019] General Audience – Catechesis on the Apostolic visit to Morocco. [Online] Available at: www.vatican.va [Accessed on: 9 September 2022]

[937] Pope Francis [2020] Encyclical Fratelli Tutti, para 277 [Online] Available at: www.vatican.va [Accessed on: 10 September 2022]

[938] Pope Francis [2021] At the service of Human Fraternity [Online] Available at: www.youtube.com [Accessed on: 9 September 2022]

[939] Pope Francis [2016] Introduction to the video of Pope Francis' prayer intentions for January 2016 [Online] Available at: www.youtube.com [Accessed on: 9 September 2022]

Every religion is a way to arrive at God. There are different languages to arrive at God, but God is God for all. And how is God God for all? We are all sons and daughters of God. But my god is more important than your god, is that true? There is only one God and each of us has a language to arrive at God. Sikh, Muslim, Hindu, Christian, they are different paths.[940]

Pope Francis' erroneous soteriologies are indicative of an underlying Indifferentism regarding other religions. Ott defines Indifferentism as follows, 'The Church rejects the dogmatic tolerance which would concede the same power of justification and the same value to all religions, or to all Christian confessions'.[941] The error of Western philosophical Indifferentism can be traced back to the 18th century French Philosopher Jean-Jacques Rousseau in his influential work on education, *Emile*:

Do not let us confuse the outward forms of religion with religion itself. The service God requires is of the heart; and when the heart is sincere that is ever the same. It is a strange sort of conceit which fancies that God takes such an interest in the shape of the priest's vestments, the form of words he utters, the gestures he makes before the altar and all his genuflections. Oh, my friend, stand upright, you will still be too near the earth. God desires to be worshipped in spirit and in truth; this duty belongs to every religion, every country, every individual.[942]

Pope Francis' assertion that non-Christians 'faithful to their own consciences, can live "justified by the grace of God"' is reminiscent of Rousseau when he writes, 'The service God requires is of the heart; and when the heart is sincere that is ever the same.' Pope Francis' indifferentism is gravely contrary to the teaching of the Church.

The Teaching of the Church
Membership of the Church is necessary for all men for salvation (**De fide.**)[943]
Christ by His Sacrifice on the Cross has ransomed us and reconciled us with God. (**De Fide**)[944]
Christ did not die for the predestined only. (**De Fide**)[945] *Christ died not for the Faithful only, but for all mankind without exception.* (**Sent. fidei proxima**)[946]
Christ is the Supreme Prophet promised in the Old Covenant and the absolute teacher of humanity. (**Sent. certa**)[947]
Since the first days of the Church, it was clearly understood that our Lord Jesus Christ is the unique and universal Saviour of mankind, who instituted the Church as absolutely necessary for the salvation of all men. The definitive expression of this soteriological imperative occurred during the Fourth Lateran Council (1215) when it declared, 'There is indeed one universal church of the faithful, outside of which nobody at all is saved [*extra quam nullus omnino salvatur*] in which Jesus Christ is both priest and sacrifice'.[948] The Council of Florence (1439 to 1445) was more explicit regarding the salvific status of non-Christians:

She firmly believes, professes, and preaches that 'none of those who are outside of the Catholic Church, not only pagans', but also Jews, heretics, and schismatics, can become sharers of eternal life, but they will go into the eternal fire 'that was prepared for the

---

[940]Haynes, M [2024] *Pope Francis: 'Every religion is a way to arrive at God'* [Online] Available at: www.lifesitenews.com [Accessed on: 21 May 2025]
[941]Ott, L *Op. cit.*, p. 313.
[942]Jean-Jacques Rousseau [1762] *Emile, Or Treatise on Education*, Book III, p.330 [Online] Available at: www.globalgreyebooks.com [Accessed on: 11 September 2022]
[943]Ott, L [1957] *Op. cit.*, p. 312
[944]*Ibid.*, p. 185
[945]*Ibid.*, p. 188
[946]*Ibid.*
[947]*Ibid.*, p.180
[948]Fourth Lateran Council [1215] *Confession of Faith.* [Online] Available at: www.papalencyclicals.net [Accessed on: 5 July 2022]

devil and his angels' [Mt 25:41] unless, before the end of their life, they are joined to her.[949]

The Second Vatican Pastoral Council proposed a modified version of the *De Fide* doctrine that the Church is necessary for salvation, possibly reflecting the influence of the heterodox theologian Karl Rahner SJ, who was one of seven periti — specialist theologians— advising on the drafting of the Dogmatic Constitution on the Church, *Lumen Gentium*. The Second Vatican Council's teaching on soteriology and non-Christians can be summarised as follows:

i)   Our Lord Jesus Christ is the unique, universal Saviour of all mankind, 'Christ, present to us in His Body, which is the Church, is the one Mediator and the unique way of salvation',[950] 'No one is freed from sin by himself and by his own power… all stand in need of Christ, their model, their mentor, their liberator, their Saviour, their source of life';[951] 'God is Saviour and Creator, Lord of human history as well as of salvation history',[952] 'His saving design extends to all men, (Wis. 8:1; Acts 14:17; Rom. 2:6-7; I Tim. 2:4) until that time when the elect will be united in the Holy City, the city ablaze with the glory of God…Christ underwent His passion and death freely, because of the sins of men and out of infinite love, in order that all may reach salvation'.[953]

ii)   The Catholic Church is 'the universal sacrament of salvation',[954] 'the Church, being the salt of the earth and the light of the world (cf. Matt. 5:13-14), is more urgently called upon to save and renew every creature'.[955]

iii) 'The Church…is necessary for salvation…In explicit terms He Himself affirmed the necessity of faith and baptism (Mk. 16:16; Jn. 3.5) and thereby affirmed also the necessity of the Church, for through baptism as through a door men enter the Church. Whosoever, therefore, knowing that the Catholic Church was made necessary by Christ, would refuse to enter or to remain in it, could not be saved',[956] 'For Christ Himself by stressing in express language the necessity of faith and baptism (cf. Mark 16:16; John 3:5), at the same time confirmed the necessity of the Church, into which men enter by baptism, as by a door. Therefore those men cannot be saved, who though aware that God, through Jesus Christ founded the Church as something necessary, still do not wish to enter into it, or to persevere in it. (LG 14)'.[957]

iv)   *Lumen Gentium 16* declared that in order to 'procure the salvation of all', the Church must 'Preach the Gospel to every creature', referencing Mark 16:16 'He that believeth and is baptized, shall be saved: but he that believeth not shall be condemned'.

v)   Non-Christian religions are dangerous, because even though some contain a degree of truth and grace, 'often men, deceived by the Evil One, have become

---

[949]Denzinger, H [2010] *Op. cit.*, p.1442, Dz 1351
[950]Second Vatican Council [1965] Dogmatic Constitution on the Church, *Lumen Gentium*, para 14 [Online] Available at: www.vatican.va [Accessed on: 12 September 2022]
[951]Second Vatican Council Decree, [1965] *Ad Gentes*, para 8. [Online] Available at: www.vatican.va [Accessed on: 12 September 2022]
[952]Second Vatican Council [1965] Pastoral Constitution on the Church in the Modern World, *Gaudium et Spes*, para 51 [Online] Available at: www.vatican.va [Accessed on: 12 September 2022]
[953]Second Vatican Council [1965] Decree, *Nostra aetate*, para 1,4 [Online] Available at: www. vatican.va [Accessed on: 12 September 2022]
[954]Second Vatican Council [1965] Dogmatic Constitution on the Church, *Lumen Gentium*, para 48. [Online] Available at: www.vatican.va [Accessed on: 12 September 2022]
[955]Second Vatican Council [1965] Decree, *Ad Gentes*, para 1 [Online] Available at: www.vatican.va [Accessed on: 12 September 2022]
[956]Second Vatican Council [1965] Dogmatic Constitution on the Church, *Lumen Gentium*, para 14 [Online] Available at: www.vatican.va [Accessed on: 12 September 2022]
[957]Second Vatican Council [1965] Decree, *Ad Gentes*, para 7 [Online] Available at: www.vatican.va [Accessed on: 12 September 2022]

vain in their reasonings and have exchanged the truth of God for a lie, serving the creature rather than the Creator (Rom. 1:21, 25). Or some there are who, living and dying in this world without God, are exposed to final despair'.[958]

vi) Christ, the author of salvation, overcomes the devil's influence manifested in non-Christian religions, thereby purifying truth or grace in the lives of non-Christian people. Through preaching the Gospel and the celebration of the sacraments, especially the Most Holy Eucharist, in every nation, God 'brings about the presence of Christ, the author of salvation'. Whatever 'truth and grace' found among the nations is 'a sort of secret presence of God' that 'frees from all taint of evil and restores to Christ its maker, who overthrows the devil's domain and wards off the manifold malice of vice.' And so, whatever good found in non-Christian 'rites and cultures' 'is healed, uplifted, and perfected for the glory of God, the shame of the demon, and the bliss of men.'[959]

vii) Non-Christian religions only serve a good purpose if they act as preparations to receive the Gospel of Christ. Whatever good or truth found non-Christian religions is not a 'source' independent from Christ but is a 'preparation for the Gospel'.[960]

viii) Only in Christ — 'the way, the truth and the life' (Jn 14:6) — will non-Christians discover the 'fullness of religious life' because it is only through Christ that 'God has reconciled all things to Himself'.[961]

ix) Vatican II re-iterated Pope Bl. Pius IX's idea of the salvation of those struggling with invincible ignorance. Like Pope Pius IX, Vatican II does not mention non-Christian religions, but restricts its comments to individuals: 'Those also can attain to salvation who through no fault of their own do not know the Gospel of Christ or His Church, yet sincerely seek God and moved by grace strive by their deeds to do His will as it is known to them through the dictates of conscience'.[962]

x)   No document of the Second Vatican Council states that 'grace' or the 'grace of justification' can be found in non-Christian religions.

Commenting on Vatican II's approach to non-Christian religions and salvation, Cardinal Aloys Grillmeier S.J., commented that the Council 'clearly affirmed that Christ is and remains the real way of salvation' and presented non-Christian religions as 'forming a disposition for salvation in Christ'.[963] It did not present non-Christian religions as equivalent to Christianity or as independent means of salvation. The question of whether Vatican II's approach to non-Christian religions is a genuine development of Church teaching on soteriology — *extra Ecclesiam nulla salus* — or is contrary to it, is for a future council and pope to decide. What is demonstrably clear, is that Pope Francis' *anonymous Christian* soteriology goes beyond Vatican II by claiming that non-Christians are justified and that their rituals are associated with sacramental sanctifying grace. Furthermore, Pope Francis' later soteriology — *God wills a pluralism and diversity of religions* — is totally contrary to Vatican II by implying that non-Christian religions are independent from Christ.

Proof from the Sources of Faith
a) Teaching from Holy Scripture
The Old Testament testifies to God's abhorrence towards those who worship other 'gods', because such idolatry masquerades the worship of demons:

> They provoked him by strange gods, and stirred him up to anger, with their abominations. They sacrificed to devils and not to God: to gods whom they knew not:

[958]Second Vatican Council [1965] Dogmatic Constitution on the Church, *Lumen Gentium*, para 16 [Online] Available at: www.vatican.va [Accessed on: 12 September 2022]

[959]*Ibid.*, para 9   [960]*Ibid.*, para 16

[961]Second Vatican Council [1965] *Decree Nostra Aetate*, para 2 [Online] Available at: www.vatican.va [Accessed on: 12 September 2022]

[962]*Lumen Gentium*, Chap. 2, para 16

[963]Vorgrimler, H [1967] *Commentary on the Documents of Vatican II*, vol. 1. New York: Herder & Herder, p.184

that were newly come up, whom their fathers worshipped not. Thou hast forsaken the God that begot thee, and hast forgotten the Lord that created thee (Deut 32:15-18)

Israel is exhorted to have nothing to do with the 'strange god's' of other nations, 'Now therefore, said he, put away strange gods from among you, and incline your hearts to the Lord the God of Israel' (Josh 24:23). The Lord demands that Israel separate herself from surrounding nations because of their worship of demons:

> The people of Israel, and the priests and Levites have not separated themselves from the people of the lands, and from their abominations, namely, of the Chanaanites, and the Hethites, and the Pherezites, and the Jebusites, and the Ammonites, and the Moabites, and the Egyptians, and the Amorrhites (Ezra 9:1).

Israel is called to reject other religions to the point of martyrdom (II Macc 6: 18-7:42). Sidrach, Misach, and Abdenago are exemplars of Israel's repudiation of other religions, 'we will not worship thy gods, nor adore the golden statue which thou hast set up' (Dan 3:18).

Israel knew that only a remnant of the just would be saved from God's anger on the Day of the Lord, foreshadowed by the remnant saved by Noah's Ark from the flood (Wis 10:4; Amos 5:15; Isa 28:5). Only those justified by God will be included in the Book of life, 'And at that time shall thy people be saved, every one that shall be found written in the book' (Dan 12:1; cf. Rev 20:15).

On numerous occasions, our Lord Jesus Christ declared that he is the only saviour of mankind, and that faith in him is necessary for salvation:

i) 'No man cometh to the Father, but by me'. (Jn 14:6)
ii) 'This is eternal life: That they may know [ginōskōsin] thee, the only true God, and Jesus Christ, whom thou hast sent'. (Jn 17:3)
iii) 'He that believeth and is baptized, shall be saved: but he that believeth not shall be condemned'. (Mk 16:16)
iv) 'Amen, amen I say unto you: Except you eat the flesh of the Son of man, and drink his blood, you shall not have life in you'. (Jn 6:54)
v) 'He that is not with me, is against me: and he that gathereth not with me, scattereth'. (Mt 12:30)

St. John uses the Greek word *ginōskōsin* (Jn 17:3) to convey the relationship necessary with Jesus in order to be saved — *ginóskó* [to know] means to have a personal relationship with our Lord that leads to intimate understanding.[964] When St. Mark writes about the 'belief' (Mk 16:16) necessary to be saved he uses the Greek word *pisteuó* which means to have a faith that enables one to be able to give oneself up to Jesus,[965] sacramentally expressed in totally giving oneself up to the waters of baptism. This salvific, intimate relationship with Jesus is predicated on being a member of the Church, and not on the indirect, unknowing relationship proposed in Rahner's *Anonymous Christian* soteriology, or repudiated by the *God wills a plurality and diversity of religions* understanding of soteriology.

The early Christians testified to the divinely revealed truth that membership of the Church is necessary for all men for salvation, 'Neither is there salvation in any other. For there is no other name under heaven given to men, whereby we must be saved' (Acts 4:12). The emphasis on the importance of knowing the name of Jesus for salvation re-iterates the necessity of having a personal relationship with our Lord.

St. Paul warned of the dangers posed by non-Christian religions that worshipped demons disguised as idols (I Cor 10:20-21) and the imperative to remain separate from the worship of non-Christians:

---
[964]*Strong's Concordance* [Online] Available at: biblehub.com [Accessed on: 13 September 2022]
[965]*Ibid.*

Bear not the yoke with unbelievers. For what participation hath justice with injustice? Or what fellowship hath light with darkness? And what concord hath Christ with Belial? Or what part hath the faithful with the unbeliever? And what agreement hath the temple of God with idols? For you are the temple of the living God; as God saith: I will dwell in them, and walk among them; and I will be their God, and they shall be my people. Wherefore, Go out from among them, and be ye separate, saith the Lord, and touch not the unclean thing: And I will receive you; and I will be a Father to you; and you shall be my sons and daughters, saith the Lord Almighty (II Cor 6:14-18).

St. Paul expressed the fundamental truth of soteriology, that it is God's general will that all men are saved, but only through his Son, our Lord Jesus Christ:

God our saviour, Who will have all men to be saved, and to come to the knowledge of the truth. For there is one God, and one mediator of God and men, the man Christ Jesus: Who gave himself a redemption for all, a testimony in due times. (I Tim 2: 3-6).

Pope Francis' inter-faith soteriologies do not proclaim this saving truth.

b) The Testimony of Tradition

The early Church described herself as The Way [*tes hodos*] (Acts 19:23; cf. 9:2; 22;4; 24:14,22), expressing the Church's self-understanding that following the narrow way to salvation set out by Jesus (Mt 7:13-14) is the only way that God offers to man. Christianity is not one way among many ways to salvation — as taught by Pope Francis — but the only way.

In the first century, St. Ignatius of Antioch referred to Jesus as the 'unerring way' that leads to the Father. He went on to describe the characteristics of those journeying on The Way, 'God-bearers, spirit-bearers, temple-bearers, bearers of holiness, adorned in all respects with the commandments of Jesus Christ'.[966] Four hundred years later, St. John Chrysostom wrote that indeed it was the way, 'the Way, that led into the kingdom of heaven'.[967]

Faced with the heresies of the syncretistic Gnostics, St. Irenaeus insisted on the importance of avoiding non-Christians in order to ensure remaining in the entrance to life, 'For she [the Church] is the entrance to life; all others are thieves and robbers. On this account are we bound to avoid them, but to make choice of the thing pertaining to the Church with the utmost diligence, and to lay hold of the tradition of the truth'.[968] St. Irenaeus identified salvation solely with the Church, and those outside the Church 'rob themselves of life… For where the Church is, there is the Spirit of God; and where the Spirit of God is, there is the Church, and every kind of grace'.[969]

Origen could not be clearer that membership of the Church is absolutely necessary for salvation, and that 'outside this house, that is, outside the Church, no one is saved [*extra ecclesiam nemo salvatur*]. For if anyone go outside, he shall be guilty of his own death'.[970]

As well as being famous for coining the phrase 'there is no salvation out of the Church [*salus extra ecclesiam non est*],[971] St. Cyprian introduced the scriptural motif of Noah's Ark to convey the imperative that salvation from the flood of evil can only

---

[966]St. Ignatius of Antioch. *The Epistle of Ignatius to the Ephesians*, longer version, Chap. IX [Online] Available at: http://www.earlychristianwritings.com [Accessed on: 14 September 2022]

[967]St. John Chrysostom. *Homily XLI. Acts XIX 8-9* [Online] Available at: http://www. documentacatholicaomnia.eu/ [Accessed on: 14 September 2022]

[968]St. Irenaeus. *Against Heresies*. Book III, Chapter 4 [Online] Available at: www.newadvent.org [Accessed on: 14 September 2022]

[969]*Ibid.*, Bk III, Chap. 24, para 1.

[970]*Extra Ecclesiam Nulla Salus* (Outside the Church there is no salvation) [Online] Available at: www.ewtn.com [Accessed on: 15 September 2022]

[971]St. Cyprian. *To Jubaianus, Concerning the Baptism of Heretics*, epistle 72, para 21 [Online] Available at: www.newadvent.org [Accessed on: 15 September 2022]

be found in the Catholic Church, 'If anyone could escape who was outside the Ark of Noah, then he also may escape who shall be outside of the Church'.[972]

Preaching on the Old Testament, St. Augustine said that non-Christians had 'fornicating souls' by which he meant 'those which in one way or another have prostituted themselves to many false gods… The pagan soul has no lawful husband; it is corrupted by prostituting itself with a variety of demons'. St. Augustine exhorted Catholics to want what God wants regarding non-Christian religions:

> That every superstition of the pagans and the Gentiles should be abolished is what God wants, God has ordered, God has foretold, God has begun to bring about, and in many parts of the world has already in great measure achieved.[973]

St. Thomas Aquinas re-iterated St. Cyprian's use of the motif of Noah's Ark to convey the truth that there is no salvation outside the Church, '…there is no entering into salvation outside the Church, just as in the time of the deluge there was none outside the Ark, which denotes the Church'.[974]

c) The Defence by the Magisterium
In the 7th century, the Sixteenth Synod of Toledo depicted the holy Catholic Church as the universal sacrament of salvation, as 'rich in signs of eminence, brilliant in virtues, and resplendent in the gifts of the Holy Spirit'. For this reason, the synod fathers declared that those who were not members of her, or who rejected her, rightly deserved damnation:

> …all those now who are not at all in her or will not be in her or have departed or will depart from her…these will be punished by the sentence of everlasting damnation, and they will be burned on flaming pyres with the devil and his associates until the end of time.[975]

During the 12th century, Pope Innocent III coined a variation of St. Cyprian's succinct formula, *salus extra ecclesiam non est* [there is no salvation out of the Church]: 'We believe in our heart and confess with our tongue the one Church…the holy Roman, catholic, and apostolic Church outside which we believe no one is saved'.[976]

Pope Boniface VIII drew on St. Cyprian's use of Noah's Ark to convey the truth of *salus extra ecclesiam non est*:

> There had been at the time of the deluge only one ark of Noah, prefiguring the one Church, which ark, having been finished to a single cubit, had only one pilot and guide, i.e., Noah, and we read that, outside of this ark, all that subsisted on the earth was destroyed.[977]

During the 16th century, Pope St. Pius V's *Catechism of the Council of Trent* referenced Acts 4:12 to teach that our Lord is the only saviour of mankind, and membership of his Church is necessary for salvation, 'outside of which there is no other name under Heaven given to men whereby we must be saved'.[978]

---

[972]St. Cyprian. *Treatise* 1, on the Unity of the Church, para 6 [Online] Available at: www.newadvent. org [Accessed on: 15 September 2022]

[973]St. Augustine. The Works of Saint Augustine: A Translation for the 21st Century [1990] *Sermons on the Old Testament*, 15:3, 24:6 New York: New City Press, p.324

[974]St. Thomas Aquinas. *Summa Theologiae*. Tertia Pars. Q 73. Art 3 [Online] [Online] Available at: www.newadvent.org [Accessed on: 15 September 2022]

[975]Denzinger, H *Op. cit.*, p. 202, Dz 575

[976]*Ibid.*, p. 263, Dz 792

[977]Pope Boniface VIII [1302] *Bull Unam Sanctam* [Online] Available at: www.papalencyclicals.net [accessed on: 16 September 2022]

[978]Pope St. Pius V [1556] *The Roman Catechism: The Catechism of the Council of Trent*, The First Petition of The Lord's Prayer 'Hallowed Be Thy Name' [Online] Available at: www.docdroid.net [Accessed on: 16 September 2022]

Sixty-two years after the French philosopher Jean-Jacques Rousseau advocated philosophical religious indifferentism based on subjective emotions, Pope Leo XII explicitly identified and condemned Indifferentism. Pope Leo XII's analysis of the error in his encyclical *Ubi Primum* (1824) is as follows:

i) Religious tolerance or indifferentism presents itself 'under the gentle appearance of piety and liberality'.

ii) This philosophy of Indifferentism preaches that 'God has given every individual a wide freedom to embrace and adopt without danger to his salvation whatever sect or opinion appeals to him on the basis of his private judgment'.

iii) 'The current indifferentism has developed to the point of arguing that everyone is on the right road', even those groups that reject Divine Revelation, such as Deists and Naturalists, those who reject the Christian belief in the supernatural.

iv) Indifferentism is a pseudo-philosophy rejected by right-thinking people because it is impossible for 'God, who is Truth Itself, the best, the wisest Provider, and the Rewarder of good men, to approve all sects who profess false teachings which are often inconsistent with one another and contradictory, and to confer eternal rewards on their members'.

v) There is no salvation outside the Church because 'no other name under heaven is given to men except the name of Jesus Christ of Nazareth in which we must be saved (Acts 4:12).[979]

Following Pope Leo XII's condemnation of the error of Indifferentism, successive 19th century popes warned of the danger it posed: 'Among these heresies belongs that foul contrivance of the sophists of this age who do not admit any difference among the different professions of faith and who think that the portal of eternal salvation opens for all from any religion' (Pope Pius VIII);[980] 'This perverse opinion is spread on all sides by the fraud of the wicked who claim that it is possible to obtain the eternal salvation of the soul by the profession of any kind of religion, as long as morality is maintained' (Pope Gregory XVI).[981]

Pope Bl. Pius IX promulgated a number of encyclicals that included condemnations of Indifferentism and defended the truth that membership of the Church was necessary for salvation. In his 1846 encyclical *Qui Pluribus*. Pope Pius IX referenced St. Paul's protestation that there can be no concord between Christ and demons of non-Christian religions (II Corinthians 6:14-18):

> Also perverse is the shocking theory that it makes no difference to which religion one belongs, a theory which is greatly at variance even with reason. By means of this theory, those crafty men remove all distinction between virtue and vice, truth and error, honourable and vile action. They pretend that men can gain eternal salvation by the practice of any religion, as if there could ever be any sharing between justice and iniquity, any collaboration between light and darkness, or any agreement between Christ and Belial.[982]

In his encyclical *Singulari Quidem* (1856) Pope Pius IX again re-iterated that 'the only hope of salvation for mankind is placed in the Christian faith'. However, he went on to add a profound change to the traditional formula, *'there is no salvation out of the Church'*, writing, 'Outside of the Church, nobody can hope for life or salvation *unless he is excused through ignorance beyond his control.* [emphasis added].

---

[979]Pope Leo XII [1824] Encyclical *Ubi primum*, para 12-14 [Online] Available at: www.papalencyclicals.net [Accessed on: 16 September 2022]

[980]Pope Pius VIII 1829] Encyclical *Traditi Humilitati*, para 4 [Online] Available at: www.papalencyclicals.net [Accessed on: 16 September 2022]

[981]Pope Gregory XVI [1832] Encyclical *Mirari Vos Arbitramur*, 13 [Online] Available at: www.papalencyclicals.net [Accessed on: 16 September 2022]

[982]Pope Bl. Pius IX [1846] Encyclical *Qui Pluribus*, para 15 [Online] Available at: www.papalencyclicals.net [Accessed on: 16 September 2022]

While upholding the revealed truth that 'no one can be saved outside the Catholic Church' Pope Pius IX made the distinction between those 'struggling with invincible ignorance' and those 'who oppose the authority and statements' of the Catholic Church and stubbornly separate themselves from the Catholic Church and the successor of St. Peter. The invincibly ignorant belong to a different category because they are not guilty of the deliberate sin of rejecting to listen to the Church, which deserves eternal punishment. Their culpability is mitigated by:

> Sincerely observing the natural law and its precepts inscribed by God on all hearts and ready to obey God, they live honest lives and are able to attain eternal life by the efficacious virtue of divine light and grace. Because God knows, searches and clearly understands the minds, hearts, thoughts, and nature of all, his supreme kindness and clemency do not permit anyone at all who is not guilty of deliberate sin to suffer eternal punishments.

Pope Pius IX points out that those struggling with invincible ignorance are very different from those who argue that it is 'possible to arrive at eternal salvation although living in error and alienated from the true faith and Catholic unity'. Furthermore, he does not mention that the invincibly ignorant are practicing members of non-Christian religions, only that they 'sincerely' observe the natural law and are 'ready to obey God'.[983]

Pope St. Pius X addressed the threat posed by Modernists seeking to introduce their development of Indifferentism into the Church in his seminal encyclical, *Pascendi Domi-nici Gregis* (1907). Pope Pius X observed that the modernist's privileging of 'experience' over doctrine, combined with their reduction of religion to symbolism resulted in the affirmation that 'every religion, even that of paganism, must be held to be true'. He pointed out the inevitable conclusion that if personal experience was given priority over divine revelation, then the personal experience of Muslims must be accepted as being as true as the personal experiences of Catholics. Pope Pius X saw this erroneous conclusion as the objective of Modernists, 'Indeed Modernists do not deny but actually admit, some confusedly, others in the most open manner, that all religions are true. That they cannot feel otherwise is clear'.[984]

Pope St. Pius X's catechism clearly set out the Church's doctrine that those outside the Church are not saved, including members of non-Christian religions:

i)   'No one can be saved outside the Catholic, Apostolic Roman Church, just as no one could be saved from the flood outside the Ark of Noah, which was a figure of the Church'.

ii)   'Jesus Christ died for all, but not all are saved, because not all will acknowledge Him; all do not observe His Law; all do not avail themselves of the means of salvation He has left us.'

iii) 'Those who are damned do not belong to the Communion of Saints in the other life; and in this life those who belong neither to the body nor to the soul of the Church, that is, those who are in mortal sin, and who are outside the true Church.'

iv)   'Outside the true Church are: Infidels, Jews, heretics, apostates, schismatics, and the excommunicated.'

v)   'Infidels are those who have not been baptised and do not believe in Jesus Christ, because they either believe in and worship false gods as idolaters do, or though admitting one true God, they do not believe in the Messiah, neither as already come in the Person of Jesus Christ, nor as to come; for instance, Mohammedans and the like.'

Pope St. Pius X, drawing on the Council of Trent's reference to the 'desire for baptism' (*Decree on Justification*, Session 6, Chap. 4), refined Pope Bl. Pius IX's teaching on the salvation of those individuals struggling with invincible ignorance:

---

[983]Pope Bl. Pius IX [1863] Encyclical *Quanto Conficiamur Moerore*, para 7-8 [Online] Available at: www.papalencyclicals.net [Accessed on: 16 September 2022]

[984]Pope St. Pius X [1907] Encyclical *Pascendi Dominici Gregis*, para 14 [Online] Available at: www.vatican.va [Accessed on: 16 September 2022]

If he is outside the Church through no fault of his, that is, if he is in good faith, and if he has received Baptism, or at least has the implicit desire of Baptism; and if, moreover, he sincerely seeks the truth and does God's will as best he can such a man is indeed separated from the body of the Church, but is united to the soul of the Church and consequently is on the way of salvation.[985]

Pope Pius XI condemned inter-religion meetings because they foster Indifferentism, 'founded as they are on that false opinion which considers all religions to be more or less good and praiseworthy, since they all in different ways manifest and signify that sense which is inborn in us all, and by which we are led to God and to the obedient acknowledgment of His rule'. He warned that such an attitude was dangerous because it distorts 'the idea of true religion', leading to individuals 'altogether abandoning the divinely revealed religion'.[986]

The magisterial concern about Indifferentism continued after the Second Vatican Council, with Pope St. Paul VI warning, 'This message [the Gospel of our Lord Jesus Christ] is indeed necessary. It is unique. It cannot be replaced. It does not permit either indifference, syncretism or accommodation. It is a question of people's salvation'. Pope Paul VI even went as far as pointing out the failure of non-Christian religions compared to Christianity, 'In other words, our religion effectively establishes with God an authentic and living relationship which the other religions do not succeed in doing, even though they have, as it were, their arms stretched out towards heaven'.[987]

Pope St. John Paul II also warned against the dangers of Indifferentism that had succeeded in infiltrating the Church by the 20th century:

i) Pope John Paul II identified Indifferentism as the cause of the widespread lack of interest in the missionary task, 'It is based on incorrect theological perspectives and is characterised by a religious relativism which leads to the belief that "one religion is as good as another"'.[988]

ii) 'A mentality has arisen in theological and ecclesial circles that tends to relativize Christ's revelation and his unique and universal mediation of salvation, as well as to diminish the need for Christ's Church as the universal sacrament of salvation'.[989]

iii) Pope John Paul II criticised the plurality of religions soteriology, 'It is a mistake, then, to regard the Church as a way of salvation along with those constituted by other religions, which would be complementary to the Church, even if converging with her on the eschatological kingdom of God'.[990]

Pope Francis' soteriologies — *Anonymous Christian and God wills a pluralism and diversity of religions* — are expressions of the grave error of Indifferentism, that is contrary to the doctrine 'no one can be saved outside the Catholic Church', modified by the speculative doctrine of mitigated culpability due to invincible ignorance.

---

[985]Pope St. Pius X [1908] *Catechism of St. Pius X*, The Fourth Article of the Creed, Question 18; Those Outside the Communion of Saints, Question 10 -12; The Ninth Article of the Creed: The Church in General, Question 27, 29 [Online] Available at: www.ewtn.com [Accessed on: 16 September 2022]

[986]Pope Pius XI [1928] Encyclical *Mortalium Animos*, para 2 [Online] Available at: www.vatican.va [Accessed on: 16 September 2022]

[987]Pope St. Paul VI [1975] Apostolic Exhortation *Evangeli Nuntiandi*, paras 5, 53 [Online] Available at: www.vatican.va [Accessed on: 16 September 2022]

[988]Pope St. John Paul II [1990] Encyclical *Redemptoris Missio*, para 36 [Online] Available at: www. vatican.va [Accessed on: 16 September 2022]

[989]Pope St. John Paul II [2000] *Address to the Members, Consultors and Staff of the Congregation for the Doctrine of the Faith*, para 4 [Online] Available at: www.vatican.va [Accessed on: 16 September 2022]

[990]*Ibid.*

The Questionable Words and Deeds of Pope Francis and His Appointees

Pope Francis' appointments of cardinals, bishops and curial officials exemplifies Morton Blackwell's principle of political activism, 'Personnel is Policy', by which he meant the deliberate appointment of individuals to key positions within an organisation in order to significantly shape the policies and outcomes of that entity.[1] Pope Francis selected and elevated many men to the Sacred College of Cardinals, Sacred College of Bishops and Vatican curia who shared his radical agenda, and in whom he could rely on to repeat, amplify and implement his rupture from the Deposit of Faith. Paying attention to what Pope Francis' appointees said and did during his twelve year pontificate is essential to get a true picture of the practical steps the Supreme Pontiff took to impose his 'new paradigm'[2] on the Church.

Here's just one example of how Pope Francis chose bishops to further his radical agenda, from many hundreds recorded in this section. Pope Francis elevated fellow Jesuit Archbishop Jean-Claude Hollerich of Luxembourg to the College of Cardinals in 2019; appointed him to the influential position of relator general of the Synod of Bishops on Synodality in 2021, and a member of his advisory Council of Cardinals in 2023. Luxembourg has a tiny Catholic population of 271,000 Catholics, of which only 6% say they go to Mass weekly, which is 16,260. So why did Pope Francis promote Archbishop Jean-Claude Hollerich to these influential positions in the Church?

In 2012 Archbishop Hollerich signed the *Charte de la Diversité Lëtzebuerg*, committing the Archdiocese of Luxembourg to promote diversity, including diversity regarding 'sexual orientation'.[3] Following his appointment to the cardinalate by Pope Francis in 2019 Jean-Claude Hollerich became notorious for his public advocacy of changing the Church's doctrine on homosexuality. In response to the question, 'How do you get around the Church's teaching that homosexuality is sin?' Hollerich replied:

> I believe that this is false. But I also believe that here we are thinking further about the teaching. So, as the Pope has said in the past, this can lead to a change in teaching. So I believe that the sociological-scientific foundation of this teaching is no longer correct, what one formerly condemned was sodomy. One thought at that time that in the sperm of the man, the whole child was kept. And one has simply transferred this to homosexual men. But there is no homosexuality at all in the New Testament. There is only discussion of homosexual acts, which were to some extent pagan cultic acts. That was naturally forbidden. I believe it is time for us to make a revision in the basic foundation of the teaching.[4]

[1]Blackwell, M [2015] *The Laws Of The Public Policy Process* [Online] Available at: leadershipinstitute. org [Accessed on: 21 July 2025]

[2]Pentin, E [2018] *Cardinal Parolin: Amoris Laetitia Represents New Paradigm, Spirit and Approach* [Online] Available at: www.ncregister.com [Accessed on: 21 July 2025]

[3]*Charte de la Diversité: Un an de diversité et plus de 90 entreprisessignataires!* [2013] [Online] Available at: www.dsm.legal [Accessed on: 21 July 2025]

[4]Caldwell, S [2022] *Cardinal Hollerich: Church teaching on gay sex is 'false' and can be changed* [Online] Available at: catholicherald.co.uk [Accessed on: 23 October 2022]

In response to Cardinal Hollerich's statement, Cardinal George Pell, during an interview with *K-TV*, the German Catholic television agency, called for the Congregation for the Doctrine of the Faith to investigate Hollerich for his 'wholesale and explicit rejection of the Catholic Church's teaching on sexual ethics.'[5] Cardinal Pell doubled down on his criticism of Cardinal Hollerich during his interview with *The Catholic Herald*, expressing grave doubts about Pope Francis appointing him the relator general of the Synod on Synodality:

> I can't see how it's possible that a man who teaches explicit heresy, for example, on sexual morality, could possibly be the relator, the principle driver of the synod. It would be absolutely unprecedented in Catholic history for a man who's explicitly heretical on some particular point to have a position like that. Undoubtedly, the evil one, the devil, will be at work in the synodal process to take it off the paths.[6]

Despite Cardinal George Pell's call for the CDF to investigate Cardinal Hollerich for heresy, Pope Francis not only retained him as the relator general of the Synod on Synodality 2023/2024, but also promoted him to his advisory Council of Cardinals one year after Cardinal Pell's warning. Consequently, a major focus at the 2023 Synod on Synodality was on listening to and accompanying people in diverse situations, including those who feel excluded due to their 'identity and sexuality' (*Final Report, Section 15*). This set the stage for Cardinal Fernández, the prefect of the Dicastery for the Doctrine of the Faith, to promulgate, two months later, the declaration *Fiducia Supplicans*, which allowed the blessing of same-sex couples.

There's also another older maxim that has guided the creation of this section, which is 'actions speak louder than words', emphasising that what people do is more revealing of their true intentions or character than what they say. It is particularly necessary to study the words and deeds of Pope Francis' appointees to build up a picture of his true intentions because of his notorious use of ambiguity and confusion. Archbishop Charles Chaput, archbishop emeritus of Philadelphia, accused Pope Francis' pontificate of 'persistent and deliberate ambiguity',

> Over the past decade ambiguity on certain matters of Catholic doctrine and practice has become a pattern for the current pontificate.[7]

Pope Francis' political use of ambiguity to hide his true intentions was frequently compared to the machiavellian political style of his fellow Argentinian politician Juan Perón (1895 to 1974). Dr. Joseph Shaw used this apocryphal tale of Perón to illustrate Pope Francis use of ambiguity,

> we need some other tool to analyse Pope Francis's strategy, perhaps one named in honor of Juan Perón, sometime military ruler of his native Argentina. An illustrative apocryphal tale of Perón tells us that one day, while driving along, his chauffeur asked him whether he should turn right or left. 'Signal left, turn right,' the great statesman replied.[8]

When, four months into his pontificate, Pope Francis told the young people at the 2013 World Youth Day, '*hagan lío*' [Go make a mess][9] he was also expressing his preferred leadership style. The premise of this section is that in order to unravel the delib-

[5]Pentin, E [2022] *Cardinal Pell Calls on Vatican to Correct 2 Senior European Bishops for Rejecting Church's Sexual Ethics* [Online] Available at: www.ncregister.com [Accessed on: 31 December 2023]

[6]Wolfe, R [2022] *Cardinal Pell: Pope 'will have to speak' against dissident German Synod* [Online] Available at: www.lifesitenews.com [Accessed on: 3 January 2024]

[7]Chaput, C [2023] *The Cost of 'Making a Mess'* [Online] Available at: firstthings.com [Accessed on: 21 July 2025]

[8]Shaw, J [2025] *Pope of Ambiguity* [Online] Available at: firstthings.com [Accessed on: 21 July 2025]

[9]*Pope to youth: shake things up, bring Church to the streets* [2013] [Online] Available at: www.catholicnewsagency.com [Accessed on: 21 July 2025]

erate mess of Pope Francis' pontificate we must look closely at the words and deeds of the men whom he chose to be his agents of change in the Church.

Here's just one example of how Pope Francis chose bishops who would work with him to create the ambiguity and confusion he wanted to further his radical agenda. In 2013 Pope Francis appointed Archbishop Bruno Forte of Chieti-Vasto, Italy, as the Special Secretary for the 2014 Extraordinary Synod of Bishops on *'The challenges of the family in the context of evangelisation'*. Archbishop Forte was known as a 'progressive' theologian, having studied under heterodox theologians such as Fr. Hans Küng and Cardinal Walter Kasper, the latter of whom proposed allowing the divorced and civilly remarried Catholics to receive Communion. During his first angelus address, Pope Francis had promoted Cardinal Kasper's proposal to overturn the Church's prohibition on the divorced and civilly remarried to receive Holy Communion.[10] Furthermore, the Supreme Pontiff invited Cardinal Kasper to address the his first consistory of cardinals on his proposals. Though many cardinals opposed Kasper, Pope Francis made it clear that Cardinal Kaiser had his backing during his closing address.[11] Therefore, it is obvious that Pope Francis appointed Archbishop Bruno Forte, a disciple of Walter Kasper, as the Special Secretary for the Synod on the Family in order to influence and shape its documents.

In 2016 Archbishop Forte admitted that Pope Francis, with his assistance, had intentionally manipulated the 2014 Synod on the Family to get the result that he wanted — allowing the divorced and civilly re-married to receive Holy Communion:

> Archbishop Forte, in fact, revealed a particular 'behind-the-scenes' detail of the Synod: 'If we explicitly talk about communion for the divorced and remarried,' Archbishop Forte recounted, quoting a quip from Pope Francis, 'you don't know what a mess they'll make for us. So, let's not talk about it directly; make sure the premises are there, and I will draw the conclusions.' 'Typical of a Jesuit,' Archbishop Forte joked.[12] [Trans]

Finally, another way this section seeks to expose Pope Francis's radical agenda to promote rupture from the Deposit of Faith is to highlight the appeals, protests and criticisms from faithful clergy and laity over the twelve years of his pontificate. The insults and ad hominem attacks this provoked from Pope Francis and his appointees are very revealing in themselves.

---

[10]Pope Francis [17 March 2013] *Angelus Address* [Online] Available at: www.vatican.va [Accessed on: 10 October 2022]

[11]Magister, S [2014] *Kasper Changes the Paradigm, Bergoglio Applauds* [Online] Available at: chiesa.espresso.repubblica.it [Accessed on: 11 October 2022]

[12]Skojec, S [2016] *Forte: Pope Did Not Want to Speak "Plainly" Of Communion for Remarried* [Online] Available at: onepeterfive.com [Accessed on: 21 July 2025]

The Questionable Words and Deeds of Pope Francis and His Appointees

2013

13th March

When Monsignor Guido Marini went to vest the new elected Francis with the traditional mozzetta worn by popes when they were presented to the Church from the loggia of St. Peter's, Pope Francis is reported as saying, 'No thank you, Monsignor. You put it on instead. Carnival time is over!'.[991] He also rejected the traditional papal pectoral cross and red shoes.[992] Francis singled out Cardinal Godfried Danneels for the honour of standing with him on the loggia. Cardinal Godfried Danneels was notorious for attempting to convince King Baudouin that he should sign the Belgian abortion bill into law in 1990,[993] covered up clergy sexual abuse of children and was a member of the 'Saint Gallen mafia' that opposed the pontificate of Pope St. John Paul II and conspired to win the election of Pope Francis.[994]

15th March

In his address to the Sacred College of Cardinals, Pope Francis compared the Holy Spirit to 'an Apostle of Babel': 'The Paraclete creates all the differences among the Churches, almost as if he were an Apostle of Babel.'[995]

16th March

Pope Francis dispensed with the apostolic blessing at the conclusion of his meeting with communications professionals, 'I respect your consciences and since you are not all Catholic, I will not bless you but pray for you in my heart'.[996]

17th March

During his first angelus address in St. Peter's Square, Pope Francis recommended the work of Cardinal Kasper, the leading proponent of allowing the divorced and civilly 're-married' to receive Holy Communion.[997]

---

[991]Willey, D [2013] *Pope Francis' first moves hint at break with past* [Online] Available at: www.bbc.co.uk [Accessed on: 10 October 2022]

[992]O'Connell, G [2013] *From the start Pope Francis has rejected status symbols* [Online] Available at: www.americamagazine.org [10 October 2022]

[993]Smits, J [2015] *Cardinal Danneels tried to convince Belgian king to sign bill legalizing abortion: former prime minister* [Online] www.lifesitenews.com [Accessed on: 10 October 2022]

[994]Chretien, C [2019] *Dissident cardinal who covered up sex abuse dies. Pope praises him as 'zealous pastor'* [Online] Available at: www.lifesitenews.com [Accessed on: 10 October 2022]

[995]Pope Francis [2013] *Audience with the Cardinals* [Online] Available at: www.vatican.va [Accessed on: 10 October 2022]

[996]Pope Francis [2013] *Audience with Communications Professionals* [Online] Available at: www.cbcew.org.uk [Accessed on: 10 October 2022]

[997]Pope Francis [17 March 2013] *Angelus Address* [Online] Available at: www.vatican.va [Accessed on: 10 October 2022]

23rd May

The publication of the *Annuario Pontificio* for 2013 revealed that Pope Francis only wanted to officially emphasise his title as 'Bishop of Rome', relegating the other traditional titles of the pope: 'Vicar of Jesus Christ; Successor of the Prince of the Apostles; Supreme Pontiff of the Universal Church; Primate of Italy; Archbishop and metropolitan of the Roman province; Sovereign of Vatican City-State, and, Servant of the Servants of God.'[998]

6th June

In a private audience with the presiding board of the CLAR — the Latin American and Caribbean Confederation of Religious Men and Women — Pope Francis downplayed the authority of the Congregation of the Doctrine of the Faith and mocked the traditional devotion of the spiritual bouquet.[999]

15th June

Pope Francis appointed Msgr. Battista Ricca to the position of Prelate of the Institute for the Vatican's Works of Religion (IOR),[1000] despite credible allegations of notorious homosexual conduct while posted to the nunciature in Montevideo, Uruguay.[1001]

19th June

Pope Francis met Cardinal Theodore McCarrick and commissioned him to undertake a mission to China. Thereby, lifting the sanctions restricting him to a private, retired life imposed by Pope Benedict XVI for his notorious homosexual corruption of seminarians.[1002] In his 2019 book *In the Closet of the Vatican the homosexual* Dr. Frédéric Martel referred to Pope Francis' relationship with the homosexual Cardinal McCarrick, based on his conversations with Vatican officials:

> Pope Bergoglio was really informed by Archbishop Carlo Maria Viganò of the past of [McCarrick's] predation towards seminarians and young priests, but he did not consider the fact so important. And consequently not only did he relieve him of the restrictions that Benedict XVI had imposed on him (whose existence was confirmed, as well as by Viganò, by Cardinal Marc Ouellet) but he also used him as an advisor for appointments in the United States (the promotion of Kevin Farrell to Camerlengo and entrusting Blase Cupich with the organization of the summit on child abuse are the more recent confirmations, if ever they were needed) and he used him as his personal representative both in the United States (with Obama) and abroad in China, Armenia, Iran and Cuba.[1003]

11th July

The Sacred Congregation for Institutes of Consecrated Life and Societies of Apostolic Life issued a Decree dissolving the General Council of the Franciscan Friars of the Immaculate, appointing Rev. Fidenzio Volpi as Apostolic Commissioner to investigate and govern the religious community, and restricting their celebration of the traditional

---

[998] *Vatican Diary / The identity cards of the last two popes* [2013] [Online] Available at: chiesa.espresso. repubblica.it [Accessed on: 10 October 2022]

[999] *Pope to Latin American Religious: Full text. Update: Religious confirm they were the source* [2013] [Online] Available at: rorate-caeli.blogspot.com [Accessed on: 10 October 2022]

[1000] *Msgr. Battista Ricca Appointed Interim Prelate of IoR* [2013] [Online] Available at: http://visnews-en.blogspot.com [Accessed on: 10 October 2022]

[1001] Pentin, E [2013] *Vaticanista Publishes Lurid Tale Surrounding Vatican Bank Appointee* [Online] Available at: www.ncregister.com [Accessed on: 10 October 2022]

[1002] *Archbishop Vigano's Testimony* [2013] [Online] Available at: www.churchmilitant.com [Accessed on: 10 October 2022]

[1003] Hickson, M [2013] *New book confirms Viganò's report that Pope Francis knew about McCarrick abuse* [Online] Available at: www.lifesitenews.com [Accessed on: 10 October 2022]

Latin Mass. These restrictive measures followed complaints to the Vatican from a group of friars who opposed the traditional Mass and complained of critiques of the Second Vatican Council as signifying an 'irreconcilable break with previous tradition'.[1004]

29th July

During the flight back from World Youth Day in Brazil, Pope Francis responded to a journalist's question about a 'gay lobby' in the Vatican by saying, 'If a person is gay and seeks God and has good will, who am I to judge?' Furthermore, in response to a journalist asking why he didn't speak to the young people about abortion and same-sex marriage in light of the Brazilian government passing permissive laws, Pope Francis replied, 'The Church has already spoken quite clearly on this. It was unnecessary to return to it, just as I didn't speak about cheating, lying, or other matters on which the Church has a clear teaching!'[1005]

19th August

Fr. Gustavo Oscar Zanchetta was consecrated bishop of Orán, Argentina, one of the first bishops of Pope Francis' pontificate. Fr. Zanchetta had worked closely with Archbishop Jorge Bergoglio when he headed the Argentine bishops' conference. In 2015 a diocesan official discovered pornographic images of young men engaged in sexual acts and nude selfies on the bishop's cellphone. In October 2015 Pope Francis summoned Bishop Zanchetta to Rome, when the latter claimed his phone had been hacked. The pontiff accepted the explanation and took no action. In 2016 three of Bishop Zanchetta's vicars general and two monsignors made a formal complaint to the Argentine nunciature alleging inappropriate behaviour with seminarians. A diocesan official again reported Bishop Zanchetta for possessing pornographic images in 2017. Resigning from his diocese in 2017 for 'health reasons', Pope Francis transferred Bishop Zanchetta to the Vatican and appointed him an advisor to the Administration of the Patrimony of the Holy See. In 2019 it became public that a complaint had been made against Bishop Zanchetta accusing him of 'problematic behaviour' with seminarians, entering their bedrooms at night to request massages and offering them alcohol. Three seminarians accused Bishop Zanchetta of abuse and later left the seminary. Ten other seminarians were intimidated to remain silent about the abuse they had witnessed. The Vatican twice insisted it knew nothing about allegations against Bishop Zanchetta until Autumn 2018. In 2021, Bishop Zanchetta was charged by Argentinean authorities with 'aggravated continuous sexual abuse' of two adult-aged seminarians, and fraud and mismanagement of funds. Denying the charges, he resigned his post as an assessor at the Vatican's Administration of the Patrimony of the Holy See. His trial was postponed until February 2022 due to the Vatican not providing the canonical file of its investigation of Bishop Zanchetta. The Vatican continued to fail to send its files on Zanchetta to Argentina, so the judges elected to proceed with the trial without them. On March 2022 an Argentine court found Bishop Gustavo Zanchetta guilty of sexually abusing seminarians, sentencing him to four and a half years in prison. Instead of serving his custodial sentence in prison, Zanchetta lived under house arrest in a retired priests' home.[1006]

[1004]*Why the Franciscan Friars of the Immaculate have been placed under the supervision of a commissioner* [2013] [Online] Available at: www.lastampa.it [Accessed on: 23 October 2022]

[1005]Pope Francis [2013] *Press conference during the return flight from the XXVIII World Youth Day.* [Online] Available at: www.vatican.va [Accessed on: 11 October 2022]

[1006]Barillas, M [2013] *Argentine bishop promoted by Pope Francis at Vatican accused of abusing seminarians* [Online] Available at: www.lifesitenews.com; Brockhaus, H [2019] Pope Francis says *Argentine bishop will go to trial for sexual misconduct* [Online] Available at: www.catholicnewsagency.com; Brockhaus, H [2021] *Argentine Bishop Zanchetta Ends Vatican Job at APSA* [Online] Available at: www.ncregister.com; San Martín, Inés [2021] *Argentinean trial of former Vatican official postponed until February* [Online] Available at: cruxnow.com; *Argentine Bishop Zanchetta sentenced for sex abuse* [2022] [Online] Available at: www.pillarcatholic.com; *Local Catholics protest Zanchetta house arrest at retired priest home.* [Online] Available at: www.pillarcatholic.com [Accessed on: 11 October 2022]

4th September

Pope Francis released an open letter in answer to Eugenio Scalfari's questions addressed to him via the pages of *La Repubblica*, the left-wing Italian newspaper Scalfari founded and edited (7th July & 7th August). In his reply Francis relativises the importance of belief in God and seeking faith by telling the atheist Scalfari that it is more important to follow one's conscience. Pope Francis' letter was posted on the Vatican website as an official document of his pontificate.[1007]

30th September

America Magazine published an interview in which Pope Francis said it's not necessary to talk all the time about abortion, gay marriage and the use of contraceptive methods. Referring to his earlier response 'Who am I to judge?' to a question about homosexual clergy, Francis explained 'it is not possible to interfere spiritually in the life of a person.'[1008]

1st October

Eugenio Scalfari, the atheist editor of the *La Repubblica*, published his first face-to-face exchange with Pope Francis. He reported that Pope Francis told him that 'The most serious of the evils that afflict the world these days are youth unemployment and the loneliness of the old.' He also recounted Pope Francis' criticism of previous pontificates, 'Heads of the Church have often been narcissists, flattered and thrilled by their courtiers. The court is the leprosy of the papacy.' He also reported that Pope Francis told him, 'And I believe in God, not in a Catholic God, there is no Catholic God.'[1009] The interview was also published in the Vatican newspaper *L'Osservatore Romano* and posted on the Vatican website.

3rd October

During a press briefing, asked whether the text of Eugenio Scalfari's interview 'accurately captured the "sense" of what the pope had said, Fr. Lombardi, the Vatican spokesman, replied that if Francis felt his thought had been "gravely misrepresented," he would have said so.'[1010]

5th October

The National Catholic Register published a letter of clarification about Eugenio Scalfari's interview with Pope Francis from Fr. Thomas Rosica, the English-language Vatican spokesman. Fr Rosica explained that 'Scalfari has stated that he showed the text to Francis for his approval, but it's not clear how closely the pope read it.'[1011]

8th October

Pope Francis announced an Extraordinary General Assembly of the Synod of Bishops on the theme 'The Pastoral Challenges of the Family in the Context of Evangelization' to be held at the Vatican between the 5th-19th October, 2014.

 La Repubblica reported the announcement from Kairos, an organization of LGBT Catholics in Florence, Italy, that Pope Francis had replied with a handwritten note to

---

[1007]Pope Francis [2013] *Letter to a non-believer: Pope Francis responds to Dr. Eugenio Scalfari, journalist of the Italian newspaper "La Repubblica"* [Online] Available at: www.vatican.va [Accessed on: 11 October 2022]

[1008]Spadaro, A [2013] *A Big Heart Open to God: An interview with Pope Francis* [Online] Available at: www.americamagazine.org [Accessed on: 11 October 2022]

[1009]Scalfari, E [2013] *The Pope: how the Church will change* [Online] Available at: www.repubblica.it [Accessed on: 11 October 2022]

[1010]Allen, J [2013] *Dolan confirms error in Scalfari interview* [Online] Available at: www.ncronline.org [Accessed on: 11 October 2022]

[1011]Pentin, E [2013] *Vatican: Scalfari Interview Misses Details, Conflates Facts* [Online] Available at: www.ncregister.com [Accessed on: 11 October 2022]

their letter sent to him in June. They also received a reply from the Vatican's Secretariat of State, telling them that Pope Francis 'really enjoyed' their letter to him. It is thought to be the first time a pontiff has replied to a group advocating homosexuality.[1012]

18th October

Archbishop Lorenzo Baldisseri, the secretary general of the Vatican's Synod of Bishops, sent the world's national bishops conferences a questionnaire to be distributed to the laity in preparation for the 2014 Extraordinary Synod on the Family. The questionnaire sought to elicit, among other things, the opinions of the laity on the Church's doctrine on contraception, so called same-sex 'marriage', co-habitation, and the divorced and civilly 're-married'.[1013]

5th November

During a visit to the Vatican Grottoes, Pope Francis mocked a young altar boy for holding his hands together in the gesture of prayer, pulling his hands apart as he chided, 'Are your hands bound together? It seems like they're stuck.'[1014]

11th November

During an interview with Fernando E. Solanas, Pope Francis referred to the Hindu false 'deity' Shiva, 'Because then we create and destroy. The God Shiva, right? The myth which tells that he created the world is a current myth. The God Shiva creates the world and then destroys it. Now, it occurs to me that we are living the myth of Shiva I think.' He also quoted positively the Chinese communist leader Zhou Enlai.[1015]

18th November

Following months of controversy, the Vatican removed the text of Eugenio Scalfari's interview with Pope Francis from the Vatican website, where it had been posted under the section for papal speeches.[1016]

24th November

Pope Francis' apostolic exhortation, *Evangelii Gaudium*, was promulgated. Among other things, Pope Francis proposed that 'genuine doctrinal authority' (*EG* 32) be de-centralised to separate national bishops' conferences.[1017] Thereby, diminishing the authority of the Congregation for the Doctrine of the Faith and undermining the unity of the Church.

8th December

Fr. Fidenzio Volpi, Apostolic Commissioner to the Franciscan Friars of the Immaculate (FFI), issued a series of sanctions against the order in the name of Pope Francis: He sent Rev. Stefano Maria Manelli, founder of the FFI, to live in a religious home; closed the FFI seminary; suspended the FFI's lay movement; suspended ordinations of new priests for a year, and required future priests to formally accept the teachings of the Second Vatican Council and the *Novus Ordo* liturgy.[1018]

[1012]Clark, K [2013] *Pope pens letter to gay Catholics* [Online] Available at: www.americamagazine.org [Accessed on: 11 October 2022]
[1013]McElwee, J [2013] *Vatican asks for parish-level input on synod document* [Online] Available at: www.ncronline.org [Accessed on: 11 October 2022]
[1014]*Pope Francis visits Vatican Grottoes to pray for deceased Pontiffs* [2013] [Online] Available at: www.romereports.com [Accessed on: 11 October 2022]
[1015]Solanas, F [2013] *Pope Francis supports anti-fracking campaign By Fernando E. Solanas* [Online] Available at: www.youtube.com [Accessed on: 11 October 2022]
[1016]*Pope's controversial interview with atheist Scalfari scrubbed from Vatican website* [2013] [Online] Available at: www.lifesitenews.com [Accessed on: 11 October 2022]
[1017]Pope Francis [2013] *Post Synodal Apostolic Exhortation Evangelii Gaudium* [Online] Available at: www.vatican.va [Accessed on: 11 October 2022]
[1018]Winfield, N [2013] *Pope's crackdown on order alarms traditionalists* [Online] Available at: apnews.com [Accessed on: 11 October 2022]

Fr. Volpi also distributed a circular letter to all the Friars of the Immaculate, accusing prominent members of the Franciscan Sisters of the Immaculate 'of having contributed to the creation of a "distorted mentality" in the Friars, strongly influencing their life-style.' Accusations that the Franciscan Sisters of the Immaculate strongly rebutted.[1019]

16th December

Pope Francis removed Cardinal Burke from the Congregation for Bishops, appointing instead Washington Cardinal Wuerl who opposed Burke on the need to deny Holy Communion to pro-abortion politicians.[1020]

2014

20 February

Pope Francis invited Cardinal Kasper to address the consistory of cardinals on his proposals for a 'penitential way' to allow divorced and civilly 're-married' Catholics to receive Holy Communion. Though many cardinals opposed Kasper's proposals, Pope Francis made it clear that he endorsed them commenting during his closing address to the cardinals:

> Yesterday, before going to sleep — although I did not do this to put myself to sleep — I read or rather re-read the work of Cardinal Kasper, and I would like to thank him because I found profound theology, and even serene thinking in theology. It is pleasant to read serene theology. And I also found what Saint Ignatius told us about, that 'sensus Ecclesiae,' love for Mother Church. It did me good and an idea came to me — excuse me, Eminence, if I embarrass you — but the idea is that this is called 'doing theology on one's knees.' Thank you. Thank you.[1021]

22nd February

Pope Francis admitted Archbishop Nichols of Westminster to the Sacred College of Cardinals, who is notorious for his support of the Soho Masses Pastoral Council that allows homosexual militants who publicly defy the Church's moral doctrine to receive Holy Communion.[1022] In January 2013, Archbishop Nichols oversaw the re-branding of the Soho Masses Pastoral Council as LGBT Catholics Westminster and re-locating them to Farm St, Mayfair.[1023]

5th March

Corriere della Sera published a wide-ranging interview with Pope Francis, during which the issue of whether the Church could support civil unions for homosexual persons was raised. In response Pope Francis obfuscated, 'It is about pacts of cohabitating of various natures, of which I wouldn't know how to list the different ways. One needs to see the different cases and evaluate them in their variety.' He also employed situation ethics in his reply to a question about *Humanae Vitae*, saying, 'The question is not that of changing the doctrine but of going deeper and making pastoral (ministry) take into account the situations and that which it is possible for people to do.'[1024]

[1019]*Franciscan Sisters of the Immaculate fight back, call Fr. Volpi's accusations 'totally unfounded', Volpi's comments 'offend our entire Institute, and consequently, we refute them completely'* [2013] [Online] Available at: rorate-caeli.blogspot.com [Accessed on: 11 October 2022]

[1020]Yardley, J & Horowitz, J [2013] *Pope Replaces Conservative U.S. Cardinal on Influential Vatican Committee* [Online] Available at: www.nytimes.com [Accessed on: 11 October 2022]

[1021]Magister, S [2014] *Kasper Changes the Paradigm, Bergoglio Applauds* [Online] Available at: chiesa.espresso.repubblica.it [Accessed on: 11 October 2022]

[1022]Dodd, L [2014] *Nichols the cardinal: 'another step on priestly journey full of surprises'* [Online] Available at: www.thetablet.co.uk [Accessed on: 11 October 2022]

[1023]*LGBT Catholics Westminster* [2016] [Online] Available at: lgbthistoryuk.org [Accessed on: 11 October 2022]

[1024]Pope Francis [2014] *Transcript: Pope Francis' March 5 interview with Corriere della Sera* [Online] Available at: www.catholicnewsagency.com [Accessed on: 11 October 2022]

21st April

Pope Francis telephoned an Argentinean woman, Jaquelina Lisbona, in response to a letter she had sent him in Autumn 2013. During a media interview Jaquelina Lisbona explained she had written to Pope Francis because her new parish priest, upholding the Church's doctrine, had denied her Holy Communion because she was civilly married to a divorcee who had a valid pre-existing marriage. Pope Francis told her that it was okay for her to receive Communion, saying, 'A little bread and wine does no harm'.[1025]

6th May

Pope Francis concelebrated Mass with the pro-homosexual Don. Michele de Paolis at the chapel of Domus Santa Martha. Fr. Michele de Paolis cofounded the homosexual activist organization, *Agedo Foggia*, that campaigns to change doctrine on homosexuality. Don Michele wrote,

> 'homosexual love is a gift from (God) no less than heterosexual…Some church people say, "It's okay to be gay, but they should not have sex, they can not love each other." This is the greatest hypocrisy. It's like saying to a plant that grows, 'You must not flourish, you must not bear fruit!' Yes, it is against nature!'

At the close of their meeting Pope Francis bowed to Don. Michele de Paolis and kissed his hands.[1026]

7th May

During an interview with the US liberal Catholic journal *Commonweal*, Cardinal Kasper stated that Pope Francis had told him that 50% of Catholic marriages were invalid, 'I've spoken to the pope himself about this, and he said he believes that 50 percent of marriages are not valid.'[1027] Eminent American canonist Dr. Edward Peters responded, 'I am stunned at the pastoral recklessness of such an assertion. Simply stunned.'[1028]

16th May

Pope Francis appointed liberal and pro-homosexual Fr. Timothy Radcliffe OP a consultor for the Pontifical Council for Justice and Peace.[1029]

19 May

João Cardinal Braz de Aviz, Prefect of the Congregation for Institutes of Consecrated Life, informed the Superior General of the Franciscan Sisters of the Immaculate (FSI) of the appointment of Sister Fernanda Barbiero as 'Visitor' with powers to impose changes to the FSI.[1030]

June

At the urging of his close collaborators Cardinal Coccopalmerio, president of the Pontifical Council for Legislative Texts and Monsignor Pio Vito Pinto, Dean of the Roman Rota, Pope Francis reversed the CDF's 2012 decision to suspend a *divinis* Fr.

[1025]McElwee, J [2014] *Pope's call to woman raises questions on divorced and remarried* [Online] Available at: www.ncronline.org; Roberts, H [2014] *A little bread and wine 'does no harm': Pope Francis goes against years of Catholic teaching and tells divorced woman it is OK to take communion* [Online] Available at: www.dailymail.co.uk [Accessed on: 11 October 2022]

[1026]*Pope kisses the hand of, concelebrates mass with pro-homosexual activist priest* [2014] [Online] Available at: www.lifesitenews.com [Accessed on: 11 October 2022]

[1027]Boudway, M & Gallicho, G [2014] *An Interview with Cardinal Walter Kasper* [Online] Available at: www.commonwealmagazine.org [Accessed on: 11 October 2022]

[1028]Peters, E [2014] *Even if the pope said it, it was reckless to repeat it* [Online] Available at: canonlawblog. wordpress.com [Accessed on: 11 October 2022]

[1029]Bourne, L [2014] *Vatican appointee says gay sex can express Christ's 'self-gift'* [Online] Available at: www.lifesitenews.com [Accessed on: 11 October 2022]

[1030]Mattei, E de [2014] *Salus animarum suprema lex?* [Online] Available at: rorate-caeli.blogspot.com [Accessed on: 11 October 2022]

Mauro Inzoli for the crimes of sexually abusing boys in the confessional, restoring his priestly status.[1031] In June 2016 Fr. Mauro Inzoli was sentenced to four years and nine months for eight incidents of sexual violence between 2004 and 2008 against five children aged 12-16. In 2017 Fr. Mauro Inzoli was again laicised.[1032]

8th June

For the first time in history, Islamic prayers and readings from the Quran were said in the Vatican at the invitation of Pope Francis.[1033]

14th June

Pope Francis asked Justin Welby, head of the Anglican ecclesial community to 'bless' him in front of the cameras.

11th-12th July

The Pontifical Council for Justice and Peace convened a two-day seminar at the Pontifical Academy of Science inside the Vatican under the theme 'The Global Common Good: Towards a More Inclusive Economy'. Keynote speakers included the world's foremost proponents of abortion and population control Ban Ki-moon and Jeffrey Sachs.[1034]

13th July

La Repubblica published the third exchange between Eugenio Scalfari and Pope Francis held in the Vatican. During the interview Pope Francis is reported as saying, 'Two per cent of paedophiles are priests, and even bishops and cardinals.' Though Fr. Lombardi, the Vatican spokesman, questioned the accuracy of this quotation, Pope Francis did not deny or repudiate it.[1035]

9th September

Pope Francis appointed Cardinal Godfried Danneels as a Synod Father for the Extraordinary Synod in October. Danneels covered up clergy sexual abuse of children and was pro-homosexual civil 'marriages'.[1036]

17th September

The French Catholic newspaper *La Croix* reported a source close to Francis saying the pope would be 'annoyed by the publication' of *Remaining in the Truth of Christ: Marriage and Communion in the Catholic Church.* (Ignatius Press, 2014). This is a collective work, including five cardinals, defending the prohibition of divorced and civilly 'remarried' receiving Holy Communion. Other Vatican sources denied this saying Francis wasn't even aware of the book.[1037]

20th September

Pope Francis appointed pro-homosexual Bishop Blaise Cupich Archbishop of Chicago. Cupich becomes an outspoken advocate of LGBT 'rights' in the Church.

[1031]Dougherty, M [2014] *A child abuse scandal is coming for Pope Francis* [Online] Available at: theweek.com [Accessed on: 11 October 2022]

[1032]*Pope Francis laicises abuser priest* [2014] [Online] Available at: catholicherald.co.uk [Accessed on: 11 October 2022]

[1033]*Islamic prayers to be held at the Vatican* [2014] [Online] Available at: english.alarabiya.net [Accessed on: 11 October 2022]

[1034]*Vatican brings together Mark Carney, Mohammad Yunus, Jeffrey Sachs to call for more person-centred economy* [2014] [Online] Available at: www.thetablet.co.uk [Accessed on: 11 October 2022]

[1035]Davies, L [2014] *Did Pope Francis really say 2% of priests are paedophiles?* [Online] Available at: www.theguardian.com [Accessed on: 11 October 2022]

[1036]Western, JH [2014] *Pope Francis and homosexuality: confusing signs* [Online] Available at: www.lifesitenews.com [Accessed on: 11 October 2022]

[1037]Fessio, J [2014] *Is Pope Francis upset about an Ignatius Press book?* [Online] Available at: /www.catholicworldreport.com [Accessed on: 11 October 2022]

30th September

Pope Francis appointed pro-homosexual John Arnold Bishop of Salford. Arnold would establish a regular LGBT Mass.

3rd October

During the first press conference of the Extraordinary Synod on the Family, Cardinal Lorenzo Baldisseri, secretary general of the Synod of Bishops, announced that, breaking with previous practice, the texts of the Synod Father's interventions would not be made public. Instead, a daily vague 'summary' was released. This was according to the wishes of Pope Francis, who wanted the Synod Fathers to have 'freedom of expression'.[1038] Cardinal Gerhard Müller, the Prefect of the CDF, protested that the faithful had the right to know what their bishop was saying.[1039] In reaction to this strict control of information, there were growing concerns about manipulation of the synod. A senior Vatican official observed that all the Synod press briefings 'were geared toward spinning a liberal angle', while speeches 'in favour of tradition were not reported'.[1040]

Two years after the synod, Archbishop Bruno Forte, the Special Secretary of the Synod, admitted that Pope Francis had instructed him about how they should manipulate the synod. Archbishop Forte claimed that the pope told him: 'If we speak explicitly about communion for the divorced and remarried, you do not know what a terrible mess we will make. So we won't speak plainly, do it in a way that the premises are there, then I will draw out the conclusions. Typical of a Jesuit.'[1041]

5th October

During his homily at the Mass for the opening on the Extraordinary Synod, Pope Francis criticised 'evil pastors' who

> lay intolerable burdens on the shoulders of others, which they themselves do not lift a finger to move...We too, in the Synod of Bishops, are called to work for the Lord's vineyard. Synod Assemblies are not meant to discuss beautiful and clever ideas, or to see who is more intelligent.[1042]

Argentina's *La Nacion* newspaper published an interview with Pope Francis in which he was asked was he 'worried' about a book released by five cardinals, including Cardinal Burke and Cardinal Pell, opposing proposals to allow the divorced and civilly 'remarried' to receive Holy Communion, titled *Remaining in the Truth of Christ: Marriage and Communion in the Catholic Church*. Avoiding answering the question directly, he replied, 'I even enjoy debating with the very conservative, but intellectually well formed bishops' but 'the world has changed and the Church cannot lock itself into alleged interpretations of dogma.'[1043]

6th October

Cardinal Burke and Fr. Dodaro arranged for the postal delivery of their book *Remaining in the Truth of Christ: Marriage and Communion in the Catholic Church*, to all the Synod

[1038]Western, JH [2014] *'You should come up here if you know everything': Cardinal fires back as press questions Synod's 'lack of transparency'* [Online] Available at: www.lifesitenews.com [Accessed on: 11 October 2022]

[1039]Craine, P [2014] *Pope's doctrinal head: Bishops' talks at family synod 'should be published'* [Online] Available at: www.lifesitenews.com [Accessed on: 11 October 2022]

[1040]Pentin, E [2015] *The Rigging of a Vatican Synod? An Investigation into Alleged Manipulation at the Extraordinary Synod on the Family.* San Francisco, Ignatius Press, p. 51

[1041]Chretien, C [2016] *Archbishop: Pope told me we must avoid speaking 'plainly' on Communion for remarried* [Online] Available at: www.lifesitenews.com [Accessed on: 11 October 2022]

[1042]Pope Francis [2014] *Homily at Mass for the Extraordinary Synod on the Family* [Online] Available at: www.vatican.va [Accessed on: 11 October 2022]

[1043]Western, JH & White, H [2014] *Pope Francis distances himself from 'very conservative' bishops* [Online] Available at: www.lifesitenews.com [Accessed on: 11 October 2022]

Fathers at the synod hall, with the compliments of Ignatius Press. These arrived at the Vatican post office four or five days later. Various sources confirm that Cardinal Baldisseri was 'furious' that the books had been sent to the Synod Fathers. He demanded that the Vatican post office block the delivery, but was told that that would be illegal. Instead, delivery was delayed as long as possible, until the middle of the second week of the synod. Even then, the books were only left in the mailboxes for two days and then removed. As a result, the majority of Synod Fathers did not receive their copy.[1044]

13th October

The publication of the *Relatio Post Disceptationem* — the mid-term report of the Synod — raised further concerns about manipulation. The report, written by Archbishop Bruno Forte, stated that the Synod Fathers:

- were open to admitting the divorced and civilly 're-married' to Holy Communion on a 'case-by-case basis';
- sought to encourage the Church to be positive about the homosexual orientation, and,
- wanted to focus on 'positive' aspects of sinful unions.[1045]

Cardinal Wilfrid Napier, O.F.M., one of the synod fathers, recalled others protesting to him about the mid-term report:

> How then could this be stated as coming from the synod when the synod hasn't even discussed it yet? and others stating, there are things said there about the synod saying this, that, and the other, but nobody ever said them. So that's when it became plain that there was some engineering going on.[1046]

In January 2015, Cardinal Lorenzo Baldisseri admitted in an interview that Pope Francis had approved the controversial *Relatio Post Disceptationem* before its publication.[1047]

16th October

When the reports of the Synod Fathers' small group discussions were handed to the synod secretariat Cardinal Baldisseri, he announced that, unlike previous synods, the reports would not be made public. It was reported this decision was booed and jeered by some of the Synod Fathers for around fifteen minutes until Pope Francis gave way and approved that the reports could be published.[1048] Cardinal Burke highlighted the significance of this victory against the manipulation of the synod, 'I consider the publication of the reports of the ten small groups of critical importance, for they demonstrate that the Synod Fathers do not accept at all the contents of the *Relatio*.'[1049]

17th October

Cardinal Burke announced that Pope Francis had demoted him from his senior position as Prefect of the Supreme Tribunal of the Apostolic Signatura — the Church's highest legal court — and assigned him patron of the Sovereign Military Order of Malta. Cardinal Burke had been outspoken in upholding the prohibition of divorced and civilly 're-married' and pro-abortion politicians receiving Holy Communion.

[1044]Pentin, E [2015] *Op. cit., ibid.*, p.61

[1045]*Family Synod: Midterm report — full text* [2014] [Online] Available at: www.indcatholicnews. com [Accessed on: 11 October 2022]

[1046]Pentin, E [2015] *Op. cit.*, p.37

[1047]White, H & Craine, P [2015] *Pope Francis approved family synod's controversial mid-term report before publication: synod chief* [Online] Available at: www.lifesitenews.com [Accessed on: 11 October 2022]

[1048]Pentin, E [2015] *Op. cit.*, p.130

[1049]*Cardinal Burke to CWR: confirms transfer, praises pushback, addresses controversy over remarks by Cardinal Kasper* [2014] [Online] Available at: www.catholicworldreport.com [Accessed on: 11 October 2022]

18th October

During the vote on the final report, the Synod Fathers did not give the sections allowing reception of Holy Communion for the divorced and civilly 'remarried' the two-thirds majority needed for them to be included. In response, Pope Francis overturned the rules governing the synod and instructed that the final report include the sections covering the overturning the traditional prohibition of Holy Communion for the divorced and re-married. By so doing, Pope Francis ensured that this attack on the indissolubility of marriage and the sanctity of the Blessed Sacrament was included on the agenda of the 2015 Synod on the Family. Pope Francis also ordered the inclusion of the section on 'pastoral attention' to homosexual persons though it also failed to get the two-thirds majority vote. Cardinal Marx, a close advisor of the pope, said that by so doing Pope Francis had 'pushed the doors open' regarding doctrine on divorce and homosexuality.[1050]

Pope Francis expressed his displeasure at those Synod Fathers who had resisted his goal of changing the doctrine of the Church during his concluding address, saying:

> a temptation to hostile inflexibility, that is, wanting to close oneself within the written word, (the letter) and not allowing oneself to be surprised by God, by the God of surprises, (the spirit); within the law, within the certitude of what we know and not of what we still need to learn and to achieve. From the time of Christ, it is the temptation of the zealous, of the scrupulous, of the solicitous and of the so-called – today – 'traditionalists' and also of the intellectuals…to transform the bread into a stone and cast it against the sinners, the weak, and the sick (cf. Jn 8:7), that is, to transform it into unbearable burdens (Lk 11:46).'[1051]

28th October

Eugenio Scalfari, the atheist editor of the *La Repubblica*, published his fourth exchange with Pope Francis in which he reported that though the Supreme Pontiff doesn't consider himself a proponent of Relativism, he does think that truth is relative:

> the Pope refuses the word 'relativism,' i.e. a real movement with aspects of religious politics; but he does not refuse the word 'relative'. No to relativism, but that truth is relative is a matter of fact that Pope Francis acknowledges.[1052]

In response to Scalfari's interview, Fr. Federico Lombardi, director of the Holy See press office stated gnomically, 'Scalfari pursues his own discourse' and, 'if there are no words published by the Holy See press office and not officially confirmed, the writer takes full responsibility for what he has written.'[1053]

30th November

During the in-flight press conference returning from his apostolic visit to Turkey, Pope Francis compared Christian fundamentalists with Muslim fundamentalists who commit acts of terrorism:

> And I sincerely believe that we cannot say all Muslims are terrorists, just as we cannot say that all Christians are fundamentalists – we also have fundamentalists among us, all religions have these small groups. I told the President [Erdogan] that it would be good to issue a clear condemnation against these kinds of groups.[1054]

[1050]White, H [2014] *Pope ordered rejected paragraph on homosexuality retained in final Synod document: Cardinal Marx* [Online] Available at: www.lifesitenews.com [Accessed on: 11 October 2022]

[1051]Pope Francis [2014] *Address for the Conclusion of the Extraordinary Synod on the Family* [Online] Available at: www.vatican.va [Accessed on: 11 October 2022]

[1052]*Are an atheist journalist's papal interviews reliable?* [Online] Available at: www.catholicnewsagency.com [Accessed on: 17 September 2022]

[1053]*Ibid.*

[1054]Pope Francis [2014] *In-flight press conference from Istanbul to Rome* [Online] Available at: www.vatican.va [Accessed on: 11 October 2022]

7th December

Argentina's major newspaper, *La Nacion*, published an interview with Pope Francis in which he called for a relaxation of the Church's prohibitions against divorced and civilly 'remarried' Catholics playing a sacramental role in the life of the Church, such as being godparents. Hinting that he approved of them receiving Holy Communion, he also criticised those Synod Fathers who insisted on upholding the Church's doctrine on the matter:

> You could ask me 'are there any that are completely stubborn and won't move from their positions?'. Yes, there surely are. But that is not my concern. It's a question of praying for the Holy Spirit to convert them, if any.[1055]

15th December

The General Secretariat of the 2015 Ordinary Synod disseminated the *Lineamenta* — guideline document — to the world's bishops. It warned them to avoid reflections that are 'based simply on an application of doctrine' because such an approach would 'not respect the conclusions of the Extraordinary Synodal Assembly and would lead their reflection far from the path already indicated.' They were instructed 'to be guided by the pastoral approach initiated at the Extraordinary Synod which is grounded in Vatican II and the Magisterium of Pope Francis', even though the final report of the 2014 synod included sections that failed to achieve two-thirds majority vote.[1056]

2015

19th January

During a mid-flight press conference returning from his apostolic visit to the Philippines, Pope Francis' responded to a question on the Church's opposition to contraception. His comment about a woman pregnant with her eighth child that was to be delivered by caesarean section was seen as critical of large Catholic families:

> That example I mentioned shortly before about that woman who was expecting her eighth (child) and already had seven who were born with caesareans. That is an irresponsibility (That woman might say) 'no but I trust in God' But God gives you methods to be responsible. Some think that, excuse me if I use that word, that in order to be good Catholics we have to be like rabbits. No. Responsible parenthood![1057]

22nd January

Through the pages of the Italian bishop's newspaper Avvenire, Archbishop Giovanni Becciu issued an apology and clarification on behalf of Pope Francis about his criticism of large families, 'The Pope is truly sorry… [The pope] absolutely did not want to disregard the beauty and the value of large families.'[1058]

24th January

Pope Francis granted a 'strictly private' audience to two women, one of whom presented herself as a man, going by the name Diego Neria Lejarraga. It was reported as the pope meeting a 'transsexual man and his fiancée.' Pope Francis had phoned the woman presenting as a man twice in December 2014 following her sending him a letter

---

[1055]Piqué, E [2014] *The synod on the family: 'The divorced and remarried seem excommunicated'* [Online] Available at: www.lanacion.com.ar [Accessed on: 11 October 2022]

[1056]White, H [2014] *'Avoid simply applying doctrine,' Vatican urges bishops preparing for 2015 family synod* [Online] Available at: www.lifesitenews.com [Accessed on: 11 October 2022]

[1057]O'Connell, G [2015] *Full transcript of pope's press conference on flight from Manila* [Online] Available at: www.americamagazine.org [Accessed on: 11 October 2022]

[1058]Western, JH [2015] *Pope Francis sorry for remarks perceived as insulting large families* [Online] Available at: www.lifesitenews.com [Accessed on: 11 October 2022]

complaining about the reaction of her parish to her 'gender reassignment'. She reported Pope Francis as saying during one of their telephone conversations, 'God loves all his children, however they are; you are a son of God, who accepts you exactly as you are. Of course you are a son of the Church!'[1059]

14th February

Among the archbishops elevated to the Sacred College of Cardinals by Pope Francis was Archbishop John Dew of New Zealand, notorious for proposing at the 2005 synod under Pope Benedict XVI, that divorced and 'remarried' should receive communion.[1060]

15th February

Members of the militant homosexual group New Ways Ministry were seated with dignitaries and special Catholics groups at Pope Francis' Wednesday audience. This singling out for special treatment happened despite Archbishop James Hickey of Washington denying New Ways Ministry approval or authorization to work as a Catholic organisation because of its vocal opposition to Church doctrine on homosexuality. Sr. Jeannine Gramick, a co-founder of the group, was also present with members of New Ways Ministry at Pope Francis' audience despite the CDF ruling in 1999 that 'permanently prohibited them from any pastoral work with homosexual persons.'[1061]

19th February

During his annual meeting with the clergy of Rome, Pope Francis criticised as 'mistaken' those bishops and priests committed to the 'reform of the reform' associated with Pope Benedict XVI. He went on to criticise bishops who accepted traditionalist seminarians:

> who were kicked out of other dioceses, without finding out information on them, because they presented themselves very well, very devout. They were then ordained, but these were later revealed to have psychological and moral problems.[1062]

6th March

Pope Francis gave an interview with Valentina Alazraki, Mexican Media Company Televisa, in which he repeated that divorced and civilly 'remarried' should be allowed to be godparents, and added, that they should also be allowed to be catechists. By so doing, Pope Francis ignored the Church's prohibition due to public scandal.[1063]

8th March

The Vatican officially hosted the second annual Voices of Faith conference of feminists, whose speakers included the pro-abortion and pro-homosexual writer, Dr. Tina Beattie, and Deborah Rose-Milavec, head of an American organization promoting female ordination.[1064]

[1059]White, H [2015] *Pope receives 'transgender' woman and female partner for private audience* [Online] Available at: www.lifesitenews.com; Ivereigh, A [2015] *'Of course you are a son of the Church', Francis tells transgender man* [Online] Available at: cvcomment.org [Accessed on: 11 October 2022]
[1060]*Pope Francis appoints 20 new cardinals* [2015] [Online] Available at: www.bbc.co.uk [Accessed on: 11 October 2022]
[1061]Pullella, P [2015] *Gay Catholic group gets VIP treatment at Vatican for first time* [Online] Available at: www.reuters.com; Congregation for the Doctrine of the Faith [1999] *Notification regarding Sister Jeannine Gramick, SSND, and Father Robert Nugent, SDS* [Online] Available at: www.vatican.va [Accessed on: 11 October 2022]
[1062]Cernuzio, S [2015] *Pope Holds Two Hour Meeting with Roman Clergy* [Online} Available at: zenit. org [Accessed on: 11 October 2022]
[1063]Alazraki, V [2015] *Pope Francis Interviewed by Mexican Media Company Televisa* [Online] Available at: www.ewtn.com [Accessed on: 11 October 2022]
[1064]*Voices of Faith brings women to Vatican on International Women's Day* [Online] Available at: http://www.archivioradiovaticana.va [Accessed on: 11 October 2022]

12th March

Pope Francis appoints pro-homosexual Bishop John Stowe, OFM Conv., as Bishop of Lexington, Kentucky. Stowe becomes an outspoken advocate of LGBT rights in the Church.

14th March

Eugenio Scalfari, the atheist editor of the *La Repubblica*, published his fifth exchange with Pope Francis in which he reported that the pope denied the immortality of souls and the existence of Hell. According to Scalfari, Francis told him that those souls who die in a state where 'egoism overpowers and suffocates his love for others', are self-condemned. When asked if such souls will be punished, Francis was reported as replying:

> there is no punishment, but the annihilation of that soul. All the others will participate in the bliss of living in the presence of the Father. The annihilated souls will not be part of that banquet; with the death of the body their journey is ended.[1065]

23rd March

Pope Francis appoints pro-homosexual Bishop Robert McElroy as Bishop of San Diego, California. McElroy becomes an outspoken advocate of LGBT rights in the Church.

24th March

In response to a request from *LifeSiteNews* for clarification of Pope Francis' exchange with Eugenio Scalfari, Fr. Thomas Rosica, English-language assistant to the Holy See Press Office, did not deny its veracity but replied, as reported by *LifeSiteNews*:

> ' "All official, final texts of the Holy Father are found on the Vatican website', and since they were never published by the Holy See Press Office they 'should not be considered official texts. They were,' said Fr. Rosica, 'private discussions that took place and were never recorded by the journalist'.[1066]

11th April

Pope Francis promulgated *Misericordiae Vultus*, his Bull of Indiction of the Extraordinary Jubilee of Mercy. In the Bull Pope Francis reduced the seriousness of sins reserved to the Holy See, such as abortion, by delegating the authority to pardon them to priests chosen to be Missionaries of Mercy.[1067]

14th April

Pope Francis appointed heterodox Cardinal John Drew to the Congregation for the Evangelization of Peoples and the Pontifical Council for Christian Unity.[1068]

28th April

The Pontifical Academy of Sciences and the Pontifical Academy of Social Sciences convened a summit on climate change at which eugenicist Ban Ki-moon delivered the keynote address.[1069]

[1065]Scalfari, E [2015] *What Pope Francis may say to Europe's Nonbelievers* [Online] Available at: rorate-caeli.blogspot.com [Accessed on: 11 October 2022]

[1066]Western, JH [2015] *About that Pope Francis 'interview' where he denied the existence of Hell* [Online] Available at: www.lifesitenews.com [Accessed on: 11 October 2022]

[1067]Pope Francis [2015] *Bull of indiction of the Extraordinary Jubilee of Mercy, Misericordiae Vultus* [Online] Available at: www.vatican.va [Accessed on: 11 October 2022]

[1068]*Voice of the Family expresses concern over appointment of Cardinal Dew to Roman dicasteries* {2015] [Online] Available at: voiceofthefamily.com [Accessed on: 11 October 2022]

[1069]Kirchgaessner, S [2015] *Vatican official calls for moral awakening on global warming* [Online] Available at: www.theguardian.com [Accessed on: 11 October 2022]

5th May

For the first time in history, a woman claiming to be an archbishop was invited by Pope Francis to a private audience in the Vatican. Antje Jackelén was invited as head of the Lutheran ecclesial community of Sweden.[1070]

9th May

Pope Francis bowed his head to receive a 'blessing' from 100 Protestant Pentecostal ministers in front of the cameras.[1071]

14th May

During a United Nations meeting, pro-homosexual Archbishop Paglia, head of the Vatican's Pontifical Council for the Family, praised the US sitcom 'Modern Family,' that features two 'married' homosexual men who adopt a baby, and an older divorced father who remarries a younger woman. When asked by EWTN journalist Raymond Arroyo whether he approved of the show or not, Archbishop Paglia replied, 'This is not the heart of the question.'[1072]

18th May

In May 2015, Bishop Marcelo Sánchez Sorondo responded to concerns of a pro-life and pro-family group about the Vatican giving a platform to the world's foremost proponents of abortion and population control in July 2014. Bishop Sorondo admitted that they had discussed 'access to family planning and sexual and reproductive health and reproductive rights', which are euphemisms for contraception, sterilization, and abortion. Bishop Sánchez Sorondo also downplayed the moral primacy of abortion, 'Unfortunately, there is not only the drama of abortion, but there are also all these other dramas'. To those who criticised his decision to collaborate with Ban Ki-moon and Jeffrey Sachs he accused them of being members of the rightwing US Tea Party and those whose income derived from oil.[1073] Bishop Sánchez Sorondo had been re-confirmed chancellor of the Vatican's Pontifical Academy of Social Sciences and chancellor of the Pontifical Academy of Sciences by Pope Francis in 2014.

25th May

Pope Francis admits in an interview that the only daily newspaper that he reads is the anticlerical Socialist paper *La Repubblica*, founded by the atheist Eugenio Scalfari.[1074]

8th June

Pope Francis appointed Bishop Heiner Koch of Dresden-Meißen to be the new Archbishop of Berlin. Bishop Koch defends the unions of homosexual persons and ending the prohibition of divorced and civilly 'remarried' receiving Holy Communion.[1075]

12th June

For the first time in history, a so-called 'married' homosexual, atheist activist was invited to a public meeting with a pope. Pope Francis met with Simón Cazal, exe-

---

[1070]*Catholics and Lutherans looking ahead to Reformation anniversary* [2015] [Online] www.archivioradiovaticana.va [Accessed on: 11 October 2022]

[1071]*Church Revolution in Pictures* [2015] [Online] Available at: www.traditioninaction.org [Accessed on: 11 October 2022]

[1072]Hickson, M [2015] *New Vatican book suggests opening door to Communion for 'remarried' Catholics* [Online] Available at: www.lifesitenews.com [Accessed on: 11 October 2022]

[1073]Baklinski, P [2015] *Vatican official to pro-life leader: 'You and your cohort [are] out in the cold'* [Online] Available at: www.lifesitenews.com [Accessed on: 11 October 2022]

[1074]Rodari, P [2015] *The Pope: I don't watch TV, I read only La Repubblica* [Online] Available at: rorate-caeli.blogspot.com [Accessed on: 11 October 2022]

[1075]Hickson, M [2015] *Pope Francis appoints new archbishop of Berlin who defends gay unions* [Online] Available at: www.lifesitenews.com [Accessed on: 11 October 2022]

cutive director of Paraguay LGBT group SomosGay during his apostolic visit to Paraguay.[1076]

18th June

Pope Francis' encyclical *Laudato Si* was released, the longest encyclical in history, presenting climate change theory and its claims as established scientific fact. Pope Francis also argued for a one-world government with the power to impose sanctions and penalties. (175; 214).[1077]

19th June

It was announced that Pope Francis had appointed Professor John Schellnhuber as an ordinary member of the Pontifical Academy of Sciences. Professor Schellnhuber is a leading proponent of climate change theory, one world government and a full member of the Club of Rome that advocates for radical population control.[1078]

23rd June

The *Instrumentum Laboris* for the ordinary synod was published on the theme 'the vocation and mission of the family in the Church and in the contemporary world.' It included sections from the final report of the Extraordinary Synod that proposed allowing divorced and 'remarried' to receive Holy Communion rejected by the Synod Fathers. It was also criticised for:

- undermining the absolute prohibition of contraception by implying that conscience can trump the doctrine that contraception is intrinsically evil depending on the situation (137);
- its neutral presentation of the morality of IVF, which undermine the Church's absolute prohibition (34);
- its presentation of Christ's teaching on the indissolubility of marriage as an 'ideal' not a command (42), and,
- highlighting 'positive aspects' of cohabitation, making no mention of the grave sin of fornication (98).[1079]

1st July

Vatican Radio's German edition uncritically published on its website an article by Father Martin Lintner, a professor at Brixen Theology College, opposing the Church's condemnation of homosexual acts as acts of grave depravity. Alongside the pro-homosexuality article, Vatican Radio posted a photograph of two lesbians kissing. The article and photograph were eventually removed by 8th July. Father Bernd Hagenkord, the editor of Vatican Radio's German edition, complained about the criticism that had led to the articles removal, 'Some people cannot bear it that some people are different. And then we are astonished…that homosexuals feel discriminated? Still today.'[1080]

9th July

In response to an Italian author's publisher sending Pope Francis a selection of her children's books which deal with lesbian, gay, bisexual and transgender issues, the pontiff sent a letter to the author:

[1076]Brydum, S {2015] *Married Gay Activist's Meeting with Pope Was 'Very Productive'* [Online] Available at: www.advocate.com [Accessed on: 11 October 2022]

[1077]Western, JH [2015] *Pope's encyclical: Pro-climate-change, but anti-population control, pro-life, and anti-gender ideology* [Online] Available at: www.lifesitenews.com [Accessed on: 11 October 2022]

[1078]Hickson, M & Western, JH [2015] *Who's that one-world climate guru who helped present the pope's encyclical at the Vatican?* [Online] Available at: www.lifesitenews.com [Accessed on: 11 October 2022]

[1079]McCusker, M [2015] *Analysis of the Instrumentum Laboris of the Ordinary Synod of the Family* [Online] Available at: voiceofthefamily.com [Accessed on: 11 October 2022]

[1080]Weatherbe, S [2015] *Vatican Radio removes photo of lesbians kissing, but editor blasts critics* [Online] Available at: www.lifesitenews.com [Accessed on: 11 October 2022]

His holiness is grateful for the thoughtful gesture and for the feelings which it evoked, hoping for an always more fruitful activity in the service of young generations and the spread of genuine human and Christian values.[1081]

10th July

During his apostolic journey to Bolivia, Pope Francis was presented with a communist hammer and sickle crucifix by Bolivian President Evo Morales. During the in-flight press conference returning to Rome the pontiff did not find it offensive and 'I'm taking it home with me.'[1082]

15th July

Attorney Elizabeth Yore accused high-level Vatican officials at the 28th April climate change summit of treating her and her fellow Heartland Institute delegates with disrespect. She wrote that due to them asking the Vatican to reconsider its support of the climate change agenda they were 'not only ignored, but we were scoffed at and demeaned by high-level Vatican officials who called us deniers, Tea Partiers, and funded by oil interests.' Even though Pope Francis claimed in his encyclical *Laudato Si* that he wanted 'to encourage an honest and open debate', Elizabeth Yore concluded, 'Based on our personal experience in Rome, there is no interest in hearing the other side of the science debate by the Vatican.'[1083]

On the same date, Bishop Marcelo Sanchez Sorondo, chancellor of the Pontifical Academy of Sciences, responded to those who criticised the Vatican's collaboration with population control proponents Ban Ki-moon and Jeffrey Sachs, 'The Holy See does not see the United Nations as the devil as certain right-wing thinkers do.'[1084]

22nd July

Jeffrey Sachs, abortion advocate, was again a key note speaker at a joint Vatican / United Nations symposium at the invitation of Bishop Marcelo Sanchez Sorondo in his role as chancellor of the Pontifical Academy of Sciences.[1085]

The Pontifical Council on the Family, headed by Archbishop Paglia, published a book *Family and Church: An Indissoluble Bond* containing the presentations of seminars hosted early in 2015. The book presents proposals to allow the divorced and 'remarried' to receive the sacrament of penance and Holy Communion.[1086]

8th September

The Vatican released Pope Francis' Motu Proprio, *Mitis Iudex Dominus*, which amended canon law, making it simpler and swifter for Catholics to secure a marriage annulment. It was hailed as the most radical reform of the Church's marriage laws for 250 years. It lessened the time for receiving a judgment of annulment to as little as 45 days, eliminated the need for a second confirming judgment and gave local bishops, rather than canonical judges, the decision on annulments.[1087]

[1081]Scammell, R [2015] *Pope Francis sends letter praising gay children's book* [Online] Available at: www.theguardian.com [Accessed on: 11 October 2022]

[1082]*Pope reveals fate of hammer-and-sickle crucifix* [2015] [Online] Available at: www.thetablet.co.uk [Accessed on: 11 October 2022]

[1083]Jalsevac, S [2015] *The Pope's climate letter urges 'Dialogue with Everyone,' so why did Vatican single out and harass us?* [Online] Available at: www.lifesitenews.com [Accessed on: 11 October 2022]

[1084]Glatz, C [2015] *The UN is not 'the devil', and the Vatican is free to work with it, says bishop* [Online] Available at: catholicherald.co.uk [Accessed on: 11 October 2022]

[1085]Western, JH & Hickson, M [2015] *Vatican bishop mocks 'right wing' critics who think UN is 'the devil'* [Online] Available at: www.lifesitenews.com [Accessed on: 11 October 2022]

[1086]Hickson, M [2015] *New Vatican book suggests opening door to Communion for 'remarried' Catholics* [Online] Available at: www.lifesitenews.com [Accessed on: 11 October 2022]

[1087]Western, JH [2015] *Cardinal Burke had grave reservations on the same annulment proposals Pope Francis just enshrined* [Online] Available at: www.lifesitenews.com [Accessed on: 11 October 2022]

10th September

The German newspaper *Die Ziet* published a seven-page dossier compiled by anonymous, senior Vatican officials about Pope Francis' Motu Proprio *Mitis Iudex Dominus*. The officials accused Pope Francis of abandoning the dogma of marital indissolubility by introducing de facto 'Catholic divorce'. They also complained that despite the pontiff introducing such serious changes of canon law, none of the Holy See's dicasteries, including the Congregation for the Doctrine of the Faith, nor any of the national bishops' conferences were consulted. They characterised such top down imposition of changes as 'Führerprinzip' — ruling by imperious decree — which contradicted Pope Francis' much vaunted advocacy of synodality and collegiality.[1088]

10th-12th September

Cardinal Óscar Rodríguez Maradiaga, the coordinator of Pope Francis' advisory body, the Council of Nine, was a key note speaker at a conference in Rome organised by the heterodox International Academy for Marital Spirituality. The conference advocated ending the Church's prohibition of divorced and 'remarried' receiving communion and the acceptance of homosexual unions.[1089]

13th September

Pope Francis' interview with Buenos Aires' *Radio Millennium* was broadcast, during which the pontiff launched an attack on those who uphold dogmatic truths that safeguard divine revelation,

> Our God is a God who is close, who accompanies. Fundamentalists keep God away from accompanying his people, they divert their minds from him and transform him into an ideology. So in the name of this ideological god, they kill, they attack, destroy, slander. Practically speaking, they transform that God into a Baal, an idol...No religion is immune from its own fundamentalisms. In every religion there will be a small group of fundamentalists whose work is to destroy for the sake of an idea, and not reality. And reality is superior to ideas.[1090]

15th September

Pope Francis announced his special appointees to the 2015 synod on the family, including Cardinal Danneels, notorious for covering up clergy sex abuse, attempting to persuade the King of Belgium to sign abortion into law, support for homosexual 'unions' and promotion of pornographic sex education materials in Catholic schools.[1091] Other special appointees included Cardinal Kasper, the architect of abolishing the prohibition of divorced and 'remarried' receiving communion, pro-homosexual Cardinal Christoph Schönborn, pro-homosexual Cardinal Raymundo Damasceno Assis, pro-homosexual Archbishop Blase Cupich of Chicago, and pro-homosexual Bishop Johan Bonny of Antwerp, Belgium.[1092]

20th September

During his speech to young people in Havana, Cuba, Pope Francis did not mention our Lord Jesus Christ once; instead, he launched an attack on those who turn religion into a 'little convent':

[1088]Pentin, E [2015] *Pope Attacked Over Motu Proprio; Cardinal Kasper Reasserts His Proposal* [Online] Available at: www.ncregister.com [Accessed on: 11 October 2022]

[1089]Hickson, M [2015] *Close papal advisor heads conference attacking Church's moral teaching* [Online] Available at: www.lifesitenews.com [Accessed on: 11 October 2022]

[1090]*For Pope Francis, religious fundamentalism diverts us from the true God* [Online] Available at: www.catholicnewsagency.com [Accessed on: 11 October 2022]

[1091]*Heterodox Cardinal embroiled in child abuse cover-up scandal is Pope's special appointee to Family Synod* [2015] [Online]] Available at: voiceofthefamily.com [Accessed on: 11 October 2022]

[1092]*Pope appoints leading opponents of Catholic doctrine to Ordinary Synod* [Online] Available at: voiceofthefamily.com [Accessed on: 11 October 2022]

When a religion becomes a 'little convent' it loses the best that it has, it loses its reality of adoring God, of believing in God. It's a little convent of words, of prayers, of 'I'm good and you're bad,' of moral regulations. I have my ideology, my way of thinking and you have yours; I close myself in this 'little convent' of ideology.[1093]

23rd September

Pope Francis held a publicised 'private' meeting at the Apostolic Nunciature, Washington, with a so called homosexual 'couple' – Yayo Grassi, an atheist, and his 'partner' of 19 years Iwan Bagus. Grassi said Pope Francis had long known that he was gay, but had never condemned his sexuality or his same-sex relationship, had never been judgmental, or said anything negative. A film of the 'private' meeting was later released.[1094]

24th September

During his address to the US Congress Pope Francis called for the abolition of the death penalty and made no direct mention of abortion, 'This conviction has led me, from the beginning of my ministry, to advocate at different levels for the global abolition of the death penalty.'[1095]

25th September

During his address to the United Nations Pope Francis made no reference to the Most Holy Name of Our Lord Jesus Christ.[1096]

Openly homosexual TV reporter and comic, Mo Rocca, was chosen to serve as one of the lectors at Pope Francis' Madison Square Garden Mass.[1097]

1st October

Francis DeBernardo, Executive Director of New Ways Ministry, was given press credentials to the Synod on the family. By so doing, the Vatican ignored the fact that Archbishop James Hickey of Washington had denied New Ways Ministry approval or authorization to work as a Catholic organisation because of its vocal opposition to Church doctrine on homosexuality. During Synod press conferences, Fr. Lombardi, the Vatican spokesman, called on DeBernardo many times to ask questions. Furthermore, Cardinal Oswald Gracias, one of the members of the Synod's final report drafting committee, gave an interview to Francis DeBernardo.[1098]

2nd October

Cardinal Baldisseri announced the ten members of the drafting committee for the synod's final document. Alarm was caused by the inclusion of five heterodox members, in addition to Cardinal Baldisseri and Archbishop Bruno Forte: Cardinal Wuerl of Washington, Cardinal Dew of Wellington, Archbishop Victor Manuel Fernandez of Argentina, Bishop Marcello Semeraro of Albano, and the Jesuit General, Father Adolfo

---

[1093]*Pope's Impromptu Speech to Youth: Don't Close Yourself Into a 'Little Convent'* [2015] [Online] Available at: aleteia.org [Accessed on: 11 October 2022]

[1094]Javers, E [2015] *Pope Francis Met With Gay Couple Yayo Grassi and Iwan Bagus During His Time in U.S.* [Online] Available at: www.nbcnews.com [Accessed on: 11 October 2022]

[1095]*In address to Congress, Pope Francis calls for the abolition of the death penalty* [2015] [Online] Available at: deathpenaltyinfo.org [Accessed on: 11 October 2022]

[1096]Pope Francis [2015] *Full text: Pope's address to the UN* [Online] Available at: aleteia.org [Accessed on: 11 October 2022]

[1097]Marans, D [2015] *Mo Rocca's Starring Role In Pope's Mass Thrills LGBT Advocates* [Online] Available at: www.huffingtonpost.co.uk [Accessed on: 11 October 2022]

[1098]*Synod Father: Church needs gays* [2015] [Online] www.churchmilitant.com [Accessed on: 11 October 2022]

Nicolás.[1099] He also announced changes to the way the synod was conducted that led to concerns that the 2015 synod would also be manipulated.[1100]

5th October

Cardinal George Pell delivered a letter to Pope Francis, signed by him and twelve other cardinals, expressing concerns about manipulation of the synod. There were allegations that Pope Francis was enraged by the letter, 'If this is the case, they can leave. The Church does not need them. I will throw them all out'…'Don't they know that I'm the one in charge here? I'll have their red hats.'[1101]

From the synod floor, Cardinal Pell also recommended that the membership of the special committee of ten persons appointed by Pope Francis to write the synod's final document should be expanded with members chosen by the Synod Fathers. He observed that the committee did not include a sufficiently broad spectrum of members, from the different regions. Pope Francis gave no response.[1102]

Cardinal Erdő, the General Relator of the Synod, delivered his opening report to the Synod Fathers that, as in previous synods, was intended to guide their deliberations. Cardinal Erdő delivered a robust defence of Catholic doctrine pertaining to human sexuality and the family. He decisively rejected the 'Kasper proposals' to end the Church's prohibition of divorced and 'remarried' receiving Holy Communion, and clearly upheld Catholic teaching on homosexuality, the indissolubility of marriage and contraception.[1103]

6th October

Pope Francis delivered an unscheduled intervention, seen as a response to the cardinals' letter, during which he warned the Synod Fathers to avoid a 'hermeneutic of conspiracy' which was 'sociologically weak and spiritually unhelpful.'[1104]

Pope Francis went on to undermine the authority of Cardinal Erdő's defence of Catholic doctrine to the synod, by directing the Synod Fathers to base their deliberations only on his own opening address at the 2014 Extraordinary Synod, the *Final Report* of the Extraordinary Synod, and his own closing address of that synod. He also underlined that the reception of Holy Communion by the divorced and 'remarried' was to be addressed by the Synod Fathers, even though it had failed to attain two-thirds majority at the 2014 synod.[1105]

13th October

Abbot Jeremias Schröder OSB, a Synod Father, was selected by the Vatican press office to address the daily press conference. During these conferences he claimed that a majority of the Synod Fathers supported allowing different regions of the Church to establish their own ways of dealing with issues such as homosexuality and divorce. Regarding 'the social acceptance of homosexuality' and dealing with 'divorced and remarried persons' Abbot Schröder went on to say that 'bishops conferences should be

[1099]McElwee, J [2015] *New process for Synod of Bishops aims at allowing more dialogue* [Online] Available at: www.ncronline.org [Accessed on: 11 October 2022]

[1100]*Voice of the Family [2015] Why we fear the Ordinary Synod on the Family is being manipulated* [Online] Available at: www.lifesitenews.com [Accessed on: 11 October 2022]

[1101]Marcantonio Colonna [2018] *The Dictator Pope: The Inside Story of the Francis Papacy*. Washington: Regnery Publishing

[1102]O'Connell, G [2015] *Pope to Synod Fathers: don't give in to the conspiracy theory* [Online] Available at: www.americamagazine.org [Accessed on: 11 October 2022]

[1103]*Full text of Cardinal Erdo's introductory report for the Synod on the Family* [2015] [Online] Available at: www.catholicnewsagency.com [Accessed on: 11 October 2022]

[1104]Ivereigh, A [2015] *From the Synod (4): why the Pope warned against conspiracy theorists* [Online} Available at: www.catholicvoices.org.uk [Accessed on: 11 October 2022]

[1105]*Has the intervention of Pope Francis returned synod to heterodox trajectory?* [2015] [Online] Available at: voiceofthefamily.com [Accessed on: 11 October 2022]

allowed to formulate pastoral responses that are in tune with what can be preached and announced and lived in a different context.'[1106]

17th October

Pope Francis used the occasion of his address commemorating the 50th Anniversary of the Institution of the Synod of Bishops to develop his concept of a 'synodal Church' that he introduced in his apostolic exhortation, *Evangelii Gaudium*:

> In a synodal Church, as I have said, 'it is not advisable for the Pope to take the place of local Bishops in the discernment of every issue which arises in their territory. In this sense, I am conscious of the need to promote a sound "decentralisation" (*EG*, 16).

By so doing, Pope Francis proposed an ecclesiology that threatened to diminish the authority of the Petrine office and its agencies to safeguard doctrine and also the catholic unity of the Church.[1107]

22nd October

Cardinal Oswald Gracias, appointed by Pope Francis as a member of the Synod's final report drafting committee, was selected by the Vatican press office to speak at the daily press conference. He supported the decentralisation of doctrinal authority over marriage and family issues to national bishops' conferences. He also said that Pope St. John Paul II's reiteration of the Church's traditional prohibition of Holy Communion for the divorced and 'remarried' — as set out in his apostolic exhortation, *Familiaris Consortio*, 84 — was outdated, because 'circumstances have changed.'[1108]

24th October

During his closing address to the synod Pope Francis again criticised those who upheld the doctrine of the Church:

> The Synod experience also made us better realise that the true defenders of doctrine are not those who uphold its letter, but its spirit; not ideas but people; not formulae but the gratuitousness of God's love and forgiveness.[1109]

25th October

The Synod Fathers voted on the sections of the Final Report of the 2015 Synod. Section 85 represented the culmination of two years of debate and manipulation over the issue of ending the absolute prohibition of divorced and 'remarried' receiving Holy Communion. In order to be approved, each paragraph required a two-thirds majority, in this case 177 votes. Section 85 received 178 votes. Section 85 partially quoted Pope St. John Paul II's apostolic exhortation on the family *Familiaris Consortio*, 84, omitting Pope John Paul's re-iteration of the prohibition of communion to the divorced and 'remarried'. Instead, section 85 devolved decisions about allowing the divorced to receive Holy Communion to the 'guidelines of bishops'.[1110]

1st November

Italian atheist Eugenio Scalfari published an account of his sixth exchange with Pope Francis conducted over the telephone on October 28h. Scalfari reported that the pontiff

---

[1106]Western, JH [2015] *Synod spokesman: Majority back letting local churches decide on how to deal with homosexuality* [Online] Available at: www.lifesitenews.com [Accessed on: 11 October 2022]
[1107]Pope Francis [2015] *Address at ceremony commemorating the 50th anniversary of the institution of the synod of bishops* [Online] Available at: www.vatican.va [Accessed on: 11 October 2022]
[1108]*DANGER AHEAD. Synod document drafting committee member: Familiaris Consortio? 'Circumstances have changed!' Divorced-and-remarried, 'decentralization' still on the agenda* [Online] Available at: rorate-caeli.blogspot.com [Accessed on: 11 October 2022]
[1109]Pope Francis [2015] *Address at conclusion of the ordinary synod on the family* [Online] Available at: www.vatican.va [Accessed on: 11 October 2022]
[1110]Synod of Bishops [2015] *The Final Report of the Synod of Bishops to the Holy Father, Pope Francis* [Online] Available at: www.vatican.va [Accessed on: 11 October 2022]

told him regarding the divorced and 'remarried' receiving Holy Communion that as a consequence of the recent synod, 'all the divorced who ask will be admitted':

> The diverse opinion of the bishops is part of this modernity of the Church and of the diverse societies in which she operates, but the goal is the same, and for that which regards the admission of the divorced to the Sacraments, [it] confirms that this principle has been accepted by the Synod. This is bottom line result, the de facto appraisals are entrusted to the confessors, but at the end of faster or slower paths, all the divorced who ask will be admitted.[1111]

The Vatican's spokesman, Father Lombardi, responded that Scalfari's story was inaccurate, but Pope Francis did not contradict or repudiate Scalfari's account.[1112]

6th November

Pope Francis appointed pro-homosexual Jozef De Kesel Archbishop of Mechelen-Brussels, Belgium.[1113]

15th November

During his participation in a service at Rome's Lutheran church, Pope Francis responded to a Lutheran's question about whether she could receive Holy Communion with her Catholic husband. The pontiff's reply was widely seen as leaving it to Lutheran to decided if she should:

> A pastor friend of mine said to me: 'We believe that the Lord is present there. He is present. You believe that the Lord is present. So what is the difference?' — 'Well, there are explanations, interpretations...'. Life is greater than explanations and interpretations. Always refer to Baptism: 'One faith, one baptism, one Lord', as Paul tells us, and take the outcome from there. I would never dare give permission to do this because I do not have the authority. One Baptism, one Lord, one faith. Speak with the Lord and go forward. I do not dare say more.[1114]

19th November

Cardinal Sarah, Prefect of the Congregation for Divine Worship and the Discipline of the Sacraments, in comments to the French Catholic magazine, *L'Homme Nouveau*, said, regarding giving Holy Communion to those who are in a state of mortal sin, such as adulterers and active homosexuals:

> Not even a pope can dispense from such a divine law: The entire Church has always firmly held that one may not receive communion with the knowledge of being in a state of mortal sin, a principle recalled as definitive by John Paul II in his 2003 encyclical *Ecclesia de Eucharistia*.[1115]

20th November

During his address to a conference on the 50th anniversary of the Conciliar Decrees on the priesthood, *Optatam Totius* and *Presbyterorum Ordinis*, Pope Francis launched an ad hominem attack against priests who uphold the doctrine and discipline of the Church:

> I will tell you sincerely I'm scared of rigid priests. I keep away from them. They bite! ... There are often young men who are psychologically unstable without knowing it and

[1111]*Bombshell: Pope to His Favorite Journalist: 'All the Divorced who ask will be admitted [to Communion]'* [2015] [Online] Available at: rorate-caeli.blogspot.com [Accessed on: 11 October 2022]

[1112]Baklinski, P [2015] *Italian journalist: Pope Francis told me 'all the divorced who ask will be admitted' to Communion* [Online] Available at: www.lifesitenews.com [Accessed on: 11 October 2022]

[1113]Smits, J [2015] *Pope appoints well-known 'progressive' protégé of Cardinal Danneels to major see of Brussels* [Online] Available at: www.lifesitenews.com [Accessed on: 11 October 2022]

[1114]Pope Francis [2015] *Address during visit to the Evangelical Lutheran church of Rome* [Online] Available at: www.vatican.va [Accessed on: 11 October 2022]

[1115]Western, JH [2015] *Vatican Chief of Sacraments: No pope can change divine law on Communion* [Online] Available at: www.lifesitenews.com [Accessed on: 11 October 2022]

who look for strong structures to support them. For some it is the police or the army but for others it is the clergy. When a youngster is too rigid, too fundamentalist, I don't feel confident (about him). Behind it there is something he himself does not understand. Keep your eyes open![1116]

21st November

During his address to the World Congress on Catholic Education organised by the Congregation in charge of Catholic Education, Pope Francis told participants that Christian schools must not seek conversions:

> Christian education is not only teaching catechism and proselytizing. Never proselytise in schools. Christian education is bringing up the young in complete reality with human values and one of these [values] is transcendence.[1117]

30th November

During the in-flight press conference returning from the apostolic visit to Africa, Pope Francis responded to a question about whether the Church should drop her opposition to condoms. Instead of upholding the Church's prohibition of immoral methods of birth control, the pontiff replied that the Church was confused over the issue, saying that 'healing' was the priority:

> Yes, this is one method. The Church's moral teaching is – I think – uncertain about whether it has to do with the fifth or the sixth commandment: protect life or keep sexual relations open to life? But that is not the problem. The problem is bigger than that. The question makes me think of what they once asked Jesus: 'Tell us, Master, is it permissible to heal on the Sabbath?' It is a duty to heal! This question… is it permissible?

Pope Francis went on to criticise those Catholics who upheld the traditional doctrine that the Catholic Church possess absolute Truth:

> Fundamentalism is a sickness which exists in all religions. We Catholics have some people – not just a few, but a lot – who believe they possess absolute truth and go around slandering and defaming everyone else; they do a lot of harm. I say this because it's my Church, but it is all of us! And we have to fight against it. Religious fundamentalism is not religious. Why? Because God is missing. It is idolatrous, just as money is idolatrous. Being political, in the sense of winning over people who have this tendency… that is the 'politics' in which we religious leaders must engage. But fundamentalism, which always ends up in tragedy or crime, is something evil, but there is a bit of it in every religion.[1118]

8th December

On the Feast of the Immaculate Conception St. Peter's Basilica was plunged into darkness so that it could become a 'screen' onto which images of the natural and human world could be projected, including the image of a Muslim woman in a burka. It was sponsored by the World Bank.[1119]

10th December

The Vatican's Commission for Religious Relations with Jews published 'The Gifts and Calling of God are irrevocable'. It explicitly stated that the Church must not conduct

---

[1116]Ong, C [2015] *Pope Francis says he's 'scared of rigid, fundamentalist' priests because 'they bite'* [Online] Available at: www.christiantoday.com [Accessed on: 11 October 2022]

[1117]*The Pope: 'No to proselytism in Catholic schools'* [2015] [Online] Available at: rorate-caeli.blogspot. com [Accessed on: 11 October 2022]

[1118]Pope Francis [2016] *In-flight press conference from the Central African Republic* [Online] Available at: www.vatican.va [Accessed on: 11 October 2022]

[1119]Socci, A [2016] *Francis Effect: the Vatican profaned* [Online] Available at: rorate-caeli.blogspot. com [Accessed on: 11 October 2022]

the mission to the Jews, 'In concrete terms this means that the Catholic Church neither conducts nor supports any specific institutional mission work directed towards Jews.'[1120]

11th December

Bishop Marcelo Sanchez Sorondo, chancellor of the Pontifical Academy of Sciences, insisted that Pope Francis' advocacy of climate change theory in his encyclical Laudato Si was part of the ordinary Magisterium and therefore binding on the faithful:

> When the Pope has assumed this, it is Magisterium of the Church whether you like it or not – it is the Magisterium of the Church just as abortion is a grievous sin – equal (it is the same)… it is Magisterium of the Church… whether you like it or not.[1121]

2016

5th January

Pope Francis' first video message to accompany his monthly prayer intentions was released by the Jesuit group Apostleship of Prayer in association with the Vatican Television Centre. On the theme of the world's religions it included a Lama, a Rabbi, an Islamic leader and a priest and showed hands holding a statue of Buddha, Muslim prayer beads, a Minora, and a statue of Baby Jesus as if they were all equal. The Crucifix was noticeable by its absence.[1122]

12th January

Pope Francis' book length interview with Andrea Tornielli was published: *The Name of God is Mercy*. In which he, again, criticised the tradition-minded faithful as 'scholars of the law' who he described as his greatest enemies. In his words, they 'represent the principal opposition to Jesus; they challenge him in the name of doctrine…This approach is repeated throughout the long history of the Church.'[1123]

15th January

Following a private audience with Pope Francis, a group of Finnish Lutherans, including their leader who claims to be a bishop, were offered Holy Communion by priests at Mass held in St. Peter's Basilica. Samuel Salmi told the media that 'I myself accepted it [Holy Communion].' He added that 'this was not a coincidence.' He continued:

> At the root of this there is, without a doubt, the ecumenical attitude of a new Vatican. The pope was not here at the Mass, but his strategic intention is to carry out a mission of love and unity. There are also theological adversaries in the Vatican, for which reason it is difficult to assess how much he can say, but he can permit practical gestures.[1124]

18th January

During his homily Pope Francis accused those who upheld the Tradition of the Church as committing the 'sin of divination' and the 'sin of idolatry':

[1120]*Vatican issues new document on Christian-Jewish dialogue* [2016] [Online] Available at: www.archivioradiovaticana.va [Accessed on: 11 October 2022]

[1121]Western, JH [2016] *Vatican bishop: Pope's view on global warming is as authoritative as the condemnation of abortion* [Online] Available at: www.lifesitenews.com [Accessed on: 11 October 2022]

[1122]Harris, H [2016] *In first prayer video, Pope stresses interfaith unity: 'We are all children of God'* [Online] Available at: www.catholicnewsagency.com [Accessed on: 12 October 2022]

[1123]Western, JH [2016] *New book-length interview shows Pope is awesomely merciful and sorely misled* [Online] Available at: www.lifesitenews.com [Accessed on: 12 October 2022]

[1124]Cullinan Hoffman, M [2016] *Lutherans receive Communion at Vatican after meeting with Pope: report* [Online] Available at: www.lifesitenews.com; Cullinan Hoffman, M [2015] *Lutheran bishop's reception of communion in Vatican was mistake, says Finnish Catholic spokesman* [Online] Available at: www.lifesitenews.com [Accessed on: 12 October 2022]

Christians who are obstinate, saying 'this is how it's always been done, this is the way, this is the path', are sinning: the sin of divination'. It is 'as if they were to go to a palm reader'. In the end, 'what has been said and what doesn't change — "by me and my closed heart" — becomes "more important" than 'the Word of the Lord'. This 'is also the sin of idolatry: stubbornness. The Christian who insists, sins. The sin of idolatry.'[1125]

19th January

Cardinal Joseph Zen Ze-kiun SDB, Bishop Emeritus of Hong Kong, released a statement expressing his concerns about negotiation between the Vatican's Secretariat of State and the Chinese communist government. He raised the question, 'Is Pope Francis' Vatican handing over her authority to China's atheist government?', giving as an example what occurred to Chinese Catholics after the Vatican delegation left:

> Shortly after the Vatican delegation left Beijing, the government organized a large gathering of Church leaders, forcing on that occasion a celebration of all the bishops, legitimate, illegitimate and excommunicated. These are all objectively schismatic acts. The government now can string along a large number of bishops, resulting in an irrecoverable loss of dignity. If the Holy See signed some agreement with the Government without clarifying all these things, it will cause a severe wound to the conscience of the faithful.[1126]

21st January

It was announced that Pope Francis had issued a decree changing the rubrics in the *Roman Missal* pertaining to the Holy Thursday's washing of the feet to include women and girls.[1127]

25th January

The journal *Scientific American* published an interview with the stem-cell scientist Juan Carlos Izpisua Belmonte in which he claimed Pope Francis had given his approval to the creation of human-animal hybrids. Juan Carlos Izpisua Belmonte said:

> Even though Spain is quite open to this stem cell research area, at the same time, Spain is a very Catholic country, so we had to go through the Pope. He very nicely said yes. This is to help people. *Scientific American*: The current Pope? JCIB: Yes. The current Pope. So the Vatican is behind this research and has no problem based on the idea is to help humankind. And in theory all that we will be doing is killing pigs.

The Pontifical Academy of Sciences, the Vatican's scientific body, did not respond to an e-mail seeking to confirm Pope Francis's position. Though Fr. Federico Lombardi, the Vatican spokesman, issued a denial, Pope Francis did not issue a public statement correcting or repudiating the claim.[1128]

8th February

During the in-flight press conference on the return from the Apostolic Visit to Mexico Pope Francis responded to a question on the threat posed by the Zika virus to unborn babies. Rejecting abortion as an option, Pope Francis replied that faced with the Zika virus it was not an 'absolute evil' to use artificial contraception:

[1125]Pope Francis [2016] *Morning Meditation in the Chapel of the Domus Sanctae Marthae*, New wineskins [Online] Available at: www.vatican.va [Accessed on: 12 October 2022]
[1126]Zen Ze-kiun, J [2016] *Cardinal Zen: Is Pope Francis' Vatican handing over her authority to China's atheist government?* [Online] Available at: www.lifesitenews.com [Accessed on: 12 October 2022]
[1127]San Martín, I [2016] *Francis changes the rules: Women can have their feet washed on Holy Thursday* [Online] Available at: cruxnow.com [Accessed on: 12 October 2022]
[1128]Gorman, C [2016] *Tissue Mash-Up: a Q&A with Juan Carlos Izpisua Belmonte* [Online] Available at: www.scientificamerican.com [Accessed on: 12 October 2022]

Regarding a 'lesser evil': preventing pregnancy is one thing — we are speaking in terms of the conflict between the 5th and 6th Commandments. The great Paul VI, in a difficult situation in Africa, allowed nuns to use a form of artificial contraception amid the violence. It is important not to confuse the evil of preventing pregnancy, in itself, with abortion… On the other hand, preventing pregnancy is not an absolute evil, and in certain cases, such as the one I mentioned of Bl. Paul VI, it was clear.

Pope Francis also said that divorced and 'remarried' Catholics need to be integrated into the parish as a condition to receive Holy Communion:

Being integrated into the Church does not mean 'taking communion'. I know remarried Catholics who go to Church once or twice a year: 'I want to receive communion!', as if communion were a commendation. It is a matter of integration... the doors are all open. But one cannot just say: from now on 'they can take communion'. This would also wound the spouses, the couple, because it won't help them on the path to integration. These two were happy! They used a really lovely expression: 'We do not take Eucharistic communion, but we do find communion by visiting people in the hospital, in this or that service...'. Their integration is there. If there is something more, the Lord will tell them, but ... it is a journey, it is a path….[1129]

8th February

Corriere Della Serra, a leading Italian newspaper, published an interview with Pope Francis during which he praised as one of Italy's 'forgotten greats' Italy's notorious abortionist and advocate Emma Bonino. Bonino conducted illegal abortions in her apartment, worked with an organisation that conducted 10,000 illegal abortions, and played a leading role in legalising abortion in Italy.[1130]

19th February

In the wake of Pope Francis' apparent relaxation of the Church's absolute ban on the use of artificial contraception, Vatican spokesman Fr. Federico Lombardi confirmed that this had been the pontiff's intention:

The contraceptive or condom, in particular cases of emergency or gravity, could be the object of discernment in a serious case of conscience. This is what the Pope said…the possibility of taking recourse to contraception or condoms in cases of emergency or special situations. He is not saying that this possibility is accepted without discernment, indeed, he said clearly that it can be considered in cases of special urgency.[1131]

21 February

During his Angelus address Pope Francis called for the international abolition of the death penalty:

Because even a criminal has the inviolable right to life, a gift of God. I appeal to the consciences of leaders, that they come to an international consensus aimed at abolishing the death penalty.[1132]

24th February

In response to Pope Francis' apparent relaxation of the Church's condemnation of artificial contraception as 'intrinsically evil', the Catholic Bishops' Conference of the Philippines called for the 're-evaluation' of the use of contraception in some cases.[1133]

[1129]Pope Francis [2016] *In-flight press conference on return from Mexico to Rome* [Online] Available at: www.vatican.va [Accessed on: 12 October 2022]

[1130]Western, JH [2016] *Pope calls Italy's foremost abortion promoter one of nation's 'forgotten greats'* [Online] Available at: www.lifesitenews.com [Accessed on: 12 October 2022]

[1131]Western, JH [2016] *Vatican affirms Pope was speaking about contraceptives for Zika* [Online] Available at: www.lifesitenews.com [Accessed on: 12 October 2022]

[1132]Pope Francis [2016] *Angelus Address* [Online] Available at: www.vatican.va [Accessed on: 12 October 2022]

[1133]Baklinski, P [2016] *In wake of Pope's remarks, Filipino bishops call for a 're-evaluation' of contraception in some cases* [Online] Available at: www.lifesitenews.com [Accessed on: 12 October 2022]

28th February

Loyola Press published the children's book '*Dear Pope Francis': The Pope Answers Letters from Children Around the World*. It contained Pope Francis' answer to a question asking if he had been an altar server. In his answer, the pontiff disclosed how he had mocked the traditional Latin Mass as an altar boy:

> The priest spoke but I didn't understand anything and neither did my friends. So, for fun we'd do imitations of the priest, messing up the words a bit to make up weird sayings in Spanish. We had fun, and we really enjoyed serving Mass.[1134]

8th April

The Vatican promulgated Pope Francis' apostolic exhortation, *Amoris Laetitia*, being his response to the 2014 Extraordinary Synod and the 2015 Ordinary Synod on marriage and the family. As expected, Pope Francis used a form of words to end the Church's prohibition of divorced and civilly 'remarried' Catholics receiving Holy Communion. Section 305, with footnote 351, was written in such a way that allowed those bishops who so wanted, to allow divorced and civilly remarried Catholics to receive the sacrament of confession and Holy Communion. Section 305, with footnote 351 stated:

> Because of forms of conditioning and mitigating factors, it is possible that in an objective situation of sin – which may not be subjectively culpable, or fully such – a person can be living in God's grace, can love and can also grow in the life of grace and charity, while receiving the Church's help to this end. (305). In certain cases, this can include the help of the sacraments. (351).

Furthermore, Dr. Josef Seifert, founding rector of the International Academy of Philosophy in Liechtenstein, would later warn that *Amoris Laetitia* section 303 was a ticking 'theological atomic bomb' that had the capacity to entirely destroy all Catholic moral teaching. Dr. Josef Seifert wrote that 'besides calling an objective state of grave sin, euphemistically, "not yet fully the objective ideal," *Amoris Laetitia* says that we can know with "a certain moral security" that God himself asks us to continue to commit intrinsically wrong acts, such as adultery or active homosexuality.'[1135]

9th April

In an interview with the *Chicago Tribune* Archbishop Cupich, a Pope Francis appointee, said that *Amoris Laetitia* was a 'game-changer' that allowed priests, on a case-by-case basis, to allow remarried divorcees to receive the sacraments:

> There is a mindset within the life of the church among Catholics that if in fact they do have marriage breakups and they get into a second marriage that its kind of over for them unless they can get an annulment. The pope is saying that's not the case.[1136]

11th April

Cardinal Burke said that Pope Francis' *Amoris Laetitia* could not change Church teaching and practice, emphasising that the apostolic exhortation is not magisterial:

> Pope Francis makes clear, from the beginning, that the post-synodal apostolic exhortation is not an act of the magisterium… a personal reflection of the Pope, while received with the respect owed to his person, is not confused with the binding faith owed to the exercise of the magisterium.[1137]

[1134]Vennari, J [2016] *Francis' Vulgar Comments on the Traditional Latin Mass* [Online] Available at: catholicfamilynews.com [Accessed on: 12 October 2022]

[1135]Baklinski, P [2016] *Amoris Laetitia is a ticking 'atomic bomb' set to obliterate all Catholic morality: philosopher* [Online] Available at: www.lifesitenews.com [Accessed on: 12 October 2022]

[1136]Brachear Pashman, M & Leventis Lourgos, A [2016] *Cupich: Pope's document on sex, marriage, family life a 'game changer'* [Online] Available at: www.chicagotribune.com [Accessed on: 12 October 2022]

[1137]Western, JH [2016] *Cardinal Burke: Pope's exhortation not magisterial, can't change Church teaching* [Online] Available at: www.lifesitenews.com [Accessed on: 12 October 2022]

13th April

La Civiltà Cattolica, a Jesuit journal approved by the Vatican prior to publication, contained an article written by its editor, Fr. Antonio Spadaro SJ, in which he confirmed that Pope Francis's *Amoris Laetitia* allowed the possibility of granting Communion to 'remarried' divorcees. He concluded:

> The pastoral practice of 'all or nothing' seems more sure to the 'rigorist' theologians, but it inevitably leads to a 'Church of the pure.' Valuing formal perfection before all else and as an end in itself brings the risk of unfortunately covering up many behaviours that are in fact hypocritical and pharisaic.[1138]

15th April

Cardinal Kasper — the architect of ending the Church's doctrine and discipline denying those committing adultery Holy Communion — said in an interview that Pope Francis' *Amoris Laetitia* 'doesn't change anything of church doctrine or of canon law – but it changes everything.' He went on to explain that *Amoris Laetitia* affirmed his permissive position:

> it seems clear to me as to many other observers, that there can be situations of divorced and remarried where on the way of inclusion, absolution and communion become possible.[1139]

16th April

During the in-flight press conference, on the return from the apostolic visit to the island of Lesbos, Pope Francis was asked about footnote 351 of *Amoris Laetitia* that was being widely understood as changing the Church's doctrine and discipline about the divorced and 'remarried. Pope Francis replied that he did not remember that footnote:

> I do not remember that footnote, but surely if something of that sort is in a footnote it is because it was said in the *Evangelii Gaudium*. I don't recall the number, but surely that is the case.[1140]

When asked if *Amoris Laetitia* 'changed the discipline that governs the access to the Sacraments' for divorced and civilly 'remarried' Pope Francis replied, 'Io posso dire, si. Punto' [I can say yes. Period.][1141]

20th April

Three German bishops — Cardinal Reinhard Marx, Archbishop Dr. Heiner Koch, and Bishop Franz-Josef Bode — stated that footnote 351 of *Amoris Laetitia* permitted divorced and civilly remarried Catholics to access the sacraments on a case-by-case basis. They concluded, regarding those committing adultery 'Hence it is [sic] can no longer simply be said that all those in any "irregular" situation are living in a state of mortal sin and are deprived of sanctifying grace.'[1142]

21st April

Fr Federico Lombardi, the Vatican spokesman, announced the suspension of the independent audit of Vatican finances by PricewaterhouseCoopers (PwC). It emerged

---

[1138]Chretien, C & Jalsevac, J [2016] *Vatican-approved magazine: Exhortation opens door to Holy Communion for remarried divorcees* [Online] Available at: www.lifesitenews.com [Accessed on: 12 October 2022]

[1139]Lamb, C [2016] *Kasper says Pope's synod document 'changes everything'* [Online] Available at: www.lastampa.it [Accessed on: 12 October 2022]

[1140]Pope Francis [2016] *In-flight press conference on return from Lesbos to Rome* [Online] Available at: www.vatican.va [Accessed on: 12 October 2022]

[1141]Jalsevac, J [2016] *Vatican website misquotes Pope Francis on Communion for the divorced and remarried* [Online] Available at: www.lifesitenews.com [Accessed on: 12 October 2022]

[1142]Chretien, C [2016] *Exhortation allows Communion for divorced/remarried on case-by-case basis, claim 3 German bishops* [Online] Available at: www.lifesitenews.com [Accessed on: 12 October 2022]

that Archbishop Angelo Becciu, an official of the Secretariat of State, had written a letter, on behalf of Cardinal Parolin – the Sectary of State – to every Vatican office on 12 April announcing the suspension. The letter announced that the authority to collect financial information given to PwC by Cardinal Pell, prefect of the Secretariat for the Economy, had been revoked by Cardinal Parolin.[1143] Cardinal Pell's instruction of PwC to conduct an independent audit followed his discovery in 2014 that 'some hundreds of millions of euros were tucked away in particular sectional accounts and did not appear on the balance sheet'. Cardinal Pell singled out the Secretariat of State as part of the Vatican that 'jealously guarded its independence.'[1144]

22nd April

Aachener Zeitung, a German newspaper, published an interview with Cardinal Kasper in the aftermath of *Amoris Laetitia*, in which he said Pope Francis' intention was 'not to preserve everything as it has been of old.' He went on to say, regarding remarried divorcees:

> The door is open. … There is also some freedom for the individual bishops and bishops' conferences. … Not all Catholics think the way we Germans think.… Here [in Germany,] something can be permissible which is forbidden in Africa. Therefore, the pope gives freedom for different situations and future developments.[1145]

2nd May

The German Catholic newspaper *Die Tagespost* published an interview with Cardinal Müller, the prefect of the Congregation for the Doctrine of the Faith. During which Cardinal Müller categorically stated that Church's teaching on remarried divorcees receiving Holy Communion cannot be changed, and *Amoris Laetitia* did not do so. Regarding the prohibition on adulterers receiving Holy Communion he said, 'What has been taught by John Paul II in *Familiaris Consortio* and by Benedict XVI in *Sacramentum Caritatis* is still valid in an unchanged way.'[1146]

7th May

Corrispondenza Romana published Prof. Roberto de Mattei's interview with Abbé Claude Barthe, an eminent theologian with connections in the Vatican. Abbé Barthe claimed that the text of the post-synodal letter *Amoris Laetitia* was broadly completed by September 2015, one month before the opening of the Synod on the Family.[1147] By so doing, adding to fears that the entire synodal process since 2014 had been manipulated to end the Church's prohibition of individuals living in a state of adultery receiving Holy Communion.

12th May

During a meeting with the International Union of Superiors General, Pope Francis announced that he intended to set up a commission to study the role of deaconesses in the early church. This was in response to a question about allowing women to be ordained permanent deacons. Pope Francis responded: 'I would like to constitute an

[1143]Kirchgaessner, S [2016] *Vatican's suspension of major PwC audit exposes internal rift* [Online] Available at: www.theguardian.com [Accessed on: 12 October 2022]
[1144]*Vatican finds hundreds of millions of euros 'tucked away': cardinal* [2016] [Online] Available at: www.reuters.com [Accessed on: 12 October 2022]
[1145]Hickson, M [2016] *Kasper: Pope Intends 'Not to Preserve Everything as it has Been'* [Online] Available at: onepeterfive.com [Accessed on: 12 October 2022]
[1146]Hickson, M [2016] *Cardinal Müller: Communion Remains Off-Limits for 'Remarried'* [Online] Available at: onepeterfive.com [Accessed on: 12 October 2022]
[1147]Mattei, R de [2016] *'An Interpretation of Amoris Laetitia From Tradition is Not Possible' – Interview With Abbé Claude Barthe* [Online] Available at: www.theeponymousflower.com [Accessed on: 12 October 2022]

official commission to study the question: I think it will do the Church good to clarify this point: I agree and I will speak about doing something of this nature.'[1148] The Vatican's International Theological Commission had already published a report of their investigation into this matter in 2003 under the title 'From the Diakonia of Christ to the Diakonia of the Apostles'.

17th May

La Croix, the French liberal Catholic newspaper, published an interview with Pope Francis in which he said that Islam and Christianity were similar: 'It is true that the idea of conquest is inherent in the soul of Islam. However, it is also possible to interpret the objective in Matthew's Gospel, where Jesus sends his disciples to all nations, in terms of the same idea of conquest.'[1149]

25th May

Monsignor Jean-Marie Mupendawatu, secretary to the Pontifical Council for the Pastoral Care of Health Care Workers, told the 69th World Health Assembly that the Holy See welcomed goal 3 of the Sustainable Development Goals (SDGs), and the goal's 13 targets. He said this despite one of the 13 targets including calls for 'universal access to sexual and reproductive health care services', which include abortion and contraception.[1150]

29th May

Pope Francis presided at the World Congress of *Scholas Occurrentes* during which he awarded an Olive Medal for Peace to George Clooney, Richard Gere and Salma Hayek in recognition of their activism against climate change, war, and terrorism. All three actors are prominent supporters of abortion, contraception and homosexual 'marriage' and publicly critical of the Church.[1151]

30th May

La Nuova Bussola Quotidiana published an interview with Cardinal Carlo Caffarra, founding president of the Pontifical John Paul II Institute for Studies on Marriage and Family, who rejected the possibility that Amoris Laetitia changed doctrine on divorce and the sacraments:

> No. He who lives a state of life which objectively contradicts the sacrament of the Eucharist, cannot receive the sacrament…Now, if the Pope had wanted to change the previous Magisterium, whose teaching is extremely clear, he would have had the duty — and the grave duty — to say so clearly and directly. One cannot change the age-old discipline of the Church with a footnote, and in an uncertain tone. I'm applying a principle of interpretation that has always been applied in theology. The uncertain Magisterium is to be interpreted in continuity with the previous one.[1152]

1st June

Women's Ordination Worldwide, a group that campaigns for the 'ordination' of women, were granted a meeting with an official of the Vatican's Secretariat of State.

[1148]Pope Francis [2016] *Full Text of Pope's Q-and-A With Women Religious* [Online] Available at: zenit. org [Accessed on: 12 October 2022]

[1149]Western, JH [2016] *Confusing even the devout: the troubling statements of Pope Francis* [Online] Available at: www.lifesitenews.com [Accessed on: 12 October 2022]

[1150]Baklinski, P [2016] *Vatican official uncritically 'welcomes' UN development goal – despite its pro-abortion language* [Online] Available at: www.lifesitenews.com [Accessed on: 12 October 2022]

[1151]Craine, P [2016] *Pope Francis' award to Hollywood pro-abortion, anti-marriage advocates endangers the family* [Online] Available at: www.lifesitenews.com [Accessed on: 12 October 2022]

[1152]Baklinski, P [2016] *Amoris Laetitia is 'objectively unclear' since even bishops have conflicting interpretations: Cardinal Caffarra* [Online] Available at: www.lifesitenews.com [Accessed on: 12 October 2022]

During the unprecedented meeting the official agreed to give a petition to Pope Francis calling for the penalty of excommunication to be lifted from 150 women who had received simulated ordination.[1153]

9th June

Pope Francis preached against striving for Christian perfection, and instead advocated gradualism and compromise:

> This is the healthy realism of Catholicism. It is not Catholic to say 'or this or nothing:' This is not Catholic, this is heretical. Jesus always knows how to accompany us, he gives us the ideal, he accompanies us towards the ideal, He frees us from the chains of the laws' rigidity and tells us: 'But do that up to the point that you are capable.' And he understands us very well. He is our Lord and this is what he teaches us.[1154]

10th June

The Vatican announced that it had cancelled a full, external audit of its finances by the accountancy firm PwC. By way of justification, the Vatican stated, 'by law, the task of performing the financial statement audit is entrusted to the [Vatican's] Office of the Auditor General', rather than an external auditor…normally the case for every sovereign state.'[1155]

16th June

During a Q&A with the Diocese of Rome's pastoral congress Pope Francis said, '… the great majority of our sacramental marriages are null. Because they say "yes, for the rest of my life!" but they don't know what they are saying. Because they have a different culture. They say it, they have good will, but they don't know.'[1156] (Confirming Cardinal Kasper's statement during 7th May 2014 interview that Pope Francis had told him that 50% of Catholic marriages were invalid.) The pontiff went on to praise couples committing fornication by cohabiting, 'I've seen a lot of fidelity in these cohabitations, and I am sure that this is a real marriage, they have the grace of a real marriage because of their fidelity.'

Recounting the episode in the Gospel of our Lord's conversation with the woman caught in adultery, Pope Francis also told the delegates Jesus 'plays the fool a bit' and that he 'was scant on morality' [ha mancato verso la morale]. He also said, incomprehensibly, that Jesus was not 'a clean one' [un pulito]. The official Vatican transcript changed Pope Francis' statement that Jesus 'plays the fool a bit' to 'pretended not to understand'.[1157]

Pope Francis also responded to criticism of his apostolic exhortation Amoris Laetitia for changing the Church's doctrine on divorce and reception of the Blessed Sacrament, insisting, against the clear facts of the case, that his innovations were sound teaching:

> For your own peace of mind, I have to tell you that everything that is written in the exhortation [Amoris Laetitia] – and here I refer to the words of a great theologian who once was a secretary of the Congregation for the Doctrine of the Faith, Cardinal Schönborn, who presented it [Amoris Laetitia] – everything is Thomistic, from the

---

[1153]Lamb, C [2016] *Campaigners for women's ordination have unprecedented meeting with Vatican representative* [Online] Available at: www.thetablet.co.uk [Accessed on: 12 October 2022]

[1154]*Pope: Those who say 'its this or nothing' are heretics not Catholics* [2016] [Online] Available at: www.indcatholicnews.com [Accessed on: 12 October 2022]

[1155]*Vatican cancels full external audit of its finances* [2016] [Online] Available at: catholicherald.co.uk [Accessed on: 12 October 2022]

[1156]Skojec, S [2016] *Pope Francis: 'The Great Majority of Our Sacramental Marriages are Null'* [Online] Available at: onepeterfive.com/ [Accessed on: 12 October 2022]

[1157]Socci, A [2016] *Pope Bergoglio: 'Jesus plays the fool a bit'. This and other inconceivable, extremely grave 'expressions' pronounced last Thursday…*[online] Available at: roratcaeli.blogspot.com [Accessed on: 12 October 2022]

beginning to the end. It is sound doctrine. But, so many times, we want it to be so that sound doctrine would have a mathematical security which does not, in fact, exist – neither in a lax and indulgent way, nor in a stiff and rigid way.[1158]

Pope Francis also called priests who refuse baptism to the children of single mothers 'animals'. He went on to explain, 'embracing, accompanying, integrating, discerning should be done without sticking one's nose into the morality of people's lives'.[1159]

17th June

The Vatican announced that Pope Francis had approved a revision of the official transcript of his Q&A with the Diocese of Rome's pastoral congress. Instead of reporting his statement that 'the great majority of our sacramental marriages are null', the transcript was changed to read that '"a portion" of sacramental marriages are null'.[1160]

22nd June

Pope Francis singled out Father Pierre Valkering to meet him following his Wednesday audience, so Father Valkering could present him with his book, a compilation of funeral homilies about the theme of homosexuality. Father Pierre Valkering recounted their encounter, saying he told Pope Francis that:

> this book can encourage the Church to give more thought to homosexuality because it contains a treasury of experience on homosexuals, their loves, their lives and their sorrows. The Pope answered that he gives them a great deal of attention and that he always carries them in his heart.[1161]

23rd June

The Irish Times published comments from Cardinal Marx, one of the council of nine cardinals chosen by Pope Francis to advise him, in which Cardinal Marx said the Catholic Church should publicly apologise to homosexuals for what he called its scandalous and terrible treatment of them:

> 'The history of homosexuals in our societies is very bad because we've done a lot to marginalise [them].' As church and society 'we've also to say "sorry, sorry"'. Until 'very recently', the church, but also society at large, had been 'very negative about gay people . . . it was the whole society. It was a scandal and terrible'.[1162]

26th June

Pope Francis misrepresented the Church's doctrine on homosexuality by giving a partial quotation of the *Catechism of the Catholic Church*:

> I will repeat what I said during my first trip, and I also repeat what the *Catechism of the Catholic Church* says, namely that they should not be discriminated against, that they should be shown respect and given pastoral assistance. We can disapprove of some ways of acting that are a little too offensive to other people, not for ideological reasons but in terms, we might say, of political propriety. But none of this has to do with the problem: if the problem is that a person is so inclined, and with good will seeks God, who are we to judge him or her? We should be helpful to them, in accordance with the teaching of the Catechism. The Catechism is clear! There are traditions in some countries, in

[1158]Western, JH [2016] *Pope: All of Amoris Laetitia is 'sound doctrine'; ban the death penalty* [Online] Available at: www.lifesitenews.com [Accessed on: 12 October 2022]

[1159]Palmer, D [2016] *Priests who refuse baptism to babies of single mothers are 'animals'* [Online] Available at: www.thetablet.co.uk [Accessed on: 12 October 2022]

[1160]*Updated: Most marriages today are invalid, Pope Francis suggests* [2016] [Online] Available at: www.catholicnewsagency.com [Accessed on: 12 October 2022]

[1161]Smits, J [2016] *Dutch priest jubilant after giving Pope Francis his book of pro-gay homilies* [Online] Available at: www.lifesitenews.com [Accessed on: 12 October 2022]

[1162]McGarry, P [2016] *Church must apologise to gay people, pope's adviser declares* [Online] Available at: www.irishtimes.com [Accessed on: 12 October 2022]

some cultures with a different approach to the problem. I think that the Church should apologise – as that 'Marxist' Cardinal said [Cardinal Reinhold Marx] – not only to this person who is gay and has been offended…

Pope Francis also praised the heresiarch Martin Luther:

I think that Martin Luther's intentions were not mistaken; he was a reformer. Perhaps some of his methods were not right, although at that time, if you read Pastor's history, for example – Pastor was a German Lutheran who experienced a conversion when he studied the facts of that period; he became a Catholic – we see that the Church was not exactly a model to emulate. There was corruption and worldliness in the Church; there was attachment to money and power. That was the basis of his protest. He was also intelligent, and he went ahead, justifying his reasons for it. Nowadays, Lutherans and Catholics, and all Protestants, are in agreement on the doctrine of justification: on this very important point he was not mistaken.[1163]

30th June

Francis appointee Bishop Robert McElroy of San Diego criticised the *Catechism of the Catholic Church* for calling homosexual sex acts 'intrinsically disordered', describing it as 'very destructive language that I think we should not use pastorally.'[1164]

3rd July

La Nacion, the Argentinian daily newspaper, published an interview with Pope Francis during which he stated that he would not allow bishops who uphold the Faith of the Church to slow him down:

They do their job and I do mine. I want a Church that is open, understanding, that accompanies wounded families. They say no to everything. I go ahead, without looking over my shoulder…Nails are removed by applying pressure to the top. Or, they are set aside to rest, when retirement age arrives.[1165]

7th July

Pope Francis appointed pro-homosexual Archbishop Cupich as a member of the Congregation for Bishops, giving him a role in recommending to the Pope candidates to be appointed bishops. Archbishop Cupich joined fellow US liberal Cardinal Donald Wuerl, who Pope Francis named to the congregation in December 2013.[1166]

The Italian newspaper *Corriere della Sera* published an interview with Cardinal Schönborn, Archbishop of Vienne in which he asserted that all prior magisterial teaching on the family must be read through *Amoris Laetitia*. Pope Francis nominated Cardinal Schönborn as the authoritative interpreter of *Amoris Laetitia*. He admitted that the apostolic exhortation clearly allows Communion for those in objective states of sin:

The Pope invites us not only to look at the outside conditions, […] but to ask ourselves, if we are thirsty for merciful forgiveness, with the mindset to respond better to the sanctifying dynamism of grace. It is therefore possible in certain cases, for those who are in an objective situation of sin to receive the help of the sacraments.[1167]

[1163]Pope Francis [2016] *In-flight press conference on return from Armenia to Rome* [Online] Available at: www.vatican.va [Accessed on: 12 October 2022]
[1164]Chretien, C [2016] *U.S. Bishop: Catechism uses 'very destructive' language on homosexuality* [Online] Available at: www.lifesitenews.com [Accessed on: 12 October 2022]
[1165]*Pope rejects conflict with 'ultraconservative' Catholics in new interview* [2016] [Online] Available at: www.catholicnewsagency.com [Accessed on: 12 October 2022]
[1166]Chretien, C [2016] *Pope names left-wing Archbishop Cupich to key role in picking future U.S. bishops* [Online] Available at: www.lifesitenews.com [Accessed on: 12 October 2022]
[1167]Kant, M [2016] *Cardinal Schönborn: All prior teaching on family must be read through Amoris Laetitia* [Online] Available at: www.lifesitenews.com [Accessed on: 12 October 2022]

9th July

Pope Francis issued the Motu Proprio *I Beni Temporali*, regarding certain competencies in economic-financial matters.[1168] This Motu Proprio reduced the power of the Secretariat for the Economy to introduce financial reforms, such as appointing PwC as the independent auditor of the Vatican.[1169]

11th July

Vatican spokesman Father Federico Lombardi dismissed Cardinal Sarah's recommendation, as the Prefect for the Congregation for Divine Worship and the Discipline of the Sacraments, that priests celebrate the Mass *ad orientem*. Fr. Lombardi went on to insist that the Traditional Latin Mass must not take the place of the *Novus Ordo*.[1170]

15th July

Pope Francis personally intervened to dissolve the recently-created Belgian Fraternity of the Holy Apostles of Brussels, an order of faithful priests that upheld the tradition of the Church. Cardinal Josef De Kesel, appointed by Pope Francis, signed the decree of dissolution on this day which stated that it had been abolished because 'most' of the seminarians were of French origin.[1171]

26th July

The Pontifical Council for the Family, headed by the pro-homosexual Archbishop Paglia, released its explicit sex education programme for young people at World Youth Day in Poland under the title 'The Meeting Point: The Adventure of Love'. Sidelining the preeminent role of parents to educate their children, it also failed to mention Christ's teaching on marriage or uphold the Church's sexual morality on fornication, prostitution, adultery, contraception, homosexual activity, and masturbation. In one lesson, it holds up notorious homosexual Elton John as 'an example of a gifted and famous person.'[1172]

27th July

Archbishop Stanislaw Gadecki, the head of the Polish Bishops' Conference, recounted that Pope Francis spoke to him and other bishops about allowing local bishops conferences to make decisions about giving Communion to those who are divorced and remarried: 'The Holy Father says that general laws are very hard to enforce in each country, and so he speaks about decentralisation'. Thereby, fracturing the Catholic unity of the Church.[1173]

2nd August

Pope Francis announced the membership of his commission convened to investigate the question of women deacons.[1174] This question was settled in 2002 by the International

[1168]Pope Francis [2016] *Apostolic Letter I beni temporali* [Online] Available at: www.vatican.va [Accessed on: 12 October 2022]

[1169]Lawler, P [2016] *Another blow to Vatican transparency and financial accountability* [Online] Available at: www.lifesitenews.com [Accessed on: 12 October 2022]

[1170]*Holy See Press Office [2016] Some clarifications on the celebration of Mass* [Online] Available at: press.vatican.va [Accessed on: 12 October 2022]

[1171]Smits, J [2016] *Pope Francis personally intervenes to dissolve flourishing, faithful priestly order* [Online] Available at: www.lifesitenews.com [Accessed on: 12 October 2022]

[1172]Baklinski, P [2016] *At World Youth Day, Vatican releases teen sex-ed program that leaves out parents and mortal sin* [Online] Available at: www.lifesitenews.com [Accessed on: 12 October 2022]

[1173]Baklinski, P [2016] *Pope spoke of 'decentralizing' decisions on Communion for divorced/remarried: Polish bishops' head* [Online] Available at: www.lifesitenews.com [Accessed on: 12 October 2022]

[1174]Chretien, C [2016] *Pope's deaconess commission includes prominent U.S. dissident* [Online] Available at: ww.lifesitenews.com; Hichborn, M [2016] *The women's ordination end-run?* [Online] Available at: www.churchmilitant.com [Accessed on: 12 October 2022]

Theological Commission with its report From the *Diakonia of Christ to the Diakonia of the Apostles*:

> With regard to the ordination of women to the diaconate, it should be noted that two important indications emerge from what has been said up to this point:
> 1. The deaconesses mentioned in the tradition of the ancient Church — as evidenced by the rite of institution and the functions they exercised — were not purely and simply equivalent to the deacons;
> 2. The unity of the sacrament of Holy Orders, in the clear distinction between the ministries of the bishop and the priests on the one hand and the diaconal ministry on the other, is strongly underlined by ecclesial tradition, especially in the teaching of the Magisterium.[1175]

17th August

Pope Francis announced the appointment of pro-homosexual Archbishop Paglia as head of the Pontifical Academy for Life and grand chancellor of the Pontifical Pope John Paul II Institute for Studies on Marriage and Family. Archbishop Paglia had spoken publicly in support of ending the prohibition of individuals in a state of sin receiving the Blessed Sacrament. Pope Francis also removed Monsignor Livio Melina as president of the Pontifical Pope John Paul II Institute for Studies on Marriage and Family, replacing him with Monsignor Pierangelo Sequeri. Monsignor Livio Melina had defended the Church's perennial teaching that divorcees committing adultery through a second marriage could not receive Holy Communion.[1176]

Pope Francis also announced the appointment of Bishop Kevin Farrell of Dallas as the prefect of the newly established Dicastery for Laity, Family and Life.[1177] As a former Legionary of Christ Bishop Farrell had known the founder of the Legionaries, Fr. Marcial Maciel, a serial sex abuser and drug addict. Bishop Farrell also shared a flat for six years with Archbishop Theodore McCarrick, the serial homosexual predator.[1178]

18th August

Bishop Vincent Long Van Nguyen of Parramatta, Australia, appointed by Pope Francis in May 2016, denounced doctrine that identifies homosexual sex acts as 'intrinsically disordered'. (*Catechism of the Catholic Church*, 2357.) Bishop Long Van Nguyen said:

> We cannot talk about the integrity of creation, the universal and inclusive love of God, while at the same time colluding with the forces of oppression in the ill-treatment of racial minorities, women, and homosexual persons… It won't wash with young people, especially when we purport to treat gay people with love and compassion and yet define their sexuality as 'intrinsically disordered.'[1179]

When challenged that he was contradicting Church teaching, the bishop issued a press statement, in which he stated, 'To accept a person's sexual identity does not mean to condone his or her behaviour which are contrary to moral norms and the church's teaching.'[1180]

[1175]International Theological Commission [2002] *From the Diakonia of Christ to the Diakonia of the Apostles* [Online] Available at: www.vatican.va [Accessed on: 28 October 2022]

[1176]Chretien, C [2016] *Archbishop who supports Communion for remarried divorcees to head Pontifical Academy for Life, JPII Institute* [Online] Available at: www.lifesitenews.com [Accessed on: 12 October 2022]

[1177]Harris, E [2016] *Bishop Kevin Farrell of Dallas to Head New Vatican Dicastery for Laity, Family and Life* [Online] Available at: www.ncregister.com [Accessed on: 12 October 2022]

[1178]Niles, C [2016] *Homosexual Bishop Funneled Millions From Hospital for Gifts, Personal Use* [Online] Available at: www.churchmilitant.com [Accessed on: 13 October 2022]

[1179]Baklinski, P [2016] *Australian bishop denounces Church teaching that homosexuality is disordered* [Online] Available at: www.lifesitenews.com [Accessed on: 13 October 2022]

[1180]Baklinski, P [2016] *Australian bishop defends call for Catholic Church to 'accept' gay orientation* [Online] Available at: www.lifesitenews.com [Accessed on: 13 October 2022]

23rd August

L'Osservatore Romano, the official newspaper of the Holy See, published an article by Fr. Salvador Pie-Ninot in which he argued that Pope Francis' *Amoris Laetitia* was an example of the 'ordinary magisterium' to which Catholics are obliged to respond with 'the basic attitude of sincere acceptance and practical implementation... calling for the religious submission of will and intellect.'[1181]

25th August

In a conversation with members of the Jesuit order from Poland, Pope Francis told them to prepare future priests not to think in terms of black and white 'ideas', but to deal with a world that is predominantly grey:

> Future priests need to be formed not with general and abstract ideas, which are (overly) clear and distinct, but this fine discernment of spirits, so that they can help people in their concrete lives...need to truly understand this: in life not everything is black and white, white and black. No! In life shades of grey predominate. We must then teach how to discern within this grey.[1182]

1st September

Pope Francis published a message for the celebration of the world day of prayer for the care of creation in which he praised the UN's Sustainable Development Goals. One of these goals calls on member states to 'ensure universal access to sexual and reproductive health' by 2030, which includes access to contraception, including abortifacient methods, and other forms of abortion. Pope Francis wrote:

> The protection of our common home requires a growing global political consensus. Along these lines, I am gratified that in September 2015 the nations of the world adopted the Sustainable Development Goals...[1183]

5th September

Pope Francis sent a private letter to the bishops of Buenos Aires praising them for the 'pastoral' document they sent to their priests outlining a set of criteria based on the eighth chapter of *Amoris Laetitia* allowing divorcees who entered a second union to receive the sacraments on a case-by-case basis. Pope Francis responded: This 'is very good and fully captures the meaning of chapter VIII of the *Amoris Laetitia*. There are no other interpretations. I am sure it will do much good'.[1184]

12th September

Vatican Radio confirms that leaked copies of Pope Francis' private letter to the bishops of Buenos Aires about their implementation of *Amoris Laetitia* are genuine. Vatican radio reported:

> Pope Francis has written a letter to the bishops of the Buenos Aires region of Argentina, praising them for their document which spells out ways in which priests should apply the teachings of his apostolic exhortation *Amoris Laetitia*.[1185]

[1181]Wooden, C [2016] *Vatican newspaper: 'Amoris Laetitia' is authoritative church teaching* [Online] Available at: www.ncronline.org [Accessed on: 13 October 2022]

[1182]Harris, E [2016] *Life isn't black and white – teach priests to discern the gray, Pope says* [Online] Available at: www.catholicnewsagency.com [Accessed on: 13 October 2022]

[1183]Pope Francis [2016] *Message for the celebration of the word day of prayer for the care of creation* [Online] Available at: www.vatican.va [Accessed on: 13 October 2022]

[1184]Tornielli, A [2016] *Pope Francis on the correct interpretation of the 'Amoris Laetitia'* [Online] Available at: www.lastampa.it [Accessed on: 13 October 2022]

[1185]Western, JH [2016] *Vatican Radio confirms Pope's leaked letter on Amoris Laetitia as authentic* [Online] Available at: www.lifesitenews.com [Accessed on: 13 October 2022]

2nd October

During the in-flight press conference returning from the apostolic visit to Georgia and Azerbaijan Pope Francis was asked about transgenderism. The pontiff replied that sexual morality for transgender individuals must be decided on a case-by-case basis. Recounting his meeting with a woman presenting herself as a man:

> She is a young woman who suffered much because she felt like a young man. She felt like a young man, but she was physically a young woman…He wrote me a letter saying that, for him, it would be a consolation to come [see me] with his wife. He that was her but is he.[1186]

5th October

Cardinal Agostino Vallini, the vicar of the Diocese of Rome, publicised the official diocesan guidelines for the implementation of *Amoris Laetitia*. The guidelines allow unmarried couples living together and engaging in a sexual relationship to receive the Sacraments without repenting if sexual continence makes the 'stability' of their relationship 'difficult' after a period of 'discernment' with their pastor. The guidelines overturned the Church's canon law on nullity by stating couples can receive the sacraments if 'there is the moral certainty that the first marriage [of one of the parties] was null but there are not the proofs to demonstrate this in a judicial setting.'[1187]

11th October

Cardinal Christoph Schönborn's cathedral published their Autumn magazine that featured two homosexual men who engaged in a 'civil union' with their adopted son under the title, 'We are Family'.[1188]

13th October

Pope Francis received a group of 1,000 Lutherans and Catholics from Germany in the Vatican's Paul VI hall where a large statue of the heresiarch Martin Luther was erected.[1189]

14th October

The *National Catholic Reporter*, a US newspaper condemned by its bishop for opposing Church teaching, published an exclusive interview with Cardinal-designate Kevin Farrell, the newly appointed prefect of the new Dicastery for Laity, Family and Life. Bishop Farrell praised *Amoris Laetitia*:

> I think that the document *Amoris Laetitia* is faithful to the doctrine and to the teaching of the church. It is carrying on the doctrine of Familiaris Consortio of John Paul II. I believe that passionately. Basically this is the Holy Spirit speaking to us…Do we believe that the Holy Spirit wasn't there in the first synod? Do we believe he wasn't in the second synod? Do we believe that he didn't inspire our Holy Father Pope Francis in writing this document? …I firmly believe [*Amoris Laetitia*] is the teaching of the church. This is a pastoral document telling us how we should proceed. I believe we should take it as it is.[1190]

[1186]McElwee, J [2016] *Francis: Sexual morality determined case-by-case, even for transgender* [Online] Available at: www.ncronline.org [Accessed on: 13 October 2022]
[1187]Chretien, C [2016] *Diocese of Rome's new guidelines allow Communion for sexually active cohabitating couples in 'limited' cases* [Online] Available at: www.lifesitenews.com [Accessed on: 13 October 2022]
[1188]Hickson, M [2016] *Cdl. Schönborn's Vienna Cathedral Bulletin Depicts Homosexual Couple with Adopted Son* [Online] Available at: onepeterfive.com [Accessed on: 13 October 2022]
[1189]Westen, JH [2016] *A statue of Luther in the Vatican and a new papal definition of 'lukewarm'* [Online] Available at: www.lifesitenews.com [Accessed on: 13 October 2022]
[1190]McElwee, J [2016] *New Cardinal Farrell: Amoris Laetitia is 'the Holy Spirit speaking'* [Online] Available at: www.ncronline.org [Accessed on: 13 October 2022]

Bishop Farrell ignored the fact that *Familiaris Consortio*, section 84, explicitly prohibits divorcees committing adultery from receiving Holy Communion in all circumstances.

25th October

Archbishop Diarmuid Martin of Dublin said in a speech preparing for the 2018 World Meeting of Families that it was hard to define what is meant by 'family', lamenting the problems caused by judging 'things in black and white' which was at odds with Pope Francis' vision of morality:

> 'Let me say something about which I feel strongly: do not allow ourselves to be become entangled in trying to produce definitions of the family,' Martin said. 'Family is such a transcultural value that it cannot be defined simply. We may find it hard to define, but we all recognize what is family…Family is about love, no matter how imperfect and failing: it is about a love which enriches lives.'[1191]

28th October

Pope Francis replaced all of the members of the Vatican's Congregation for Divine Worship, appointing 27 new members. Tradition-minded prelates were removed and replaced with innovators. Though tradition-minded Cardinal Robert Sarah remained prefect, Pope Francis' move was seen to curtail his power and influence.[1192]

31st October

Pope Francis visited Sweden to commemorate the 500th anniversary of the beginning of the Reformation. During one of his addresses Pope Francis praised the heresiarch Martin Luther and the Reformation:

> With gratitude we acknowledge that the Reformation helped give greater centrality to Sacred Scripture in the Church's life…The spiritual experience of Martin Luther challenges us to remember that apart from God we can do nothing.[1193]

4th November

Pope Francis published new statutes of the Pontifical Academy for Life with the purpose of fundamentally changing the body founded by Pope St. John Paul II to defend the sanctity of life. Pope Francis dispensed future members of the Academy from taking the Lejeune Oath, a vow expressing members willingness to follow doctrine on the sacredness of human life and an obligation to not perform 'destructive research on the embryo or foetus, elective abortion, or euthanasia.' Pope Francis also dismissed all members of the Academy, including those who had been appointed for life, and excluded the Congregation for the Doctrine of the Faith from its participation in the work of the Academy.[1194] The homosexualist Archbishop Paglia, as the newly appointed president of the Pontifical Academy for Life, was charged with implementing the new statutes and appointing new members from the 1st January 2017.

8th November

Having praised notorious abortionist Emma Bonino in February 2016 as one of the 'forgotten greats' of Italy, Pope Francis held a private audience with her to discuss asylum seekers and the integration of migrants.[1195]

[1191]Chretien, C [2016] *Irish archbishop refuses to define family, opening door to confusion* [Online] Available at: www.lifesitenews.com [Accessed on: 13 October 2022]

[1192]*Pope makes complete overhaul of Vatican liturgical congregation* [2016] [Online] Available at: www.catholicculture.org [Accessed on: 13 October 2022]

[1193]Lamb, C [2016] *Pope Francis expresses gratitude to Martin Luther but swerves eucharist question in first address in Sweden* [Online] Available at: www.thetablet.co.uk [Accessed on: 13 October 2022]

[1194]Bentz, J [2016] *Pope: Pontifical Academy for Life members no longer required to sign pro-life declaration* [Online] Available at: www.lifesitenews.com [Accessed on: 13 October 2022]

[1195]*Pope receives Emma Bonino* [2016] [Online] Available at: www.ansa.it [Accessed on: 13 October 2022]

11th November

The book *Nei tuoi occhi è la mia parola* [In Your Eyes Are My Word] was published containing an interview with Pope Francis. During the interview, Pope Francis criticised the liturgical 'Reform of the reform' and young people who preferred the Traditional Latin Mass:

> Pope Francis insisted the Mass reformed after the Second Vatican Council is here to stay and 'to speak of a "reform of the reform" is an error.' In authorising regular use of the older Mass, now referred to as the 'extraordinary form,' Pope Benedict XVI was 'magnanimous' toward those attached to the old liturgy, he said. 'But it is an exception.' Pope Francis wonders why some young people, who were not raised with the old Latin Mass, nevertheless prefer it. 'And I ask myself: Why so much rigidity? Dig, dig, this rigidity always hides something, insecurity or even something else. Rigidity is defensive. True love is not rigid.'[1196]

Eugenio Scalfari, the atheist editor of the Italian newspaper *La Repubblica*, published his seventh exchange with Pope Francis during which the pontiff praised Marxist socialism. In response to Scalfri asking, 'Are you therefore thinking of a Marxist type of society?' The pontiff replied, 'It has been said many times and my response has always been that, if anything, it is the communists who think like Christians.'[1197]

14th November

Four Cardinals announced their formal call to Pope Francis to answer *dubia* requesting clarification about aspects of *Amoris Laetitia*. Privately delivering their *dubia* to him on the 19th September, cardinals Carlo Caffarra, Raymond Burke, Walter Brandmüller and Joachim Meisner decided to go public when Pope Francis failed to respond. Submitting a *dubium* to a pontiff is a traditional way of establishing clarity about doctrine. The cardinals explained that they felt impelled to submit their *dubia* because paragraphs 300-305 in Chapter 8 of *Amoris Laetitia* 'allude to or even explicitly teach a change in the discipline of the Church with respect to the divorced who are living in a new union.'

- The first *dubium* asked whether following the publication of *Amoris Laetitia* it was now possible for remarried divorcees to receive the sacraments, even though they were engaging in sexual relations in contradiction of previous doctrine set out in *Familiaris Consortio* 84.
- The second *dubium* asked if Pope St. John Paul II's reiteration of the Church's perennial doctrine 'on the existence of absolute moral norms that prohibit intrinsically evil acts and that are binding without exceptions,' (*Veritatis Splendor*, 79) was still valid.
- The third *dubium* asked whether following *Amoris Laetitia*, it remained possible to affirm that a person who 'habitually lives in contradiction to a commandment of God's law, as for instance the one that prohibits adultery' is living 'in an objective situation of grave habitual sin.'
- Their fourth *dubium* asked Pope Francis to clarify whether it was still valid to teach that 'circumstances or intentions can never transform an act intrinsically evil by virtue of its object into an act 'subjectively' good or defensible as a choice.'(*Veritatis Splendor*, 81).
- The fifth *dubium* asked Pope Francis to clarify that Veritatis *Splendor*, 56 remained valid, 'that conscience can never be authorized to legitimate exceptions to absolute moral norms that prohibit intrinsically evil acts by virtue of their object.'

[1196]*Pope, in interview, laments 'rigidity' of youth who prefer Latin Mass* [2016] [Online] Available at: www.catholicculture.org [Accessed on: 13 October 2022]
[1197]Scalfari, E [2016] *Pope Francis: 'Trump? I do not judge. I care only if he makes the poor suffer'* [Online] Available at: www.repubblica.it [Accessed on: 13 October 2022]

Throughout the *dubia* the cardinals highlighted that *Veritatis Splendor* was 'based on sacred Scripture and on the Tradition of the Church'.[1198]

15th November

Catholic News Service published an interview with Cardinal-elect Kevin Farrell in which he criticised Archbishop Chaput on Philadelphia's implementation of *Amoris Laetitia* for re-iterating the Church's teaching that couples committing adultery cannot receive the sacraments. Farrell stated:

> I don't share the view of what Archbishop Chaput did, no…It is better to say to the couple, 'Let's work together and let's walk together' – as Pope Francis would say – 'through this process and see how far we arrive.' [The Catholic Church cannot react by] closing the doors before we even listen to the circumstances and the people. That's not the way to go.

To which Archbishop Chaput replied:

> In response, Archbishop Chaput told Catholic News Service: 'I wonder if Cardinal-designate Farrell actually read and understood the Philadelphia guidelines he seems to be questioning. The guidelines have a clear emphasis on mercy and compassion. This makes sense because individual circumstances are often complex. Life is messy. But mercy and compassion cannot be separated from truth and remain legitimate virtues. The Church cannot contradict or circumvent Scripture and her own magisterium without invalidating her mission. This should be obvious. The words of Jesus himself are very direct and radical on the matter of divorce.'[1199]

16th November

Mons. Vito Pinto, the Dean of the Apostolic Tribunal of the Roman Rota, vehemently criticised the *dubia* cardinals during a conference in the Ecclesiastical University of San Dámaso in Madrid, Spain:

> The action of the Holy Spirit cannot be doubted. [The Cardinals] question not one synod but two! The ordinary and the extraordinary. Which Church do these Cardinals defend? The Pope is faithful to the doctrine of Christ.[1200]

17th November

Pope Francis unusually cancelled his pre-Consistory Meeting of Cardinals, reportedly because he wanted to avoid cardinals resubmitting dubia over Amoris Laetitia.[1201]

18th November

Avvenire, the official newspaper of the Italian hierarchy, published an interview with Pope Francis in which he dismissed critics of his apostolic exhortation *Amoris Laetitia*: 'Some people — I am thinking of certain responses to *Amoris Laetitia* — continue to misunderstand. It's either black or white [to them], even if in the flow of life you have to discern.' Asked about critics who accuse the pope of 'Protestantising' the Catholic Church, Pope Francis replied:

> I don't lose sleep over it…When not given in bad faith, they help with the way forward. Other times you see right away that the critics pick bits from here and there to justify a pre-existing viewpoint; they are not honest, they are acting in bad faith to

---

[1198]Pentin, E [2016] *Four Cardinals Formally Ask Pope for Clarity on 'Amoris Laetitia'* [Online] Available at: www.ncregister.com [Accessed on: 13 October 2022]

[1199]*Pope criticises 'legalism' after cardinals' request for clarification* [2016] [Online] Available at: catholicherald.co.uk [Accessed on: 13 October 2022]

[1200]Bentz, J [2016] *Four Cardinals' 'dubia' is a 'very serious scandal': Dean of Vatican's top appeals court* [Online] Available at: www.lifesitenews.com [Accessed on: 13 October 2022]

[1201]Pentin, E [2016] *Pope Francis Decides Not to Hold Pre-Consistory Meeting of Cardinals* [Online] Available at: www.ncregister.com [Accessed on: 13 October 2022]

foment divisions. You see right away that a certain 'rigourism' is born out of a lack of something, from a desire to hide inside the armour of one's own sad dissatisfaction behind some kind of body armour. If you watch *Babette's Feast*, you see this rigid form of behaviour.[1202]

The Tablet, the English heterodox Catholic newspaper, published an interview with the pro-homosexual cardinal-elect Joseph Tobin in which he criticised the cardinals who submitted the *dubia* to Pope Francis:

> *Amoris Laetitia* cannot simply be reduced to a question of 'yes or no' in a specific pastoral situation. The Holy Father is capturing the work of two synods so if four cardinals say that two synods were wrong, or that somehow the Holy Father didn't reflect what was said in those synods, I think that should be questioned. He believes that what he published is rooted deeply in that reflection, which was not an easy one. I was not a member of that synod but reading the documents and knowing a little about the participants, I realise it was not easy but you are dealing with difficult pastoral questions. Just to simply reduce it to a '*dubium*', I think it is at best naive.[1203]

Edward Pentin, the US *National Catholic Register's* Rome Correspondent, told EWTN's *The World Over Live* show about Pope Francis' response to the publication of the *dubia*,

> 'I do understand from sources within Santa Marta that the pope is not happy at all. In fact, he's…boiling with rage. He's really not happy at all with this.'[1204]

Archbishop Becciu, the Substitute for General Affairs to the Secretary of State, gave an interview to the Italian newspaper *La Stampa* in reaction to the controversy around the *dubia* and *Amoris Laetitia*. In response to a question about 'those who continue to fuel controversy over the interpretation of the *Amoris Laetitia*,' Archbishop Becciu replied:

> The Pope is a very peaceful man, he is always good-spirited, but obviously, every form of division causes him distress and pain. I will not go into the controversies but I do wish to reiterate the principles I have always been taught by the healthy tradition of the Church: as the Pope's humble collaborator, I feel I have a duty to loyally tell him what I think when a decision is being taken. Once it is taken, I obey the Holy Father fully. The unity of the Church, for which Jesus sweated blood and gave his life, comes before my own ideas, however good they may be. Ideas that have involved disobedience have ruined the Church.[1205]

19th November

Pope Francis elevated to the Sacred College of Cardinals pro-homosexual Archbishop Cupich, pro-homosexual Joseph Tobin and Archbishop Kevin Farrell, former long-time flatmate of serial homosexual predator Cardinal McCarrick.

During a Q&A after his elevation to the College of Cardinal pro-homosexual Cardinal Cupich defended *Amoris Laetitia* as a magisterial document and that, therefore, Pope Francis need not respond to those who had doubts:

> All I know is that the doubts that are there, that are expressed, aren't my doubts, and I think they're not the doubts of the universal Church. The document that they're having doubts about is the fruit of two synods, and the fruit of propositions that were voted on by two-thirds of the bishops who were there. It is a post-synodal apostolic exhortation and so it stands on the same level as all the other post-synodal apostolic exhortations

[1202]Gibson, D [2016] *Pope Francis dismisses critics of his teachings* [Online] Available at: www. ncronline.org [Accessed on: 13 October 2022]

[1203]Lamb, C [2016] *US Church must become 'agent of healing' post-Trump, says Cardinal-elect* [Online] Available at: www.thetablet.co.uk [Accessed on: 13 October 2022]

[1204]Chretien, C [2016] *Vatican expert: Sources say Pope Francis 'boiling with rage' over Amoris criticism* [Online] Available at: www.lifesitenews.com [Accessed on: 13 October 2022]

[1205]Tornielli, A [2016] *Amoris Laetitia, Becciu: 'The unity of the Church comes before one's own ideas'* [Online] Available at: www.lastampa.it [Accessed on: 13 October 2022]

as a magisterial document. I think that if you begin to question the legitimacy of what is being said in such a document, do you then throw into question then all of the other documents that have been issued before by the other popes? So I think really it's not for the Pope to respond to that. I think it's a moment for anyone who has doubts to examine how is it they have got to that position because it is a magisterial document of the Church.

However, as critics pointed out, Cardinal Cupich was mistaken in that the Synod Fathers rejected communion for remarried divorcees, when that proposition failed to attain a two-third majority.[1206]

2nd December

Monsignor Vito Pinto, the Dean of the Apostolic Tribunal of the Roman Rota, continued his vehement criticism of the cardinals for submitting their *dubia* to Pope Francis, even though it is a well-established means to seek clarification from the Apostolic See:

> They gave the Pope a slap in the face. The Pope can receive counsel from his Cardinals, that is something else than forcing a counsel upon him. They are no institution that is qualified for anything. On what do they base themselves? That they are four Cardinals? That is not enough. Please. Of course they can write their questions, but to urge him to answer and to publish the thing, that is a scandal. The absolute majority of the first synod and a two-thirds majority in the second, in which the members of the bishops' conferences were present, have exactly approved these theses that now the four Cardinals contest. This is crazy. There is no College of Cardinals that could hold the Pope accountable. The task of the Cardinals is to help the Pope in the exercise of his office and not to impede him or to give him instructions. The fact is, Francis is not only in full accordance with the teaching, but also with all of his predecessors in the 20th century, and that was a Golden Age with excellent Popes, starting with Pius X. I am shocked, especially about the gesture of Meisner. [...] Meisner a great supreme shepherd! That he would go this far, I would have not expected. He was very close to John Paul II and Benedict XVI. [...] And Burke – we have worked together. [...] Now I would ask him: 'Eminence, why have you done this?' Officially this action has no value. The Church needs unity not walls, says the Pope. He will not take the Cardinalate away from the four. We know how Francis is. He believes that men can convert. I know that he prays for them.[1207]

7th December

The Belgian Catholic weekly *Tertio* published an interview with Pope Francis in which he claimed that the contents of *Amoris Laetitia* received two-thirds majority vote of the Synod Fathers: 'It is interesting that all that (the document) contains, it was approved in the Synod by more than two thirds of the fathers. And this is a guarantee.' By making this claim, the pontiff glossed over the fact that the proposition to allow those divorcees committing adultery in second 'marriages' did not receive two-thirds majority at the 2014 synod.[1208]

He also described the media's fascination with scandal in terms of the sexual pathology of those with abnormal interest in faeces:

> I believe that the media should be very clear, very transparent, and not fall prey — without offence, please — to the sickness of coprophilia, which is always wanting to communicate scandal, to communicate ugly things, even though they may be true.[1209]

[1206]Pentin, E [2016] *Cardinal Cupich is Mistaken: Synod Fathers Did Reject Communion for Remarried Divorcees* [Online] Available at: www.ncregister.com [Accessed on: 13 October 2022]

[1207]Bentz, J [2016] *Top Vatican judge doubles down against four Cardinals: 'They gave the Pope a slap in the face'* [Online] Available at: www.lifesitenews.com [Accessed on: 13 October 2022]

[1208]Winfield, N [2016] *Pope insists suggestion on remarried has church backing* [Online] Available at: apnews.com [Accessed on: 13 October 2022]

[1209]Chappell, B [2016] *Pope Francis Warns Media Against Infatuation With Scandal, Citing 'Coprophilia'* [Online] Available at: www.npr.org [Accessed on: 13 October 2022]

9th December

During a homily Pope Francis mocked priests who wore traditional clerical accoutrements:

> Actually, 'on the subject of rigidity and worldliness', Pope Francis shared an anecdote, something that 'happened some time ago: an elderly monsignor came to me', a member 'of the curia, who worked, a normal man, a good man, in love with Jesus; and he told me that he had gone to Euroclero to buy a couple of shirts and saw a young man in front of the mirror – he couldn't have been more than 25; he was either a young priest or was about to become a priest – in front of the mirror, with a large, ample, velvet cloak with a silver chain, and he was looking at himself. Then he picked up a "saturno" hat, put it on and looked at himself: a worldly, rigid man'. And the 'very wise monsignor', Pope Francis continued, 'managed to overcome his pain' with a dose of 'healthy humour and added: "and they say the Church doesn't allow women in the priesthood!"'. Thus, 'when a priest becomes a functionary', in the end things become 'ridiculous, always'.[1210]

22nd December

During his Christmas address to the Curia Pope Francis criticised those who he characterised as offering 'malicious resistance' to his so called reforms:

> There are also cases of malicious resistance, which spring up in misguided minds and come to the fore when the devil inspires ill intentions (often cloaked in sheep's clothing). This last kind of resistance hides behind words of self-justification and, often, accusation; it takes refuge in traditions, appearances, formalities, in the familiar, or else in a desire to make everything personal, failing to distinguish between the act, the actor, and the action.[1211]

Cardinal Kasper, a close ally of Pope Francis and architect of allowing divorced adulterers to receive the sacraments, gave an interview to Vatican Radio about the *dubia* concerning *Amoris Laetitia*. In which he responded:

> Of course, anyone can ask the pope questions and questions – any cardinal can do that. Whether it was a good idea to make them public is a completely different question. I doubt it was. In my opinion, the Apostolic Letter is clear. There are also statements by the pope himself, such as his letter to the Argentine bishops, or explanations by the Cardinal Vicar of Rome. There it is clarified what the pope means and how he understands it. Others have shown that there is no contradiction [in Amoris] to the testimony of John Paul II, but a homogeneous development. This is my position, so I see it this way. In this respect, for me, these *dubia*, these doubts do not exist.[1212]

Cardinal Kasper's reference to Pope St. John Paul II glosses over the fact that *Amoris Laetitia* absolutely contradicts his apostolic exhortation *Familiaris Consortio*, 84 and his *Catechism of the Catholic Church*, 1650.

Pope Francis appointed a commission to investigate the removal of Albrecht von Boeselager as the Grand Chancellor of the Sovereign Military Order of Malta. Von Boeselager had been dismissed by Grand Master Matthew Festing after twice refusing orders to resign due to his 'turning a blind eye' to the distribution of condoms in facilities run by the order in the developing world.[1213] In taking this action, Grand Master Matthew Festing was advised by Cardinal Burke, the incumbent patron of the Sovereign Military Order of Malta.

[1210]Pope Francis [2016] *Morning Meditation in the Chapel of the Domus Sanctae Marthae, Mediators or intermediaries* [Online] Available at: www.vatican.va [Accessed on: 13 October 2022]
[1211]Pope Francis [2016] *Christmas address to the Roman Curia* [Online] Available at: www.vatican.va [Accessed on: 13 October 2022]
[1212]Baklinski, P [2016] *Cardinal Kasper: Amoris Laetitia is 'clear,' so 'these dubia … do not exist'* [Online] Available at: www.lifesitenews.com [Accessed on: 13 October 2022]
[1213]Pullella, P [2016] *Pope orders probe over dismissal of Knights of Malta deputy head* [Online] Available at: www.reuters.com [Accessed on: 13 October 2022]

23rd December

The German magazine *Der Spiegel* reported that Pope Francis had confided to a small group that he may split the Church:

> In a very small circle, Pope Francis is said to have self-critically further explained himself as follows: 'It is not to be excluded that I will enter history as the one who split the Catholic Church'.

Der Spiegel also reported the assessment of Cardinal Brandmüller, one of the signatories of the *dubia*, of what is at stake with *Amoris Laetitia*:

> It is about all or nothing to speak in colloquial terms; that is to say, it is about the kernel of the whole, about the teaching of doctrine. Whoever thinks that persistent adultery and the reception of Holy Communion are compatible is a heretic and promotes schism.[1214]

The Grand Magistry of the Sovereign Order of Malta published their rejection of Pope Francis' investigation into the dismissal of Albrecht von Boeselager for allowing the distribution of condoms:

> The replacement of the former Grand Chancellor is an act of internal governmental administration of the Sovereign Order of Malta and consequently falls solely within its competence.[1215]

In an interview with *Die Presse*, Bishop Benno Elbs of the Diocese of Feldkirch, Austria, appointed by Pope Francis in May 2013, contradicted Church doctrine on divorce and remarriage, and contraception. About remarried divorcees receiving Holy Communion he said:

> The teaching has changed insofar as she has opened the door. People have made decisions of conscience in the past, but now they can do it – so to say – with the blessing of the Pope. That is an essential progress.

About contraception he said:

> The Synod paper recommends natural methods of regulating conception. Recommends. The regulation of conception is a decision of conscience of the couple.[1216]

26th December

Marco Tosatti, Vaticanista journalist, reported that Pope Francis had ordered Cardinal Gerhard Ludwig Müller, Prefect of the Congregation for the Doctrine of the Faith, to dismiss three priests, whom Cardinal Müller protested were some of his best collaborators. Marco Tosatti gave an account of Cardinal Müller's meeting with the pontiff:

> Finally, he was received in an audience. And he said: 'Your Holiness, I have received these letters, but I did not do anything because these persons are among the best of my dicastery… what did they do?' The answer was, as follows: 'And I am the pope, I do not need to give reasons for any of my decisions. I have decided that they have to leave and they have to leave.' He got up and stretched out his hand in order to indicate that the audience was at an end. On 31 December, two of the three [men] will leave the dicastery in which they have worked for years, and without knowing the why. For the third, there seems to be a certain delay. But then, there is another implication which, if true, would be even more unpleasant. One of the two had freely spoken about certain decisions of the pope – perhaps a little bit too much. A certain person – a friend of

[1214]Donnelly, N [2016] *Pope Says He May Split the Catholic Church, According to Der Spiegel* [Online] Available at: www.churchmilitant.com [Accessed on: 13 October 2022]

[1215]Chretien, C [2016] *Knights of Malta rebuff Vatican: Investigation of our 'internal' matters is 'unacceptable'* [Online] Available at: www.lifesitenews.com [Accessed on: 13 October 2022]

[1216]Bentz, J [2016] *Austrian bishop: 'Remarried' Catholics now have 'blessing of the Pope' to receive Communion* [Online] Available at: www.lifesitenews.com [Accessed on: 13 October 2022]

a close collaborator of the pope – heard this disclosure and passed it on. The victim received then a very harsh telephone call from Number One [i.e., the pope]. And then soon came the dismissal.[1217]

Sandro Magister, another Vaticanista journalist, later confirmed, 'One of the priests, likely Kruijen', was 'reprimanded harshly by telephone for having expressed criticisms against him [Pope Francis], which had come to the pope's ear through an informant.'[1218]

2017

2nd January

For the first time in history, Pope Francis appointed a Protestant as editor of the Vatican newspaper *L'Osservatore Romano* for the Argentina edition. Marcelo Figueroa is a pastor of the Presbyterian Church and director of the Argentine Biblical Society for twenty-five years. He is also a personal friend of Pope Francis.[1219]

5th January

The Vatican's Pontifical Council for Christian Unity and the World Council of Churches issued a joint document to promote the 2017 'Week of Prayer for Christian Unity' with the theme 'Reconciliation: The love of Christ compels us.' It stated:

> Lutheran and Catholic Christians will for the first time commemorate together the beginning of the Reformation…Catholics are now able to hear Luther's challenge for the Church of today, recognising him as a 'witness to the gospel.'[1220]

Catholics traditionally recognised the apostate priest Martin Luther as a heresiarch.

13th January

The bishops in the Archdiocese of Malta and the Diocese of Gozo issued guidelines allowing divorced and 'remarried' Catholics living in a state of objective sin to receive the sacraments. Archbishop Charles Scicluna of Malta and Bishop Grech stated that such couples could receive Holy Communion when 'with an informed and enlightened conscience … acknowledge and believe that he or she are at peace with God.' Bishop Grech was later promoted by Pope Francis when he appointed him Secretary General of the Synod of Bishops and elevated him to the Sacred College of Cardinals.[1221]

The Synod Secretariat released the lineamenta for the 2018 ordinary synod on youth, *Young People, the Faith and Vocational Discernment*. A characteristic of the document is its hostility towards Tradition:

> 'the goal of every serious pastoral vocational programme is truly free and responsible choices, fully removed from practices of the past' (II.2); 'the old approaches no longer work and the experience passed on by previous generations quickly becomes obsolete' (I. 3).

It also privileged the experience of young people over doctrinal authority and formation.[1222]

[1217]Hickson, M [2016] *Pope Orders Cardinal Müller to Dismiss Three CDF Priests* [Online] Available at: onepeterfive.com [Accessed on: 13 October 2022]

[1218]Magister, S [2016] *A Firing, a Demolition: Behold the New Curia* [Online] Available at: magister. blogautore.espresso.repubblica.it [Accessed on: 13 October 2022]

[1219]Kelly, B [2017] *Pope Appoints Protestant Friend Director of Vatican Newspaper in Argentina* [Online] Available at: catholicism.org [Accessed on: 13 October 2022]

[1220]Westen, JH [2017] *Vatican: Catholics now recognize Martin Luther as a 'witness to the gospel'* [Online] Available at: www.lifesitenews.com [Accessed on: 13 October 2022]

[1221]Bourne, L [2017] *Vatican newspaper publishes Maltese bishops' guidelines endorsing Communion for 'remarried'* [Online] Available at: www.lifesitenews.com [Accessed on: 13 October 2022]

[1222]McCusker, M [2017] *Vatican's youth synod looks like another assault on the Catholic faith* [Online] Available at: www.lifesitenews.com [Accessed on: 13 October 2022]

14th January

The Vatican's official newspaper, *L'Osservatore Romano*, published in full the Archdiocese of Malta and the Diocese of Gozo's guidelines on allowing divorced and 'remarried' Catholics living in a state of objective sin to receive the sacraments.

The Italian newspaper *Il Foglio* published an interview with Carlo Cardinal Caffarra, one of the *dubia* cardinals, in which he explained the fifth *dubium* was the most important:

> That is why among the five *dubia*, *dubium* number five is the most important. There is a passage of *Amoris Laetitia*, at n. 303, which is not clear; it seems – I repeat: it seems – to admit the possibility that there is a true judgment of conscience (not invincibly erroneous; this has always been acknowledged by the Church) in contradiction to that which the Church teaches as pertaining to the deposit of divine Revelation. It seems. And so, we put the *dubium* to the Pope.[1223]

17th January

The Vatican's Philatelic and Numismatic Office confirmed that it would be issuing a stamp featuring the heresiarch Martin Luther to commemorate the 500-year anniversary of the Protestant heresy and schism.[1224]

19th January

Pope Francis praised the heresiarch and schismatic Martin Luther during a meeting with members of the Ecumenical Delegation from Finland: 'the intention of Martin Luther five hundred years ago was to renew the Church, not divide her.'[1225]

The Italian traditional website *Messa in Latino* reported that Bishop Mario Grech of Gozo had threatened to suspend the faculties of priests who refused to administer the sacraments to divorcees committing adultery:

> We have been told by reliable sources, whose identity we know but for obvious reasons we cannot divulge, that in recent days Bp. Mario Grech returned from Rome and threatened priests of his diocese of Malta that he would 'prohibit [their ability to offer] Mass if you do not support the directives of *Amoris Laetitia* authored with Bishop Sciucluna.'

The Gozo diocese's Facebook page posted a denial. A Maltese priest later confirmed that Grech 'did indeed threaten a priest on the subject of Holy Communion to the divorced and remarried.'[1226] Bishop Mario Grech was later elevated to the Sacred College of Cardinals by Pope Francis and Secretary General of the Synod of Bishops.

25th January

Pope Francis imposed a 'junta' administration on another sovereign entity. The Vatican announced that it was taking control of the Sovereign Order of the Knights of Malta following the Grand Master Matthew Festing publicly defying Pope Francis. Under Festing the Knights of Malta refused to cooperate with the Vatican's illegitimate investigation into the dismissal of Albrecht von Boeselager as the Grand Chancellor for distributing condoms.[1227] Eminent canon lawyer Ed Condon observed, 'Under

[1223]Matzuzzi, M [2017] *'Only a blind man can deny that there is great confusion in the Church.' An interview with Carlo Cardinal Caffarra* (Trans. by Andrew Guernsey)[Online] Available at: docs. google.com/document [Accessed on: 13 October 2022]

[1224]Bentz, J [2017] *Vatican to issue stamp featuring Martin Luther* [Online] Available at: www. lifesitenews.com [Accessed on: 13 October 2022]

[1225]*Pope: Luther's intention was to renew the Church, not divide her* [2017] [Online] Available at: http:// www.archivioradiovaticana.va [Accessed on: 13 October 2022]

[1226]Eli, B [2017] *Malta Bishop Threatens to Suspend Priests Who Refuse Communion to Civilly Remarried*; Niles, C [2017] *Priest Confirms: Malta Bishop Mario Grech Did Threaten Priest* [Online] Available at: www.churchmilitant.com [Accessed on: 13 October 2022]

[1227]Pentin, E [2017] *Grand Master of the Order of Malta Offers Resignation* [Online] Available at: www. ncregister.com [Accessed on: 13 October 2022]

international law, what we are seeing is effectively the annexation of one country by another.'[1228]

28th January

Under the control of the Vatican, the 'Sovereign' Order of the Knights of Malta reinstated their former Grand Chancellor, Albrecht Freiherr von Boeselager. His dismissal in 2016 for distributing condoms under the auspices of the Knights of Malta triggered Pope Francis' unprecedented and illegal intervention in the internal affairs of a sovereign entity.[1229]

30th January

Bishop Robert Barron, appointed auxiliary bishop of Los Angeles by Pope Francis in 2015, gave an interview in which he said that he wouldn't press to reverse the Supreme Court's decision to legalise so called 'gay marriage'. He also misrepresented the Church's teaching on homosexuality when he said, 'if the only thing a gay person hears from the Catholic Church is, 'you're intrinsically disordered,' we've got a very serious problem, if that's what the message has become.' The Church teaches that homosexual sex acts are 'intrinsically disordered', not persons. (CCC 2357)[1230]

1st February

The German bishops published guidelines on *Amoris Laetitia* allowing divorced and 'remarried' Catholics committing adultery to receive Holy Communion on a case-by-case basis.[1231]

5th February

Pope Francis used a euphemism popular with pro-abortion advocates to describe abortion in his message to mark the Italian 'Day for Life':

> Let us promote the culture of life as a response to the logic of rejected and to the falling birth rate; let us be close to and together pray for the babies who are at risk of the interruption of pregnancy...

Pope St. John Paul II condemned the use of 'interruption of pregnancy':

> In this regard the reproach of the Prophet is extremely straightforward: 'Woe to those who call evil good and good evil, who put darkness for light and light for darkness' (Isa 5:20). Especially in the case of abortion there is a widespread use of ambiguous terminology, such as 'interruption of pregnancy', which tends to hide abortion's true nature and to attenuate its seriousness in public opinion. (*Evangelium Vitae*, 58).[1232]

8th February

In an interview with Edward Pentin of the National Catholic Register, Cardinal Marx of Munich and Freising, said in response to a question about allowing divorced and 'remarried' Catholics committing adultery to receive Holy Communion: 'I think there is a clear position and the line of the Pope is very clear.'[1233]

[1228]Lawler, P [2017] *The ideological purge at the Vatican* [Online] Available at: www.catholicculture. org [Accessed on: 13 October 2022]

[1229]Harris, E [2017] *Knights of Malta appoint interim leader, reinstate Grand Chancellor* [Online] Available at: www.catholicnewsagency.com [Accessed on: 13 October 2022]

[1230]Pelletier, R [2017] *Bishop Robert Barron Does Not Want to Reverse Gay 'Marriage'* [Online] Available at: www.churchmilitant.com [Accessed on: 13 October 2022]

[1231]Harris, E [2017] *German bishops say the divorced-and-remarried may receive Communion* [Online] Available at: www.lifesitenews.com [Accessed on: 13 October 2022]

[1232]Pope Francis [2017] *The Pope greets all those who work to promote life* [Online] Available at: press. vatican.va; McCusker, M [2017] *Pope Francis marks 'Day for Life' with abortion euphemism condemned by St. John Paul II* [Online] Available at: ww.lifesitenews.com [Accessed on: 13 October 2022]

[1233]Pentin, E [2017] *Cardinal Marx: Pope's Line in Amoris Laetitia is 'Very Clear'* [Online] Available at: www.ncregister.com [Accessed on: 13 October 2022]

13th February

La Civilta Cattolica, the Jesuit journal edited by Pope Francis' close collaborator, Fr. Antonio Spadaro SJ, and vetted by the Vatican's Secretariat of State, published an essay by its deputy editor, Father Giancarlo Pani, which sought to reopen the possibility of ordaining women to the priesthood. Immediately following the publication of the essay Pope Francis strongly commended the staff of *La Civilta Cattolica*; '...the Pope told its current contributors never to be afraid of the storms, but to proceed courageously, guided by the Spirit, into uncharted waters.'[1234]

14th February

Cardinal Francesco Coccopalmerio, President of the Pontifical Council for the Interpretation of Legal Texts, spoke at the launch of his book, *The Eighth Chapter of the Post-Synodal Apostolic Exhortation Amoris Laetitia*. During his address he insisted that those living in objectively sinful situations 'must be given Holy Communion':

> Divorced and remarried, unmarried couples living together, are certainly not models of unions in harmony with Catholic doctrine, but the Church cannot look the other way. For which reason the sacraments of Reconciliation and Communion ought to be given also to so-called wounded families and to those who, even though living in situations not in line with the traditional canons on matrimony, express a sincere desire to draw closer to the sacraments after an adequate period of discernment.[1235]

Pro-homosexual Cardinal Cupich of Chicago posted a tweet supporting Cardinal Coccopalmerio's interpretation of *Amoris Laetitia*:

> Amoris Laetitia expresses with 'absolute clarity' marriage doctrine in full fidelity to traditional Church teaching.[1236]

15th February

Cardinal Zen, the Bishop Emeritus of Hong Kong and China, warned in an interview with *LifeSiteNews* against the danger of the Vatican selling out the Chinese underground Church in a deal with the Chinese Communist Party:

> We are very much worried because it seems that the Vatican is going to make a very bad agreement with China. And I can understand that the pope is really naive... He doesn't know the Chinese communists. But unfortunately the people around him are not good at all. They have very wrong ideas. And I'm afraid that they may sell out our underground Church. That would be very sad.[1237]

18th February

Fr. Arturo Sosa Abascal SJ, the newly elected Superior General of the Jesuits, gave an interview to the website *Rossoporpora*. Asked about Church doctrine on marriage and divorce being founded on the teaching of our Lord Jesus Christ, he responded that the 'words of Jesus against divorce are 'relative':

[1234]Mirus, J [2017] *Reopening the question of women priests: A theological travesty and a spiritual tragedy* [Online] Available at: www.catholicculture.org [Accessed on: 13 October 2022]
[1235]Baklinski, P [2017] *Vatican Cardinal: Catholics in adulterous unions 'must be given' Communion* [Online] Available at: www.lifesitenews.com [Accessed on: 13 October 2022]
[1236]Bourne, L [2017] *Twitter erupts with dubious reaction to Cardinal Cupich's post on marriage document's 'absolute clarity'* [Online] Available at: www.lifesitenews.com; Niles, C [2017] *Chicago Cardinal Roundly Mocked on Twitter for Defense of Amoris Laetitia* [Online] Available at: www. churchmilitant.com [Accessed on: 13 October 2022]
[1237]Chretien, C [2017] *EXCLUSIVE: Cardinal Zen says 'naïve' Pope and bad advisors are betraying underground Church in China* [Online] Available at: www.lifesitenews.com [Accessed on: 13 October 2022]

At that time, no one had a recorder to take down his words. What is known is that the words of Jesus must be contextualised, they are expressed in a language, in a specific setting, they are addressed to someone in particular.[1238]

22nd February

In an interview with *The Irish Catholic* newspaper Cardinal Nichols, raised to the Sacred College by Pope Francis in 2014, disingenuously proposed that *Amoris Laetitia* didn't change doctrine:

> The issues raised by *Amoris Laetitia* are not core doctrinal issues, these are about how do we live, in very traditional terms actually, everything in *Amoris Laetitia* is drawn from the tradition of the Church: how do we live the mercy of God and how do we enable people who feel judged, feel excluded, feel as if they have no place, to begin to explore that.

Asked about Cardinal Burke raising the possibility of a formal correction of Pope Francis over *Amoris Laetitia*, Cardinal Nichols replied:

> The pope is the one who has been chosen under the influence of the Holy Spirit to lead the Church, and we will follow his lead. The pope's patience and reserve about this whole matter is exactly what we should observe.[1239]

Archbishop Vincenzo Paglia, head of the Pontifical Academy for Life, delivered a fulsome eulogy for the recently deceased Italian Radical Party founder Marco Pannella. Pannella was a bisexual atheist who publicly advocated the legalisation of abortion, gay 'marriage,' blasphemy, free love, and transgender rights. Among other things Archbishop Paglia said:

> His [Pannella's] story shows how a man can help history to go forward towards the defence of each and every person's dignity, specially those who are marginalized. … I take great pleasure in saying that Marco was truly a spiritual man who fought and hoped against all hope …[1240]

25th February

Pope Francis told participants at a Roman Rota course on marriage preparation to welcome couples cohabiting, ignoring the fact that they are committing the grave sin of fornication:

> At the same time, reach out in the Gospel way by meeting and welcoming young people who prefer to live together without being married.[1241]

27th February

Dr. Paul Ehrlich, a proponent of sex-selective abortions and mass sterilisation, was a keynote speaker, at the invitation of Bishop Marcelo Sánchez Sorondo, at the Vatican conference, *Biological Extinction*, hosted by the Pontifical Academy of Sciences. Dr. Paul Ehrlich, author of the 1968 bestseller, *The Population Bomb*, has been described as 'the undisputed father of the modern, pro-abortion population control movement'. In 2014 Ehrlich wrote that the most unethical thing going on now in religion is the Catholic

[1238]Baklinski, P [2017] *New Jesuit chief claims Jesus' own words against divorce are 'relative,' subject to 'interpretation'* [Online] Available at: www.lifesitenews.com; Magister, S [2017] *Marriage and Divorce. The General of the Jesuits: 'Jesus Too Must Be Reinterpreted'* [Online] Available at: magister.blogautore.espresso.repubblica.it [Accessed on: 13 October 2022]
[1239]Ivereigh, A [2017] *UK cardinal says on 'Amoris', we follow the pope's lead* [Online] Available at: cruxnow.com [Accessed on: 13 October 2022]
[1240]Smits, J [2017] *Pontifical Academy for Life chief glorifies radical culture of death devotee* [Online] Available at: www.lifesitenews.com [Accessed on: 13 October 2022]
[1241]Pope Francis [2017] *Address to participants in the course on the marriage process* [Online] Available at: www.vatican.va [Accessed on: 13 October 2022]

Church's 'opposition to the use of contraception.' Also speaking at the conference was Professor John Bongaarts, vice president of the Population Council, who promotes a global reduction in births and the wide distribution of artificial contraceptives. Bishop Sanchez Sorondo has a history of inviting eugenicists to speak at the Vatican.

Dr. Paul Ehrlich told *LifeSiteNews* that he was thrilled with the direction taken by Pope Francis:

> I think the Pope recognises the threat to future lives, and to the persistence of society, posed by overpopulation… Family planning with modern contraception is the only ethical solution, and if made universally available would greatly reduce the frequency of abortion. It also would generally improve women's health and education. Francis is a brilliant and compassionate man – draw your own conclusions.[1242]

Bishop Marcelo Sánchez Sorondo, Chancellor of the Pontifical Academy of Sciences and the Pontifical Academy of Social Sciences said at the Vatican conference:

> Many times, we don't know exactly what is the doctrine of the Church – we know some part but not all the doctrine of the Church about the question of the fecundity.[1243]

6th March

Cardinal Reinhard Marx, the President of the German Bishops' Conference and member of Pope Francis' Advisory Council of Cardinals, spoke at a press conference about the pontiff's response to the German Bishops' guidelines allowing divorced and 'remarried' adulterers to receive communion. He said Pope Francis was 'overjoyed':

> I gave to the pope the text which we have made with regard to *Amoris Laetitia*, and he has received it with joy; I was able to speak with him about it, and he considers it to be right that the local churches make their own statements once more, and that they therein draw their own pastoral conclusions; and [he] is very positive about this and he received it very positively that we as the German Bishops' Conference have written such a text.[1244]

8th March

The German newspaper *Die Zeit* published an interview with Pope Francis in which he admitted that he was open to the possibility of ordaining married Latin-rite Catholic men to the priesthood in response to the priest shortage in some countries:

> We have to think about if the *viri probati* are a possibility. Then we also have to discern which tasks they can take on, for example, in forlorn communities.[1245]

13th March

For the first time in history, an Anglican Liturgy was celebrated in St. Peter's Basilica, Rome. Merton College Choir, Oxford University, sang the first ever Anglican Evensong to be celebrated at the altar of the Chair of St. Peter.[1246]

[1242]Baklinski, P [2017] *He supports forced abortion, sterilization. Next month, he's speaking at the Vatican* [Online] Available at: www.lifesitenews.com; Gamble, R [2017] *Outspoken advocate of reducing human population by abortion speaks at Vatican conference* [Online] Available at: www.thetablet.co.uk [Accessed on: 13 October 2022]

[1243]Chretien, C [2017] *Vatican bishop: 'We don't know exactly' what the Church teaches on procreation; 'education' will help women have one kid instead of seven* [Online] Available at: www.lifesitenews.com [Accessed on: 13 October 2022]

[1244]Hickson, M [2017] *Cardinal Marx: Pope Francis Was Joyful that the German Bishops Wrote Guidelines about Amoris Laetitia* [Online] Available at: onepeterfive.com [Accessed on: 12 October 2022]

[1245]Bourne, L [2017] *Pope Francis: 'We have to think about' married priests in Catholic Church* [Online] Available at: www.lifesitenews.com [Accessed on: 13 October 2022]

[1246]*Choir to sing first ever Anglican Evensong at St. Peter's, Rome* [2017] [Online] Available at: www. merton.ox.ac.uk [Accessed on: 13 October 2022]

7th April

Cardinal Kevin Farrell, appointed by Pope Francis Prefect of the Dicastery for Laity, Family and Life publicly praised pro-homosexual Fr. James Martin's book on LGBT ministry, *Building A Bridge*. Cardinal Farrell said, 'It will also help LGBT Catholics feel more at home in what is, after all, their church.'[1247]

12th April

Pope Francis appointed pro-homosexual Fr. James Martin SJ consultor to the Secretariat for Communications.[1248]

17th April

Archbishop Charles Scicluna of Malta said on TV that non-abortifacient contraceptives can be used, 'What we are saying is that if you have to use a contraceptive make sure it is not one that kills life'.[1249]

19th April

Pope Francis appointed pro-homosexual Fr. John Dolan to be an auxiliary bishop in the Diocese of San Diego.[1250]

25th April

The *dubia* cardinals delivered a letter to Pope Francis requesting a private audience to discuss the 'confusion and disorientation' following the publication of *Amoris Laetitia*. Cardinals Caffarra, Walter Brandmüller, Raymond Burke, and Joachim Meisner also requested that during the private audience Pope Francis discuss the five *dubium* they submitted to him in 2016. Having received no reply from Pope Francis to their request, the cardinals made their letter to him public two months latter.[1251]

28th-30th April

Bishop John Stowe of Kentucky, appointed by Pope Francis, delivered addresses at the militant LGBT New Ways Ministry conference. (Cardinal Francis George of Chicago, president of the United States Conference of Catholic Bishops, condemned the LGBT group in 2010 for not adhering to doctrine on homosexuality). Among other things, Bishop John Stowe said:

> Christian morality is more concerned with the well-being and dignity of the person than with rules, norms or commandments. Jesus seems to teach this on many occasions.[1252]

5th May

Fr. James Martin SJ, appointed a consultor to the Secretariat for Communications by Pope Francis, posted a comment on his Facebook page saying some saints were probably homosexual:

[1247]Chretien, C [2017] *Francis-appointed Cardinals back Jesuit's pro-LGBT book* [Online] Available at: ww.lifesitenews.com [Accessed on: 13 October 2022]
[1248]Chretien, C [2017] *Vatican names pro-gay Fr. James Martin as communications consultant* [Online] Available at: www.lifesitenews.com [Accessed on: 13 October 2022]
[1249]Niles, C [2017] *Malta Archbishop Offers Ambiguous Comments on Contraception* [Online] Available at: www.churchmilitant.com [Accessed on; 14 October 2022]
[1250]Shine, R [2017] *Pope Francis Appoints LGBT-Positive Priest as Auxiliary Bishop in San Diego* [Online] Available at: www.newwaysministry.org [Accessed on: 13 October 2022]
[1251]Baklinski, P [2017] *Four Cardinals release letter asking to meet Pope about 'confusion and disorientation' in Church* [Online] Available at: www.lifesitenews.com [Accessed on: 13 October 2022]
[1252]Niles, C [2017] *Kentucky Bishop Insists on Speaking at Pro-LGBT Symposium*; [2016] *KY Bishop Responds to Church Militant, Justifies Talk at Pro-Gay Symposium* [Online] Available at: www. churchmilitant.com [Accessed on: 13 October 2022]

Some of them were probably gay. A certain percentage of humanity is gay, and so were most likely some of the saints. You may be surprised when you get to heaven to be greeted by LGBT men and women'. Fr. James Martin SJ later deleted his post.[1253]

7th May

Cardinal Joseph Tobin of Newark, appointed by Pope Francis, expressed his delight that an openly LGBT group was making a pilgrimage to his cathedral: 'I am delighted that you and the LGBTQ brothers and sisters plan to visit our beautiful cathedral. You will be very welcome!'[1254]

10th May

Pro-homosexual Fr. Timothy Radcliffe OP, appointed by Pope Francis a consultor for the Pontifical Council for Justice and Peace in 2014, gave a speech in Brisbane, Australia, in which he criticised the 'tyranny of Tradition'. He also spoke in favour of *Amoris Laetitia* allowing people committing adultery to receive Holy Communion:

> If divorced people can face their own responsibility and failure, if they faced up to what they had done and been, then maybe the best thing was for them to come back to the medicine of the Eucharist.'[1255]

16th May

Pope Francis appointed forty-five ordinary members and five honorary members to the Pontifical Academy for Life, following his dismissal of all previous members, including those appointed for life. Among the pontiff's new appointees was Professor Nigel Biggar of Oxford University, an Anglican minister who supports legalised abortion up to 18 weeks and has expressed qualified support for euthanasia. Pope Francis also appointed Professor Maurizio Chiodi, an Italian priest and moral theologian who publicly criticised fundamental magisterial documents on life issues, including Pope St. Paul VI's *Humanae Vitae*, Pope St. John Paul II's *Evangelium Vitae* and the CDF's *Donum Vitae*.[1256] Four other new members have voiced opposition to *Humane Vitae*, including Monsignor Pierangelo Sequeri; Anne-Marie Pelletier; Father Alain Thomasset, SJ; and Fr. Humberto Miguel Yanez SJ.[1257] Archbishop Vincenzo Paglia, the head of the Pontifical Academy for Life accused those Catholics and Catholic journalists scandalised by the appointment of pro-abortion Professor Nigel Biggar of 'sensationalism': '[W]e pray that Catholics and Catholic media not fall victim to sensationalism. Love for life must mean love for each other.'[1258]

18th May

The Catholic Education Service (CES), an agency of the Bishops' Conference of England and Wales, published a program promoting radical LGBT propaganda in Catholic schools. The program, titled *Made in God's Image: Challenging homophobic and biphobic bullying in Catholic Schools*, containing material taken from the militant gay activist

[1253]Baklinski, P [2017] *Some saints 'were probably gay': Pro-gay Vatican advisor* [Online] Available at: www.lifesitenews.com [Accessed on: 13 October 2022]

[1254]Santora, A [2017] *N.J. cardinal offers historic welcome to LGBT community* [Online] Available at: www.nj.com [Accessed on: 14 October 2022]

[1255]Chretien, C [2017] *Pro-gay Vatican advisor slams the 'tyranny of tradition' that forbids Communion for adulterers* [Online] Available at: www.lifesitenews.com [Accessed on: 13 October 2022]

[1256]Bourne, L [2017] *Pope Francis guts Vatican pro-life academy of members chosen by St. John Paul II* [Online] Available at: www.lifesitenews.com [Accessed on: 13 October 2022]

[1257]Cummings McLean, D [2017] *Vatican appoints opponents of Church teaching on birth control to pro-life academy* [Online] Available at: www.lifesitenews.com [Accessed on: 14 October 2022]

[1258]Baklinski, P [2017] *Vatican pro-life academy head defends appointment of abortion supporter* [Online] Available at: www.lifesitenews.com; Eli, B [2017] *Abp. Paglia Upholds Appointment of Pro-Abort Anglican* [Online] Available at: www.churchmilitant.com [Accessed on: 14 October 2022]

groups Stonewall and LGBT Youth Scotland. Stonewall has a reputation for being anti-Catholic, in particular through its 'Bigot of the Year' award.[1259]

19th May

Pope Francis gave a homily that was seen as a thinly veiled attack on the four cardinals, three of whom were retired, who submitted a *dubia* seeking clarity about sections of *Amoris Laetitia*. Pope Francis said:

> But there have always been those people who, without any official title, go about disturbing the Christian community with discourses which unsettle souls: 'Ah, no, what he said is heretical; that cannot be said, not that, the doctrine of the Church is this. In reality, they are fanatics about things which are not clear, like those fanatics who went about sowing weeds to divide the Christian community. So, this is the problem: when the doctrine of the Church, which comes from the Gospel, which the Holy Spirit inspires — because Jesus said 'He will teach you and will help you to recall all that which I have taught' — becomes ideology. Thus, we see the great error of these people: those who were going there were not believers; they were 'ideologized'; they had an ideology which closed their heart to the work of the Holy Spirit.... Today I am inspired to ask for the grace of mature obedience to the Magisterium of the Church, the obedience to what the Church has always taught and continues to teach us. With this obedience, one develops the Gospel; explains it better each time, in fidelity to Peter, to the bishops and, ultimately, to the Holy Spirit who guides and sustains this process...pray for those who transform doctrine into ideology, so that the Lord may give them the grace of conversion to the unity of the Church, to the Holy Spirit, and to true doctrine.[1260]

Cardinal Óscar Rodríguez Maradiaga, the head of Pope Francis' advisory group of nine Cardinals launched an ad hominem attack against Cardinal Burke in response to the *dubia*. In the book length interview, *Solo il Vangelo è rivoluzionario*, Cardinal Maradiaga said Cardinal Burke:

> is a disappointed man, in that he wanted power and lost it. He thought he was the maximum authority in the United States. He's not the magisterium . . . The Holy Father is the magisterium, and he's the one who teaches the whole Church. This other [person] speaks only his own thoughts, which don't merit further comment. They are the words of a poor man. These currents of the Catholic right are persons who seek power and not the truth, and the truth is one . . . If they claim to find some 'heresy' in the words of Francis, they're making a big mistake, because they're thinking only like men and not as the Lord wants. What sense does it have to publish writings against the pope, which don't damage him but ordinary people? What does a right-wing closed on certain points accomplish? Nothing! Ordinary people are with the pope, this is completely clear. I see that everywhere. Those who are proud, arrogant, who believe they have a superior intellect ... poor people! Pride is also a form of poverty.[1261]

20th May

Pro-homosexual Bishop McElroy of San Diego, appointed by Pope Francis, gave a commencement address at the Jesuit School of Theology at Santa Clara University. During his address he told theology students Pope Francis' teaching represented 'a new theological tradition' that 'does not first demand a change of life':

[1259]Donnelly, N [2017] *UK bishops' group pushing radical LGBT propaganda in Catholic schools; INTERVIEW: UK bishop questions LGBT involvement in Catholic schools' sex-ed program* [Online] Available at: www.lifesitenews.com [Accessed on: 14 October 2022]
[1260]Pope Francis [2017] Pope Francis [2016] *Morning Meditation in the Chapel of the Domus Sanctae Marthae, Doctrine and ideology* [Online] Available at: www.vatican.va [Accessed on: 14 October 2022]
[1261]Niles, C [2017] *Head of Gang of Nine Trashes Cdl. Raymond Burke* [Online] Available at: www.churchmilitant.com [Accessed on: 14 October 2022]

There has emerged in the last three years a vibrantly transformed branch of Catholic theology which is rightfully claiming its place as a central element of Catholic doctrine and practice — the pastoral theology which is contained in the teachings of Pope Francis… It demands that moral theology proceed from the actual pastoral action of Jesus Christ, which does not first demand a change of life.[1262]

An approach that appears contrary to the preaching of our Lord Jesus Christ, 'The time is accomplished, and the kingdom of God is at hand: repent, and believe the gospel.' (Mark 1:15).

23rd May

Archbishop Charles Scicluna of Malta condemned as 'propaganda' a full page advertisement in a national newspaper that defended marriage from LGBT activists seeking to legalise so called homosexual 'marriage'. Archbishop Scicluna's diocesan website posted the following condemnation:

> The Archdiocese of Malta categorically states that, while respecting the right of freedom of expression of every person or any other entity, it is not in any way involved with the propaganda by the Maltese Catholics United for the Faith.[1263]

5th June

The Rt. Rev. Gerard de Korte, appointed Bishop of Den Bosch by Pope Francis in 2016, confirmed that he would give a blessing at the end of a service in his cathedral celebrating *Roze Zaterdag* [Pink Saturday], the Dutch version of so called Gay Pride parades.[1264]

6th June

In an interview with Religion News Service, Fr. James Martin SJ, Pope Francis' appointee to the Secretariat for Communications, criticised the *Catechism of the Catholic Church*'s reiteration of the Church's doctrine on homosexuality:

> I'm no theologian, but I would say that some of the language used in the catechism on that topic needs to be updated, given what we know now about homosexuality. Earlier, for example, the catechism says that the homosexual orientation is itself 'objectively disordered.' But, as I say in the book, saying that one of the deepest parts of a person — the part that gives and receives love — is disordered is needlessly hurtful. A few weeks ago, I met an Italian theologian who suggested the phrase 'differently ordered' might convey that idea more pastorally.[1265]

Archbishop Paglia defended the homoerotic mural he commissioned for his cathedral, painted by the homosexual artist Ricardo Cinalli and featuring an image of our Lord Jesus Christ modelled on a local male hairdresser. The mural depicts Jesus pulling in nets filled with naked and semi-nude homosexuals, transsexuals, prostitutes, and drug dealers in depraved interactions. Catholic art critics have called the mural 'blasphemous,' 'disgusting,' and even 'demonic'. Archbishop Paglia defended it saying:

> One great theme of my preaching in such circumstances was reliance on God's mercy to deliver us from eternal punishment, and in that context I was presented with a project for a mural that would show the risen Christ gathering into nets all of wounded and

---

[1262]Bourne, L [2017] *Pope's 'new' theology 'does not first demand a change of life': bishop* [Online] Available at: www.lifesitenews.com [Accessed on: 14 October 2022]

[1263]Baklinski, P [2017] *Malta's bishops denounce newspaper ad opposing gay 'marriage'* [Online] Available at: www.lifesitenews.com [Accessed on: 14 October 2022]

[1264]Smits, J [2017] *Catholic cathedral welcomes 'Pink Saturday' gay pride gathering with bishop's blessing* [Online] Available at: www.lifesitenews.com [Accessed on: 14 October 2022]

[1265]Merritt, J [2017] *This Vatican adviser is moving Catholics toward LGBT inclusion* [Online] Available at: religionnews.com [Accessed on: 14 October 2022]

suffering humanity and, as their Redeemer, bringing them with him as he ascended to Heaven and the Father.[1266]

9th June

Cardinal Blase Cupich, Pope Francis appointee, wrote a forward to a book approving Holy Communion to adulterers. The forward is contained in the English translation of Cardinal Coccopalmerio's book, *A Commentary on Chapter Eight of Amoris Laetitia*. In light of the Church's constant prohibition of allowing adulterers to receive the sacraments, Cardinal Cupich bizarrely wrote, that the book:

> fully complies with traditional Church teaching on marriage but is also in conformity with accepted standards of a pastoral approach that is positive and constructive.[1267]

11th June

To celebrate the Solemnity of the Most Holy Trinity, Bishop Angel José Macin of the Diocese of Reconquista, Argentina — appointed by Pope Francis in 2013 — celebrated a special Mass for divorced and civilly 'remarried' couples. During the Mass the thirty plus couples received Holy Communion while relatives and friends took photographs. Bishop Macin claimed that *Amoris Laetitia* allowed such couples to receive Holy Communion.[1268]

20th June

Libero Milone resigned from his post as the Vatican's first Auditor General after two years in the role. It later emerged that Libero Milone — a former partner with Deloitte, a multinational auditing and consultancy firm — was forced to resign by the head of the Gendarmerie [Vatican police]. Libero Milone told journalists:

> I was threatened with arrest. The head of the Gendarmerie (Vatican police) intimidated me to force me to sign a resignation letter that they had already prepared weeks in advance.

A source told the National Catholic Register that the reason why Milone was removed was because he 'had apparently stumbled upon certain and clear abuses of funds.' Cardinal Giovanni Angelo Becciù, the former Vatican's undersecretary of state and prefect of the Congregation for the Causes of Saints, made serious allegations against Milone:

> He went against all the rules and was spying on the private lives of his superiors and staff, including me. If he had not agreed to resign, we would have prosecuted him.

An inquiry conducted by the Vatican promoter of justice came to the conclusion that no evidence existed to support these accusations.[1269]

22nd June

Pope Francis conferred on Liliane Ploumen, a Dutch politician and international abortion activist, a pontifical order, receiving her into the Pontifical Equestrian Order of St. Gregory, usually bestowed for 'meritorious service to the Church.' In response to President Trump cutting US funding of international abortions in January 2017, Liliane Ploumen set up the abortion group, *She Decides*, that raised $200 million to make up the

---

[1266]Baklinski, P [2017] *Vatican archbishop defends cathedral's pornographic, homoerotic mural as 'evangelizing' tool* [Online] Available at: www.lifesitenews.com [Accessed on: 14 October 2022]

[1267]Baklinski, P [2017] *U.S. cardinal writes foreward to new book approving Communion for adulterers* [Online] Available at: www.lifesitenews.com [Accessed on: 14 October 2022]

[1268]Cummings McLean, D [2017] *Argentinian bishop offers special Mass to give Communion to adulterers* [Online] Available at: www.lifesitenews.com [Accessed on: 14 October 2022]

[1269]Pentin, E [2017] *Vatican Withdraws Charges Against Former Auditor General* [Online] Available at: www.ncregister.com [Accessed on: 14 October 2022]

shortfall in funds for the killing of babies. Three months later Pope Francis gave her one of the Holy See's highest honours for laity. In January 2018 Liliane Ploumen told a Dutch radio show that she believed the Vatican was aware of her work for *She Decides* and that she saw this as confirmation of her work. She said: '…the Vatican probably knows that I started *She Decides* and they gave me this prize – very special.' The interviewer asked, 'Do you see it as confirmation of what you are doing for girls and women, for abortion?' To which she replied, 'Yes, that, and also, the last couple of years I invested a lot of time in establishing contacts with the Vatican.'[1270] In response, Paloma García Ovejero, deputy spokesperson of the Holy See Press Office, said that the honour awarded to Lilianne Ploumen was part of an exchange of honours between delegations after she took part in an official state visit of the Dutch monarchs. He said: 'Therefore, it is not in the slightest a placet [an expression of assent] to the politics in favour of abortion and of birth control that Mrs Ploumen promotes.'[1271]

2nd July

Pope Francis removed Cardinal Gerhard Müller from his position as prefect of the Congregation for the Doctrine of the Faith, breaking the precedent that holders of this office held it until retirement at 75, if not longer. Cardinal Müller opposed liberal interpretations of *Amoris Laetitia* favoured by Pope Francis. Cardinal Müller complained that Pope Francis dismissed him in a one-minute conversation, without giving a reason for his termination, saying 'This style [sic] I cannot accept. The Church's social teaching should be applied.'[1272] *America Magazine*, edited by pro-homosexual Fr. James Martin SJ, reported that cardinals had complained to Pope Francis about Cardinal Gerhard Müller:

> …a number of cardinals had asked Francis to remove Cardinal Müller from that post because he had on a number of occasions publicly disagreed with or distanced himself from the pope's positions, and they felt this was undermining the papal office and Magisterium.[1273]

6th July

The news broke in the English press that two months previously a high-ranking Vatican monsignor had been arrested for possession of illegal drugs by Vatican police after they caught him hosting a homosexual orgy in an apartment in the Palazzo del Sant'Ufficio. This Vatican property also houses the offices of the Congregation for the Doctrine of the Faith. Monsignor Luigi Capozzi was secretary to Cardinal Francesco Coccopalmerio, prefect of the Pontifical Council for the Interpretation of Legal Texts, one of Pope Francis' closest collaborators. Capozzi was hospitalised for detoxification at the Pius XI clinic in Rome, before undertaking a spiritual retreat at a convent in Italy. Cardinal Coccopalmerio had recommended Monsignor Capozzi to Pope Francis as a future bishop. A Vatican source later informed *LifeSiteNews* that Pope Francis had allocated the apartment to Monsignor Capozzi, 'in spite of the fact that someone had warned the Pope about Capozzi's grave problems.'[1274] A highly placed Vatican source

[1270]Hichborn, M [2017] *Dutch abortion activist: Pope Francis honoring me is a 'confirmation' of my abortion work* [Online] Available at: www.lifesitenews.com [Accessed on: 14 October 2022]
[1271]Pentin, E [2017] *Vatican: Papal Honor for Pro-Abortion Politician Not a Sign of Support* [Online] Available at: www.ncregister.com [Accessed on: 14 October 2022]
[1272]Western, JH [2017] *Former Vatican doctrine chief criticizes how Pope dismissed him: 'I cannot accept' his style* [Online] Available at: www.lifesitenews.com [Accessed on: 14 October 2022]
[1273]O'Collins, G [2017] *Update: Vatican announces Pope Francis has not reconfirmed Muller as head of the CDF* [Online] Available at: www.americamagazine.org [Accessed on: 14 October 2022]
[1274]Freitag, J [2017] *Vatican Monsignor Busted in Sex Sting Protected by Powerful Clergy* [Online] Available at: www.churchmilitant.com; Hickson, M [2017] *Vatican Source: Pope dismissed Cdl. Müller for following Church rules on abuse cases* [Online] Available at: www.lifesitenews.com [Accessed on: 15 October 2022]

also informed *LifeSiteNews* that Cardinal Coccopalmerio was 'presiding' over the cocaine-fuelled homosexual orgy 'when the Vatican Gendarmes broke in, and that they instructed him to absent himself before they started making arrests.' The source also said that Pope Francis knew of Cardinal Coccopalmerio's presence at the homosexual orgy.[1275]

7th July

Marco Tosatti, a journalist specialising in reporting on the Vatican, revealed that Pope Francis interrupted Cardinal Gerhard Müller's celebration of the Mass to order him to stop investigating one of his friends. Marco Tosatti gave an account of the event that occurred in 2013:

> The cardinal was celebrating Mass in the church attached to the congregation palace, for a group of German students and scholars. His secretary joined him at the altar: 'The pope wants to speak to you.' 'Did you tell him I am celebrating Mass?' asked Müller. 'Yes,' said the secretary, 'but he says he does not mind — he wants to talk to you all the same.' The cardinal went to the sacristy. The pope, in a very bad mood, gave him some orders about a dossier concerning one of his friends, a cardinal. (This is a very delicate matter. I have sought an explanation of this incident from the official channels. Until the explanation comes, if it ever comes, I cannot give further details.) Obviously, Müller was flabbergasted.[1276]

It later emerged that Pope Francis stopped Cardinal Müller investigating allegations of sex abuse against Cardinal Cormac Murphy-O'Connor. Murphy-O'Connor had played a role in the election of Jorge Bergoglio to the papacy.[1277]

Eugenio Scalfari published an account of his eighth engagement with Pope Francis in his newspaper *La Repubblica*. He made the allegation that Pope Francis believed that the Son of God abandoned his divinity at the Incarnation and was only a man until the Resurrection when he became God again. Scalfari wrote 'We have said these things to each other many times and it is the reason that made the friendship between the Head of the Church and an unbeliever'. Scalfari went on to allege that in previous conversations Pope Francis and he agreed that in a few millennium the human race would become extinct, at which point:

> the souls who now enjoy the bliss of contemplating God but remain distinct from him will merge with him. At this point the distance between transcendent and immanent will no longer exist.[1278]

10th July

Pope Francis sent his congratulations and apostolic blessing to two homosexual men on the occasion of the baptism of their three adopted children.[1279]

14th July

Cardinal Zen, Archbishop Emeritus of Hong Kong, denounced a new Vatican agreement with the Chinese atheistic Communist government:

> On the surface the authority of the Pope is safe because they say the Pope has the last word. But the whole thing is fake. They are giving decisive power to the government

[1275]Hickson, M & Western, JH [2017] *Source: Vatican cardinal was at drug-fueled homosexual party, and Pope knows it* [Online] Available at: www.lifesitenews.com [Accessed on: 15 October 2022]

[1276]Tosatti, M [2017] *The Good Soldier* [Online] Available at: www.firstthings.com [Accessed on: 15 October 2022]

[1277]Hickson, M [2017] *Source: Pope blocked investigation of abuse allegations against cardinal who helped elect him* [Online] Available at: www.lifesitenews.com [Accessed on: 15 October 2022]

[1278]Scalfari, E [2017] *Scalfari intervista Francesco: 'Il mio grido al G20 sui migranti'* [Online] Available at: www.repubblica.it [Accessed on: 17 September 2022]

[1279]DeBernardo, F [2017] *Pope Congratulates, Blesses Gay Couple on the Baptism of Their Adopted Children* [Online] Available at: www.newwaysministry.org [Accessed on: 15 October 2022]

... how can the initiative of choosing bishops be given to an atheistic government? Incredible. Incredible.[1280]

In an interview with the German newspaper *Augsburger Allgemeine* Cardinal Marx of Munich said he was not concerned about Germany's legalisation of called 'gay marriages' in 30th June 2017. He said: 'The Christian position is one thing. It's another thing to ask if I can make all the Christian moral concepts (state) laws.'[1281]

25h July

The Italian newspaper *Il Foglio*, published an interview with Cardinal Gerhard Müller, following his removal as prefect for the Congregation for the Faith. When asked about *Amoris Laetitia*, he answered:

> I think that the words of Jesus Christ must always be the foundation of the Church's doctrine. And nobody — until yesterday — could say that this was not true. It is clear: we have the irreversible revelation of Christ. And the Church has been entrusted with the *depositum fidei*, i.e. the entire content of revealed truth. The Magisterium does not have the authority to correct Jesus Christ. It is He, if anyone, Who corrects us. And we are obliged to obey Him; we must be faithful to the doctrine of the apostles, clearly developed in the spirit of the Church.[1282]

30th July

Pro-homosexual Bishop Antônio Carlos Cruz Santos of Caicó, appointed by Pope Francis in 2014, gave a homily in which he said that homosexuality was a 'gift from God'. He said:

> ...when you look at homosexuality, you cannot say it's an option. If it is not a choice, if it is not a disease, in the perspective of faith it can only be a gift. A gift from God. It's given by God. But perhaps our prejudices do not get the gift of God.[1283]

11th August

A group of clergy and lay scholars from around the world presented Pope Francis with a formal filial correction, accusing him of propagating heresies, entitled *Correctio Filialis de Haeresibus Propagatis*, meaning 'A Filial Correction Concerning the Propagation of Heresies'. It stated 'that the pope has, by his apostolic exhortation *Amoris Laetitia*, and by other, related, words, deeds and omissions, effectively upheld 7 heretical positions about marriage, the moral life, and the reception of the sacraments, and has caused these heretical opinions to spread in the Catholic Church.' In response to Pope Francis failing to respond to the filial correction, it was published with the additional support of other clergy and lay scholars.[1284]

13th August

The *Times of Malta* published Bishop Grech of Gozo's pastoral letter in which he attacked critics of his guidelines allowing adulterers to receive Holy Communion. Bishop Grech was later promoted by Pope Francis when he appointed him Secretary General of the Synod of Bishops and elevated him to the Sacred College of Cardinals. He said:

[1280]Western, JH [2017] *Cardinal Zen: Pope Francis' Vatican is backing a 'fake' church in China* [Online] Available at: www.lifesitenews.com [Accessed on: 15 October 2022]

[1281]*Same-sex marriage not a major concern for Church, says German Cardinal Marx* [2017] [Online] Available at: www.catholicculture.org [Accessed on: 15 October 2022]

[1282]Matzuzzi, M [2017] *Extensive Interview with Cardinal Müller: 'I'm loyal to the Pope, not an adulator'* [Online] Available at: rorate-caeli.blogspot.com [Accessed on: 15 October 2022]

[1283]San Martín, I [2019] *Bishop calls homosexuality 'gift from God,' seeks to end 'prejudices that kill'* [Online] Available at: cruxnow.com [Accessed on: 15 October 2022]

[1284]Pentin, E [2017] *Clergy and Lay Scholars Issue Filial Correction of Pope Francis* [Online] Available at: www.ncregister.com [Accessed on 12 October 2022]; *Correctio filialis de haeresibus propagatis'* [2017] Available at: www.correctiofilialis.org [Accessed on: 12 October 2022]

Unfortunately, there exist prophets of doom, who in their religious zeal, are more prone to focus on the defect rather than the much good there is in man; they get stuck in considering the mistake rather than appreciating the efforts, however small but sincere, that a person tries to make to rise up on his feet; they are more interested in defending the letter of the law than the person. Attitudes of this type annihilate all hope in people and make the Church what it is not, and what it should never be.[1285]

18th August

Fr. James Martin SJ, appointed by Pope Francis a consultor to the Vatican's Secretariat for Communications, responded to receiving an award from a pro-homosexual group that God made LGBTQ people who they are. Martin said:

I hope that the award serves as another reminder that all LGBTQ people are beloved children of God, that God made them who they are, and that they have as much place in our churches as anyone else.[1286]

21st August

The Italian magazine *Tempi* published an interview with the newly elected Superior General of the Jesuits, Fr. Arturo Sosa, SJ in which he denied the objective existence of the devil. Fr. Sosa said that Satan was a symbol of human evil:

[The devil] exists as the personification of evil in different structures, but not in persons, because he is not a person, he is a way of acting evil. He is not a person like a human person. It is a way of evil to be present in human life. Good and evil are in a permanent war in the human conscience and we have ways to point them out. We recognize God as good, fully good. Symbols are part of reality, and the devil exists as a symbolic reality, not as a personal reality.[1287]

24th August

Pope Francis invoked magisterial authority regarding the post-Vatican II liturgical innovations when delivering an address to the 68th Italian National Liturgical Week in Italy. The pontiff said: 'After this magisterium, after this long journey, We can affirm with certainty and with magisterial authority that the liturgical reform is irreversible.'[1288]

30th August

The National Conference of Brazilian Bishops issued guidelines regarding divorced and invalidly 'remarried' couples that proposed 'excuses' for adulterous sexual relations. Claiming the authority of Pope Francis' *Amoris Laetitia* the Brazilian Bishops stated:

There are extreme cases in which the existence of excuses for not interrupting conjugal interactions, for example, the existence of children and of certain moral circumstances, can reduce or even eliminate the moral responsibility and imputability of illicit acts.[1289]

31st August

Archbishop Javier Martínez Fernández issued a statement announcing that he had dismissed the eminent Catholic philosopher Dr. Josef Seifert from his post at the

---

[1285]Sansone, K [2017] *Gozo Bishop warns against 'cheap hope' and 'prophets of doom'* [Online] Available at: timesofmalta.com [Accessed on: 15 October 2022]

[1286]*Vatican advisor scraps catholic teaching says God made gays who they are* [2017] [Online] Available at: www.lifesitenews.com [Accessed on: 15 October 2022]

[1287]*Jesuit superior general: Satan is a 'symbolic reality'* [2017] [Online] Available at: www. catholicnewsagency.com [Accessed on: 15 October 2022]

[1288]Pope Francis [2017] *Address to participants in the 68th National Liturgical Week in Italy* [Online] Available at: www.vatican.va [Accessed on: 15 October 2022]

[1289]Cullinan Hoffman, M [2017] *Brazilian bishops claim that sex outside of marriage can sometimes be justified* [Online] Available at: www.lifesitenews.com; Domingues, F [2017] *On Amoris guidelines, Brazil bishops leave sacraments open for some divorced and remarried* [Online] Available at: cruxnow. com [Accessed on: 15 October 2022]

International Academy of Philosophy in Granada. Archbishop Fernández removed Professor Seifert for publishing criticism of Pope Francis' *Amoris Laetitia* in which he accused it of containing 'a moral theological atomic bomb that threatens to tear down the whole moral edifice of the Ten Commandments and of Catholic moral teaching.' Archbishop Fernández wrote that Dr. Seifert's article:

> damages the communion of the Church, confuses the faith of the faithful, and sows distrust in the successor of Peter, which, in the end, does not serve the truth of faith, but, rather, the interests of the world.[1290]

3rd September

Pope Francis issued the Motu Proprio *Magnum Principium* to change the rules for liturgical translation into vernacular languages in the Roman Rite. By so doing, Pope Francis transferred responsibility for assessing a vernacular translation's fidelity to the Latin away from the Congregation for Divine Worship and the Discipline of the Sacraments to the national bishops' conferences. This abrogated key principles of Pope St. John Paul II's Motu Proprio *Liturgiam Authenticam* that required that vernacular translations follow the Latin accurately instead of being paraphrases. After the promulgation of *Magnum Principium* Cardinal Sarah, the prefect of the Congregation for Divine Worship, insisted that *Liturgiam Authenticam* remained the basis for new translations proposed by bishops' conferences. However, on 15th October Pope Francis publicly rebuked Cardinal Sarah for attempting to circumvent his decentralisation to Bishops' Conferences.[1291] Cardinal Gerhard Müller, the former prefect of the CDF, warned that the unity of the Church would be destroyed if bishops' conferences, not the Vatican, had the final word over translations of liturgical texts.[1292]

10th September

The divorced and civilly 'remarried' spouse of Colombian president Juan Manuel Santos claimed that Pope Francis blessed her union with Santos during his state visit to Colombia, and published a video of the event.[1293]

13th September

Pro-homosexual Bishop Vincent Long Van Nguyen of Parramatta, Australia, — appointed by Pope Francis in 2016 — issued a pastoral letter about the referendum of legalising so called 'gay marriage'. In the letter he appeared to suggest that Catholics could vote for gay marriage:

> It should not be a matter of a simple answer Yes or No to the postal survey... should also be an opportunity for us to listen to what the Spirit is saying through the signs of the times... It is important to remember from the very outset that the postal survey is about whether or not Australians want the legal definition of civil marriage changed to include same-sex couples. It is not a referendum on sacramental marriage as understood by the Catholic Church.[1294]

[1290]Hickson, M [2017] *Spanish Archbishop Fires Professor Seifert for Amoris Laetitia Critique* [Online] Available at: onepeterfive.com [Accessed on: 15 October 2022]

[1291]Skojec, S [2017] *Cardinal Sarah Publicly Refuted by Pope Francis on Liturgy Changes* [Online] Available at: onepeterfive.com [Accessed on: 15 October 2022]

[1292]Baklinski, P [2017] *Giving bishops final word on Mass translations would 'destroy' Church unity: Cardinal Muller* [Online] Available at: www.lifesitenews.com [Accessed on: 15 October 2022]

[1293]Cullinan Hoffman, M [2017] *Pope Blessed Our Union, Claims Wife of Divorced and Remarried Colombian President* [Online] Available at: www.lifesitenews.com [Accessed on: 15 October 2022]

[1294]Baklinski, P [2017] *Did this bishop just tell Catholics they could vote for gay 'marriage'?* [Online] Available at: www.lifesitenews.com; San Martín, I [2017] *Australian bishop on same-sex marriage: Listen to 'signs of the times'* [Online] Available at: cruxnow.com [Accessed on: 15 October 2022]

14th September

Pope Francis told a group of newly ordained bishops that when it came to dealing with moral issues not to be 'imprisoned by nostalgia for being able to give just one answer to apply in all cases.' He also said: 'Discernment can't be reduced to repeating formulas such as 'high clouds send little rain' to a concrete person, who's often immersed in a reality that can't be reduced to black and white.'[1295]

19th September

Pope Francis issued a motu proprio announcing his replacement of the renowned John Paul II Institute for Studies on Marriage and the Family, established by Pope John Paul II in 1981, with the John Paul II Pontifical Theological Institute for Marriage and Family Sciences. The purpose of the new body was to promote *Amoris Laetitia*.[1296] The website of German Catholic bishops' conference celebrated the Pope's dissolution of the John Paul II Institute criticising it as 'a stronghold of resistance against Francis' agenda of mercy.'[1297]

25th September

Cardinal Marc Ouellet, Prefect of the Congregation for Bishops, reversed his position of upholding the Church perennial prohibition of adulterers receiving Holy Communion. In his 2015 book *Mystery and Sacrament of Love*, Cardinal Ouellet wrote:

> Despite pressure from various cultures and theological opinions, the Holy See does not permit Eucharistic communion to persons who have contracted a sacramental bond and then abandoned it to form another, non-sacramental bond.

But in 2017 he reversed his position in a talk to 80 bishops and eparchs attending the plenary of the Canadian Conference of Catholic Bishops in which he said regarding *Amoris Laetitia*:

> And all of this may open a door to receiving the help of the sacraments of penance and Eucharist in certain cases, as we read in the footnote [of *Amoris Laetitia*], not in such a way as to generalise or trivialise, but in a way that discerns carefully with a logic of pastoral mercy.[1298]

6th October

Fr. Antonio Spadaro SJ, confident of Pope Francis and editor of *La Civiltà Cattolica*, gave an address at a conference about implementing *Amoris Laetitia* at Boston College. Fr. Spadaro said:

> We must conclude that the Pope realises that one can no longer speak of an abstract category of persons and … [a] praxis of integration in a rule that is absolutely to be followed in every instance. Since the degree of responsibility is not equal in all cases, the consequences or effects of a rule need not necessarily always be the same. It is no longer possible to judge people on the basis of a norm that stands above all.[1299]

9th October

Archbishop Paglia, president of the newly reconstituted Pontifical Academy for Life, told a press conference that he was widening the remit of the Academy away from

[1295] *Pope calls new bishops to avoid 'nostalgia' for one-size-fits-all answers* [2017] [Online] Available at: cruxnow.com [Accessed on: 15 October 2022]

[1296] Lamb, C [2017] *Pope re-founds John Paul II institute on marriage and family with new focus on contemporary realities* [Online] Available at: www.thetablet.co.uk [Accessed on: 15 October 2022]

[1297] Hickson, M [2017] *German Bishops' Website Comments on the New John Paul II Institute* [Online] Available at: onepeterfive.com [Accessed on: 15 October 2022]

[1298] Gyapong, D [2017] *Cardinal Ouellet denounces 'alarmist' interpretations of 'Amoris Laetitia'* [Online] Available at: www.americamagazine.org [Accessed on: 15 October 2022]

[1299] Ascik, T [2017] *Church teaching and sexuality: What 'no longer' holds?* [Online] Available at: www.catholicworldreport.com [Accessed on: 15 October 2022]

Pope St. John Paul II's focus on medical and bioethical matters such as abortion and IVF to include 'the environment, immigration, and arms control.'[1300]

11th October

During his speech to the Pontifical Council for the Promotion of the New Evangelization Pope Francis said that the death penalty was contrary to the Gospel and indicated that he wanted to change the *Catechism of the Catholic Church* on this matter. He said:

> I would like now to bring up a subject that ought to find in the *Catechism of the Catholic Church* a more adequate and coherent treatment in the light of these expressed aims. I am speaking of the death penalty. This issue cannot be reduced to a mere résumé of traditional teaching without taking into account not only the doctrine as it has developed in the teaching of recent Popes, but also the change in the awareness of the Christian people which rejects an attitude of complacency before a punishment deeply injurious of human dignity. It must be clearly stated that the death penalty is an inhumane measure that, regardless of how it is carried out, abases human dignity. It is per se contrary to the Gospel, because it entails the wilful suppression of a human life that never ceases to be sacred in the eyes of its Creator and of which – ultimately – only God is the true judge and guarantor. [...] Here we are not in any way contradicting past teaching, for the defence of the dignity of human life from the first moment of conception to natural death has been taught by the Church consistently and authoritatively.[1301]

Pro-homosexual Fr. James Martin SJ's publisher released the names of cardinals and bishops who had publicly endorsed his book promoting LGBT in the Church. These included the three US bishops elevated to the Sacred College of Cardinals by Pope Francis: Cardinal Cupich, Cardinal Farrell and Cardinal Tobin. They also included the following appointed by Pope Francis — Archbishop John Wester of Santa Fe, Bishop John Stowe of Lexington and Bishop McElroy of San Diego.[1302]

15th October

Cardinal Barbarin, Archbishop of Lyons in France and Primate of the Gauls, held a service for Catholics with broken marriages. During the service he encouraged divorced and civilly 'remarried' Catholics to receive Holy Communion:

> When someone is living in that situation and decides in conscience to go and receive communion, no one judges them. It is not to be lax to say that it means welcoming and loving each person as they are, at the point they have reached, it means accompanying them personally in their spiritual combat, and above all, I hope, to pray for them 'in secret.[1303]

17th October

A program to prepare families for the 2018 World Meeting of Families in Ireland was released with the authority of Archbishop Diarmuid Martin of Dublin. The six part program *'Amoris: Let's talk Family! Let's be Family!'* contained explicit promotion of homosexual relationships as a form of family, including a photograph of two lesbians embracing with the caption:

[1300]Gallagher, J [2017] *Pro-Life Redefined at the Vatican* [Online] Available at: www.crisismagazine.com [Accessed on: 15 October 2022]

[1301]Pope Francis [2017] *Address to participants in the meeting promoted by the Pontifical Council for Promoting the New Evangelization* [Online] Available at: www.vatican.va [Accessed on: 15 October 2022]

[1302]*Top Catholic Church Officials Provide New Support for Father James Martin's Latest Book Building a Bridge* [2017] [Online] Available at: d1swt8v074cpkh.cloudfront.net [Accessed on: 15 October 2022]

[1303]Smits, J [2017] *Ban on Communion for divorced and remarried is 'absurd and inhuman': Cardinal* [Online] Available at: www.lifesitenews.com; Tosseri, B [2017] *Listening to Catholic divorced and remarried couples* [Online] Available at: /international.la-croix.com [Accessed on: 15 October 2022]

> While the Church upholds the ideal of marriage as a permanent commitment between a man and a woman, other unions exist which provide mutual support to the couple. Pope Francis encourages us never to exclude but to accompany these couples also, with love, care and support.[1304]

27th October

Cardinal Cupich delivered an address to the US Catholic Theological Union in which he said that in order to be able to 'discern' like Pope Francis Catholics must be prepared to 'give up cherished beliefs':

> It is our job to take up that discernment. It takes time. It involves discipline. Most importantly it requires that we be prepared to let go of cherished beliefs and long-held biases. It is this willingness of Francis to let go of the unnecessary and explore unchartered waters that gives him internal freedom, while unsettling some.[1305]

1st November

The United States Conference of Catholic Bishops dismissed Fr. Thomas Weinandy OFM, Cap., as a consultant to the USCCB Committee on Doctrine. The reason for his dismissal was his publication of a letter he'd sent privately to Pope Francis which the pontiff had failed to answer. Father Weinandy's letter said Pope Francis' papacy was marked by 'chronic confusion' and that the faithful were losing confidence in him because he was appointing bishops who not only 'hold views counter to Christian belief but who support and even defend them.' He also wrote:

> Your critics have been accused, in your own words, of making doctrine an ideology. But it is precisely Christian doctrine – including the fine distinctions made with regard to central beliefs like the Trinitarian nature of God; the nature and purpose of the Church; the Incarnation; the Redemption; and the sacraments – that frees people from worldly ideologies and assures that they are actually preaching and teaching the authentic, life-giving Gospel. Those who devalue the doctrines of the Church separate themselves from Jesus, the author of truth.

In response to Fr. Weinandy's letter the US bishops publicly professed their 'strong unity with and loyalty to the Holy Father, Pope Francis.'[1306]

2nd-4th November

Bishop Sorondo's Pontifical Academy of Science held another conference that included population control experts, under the title *Health of People, Health of Planet and Our Responsibility: Climate Change, Air Pollution and Health*. Speakers included Sir Partha Dasgupta, who praised China's population control index and Jeffrey Sachs who promotes abortion as a population control measure. He co-hosted the Vatican's 2015 conference on climate change.[1307]

2nd November

The Italian newspaper *Il Messaggero* reported that Pope Francis had given the Brazilian bishops permission to discuss overturning the discipline of mandatory priestly celibacy among Latin-rite Catholics to make up for a shortage of priests. The pontiff's permission was given in response to a request from the head of the Episcopal Commission for

---

[1304]Baklinski, P [2017] *Bishops use Pope's teaching to push homosexuality at 2018 World Meeting of Families* [Online] Available at: www.lifesitenews.com [Accessed on: 17 October 2022]
[1305]Baklinski, P [2017] *Catholics must let go of 'cherished beliefs' to 'discern' like Pope Francis: U.S. Cardinal* [Online] Available at: www.lifesitenews.com [Accessed on: 15 October 2022]
[1306]Flynn, JD [2017] *Theologian resigns from USCCB committee after publishing letter to Pope Francis* [Online] Available at: www.boston-catholic-journal.com [Accessed on: 15 October 2022]
[1307]*Health of People, Health of. Planet and Our Responsibility: Climate Change, Air Pollution and Health* [2017] [Online] Available at: www.pas.va [Accessed on: 15 October 2022]

the Amazon, Cardinal Claudio Hummes, former Prefect for the Congregation for the Clergy.[1308]

6th November

Pro-homosexual Cardinal Blase Cupich, appointed by Pope Francis, said that LGBT activist Fr. James Martin SJ, was the foremost evangeliser of young people. Giving an address at the University of Chicago Institute of Politics Cardinal Cupich said about Fr. James Martin SJ:

> He really is one of the, if not the foremost evangeliser in the Church today, especially for young people. I appreciate what he's doing. I think he has a wonderful message and the way that he brings that message to people.[1309]

13th November

Cardinal John Dew of Wellington, New Zealand, broke with the perennial discipline of the Church by allowing lay people to proclaim the Gospel at the celebration of the Mass. Elevated to the Sacred College of Cardinals by Pope Francis in 2015, Archbishop John Drew said his innovation was inspired by Pope Francis.[1310]

16th November

The Vatican's official newspaper *L'Osservatore Romano* published an article claiming that Pope Francis' emphasis in *Amoris Laetitia* on mercy over law allows a so called 'second marriage' after a first valid marriage not to be viewed as the scandalously public habitual sin of adultery. Father Gerald Bednar, Vice Rector and Professor of Systematic Theology at Saint Mary Seminary in the U.S. Diocese of Cleveland wrote that:

> The issue is not whether divorce is permissible. Clearly it is not. The issue is whether a second marriage must be characterised continuously as adultery. That precise question has not been addressed before, not even in *Familiaris Consortio*....[Pope Francis] proposes that in appropriate cases, partners already in a second marriage may enter a period of discernment, accompanied by an experienced priest, so they can reflect on relevant issues. After a suitable period of time, they may celebrate a sacramental confession in which they accept an appropriate penance and receive absolution. Communion may follow that discernment and penance (*AL* 305).

Of course, this is totally contrary to our Lord teaching on divorce as adultery and on its traditional hermeneutic. (cf. Mark 10:11).[1311]

16th-17th November

The Vatican's Pontifical Academy for Life co-hosted a conference on End-of-Life Questions with the World Medical Association and German Medical Association. Speakers included Dr. Yvonne Gilli, president of the board of Switzerland's abortion provider Planned Parenthood affiliate, and the president of the pro-euthanasia Royal Dutch Medical Association.[1312]

17th November

Cardinal Nichols of Westminster, elevated to the Sacred College of Cardinals by Pope Francis, welcomed the militant LGBT group Quest back into the Archdiocese of

---

[1308]Philips, J [2017] *Pope raises prospect of married men becoming priests* [Online] Available at: www.telegraph.co.uk [Accessed: 15 October 2022]

[1309]Baklinski, P [2017] *Francis-appointed cardinal praises pro-LGBT priest as 'foremost evangelizer' of youth* [Online] Available at: www.lifesitenews.com [Accessed on: 15 October 2022]

[1310]Bourne, L [2017] *Cardinal says Pope Francis inspired him to get 'creative' in liturgy, lets lay people read Gospel* [Online] Available at: www.lifesitenews.com [Accessed on: 15 October 2022]

[1311]Baklinski, P [2017] *Mercy for Pope means 'second marriage' isn't adultery: priest in Vatican newspaper* [Online] Available at: www.lifesitenews.com [Accessed on: 15 October 2022]

[1312]Cullinan Hoffman, M [2017] *Swiss Planned Parenthood president invited to speak at Vatican* [Online] Available at: www.lifesitenews.com [Accessed on: 15 October 2022]

Westminster that had been banned by one of his predecessors for contravening doctrine on homosexuality.[1313]

23rd November

The Vatican's Philatelic and Numismatic Office released a stamp marking the 500th anniversary of the Protestant schism. The stamp featured the heresiarchs Martin Luther and Philip Melanchthon.[1314]

29th November

Pope Francis addressed the Supreme Sangha Council of Buddhist Monks in Yangon during his Apostolic Journey to Myanmar. Even though the founder of a false religion, Pope Francis recommended the Buddha as a spiritual guide: 'To realise that we cannot be isolated from one another. If we are to be united, as is our purpose, we need to surmount all forms of misunderstanding, intolerance, prejudice and hatred. How can we do this? The words of the Buddha offer each of us a guide'.[1315]

2nd December

Cardinal Pietro Parolin, the Secretary of State — on the orders of Pope Francis — published in the *Acta Apostolicae Sedis* (AAS) the pontiff's letter praising the Argentinian bishops implementation of *Amoris Laetitia* to allow adulterers to receive Holy Communion with their guidelines. By putting two capitalised Latin words in bold type — EPISTULA APOSTOLICA — Pope Francis deliberately sought to raise the authority of his corruption of doctrine to the level of magisterial teaching as 'Magisterium authenticum'.[1316]

6th December

Agencia Ecclesia, the official news service of the Portuguese bishops, published a statement from Cardinal Manuel Clemente, the Cardinal Patriarch of Lisbon. Cardinal Clemente encouraged priests to allow divorced and 'remarried' committing adultery to receive Holy Communion on a case-by-case basis after a period of discernment.[1317]

7th December

During an interview on the Italian bishops' television channel, TV2000, Pope Francis claimed that the clause 'lead us not into temptation' of the Lord's Prayer was not a good translation and should be changed to his preferred version, 'do not let us fall into temptation'. He said:

> The French have changed the text with a translation that says 'do not let me fall into temptation.' I am the one who falls, but it isn't He who throws me into temptation and then looks on to see how I fell. A father does not do this; a father helps us get up immediately. The one who leads you into temptation is Satan, that's Satan's role.[1318]

[1313]Pelletier, R [2017] *UK Cardinal Reinstates Dissenting LGBT Group* [Online] Available at: www.churchmilitant.com; Baklinski, P [2017] Cardinal welcomes previously banned pro-LGBT group back to archdiocese [Accessed on: 15 October 2022]
[1314]*Vatican issues stamp featuring Martin Luther for Reformation anniversary* [2017] [Online] Available at: cruxnow.com [Accessed on: 15 October 2022]
[1315]*Pope addresses Sangha Council of Buddhist Monks: Full text* [2017] [Online] www.vaticannews.va [Accessed on: 15 October 2022]
[1316]Harrison, B [2017] *Authentic confusion over Pope Francis' 'authentic magisterium'* [Online] Available at: www.lifesitenews.com [Accessed on: 15 October 2022]
[1317]Cullinan Hoffman, M [2017] *Lead Portuguese cardinal: divorced and remarried couples can 'return to the sacramental life'* [Online] Available at: www.lifesitenews.com [Accessed on: 15 October 2022]
[1318]*Pope Francis suggests translation change to the 'Our Father'* [Online] Available at: www.americamagazine.org [Accessed on: 15 October 2022]

However, contrary to Pope Francis' idiosyncratic opinion, Dame Mary Beard, Regius Professor of Classics at the University of Cambridge, stated that the traditional version of the Our Father is 'as close as you can get to the earliest (Greek) version we have'.[1319]

Cardinal Kaspar, the architect of ending the Church's prohibition of adulterers receiving Holy Communion based on our Lord's teaching (Mark 10:11), responded to Pope Francis' publication of his letter on the Argentinian bishops' implementation of *Amoris Laetitia*. The German edition of Vatican Radio published his reaction:

> With the official publication of the letter from Pope Francis to the bishops of the Buenos Aires region, the painful dispute over the apostolic exhortation *Amoris Laetitia* is hopefully over.

Cardinal Kasper bizarrely claimed:

> it is not a novelty, but a renewal of an old tradition against neo-scholastic constrictions. As proven experts of the doctrine of Pope John Paul II have shown, there is no contradiction with the two predecessors of Pope Francis.

He went on to criticise the obligation to live by God's absolute commandments:

> But universally valid objective commandments (...) cannot be applied mechanically or by purely logical deduction to concrete, often complex and perplexing, situations. [This] has nothing to do with situational ethics that knows no universal commandments, it is not about exceptions to the commandment, but about the question of understood as situational conscience cardinal virtue of prudence.[1320]

12th December

The Vatican's controversial homoerotic nativity crèche was unveiled, donated by the ancient Abbey of Montevergine in the Campania. The Abbey of Montevergine houses a Marian image that has been blasphemously adopted as patroness by LGBT activists in Italy and is the annual destination of a gay pride pilgrimage. The creche included the prone figure of a naked man. In response to the controversy, Antonello Sannini, president of homosexual activist group Arcigay Naples, said:

> The presence of the Vatican Nativity Scene for us is a reason to be even happier this year. For the homosexual and transsexual community in Naples, it is an important symbol of inclusion and integration.[1321]

14th December

Fr. Maurizio Chiodi, newly appointed by Pope Francis as a member of the 'reformed' Pontifical Academy for Life, gave a lecture entitled 'Re-reading *Humanae Vitae* (1968) in light of *Amoris Laetitia* (2016)'. The lecture was part of the Pontifical Gregorian University's series of talks from October until May 2018 to mark the 50th anniversary of Pope Paul VI's promulgation of *Humanae Vitae*. According to philosopher Professor Josef Seifert's account of Fr. Maurizio Chiodi's lecture:

> Chiodi invokes Pope Francis' apostolic exhortation on the family, *Amoris Laetitia*, as a new model and paradigm for moral theology that eliminates the notion (solemnly and magisterially laid down in *Humanae Vitae, Familiaris Consortio*, and *Veritatis Splendor*) that contraception is an intrinsically evil human act that is wrong anywhere and at any time. Chiodi adds, in radical and direct contradiction to the teaching of the Magisterium of the Church in *Humanae Vitae*, that there are 'circumstances — I refer to Amoris Laetitia, Chapter 8 — that precisely for the sake of responsibility, require contraception.' When

[1319]Montagna, D [2017] *Acclaimed Cambridge professor critiques Pope Francis' approval of new 'Our Father'* [Online] Available at: www.lifesitenews.com [Accessed on: 15 October 2022]
[1320]*Cardinal Kasper: The controversy surrounding Amoris Laetitia has come to an end* [2017] [Online] Available at: www.catholicnewsagency.com [Accessed on: 15 October 2022]
[1321]Montagna, D [2017] *Vatican's 'sexually suggestive' nativity has troubling ties to Italy's LGBT activists* [Online] Available at: www.lifesitenews.com [Accessed on: 15 October 2022]

'natural methods are impossible or unfeasible, other forms of responsibility need to be found,' Fr. Chiodi argued.[1322]

21st December

The Italian newspaper *L'Espresso* reported that Pope Francis had been given a dossier in May 2017 that outlined evidence of a massive financial scandal of one of his closest advisors, Cardinal Óscar Andrés Rodríguez Maradiaga, the archbishop of Tegucigalpa, Honduras. Cardinal Maradiaga was also the chairman of the Pope's Council of Cardinal Advisers charged with reforming the Roman Curia. The evidence in the dossier was gathered from about fifty witnesses, including diocesan administrators, clergymen, the cardinal's secretary and chauffeur. There were also allegations that Cardinal Maradiaga funnelled money to an intimate male friend who lives with the auxiliary bishop Juan José Pineda in an apartment close to Cardinal Maradiaga's residence.[1323] *L'Espresso* later published Cardinal Maradiaga's denial of financial corruption.

Pope Francis delivered his Christmas message to the Curia in which he scathingly criticised those clergy he had dismissed from their position for obstructing his agenda to change the Church:

> Another danger is those who betray the trust put in them and profiteer from the Church's motherhood. I am speaking of persons carefully selected to give a greater vigour to the body and to the reform, but – failing to understand the lofty nature of their responsibility – let themselves be corrupted by ambition or vainglory. Then, when they are quietly sidelined, they wrongly declare themselves martyrs of the system, of a 'Pope kept in the dark', of the 'old guard'…, rather than reciting a mea culpa. Alongside these, there are others who are still working there, to whom all the time in the world is given to get back on the right track, in the hope that they find in the Church's patience an opportunity for conversion and not for personal advantage.[1324]

22nd December

The New York Times published an interview with Cardinal Joseph Tobin, appointed by Pope Francis, in which he proposed that the pontiff could elevate a woman to the Sacred College of Cardinals. Cardinal Joseph Tobin said: 'Maybe my theology isn't sophisticated enough, but I don't believe that there's a compelling theological reason why the pope couldn't name a woman cardinal.'[1325]

2018

11th January

Vatican News published an interview with Cardinal Parolin, Vatican's Secretary of State, in which he explained that Pope Francis was imposing a 'new paradigm' on the Church. He said:

> …ultimately *Amoris Laetitia* arose from a new paradigm that Pope Francis is carrying out with wisdom, prudence and even patience. A change in paradigm, inherent in the text itself, that is asked of us: this new spirit, this new approach! […] Probably the difficulties that have arisen and still exist in the Church are due, in addition to some aspects of the content, to this change in attitude that the Pope asks of us. The pope goes slow because he wants to be sure that the changes have a deep impact. The slow

[1322]Hickson, M [2017] *Professor Seifert Comments on Fr. Chiodi's 'Re-Reading of Humanae Vitae'* [Online] Available at: onepeterfive.com [Accessed on: 15 October 2022]

[1323]Niles, C [2017] *'Vice Pope' Investigated for Financial Mismanagement* [Online] Available at: www.churchmilitant.com [Accessed on: 15 October 2022]

[1324]Pope Francis [2017] *Address at Christmas greetings of the Roman Curia* [Online] Available at: www.vatican.va [Accessed on: 15 October 2022]

[1325]Kristof, N [2017] *Cardinal Tobin, am I a Christian?* [Online] Available at: www.nytimes.com [Accessed on: 15 October 2022]

pace is necessary to ensure the effectiveness of the changes. He knows there are those hoping that the next pope will turn everything back around. If you go slowly it's more difficult to turn things back… You have to realise that he is aiming at reform that is irreversible.[1326]

16th January

Pope Francis engaged in a conversation with 90 Jesuits in Santiago de Chile during his apostolic visit to South America. When asked about what resistance he has encountered during this pontificate, and how he is handling it the pontiff replied:

> …when I realise that there is real resistance, of course it displeases me. Some people tell me that resistance is normal when someone wants to make changes. The famous 'we've always done it this way' reigns everywhere, it is a great temptation that we have all faced. I cannot deny that there is resistance. I see it and I am aware of it. There is doctrinal resistance, which you all know better than I do. For the sake of mental health I do not read the websites of this so-called 'resistance.' I know who they are, I am familiar with the groups, but I do not read them, simply for my mental health. If there is something very serious, they inform me so that I know about it. You all know them … It is a displeasure, but we must move ahead. Historians say that it takes a century before a Council puts down roots. We are halfway there. When I perceive resistance, I try to dialogue, when dialogue is possible. But some resistance comes from people who believe they possess the true doctrine and accuse you of being a heretic. When I do not find spiritual goodness in these people, because of what they say or write, I simply pray for them. It pains me, but I do not dwell on this feeling for the sake of mental hygiene.[1327]

19th January

During his apostolic visit to Chile Pope Francis caused controversy by publicly accusing sex abuse survivors of slander against Bishop Barros for claiming he covered up the crimes of the notorious paedophile Fr. Fernando Karadima. The pontiff said:

> The day they bring me proof against Bishop Barros, I'll speak. There is not one shred of proof against him. It's all calumny. Is that clear?[1328]

However, *Associated Press* was later to publish claims that Pope Francis had been handed survivor testimony regarding the complicity of Bishop Barros in covering up child sex abuse. In 2015 the pontiff had been handed evidence by Cardinal O'Malley — the head of the Vatican's Commission for the Protection of Minors — implicating Barros. *Associated Press* stated:

> Pope Francis received a victim's letter in 2015 that graphically detailed how a priest sexually abused him and how other Chilean clergy ignored it, contradicting the pope's recent insistence that no victims had come forward to denounce the cover-up.[1329]

22nd January

The book *Tutti gli Uomini di Francesco* [All Francis's Men] was released in which Cardinal Beniamino Stella, prefect of the Congregation for Clergy, expressed support for married priests in the Latin rite. He wrote:

[1326]Cummings McLean, D [2018] *Vatican Cardinal: Amoris Laetitia arose from Pope's 'new paradigm' for Catholic Church* [Online] Available at: www.lifesitenews.com; Pentin, E [2018] *Cardinal Parolin: Amoris Laetitia Represents New Paradigm, Spirit and Approach* [Online] Available at: www.ncregister.com [Accessed on: 16 October 2022]
[1327]Montagna, D [2018] *Pope Francis: I avoid reading heresy accusations 'for the sake of my mental health'* [Online] Available at: www.lifesitenews.com [Accessed on: 16 October 2022]
[1328]Winfield, N [2018] *Pope shocks Chile by accusing sex abuse victims of slander* [Online] Available at: apnews.com [Accessed on: 16 October 2022]
[1329]Cullinan Hoffman, M [2018] *Pope Francis' claim he never heard from abuse victims regarding Chilean bishop is false, AP reports* [Online] Available at: www.lifesitenews.com [Accessed on: 16 October 2022]

...there is acute suffering because of a real 'sacramental emergency,' which the few priests present are not able to accommodate... Continuing to maintain their family and jobs and receiving a formation contextualised for their environment [married priests] could offer part-time service to the community they come from in order to guarantee the sacraments, especially by presiding at the Eucharistic celebration.[1330]

Asia News reported that the Vatican has asked legitimate bishops in China to step aside in favour of illegitimate ones of the Communist puppet Chinese Patriotic Catholic Association:

Last December, Mgr. Peter Zhuang Jianjian of Shantou (Guangdong) was forced to go to Beijing where 'a foreign prelate' from the Vatican asked him to leave his see to illicit bishop Joseph Huang Bingzhang. He had received the same request last October. Mgr Joseph Guo Xijin, ordinary bishop of Mindong, is expected to become the auxiliary or coadjutor of illicit Bishop Vincent Zhan Silu.[1331]

29th January

Cardinal Zen, Archbishop Emeritus of Hong Kong, addressed a letter to the media warning that the Vatican was 'selling out the Catholic Church in China [and] giving its blessing on the new...schismatic Church' created by the Communists. Cardinal Zen wrote:

Some say that all the efforts to reach an agreement is to avoid the ecclesial schism. How ridiculous! The schism is there, in the Independent Church! The Popes avoided using the word 'schism' because they knew that many in the official Catholic community were there not by their own free will, but under heavy pressure. The proposed 'unification' would force everybody into that community. The Vatican would be giving the blessing on the new strengthened schismatic Church, taking away the bad conscience from all those who are already willing renegades and those others who would readily join them.[1332]

3rd February

Cardinal Reinhard Marx, appointed by Pope Francis a member of his advisory council of cardinals, said during a German radio interview that he supported the blessing of homosexual 'unions'. He said that:

closer pastoral care must also apply to homosexuals... one must also encourage priests and pastoral workers to give people in concrete situations [of homosexual unions] encouragement. I do not really see any problems there.

Asked by the interviewer if he could 'imagine a way to bless homosexual couples in the Catholic Church,' Cardinal Marx responded 'yes', adding 'There are no general solutions. I don't think that's right, because this is pastoral care for individual cases, which I have to leave to the pastor . . . there are things that cannot be regulated.'[1333]

5th February

The *Global Times* newspaper, an organ of the Chinese Communist Party, praised Pope Francis for making 'substantive concessions to China on bishop appointments.' This

[1330]Chretien, C [2018] *Vatican cardinal: Church should consider married priests in some cases* [Online] Available at: www.lifesitenews.com; Tornielli, A [2018] Stella, *'The hypothesis of allowing older married men to become priests is being studied'* [Online] Available at: www.lastampa.it [Accessed on: 16 October 2022]

[1331]Lin, JB [2018] *The Vatican asks legitimate bishops to step aside in favour of illegitimate ones* [Online] Available at: www.asianews.it [Accessed on: 16 October 2022]

[1332]Zen Ze-kiun, J [2018] *Dear Friends in the Media* [Online] Available at: oldyosef.hkdavc.com [Accessed on: 16 October 2022]

[1333]Hickson, M [2018] *Cardinal Marx: I did not propose a blessing for gay couples, only 'spiritual encouragement'* [Online] Available at: www.lifesitenews.com; Olson, C [2018] *Cardinal Marx promotes false news about blessings and 'homosexual unions'* [Online] Available at: www.catholicworldreport.com [Accessed on: 16 October 2022]

was a reference to Pope Francis legitimising excommunicated bishops loyal to the Chinese Communist party while forcing legitimate bishops of the underground Church into retirement.[1334]

Pope Francis appointed Father José Tolentino Calaça de Mendonça, vice rector of the Catholic University of Lisbon, to preach the Vatican's 2018 Lenten Retreat. Fr. Tolentino de Mendonça wrote the preface to Sr. Teresa Forcades' book *Feminist Theology in History*. Known as 'Europe's most radical nun', Sr. Teresa Forcades advocates the legalisation of abortion and homosexual 'marriage' and adoptions. Fr. Tolentino de Mendonça had been vocal in his support of Pope Francis' changes to doctrine regarding adultery and homosexuality:

> No one can be excluded from the love and mercy of Christ. And that experience of mercy has to be taken to everyone, whether they be Christians who are remarried, wounded by disastrous matrimonial experiences, whether it be the reality of new families, whether it be homosexual persons, who in the Church must find a space to be heard, a place of welcome and mercy.[1335]

6th February

The Cardinal Patriarch of Lisbon, Manuel Clemente, published his endorsement of giving Holy Communion to the divorced and civilly 'remarried' living in a state of adultery on a case-by-case basis. He asserted that there are 'exceptional circumstances' when there is the 'sacramental possibility in conformity with the apostolic exhortation [*Amoris Laetitia*] and the above-cited documents.'[1336]

Archbishop Marcelo Sánchez Sorondo, the head of the Vatican's Pontifical Academies for Sciences and Social Sciences, praised Communist China in an interview with the Spanish-language version of Vatican Insider. He said that China's communist regime was the 'best [at] implementing the social doctrine of the Church.'[1337]

7th February

The Vatican's Pontifical Academy of Sciences tweeted without comment a pro-contraception *New York Times* article about people using birth control to stop having children because of 'climate change' fear. Under Archbishop Marcelo Sánchez Sorondo the Vatican's Academy of Sciences has hosted a number of conferences to which the world's leading proponents of contraception and abortion had been invited to speak.[1338]

The New York Times columnist Frank Bruni published an op-ed quoting pro-homosexual Bishop Robert McElroy, appointed by Pope Francis, attacking critics of the pro-homosexual Fr. James Martin SJ. Bishop Robert McElroy said:

> We have to face the fact that there is a group of people across all religious views that are particularly antagonistic to LGBT people. That comes from deep within the human soul, and it's really corrosive and repugnant.[1339]

[1334]Cummings McLean, D [2018] *China's state-run paper praises Pope Francis' 'wisdom' in making concessions on bishop appointments* [Online] Available at: www.lifesitenews.com [Accessed on: 16 October 2022]

[1335]Cullinan Hoffman, M [2018] *Pope Francis chooses priest to guide Lent retreat who holds Jesus didn't 'establish rules'* [Online] Available at: www.lifesitenews.com Glori, L [2018] *Is Pope Francis Opening the Doors of the Church to 'Queer Theology'?* [Online] Available at: onepeterfive.com [Accessed on: 16 October 2022]

[1336]Cullinan Hoffman, M [2018] *Portuguese Cardinal declares acceptance of communion for adulterously remarried couples* [Online] Available at: www.lifesitenews.com [Accessed on: 16 October 2022]

[1337]Littlejohn, R [2018] *Praise of China's Adherence to Catholic Social Doctrine Flies in the Face of Facts* [Online] Available at: www.ncregister.com [Accessed on: 16 October 2022]

[1338]Chretien, C [2018] *Vatican science academy tweets New York Times story supporting population control* [Online] Available at: www.lifesitenews.com [Accessed on: 16 October 2022]

[1339]Bourne, L [2018] *San Diego bishop: Some Catholics have 'corrosive and repugnant' views on homosexuality* [Online] Available at: www.lifesitenews.com [Accessed on: 16 October 2022]

9th February

Cardinal Cupich delivered a lecture at the Von Hügel Institute for Critical Catholic Inquiry at Cambridge University. Cardinal Cupich, appointed by Pope Francis, told his audience that *Amoris Laetitia* was 'nothing short of revolutionary,' a 'hermeneutical shift,' and is '[forcing] a paradigm shift' on the Church. It broke with the universal application of moral principles that all people are called to obey:

> [*Amoris Laetitia* rejects] an authoritarian or paternalistic way of dealing with people that lays down the law, that pretends to have all the answers, or easy answers to complex problems, that suggests that general rules will seamlessly bring immediate clarity or that the teachings of our tradition can pre-emptively be applied to the particular challenges confronting couples and families.

He also insisted that the publication of Pope Francis' endorsement of the Argentinian bishops implementation of *Amoris Laetitia* raised it to the level of binding magisterial teaching:

> [T]he publication in *Acta Apostolicae Sedes* [*sic*] of his letter to the bishops of Buenos Aires…confirms that their interpretation of Amoris authentically reflects his mind as being official Church teaching. It will now be up to all in the Church … to respond in a spirit of affective and effective collegiality with the Successor of Peter.[1340]

10th January

The German regional newspaper *Neue Osnabrücker Zeitung* published an interview with Bishop Franz-Josef Bode, the Vice President of the German Bishops' Conference, in which he praised 'positive' elements in homosexual relationships. He said:

> We have to reflect upon the question as to how to assess in a differentiated manner a relationship between two homosexual persons. Is there not so much positive and good and right so that we have to be more just.[1341]

29th January

Pro-homosexual Cardinal Cupich, appointed by Pope Francis, gave an address at the North Shore Congregation Israel synagogue that describes itself as 'We are interfaith. We are LGBTQ.' Cardinal Cupich said that evangelisation doesn't mean converting Jews to the Catholic Faith which he criticised as 'proselytism'.[1342]

11th February

Rabbi Dr. Fishel Szlajen, newly appointed as a member of the reformed Pontifical Academy for Life by Pope Francis, wrote that abortion was allowed in some circumstances, such as threats to the mother's own life or psychological wellbeing in cases of rape or disability:

> In only one case does the Bible call for abortion: when the life of the conceptus [the unborn child] inexorably threatens that of its mother.

This is contrary to Catholic moral doctrine.[1343]

13th February

Cardinal Zen, Archbishop Emeritus of Hong Kong, posted a response to Cardinal Parolin's comments about the Vatican's negotiations with the Chinese Communist

[1340]Roberts, J [2018] *Cupich: Amoris Laetitia is Pope Francis' 'revolutionary' vision for the Church* [Online] Available at: www.thetablet.co.uk [Accessed on: 16 October 2022]

[1341]Hickson, M [2018] *VP of German Bishops Conference wants to bless homosexual couples* [Online] Available at: www.lifesitenews.com [Accessed on: 16 October 2022]

[1342]Chretien, C [2018] *Cardinal Cupich: 'Evangelization' doesn't mean converting Jews to Catholicism* [Online] Available at: www.lifesitenews.com [Accessed on: 16 October 2022]

[1343]*Member of Vatican pro-life academy says Bible justifies abortion in exceptional cases* [2018] [Online] Available at: catholicherald.co.uk [Accessed on: 16 October 2022]

Party. Cardinal Zen said Parolin's statement 'disgusts me', accusing him of shedding 'crocodile tears' for persecuted Catholics in China, saying in reality he 'despises the genuine faith of those who firmly defend the Church, founded by Jesus on the Apostles.' He continued:

> There is no reason to fear a schismatic church created by the [Communist] party. It will fade with the collapse of the regime. But a schismatic church with the Pope's blessing will be horrible![1344]

14th February

The Diocese of Linz, Austria, invited homosexual 'couples' to attend two parishes to receive a blessing on St. Valentine's Day. The official diocesan newspaper, *KirchenZeitung*, had announced beforehand:

> St. Valentine is known as the saint of friendship and of love. In many parishes and ecclesial institutions, it is already tradition to offer blessings of couples around the time of his feast day. People in homosexual relationships are welcome at the blessing ceremonies in Wels-St. Franziskus [Church] and in the Ursulinenki... The blessing expresses that one is welcomed by one's partner and by God.[1345]

20th February

LifeSiteNews, the Catholic online media organisation, published details of leaked documents they had received showing Pope Francis' direct involvement in a Vatican financial scandal. During the summer of 2017 Pope Francis personally requested, and obtained in part, a $25 million grant from the U.S.-based Papal Foundation for the Istituto Dermopatico dell'Immacolata, a Church-owned hospital in Rome accused of money laundering by the Italian Finance police. On January 6 the chairman of the Papal Foundation's audit committee resigned in protest of the grant, as did two other members.[1346]

Cardinal Müller published an essay in the US Catholic journal *First Things* in which he challenged Cardinal Parolin's statement that Pope Francis was introducing a 'paradigm shift' to the Church. He wrote that a '"paradigm shift"...by which the Church takes on the criteria of modern society to be assimilated by it' isn't a 'development' of doctrine, but 'a corruption' of it.[1347]

21st February

Cardinal Joseph Tobin, appointed by Pope Francis, posted a tweet in which he wrote, 'Supposed to be airborne in 10 minutes. Nighty-night, baby. I love you' which he then deleted. It later emerged that an Italian actor, Francesco Castiglione, was living in Cardinal Tobin's rectory. George Neumayr, an investigative reporter with *American Spectator*, asked Cardinal Tobin about this:

> Was Castiglione living at the rectory until I reported it?...Tobin responded that, yes, Castiglione was living at his rectory 'temporarily.' I asked him why. He said that Castiglione was taking 'language classes' at Seton Hall. Asked why he would provide temporary housing to a random Seton Hall student, Tobin couldn't offer an explanation.[1348]

[1344]Montagna, D [2018] *Cardinal Zen: 'A schismatic church with the Pope's blessing will be horrible!'* [Online] Available at: www.lifesitenews.com [Accessed on: 16 October 2022]

[1345]Shine, R [2018] *In Midst of Debate, Austrian Parishes Bless Same-Gender Couples' Love* [Online] Available at: www.newwaysministry.org [Accessed on: 16 October 2022]

[1346]Bourne, L [2018] *Pope's request for $25 million to corruption-plagued hospital makes major media* [Online] Available at: www.lifesitenews.com [Accessed on: 16 October 2022]

[1347]Müller, G [2018] *Development, or Corruption?* [Online] Available at: www.firstthings.com [Accessed on: 16 October 2022]

[1348]Wynne, S [2018] *Cdl. Joseph Tobin Tweets: 'Nighty-night, baby. I love you'* [Online] Available at: www.churchmilitant.com; Mainwaring, D [2018] *Cardinal Tobin admits to 'temporarily' housing Italian actor known for posing shirtless* [Online] Available at: www.lifesitenews.com [Accessed on: 16 October 2022]

22nd February

Cardinal Reinhard Marx, president of the German Bishops Conference, announced that the German bishops had decided that Protestant spouses of Catholics could receive Holy Communion in individual cases without the need to convert to the Catholic Church. The German bishops concluded:

> A precondition is that the Protestant partner 'after a deep discernment in a spiritual conversation with the priest or another pastoral worker comes to the decision of conscience to affirm the Faith of the Catholic Church, as well as to end a serious spiritual situation of emergency' and to wish to fulfil the yearning for the Eucharist.[1349]

23rd February

The Irish Bishops' conference published a video to prepare families for the upcoming World Meeting of Families in Ireland. It featured a lesbian saying she was upset about the Church's teaching on homosexuality and the mother of a homosexual son who works for the normalisation of homosexuality in the Church. The latter said:

> I was quite ignorant at the time as regards gay people and didn't really understand. I got involved with a group of parents in the north of Ireland and spent quite a lot of time with them and those very words 'intrinsically evil' and 'disordered' really upset us.[1350]

4th March

The *National Catholic Register* published a report concerning testimonies, submitted by former seminarians to a Vatican investigator, which detailed allegations of serious homosexual misconduct by Auxiliary Bishop Juan José Pineda Fasquelle of the Archdiocese of Tegucigalpa, Honduras. Bishop Pineda Fasquelle was the auxiliary of Cardinal Maradiaga, Pope Francis' confident and chairman of his advisory council of cardinals. One seminarian testified: Bishop Pineda Fasquelle

> attempted to have sexual relations ... without my authorization, during the period I was in service with him. In the night he came close to me and touched my intimate parts and chest. I tried to stop him; on several occasions, I got out of bed and went out. Sometimes I went to the Blessed Sacrament to pray to ask God that that should stop happening.

There were also credible claims that Bishop Pineda Fasquelle had a series of homosexual partners. Though this evidence had been presented to Pope Francis, Bishop Pineda Fasquelle had been left in charge of the Archdiocese of Tegucigalpa while Cardinal Maradiaga received medical treatment.[1351]

6th March

Cardinal Kasper, the architect of ending the prohibition of adulterers receiving Holy Communion, made bizarre claims when he told *Vatican News* that people should stop calling Pope Francis' changes of Church doctrine in *Amoris Laetitia* 'heresy':

> There is a very bitter debate [about the Pope's teaching], way too strong, with accusations of heresy. A heresy is a tenacious disagreement with formal dogma. The doctrine of the indissolubility of marriage has not been called into question on Pope Francis' part!/[1352]

[1349]Hickson, M [2018] *Germany's bishops approve Communion for Protestant spouses* [Online] Available at: www.lifesitenews.com; *German bishop announces communion for Protestant spouses in 'individual cases'* [2018] [Online] Available at: www.catholicworldreport.com [Accessed on: 16 October 2022]
[1350]*Irish bishops feature lesbian, LGBT activist in World Meeting of Families video* [2018] [Online] Available at: www.lifesitenews.com [Accessed on: 16 October 2022]
[1351]Montagna, D [2018] *Will Pope Francis respond to 'extremely grave testimonies' alleging sexual abuse by Honduran bishop?* [Online] Available at: www.lifesitenews.com; Pentin, E [2018] *Former Seminarians Allege Grave Sexual Misconduct by Honduran Bishop Pineda* [Online] Available at: www. ncregister.com [Accessed on: 16 October 2022]
[1352]Cullinan Hoffman, M [2018] *Cardinal Kasper: Stop calling it 'heresy' to allow Communion for adulterers* [Online] Available at: www.lifesitenews.com]Accessed on: 16 October 2022]

13th March

Bishop Marcello Semeraro of the Italian diocese of Albano, and one of Pope Francis' closest advisors, issued a decrees allowing individuals in adulterous relationships to assume official positions in the Church. He wrote that 'after a careful evaluation by the pastor' such individuals may 'actively participate in the Liturgy of the Word during the celebration' of Mass as lectors who publicly read the epistle. They may be deemed ideal for the teaching of the Catholic religion in schools, even to be 'educators of the faith together with other catechists of Christian initiation.' Regarding allowing individuals committing adultery to receive Holy Communion, Bishop Semeraro wrote:

> Do not forget that the imputability and the responsibility of an action can be diminished or eliminated by ignorance, inadvertance, violence, fear, habits, immoderate affections, and by other psychic or even social factors.[1353]

14th March

Cardinal Kasper published a booklet, *The Message of Amoris Laetitia: A Fraternal Discussion*, in which he claimed that homosexual 'unions' contained elements of marriage. He wrote:

> The pope does not leave room for doubt over the fact that civil marriages, de facto unions, new marriages following a divorce (*Amoris Laetitia* 291) and unions between homosexual persons (*Amoris Laetitia* 250) do not correspond to the Christian conception of marriage. He says, however, that some of these partners can realise in a partial and analogous way some elements in Christian marriage (*Amoris Laetitia* 292). Just as outside the Catholic Church there are elements of the true Church, in the above-mentioned unions there can be elements present of Christian marriage, although they do not completely fulfil, or do not yet completely fulfil, the ideal.[1354]

23rd March

Eugenio Scalfari published an account of his ninth engagement with Pope Francis in his newspaper *La Repubblica* in which the pontiff again expressed doubts about the existence of hell. According to Scalfari, Pope Francis told him that hell does not exist and that unrepentant souls in mortal sin disappear after death:

> They are not punished, those who repent obtain God's forgiveness and join the ranks of souls who contemplate him, but those who do not repent and cannot therefore be forgiven disappear. Hell does not exist; the disappearance of sinful souls exists.[1355]

Archbishop Vincenzo Paglia, the head of the Pontifical Academy for Life, gave an address at the seminary of the Mexican diocese of Queretaro during which he expressed frustration at the continued criticism of *Amoris Laetitia*. He shouted: 'Enough of debating all of this! Enough!…it's time to put an end to this discussion and to begin to receive people.'[1356]

24th March

Archbishop Vincenzo Paglia, President of the Vatican's Pontifical Academy for Life, gave an address at the major seminary of the Mexican diocese of Queretaro in which he criticised the family as a 'domestic church' (*Lumen Gentium* 11; cf. *Familiaris Consortio* 23, *Catechism of the Catholic Church* 2204). Archbishop Paglia said:

[1353]Cullinan Hoffman, M [2018] *Pope Francis adviser invites adulterous couples to be godparents, teach religion* [Online] Available at: www.lifesitenews.com]Accessed on: 16 October 2022]

[1354]Cullinan Hoffman, M [2018] *Cardinal Kasper: Homosexual unions are 'analogous' to Christian marriage* [Online] Available at: www.lifesitenews.com]Accessed on: 16 October 2022]

[1355]Montagna, D [2018] *Hell 'does not' exist…sinful souls 'disappear,' Pope Francis allegedly tells favorite interviewer* [Online] Available at: www.lifesitenews.com]Accessed on: 16 October 2022]

[1356]Cullinan Hoffman, M [2018] *'Enough debating!' Vatican archbishop says it's time to accept Amoris Laetitia* [Online] Available at: www.lifesitenews.com]Accessed on: 16 October 2022]

The Church, which is a familial Church, for me, it isn't very clear, it's dangerous, for example, to define the individual family as a little church. It's very dangerous, because it can encourage an egoism of the family. I'm complete. I'm a little church. No?[1357]

26th March

The *Instrumentum Laboris* for the October 2018 Synod on young people was presented to Pope Francis. The working document stated that doctrine on 'contraception, abortion, homosexuality, cohabitation' was 'especially controversial' and that 'they may want the Church to change her teaching.'[1358]

28th March

Bishop Manuel Linda of Porta, Portugal, newly appointed by Pope Francis, criticised divorced and civilly 'remarried' couples who abstained from sexual relations according to Church teaching. He said:

I know that there are some remarried couples, who were previously in a canonical marriage and who later reconstructed their lives and are in another marriage that is not canonical, who for motives of faith and of interior conviction and of conscience, in fact live in sexual abstinence. But we have to ask ourselves: is that itself a family? I'm convinced that it isn't really a family....It's one thing to have a living arrangement like I have here in the house with other people, but we're not a family. It's another thing to be a family. Therefore, I would not insist much on this matter of de facto sexual abstinence.[1359]

29th March

During his homily at the Chrism Mass, Pope Francis attacked the Catholic tradition safeguarding God's revelation of observing 'abstract truths' such as God's commandments. The pontiff said:

We must be careful not to fall into the temptation of making idols of certain abstract truths. They can be comfortable idols, always within easy reach; they offer a certain prestige and power and are difficult to discern. Because the 'truth-idol' imitates, it dresses itself up in the words of the Gospel, but does not let those words touch the heart. Much worse, it distances ordinary people from the healing closeness of the word and of the sacraments of Jesus.[1360]

30th March

On Good Friday the German newspaper, *Augsburger Allgemeine*, published an interview with Fr. Anselm Grün, an author Pope Francis has expressed his admiration for and who he recommended to the clergy of Rome. During the interview Fr. Grün expressed support for the ordination of women 'deacons' as a step towards the ordination of woman 'priests' and eventually a woman 'pope':

There are no theological reasons that speak against an abolishment of priestly celibacy or against female priests, female bishops, or a female pope. Only here it is about historical processes...the first step has to be now the ordination of women as deaconesses.[1361]

[1357]Cullinan Hoffman, M [2018] *Vatican archbishop: It's 'very dangerous' to speak of the family as a 'little church'* [Online] Available at: www.lifesitenews.com]Accessed on: 16 October 2022]

[1358]Bourne, L [2018] *Catholic Youth Synod working document calls abortion, homosexuality 'especially controversial'* [Online] Available at: www.lifesitenews.com]Accessed on: 16 October 2022]

[1359]Cullinan Hoffman, M [2018] *Bishop promoted by Francis: 'Remarried' couples must have sex to be 'family'* [Online] Available at: www.lifesitenews.com]Accessed on: 16 October 2022]

[1360]Pope Francis [2018] *Homily at Chrism Mass* [Online] Available at: www.vatican.va [Accessed on: 16 October 2022]

[1361]Hickson, M [2018] *A Priest Praised by the Pope: A Female Pope is a Possibility in the Future* [Online] Available at: onepeterfive.com [Accessed on: 16 October 2022]

3rd April

Carmelite missionary sister Martha Pelloni gave an interview to the Argentinian radio program *Crónica Anunciada* in which she reported that Pope Francis had told her some forms of contraception were acceptable. Sr. Martha Pelloni told listeners that Pope Francis said various forms of contraception could be permissible to prevent poor women from choosing abortion:

> Pope Francis said three words to me in this regard: 'condom, transitory, and reversible,' meaning by the second word the 'diaphragm' and by the third 'tubal ligation', which 'we recommend to the women of the fields'.[1362]

Pope Francis did not issue a public correction or repudiation.

5th April

Bishop Marcelo Sanchez Sorondo, chancellor of the Pontifical Academies of sciences and social sciences, issued a letter rebuking doctors, lawyers and academics who had written to him about their concerns that Chinese authorities were illegally harvesting organs from convicts. Bishop Sorondo accused them of attempting to interfere with the negotiations being conducted between the Vatican and the Chinese Communist Party. He wrote:

> [There are groups who] for various reasons do not want to understand that the Church, the United Nations, and the people of the earth must follow the evolution of a country with a population of 1,300 million and 31 million Christians, which is becoming one of the most important protagonists of the new world scenario that is passing from the Atlantic to the Pacific, like it went from the Mediterranean to the Atlantic in the past.[1363]

9th April

Pope Francis published his apostolic exhortation *Gaudete et Exsultate* in which he criticised Catholics who see abortion as a more important issue than migration, arguing that immigration was as important as the worldwide murder of tens of millions of pre-born babies every year. The pontiff wrote:

> Our defence of the innocent unborn, for example, needs to be clear, firm and passionate, for at stake is the dignity of a human life, which is always sacred and demands love for each person, regardless of his or her stage of development. Equally sacred, however, are the lives of the poor, those already born, the destitute, the abandoned and the underprivileged, the vulnerable infirm and elderly exposed to covert euthanasia, the victims of human trafficking, new forms of slavery, and every form of rejection… We often hear it said that, with respect to relativism and the flaws of our present world, the situation of migrants, for example, is a lesser issue. Some Catholics consider it a secondary issue compared to the 'grave' bioethical questions. That a politician looking for votes might say such a thing is understandable, but not a Christian, for whom the only proper attitude is to stand in the shoes of those brothers and sisters of ours who risk their lives to offer a future to their children. Can we not realize that this is exactly what Jesus demands of us, when he tells us that in welcoming the stranger we welcome him (cf. Mt 25:35)? (*GE* 101-102).

Pope Francis also appeared to criticise those who disagreed with his attempt to change doctrine on the indissolubility of marriage and the gravity of the sin of adultery in his apostolic exhortation Amoris Laetitia. The Pontiff wrote:

> Not infrequently, contrary to the promptings of the Spirit, the life of the Church can become a museum piece or the possession of a select few. This can occur when some

[1362]Skojec, S [2018] *Argentinian Nun Says Pope Advocates Contraception. Again* [Online] Available at: onepeterfive.com [Accessed on: 16 October 2022]

[1363]*Vatican bishop defends China on organ harvesting* [2018] [Online] Available at: catholicherald. co.uk [Accessed on: 16 October 2022]

groups of Christians give excessive importance to certain rules, customs or ways of acting. The Gospel then tends to be reduced and constricted, deprived of its simplicity, allure and savour. This may well be a subtle form of pelagianism, for it appears to subject the life of grace to certain human structures … only to end up fossilized … or corrupt. (*GE* 58).[1364]

10th April

Konbini News broadcast a TV interview with Fr. Daniel Duigou in which he said that during a 45 minute private meeting with Pope Francis the pontiff approved of his blessing homosexual 'couples'. Fr. Daniel Duigou said:

> Immediately [the pope's] first question was: 'So, do you bless the divorced and remarried?', which is one of the great questions today in the Church... And I say to him: 'And I listen, and I bless them and I also bless homosexual couples.' And he answers: 'Yes, because blessing means God thinks of the good of the [human person] and God thinks well of [all people].'

When asked if Pope Francis supports blessing same-gender couples, Fr. Duigou replied, 'Yes, absolutely.' Pope Francis did not clarify or repudiate Fr. Daniel Duigou's account of their meeting.[1365]

12th April

Pro-homosexual Cardinal Joseph Tobin, appointed by Pope Francis, gave an address at the Villanova University conference celebrating five years of the Bergoglian pontificate, *Pope Francis, a Voice Crying Out in the World: Mercy, Justice, Love, & Care for the Earth.* Cardinal Tobin said the Church was changing her position on same-sex relationships:

> ...the Church is moving on the question of same-sex couples, albeit not as quickly as some people would like. Dialogue is key. What I say to people in same-sex relationships and want to teach, I say, 'How do you do it?' Help me understand. How do you communicate the fullness of the Catholic position on the moral question and justify... the choices you've made with your life? Just help me understand that... Sometimes people do.[1366]

26th - 28th April

The Pontifical Council for Culture and the CURA Foundation held a three day conference on the theme 'Unite to Cure — How Science, Technology and the 21st Century Will Impact Culture and Society.' It featured controversial pop-star Katy Perry speaking on teaching children transcendental meditation. Katy Perry is an LGBT activist, promotes the abortion provider Planned Parenthood, and said she sold her soul to the devil.[1367]

2nd May

The Belgian LGBT magazine, *Zizo-Online*, published an account of a private meeting with Cardinal Josef De Kesel — appointed by Pope Francis — in which Cardinal Josef De Kesel expressed approval of homosexuality. Cardinal De Kesel is reported as saying:

> The church must respect gays and lesbians more, including in the way they live out that sexuality...Twenty years ago I would have spoken differently from what is now the case. At that time I would have followed the official teaching of the Church more. My attitude has become much more 'understanding'… respect takes the central place… The

---

[1364]Pope Francis [2018] *Apostolic Exhortation Gaudete et Exsultate* [Online] Available at: www. vatican.va [Accessed on: 17 October 2022]

[1365]Shine, R [2018] *French Priest Says Pope Francis Approved Blessing Gay Couples* [Online] Available at: www.newwaysministry.org [Accessed on: 16 October 2022]

[1366]O'Loughlin, M [2018] *Cardinal Tobin warns against temptation to shrink Catholic community to pure members* [Online] Available at: www.americamagazine.org [Accessed on: 16 October 2022]

[1367]Montagna, D [2018] *Vatican invites Katy Perry to talk about Transcendental Meditation* [Online] Available at: www.lifesitenews.com [Accessed on: 16 October 2022]

official viewpoint of Rome is that homosexuality is 'a disordered behaviour' because it does not follow the normal order, where sexuality is oriented towards procreation... Everyone can clearly feel that the official viewpoint is no longer sustainable. Some time ago Pope Francis said about LGBT's: 'Who am I to judge people who are searching for God?' Those words are not nothing. Those words were unthinkable ten years ago. They bear witness to what he personally believes. Francis has made his mark. It will not be easy to turn back. Not even under a new pope. Although I do admit that Francis' words did not fall on good earth everywhere.[1368]

3rd May

Archbishop Luis Ladaria, SJ, prefect of the Congregation for the Doctrine of the Faith, released a statement after his meeting with German bishops regarding their decision to allow Protestant spouses to receive Holy Communion. Archbishop Ladaria stated that Pope Francis 'appreciates the ecumenical commitment of the German bishops and asks them to find, in a spirit of ecclesial communion, a unanimous result if possible.' Cardinal Willem Jacobus Eijk of Holland called Pope Francis' directive 'completely incomprehensible':

> The Church's doctrine and practice regarding the administration of the Sacrament of the Eucharist to Protestants is perfectly clear... The practice of the Catholic Church, based on her faith, is not determined and does not change when the majority of an episcopal conference votes in favour of it, not even if unanimously.[1369]

4th May

Pope Francis gave an address to the International Convention promoted by the Congregation for the Institutes of Consecrated Life and the Societies of Apostolic Life. During his address the pontiff said:

> ...this Holy Spirit is a disaster because He never tires of being creative! Now, with the new forms of consecrated life, He is truly creative, with the charisms... It is interesting: He is the Author of diversity but at the same time the Creator of unity.[1370]

7th May

Pro-homosexual Fr. James Martin SJ — appointed consultor to the Secretariat for Communications by Pope Francis — tweeted that a fellow attendee at the Met Gala told him 'I love that you got dressed up as a sexy priest.'[1371] The Met Gala is an annual fundraising gala for the benefit of the Metropolitan Museum of Art's Costume Institute.

8th May

Three German judges delivered their verdict regarding Albrecht von Boeselager's legal action against the Austrian Catholic news service *Kath.net* to stop them reporting his distribution of condoms when he was the Grand Hospitaller of the Order of the Knights of Malta. Pope Francis had ordered the resignation of Grand Master Matthew Festing for dismissing Albrecht von Boeselager for distributing condoms. Von Boeselager was re-instated and appointed Grand Chancellor. The three judges of the Hamburg District Court ruled that Boeselager knowingly lied:

[1368]Smits, J [2018] *Belgian diocese won't deny cardinal endorsed homosexuality* [Online] Available at: www.lifesitenews.com; Slavsky, A [2018] *Belgian Bishop Affirms Gay Sex* [Online] Available at: www.churchmilitant.com [Accessed on: 16 October 2022]

[1369]Montagna, D [2018] *Pope Francis asks German bishops for 'unanimous' decision on intercommunion with Protestants* [Online] Available at: www.lifesitenews.com; Pentin, E [2018] *Cardinal Eijk: Pope Francis Needed to Give Clarity on Intercommunion* [Online] Available at: www.ncregister.com [Accessed on: 16 October 2022]

[1370]Fair, J [2018] *Pope Francis: Consecrated Need Authentic Guide* [Online] Available at: zenit.org [Accessed on: 16 October 2022]

[1371]Cullinan Hoffman, M [2018] *Pro-LGBT Vatican advisor Fr. James Martin: They called me 'sexy' at Met Gala* [Online] Available at: www.lifesitenews.com]Accessed on: 16 October 2022]

the judges found that Boeselager's denial of knowledge about the condom distribution was untruthful and that he had 'knowingly procured' it with 'full knowledge and will.'[1372]

11th May

Archbishop Stefan Hesse of Hamburg — appointed by Pope Francis in 2015 — told the Central Committee of German Catholics (ZdK) that Pope Francis had given the nod of approval to the German bishops' intercommunion proposal. Archbishop Hesse said that by referring the matter back to the German bishops, the pontiff signalled that they had the competence to decide the matter by majority vote.[1373]

20th May

The UK *Guardian* newspaper published an account of Pope Francis' private audience with Juan Carlos Cruz. According to Juan Carlos Cruz the pontiff told him:

> Juan Carlos, that you are gay does not matter. God made you like this and loves you like this and I don't care. The pope loves you like this. You have to be happy with who you are.

Pope Francis did not clarify or repudiate Juan Carlos Cruz's account of their meeting.[1374]

7th -10th June

Cardinal Parolin, the Vatican's Secretary of State, attended the 66th Bilderberg Meeting in Turin, Italy. The behind-closed doors meeting between 'invite only' attendees is known as one of the agencies of elitist globalism.[1375]

8th June

The Vatican published the *Lineamenta* for the 2019 Synod of Bishops Special Assembly for the Pan-Amazon Region. Among other things, it called for official ministry to be conferred on women:

> Along these lines, it is necessary to identify the type of official ministry that can be conferred on women....

Bishop Erwin Kräutler, appointed by Pope Francis as one of the organisers of the October 2019 Synod, is a militant proponent of the 'ordination' of women to the diaconate and priesthood.[1376]

11th June

The Holy See Press Office published Pope Francis' Ireland schedule with what it called 'Highlights from the Pastoral Programme for the 9th World Meeting of Families in Dublin.' These highlights included the announcement that pro-homosexual Fr. James Martin SJ was to feature as a speaker. Fr. Martin later posted on Facebook, 'At the invitation of the Vatican's Dicastery for Laity, Family and Life, and the Archdiocese of Dublin, I'll be speaking at the World Meeting of Families.' He also told *America Magazine*, of which he is the editor:

[1372]Niles, C [2018] *Knights of Malta Demand That Chancellor Resign* [Online] Available at: www.churchmilitant.com [Accessed on: 16 October 2022]
[1373]Pentin, E [2018] *German Bishop: Pope Francis Has Clearly Hinted Support for Intercommunion Proposal* [Online] Available at: www.ncregister.com [Accessed on: 16 October 2022]
[1374]Kirchgaessner, S [2018] *Pope Francis tells gay man: 'God made you like this'* [Online] Available at: www.theguardian.com [Accessed on: 16 October 2022]
[1375]*Analysis: Cardinal Parolin at the elite Bilderberg meeting* [2018] [Online] Available at: www.catholicworldreport.com [Accessed on: 16 October 2022]
[1376]Hickson, M [2018] *Papal advisor claims Francis would not give 'strict no' to women's ordination* [Online] Available at: www.lifesitenews.com [Accessed on: 16 October 2022]

I'm tremendously grateful for this invitation, not so much for what it says about my own ministry or writing but what it says to L.G.B.T. Catholics, a group of people who have for so long felt excluded. I hope they see this invitation, which had to be approved by the Vatican, as an unmistakable sign of welcome from the Church.[1377]

18th June

Cardinal Christoph Schönborn, a close advisor of Pope Francis, gave an interview to the Austrian news outlet *OE24* in which he discussed the 'ordination' of women. Cardinal Schönborn said:

There were deaconesses in the first centuries which could be reintroduced, but there have never been priestesses in the Catholic Church.[1378]

Cardinal Schönborn's endorsement of women deacons ignored the findings of the International Theological Commission (2003) that women 'deaconesses' were not ordained ministers of the Church.[1379]

19th June

The *Instrumentum Laboris* — working document — of the XV ordinary synod of bishops on *Young People, The Faith and Vocational Discernment* was published. It was the first Vatican document to include the activist homosexual term LGBT:

Some LGBT youths, through various contributions that were received by the General Secretariat of the Synod, wish to 'benefit from greater closeness' and experience greater care by the Church, while some BC [Bishops' Conferences] ask themselves what to suggest 'to young people who decide to create homosexual instead of heterosexual couples and, above all, would like to be close to the Church.'[1380]

When asked at the press conference why the acronym 'LGBT' appeared in the *Instrumentum Laboris*, Cardinal Baldisseri, the Secretary General of the Synod of Bishops, replied that 'LGBT' was taken from the pre-synodal document compiled by young people at their meeting with the Pope and Synod organisers, March 19-24, 2018. He said, 'They provided us with a document, and we quoted it. This is the explanation for this.' However, it later emerged that the acronym LGBT was not included in the final document of the pre-synodal meeting with youth.[1381]

20th June

New York Cardinal Timothy Dolan released a press statement announcing that a review board had found that allegations that Cardinal McCarrick had sexually abused a child were 'credible and substantiated.' Pope Francis had rehabilitated Cardinal McCarrick in 2013, releasing him from constraints imposed on him by Pope Benedict XVI in response to allegations of depraved sexual conduct.[1382]

[1377]O'Loughlin, M [2018] *Father James Martin SJ to speak on welcoming LGBT Catholics at World Meeting of Families* [Online] Available at: www.americamagazine.org [Accessed on: 16 October 2022]

[1378]Bourne, L [2018] *Cardinal close to Pope Francis pushes possibility of female deacons* [Online] Available at: www.lifesitenews.com; *For Austrian cardinal, female deacons an 'open question'* [2018] [Online] Available at: www.catholicnewsagency.com [Accessed on: 16 October 2022]

[1379]*International Theological Commission [2002] From the Diakonia of Christ to the Diakonia of the Apostles* [Online] Available at: www.vatican.va [Accessed on: 16 October 2022]

[1380]Synod of Bishops [2018] *Instrumentum Laboris, young people, the faith and vocational discernment* [Online] Available at: www.vatican.va [Accessed on: 16 October 2022]

[1381]Montagna, D [2018] *Why is the Vatican highlighting 'LGBT youth' in lead up to Youth Synod?* [Online] Available at: www.lifesitenews.com [Accessed on: 16 October 2022]

[1382]Niles, C [2018] *High-Ranking US Cardinal Accused of Sex Abuse* [Online] Available at: www. churchmilitant.com [Accessed on: 16 October 2022]

21st June

During the in-flight press conference returning from Geneva, Switzerland, Pope Francis said that it was up to individual bishops, and not bishops' conferences, to determine whether a Protestant spouse who is married to a Catholic may receive the Holy Eucharist. The pontiff said:

> However, the Code [of canon law] says that the bishop of the particular Church — this word is important, particular, if it is a diocese — has to handle this: it's in his hands.[1383]

27th June

The German bishops published their pastoral 'guidance' that allows Protestant spouses of Catholics, in certain cases, to receive Holy Communion. Even though the CDF sent the German bishops a letter on the 25th May, with the authority of the Pope Francis, blocking the publication of this 'guidance', Cardinal Marx indicated that the publication of the 'guidance' had the support of Pope Francis. Cardinal Marx released a 'note' signed by Pope Francis, following their meeting of the 12th June that stated, 'the 25 May CDF letter 'gives some recommendations', but 'does not give instructions' to the German bishops. The 'note' also stated that 'the Holy Father does not wish that the text appears as a text of the bishops' conference, because it relates to a dimension of the Universal Church.' Therefore, to meet this technical requirement, the 'guidance' is not attributed to a named author or a named organisation.[1384]

29th June

Pope Francis appointed Bishop Nunzio Galantino as the new president of the Administration of the Patrimony of the Apostolic See. Bishop Galantino has questioned the Church's opposition to abortion and euthanasia and has criticised pro-life witness outside abortion clinics. He said:

> In the past, we have concentrated exclusively on (saying) 'No' to abortion and euthanasia. It can't be like this, between (birth and death) there is a developing existence.

He also said:

> I do not identify with the expressionless faces of those who recite the rosary outside the clinics who practice interruption of pregnancy ('l'interruzione della gravidanza'), but with those young people who are opposed to this practice and strive for the quality of life of the people, for their right to health, to work.

Bishop Galantino also spoke approvingly of the heresiarch Martin Luther: 'The Reformation carried out by Martin Luther 500 years ago was an event of the Holy Spirit.'[1385]

3rd July

Cardinal Kevin Farrell, prefect of the Vatican's Dicastery for Laity, Family and Life — appointed by Pope Francis — gave an interview to *Intercom* magazine, a publication of the Irish Catholic Bishops' Conference. During the interview he said that priests should not be involved in the preparation of couples for the sacrament of marriage. Cardinal Farrell said:

> They have no credibility, they have never lived the experience; they may know moral theology, dogmatic theology in theory, but to go from there to putting it into practice every day…. they don't have the experience.[1386]

[1385]Cummings McLean, D [2018] *New Vatican investments chief opposes pro-life witness, admires Luther* [Online] Available at: www.lifesitenews.com [Accessed on: 16 October 2022]
[1386]Bourne, L [2018] *Pope-Francis-appointed cardinal: Priests have 'no credibility' to do marriage prep* [Online] Available at: www.lifesitenews.com [Accessed on: 17 October 2022]

The Diocesan spokesman of pro-homosexual Bishop John Stowe — appointed by Pope Francis — told a local radio that it was up to each parish of the Diocese of Lexington to decide to promote homosexuality. This was in response to the parish of St. Paul displaying the pro-LGBT rainbow banner outside their Catholic Church in Lexington. Also, the Church of St. Francis of Assisi, New York City, a well-known pro-gay parish run by Franciscan priests, celebrating a 'Pre-Pride' Mass as part of New York City's Gay Pride Parade.[1387]

Katholische.de reported that four German bishops approved limited intercommunion with Protestants — Bishops Gerhard Feige of Magdeburg, Archbishop Stefan Hesse of Hamburg, Bishop Franz-Josef Bode of Osnabrück, and Archbishop Becker of Paderborn.[1388]

11th July

Pope Francis sent a letter to the participants in the 3rd International conference of 'Catholic Theological Ethics in the World Church'. The conference featured many feminist and pro-LGBT speakers, and was co-organised by Fr. James Keenan, who campaigns for same-sex 'marriage'.[1389]

12th July

Pope Francis wrote a letter of thanks to the Patriarch of Lisbon, Cardinal Manuel Clemente, regarding his recent instructional note implementing *Amoris Laetitia*, allowing divorced and civilly 'remarried' to receive Holy Communion. The pontiff wrote that the note 'filled him with joy'.[1390]

20th July

The Vatican announced in passing the resignation of Honduran Auxiliary Bishop Juan José Pineda Fasquelle. Seminarians had submitted allegations of homosexual misconduct to a Vatican investigator. In March Bishop Pineda Fasquelle had been left in charge of the Archdiocese of Tegucigalpa while Cardinal Maradiaga received medical treatment.

26th July

Cardinal Óscar Rodríguez Maradiaga, confident of Pope Francis and chairman of Pope Francis' Council of Nine cardinals, was reported as vehemently criticising his own seminarians of the Honduran Diocese of Santa Rosa de Copán. Cardinal Maradiaga attacked fifty seminarians for speaking out against their seminary's rampant homosexual subculture. He accused them of being '"gossipers" who wish to portray their fellow seminarians in a bad light.'[1391]

27th July

Pope Francis received a letter from homosexual Cardinal Theodore McCarrick, Archbishop Emeritus of Washington, resigning from the Sacred College of Cardinals. The pontiff re-established the constraints Pope Benedict XVI had imposed on Cardinal McCarrick. In 2013 Pope Francis had removed Pope Benedict's constraints on McCarrick when he commissioned him to undertake a mission to China, despite being informed of the allegations of his depraved sexual behaviour.

[1387]Nussman, D [2018] *Pro-Gay Parishes Causing Scandal* [Online] Available at:: www.churchmilitant. com [Accessed on: 17 October 2017]

[1388]*Now four German dioceses approve limited intercommunion with Protestants* [2018] [Online] Available at: www.praytellblog.com [Accessed on: 16 October 2022]

[1389]Hickson, M [2018] *Pope Francis endorses conference featuring dissident, pro-LGBT speakers* [Online] Available at: www.lifesitenews.com [Accessed on: 17 October 2022]

[1390]Hickson, M [2018] *Pope Praises Cardinal Who Now Admits Remarried Divorcees to Communion* [Online] Available at: www.lifesitenews.com [Accessed on: 17 October 2022]

[1391]Mainwaring, D [2018] *Pope Francis' top 'reform' cardinal slams seminarians for exposing homosexuality inside seminary* [Online] Available at: www.lifesitenews.com [Accessed on: 17 October 2022]

1st August

The CDF sent a letter to the world's bishops informing them that Pope Francis had issued a re-script overturning the Church's perennial doctrine on the moral permissibility of the death penalty. Pope Francis revised the 1992 Catechism to teach that the death penalty was 'inadmissible' and advocating that the Church 'works with determination for its abolition worldwide.' Paragraph 2267 was changed to read:

> Consequently, the Church teaches, in the light of the Gospel, that 'the death penalty is inadmissible because it is an attack on the inviolability and dignity of the person', and she works with determination for its abolition worldwide.

This change is contrary to natural law, Sacred Scripture, Sacred Tradition, and the Magisterium of the Church.[1392]

4th August

Edward Pentin, the Vatican correspondent for the US National Catholic Register, reported allegations regarding Cardinal Oscar Rodriguez Maradiaga, a close confident of Pope Francis, and his 'protection' of homosexual seminarians. Though the Congregation for the Clergy had instructed the bishops of Honduras to remove homosexual seminarians, Cardinal Maradiaga had not acted on the instruction from the Vatican. Pentin reported, 'about 40 seminarians [out of a total of 180] are actively homosexual, and about 20 more who are in the closet. Many repress it to be able to reach ordination but once ordained, they are "free and unbridled".'[1393]

6th August

Vatican News published an interview with Archbishop Rino Fisichella, president of the Pontifical Council for the New Evangelization, to mark the 25th anniversary of the promulgation of Pope St. John Paul II's encyclical on fundamental moral principles, *Veritatis Splendor*. Archbishop Fisichella criticised Catholics who accused Pope Francis of teaching errors against the magisterium of the Church:

> The magisterium must never be used instrumentally to place a contrast in the development of the doctrine. When there is an instrumental use, then I fear there is no desire for a discovery of the truth, and also that there is no fidelity to the tradition of the Church. I don't think there are any grounds that justify challenging the teaching of Pope Francis in the light of the previous magisterium. On the contrary, we need to reiterate how much continuity there is in development. I think, however, that it is also important to carefully consider the whole teaching of Pope Francis and not just a single particular aspect of it: the mosaic is produced by the whole deck, not by a single card.[1394]

The German bishops' national conference website celebrated the Diocese of Stuttgart's Catholic youth group *Katholische junge Gemeinde* winning an award after participating in a pro-LGBT parade. The youth group had displayed pro-LGBT signs, quoting Pope Francis' reported words to homosexual Juan Carlos Cruz:

> God made you like that and he loves you like that and I do not care. The Pope loves you as you are, you have to be happy with who you are. You should not think about what others think about you.

Another sign displayed by the youth group stated, 'Jesus had…two fathers.'[1395]

[1392]Pentin, E [2018] *Pope Francis Changes Catechism to Say Death Penalty 'Inadmissible'* [Online] Available at: www.ncregister.com [Accessed on: 17 October 2022]
[1393]Montagna, D [2018] *Report: Cardinal close to Pope is protecting cadre of homosexual seminarians in Honduras* [Online] Available at: www.lifesitenews.com [Accessed on: 17 October 2022]
[1394]Lomonaco, A [2018] *Abp Fisichella reflects on 25 years of Veritatis splendor* [Online] Available at: www.vaticannews.va/ [Accessed on: 17 October 2022]
[1395]Hickson, M [2018] *German bishops' website touts Catholic youth group's 'gay pride' award* [Online] Available at: www.lifesitenews.com [Accessed on: 17 October 2022]

9th August

Pope Francis' book length interview with Dominique Wolton was published with the title *The Path to Change: Thoughts on Politics and Society*. During the interview Pope Francis accepted the term 'civil union' for the immoral bondings between homosexuals:

> But let's say things as they are: Marriage is between a man and a woman. This is the precise term. Lets call unions between the same sex 'civil unions'.[1396]

14th August

Fr. Thomas Rosica CSB, the Vatican's English language spokesperson appointed at the beginning of Pope Francis' pontificate, issued a statement asserting that the Church had entered a new phase with Pope Francis that went beyond sacred Scripture, sacred Tradition and the perennial Magisterium. Fr. Thomas Rosica wrote:

> Pope Francis breaks Catholic traditions whenever he wants because he is free from disordered attachments. Our Church has indeed entered a new phase. With the advent of this first Jesuit pope, it is openly ruled by an individual rather than by the authority of Scripture alone or even its own dictates of tradition plus Scripture. The pope's openness, however, also a signature of his Jesuit training and development, means that not even he is sure where the spirit will lead. I don't have all the answers. I don't even have all the questions. I always think of new questions, and there are always new questions coming forward.[1397]

It later emerged that Fr. Rosica had plagiarised this assessment of Pope Francis from a post by the fundamentalist Protestant Richard Bennett, a former Dominican and laicised priest, originally written as a criticism of Pope Francis.[1398]

16th August

Pope Francis consecrated as bishop pro-homosexual José Tolentino Mendonça, appointing him head of the Vatican Secret Archives. The pontiff had previously selected Fr. Mendonça to deliver the 2018 Vatican Lenten retreat. Fr. Mendonça was associated with the work of Sr. Teresa Forcades, a Spanish nun notorious for advocating the legalisation of homosexual 'marriage' and the right of women to murder their babies through abortion. Fr. Mendonca claimed that Forcades' work conformed with the teaching of our Lord Jesus Christ:

> Teresa Forcades i Vila reminds of that which is essential: that Jesus of Nazareth did not codify, nor did he establish rules. Jesus lived. That is, he constructed an ethos of relation, somatized the poetry of his message in the visibility of his flesh, expressed his own body as a premise.[1399]

17th August

Pope Francis appointed Venezuelan Archbishop Edgar Peña Parra as the Vatican's Deputy Secretary of State. Archbishop Peña Parra is a 'very close friend' of pro-homosexual papal collaborator Cardinal Óscar Rodríguez Maradiaga and disgraced homosexual bishop, Juan José Pineda Fasquelle.[1400] Credible allegations later emerged that Archbishop Peña Parra had been removed from his first seminary because he had

---

[1396]DeBernardo, F [2018] *Pope Francis Allows For Civil Unions for Lesbian and Gay Couples* [Online] Available at: www.newwaysministry.org [Accessed on: 17 October 2022]

[1397]Cullinan Hoffman, M [2018] *'Pope Francis breaks Catholic traditions whenever he wants': Vatican advisor Fr. Rosica* [Online] Available at: www.lifesitenews.com [Accessed on: 17 October 2022]

[1398]*Pope Francis: Master of Jesuit Spiritual Exercises* [2018] [Online] Available at: bereanbeacon.org [Accessed on: 17 October 2022]

[1399]Cullinan Hoffman, M [2018] *Pope names new Vatican bishop who claims Jesus didn't 'establish rules'* [Online] Available at: www.lifesitenews.com [Accessed on: 17 October 2022]

[1400]Montagna, D [2018] *New top official at Vatican is 'close friends' with Cardinal Maradiaga, disgraced auxiliary bishop* [Online] Available at: www.lifesitenews.com [Accessed on: 17 October 2022]

a homosexual orientation and was, 'a sexually sick person.'[1401] Archbishop Viganò accused Pope Francis of ignoring a dossier of evidence outlining Archbishop Peña Parra's sexual abuse of seminarians and other depraved acts.[1402]

21st August

The *Crux* news website published Pope Francis' letter to English author Stephen Walford in response to his new book, an apologia of *Amoris Laetitia*. In his letter Pope Francis claimed that his apostolic exhortation allowing couples committing adultery through second civil 'marriages' followed St. Thomas Aquinas 'without rupture'. The pontiff wrote:

> With respect to the problems that involve ethical situations, the Exhortation follows the classical doctrine of St. Thomas Aquinas.[1403]

However, St. Thomas Aquinas condemned sins against marriage such as fornication and adultery, and upheld the moral and sacramental principle, contradicted by *Amoris Laetitia*, that in order to receive the sacraments one needed to repent and make a firm purpose to amend one's life (*ST* III, q. 90, a. 4; cf. ST II-II, q. 43, a. 1).[1404]

20th August

Pope Francis issued a letter addressed to the entire people of God about the sexual abuse of children and young people by clergy. This was in response to a Pennsylvania grand jury report that exposed 70 years of clergy sex abuse of 1,000 victims on the part of some 300 priests. The 2022 word letter did not once mention the role of 'homosexuality' in the sexual abuse or the part played by bishops in the perpetration and/or cover-up of the sexual abuse. Instead Pope Francis blamed 'clericalism' for the crimes:

> Clericalism, whether fostered by priests themselves or by lay persons, leads to an excision in the ecclesial body that supports and helps to perpetuate many of the evils that we are condemning today. To say 'no' to abuse is to say an emphatic 'no' to all forms of clericalism.[1405]

22nd August

Archbishop Carlo Maria Viganò, the former U.S. nuncio, released detailed testimony about the episcopal cover-up of former Cardinal McCarrick's homosexual abuse of seminarians. Archbishop Viganò's personal testimony directly implicated Pope Francis, accusing him of knowing involvement in the cover-up of McCarrick's sexual perversity. Archbishop Viganò stated:

> The Pope learned about it from me on June 23, 2013 and continued to cover for him. He did not take into account the sanctions that Pope Benedict had imposed on him and made him his trusted counselor ...He knew from at least June 23, 2013 that McCarrick was a serial predator. Although he knew that he was a corrupt man, he covered for him to the bitter end.

With Pope Francis' patronage, the homosexually active Cardinal McCarrick 'had become the kingmaker for appointments in the Curia and the United States, and the most listened to advisor in the Vatican for relations with the Obama administration.'

[1401]*Questions arise about Vatican official mentioned in Vigano report* [2018] [Online] Available at: www.catholicnewsagency.com [Accessed on: 17 October 2022]
[1402]Cullinan Hoffman, M [2018] *Pope Francis ignored 'terrifying dossier' on top Vatican official's sex abuse: Abp. Viganò* [Online] Available at: www.lifesitenews.com [Accessed on: 17 October 2022]
[1403]*Pope: No 'rupture' in 'Amoris,' which is rooted in 'classical doctrine' of Aquinas* [2018] [Online] Available at: cruxnow.com [Accessed on: 17 October 2017]
[1404]Pentin, E [2018] *Is 'Amoris Laetitia' Really Thomistic?* [Online] Available at: www.ncregister.com [Accessed on: 17 October 2017]
[1405]Pope Francis [2018] *Letter to the People of God* [Online] Available at: press.vatican.va [Accessed on: 17 October 2022]

Archbishop Viganò also testified that a number of pro-homosexual episcopal appointments and elevations to the Sacred College of Cardinals was due to Pope Francis accepting the advice of Cardinal McCarrick:

> The appointments of Blase Cupich to Chicago and Joseph W. Tobin to Newark were orchestrated by McCarrick, Maradiaga and Wuerl, united by a wicked pact of abuses by the first, and at least of cover-up of abuses by the other two. Their names were not among those presented by the Nunciature for Chicago and Newark... The appointment of (Bishop Robert) McElroy in San Diego was also orchestrated from above, with an encrypted peremptory order to me as Nuncio, by Cardinal Parolin: 'Reserve the See of San Diego for McElroy....' McElroy was also well aware of McCarrick's abuses as can be seen from a letter sent to him by Richard Sipe on July 28, 2016.

Archbishop Viganò named several high-ranking prelates who had acted to promote homosexuals into positions of responsibility in the Church and/or who favour of subverting Catholic doctrine on homosexuality. These prelates included: Cardinal Maradiaga, appointed by Pope Francis as the head of his advisory council of cardinals, Cardinal Tarcisio Bertone — former Vatican Secretary of State — Cardinal Francesco Coccopalmerio — former head of the Pontifical Council for the Interpretation of Legal Texts — Archbishop Vincenzo Paglia — the president of the Pontifical Academy for Life.

Archbishop Viganò also testified against the pro-homosexual Fr. James Martin SJ, a rising star in Pope Francis' pontificate:

> Father James Martin SJ, acclaimed by the people mentioned above, in particular Cupich, Tobin, Farrell and McElroy, appointed Consultor of the Secretariat for Communications, well-known activist who promotes the LGBT agenda, chosen to corrupt the young people who will soon gather in Dublin for the World Meeting of Families, is nothing but a sad recent example of that deviated wing of the Society of Jesus.[1406]

24th August

A pro-homosexual activist permanent deacon was chosen to assist Cardinal Kevin Farrell at Mass for the World Meeting of Families in Dublin. A homosexual website announced:

> Deacon Ray Dever of Tampa, Fla., and his 25-year-old bi daughter, Emily Dever, plan to be 'a visible presence' at the church event, according to a press release from New Ways Ministry, which advocates for LGBTQ equality in Catholicism.[1407]

Cardinal Farrell is the prefect for the Dicastery for Laity, Family and Life.

26th August

In an interview with Chicago's *NBC 5's TV News*, Cardinal Cupich responded to accusations that Pope Francis had covered-up Cardinal McCarrick's homosexual depravity:

> For the Holy Father, I think to get into each and every one of those aspects, in some way is inappropriate and secondly, the pope has a bigger agenda. He's gotta get on with other things of talking about the environment and protecting migrants and carrying on the work of the Church. We're not going to go down a rabbit hole on this.[1408]

29th August

At a meeting with 200 seminarians at Mundelein Seminary, pro-homosexual Cardinal Cupich — appointed by Pope Francis — responded to concerns about the sex abuse

[1406]Viganò, CM [2018] *Testimony* [Online] Available at: www.documentcloud.org [Accessed on: 17 October 2022]

[1407]Sciambra, J [2018] *LGBT activist deacon assists Cardinal Farrell in closing Mass at Vatican-run family meeting* [Online] Available at: www.lifesitenews.com [Accessed on: 17 October 2022]

[1408]Cullinan Hoffman, M [2018] *Cdl. Cupich: Pope's 'bigger agenda' focuses on environment, migrants, not sex abuse* [Online] Available at: www.lifesitenews.com [Accessed on: 17 October 2022]

scandals and the homosexual predations of former Cardinal McCarrick rocking the Church. He told the seminarians that he didn't 'buy the argument advanced by some in the church that homosexuality is at the root of much of the sexual abuse by priests... facts don't bear that out, and it's wrong' to blame a group of people that way.'

He also said that the Church had a bigger agenda that dealing with the sex abuse of children, 'While the church's "agenda" certainly involves protecting kids from harm, we have a bigger agenda than to be distracted by all of this, including helping the homeless and sick.'[1409]

11th September

Pro-homosexual Bishop Vincent Long Van Nguyen of Parramatta — appointed by Pope Francis — gave an address to the National Council of Priests, Canberra, Australia. During his address he expressed openness to the 'ordination' of women:

> In fact, important as it is to consider the question of women ordained ministries in the Church (for which the Study Commission on Women's Diaconate was set up), it is far worse to persist with structures that fail to convey the message of the Gospel to the deep yearnings of men and women of today.

He went on to criticise St. John Vianney, the patron saint of parish priests, as an outdated model of the priesthood:

> Ironically, the whole clerical culture is often geared towards individual heroism and male chauvinism. The Curé of Ars, John Vianney, blessed John, he was a hard man wasn't he? He denounced dancing among other things. He is a patron saint par excellence for this kind of priestly individual heroism. No wonder many of us suffer from ministerial burn out, depression, and loneliness.[1410]

13th September

Pope Francis rejected a request from the US bishops to order an apostolic visitation of the North American Church to investigate how former Cardinal Theodore McCarrick was able to reach the most senior position in the hierarchy despite the Vatican and US bishops knowing of allegations of his homosexual depravity. US journalist Phil Lawler observed that this made it clear that Pope Francis did not want a full and honest investigation into the McCarrick homosexual abuse scandal.[1411]

14th September

Andrea Tornielli, (later appointed by Pope Francis editorial director of the Dicastery for Communication in December 2018) published an article in the Italian newspaper *La Stampa*. Tornielli made the bizarre claim that the scandal about Cardinal McCarrick was not about homosexuality but clericalism. He wrote:

> The McCarrick disaster...is an obvious case of psychological abuse, abuse of power and conscience and sexual abuse. It has been treated for too long only as a case of homosexual practice. No, McCarrick did not have homosexual relations. He harassed and abused seminarians in the name of his episcopal power, making them understand that going to the beach house with him and submitting to his attention was an obligatory step to be better known to him and to land a priestly ordination.[1412]

[1409]Mainwaring, D [2018] *Cdl. Cupich on abuse crisis: We shouldn't be 'distracted' by this, Church has 'bigger agenda'* [Online] Available at: www.lifesitenews.com [Accessed on: 17 October 2022]

[1410]Cummings McLean, D [2018] *Australian bishop touts women's ordination: 'transformation of priesthood' is underway* [Online] Available at: www.lifesitenews.com [Accessed on: 17 October 2022]

[1411]Lawler, P [2018] *Does the Pope want the truth? Now we know* [Online] Available at: www.catholicculture.org [Accessed on: 17 October 2022]

[1412]Tornielli, A [2018] *McCarrick case: abuse and clericalism. Doubts on his appointment* [Online] Available at: www.lastampa.it [Accessed on: 17 October 2022]

18th September

Pope Francis announced his appointment of 39 special delegates to the Synod on young people, including many who were pro-homosexual and with records of advocating erroneous teaching — Cardinal Marx, Cardinal Cupich, Cardinal Tobin, Archbishop Vincenzo Paglia and Father Antonio Spadaro.[1413]

The Vatican released Pope Francis' new apostolic constitution entitled *Episcopalis Communio* [Episcopal Communion]. The apostolic constitution transformed the synod of bishops into a deliberative, legislative body rather than a consultative one with the final synod document elevated to form part of the 'ordinary magisterium of the Successor of Peter,' subject to papal approval:

> If it is expressly approved by the Roman Pontiff, the Final Document participates in the ordinary Magisterium of the Successor of Peter. If the Roman Pontiff has granted deliberative power to the Synod Assembly, according to the norm of canon 343 of the *Code of Canon Law*, the Final Document participates in the ordinary Magisterium of the Successor of Peter once it has been ratified and promulgated by him. (art.18)[1414]

22nd September

The Vatican and People's Republic of China issued a joint statement announcing they had signed a 'provisional' agreement on the procedure for appointing Chinese Catholic bishops. The text of the agreement was not released and the content remained unknown. Cardinal Joseph Zen, emeritus Bishop of Hong Kong, responded:

> So, what is the result of all this work? What is the answer to our long wait? Nothing is said! Is it secret? The whole statement boils down to 'There was the signing of an agreement between the Holy See and the People's Republic of China on the appointment of Bishops'. All the rest are meaningless words. So, what is the message the Holy See intends to send to the faithful in China with this statement? 'Have faith in us, accept what we have decided'(?) And what will the government say to Catholics in China? 'Obey us, the Holy See already agrees with us'(?) Are we to accept and obey without knowing what must be accepted, to what one must obey?[1415]

Cardinal Zen also said:

> They're [sending] the flock into the mouths of the wolves. It's an incredible betrayal. The consequences will be tragic and long lasting, not only for the church in China but for the whole church because it damages the credibility.[1416]

Just an hour after the announcement, the communist government-approved Chinese Patriotic church declared its 'independence' from Rome, stating that it would remain loyal to the Communist Party.[1417]

In an exclusive interview with the *Global Times*, a daily tabloid owned by China's Communist Party, Bishop Marcelo Sánchez Sorondo, chancellor of the Vatican's Pontifical Academies for Sciences and Social Sciences, rebuked critics of the Vatican-China deal. He said:

> [The critics] are very strong in their position. They are loud, but there are not very many of them. They are a loud minority. In our interpretation, the critics are a little minority group of people, people who wanted to create trouble.

[1413]Kwasniewski, P [2018] *Pope Francis is no longer hiding his strategy for manipulating outcome of Youth Synod* [Online] Available at: www.lifesitenews.com [Accessed on: 17 October 2022]

[1414]Pope Francis [2018] *Apostolic Constitution Episcopalis communio* [Online] Available at: www. vatican.va [Accessed on: 17 October 2022]; Pentin, E [2018] *Pope Francis Boosts Authority of the Synod of Bishops* [Online] Available at: www.ncregister.com [Accessed on: 17 October 2022]

[1415]Mattei, R de [2018] *Is Pope Francis trying to fundamentally change the papacy?* [Online] Available at: www.lifesitenews.com [Accessed on: 17 October 2022]

[1416]Sherwood, H [2018] *Vatican signs historic deal with China – but critics denounce sellout* [Online] Available at: www.theguardian.com [Accessed on: 17 October 2022]

[1417]Mainwaring, D [2018] *China's communist-run church declares 'independence' immediately after deal with Vatican* [Online] Available at: www.lifesitenews.com [Accessed on: 17 October 2022]

He went on to praise the communist government of China, 'The country has a large population with good quality people, it observes the common good and it has proved its ability to great missions like fighting against poverty and pollution.'[1418]

Cardinal Cupich — appointed by Pope Francis — removed Fr. Paul Kalchik from Resurrection parish in Chicago in retaliation for the priest burning a homosexualist 'rainbow pride flag' previously used by the parish to promote the homosexual agenda. A member of the parish staff told *Church Militant*, 'Cardinal Cupich just sent an ultimatum — go, or the police will come. We could not stand for him to be taken away in handcuffs like a criminal. So he's gone.'[1419]

During his apostolic journey to Lithuania Pope Francis was presented with a book of photographs of Pope St. John Paul II. The pontiff responded, '[Pope John Paul II] was a saint, I am the devil.'[1420]

25th September

Following the release of the German bishops' report into clergy sex abuse — that revealed a high percentage of homosexual abuse — *Katholisch.de*, the news website of the German Bishops' Conference, published several articles denying the connection between homosexuality and priestly sex abuse.[1421]

29th September

Archbishop Carlo Maria Viganò issued a second testimony in response to Pope Francis refusing to respond to his first testimony accusing him of knowingly covering up Cardinal McCarrick's homosexual depravity and appointing him 'one of his principal agents in governing the Church':

> The center of my testimony was that since at least June 23, 2013, the pope knew from me how perverse and evil McCarrick was in his intentions and actions, and instead of taking the measures that every good pastor would have taken, the pope made McCarrick one of his principal agents in governing the Church, in regard to the United States, the Curia, and even China, as we are seeing these days with great concern and anxiety for that martyr Church.[1422]

1st October

Pro-homosexual Fr. Peter Beer, the Vicar General of Cardinal Marx's Archdiocese of Munich, praised the contribution of homosexual clergy and employees in an interview posted on the German bishops' website. He said:

> We have homosexual priests and homosexual employees, and these persons with homosexual inclinations [and acts?] render an important and good service and are an important part of the community of service, in which we together work for (and in the context of) the mission of Jesus.

Fr. Beer also denied that there was any link between homosexuality and clergy sexual abuse of teenagers and children:

> There are now, repeatedly, those claims that the studies [on clerical abuse in Germany] have shown that the abuse victims are mostly boys and the offenders mostly men. I wish

---

[1418]Craine, P [2018] *Vatican bishop rebukes critics of China deal: Communist nation 'observes the common good'* [Online] Available at: www.lifesitenews.com [Accessed on: 17 October 2022]

[1419]Niles, C [2018] *Chicago Priest Goes Into Hiding to Escape Cdl. Cupich's Punishment* [Online] Available at: www.churchmilitant.com [Accessed on: 17 October 2022]

[1420]*The Latest: Pope quips 'I am the devil' next to John Paul* [2018] [Online] Available at: apnews.com [Accessed on: 17 October 2022]

[1421]Hickson, M [2018] *German bishops' website quotes pro-gay Fr. Martin to refute link between homosexuality and sex abuse* [Online] Available at: www.lifesitenews.com [Accessed on: 17 October 2022]

[1422]*Archbishop Viganò issues new letter on Pope Francis and McCarrick* [2018] [Online] Available at: cruxnow.com [Accessed on: 17 October 2022]

to give a warning, not to draw – because of this observation – a direct connection between homosexuality and abuse… [This would] constitute an unbearable discrimination of persons with homosexual inclinations. I explicitly reject that and I ask us all, not to follow here such slogans.[1423]

4th October

Pro-homosexual Bishop Robert McElroy of San Diego — appointed by Pope Francis — held the third in a series of eight 'listening sessions'. A women accused Bishop McElroy of promoting homosexuality and supporting employees promoting homosexuality in his diocese:

Bishop McElroy, the reason that we think that you are promoting LGBT is because you use that nomenclature…You use the nomenclature of the homosexual activist agenda… You're advocating for removing the term 'intrinsically disordered' from the catechism with regards to homosexual acts. You're supporting what's going on down at St. John the Evangelist, because you came and concelebrated at the 'Always our Children' mass last October with Auxiliary Bishop Dolan, and all of the homosexual activists from San Diego were given front row seats.

When she referred to an openly homosexual man 'running the show' at the parish of St. John the Evangelist Bishop Robert McElroy cut her off:

Alright, you've gone far enough now. You're not going to stand here and disparage an employee of the diocese. You can leave if you're going to do that. The other things you can say — you cannot attack an employee of the diocese…I owe it to the employees of the Archdiocese [sic] not to let those calumnies be said.[1424]

16th October

A group of Synod Fathers at the Youth Synod led by pro-homosexual Cardinal Oscar Rodriguez Maradiaga — a close confident of Pope Francis — called for the Church to be open to the 'realities' of the lives of homosexuals:

There is the issue of what to do and how to act with homosexuals, which cannot remain outside of our pastoral activity and other realities such as marriages between homosexuals, wombs for rent, adoption on the part of couples of the same sex, all of which are current issues and favoured and sponsored by international governmental institutions.[1425]

19th October

Archbishop Carlo Maria Viganò, the former nuncio to the USA, released his third testimony in which he criticised the silence among the hierarchy about the scourge of clerical homosexuality. Archbishop Viganò wrote:

As to the second silence, this very grave crisis cannot be properly addressed and resolved unless and until we call things by their true names. This is a crisis due to the scourge of homosexuality, in its agents, in its motives, in its resistance to reform. It is no exaggeration to say that homosexuality has become a plague in the clergy, and it can only be eradicated with spiritual weapons. It is an enormous hypocrisy to condemn the abuse, claim to weep for the victims, and yet refuse to denounce the root cause of so

[1423]Hickson, M [2018] *With Cardinal Marx at Youth Synod, his vicar general says Munich diocese has 'homosexual priests'* [Online] Available at: www.lifesitenews.com [Accessed on: 17 October 2022]

[1424]O'Neill, T [2018] *'I have no faith in your will or your character,' abuse victim tells pro-LGBT Bishop McElroy* [Online] Available at: www.lifesitenews.com; Nussman, D [2018] *San Diego Bishop Kicks Out Young Orthodox Catholics* [Online] Available at: www.churchmilitant.com [Accessed on: 17 October 2022] [Accessed on: 17 October 2022]

[1425]Meloni, J [2018] *Is the Youth Synod's Final Document Already Written?* [Online] Available at: www.crisismagazine.com; Cummings McLean, D [2018] *Youth Synod group calls Church to attend to 'realities' of gay 'marriage', surrogacy, adoption* [2018] [Online] Available at: www.lifesitenews.com [Accessed on: 17 October 2022]

much sexual abuse: homosexuality. It is hypocrisy to refuse to acknowledge that this scourge is due to a serious crisis in the spiritual life of the clergy and to fail to take the steps necessary to remedy it.[1426]

22nd October

The Jesuit journal *America Magazine*, edited by pro-homosexual Fr. James Martin SJ — appointed by Pope Francis a consultor to the Vatican's Dicastery for Communication — published an article denying the link between homosexuality and clergy sex abuse of teenagers and children. Despite incontrovertible evidence to the contrary, Dr. Thomas G. Plante, a professor of psychology at the Jesuit Santa Clara University, asserted that sexual orientation was 'simply' not a factor in the clerical sex-abuse of minors.[1427]

23rd October

Vatican News, the Holy See's news agency, referred to Pope Francis as the 'successor of Christ' for the third time since the 29th August, when describing the pontiff's address in Dublin it stated, 'In the Procathedral of Dublin, the successor of Christ declared …'. On the 14th October *Vatican News* posted about Pope Francis, 'This person spoke in the terms of supply and demand, specified the successor of Christ …'. And on the 23rd October *Vatican News* listed Pope Francis' engagements for November to January, including the sentence, 'on Sunday, January 13, on the Feast of the Nativity of the Lord, the successor of Christ will celebrate Holy Mass and the baptism for children in the Sistine Chapel at 9:30.'[1428]

27th October

The Synod on 'Young People, the Faith and Vocational Discernment' concluded with the final document passing by the required two-thirds majority. As well as including the LGBT term 'sexual inclination' it called for changes to the Church's teaching on sexual morality:

> There are questions concerning the body, affectivity and sexuality which require a deepened anthropological, theological and pastoral elaboration, to be carried out in the most appropriate ways and at the most appropriate levels, from the local to the universal. (150).

The reference to the *Instrumentum Laboris*, with its inclusion of the acronym 'LGBT' was seen as a Machiavellian way of inserting the term into the ordinary magisterium of the Church:

> It is important to clarify the relationship between the *Instrumentum Laboris* and the Final Document. The former is the unitary and synthetic reference framework that emerged from the two years of listening; the second is the fruit of the discernment carried out and brings together the generative thematic nuclei on which the Synod Fathers concentrated with particular intensity and passion. We therefore recognize the diversity and complementarity of these two texts.[1429]

3rd November

Pro-homosexual Fr. James Martin SJ, appointed by Pope Francis a Vatican consultor and speaker at the 2018 International Meeting of Families, gave an address at the Ignatian Family Teach-in for Justice. He lauded the LGBT achievements of Pope Francis:

[1426]Montagna, D [2018] *Archbishop Viganò issues third testimony, refutes accusations of Cardinal Ouellet* [Online] Available at: www.lifesitenews.com [Accessed on: 17 October 2022]
[1427]Cummings McLean, D [2018] *Jesuit-run America mag runs article denying link between homosexuality and clergy sex abuse* [Online] Available at: www.lifesitenews.com [Accessed on: 17 October 2022]
[1428]Nardi, G [2018] *Vatican News Styles Pope as 'Successor of Christ'* [Online] Available at: www.theeponymousflower.com [Accessed on: 17 October 2022]
[1429]Montagna, D [2018] *Vatican Youth Synod final doc approved. Read the most controversial passages* [Online] Available at: www.lifesitenews.com [Accessed on: 17 October 2022]

Just look at what has happened in the last five years — since Pope Francis has been elected. First of all, Pope Francis's comments about LGBT people like 'Who am I to judge'. His five most famous words were in response to questions about gay people, right? He's the first pope to use the word 'gay', you know, in a sentence. He has gay friends. He's talked about wanting gay people to feel welcome in the Church. That's a big deal. He has also appointed gay-friendly bishops and archbishops and cardinals, like Cardinal Tobin, the archbishop of Newark who, for example, held a 'Welcome Mass' for LGBT people in his Cathedral… So that's one trend. Last week, for example, at the Synod of Youth [sic] at the Vatican, they had a whole gathering of bishops and experts … to talk about young people. And LGBT issues were discussed there more openly than at any Synod in the past, right? That's a big step forward. In their final document, the Synod delegates talked about accompaniment of LGBT people, listening to them, and acknowledge the work that many people in the Church do in ministering to this community. … The Synod couldn't quite bring itself to use the term LGBT, preferring to stick with 'sexual orientation' in quotes, thanks to opposition mainly from places where LGBT rights aren't as far along, in some diocese in the US and particularly in sub-Saharan Africa and India. Overall, though, the Church has moved ahead on these issues…and is learning. The Church is learning.[1430]

7th November

The traditional community of nuns, *Les Petites Sœurs de Marie, Mère du Rédempteur* [Little Sisters of Mary, Mother of the Redeemer] issued a statement following the Dicastery for Religious attempting to remove their superior general and impose three commissioners. The majority of nuns, who serve the elderly in French nursing homes, requested that they be released from their vows:

> After having acquired the moral certainty throughout this year that the reception of the apostolic commissioner within our Institute would cause serious and certain harm, both regarding the understanding of the charisma bequeathed by God to Mother Mary of the Cross, our Foundress, and the way of living it, after many times proposing solutions of appeasement without any answer ever having been given to us, after consulting with authorized and competent persons, after having prayed much and always with the desire to remain daughters of the Church, wanting to remain faithful and obedient to the truth, it seemed to us that we had no choice but to renounce our vows. We are therefore 34 out of 39 Sisters who are members of the Institute, who have asked to be relieved of our vows by the Dicastery for Religious….We do not make this sacrifice lightly: we desire to remain in full communion with the Church, but we cannot indicate more clearly, nor more painfully, our impossibility, in conscience, to obey what is imposed.[1431]

8th November

In an interview with the *Union of Catholic Asian News* Cardinal Zen, emeritus archbishop of Hong Kong, announced that he'd travelled to Rome at the end of October to deliver a seven-page letter to Pope Francis outlining the crisis engulfing the Church in China since the Vatican signed a secret deal with the Chinese Communist government. Cardinal Zen was not granted a meeting with the pontiff. The letter gave details of the persecution of underground priests including confiscated money, harassment by civil authorities, imprisonment, and even execution. He testified that:

> the Holy See does not support them and regards them as trouble, referring to them causing trouble and not supporting unity. This is what makes them most painful. The 'underground clerics have cried to him' as a result of the deal with the communists about

---

[1430]Cummings McLean, D [2018] *Fr. James Martin: Pope appoints 'gay-friendly' bishops, cardinals to change Church on LGBT* [Online] Available at: www.lifesitenews.com [Accessed on: 17 October 2022]

[1431]Cullinan Hoffman, M [2018] *Conservative order of nuns on verge of destruction following Vatican interventions* [Online] Available at: www.lifesitenews.com [Accessed on: 18 October 2022]

the appointment of bishops. Cardinal Zen also said: 'They said officials have forced them to become open, to join the (schismatic) Chinese Catholic Patriotic Association and to obtain a priest's certificate with the reason that the pope has signed the Sino-Vatican provisional agreement. Some priests have escaped, and some have disappeared because they do not know what to do and are annoyed. The agreement is undisclosed, and they do not know if what officials say is true or not.'[1432]

Vatican News — the 'information system of the Holy See' — posted an interview with the pro-abortion US nun Sister Simone Campbell, leader of the left-wing 'Nuns on the Bus'. In 2016 Sr. Campbell stated:

> If we were really serious about being pro-life, we wouldn't look just at birth. From my perspective, I don't think it's a good policy to outlaw abortion. I think, rather, let's focus on economic development for women and economic opportunity. That's what really makes the change.[1433]

9th November

Bishop Pietro Shao Zhumin of Wenzhou was kidnapped for the fifth time by Chinese communist police to undergo isolation and indoctrination for 10-15 days. Bishop Shao belongs to the underground church not recognized by the communists. When kidnapped in 2017 he was imprisoned for seven months.[1434]

13th November

Pro-homosexual Cardinal Cupich — appointed by Pope Francis — made an intervention from the floor of the US bishops' conference meeting. Cardinal Cupich told his fellow bishops that examinations of offences against minors should be separated from clergy sex acts with adults:

> Because in some of the cases with adults … involving clerics, it could be consensual sex, anonymous, but also involve adult pornography. There's a whole different set of circumstances that need to come into play here. In some of the cases with adults involving clerics, it could be consensual sex … there's a whole different set of circumstances.[1435]

17th November

Pro-homosexual Fr. Ansgar Wucherpfennig SJ, re-instated by the Vatican as the rector of the Jesuit graduate school in Frankfurt, Germany, gave an interview on the German bishops' website. Fr. Wucherpfennig explained that in order to be re-appointed he had not withdrawn his statements in favour of the blessing of homosexual bondings or his support for the 'ordination' of women, 'No, I did not recant.'[1436]

22nd November

La Croix International — the French Catholic website — published an interview with Cardinal Zen about his reaction to the Vatican-Chinese Communist 'secret' deal. Cardinal Zen said:

[1432]Cummings McLean, D [2018] *Cardinal Zen delivers new letter on China to Pope Francis: 'Underground clerics have cried'* [Online] Available at: www.lifesitenews.com [Accessed on: 18 October 2022]
[1433]Bordoni, L [2018] *'Nuns on the Bus' celebrate more women in power after US midterm elections* [Online] Available at: www.vaticannews.va ; Cummings McLean, D [2018] *Vatican's own news website profiles pro-abortion 'nun' praising US midterm election results* [Online] Available at: www.lifesitenews.com [Accessed on: 17 October 2022]
[1434]Cervellera, B [2018] *Wenzhou's bishop Shao Zhumin taken by police* [Online] Available at: www.asianews.it [Accessed on: 18 October 2022]
[1435]Bourne, L [2018] *Consensual' sex between clergy and adults 'different' than child sex abuse: Cupich* [Online] Available at: www.lifesitenews.com [Accessed on: 18 October 2022]
[1436]Hickson, M [2018] *Vatican-approved Jesuit rector: I still want to see homosexual couples blessed and women ordained* [Online] Available at: www.lifesitenews.com [Accessed on: 18 October 2022]

The Pope didn't get anything from this agreement, it's a 'fake,' an illusion, and Beijing made him lose his authority. The Chinese authorities still consider they are in charge of the Chinese Church and they will still choose the bishops. The Pope will only have the last word… As this agreement is secret, the Chinese think that all the process now is legalised and they can choose the bishops. They think the Holy See signed a white paper (blank check) and that they can do what they want.[1437]

23rd November

Pope Francis appointed pro-homosexual Cardinal Cupich to organise the Vatican summit on clergy sex abuse, held between February 21-24 2019. In a meeting with seminarians on the 29th August, despite the evidence, Cardinal Cupich had denied any links between homosexuality and clergy sex abuse. Instead, Cardinal Cupich blamed 'clericalism':

> … this crisis is about the abuse of power and a culture of protection and privilege, which have created a climate of secrecy, without accountability for misdeeds.[1438]

29th November

The German bishops' news website published an article by pro-homosexual Gerhard Kruip, a Catholic German ethics professor, in which he claimed many German bishops don't believe homosexual sex acts are morally depraved. Professor Kruip wrote:

> …most Catholics, theologians, and more and more bishops (even if they do not dare to say it in public) in Germany have come to the conviction that homosexual acts – at least then, when they are an expression of a loving relationship, in which the partners take responsibility for one another – are not something that is generally 'intrinsically disordered'.[1439]

12th December

Underground Bishop Vincent Guo Xijin of Mindong told his priests that Pope Francis had requested that he cede his diocese to the formerly excommunicated, communist-approved cleric Vincenzo Zhan Silu. He officially abdicated his position as the ordinary of the Diocese of Mindong in the presence of Msgr. Claudio Maria Celli, head of a Vatican delegation. Msgr. Celli informed Bishop Guo that Pope Francis expected him to agree as a 'gesture of obedience and of sacrifice for the general situation of the Chinese Church.' Msgr. Celli also announced that the underground bishop of Shantou, Msgr. Pietro Zhuang Jianjian would abdicate in favour of the formerly excommunicated Giuseppe Huang Bingzhang, also recently reconciled with the Holy See. Priests protested that the Vatican has consigned the Church into the hands of the communist government.[1440]

13th December

The regional German newspaper *Kölner Stadt-Anzeiger* published an interview with Bishop Heiner Wilmer of Hildesheim — newly appointed by Pope Francis — in which he said that it could no longer be claimed that the Church was 'pure and immaculate'. Bishop Wilmer said:

> I believe the abuse of power is in the DNA of the Church. We cannot any more shrug this off as something minor, but we have to rethink (the hierarchy) in a radical way.

[1437]Malovic, D [2018] *Pope Francis should stop negotiations with Beijing'* [Online] Available at: international.la-croix.com [Accessed on: 18 October 2022]

[1438]Montagna, D [2018] *Pope Francis appoints Cardinal Cupich to organize Vatican summit on clergy sex abuse* [Online] Available at: www.lifesitenews.com [Accessed on: 18 October 2022]

[1439]Hickson, M [2018] *Pro-LGBT Catholic prof: Many German bishops don't believe homosexual acts are wrong* [Online] Available at: www.lifesitenews.com [Accessed on: 18 October 2022]

[1440]*Mindong: Msgr. Guo Xijin, underground bishop, gives way to formerly excommunicated Msgr. Zhan Silu* [2018] [Online] Available at: www.asianews.it [Accessed on: 18 October 2022]

> We do not yet have any idea of what the consequences should be for theology....In the future, we will only then be able to confess the faith in the 'holy Church' when we also confess at the same time: This Church is also a sinful Church....[About the ecclesiological doctrine that there are in the Church individual sinners, but the Church herself is pure and immaculate:] We have to say good-bye to this and accept that there are 'structures of evil' in the Church as a community.[1441]

By so saying, Bishop Wilmer contradicts the Nicene Creed, which states, 'I believe in one, holy, catholic and apostolic Church.'

14th December

The German bishops' news website *Katholisch.de* posted an account of an address by Professor Marie-Jo Thiel at the Catholic Academy in Freiburg. Professor Thiel was appointed by Pope Francis as a member of his 'reformed' Pontifical Academy for Life. During her address she said that the Church's teachings on sexuality have been a 'complete failure', rejected the doctrine that homosexual acts are intrinsically disordered and can never be approved, and firmly rejected the Church's ban on contraception.[1442]

17th December

Pope Francis condemned all previous popes who employed the death penalty, though their acts were in conformity with sacred Scripture, sacred Tradition, and the perennial Magisterium. In his address to a delegation from the International Commission against the Death Penalty, the pontiff said:

> Even in the Papal State, this inhuman form of punishment was resorted to, ignoring the primacy of mercy over justice.[1443]

18th December

Chinese police raided an underground convent in the city of Qiqihar, Heilongjiang Province, evicted the nuns and set about destroying the convent. The local faithful suspected that the operation was designed to put pressure on the underground Catholic community to register under the government.[1444]

20th December

Cardinal Marx of Munich — a member of Pope Francis' advisory council of cardinals — spoke at the Munich Press Club in which he said that Pope Francis did not take a 'fixed position' on sexual morality. Cardinal Marx said:

> the Church has so far only spoken about sexuality in an 'odd and touchy [verschroben]' way, and now she needs 'to speak about sexuality in a different manner, also about homosexuality. As you know, this is highly controversial also theologically and dogmatically. We have to address it how, we do not yet fully know. To silence it, does not work anymore.'

About Pope Francis's position on sexual morality, Cardinal Marx said, 'I see that he is not so fixed here.' Despite the evidence, Cardinal Marx also rejected the claim that there is a link between homosexuality and clerical abuse, 'Priests with a homosexual

---

[1441]Hickson, M [2018] *New German bishop: Abuse crisis means 'goodbye' to Church as 'pure and immaculate'* [Online] Available at: www.lifesitenews.com [Accessed on: 18 October 2022]
[1442]Hickson, M [2018] *New Pontifical Academy for Life member questions Church teaching on homosexuality, contraception* [Online] Available at: www.lifesitenews.com [Accessed on: 18 October 2022]
[1443]Pope Francis [2018] *Audience with the Delegation of the International Commission against the Death Penalty* [Online] Available at: press.vatican.va [Accessed on: 18 October 2022]
[1444]Zhicheng, W [2018] *Nuns convent half demolished in Qiqihar* (Video) [Online] Available at: www.asianews.it [Accessed on: 18 October 2022]

inclination do not "endanger" others more than heterosexually inclined priests when it comes to clerical abuse.'[1445]

21st December

The US *Wall Street Journal* published an article accusing the appeals panel of the Congregation for the Doctrine of the Faith, established by Pope Francis, of showing leniency towards priests guilty of sex abuse. The *Wall Street Journal* reported, 'Previously most were handled by the full assembly of the Congregation for the Doctrine of the Faith, roughly two dozen cardinals and bishops. Appellants were almost never successful in winning reduced punishments.' By contrast, regarding the appeals panel:

> In its three years of operation, the college has reduced the penalties of at least 15 clerical sex abusers in Argentina, Mexico, Peru and other countries from defrocking—or removal from the priesthood—to temporary suspensions, ranging from three to five years, according to people familiar with the matter.[1446]

2019

1st January

A letter from Pope Francis to the American bishops concerning the clergy sex abuse crisis was published without mentioning 'homosexuality' or 'Cardinal McCarrick.' The pontiff instead criticised approaching the problem of pederasty and ephebophilia from a position of moral certainties and rigid formulations:

> This collegial awareness of our being sinners in need of constant conversion, albeit deeply distressed and pained by all that that has happened, allows us to enter into affective communion with our people. It will liberate us from the quest of false, facile and futile forms of triumphalism that would defend spaces rather than initiate processes. It will keep us from turning to reassuring certainties that keep us from approaching and appreciating the extent and implications of what has happened. It will also aid in the search for suitable measures free of false premises or rigid formulations no longer capable of speaking to or stirring the hearts of men and women in our time.

Pope Francis even went so far as to reject approaching the moral crisis from the position of Catholic doctrine and morality:

> The catholicity of the Church cannot be reduced merely to a question of doctrine or law; rather, it reminds us that we are not solitary pilgrims: 'If one member suffers, all suffer together' (I Cor 12:26).'[1447]

2nd January

Pope Francis criticised faithful who attended Mass daily but who failed to live the virtue of love, saying it would be better if they stopped going to church and became atheists. The pontiff said:

> How many times have we witnessed the scandal of those who go to church and spend all day there or attend every day, and later go on hating others or speaking ill of people. This is a scandal. It would be better to not go to church. Live like an atheist.[1448]

[1445]Hickson, M [2018] *Cdl. Marx: Pope Francis is 'not so fixed,' he's open to discussing sexual morality* [Online] Available at: www.lifesitenews.com [Accessed on: 18 October 2022]
[1446]Rocca, F [2018] *Vatican Panel Faces Criticism Over Leniency for Priests Guilty of Abuse* [Online] Available at: www.wsj.com [Accessed on: 18 October 2022]
[1447]Pope Francis [2019] *Letter to the Bishops of the United States of America Conference of Catholic Bishops* [Online] Available at: www.vatican.va [Accessed on: 18 October 2022]
[1448]Barillas, M [2019] *Pope Francis: It's better to be 'atheist' than attend daily mass as hypocrite* [Online] Available at: www.lifesitenews.com [Accessed on: 18 October 2022]

8th January

The Vatican released a new logo in advance of Pope Francis's visit to Morocco in March, featuring the syncretic fusion of the crescent of Islam encompassing the cross of Christ.[1449]

13th January

Pro-homosexual Cardinal Vincent Nichols of Westminster — elevated to the Sacred College of Cardinals by Pope Francis — celebrated a Mass for homosexuals at the Jesuit's Church of the Immaculate Conception, Farm Street, London. Cardinal Nichols was steadfast in his support for the notorious Soho Masses organised by LGBT militants. He told Catholics witnessing against these Masses to 'hold their tongues'.[1450]

16th January

The Vatican issued a statement about February's summit of bishops on clerical sex abuse that made it clear that it would only examine the sexual abuse of children by clergy. Many faithful expressed concern and dismay that it would not examine all cases of sexual abuse in the Church, including the homosexual abuse of young men and seminarians that typified the depravity committed by Cardinal McCarrick and other senior clergy.[1451]

24 January

Pope Francis delivered an address to the Central American Bishops during his apostolic journey to World Youth Day held in Panama. During his address the pontiff criticised the denouncing of heresy:

> Even in the Catholic media there is a lack of compassion. There is schism, condemnation, cruelty, exaggerated self-praise, the denouncing of heresy... May compassion never be lost in our Church and may the centrality of compassion never be lost in the life of a bishop.[1452]

25th January

The Diocese of Innsbruck, Austria, announced that it would host a set of 'seminars' for divorced and civilly 'remarried' couples with the purpose of allowing them, at the end of the seminar, to receive the sacraments of Reconciliation, Holy Communion and the blessing of their adulterous union. The Diocese of Innsbruck highlighted that Pope Francis' apostolic exhortation *Amoris Laetitia* was the inspiration of these seminars.

The Vatican announced Pope Francis' appointment of Fr. Carlos Castillo Mattaso-glio as the new Archbishop of Lima, Peru. During an interview with the Peruvian magazine *Caretas* in February 2019 Archbishop Mattasoglio said that he was against the Church opposing the legalisation of abortion:

> On the juridical level — I haven't studied the topic much — it does seem to me to be problematical when someone wishes to make laws and the Church seeks to impede it. What is necessary to do is to have a clarifying dialogue, not to make a political struggle out of it, because [the value of] life is an educational issue. I believe that people must

[1449]Montagna, D [2019] *Tashlan comes to town: Vatican releases combined cross and crescent logo for Pope's trip to Morocco* [Online] Available at: www.lifesitenews.com [Accessed on: 18 October 2022]
[1450]*Cardinal Nichols presides at Mass welcoming LGBT+ Catholics, parents and families* [2019] [Online] Available at: www.indcatholicnews.com; Jones, S [2014] *Vincent Nichols: enigmatic archbishop stepping into pope's inner circle* [Online] Available at: www.theguardian.com [Accessed on: 18 October 2022]
[1451]Dail, B [2019] *Catholic whistleblower criticizes Vatican abuse summit for only addressing minor abuse* [Online] Available at: www.lifesitenews.com [Accessed on: 18 October 2022]
[1452]Pope Francis [2019] *Address to Bishops of Central America* [Online] Available at: www.vatican.va [Accessed on: 18 October 2022]

reflect on it and decide in freedom. If they make a mistake, we continue to explain, helping them to become aware of it.[1453]

27th January

During the in-flight press conference on the return from World Youth Day in Panama, Pope Francis expressed his openness to abandon the Latin-rite tradition of priestly celibacy. The Pontiff admitted he was open to the ordination of *viri probati* in some circumstances:

> And [Bishop] Lobinger says: one can ordain an elderly man, married – that is his thesis – one could ordain an elderly married man, but only so that he exercises the *munus sanctificandi*, that is, that he celebrates Mass, that he administers the sacrament of Reconciliation and performs the Anointing of the Sick. Priestly ordination gives the three *munera: regendi* – to govern, the pastor –; *docendi* – to teach –, and, *sanctificandi*. This comes with ordination. The bishop would only give the faculties for the *munus sanctificandi*: this is the thesis. The book is interesting. Perhaps this can help in considering the problem. I believe that the problem must be opened in this sense, where there is a pastoral problem, because of the lack of priests. I'm not saying that it should be done, because I have not reflected, I have not prayed sufficiently about it.[1454]

31st January

The German magazine *Stern* published an interview with Cardinal Christoph Schönborn of Vienna, theological advisor to Pope Francis. During the interview Cardinal Schönborn asserted that the Church now accepted the State legalising homosexuals to enter 'civil marriages':

> To be honest, we have accepted it already for a long time... we define it differently and that we raise our voice when we believe that this path for the whole of society is not good. We may enter into the discussion, too.

He went on to praise the homosexual witness to 'marriage':

> I personally am moved that, at a time where marriage is losing its attraction, those couples who feel and live out a same-sex attraction yearn to have thus the highest form of partnership.

In his eyes, these couples thereby give 'witness that marriage is an important good.'[1455] Cardinal Schönborn's assertion that the Church had accepted homosexual 'civil marriage' contradicted the 2003 Congregation for the Doctrine of the Faith statement *Considerations Regarding Proposals to Give Legal Recognition to Unions Between Homosexual Persons*.[1456]

4th February

During his apostolic journey to the United Arab Emirates, Pope Francis signed with the Grand Imam of Egypt's al-Azhar mosque the *Document on Human Fraternity for World Peace and Living Together*. It included the controversial passage that a 'pluralism and diversity' of religions is 'willed by God', which is the heresy of Indifferentism. The document states:

[1453]Cullinan Hoffman, M [2018] *Massive annual March for Life in Lima postponed without explanation by new Francis-appointed archbishop* [Online] Available at: www.lifesitenews.com [Accessed on: 18 October 2022]

[1454]Pope Francis [2019] *In-flight press conference on return from World Youth Day at Panama* [Online] Available at: www.vatican.va [Accessed on: 18 October 2022]

[1455]Hickson, M [2019] *Cardinal Schönborn: 'Married' gays give 'witness that marriage is an important good'* [Online] Available at: www.lifesitenews.com [Accessed on: 18 October 2022]

[1456]*Congregation for the Doctrine of the Faith [2019] Considerations Regarding Proposals to Give Legal Recognition to Unions Between Homosexual Persons* [Online] Available at: www.vatican.va [Accessed on: 18 October 2022]

Freedom is a right of every person: each individual enjoys the freedom of belief, thought, expression and action. The pluralism and the diversity of religions, colour, sex, race and language are willed by God in His wisdom, through which He created human beings. This divine wisdom is the source from which the right to freedom of belief and the freedom to be different derives. Therefore, the fact that people are forced to adhere to a certain religion or culture must be rejected, as too the imposition of a cultural way of life that others do not accept.[1457]

During the in-flight press conference returning from the United Arab Emirates, Pope Francis claimed that the *Document on Human Fraternity for World Peace* had been approved by the papal theologian:

I had some theologians read [the document] and even [had it read] officially by the theologian of the Pontifical Household, that is a Dominican, and with the beautiful tradition of the Dominicans not to go on a witch-hunt, but to see where is the right thing... and he approved it.[1458]

However, it later emerged that the papal theologian, Fr. Wojciech Giertych OP was consulted but did not see the final draft of the controversial document.'[1459]

8th February

Bishop Schneider of Astana, Kazakhstan, warned that the Vatican's sex abuse summit would be 'doomed to failure' if it failed to address homosexuality among the clergy, and such an omission would display 'a peculiar form of clericalism'. Bishop Schneider wrote:

If it will not highlight the predominant role of homosexual behaviour in the clerical sexual abuse cases, the Summit will give a highly irresponsible answer and will be doomed to failure from the start, manifesting thereby also a peculiar form of clericalism... the overwhelming majority of the cases of clerical sexual abuse were of a homosexual nature. The predominant cause of sexual abuses on the part of the clergy is consequently and undeniably homosexual or sodomite vice.[1460]

10-12 February

Pope Francis sent a video message of support to the World Government Summit taking place in Dubai, United Arab Emirates, the main objective being to implement the UN's 'Sustainable Development Goals'. The Sustainable Development Goals include ensuring 'universal access to sexual and reproductive health and reproductive rights', including contraception and legal abortion.[1461]

The *National Catholic Register* published an essay written by Archbishop Carlo Viganò expressing his concerns about the Vatican's sex abuse summit. Archbishop Carlo Viganò wrote:

Why will the meeting focus exclusively on the abuse of minors? These crimes are indeed the most horrific, but the crises in the United States and Chile that have largely precipitated the upcoming summit have to do with abuses committed against young adults, including seminarians, not only against minors. Almost nothing has been said

[1457]Pope Francis [2019] *The Document on Human Fraternity for World Peace and Living Together* [Online] Available at: www.vatican.va [Accessed on: 18 October 2022]
[1458]Pope Francis [2019] *In-flight press conference on return from Abu Dhabi* [Online] Available at: www.catholicnewsagency.com [Accessed on: 18 October 2022]
[1459]Montagna, D [2019] *Papal theologian never saw final draft of controversial doc with Muslims, contrary to Pope's claims* [Online] Available at: www.lifesitenews.com [Accessed on: 18 October 2022]
[1460]Barillas, M [2019] *Bishop Schneider: Abuse summit will be 'doomed' if it doesn't address homosexuality* [Online] Available at: www.lifesitenews.com [Accessed on: 18 October 2022]
[1461]Pope Francis [2019] *Video message of his holiness pope francis to the participants in the World Government Summit* [Online] Available at: www.catholicnewsagency.com [Accessed on: 18 October 2022]

about sexual misconduct with adults, which is itself a grave abuse of pastoral authority, whether or not the relationship was 'consensual.' Why does the word 'homosexuality' never appear in recent official documents of the Holy See? This is by no means to suggest that most of those with a homosexual inclination are abusers, but the fact remains that the overwhelming majority of abuse has been inflicted on post-pubescent boys by homosexual clerics. It is mere hypocrisy to condemn the abuse and claim to sympathise with the victims without facing up to this fact honestly. A spiritual revitalisation of the clergy is necessary, but it will be ultimately ineffectual if it does not address this problem. Why does Pope Francis keep and even call as his close collaborators people who are notorious homosexuals? Why has he refused to answer legitimate and sincere questions about these appointments? In doing so he has lost credibility on his real will to reform the Curia and fight the corruption.[1462]

14th February

Pope Francis appointed Cardinal Kevin Farrell as papal camerlengo, making him responsible for administering the Vatican when the pontiff dies or resigns and before the election of a successor. Cardinal Kevin Farrell was a close associate of the disgraced homosexual predator Cardinal McCarrick, even sharing an apartment with him for six years when he served as McCarrick's auxiliary bishop.[1463]

16th February

The German news magazine *Der Spiegel* published an interview with Cardinal Gerhard Müller, the former prefect of the Congregation for the Doctrine of the Faith. Cardinal Müller said that Pope Francis allowed himself to be dependent upon his counsellors who had 'base motives':

> Unfortunately, he is surrounded by people who have little understanding of theology and of the Church's social teaching, but who do not wish to abandon the century-old mentality of a courtier.

Cardinal Gerhard Müller also objected to the intention of the Vatican's Sexual Abuse Summit to ignore the role of homosexuality in these crimes:

> In the Congregation for the Faith, we had the statistically perfect overview. Far more than 80% of the victims of sexual abuse under 18 years of age were young men in puberty or post-puberty. But at the upcoming Abuse Summit starting Thursday, these data are not to play any role, which is unreasonable.[1464]

18th February

Pope Francis removed the canonical sanctions imposed in 1984 by Pope St. John Paul II against the communist Nicaraguan priest Ernesto Cardenal. Pope St. John Paul II had suspended Fr. Cardenal's priestly faculties due to his political militancy and his serving as a member of the cabinet of the Nicaraguan dictator José Daniel Ortega. Canon law prohibits priests participating in political office. (Can. 285). Pope Francis restored Fr. Cardenal's faculties despite the fact that he had not repented his disobedience.[1465]

Pro-homosexual Cardinal Cupich participated in a press conference ahead of the Vatican's sex abuse summit. Diane Montagna asked whether homosexuality among the clergy would be discussed in the light of more than 80% of the victims of these sexual

[1462]Viganò, C [2019] *Despite Grave Problems, the Lord Will Never Abandon His Church* [Online] Available at: www.ncregister.com [Accessed on: 18 October 2022]
[1463]Barillas, M [2019] *Pope Francis names Cardinal with close ties to McCarrick as key figure in next papal election* [Online] Available at: www.lifesitenews.com [Accessed on: 18 October 2022]
[1464]Hickson, M [2019] *Vatican's former doctrine chief: Pope is 'surrounded' by people who don't know much theology* [Online] Available at: www.lifesitenews.com [Accessed on: 18 October 2022]
[1465]Barillas, M [2019] *Pope Francis lifts Pope St. John Paul's sanction on Communist priest* [Online] Available at: www.lifesitenews.com [Accessed on: 18 October 2022]

offenders being teenagers of the male sex. Cardinal Cupich admitted that the majority were 'male on male sex abuse' but refused to call it 'homosexuality':

> Yes, I believe that it's important to admit the fact and recognize the fact of what you said in terms of the percentage of abuse involving male on male sex abuse. That is important. I think that has to be recognized. At the same time, as professional organizations studied the causes and contexts — such as the John Jay School of Criminal Justice and also the Royal Commission's report in Australia — indicated that homosexuality itself is not a cause. It is a matter however of opportunity and also a matter of poor training on the part of people.

Italian journalist Sandro Magister referred to Cardinal Cupich's earlier reference to a sharp drop in recent years in American cases of abuse against minors, against teenagers due to 'very strong screening in seminaries.' He asked Cardinal Cupich to, therefore, confirm that 'the elimination of the presence of homosexual tendencies in aspirants to the priesthood and then in the clergy' went to the root of the problem of clergy sex abuse. Cardinal Cupich denied that the purpose of the screening was to identify and remove candidates with homosexual tendencies:

> The screening is important, not in terms of the issue of homosexuality but in terms ... [of] an attitude about human sexuality that is not in keeping with the Church...it is not a particular screening that has to do with one's sexual orientation as the major factor.[1466]

By saying this, Cardinal Cupich contradicted the 2005 Instruction *Concerning the Criteria for the Discernment of Vocations with regard to Persons with Homosexual Tendencies in view of their Admission to the Seminary and to Holy Orders.*[1467]

19th February

Cardinal Raymond Burke and Cardinal Walter Brandmüller published an open letter to the presidents of bishops' conferences attending the Vatican's clergy sex abuse summit. The cardinals criticised the summit for planning to ignore the role of homosexuality in the crisis and instead blame it on 'clericalism':

> The plague of the homosexual agenda has been spread within the Church, promoted by organised networks and protected by a climate of complicity and a conspiracy of silence. The roots of this phenomenon are clearly found in that atmosphere of materialism, of relativism and of hedonism, in which the existence of an absolute moral law, that is without exceptions, is openly called into question. Sexual abuse is blamed on clericalism. But the first and primary fault of the clergy does not rest in the abuse of power but in having gone away from the truth of the Gospel. The even public denial, by words and by acts, of the divine and natural law, is at the root of the evil that corrupts certain circles in the Church.[1468]

20th February

On the eve of the Vatican's sex abuse summit Pope Francis launched an impromptu attack on his critics when he departed from his prepared text. The pontiff said:

> One cannot live one's whole life accusing, accusing, accusing the Church. Whose office is it to accuse? Who is the one the Bible calls the Great Accuser? The devil! And those who spend their lives accusing, accusing, accusing, are — I will not say children, because the devil doesn't have any — but friends, cousins, relatives of the devil.

[1466]Montagna, D [2019] *Cardinal Cupich: Vast majority of clergy abuse is homosexual, but homosexuality 'not a cause'* [Online] Available at: www.lifesitenews.com [Accessed on: 18 October 2022]
[1467]Congregation for Catholic Education [2005] *Instruction Concerning the Criteria for the Discernment of Vocations with Regard to Persons with Homosexual Tendencies in View of Their Admission to the Seminary and to Holy Orders* [Online] Available at: www.vatican.va [Accessed on: 18 October 2022]
[1468]Pentin. E [2019] *Cardinals Burke and Brandmüller: 'End the Conspiracy of Silence'* [Online] Available at: www.ncregister.com [Accessed on: 18 October 2022]

Since December 2018 Andrea Tornielli, appointed by Pope Francis editorial director of Vatican communications, had publicly identified Archbishop Viganò and Cardinal Joseph Zen of Hong Kong the 'Great Accuser' and 'another great accuser' respectively.[1469]

21st February

Archbishop Charles Scicluna of Malta, one of the organisers of the Vatican's sex abuse summit, answered journalists questions on the opening day. Sandro Magister, the Italian journalist, asked him about the complete absence of any reference to 'homosexuality', particularly in light of the fact that over 80 percent of clerical abuse victims were post-pubescent boys. In his reply Archbishop Scicluna equated homosexuality with heterosexuality, despite sacred Scripture and Tradition's condemnation of homosexual sex acts:

> You spoke about one category, someone else could speak about heterosexuality. These are human conditions that we recognize, that exist. But they aren't something that really predisposes to sin... But I would never dare point to a category as one that has the propensity to sin. We all have the same propensity.[1470]

During a later press conference *LifeSiteNews* asked Archbishop Scicluna about the connection between a homosexual subculture among the clergy, and the sex abuse crisis. The Maltese archbishop tersely replied that homosexuality among the clergy 'has nothing to do with sexual abuse of minors. You cannot not address misconduct of that nature, which is sinful, but this is not about the sexual abuse of minors.'[1471]

The Pontifical Council for Interreligious Dialogue sent a letter to Catholic university professors in Rome informing them of Pope Francis' request for the 'widest possible dissemination' of the *Document on Human Fraternity for World Peace and Living Together* signed by Pope Francis and by Ahmad el-Tayeb, Grand Imam of Egypt's al-Azhar Mosque. The document was heavily criticised for containing the heretical statement, 'The pluralism and the diversity of religions, colour, sex, race and language are willed by God in His wisdom, through which He created human beings.'[1472]

24th February

During his closing address to the Vatican sex abuse summit Pope Francis failed to mention the homosexual nature of the majority of crimes, instead blaming 'clericalism':

> It is difficult to grasp the phenomenon of the sexual abuse of minors without considering power, since it is always the result of an abuse of power, an exploitation of the inferiority and vulnerability of the abused, which makes possible the manipulation of their conscience and of their psychological and physical weakness. [...] It will be precisely this holy People of God to liberate us from the plague of clericalism, which is the fertile ground for all these disgraces.[1473]

1st March

Archbishop Charles Scicluna of Malta sent a personal representative — whom he highly recommended — to take part in a discussion on the LGBT lifestyle on the Maltese TV show *Xarabank*. Fr. Kevin Schembri, a theologian and jurist at the University of Malta

[1469]Montagna, D [2019] *Pope says on eve of abuse summit: Those who spend lives accusing Church are 'relatives of the devil'* [Online] Available at: www.lifesitenews.com [Accessed on: 18 October 2022]

[1470]Montagna, D [2019] *Archbishop at Vatican abuse summit: Homosexuality isn't 'something that really predisposes to sin'* [Online] Available at: www.lifesitenews.com [Accessed on: 18 October 2022]

[1471]Montagna, D [2019] *Vatican summit organizer: Gay subculture in seminaries has 'nothing to do with sex abuse of minors'* [Online] Available at: www.lifesitenews.com [Accessed on: 18 October 2022]

[1472]Hickson, M [2019] *Pope asks universities to disseminate his claim 'diversity of religions' is 'willed by God'* [Online] Available at: www.lifesitenews.com [Accessed on: 18 October 2022]

[1473]Pope Francis [2019] *Address at the close of the meeting on the protection of minors in the Church* [Online] Available at: www.vatican.va [Accessed on: 18 October 2022]

made various statements contrary to the Church's doctrine on homosexuality. His response to the question, is being 'gay' 'bad' in the eyes of God? Fr. Schembri responded:

> It cannot be something bad, because he created it. God created it, and he created it in his plan. Therefore to be gay, meaning when a person in the depth of their heart recognises that he or she is a person who is gay or lesbian, that person is recognising how God created them.

In response to the question, do those who are gay and Catholic, need to change? Fr. Schembri responded,

> No. If he recognises that he is a gay person as created by God, he does not need to change. Rather, I would dare say, he would be harming himself if he tries not to accept himself or herself as they are as a gay person, and sometimes this, but this would take much more time to discuss, this is where what we call 'internalised homophobia' comes in.

In response to the question, does the Bible condemn sodomy, quoting I Corinthians 6:9?, Archbishop Scicluna's personal representative responded:

> St. Paul was not writing there to the Corinthians about gays as we understand them today, when we are talking about persons who acknowledge that they had a different sexual orientation, or persons who for example, are living an experience of love, which is sincere, and who are authentic towards themselves.

Fr. Schembri's eisegesis of the Bible contradicts the *Catechism of the Catholic Church*'s condemnation of homosexual sex acts:

> Basing itself on Sacred Scripture, which presents homosexual acts as acts of grave depravity, tradition has always declared that 'homosexual acts are intrinsically disordered.' (CCC 2357).[1474]

6th March

Pope Francis met, and was photographed with, members of LGBT+ Catholics Westminster, the latest manifestation of the militant homosexual group, the Soho Masses Pastoral Council. The group included LGBT activists Julian Filochowski, the former director of CAFOD, an agency of the Bishops' Conference of England and Wales, and Martin Pendergast, a former Carmelite priest. They entered into a civil 'union' in 2006. Pro-homosexual Cardinal Nichols of Westminster, elevated to the Sacred College of Cardinals by Pope Francis, published a letter expressing his support for the homosexuals meeting Pope Francis, which included the following exhortation:

> May St. Peter and St. Paul, and indeed all the Apostles, continue to guide you on your way, and may you never fail to be inspired by their witness as faithful servants of our Lord and Saviour, Jesus Christ.[1475]

11th March

Vatican News published the opinion of a member of the Bergoglian Pontifical Academy for Life that in some circumstances children should be prescribed 'puberty blockers.' Laura Palazanni, Professor of Law at the University of Rome, argued that the puberty blocker triptorelin should be used 'only briefly' to create 'a window of opportunity' to allow medical assessments. Triptorelin is used to treat prostate cancer and is also used to cause 'chemical castration'.[1476]

[1474]Cullinan Hoffman, M [2018] *God makes people 'gay', says priest standing in for Maltese archbishop in TV interview* [Online] Available at: www.lifesitenews.com [Accessed on: 18 October 2022]

[1475]Gamble, R [2019] *LGBT Catholics Westminster meet Pope Francis* [Online] Available at: www.thetablet.co.uk [Accessed on: 18 October 2022]

[1476]Cummings McLean, D [2019] *Vatican News runs interview claiming puberty blockers okay in 'very restricted cases'* [Online] Available at: www.lifesitenews.com [Accessed on: 18 October 2022]

14th March

The Vatican published Pope Francis' telegram of condolence for the death of pro-homosexual Cardinal Godfried Danneels, Archbishop Emeritus of Mechelen-Brussel. Though Cardinal Danneels supported the legalisation of abortion and homosexual 'marriage' and covered up clergy sex abuse of children, Pope Francis praised him as a 'zealous pastor' who 'served the Church with dedication.'[1477]

Cardinal Marx of Munich — a member of Pope Francis' advisory group of cardinals — gave a press conference at the close of the German Bishops' Conference's spring assembly. Cardinal Marx announced that the Church in Germany would begin a 'synodal path' led by the heterodox lay group, the Central Committee of German Catholics (ZdK) that would re-evaluate doctrine on the Church, celibacy, and sexual morality. Cardinal Marx also referred to the proposals made to the German bishops by Professor Eberhard Schockenhoff who advocated that the Church change her doctrine on contraception, cohabitation, gender theory, and homosexual couples. In the light of this, Cardinal Marx concluded that there is 'a need for discussion about the Catechism.'[1478]

25th March

Pope Francis visited the Marian shrine of Loreto. A video was released showing the pontiff grimacing as he repeatedly snatched his hand away as a queue of faithful attempted to kiss the papal ring. The Vatican later issued a statement explaining he did it for reasons of 'hygiene'.[1479]

2nd April

Pope Francis' apostolic exhortation to young people *Christus Vivit* [Christ is Alive] in response to the Youth synod contained yet another attack on Tradition. The pontiff wrote:

> Let us ask the Lord to free the Church from those who would make her grow old, encase her in the past, hold her back or keep her at a standstill.

He also gave a platform to those who questioned the Church's sexual morality, highlighting 'homosexuality':

> … sexual morality often tends to be a source of 'incomprehension and alienation from the Church, inasmuch as she is viewed as a place of judgment and condemnation'. Nonetheless, young people also express 'an explicit desire to discuss questions concerning the difference between male and female identity, reciprocity between men and women, and homosexuality'.[1480]

During his apostolic journey to Morocco Pope Francis delivered a homily at Rabat's Cathedral of Saint Peter. The pontiff told the faithful not to 'proselytise' and increase the members of their Church:

> For Jesus did not choose us and send us forth to become more numerous! He called us to a mission. He put us in the midst of society like a handful of yeast: the yeast of the Beatitudes and the fraternal love by which, as Christians, we can all join in making present his kingdom.[1481]

[1477]Pope Francis [2019] *Telegram of condolences for the death of His Eminence Cardinal Godfried Danneels* [Online] Available at: www.vatican.va [Accessed on: 18 October 2022]

[1478]Hickson, M [2019] *'Need for change': Cdl. Marx says German bishops will revisit Catholic sexual teaching* [Online] Available at: www.lifesitenews.com [Accessed on: 19 October 2022]

[1479]Montagna, D [2019] *Disturbing video: Pope Francis refuses to let Catholic faithful kiss his papal ring* [Online] Available at: www.lifesitenews.com [Accessed on: 19 October 2022]

[1480]Pope Francis [2019] *Post Synodal Apostolic Exhortation Christus Vivit* [Online] Available at: www.vatican.va [Accessed on: 19 October 2022]

[1481]Cummings McLean, D [2019] *Pope Francis warns Moroccan Christians against 'proselytism'* [Online] Available at: www.lifesitenews.com [Accessed on: 19 October 2022]

4th April

Pope Francis appointed pro-homosexual Archbishop Wilton D. Gregory of Atlanta as the Archdiocese of Washington D.C. Archbishop Gregory permitted the Shrine of the Immaculate Conception (Atlanta, GA) to act as a centre for LGBT events and appointed a pro-homosexual priest to be the diocesan spiritual director for victims of sexual abuse by clergy.[1482]

5th April

Cardinal Pietro Parolin, Pope Francis' Secretary of State, met with a pro-homosexual international delegation of judges, financiers, legal experts, politicians and LGBT militants. The purpose of the meeting was to elicit the Holy See's support for the decriminalisation of homosexuality. The delegates praised Pope Francis' intervention with the Bishops of Belize who had initially opposed the repeal of the country's law that criminalised sodomy, but unexpectedly dropped their support of the appeal against changing the law. The delegates state:

> We humbly request the Vatican to consider issuing a public statement in which the official policy of the Holy See is clarified, noting the active steps taken by Pope Francis to resolve the matter in Belize and the opinion of the UN Independent Expert on SOGI [sexual orientation and gender identity] sent to us for the purpose of this meeting: 'I am convinced that a pronouncement of His Holiness would have been of fundamental importance in the work of fighting violence and discrimination that affects hundreds of millions of people every day.'[1483]

7th May

During the in-flight press conference returning from the apostolic journey to Bulgaria and North Macedonia, Pope Francis said that the commission on women 'deacons' did not reach agreement.[1484] Though the pontiff did not make public the report of the commission, others revealed some of its contents. Professor Peter Hünermann, a prominent German theologian in favour of women's 'ordination' to the diaconate told *LifeSiteNews* that the commission's report found that 'there is no historical evidence that in the patristics women were ordained as deacons.' He concluded that the fact that Pope Francis 'has withheld the results for months now' was 'a sign for me that he does not agree with this statement as it stands.'[1485]

12th April

Cardinal John Dew of New Zealand — elevated to the Sacred College of Cardinals by Pope Francis — published a newsletter addressed to all the faithful urging them to stop referring to their priests as 'Father' in the name of fighting 'clericalism' in the Church. Pope Francis had identified 'clericalism' as the cause of sex abuse, despite the evidence showing homosexuality involved in 80% of sex abuse crimes. Cardinal Dew wrote:

> Being called 'Father' may seem important to some priests, but is it really that important? Making a choice to tell the people we serve not to call us Father (or for me 'Your Eminence' or 'Cardinal') might seem a very small thing to do, but it may be the beginning of the reform in the Church which we have been asked to do by Pope Francis.[1486]

[1482]Bourne, L [2019] *US archbishop appoints pro-gay priest as 'spiritual guide' for sex abuse victims: report* [Online] Available at: www.lifesitenews.com [Accessed on: 19 October 2022]
[1483]Barillas, M [2019] *LGBT activists claim Pope Francis helped to ensure decriminalisation of gay sex acts in Belize* [Online] Available at: www.lifesitenews.com [Accessed on: 19 October 2022]
[1484]O'Connell, G [2019] *Pope says commission of women deacons did not reach agreement* [Online] Available at: www.americamagazine.org [Accessed on: 19 October 2022]
[1485]Hickson, M [2019] *Theologian claims Vatican commission on female deacons found no evidence they existed* [Online] Available at: www.lifesitenews.com [Accessed on: 19 October 2022]
[1486]Barillas, M [2019] *New Zealand cardinal asks laity to stop calling priests 'Father' to fight 'clericalism'* [Online] Available at: www.lifesitenews.com [Accessed on: 19 October 2022]

17th April

Pro-homosexual Cardinal Joseph Tobin of Newark, New Jersey — elevated to the Sacred College of Cardinals by Pope Francis — gave an interview to NBC's *Today Show* in which he questioned the Church's doctrine on homosexuality. When mistakenly challenged about the *Catechism of the Catholic Church* referring to homosexuality as 'intrinsically disordered' (The Catechism refers to homosexual acts as 'intrinsically disordered' *CCC* 2357) Cardinal Tobin responded: 'That is…it's very unfortunate language. Let's hope that eventually that language is a little less hurtful.'[1487]

30th April

An international group of 19 Catholic academics and clergy published an open letter addressed to the world's bishops requesting that they investigate Pope Francis for the canonical delict of heresy. It was the follow up to the 2017 Filial Correction delivered to Pope Francis, *Correctio Filialis de Haeresibus Propagatis*.[1488] The letter to the bishops accusing Pope Francis of heresy stated, among other things:

> We take this measure as a last resort to respond to the accumulating harm caused by Pope Francis's words and actions over several years, which have given rise to one of the worst crises in the history of the Catholic Church [...] Since Pope Francis has manifested heresy by his actions as well as by his words, any abjuration must involve repudiating and reversing these actions, including his nomination of bishops and cardinals who have supported these heresies by their words or actions. Such an admonition is a duty of fraternal charity to the Pope, as well as a duty to the Church. If – which God forbid! – Pope Francis does not bear the fruit of true repentance in response to these admonitions, we request that you carry out your duty of office to declare that he has committed the canonical delict of heresy and that he must suffer the canonical consequences of this crime.

Pope Francis later responded to these allegations of heresy by saying he found them 'humorous'.[1489] Cardinal Gerhard Müller, former Prefect of the Congregation for the Doctrine of the Faith, responded that as some of the signatories were 'renowned theologians' it was important that Pope Francis responded to their allegations:

> …it would be important that the Holy Father makes the Congregation for the Faith issue a response, and not the Secretary of State or any of his friendly journalists or theologians.

There was no such response.[1490]

2nd May

Katholische.de, the website of the German Catholic Bishops, posted an interview with pro-homosexual Bishop Franz-Josef Overbeck of Essen about the October 2019 Amazonian synod. Bishop Overbeck enthusiastically predicted that the synod would lead to a 'break' in the Church and that 'nothing will be the same as it was.' He expected and welcomed radical changes to the Church's doctrine on sexual morality, the male priesthood, and priestly celibacy.[1491]

[1487]Mainwaring, D [2019] *Cardinal Tobin calls Catholic teaching on homosexuality 'unfortunate… hurtful'* [Online] Available at: www.lifesitenews.com [Accessed on: 19 October 2022]

[1488]*Correctio Filialis de haeresibus propagatis* [2019] [Online] Available at: www.correctiofilialis.org [Accessed on: 19 October 2022]

[1489]Hickson, M [2019] *Prominent clergy, scholars accuse Pope Francis of heresy in open letter* [Online] Available at: www.lifesitenews.com [Accessed on: 19 October 2022]; Gledhill, R [2019] *Scholars and priests accuse Pope of heresy* [Online] Available at: www.thetablet.co.uk [Accessed on: 19 October 2022]

[1490]Hickson, M [2019] *Vatican's former doctrine chief: open letter accusing pope of heresy deserves 'response'* [Online] Available at: www.lifesitenews.com [Accessed on: 19 October 2022]

[1491]Cummings McLean, D [2019] *Pro-LGBT German bishop: 'Nothing will be the same' in Church after Amazon Synod* [Online] Available at: www.lifesitenews.com [Accessed on: 19 October 2022]

4th May

In an address to the Swiss Guard Pope Francis told them that 'religious diversity' was a 'human wealth'. The pontiff said:

> This will help you to live in society with the right attitude, recognising cultural, religious, and social diversity as human wealth and not as a threat. This is particularly important in a world where there are, as never before, large movements of populations and people searching for security and a dignified life.[1492]

6th May

Pope Francis appointed Cardinal Claudio Hummes, emeritus archbishop of São Paulo, to serve as 'relator general' of the Amazon Synod. Cardinal Hummes was an outspoken advocate of the end of mandatory celibacy for priests in the Latin-rite and the priestly ordination of married men.[1493]

8th May

The regional German newspaper *Osnabrücker Zeitung* published an interview with pro-homosexual Bishop Franz-Josef Bode of Osnabrück and Vice-President of the German Bishops' conference about his hopes for the Amazonian synod. He wanted to see the end of mandatory priestly celibacy in the Latin-rite Catholic Church and the introduction of married, part-time priests. He could 'very well imagine that there are also priests with family and [civil] job, similar to our deacons, some of whom are married and have a job.'[1494]

10th May

Pope Francis took part in a Q & A with the International Union of Superiors General in which he gave a modernist interpretation of the 'development of doctrine'. The pontiff said:

> The Church is not only Denzinger, that is, the collection of dogmatic passages, of historical things. This is true, but the Church develops on her journey in fidelity to Revelation. We cannot change Revelation. It's true the Revelation develops. The word is 'development' — it develops with time. And we with time understand the faith better and better. The way to understand the faith today, after Vatican II, is different from the way of understanding the faith before Vatican II. Why? Because there is a development of knowledge. You are right. And this isn't something new, because the very nature — the very nature — of Revelation is in continual movement to clarify itself.[1495]

The Catholic news website *Crux* published an edited note from a prominent advocate in the fight against clerical abuse concerning his meeting with Pope Francis. During their meeting Pope Francis told him he'd read Frédéric Martel's book about homosexuals in the Vatican, *Inside the Closet of the Vatican: Power, Homosexuality, Hypocrisy*. The source sent a message to Martel which *LifeSite*News published in full. It stated:

> After I met you [Frédéric Martel] in Rome, I met with the Pope and asked him about your book [...] He said he had read it. He said it was good. That he knew of many of them. He told me being gay is not a problem. We discussed good gays and those gays that are evil but because of power.[1496]

[1492]*Shrinking Swiss Guards implored by pope to embrace diversity* [2019] [Online] Available at: cruxnow. com [Accessed on: 19 October 2022]

[1493]Barillas, M & Mainwaring, D [2019] *Pope Francis' choice to oversee Amazon Synod suggests married priests on the horizon* [Online] Available at: www.lifesitenews.com [Accessed on: 19 October 2022]

[1494]Hickson, M [2019] *German bishops' vice president expects Amazon synod to propose married priests 'with civil job'* [Online] Available at: www.lifesitenews.com [Accessed on: 19 October 2022]

[1495]Hickson, M [2019] *Vatican media official: No, Pope Francis did not nix possibility of female deacons* [Online] Available at: www.lifesitenews.com [Accessed on: 19 October 2022]

[1496]Giangravè, C [2019] *Advocate says pope read, liked new book on gays in the Vatican* [Online] Available at: cruxnow.com [Accessed on: 19 October 2022]

11th May

The German daily newspaper *Der Tagesspiegel* published an interview with Pro-homosexual Bishop Franz-Josef Bode of Osnabrück and Vice-President of the German Bishops' conference. Bishop Bode expressed his support for feminist Catholics breaking the obligation of assisting Mass on Sunday. He said:

> I like this initiative, in order to set an example for [the promotion of] more participation of women in the Catholic Church. One has really to take into account the impatience of many women in the Catholic Church. Behind it, there is to be found a deep wound that they are not being properly welcomed in accordance with their service.

14th-15th May

The Pre-Synodal Council of the Special Assembly of the Synod of Bishops for the Pan-Amazon Region approved the *Instrumentum Laboris* of the October Synod. The working document promoted indigenous pagan religions:

> For the indigenous peoples of the Amazon Basin, the good life comes from living in communion with other people, with the world, with the creatures of their environment, and with the Creator. Indigenous peoples, in fact, live within the home that God created and gave them as a gift: the Earth. Their diverse spiritualities and beliefs motivate them to live in communion with the soil, water, trees, animals, and with day and night. Wise elders – called interchangeably '*payés, mestres, wayanga* or *chamanes*', among others – promote the harmony of people among themselves and with the cosmos.(6).

Furthermore, it celebrated belief in 'earth' spirits:

> the life of the Amazonian community has not yet been influenced by Western civilization. This is reflected in the beliefs and rites regarding the action of spirits and the divinity — named in many different ways — with and in the territory, with and in relation to nature. This cosmo-vision is picked up in Francis's 'mantra': 'everything is connected'.(25).

It also promoted pagan pantheism:

> The Creator Spirit which fills the universe (cf. Wisdom 1:7) is the Spirit that for centuries has nurtured the spirituality of these peoples even before the proclaiming of the Gospel and spurs them onto accepting it, from the base of their [own] cultures and traditions. (n.120).

It also advocated the development of ministerial roles for women:

> Another is to propose new ministries and services for the different pastoral agents, ones which correspond to activities and responsibilities within the community. Along these lines, it is necessary to identify the type of official ministry that can be conferred on women, taking into account the central role which women play today in the Amazonian Church. It is also necessary to foster indigenous and local-born clergy, affirming their own cultural identity and values. Finally, new ways should be considered for the People of God to have better and more frequent access to the Eucharist, the center of Christian life (cf. *DAp* 251). (14).[1497]

17th May

Katholische.de, the website of the German Catholic Bishops, posted an address of Bishop Ulrich Neymeyr of Erfurt, Germany — appointed by Pope Francis — in which he supported the 'ordination' of women. Bishop Neymeyr questioned the reservation of the priesthood to men, asking 'what does representation [of Christ] mean? How far

---

[1497]Pre-Synodal Council of the Special Assembly of the Synod of Bishops for the Pan-Amazon Region [2019] '*Amazonia: New Paths for the Church and for an Integral Ecology*': *Preparatory Document of the Synod of Bishops for the Special Assembly for the Pan-Amazon Region* [Online] Available at: press.vatican.va [Accessed on: 19 October 2022]

does it go? And does it need to be related to [biological] sex?' He added, in Germany 'there might already be a majority of people who can imagine female ordination. I, too.'[1498] By saying this, Bishop Neymeyr contradicted Pope St. John Paul II's Apostolic Letter *Ordinatio Sacerdotalis*.[1499]

28th May

The Latin American media group *Televisa* published Valentina Alazraki's extensive interview with Pope Francis. During the interview the pontiff said that accusations of heresy made against him by nineteen Catholic academics and clergy were 'humorous'. When asked how he took the accusation that he was a heretic, he responded:

> With a sense of humour, my daughter. It does not hurt me at all. Hypocrisy and lies hurt me, these hurt me. But such a mistake, where there are even people who have filled their heads with … no, please, you have to take care of them too. I also pray for them because they are wrong and poor people, some are manipulated. And who are those who signed…?

Pope Francis went on to talk about the Catholic Church's relations with the communist government of China, that was intensifying its persecution of the underground church:

> I love the Chinese very much. Relations with China are good, very good. The other day two Chinese bishops came to me, one who came from the underground church and the other from the patriotic church, already recognized as brothers. They came here to visit us. This is an important step. They know that they must be good patriots and that they must take care of the Catholic flock.

When asked about his knowledge of the homosexual depravity of Cardinal McCarrick Pope Francis replied, 'I didn't know anything … nothing, nothing.'[1500] In response to Pope Francis' emphatic denial of any knowledge regarding Cardinal McCarrick's homosexual abuse of seminarians Archbishop Viganò said:

> What the Pope said about not knowing anything is a lie. […] He pretends not to remember what I told him about McCarrick, and he pretends that it wasn't him who asked me about McCarrick in the first place.[1501]

3rd June

During his in-flight press conference returning from his apostolic journey to Romania, Pope Francis praised an unnamed Catholic archbishop for leading Lutheran worship in a Lutheran cathedral. The pontiff said:

> In one European city, there is a good relationship between the Catholic archbishop and the Lutheran archbishop. The Catholic archbishop was scheduled to come to the Vatican on Sunday evening, and he called me to say that he would arrive on Monday morning. When he arrived, he told me: 'Excuse me, but yesterday the Lutheran archbishop had to go to one of their meetings, and he asked me: "Please, come to my cathedral and lead the worship."' Eh, there's fraternity. Coming this far is a lot. And the Catholic bishop preached. He did not do the Eucharist, but he preached. This is fraternity.

Pope Francis went on to deny that the Orthodox were in schism from the Catholic Church:

[1498]Hickson, M [2019] *German bishop laments 'shackle' of Church's refusal to ordain women* [Online] Available at: www.lifesitenews.com [Accessed on: 19 October 2022]

[1499]Pope St. John Paul II [1994] *Apostolic Letter Ordinatio sacerdotalis* [Online] Available at: www. vatican.va [Accessed on: 18 October 2022]

[1500]Mares, C [2019] *Pope Francis responds to heresy accusation, China concerns* [Online] Available at: www.catholicnewsagency.com [Accessed on: 19 October 2022]

[1501]Montagna, D [2019] *Abp Viganò says Pope is lying in latest denial about McCarrick* [Online] Available at: www.lifesitenews.com [Accessed on: 19 October 2022]

> We Catholics also have closed people who do not want [to pray together] and say that the Orthodox are schismatics. That's old business. The Orthodox are Christians. But there are some Catholic groups that are a bit fundamentalist. We have to tolerate them, and pray for them, that the Lord by the Holy Spirit softens their hearts.

The pontiff yet again criticised Catholic who upheld Tradition as 'fundamentalists':

> In an interview made by Andrea Monda in *L'Osservatore* Romano a few days ago (do you read *L'Osservatore Romano*?) there was a quotation of the musician Gustav Mahler that I liked so much. Speaking of tradition, he said that tradition is the guarantee of the future and not the keeper of ashes. It is not a museum. Tradition does not preserve ashes; the nostalgia of fundamentalists [is] to return to the ashes. No, tradition is the roots that guarantee the tree grows, flowers and gives fruit. I repeat with that piece by the Argentine poet I like so much: 'All that the tree has in bloom comes from that which it has underground.'[1502]

[What Mahler actually said is practically a contradiction of Pope Francis' position: 'Tradition is not the worship of ashes but the preservation of the flame'.]

In an interview in the US Jesuit journal *America Magazine* Archbishop Rino Fisichella discussed his revision of the 1993 *Theological Commentary on the Catechism of the Catholic Church*. Archbishop Fisichella explained the radical change to the Commentary's section on the death penalty to be in accord with Pope Francis' rescript declaring the death penalty 'inadmissible' and 'contrary to the gospel':

> Sometimes we are guilty of giving the impression that tradition is an exercise akin to an athletics relay in which the aim is to pass the gold baton of the faith onto the next runner just exactly as it was received. But this conception risks reducing tradition to a fly in amber and ends up negating its very origin and purpose. Tradition has its origin in the Gospel which the living Christ ordered the Apostles to preach and to hand on to their successors, the bishops. It is precisely tradition which allows the church to confront new situations and evaluate them in the light of the Gospel. To deny this dynamic nature of tradition is tantamount to denying the contemporaneity of the Christian faith.[1503]

However, Archbishop Rino Fisichella ignores the fact that any development of doctrine is not allowed to contradict the original doctrine, as Pope Francis' change does.

4th June

The German daily *Frankfurter Rundschau* published an interview with Cardinal Walter Kasper, Emeritus bishop of Rottenburg-Stuttgart and adviser to Pope Francis, which discussed his expectations of the Amazonian synod. Cardinal Kasper said that if the synod proposed that married men should be ordained to the priesthood, Pope Francis would 'in principle probably accept it.' He added, 'celibacy is not a dogma, it is not an unalterable practice.'[1504]

6th June

Pope Francis appointed pro-homosexual Cardinal Joseph Tobin of Newark, New Jersey, as a member of the Vatican's Congregation for Catholic Education. Cardinal Tobin publicly criticised on US TV the *Catechism of the Catholic Church*'s presentation of homosexuality, saying that it contained 'very unfortunate language. Let's hope that eventually that language is a little less hurtful.'[1505]

[1502]Pope Francis [2019] *In-flight press conference on return from Romania* [Online] Available at: www. catholicnewsagency.com [Accessed on: 19 October 2022]

[1503]Salai, S [2019] *Meet the Bishop behind the updated catechism* [Online] Available at: www. americamagazine.org [Accessed on: 19 October 2022]

[1504]Montagna, D [2019] *Cardinal Kasper: Pope Francis will 'probably accept' married priests if Amazon synod proposes it* [Online] Available at: www.lifesitenews.com [Accessed on: 19 October 2022]

[1505]Barillas, M [2019] *Pope Francis appoints pro-LGBT Cdl. Tobin to oversee Catholic education* [Online] Available at: www.lifesitenews.com [Accessed on: 19 October 2022]

10th June

Following the Vatican's takeover of the Sovereign Military Order of Malta, the Grand Master of the Order issued a letter banning the Extraordinary Form of the Roman Rite of the Mass. Fra Dalla Torre stated:

> Henceforth, all the liturgical ceremonies within our Order must be performed according to the ordinary rite of the Church (rite of St. Paul VI) and not the extraordinary rite (Tridentine rite)… This decision applies to all the official liturgical celebrations such as investitures, Masses during our pilgrimages, memorial masses, as well as the feasts and solemnities of the Order.

He banned the traditional Latin Mass in the name of 'cohesion and communion'.[1506] Henry Sire, expelled from the Order for penning *The Dictator Pope*, commented:

> The first thing to understand about the Grand Master banning celebrations in the traditional rite is that its real author is likely Baron von Boeselager who has just obtained his re-election as Grand Chancellor for another five years. The move is another step in the programme of revenge that Boeselager has pursued against the traditionalist party — who were strong in the Order's government until he forced Fra' Matthew Festing out in 2017. The appeal to the rule about 'keeping liturgical uniformity in a religious order' is completely spurious. It would be understandable in a uniform order such as the Jesuits (although even they have priests who say the traditional Mass), but the Order of Malta has always been a very decentralised organization, in which each country was allowed to set its own way of doing things. That, however, is not to Boeselager's liking. He wants an absolute dictatorship in the Order, and he has pretty well achieved it.[1507]

15th June

The Catholic news website *Crux* posted an interview with Sister María Luisa Berzosa, appointed by Pope Francis as a Consultor of the General Secretariat of the Synod of Bishops, one of four nuns appointed to this role in a historic first. Sister Berzosa expressed her hope that women would one day be 'ordained' priests:

> Things would have to change [she said.] But I think that if steps are taken, processes are made, responsibilities are assumed, the [ordination of women] can be at the end of this process, without much ado, as a natural progression. It is true that when I accompany a person spiritually, I can't hear their confession, and I have to call somebody else to lead the liturgy. And sometimes I wish I was able to do that.[1508]

20th June

The United States Conference of Catholic Bishops approved a revision to its *U.S. Catechism for Adults* implementing Pope Francis' ban on the death penalty, in contradiction to sacred Scripture and sacred Tradition. In 2017 Pope Francis declared that the death penalty was 'inadmissible' and 'contrary to the gospel'. Bishop Robert Barron — appointed by Pope Francis — spoke in support of the radical break with the Church's perennial doctrine:

> To my mind, the pope maintains and our version imitates a certain, if you want, eloquent ambiguity on that point. Where it doesn't use the language of intrinsic evil for example. But it uses language like that, inadmissible, morally unacceptable… So we're just trying to imitate as much as we can what's found in the way the pope revised this teaching. But I wouldn't dare speak to what the mind of the pope on that is, but that's

[1506]Barillas, M [2019] *Order of Malta bans traditional Latin Mass for its liturgical ceremonies* [Online] Available at: www.lifesitenews.com [Accessed on: 19 October 2022]

[1507]Dail, B [2019] *Knights of Malta members suspect Latin Mass banned to 'cleanse' order of traditionalists* [Online] Available at: www.lifesitenews.com [Accessed on: 19 October 2022]

[1508]San Martín, I [2019] *New member of Synod office says pope making 'small steps' for women* [Online] Available at: cruxnow.com [Accessed on: 19 October 2022]

just my assessment of why that language is used. We just tried for the most part to imitate it.[1509]

28th June

Pro-homosexual Bishop John Stowe of Lexington, Kentucky — appointed by Pope Francis — issued a 'prayer card celebrating homosexual 'pride' and included an image of a crucifix with rainbow colours coming from it. Bishop Stowe wrote on the card:

> Dear sisters and Brothers, I greet you warmly and offer you my prayers on your behalf during this celebration of Pride. You are God's beloved.[1510]

The Vatican published *Pastoral Orientations for Bishops and Priests in the People's Republic of China* which, among other things, recommended that priests of the underground church register with the Chinese communist government. It states:

> If a Bishop or a priest decides to register civilly, but the text of the declaration required for the registration does not appear respectful of the Catholic faith, he will specify in writing, upon signing, that he acts without failing in his duty to remain faithful to the principles of Catholic doctrine. Where it is not possible to make such a clarification in writing, the applicant will do so at least orally and if possible in the presence of a witness. In each case, it is appropriate that the applicant then certify to his proper Ordinary with what intention he has made the registration. The registration, in fact, is always to be understood as having the sole aim of fostering the good of the diocesan community and its growth in the spirit of unity, as well as an evangelisation commensurate to the new demands of Chinese society and the responsible management of the goods of the Church.[1511]

Cardinal Joseph Zen — archbishop emeritus of Hong Kong — presented nine criticisms of the document to Pope Francis and Cardinal Pietro Parolin. Cardinal Zen wrote:

> A text is signed against the faith and it is stated that the intention is to promote the good of the community, a more suitable evangelisation, and the responsible management of Church assets. This general rule is obviously against all fundament[al] moral theology! If valid, [it] would justify even apostasy! […] This document has radically turned upside what is normal and what is abnormal, what is rightful and what is pitiable. Those who wrote it hope perhaps that the pitied minority will die a natural death. By this minority I mean not only underground priests, but also the many brothers in the official community who have worked with great tenacity to achieve change, hoping for the support of the Holy See.[1512]

29th June

On the Feast of the Apostles Sts. Peter and Paul, Pope Francis gave away precious relics of St. Peter the Apostle to the Orthodox Ecumenical Patriarch Bartholomew of Constantinople. The reliquary was kept in the papal chapel in the Apostolic Palace. Pope Francis justified his action by saying:

> I no longer live in the Apostolic Palace, I never use this chapel, I never [celebrate] Holy Mass here, and we have St. Peter's relics in the basilica itself, so it will be better if they will be kept in Constantinople. This is my gift to the Church of Constantinople. Please take this reliquary and give it to my brother Patriarch Bartholomew.[1513]

[1509]Bourne, L [2019] *US bishops follow Pope in calling death penalty 'inadmissible,' admit they don't know what it means* [Online] Available at: www.lifesitenews.com [Accessed on: 19 October 2022]

[1510]Moyski, M [2019] *KY Bishop John Stowe Aggressively Pushes LGBT Agenda* [Online] Available at: www.churchmilitant.com [Accessed on: 19 October 2022]

[1511]Tornielli, A [2019] *Orientations for the Chinese Clergy, respecting their freedom of conscience* [Online] Available at: www.vaticannews.va [Accessed on: 19 October 2022]

[1512]Dail, B [2019] *Cdl. Zen warns Pope Francis that Vatican directives for China church may lead to 'death of true faith'* [Online] Available at: www.lifesitenews.com [Accessed on: 19 October 2022]

[1513]Montagna, D [2019] *Pope Francis gives away relics of St. Peter to Orthodox patriarch* [Online] Available at: www.lifesitenews.com [Accessed on: 19 October 2022]

3rd July

In an interview with *LifeSiteNews*, Cardinal Kasper — a theological adviser to Pope Francis — called for women to be commissioned as lectors, extraordinary Eucharistic ministers, and leaders of liturgies of the word. Cardinal Kasper said:

> The Church is free to put into effect the vocation of women to these offices with the help of a non-sacramental, liturgical blessing – in the presence of the whole congregation and within the celebration of the Holy Eucharist (for example in the context of the Prayers of the Faithful) – and to do so in such a form that there is no confusion with a sacramental ordination. In similar ways, it is done in the case of the blessing of an abbot or an abbess, of a religious profession, of the Sacrament of Matrimony, and so on.[1514]

On the 23rd January 2022 Pope Francis formally conferred the ministries of lector and catechist on women during the celebration of Mass of the Word of God.[1515]

10th July

The Paraguayan newspaper *ABC Color* daily published an interview with Cardinal João Braz de Aviz, prefect of the Congregation for Institutes of Consecrated Life and Societies of Apostolic Life. Cardinal Braz de Aviz revealed that Pope Francis had directed that bishops at the upcoming Amazon Synod discuss ordaining married men to the priesthood for remote regions such as the Amazon, 'Francis launched that idea to be verified and studied, not for the entire Church, which has its problems, but at the same time is not the great central problem.'[1516]

24th July

Pro-homosexual Archbishop Vincenzo Paglia, Grand Chancellor of the John Paul II Pontifical Theological Institute for the Sciences of Marriage and the Family, sent a letter to all professors informing them that they had been suspended. Archbishop Vincenzo Paglia also eliminated courses viewed by many as central to the legacy of John Paul II. His action was part of the implementation of Pope Francis' re-modelling of the Institute according to *Amoris Laetitia*, as set out in his 2017 Motu Proprio *Summa Familiae Cura*.[1517] This act marked the de facto suppression of Pope St. John Paul II's world famous Institute and its replacement by Pope Francis' Pontifical John Paul II Theological Institute for Matrimonial and Family Science.

Monsignor Livio Melina, who held the Chair of Fundamental Moral Theology, along with Father José Noriega, who held the Chair of Specialised Moral Theology, were sacked as part of a purge of faithful Catholic professors. Monsignor Livio Melina, was the successor of the John Paul II Institute's founding president, Cardinal Carlo Caffarra, and, along with Father Noriega, staunchly upheld the Church's moral doctrine.[1518] In an interview Monsignor Livio Melina said to the Italian daily *La Verità*:

> If the decisions taken by Archbishop Paglia are not revoked, then what they are saying is: 'The interpretation of the magisterium of Pope Francis in continuity with the previous Magisterium is intolerable in the Church'... There is a paradox in all of this. Some dissenting theologians from Catholic moral theology, who clearly opposed the Magisterium, have been banned from teaching, but this happened after a regular trial. But what happened in the case of the professors of the John Paul II Institute?

[1514]Hickson, M [2019] *Cdl. Kasper calls for 'non-sacramental, liturgical blessings' for female Eucharistic ministers, lectors* [Online] Available at: www.lifesitenews.com [Accessed on: 19 October 2022]
[1515]*Pope to install catechists, lectors at Word of God celebration* [2019] [Online] Available at: www.ncronline.org [Accessed on: 19 October 2022]
[1516]Barillas, M [2019] *Vatican religious life chief: Pope wants priestly celibacy questioned at Amazon Synod* [Online] Available at: www.lifesitenews.com [Accessed on: 19 October 2022]
[1517]Pope Francis [2019] *Apostolic Letter Summa Familiae Cura* [Online] Available at: www.vatican.va [Accessed on: 18 October 2022]
[1518]Montagna, D [2019] *All profs suspended, president dismissed as part of 'destruction' of John Paul II Institute* [Online] Available at: www.lifesitenews.com [Accessed on: 19 October 2022]

The accusation is not that of denying Catholic doctrine, but only of not following a particular interpretation of the Magisterium of Pope Francis. But, above all, we have been deprived of our professorship without any possibility of defending ourselves, without us even having heard … what we are really accused of.[1519]

Archbishop Vincenzo Paglia also dismissed Professor Stanisław Grygiel, a former student of the then Father Karol Wojtyła at the Catholic University of Lublin, and friend of Pope John Paul II. Professor Grygiel observed:

Some professors have been removed from the Institute, some professors who read *Amoris Laetitia* in the light of the faith of the Church rooted in the Gospel and Tradition, and not, as Cardinal Christoph Schönborn of Vienna demanded in his discussion with Cardinal Carlo Caffarra, read the Tradition present in the teaching of the previous popes in the light of that document […] As a result of reading the revealed truth about man only in the light of today's here and now, it is very easy to descend to the level of flattering those truths that one's career depends on.[1520]

30th July

Pro-homosexual Archbishop Vincenzo Paglia, Grand Chancellor of the John Paul II Pontifical Theological Institute for the Sciences of Marriage and the Family, appointed a pro-contraception Italian priest to direct moral theology at the Bergoglian 'reformed' Institute. Pro-homosexual Fr. Maurizio Chiodi, a professor of moral theology at the Northern University of Milan and new member of Paglia's Pontifical Academy for Life, declared in a 2018 lecture, entitled *Re-reading Humanae Vitae (1968) in light of Amoris Laetitia* (2016):

There are circumstances — I refer to *Amoris Laetitia*, Chapter 8 — that precisely for the sake of responsibility, require contraception… an artificial method for the regulation of births could be recognized as an act of responsibility that is carried out, not in order to radically reject the gift of a child, but because in those situations responsibility calls the couple and the family to other forms of welcome and hospitality.

In an interview published on July 29, 2019 by the Italian bishops' conference newspaper, *Avvenire*, Fr. Chiodi said that, on the basis of *Amoris Laetitia*, sexual acts within a homosexual relationship can be good, at least in certain circumstances:

As Pope Francis recalled, even if regarding another issue — the 'divorced and remarried' — it is clear that, within a historical perspective, each person is asked not only what is possible for him, but also what is possible for him in a specific moment of life. […] I would not exclude that, under certain conditions, a homosexual couple's relationship is, for that subject, the most fruitful way to live good relationships, considering their symbolic meaning, which is both personal, relational and social. This, for example, happens when the stable relationship is the only way to avoid sexual vagrancy or other forms of humiliating and degrading erotic relationships or when it is help and stimulus to walk on the road to good relationships.[1521]

Pro-homosexual Paglia also invited pro-homosexual Fr. Pier Davide Guenzi to teach at the 'reformed' Institute. In an interview with the Italian bishops' conference newspaper, Fr. Guenzi advocated homosexual sex acts praising the 'potentialities for 'mutual enrichment' embedded in same-sex relationships, observing that 'the man-woman bond does not exhaust all forms of human expression even from the affective point

---

[1519]Montagna, D [2019] *JPII Institute profs dismissed for interpreting Francis in line with Tradition? Former president speaks out* [Online] Available at: www.lifesitenews.com; Nussman, D [2019] *John Paul II Institute: Dismissed Professor Speaks Out* [Online] Available at: www.churchmilitant.com [Accessed on: 19 October 2022]

[1520]Cummings McLean, D [2019] *Ousted JP2 Institute prof links institute's gutting to Amazon synod* [Online] Available at: www.lifesitenews.com [Accessed on: 19 October 2022]

[1521]Montagna, D [2019] *Pro-contraception priest invited to teach at new John Paul II Institute in Rome* [Online] Available at: www.lifesitenews.com [Accessed on: 19 October 2022]

of view.'[1522] Both Fr. Maurizio Chiodi and Fr. Pier Davide Guenzi contradict Catholic moral doctrine safeguarded and expressed by Pope St. John Paul II.

1st August

The German publisher *Herder Verlag* released the book *With the Blessing of the Church? Same-Sex Partnership in the Focus of Pastoral Care* with the support of two German bishops. Pro-homosexual Bishop Franz-Josef Bode of Osnabrück and pro-homosexual Archbishop Stefan Hesse of Hamburg wrote the preface to the book, in which they state:

> When homosexual men and lesbian women confess themselves as believing Christians – in spite of the experiences of rejection – and ask for pastoral care on their path of life, then this is very impressive and challenges us to develop together perspectives. Here, the 'wish for a blessing for same-sex partnerships as an expression of a faithful trust that God's love and fidelity toward us men is being effective in it' is to be mentioned.

The book includes a contribution by Jens Ehebrecht-Zumsande, an employee of the Archdiocese of Hamburg's pastoral department, who is very public about his homosexual relationship with the head of homosexual activist group *Pride Hamburg*.[1523]

13th August

Pro-homosexual Archbishop Wilton Gregory of Washington — appointed by Pope Francis — held a public Q & A during which he was asked a question by a woman who was presenting 'himself' as a 'man'. After saying that she 'worships' with the pro-homosexual group Dignity Washington, 'Rory' asked Archbishop Gregory, 'what place do I, as a confirmed transgender Catholic – what place do my queer friends have here at this diocese?' Gregory responded:

> You belong to the heart of this Church. And there is nothing that you may do, may say, that will ever rip you from the heart of this Church. There is a lot that has been said to you, about you, behind your back, that is painful and is sinful.[1524]

Archbishop Gregory made no reference to the danger of losing sanctifying grace through mortal sin.

14th August

Katholisch.de, the news website funded by the German bishops, posted an article by Abbot Jeremias Schröder OSB, arguing for the appointment of women as apostolic nuncios, which is traditionally reserved to clerics. This follows his post in July arguing that women should be allowed to preach at Mass. Abbot Jeremias Schröder was an outspoken supporter of Pope Francis' agenda to allow adulterers to receive Holy Communion at the 2015 synod.[1525]

20th August

Vatican News announced the creation of The Higher Committee of Human Fraternity established to promote the *Document on Human Fraternity for World Peace and Living Together* signed by Pope Francis and Grand Imam Al-Tayeb of Al-Azhar in Abu Dhabi in February 2019. The *Document on Human Fraternity* included the heretical statement that God willed the diversity of religions. Membership of The Higher Committee

---

[1522]Spinello, R [2019] *Meet the New Faculty at the John Paul II Institute* [Online] Available at: www.crisismagazine.com [Accessed on: 19 October 2022]

[1523]Hickson, M [2019] *Two German bishops endorse book calling for Church blessing for homosexual couples* [Online] Available at: www.lifesitenews.com [Accessed on: 19 October 2022]

[1524]Cummings McLean, D & Baklinski, P [2019] *New D.C. archbishop: transgender Catholics are in 'heart' of Church, part of 'the family'* [Online] Available at: www.lifesitenews.com [Accessed on: 19 October 2022]

[1525]Hickson, M [2019] *German bishops' website publishes piece proposing female papal nuncios* [Online] Available at: www.lifesitenews.com [Accessed on: 19 October 2022]

included Bishop Miguel Ángel Ayuso Guixot, President of the Pontifical Council for Interreligious Dialogue and Monsignor Yoannis Lahzi Gaid, Personal Secretary of Pope Francis.[1526] In an interview with *Vatican News*, Bishop Ayuso Guixot responded to the criticism that the Document was syncretistic without dealing with the even more serious accusation of the heresy of indifferentism:

> While respecting the opinions of those who may think that the Abu Dhabi Declaration may slip into syncretism or relativism, even in good faith, I believe that fear is the number one enemy of inter-religious dialogue. The Catholic Church recalls the value of its own identity, the courage of otherness and the sincerity of intentions. It is not a matter of making a 'melting pot' in which all religions are considered equal, but that all believers, those who seek God and all people of good will without religious affiliation, have equal dignity. We must therefore commit ourselves so that God, who created us, is not a reason for division, but for unity.[1527]

21st August

The Italian magazine *Tempi* published an interview with Fr. Arturo Sosa SJ, the Superior General of the Society of Jesus, in which he again denied an article of the Faith — the existence of the devil. Describing Satan as a 'symbolic reality', Fr. Arturo Sosa said:

> The devil exists as the evil personified in different structures but not in people, because it is not a person, it is a way of implementing the bad. He is not a person like a human person. It is a way of evil to be present in human life. Good and evil are in a permanent struggle in human consciousness, and we have ways to indicate them. We recognize God as good, entirely good. Symbols are part of reality, and the devil exists as a symbolic reality, not as a personal reality.

Prominent canon lawyer Ed Peters highlighted the seriousness of Sosa's denial of an article of Faith:

> Denial of an article of faith is an element of the canonical crime of heresy (1983 CIC 751), an act punishable by measures up to and including excommunication, dismissal from the clerical state, and/or loss of ecclesiastical office (1983 *CIC* 1364, 194). Failure to act on such information as is available in the public forum would constitute, in my view, a dereliction of governing duty. (see 1983 *CIC* 392, 1389).

Pope Francis had the duty to act in this case, which he chose not to exercise.[1528]

30th August

Luzerner Zeitung, a Swiss daily newspaper, quoted Hansruedi Huber, the official spokesman of the Diocese of Basel expressing the diocese's support for the legalisation of homosexual 'civil marriage.' The official spokesman said:

> We welcome the planned regulations that provide homosexual partnerships with stable and reliable legal security. It is important to us that children who grow up in same-sex partnerships are given a legal framework that serves the welfare of the child.[1529]

1st September

Pope Francis announced his elevation of 13 bishops to the Sacred College of Cardinals. Among the 13 were bishops who had expressed support for homosexuality, abortion, and indifferentism.

[1526]*Committee created to promote document on Human Fraternity* [2019] [Online] Available at: www.vaticannews.va [Accessed on 19 October 2022]

[1527]Smits, J [2019] *Pope Francis welcomes interfaith committee, controversial Abu Dhabi document* [Online] Available at: www.lifesitenews.com [Accessed on: 19 October 2022]

[1528]Bourne, L [2019] *Leader of Jesuit order: Satan exists only as a 'symbolic reality'* [Online] Available at: www.lifesitenews.com [Accessed on: 19 October 2022] ; Peters, E [2019] *Rev. Sosa's remarks on the devil warrant official response* [Online] Available at: canonlawblog.wordpress.com [Accessed on: 19 October 2022]

[1529]Smits, J [2019] *Swiss diocese officially applauds govt's efforts to legalize same-sex 'marriage'* [Online] Available at: www.lifesitenews.com [Accessed on: 19 October 2022]

- Archbishop Matteo Zuppi of Bologna, who wrote the preface for the Italian translation of the LGBT manifesto of pro-homosexual Fr. James Martin SJ;
- Archbishop José Tolentino de Mendonça, the archivist and librarian of the Holy Roman Church, who expressed support for the pro-homosexual, pro-abortion nun Sister Maria Teresa Forcades, and,
- Archbishop Miguel Angel Ayuso Guixot, who played a key role in drawing up the Abu Dhabi Declaration that contained the heresy of indifferentism.[1530]

3rd September

Archbishop Vincenzo Paglia, president of the Pontifical Academy for Life and Grand Chancellor of the John Paul II Institute delivered an address at Loyola Marymount, a Jesuit university in Los Angeles. During his address he made it clear that he wanted both institutions to abandon absolute, objective moral norms in their work and to re-define the Catholic understanding of human 'life':

> [Francis] warns us that it is risky to look at human life in a way that detaches it from experience and reduces it to biology or to an abstract universal, separated from relationships and history. Rather, the term 'life' must be redefined, moving from an abstract conception to a 'personal' dimension: life is people, men and women, both in the individuality of each person and in the unity of the human family.[1531]

4th September

Nicholas Seneze of the French heterodox Catholic *La Croix* magazine presented Pope Francis with a copy of his book *Comment l'Amerique veut changer de pape*, [How America Wants to Change Pope]. The pontiff responded: *'Per me è un onore che mi attaccano gli americani* [I think it's an honour that Americans attack me]'.[1532]

8th September

The German newspaper *Frankfurter Allgemeine Sonntagszeitung* published an interview with Cardinal Reinhard Marx, the President of the German Bishops' Conference. During the interview Cardinal Marx expressed the hope that the Amazonian synod would approve ending mandatory priestly celibacy to allow married priests. The German Bishops' Conference, which has heavily financed the Amazon Synod, is also considering married priests as part of its 'synodal path' discussions.[1533]

10th September

During the in-flight press conference returning from the apostolic journey to South Africa, Pope Francis admitted that he was not afraid of schism in the Church, before going on to criticise 'rigid' Catholics. The pontiff said:

> A schism is always an elitist separation stemming from an ideology detached from doctrine. It is an ideology, perhaps correct, but that engages doctrine and detaches it…. And so I pray that schisms do not happen, but I am not afraid of them. This is one of the results of Vatican II, not because of this or that Pope. For example, the social things that I say are the same things that John Paul II said, the same things! I copy him. But they say: the Pope is a communist…. Ideologies enter into doctrine and when doctrine slips into ideology that's where there's the possibility of a schism. There's the ideology

[1530]Montagna, D [2019] *Pope Francis raises concerns with surprise appointment of 13 new cardinals* [Online] Available at: www.lifesitenews.com [Accessed on: 19 October 2022]
[1531]Cummings McLean, D [2019] *'The term 'life' must be redefined,' new head of Vatican Life Academy declares* [Online] Available at: www.lifesitenews.com [Accessed on: 19 October 2022]
[1532]Pentin, E [2019] *Pope Francis Says It's an 'Honor' to be Criticized by Americans* [Online] Available at: www.ncregister.com [Accessed on: 19 October 2022]
[1533]Hickson, M [2019] *Cardinal Marx to attend Amazon Synod in October, says he can 'picture' it approving married priests* [Online] Available at: www.lifesitenews.com [Accessed on: 19 October 2022]

of the primacy of a sterile morality regarding the morality of the people of God. The pastors must lead their flock between grace and sin, because this is evangelical morality. Instead, a morality based on such a pelagian ideology leads you to rigidity, and today we have many schools of rigidity within the Church, which are not schisms, but pseudo-schismatic Christian developments that will end badly. When you see rigid Christians, bishops, priests, there are problems behind that, not Gospel holiness. So, we need to be gentle with those who are tempted by these attacks, they are going through a tough time, we must accompany them gently.[1534]

Responding to Pope Francis' comments about schism, Archbishop Vigano observed:

Pope Francis is saying that because he knows the Amazon Synod may provoke a schism. He is ready to say others are making the schism, but (by his actions in continuing to support the Amazon Synod) he is provoking it himself. Is this the attitude of a pastor who cares for the faithful? It is his own duty to prevent a schism.[1535]

Pope Francis also called on Catholics to 'obey' international organisations, such as the United Nations, ignoring its pro-abortion, pro-contraception, pro-homosexual agenda:

I would like to repeat what the Doctrine of the Church says about this: When we acknowledge international organisations and we recognise their capacity to give judgment, on a global scale – for example the international tribunal in The Hague, or the United Nations. If we consider ourselves humanity, when they make statements, our duty is to obey. It is true that not all things that appear just for the whole of humanity will also be so for our pockets, but we must obey international institutions. That is why the United Nations were created.[1536]

12th September

The Vatican posted a video message from Pope Francis inviting international organisations to participate in a 2020 conference held at the Vatican, *Reinventing the Global Educational Alliance*. During the video the pontiff said: 'A global educational pact is needed to educate us in universal solidarity and a new humanism.'[1537]

14h September

In an address to prison workers Pope Francis again expressed his opposition to life-sentences. The pontiff said:

Life imprisonment is not the solution to problems, but a problem to be solved. Because if hope is locked up, there is no future for society. Never deprive anyone of the right to start over! You, dear brothers and sisters, with your work and your service are witnesses of this right: the right to hope, the right to start anew.[1538]

Pope Francis made no reference to the victims of crimes or the requirement of justice. The pope's advocacy of leniency towards those who commit grave crimes follows his re-writing of the Catechism to state that the death penalty is 'inadmissible', overturning sacred Scripture and tradition.

19th September

ACI Prensa published an interview with Andrea Tornielli, appointed by Pope Francis the editorial director of the Vatican's Dicastery for Communications. Mr. Tornielli

---

[1534]Pope Francis [2019] *In-flight press conference on return from South Africa* [Online] Available at: www.vaticannews.va [Accessed on: 19 October 2022]

[1535]Moynihan, R [2019] *Letter #49, 2019: The Matter of Schism* [Online] Available at: insidethevatican.com [Accessed on: 19 October 2022]

[1536]Pope Francis [2019] *In-flight press conference on return from South Africa Op. cit.*

[1537]Montagna, D [2019] *Pope Francis invites religious, political leaders to sign 'Global Pact' for 'new humanism'* [Online] Available at: www.lifesitenews.com [Accessed on: 19 October 2022]

[1538]Cummings McLean, D [2019] *Pope Francis repeats opposition to life imprisonment: 'Not the solution'* [Online] Available at: www.lifesitenews.com [Accessed on: 19 October 2022]

confirmed that the Amazonian synod would discuss ending mandatory celibacy of priests in the Latin-rite:

> The synod will discuss the possibility, for territories like the Amazon, to propose the ordination of married men. That is, the ordination of catechists, older persons who already have a role of responsibility in several communities. But it's not a decision already made, nor is it certain that [the] synod will arrive at that decision. In any case it would not be a decision of the synod but it would be a decision of the pope.[1539]

Archbishop Chaput of Chicago issued a warning about the writings and activities of the pro-homosexual Fr. James Martin SJ, appointed by Pope Francis as a consultor to the Vatican. Archbishop Chaput wrote:

> At the same time, a pattern of ambiguity in his teachings tends to undermine his stated aims, alienating people from the very support they need for authentic human flourishing. Due to the confusion caused by his statements and activities regarding same-sex related (LGBT) issues, I find it necessary to emphasize that Father Martin does not speak with authority on behalf of the Church, and to caution the faithful about some of his claims.

Archbishop Chaput also challenged bishops who supported Fr. Martin:

> Supporters of Father Martin's efforts will note, correctly, that several Church leaders have endorsed his work. Those Churchmen are responsible for their words — as I am for mine, as pastor of the Church in Philadelphia. And specifically in that role as pastor, I want to extend the CDF's caution to all the faithful of the Church in Philadelphia, regarding the ambiguity about same-sex related issues found throughout the statements and activities of Father James Martin.[1540]

In response to Archbishop Chaput's warning about Fr. James Martin Pope Francis held a much publicised 'private' meeting with Fr. Martin on the 30th September. Fr Martin tweeted a photograph of his meeting Pope Francis, writing:

> Dear friends: Today Pope Francis received me for a private 30-minute audience in the Apostolic Palace, where I shared with him the joys and hopes, and the griefs and anxieties, of LGBT Catholics and LGBT people worldwide. I was so grateful to meet with this wonderful pastor. The only other person in the room during our meeting was his translator.[1541]

21st September

Pope Francis invited two notorious pro-abortionists as guests at the Amazonian synod, American economist Jeffrey Sachs, and Korean former Secretary-General of the United Nations Ban Ki-moon.[1542]

23rd September

Cardinal Reinhard Marx gave a press conference during which he disclosed that following his meeting with Pope Francis in Rome the pontiff had given permission for the German bishops to continue with their 'synodal path'. Pope Francis gave his permission even though the German synodal path intended to discuss female ordination, celibacy, and changing Church doctrine on sexual morality.[1543]

[1539]Cummings McLean, D [2019] *Married priests will be discussed at Amazon Synod: Vatican spokesman* [Online] Available at: www.lifesitenews.com [Accessed on: 19 October 2022]

[1540]Chaput, C [2019] *Father James Martin and Catholic belief* [Online] Available at: catholicphilly.com [Accessed on: 19 October 2022]

[1541]Cummings McLean, D [2019] *Pope Francis meets privately with pro-homosexual celebrity priest James Martin* [Online] Available at: www.lifesitenews.com [Accessed on: 19 October 2022]

[1542]Cummings McLean, D [2019] *Pope invites pro-abortion UN leaders to Amazon Synod* [Online] Available at: www.lifesitenews.com [Accessed on: 19 October 2022]

[1543]Hickson, M [2019] *Cdl Marx: 'no stop sign' from Pope Francis for our German synodal path on celibacy, sexual morality* [Online] Available at: www.lifesitenews.com [Accessed on: 19 October 2022]

24th September

The Vatican's Congregation for Catholic Education intervened to suspend a US archbishop's decision to cut diocesan ties with a Jesuit school that refused to sack a teacher who was openly homosexual. Archbishop Charles C. Thompson ruled that the school could no longer call itself 'Catholic' and ordered the Indianapolis archdiocese to cut official ties with Brebeuf Jesuit Preparatory School after it refused to fire Layton Payne-Elliott, a teacher who had contracted a same-sex 'marriage' to another teacher, Joshua Payne-Elliott, who had been fired by Indianapolis Cathedral High School. Brebeuf Jesuit Preparatory School, with the assistance of the Provincial of the USA Midwest Province of the Society of Jesus, appealed to the Congregation for Catholic Education to rescind and permanently set aside the Archbishop's decision. In 2020 the Vatican appointed pro-homosexual Cardinal Joseph Tobin of Newark to mediate between the archbishop and the school. The issue remains unresolved and the archbishop's decision remains suspended.[1544]

America Magazine broadcast an interview with pro-homosexual Cardinal Joseph Tobin of Newark in which he touched upon the Church's doctrine on sexual morality. He said, 'A rethinking of the mystery of human sexuality is important, is incumbent. It is not going to be done in a weekend'.[1545]

26th September

The heterodox English Catholic weekly magazine *The Tablet* published openly homosexual James Alison's account of a phone call from Pope Francis. James Alison had received the penalty of laicisation in 1990's from the Congregation for the Doctrine of the Faith. According to James Alison Pope Francis affirmed his priestly ministry during the phone call, giving an account of their conversation. According to Alison Pope Francis said:

> 'I want you to walk with deep interior freedom, following the Spirit of Jesus. And I give you the power of the keys. Do you understand? I give you the power of the keys.' I said, 'Yes', though in retrospect, how, in my daze, I thought I had understood the gift is beyond me. The conversation went on, talking with humour, and even a certain piquancy, about friends and acquaintances in common. In the background a hint of lyric opera, which I strained to recognise. After urging me to discretion, not to cause problems for good bishops, he ended with 'Pray for me. I'll look up your dossier and get back to you.'

This was seen by the militant homosexual group New Ways Ministry as Pope Francis restoring James Alison to priestly ministry.[1546]

27th September

During a Q & A with fellow Jesuits in Mozambique, Pope Francis admitted he felt bitterness when introduced to a woman who told him about converting two young people to the Catholic Faith. The pontiff said in front of the two young converts:

> Today I felt a certain bitterness after a meeting with young people. A woman approached me with a young man and a young woman. I was told they were part of a slightly fundamentalist movement. She said to me in perfect Spanish: 'Your Holiness, I am from South Africa. This boy was a Hindu and converted to Catholicism. This girl was Anglican and converted to Catholicism.' But she told me in a triumphant way, as

[1544]Mainwaring, D [2019] *Vatican suspends US archbishop's decision to strip 'Catholic' label from pro-gay 'marriage' Jesuit school* [Online] Available at: www.lifesitenews.com; Cardinal Tobin asked to mediate Indy high school standoff [2021] [Online] Available at: www.pillarcatholic.com [Accessed on: 19 October 2022]

[1545]Mahoney, W [2019] *Cdl. Tobin: 'Rethinking of the Mystery of Human Sexuality Is Important'* [Online] Available at: www.churchmilitant.com [Accessed on: 19 October 2022]

[1546]Shine, R [2019] *Pope Francis Phones Prominent Gay Theologian and Priest James Alison, Restores Him to Ministry* [Online] Available at: www.newwaysministry.org [Accessed on: 19 October 2022]

though she was showing off a hunting trophy. I felt uncomfortable and said to her, 'Madam, evangelization yes, proselytism no.'

Pope Francis also criticised young priests for dressing in traditional style, saying it indicated moral problems and imbalances:

> Have you never seen young priests all stiff in black cassocks and hats in the shape of the planet Saturn on their heads? Behind all the rigid clericalism there are serious problems. I had to intervene recently in three dioceses with problems that expressed themselves in these forms of rigidity that concealed moral problems and imbalances.

The pontiff went on to criticise priests who focused on sins that broke the sixth commandment:

> One dimension of clericalism is the exclusive moral fixation on the sixth commandment. Once a Jesuit, a great Jesuit, told me to be careful in giving absolution, because the most serious sins are those that are more angelical: pride, arrogance, dominion…. And the least serious are those that are less angelical, such as greed and lust. We focus on sex and then we do not give weight to social injustice, slander, gossip and lies. The Church today needs a profound conversion in this area.[1547]

Cardinal Joseph Zen, emeritus bishop of Hong Kong, sent a letter to the Sacred College of Cardinals beseeching them to denounce the Vatican's secret deal with the Chinese communist government. Cardinal Zen wrote:

> Pardon the inconvenience my letter will cause you. It is just that, in conscience, I believe that the problem I present here concerns not only the Church in China, but the whole Church, and we cardinals have the grave responsibility to help the Holy Father in guiding the Church. From my analysis of the document of the Holy See (June 28, 2019), 'Pastoral guidelines of the Holy See concerning the civil registration of clergy in China,' it is quite clear that it encourages the faithful in China to enter a schismatic church (independent of the pope and under the orders of the Communist Party) […] Your Eminence, can we passively witness the murder of the Church in China by those who should protect and defend her from her enemies? Begging on my knees, your brother.[1548]

1st October

The Argentinean newspaper *La Nación* published an article by Archbishop Victor Manuel 'Tucho' Fernández of La Plata, appointed by Pope Francis in 2018. Archbishop Fernández called on Catholics not to defend their churches from attacks by tens of thousands of feminists during the annual National Women's Encounter. In the past the event had led to churches being graffitied and set on fire in violent protests against the Church's teaching on abortion and contraception. Archbishop Fernández wrote:

> I ask all Catholics to avoid any form of verbal aggression and any initiative that ends up being provocative. Catholic women can give their opinion in the workshops (of the feminists), or just pray at home. But during this time it's not appropriate to engage in activities that, with the excuse of protecting churches, can be interpreted as a Christian 'resistance'…. As archbishop of La Plata, I have made the commitment to seek to avoid any act, mobilization or expression that appears to be a counter-offensive, which would useless, ineffective, and imprudent.[1549]

Pro-homosexual Fr. James Martin SJ, shown many marks of special favour by Pope Francis, posted a series of tweets giving details of his meeting with senior officials of the Congregation for Catholic Education. He had requested a meeting about the

[1547]Spadaro, A [2019] *Pope's meeting with Jesuits in Mozambique and Madagascar* [Online] Available at: www.vaticannews.va [Accessed on: 19 October 2022]

[1548]Montagna, D [2019] *Cdl. Zen urges cardinals to stop the 'murder of the Church in China'* [Online] Available at: www.lifesitenews.com [Accessed on: 19 October 2022]

[1549]Cullinan Hoffman, M [2019] *Francis-appointed bishop urges Catholics not to oppose violent feminists who attack churches, defends feminists* [Online] Available at: www.lifesitenews.com [Accessed on: 19 October 2022]

Congregation's document 'Male and Female He Created Them: Towards a Path of Dialogue on the Question of Gender Theory in Education.' According to Fr Martin, and not contradicted by the Congregation, he got Cardinal Giuseppe Versaldi, the Prefect of the Congregation, to apologise to gender confused people for the document. Fr. Martin tweeted:

> His Eminence (Cardinal Versaldi) expressed sorrow if people thought the Congregation was accusing people of being ideologically distorted, and they wish to share their care for transgender people and want to continue dialogue to reflect on their experiences.[1550]

4th October

On the eve of the Amazonian synod, Pope Francis participated in a shamanistic ritual held in the Vatican Gardens venerating idols representing the pagan 'goddess' Pachamama. The ritual included deep prostrations towards the idols by Catholics, including a Franciscan friar, who formed a circle around the idols. Pope Francis was among a group of seated participants. At the conclusion of the ritual a woman shaman presented the pontiff with the Pachamama idol. They bowed to each other. She then blessed herself. The Pope then imitated her and blessed himself. She reached for his hand and shook it. The Pope then appeared to reach out and touch the statue before proceeding to bless it.[1551]

Pope Francis again venerated a Pachamama idol during a service held in St. Peter's Basilica, and welcomed the idol into the Paul VI Hall after it was carried in procession on the shoulders of bishops across St. Peter's Square, where it was enthroned at the base of the podium from which the pontiff addressed the Synod Fathers. Later during the synod, the Pachamama idol was taken in procession during the stations of the cross, beginning at the foot of Castel Sant'Angelo and processing toward St. Peter's Square.[1552]

When a set of identical idols were removed from the Church of Santa Maria in Traspontina and thrown into the Tiber by faithful Catholics Pope Francis issued a statement in the Synod Hall confirming that the statues were indeed of the idol Pachamama, which had been disputed. The Pontiff said:

> Good afternoon, I would like to say a word about the pachamama statues that were removed from the Church at Traspontina, which were there without idolatrous intentions and were thrown into the Tiber. First of all, this happened in Rome and, as bishop of the diocese, I ask pardon of the people who were offended by this act. Then, I can inform you that the statues which created so much media clamour were found in the Tiber. The statues are not damaged.[1553]

The Vatican even considered bringing criminal charges against those who threw the pagan idols in the River Tiber.[1554]

During the closing Mass for the Amazon Synod, during the offertory procession, Pope Francis received a ritual bowl of plants associated with Pachamama from a member of the indigenous Satere-Mawe people of Brazil. Pope Francis gave the black bowl containing earth, green plants and red flowers to Master of Ceremonies Monsignor Guido Marini who, following the pontiff's instructions, placed the Pachamama

---

[1550]Cummings McLean, D [2019] *LGBT activist priest meets with Vatican education chief to discuss doc critical of 'gender theory'* [Online] Available at: www.lifesitenews.com [Accessed on: 19 October 2022]

[1551]Hickson, M [2019] *WATCH: Pope Francis blesses controversial 'Pachamama' statue before opening Amazon synod* [Online] Available at: www.lifesitenews.com [Accessed on: 19 October 2022]

[1552]Gomes, J [2019] *Amazon synod's stations of the cross fuse politics and paganism with piety* [Online] Available at: www.churchmilitant.com [Accessed on: 19 October 2022]

[1553]*Full transcript of the Pope's comments on pagan 'Pachamama' statues* [2019] [Online] Available at: www.lifesitenews.com [Accessed on: 19 October 2022]

[1554]Gomes, J [2019] *Vatican considers pressing charges over 'Pachamama' theft* [Online] Available at: www.churchmilitant.com [Accessed on: 19 October 2022]

bowl on the altar, in violation of liturgical norms for the celebration of the Mass. (*The General Instruction of the Roman Missal*, 305).[1555]

Vatican News published an interview with German Fr. Paulo Suess, the main author of the Amazon Synod's *Instrumentum Laboris*, in which he discussed the veneration of Pachamama. In response to the criticism that it was a 'pagan rite' he answered:

> So what. Even if it would have been a pagan rite, then it is nevertheless a pagan worship of God. A rite always has something to do with worship of God. One cannot dismiss the pagan [rite] as nothing. What is pagan? In our big cities, we are not less pagan than those there in the jungle. One should reflect upon this.[1556]

Bishop Emeritus José Luis Azcona Hermoso of the Brazilian city of Marajó condemned the veneration of Pachamama in the Vatican during a homily. He told the congregation:

> Pachamama is not and never will be the Virgin Mary. To say that this statue represents the Virgin is a lie. She is not Our Lady of the Amazon because the only Lady of the Amazon is Mary of Nazareth. Let's not create syncretistic mixtures. All of that is impossible: the Mother of God is the Queen of Heaven and earth. The invocation of the statues before which even some religious bowed at the Vatican (and I won't mention which congregation they belong to) is an invocation of a mythical power, of Mother Earth, from which they ask blessings or make gestures of gratitude. These are scandalous demonic sacrileges, especially for the little ones who are not able to discern.[1557]

Archbishop Carlo Maria Viganò called for the re-consecration of St. Peter's Basilica following Pope Francis conducting idolatrous worship near the Tomb of St. Peter:

> The barque of the Church is in the grip of a raging storm. To quell the tempest, those Successors of the Apostles who have tried to leave Jesus on the shore, and who no longer perceive His presence, have begun to invoke the Pachamama! Jesus prophesied: 'When you see the desecrating sacrilege … there will be a great tribulation, such as has not been from the beginning of the world until now, no, and never will be' (Mt 24:15;21). The abomination of idolatrous rites has entered the sanctuary of God and has given rise to a new form of apostasy, whose seeds — which have been active for a long time — are growing with renewed vigour and effectiveness.[1558]

8th October

Eugenio Scalfari, the atheist founder of *La Repubblica*, published his tenth engagement with Pope Francis in which he claimed that Pope Francis denied the divinity of Jesus Christ. (He first reported Pope Francis' erroneous kenotic Christology in 7th July 2017). Eugenio Scalfari wrote the following, even putting some of Francis's reported speech in quotation marks:

> Those who have had the chance, as I have had different times, to meet him [Pope Francis] and speak to him with the greatest cultural confidence, know that Pope Francis conceives Christ as Jesus of Nazareth, a man, not God incarnate. Once incarnated, Jesus ceases to be a God and becomes a man until his death on the cross…. When I happened to discuss these phrases, Pope Francis told me: 'They are the definite proof that Jesus of Nazareth, once he became a man, even if he was a man of exceptional virtue, was not God at all.'

Though the Vatican denied the general accuracy of Scalfari's report, Francis did not issue a public repudiation of Scalfari's account of his Christological beliefs and affirm

---

[1555]Cummings McLean, D [2019] *Vatican newspaper features 'Pachamama' bowl used at Amazon Synod's closing Mass* [Online] Available at: www.lifesitenews.com [Accessed on: 19 October 2022]
[1556]Hickson, M [2019] *If 'pagan' rites are part of Amazon synod, they're still 'worship of God': synod working doc writer* [Online] Available at: www.lifesitenews.com [Accessed on: 19 October 2022]
[1557]Barillas, M [2019] *'Demonic sacrilege': Brazilian bishop condemns Vatican gardens' 'Pachamama' ritual* [Online] Available at: www.lifesitenews.com [Accessed on: 19 October 2022]
[1558]Montagna, D [2019] *Abp Viganò: 'The abomination of idolatrous rites has entered the sanctuary of God'* (Exclusive) [Online] Available at: www.lifesitenews.com [Accessed on: 19 October 2022]

that he fully upheld that our Lord Jesus Christ was true God and true man throughout his earthly life. Archbishop Carlo Maria Viganò urged the Pope himself to give a 'clear answer':

> Christians expect a clear answer from the Pope himself. The thing is too important; it is essential: Yes, I believe that Christ is the Son of God made Man, the only Saviour and Lord. All Christians await this clarification from him, not from others, and by virtue of their baptism have the right to have this response.[1559]

Cardinal Müller, the former Prefect of the CDF, also criticised the Vatican's lukewarm response.[1560]

15th October

The Pontifical Academy of Sciences — led by the pro-communist Bishop Marcelo Sánchez Sorondo — held a youth symposium titled: 'Intergenerational Leadership: *Laudato Si'* and the Sustainable Development Goals.' The symposium was conducted in partnership with the Sustainable Development Solutions Network (SDSN), directed by pro-abortion eugenicist, Jeffrey Sachs. The SDSN was founded by pro-abortion former United Nations General Secretary Ban Ki-moon and funded by the pro-abortion Bill and Melinda Gates Foundation.[1561]

26th October

The Final Document of the Amazon Synod called for women to be formally instituted into the ministries of Lector and Acolyte, that have been traditionally reserved to men due to their service of the sacred liturgy and Apostolic Ministry instituted by our Lord Jesus Christ — bishops, priests and deacons. The Final Document stated:

> We ask that the Motu Propio of St. Paul VI, *Ministeria Quaedam* (1972) be revised, so that women who have been properly trained and prepared can receive the ministries of Lector and Acolyte, among others to be developed. (102). The Final Document also stated: 'It is urgent for the Church in the Amazon to promote and confer ministries for men and women in an equitable manner.' (95).

The Final Document also called for the 'ordination' of women to the permanent diaconate:

> In the many consultations carried out in the Amazon, the fundamental role of religious and lay women in the Church of the Amazon and its communities was recognized and emphasised, given the multiple services they provide. In a large number of these consultations, the permanent diaconate for women was requested. For this reason the theme was important during the Synod. (103)

The Final Document called for the ordination of married, permanent deacons to the priesthood, thereby ending the universal requirement of celibacy for priestly ministry in the Latin-rite:

> We proposed to establish criteria and dispositions on the part of the competent authority, within the framework of *Lumen Gentium* 26, to ordain priests suitable and esteemed men of the community, who have had a fruitful permanent diaconate and receive an adequate formation for the priesthood, having a legitimately constituted and

[1559]Barillas, M [2019] *Pope's favored interviewer claims Francis denies Christ's divinity*; Montagna, D [2019] *Abp Viganò urges Pope to personally answer claims he doesn't believe in divinity of Christ* [Online] Available at: Available at: www.lifesitenews.com; Donnelly, N [2019] *'Jesus, only a Man — Does Francis want to blow up Christology?'* [Online] Available at: rorate-caeli.blogspot.com [Accessed on: 20 October 2022]

[1560]Harrison, B [2019] *Cardinal Müller denounces Roman 'Pachamama' events* [Online] Available at: www.lifesitenews.com [Accessed on: 20 October 2022]

[1561]Montagna, D [2019] *Vatican hosts youth conference with pro-abortion UN activists* [Online] Available at: www.lifesitenews.com [Accessed on: 20 October 2022]

stable family to sustain the life of the Christian community through the preaching of the Word and the celebration of the Sacraments in the most remote areas of the Amazon region. In this regard, some were in favour of a more universal approach to the subject. (111).

The Final Document also uncritically praised pagan religions:

In the Amazon, inter-religious dialogue takes place especially with indigenous religions and afro-descendant cults. These traditions deserve to be known, understood in their own expressions and in their relationship with the forest and mother earth. Together with them, Christians, secure in their faith in the Word of God, can enter into dialogue, sharing their lives, their concerns, their struggles, their experiences of God, to deepen each other's faith and to act together in defence of our common home. (25)....The ancestral wisdom of the aboriginal peoples affirms that mother earth has a feminine face. (101)

The Final Document proposed incorporating such pagan religion into an 'Amazonian' rite:

The new organism of the Church in the Amazon must constitute a competent commission to study and dialogue, according to the habits and customs of the ancestral peoples, the elaboration of an Amazonian rite that expresses the liturgical, theological, disciplinary and spiritual patrimony of the Amazon…It could also study and propose how to enrich ecclesial rites with the way in which these peoples care for their territory and relate to its waters.[1562]

28th October

Many bishops, priests and member of the laity in Germany welcomed the recommendations of the Amazonian Synod's Final Document as signifying revolutionary change in the Church. In response, the German Bishops' Conference immediately published the controversial statutes of the 'synodal path' that formally established the process to question the Church's teaching on priestly celibacy, human sexuality, and the role of women in the Church. In an interview with the German bishops' news website pro-homosexual Bishop Franz-Josef Overbeck of Essen said it was time to consider 'women priests':

Can one, for example, make a link between the access to the priesthood and the Y chromosome by justifying it with the Will of Jesus?…Most people do not understand this anymore and also do not believe in it. I myself am also more than pensive.

The German Bishops' website also published a reflection by pro-homosexual Fr. Wunibald Müller SJ:

[The Amazon Synod] will go down in history as the synod with which the end of obligatory celibacy was heralded. With the [Amazon Synod's] recommendation to ordain morally proven, married men to the priesthood, the dam finally broke which heretofore hindered the abolishment of obligatory celibacy.[1563]

In an interview with *Catholic News Service* pro-homosexual Bishop Robert McElroy of San Diego — appointed by Pope Francis — said most bishops at the Amazonian synod supported the 'ordination' of women to the diaconate. Bishop McElroy said:

The sentiment among the bishops of the synod was in favour, the majority of bishops, were in favour of admitting women to the permanent diaconate. My own view is that I'm in favour of opening any ministry we have in the Church to women which is not clearly precluded doctrinally. My own assessment of it is…that what has come out so far indicates the current diaconate for women is not clearly prohibited by doctrinal

---

[1562]Synod Secretariat [2019] *Amazonia: New Paths for the Church and for an Integral Ecology* [Online] Available at: secretariat.synod.va [Accessed on: 20 October 2022]
[1563]Hickson, M [2019] *German bishops' website overflows with praise for Amazon Synod's final doc* [Online] Available at: www.lifesitenews.com [Accessed on: 20 October 2022]

considerations. My hope would be that they would find a pathway to make that a reality. I think there's a good possibility that's the direction it's going to head into. The Pope added his comments yesterday. The fact he did that, makes me think there's a good chance that some positive action will come out of that.[1564]

1st November

The Holy See press office issued a statement announcing that Vatican police had raided the offices of the Secretariat of State and the Vatican's financial watchdog office. The focus of their investigation was evidence relating to a 2014 Vatican property investment in luxury apartments at 60 Sloane Ave, London. The investment had been authorized by Cardinal Angelo Becciu — a close associate of Pope Francis — during his tenure as sostituto at the Holy See's Secretariat of State. It emerged that a substantial part of the $200 million investment came through credit extended by BSI, a Swiss bank with a record of violating money-laundering and fraud safeguards. The Vatican's Prefecture for the Economy, headed by Cardinal Pell, discovered that the then Archbishop Becciu attempted to hide the loans off-books and demanded details of the loans. Archbishop Becciu summoned Cardinal Pell in order to reprimand him. According to a highly placed source:

> Becciu summoned the cardinal — summoned him. Pell was supposed to be the ultimate authority in monitoring and authorizing all Vatican financial business, answerable only to Pope Francis, but Becciu shouted at him like he was an inferior. Becciu reportedly told Pell the cardinal was 'interfering in sovereign business' by looking into the Secretariat's dealings with BSI. Cardinal Pell was given to understand that as far as [Becciu] was concerned, the prefect was basically an administrative clerk and a rubber stamp, no more.

Cardinal Pell tried to raise Becciu's attempt to disguise the loans at the Council for the Economy, an agency led by Cardinal Reinhard Marx of Münich — another close collaborator with Pope Francis — but Cardinal Reinhard Marx took no action.[1565]

In 2020 the Italian news program, *La Iene*, broadcast information that it had received showing the Vatican Secretariat of State sent an estimated 500,000 euros ($587,900) over a period of five years to a 'humanitarian organization' in Slovenia run by Cecilia Marogna, hired as a security consultant by Cardinal Becciu. Marogna was later arrested and charged with embezzlement and misappropriation of funds by the Italian financial police after an international warrant was issued by Interpol at the Vatican's request.[1566] Cardinal Becciu was forced to resign amid investigations that he embezzled 100,000 euros of Vatican funds, redirecting them to Spes, a Caritas organization run by his brother, Tonino Becciu, in his home Diocese of Ozieri, Sardinia.[1567]

In 2021 Cardinal Becciu was indicted with nine others with charges of money laundering, fraud and abuse of office in relation to the London investment and other investments in which it lost millions.[1568] A witness for the prosecution — Msgr. Alberto Perlasca, who 'shepherded' the $400 million Sloane Ave., London, development — testified that 'Pope Francis himself had authorized the machinations' they were now saying were part of a 'criminal shakedown of the Vatican'.[1569] The trial was suspended

[1564]Kokx, S [2019] *Pro-gay US bishop: Majority of bishops at Amazon Synod 'favor' female deacons* [Online] Available at: www.lifesitenews.com [Accessed on: 20 October 2022]

[1565]Condon. E [2019] *Vatican officials: Swiss bank suspected of money laundering led to Pell conflict* [Online] Available at: www.catholicnewsagency.com [Available at: 20 October 2022]

[1566]Arocho Esteves, J [2020] *Reports: Analyst linked to Cardinal Becciu is arrested* [Online] Available at: angelusnews.com [Accessed on: 20 October 2022]

[1567]Wooden, C & Arocho Esteves, J [2020] *Cardinal Becciu resigns as prefect, renounces rights as cardinal* [Online] Available at: catholicnews.com [Accessed on: 20 October 2022]

[1568]*Vatican judge orders cardinal and nine others to stand trial for alleged financial crimes* [2021] [Online] Available at: www.theguardian.com [Accessed on: 20 October 2022]

[1569]Altieri, C [2021] *Cardinal Becciu's trial is a dysfunctional show with serious repercussions* [Online] Available at: www.catholicworldreport.com [Accessed on: 20 October 2022]

in November 2021. When the trial recommenced in 2022, confronted with incriminating messages he sent and official documents bearing his signature, Cardinal Becciu blamed Pope Francis, his staff and a bad memory.[1570] In August 2022, Pope Francis invited Cardinal Becciu to attend the consistory of cardinals later in the month, which many saw as the Supreme Pontiff's first steps in re-habilitating his former right-hand man.[1571]

5th November

Eugenio Scalfari, the atheist founder of the Italian daily newspaper *La Repubblica*, published the eleventh account of his engagement with Pope Francis. According to Scalfari, Pope Francis told him he does not believe in the bodily Resurrection of our Lord Jesus Christ. Scalfari recounted the words of Pope Francis about the Resurrection:

> He was a man until he was placed in the tomb by the women who recomposed his body. That night, in the tomb, the man disappeared and came forth from the grotto in the semblance of a spirit that met the women and the Apostles while still preserving the shadow of the person, and then he definitely disappeared.

Pope Francis did not repudiate or contradict Scalfari's account of their conversation.[1572]

11th November

Thomas Stanzer, a spokesman from the Austrian Diocese of Graz-Seckau confirmed that Fr. Michael Kopp presided over a church service for two women in a homosexual civil union, referring to Pope Francis' *Amoris Laetitia* to justify his actions. Thomas Stanzer said:

> The basic question is if homosexual people can feel themselves at home in the Church. Family spiritual advisor Michael Kopp answered 'yes' to this question. [Father Kopp] celebrated a liturgy of thanksgiving with two civilly married [sic] women who are both believing Christians and who had both found their way out of personal crises with the help of the Catholic Church. Every person, regardless of sexual orientation, ought to be respected in his or her dignity and treated with consideration, while 'every sign of unjust discrimination' is to be carefully avoided, the Post-Synodal Apostolic Exhortation *Amoris Laetitia* (250) states.[1573]

12th November

Pro-homosexual Bishop Robert McElroy of San Diego — appointed by Pope Francis — objected to the US bishops conference stating that abortion remains their 'pre-eminent' social justice priority. Bishop McElroy told his fellow bishops that this statement was 'at least discordant with the pope's teaching if not inconsistent and that it is a grave disservice to our people if we're trying to communicate to them what the Magisterium teaches.'[1574]

An international group of priests, deacons and lay scholars published a statement calling on Pope Francis to 'repent publicly and unambiguously' for the objectively grave sins of allowing, and participating in, the pagan worship of the Peruvian pagan idol Pachamama that took place during the Amazon Synod in Rome.[1575]

[1570]*Becciu blames Pope Francis, staff, bad memory in Vatican trial* [2022] [Online] Available at: www.pillarcatholic.com [Accessed on: 20 October 2022]

[1571]Arocho Esteves, J [2022] *Cardinal Becciu says pope invited him to August consistory* [Online] Available at: www.osvnews.com [Accessed on: 20 October 2022]

[1572]Barillas, M [2019] *Pope's go-to interviewer now claims Francis denies Jesus' bodily resurrection* [Online] Available at: www.lifesitenews.com [Accessed on: 19 October 2022]

[1573]Cummings McLean, D [2019] *Austrian diocese confirms that Catholic priest held liturgy celebrating lesbian union* [Online] Available at: www.lifesitenews.com [Accessed on: 19 October 2022]

[1574]Cummings McLean, D [2019] *1 in 3 US bishops at fall meeting vote to downplay abortion by citing Pope Francis* [Online] Available at: www.lifesitenews.com [Accessed on: 19 October 2022]

[1575]Hickson, M [2019] *100 priests, lay scholars call Pope Francis to repent for Pachamama idolatry at Amazon Synod* [Online] Available at: www.lifesitenews.com [Accessed on: 20 October 2022]

14th November

Pope Francis had a private audience with Jayne Ozanne, a homosexual activist who campaigns for the ban of 'conversion therapies' designed to help individuals free themselves from unwanted same-sex attractions.[1576]

Cardinal Walter Kasper — a theological adviser of Pope Francis — spoke at the Spanish conference titled, *The Contributions of Pope Francis to Theology and Pastoral Care*. During his talk Cardinal Kasper said Pope Francis felt called by the Holy Spirit to 'change' the Church:

> The Pope is quite serene because he has great interior confidence, an interior compass: the strength of the Holy Spirit. Francis is convinced that the Holy Spirit has called on him to change or, in other words, renew the Church. He is working on that.

Cardinal Kasper also gave a convoluted response to the possibility of the ordination of women:

> It is difficult to explain that today, but I believe that it is an ancient tradition that we share with the Eastern churches. But I think that, in time, the doors will be opened. Besides, there are already many ministries of the Church for which ordination is not necessary. But women are not content with that. Clearly, there are some who are raising their voice and have the right to be heard.[1577]

15th November

Pope Francis gave his approval to the 'House of Abraham' project which will house a mosque, a synagogue, and a church symbolically united on one foundation. The project was presented to Pope Francis by the Grand Imam Ahmed Al-Tayeb, Sheik of Al-Azhar, members of the Abu Dhabi government, and representatives of the Higher Committee for achieving the goals contained in the Document on Human Fraternity for World Peace and Living Together. Archbishop Viganò denounced the plans:

> The building of the House of the Abrahamic Family appears like a Babelesque enterprise, designed by the enemies of God, of the Catholic Church and of the only true religion capable of saving man and the whole created from destruction, both present as well as eternal and definitive. The foundations of this 'House,' destined to give way and crumble, precisely where, at the hands of the same builders, the Only Corner Stone is incredibly about to be removed: Jesus Christ, Saviour and Lord, on whom stands the House of God. 'Therefore,' warns the Apostle Paul, 'let each one take care how he builds upon it. For no other foundation can anyone lay than that which is laid, which is Jesus Christ. (I Cor 3:10)' In the garden of Abu-Dhabi, the Temple of the World Syncretic Neo-Religion is about to arise with its anti-Christic dogmas. Not even the most hopeful of the Freemasons would have imagined so much![1578]

18th November

Pope Francis addressed participants at the meeting promoted by the Instituto para el Dialogo Interreligioso de la Argentina. During his address, the pontiff praised the Yalta Pact between the allies at the end of the Second World War that consigned millions to the communist tyranny of the Soviet Union. Pope Francis made his comments in the context of discussing the Abu Dhabi document he signed in February 2019:

> Once, at the beginning of last February, a very wise man, a very wise European politician, told me about this document: 'it goes beyond the methodology of the pact to maintain

---

[1576]Gomes, J [2019] *Pope Meets With Notorious Anglican Lesbian Activist* [Online] Available at: / www.churchmilitant.com [Accessed on: 20 October 2022]

[1577]Barillas, M [2019] *Cardinal Kasper: Pope Francis feels called to 'change' Church, door will 'open' to women at altar* [Online] Available at: www.lifesitenews.com [Accessed on: 19 October 2022]

[1578]Montagna, D [2019] *Abp Viganò decries Pope-approved plan to build 'Abrahamic' religious site with Muslims, Jews* [Online] Available at: www.lifesitenews.com [Accessed on: 20 October 2022]

balance and peace, which is very good, but these documents go further'. And he gave me this example: 'let us think of the end of the Second World War, let us think of Yalta; in Yalta a balance was struck in order to break the impasse, a balance that was weak but possible. The cake was shared, and a period of peace was maintained, but these documents, this attitude that goes towards dialogue among the transcendent, creates fraternity, surpasses pacts, surpasses the political; it is political in that it is human, but it surpasses this, it transcends this, it makes it nobler'. This is the way. And meanwhile, yes, at the political level, doing what can be done, because it is also important.[1579]

19th November

During his apostolic journey to Thailand, Pope Francis asked for a 'blessing' from the Buddhist 'Supreme Patriarch' at the Wat Ratchabophit Sathit Maha Simaram Temple, Bangkok. The pontiff also referred to all religions as 'beacons of hope':

Occasions like this remind us how important it is for religions to become more and more beacons of hope, as promoters and guarantors of fraternity.[1580]

22nd November

Pro-homosexual Fr. James Martin SJ — singled out by Pope Francis for many signs of favour — posted on twitter a painting drawn from a series of blasphemous homoerotic works depicting the life of our Lord Jesus Christ as a homosexual man. The paintings are the work of the homosexual artist Douglas Blanchard, illustrating the book titled, *The Passion of Christ: A Gay Vision* According to the promotional description of the book:

Meet Jesus as a gay man of today in a contemporary city with *The Passion of Christ: A Gay Vision*. In stunning new images, the modern Christ figure is jeered by fundamentalists, tortured by Marine look-alikes, and rises again to enjoy homoerotic moments with God.[1581]

25th November

Bishop Renato Marangoni of Belluno-Feltre, Italy, issued a pastoral letter apologising to individuals who had entered into adulterous civil unions in response to Pope Francis' *Amoris Laetitia*. Bishop Marangoni described the adulterous relationships as 'new experiences of union for which some have chosen to remarry civilly or not to marry'. He continued:

There is a first word I wish to confide to you: Sorry! This word contains our awareness that we have often ignored you in our parish communities. Perhaps you have also suffered from attitudes among us of judgment and criticism towards you. For a long time, we have also said that you could not be fully admitted to the sacraments of Penance and the Eucharist, while in many of you there was a desire to be sustained by the gift of the sacraments and by the warmth and affection of a community.[1582]

3rd December

New Bloom website published an interview with Cardinal Zen, Emeritus bishop of Hong Kong, in which he accused Pope Francis of 'legitimising' a schism within the Church in China. Cardinal Zen said:

Recently I learned that the Holy Father, on a flight back from (I don't remember where) said, 'Sure, I don't want to see a schism. But I'm not afraid of a schism.' And I'm going

---

[1579]Pope Francis [2019] *Address to participants at the meeting promoted by the Instituto para el Dialogo Interreligioso de la Argentina (IDI)* [Online] Available at: www.vatican.va [Accessed on: 20 October 2022]

[1580]*Pope in Thailand: Catholics and Buddhists can live as 'good neighbours'* [2019] [Online] Available at: www.vaticannews.va [Accessed on: 20 October 2022]

[1581]Mainwaring, D [2019] *Fr. James Martin touts blasphemous image of Jesus as a homosexual* [Online] Available at: www.lifesitenews.com [Accessed on: 20 October 2022]

[1582]Montagna, D [2019] *Bishop apologizes to unrepentant adulterers, invites them back to the sacraments* [Online] Available at: www.lifesitenews.com [Accessed on: 20 October 2022]

to tell him 'you are encouraging a schism. You are legitimising the schismatic church in China.' Incredible.[1583]

4th December

Pro-homosexual Fr. James Martin SJ posted a tweet about same-sex sex acts in animals. Fr. Martin tweeted:

> Scientists in new study: 'The researchers suggest that same-sex behaviour is bound up in the very origins of animal sex. It hasn't had to continually re-evolve: It's always been there.'

In response to the reply, 'Show us a monkey that created a cathedral and we'll start paying attention', the priest tweeted:

> Instead I can show you some gay architects, painters, sculptors, musicians, writers and poets, many of whom have created works of art that praise and exalt God. Maybe then you'll start paying attention.[1584]

The Italian newspaper *Corriere Della Sera* reported that the Vatican's Secretariat of State invested one million euros in the film *Rocketman*, a biography of the notorious homosexual Elton John. The film contained an explicit depiction of homosexual sex acts.[1585]

5th December

During his apostolic journey to Thailand and Japan Pope Francis addressed a group of Jesuits from Southeast Asia. He indicated that he considered Chapter 8 of his apostolic letter *Amoris Laetitia* — which he interprets as allowing adulterers to receive Holy Communion — as part of the binding Magisterium of the Church. The pontiff said:

> I could answer you in two ways: in a casuistic way, which however is not Christian, even if it can be ecclesiastical; or according to the Magisterium of the Church as in the eighth chapter of *Amoris Laetitia*, that is, journey, accompany and discern to find solutions....And this has nothing to do with situation ethics, but with the great moral tradition of the Church.'[1586]

The Commission for Marriage and Family of the German Bishops' Conference published a press release giving details of its expert consultation on the topic 'The sexuality of man: how to discuss it scientifically-theologically, and how to assess it ecclesiastically?' The press release stated that they concluded that homosexuality was as 'normal' as heterosexuality:

> There was also agreement that the sexual preference of man expresses itself in puberty and assumes a hetero- or homosexual orientation. Both belong to the normal forms of sexual predisposition, which cannot or should not be changed with the help of a specific socialisation.

This conclusion is totally contrary to God's revelation contained in sacred Scripture and Tradition.[1587]

[1583]Haggerty, N [2019] *Interview: Cardinal Joseph Zen* (陳日君) [Online] Available at: newbloommag.net [Accessed on: 20 October 2022]
[1584]Laurence, L [2019] *Pro-LGBT priest James Martin tweets about study normalizing animal 'same-sex behavior'* [Online] Available at: www.lifesitenews.com [Accessed on: 20 October 2022]
[1585]Gerevini, M di & Massaro, F [2019] *Vatican invested in Lapo Elkann and Elton John film* [Online] Available at: www.corriere.it [Accessed on: 20 October 2022]
[1586]Pope Francis [2019] *'Our Little Path': Pope Francis with the Jesuits in Thailand and Japan* [Online] Available at: www.laciviltacattolica.com [Accessed on: 20 October 2022]
[1587]Cummings McLean, D [2019] *German bishops proclaim homosexuality 'normal,' adultery 'not grave'* [Online] Available at: www.lifesitenews.com [Accessed on: 20 October 2022]

8th December

Pope Francis appointed pro-homosexual, pro-adultery Cardinal Luis Antonio Gokim Tagle, Archbishop of Manila, as the Prefect of the Congregation for the Evangelization of Peoples (Propaganda Fide). During the 2015 Extraordinary Synod on the family Cardinal Tagle criticised the Church's 'harsh' language regarding homosexuality and adultery, saying:

> Yes, I think even the language has changed already, the harsh words that were used in the past to refer to gays and divorced and separated people, the unwed mothers etc., in the past they were quite severe....But we are glad to see and hear shifts in that.[1588]

12th December

During his homily for the Feast of Our Lady of Guadalupe Pope Francis criticised the doctrine of the Blessed Virgin Mary as Co-Redemptrix. The pontiff said:

> She never wanted for herself something that was of her son. She never introduced herself as co-redemptrix. No. Disciple. Mary, never stole for herself anything that was of her son, instead serving him. Because she is mother. She gives life. When they come to us with the story of declaring her this or making that dogma, let's not get lost in foolishness.

In response to Pope Francis' attack on this Marian doctrine Archbishop Viganò wrote:

> The tragic story of this failed pontificate advances with a pressing succession of twists and turns. Not a day passes: from the most exalted throne the Supreme Pontiff proceeds to dismantle the See of Peter, using and abusing its supreme authority, not to confess but to deny; not to confirm but to mislead; not to unite but to divide; not to build but to demolish. Material heresies, formal heresies, idolatry, superficiality of every kind.[1589]

14th December

The Vatican's Congregation for Catholic Education sponsored a Christmas concert to raise funds to support 'the presence, tradition and culture of the indigenous populations of the Amazon'. The audience included Cardinal Giuseppe Versaldi, Prefect of the Congregation for Catholic Education, and deputy Secretary of State, Archbishop Edgar Pena Parra. During the concert a young indigenous woman was welcomed onto the stage from where she addressed the audience. She invited people to cross their arms over their heart and 'feel a strong vibration':

> This is the heart – your heart, but also the heart of Mother Earth. In another place, where you feel silence, there is the spirit, the spirit that allows us to understand the message of the Mother. For us, the indigenous peoples, above all for my people, Mother Earth, the 'Hicha Guaia,' is everything. It is this Mother who provides us with nourishment. She is the one who gives us the sacred water, she is the one who gives us the medicinal plants, and she is the one who reminds us of our origin, the origin of [our] creation. Therefore, we give to her our birth placenta and our first cutting of hair. Our connection with her is constant. That's how the pulse feels, that's how the heart feels, it vibrates.

A widely published photograph shows Cardinal Giuseppe Versaldi and Archbishop Pena Parra taking part in the pagan ritual.[1590]

16th December

The Vatican's Pontifical Biblical Commission published the book *What Is Man? An Itinerary of Biblical Anthropology [Che cosa è l'uomo? Un itinerario di antropologia biblica].*

[1588]Montagna, D [2019] *Pope appoints cardinal critical of Church's 'severe' language to gays to head major Vatican office* [Online] Available at: www.lifesitenews.com [Accessed on: 20 October 2022]

[1589]San Martín, I [2019] *Pope calls idea of declaring Mary co-redemptrix 'foolishness'* [Online] Available at: cruxnow.com [Accessed on: 20 October 2022]

[1590]Montagna, D [2019] *WATCH: Vatican Christmas concert features indigenous woman teaching audience to channel 'mother earth'* [Online] Available at: www.lifesitenews.com [Accessed on: 20 October 2022]

In its treatment of homosexuality the Pontifical Biblical Commission contradicted the Church's traditional hermeneutic of the 'sin of Sodom' stating that God punished the city not for homosexual acts of grave depravity but due to sins against hospitality. The book states:

> The story, however, is not intended to present the image of an entire city dominated by irrepressible homosexual cravings; rather, it denounces the conduct of a social and political entity that does not want to welcome the foreigner with respect, and therefore claims to humiliate him, forcing him to undergo an infamous treatment of submission… We must therefore say that the story about the city of Sodom (as well as that of Gabaa) illustrates a sin that consists in the lack of hospitality, with hostility and violence towards the stranger, a behaviour judged very serious and therefore deserving to be sanctioned with the utmost severity, because the rejection of the different, of the needy and defenseless stranger, is a principle of social disintegration, having in itself a deadly violence that deserves an adequate punishment.

Jesuit Father Pietro Bovati, secretary for the Pontifical Biblical Commission, said the book was undertaken at the express wish of Pope Francis.[1591]

20th December

Pope Francis participated in a Q & A with schoolchildren of Rome's Pilo Albertelli classical secondary school. In response to a schoolboy asking him how one ought to give a reason for one's own faith the pontiff responded:

> With a non-believer the last thing I have to do is try to convince him. Never. The last thing I have to do is talk. I have to live in accordance with my faith… I have to live in accordance with my faith. And it will be my testimony that will awaken the curiosity of the other who says: 'But why do you do this?' And that's where I can talk. But listen, never, ever advance the Gospel through proselytism. If someone says he is a disciple of Jesus and comes to you with proselytism, he is not a disciple of Jesus. We shouldn't proselytise, the Church does not grow from proselytizing.[1592]

Roberto Mancini, manager of Italy's national football team, explained to Italian television *TG5* that he no longer made the sign of the cross before each match following a conversation with Pope Francis. Asked why he didn't make the sign of the cross like other footballers Roberto Mancini replied:

> I used to do that too, you know, hoping nothing happened during the game, then we went to the pope. Pope Francis said, 'Why are you making the sign of the cross, don't you have other thoughts in this moment?' So since that time I don't do it anymore. I don't want the pope to get angry.[1593]

21st December

During his Christmas greetings to the Roman curia, Pope Francis quoted heterodox fellow Jesuit the late Cardinal Martini of Milan to support his theme that the Church must be changed. The pontiff said:

> Cardinal Martini, in his last interview, a few days before his death, said something that should make us think: 'The Church is two hundred years behind the times. Why is she not shaken up? Are we afraid? Fear, instead of courage? Yet faith is the Church's foundation. Faith, confidence, courage… Only love conquers weariness'.

He also again criticised those who opposed his radical agenda as 'imbalanced':

[1591]Montagna, D [2019] *Vatican publishes new book reducing 'sin of Sodom' to 'lack of hospitality'* [Online] Available at: www.lifesitenews.com [Accessed on: 20 October 2022]

[1592]Montagna, D [2019] *Pope Francis tells teens they're not a 'disciple of Jesus' if they try to convert non-believers* [Online] Available at: www.lifesitenews.com [Accessed on: 20 October 2022]

[1593]*Francis Asked Football Manager Not To Make Sign Of The Cross* [2019] [Online] Available at: www.gloria.tv [Accessed on: 20 October 2022]

Here, there is a need to be wary of the temptation to rigidity. A rigidity born of the fear of change, which ends up erecting fences and obstacles on the terrain of the common good, turning it into a minefield of incomprehension and hatred. Let us always remember that behind every form of rigidity lies some kind of imbalance. Rigidity and imbalance feed one another in a vicious circle. And today this temptation to rigidity has become very real.[1594]

23rd December

The German magazine *Der Stern* published an interview with Cardinal Marx of Munich and Freising — a member of Pope Francis' advisory council of cardinals and, at the time, president of the German bishops' conference. During the interview Cardinal Marx said:

I insist: we welcome homosexuals, they belong to the Church, also to the sacramental community. [Homosexual couples can receive] a blessing in the sense of a pastoral accompaniment, we can pray together.... When people in a homosexual relationship are loyal to one another over years, are available to one another, and even take care of each other until death; then we as Church cannot make a bracket around this entire life, placing a minus sign in front of it and say that all of this has no worth because it takes place in a homosexual relationship.[1595]

2020

3rd January

Archbishop Edmundo Valenzuela of Paraguay delivered a homily on the Feast of the Holy Family during which he singled out the needs of homosexual 'families'. Archbishop Valenzuela told the congregation:

Today we find that there are homosexual couples who form families. We cannot ignore that reality. They require a particular competence and preparation on the part of family movements to accompany these people, in order to show them mercy and understanding. We should not denigrate them. We should not simply accuse them of a morally irregular situation, which is true, because we do not achieve anything with that; but we must propose that they live properly, reintegrate, pray, and that they be in solidarity and sensitive to the poor and the most needy. So this tells us about a variety of families in our globalized society in which we are all immersed.[1596]

6th January

During the celebration of the Mass for the Solemnity of the Epiphany Bishop Derio Olivero of Pinerolo, Italy — appointed by Pope Francis in 2017 — announced that the Nicene creed would not be recited in case it caused offence. Bishop Olivero said:

Since there are also non-believers, everyone will say it in silence. Those who believe can say it and those who do not believe or are of other faiths will say in silence the reasons for their belief.[1597]

7th January

The official Catholic website of French-speaking Belgium bishops published an interview with pro-homosexual Cardinal Jozef De Kesel of Mechelen-Brussels, appointed by Pope Francis. During the interview he expressed half-hearted opposition to the abortion of babies, saying killing them at twelve weeks was better than eighteen weeks:

[1594]Pope Francis [2019] *Address at Christmas Greetings to the Roman Curia* [Online] Available at: www.vatican.va [Accessed on: 20 October 2022]
[1595]Hickson, M [2019] *Cdl Marx: Homosexual couples can receive 'blessing' from Church* [Online] Available at: www.lifesitenews.com [Accessed on: 20 October 2022]
[1596]Barillas, M [2020] *South American archbishop tells Catholics to 'accompany' homosexual couples and their 'families'* [Online] Available at: www.lifesitenews.com [Accessed on: 20 October 2022]
[1597]Montagna, D [2020] *Bishop nixes Nicene Creed at Epiphany Mass to avoid offending unbelievers* [Online] Available at: www.lifesitenews.com [Accessed on: 20 October 2022]

The period within which an abortion can be carried out is not a trivial matter: there is a big difference between twelve and eighteen weeks. At eighteen weeks, the operation is much more burdensome for both the woman and the doctor. Furthermore, it should be remembered that abortion is always a failure and will never be an ordinary medical procedure.[1598]

8th January

The U.S. Congressional-Executive Commission on China (CECC) released its annual report reporting that there was an 'intense spike' in persecution of Christians that corresponded with the Vatican signing its secret deal with the Chinese communists:

> In September 2018, the Chinese Ministry of Foreign Affairs signed an agreement with the Holy See, paving the way for the unification of state-sanctioned and underground Catholic communities. Subsequently, local Chinese authorities subjected Catholic believers in China to increased persecution by demolishing churches, removing crosses, and continuing to detain underground clergy. The Party-led Catholic national religious organizations also published a plan to 'sinicize' Catholicism in China.[1599]

10th January

Through the pages of the Portuguese daily *Jornal de Noticias* Cardinal Antonio Dos Santos Marto of Leiria-Fatima announced that couples committing adultery through divorce and civil 'marriage' had received Holy Communion. Cardinal Marto announced that two divorced and 'remarried' couples and a divorced and 'remarried' woman have been allowed to receive Holy Communion in his diocese 'like any Catholic'.[1600]

12th January

The French daily newspaper *Le Figaro* published extracts from a book defending priestly celibacy co-authored by Benedict XVI and Cardinal Robert Sarah, with the title, *From the Depths of Our Hearts*. Pope Benedict XVI wrote:

> The ability to renounce marriage in order to place oneself totally at the Lord's disposal is a criterion for the priestly ministry. As for the concrete form of celibacy in the ancient Church, it should also be pointed out that married men could only receive the sacrament of Holy Orders if they had committed themselves to sexual abstinence, that is to say, to a Josephite marriage. Such a situation seems to have been quite normal during the first centuries.

Cardinal Sarah wrote:

> I cannot in conscience, as a son of Africa, support the idea that the peoples on the road to evangelization should be deprived of this encounter with a priesthood lived to the full. The peoples of Amazonia have the right to a full experience of Christ the Bridegroom. They cannot be offered 'second class' priests. On the contrary, the younger a Church is, the more it needs to meet the radical nature of the Gospel.[1601]

Antonio Socci, an Italian Catholic journalist, reported that Pope Francis was infuriated by the texts in *From the Depths of Our Hearts* supporting priestly celibacy. Socci wrote:

> The day before yesterday… the end of the world broke out in the Vatican because Bergoglio was furious. In fact, that very authoritative pronouncement of Benedict XVI

[1598]Smits, J [2020] *Leading cardinal of Belgium reflects on 2019: Brexit bad, atheism fully respectable* [Online] Available at: www.lifesitenews.com [Accessed on: 20 October 2022]

[1599]Barillas, M & Baklinski, P [2020] *'Intense' spike in Christian persecution after China's secret deal with Vatican: US gov't report* [Online] Available at: www.lifesitenews.com [Accessed on: 20 October 2022]

[1600]Smits, J [2020] *Portuguese cardinal allows divorced and 'remarried' Catholics to receive Communion* [Online] Available at: www.lifesitenews.com [Accessed on: 20 October 2022]

[1601]Montagna, D [2020] *'I cannot keep silent': Benedict XVI and Cdl. Sarah defend priestly celibacy in new book* [Online] Available at: www.lifesitenews.com [Accessed on: 20 October 2022]

prevents him from taking a pickaxe to ecclesiastical celibacy as he had planned to do in the next post-synodal exhortation. Thus, [Pope Francis] personally called Archbishop Gänswein, the secretary of Benedict XVI as well as the prefect of Bergoglio's pontifical household, and — furious — ordered him to remove the name of Benedict XVI from the cover of the book....

Archbishop Georg Gänswein denied Socci's account of events.[1602] However, Pope Francis promptly 'removed' Archbishop Gänswein from his role as the prefect of of the papal household due to his involvement in Pope Benedict XVI and Cardinal Sarah's book.[1603] The book continues to list Pope Benedict XVI as the co-author.

16th January

Asia News website posted the news that Msgr. Vincenzo Guo Xijin, the former bishop of Mindong, Fujian, China was sleeping on the street having been made homeless by the Vatican-Chinese Communist government secret deal. At least five parishes and a home for the elderly kept by the nuns were also closed, with electricity and water supplies cut off. Their 'crime' was refusing to sign up to the 'independent' communist 'church'.[1604]

The Swiss Protestant news agency website *Protestinfo* announced that the first Catholic Mass in Geneva's cathedral since the Reformation would be celebrated on the 29th February and that Protestants had been invited to attend and receive Holy Communion. About Protestants receiving the Catholic sacrament of Holy Communion the article explained:

> This is nothing special in Geneva. This is already done locally in many parishes during ecumenical celebrations where Protestants and Catholics invite each other to the Lord's Supper and to Communion.[1605]

Postponed due to the COVID pandemic, it took place on 5th March 2022, the first Saturday of Lent.

17th January

Bishop Barry Knestout of Richmond, USA, released a statement expressing his 'sadness' that the female 'ordination' of an Episcopalian 'bishop' would no longer be held in a Catholic church of his diocese. Bishop Knestout wrote:

> It is with great sadness that I have received a letter from Bishop-Elect Susan Haynes stating that, due to the controversy of the proposed use of St. Bede Catholic Church for her consecration as the bishop for the Episcopal Diocese of Southern Virginia, she has decided to find another location for the ceremony to take place.[1606]

25th January

The Italian news service *Umbria 24* published remarks made by Cardinal Gualtiero Bassetti — elevated to the Sacred College of Cardinals by Pope Francis in 2014 and elected president of the Italian bishops' conference in 2017. Cardinal Bassetti told the media that Catholics who didn't like Pope Francis could become Protestant:

[1602]Cummings McLean, D [2020] *Vatican insider: 'Furious' Francis demanded Benedict retract name from priestly celibacy book* [Online] Available at: www.lifesitenews.com [Accessed on: 20 October 2022]

[1603]Mickens, R [2020] *The shadow pontificate is drawing to a close* [Online] Available at: international.la-croix.com [Accessed on: 20 October 2022]

[1604]Cervellera, B [2020] *Mindong's Msgr. Guo evicted from the curia: he will sleep on the street. Several priests and elderly also made homeless (Video)* [Online] Available at: www.asianews.it [Accessed on: 20 October 2022]

[1605]Laurence, L [2020] *Protestants to receive Communion at first Catholic Mass in Geneva Cathedral since Reformation* [Online] Available at: www.lifesitenews.com [Accessed on: 20 October 2022]

[1606]*Bishop Knestout Statement Following the Episcopal Diocese of Southern Virginia's Decision to Change Consecration Location* [2020] [Online] Available at: richmonddiocese.org [Accessed on: 20 October 2022]

Criticism is fine, but this destructivism, no. If someone doesn't like this pope let him say so, because he's free to choose other paths. There are too many people talking about the pope. I said to someone, 'Make the choice to be evangelical, if you don't like the Catholic Church, if this boat is too tight.' Our Protestant brethren have neither pope nor bishop; let everyone make their own choices. Enough complaining, it's useless anyway. Excuse the outburst, but everyone's objective ought to be to look for answers for the good of the Church and humanity.[1607]

29th January

The German bishops released the working document on sexual morality for their so called Synodal Path. Pro-homosexual Bishop Georg Bätzing of Limburg – appointed by Pope Francis and elected President of the German bishop's conference later in 2020 – was responsible for the contents of the document that approved the use of contraception, the practice of masturbation, and sodomy. It deliberately replaced divine revelation on sexual morality, 'which sees sexual activity only within marriage, and still directed strongly towards procreation', with 'insights' from psychology, sociology, anthropology. It praised masturbation as 'responsible' behaviour, 'The joyful experience of one's own body (self sex) can also mean a responsible approach to one's own sexuality'. Against the universal testimony of divine revelation, it recommended that homosexual acts should no longer be considered 'intrinsically evil': 'homosexual acts also realise positive meaningful values, insofar as they are an expression of friendship, reliability, loyalty and support in life.' And it directly repudiated doctrine prohibiting contraception:

> Not every sexual act must remain open to procreation: the principle of responsible parenthood is extended to include the element of family planning through the free choice of a means of contraception appropriate to the respective life situation. Family planning, even by means of artificial contraception, is not a hostile act, but supports the right of a couple to make a responsible joint decision on the number of children, the intervals between births and the concrete means of family planning.[1608]

31st January

Following a meeting with Pope Francis, pro-abortion, divorcee and adulterer President Alberto Fernandez of Argentina, 61, and his concubine, actress Fabiola Yañez, 38, received Holy Communion from pro-eugenics Bishop Marcelo Sanchez Sorondo during Mass in Saint Peter's Basilica.[1609] Bishop Sorondo later defended giving Holy Communion to the pro-abortion adulterer. Diane Montagna asked Bishop Sorondo, 'How can you give them Communion? It's Jesus. It's Jesus. They're living openly in adultery and he supports abortion.' To which Bishop Sorondo replied:

> Sorry, sorry, do you know the canon law? Do you know the canon law? We need to follow canon law, not the opinion of some bishops. And the canon law says that you cannot not give – you are obliged to give Communion if somebody asks you for Communion. Only in the case that he is excommunicated. The President is not excommunicated, so I can give Communion if he asks me for Communion.

To which Diane Montagna responded: ' But if he is pro-abortion…'. He replied:

> Nothing to do [with it]. They don't say that we shouldn't give Communion to a politician who is pro-abortion. This is the opinion of some bishops of your country, but it is not the opinion of the bishops' conference.

[1607]Montagna, D [2020] *Italian cardinal: Catholics who don't like Pope Francis can become Protestant* [Online] Available at: www.lifesitenews.com [Accessed on: 20 October 2022]

[1608]Bürger, M [2020] *German bishops' synod working doc calls for approval of contraception, homosexuality, women's ordination* [Online] Available at: www.lifesitenews.com [Accessed on: 20 October 2022]

[1609]Smits, J [2020] *Pro-abortion Argentina president receives Holy Communion along with mistress at Vatican* [Online] Available at: www.lifesitenews.com [Accessed on: 20 October 2022]

Later Diane Montagna again pressed, 'But the Eucharist is Jesus. How can you give Jesus …' To which he insisted:

> I believe in the conscience of the people. If the people ask me for Communion; I don't know if he is really in sin, or not. I don't have the possibility to say. Maybe this day they went to confession, and he doesn't want to have relations with his lady. So, there are many questions that are impossible to resolve in this form.

Even though he is an Argentinian, Bishop Sorondo claimed he didn't know that President Fernandez was publicly living with his mistress.[1610]

12th February

Pope Francis released his post-synodal apostolic exhortation *Querida Amazonia* in response to the 2019 Amazonian synod. It includes sections that were seen as attempted justifications for the veneration of the pagan idol Pachamama:

> Let us not be quick to describe as superstition or paganism certain religious practices that arise spontaneously from the life of peoples. Rather, we ought to know how to distinguish the wheat growing alongside the tares, for 'popular piety can enable us to see how the faith, once received, becomes embodied in a culture and is constantly passed on'… It is possible to take up an indigenous symbol in some way, without necessarily considering it as idolatry. A myth charged with spiritual meaning can be used to advantage and not always considered a pagan error. Some religious festivals have a sacred meaning and are occasions for gathering and fraternity, albeit in need of a gradual process of purification or maturation.(78-79).

Again, as happened in *Amoris Laetitia*, Pope Francis used a footnote to plant the seeds for radical changes with a footnote reference to an 'Amazonian Rite' in the section on 'The inculturation of the liturgy': 'During the Synod, there was a proposal to develop an "Amazonian rite".' (120). Archbishop Víctor Manuel Fernández of La Plata — appointed by Pope Francis — commented that the question of the married priesthood and other proposals of the synod are not 'off the table,' but, instead, will come up again with respect to a new 'Amazonian rite' to be developed.[1611] Fr. Víctor Codina SJ proposed that footnote 120's approval of an Amazonian Rite was a breakthrough because papal approval for the creation of an Amazonian Rite would allow for both married clergy and female ministers as proposed by the Amazon Synod's Final Document.[1612] In July 2020 Pope Francis, and his collaborators, established the Amazon Ecclesial Conference, one of the goals of which is to create the Amazonian rite.[1613]

25th February

LifeSiteNews published an interview with Archbishop Vincenzo Zani, secretary of the Congregation for Catholic Education, who was appointed by Pope Francis to organise the Global Education Pact. Archbishop Zani explained that Pope Francis wanted to create a new humanism in which God withdraws:

> God creates but then withdraws. He leaves man, saying, 'Go!'… At this point, then, we find the specifically Christian dimension, where God himself becomes nothing in order to elevate humanity. This is the new humanism. This is the new humanism; that is, it is the humanism that gets back on its feet, resumes the journey of relationship to God,

[1610]Montagna, D [2020] *EXCLUSIVE: Vatican bishop defends giving Communion to pro-abortion Argentine president and mistress* [Online] Available at: www.lifesitenews.com [Accessed on: 20 October 2022]
[1611]Hickson, M [2020] *Pope's ghostwriter, advisor claims Francis blazed path to married priests in Amazon exhortation* [Online] Available at: www.lifesitenews.com [Accessed on: 20 October 2022]
[1612]Twomey, V [2020] *What's wrong with an Amazonian Rite?* [Online] Available at: www. catholicworldreport.com [Accessed on: 20 October 2022]
[1613]Lamb, C [2020] *New Amazon body points to Pope's vision for Church* [Online] Available at: www. thetablet.co.uk [Accessed on: 20 October 2020]

doesn't cut off this relationship, but strengthens it, and especially — since man is made in the image and likeness of God — this impression of God in the soul of man has to be understood and developed.[1614]

28th February

The news website of the German bishops publicised the 'blessing of departure' for couples getting divorced, copied from practices in Protestant churches. Examples of blessings of departure included:

> a baking pan, shaped like a heart, filled with frozen water, which is passed around in the pews, the ice melting with each touch or a curtain at the church door, which is ripped up as the participants leave the church, as a sign for what they left behind.

This practice is contrary to our Lord's teaching on the indissolubility of marriage.[1615]

4th March

Monsignor Pirmin Spiegel, the head of the German bishops' relief agency *Misereor*, announced that in response to Pope Francis' apostolic letter *Querida Amazonia* a number of Latin American bishops would soon request that Pope Francis would grant them permission to ordain married priests.[1616]

5th March

Pope Francis released a video communicating his prayer intentions for March which focused on Catholics in China. The pontiff said: 'Today, the Church in China looks to the future with hope. The Church wants Chinese Christians to be truly Christians, and to be good citizens.' By so saying, Pope Francis ignored the intensifying persecution of the underground Catholic Church at the hands of the Chinese Communist Party. He also ignored the significance of the phrase 'good citizen' in the context of the communist agenda inimical to the Catholic Faith.[1617]

7th March

On behalf of Pope Francis, Cardinal Lorenzo Baldisseri, the secretary general of the synod of bishops, announced that the next synod of bishops would be on synodality. The theme of the synod of bishop would be, 'For a synodal Church: communion, participation, and mission.' The term 'synodality' as used by Pope Francis has been criticised for signifying the 'democratisation' of the Church and the re-emergence of the heresy of Gallicanism.[1618]

The Vatican announced that Pope Francis' public recitation of the Angelus prayer and weekly general audience would cease due to the coronavirus. Instead, they would be live-streamed from the papal library.[1619]

Cardinal Luis Ladaria Ferrer, the prefect of the Congregation for the Doctrine of the Faith, sent a letter to the presidents of bishops' conferences, including a questionnaire inquiring about the local church's 'experience' with Pope Benedict XVI's recognition

[1614]Montagna, D [2020] *Vatican Abp organizing Global Education Pact touts pope's 'new humanism' where God 'withdraws'* [Online] Available at: www.lifesitenews.com [Accessed on: 20 October 2022]

[1615]Bürger, M [2020] *German bishops publicize 'blessing of departure' for couples getting divorced* [Online] Available at: www.lifesitenews.com [Accessed on: 20 October 2022]

[1616]Hickson, M [2020] *Latin American bishops to ask Pope for married priests in wake of new Amazon exhortation* [Online] Available at: www.lifesitenews.com [Accessed on: 20 October 2022]

[1617]*Pope's March prayer intention: 'For Catholics in China'* [2020] [Online] Available at: www.vaticannews.va [Accessed on: 20 October 2022]

[1618]Bürger, M [2020] *Pope Francis calls for next world meeting of bishops to focus on 'synodality'* [Online] Available at: www.lifesitenews.com [Accessed on: 20 October 2022]

[1619]Wooden, C [2020] *After leading 'virtual' Angelus, pope blesses crowd in St. Peter's Square* [Online] Available at: catholicnews.com [Accessed on: 20 October 2022]

of priests' right to celebrate the traditional Latin Mass expressed in his Motu Proprio *Summorum Pontificum*. The letter stated:

> Thirteen years after the publication of the Motu Proprio *Summorum Pontificum* issued by Pope Benedict XVI, His Holiness Pope Francis wishes to be informed about the current application of the aforementioned document.

The questionnaire included questions asking:

- whether the practice of the it 'corresponds to a true pastoral need' or whether 'it is promoted by a single priest';
- whether there are 'positive or negative aspects' of the 'extraordinary form' of the Mass;
- whether other Sacraments are being administered in the traditional form;
- whether the seminarians are being influenced by it;
- whether the *Roman Missal* of the year 1962 has been in use in this rite.

The ninth question read: 'Thirteen years after the Motu Proprio *Summorum Pontificum*, what is your advice about the extraordinary form of the Roman Rite?' Professor Brian McCall, the Editor-in-Chief of the traditional Catholic newspaper *Catholic Family News*, commented:

> I cannot help but be suspicious that there may be a nefarious motive behind these questions. A common technique of revolutionary dictatorships is to gather data and then selectively use it to justify repression. It is therefore possible that this survey will be revealed to be a prelude to rescinding or severely restricting the legal guarantees of *Summorum Pontificum*. We know from public statements that Pope Francis bears no love for the Traditional Mass and the millions of laity and clergy attached to it.[1620]

8th March

Cardinal Angelo De Donatis, Vicar General of Pope Francis responsible for the diocese of Rome, announced that all public Masses and liturgical celebrations would be prohibited in response to the pandemic. Cardinal De Donatis stated:

> The Church of Rome... assumes an attitude of full responsibility towards the community in the awareness that protection from contagion requires even drastic measures, especially in interpersonal contact. Therefore, until the same date of April 3, the communal liturgical celebrations are suspended. The season of Lent helps us to live this great trial evangelically. I bless you by entrusting you all to Our Lady of Divine Love.[1621]

Westdeutscher Rundfunk Köln, the German broadcaster, released an interview with pro-homosexual Bishop Georg Bätzing of Limburg — appointed by Pope Francis in 2016. The new president of the German Bishops' Conference said he would be open to request permission from Pope Francis to 'ordain' women deacons. He would ask Pope Francis for an indult allowing female 'deacons' in Germany once the 'synodal path' was completed:

> A very powerful demeanour is needed here. And it is more powerful if it is formulated jointly by the well-represented people of God in this synodal assembly of bishops and laity. That has more weight. [The female 'diaconate'] could be one of the decisions at the end of the Synodal Path. And if that is decided, I am ready to do so, and as a member of the steering committee I am even obliged to transport it to Rome.[1622]

[1620]Hickson, M [2020] *Pope Francis surveys bishops worldwide on Traditional Latin Mass* [Online] Available at: www.lifesitenews.com [Accessed on: 20 October 2022]

[1621]Mares, C [2020] *Diocese of Rome cancels all public Masses, announces day of fasting and prayer* [Online] Available at: www.catholicnewsagency.com [Accessed on: 20 October 2022]

[1622]Bürger, M [2020] *President of German Bishops' Conference signals openness to female 'deacons'* [Online] Available at: www.lifesitenews.com [Accessed on: 20 October 2022]

9th March

The Italian Bishop's Conference announced that all public Masses would be prohibited until the 3rd April in response to the coronavirus pandemic. The Italian bishops accepted the Italian government's decree of the 8th March that called for the suspension of 'civil and religious ceremonies, including funeral ceremonies.' Catholic historian Prof Roberto de Mattei criticised the closure of churches:

> In reality, it is not anti-Christian persecutions that we should speak of, but of 'auto-persecution' among Churchmen, who, by closing the churches and suspending Masses, seem to be bringing to its ultimate coherence a process of auto-demolition begun in the 1960s with the Second Vatican Council. And unfortunately, individual exceptions apart, even the traditionalist clergy, who are closed up in their houses, appear victim to this auto-persecution.[1623]

12th March

Following consultations with Pope Francis, Cardinal Angelo De Donatis, the vicar general of Rome, announced the closure of all Roman churches to the public due to the coronavirus pandemic. However, Cardinal Konrad Krajewski, the papal almoner, refused to comply, announcing that he would keep Santa Maria Immacolata open. Cardinal Krajewski said:

> It is the act of disobedience, yes, I myself put the Blessed Sacrament out and opened my church. It did not happen under fascism, it did not happen under the Russian or Soviet rule in Poland – the churches were not closed. This is an act that should bring courage to other priests. Home should always be open to its children. I don't know whether people will come or not, how many of them, but their home is open.[1624]

The next day Cardinal De Donatis modified the restriction, stating that the decision to close or keep open parish churches would be left to parish pastors:

> [The decree] is therefore modified, placing the ultimate responsibility of entering the places of worship in the hands of priests and all the faithful, so as not to expose the population to any danger of contagion and at the same time avoid the sign of a physical prohibition on access to a place of worship by closing it, which could create disorientation and a greater sense of insecurity.

However, non-parish churches and other religious buildings remained closed.[1625]

25th March

Cardinal Sarah, the Prefect of the Congregation for Divine Worship and the Discipline of the Sacraments, issued a decree restricting the liturgies for Holy Week due to the coronavirus pandemic. Palm Sunday processions outside were banned; the Mass of the Lord's Supper on the evening of Holy Thursday would not include the rite of feet washing and would not end with a procession of the Blessed Sacrament; there were to be no baptisms during the Easter Vigil.[1626]

27 March

During a special Urbi et Orbi for the COVID pandemic, Pope Francis said a prayer that denied that the pandemic was God's judgement on the world, but was a time for human beings to make judgements about how they lived:

[1623]Mattei, R di [2020] *Church is 'auto-persecuting' its own members in coronavirus pandemic* [Online] Available at: www.lifesitenews.com [Accessed on: 20 October 2022]

[1624]Guzik, P [2020] *Papal Almsgiver breaks decree, opens Rome church for prayer and adoration* [Online] Available at: cruxnow.com [Accessed on: 20 October 2022]

[1625]Mares, C [2020] *Rome's churches closed, then opened again. What happened?* [Online] Available at: www.catholicnewsagency.com [Accessed on: 20 October 2022]

[1626]Congregation for Divine Worship and the Discipline of the Sacraments [2020] *Decree in time of COVID 19* [Online] Available at: press.vatican.va [Accessed on: 20 October 2022]

Lord, you are calling to us, calling us to faith. Which is not so much believing that you exist, but coming to you and trusting in you. This Lent your call reverberates urgently: 'Be converted!', 'Return to me with all your heart' (Joel 2:12). You are calling on us to seize this time of trial as a time of choosing. It is not the time of your judgement, but of our judgement: a time to choose what matters and what passes away, a time to separate what is necessary from what is not. It is a time to get our lives back on track with regard to you, Lord, and to others.[1627]

The US *Remnant* newspaper published an interview with Bishop Athanasius Schneider, auxiliary bishop of Astana, Kazakhstan. He encouraged priests to continue offering the Most Holy Sacrifice of the Mass to the faithful during the pandemic, even if bishops or the government prohibited it:

If a priest observes in a reasonable manner all the necessary health precautions and uses discretion, he has not to obey the directives of his bishop or the government to suspend Mass for the faithful. Such directives are a pure human law; however, the supreme law in the Church is the salvation of souls. Priests in such a situation have to be extremely creative in order to provide for the faithful, even for a small group, the celebration of Holy Mass and the reception of the sacraments. Such was the pastoral behaviour of all confessor and martyr priests in the time of persecution.

Bishop Schneider criticised his fellow bishops for closing the churches:

My general impression is that the prevailing majority of bishops reacted precipitously and out of panic in prohibiting all public Masses and — what is even more incomprehensible — in closing churches. Such bishops reacted more like civil bureaucrats than shepherds. In focusing too exclusively on all the hygienic protective measures, they have lost a supernatural vision and have abandoned the primacy of the eternal good of souls.

Bishop Schneider concluded:

It is revealing the loss of supernatural vision. In recent decades, many members of the Church's hierarchy have been immersed predominantly in secular, inner-worldly and temporal affairs and have thus become blind to supernatural and eternal realities. Their eyes have been filled with the dust of earthly occupations, as St. Gregory the Great once said (see *Regula Pastoralis* II, 7). Their reaction in handling the coronavirus epidemic has revealed that they give more importance to the mortal body than to the immortal soul of men, forgetting the words of our Lord: 'For what shall it profit a man, if he gains the whole world, and suffer the loss of his soul?' (Mk 8:36). The same bishops who now try to protect (sometimes with disproportionate measures) the bodies of their faithful from contamination with a material virus, tranquilly allowed the poison virus of heretical teachings and practices to spread among their flock.[1628]

31st March

Vatican News, the Holy See's official news service, published an article celebrating the ecological 'benefits' of the coronavirus pandemic. Fr. Benedict Mayaki SJ's article was published under the title 'Coronavirus: Earth's unlikely ally: The changes in human behaviour due to the Covid-19 virus pandemic are yielding unintended benefits to the planet.' Only referring to the impact on human beings as 'a global health concern' Fr Mayaki went on to write:

Earth is healing itself. In Italy, fish have returned to the canals in Venice. Less tourism and water transport have allowed the murky waters to settle. Migratory birds, including swans have been sighted gliding through the city's waterways.

This crass ecological perspective on the pandemic echoed Pope Francis' earlier statement on the 22nd March when he said:

[1627]Pope Francis [2020] *Extraordinary moment of prayer and 'Urbi et Orbi' Blessing* [Online] Available at: www.vatican.va [Accessed on: 20 October 2022]

[1628]Montagna, D [2020] *Bishop Athanasius Schneider on Church's handling of Coronavirus* [Online] Available at: remnantnewspaper.com [Accessed on: 20 October 2022]

Curiously the planet hasn't been very clean for a long time…There's a saying that you surely know: God always forgives, we forgive sometimes, [but] nature never forgives. Fires, earthquakes. . . that is, nature is having a fit, so that we will take care of nature.

Following an outcry at its insensitivity to the suffering and grief of thousands *Vatican News* deleted Fr. Mayaki's article.[1629]

1st April

The Congregation for Divine Worship and the Discipline of the Sacraments, invoking the authority delegated to it by Pope Francis, issued the Decree on the Mass in Times of Pandemic. Revising Pope Clement VI's Votive Mass for the Deliverance from Death in Time of Pestilence it removed all references to pestilence as an expression of the 'wrath of God' at the human race sunk in the depths of sinful depravity and the need for conversion and repentance. Instead it only asks God for help during the pandemic, as expressed in its collect:

Almighty and eternal God, our refuge in every danger, to whom we turn in our distress; in faith we pray, look with compassion on the afflicted, grant eternal rest to the dead, comfort to mourners, healing to the sick, peace to the dying, strength to healthcare workers, wisdom to our leaders, and the courage to reach out to all in love, so that together we may give glory to your holy name. Through our Lord Jesus Christ your Son, who lives and reigns with you in the unity of the Holy Spirit, God forever and ever.[1630]

2nd April

The Vatican published *The Annuario Pontificio* — the Holy See's Directory — which revealed that Pope Francis had dropped the ancient papal title 'Vicar of Jesus Christ', simply listing the name *Jorge Mario Bergoglio* in large, block capitals. The title 'Vicar of Jesus Christ' is relegated to a footnote on historical titles:

Vicar of Jesus Christ, Successor of the Prince of the Apostles, Supreme Pontiff of the Universal Church, Primate of Italy, Archbishop and Metropolitan of the Roman province, Sovereign of the State of the Vatican City, and Servant of the Servants of God.

Cardinal Gerhard Müller, the former prefect of the Congregation for the Doctrine of the Faith, commented on the 'embarrassment' that the *Annuario Pontificio* had 'demeaned essential elements of the Catholic teaching on the primacy [of the Pope] as mere historical appendix.' He described it as 'a theological barbarism to demean as historical burden the titles of the Pope "Successor of Peter, Representative of Christ, and visible head of the entire Church."' Archbishop Carlo Maria Viganò, the former papal nuncio to the USA, observed:

This change in the layout and content of an official text of the Catholic Church cannot be ignored, nor is it possible to attribute it to a gesture of humility on the part of Francis, which is not in keeping with his name being so prominently featured. Instead, it seems possible to see in it the admission — passed over in silence — of a sort of usurpation, whereby it is not the *'Servus servorum Dei'* [The Servant of the Servants of God] who reigns, but the person of Jorge Mario Bergoglio, who has officially disavowed being the Vicar of Christ, the Successor of the Prince of the Apostles and the Supreme Pontiff, as if they were annoying trappings of the past: only mere 'historical titles'.[1631]

[1629]Cullinan Hoffman, M [2020] *Vatican News pulls article calling coronavirus 'ally' of the Earth because of environmental benefits* [Online] Available at: www.lifesitenews.com [Accessed on: 20 October 2022]

[1630]Gomes, J [2020] *Pope Francis Strips God's Wrath From Mass for Pandemic* [Online] Available at: www.churchmilitant.com: Cullinan Hoffman, M [2020] *Vatican's new special Mass for pandemic doesn't mention God's wrath, unlike original* [Online] Available at: www.lifesitenews.com [Accessed on: 20 October 2022]

[1631]Hickson, M [2020] *Pope Francis drops 'Vicar of Christ' title in Vatican yearbook* [Online] Available at: www.lifesitenews.com [Accessed on: 20 October 2022]

8th April

The Vatican released a memo announcing that Pope Francis had instructed Cardinal Ladaria Ferrer, Prefect of the Congregation for the Doctrine of the Faith, to appoint a new commission on the 'study of the female diaconate.' There was no reference to Pope Francis' first commission to study the female 'diaconate', nor was information released about the findings of the first commission.[1632]

During his homily at morning Mass, Pope Francis said he didn't know if Judas was in hell, preferring to focus on Jesus referring to Judas as 'friend'. The pontiff said:

> Something that calls my attention is that Jesus never calls him 'traitor': [Jesus] says he will be betrayed, but he doesn't say to [Judas], 'traitor.' He never says, 'Go away, traitor'. Never. In fact, he calls him, 'Friend', and he kisses him. The mystery of Judas … What is the mystery of Judas. I don't know … Don Primo Mazzolari explains it better than me … Yes, it consoles me to contemplate that capital [of the column] of Vezelay: How did Judas end up? I don't know. Jesus threatens forcefully here; he threatens forcefully: 'woe to that man by whom the Son of Man is betrayed. It would be better for that man if he had never been born.' But does that mean that Judas is in Hell? I don't know. I look at that capital. And I listen to the word of Jesus: 'Friend.'[1633]

9th April

In various interviews with local media, pro-homosexual Cardinal Cupich of Chicago — shown many signs of favour by Pope Francis — dismissed the power of prayer in response to the coronavirus pandemic. He told listeners to *WBBM Newsradio*: 'Religion is not magic where we just say prayers and think things are going to change. God gave us a brain and the gift of intelligence and we have to use it in this moment.' During an interview on *ABC7 Chicago* Cardinal Cupich said:

> God doesn't allow us to have a religion into a magic formula where we say a prayer and think things are going to go away. We have to take responsibility for our actions and we have to make sure we keep each other safe.'

Implicit in this is dismissal of the power of prayer, contrary to the teachings of our Lord Jesus Christ.[1634]

12th April

The German newspaper *Frankfurter Allgemeine Sonntagszeitung* published an interview on Easter Sunday with the new president of the German bishops' conference, pro-homosexual Bishop Georg Bätzing of Limburg — appointed by Pope Francis in 2016. During the interview Bishop Bätzing called for the Church to change her condemnation of sodomy, founded on God's revelation. He said:

> Here the statement of the Catechism is first of all that these people are to be met with esteem and respect. But every single sexual act is seen as evidence of a disordered sexual life. This is something that many people no longer want or can understand.[1635]

In an interview with the German magazine, *Bunte*, in March 2022 Bishop Georg Bätzing responded to a question about the permissibility of sodomy:

> Yes, it's OK if it's done in fidelity and responsibility. It doesn't affect the relationship with God. How someone lives their personal intimacy is none of my business.

[1632]Cummings McLean, D [2020] *Pope Francis appoints another commission to study female deacons* [Online] Available at: www.lifesitenews.com [Accessed on: 20 October 2022]

[1633]Hattrup, K [2020] *Satan pays badly, warns pope, calling us to find the 'Little Judas' we have within* [Online] Available at: aleteia.org [Accessed on: 20 October 2022]

[1634]Bürger, M [2020] *US cardinal dismisses prayer power during pandemic: We can't just pray and think things will change* [Online] Available at: www.lifesitenews.com [Accessed on: 20 October 2022]

[1635]Bürger, M [2020] *In Easter interview, German bishops' head calls for changing Church teaching on homosexuality* [Online] Available at: www.lifesitenews.com [Accessed on: 20 October 2022]

To the journalist's assertion that no one adhered to the Church's teaching that sexuality should only be practiced within marriage Bishop Bätzing replied:

> That's true. And we have to somewhat change the Catechism on this matter. Sexuality is a gift from God. And not a sin.[1636]

14th April

Australia's *Sky News* released Andrew Bolt's interview with Cardinal George Pell following the High Court of Australia's unanimous judgment quashing Cardinal Pell's convictions for child sexual abuse and determining that judgments of acquittal be entered in their place. Referring to Cardinal Pell's former role as prefect of the Secretariat for the Economy, Andrew Bolt asked Cardinal Pell whether he had ever considered that 'the trouble he was causing to corrupt officials in the Vatican was related to the troubles he has since experienced in Australia'. Cardinal Pell responded: 'Most of the senior people in Rome who are in any way sympathetic to financial reform believe that they are.'[1637]

In a later interview Cardinal Pell raised concerns about the $2,300,000 [AUD] sent by Cardinal Angelo Becciu — a close associate of Pope Francis — from the Vatican Secretary of State to Australia. Monsignor Alberto Perlasca, a former senior official at the Secretariat of State, said that the funds were sent to the Australian Conference of Bishops for Cardinal Pell's expenses during his trial and imprisonment. However, the Australian Conference of Bishops disputed this claim, saying it did not receive the money. About this, Cardinal Pell said:

> We have one basic unanswered question [Pell told CNA in a phone interview]. We do know — this has been confirmed by Cardinal Becciu — that $2,300,000 [AUD] was sent from the Vatican Secretary of State to Australia. The conference of bishops has said 'no such money ever arrived, certainly, we didn't receive it.' So the unanswered question is: If the money wasn't sent for something to do with my case, why was it sent? But it's a major unanswered question. And as I said, Cardinal Becciu confirms that the money was sent, and he believes it's none of my business as to why it was sent.[1638]

It was speculated in the media that disgraced Cardinal Becciu, facing trial for financial corruption, sent the $2,300,000 to recipients in Australia 'who helped to ensure false, hostile testimony in the abuse trial of Cardinal Pell'.[1639]

15th April

During his interview with US *Fox News*' Tucker Carlson, Democratic New Jersey Governor Phil Murphy revealed that he had worked closely in suppressing the public celebration of the Mass with pro-homosexual Cardinal Joseph Tobin of Newark — shown many signs of favour by Pope Francis. Governor Murphy related a phone call he had with Cardinal Tobin:

> 'I said, listen, I'm really concerned about drive-through Holy Communion because we had heard some stories about priests who unwittingly had the virus and unwittingly passed it on to parishioners.' According to Murphy Cardinal Tobin declared: 'We're not doing that. I promise you. And I'll confirm that with my fellow bishops.'[1640]

[1636]*German Catholic bishops' leader calls for change to Catechism on sexuality* [2020] [Online] Available at: www.catholicnewsagency.com [Accessed on: 20 October 2022]

[1637]Smeaton, P [2020] *Cardinal Pell: 'Senior people in Rome' believe Vatican officials linked to my imprisonment* [Online] Available at: www.lifesitenews.com [Accessed on: 20 October 2022]

[1638]Rousselle, C [2020] *Cardinal Pell to Becciu: What was that $2M payment actually for?* [Online] Available at: www.catholicnewsagency.com [Accessed on: 20 October 2022]

[1639]Kington, T [2020] *Cardinal Becciu 'stole funds to bribe witnesses' in sex abuse case against rival George Pell* [Online] Available at: www.thetimes.co.uk [Accessed on: 20 October 2022]

[1640]Bürger, M [2020] *Dem governor tells Tucker Carlson how he worked closely with top US cardinal to ban sacraments* [Online] Available at: www.lifesitenews.com [Accessed on: 20 October 2022]

21st April

The Australian newspaper published an interview with Cardinal Burke, the former Prefect of the Apostolic Signatura, in which he criticised the Vatican for thanking the Chinese Communist Party for COVID medical supplies, but ignoring the help given by Taiwan. Taiwan donated 280,000 medical masks to the Vatican, the Italian bishops, Italian hospitals, and various religious institutes in Italy. Cardinal Burke said:

> Something is badly wrong [with China seemingly enjoying] a place of privilege with the Vatican. The Holy See made a point to praise the People's Republic of China for sending masks and medical equipment to the Vatican, while it has not acknowledged in any public way the generous help received from Taiwan. The agreement which the Vatican made with the People's Republic of China in 2018 – of which there is still no public record – has been, in practice, a repudiation of the tremendous suffering of countless Chinese confessors of the faith and martyrs for the faith at the hands of the atheistic communist government and has only resulted in a greater ongoing persecution of faithful Chinese Catholics.[1641]

23rd April

The Diocese of Limburg published a sermon by pro-homosexual Bishop Georg Bätzing repudiating the idea that the coronavirus pandemic was 'punishment' from God, which is the traditional understanding of times of pestilence. In response to people considering COVID-19 as God's punishment Bishop Bätzing said: 'My God has not known such thoughts since Jesus died for us. That is when God made his decision for life. God does not punish.'[1642]

27th April

The Spanish news outlet *Religión Digital* published an interview with Archbishop Víctor Manuel Fernández — appointed by Pope Francis and one of his personal confidants. Reflecting on the suspension of public worship due to the coronavirus pandemic, Archbishop Fernández said that Pope Francis might consider abandoning the precept of the Catholic Church that Catholics go to church on Sundays and Holy Days of obligation, saying it 'is not indispensable' and 'is something that could fall.'[1643]

28th April

During his homily at morning Mass, Pope Francis called on Italian Catholics to obey the continuing ban on public Mass enforced by phase two of the Italian government's COVID restrictions. The pontiff said:

> At this time when measures for leaving the quarantine are beginning, let us pray to the Lord that He will give his people, to all of us, the grace of prudence and obedience, so that the pandemic does not return.

By so doing, Pope Francis contradicted the position taken by the Italian bishops' conference who had criticised the Italian government for extending the ban on public worship. A criticism expressed by Bishop Massimo Camisasca of Reggio Emilia:

> The decision of the [government] expresses an arbitrary violation of religious freedom, sanctioned by the Constitution. At this time, the Church insists on the ability to return to her pastoral activities with the autonomy she deserves under the law.[1644]

[1641]Mainwaring, D [2020] *Cardinal Burke criticizes Vatican for thanking China but not Taiwan* [Online] Available at: www.lifesitenews.com [Accessed on: 20 October 2022]
[1642]Bürger, M [2020] *Head of German bishops: Coronavirus not divine punishment since 'God does not punish'* [Online] Available at: www.lifesitenews.com [Accessed on: 20 October 2022]
[1643]Hickson, M [2020] *Pope Francis' confidant: Sunday Mass obligation isn't 'indispensable,' it 'could fall'* [Online] Available at: www.lifesitenews.com [Accessed on: 20 October 2022]
[1644]Cummings McLean, D [2020] *Pope Francis calls for 'obedience' to Italian 'phase 2' restrictions that continue ban on Mass* [Online] Available at: www.lifesitenews.com [Accessed on: 20 October 2022]

18th May

Archbishop Coleridge, president of the Australian Catholic Bishops' Conference, issued a statement welcoming the report 'The Light from the Southern Cross' that proposed separating the priesthood from governance of the Church. Among other things, the report recommended the appointment of lay women and men to senior decision-making bodies and agencies be accelerated so that they could exercise greater influence in ecclesial matters. By so doing, Archbishop Coleridge expressed approval of the Church in Australia abandoning the Apostolic nature of the Church in which clergy, through the sacrament of ordination, participate in the triple *munera* of Christ, including the *munus regendi* — Christ's power to rule the Church.[1645]

27th May

The German online journal *Publik-Forum* published an interview with pro-homosexual Bishop Georg Bätzing of Limburg and president of the German bishops' conference — appointed by Pope Francis. Bishop Bätzing expressed the hope that the German synodal path's radical agenda on sexual morality and other ecclesial matters, such as the faux ordination of women, would be 'transported' on 'the level of the Universal Church.' Bishop Bätzing said:

> What is being developed by way of a synod also needs to be clarified and responded to with the help of a synod, because that is the new element that has become strong under Pope Francis... among the people of God, the arguments for the 'no' to female ordination are often not anymore accepted. That is why I am very much in favour of transporting the insights and decisions which we collect at the synodal path — also concerning women and offices — to Rome, onto the level of the Universal Church. What is being developed by way of a synod, also needs to be clarified and responded to with the help of a synod because that is the new element that has become strong under Pope Francis.

On sexual morality he said:

> It seems to many people merely to be a morality of interdictions. I hope we will further develop certain formulations as they are now in the Catechism and as they reflect the current state of the doctrine. Indeed for quite some time now, there is a tension between the life realities of the people and the life realities of the Church. Many experience a sort of alienation.

About blessing homosexual bondings Bishop Bätzing said:

> We have talked with people. Not few are suffering under the fact that their relationship does not receive full ecclesial recognition, for example because they are civilly divorced and remarried people or because they live in a same-sex partnership. They are waiting for signs.[1646]

4th June

The German Catholic weekly newspaper *Die Tagespost* published an interview with the former apostolic nuncio to Germany, Archbishop Erwin Josef Ender. Archbishop Ender expressed alarm at the prospect that the German bishops intended to 'reinvent' the Church through their 'synodal way':

> If one were to believe some media reports, then a Reformation-like 'revolution' is imminent. Without any consideration for the genuine sources of faith and revelation, namely Scripture and Tradition, Church is supposed to reinvent itself, so to speak. I have read the drafts for the four forums of the 'Synodal Way' and am alarmed at the direction

[1645]Smeaton, P [2020] *Australian bishops' commissioned report calls for Church governance by lay women* [Online] Available at: www.lifesitenews.com [Accessed on: 20 October 2022]
[1646]Hickson, M [2020] *German bishops' head: We need to speak about female ordination, 'transport' discussion to Rome* [Online] Available at: www.lifesitenews.com [Accessed on: 20 October 2022]

that the discussion seems to be taking. It would appear that Scripture and Tradition have been ousted and their place taken by so-called 'modern' theology and the human sciences. This bears no similarity at all to the perspective of faith of the Council texts.[1647]

Die Tagespost also published Cardinal Rainer Maria Woelki of Cologne's criticism of the German 'synodal way'. Cardinal Woelki said:

> The problem with the 'synodal path' in Germany is that for many people, it is not an open-ended path at all, but a project whose only satisfying result has to be the abolition of obligatory celibacy, women deacons, and the reduction of Catholic sexual morality to the sentence: Between adults, voluntary sexual relations of whatever kind are not to be objected to.[1648]

5th June

Katholisch.de, the website of the German Bishops' conference, published an interview with Fr. Ewald Volgger about the pro-homosexuality book he edited for the Austrian bishops. Fr. Volgger asserted that the Church must recognise the 'sacramental character' of sodomite unions:

> When the Church's magisterium recognises a same-sex relationship as a common development of the baptismal vocation, it expresses that God is present and active in Jesus Christ. This constitutes the sacramental character of the relationship. The designation is not the primary goal; what is essential is the recognition of the common way of life of two same-sex partners whom God brings together.... By blessing homosexual relationships the Church would show an appreciation for this relationship, and would symbolically express the love of God for man. Fr. Volgger pointed out that homosexual people were already integrated into the life of the Church, from the parish to the highest levels of the ecclesiastical hierarchy. If the Church openly acknowledges this and recognises the character of these people, then the Church will also open the way to a life in same-sex partnership.

In an earlier interview published on the Diocese of Linz website Fr. Volgger argued for the Church recognising equivalence between homosexuality and heterosexuality:

> Just as marriage between a man and a woman is an image of God's creative love, so is a same-sex relationship an image of God's attention to human beings.... If partners live the gift of mutual love in faithfulness to one another and live their lives with the spiritual gifts of God such as kindness, forbearance, patience, reconciliation, etc., their relationship is also an image of God's goodness and humanity.

By so doing, Fr. Volgger ignores God's explicit condemnation in Scripture and Tradition of homosexual sex acts as acts of grave depravity.[1649]

20th June

Pope Francis delivered an address on the Church's response to coronavirus to bishops, doctors, nurses, and other healthcare workers from the Italian region of Lombardy. During his address he criticised priests who did not conform to the restrictions imposed on the Church as 'adolescents'. This was taken as the pontiff criticising those priests who continued to offer the sacraments to the faithful. Pope Francis said:

> The pastoral zeal and creative solicitude of priests helped people to follow the way of faith and not to remain alone before sorrow and fear. This priestly creativity... overcame... a few, 'adolescent' expressions against the measures of the authority having the duty of protecting the health of the people. I admired the apostolic spirit of many

[1647]Bürger, M [2020] *Former apostolic nuncio to Germany 'alarmed' at bishops' plan to 'reinvent' Church* [Online] Available at: www.lifesitenews.com [Accessed on: 21 October 2022]
[1648]Bürger, M [2020] *German cardinal criticizes 'synodal path,' exhorts German Church to 'remain Catholic'* [Online] Available at: www.lifesitenews.com [Accessed on: 21 October 2022]
[1649]Bürger, M [2020] *Austrian priest: Church must recognize 'sacramental character' of gay partnerships* [Online] Available at: www.lifesitenews.com [Accessed on: 21 October 2022]

priests who visited by telephone, knocked on doors, called by homes (saying): 'Do you need something? I will do your shopping. A thousand things. Closeness, creativity, without shame.... They were a sign of the consoling presence of God. [These priests were] fathers, not adolescents.[1650]

During an interview on Steve Bannon's US show *The War Room* Chinese Billionaire Guo Wengui claimed the Vatican had been bribed by the Chinese Communist government to be silent about its intensifying persecution of faithful Catholics. Guo Wengui said:

2014, the CPC, inside, made the decision: Every year, they want 2 billion dollars to pay to the Vatican, to influence the Vatican policy about China/Vatican — and [regarding] the Christian and Catholic [mistreatment], they wanted Vatican to shut up, to follow the CPC about religion, you know the policy – that's disaster.[1651]

27th June

The German bishops' conference published a report from pro-homosexual Bishop Georg Bätzing's meeting with Pope Francis. Bishop Georg Bätzing's of Limburg and president of the German bishops' conference was appointed by Pope Francis. Bishop Bätzing recounted that Pope Francis encouraged the German Church to continue its 'synodal way' despite it recommending masturbation, the use of contraception, changing the Church's doctrine on homosexuality, and the faux-ordination of women. Bishop Bätzing said:

I feel strengthened by the intensive exchange with the Holy Father to continue on the path we have taken. The Pope appreciates this project, which he connects closely with the concept of 'synodality' that he coined. It was a matter of concern to me to make it clear that the Church in Germany is taking this path and always knows that it is bound to the universal Church.[1652]

28th June

The Spanish newspaper *El Confidencial* published an interview with Archbishop Santiago Agrelo Martínez OFM, retired bishop of Tangiers, in which he said that not all abortions were 'immoral'. Asked about coronavirus vaccine research that used cells harvested from a baby murdered through abortion Archbishop Martínez said:

If they are experimenting on a vaccine with aborted fetal cells, what I won't do is to say that it is immoral, since even an ignoramus like me knows that there are abortions that have nothing immoral about them... that is something that everyone in the Church knows, that there are abortions that in no way can be morally condemned. Look, in the end we are not here, I am not authorized to think that any woman who aborted, did so under immoral conditions, without having a right to do so. I cannot think that, ever, because it would be to judge in a way that isn't proper for me. Theoretically, I can condemn the woman, or her family, when they intentionally provoke an abortion. But that is the theory, the pages of a book, they are not the pages of life, and that is why I cannot condemn her, never.

Archbishop Santiago Agrelo Martínez OFM's statement is totally contrary to Church doctrine on the 'abominable crime' of abortion. (*Gaudium est Spes* 51). Neither Pope Francis or the Congregation for the Doctrine of the Faith issued a correction.[1653]

[1650]Cummings McLean, D [2020] *Pope Francis belittles as 'adolescent' priests who defied COVID lockdowns to give faithful sacraments* [Online] Available at: www.lifesitenews.com [Accessed on: 21 October 2022]
[1651]Mosher, S [2020] *Why Chinese whistleblower may be right that Communists paid Vatican to 'shut up' about its war on Catholics* [Online] Available at: www.lifesitenews.com [Accessed on: 21 October 2022]
[1652]Bürger, M [2020] *Pope Francis exhorts German Catholics to continue on 'Synodal Path'* [Online] Available at: www.lifesitenews.com [Accessed on: 21 October 2022]
[1653]Laurence, L [2020] *Some abortions 'have nothing immoral about them': retired archbishop* [Online] Available at: www.lifesitenews.com [Accessed on: 21 October 2022]

20th July

The Vatican's Congregation for Clergy published the instruction 'The pastoral conversion of the parish community in the service of the evangelizing mission of the Church'. The new instruction clarifies that in some circumstances a bishop may entrust the pastoral care of a parish to a woman. The instruction states that in dioceses facing a shortage or lack of priests:

> [A bishop] may entrust the pastoral care of a parish to a deacon, to a consecrated religious or layperson, or even to a group of persons.

Those so entrusted 'will be directed by a priest with legitimate faculties, who will act as a "moderator of pastoral care," with the powers and functions of a parish priest, albeit without an office with its duties and rights'.

Those lay women delegated to undertake pastoral care in a parish would be able to celebrate a Liturgy of the Word on Sundays and Holy Days of obligation in the extraordinary circumstance that no priest is available; provide baptism; celebrate funeral rites; and assist at marriages.[1654]

22nd July

The Pontifical Academy for Life published 'Humana Communitas in the Age of Pandemic: Untimely Meditations on Life's Rebirth'.[1655] A meditation on the coronavirus pandemic, it was notable for its lack of reference to 'God, Jesus Christ, the Holy Spirit, the Church, the sacraments, prayer, or even charity'. It was also remarkable for its nihilistic perspective:

> We emerge from a night of mysterious origins: called into being beyond choice, we come soon to presumption and complaint, asserting as ours what we have only been vouchsafed. Too late do we learn consent to the darkness from which we came, and to which we finally return.[1656]

In response to criticisms about the lack of Christian references Fabrizio Mastrofini, a spokesman of the Pontifical Academy for Life, said:

> We are interested in entering into human situations, reading them in the light of faith, and in a way that speaks to the widest possible audience, to believers and non-believers, to all men and women 'of good will'. I do not know, at this point, whether a philological 'accounting' work on how many times a few key words recur in a text is useful.[1657]

28th July

Father José Antonio Álvarez, spokesman for the Diocese of San Rafael, Argentina, posted a video on Facebook announcing that the Vatican's Congregation for Clergy supported Bishop Eduardo Maria Taussig's decision to close down his seminary. The San Rafael seminary was one of the most successful in Argentina and in all of Latin America, with a large number of vocations. Bishop Taussig had ordered that communion could only be received in the hand at the seminary, despite the seminary, and diocese, observing the practice of only receiving Holy Communion on the tongue, kneeling down. When the rector and other clergy on the staff of the seminary refused to obey his instruction, he sacked them and closed the seminary. The spokesman for the Diocese of San Rafael said on his Facebook video:

[1654]Laurence, L [2020] *Vatican legal clarification allows bishops to 'entrust...care of a parish' to women* [Online] Available at: www.lifesitenews.com [Accessed on: 21 October 2022]
[1655]*Pontifical Academy for Life [2020] Humana Communitas in the age of Pandemic untimely meditations on life's re-birth* [Online] Available at: www.academyforlife.va [Accessed on: 21 October 2022]
[1656]Gomes, J [2020] *Vatican on Pandemic: 'God Is Dead'* [Online] Available at: www.churchmilitant. com [Accessed on: 21 October 2022]
[1657]Bürger, M [2020] *Vatican academy defends dropping 'God' from pandemic document to reach 'widest possible audience'* [Online] Available at: www.lifesitenews.com [Accessed on: 21 October 2022]

The measure taken by the Congregation for the Clergy, which is just the dicastery of the Holy Father that has jurisdictions over these cases, takes into consideration that due to the undisciplined reaction of a good portion of the clergy of the diocese, at this moment, this diocese is not able to put together a group of teachers who will conform to the church's discipline. Since that is something that cannot be resolved immediately… Well … to safeguard the formation of the seminarians so that they can continue with their formation, they will be sent to other seminaries. That is something that will be the subject of an ongoing dialogue in the remaining months of the academic year.[1658]

Following his meeting with Pope Francis in October 2020, Bishop Taussig said that the Vatican's decision to close the seminary was 'not up for discussion.' Due to prolonged resistance in the diocese to his order to receive communion in the hand, Bishop Taussig resigned on the 5th February 2020.[1659]

30th July

Eugenio Scalfari, the atheist founder of *La Repubblica*, published his twelfth engagement with Pope Francis based on an hour long discussion they held together in the Vatican on the 30th July. They discussed environmental issues.[1660]

14th August

Yahoo News reported that Pope Francis had written to Sister Mónica Astorga Cremona, known as the 'Nun of the Trans' to congratulate her for opening in Argentina a residence for 'trans women' — men who choose to identify as women. The pontiff wrote:

> Dear Monica, God who did not go to the seminary or study theology will repay you abundantly. I pray for you and your girls. Do not forget to pray for me. May Jesus blesses (sic) you and may the Holy Virgin take care of you.[1661]

16th August

The Australian newspaper the *Daily Telegraph* published a report that the Diocese of Parramatta had adopted a new religious curriculum that includes LGBT studies, gender fluidity, identity politics, and atheism. Pro-homosexual Bishop Vincent Long — appointed by Pope Francis — defended introducing children in Catholic schools to beliefs and behaviours contrary to Catholic doctrine:

> The new curriculum is not just a one way street. It's not just our teachers proclaiming tenets of the Christian faith and doctrines we believe in. Young people engage much better with the Christian faith much more meaningfully, personally and seriously when their questions, concerns and issues are taken up. Religious education teachers must not just learn from the textbook or the teachings of the Church or the Bible for that matter. The onus is on them to dialogue with the young people, instead of just teaching them or proclaiming the faith to them.[1662]

20th August

DOMRADIO.DE, the Catholic multimedia portal of the Archdiocese of Cologne, published an interview with Archbishop Stefan Heße of Hamburg, appointed by Pope

[1658]Cummings McLean, D [2020] *Vatican backs bishop in closing down seminary over priests' resistance to giving Communion on hand* [Online] Available at: www.lifesitenews.com [Accessed on: 21 October 2022]

[1659]Ramos, D [2022] *Resignation of Argentine bishop accepted after controversy over seminary closure* [Online] Available at: www.catholicnewsagency.com [Accessed on: 21 October 2022]

[1660]O'Connell, G [2020] *Pope Francis discusses climate crisis with well-known Italian journalist* [Online] Available at: www.americamagazine.org [Accessed on: 21 October 2022]

[1661]Mainwaring, D [2020] *Pope Francis praises nun for opening 'trans home' for men claiming to be women, calls them 'girls'* [Online] Available at: www.lifesitenews.com [Accessed on: 21 October 2022]

[1662]Mainwaring, D [2020] *Australian diocese to teach kids LGBT studies, gender fluidity, atheism in new religion class* [Online] Available at: www.lifesitenews.com [Accessed on: 21 October 2022]

Francis in 2015. Archbishop Heße asserted that Pope St. John Paul II's Apostolic Letter *Ordinatio Sacerdotalis* could not stop debate on the faux-ordination of women 'priests'. He said:

> You have to be allowed to think and discuss the issues. The discussion is still there, it is alive, and it cannot be stifled by a paper. The historical perspective is one thing — but it's not everything.

According to *LifeSiteNews*:

> Archbishop Heße pointed out that modern theologians are asking whether in the incarnation of Christ the decisive thing was the Second Person of the Trinity becoming a man or becoming a person [Personwerden].[1663]

This contradicts the Church's Christological doctrine that defines the Incarnation as the Person of the Son of God assuming a human nature united to His divine nature. To propose that there are two persons in Jesus — a divine Person and a human person — is the heresy of Nestorianism.

1st September

The Office for Peace and Justice in the Diocese of Lexington requested that all parishes promote so called 'LGBT ministry' through their parish newsletters. The Diocese of Lexington is headed by pro-homosexual Bishop Bishop John Stowe OFM. Pro-homosexual Fr. James Martin SJ — shown many signs of favour by Pope Francis — applauded the move on twitter.[1664]

3rd September

Newsweek, the US weekly news magazine, published a report about the pro-homosexual priest Fr. James Martin SJ telling other priests to stop saying voting for pro-abortion, self-described Catholic, Democrat Presidential candidate Joe Biden was a 'mortal sin'. *Newsweek* reported:

> Posting to social media, Martin said he has overheard an increasing number of priests and U.S. Catholic leaders making the claim that a vote for Biden — who is Catholic — amounts to one of the most grave offences against God. Father Martin told Newsweek Thursday that he and fellow Catholics feel compelled to help on 'any issues where life is endangered,' which he said should include caring for the poor, the homeless and LGBTQ community — not just abortion. Dear friends: I'm seeing more priests saying that voting for Joe Biden is a mortal sin. It is not.[1665]

10th September

Pro-homosexual Bishop John Stowe OFM of Lexington, Kentucky — appointed by Pope Francis — participated in a webinar hosted by Catholic Climate Covenant. Bishop Stowe expressed criticism of the US Bishops' Conference's 2020 US election document 'Forming Consciences for Faithful Citizenship' for identifying abortion as the 'preeminent priority' for voters to be concerned about. He referenced Pope Francis' approach as justifying his 'demotion' of abortion as an electoral priority. Bishop Stowe said:

> I voted against the inclusion of that language. I do understand the logic of it being preeminent, because without the right to life the other human rights don't come

[1663]Bürger, M [2020] *German archbishop: John Paul II's teaching can't 'stifle' debate on female priests* [Online] Available at: www.lifesitenews.com [Accessed on: 21 October 2022]

[1664]Mainwaring, D [2020] *Diocese asks parishes to promote Catholic LGBT Ministry in parish bulletins* [Online] Available at: www.lifesitenews.com [Accessed on: 21 October 2022]

[1665]Fearnow, B [2020] *Vatican Consultant Urges U.S. Priests To Refrain from Telling People Voting for Joe Biden Is a 'Mortal Sin'* [Online] Available at: www.newsweek.com [Accessed on: 21 October 2022]

into existence. So I do understand it on one level, but unfortunately it gives people the permission to think it's the only one that matters, and I don't think that was the intention of the document. It goes against other parts of the document that tell us not to be single issue voters, so if we do take that web of life kind of spirituality, we see the interconnectedness of all these issues. Pope Francis has done a great job of leading us towards that. I think the unnecessary inclusion of that word took a step backward.[1666]

17th September

Pope Francis met with members of the pro-homosexual group *Tenda di Gionata* [Jonathan's Tent] (There reference to the Biblical figure of Jonathan is a common eisegesis among homosexual groups who scandalously misrepresent the friendship between David and Jonathan in terms of a homosexual sin). Mara Grassi, the vice president of the association, reported that the pontiff said, regarding their children who identify as homosexual: 'God loves your children as they are.'[1667]

18th September

The German bishops' conference official news website, *katholisch.de*, published an interview with pro-homosexual Cardinal Hollerich of Luxembourg, elevated to the Sacred College of Cardinals by Pope Francis in 2019. Cardinal Hollerich expressed his support for the faux-ordination of women:

> I am not saying that they have to become priestesses; I simply do not know. But I am open to it. But it is clear that the current situation is not enough. You have to see and realise that women have a say in the church. What I like about the Synodal Path is that it is a way of which one does not always know how it will continue. One takes steps and looks together for the next.[1668]

4th October

Pope Francis promulgated his encyclical *Fratelli Tutti: On Fraternity and Social Friendship*. Pope Francis misrepresented St. Francis of Assisi's approach to the evangelisation of 'Saracens and other nonbelievers' through a partial quotation of the Early Rule that omitted the importance St. Francis gave to proclaiming to Muslims the doctrine of the Most Holy Trinity, Jesus as the Redeemer and Saviour, and to the necessity of Baptism.[1669] The pontiff wrote:

> Unconcerned for the hardships and dangers involved, Francis went to meet the Sultan with the same attitude that he instilled in his disciples: if they found themselves 'among the Saracens and other nonbelievers', without renouncing their own identity they were not to 'engage in arguments or disputes, but to be subject to every human creature for God's sake'. (*Early Rule*, Chap. 16, 6). In the context of the times, this was an extraordinary recommendation. We are impressed that some eight hundred years ago Saint Francis urged that all forms of hostility or conflict be avoided and that a humble and fraternal 'subjection' be shown to those who did not share his faith. Francis did not wage a war of words aimed at imposing doctrines; he simply spread the love of God. In this way, he became a father to all and inspired the vision of a fraternal society. Indeed, 'only the man who approaches others, not to draw them into his own life, but to help them become ever more fully themselves, can truly be called a father.' (*FT* 3).

Pope Francis also continued to appear to promote religious indifferentism:

[1666]Bürger, M [2020] *US bishop says environment should be 'preeminent issue' for voters, not abortion* [Online] Available at: www.lifesitenews.com [Accessed on: 21 October 2022]
[1667]O'Connell, G [2020] *Pope Francis to parents of L.G.B.T. children: 'God loves your children as they are.'* [Online] Available at: www.americamagazine.org [Accessed on: 21 October 2022]
[1668]Smits, J [2020] *Cardinal: 'I am open' to female 'priests'* [Online] Available at: www.lifesitenews.com [Accessed on: 21 October 2022]
[1669]Gomes, J [2020] *'Fratelli Tutti' Falsifies St. Francis' Mission* [Online] Available at: www.churchmilitant.com [Accessed on: 21 October 2022]

From our faith experience and from the wisdom accumulated over centuries, but also from lessons learned from our many weaknesses and failures, we, the believers of the different religions, know that our witness to God benefits our societies. The effort to seek God with a sincere heart, provided it is never sullied by ideological or self-serving aims, helps us recognize one another as travelling companions, truly brothers and sisters. (*FT* 274).[1670]

Pope Francis' encyclical was criticised for omitting any reference to abortion in his list of evils that comprise the phenomenon of social and economic exclusion. The pontiff wrote:

The biggest concern should not be about a drop in the polls, but about finding effective solutions to the phenomenon of social and economic exclusion, with its baneful consequences: human trafficking, the marketing of human organs and tissues, the sexual exploitation of boys and girls, slave labour, including prostitution, the drug and weapons trade, terrorism and international organised crime. Such is the magnitude of these situations, and their toll in innocent lives, that we must avoid every temptation to fall into a declarationist nominalism that would assuage our consciences. (*FT* 188).

Archbishop Carlo Maria Viganò, former papal nuncio to the USA, commented:

This encyclical is the ideological manifesto of Bergoglio, his profession of masonic faith, and his candidacy for the presidency of the Universal Religion, handmaid of the New World Order. So much … subordination to mainstream thought may bring him the applause of the enemies of God, but it confirms the inexorable abandonment of the evangelising mission of the Church.[1671]

6th October

Pope Francis appointed Cardinal Kevin Farrell head of the Commission for Reserved Matters, (charged with overseeing the Vatican's financial transactions). Cardinal Kevin Farrell was a prominent associate of the sex predator Fr. Marcial Maciel, (founder of the Legion of Christ), and a prominent associate and flatmate of sex predator Cardinal Theodore McCarrick. A recipient of many favours, Pope Francis had already appointed Cardinal Farrell the Camerlengo of the Holy Roman Church and the Prefect of the super dicastery for Laity, Family and Life.[1672]

15th October

Pope Francis released a video calling for a Global Compact on Education. It was notable more for its omissions than its content. The pontiff made no reference to our Lord Jesus Christ, and in his list of injustices facing children Pope Francis did not mention abortion or gender ideology. He made man and the world the centre of his vision for education, from which God and His revelation was absent:

To make human persons in their value and dignity the centre of every educational programme, both formal and informal, in order to foster their distinctiveness, beauty and uniqueness, and their capacity for relationship with others and with the world around them, while at the same time teaching them to reject lifestyles that encourage the spread of the throwaway culture.[1673]

[1670]Pope Francis [2020] *Encyclical Fratelli Tutti* [Online] Available at: www.vatican.va [Accessed on: 21 October 2022]

[1671]Cummings McLean, D [2020] *Faithful Catholics as well as dissidents react to Pope Francis' new 'brotherhood' encyclical 'Fratelli tutti'* [Online] Available at: www.lifesitenews.com [Accessed on: 21 October 2022]

[1672]Mainwaring, D [2020] *Pope Francis appoints cardinal with McCarrick, Fr. Martin connections to monitor Vatican finances* [Online] Available at: www.lifesitenews.com [Accessed on: 21 October 2022]

[1673]Cummings McLean, D [2020] *Pope Francis calls for a global education pact with humanity at its center* [Online] Available at: www.lifesitenews.com [Accessed on: 21 October 2022]

16th October

The Vatican City State Mint issued a 10 euro silver coin depicting an Amazonian indigenous woman carrying the world in her womb. Coinciding with the anniversary of the veneration of the Pachamama pagan idol in the Vatican, the German bishop's conference website *katholisch.de* highlighted the coins connection with the notorious event:

> The coin recalls the Pachamama statues set up at the Amazon synod in the previous year, which according to the prefect of the Vatican communication dicastery, Paolo Ruffini, 'stand for life, fertility and mother earth' and should bring the culture of the Amazon region also objectively to the synod.[1674]

21st October

Openly homosexual filmmaker Evgeny Afineevsky's documentary film about Pope Francis, *Francesco*, was premiered in Rome. During the film the pontiff called for the legalisation of civil unions for homosexuals, contradicting the doctrine of the Church:

> Homosexuals have a right to be a part of the family. They're children of God and have a right to a family. Nobody should be thrown out, or be made miserable because of it. What we have to create is a civil union law. That way they are legally covered. I stood up for that.[1675]

The controversy that followed Pope Francis' endorsement of civil unions for homosexual persons resulted in the Vatican press office ordering its journalists not to comment. Massimiliano Menichetti, the head of Radio Vaticana – *Vatican News* sent an email to staff stating:

> Good day everyone, in reference to the uproar stirred up by the film *Francesco* by the Russian director Evgeny Afineevsky, for now we are not coming out with ANY news, either on the radio or on the web. Nothing also about the film or the award given today in the Vatican. There is an active discussion about how to address the current media crisis. A statement from the Press Office is not excluded.[1676]

Active homosexual Evgeny Afineevsky was presented with the Italian government's Kinéo Award for his film about Pope Francis in the Vatican Gardens, in the presence of curial officials.[1677]

The film *Francesco* also featured the 'union' of two homosexual men, Andrea Rubera and Dario De Gregorio, who were favoured by a phone call from Pope Francis in April 2015. The active homosexuals are credited with convincing the pope that 'homosexuals have the right to have a family'. To this end, they 'rented the womb' of a lesbian surrogate in Canada in order to father children, contravening Italian law which bans surrogacy.[1678]

22nd October

Despite evidence of the intensified persecution in China of Catholics, and other Christians, following its secret deal with the Chinese communist government, the Vatican celebrated the extension of the deal for another two years. In a communique the Vatican announced:

[1674]Gomes, J [2020] *Vatican Mints Mother Earth Coin* [Online] Available at: www.churchmilitant.com; Bürger, M [2020] *Vatican issues coin of mother carrying 'earth in her womb' one year after Pachamama scandal* [Online] Available at: www.lifesitenews.com [Accessed on: 21 October 2022]

[1675]*Pope Francis calls for civil union law for same-sex couples, in shift from Vatican stance* [2020] [Online] Available at: www.catholicnewsagency.com [Accessed on: 21 October 2022]

[1676]Haynes, M [2020] *Vatican press office orders silence about Pope's same-sex union comments* [Online] Available at: www.lifesitenews.com [Accessed on: 21 October 2022]

[1677]Bürger, M [2020] *Vatican hosts award ceremony for gay director of film in which Pope endorsed gay civil unions* [Online] Available at: www.lifesitenews.com [Accessed on: 21 October 2022]

[1678]Gomes, J [2020] *Pope Backs 'Married' Gays Who Rented Uterus* [Online] Available at: www.churchmilitant.com [Accessed on: 21 October 2022]

The Holy See considers the initial application of the Agreement – which is of great ecclesial and pastoral value – to have been positive, thanks to good communication and cooperation between the Parties on the matters agreed upon, and intends to pursue an open and constructive dialogue for the benefit of the life of the Catholic Church and the good of Chinese people.[1679]

26th October

Pope Francis appointed thirteen new cardinals, some of whom were pro-homosexual, pro-adultery, including:

- Archbishop Wilton D. Gregory of Washington, D.C.;
- the Maltese Bishop Mario Grech of the Vatican-based Secretary of the Synod of Bishops;
- Italian Archbishop Marcello Semeraro, prefect of the Vatican's Congregation for the Causes of Saints, and,
- Archbishop Celestino Aós Braco of Santiago, Chile.[1680]

2nd November

Archbishop Carlo Maria Viganò published a statement revealing details about the homosexual coterie with whom Pope Francis surrounds himself:

Bergoglio's recent utterances about homosexual civil unions; the impressive number of homosexual prelates with whom he has surrounded himself even in his residence at Santa Marta, beginning with his personal secretary Msgr. Fabian Pedacchio, who was suddenly removed and vanished into thin air; and the scandals that emerge daily about the homosexual lobby in the Vatican: all of these elements suggest that the Argentine wants to legitimise LGBTQ ideology not only in order to support the globalist agenda and demolish the immutable principles of Catholic morality, but also in order to decriminalise the crimes and abuses of his collaborators, protecting the magic circle that involves Maradiaga, Pineda, Peña Parra, Zanchetta, and the entire Vatican lavender mafia.

I wonder if Bergoglio himself, who was unknown to many people until March 13, 2013, is not being blackmailed by those who benefit with such impunity from his clemency. This would explain the motive that leads the one who sits on the Throne to rage with so much ruthlessness against the Church of Christ, while showing the greatest respect for people who are notoriously corrupt, perverted, and almost always implicated in sexual and financial scandals. The alternative – the plausibility of which is supported by disturbing elements that continue to be gathered with each passing day – is that Bergoglio's choice to surround himself with people given over to vice, who are therefore blackmailable, is a deliberate one, and that the ultimate goal that he pursues consists in the demolition of the Catholic Church, replacing it with a sort of philanthropic and ecumenical NGO that is subservient to the globalist élite. Faced with this betrayal by the one who holds the Papacy, any effort at transparency and clarity, if it is to be effective, cannot exclude the one who for over seven years has proclaimed by his words that he wants to clean up the Vatican and the Church.[1681]

10th November

The Secretariat of State of the Holy See published its investigation into the homosexual predator Cardinal McCarrick, 'Report on the Holy See's Institutional Knowledge and

---

[1679]*Communiqué on the extension of the Provisional Agreement between the Holy See and the People's Republic of China regarding the appointment of Bishops, 22 October 2020* [Online] Available at: press. vatican.va [Accessed on: 21 October 2022]

[1680]Mangiaracina, E [2020] *Pope Francis appoints 13 new cardinals, some of whom are pro-LGBT, back communion for adulterers* [Online] Available at: www.lifesitenews.com [Accessed on: 21 October 2022]

[1681]Viganò, C [2020] *Viganò reveals details – including names – about homosexual lobby in the Vatican* [Online] Available at: www.lifesitenews.com [Accessed on: 21 October 2022]

Decision-Making Related to Former Cardinal Theodore Edgar McCarrick (1930 To 2017).' Despite equivocation and ambiguity, the report makes clear that Pope Francis knew about 'rumours' of Cardinal McCarrick's sex abuse and did nothing about it. The report does not refer to the fact that the pontiff used McCarrick as his personal representative both in the United States and abroad in China, Armenia, Iran and Cuba. The report also indicates that Cardinal Parolin, Pope Francis' secretary of state, didn't treat Cardinal McCarrick's history of homosexual activity with seminarians and priests as a serious matter:

> After the letter from McCarrick, Cardinal Parolin stated that he mentioned in a brief conversation with Pope Francis that McCarrick was 'gossiped about' regarding past imprudent acts with adults and that the Congregation for Bishops had previously indicated to McCarrick that he should lead a more reserved life and not travel so much. Cardinal Parolin recalled that he 'did not present it as a matter of grave concern, or as something very serious,' but that he asked if anything should be done, noting, 'He keeps writing. He continues to travel. He continues to meet people.' Cardinal Parolin recollected that, during this exchange, Pope Francis commented that 'maybe McCarrick could still do something useful.[1682]

Pope Francis denied Archbishop Viganò's claim to have told him about Cardinal McCarrick's homosexual abuse of seminarians:

> Pope Francis did not recollect what Viganò said about McCarrick during these two meetings. However, because McCarrick was a cardinal known personally to him, Pope Francis was certain that he would have remembered had Viganò spoken about McCarrick with any 'force or clarity'.[1683]

The report failed to mention the name of McCarrick's primary victim James Grein, who alleged that Theodore McCarrick abused him for two decades.[1684]

In response to Pope Francis' denial Archbishop Viganò responded:

> This statement is absolutely false. First of all, it was Bergoglio himself, on June 23, 2013, who explicitly asked me my opinion of McCarrick. As I testified in my 2018 Memoir: 'I answered him with complete frankness […]: "Holy Father, I don't know if you know Cardinal McCarrick, but if you ask the Congregation for Bishops there is a dossier this thick about him. He corrupted generations of seminarians and priests and Pope Benedict ordered him to withdraw to a life of prayer and penance." The Pope did not make the slightest comment about those very grave words of mine and did not show any expression of surprise on his face, as if he had already known the matter for some time, and he immediately changed the subject. But then, what was the Pope's purpose in asking me that question: "What is Cardinal McCarrick like?" He clearly wanted to find out if I was an ally of McCarrick or not.'
>
> It should be noted that I had learned from McCarrick himself that Bergoglio had received him four days before my audience, and that Bergoglio had authorized him to go to China. What was the point of asking me for an opinion, when Bergoglio already held McCarrick in the highest esteem?[1685]

The Italian journalist Marco Tosatti observed that the Vatican report's account of Pope Francis' knowledge of the allegations against Cardinal McCarrick contradicted the pontiff's categorical denial of any knowledge in his 28 May 2019 interview with Valentina Alazraki published on the *Vatican News* website. Pope Francis stated:

[1682]Secretariat of State of the Holy See [2020] *Report on the Holy See's Institutional Knowledge and Decision-Making Related to Former Cardinal Theodore Edgar McCarrick (1930 to 2017)* [Online] Available at: www.vatican.va [Accessed on: 21 October 2022]

[1683]Hickson, M [2020] *McCarrick report confirms Pope Francis knew about rumors of ex-Cardinal's sex abuse and did nothing* [Online] Available at: www.lifesitenews.com [Accessed on: 21 October 2022]

[1684]Gomes, J [2020] *McCarrick Report: Pope Hero, Viganò Villain* [Online] Available at: www. churchmilitant.com [Accessed on: 21 October 2022]

[1685]*Viganò's full interview with EWTN's Raymond Arroyo on what Vatican got wrong in McCarrick Report* [Online] Available at: www.lifesitenews.com [Accessed on: 21 October 2022]

I knew nothing, obviously, of McCarrick. Nothing, nothing. I said several times that I didn't know, that I had no idea. You know that I didn't know anything about McCarrick; otherwise, I would not have stayed quiet.[1686]

The UK Independent Inquiry into Child Sexual Abuse published its report on the Catholic Church's response to child sex abuse in England and Wales. The report singled out pro-homosexual Cardinal Vincent Nichols — elevated to the Sacred College of Cardinals by Pope Francis in 2014 — for criticism. The report concluded that Cardinal Nichols did not 'demonstrate compassion towards victims in the recent cases which we examined.' Regarding his response to the leak to the media of allegations made by a woman against Cardinal Murphy O'Connor, (a friend of Pope Francis), the report concluded:

[Cardinal Nichols] was particularly concerned about the impact the leak would have on the reputation of Cardinal Murphy-O'Connor, rather than the impact the disclosure of RC- A710's personal information had on her. In the 13 months between the leak and the final public hearing, RC-A710 had not received an apology from Cardinal Nichols. It appears that he did not do so as a result of his misplaced desire to give priority to the protection of the reputation of the Church, the Pope and Cardinal Murphy-O'Connor.

The report also highlighted the lack of co-operation from the Holy See in its investigation:

The Holy See's stance was contrary to the spirit of its public statements…The Holy See's limited response on this matter manifestly did not demonstrate a commitment to taking action. Their lack of cooperation passes understanding.[1687]

13th November

The Congregation for Divine Worship and the Discipline of the Sacraments ruled that bishops had the right to ban the faithful receiving Holy Communion on the tongue during 'times of difficulty'. The ruling was in response to the faithful petitioning to overturn Bishop Richard Stika of Knoxville's decision to ban Holy Communion on the tongue during the COVID-19 pandemic. The ruling stated

As has already been enunciated in the circular letter of Card. Robert Sarah of August 15, 2020, and approved for publication by His Holiness Pope Francis, 'in times of difficulty (e.g., wars, pandemics), Bishops and Episcopal Conferences can give provisional norms which must be obeyed', even clearly, as in this case, to suspend for whatever time might be required, reception of Holy Communion on the tongue at the public celebration of the Holy Mass. This Dicastery does hereby therefore act to confirm the decision of Bishop Stika and thereby rejects your petition seeking its modification.

The letter was signed by Arthur Roche, Archbishop Secretary of the Vatican's Congregation for Worship and the Sacraments, but not by Cardinal Robert Sarah, the prefect of the Congregation.[1688]

24th November

Archbishop Wilton D. Gregory of Washington, D.C. — elevated to the Sacred College of Cardinals by Pope Francis— attempted to justify to *Catholic News Service* why he would be giving Holy Communion to radical pro-abortion Joe Biden:

I hope it's a real dialogue, because I think that's the mantra of Pope Francis — that we should be a church in dialogue, even with those with whom we have some serious

---

[1686]Tosatti, M [2020] *Oops. Vatican's McCarrick report catches Pope Francis taking 'tiny liberties with the truth'* [Online] Available at: www.lifesitenews.com [Accessed on: 21 October 2022]
[1687]Haynes, M [2020] *Report shows Cdl. Nichols prioritized reputation of Pope Francis over allegations of child sex abuse* [Online] Available at: www.lifesitenews.com [Accessed on: 21 October 2022]
[1688]Baklinski, P [2020] *Cdl. Sarah's signature absent from Vatican letter backing ban of Communion on tongue during COVID* [Online] Available at: www.lifesitenews.com [Accessed on: 21 October 2022]

disagreements… On my part, it's a matter of the responsibility that I have as the archbishop to be engaged and to be in dialogue with him, even in those areas where we obviously have some differences. The capacity to have civil disagreements — serious disagreements, you know, really pointed disagreements — but done in such a way that the focus is on the argument, not on the demonization of the people with whom we disagree.[1689]

11th December

Reuters published a report on Cardinal Carlos Aguiar Retes of Mexico's support for 'civil unions' for homosexuals. Cardinal Retes expressed agreement with Pope Francis' endorsement of the legalisation of homosexual 'unions':

I completely agree. All of us are children of God, all are members of the family, and if we're fighting so that families are united, regardless of their conduct, they don't stop being our children. And that's what Pope Francis said, everyone has the right to family.

Cardinal Retes also criticised parents for rejecting children who entered into homosexual bondings:

Because if, as it happens unfortunately, a son in a family declares himself openly homosexual, then they don't want to have anything to do with him. And that can't be, it just can't be. If they decide as a matter of free choice to be with another person, to be in a union, that's freedom.[1690]

16th December

Pope Francis launched a new partnership between the Vatican and pro-abortion, pro-homosexual United Nations (UN) during the Vatican's Youth Symposium, co-hosted by the Pontifical Academy of Social Sciences led by Archbishop Marcelo Sánchez Sorondo. The joint initiative, Mission 4.7, is headed by pro-abortion Audrey Azoulay and Ban Ki-moon. Ignoring their promotion of abortion, the pontiff told participants:

The Global Compact on Education and Mission 4.7 will work together for the civilisation of love, beauty and unity. Allow me to tell you that you are the poets of a new human beauty, a new fraternal and friendly beauty, as well as of the preservation of the earth we tread.[1691]

21st December

During his Christmas address to the curia Pope Francis claimed the authority of the Holy Spirit, to justify his introduction of 'newness' into the Church:

The newness born of crisis and willed by the Spirit is never a newness opposed to the old, but one that springs from the old and makes it continually fruitful. Jesus explains this process in a simple and clear image: 'Unless a grain of wheat falls into the earth and dies, it remains just a single grain; but if it dies, it bears much fruit' (Jn 12:24). The dying of a seed is ambivalent: it is both an end and the beginning of something new. It can be called both 'death and decay' and 'birth and blossoming', for the two are one. We see an end, while at the same time, in that end a new beginning is taking shape…Everything evil, wrong, weak and unhealthy that comes to light serves as a forceful reminder of our need to die to a way of living, thinking and acting that does not reflect the Gospel. Only by dying to a certain mentality will we be able to make room for the newness that the Spirit constantly awakens in the heart of the Church.

[1689]Haynes, M [2020] *BREAKING: DC archbishop affirms he will give Holy Communion to pro-abortion Joe Biden* [Online] Available at: www.lifesitenews.com [Accessed on: 21 October 2022]

[1690]Alire Garcia, D [2020] *Mexico's senior Catholic leader backs civil unions for gay couples* [Online] Available at: www.reuters.com [Accessed on: 21 October 2022]

[1691]Haynes, M [2020] *Pope Francis teams up with UN to educate world on sustainable lifestyles, gender equality, global citizenship* [Online] Available at: www.lifesitenews.com [Accessed on: 21 October 2022]

The pontiff criticised those who opposed his agenda as being like King Herod:

> Each of us, whatever our place in the Church, should ask whether we want to follow Jesus with the docility of the shepherds or with the defensiveness of Herod, to follow him amid crisis or to keep him at bay in conflict.[1692]

27th December

During his angelus address Pope Francis announced that a year of reflection on his pro-adultery, pro-fornication exhortation *Amoris Laetitia* would begin on March 19, 2021 – the Feast of St. Joseph and conclude during June 2022.[1693]

30th December

The German magazine *Herder Korrespondenz* published an interview with pro-homosexual Bishop Georg Bätzing of Limburg and president of the German Bishops' conference. Bishop Bätzing was appointed by Pope Francis in 2016. Bishop Bätzing rejected the Church's Magisterium in various areas. As well as wanting to change Church doctrine on sodomy, he wanted the Church to bless homosexual and adulterous 'unions': 'We need solutions that are not only effective in private, but also have public visibility — yet make it clear that no marriage is being solemnised.' Bishop Bätzing also expressed support for the faux-ordination of women to the diaconate, presbyterate and episcopate:

> [It was important to him to] honestly state the church's arguments as to why the sacramental ministry can only be given to men. But I must honestly say that I am also aware that these arguments are becoming less and less convincing and that there are well-developed arguments in theology in favour of opening up the sacramental ministry to women as well.

He also supported Protestants receiving Holy Communion in the Catholic Church, ignoring the fact of their schismatic status.[1694]

Edward Pentin, Vatican correspondent for the *National Catholic Register*, reported that in January 2021 Pope Francis overruled two senior cardinals who wanted to summon Bishop Georg Bätzing to Rome to be corrected over his public dissent from the Magisterium in his interview with *Herder Korrespondenz*. Sources told Edward Pentin that Cardinal Luis Ladaria, prefect of the Congregation for the Doctrine of the Faith, and Cardinal Kurt Koch, the Swiss president of the Pontifical Council for Promoting Christian Unity wanted to ask Bishop Bätzing to come to Rome to correct him. 'Santa Marta said "No",' one of the sources told Pentin referring to the Pope's official residence.[1695]

2021

2nd January

The *Irish Times* published an interview with pro-homosexual archbishop-elect Dermot Farrell of Dublin, (appointed by Pope Francis), in which he expressed support for the faux-ordination of women and the blessing of homosexual bondings. Regarding 'ordaining' women archbishop-elect Farrell said:

> I think that the big issue for women priests for me is that the two pillars of our faith and the Church are scripture and tradition and the biggest barrier to that (women priests) is

---

[1692]Pope Francis [2020] *Address to the Roman* Curia [Online] Available at: www.vatican.va [Accessed on: 21 October 2022]

[1693]*Pope Francis to mark fifth anniversary of 'Amoris Laetitia' with year dedicated to family* [2020] [Online] Available at: www.catholicnewsagency.com [Accessed on 21 October 2022]

[1694]*Head of German bishops, self-described conservative, calls for change* [2020] [Online] Available at: cruxnow.com [Accessed on: 21 October 2022]

[1695]Pentin, E [2020] Pentin, E [2020] *Vatican Now in Crisis Management Mode with German Bishops* [Online] Available at: www.ncregister.com [Accessed on: 21 October 2022]

probably tradition, not the scriptures. That's the hurdle that has to be overcome. Would I like to see women deacons[?] I would.

About blessing homosexual bondings he said:

The difficulty with blessings is that they are very often misconstrued as marriage. Priests have given these blessings in the past. I remember one colleague of mine. I had said to him – he used to have this ceremony of the blessing of rings – I said to him I don't have a difficulty with blessing rings if you're doing that here in the house but if you go out into the public domain, in a church, and bless rings as you see it …they turned up with 200 people and they saw it as a marriage. Sometimes people use that phraseology … you're into confusion there. It can be misconstrued as 'yes, the priest married us'.

He also criticised the faithful he characterised as 'traditional Catholics':

They're hostile towards anyone that doesn't agree with them, they're almost close to being intolerant. They're everywhere. I'd be respectful of them, they have a view and probably want to impose that view on everyone. That's disrespectful. They have to respect the views of other people in the Catholic faith who for various reasons may not have the same commitment they have. That doesn't mean they're any less sincere. Why should that (irregular) person be ostracised?[1696]

5th January

The Worldwide Prayer Network (PWPN) released the latest video of Pope Francis' prayer intentions. The video promoted religious indifferentism showing a woman praying the rosary, a Muslim woman and a Jewish man performing their respective prayers, before moving to an address delivered by Pope Francis. The pontiff said:

When we pray to God following Jesus, we come together as brothers and sisters with those who pray according to other cultures, other traditions and other beliefs. We are brothers and sisters who pray. Fraternity leads us to open ourselves to the Father of all and to see in the other a brother or sister, to share our lives or to support, to love, and to know each other. The Church values God's action in other religions, without forgetting that for us Christians, the wellspring of human dignity and fraternity, is in the Gospel of Jesus Christ. We believers must return to our sources and concentrate on what is essential. What is essential to our faith is the adoration of God and love of neighbour.[1697]

The Vatican promulgated Pope Francis' Motu Proprio *Spiritus Domini* that changed canon law to permit women to be formally instituted into the ministries reserved solely to men by apostolic tradition, those of lector and acolyte. The pontiff ignored the close association of lector and acolyte with the episcopate, presbyterate and diaconate, reflected in the fact that their reception remains a necessary requirement for candidates to Holy Orders.[1698]

Dr. Peter Kwasniewski commented:

Pope Francis's decision, with his Motu Proprio *Spiritus Domini*, to modify canon law so that the 'ministries' of lector and acolyte are now open to women fits snugly into this larger pattern of rupture from Catholic tradition. While previously women were allowed to read the readings and assist at the altar, canon law permitted only men (*viri*) to be 'installed,' in a permanent and stable way, as lectors and acolytes. It is, one might say, another nail in the coffin of the *Novus Ordo*, detaching it still further from the

[1696]*Archdiocese of Dublin may need major organizational changes says Archbishop-elect in Irish Times interview* [2021] Available at: www.catholicnewsagency.com [Accessed on: 22 October 2022]
[1697]Gomes J [2021] *Pope's Epiphany Video Cancels Evangelism* [Online] Available at: www.churchmilitant.com; Haynes, M [2020] *Pope Francis's latest video promotes religious indifferentism 'at the service of human fraternity'* [Online] Available at: www.lifesitenews.com [Accessed on: 22 October 2022]
[1698]McLoone, D [2021] *Pope Francis opens up formerly male liturgical roles to women* [Online] Available at: www.lifesitenews.com [Accessed on: 22 October 2022]

patrimony of Latin-rite worship. [...] while Pope Francis's Motu Proprio may look like a technicality — and surely would have no effect on all those places in the world where the sanctuary is already overrun with females — it represents, in fact, a tectonic shift both in theology and in praxis. For the first time ever, Francis is saying that the Catholic Church should officially institute women as liturgical ministers, i.e., not as substitutes for ministers, but as ministers simply speaking.[1699]

13th January

The radical heterodox US newspaper the *National Catholic Reporter* published an interview with the openly homosexual Andrea Rubera in which he discussed Pope Francis' phone call to him in April 2015. Andrea Rubera and Dario formed a homosexual pairing in which they are raising three children conceived through *in vitro fertilisation* through a surrogate 'mother.' The pontiff phoned Andrea Rubera in response to a letter he had sent outlining his desire to enrol their oldest child in a catechetical program at a Rome-area parish, concerned that their child might be subject to prejudice. According to Andrea Rubera Pope Francis said:

> Mr. Rubera, is that you? I think you should do it. Go to the pastor, ask for a meeting, introduce yourself transparently and I'm quite confident that everything is going to be all right.[1700]

On the publication of his phone call to Andrea Rubera, Pope Francis did not issue a statement upholding the Church's doctrine on the grave sins associated with homosexuality, homosexual 'unions', IVF or surrogacy.

20th January

The Vatican temporarily embargoed the U.S. Bishops' Conference's statement criticising incoming President Joe Biden, who presented himself as a faithful Catholic. The statement by the USCCB's President Archbishop José Gómez criticised Biden's radical abortion agenda:

> I must point out that our new President has pledged to pursue certain policies that would advance moral evils and threaten human life and dignity, most seriously in the areas of abortion, contraception, marriage, and gender. Of deep concern is the liberty of the Church and the freedom of believers to live according to their consciences. For the nation's bishops, the continued injustice of abortion remains the 'preeminent priority'.

Sources close to the bishops' conference revealed that the Vatican spiked the criticism of Biden following objections made to them by Cardinal Joseph Tobin of Newark, New Jersey and Cardinal Blase Cupich of Chicago, both recipients of Pope Francis' patronage.[1701] The statement was later released the same day. Cardinal Cupich publicly rebuked the US bishops' conference for their criticism of pro-abortion Biden:

> Today, the United States Conference of Catholic Bishops issued an ill-considered statement on the day of President Biden's inauguration. Aside from the fact that there is seemingly no precedent for doing so, the statement, critical of President Biden came as a surprise to many bishops, who received it just hours before it was released.[1702]

[1699]Kwasniewski, P [2021] *Pope Francis's inclusion of 'female ministries' continues his pattern of rupture* [Online] Available at: www.lifesitenews.com [Accessed on: 22 October 2022] Cf. Kwasniewski, P [2021] *Ministers of Christ: Recovering the Roles of Clergy and Laity in an Age of Confusion.* Manchester, New Hampshire: Crisis Publications

[1700]McElwee, J [2021] *Pope's phone call helps children of Italian gay couple become Catholic* [Online] Available at: www.ncronline.org [Accessed on: 22 October 2022]

[1701]Westen, JH [2021] *Vatican delays US Bishops' criticism of Biden's abortion stance till Pope can praise Biden unconditionally* [Online] Available at: www.lifesitenews.com [Accessed on: 22 October 2022]

[1702]Baklinski, P [2021] *Cardinal Cupich rebukes US bishops' statement condemning Biden's plan to pursue 'evil' abortion, gender policies* [Online] Available at: www.lifesitenews.com [Accessed on: 22 October 2022]

25th January

Fourteen US bishops, including one cardinal and one archbishop, signed a pro-homosexual declaration stating 'God is on your side' issued by a pro-homosexual advocacy group. The declaration partially quoted the *Catechism of the Catholic Church*, omitting the reference to homosexual sex acts being acts of grave depravity and intrinsically disordered. The pro-homosexual bishops included:

- Cardinal Joseph Tobin of Newark, elevated to the Sacred College of Cardinals by Pope Francis in 2016;
- Archbishop John Wester of Santa Fe, appointed by Pope Francis in 2015;
- Bishop Steven Biegler of Cheyenne, appointed by Pope Francis in 2017;
- Bishop John Dolan, auxiliary of San Diego, appointed by Pope Francis in 2017;
- Bishop Joseph Kopacz of Jackson, appointed by Pope Francis in 2013;
- Bishop Robert McElroy of San Diego, appointed by Pope Francis in 2015;
- Bishop Alberto Rojas, Coadjutor bishop of San Bernardino, appointed by Pope Francis in 2019;
- Bishop Oscar Azarcón Solís of Salt Lake City, appointed by Pope Francis in 2017;
- Bishop John Stowe of Lexington, appointed by Pope Francis in 2015;
- Bishop Anthony Taylor of Little Rock;
- Bishop Edward Weisenburger of Tucson, appointed by Pope Francis in 2017;
- Bishop Thomas Gumbleton;
- Bishop Denis Madden, and,
- Bishop Ricardo Ramirez.[1703]

29th January

Pope Francis delivered his annual address to the officials of the Tribunal of the Roman Rota for the inauguration of the judicial year. During his address, the Pontiff presented the dubious argument that the perplexity of children should be a reason why divorced parents should receive Holy Communion:

> However, how can it be explained to children that, for example, their mother, abandoned by their father and often without the intention of establishing another matrimonial bond, may receive the Eucharist with them on Sunday, whereas their father, living with them or awaiting the declaration of nullity of marriage, cannot participate at the Eucharistic table?[1704]

1st February

Georgetown Initiative on Catholic Social Thought facilitated an online forum on 'President Biden, U.S. Bishops and Pope Francis: How to Promote Catholic Principles in a Divided Church and Nation.' During the forum, pro-homosexual Bishop Robert W. McElroy of San Diego — appointed by Pope Francis — argued that pro-abortion, pro-homosexual President Biden must be allowed to receive Holy Communion:

> I do not see how depriving the president or other political leaders of Eucharist based on their public policy stance can be interpreted in our society as anything other than the weaponisation of Eucharist and an effort not to convince people by argument and by dialogue and by reason, but, rather, to pummel them into submission on the issue. It would be very destructive. It would also cast the (U.S. bishops') conference more significantly into the role of being partisan, as being associated with one party rather than the other.[1705]

[1703]*'God is on your side': A statement from Catholic Bishops on Protecting LGBT Youth* [2021] [Online] Available at: tylerclementi.org [Accessed on: 22 October 2022]

[1704]Pope Francis [2021] *Address to the officials of the Roman Rota at Inauguration of the Judicial Year* [Online] Available at: www.vatican.va [Accessed on: 21 October 2022]

[1705]Pattison, M [2021] *Bishop warns against 'weaponization of Eucharist' with elected officials* [Online] Available at: www.ncronline.org [Accessed on: 22 October 2022]

2nd February

During a meeting with journalists from the press agency of the US Bishops' Conference Pope Francis again talked about coprophilia, a sexual perversion associated with homosexuality. The pontiff condemned 'coprophilia' in the media, which he described as their 'love of filth'. Pope Francis also heavily condemned those Catholics he characterised as 'fundamentalists':

> All religions have fundamentalist groups. All of them. We do too. And they destroy, starting from their fundamentalism. But these are small religious groups that have distorted and have 'sickened' their religion, and as a result they fight, they wage war, or they cause division in communities, which is a form of war. But these are the fundamentalist groups we have in all religions.[1706]

4th February

The Vatican issued a video message from Pope Francis celebrating the first International Day of Human Fraternity, the anniversary of the 'Document on Human Fraternity for World Peace and Living Together,' which was co-signed by Pope Francis and the Grand Imam Ahmad al-Tayyeb on February 4, 2019. The Abu Dhabi declaration was notorious for its promotion of religious indifferentism. Pope Francis' video message made no mention of our Lord Jesus Christ or any Christian references. The pontiff also bestowed an award for peace and fraternity on the pro-abortion and pro-LGBT, United Nations Secretary General Antonio Guterres.[1707] The Gran Logia de España, Spain's main masonic lodge, expressed its profound satisfaction at Pope Francis's involvement in the 'Human Fraternity' initiative.[1708]

10th February

Pope Francis appointed pro-homosexual Sr. Nathalie Becquart as an undersecretary of the General Secretariat of the Synod of Bishops. Her appointment made Sr. Becquart the first woman in the history of the Church to have the right to vote in the Synod of Bishops.[1709] Sr. Becquart delivered the 2022 Father Robert Nugent Memorial Lecture for the heretical New Ways Ministry.[1710] In 1999 the Congregation for the Doctrine of the Faith imposed canonical penalties on Father Robert Nugent for his failure to uphold the Church's doctrine on homosexuality.[1711] The United States Conference of Catholic Bishops issued a warning to the faithful that New Ways Ministry was not to be considered a Catholic organisation for advocating homosexual sex.[1712]

The following year in 2022, *The New York Times* published an interview with Sr. Nathalie Becquart in which she spoke of Pope Francis' agenda to separate leadership in the Church from the sacrament of Holy Orders:

> The vision of Pope Francis, through this synod, is to get rid of a clerical church and move to a synodal church — to disconnect participation in the leadership of the church from

[1706]Ceraso, G [2021] *Pope Francis speaks with Catholic News Service about US Church, journey to Iraq* [Online] Available at: www.vaticannews.va [Accessed on: 22 October 2022]

[1707]Haynes, M [2021] *Pope Francis commemorates Abu Dhabi document, gives peace award to pro-abortion UN chief* [Online] Available at: www.lifesitenews.com [Accessed on: 22 October 2022]

[1708]Smits, J [2021] *Spanish Freemasons praise Pope Francis, laud 'International Fraternity Day'* [Online] Available at: www.lifesitenews.com [Accessed on: 22 October 2022]

[1709]*'A door has opened': Pope Francis appoints first woman to senior synod post* [2021] [Online] Available at: www.theguardian.com [Accessed on: 22 October 2022]

[1710]Gomes, J [2021] *Feminist Vatican Nun Endorses LGBT+ Caucus* [Online] Available at: www.churchmilitant.com [Accessed on: 22 October 2022]

[1711]Congregation for the Doctrine of the Faith [1990] *Notification regarding Sr. Jeannine Gramick, SSND, and Fr Robert Nugent, SDS* [Online] Available at: www.vatican.va [Accessed on: 21 October 2022]

[1712]*USCCB President Clarifies Status of New Ways Ministry* [2010] [Online] Available at: www.usccb.org [Accessed on: 21 October 2022]

ordination. We can say that the way now opening up is to listen to all different views; for instance, not everyone thinks ordination of women is a good path. You have some groups calling for that, but you also have some groups calling for new ministries.[1713]

This signifies a break with the sacramental doctrine of the Church that sees the sacrament of Holy Orders as necessary to participate in the triple *munera* of Christ, including the *munus regendi* – the power to rule the Church originating in Christ's role as King.

13th February

Vatican News — the Catholic news website provided by the Vatican's Dicastery for Communication — published an interview with the pro-abortion Catholic poet Amanda Gorman, following her reading a poem at pro-abortion, pro-homosexual Catholic President Joe Biden's inauguration. In 2019 Gorman delivered a poetic address in which she called on people to 'fight to keep Roe v. Wade alive,' and outlined 'eight reasons to stand up today against abortion bans in the United States.'[1714]

15th February

Pope Francis appointed pro-homosexual Fr. Joseph Maria Bonnemain as the bishop of the traditionalist Diocese of Chur, Switzerland. Bishop-elect Bonnemain had published a document in 2017 enthusiastically endorsing Pope Francis's post-synodal exhortation *Amoris Laetitia* for allowing adulterers to receive Holy Communion.[1715] Later in the year, Bishop Bonnemain frequently expressed support for homosexual civil 'unions' and 'marriages' during Switzerland's referendum on the issue. He participated in a discussion hosted by the Swiss public broadcast channel *SRF* in which he was asked if he would oppose a certain woman (Miss S.) who wished to marry her female partner. He answered:

> I have nothing against it. I am only of the opinion that any form of discrimination should be removed and that, at the same time, there takes place a reasonable differentiation whether different things are being called the same name.

Later he wrote:

> I think it is good and right that, in the realm of the state, different forms of stable relationships are given rights and duties and, at the voting booth, everybody (male and female) should decide freely and based on one's own conviction what is best to protect and promote these partnerships. It is for me self-evident that other forms of partnership can be oriented toward an enduring love, as well. My only concern is – and here I am neither judging nor dismissing: I plead for maintaining this difference when naming [these different 'marriages'].[1716]

During the Mass for his consecration Bishop Joseph Maria Bonnemain gave Holy Communion to three Protestants, Rita Famos, president of the Evangelical Reformed Swiss church, Michel Müller, president of the Zürich church council, and Mario Fehr, socialist councillor of the canton of Zürich.[1717]

[1713]Haynes, M [2021] *Pope Francis is using Synod to separate Church 'leadership' from 'ordination': liberal Vatican nun* [Online] Available at: www.lifesitenews.com [Accessed on: 22 October 2022]

[1714]Haynes, M [2021] *Vatican News praises pro-abortion 'Catholic' woman who recited poem at Biden's inauguration* [Online] Available at: www.lifesitenews.com [Accessed on: 22 October 2022]; Gisotti, A [2021] *Amanda Gorman: poetry is the language of reconciliation* [Online] Available at: www.vaticannews.va [Accessed on: 22 October 2022]

[1715]Hickson, M [2021] *Newly appointed Swiss bishop declines to have his own episcopal coat of arms* [Online] Available at: www.lifesitenews.com [Accessed on: 22 October 2022]

[1716]Hickson, M [2021] *Swiss Opus Dei bishop: 'I have nothing against' one woman 'marrying' another* [Online] Available at: www.lifesitenews.com [Accessed on: 22 October 2022]

[1717]Smits, J [2021] *New Swiss bishop gives Holy Communion to non-Catholics* [Online] Available at: www.lifesitenews.com [Accessed on: 22 October 2022]

18th February

The Pontificia Academia Mariana Internationalis and the Franciscan pontifical University of Rome, the 'Antonianum,' organised a ten weekly series of online webinars, *Mary, a model for faith and life for Christianity and Islam*. The Italian weekly *Famiglia Christiana* published an article by Gian Matteo Roggio explaining that Pope Francis' Abu Dhabi Declaration was the inspiration of the webinars:

> Belonging to these three religious and multi-cultural worlds (Judaism, Christianity, Islam), the figure of Mary is in itself a pressing and constant invitation to intersect and interconnect these same worlds, even making them a model of plural coexistence where the boundaries of each are made to allow communication, passage, exchange; and not to be closed, according to the many figures of exclusion that have, as their fruit, the culture, psychology, politics and economics of war, hatred and inhumanity.[1718]

22nd February

Pro-homosexual Msgr. Philippe Bordeyne was appointed as the new president of the Pontifical John Paul II Theological Institute for Matrimonial and Family Science. Msgr. Philippe Bordeyne also supports the use of artificial contraception:

> The encyclical *Humanae Vitae* teaches that only natural methods of fertility control are licit. However, it must be recognized that the distance between the practice of the faithful and the magisterial teaching has increased. Is this plain deafness to the calls of the Spirit or the fruit of a work of discernment and responsibility among Christian couples subjected to the pressure of new lifestyles? [...] The other way, whose moral licitness could be admitted, and the choice entrusted to the wisdom of the spouses, would consist in using non-abortive contraceptive methods. If they decide to introduce this medicine into the intimacy of their sexual life, the spouses would be invited to redouble their mutual love. This is the only way to humanise the use of technology, in the service of a 'human ecology of reproduction.'[1719]

Transversalités, the magazine of the Institut Catholique of Paris, published a short essay by Msgr. Philippe Bordeyne under the title, 'The Catholic Church in the work of discernment in the face of homosexual unions'. In this essay Msgr. Philippe Bordeyne sets out guidance about how to bless homosexual bondings. Msgr. Bordeyne wrote:

> In the event that a blessing prayer should be foreseen, it would be better to limit oneself to a blessing of the persons, discarding formulations that would evoke their union too directly, in order to avoid confusion with the ritual blessing of a man and a woman united in marriage. [...] The ecclesial sign of the blessing, performed by a minister of the Church, would therefore be granted to two persons who, each having formed a judgment of conscience taking into account their own limitations, seek the Church's help to grow in openness to grace. In concrete terms, it would be desirable that the minister subsequently proceed with two personal prayers of blessing.

Msgr. Bordeyne also proposed liturgical formulas to be used in blessing homosexual pairings.[1720]

4th March

Pope Francis appointed pro-homosexual Cardinal Joseph Tobin, C.SS.R, of Newark, USA, to the Congregation for Bishops, tasked with the responsibility of advising the

---

[1718]Smits, J [2021] *Vatican to organize conference promoting Mary as 'model for faith' for both Christianity and Islam* [Online] Available at: www.lifesitenews.com [Accessed on: 22 October 2022]

[1719]Smits, J [2021] *Next head of Pope's marriage and family institute is pro-contraception* [Online] Available at: www.lifesitenews.com [Accessed on: 22 October 2022]

[1720]Magister, S [2021] *Family Feud. On the Blessing of Homosexual Couples the Vatican Has an Enemy in the House* [Online] Available at: magister.blogautore.espresso.repubblica.it [Accessed on: 22 October 2022]

pontiff about potential episcopal candidates for dioceses across the world. Dr. Peter Kwasniewski observed:

> This new assignment of a cardinal whom Archbishop Vigano has repeatedly demonstrated to be part of the McCarrick cabal indicates that the 'bishop factory' will continue to produce predominantly Bergoglian 'magic circle' candidates, doctrinally progressive, morally compromised, who will promote the 'new paradigm' that dissolves the Catholic religion.[1721]

The Vicar of Opus Dei in Côte d'Ivoire sent a letter to Abbé Janvier Gbénou informing him that due to his public criticism of Pope Francis' advocacy of the legalisation of homosexual pairings he was banned from celebrating public Masses, hearing confessions, preaching, and was also told to leave the Opus Dei residence. Fr. Janvier Gbénou explained the reason for his criticism of the pontiff:

> It is because there is an apparent victory of homosexuality over the papacy, which is considered the last moral bulwark of humanity. Of the 266 Popes the Catholic Church has had, Pope Francis is the first to have accepted homosexual civil coexistence laws. The problem is that Christians live in civil society and not only in ecclesial society. If homosexuality becomes established in civil law, there will be many negative consequences for the Catholic Church in the short, medium, and long term: the loss of value of the Sacrament of Marriage, the loss of value of the Sacrament of the Eucharist, the difficulty of educating children to true love between man and woman as willed by God the Creator, future priestly and religious vocations, the security of Christians against terrorism, the moral coherence of Christian doctrine, the faith of the Christian faithful, the unity of the Church, etc.[1722]

On the 25th February 2022 Abbé Janvier Gbénou was informed by his superior, Abbé Serge Abdoulaye Sissoko, that his appeal had failed and that he had been expelled from Opus Dei. He was also informed that he could 'make an appeal before the Holy See in accordance with canons 1735 and 1737 of the *Code of Canon Law*.'[1723]

6th March

During his apostolic journey to Iraq, Pope Francis addressed an 'interreligious' service at the ruins of Ur, the birthplace of Abraham. During his address the pontiff made no reference to our Lord Jesus Christ, but instead presented the world's religions as if they were on an equal footing:

> Today we, Jews, Christians and Muslims, together with our brothers and sisters of other religions, honour our father Abraham by doing as he did: we look up to heaven and we journey on earth.[1724]

8th March

During the in-flight press conference returning from his apostolic journey to Iraq, Pope Francis admitted he considered the risk of being accused of heresy was a price he was willing to pay. The pontiff said in defence of his 'human fraternity' project:

> You know that there are some criticisms: that the pope is not courageous, he is a reckless person who is taking steps against Catholic doctrine, that he is one step away

[1721]Cummings McLean, D [2021] *Pope Francis names Cardinal Joseph Tobin to the Congregation for Bishops* [Online] Available at: www.lifesitenews.com [Accessed on: 22 October 2022]

[1722]Hickson, M [2021] *Exclusive interview: Courageous priest sidelined for challenging Pope Francis' support of gay civil unions* [Online] Available at: www.lifesitenews.com [Accessed on: 22 October 2022]

[1723]Hickson, M [2021] *Opus Dei expels African priest for criticizing Pope's endorsement of same-sex civil unions* [Online] Available at: www.lifesitenews.com [Accessed on: 22 October 2022]

[1724]Pope Francis [2021] *Full text: Pope Francis' address at an interreligious meeting in the Plain of Ur* [Online] Available at: www.catholicnewsagency.com; Gomes, J [2021] *No Jews, No Jesus at Pope's 'Abrahamic' Event* [Online] Available at: www.churchmilitant.com [Accessed on: 22 October 2022]

from heresy, there are risks. But these decisions are always made in prayer, in dialogue, in asking for advice, in reflection. They are not a whim and also are the line that the Council taught.[1725]

12th March

The Vatican's Secretariat of State circulated a note announcing restrictions to all 'individual' Masses in Saint Peter's Basilica, including stringent restrictions for the traditional Latin Mass. The note stipulated that all priests and faithful will be required to join two 'concelebrated' Masses at fixed times between 7 and 9 a.m. Only authorised priests are able to celebrate the traditional Latin rite, confined to four time slots between 7 and 9 a.m., at only one altar: the Clementine Chapel of the Crypt.[1726]

Cardinal Burke, the former prefect of the Apostolic Signatura, issued a statement protesting the banning of individual Masses at St. Peter as contrary to and in direct violation of universal Church law. Cardinal Burke wrote:

> The document imposes concelebration upon priests who wish to offer the Holy Mass in Saint Peter's Basilica, which is contrary to universal Church law and which unjustly conditions the primary duty of the individual priest to offer the Holy Mass daily for the salvation of the world (can. 902). In what church more than in the Basilica of Saint Peter would a priest desire to offer the Holy Mass, which is the most perfect and fullest way in which he carries out his priestly mission? If an individual priest wishes to offer the Holy Mass in the Basilica, once the directives in question are in force, he will be constrained to concelebrate, in violation of his freedom to offer the Holy Mass individually.[1727]

Cardinal Gerhard Müller, the former prefect of the Congregation for the Doctrine of the Faith, denounced the restrictions, saying:

> Nobody is obliged to obey it. Nobody can be forced to concelebrate, because the normal form of the holy Mass is one priest is celebrating, representing Christ. Perhaps [there is] the possibility of concelebration of the bishop and his priest in the diocese and the cathedral, but the concelebration only of priests together is not a normal form...This letter is very strange, and this argumentation and the terminology — holy Masses are 'suppressed' — doesn't sound very Catholic.[1728]

The German Catholic newspaper *Die Tagespost* published an essay by Cardinal Walter Brandmüller, the retired president of the Papal Committee for Historical Sciences, criticising the restrictions:

> The suggestion has already been made that this was a *'ballon d'essai'* [trial balloon] intended to explore the reactions to be expected to intended innovations. If this were true, however, the very serious question would have to be asked whether this could be the way in which the power of the keys should be exercised in the Church of Jesus Christ. [...] The basilica above the tomb of Peter, the Prince of the Apostles, and the tombs of many saints, are unique in the world, the centre of the universal Church and, from the earliest times, a pilgrimage destination for the faithful from all over the world. To deprive the many pilgrims, especially the priests, who come to Rome in large numbers from distant parts of the world, of the opportunity to celebrate Holy Mass in the Father's house, as it were, would be absolutely unjustifiable.[1729]

[1725]Pope Francis [2021] *In-flight press conference on return from Iraq* [Online] Available at: www.vaticannews.va [Accessed on: 22 October 2022]

[1726]Gomes, J [2021] *St. Peter's Basilica Bans 'Private' Masses* [Online] Available at: www.churchmilitant.com [Accessed on: 22 October 2022]

[1727]Burke, R [2021] *Statement on the Offering of the Holy Mass in the Papal Basilica of Saint Peter* [Online] Available at: www.cardinalburke.com [Accessed on: 22 October 2022]

[1728]Mangiaracina, E [2021] *'Nobody is obliged to obey' decree suppressing individually said Masses at St. Peter's: Cardinal Müller* [Online] Available at: www.lifesitenews.com [Accessed on: 22 October 2022]

[1729]Hickson, M [2021] *Third cardinal publicly opposes Vatican letter banning private Masses at St. Peter's basilica* [Online] Available at: www.lifesitenews.com [Accessed on: 22 October 2022]

15th March

The Congregation for the Doctrine of the Faith published its responsum to a *dubium* regarding the blessing of the unions of persons of the same sex. To the question, 'does the Church have the power to give the blessing to unions of persons of the same sex?' The CDF answered, 'Negative'. Though recognising the existence of 'positive elements' in homosexual bondings the CDF ruled that the Church did not have the power to bless homosexual 'unions':

> The presence in such relationships of positive elements, which are in themselves to be valued and appreciated, cannot justify these relationships and render them legitimate objects of an ecclesial blessing, since the positive elements exist within the context of a union not ordered to the Creator's plan…the blessing of homosexual unions cannot be considered licit. This is because they would constitute a certain imitation or analogue of the nuptial blessing, invoked on the man and woman united in the sacrament of Matrimony, while in fact 'there are absolutely no grounds for considering homosexual unions to be in any way similar or even remotely analogous to God's plan for marriage and family. (*Amoris Laetitia* 251)'

The CDF concluded that, '[God] does not and cannot bless sin'.[1730]

Within hours of the CDF publishing the response to the *dubium* Bishop Georg Bätzing, the Chairman of the German Bishops' Conference, posted his defiance of the Sacred Congregation's answer upholding the doctrine of the Church. He wrote that the CDF had responded to the *dubium* 'in the negative' on the basis of 'Church teaching as reflected in several Roman documents'. However, Bishop Bätzing continued:

> In Germany and in other parts of the Universal Church there have been discussions for a long time as to how this teaching and teaching development can generally be advanced with sound arguments — on the basis of fundamental truths of faith and morality, ongoing theological reflection and also in openness to newer results of the human sciences and the living situations of today's people.[1731]

Pro-homosexual Cardinal Blase Cupich of Chicago — recipient of signs of favour from Pope Francis — issued a statement about the CDF statement on blessing homosexual unions. Cardinal Cupich wrote:

> Today's response, issued by the Congregation for the Doctrine of the Faith, offers nothing new on the Church's teaching on the Sacrament of Matrimony. Regardless, it needs to be read in the context of the teachings in the Catechism and the encouraging statements of Pope Francis to LGBTQ persons about their relationship to the church, as well as his urging that pastors welcome them with respect and sensitivity, recognising, as the Congregation response does today, the many positive elements in same-sex relationships, 'which are in themselves to be valued and appreciated.' Yet, the understandable reaction among many to this response will be disappointment. This should prompt us in the Church and in the archdiocese to redouble our efforts to be creative and resilient in finding ways to welcome and encourage all LGBTQ people in our family of faith.[1732]

Pro-homosexual Fr James Martin SJ — the recipient of many signs of favour from Pope Francis — posted a series of tweets addressed to active homosexuals protesting the CDF upholding the Church's ban on blessing homosexual bondings:

> Dear friends: Today I received dozens of messages from #LGBTQ people, as well as their friends, families and allies, who told me they were disappointed, discouraged

---

[1730]Congregation for the Doctrine of the Faith [2021] *Responsum of the Congregation for the Doctrine of the Faith to a dubium regarding the blessing of the unions of persons of the same sex* [Online] Available at: press.vatican.va [Accessed on: 22 October 2022]

[1731]Gomes, J [2021] *Vatican Bars Blessings for Same-Sex Couples* [Online] Available at: www.churchmilitant.com [Accessed on: 22 October 2022]

[1732]*Statement of Cardinal Blase J. Cupich, archbishop of Chicago, on Same Sex Unions* [2021] [Online] Available at: www.archchicago.org [Accessed on: 22 October 2022]

and disheartened by the Vatican's latest pronouncement on barring the blessings of same-sex marriages... For many of them, the document was profoundly discouraging, though it was perhaps not surprising, given the CDF's longstanding position on this topic... Many people, encouraged by several German bishops, and other priests in the West who have ventured to give such blessings, were hoping that such blessings might represent a small way that the church might recognize what the CDF's document called the 'positive elements...'...of these couples, even if they could not be married within the church, in a sacramental union. Especially painful for many LGBTQ people who contacted me today was the statement that God 'does not and cannot bless sin' [...] Most of all, never despair. That voice is not coming from God. The voice of hope is. After all, what are the dark 40 days of Lent other than a preparation for a light-filled Easter? On Easter Christ upended all expectations and reminded us that nothing is impossible with God... Besides, what is the alternative? To lock ourselves behind closed doors like the disciples on Good Friday and Holy Saturday? To live in fear of the future that God has in store for us? To shrink in terror from the hard work that all disciples are called to do?... to doubt that Jesus is on the side of those who feel in any way marginalized? To leave the community into which Christ himself called us at our baptism?... As Christians we live in hope and in the trust that Easter is always before us, not matter how cold the winter or how difficult the Lent. Blessed be the name of the Lord.[1733]

During his Angelus Address on the 21st March 2021, Pope Francis appeared to distance himself from the Congregation for the Doctrine of the Faith upholding the ban on the blessing of homosexual bondings. The pontiff said:

We too must respond with the witness of a life that is given in service, a life that takes upon itself the style of God – closeness, compassion and tenderness – and is given in service. It means sowing seeds of love, not with fleeting words but through concrete, simple and courageous examples, not with theoretical condemnations, but with gestures of love. Then the Lord, with his grace, makes us bear fruit, even when the soil is dry due to misunderstandings, difficulty or persecution, or claims of legalism or clerical moralism. This is barren soil.[1734]

Pope Francis later demoted the author of the CDF statement, Archbishop Giacomo Morandi from his post as secretary of the CDF. It was reported that Archbishop Morandi had insisted that the CDF respond to calls by several German bishops for the liturgical blessing of homosexual bondings.[1735]

16th March

The German broadcaster, *Deutsche Welle*, reported that 60 German priests had signed a letter stating that they would defy the CDF's ban and bless homosexual couples:

In view of the refusal of the Congregation for the Doctrine of the Faith to bless homosexual partnerships, we raise our voices and say: We will continue to accompany people who enter into a binding partnership and bless their relationship in the future. We do not refuse a blessing ceremony.

Kath.ch, the Catholic news service of the Church in Switzerland, reported that 350 priests, led by Fr Helmut Schülle issued 'Call to Disobedience 2.0' that stated they would

continue to bless same-sex couples...[and] vehemently protests against the assumption that same-sex loving couples are not part of the divine plan. Here the attempt is made to undermine the reality of creation with dogmatising presumptions.[1736]

[1733]Martin, J [2021] *Tweets posed on Mar 15, 2021* [Online] Available at: twitter.com/JamesMartinSJ [Accessed on: 22 October 2022]
[1734]Pope Francis [2021] *Angelus Address* [Online] Available at: www.vatican.va [Accessed on: 22 October 2022]
[1735]Caldwell, S [2021] *Pope demotes Vatican official who championed statement against blessings of same-sex couples* [Online] Available at: catholicherald.co.uk [Accessed on: 22 October 2022]
[1736]Baklinski, P [Online] *Pro-LGBT Catholic bishops, priests decry, defy Vatican's ban on blessings for homosexual couples* [Online] Available at: www.lifesitenews.com [Accessed on: 22 October 2022]

17h March

The Flemish daily *Het Laatste Nieuws* published an op ed by, and an interview with, the pro-homosexual Bishop Johan Bonny of Antwerp. In his op ed Bishop Bonny wrote:

> This week, the Congregation for the Doctrine of the Faith responded negatively to the question of whether priests may bless same-sex unions. How do I feel after the 'responsum?' Bad. I feel vicarious shame for my Church (…). And I especially feel intellectual and moral incomprehension. I want to apologise to all those for whom this 'responsum' is hurtful and incomprehensible: believing gay couples who are active in the Catholic Church, parents and grandparents of gay couples and their children, pastoral staff and counsellors of gay couples. Their pain over the Church is mine today.

In his interview Bishop Bonny said:

> I read this last Monday. I was very disappointed, very angry, and this for many reasons. Regarding the concept of sin: I was at the 2015 synod on the family. The important thing there was that they were trying to avoid any discussion around the word sin because it's such a difficult concept to handle. You don't so easily commit a sin even when you want to. You have to take into account who is who, how was that particular person born, what kind of relationship can he or she have, what is the degree of care and permanence of a relationship, what is its degree of openness to children, to society, what kind of responsibility do these people take on. It is not possible to hold on to one aspect of life in order to hang the label 'sin' on everything. The great classical moral theology is always much more careful and nuanced in this regard. What disappoints me is the defective theological quality of the people in this Roman department.[1737]

18th March

Cardinal Kevin Farrell — recipient of many signs of favour from Pope Francis — gave a press conference to mark the opening of the *Amoris Laetitia* Family Year in his role as prefect of the Dicastery for the Laity, Family and Life. Asked about the CDF upholding the ban on blessing homosexual bondings, Cardinal Farrell made a distinction between sacramental marriages and homosexual civil 'marriages' and 'unions':

> The pastoral life of the Church is open to all people. It is essential and very important that we always open our arms to receive and to accompany all people in their different stages of life and in their different life situations. Sometimes we fail to understand also a distinction that must be made, and that is that when the Church speaks about marriage it speaks about sacramental marriage, it doesn't speak about civil unions. It doesn't speak about other forms of marriage. It speaks to the issue of sacramental marriage, and *Amoris Laetitia* speaks to that sacramental marriage.

Cardinal Kevin Farrell misspoke when he stated that the Church didn't speak about civil unions. In 2003 the Congregation for the Doctrine of the Faith promulgated the document *Considerations Regarding Proposals to Give Legal Recognition to Unions Between Homosexual Persons*. This CDF document declared that placing homosexual unions on the same level as marriage would not only approve of 'deviant behaviour' but also obscure basic values of humanity.[1738]

24th March

During his general audience address Pope Francis once again repudiated the Marian role as Co-redemptrix:

> Our Lady, who, as the Mother to whom Jesus entrusted us, 'enfolds' us all; but as a Mother, not as a goddess, not as co-redeemer: as a Mother. It is true that Christian piety has always given her beautiful titles, as a child gives his or her mom: how many

[1737]Smits, J [2021] *'Angry' Belgian bishop slams Vatican for rejecting same-sex blessings* [Online] Available at: www.lifesitenews.com [Accessed on: 22 October 2022]
[1738]Haynes, M [2021] *Leading Vatican cardinal hints at way to avoid ban on same-sex blessings* [Online] Available at: www.lifesitenews.com [Accessed on: 22 October 2022]

beautiful things children say to their mom whom they love so much! But let us be careful: the beautiful things that the Church, the Saints, say about Mary, take nothing away from Christ's sole Redemption. He is the only Redeemer. They are expressions of love like a child for his or her mom — some are exaggerated. But love, as we know, always makes us exaggerate things, but out of love.[1739]

24th March

Pope Francis appointed Juan Carlos Cruz, an openly homosexual man, to the Pontifical Commission for the Protection of Minors.[1740] On the 20th May 2018, Juan Carlos Cruz revealed that Pope Francis had told him during a private meeting that God has made him a homosexual. According to Cruz Pope Francis said: 'Juan Carlos, that you are gay does not matter. God made you like this and loves you like this and I don't care. The pope loves you like this. You have to be happy with who you are.'[1741] Pope Francis was later photographed embracing Juan Carlos Cruz when he came to Rome to thank the pontiff for his appointment.[1742]

Kathpress and the Austria archdiocesan media outlet *Der Sonntag* published an interview with Cardinal Christoph Schönborn — a theological advisor to Pope Francis — in which he expressed objections to the CDF ban on blessing homosexual bondings. Cardinal Schönborn

> [placed the question of blessing homosexual relationships] in the same category as the question of whether this (blessing) is possible for remarried or unmarried partnerships…(if) the request for a blessing is sincere and desired by a couple from God to aid a life path homosexual or otherwise, then such a blessing will not be refused… this declaration has hit many so particularly painfully, because they have the feeling that they are being rejected by the Church. [The Church] must teach, but she is first a mother. And many same-sex sentient and living people are particularly sensitive to this very question: 'Is the Church mother to us? A mother will not refuse the blessing. A blessing is not a reward for good behaviour, but a plea for help from above… first ask exactly about their living conditions and situation, yet will still gladly give them this blessing.'[1743]

1st April

The Vatican newspaper *L'Osservatore Romano's* Holy Thursday edition featured a photograph of a homoerotic painting depicting a nude resurrected Jesus embracing and ministering to the dead body of Judas. The editorial explained that the painting was inspired by Pope Francis' book *Our Father: Reflections on the Lord's Prayer* that suggested Judas may not be in hell. The artist gave it to Pope Francis 'who had placed it behind his desk in his personal study along with a statue of Jesus carrying Judas as a lost sheep.'[1744]

The US pro-LGBT Human Rights Campaign released a letter supporting men presenting themselves as women containing the signatures of an archbishop along with a bishop and several priests. Signatories included Archbishop John Wester, of Santa Fa,

---

[1739]Pope Francis [2021] *General Audience Address* [Online] Available at: www.vatican.va [Accessed on: 22 October 2022]

[1740]McLoone, D [2021] *Pope appoints open homosexual to Pontifical Commission for the Protection of Minors* [Online] Available at: www.lifesitenews.com [Accessed on: 22 October 2022]

[1741]Kirchgaessner, S [2021] *Pope Francis tells gay man: 'God made you like this'* [Online] Available at: www.theguardian.com [Accessed on: 22 October 2022]

[1742]Mainwaring, D [2021] *Pope Francis greets homosexual activist appointed to Pontifical Commission for the Protection of Minors* [Online] Available at: www.lifesitenews.com [Accessed on: 22 October 2022]

[1743]McLoone, D [2021] *Cardinal opposes Church's ban on blessing same-sex unions: 'I was not happy about the declaration'* [Online] Available at: www.lifesitenews.com [Accessed on: 22 October 2022]

[1744]Western, JH [2021] *Why is there a painting of a nude Jesus ministering to Judas in Pope Francis' study?* [Online] Available at: www.lifesitenews.com [Accessed on: 22 October 2022]

appointed by Pope Francis in 2016, and Bishop John Stowe of Lexington, appointed by Pope Francis in 2015.[1745]

14th April

Pro-homosexual Cardinal Cupich of Chicago — recipient of many signs of favour from Pope Francis — wrote a letter to Archbishop Samuel Aquila of Denver to criticise his article published in *America Magazine* under the title 'For the church to live in eucharistic coherence, we must be willing to challenge Catholics persisting in grave sin.' As well as being pro-homosexual, Cardinal Cupich is a vocal defender of the right of radical pro-abortion politicians, such as President Joe Biden to receive Holy Communion. Archbishop Aquila called it erroneous to hold that:

> Any baptized Catholic can receive Communion if he or she simply desires to do so… None of us have the freedom to approach the altar of the Lord without a proper examination of conscience and proper repentance if grave sin has been committed. The Eucharist is a gift, not an entitlement, and the sanctity of that gift is only diminished by unworthy reception.

To which Cupich responded in his letter:

> I respectfully note that to claim that we can do anything to diminish the Eucharist, or its effects, is contrary to the church's longstanding teaching. Catholic sacramental theology is based on the premise that the sacraments are the work of Christ, which is the meaning of the Church's affirmation at Trent (DS 1608) that the sacraments act *ex opere operato*, or, as St. Thomas wrote in the Summa, III, 68,8: 'The sacrament is not wrought by the righteousness of either the celebrant or the recipient, but by the power of God.' Owing to the nature of God, Christ and his works can never be diminished by any act on our part.

Archbishop Samuel Aquila published a further article dealing with Cardinal Cupich's partial presentation of Church teaching on the reception of Holy Communion:

> Thus, neither the minister of the sacrament or the person partaking of the sacrament can dimmish the grace of the sacrament. However, how it is received (*ex opere operantis*), that is, the benefit of receiving the sacrament, is dependent upon the condition of the subject's spiritual disposition […] When one partakes of the Eucharist, one is stating by one's very action that one is in communion with Christ and his Church. However, if one is in mortal sin when receiving Communion, one is telling a lie, for, in being in a state of mortal sin, one is neither in communion with Christ nor his Church.[1746]

20th April

Pope Francis appointed pro-homosexual Bishop Robert McElroy of San Diego to the Dicastery for Promoting Integral Human Development, one of the largest dicasteries in the Vatican. It was created by Pope Francis in 2016 through the amalgamation of the Pontifical Council for Justice and Peace, the Pontifical Council for the Pastoral Care of Migrants and Itinerant People, the Pontifical Council *Cor Unum*, and the Pontifical Council for Health Care Workers.[1747] Bishop McElroy was made Bishop of San Diego by Pope Francis in 2016.

[1745]Baklinski, P [2021] *Two US bishops back pro-LGBT campaign calling for acceptance of men who claim to be female* [Online] Available at: www.lifesitenews.com [Accessed on: 22 October 2022]

[1746]*Cardinal Cupich asked Archbishop Aquila for 'public clarification' over Eucharistic doctrine* [2021] [Online] Available at: www.pillarcatholic.com; Baklinski, P [2021] Cdl. *Cupich tries to torpedo bishop's airtight argument for denying pro-abortion politicians like Biden communion* [Online] Available at: www.lifesitenews.com [Accessed on: 22 October 2022]

[1747]Haynes, M [2021] *Dissident San Diego bishop elevated to Vatican position* [Online] Available at: www.lifesitenews.com [Accessed on: 22 October 2022]

5th May

Pro-homosexual Cardinal Joseph Tobin — recipient of many signs of favour from Pope Francis — delivered the 2021 Cardinal Bernardin Common Cause Lecture, Loyola University of Chicago. Cardinal Tobin criticised previous Ecumenical Councils of the Church, apart from the Second Vatican Council and explained how Pope Francis planned to 'change' the Church. Cardinal Tobin said:

> We cannot deny that for centuries [in] our existence as a Church, synodality was, in fact, used to kick people out … With the early councils, we would come together to repudiate this heresy, to define that dogma, and the body of Christ could lumber through history. But, I would posit that we've entered a new stage of the journey, one in which the acts of synodality do not look so much like sweeping dogmatic definitions as they do fine-tuning how the Gospel is applied to the signs of the times… Francis has rightly decried the mindset of 'but we've always done it this way.' When you're towing two millennia of baggage after you on the journey, it behoves you to be intentional about which tools you have at the ready and which tools you've stocked away in some forgotten luggage compartment… Folks who seem most threatened [by Francis' plans for the Church] from the beginning have been the ones with the most engineered grasp of all the norms and canons. If A equals 'irregular union,' and B equals 'not living as brother and sister,' then A plus B equals 'never can be admitted to the Eucharist.' To this I would posit that you can be the most knowledgeable mechanic on earth and still be a rotten driver.[1748]

The far left online Catholic magazine *Publik-Forum* published an interview with pro-homosexual Cardinal Reinhard Marx of Munich and Freising, a close associate of Pope Francis. Cardinal Marx ruled out an 'ecumenism of return', meaning the return of schismatic Protestant ecclesial communities to the communion of the Catholic Church:

> An ecumenism of return is completely impossible and was neither a goal of the ecumenical movement nor of the popes. What is clear is that we want to walk a common path. What a differentiated consensus means remains open. We do not have a clear model of unity to strive for. Mere mutual recognition is not enough. Together with Heinrich Bedford-Strohm, Chairman of the Council of the Evangelical Church in Germany, I put it like this: We need visible unity in reconciled diversity.

Cardinal Marx also expressed support for Protestants to receive Holy Communion:

> As the young bishop I was at the time, I wanted to stick closely to the rules. In ecumenism, moreover, many things have relaxed and changed. If someone goes to the Eucharist or the Lord's Supper of the other denomination after a decision of conscience, I will have to accept that. My longing at some point would be a 'reciprocity,' that we could communicate reciprocally at the services.

Cardinal Marx also expressed strong criticism of the CDF statement upholding the Church's ban on the blessing of homosexual bondings:

> The way of communication has to be fundamentally different. It is very irritating. You are informed shortly beforehand that a letter from the Congregation for the Doctrine of the Faith prohibiting the blessing of homosexual couples will be published. That is not how it should be done. We bishops are not merely the extended arm of the Congregation for the Doctrine of the Faith, we should also be heard. But it is clear to us: The guarantor of unity is the Pope. And the universal Church is more than a Roman authority.[1749]

The heterodox *America Magazine* published an article by pro-homosexual Bishop McElroy of San Diego — appointed by Pope Francis — in which he misrepresents the *Catechism of the Catholic Church* to support his view that pro-abortion politicians must

---

[1748]Baklinski, P [2021] *Cardinal Tobin: 'Synodality' is Pope Francis' 'long-game' plan to change Catholic Church* [Online] Available at: www.lifesitenews.com [Accessed on: 22 October 2022]
[1749]Smits, J [2021] *German cardinal: Ecumenism of return to Catholicism 'is completely impossible'* [Online] Available at: www.lifesitenews.com [Accessed on: 22 October 2022]

allowed to receive Holy Communion. Citing paragraph 1323 of the Catechism that describes the Eucharist as 'a sacrament of love, a sign of unity, a bond of charity, a Paschal banquet', Bishop McElroy fallaciously argued that 'A national policy of excluding pro-choice political leaders from the Eucharist will constitute an assault on that unity, on that charity.' Bishop McElroy went on to argue that if pro-abortion politicians were denied Holy Communion because 'worthiness requires integral union with all of the major teachings of Catholic faith,' then very few politicians, and parishioners, would be able to receive Holy Communion. He continued:

> …failure in fulfilling that obligation in its fullness cannot be the measure of eucharistic worthiness in a church of sinners and questioners, who must face intense pressures and complexities in their daily lives.[1750]

7th May

Cardinal Luis F. Ladaria, Prefect of the Congregation for the Doctrine of the Faith, sent a letter in response to a letter from Archbishop José H. Gomez, president of the U.S. Conference of Catholic Bishops. Archbishop Gomez informed the CDF that the US bishops were drawing up a policy on Holy Communion and pro-abortion politicians. For the first time in the history of the Church Cardinal Ladaria used abortionists preferred phrase 'pro-choice' in a Church document; referring to 'pro-choice politicians', as well as 'pro-choice legislation' and a 'pro-choice position.' Deacon Nick Donnelly commented:

> Only five months ago the CDF issued a statement trumpeted around the world as the Church accepting 'vaccines' from babies murdered through abortion. Now it has adopted the euphemism 'pro-choice' used to hide the abominable reality of abortion. That the CDF could use such a phrase shows how far the curial officials have abandoned even Vatican II's understanding of abortion as an 'unspeakable crime.' (GS 51) For the two billion-plus babies murdered in the 'silent holocaust' of abortion, this was 'no-choice.'[1751]

17th May

Pro-homosexual Bishop Johan Bonny of Antwerp, Belgium, signed a parliamentary Charter which committed all to fight 'discrimination' against the 'LGBTQ+' community and its members at a ceremony to mark the International Day against Homophobia and Transphobia.[1752]

20th May

Pro-homosexual Cardinal Mario Grech, the Secretary General of the Synod of Bishops, sent a letter to the world's bishops announcing Pope Francis' plans for an unprecedented multi-stage international synodal process that would conclude with an Ordinary General Assembly of the Synod of Bishops held in Rome in two sessions, October 2023 and October 2024. In an interview with Andrea Tornielli for *Vatican News*, Cardinal Grech misrepresented the Church's teaching on the *sensus fidei* to justify a wide consultation as part of the synodal process:

> This traditional aspect of doctrine throughout the history of the Church professes that 'the entire body of the faithful … cannot err in matters of belief' by virtue of the light that comes from the Holy Spirit given in baptism. The Second Vatican Council teaches that the People of God participate in the prophetic office of Christ. Therefore, we must listen to the People of God, and this means going out to the local churches.[1753]

[1750]Hichborn, M [2021] *Bishop McElroy erroneously defends giving Communion to pro-abortion politicians* [Online] Available at: www.lifesitenews.com [Accessed on: 22 October 2022]
[1751]Hayne, M [2021] *Vatican uses pro-abortion terminology 'pro-choice' for first time in 'abdication of moral authority'* [Online] Available at: www.lifesitenews.com [Accessed on: 22 October 2022]
[1752]Smits, J [2021] *Belgian Catholic bishop co-signs LGBT protection charter* [Online] Available at: www.lifesitenews.com [Accessed on: 22 October 2022]
[1753]Cummings McLean, D [2021] *Vatican turns synod on 'synodality' into yearlong international process with lay participation* [Online] Available at: www.lifesitenews.com [Accessed on: 22 October 2022]

Cardinal Grech omitted the conditions set out by Vatican II to guarantee the authentic exercise of the *sensus fidei* — obedient adherence to the Fidei Depositum, 'the people of God adheres unwaveringly to the faith given once and for all to the saints' (*Lumen Gentium* 12).[1754]

23rd May

Pope Francis delivered his homily for the Solemnity of Pentecost in which he expressed the desire that the Church would no longer challenge paganism or inculcate rules and regulations. The pontiff said:

> The Paraclete is telling the Church that today is the time for comforting. It is more the time for joyfully proclaiming the Gospel than for combatting paganism. It is the time for bringing the joy of the Risen Lord, not for lamenting the drama of secularisation. It is the time for pouring out love upon the world, yet not embracing worldliness. It is more the time for testifying to mercy, than for inculcating rules and regulations. It is the time of the Paraclete! It is the time of freedom of heart, in the Paraclete.[1755]

24th May

Pope Francis delivered an address to the General Assembly of the Italian Bishops in which he expressed criticisms of the Traditional Latin Mass. The pontiff also expressed criticism of young priests who desired to celebrate the Traditional Latin Mass. According to sources, Pope Francis claimed that 'there are many young priests who want to celebrate the "Tridentine Mass" even if they don't know Latin'. The sources also claimed that the pontiff told a 'characteristic story about a supposedly rigid young priest and his wise, in the eyes of Francis, bishop':

> To illustrate he told the story of a bishop to whom a young priest had turned to express his intention to celebrate in the Extraordinary Form. When asked if he know Latin, the young priest told the bishop that he was learning it. At that the bishop told him that it would be better to learn Spanish or Vietnamese because there were many Hispanics and Vietnamese people in the diocese.[1756]

27th May

Pope Francis appointed Archbishop Arthur Roche as the new Prefect of the Congregation for Divine Worship and the Discipline of the Sacraments. As the Secretary of the Congregation Archbishop Roche had distributed an essay in 2020 criticising traditional doctrine and the Traditional Latin Mass to all the bishops of the world under the title, '*The Roman Missal* of St. Paul VI: A witness to unchanging faith and uninterrupted tradition'. The essay re-hashed old canards such as the falsehood that the traditional Latin Mass reduced the laity to a state of unengaged passivity. His appointment was seen as a threat to Pope Benedict XVI's Motu Proprio *Summorum Pontificum* that encouraged, and protected, the celebration of the traditional Latin Mass and sacraments.[1757]

6th June

During his angelus address Pope Francis referred to the Most Holy Eucharist as the 'bread of sinners':

[1754]Second Vatican Council [1964] *Dogmatic Constitution on the Church, Lumen Gentium* [Online] Available at: www.vatican.va [Accessed on: 22 October 2022]

[1755]Pope Francis [2021] *Homily for the Solemnity of Pentecost* [Online] Available at: www.vatican.va [Accessed on: 22 October 2022]

[1756]Cummings McLean, D [2021] *Fears Traditional Latin Mass will be suppressed renewed in wake of Pope's alleged comments to Italian bishops* [Online] Available at: www.lifesitenews.com [Accessed on: 22 October 2022]

[1757]Haynes, M [2021] *Pope Francis appoints UK bishop known for criticizing traditional liturgy as head of the Congregation for Divine Worship* [Online] Available at: www.lifesitenews.com [Accessed on: 22 October 2022]

> It is on the night he is betrayed that Jesus gives us the Bread of Life. He gives us the greatest gift while he feels the deepest abyss in his heart: the disciple who eats with Him, who dips the morsel in the same plate, is betraying Him. And betrayal is the worst suffering for one who loves. And what does Jesus do? He reacts to the evil with a greater good. He responds to Judas' 'no' with the 'yes' of mercy. He does not punish the sinner, but rather gives His life for him; He pays for him. When we receive the Eucharist, Jesus does the same with us: he knows us; he knows we are sinners; and he knows we make many mistakes, but he does not give up on joining his life to ours. He knows that we need it, because the Eucharist is not the reward of saints, no, it is the Bread of sinners. This is why he exhorts us: 'Do not be afraid! Take and eat'.[1758]

As usual, Pope Francis made no reference for the need for repentance in order for the worthy reception of Holy Communion, thereby contradicting the Council of Trent, Session XIII, Canon 11; *Dz* 893.[1759]

21st June

Pope Francis announced the appointment of pro-homosexual Cardinal Joseph Tobin of Newark to the Supreme Tribunal of the Apostolic Signatura, the Vatican's highest court. This was the latest sign of Pope Francis' favouring Cardinal Joseph Tobin, who he only recently appointed as a member of the Congregation of Bishops.[1760]

24th June

The German Bishops' Conference released a statement following the meeting between its chairman Bishop Bätzing and Pope Francis to inform him about the German's Synodal Way. Bishop Bätzing wrote:

> The Pope encouraged us to continue to walk the Synodal Path as chosen by us, to discuss openly and honestly the open questions and to come to recommendations for another conduct of the Church. At the same time, he invited the Church in Germany to help shape the Path of Synodality that will lead to the Synod of Bishops in 2023, as announced by him [Pope Francis].

The pontiff gave his encouraging response despite the German Synodal Way members voting for radical changes to the Church's doctrine on sexual morality, including recommending masturbation, the use of contraception, changing the Church's doctrine on homosexuality, and the faux-ordination of women and ending priestly celibacy. Cardinal Gerhard Müller, former Prefect of the Congregation for the Doctrine of the Faith, responded:

> But only those who enjoy the gift of infinite naiveté still believe in the fairy tale of the good, forward-pushing Pope and his evil, slowing-down collaborators (Ladaria, Koch and even Kasper). Does this mean that they just wanted to test how far they could go, or has the realisation grown that the agenda of the Synodal Path is diametrically opposed to the Catholic faith in form and content? What is Catholic does not result from the combined majority of subjective opinions, but objectively from the binding doctrinal documents of the Catholic Church guided by the Pope and the bishops in communion with him (*Lumen Gentium* 8).[1761]

[1758]Pope Francis [2021] *Angelus Address* [Online] Available at: www.vatican.va [Accessed on: 22 October 2022]

[1759]McLoone, D [2021] *Pope Francis calls Eucharist 'bread of sinners' as USCCB considers denying pro-abort politicians Communion* [Online] Available at: www.lifesitenews.com [Accessed on: 22 October 2022]

[1760]McLoone, D [2021] *Pope appoints liberal Cardinal Tobin to Vatican's highest court* [Online] Available at: www.lifesitenews.com [Accessed on: 22 October 2022]

[1761]Hickson, M [2021] *After meeting with Pope Francis, the head of German bishops says pontiff invited them to help the Church* [Online] Available at: www.lifesitenews.com [Accessed on: 22 October 2022]

The Italian newspaper *La Stampa* published an interview with pro-homosexual Archbishop Paglia, the head of the Pontifical Academy for Life. Archbishop Paglia criticised the note sent by Cardinal Paul Gallagher to the Italian Embassy to the Holy See asking the Italian government to block a bill that would make 'homophobic' discrimination a crime punishable by jail time. Cardinal Gallagher protested 'the effect of negatively affecting the freedoms guaranteed to the Catholic Church and its faithful by the current concordat regime.' Archbishop Paglia said that the Vatican 'shouldn't have written' the note. Archbishop Paglia also appeared to support changing the Church's doctrine on homosexuality as presented in the *Catechism of the Catholic Church*: '... long live Pope Francis because his message goes beyond the thinking of many Italians,' said Paglia. 'It is an important process and I would not stop at catechism. A few months ago the catechism was changed on the death penalty. The Church is a living body and it goes on.[1762]

27th June

Pro-homosexual Fr. James Martin SJ — recipient of many signs of favour from Pope Francis — posted on twitter a handwritten letter sent to him by Pope Francis praising his 'ministry' promoting homosexuality in the Church. The pontiff wrote:

> Regarding your P.S. [about the Outreach LGBT Ministry Conference], I want to thank you for your pastoral zeal and your ability to be close to people, with that closeness that Jesus had and that reflects the closeness of God. Our Heavenly Father approaches with love every one of his children, each and everyone. His heart is open to each and everyone. He is Father. God's 'style' has three aspects: closeness, compassion and tenderness. This is how he draws closer to each one of us. Thinking about your pastoral work, I see that you are continuously looking to imitate this style of God. You are a priest for all men and women, just as God is the Father for all men and women. I pray for you to continue in this way, being close, compassionate and with great tenderness. And I pray for your faithful, your 'parishioners', and anyone whom the Lord places in your care, so that you protect them, and make them grow in the love of Our Lord Jesus Christ.

In his 'ministry' to individuals with the inclination to homosexual sins, Fr. James Martin SJ omits the Church's teaching on the 'grave depravity' of homosexual sex acts and the need for chastity (*Catechism of the Catholic Church*, 2357).

Archbishop Viganò, former papal nuncio to the USA, published a response to Pope Francis's praise of Fr. James Martin:

> The one who sits in Rome is surrounded by immoral persons who wink at LGBTQ+ movements and hypocritically simulate a welcome and an inclusivity that betrays their choice of field and their sinful tendencies. There is no more courage; there is no more fidelity to Christ; and it has reached the point of insinuating that, if Bergoglio was able to change the doctrine on capital punishment – an unheard of and absolutely impossible thing – he will certainly also be able to make sodomy licit in the name of a charity which has nothing Catholic about it and which is repugnant to Divine Revelation [...] And while the good Bishops and priests are daily confronted with the demolition that comes from above, we see published the enchanting and seductive words written by Bergoglio to James Martin SJ in support of a perverse and perverting ideology that offends the Majesty of God and humiliates the mission of the Church and the sacred authority of the Vicar of Christ.[1763]

The US Catholic publication, *The Pillar*, released a report detailing extensive use of the Chinese owned homosexual hookup app *Grindr* at the Vatican:

[1762]Mangiaracina, E [2021] *Head of Pontifical Academy for Life: Vatican 'shouldn't have' protested Italy's 'homophobia' bill* [Online] Available at: www.lifesitenews.com [Accessed on: 22 October 2022]
[1763]Viganò, C [2021] *Abp. Viganò issues 'severe warning' to Pope Francis in wake of his support for Fr. James Martin* [Online] Available at: www.lifesitenews.com [Accessed on: 22 October 2022]

Extensive location-based hookup or dating app usage is evident within the walls of Vatican City, in restricted areas of St. Peter's Basilica, inside Vatican City government and Holy See's administration buildings including those used by the Vatican's diplomatic staff, in residential buildings, and in the Vatican Gardens, both during daytime hours and overnight… at least 32 mobile devices emitted serially occurring hookup or dating app data signals from secured areas and buildings of the Vatican… At least 16 mobile devices emitted signals from the hookup app *Grindr* on at least four days between March to October 2018 within the non-public areas of the Vatican City State, while 16 other devices showed use of other location-based hookup or dating apps, both heterosexual and homosexual, on four or more days in the same time period.[1764]

29th June

During his homily for the solemnity of St. Peter and St. Paul, Pope Francis launched yet another attack on those who defended the Tradition of the Church, comparing them to Saul, the persecutor of the first Christians. The pontiff said, describing Saul:

He was also set free from the religious fervour that had made him a zealous defender of his ancestral traditions (cf. Gal 1:14) and a cruel persecutor of Christians. Set free. Formal religious observance and the intransigent defence of tradition, rather than making him open to the love of God and of his brothers and sisters, had hardened him: he was a fundamentalist.[1765]

1st July

The Pontifical Academy for Life held an online *International Roundtable on Vaccination*, in association with the German Medical Association and the World Medical Association, (despite the latter group lobbying for the legalisation of abortion in a pro-life country). The Pontifical Academy for Life praised the COVID gene-therapies as if there were no moral issues with the use of cell lines from babies murdered through abortion:

One of the greatest achievements of modern medicine, vaccines have been proven to save millions of lives and protect millions more from getting sick each year. And never in our lifetimes has the development of safe, effective vaccines taken centre stage in the global arena as prominently as it has during the devastating COVID-19 pandemic. The current pandemic has amplified some of the challenges already associated with vaccination – from the hurdles that impede equitable global distribution of vaccine doses to unfounded vaccine skepticism and mistrust.[1766]

6th July

Cardinal Zen, Emeritus Bishop of Hong Kong, published on his blog his protest about Pope Francis not answering his various *dubia* about the Vatican's secret deal with the Chinese communists and the Vatican document, 'Pastoral guidance for the civil registration of clergy in China':

Pope Francis has still not responded to his several '*dubia*' or criticisms of the document that Zen described as 'the most cruel thing' the Vatican has done concerning the Catholic Church in China, and 'absolutely against the doctrine of the Church, because it encourages people to be part of a schismatic Church.'

He went on to accuse Cardinal Parolin, Pope Francis' secretary of state, of 'murdering' the Church in China:

Parolin single-handedly completes now the trilogy of murdering the Church in China. He encourages those from the underground to join the Patriotic Association, thus

---

[1764]*Location-based apps pose security risk for Holy See* [2021] [Online] Available at: www.pillarcatholic. com [Accessed on: 22 October 2022]

[1765]Pope Francis [2021] *Homily on the solemnity of Saints Peter and Paul, Apostles* [Online] Available at: www.vatican.va [Accessed on: 22 October 2022]

[1766]Cummings McLean, D [2021] *Vatican academy to co-host pro-vaccination conference with secular medical associations* [Online] Available at: www.lifesitenews.com [Accessed on: 23 October 2022]

becoming members of a schismatic Church, to sing the song of Sion in the bird-cage (like the Hebrew slaves beside the rivers of Babylon). He allows the government to confiscate the churches of the underground, to prevent the priests from saying Mass in their private homes and to bar from church functions and religious activities those under eighteen years of age. Since the Holy See will appoint no more bishops in the underground, the community will die by natural dead [sic] (but the faith can survive in the 'catacombs').[1767]

8th July

Pope Francis appointed pro-homosexual Cardinal Jean-Claude Hollerich, S.J. as the relator general of the 2023-2024 Synod of Bishops on Synodality — the climax of the pontiff's three-year synodal process.[1768] Cardinal Hollerich was an enthusiast of the heterodox German synodal process. As well as expressing support for the end of mandatory priestly celibacy, and openness to the faux-ordination of women, Cardinal Hollerich called for the Church to change her doctrine on homosexuality. Germany's *Catholic News Agency* published an interview in 2022 in which Cardinal Hollerich said he believed the Church's teaching on homosexuality was wrong. In response to the question: 'How do you get around the Church's teaching that homosexuality is sin?' Hollerich replied:

> I believe that this is false. But I also believe that here we are thinking further about the teaching. So, as the Pope has said in the past, this can lead to a change in teaching. So I believe that the sociological-scientific foundation of this teaching is no longer correct, what one formerly condemned was sodomy. One thought at that time that in the sperm of the man, the whole child was kept. And one has simply transferred this to homosexual men. But there is no homosexuality at all in the New Testament. There is only discussion of homosexual acts, which were to some extent pagan cultic acts. That was naturally forbidden. I believe it is time for us to make a revision in the basic foundation of the teaching.[1769]

By so saying, Hollerich contradicts sacred Scripture, Tradition and the Magisterium, as summarised by the *Catechism of the Catholic Church*:

> Basing itself on Sacred Scripture, which presents homosexual acts as acts of grave depravity (Cf. Genesis 19:1-29; Romans 1:24-27; I Corinthians 6:10; I Timothy 1:10), tradition has always declared that 'homosexual acts are intrinsically disordered.' (Congregation for the Doctrine of the Faith, *Persona Humana* 8). They are contrary to the natural law. They close the sexual act to the gift of life. They do not proceed from a genuine affective and sexual complementarity. Under no circumstances can they be approved. (*CCC* 2357).

9th July

The Vatican newspaper *L'Osservatore Romano* referred to radical pro-abortion, pro-homosexuality President Joe Biden as a 'practicing Catholic'.[1770]

16h July

Pope Francis issued his Motu Proprio *Traditionis Custodes*, and accompanying letter, restricting the celebration of the traditional Latin Mass, claiming to abrogate Pope Benedict XVI's Motu Proprio *Summorum Pontificum*. The pontiff declared the Mass of

[1767]Zen Ze-kiun, J [2021] *The Third of July, Today and One Year Ago* [Online] Available at: /oldyosef. hkdavc.com [Accessed on: 23 October 2022]

[1768]Pentin, E [2021] *Pope Appoints Cardinal Jean-Claude Hollerich the Synod's New Relator General* [Online] Available at: www.ncregister.com [Accessed on: 23 October 2022]

[1769]Caldwell, S [2022] *Cardinal Hollerich: Church teaching on gay sex is 'false' and can be changed* [Online] Available at: catholicherald.co.uk [Accessed on: 23 October 2022]

[1770]Mangiaracina, E [2021] *Vatican newspaper calls pro-abortion Biden a 'practicing Catholic'* [Online] Available at: www.lifesitenews.com [Accessed on: 23 October 2022]

Pope Paul VI, known as the *Novus Ordo Missae*, the 'unique expression of the *lex orandi* of the Roman Rite':

> The liturgical books promulgated by Saint Paul VI and Saint John Paul II, in conformity with the decrees of Vatican Council II, are the unique expression of the *lex orandi* of the Roman Rite'. (Art.1). Pope Francis instructed bishops to remove Latin Mass groups out of parochial parishes into 'designated locations'. (Art.3 §2). Bishops were also instructed to undertake an inquisition of Latin Mass groups to determine 'that these groups do not deny the validity and the legitimacy of the liturgical reform, dictated by Vatican Council II and the Magisterium of the Supreme Pontiffs. (Art.3 §1).

While *Summorum Pontificum* recognised the right of all priests to celebrate the traditional Latin Mass, Pope Francis claimed the authority to remove that right, requiring all priests to apply to their bishops for his permission. Furthermore, Pope Francis insisted that priests ordained after the promulgation of *Traditionis Custodes* had to apply to the Vatican, via their bishop, to celebrate the traditional Latin Mass. (Art. 4 & 5).[1771]

In his accompanying letter, Pope Francis attempted to justify his draconian restrictions in the name of protecting the communion of the Church:

> In defence of the unity of the Body of Christ, I am constrained to revoke the faculty granted by my Predecessors. The distorted use that has been made of this faculty is contrary to the intentions that led to granting the freedom to celebrate the Mass with the *Missale Romanum* of 1962. He further attempted to justify his mean-spirited restrictions by making unsubstantiated allegations:

> But I am nonetheless saddened that the instrumental use of *Missale Romanum* of 1962 is often characterised by a rejection not only of the liturgical reform, but of the Vatican Council II itself, claiming, with unfounded and unsustainable assertions, that it betrayed the Tradition and the 'true Church'.

Pope Francis also expressed his determination that, eventually, bishops would enforce his will that everyone in the Church would solely celebrate the reformed *Novus Ordo* Mass:

> ...to provide for the good of those who are rooted in the previous form of celebration and need to return in due time to the Roman Rite promulgated by Saints Paul VI and John Paul II.[1772]

Cardinal Gerhard Müller, former prefect for the Congregation of the Faith, responded:

> Without the slightest empathy, one ignores the religious feelings of the (often young) participants in the Masses according to the Missal John XXIII (1962). Instead of appreciating the smell of the sheep, the shepherd here hits them hard with his crook. It also seems simply unjust to abolish celebrations of the 'old' rite just because it attracts some problematic people: *abusus non tollit usum* [Misuse does not nullify proper use] [....] For the unity in the confession of the revealed faith and the celebration of the mysteries of grace in the seven sacraments by no means require sterile uniformity in the external liturgical form, as if the Church were like one of the international hotel chains with their homogenous design. The unity of believers with one another is rooted in unity in God through faith, hope, and love and has nothing to do with uniformity in appearance, the lockstep of a military formation, or the groupthink of the big-tech age.[1773]

Bishop Robert Mutsaerts, auxiliary of 's-Hertogenbosch, Netherlands, responded:

[1771]Pope Francis [2021] *Apostolic letter Traditionis custodes* [Online] Available at: www.vatican.va [Accessed on: 23 October 2022]

[1772]Pope Francis [2021] *Letter of the Holy Father to the Bishops of the whole world, that accompanies the Apostolic Letter Motu Proprio data 'Traditionis Custodes'* [Online] Available at: www.vatican.va [Accessed on: 23 October 2022]

[1773]Müller, G [2021] *Cardinal Mueller on the New TLM Restrictions* [Online] Available at: www. thecatholicthing.org [Accessed on: 23 October 2022]

Francis has slammed the door hard by means of *Traditionis Custodes*. It feels like treason and is a slap in the face of his predecessors. By the way, the Church has never abolished liturgies. Not even Trent. Francis breaks completely with this tradition. The concise and powerful Motu Proprio contains a small number of propositions and commands. [...] Pope Francis is now pretending that his Motu Proprio is part of the organic development of the Church, which is completely at odds with reality. By making the Latin Mass practically impossible, he is radically breaking with the centuries-old liturgical tradition of the Roman Catholic Church. Liturgy is not a toy of popes, but the heritage of the Church. The Old Mass is not about nostalgia or taste. The Pope should be the guardian of Tradition; the Pope is the gardener, not the manufacturer. Canon law is not merely a matter of positive law, there is also such a thing as natural law and divine law, and moreover, there is such a thing as Tradition which cannot simply be set aside. What Pope Francis is doing has nothing to do with evangelization and even less to do with mercy. It is more of an ideology. [...] About the many liturgical abuses that exist all over the place in countless parishes, I never hear Bergoglio. In parishes everything is possible except the Tridentine Mass. All weapons are being thrown into the battle to eradicate the Old Mass. Why? For God's sake, why? What is this obsession of Francis to want to obliterate that small group of traditionalists? The Pope should be the guardian of tradition; not the jail-keeper of tradition. While *Amoris Laetitia* excelled in vagueness, *Traditionis Custodes* is a perfectly clear declaration of war.[1774]

22nd July

Pope Francis appointed pro-homosexual Bishop Jorge Ignacio García Cuerva of Rio Gallegos, Argentina, to the Congregation of Bishops. Bishop Cuerva was appointed bishop by Pope Francis in 2017. Bishop Cuerva was notorious for baptizing the twins of a homosexual pairing composed by two men, one a transsexual, and failing to adequately sanction a priest who organised the faux-marriage of homosexual-transexual individuals in his church. Bishop Cuerva failed to issue a condemnation of the public scandal and sacrilege.[1775]

17th August

Bishop Daniel Fernández Torres of Arecibo, Puerto Rico, recognised the right of Catholics to conscientious object to COVID gene-therapy vaccination, and gave permission to clerics to sign religious exemptions. Bishop Torres wrote:

It is possible for a faithful Catholic to have conscientious objection to the supposed obligatory nature of the vaccine against Covid-19. Consistent with what is stated here, in our Diocese of Arecibo, if the signature of an ordained minister is legitimately required to assert conscientious objection, the priests and permanent deacons who are freely willing to sign (the exemption) for the Catholic parishioner, who with a well-formed conscience thus asks for it, they can do it or it can be referred the Diocese of Arecibo... it is legitimate for a faithful Catholic to have doubts about the safety and efficacy of a vaccine given that what the pharmaceutical companies or drug regulatory agencies say is in no way a dogma of faith. And that safety and efficacy are relevant and necessary data for moral judgement... following the moral doctrine of the Church, in the face of difficult, sudden and morally debated cases, the shepherds of souls should not impose univocal solutions, but rather, following St. Alphonsus, we must leave each one to act accordingly to his right conscience.[1776]

Bishop Torres also refused to sign a joint statement issued by the Puerto Rican bish-ops that said that 'there is a duty to be vaccinated and that we do not see how a consci-

[1774]Smits, J [2021] *Dutch bishop on Pope's Latin Mass edict: 'How dictatorial, how unpastoral, how unmerciful'* [Online] Available at: www.lifesitenews.com [Accessed on: 23 October 2022]
[1775]Smits, J [2021] *Pope names leftist bishop to Vatican Congregation for Bishops* [Online] Available at: www.lifesitenews.com [Accessed on: 23 October 2022]
[1776]Ramos, D [2021] *Puerto Rican bishop recognizes right to conscientious objection to COVID vaccines* [Online] Available at: www.catholicnewsagency.com [Accessed on: 23 October 2022]

entious objection can be invoked from Catholic morality.' In March 2022 Pope Francis removed Bishop Daniel Fernández Torres from office when Bishop Torres refused to resign. This was the first time in this pontificate that a bishop had been removed from office without first having offered his resignation.[1777] Bishop Torres issued a statement protesting his removal by Pope Francis:

> I deeply regret that in the Church where mercy is so much preached, in practice some lack a minimum sense of justice. No process has been made against me, nor have I been formally accused of anything and simply one day the apostolic delegate verbally communicated to me that Rome was asking me to resign. A successor of the apostles is now being replaced without even undertaking what would be a due canonical process to remove a parish priest. I was informed that I had committed no crime but that I supposedly 'had not been obedient to the pope nor had I been in sufficient communion with my brother bishops of Puerto Rico.' It was suggested to me that if I resigned from the diocese I would remain at the service of the Church in case at some time I was needed in some other position; an offer that in fact proves my innocence. However, I did not resign because I did not want to become an accomplice of a totally unjust action and that even now I am reluctant to think that it could happen in our Church.[1778]

18th August

During his general audience address Pope Francis stated that he observed the Ten Commandments but not as 'absolutes': 'do I scorn the Commandments? No. I observe them, but not as absolutes, because I know that it is Jesus Christ who justifies me.' Bishop Athanasius Schneider, auxiliary of Astana, Kazakhstan, responded that Francis' statement 'contradicts the teaching of the Church and is very much a kind of sola fide teaching of Martin Luther.'[1779]

1st September

COPE radio, the network owned by the Spanish Catholic Episcopal Conference, broadcast an interview with Pope Francis. During the interview the pontiff mistakenly referred to the Traditional Latin Mass in the context of Biritualism, even though it is an integral part of the one Latin rite. Biritualism refers to the permission given to a priest to use a non-Latin rite. Pope Francis said:

> After this Motu Proprio, a priest who wants to celebrate that is not in the same condition as before — that it was for nostalgia, for desire, &c. — and so he has to ask permission from Rome. A kind of permission for bi-ritualism, which is given only by Rome. [Like] a priest who celebrates in the Eastern Rite and the Latin Rite, he is bi-ritual but with the permission of Rome. That is to say, until today, the previous ones continue but a little bit organised.'

Though his Motu Proprio *Traditionis Custodes* explicitly abrogated Pope Benedict XVI's *Summorum Pontificum*, Pope Francis claimed he was intending to support it: 'And on the other hand, to support and consolidate *Summorum Pontificum*.' He went on to say that having sacred Scripture in Latin was like 'laughing at the Word of God': '...that the proclamation of the Word be in a language that everyone understands; otherwise it would be like laughing at the Word of God.'[1780]

[1777]San Martín, I [2021] *Pope removes Puerto Rican bishop from office after he refused to resign* [Online] Available at: cruxnow.com [Accessed on: 23 October 2022]

[1778]*Catholic bishop in Puerto Rico says his removal by Pope Francis is 'totally unjust'* [2021] [Online] Available at: www.catholicnewsagency.com [Accessed on: 23 October 2022]

[1779]McLoone, D [2021] *Bishop Schneider: Pope Francis 10 Commandments comments contradict Church teaching, akin to teaching of Martin Luther* [Online] Available at: www.lifesitenews.com [Accessed on: 23 October 2022]

[1780]Herrera, C [2021] *Pope after operation: 'It never crossed my mind to resign'* [Online] Available at: www.vaticannews.va [Accessed on: 23 October 2022]

5th September

Pope Francis approved the appointment of Father Francis Joseph Cui Qingqi, OFM as the Bishop of Wuhan, China, under the terms of the secret Vatican-Chinese Government deal. Father Cui Qingqi is a well-known collaborator with the Chinese Communist Party and the only candidate put forward by the Chinese Communist government.[1781]

7th September

Cardinal Mario Grech, Secretary General of the General Secretariat of the Synod of Bishops, introduced the *vademecum* and the preparatory document for the multi-year Synod on Synodality. The *vademecum* included the instruction that everyone — including apostate Catholics and non-Catholics — must be included in the synodal process:

> Whatever the local circumstances, the Diocesan Contact Person(s) are encouraged to focus on maximum inclusion and participation, reaching out to involve the greatest number of people possible, and especially those on the periphery who are often excluded and forgotten [including] Catholics who rarely or never practice their faith, etc.... No one – no matter their religious affiliation – should be excluded from sharing their perspective and experiences, insofar as they want to help the Church on her synodal journey of seeking what is good and true.

It was observed that the *vademecum*'s truncated presentation of *Lumen Gentium* 12's definition of the *sensus fidelium* omitted the most essential element necessary for its authentic exercise — the obedience of faith. The omitted section of *LG* 12 refers to the importance of:

> ...faithful and respectful obedience to which the people of God accepts that which is not just the word of men but truly the word of God. Through it, the people of God adheres unwaveringly to the faith given once and for all to the saints, penetrates it more deeply with right thinking, and applies it more fully in its life.

Therefore, 'those people who have left the practice of the faith, people of other faith traditions, people of no religious belief [could] have no part in expressing the *sensus fidelium*.'[1782]

In response to a complaint from the pro-homosexual Bishop Felix Genn of Münster, the Priestly Fraternity of St. Peter moved Fr. Michael Ramm FSSP from St. Michael Catholic Church in Recklinghausen. Members of the parish council sent a letter to the vicar general of the Diocese of Münster complaining that Fr. Ramm had questioned mainstream narratives about the COVID-19 vaccine, homosexuality, and gender ideology in the parish newsletter. Fr. Ramm had written:

> What do we think today about the zeitgeist that prevailed in the Third Reich? And what will future generations say about our present zeitgeist? … How will they judge this entire COVID panic in the future? How will future generations judge this 'voluntary compulsory vaccination'? What will they say about the fact that perfectly healthy people are being vaccinated with a genetic vaccine, for the production of which people were murdered? What will people say later about the fact that today the whole world is exposed to such an unnecessary risk through vaccination? What will people say later about this gender ideology to which everyone is bowing today? Will it be celebrated in the future as a heroic deed that soccer stadiums are illuminated in rainbow colours?'

Fr. Klaus Winterkamp, the Diocese of Münster's vicar general, wrote on behalf of Bishop Felix Genn to the superior of the Priestly Fraternity of St. Peter to complain:

[1781]McLoone, D [2021] *Pope Francis approves appointment of Communist bishop to Wuhan* [Online] Available at: www.lifesitenews.com [Accessed on: 23 October 2022]
[1782]Haynes, M [2021] *ANALYSIS: Vatican's Synod on Synodality will consult non-Catholics, lapsed Catholics* [Online] Available at: www.lifesitenews.com [Accessed on: 23 October 2022]

By no means is it acceptable that the proclamation within the liturgical celebration is used to express private opinions with regard to the coronavirus pandemic or the COVID vaccine or other socio-political problems/challenges. It is also totally unacceptable in this context to accuse Pope Francis of expressing his own opinion when the proclamation, of all things, is used to disseminate private opinions.

He wrote this, despite the fact that Bishop Genn had promoted the 'blessing' of homosexual pairings in six churches within his diocese.[1783]

11th September

Pro-homosexual Bishop John Stowe of Lexington forced clergy to announce their personal medical information to the congregation at the end of Mass at Christ the King Cathedral. Deacon Tim Weinmann stated from the pulpit:

The bishop has asked that Fr. David and I, Fr. John – I'm speaking for Fr. John – make an announcement that we are not vaccinated, so people can decide if they wanted to attend Masses where they were celebrating.

In the presence of Bishop Stowe, Deacon Tim Weinmann also declared:

And also the priests, and this has been done throughout the diocese, those priests that are not vaccinated are to follow the COVID protocol in the liturgy and they are not allowed to visit the sick or elderly that are homebound. Fr. John and Fr. David, again, have not been vaccinated.[1784]

12th September

During his apostolic journey to Slovakia, Pope Francis answered questions from fellow Jesuits. In response to the question, 'How do you deal with people who look at you with suspicion?', the pontiff responded his critics did the work of the devil:

There is, for example, a large Catholic television channel that has no hesitation in continually speaking ill of the pope. I personally deserve attacks and insults because I am a sinner, but the Church does not deserve them. They are the work of the devil. I have also said this to some of them. Yes, there are also clerics who make nasty comments about me. I sometimes lose patience, especially when they make judgments without entering into a real dialogue. I can't do anything there. However, I go on without entering their world of ideas and fantasies. I don't want to enter it and that's why I prefer to preach, preach....

Pope Francis again bizarrely referred to the Traditional Latin Mass in the context of biritualism. The pontiff said:

Now I hope that with the decision to stop the automatism of the ancient rite we can return to the true intentions of Benedict XVI and John Paul II. My decision is the result of a consultation with all the bishops of the world made last year. From now on those who want to celebrate with the *vetus ordo* must ask permission from as is done with biritualism. But there are young people who after a month of ordination go to the bishop to ask for it. This is a phenomenon that indicates that we are going backward.[1785]

14th September

During his apostolic journey to Hungary and Slovakia Pope Francis addressed a meeting with young people at which he said that sins should not be the focus of confession. The pontiff said:

[1783]Bürger, M [2021] *German priest challenges COVID jabs and LGBT agenda, gets forced out of parish* [Online] Available at: www.lifesitenews.com [Accessed on: 23 October 2022]

[1784]Haynes, M [2021] *Pro-LGBT bishop bans unvaccinated clergy from ministering to sick, orders revealing of vaccine status* [Online] Available at: www.lifesitenews.com [Accessed on: 23 October 2022]

[1785]Spadaro, A [2021] *'Freedom Scares Us': Pope Francis' conversation with Slovak Jesuits* [Online] Available at: www.laciviltacattolica.com [Accessed on: 23 October 2022]

If I were to ask all of you what you think about when you go to Confession – don't answer out loud – I am quite sure your answer will be 'our sins'. But let me ask you, and please answer me, are sins really the centre of Confession? Does God want you to approach him thinking just about yourself and your sins; or about him? What does God want? That you approach him thinking about him or about your sins? What does he want? What is central, our sins or the Father who forgives everything? It is the Father. We do not go to confession to be punished and humiliated, but as children who run towards the Father's loving arms. And the Father lifts us up in every situation, he forgives all our sins. Listen well to this: God always forgives! Understood? God always forgives![1786]

15th September

During the in-flight press conference returning from his apostolic journey to Hungary and Slovakia, Pope Francis again expressed his support for the legalisation of homosexual pairings. The pontiff said:

I have spoken clearly about this: marriage is a sacrament, marriage is a sacrament. And the Church does not have the power to change the sacraments. They are thus, as the Lord has instituted [for] us. These are laws that try to help the situation of many people of different sexual orientations. And this is important, to help these people, but without imposing things that by their nature do not enter in the Church. But if they want to support a homosexual couple in life together, states have the possibility of civilly supporting them, of giving security through inheritance, health [insurance]. But the French have a law on this not only for homosexuals, but for all people who want to associate with each other [in a legally recognized relationship].

Pope Francis went on to claim that God will save everyone: 'All the same, respect everyone. The good Lord will save everyone — do not say this aloud [laughs] — but the Lord wants to save everyone.'

In response to a question about the US bishops considering denying Holy Communion to pro-abortion politicians Pope Francis characterised such considerations as 'political' and not the rightful concern of pastors:

You can tell me: but if you are close, and tender, and compassionate with a person, you have to give Communion — but that's a hypothetical. Be a pastor and the pastor knows what he has to do at all times, but as a shepherd. But if he stops this shepherding of the Church, immediately he becomes a politician. And you will see this in all the denunciations, in all the non-pastoral condemnations that the Church makes. With this principle, I believe a pastor can act well. The principles are from theology, the pastoral care is theology and the Holy Spirit, who leads you to do it with the style of God. I would venture to say up to this far…If you say to me: but can you give or cannot give [Communion]? It is casuistry, as the theologians say.

In response to a question about why some people refused the COVID gene-therapy vaccine Pope Francis made no reference to the reason why many Catholics, and Christians, conscientious refused to get jabbed — the use of cell lines from babies murdered through abortion. The pontiff referred to such people as 'deniers':

Humanity has a history of friendship with vaccines. As children, we got them for measles, for other things, for polio. All the children were vaccinated and no one said anything. Then this [opposition] happened. This was perhaps due to the virulence, the uncertainty not only about the pandemic, but also about the different vaccines, and also the reputation of some vaccines which are nothing more than distilled water. This created fear in people. Then others who say that it is a danger because with the vaccine you are infected. So many arguments that have created this division. Even in the College of Cardinals there are some deniers and one of these, poor guy, is hospitalised with the virus. I do not know how to explain [the opposition] well. Some say it comes from the

[1786]Pope Francis [2021] *Address to Young People during International Eucharistic Congress, Slovakia* [Online] Available at: www.vatican.va [Accessed on: 23 October 2022]

diversity of where the vaccines come from, which are not sufficiently tested and they are afraid. We must clarify and speak with serenity about this. In the Vatican, everyone is vaccinated except a small group which they are studying how to help.[1787]

17th September

Pope Francis praised radical pro-abortion, pro-homosexual President of Ireland, Michael D. Higgins as a 'wise man'. The pontiff said: 'Today, I did not just meet a man, a president; I met a wise man of today. I thank God that Ireland has such a wise man as its Head.' In 2018, Higgins signed a bill that legalised abortion-on-demand up until twelve weeks, with abortion up until birth allowed if the baby is found to have a life-limiting condition.[1788]

The Italian news outlet *Il Messaggero* reported that Pope Francis had abandoned the tradition of reserving the high altar — Altar of the Confessio — in St. Peter's Basilica solely for the use of the Successor of St. Peter:

> As a result of the revolution started by Pope Francis in the heart of Christianity, for the first time a simple priest – the biblical scholar Fabio Rosini – will celebrate Mass at the central altar, under Bernini's Baldacchino, which for centuries was reserved only for Popes.

Dr. Peter Kwasniewski commented:

> Sociologically speaking, what's going on here is very obvious. It is another 'taboo' that Francis wants to violate publicly, another 'line' he wants to cross in his enterprise of cancelling all traditions. Revolutionaries have to destroy any vestige of the sacred, the set-apart, the privileged, the untouchable, the elevated, the off-limits. It's what we saw in the family synods, the youth synod, and the Amazon synod: continual transgressions of boundaries, to clear the way for perpetual change, for assimilation into modernity, which is identified with Absolute Spirit in a Hegelian sense: it is where humanity is destined to go, so the Church must shatter any customs of the past that might suggest that she is either ancient or timeless or embraces all ages without essentially changing.[1789]

27th to 29th September

The Pontifical Academy for Life held the three day conference, *Public Health in Global Perspective: Pandemic, Bioethics, Future*. The Vatican conference featured many pro-abortion advocates as speakers — Dr. David Barbe the president of the pro-abortion World Medical Association (WMA); Dr. Carissa Etienne the director of the pro-abortion Pan American Health Association, Rabbi Avraham Steinberg and Dr. Daniel Sulmasy, who holds that 'the question of whether the embryo or fetus is a person ... is not answerable by science.' Deacon Nick Donnelly commented:

> If you want to know the Truth about this pontificate's curia don't listen to their words, look at their actions. By giving a platform to pro-abortion speakers and those who promote mandatory abortion tainted 'vaccines', the Vatican is signalling to the world that it no longer opposes, in any meaningful way, the murder of babies through abortion... What we are witnessing in these Vatican conferences' promoting abortion tainted 'vaccines' is a rupture with the Catholic Church's two thousand years of absolute opposition to the 'unspeakable crime' of abortion (*Gaudium et Spes* 51).'[1790]

[1787]Pope Francis [2021] *In-flight press conference on return from Slovakia* [Online] Available at: www.ncregister.com [Accessed on: 23 October 2022]

[1788]Jackson, T [2021] *Pope Francis hails pro-abortion Irish president as a 'wise man of today'* [Online] Available at: www.laciviltacattolica.com [Accessed on: 23 October 2022]

[1789]Haynes, M [2021] *Pope to 'deface' tradition and allow minor clergy use of Papal Altar in St. Peter's* [Online] Available at: www.lifesitenews.com [Accessed on: 23 October 2022]

[1790]Haynes, M [2021] *In 'rupture' with Church's 'absolute opposition' to abortion, Vatican hosting pro-aborts at pro-COVID jab conference* [Online] Available at: www.lifesitenews.com [Accessed on: 23 October 2022]

4th October

Fr. Maximilian Mary Dean, chaplain to the traditional Carmelite nuns in Fairfield, Pennsylvania, and their motherhouse in Valparaiso, Nebraska, revealed details concerning the Apostolic Visitation imposed on the nuns in September 2021. Fr. Dean reported that the aim of the Visitation was the destruction of this traditional order:

> The Co-Visitators actually sent spies; they discussed the need to stop me from bringing the Sacraments and to switch the Nuns over to the *Novus Ordo* Mass; they discussed strategies for turning the benefactors away from these traditional communities. I am not permitted to write here what they actually did during the Visitation itself, but let's just say that I was 100% correct in my assessment and that the Nuns pulling from Philadelphia was used as a pretext by the Congregation to go after these traditional Monasteries.[1791]

9th October

Pope Francis met with pro-abortion, pro-homosexuality Catholic Nancy Pelosi, the Speaker of the U.S. House of Representatives. Though her own bishop, Archbishop Salvatore Cordileone of San Francisco, had called on fellow Catholics to pray and fast for the conversion of Mrs. Pelosi due to her prominent advocacy of extreme positions on the murder of babies through abortion, Pope Francis made no mention of abortion in his discussions with her. In contrast to Pope Francis' silence, Pope Benedict raised the immorality of abortion with Mrs. Pelosi when she met with him in 2009. The Holy See's press office released a statement explaining that Pope Benedict 'took the opportunity to speak of… the Church's consistent teaching on the dignity of human life from conception to natural death which enjoin all Catholics, and especially legislators … in creating a just system of laws capable of protecting human life at all stages of its development.'[1792]

In 2022, Archbishop Cordileone of San Francisco issued a public declaration that Nancy Pelosi 'was not to be admitted to Holy Communion unless and until she publicly repudiate her support for abortion "rights" and confess and receive absolution for her cooperation in this evil in the sacrament of Penance'.[1793]

However, within a week of Archbishop Cordileone taking this canonical action, Pope Francis invited Nancy Pelosi to the Vatican for a private audience, after which she received Holy Communion during a papal Mass.[1794]

Pope Francis delivered a reflection at an event marking the commencement of the multi-year Synod on Synodality during which he expressed his purpose of creating a 'different Church'. The pontiff quoted the liberal French theologian Yves Marie-Joseph Congar OP to convey his purpose:

> 'There is no need to create another Church, but to create a different Church' (*True and False Reform in the Church*). That is the challenge. For a 'different Church', a Church open to the newness that God wants to suggest, let us with greater fervour and frequency invoke the Holy Spirit and humbly listen to him, journeying together as he, the source of communion and mission, desires: with docility and courage. Come, Holy Spirit! You inspire new tongues and place words of life on our lips: keep us from becoming a 'museum Church', beautiful but mute, with much past and little future.[1795]

[1791]Hickson, M [2021] *Hermit priest doubles down on claim that Pope's plans will 'destroy' contemplative orders* [Online] Available at: www.lifesitenews.com [Accessed on: 24 October 2022]

[1792]Mangiaracina, E [2021] *Pope Francis meets with pro-abortion Nancy Pelosi ahead of UN Climate Change Conference* [Online] Available at: www.lifesitenews.com [Accessed on: 24 October 2022]

[1793]Cordileone, S [2022] *Letter to the faithful on the Notification sent to Speaker Nancy Pelosi* [Online] Available at: sfarchdiocese.org [Accessed on: 24 October 2022]

[1794]Winfield, N [2022] *Nancy Pelosi receives Communion and meets with Pope Francis at the Vatican amid abortion debate* [Online] Available at: www.americamagazine.org [Accessed on: 24 October 2022]

[1795]Pope Francis [2021] *Address for the opening of the synod* [Online] Available at: www.vatican.va [Accessed on: 23 October 2022]

12th October

Pro-homosexual Bishop Paul Dempsey of Achonry — appointed by Pope Francis in 2020 — gave an address to the heretical group *We Are Church Ireland*, which advocates for abortion, sodomy, woman priests, divorce and communion for adulterers. Bishop Dempsey told the group:

> Critically and very importantly, and maybe this wasn't emphasised at the time, the door is not closed on that question [of married priests] and the Pope hasn't closed the door on that question, but maybe it's for another time.[1796]

16th October

Vatican News — the official news outlet of the Holy See — posted a video about the IV World Meeting of Popular Movements containing Pope Francis' address to these groups that include openly revolutionary Marxist organisations, such as Movimento dos Trabalhadores Rurais Sem Terra. The pontiff told them, among other things:

> You are, as I said in the letter I sent you last year, a veritable invisible army; you are a fundamental part of that humanity that fights for life against a system of death [...] Know that you are called to participate in great processes of change, as I said to you in Bolivia: 'the future of humanity is in great measure in your own hands, through your ability to organise and carry out creative alternatives' in your hands [...] I often hear, 'Father, we agree, but in real terms, what must we do?' I do not have the answer, and so we must dream together and find it together. There are, however, some concrete measures that may allow for significant changes. These measures are present in your documents, in your speeches, and I have taken them very much into account; I have reflected on them and consulted specialists.

Michael Hichborn, founder and president of the Lepanto Institute, observed:

> The promotion of self-professed Marxists in a video produced and published by the Vatican is a gravely serious matter, but most disturbing of all are the words of Pope Francis himself, in addressing these Marxist organizations... or Pope Francis to say such things to avowed revolutionary Communists – professed enemies of the Catholic Church and Her faithful children – is shocking beyond words![1797]

25th October

Pope Francis appointed prominent abortion and eugenics advocate Professor Jeffrey Sachs an ordinary member of the Pontifical Academy of Social Sciences. At the enthusiastic invitation of pro-communist Bishop Marcelo Sánchez Sorondo, Jeffrey Sachs was a regular speaker at Vatican conferences since the beginning of the Bergoglian pontificate. In his book *Commonwealth: Economics for a Crowded Planet* (2009), Sach's called for legalizing abortion as a cost-effective way to eliminate 'unwanted children': '...to accelerate the decline in fertility ... abortion should be legalised.'[1798]

For the second time during his pontificate Pope Francis allowed a statue of the heresiarch Martin Luther to be displayed in his presence in the Vatican.[1799]

29th October

Pope Francis met with radical pro-abortion Catholic US President Joe Biden. The White House informed journalists that 'there was laughter and clear rapport between President Biden and Pope Francis.' The murder of babies through abortion remained

---

[1796]Jackson, T [2021] *LGBT-friendly Irish bishop gives talk to dissident 'Catholic' group pushing for women priests* [Online] Available at: www.lifesitenews.com [Accessed on: 24 October 2022]

[1797]Hichborn, M [2021] *Pope Francis celebrates five openly Marxist organizations: 'You are...a veritable invisible army'* [Online] Available at: www.lifesitenews.com [Accessed on: 24 October 2022]

[1798]Haynes, M [2021] *Pope Francis appoints population control activist Jeffrey Sachs to Pontifical Academy of Social Sciences* [Online] Available at: www.lifesitenews.com [Accessed on: 24 October 2022]

[1799]Boralevi, P [2021] *Statue of Martin Luther displayed at Vatican for second time as pope addresses German protestants* [Online] Available at: www.lifesitenews.com [Accessed on: 24 October 2022]

unmentioned according to official press releases. In response to a journalist asking if abortion came up in his discussion with Pope Francis President Biden said: 'No, it didn't. It came up — we just talked about the fact that he was happy I was a good Catholic and keep receiving Communion.'[1800] Following his meeting with the pontiff, President Biden's administration convened a task force in 2022 devoted to maintaining and expanding 'access' to abortion-on-demand. Through The Women's Health Protection Act, President Biden also sought to enshrine abortion-on-demand until birth into federal law, which would have abrogated pro-life state laws across the USA. It was defeated in the Senate, when Catholic Democrat Senator Joe Manchin joined Senate Republicans in voting against the Act.[1801]

BBC Radio Four broadcast a short reflection by Pope Francis for its *Thought for the Day* segment during which he focused on climate change and the COVID pandemic, making no reference to our Lord Jesus Christ or anything to do with Christianity. This was contrasted with Pope Benedict XVI's reflection broadcast by BBC Radio Four in 2010 which spoke of our Lord Jesus Christ's death and resurrection.[1802]

3rd November

Cardinal Pietro Parolin, the Vatican Secretary of State, delivered Pope Francis' address to the UN Climate Change Conference UK 2021 — Conference of the Parties 26 [COP26]. The pontiff made no references to our Lord Jesus Christ, God, the Catholic Church, the Catholic faith or even Christian doctrine.[1803]

9th November

Cardinal Angelo De Donatis, the Vicar General for the Diocese of Rome, issued a decree restricting the celebration of the Traditional Latin Mass, including a ban on the faithful participating in the traditional Holy week Triduum previously celebrated in Rome by the Priestly Fraternity of Saint Peter (FSSP) at the Santissima Trinità dei Pellegrini. The decree states: 'every day, except the Easter Triduum, the faithful may participate in the celebration of the Eucharist according to the *Missale Romanum* of 1962 in the parish of Santissima Trinità dei Pellegrini (cf. art. 3 §5, *Traditionis Custodes*).' The decree also banned the use of the *Roman Ritual* and the *Ordines*, used for the traditional celebration of the sacraments of baptism and penance, or sacramentals.[1804]

12th November

Pope Francis delivered an address — via video — to participants attending the 75th anniversary conference of the pro-abortion, pro-homosexuality United Nations Educational, Scientific and Cultural Organization (UNESCO). The pontiff praised UNESCO as a 'privileged partner of the Holy See in the common service to peace and solidarity among peoples.'[1805]

[1800]Nagle, M [2021] *Biden says Pope Francis told him he's a 'good Catholic' amid criticism over his abortion views* [Online] Available at: abcnews.go.com; McLoone, D [2021] *Pope Francis and Biden meet in Vatican to discuss climate and COVID shots, not abortion* [Online] Available at: www.lifesitenews. com [Accessed on: 24 October 2022]

[1801]Haynes, M [2021] *Senate Republicans plus one Democrat defeat radical bill allowing abortion-on-demand until birth* [Online] Available at: www.lifesitenews.com [Accessed on: 24 October 2022]

[1802]Haynes, M [2021] *Pope uses spiritual segment on BBC radio to discuss laundry-list of social justice issues* [Online] Available at: www.lifesitenews.com [Accessed on: 24 October 2022]

[1803]Pope Francis [2021] *Pope's Address to COP26 President and Leaders* [Online] Available at: www. cbcew.org.uk [Accessed on: 24 October 2022]

[1804]Boralevi, P & Cummings McLean, D [2021] *'Traditionis Custodes' implemented in the Diocese of Rome, Latin Mass heavily restricted* [Online] Available at: www.lifesitenews.com [Accessed on: 24 October 2022]

[1805]Haynes, M [2021] *Pope praises pro-abortion UN agency, highlights 'privileged relationship' with Church* [Online] Available at: www.lifesitenews.com [Accessed on: 24 October 2022]

Bishop Robert E. Guglielmone of Charleston, USA, sent a letter to all priests and deacons instructing them that he was banning the traditional Triduum, including the Easter vigil, that the Latin Mass could only be celebrated if the *Novus Ordo* Mass was celebrated on the same day, and that he was prohibiting the celebration of the traditional sacraments of confirmation and the anointing of the sick.[1806]

14th November

The Italian language Swiss TV channel, *Tvsvizzera*, broadcast an interview with Archbishop Arthur Roche, the Prefect for the Congregation for Divine Worship and the Discipline of the Sacraments appointed by Pope Francis. Cardinal Roche said:

> It's clear that *Traditionis Custodes* is saying 'okay, this experiment has not entirely been successful,' and so let us go back to what the [Second Vatican] Council required of the Church...And we've got to remember that this [the liturgical reform] wasn't the will of the Pope. This was the will of the vast majority of the bishops of the Catholic Church, who were gathered together in the 21st ecumenical council, guiding the Pope with regard to the future.[1807]

The Second Vatican Council's Constitution on the Sacred Liturgy, *Sacrosanctum Concilium*, made no reference to abrogating the Mass of the Ages. For example, paragraph 36§1 stated, 'Particular law remaining in force, the use of the Latin language is to be preserved in the Latin rites.'[1808]

8th December

The heterodox US newspaper *National Catholic Reporter* reported that Pope Francis had sent two letters in May and June 2021 to the radical US homosexual activist group *New Ways Ministry* to praise their work. The pontiff affirmed this militant homosexual group despite the Congregation for the Doctrine of the Faith in 1999 imposing canonical penalties on its founders, Sr. Jeannine Gramick and Fr. Robert Nugent, and the fact that in 2010 Cardinal Francis George, Archbishop of Chicago, re-iterated the CDF's condemnation of the group, writing 'like other groups that claim to be Catholic but deny central aspects of Church teaching, New Ways Ministry has no approval or recognition from the Catholic Church and that they cannot speak on behalf of the Catholic faithful in the United States.'[1809]

Though the group advocates sodomy the pontiff praised them for displaying a discernible 'attitude of shepherd closeness' and thanking them for their 'neighbourly work...[your] heart, open to your neighbour.' Pope Francis also praised Sr. Jeannine Gramick, who flagrantly ignored the CDF's restrictions on her involvement with *New Ways Ministry*, writing, 'I know how much she has suffered. She is a valiant woman who makes her decisions in prayer.' Pro-homosexual Fr. James Martin SJ — recipient of many signs of favour from Pope Francis — praised the pontiff's letters to *New Ways Ministry*:

> The Holy Father's warm letter to New Ways Ministry is not only another step in his outreach to LGBTQ people, but the beginning of a kind of rehabilitation for New Ways, and for Sister Jeannine as well, in recognition of their important ministry in our church.[1810]

[1806]Haynes, M [2021] *South Carolina bishop restricts Latin Mass, bans some traditional sacraments altogether* [Online] Available at: www.lifesitenews.com [Accessed on: 24 October 2022]

[1807]Haynes, M [2021] *Vatican liturgy chief hails Traditionis Custodes' crackdown on Latin Mass 'experiment'* [Online] Available at: www.lifesitenews.com [Accessed on: 24 October 2022]

[1808]Second Vatican Council [1963] *Constitution on the sacred liturgy, Sacrosanctum concilium, para 36§1* [Online] Available at: www.vatican.va [Accessed on: 23 October 2022]

[1809]George, F [2010] *USCCB President Clarifies Status of New Ways Ministry* [Online] Available at: www.usccb.org [Accessed on: 24 October 2022]

[1810]Fraga, B [2021] *Pope Francis thanks New Ways Ministry in recent correspondence* [Online] Available at: www.ncronline.org [Accessed on: 24 October 2022]

10th December

Pope Francis sent a letter to the pro-homosexual activist Sr. Jeannine Gramick, congratulating her on fifty years of ministry, most of which was spent seeking to overturn the Church's doctrine on homosexuality and sodomy. Since 1999 Sr. Gramick has disobeyed the Congregation for the Doctrine of the Faith's order to cease her advocacy of the homosexual lifestyle. The pontiff wrote:

> Your letter reminded me of 'the style' of God... God has his own style to communicate with us. And we could summarise that style in three words: closeness, compassion, tenderness...You have not been afraid of closeness, and in getting close you did it 'feeling the pain' and without condemning anyone, but with the 'tenderness' of a sister and a mother. Thank you, Sister Jeannine, for all your closeness, compassion and tenderness.[1811]

12th December

Thierry Bonaventura, the communications manager of the General Secretariat of the Synod of Bishops, Rome, issued a public apology to the militant US pro-homosexual group, *New Ways Ministry*, for removing a link to their video on the Vatican's resource site for the multi-year Synod on Synodality. Bonaventure had removed the link when he learnt of Cardinal Francis George's condemnation of the group in 2010 in his role as President of the United States Conference of Catholic Bishops. Re-instating the link to New Ways Ministry's video Thierry Bonaventura apologised:

> I feel that I must apologise to all LGBTQ people and to the members of New Ways Ministries [sic] for the pain caused, testifying … the firm will — not only mine but of the entire General Secretariat of the Synod — not to exclude those who wish to carry out this synodal process with a sincere heart and a spirit of dialogue and real discernment.

He concluded by inviting pro-homosexual activists to write directly to the Synod Secretariat, in order to 'share' their thoughts and ideas.[1812]

15h December

The Vatican launched the *Fratelli Tutti* Foundation attached to Saint Peter's Basilica in Rome, an entity established by Pope Francis to promote his encyclical, *Fratelli Tutti*. The Foundation's mission areas are:

- to support and design pathways of art and faith;
- to invest in cultural and spiritual formation through events, experiences, paths, and spiritual exercises;
- to promote dialogue with cultures and other religions to build a 'social alliance.'

Making no references to God, the Holy Trinity, our Lord Jesus Christ, and the Blessed Virgin Mary, the purposes of the Foundation are expressed in the Masonic language of the French Revolution:

> To this end, the Foundation… nurtures initiatives aimed at fostering the development of fraternal humanism, through the promotion of the principles of liberty, equality and fraternity, conditions for building a 'universal love' that recognises and protects the dignity of persons. (VI).[1813]

[1811]McDermott, J [2021] *Pope Francis praises Sister Jeannine Gramick's 50 years of L.G.B.T. ministry in handwritten letter* [Online] Available at: www.americamagazine.org [Accessed on: 24 October 2022]

[1812]Haynes, M [2021] *Vatican apologizes to dissident pro-LGBT group, offers involvement in synodal process* [Online] Available at: www.lifesitenews.com [Accessed on: 24 October 2022]

[1813]Smits, J [2021] *Pope Francis' new foundation appears to have more in common with French Revolution than with Catholicism* [Online] Available at: www.lifesitenews.com [Accessed on: 24 October 2022]

18th December

Archbishop Arthur Roche, the Prefect for the Congregation for Divine Worship and the Discipline of the Sacraments, issued a *Responsa ad Dubia*, on certain provisions of the apostolic letter *Traditionis Custodes*. It imposed further restrictions on the Traditional Latin Mass, and the traditional rites for the sacraments. Regarding the sacraments the *Responsa* states in the question-and-answer format of *dubia*:

> On the proposed question: Is it possible, according to the provisions of the Motu Proprio *Traditionis Custodes*, to celebrate the sacraments with the *Rituale Romanum* and the *Pontificale Romanum* which predate the liturgical reform of the Second Vatican Council? The answer is: Negative.

The *Responsa* made concelebration – a novelty imposed after Vatican II – a condition for priests to be allowed to celebrate the Traditional Latin Mass:

> On the proposed question: If a Priest who has been granted the use of the *Missale Romanum* of 1962 does not recognise the validity and legitimacy of concelebration - refusing to concelebrate, in particular, at the Chrism Mass - can he continue to benefit from this concession? The answer is: Negative.

Archbishop Arthur Roche, on behalf of Pope Francis, imposed this condition, knowing full well that many tradition-minded priests refused to participate in the novelty of concelebration.

The *Responsa* also made it clear that the purpose of *Traditionis Custodes* was to eventually end the celebration of the Traditional Latin Mass:

> The Motu Proprio *Traditionis Ccustodes* intends to re-establish in the whole Church of the Roman Rite a single and identical prayer expressing its unity, according to the liturgical books promulgated by the Popes St. Paul VI and St. John Paul II, in conformity with the decrees of the Second Vatican Council and in line with the tradition of the Church.[1814]

21st December

Bishop Michael Burbidge of Arlington, USA – appointed by Pope Francis – sent an email to priests informing them that he no longer gave permission for the traditional celebration of baptism, confirmation and marriage.[1815]

27th December

Pope Francis appointed Bishop Jean-Paul Vesco OP of Oran, Algeria the Archbishop of Alger, Algeria. In February 2022 the Swiss Catholic site *Cath.ch* published an interview in which Archbishop Vesco, faced with a majority Muslim country, implicitly rejected the missionary mandate given to the Church by Christ when he spoke of the need to 'get rid of the idea that we have to evangelize and bring people to our truth.' He went on to deny the necessity of baptism for salvation, citing Pope Francis:

> He thus shows that evangelization is done in fraternity and not in conversion. It's revolutionary! He affirms in a way that baptism is not the condition of salvation.[1816]

Pro-homosexual Cardinal Cupich of Chicago – recipient of many signs of favour from Pope Francis – issued sweeping restrictions on the Traditional Latin Mass and traditional sacraments, requiring all priests, deacons, and instituted ministers to request permission to celebrate the Latin Mass either publicly or privately. Cardinal Cupich,

[1814]Haynes, M [2021] *Vatican announces harsh restrictions on traditional Mass, sacraments* [Online] Available at: www.lifesitenews.com [Accessed on: 24 October 2022]
[1815]Haynes, M [2021] *Virginia diocese announces massive restrictions on traditional sacraments following Vatican crackdown* [Online] Available at: www.lifesitenews.com [Accessed on: 24 October 2022]
[1816]Gomes, J [2021] *Archbishop of Algiers Abandons Evangelism* [Online] Available at: www.churchmilitant.com [Accessed on: 24 October 2022]

known for his permissive attitude towards homosexuality, also banned the celebration of Latin Mass on Christmas day, the Triduum, Easter Sunday, Pentecost Sunday, and the first Sunday of each month.[1817]

2022

6th January

During his homily for the Solemnity of the Epiphany Pope Francis again criticised the traditional Latin Mass and priests who celebrated it:

> Have we been stuck all too long, nestled inside a conventional, external and formal religiosity that no longer warms our hearts and changes our lives? Do our words and our liturgies ignite in people's hearts a desire to move towards God, or are they a 'dead language' that speaks only of itself and to itself? It is sad when a community of believers loses its desire and is content with 'maintenance' rather than allowing itself to be startled by Jesus and by the explosive and unsettling joy of the Gospel. It is sad when a priest has closed the door of desire, sad to fall into clerical functionalism, very sad.[1818]

7th January

In an interview with *Gloria TV* Dr. José Arturo Quarracino, nephew of the late Cardinal Antonio Quarracino, accused Pope Francis of covering up homosexual clerical abuse after he succeeded as Archbishop of Buenos Aires. According to Dr. José Quarracino, Bergoglio often covered up homosexual abuse and misconduct:

> *Is it true that Bergoglio is said to have 'covered up' homosexual abuses?* Unfortunately, yes, because this often concerned people who were close to him. The case of a priest whom he trusted very much and who was known for his homosexual tendencies was much talked about. Bergoglio 'helped' him by sending him to Rome a few years before he became Pope, among other things because this allowed him to learn a lot of confidential information from the Holy See. One must not forget that these kinds of personalities tend to gather information of all kinds, information in which Bergoglio was interested [....] priests who displayed such behaviour and could always rely on Bergoglio's discreet protection [....] [Bergoglio deliberately chose scandal-ridden collaborators] at all levels, apart from the fact that he has always surrounded himself with mediocre, submissive, and servile personalities. Bergoglio's leadership style is that of a despot who allows neither contradiction nor independent judgment.'[1819]

10th January

Pope Francis demoted Archbishop Giacomo Morandi, removing him from his position as Secretary of the Congregation for the Doctrine of the Faith. The Vatican announced that Archbishop Morandi has been appointed the ordinary of the small Italian diocese of Reggio Emilia-Guastalla, even though as archbishop he would be expected to preside over an archdiocese. Commentators, including Vatican insiders, observed that this demotion was due to Archbishop Morandi penning the *Responsum to a dubium regarding the blessing of the unions of persons of the same sex* that maintained the prohibition against such 'blessings' and also to him being less than enthusiastic about *Traditionis Custodes*.[1820]

[1817]Wolfe, R [2021] *Cardinal Cupich under fire for banning Latin Mass, allowing 'blasphemous' liturgies* [Online] Available at: www.lifesitenews.com [Accessed on: 24 October 2022]
[1818]Pope Francis [2022] *Homily for the Solemnity of the Epiphany* [Online] Available at: www.vatican. va [Accessed on: 20 December 2023]
[1819]*'Bergoglio is not a Peronist' - Gloria.tv-Interview with José Arturo Quarracino, Buenos Aires* [Online] Available at: www.gloria.tv[Accessed on: 20 December 2023]
[1820]Mainwaring, D [2022] *Pope Francis fires Vatican official who opposed 'blessings' for same-sex couples* [Online] Available at: www.lifesitenews.com [Accessed on: 20 December 2023]

12th January

In an interview with *Crux* the pro-LGBT activist Sister Jeannine Gramick described Pope Francis' recent letters of support for her ministry as a 'very significant step', signifying a 'new era in the church'. Sr. Gramick was formerly banned by the CDF from ministering to homosexuals due to her rejecting the Church's doctrine on homosexuality. She expressed the hope that Pope Francis would eventually change the Church's doctrine to accord with her own personal beliefs:

> Pope Francis is wonderful, but he hasn't changed the teaching of the church. Well, that is not his job right now. Eventually, it's his job, but right now it's up to us, the people, to articulate the faith. What do we believe?[1821]

13th January

La Civiltà Cattolica, the Jesuit journal reviewed and approved by the Vatican's Secretariat of State before publication, published an article supporting a bill before the Italian legislature that would effectively legalise assisted suicide. Fr. Carlo Casalone, a member of Pope Francis' revised Pontifical Academy for Life, argued that though the bill legalised assisted suicide, it 'could constitute a barrier, albeit imperfect and itself problematic' without stipulating the nature of this 'barrier'. Casalone supported the bill even though he admitted it had 'huge flaws' and 'diverges' from Catholic teaching on the sanctify of human life and the immorality of euthanasia. 60 Italian civil society organisations protested *La Civiltà Cattolica's* publication of the 'pro-euthanasia' article.[1822]

19th January

The Women's Ordination Conference (WOC) — a campaign group for the ordination of women to the diaconate, presbyterate and episcopacy — announced that the General Secretariat of the Synod of Bishops had included their campaign material on the Vatican's Synod Resource website for the Synod on Synodality. Deacon Nick Donnelly condemned the Vatican's link to the group as a 'scandal' because it 'supports the sacrilegious simulation of priestly ministry among women.'[1823]

20th January

During his interview with Raymond Arroyo on EWTN's *World Over Live*, Cardinal Raymond Burke, former prefect of the Supreme Tribunal of the Apostolic Signatura — the Church's highest court — commented on Pope Francis' praise of the LGBT activist Sr. Jeannine Gramick and the heterodox New Ways Ministry:

> What these personal acts of the pope are, are exactly that: these are acts that he is taking on personally, but they have nothing to do with the Church's teaching as far as I'm concerned. What I read that was quoted in the media of the letter - or letters, I'm not sure - which is written to Sister Jeanine, these are simply the opinions of a man, but they have nothing to do with the Magisterium of the Church.[1824]

23rd January

Pope Francis instituted the first women to the minor order of lector during a ceremony at St. Peter's, a ministry traditionally reserved to men in preparation for ordination to

[1821]Pattison, M [2022] *Sister Gramick reflects on series of letters from Pope Francis* [Online] Available at: cruxnow.com [Accessed on: 20 December 2023]

[1822]Knuffke, L [2022] *Italy's high court set to rule on referendum to legalize euthanasia* [Online] Available at: www.lifesitenews.com; Respinti, M [2022] *Pro-euthanasia Jesuits? Clarify now* [Online] Available at: www.ifamnews.com [Accessed on: 20 December 2023]

[1823]Haynes, M [2022] *Synod on Synodality website includes link to heretical group that wants female priests* [Online] Available at: www.lifesitenews.com [Accessed on: 20 December 2023]

[1824]McLoone, D [2022] *'Opinions of a man,' not the Church: Cardinal Burke criticizes Pope Francis' praise for LGBT group leader* [Online] Available at: www.lifesitenews.com [Accessed on: 20 December 2023]

the diaconate. Thereby enacting his January 2021 Motu Proprio, *Spiritus Domini*, that changed canon law to permit women to be instituted into the minor orders of lector and acolyte.[1825]

In an interview published by the Italian newspaper *La Stampa*, Bishop Derio Olivero of Pinerolo, appointed by Pope Francis is 2017, expressed his support for euthanasia. When asked if he was against a law for assisted suicide, the head of the Italian Bishops Conference's Commission for Ecumenism and Dialogue stated, 'Not so'. Bishop Olivero continued,

> At the same time, it is true that we must behave more like Pope Francis indicates: leave the sacristies and learn from others, from history that has changed…It is exaggerated to insist only on sacredness as an absolute term without combining quality of life and conscience. Each of these concepts taken alone becomes ideological exasperation.[1826]

24th January

The Latin Mass Society of England and Wales announced in a press release that Cardinal Nichols, elevated to the Sacred College of Cardinals in 2014 by Pope Francis, had banned any confirmations in the traditional rite in his Archdiocese of Westminster. This ban included the annual celebration of traditional confirmations organised by the Latin Mass Society at St James' Spanish Place, London.[1827]

25th January

It was revealed that Pope Francis' delegate to the Sovereign Order of the Knights of Malta, Cardinal Silvano Tomasi, had refused to recognise the Order's appointed representative to a committee reviewing the order's revised constitution. Marwan Sehnaoui, president of the order's Lebanese association, had been appointed chairman of the steering committee for the order's constitutional reform by the Lieutenant of the Grand Master. However, Cardinal Tomasi, unilaterally replaced Marwan Sehnaoui as chairman with a personal appointee. In a letter to the knights' leaders and membership Sehnaoui stated that this 'is clearly a direct attack on the sovereignty of our Order.' Even though he left a private audience with Pope Francis he'd requested to help resolve the impasse 'hopeful and confident,' Cardinal Tomasi adamantly refused to allow him to attend the constitutional revision meeting. It was observed that Tomasi's refusal to recognise the order's own delegates to their own constitutional process signalled 'a total takeover of the governance of the knights', even though Tomasi had previous told them, 'it was never the intention of this commission, nor of the Holy Father, to undermine the sovereignty of the Order, which will be totally preserved.' Marwan Sehnaoui warning his fellow knights that 'our Order is not respected, that our dignity is violated, and our future is in danger'.[1828]

Bishop Frank Dewane of Venice, Florida, issued a directive to his priests banning them from celebrating the Mass *ad orientem* – facing the East or facing the tabernacle or apse – without his permission. In his letter Bishop Dewane twice misspelled '*ad orientem*' as '*ad orientum*'. His ban of *ad orientem* was contrary to the Congregation for the Divine Worship and the Discipline of the Sacraments' letter that stated, 'Holy Mass may be celebrated *versus populum* or *versus apsidem*. Both positions are in accord with liturgical law; both are to be considered correct.'[1829]

[1825]Haynes, M [2022] *Pope Francis institutes first female lectors, catechists at Vatican in apparent 'attack' on all-male priesthood* [Online] Available at: www.lifesitenews.com [Accessed on: 22 De-cember 2023]

[1826]Haynes, M [2022] *Dissident Italian bishop backs euthanasia, suggests 'quality of life' determines its 'sacredness'* [Online] Available at: www.lifesitenews.com [Accessed on: 22 December 2023]

[1827]Haynes, M [2022] *UK cardinal bans traditional confirmations in his archdiocese following Traditionis Custodes* [Online] Available at: www.lifesitenews.com [Accessed on: 22 December 2023]

[1828]'*A direct attack': Knights of Malta delegate locked out of order's constitutional committee* [2022] [Online] Available at: www.pillarcatholic.com [Accessed on: 22 December 2023]

[1829]Wolfe, R [2022] *Florida bishop forbids priests to celebrate Mass facing the tabernacle* [Online] Available at: www.lifesitenews.com [Accessed on: 22 December 2023]

26th January

ARD, the German TV company, broadcast a documentary about homosexual clergy and laity working in the German Catholic Church entitled 'As God created us', described as 'the biggest coming out in the Catholic Church'. Over 125 employees of the German Church demanded that the Church change her doctrine on homosexuality, 'Entering into a non-heterosexual relationship or marriage must never be considered a breach of loyalty and, consequently, an obstacle to employment or a reason for dismissal.'

During an interview Bishop Helmut Dieser of Aachen, the head of the Forum for Sexuality and Partnership for *Der Synodale Weg*, responded that the Church needs to change its biblical position and laws regarding the question of homosexuality, and offered an apology, 'I apologise on behalf of the Church for people who have been hurt in their pastoral encounters with the Church'.[1830] The group of homosexual employees also issued a list of seven demands, including, 'Defamatory and outdated statements of church doctrine on sexuality and gender needs to be revised on the basis of theological and human-scientific findings. This is of utmost relevance especially in view of world-wide church responsibility for the human rights of LGBTIQ+ persons; the Church must not withhold the blessing of God and access to the sacraments from LGBTIQ+ persons and couples; In dealing with LGBTIQ+ persons, the Church has caused much suffering throughout its history. We expect the bishops to take responsibility for this on behalf of the Church, to address the institutional history of guilt, and to advocate for the changes we call for.'[1831]

The German Bishops' Conference officially supported the LGBT campaign 'Out in the Church'. Bishop Franz-Josef Bode von Osnabrück, the vice president of the German Bishops' Conference. said he saw the campaign as 'a courageous step by 125 homosex-ual employees of the Catholic Church throughout the country.'[1832]

During the Wednesday audience Pope Francis instructed parents to 'accompany' their children if they claimed to have a different 'sexual orientation': '…parents who see different sexual orientations in their children; how to deal with this and accompany their children and not hide in an attitude of condemnation.'[1833]

27th January

During a press conference pro-homosexuality Cardinal Reinhard Marx, a member of Pope Francis' Council of Cardinals, contradicted the Church's prohibition of men with 'deep seated homosexual tendencies' entering seminary to become priests. Cardinal Marx said,

> How do we deal with the homosexuality of priests? Not everyone is forced to declare [to others] their own sexual inclination, whether he is heterosexual or homosexual. He must decide that [whether to declare it] for himself. But if he does [declare it], then that is to be respected and then this is not a restriction on his ability of becoming a priest. That is my position and we have to stand up for it.[1834]

1st February

In an interview with *EWTN* show *Cara a Cara* Cardinal Gerhard Müller, the former Prefect of the Congregation for the Doctrine of the Faith criticised priests who were

---

[1830]*Over 100 German Catholic church employees including priests come out as LGBT in new documentary* [2022] [Online] Available at: www.lifesitenews.com [Accessed on: 22 December 2023]

[1831]*Demands* [2022] [Online] Available at: www.outinchurch.de [Accessed on: 22 December 2023]

[1832]Mangiaracina, E [2022] *German bishops back LGBT campaign to change Church teaching on homosexuality, gender identity* [Online] Available at: www.lifesitenews.com [Accessed on: 23 December 2023]

[1833]Mainwaring, D [2022] *Pope Francis tells parents to embrace, not condemn, children with 'differ-ent sexual orientations'* [Online] Available at: www.lifesitenews.com [Accessed on: 22 December 2023]

[1834]Jackson, T [2022] *German Cdl. Marx says homosexuality is 'not a restriction' on a man's ability to become a priest* [Online] Available at: www.lifesitenews.com [Accessed on: 22 December 2023]

campaigning for the Church to be more 'gay-friendly'. He stated that the current 'speculation' over whether the Church would offer blessings or marriages to same-sex couples 'has no basis in Revelation',

> It is a human thought, but it is not in accordance with the Word of God. God created man, not these priests who think like the world of today, according to this materialistic anthropology, who distinguish sexuality, sexual pleasure, from the responsibility to procreate sons and daughters…There are many who have totally distanced themselves from the Catholic faith. They present themselves as if they are priests, but they are not faithful. […] The doctrine of the Church is absolutely clear. This doctrine has its foundation in the anthropology revealed in the Old and New Testament, in creation and also in the institution of marriage as a sacrament, marriage made up of one man and one woman. […]The doctrine of the Church is not defined by the Pope, by this or any other Pope, or by the bishops. The doctrine of the Church has its foundation in the eschatological Revelation in Jesus Christ. The Church and Her members have to be faithful to Revelation, to the Word of God and it is not a political party.[1835]

2nd February

During the Wednesday audience Pope Francis claimed that apostates, blasphemers and persecutors of the Church are members of the Communion of Saints, because we are all 'saved sinners', without any reference to the need for repentance and absolution:

> What does this mean? That the Church is reserved for the perfect? No. It means that it is the community of saved sinners. The Church is the community of saved sinners. This is a beautiful definition. No one can exclude themselves from the Church. We are all saved sinners [….] 'Father, let us think about those who have denied the faith, who are apostates, who are the persecutors of the Church, who have denied their baptism: Are these also at home?'. Yes, these too, even the blasphemers, everyone. We are brothers. This is the communion of saints. The communion of saints holds together the community of believers on earth and in heaven.[1836]

Pro-homosexuality Bishop John Stowe of Lexington, appointed by Pope Francis in 2015, banned the celebration of the Mass 'ad orientem' and other elements of the traditional Latin Mass that he singled out for criticism as 'eccentricities':

> Within that description I would include the addition of rites and gestures that are not included in the *Roman Missal* (e.g. priests and ministers kneeling at the foot of the altar during the introductory rites), the alteration of the text of the Eucharistic Prayer by the celebrant, the use of vesture previously discontinued (e.g. birettas, maniples) and unauthorised adaptations on the posture for receiving communion (kneeling at the communion rail). Of more concern is the celebration of the mass 'ad orientem,' especially when done because of the preference of the priest celebrant.[1837]

3rd February

In an interview with the German newspaper *Sueddeutsche Zeitung* Cardinal Reinhard Marx, a member of Pope Francis' Council of Cardinals, called for the ending of mandatory priestly celibacy,

> it would be better for everyone to create the possibility of celibate and married priests. For some priests, it would be better if they were married — not just for sexual reasons, but because it would be better for their life and they wouldn't be lonely. We must hold this discussion.[1838]

[1835]Haynes, M [2022] *Cdl. Müller rejects 'political' push for LGBT ideology in the church, says it's against 'the Word of God'* [Online] Available at: www.lifesitenews.com [Accessed on: 23 December 2023]
[1836]Pope Francis [2022] *General Audience, 2 February 2022* [Online] Available at: www.vatican.va [Accessed on: 22 December 2023]
[1837]Haynes, M [2022] *Pro-LGBT US bishop bans 'ad orientem' liturgy, says Latin Mass goes against Church 'unity'* [Online] Available at: www.lifesitenews.com [Accessed on: 23 December 2023]
[1838]Jackson, T [2022] *German cardinal calls for church's celibacy rule to be dropped, priests be allowed to marry* [Online] Available at: www.lifesitenews.com [Accessed on: 23 December 2023]

In an interview with the German Catholic news agency *KNA*, Cardinal Jean-Claude Hollerich SJ, appointed by Pope Francis as Relator General of the 2021–2024 Synod on Synodality, supported demands for the Church to change her doctrine on homosexuality:

> *How do you get around the Church's teaching that homosexuality is sin?* I believe that this is false. But I also believe that here we are thinking further about the teaching. So, as the Pope has said in the past, this can lead to a change in teaching. So I believe that the sociological-scientific foundation of this teaching is no longer correct, what one formerly condemned was sodomy. One thought at that time that in the sperm of the man, the whole child was kept. And one has simply transferred this to homosexual men. But there is no homosexuality at all in the New Testament. There is only discussion of homosexual acts, which were to some extent pagan cultic acts. That was naturally forbidden. I believe it is time for us to make a revision in the basic foundation of the teaching. The change in civilisation we are witnessing today is the greatest change since the invention of the wheel. The Church has always moved with the times and has always adapted. But one always had much more time to do that. Today we must be faster. Otherwise, we lose contact and can no more be understood.[1839]

3rd-4th February

The German *Der Synodale Weg* [The Synodal Way] convened over two days to conduct preliminary votes on various controversial issues. On Friday participants voted on a document entitled 'Women in Ministries and Offices in the Church', that stated 'it is not the participation of women in all church ministries and offices that requires justification, but the exclusion of women from sacramental office.' 174 votes in favour of the ordination of women, 30 against, and 6 abstained. On Saturday, participants voted on two documents regarding homosexuality, 'Blessing celebrations for couples who love each other' and 'Magisterial reassessment of homosexuality'. The second document called for a revision of paragraphs of the Catechism of the Catholic Church on homosexuality and chastity. Both received an overwhelming majority of favourable votes.[1840]

12th February

During an interview with the Swiss Catholic news website *Cath.ch* Archbishop Jean-Paul Vesco, newly appointed to the Archdiocese of Algiers, said Catholics 'must abandon the idea that we have to evangelise and bring people to our truth'. He continued, 'At the same time, we have to accept that there might be in Islam some truth that escapes us'. Archbishop Jean-Paul Vesco praised Pope Francis' novel approach to evangelisation by not seeking to convert people to the Gospel,

> That way, [Pope Francis] shows us that evangelisation happens through fraternity, not conversion. It's revolutionary! In a sense, he asserts that baptism is not the condition for salvation.[1841]

21st February

Asia News, a news agency promoted by the Pontifical Institute for Foreign Missions, published the protest of the faithful over the continued detention of a bishop of the Chinese underground Church, Mgr. Joseph Zhang Weizhu, bishop of Xinxiang. Marking nine months since the bishop's disappearance in police custody, anonymous members of Bishop Zhang Weizhu expressed the concern that Chinese authorities had betrayed the provisional agreement between China and the Holy See. 'The persecution

[1839] Caldwell, S [2022] *Cardinal Hollerich: Church teaching on gay sex is 'false' and can be changed* [Online] Available at: www.catholicherald.co.uk [Accessed on: 23 December 2023]

[1840] *German 'Synodal Path' calls for blessing of same-sex couples, women's ordination* [2022] [Online] Available at: www.lifesitenews.com [Accessed on: 23 December 2023]

[1841] *Archbishop of Algiers says Catholics 'must abandon the idea that we have to evangelize'* [2022] [Online] Available at: www.lifesitenews.com [Accessed on: 23 December 2023]

of Catholics — especially non-official Catholics — has increased since the agreement, which was not respected in its terms.[1842]

22nd February

Archbishop Stanislaw Gądecki, the President of the Polish Bishops' Conference, wrote an open letter to Bishop Georg Bätzing, the President of the German Bishops' Conference, warning about the dangers to the Faith presented by *Der Synodale Weg* — The Synodal Way:

> I would like to express my deep concern and anxiety regarding the information that has been recently received from some spheres of the Catholic Church in Germany [....] I look with unease at the actions of the German 'synodal path' so far. Observing its fruits, one can get the impression that the Gospel is not always the basis for reflection [....] One of the temptations in the Church today is to constantly compare Jesus' teaching with the current developments in psychology and the social sciences. If something in the Gospel does not agree with the current state of knowledge in these sciences, the disciples, wanting to save the Master from being compromised in the eyes of his contemporaries, try to 'update' the Gospel. The temptation to 'modernise' concerns in a particular way the sphere of sexual identity. It is forgotten, however, that the state of scientific knowledge changes frequently and sometimes dramatically, e.g., due to paradigm shifts. Changeability is inherent in the very nature of science, which has only a fragment of all possible knowledge. Discovering errors and analysing them is the driving force of progress in science. [....] Faithful to the Church's teaching, we should not yield to the pressures of the world or to the patterns of the dominant culture since this can lead to moral and spiritual corruption. Let us avoid the repetition of worn-out slogans, and standard demands such as the abolition of celibacy, the priesthood of women, communion for the divorced, and the blessing of same-sex unions. The 'updating' of the definition of marriage in the EU Charter of Fundamental Rights is no reason to tamper with the Gospel.[1843]

24th February

During an interview with the heterodox UK catholic newspaper *The Tablet*, Archbishop Arthur Roche, the Prefect of the Congregation for Divine Worship and the Discipline of the Sacraments, criticised the resurgence of the Latin Mass and the promotion of the pre-conciliar Faith as incompatible with Vatican II: 'The promotion to return to what existed before the Second Vatican Council couldn't be tolerated because the Council had changed the way in which we're going forward. That's just a simple matter.'[1844]

25th February

In a guest article for the daily German newspaper *Fuldaer Zeitung*, Archbishop Ludwig Schick of Bamberg supported the end of mandatory priestly celibacy and for the ordination of women,

> it is just as important for the reform of the Church that women take on even more leadership offices — also in pastoral ministries [....] Women have to come in, married people have to come in, and celibates have to come in. Then sources of error could also be discovered sooner.[1845]

26th February

Bishop Rudolf Voderholzer of Regensburg strictly implemented the directives from Cardinal Roche's *Responsa Ad Dubia*. As well as banning the celebration of the traditional

[1842]*Henan's Msgr Zhang Weizhu in prison for 9 months* [2022] [Online] Available at: www.asianews.it [Accessed on: 23 December 2023]

[1843]*Letter of Fraternal Concern from the Episcopate's President regarding the German 'Synodal Path'* [2022] [Online] Available at: www.episkopat.pl [Accessed on: 27 December 2023]

[1844]Lamb, C [2022] *Arthur Roche: prefect under pressure* [Online] Available at: www.thetablet.co.uk [Accessed on: 27 December 2023]

[1845]Haynes, M [2022] *German archbishop says female deacons, 'married priests' needed to help solve 'error' in the Church* [Online] Available at: www.lifesitenews.com [Accessed on: 23 December 2023]

Latin Mass in parish churches in the Diocese of Regensburg, Bishop Voderholze also banned the traditional celebration of Baptism and Extreme Unction.[1846]

2nd March

Cardinal Mario Grech, the Secretary General of the Synod of Bishops appointed by Pope Francis in 2019, praised the German *Der Synodale Weg* despite it advocating the ordination of women, the blessing of homosexual bondings and changing doctrine on homosexuality. Cardinal Mario Grech described the *Der Synodale Weg* as a

> synodal experience on a national level…Synodality is considered an important dimension of the Church, and so every Church, even a local, a particular Church is encouraged to assume this synodal style. Yet every synod has its own level of importance.[1847]

4th March

Bishop Gustavo Zanchetta, appointed by Pope Francis in 2013 and defended by the Supreme Pontiff when allegations were first made against him in 2015, was sentenced to four and half years in prison after having been found guilty of sexually abusing two seminarians.[1848] One of Zancetta's survivors testified,

> He always bragged about being a friend of the Pope and that he talked to him about us. That put pressure on us, because he said, 'I can close this seminary,' [and] 'Don't contradict me because I'm the bishop.'[…] We were practically nothing to him. He also discriminated against seminarians for being fat or for being 'old'; there were 30-year-old seminarians and he treated them like old men who were useless.[1849]

7th March

In an interview with *The New York Times* Sister Nathalie Becquart, appointed by Pope Francis as the first female member of the Roman Curia with synodal voting rights, admitted that the Supreme Pontiff planned to attack the *munus regendi* — the office of governing — of the priesthood instituted by our Lord:

> The vision of Pope Francis, through this synod, is to get rid of a clerical church and move to a synodal church — to disconnect participation in the leadership of the church from ordination.[1850]

9th March

The Holy See announced that Pope Francis had deposed Bishop Daniel Fernández Torres of the Diocese of Arecibo in Puerto Rico. Bishop Torres had publicly opposed COVID vaccine mandates being imposed by fellow Puerto Rican bishops, refusing to sign a joint statement announcing that the faithful would be segregated at Mass based on their COVID-19 vaccination status. In a statement Bishop Torres explained,

> No process has been made against me, nor have I been formally accused of anything, and simply one day the apostolic delegate verbally communicated to me that Rome was asking me to resign. A successor of the apostles is now being replaced without even undertaking what would be a due canonical process to remove a parish priest. I was informed that I had committed no crime but that I supposedly had not been obedient

---

[1846]Hall, K [2022] *Another German bishop all but eliminates the Traditional Latin Mass in his diocese* [Online] Available at: www.lifesitenews.com [Accessed on: 23 December 2023]

[1847]Brockhaus, H [2022] *Cardinal Grech: Synod on Synodality 'is not sociological analysis of the Church'* [Online] Available at: www.catholicnewsagency.com [Accessed on: 29 December 2023

[1848]*Argentinian bishop previously defended by Pope found guilty of sexually abusing seminarians* [2022] [Online] Available at: www.lifesitenews.com [Accessed on: 23 December 2023]

[1849]*'We Were Practically Nothing to Him,' Ex-Seminarian Says of Bishop Zanchetta's Abusive Behavior* [2022] [Online] Available at: www.ncregister.com [Accessed on: 23 December 2023]

[1850]Haynes, M [2022] *Pope Francis is using Synod to separate Church 'leadership' from 'ordination': liberal Vatican nun* [Online] Available at: www.lifesitenews.com [Accessed on: 29 December 2023]

to the pope nor had I been in sufficient communion with my brother bishops of Puerto Rico. 'It was suggested to me that if I resigned from the diocese I would remain at the service of the Church in case at some time I was needed in some other position; an offer that in fact proves my innocence. However, I did not resign because I did not want to become an accomplice of a totally unjust action and that even now I am reluctant to think that it could happen in our Church. I deeply regret that in the Church where mercy is so much preached, in practice some lack a minimum sense of justice. I express my communion in the Catholic faith, with the Pope and my brothers in the episcopate, despite my perplexity at an incomprehensible arbitrariness.'

Archbishop Héctor Aguer, Archbishop Emeritus of La Plata in Argentina, issued a statement in support of Bishop Torres, accusing the Vatican under Pope Francis of being more concerned with imposing the agenda of the New World Order than proclaiming the Gospel.[1851]

The bishops of the Nordic Bishops' Conference — including the bishops of Sweden, Denmark, Norway, Finland, and Iceland — wrote an open letter to Bishop Georg Bätzing, appointed by Pope Francis and the president of the German Bishops' Conference. Expressing their alarm at the direction of the *Der Synodale Weg*, the Nordic bishops cautioned against 'capitulation to the Zeitgeist' and the resulting 'impoverishment of the content of our faith.'

It has ever been the case that true reforms in the Church have set out from Catholic teaching founded on divine Revelation and authentic Tradition, to defend it, expound it, and translate it credibly into lived life — not from capitulation to the Zeitgeist. How fickle the Zeigeist is, is something we verify on a daily basis.[1852]

11th March

K-TV, the German Catholic television agency, broadcast an interview with Cardinal George Pell, former prefect of the Secretariat for the Economy, in which he called for the CDF to investigate Cardinal Jean-Claude Hollerich and Bishop Georg Bätzing, for their 'wholesale and explicit rejection of the Catholic Church's teaching on sexual ethics.' Cardinal Pell also criticised the German *Der Synodale Weg*:

The Catholic Church is not a loose federation where different national synods or gatherings and prominent leaders are able to reject essential elements of the Apostolic Tradition and remain undisturbed. This must not become a normal and tolerated situation. Catholic unity around Christ and His teaching requires unity on the major elements in the hierarchy of truths. This rejection is a rupture, not compatible with the ancient teaching of Scripture and the Magisterium, not compatible with any legitimate doctrinal developments.[1853]

13th March

The pro-homosexual Cardinal Marx of Munich, appointed by Pope Francis to the Council of Cardinal Advisers, celebrated a Mass for the *Munich Queer Community* marking '20 years of queer worship and pastoral care.' During his homily Cardinal Marx launched a thinly veiled attack against the Church's doctrine on homosexuality:

[The Catholic Church has] many limits that once had a meaning, but are now disturbing since they no longer reflect what was actually intended by him [Christ]. [...] I desire an inclusive Church. A Church that includes all who want to walk the way of Jesus. Christ speaks in a special way against those who exclude. He wants to invite everyone with

[1851]Wolfe, R [2022] *Pope Francis abruptly removes faithful bishop who opposed COVID vaccine mandates* [Online] Available at: www.lifesitenews.com [Accessed on: 30 December 2023]
[1852]*Nordic Catholic bishops: German 'Synodal Way' fills us with worry* [2022] [Online] Available at: www.catholicnewsagency.com [Accessed on: 3 January 2024]
[1853]Pentin, E [2022] *Cardinal Pell Calls on Vatican to Correct 2 Senior European Bishops for Rejecting Church's Sexual Ethics* [Online] Available at: www.ncregister.com [Accessed on: 31 December 2023]

the primacy of love…the kingdom of God is to discover that God is love — in all its dimensions, in the question of what we have to say about sexuality and what we have to say about people's relationships. All human relationships must be marked by the primacy of Love. Then they can be accepted by God.[1854]

16th March

Bishop Georg Bätzing, President of the German Bishops' Conference, sent a letter in response to the criticisms of *Der Synodale Weg* by Archbishop Dr Stanisław Gądecki, President of the Polish Bishops' Conference. Rejecting the criticism that the German Synodal Way was dependent on psychology and social sciences rather than on Holy Scripture, Bishop Georg Bätzing retorted that *Der Synodale Weg* had the support of Pope Francis:

We do not walk the path of conversion and renewal carelessly and certainly not outside the universal Church. Several times I was able to speak about the Synodal Path with Pope Francis. Above all, however, we are walking the Synodal Path, as Pope Francis expressly urged us to do in his letter to the pilgrim people of God in Germany, not only as a search 'for a frank response to the present situation', but as a spiritual path requesting guidance from the Holy Spirit.[1855]

28th March

Bishop Georg Bätzing, President of the German Bishops' Conference, sent a letter in response to the criticisms of *Der Synodale Weg* by the Nordic Bishops' Conference. Rejecting their concerns as not corresponding to the 'actual deliberations, discussions, and decisions of our Synodal Way', Bishop Georg Bätzing attacked the notion of the Deposit of Faith:

I would also like to make it clear here that the unchangeable and unalterable *depositum fidei* [deposit of faith] must not be understood in such a way that every ecclesiastical practice, every regulation and every social form of Church, which have been developed in the course of history and under very specific circumstances of time, of themselves already represent this unchangeable depositum.[1856]

1st April

Pro-homosexuality Archbishop Malcolm McMahon of Liverpool, appointed by Pope Francis in 2014, told *LifeSiteNews* that he had 'no intention' of canceling the LGBTQ+ Mass held at St. Wilfrid's parish, Widnes. In response to the question, *if the Mass would be an endorsement of LGBT ideology, or, in contrast, a promotion of Catholic teaching on sexuality, chastity, conversion of heart, and the defense of marriage between man and woman?* Archbishop McMahon replied:

I note the comments you make, but I have no intention of asking Fr. Mark Moran to cancel this Mass. I would direct you to Pope Francis' comment that 'the LGBTQ+ community are at the heart of the church.'[1857]

In April 2021, in response to the CDF's *Responsum* to a dubium regarding the blessing of the unions of persons of the same sex Archbishop McMahon focused on the 'hurt' caused to the LGBT community rather than on the Divine Truth about homosexual sex acts safeguarded by the CDF:

[1854]Haynes, M [2022] *Cdl. Marx offers anniversary Mass for 'Munich Queer Community,' calls for 'primacy of love'* [Online] Available at: www.lifesitenews.com [Accessed on: 30 December 2023]
[1855]*Letter by Bishop Bätzing in response to the letter by Archbishop Gadecki, President of the Polish Bishops' Conference, on the Synodal Path* [2022] [Online] Available at: www.dbk.de [Accessed on: 3 January 2023]
[1856]*German Catholic bishops' leader replies to Nordic bishops' 'Synodal Way' critique* [2022] [Online] Available at: www.catholicnewsagency.com [Accessed on: 3 January 2024]
[1857]Haynes, M [2022] *English archbishop says he has 'no intention' of canceling LGBT Mass* [Online] Available at: www.lifesitenews.com [Accessed on: 1 January 2024]

The recent response by the CDF to a dubium on the blessing of same-sex unions has caused some hurt amongst the faithful of the archdiocese and beyond. I have received correspondence myself on the issue, with one father writing in a letter that his son, who is gay, 'is suffering because he has read about the recent pronouncement.' I am sure that the sentiment of this parent will echo the sentiments of many parents, and I have no doubt that this suffering is felt acutely. I also know that some of you will have heard similar sentiments from people you minister to and, perhaps, you have felt it yourselves. It is important therefore that we reach out to all our LGBT+ brothers and sisters, to show them that they have a place at the heart of our Church, and our archdiocese.[1858]

8th April

The Archdiocese of Turin instructed the parish priest of the Stigmata of San Francesco d'Assisi church that it was permissible for a transgender woman who identifies as a male to receive the sacrament of confirmation with a name that corresponds to her new 'sex'. The archdiocesan curia informed Don Antonio Borio:

Confirm the person with their new name but record the natural baptismal name in the register, adding at the bottom the date and protocol number of the sentence of the civil court which certifies the occurrence of the sexual reassignment.[1859]

The Archdiocese of Turin's instruction to Don Borio is contrary to Church doctrine (CCC 2297; 2333; 2393).

12th April

A fraternal open correction of the German bishops regarding *Der Synodale Weg* [The Synodal Way] was made public, signed by over one hundred cardinals, archbishops and bishops from around the world, including cardinals Arinze, Burke, Napier, Pell, Ruini and Zen. The fraternal correction warned of the danger of schism, accusing the German bishops of abandoning Divine Revelation for sociology and fashionable political agendas, and presenting a false understanding of religious freedom and conscience, among other things:

While they display a patina of religious ideas and vocabulary, the German Synodal Path documents seem largely inspired not by Scripture and Tradition — which, for the Second Vatican Council, are 'a single sacred deposit of the Word of God' — but by sociological analysis and contemporary political, including gender, ideologies. They look at the Church and her mission through the lens of the world rather than through the lens of the truths revealed in Scripture and the Church's authoritative Tradition.[1860]

13th April

During his Chrism Mass homily, Bishop Stephen Chow S.J. of Hong Kong, China, appointed by Pope Francis in 2021, expressed his hope that the Church will 'one day' ordain women. The Hong Kong diocese did not clarify whether Bishop Chow was referring to the ordination of women as deacons or priests.[1861]

16th April

Bishop Georg Bätzing of Limburg, appointed by Pope Francis in 2026 and president of the German bishops' conference, responded to the fraternal correction from over

---

[1858]*Catholic Record. 18 April 2021* [2022] [Online] Available at: www.liverpoolmetrocathedral.org. uk [Accessed on: 1 January 2024]

[1859]Zambrano, A [2022] *"I baptise you female and confirm you male." Turin Church break rules for trans* [Online] Available at: www.newdailycompass.com [Accessed on: 3 January 2024]

[1860]*Bishops sign letter warning that Germany's 'Synodal Path' could lead to schism* [2022] [Online] Available at: www.catholicnewsagency.com [Accessed on: 3 January 2024]

[1861]*Hong Kong bishop 'hopes' for women's ordination 'one day'* [2022] [Online] Available at: www. pillarcatholic.com [Accessed on: 3 January 2024]

100 cardinals, archbishops and bishops. Rejecting the criticisms that *Der Synodale Weg* was replacing Divine Revelation with sociology thereby bringing schism to the Church, Bishop Bätzing again claimed that the German synodal process had the support of Pope Francis:

> I was able to speak several times with the Holy Father about the Synodal Path. In his *Letter to the pilgrim people of God in Germany*, he has asked us explicitly to walk on this path as on a search for 'a frank response to the present situation'.[1862]

18th April

The Vatican, with the Italian Bishops' Conference, held a papal concert for 80,000 young people in St. Peter's Square, featuring the teenage 'gay icon' Blanco. Riccardo Fabbriconi, aka Blanco, shot to fame when he won the Sanremo 2022 music festival with the sexually suggestive song *'Brividi'* [Chills], a duo he sang as a 19 year old teenager with a 29-year-old man. Pope Francis personally introduced the pop concert.[1863]

21st April

During an interview on the UK *Catholic Herald's Merely Catholic* podcast Cardinal Pell again expressed criticism of the German *Der Synodale Weg* and Bishop Bätzing and Cardinal Hollerich. Cardinal Pell criticised the German Synodal Way

> [for thinking] that by adopting the teachings of the world around them, they are going to help Church. They're heading and facing in the wrong direction, they're making a bad situation worse. We appeal to Christ, we appeal to Revelation, to our Judaeo-Christian tradition, not to sociology or medicine.

Cardinal Pell renewed his criticism of Cardinal Hollerich for teaching heresy about homosexuality, appointed by Pope Francis the Relator General of the 2023 Synod on Synodality:

> I can't see how it's possible that a man who teaches explicit heresy, for example, on sexual morality, could possibly be the relator, the principle driver of the synod. It would be absolutely unprecedented in Catholic history for a man who's explicitly heretical on some particular point to have a position like that. Undoubtedly, the evil one, the devil, will be at work in the synodal process to take it off the paths.[1864]

28th April

A group of Swiss diocesan priests, led by Fr. Franz Imhof and Fr. Dr. Roland Graf, published a statement announcing they would not sign the new mandatory code of conduct because it 'violates the doctrine and discipline of the Catholic Church.' The new Code of Conduct was issued by Joseph Bonnemain, the pro-homosexuality bishop of the Diocese of Chur, appointed by Pope Francis in 2021. The priests objected that the code of conduct made it mandatory for priest to agree to 'refrain from sweeping negative assessments of allegedly unbiblical behaviour based on sexual orientation.' They also objected to the prohibition on actively taking up during pastoral conversations 'topics related to sexuality, and to refrain from offensive questioning about intimate life and relationship status'. The priests objected that such a prohibition would prevent them from asking necessary questions during marriage preparation that ensure the couple agree with the Church's teaching that marriage is a 'sacramental community of life and love between a man and a woman.' They also pointed out that this prohibition would stop seminary staff from asking questions necessary to ensure candidates

---

[1862]*Head of German bishops' conference defends controversial 'Synodal Path' against critics* [2022] [Online] Available at: www.lifesitenews.com [Accessed on: 3 January 2024]

[1863]Knuffke, L [2022] *Vatican hosts youth concert with pro-LGBT singer, Pope Francis makes appearance* [Online] Available at: www.lifesitenews.com [Accessed on: 3 January 2024]

[1864]Wolfe, R [2022] *Cardinal Pell: Pope 'will have to speak' against dissident German Synod* [Online] Available at: www.lifesitenews.com [Accessed on: 3 January 2024]

were not afflicted with 'deep-seated homosexual tendencies', or supported so-called 'homosexual culture'.[1865]

3rd May

In an interview with the Italian daily newspaper *Corriere Della Sera* Pope Francis again expressed admiration for the abortionist and left-wing politician Emma Bonino. Though Bonino was responsible for over 10,000 illegal abortions, some conducted in her apartment, and the legalisation of abortion in Italy, Pope Francis said, 'I have great respect for Emma Bonino: I don't share her ideas but she knows Africa better than anyone. In front of this woman I doff my hat'.

Pope Francis praised Bonino in 2016, calling her one of Italy's 'forgotten greats', receiving her later in the year in a private audience.[1866]

Archbishop Samuel Aquila of Denver wrote again to Bishop Georg Bätzing, the head of the German bishops' conference, accusing *Der Synodale Weg* of repudiating the Deposit of Faith:

> The Synodal Path does not simply address 'structural' concerns: it challenges, and in some instances repudiates, the deposit of faith. Documents of the Synodal Path cannot be read in any other way than as raising the most serious questions about the nature and binding authority of divine revelation, the nature and efficacy of the sacraments, and the truth of Catholic teaching on human love and sexuality [....] Why must Catholic teaching on fundamental issues of doctrine and the moral life change because German bishops have failed to teach effectively and govern honestly? The Church's faith did not lead to the clergy abuse scandal!' [...] There can be no concordat of mutual acceptance between the truth of divine revelation and Catholic doctrine, on the one hand, and the distorted anthropology of today's advanced secular culture, which promotes an increasingly dysfunctional sexuality, on the other. There is nothing salvific in blessing destructive thought and behaviour. To surrender to the Zeitgeist is not a matter of reading the signs of the times; it is a betrayal of the Gospel.[1867]

6th May

The General Secretariat of the Synod of Bishops led by Francis' appointee pro-homosexuality Cardinal Mario Grech, posted on its website three testimonies celebrating homosexual 'couples' adopting children. The first testimony praised two homosexual men for adopting a boy who otherwise would have been aborted. The second described the 'marriage' of two homosexual men who adopted disabled teenagers as 'The story of a sexuality that gives life'. And the third testimony celebrated two homosexual men as a 'married' couple who adopted children from impoverished countries to improve their lives. The post concluded with an attack on the Church's teaching on homosexuality:

> Matthew's greatest sadness is that he has to hide his sexuality in order to keep his job in a church institution and that he does not feel welcome in the Catholic Church precisely because of his sexuality which he considers God-given, and this despite his attempt to love the poor and destitute through his pro-life decision to adopt.[1868]

8th May

The militant Catholic LGBT group *Outreach* announced that its founder Fr. James Martin S.J. had received a letter from Pope Francis in response to three questions he submitted to the Supreme Pontiff. Instead of re-iterating the call to chastity and that under no

---

[1865]*Swiss Catholic priests refuse to sign new diocesan code of conduct, claim it contains 'LGBT ideology'* [2022] [Online] Available at: www.lifesitenews.com [Accessed on: 3 January 2024]

[1866]Haynes, M [2022] *Pope Francis again praises notorious abortionist Emma Bonino: 'I have great respect for' her* [Online] Available at: www.lifesitenews.com [Accessed on: 4 January 2024]

[1867]*Archbishop Aquila: German synodal path repudiates the deposit of faith* [2022] [Online] Available at: www.catholicnewsagency.com [Accessed on: 4 January 2024]

[1868]*Three testimonies of homosexual couples* [2022] [Online] Available at: www.synodresources.org [Accessed on: 4 January 2024]

circumstances can homosexual sex acts be approved because they are 'intrinsically disordered' (CCC 2357-2358) Pope Francis expressed unconditional approval of active homosexuals:

> *Outreach*: What would you say is the most important thing for LGBT people to know about God? Pope Francis: God is Father and he does not disown any of his children. And 'the style' of God is 'closeness, mercy and tenderness.' Along this path you will find God [....]
> *Outreach*: What do you say to an LGBT Catholic who has experienced rejection from the church? Pope Francis: I would have them recognise it not as 'the rejection of the church,' but instead of 'people in the church.' The church is a mother and calls together all her children. Take for example the parable of those invited to the feast: 'the just, the sinners, the rich and the poor, etc.' [Matthew 22:1-15; Luke 14:15-24]. A 'selective' church, one of 'pure blood,' is not Holy Mother Church, but rather a sect.[1869]

13th May

Vatican News reported that Cardinal Parolin, the Secretary of State, told reporters he hoped that Cardinal Zen's arrest by the Chinese communists should not be read as '"a disavowal" of the agreement between the Holy See and the People's Republic of China on the appointments of bishops, originally agreed in 2018 and later extended for an additional two years': 'Cardinal Parolin said, "The most concrete hope is that initiatives such as this one will not complicate the already complex and not simple path of dialogue."'[1870]

15th May

An Italian archbishop, an Italian bishop and one Maltese archbishop, in partnership with dissident Catholic LGBT organisations, marked International Day Against Homophobia and Transphobia through participating in ecumenical prayer vigils. Archbishop Corrado Lorefice of Palermo, appointed by Francis in 2015, composed a prayer urging people to welcome unrepentant homosexual persons by assuming and imitating 'the style of God that Jesus of Nazareth manifested to us: he leaves no one behind, no one is a stranger to him, all reach out, all welcome, all are recipients of his compassionate love, of the quivering of his fatherly womb.' Bishop Enrico Solmi of Parma also attended the ecumenical vigils. During his homily at the LGBT vigil pro-homosexuality Archbishop Charles Scicluna of Malta exhorted parents to unconditionally accept their homosexual children,

> Accept your children as God the Father has done. Jesus is looking at your children – as he looks at each and every one of us – when he tells us that he is giving us a new commandment to love one another.[1871]

17th May

Pro-homosexuality Archbishop Heiner Koch, appointed by Pope Francis in 2015, asked for forgiveness for the Church's discrimination against people with the disordered homosexual inclination. During a pro-LGBT prayer service at the Protestant Twelve Apostles church in Berlin, Archbishop Koch went on to say that 'homophobia' is an 'unholy line of tradition in the Church'. He also announced that he had appointed commissioners in each of the 35 parishes of the Archdiocese of Berlin to fight discrimination against homosexual persons.[1872]

[1869]Martin, J [2022] *A mini-interview with the Holy Father* [Online] Available at: www.outreach.faith [Accessed on: 4 January 2024]
[1870]Knuffke, L [2022] *Vatican says Cardinal Zen's arrest should not affect deal with China on appointment of bishops* [Online] Available at: www.lifesitenews.com [Accessed on: 4 January 2024]
[1871]Haynes, M [2022] *Italian bishops join dissident 'Catholic' groups for ecumenical LGBT 'prayer vigils'* [Online] Available at: www.lifesitenews.com [Accessed on: 4 January 2024]
[1872]*Berlin Archbishop 'Apologises' For Catholic Morality* [2022] [Online] Available at: www.gloria.tv; *Berlin archbishop asks forgiveness for homophobia in the church* [Online] Available at: cruxnow.com [Accessed on: 4 January 2024]

18th May

Bishop Felipe J. Estevez of the Diocese of St. Augustine, Florida, issued a decree fully implementing *Traditionis Custodes*. Bishop Estevez banned the traditional Latin Mass at Jacksonville's Basilica of the Immaculate Conception and effectively banned most traditional rite sacraments. The celebration of the traditional Latin Mass was to two churches where it is already celebrated, though one of them only celebrated the traditional Latin Mass on the third Sunday of the month.[1873]

20th May

Archbishop Salvatore Cordileone of San Francisco announced that he had instructed militant pro-abortion Nancy Pelosi, Democrat Speaker of the House, not to present herself for Holy Communion in his diocese:

> As you have not publicly repudiated your position on abortion, and continue to refer to your Catholic faith in justifying your position and to receive Holy Communion, that time has now come. Therefore, in light of my responsibility as the Archbishop of San Francisco to be 'concerned for all the Christian faithful entrusted to [my] care' (*Code of Canon Law*, can. 383, §1), by means of this communication I am hereby notifying you that you are not to present yourself for Holy Communion and, should you do so, you are not to be admitted to Holy Communion, until such time as you publicly repudiate your advocacy for the legitimacy of abortion and confess and receive absolution of this grave sin in the sacrament of Penance.[1874]

During an interview on MSNBC's *Morning Joe* TV show (24th May 2022) Nancy Pelosi rejected Archbishop Cordileone's instruction not to receive Holy Communion, arguing that abortion had been weaponised by the 'far right' which also opposed 'family planning, *in vitro fertilisation* (IVF), and contraception.' She also said,

> We just have to be prayerful, we have to be respectful. I come from a largely pro-life Italian American Catholic family, so I respect people's views about that, but I don't respect us foisting it onto others.[1875]

Nancy Pelosi went on to receive Holy Communion during Mass, at which Pope Francis presided, for the Solemnity of Saint Peter and Paul (29th June 2022), in St. Peter's Basilica. Witnesses reported that Nancy Pelosi was seated in the section reserved for diplomats, and received Communion. Following Mass Pope Francis was photographed enjoying a convivial meeting with Nancy Pelosi and her husband.[1876]

22nd May

During an interview with the German public-broadcasting radio station *Deutschlandfunk*, Bishop Georg Bätzing, appointed by Pope Francis in 2016 and president of the German Bishop's Conference, demanded changes to the Church's doctrine on homosexuality and the role of women. On issues around homosexuality Bishop Bätzing said: 'I will not discipline anyone who performs a blessing [blessing of homosexual bondings].... The teaching of the Catholic Church must be changed on these points.' On the 'ordination' of women he said:

> Can women be ordained priests? There I try to keep the balancing act in such a way that I say, I state, that is my task, what is the teaching of the Church, and at the same

---

[1873]Mangiaracina, E [2022] *Florida bishop cracks down on Latin Mass and sacraments in full conformity to Pope's directive* [Online] Available at: www.lifesitenews.com [Accessed on: 4 January 2024]
[1874]Archbishop Cordileone [2022] *Notification to the Speaker of the House of Representatives of the United States Congress Nancy Pelosi* [Online] Available at: www.sfarchdiocese.org [Accessed on: 4 January 2024]
[1875]Sadler, A [2022] *Pelosi responds to Holy Communion ban, says she doesn't respect 'foisting' pro-life views on others* [Online] Available at: www.lifesitenews.com [Accessed on: 4 January 2024]
[1876]Brockhaus, H [2022] *Nancy Pelosi reportedly receives Communion at papal Mass* [Online] Available at: www.catholicnewsagency.com [Accessed on: 4 January 2024]

time I perceive that this teaching no longer finds acceptance among the faithful, not only in a social context, among the faithful. The *sensus fidelium*, that is, the sense of the faithful continues. This is a sign that we must take up theologically and that leads to change. And that's what I'm committed to. So, I don't sit in the armchair and say this is the way it is now, but I really give a lot of my energy to that. And I believe that change will happen.[1877]

24th May

Pope Francis appointed pro-homosexuality Cardinal Matteo Maria Zuppi as the new president of the Italian Bishops Conference. The Rt. Rev Matteo Zuppi had been appointed bishop by Pope Francis in 2012, Archbishop of Bologna in 2015, and elevated to the Sacred College of Cardinals in 2019. In 2018 Archbishop Zuppi provided an introduction for the Italian translation of Father James Martin's pro-homosexuality book, *Building a Bridge: How the Catholic Church and the LGBT Community Can Enter Into a Relationship of Respect, Compassion and Sensitivity*. Archbishop Zuppi also wrote a preface in support of a pro-homosexuality book that called on the Church to change her doctrine on homosexuality. He wrote:

> But even in the case where a person leads a lifestyle contrary to God's law, should we not welcome him or her? What does it mean to welcome? Does it mean to justify? If Jesus had this criterion, before entering Zacchaeus' house he would have demanded his conversion.[1878]

The Hong Kong *Free Press* announced that the Diocese of Hong Kong had cancelled the annual Mass commemorating the Tiananmen Square Massacre, citing fears over the Beijing-imposed national security law. This marked the first time in thirty years that events in memory of the 10,000 people killed in Tiananmen Square would not be held. The Diocese of Hong Kong's cancellation of the Mass occurred in the context of the Chinese communists arresting Cardinal Joseph Zen and the secret Rome-Beijing pact.[1879]

27th May

German bishops gave Holy Communion to a Muslim and Protestant during Masses to celebrate 'Catholics Day'. Bishop Georg Bätzing of Limburg, appointed by Pope Francis in 2016 and chairman of the German bishops' conference, gave Holy Communion to Thomas de Maizière, a prominent Protestant. While Bishop Gebhard Fürst of Rottenburg-Stuttgart gave Holy Communion to Muhterem Aras, a Muslim politician.[1880]

29th May

Pope Francis announced his intention to create 21 new cardinals in the August consistory, including Bishop Robert McElroy of San Diego, notorious for his advocacy of homosexuality and his support for pro-abortion politician receiving Holy Communion. McElroy had been singled out to receive Pope Francis' favour, appointing him Bishop of San Diego in 2015, synod father for the 2019 Pan-Amazon Synod, and in 2021 appointing him a member of the Dicastery for Promoting Integral Human Development. In 2016 Bishop McElroy called for changes to the Catechism of the Catholic Church regarding

---

[1877]Haynes, M [2022] *Head of German bishops: Church teaching on homosexuality, female ordination 'must be changed'* [Online] Available at: www.lifesitenews.com [Accessed on: 4 January 2024]

[1878]Haynes, M [2022] *Pope Francis appoints pro-LGBT cardinal praised by top Freemason as president of Italian bishops' conference* [Online] Available at: www.lifesitenews.com [Accessed on: 4 January 2024]

[1879]Chau, C [2022] *Hong Kong Catholic group will not hold Tiananmen crackdown masses citing fears over national security law* [Online] Available at: www.hongkongfp.com [Accessed on: 4 January 2024]

[1880]Mangiaracina, E [2022] *German Catholic bishops give Eucharist to Muslim and Protestant while barring pro-life group* [Online] Available at: www.lifesitenews.com [Accessed on: 5 January 2024]

homosexuality, including removing the use of the phrase 'intrinsically disordered'.[1881] In 2017 Bishop McElroy concelebrated an LGBT Mass with his auxiliary, Bishop John Dolan, involving openly homosexual politicians and 'married' same-sex partners with children.[1882] In 2021 Bishop McElroy signed a statement with 7 other US Catholic bishops encouraging young people to identify as homosexuals, under the slogan, 'God is on your side'.[1883] Bishop McElroy has consistently insisted that abortion should not be the preeminent issue for Catholics in US elections, arguing in 2020:

> It is not Catholic that abortion is the preeminent issue that we face as a world in Catholic social teaching. It is not. For us to say that, particularly when we omit the pope's articulation of this question, I think is a grave disservice of our people.[1884]

Bishop Michael Barber, S.J., of Oakland criticised Cardinal-elect McElroy of thinking 'abortion is not wrong enough that you need say or do anything about it or interact with the politicians who are publicly promoting it.'[1885] Cardinal Gerhard Müller criticised the appointment of Bishop McElroy to the sacred College of Cardinals because he has 'taken stances on life, on family … on homosexuality that are at odds with the Church's teaching…[with a] horrifying record on homosexuality and abortion.… Nobody can understand this appointment.'[1886]

1st June

The Vatican announced that Pope Francis had appointed 22 new members to Congregation for Divine Worship and the Discipline of the Sacraments, including anti-tradition, pro-homosexuality cardinals, such as Blaise Cupich, Kevin Farrell, Luis Tagle, Mario Grech.[1887]

2nd June

Pope Francis elevated pro-homosexuality Archbishop Leonardo Steiner, O.F.M., of Manaus, Brazil, to the sacred College of Cardinals. Cardinal-elect Steiner publicly supported homosexual civil bondings, saying, 'There needs to be a dialog on the rights of shared life between people of the same sex who decide to live together. They need legal support from society.'[1888]

5th June

During his homily for the solemnity of Pentecost Pope Francis again referred to the Holy Spirit as the 'author of division' in the Church:

> And finally, oddly, the Holy Spirit is the author of division, of ruckus, of a certain disorder. Think of the morning of Pentecost: He is the author … he creates division of languages and attitudes … it was a ruckus, that! Yet at the same time, he is the author of harmony. He divides with the variety of charisms, but it is a false division, because true

---

[1881]Eli, B [2016] *San Diego bishop builds gay agenda from papal spin* [Online] Available at: www.churchmilitant.com [Accessed on: 5th January 2024]
[1882]Baklinski, P [2017] *Pro-gay bishop pushes homosexual agenda at LGBT 'Family Mass'* [Online] Available at: www.lifesitenews.com [Accessed on: 5 January 2024]
[1883]Baklinski, P [2021] *Cardinal joins 7 US Catholic bishops in affirming youths who identify as LGBT: 'God is on your side'* [Online] Available at: www.lifesitenews.com [Accessed on: 5 January 2024]
[1884]Rousselle, C [2020] *Bishop McElroy: Abortion and climate change both crucial, voters must be prudent* [Online] Available at: www.catholicnewsagency.com/ [Accessed on: 5 January 2024]
[1885]Summers, J [2022] *California bishop blasts Cardinal-elect McElroy for thinking abortion 'not wrong enough' to discuss* [Online] Available at: www.lifesitenews.com [Accessed on: 6 January 2024]
[1886]Hall, K [2022] *'Nobody can understand this': Cdl. Müller criticizes promotion of 'politician' Bishop McElroy* [Online] Available at: www.lifesitenews.com [Accessed on: 6 January 2024]
[1887]Haynes, M [2022] *Pope Francis appoints pro-LGBT, anti-Latin Mass cardinals to Vatican liturgy office* [Online] Available at: www.lifesitenews.com [Accessed on: 5 January 2024]
[1888]Knuffke, L [2022] *Pope announces pro-LGBT Brazilian bishop will be elevated to cardinal* [Online] Available at: www.lifesitenews.com [Accessed on: 5 January 2024]

division is part of harmony. He creates division with charisms and he creates harmony with all this division. This is the richness of the Church.[1889]

On the 15th March 2013 the Supreme Pontiff referred to the Holy Spirit as 'an Apostle of Babel'.[1890]

6th June

In his address to the Dicastery for Interreligious Dialogue Pope Francis continued expressing his implicit religious indifferentism exhorting those engaged in interreligious dialogue to leave their non-Christian interlocutors as they are rather than 'colonising' them:

> Being convivial with someone also means imagining and building a happy future with the other. Indeed, conviviality echoes the desire for communion that resides in the heart of every human being, thanks to which all people can speak to each other, exchange projects and outline a future together. Conviviality unites socially, but without colonising the other and preserving his or her identity. In this sense, it has political relevance as an alternative to social fragmentation and conflict.[1891]

8th June

The Franciscans of the German province elected Fr. Markus Fuhrmann, who openly admitted his homosexuality, to be their provincial superior. During an interview after his election, Fr. Fuhrmann expressed his desire to change Church doctrine on homosexuality to accord with his choices:

> I would like to promote seeing this as an opportunity that we as a church are colourful, that the church is also queer, that this is what God wants, that this corresponds to the diversity of creation and is therefore quite normal…[Catholic sexual morality that] has been officially taught up to now does not serve life.[1892]

10th June

Pope Francis announced that he was replacing the staunchly pro-life, pro-family Bishop Thomas J. Olmsted of the Diocese of Phoenix with the militant pro-homosexuality Bishop John P. Dolan, auxiliary bishop of San Diego. As parish priest of a 'scandalously pro-LGBT parish' Bishop Dolan employed an openly homosexual man as pastoral associate and director of young adult ministry and parish's social media pages display a cross superimposed on a rainbow flag.[1893]

11th June

Fr. Gabriele Davalli publicly 'blessed' a homosexual bonding in the church of San Lorenzo, Bologna, with the knowledge of pro-homosexuality Cardinal Archbishop Matteo Zuppi, fast tracked appointee of Pope Francis. The homosexuals Pietro Morotti and Giacomo Spagnoli were first registered in a civil union and then they were welcomed by a large group of priests in San Lorenzo to celebrate Mass for the pair during which Fr. Gabriele Davalli blessed the 'couple'. The Mass of Thanksgiving was accompanied by the 'typical paraphernalia of weddings: the flowers, the formal suits,

[1889]Pope Francis [2022] *Santa Messa nella Domenica di Pentecoste, 05.06.2022* [Online] Available at: www.press.vatican.va [Accessed on: 4 January 2024]

[1890]Pope Francis [2013] *Audience with the Cardinals* [Online] Available at: www.vatican.va [Accessed on: 10 October 2022]

[1891]Haynes, M [2022] *Pope Francis emphasises friendliness in religious dialogue over need for conversion* [Online] Available at: www.lifesitenews.com [Accessed on: 5 January 2024]

[1892]Gomes, J [2022] *Franciscans vote for an openly gay provincial* [Online] Available at: www.churchmilitant.com [Accessed on: 5 January 2022]

[1893]Bingham, J [2022] *Pope Francis appoints pro-LGBT bishop to replace faithful Phoenix prelate* [Online] Available at: www.lifesitenews.com [Accessed on: 5 January 2024]

the songs, the photographer and the two 'newlyweds', protagonists of the celebration, in the front row.' Pietro Morotti and Giacomo Spagnoli are members of the Catholic LGBT group *in cammino* [on the way]. After Holy Communion Fr. Gabriele Davalli presented the 'couple' with an apron. When asked, *and was the Archbishop of Bologna Matteo Maria Zuppi aware of all this*? Fr. Gabriele Davalli replied 'Yes, I informed him myself'.[1894]

13th June

The UK heterodox newspaper *The Tablet* reported that Pope Francis told a divorced man who was now identifying as a homosexual person that he could receive Holy Communion:

> One of the group, Chris Speight, handed a letter about his life story to the Pope explaining that he is a divorced gay man who was previously married to a woman. Various priests, he said, had told him that he could not receive communion because he was divorced and because he was gay. As a result, for 26 years he didn't go to Church. 'The last two words that Pope Francis said to me as he shook my hand was "take communion"', Mr Speight said with tears in his eyes.[1895]

14th June

During an interview with editors of European Jesuit journals, Pope Francis again criticised Tradition and the faithful who upheld Tradition, referring to them disparagingly as 'restorers':

> It is very difficult to see spiritual renewal using old-fashioned criteria. We need to renew our way of seeing reality, of evaluating it. In the European Church I see more renewal in the spontaneous things that are emerging: movements, groups, new bishops who remember that there is a Council behind them. Because the Council that some pastors remember best is that of Trent. What I'm saying is not nonsense [....] Restorationism has come to gag the Council. The number of groups of 'restorers' – for example, in the United States there are many – is significant. An Argentine bishop told me that he had been asked to administer a diocese that had fallen into the hands of these 'restorers.' They had never accepted the Council. There are ideas, behaviours that arise from a restorationism that basically did not accept the Council. The problem is precisely this: in some contexts the Council has not yet been accepted. It is also true that it takes a century for a Council to take root. We still have forty years to make it take root, then![1896]

15th June

The Dicastery for Institutes of Consecrated Life and Societies of Apostolic Life issued a rescript signed by Pope Francis restricting the powers of bishops to establish religious institutes or societies. This move was seen as an attempt to prevent any new traditional institutes or societies being formed. From this date, in order to establish these communities bishops must seek the written permission of the Dicastery for Institutes of Consecrated Life and Societies of Apostolic Life.[1897]

16th June

During an interview with *Vatican News* Cardinal-elect Arthur Roche, Prefect of the Vatican's Dicastery for Divine Worship and Discipline of the Sacraments, sought to

---

[1894]Zambrano, A & Scrosati, L [2022] *First gay blessing in Italy, diocese of Italian bishops' president* [Online] Available at: www.newdailycompass.com [Accessed on: 5 January 2024]
[1895]Lamb, C [2022] *Pope apologises to Comboni survivors* [Online] Available at: www.thetablet.co.uk [Accessed on: 5 January 2024]
[1896]Spadaro, A [2022] *Pope Francis in Conversation with the Editors of European Jesuit Journals* [Online] Available at: www.laciviltacattolica.com [Accessed on: 5 January 2024]
[1897]Haynes, M [2022] *Pope restricts new traditional groups by ordering Vatican approval for associations of the faithful* [Online] Available at: www.lifesitenews.com [Accessed on: 5 January 2024]

justify Pope Francis' restrictions of the traditional Latin Mass. He decried faithful Catholics wanting to celebrate the traditional Latin Mass as resisting the liturgical changes mandated by the Second Vatican Council despite the fact that the Novus Ordo was not mandated by the Decree on the Liturgy, *Sacrosanctum Concilium*:

> And the resistance to this is quite a serious matter, which the Pope has pointed out in his document on the liturgy, *Traditionis Custodes*. So, all that is taking place is the regulation of the former liturgy of 1962 Missal by stopping the promotion of that, because it was clear that the Council, the Bishops of the Council, under the inspiration of the Holy Spirit, were putting forward a new liturgy for the vital life of the Church, for its vitality. And that's really very important. And to resist that is, is something that is really quite serious, too.[1898]

20th June

Pope Francis held a private audience with Fr. Richard Rohr, O.F.M., known for his advocacy of homosexuality and promotion of New Age pagan practices. Fr. Richard Rohr also explicitly expresses religious indifferentism, writing that the historical Jesus isn't necessary for salvation, but the 'spirit can also be found through the practices of other religions, like Buddhist meditation, or through communing with nature...."This is not heresy, universalism, or a cheap version of Unitarianism. This is the Cosmic Christ, who always was, who became incarnate in time, and who is still being revealed."'[1899]

22nd June

Pope Francis met a group of 'transgender' persons who presented themselves to the Supreme Pontiff as the sex opposite to their biological sex. The group was led by Sister Genevieve Jeanningros and Father Andrea Conocchia. Pope Francis praised Alessia Nobile – a 43-year-old man and prostitute who now presents himself as a woman — for writing an autobiography, saying 'You did well to write your story. Bravo!' Nobile recounted that Pope Francis told him to 'always be myself, but not to be wrapped up in prejudice against the Church.'[1900]

Pro-homosexuality Fr. James Martin S.J., recipient of many signs of approval and promotion by Pope Francis, posted on twitter that 'Homosexuality is not an "abnormal lifestyle choice." It is the way that God created a part of the human race.'[1901]

During an interview with the Canadian Catholic pro-life *LifeSiteNews* Cardinal Gerhard Müller, former head of the CDF, felt it necessary to affirm Church teaching that no one – not even the pope – could change the teaching of the Church on homosexuality:

> This is absolutely clear, and nobody can change the doctrine of our Catholic faith that homosexual behaviour is a grave sin.... And it is absolutely clear that for every priest, cardinal, and the pope, every bishop must be absolutely faithful to the revealed faith and to the natural law which is given to us. Nobody has authority to change or to falsify the revealed Catholic faith according to the Word of God and the doctrine of the Church.... What he [Fr. James Martin S.J.,] is doing, that is a heresy, absolutely heresy. Nobody can justify it.[1902]

23rd June

Argentinian news outlets reported that Pope Francis had appointed Javier Belda Iniesta, the canon lawyer who had defended Bishop Gustavo Zanchetta during his

---

[1898]Castellano Lubov, D [2022] *A conversation with future Cardinal Roche, Prefect of Divine Liturgy, Sacraments* [Online] Available at: www.vaticannews.va [Accessed on:5 January 2022]

[1899]Haynes, M [2022] *Pope Francis gives private audience to pro-LGBT priest known for pagan practices* [Online] Available at: www.lifesitenews.com [Accessed on: 5 January 2024]

[1900]Haynes, M [2022] *'We felt welcomed': Francis personally meets group of 'transgender' individuals in papal audience* [Online] Available at: www.lifesitenews.com [Accessed on: 5 January 2024]

[1901]Hall, K [2022] *Fr. James Martin says homosexuality is 'the way God created a part of the human race'* [Online] Available at: www.vaticannews.va [Accessed on:6 January 2022]

[1902]Wolfe, R [2022] *Cdl. Müller: 'Nobody can change' Catholic doctrine that homosexuality is 'grave sin'* [Online] Available at: www.lifesitenews.com [Accessed on: 6 January 2024]

ecclesiastical trial to investigate the priests, deacons and seminarians who had testified against Zanchetta during his civil trial. Zanchetta had been sentenced to four years and six months 'house arrest' for aggravated continuous sexual abuse of two former seminarians. A former seminarian said Pope Francis' appointment of Zanchetta's defence lawyer was seen as intimidation of the witnesses, 'they are trying to make them [the witnesses] understand that what they testified is not so; it is a kind of pressure… and they are afraid.'[1903]

26th June

In response to the U.S. Supreme Court overturning the federal abortion ruling Roe vs Wade, Fr. James Martin S.J., recipient of Pope Francis' patronage, expressed his dissent from the Church's doctrine on the absolute sanctity of human life from the moment of conception. Martin posted, 'a one-minute-old zygote is not the same as a nine-month-old baby about to be born'. He also implied that women's consciences must be given priority in deciding the morality of abortion, 'women have consciences that must be heard, listened to and respected.'[1904]

29th June

Pope Francis issued his apostolic letter *Desiderio desideravi* in which he sought to justify his restrictions on the celebration of the traditional Latin Mass. He further expressed his determination to get to a position where the *Novus Ordo* is the only liturgical Roman rite celebrated throughout the worldwide Church:

> …we cannot go back to that ritual form which the Council fathers, *cum Petro et sub Petro*, felt the need to reform, approving, under the guidance of the Holy Spirit and following their conscience as pastors, the principles from which was born the reform…. For this reason I wrote *Traditionis Custodes*, so that the Church may lift up, in the variety of so many languages, one and the same prayer capable of expressing her unity. As I have already written, I intend that this unity be re-established in the whole Church of the Roman Rite. (para 61).[1905]

On the Solemnity of St. Peter and St. Paul Bishop Paul Lei Shiyin of Diocese of Jiading, China, celebrated the 101st anniversary of the founding of the Chinese Communist Party. Pope Francis lifted his excommunication for being illicitly consecrated as part of the secret Vatican-Chinese deal. During his homily in the Cathedral of the Sacred Heart of Jesus in Leshan, Bishop Paul Lei Shiyin said, 'listen to the word of the Party, feel the grace of the Party, and follow the Party'. An anonymous Chinese source observed,

> it is no longer a question of listening to the Lord, of feeling his grace and following him. This is the root of the disease of the Chinese Church today, it is difficult to get away from the influence of ideology. Politics has entered the Church.

1st July

Militant pro-homosexuality Bishop John Stowe of Lexington, appointed by Pope Francis in 2015, allowed one of his parishes to hold a 'service of atonement and apology to the LGBTQ+ community.' JR Zerkowski, the LGBTQ+ Ministry Director of St. Paul's Catholic church, wrote in the service booklet of his hopes that the Church would change her doctrine on homosexuality: 'The words the Church uses to describe me still sting, but I believe we are witnessing the evolution of doctrine, so I have hope.'[1906]

[1903]Hall, K [2022] *Pope appoints jailed bishop's canon lawyer to investigate priests who testified to abuse* [Online] Available at: www.lifesitenews.com [Accessed on: 6 January 2024]

[1904]Hall, K [2022] *Fr. James Martin on Roe reversal: 'Minute-old zygote' is 'not the same' as 9-month-old preborn baby* [Online] Available at: www.lifesitenews.com [Accessed on: 6 January 2024]

[1905]Pope Francis [2022] *Desiderio desideravi* [Online] Available at: www.vatican.va [Accessed on:5 January 2022]

[1906]Summers, J [2022] *Catholic church in Kentucky hosts 'apology service' for LGBT people* [Online] Available at: www.lifesitenews.com [Accessed on: 8 January 2024]

2nd July

During an interview with Philip Pullella of *Reuters* Pope Francis criticised those bishops who denied Holy Communion to pro-abortion politicians, in the context of Archbishop Cordileone of San Francisco banning militant pro-abortion Catholic Nancy Pelosi: 'When the Church loses its pastoral nature, when a bishop loses his pastoral nature, it causes a political problem. That's all I can say.'[1907]

Despite the faithful of the persecuted underground Church in China protesting that the Vatican had abandoned them, Pope Francis expressed the hope of renewing the controversial, secret deal with the Chinese Communist Party:

> The agreement is moving well, and I hope that in October it can be renewed. Diplomacy is like that. When you face a blocked situation, you have to find the possible way, not the ideal way, out of it. Diplomacy is the art of the possible and of doing things to make the possible become a reality… [the appointment of bishops in China since 2018] is going slowly, but they are being appointed.[1908]

Cardinal Marx of Munich and Freising expressed his hope for the ordination of women deacons. During his homily on the 150th birthday of Ellen Ammann, a leading figure in the Catholic women's movement, Cardinal Marx said,

> I believe that the time has come that it must and should be open to men and women. May the great Frau Ellen Ammann accompany us on this path. The diaconate is an office that is intended to make the connection between prayer and commitment for the poor visible in a special way, and I very much hope that we can find a way to make this office stand out even more. There is still a lot of theological and practical work to be done. I am convinced that this renewal can be a great gift for the Church.[1909]

5th July

The Italian Catholic media outlet *The Daily Compass* broke the news that Pope Francis' reformed Pontifical Academy for Life was publishing a book that legitimised contraception and IVF. *Theological Ethics of Life. Scripture, Tradition, Practical Challenges*, published by Libreria Editrice Vaticana, the Vatican Publishing House, argues for a 'paradigm shift' in the Church's reproductive ethics. Regarding contraception, the Vatican book states,

> There are situations, in which two spouses, who have decided or will decide to welcome children, can make a wise discernment in the concrete case, which without contradicting their openness to life, at that moment, does not provide for it. The wise choice will be made by appropriately evaluating all possible techniques with reference to their specific situation and obviously excluding abortifacient ones.

Regarding artificial insemination, the Vatican book states,

> …generation is not artificially separated from the sexual relationship, because the latter is, in itself, infertile. On the contrary, the technique makes available an intervention that makes it possible to remedy sterility, without supplanting the relationship, but rather making generation possible bringing to completion what the sexual relationship of these spouses cannot achieve. Technique cannot be rejected a priori in medicine: it must be made the subject of discernment, to ascertain whether it fulfils the function of a form of care for the person.[1910]

[1907]Pullella, P [2022] *Pope Francis denies he is planning to resign soon* [Online] Available at: www.reuters.com [Accessed on: 8 January 2022]

[1908]Pullella, P [2022] *Pope hopes China deal on bishops will be renewed soon* [Online] Available at: www.reuters.com [Accessed on: 8 January 2022]

[1909]*Cardinal Marx advocates women's diaconate: 'I believe the time is right'* [2022] [Online] Available at: www.newsrnd.com [Accessed on: 8 January 2022]

[1910]Scrosati, L [2022] *Vatican finds way to approve contraception and assisted fertilisation* [Online] Available at: www.newdailycompass.com [Accessed on: 8 January 2024]

8th July

The Holy See Press Office announced that the Vatican had formally joined the Paris Climate Agreement, despite its underlying eugenics agenda of promoting abortion, contraception, and sterilisation:

> The Holy See in the name and on behalf of Vatican City State, intends to contribute and to give its moral support to the efforts of all states to cooperate … in an effective and appropriate response to the challenges posed by climate change to humanity and to our common home.[1911]

12th July

During his interview with the Spanish TV network *Univision* Pope Francis was asked about US Catholic president Joe Biden's militant support of abortion. Abdicating his role as the Supreme Teacher of Faith and morals Pope Francis replied,

> 'I leave it to his conscience and that he speaks to his bishop, his pastor, his parish priest about that inconsistency.'[1912]

14th July

Eugenio Scalfari, the prominent Italian journalist and atheist, died at the age of 98, notorious for making public the heretical beliefs of Pope Francis regarding the divinity of Christ, the immortality of the soul, and the existence of Hell; accounts which Pope Francis never personally repudiated. Pope Francis responded to the news of Scalfari's death, saying that he cherished

> with affection the memory of the meetings — and the deep conversations on the ultimate questions of humankind — that he had with him over the years, and he entrusts his soul to the Lord in prayer, so that He may receive him and console those who were close to him.[1913]

15th July

Bishop Stephen D. Parkes of Diocese of Savannah, appointed by Pope Francis in 2020, announced the ruling by the Dicastery for Divine Worship and Discipline of the Sacraments that all regular celebrations of the traditional Latin Mass must end by May 2023, and parishioners 'helped' to transition to the *Novus Ordo*:

> I am also aware that the eventual cessation of these Masses will be difficult for many of the faithful in our Diocese. Please know of my pastoral concern for you. Along with Fr. Allan McDonald (Bishop's Delegate for Mass in the Extraordinary Form), the Priests who celebrate these Masses will accompany the attendees in the coming months as the transition is made to Mass in conformity with the decrees of the Second Vatican Council.[1914]

17th July

In comments to the German newspaper *Die Zeit* Irme Stetter-Karp, Catholic lay woman and co-president of *Der Synodale Weg*, praised by Pope Francis, demanded increased abortion access:

[1911]Merlo, F [2022] *Holy See: Accession to Climate Convention and Paris Agreement* [Online] Available at: www.vaticannews.va [Accessed on: 8 January 2022]

[1912]Haynes, M [2022] *Pope Francis: Biden's support for abortion is a matter for his 'conscience' and 'pastor'* [Online] Available at: www.lifesitenews.com [Accessed on: 8 January 2024]

[1913]Haynes, M [2022] *Eugenio Scalfari, atheist journalist and 'friend' of Pope Francis, dies at 98* [Online] Available at: www.lifesitenews.com [Accessed on: 8 January 2024]

[1914]Haynes, M [2022] *Georgia bishop says the Vatican ordered him to end all Latin Masses in his diocese by May 2023* [Online] Available at: www.lifesitenews.com [Accessed on: 8 January 2024]

At the same time, a nationwide provision of the medical intervention of abortion must be ensured. This is not the case at present because gynaecological care is lacking in rural areas in particular.[1915]

21st July

The Vatican released a statement regarding the German *Der Synodale Weg* announcing its intention to incorporate its decisions into the deliberations of the Synod on Synodality. The Holy See directed the German dioceses not to 'adopt new forms of governance and new orientations of doctrine and morals' — including decisions about the ordination of women and changing doctrine on homosexuality — without the approval of the universal Church:

> Therefore, it is desirable that the proposals of the Way of the particular Churches in Germany may be incorporated into the synodal process on which the universal Church is traveling, in order to contribute to mutual enrichment and to bear witness to the unity with which the Body of the Church manifests its fidelity to Christ the Lord.[1916]

Bishop Georg Bätzing, chairman of the German Bishops' Conference overseeing the Synodal Way, and Irme Stetter-Karp, the militant pro abortion co-president, expressed their annoyance at the Vatican's intervention:

> We regret with irritation that this direct communication has not taken place so far. In our understanding, a synodal church is different! This also applies to the way of communication today, which astonishes us. It does not testify to a good style of communication within the church if statements are not published by name.[1917]

22nd July

Pro-homosexuality Cardinal Wilton Gregory of the Archdiocese of Washington, elevated to the sacred College of Cardinals by Pope Francis in 2020, issued a decree severely restricting the Latin Mass, and banning traditional sacraments. Cardinal Gregory decreed that all clerics seeking to celebrate the traditional Latin Mass, 'explicitly affirm in writing "the validity and the legitimacy of the liturgical reform, dictated by Vatican Council II and the Magisterium of the Supreme Pontiffs"' and 'demonstrate an appreciation "of the value of concelebration, particularly at the Chrism Mass"'. He also banned the traditional administration of the sacraments, '[a]ll other sacraments [that is, baptism, confirmation, marriage, etc.] are to be celebrated using the liturgical books promulgated by Pope St Paul VI and Saint John Paul II.'[1918]

25th July

During his apostolic visit to Canada Pope Francis, wearing a native headdress, attended an indigenous pagan ritual expressing worship of 'Mother Earth'. During the ritual the following pagan invocation was offered:

> 'From the west side we have the wind, the oxygen that we breathe, this is the government of Mother Earth. And on the north side we have Mother Earth, Mother Earth is who we are,' continued the Indigenous leader. 'Mother Earth is all the plant life, Mother Earth, our mother, is also the mother of all insect life, Mother Earth is also the mother of all animals on the ground, in the water, in the air. Mother Earth, is of course, the Mother of all humanity. We are the people of Mother Earth, hi, hi.'[1919]

[1915]Merkowsky, C M [2022] *Female co-president of German 'Synodal Way' demands increased nationwide abortion access* [Online] Available at: www.lifesitenews.com [Accessed on: 9 January 2024]

[1916]Knuffke, L [2022] *Pope taps brakes on German bishops' 'Synodal Way' until universal Church considers proposals* [Online] Available at: www.lifesitenews.com [Accessed on: 8 January 2024]

[1917]Haynes, M [2022] *German 'Synodal Way' leaders express 'irritation' over Vatican criticism* [Online] Available at: www.lifesitenews.com [Accessed on: 8 January 2024]

[1918]Gregory, W [2022] *Traditionis Custodes in The Roman Catholic Archdiocese of Washington* [Online] Available at: www.adw.org [Accessed on: 8 January 2024]

[1919]Bingham, J [2022] *Pope Francis attends Indigenous 'healing dance' to 'Mother Earth' during Canada trip* [Online] Available at: www.lifesitenews.com [Accessed on: 8 January 2024]

28th July

During an interview with *Vatican News*, Father Gilles Mongeau S.J., Vicar Provincial of the Jesuits of Canada, discussed his plans to incorporate pagan 'spiritualities' with the Catholics Faith:

> We are also exploring with Indigenous and non-Indigenous Christians ways to decolonize the practice of the Christian faith and to encourage Catholics in Canada to appreciate the richness of Indigenous spiritualities [....] Indigenous spiritualities are particularly alive with an awareness of deep relationship with the natural environment, and the dialogue with these traditional spiritualities has taught us much about what an ecological spirituality in the Church could be.[1920]

30th July

During the inflight press conference on the return from the apostolic journey to Canada Pope Francis was asked about the possibility of re-evaluating the Church's prohibition on contraception. The Supreme Pontiff replied, distorting the teaching of St. Vincent of Lerin's by partial quotation:

> This is something very timely. But know that dogma, morality, is always on a path of development, but always developing in the same direction. To use something thing that is clear, I think I've said it other times here: for the theological development of a moral or dogmatic issue, there is a rule that is very clear and illuminating. It's more or less what Vincent of Lerins did in the 10th century. He says that true doctrine, in order to go forward, to develop, must not be quiet, it develops *ut annis consolidetur, dilatetur tempore, sublimetur aetate*. That is, it is consolidated over time, it expands and consolidates, and becomes always more solid, but always progressing.[1921]

Pope Francis took the opportunity to further criticise Tradition and the faithful who uphold the apostolic Tradition of the Church on morality:

> To be clear: it's ok when dogma or morality develops, but in that direction, with the three rules of Vincent of Lerins. I think this is very clear: a Church that does not develop its thinking in an ecclesial sense, is a Church that is going backward. This is today's problem, and of many who call themselves traditional. No, no, they are not traditional, they are people looking to the past, going backward, without roots — it has always been done that way, that's how it was done last century. And looking backward is a sin because it does not progress with the Church. Tradition, instead, someone said (I think I said it in one of the speeches), tradition is the living faith of those who have died. Instead, for those people who are looking backward, who call themselves traditionalists, it is the dead faith of the living. Tradition is truly the root, the inspiration by which to go forward in the Church, and this is always vertical. And looking backward is going backward, it is always closed. It is important to understand well the role of tradition, which is always open, like the roots of the tree, and the tree grows.... A musician used a very beautiful phrase. Gustav Mahler used to say that tradition in this sense, is the

[1920]Mutual, G [2022] *Canadian Jesuit:'Trauma is intergenerational' for Indigenous communities* [Online] Available at: www.vaticannews.va [Accessed on: 9 January 2024]
[1921]'In like manner, it behooves Christian doctrine to follow the same laws of progress, so as to be consolidated by years, enlarged by time, refined by age, and yet, withal, to continue uncorrupt and unadulterate, complete and perfect in all the measurement of its parts, and, so to speak, in all its proper members and senses, admitting no change, no waste of its distinctive property, no variation in its limits [...] On the other hand, if what is new begins to be mingled with what is old, foreign with domestic, profane with sacred, the custom will of necessity creep on universally, till at last the Church will have nothing left untampered with, nothing unadulterated, nothing sound, nothing pure; but where formerly there was a sanctuary of chaste and undefiled truth thenceforward there will be a brothel of impious and base errors. May God's mercy avert this wickedness from the minds of his servants; be it rather the frenzy of the ungodly.' St. Vincent of Lerins. *Commonitory*, Chap. 23 [Online] Available at: www.newadvent.org [Accessed on: 9 January 2024]

guarantee of the future, it is not a museum piece.[1922] If you conceive of tradition as closed, that is not Christian tradition... it is always the sap of the root that carries you forward, forward, forward. So for that reason, regarding what you are saying, thinking and carrying forward faith and morals, as long as it is going in the direction of the roots, of the sap, that's ok.[1923]

31st July

Pro-homosexuality Archbishop John Wester of Santa Fe, appointed by Pope Francis in 2015, published an essay advocating the baptism of children of 'same-sex couples', defending homosexual relationships and parenting. Archbishop Wester's essay, published on the website of the militant Catholic LGBT group *Outreach*, went so far as to equate homosexual bondings with the 'domestic church'. Even though the homosexuals are openly defying Divine Revelation, Archbishop Wester asserts that such 'couples' can bring their children up in the Faith, 'Just the same, there are substantial, foundational and critical elements in the same-sex couples' relationship that do offer strong assurances that the child will be raised in the faith.'[1924]

2nd August

The militant Catholic LGBT group *Outreach* announced that its founder Fr. James Martin S.J., had received another letter from Pope Francis praising their recent conference, *Outreach 2022 LGBTQ Catholic Ministry*. The conference featured speakers who rejected the Church's doctrine on homosexuality. Making no reference to the promotion of dissent at the conference the Supreme Pontiff wrote:

> I encourage you all to keep working in the culture of encounter, which shortens the distances and enriches us with differences, in the same manner of Jesus, who made himself close to everyone.[1925]

4th August

During his meeting with Canadian Jesuits Pope Francis again criticised Tradition and the faithful who uphold the apostolic Tradition of the Church:

> The vision of the doctrine of the Church as monolithic, to be defended without nuance is wrong. That is why it is important to have respect for tradition, the authentic one. Someone once said that tradition is the living memory of believers. Traditionalism instead is the dead life of our believers. Tradition is the life of those who have gone before us and who go on. Traditionalism is their dead memory. From root to fruit, in short, that is the way. We must take the origin as a reference, not a particular historical experience taken as a perpetual model, as if we had to stop there. 'Yesterday it was done like this' becomes 'it always has been done like this.' But this is a paganism of thought! What I have said also applies to legal matters, to law.[1926]

5th August

The Canadian Catholic pro-life media outlet *LifeSiteNews* published an exchange between the militant pro-homosexuality Cardinal Hollerich, and layman Richard Smaglick. Cardinal Hollerich was elevated to the Sacred College of Cardinals by Pope Francis 2019 and appointed the Relator General of the 2023/2024 Synod on Synodality.

[1922]What Mahler actually said was 'Tradition is not the worship of ashes but the preservation of the flame.'

[1923]*Pope Francis: It was a genocide against indigenous peoples* [2022] [Online] Available at: www.vaticannews.va [Accessed on: 9 January 2024]

[1924]Wester, J [2022] *Archbishop John C. Wester: The church should baptize children of same-sex couples* [Online] Available at: www.outreach.faith [Accessed on: 9 January 2024]

[1925]Martin, J [2022] *In new letter to Outreach, Pope Francis calls Catholics to foster a 'culture of encounter'* [Online] Available at: www.outreach.faith [Accessed on: 9 January 2024]

[1926]Spadaro, A [2022] *Walking Together: Francis in conversation with Jesuits in Canada* [Online] Available at: www.laciviltacattolica.com [Accessed on 9th January 2024]

In response to Smaglick saying that the Sacred Scriptures and the Tradition of the Church have 'taught for 2,000 years that sodomy is a sin, an abomination that cries out to heaven' Cardinal Hollerich replied,

> …the Bible also said we should stone the woman who is adulterous. The Bible said that the sun turns around the earth. So, the Bible is … [we] have to give an interpretation to the Bible.

When Richard Smaglick questioned him on whether the 'fundamental scriptural teaching on sin is being changed, Cardinal Hollerich repeatedly said 'no' before claiming, 'I know that I am in full agreement with Pope Francis.'[1927]

10th August

Pope Francis received in audience at the Vatican for a fourth time in 2022 members of a 'transgender' group of individuals, including those who have undergone a 'sex-change' surgery or who simply identify as the opposite of their actual sex. The Supreme Pontiff previously met them on April 27, June 22, and Aug. 3. The group was led by Sister Genevieve Jeanningros and Father Andrea Conocchia.[1928]

19th August

The Italian religious news site *SettimanaNews* published an interview with pro-contraception and pro-homosexuality Fr. Maurizio Chiodi, appointed by Archbishop Paglia in 2017 as a member of the 'reformed' Pontifical Academy for Life. During the interview Fr. Maurizio Chiodi expressed his belief that the Church's prohibition on contraception could be changed:

> When it comes to *Humanae Vitae*, and the earlier stance contained in *Casti Connubii* — which was even stronger — we are in the realm of *doctrina reformabilis* ('reformable doctrine'). This does not legitimise hastily substituting one's own idea with the teaching of the magisterium, claiming for oneself an infallibility denied to the magisterium, but it does open up theological discussion, within the Church, and even the possibility of dissent, both for the individual believer and the theologian.[1929]

Pope Francis demoted a Roman Curia appointee after learning that the priest had occasionally offered the Traditional Latin Mass for pilgrims prior to his promulgation of *Traditionis Custodes*. Monsignor Schroeder was due to take up the post of office head of the Disciplinary Section of the Dicastery for the Doctrine of the Faith until Pope Francis intervened and the priest promptly resigned.[1930]

24th August

Pope Francis issued a Message celebrating the fiftieth anniversary of Pope St. Paul VI's promulgation of *Ministeria Quaedam* abolishing the traditional minor orders. Reflecting on it, and his own motu proprio, *Spiritus Domini*, permitting women to be instituted into ministries traditionally seen as preparatory to ordination as deacon and priest, Pope Francis wrote:

> These two interventions should not be interpreted as an overcoming of previous doctrine, but as a further development made possible because it is based on the same principles — consistent with the reflection of the Second Vatican Council.[1931]

[1927]McLoone, D [2022] *Pro-LGBT cardinal claims Pope Francis is in 'full agreement' with his stance* [Online] Available at: www.lifesitenews.com [Accessed on: 9 January 2024]

[1928]Knuffke, L [2022] *Pope welcomes transgender group to Vatican for the fourth time this year* [Online] Available at: www.lifesitenews.com [Accessed on: 9 January 2024]

[1929]Mastrofini, F [2022] *Infallibility on Moral Issues* [Online] Available at: www.academyforlife.va/ [Accessed on: 9 January 2024]

[1930]Gagliarducci, A [2022] *How Pope Francis is changing the shape of the Roman Curia* [Online] Available at: www.catholicnewsagency.com [Accessed on: 9 January 2024]

[1931]Pope Francis [2022] *Message of the Holy Father Francis to Bishops, Priest and Deacons, Consecrated Persons and the Lay Faithful on the Fiftieth Anniversary of the Apostolic Letter Issued 'Motu Proprio' Ministeria Quaedam of Saint Paul VI* [Online] Available at: www.vatican.va [Accessed on: 9 January 2024]

25th August

Pope Francis re-appointed the militant pro-homosexuality Jesuit priest, James Martin, to serve for another five years as a consultor for the Vatican's Dicastery for Communication. The re-appointment publicly confirmed the increasing ties between Pope Francis and Fr. James Martin S.J.[1932]

26th August

During a press conference in the Vatican in preparation for the Synod on Synodality, militant pro-homosexual Cardinal Hollerich, the Relator General appointed by Pope Francis. When asked directly about his repeated admission that he wanted to change the Church's teaching on the sinfulness of homosexual acts, Cardinal Hollerich equivocated:

> I fully believe in the Tradition of the Church. What is important, I think, in this process is not a change of doctrine … And to have not a change of doctrine but a change of attitude … that we are a Church in which everybody can feel at home. I'm not in favour of changing any doctrine. [I'm in favour of] a Church in which everybody can feel welcome.[1933]

Pro-homosexuality Archbishop Paglia gave an interview to the Italian state television channel *Rai Tre* in which he said that Italy's abortion law was 'a pillar of our society'. Archbishop Paglia was appointed by Pope Francis in 2016 president of the 'reformed' Pontifical Academy of Life and Grand Chancellor of the John Paul II Pontifical Theological Institute for Marriage and Family Sciences. Archbishop Paglia said: 'I believe that at this point Law 194 is a pillar of our society.' When asked if Italian abortion law was up for debate, Archbishop Paglia responded, 'No, absolutely not.'[1934]

28th August

During an interview with the heterodox UK Catholic journal *The Tablet*, Cardinal Arthur Roche, the prefect of the Congregation for Divine Worship and the Discipline of the Sacraments further criticised traditional Catholics:

> 'The [Second Vatican] council is the highest legislation that exists in the Church. If you disregard that, you are putting yourself sideways, to the edges of the Church. You are becoming more Protestant than you are Catholic. […] That reform is taking place, but it's a slow process because there are those who are dragging their feet with regard to this and not only dragging their feet but stubbornly opposing what the Church has actually decreed. That's a very serious matter. In the end, people have to ask themselves: am I really a Catholic, or am I more of a Protestant?[1935]

A Mass was held in the parish of St. Martin in Illnau-Effretikon, Switzerland during which a woman simulated the priestly act of delivering the homily and concelebration. Monika Schmid, the pastoral leader mandated by the Bishop of Chur, prayed the canon of the Mass, including modified prayers of consecration.[1936] The pro-homosexual Bishop Joseph Bonnemain of Chur, appointed by Pope Francis, conducted an investigation and issued a simple warning, while at the same time downplaying the gravity of the

---

[1932]Haynes, M [2022] *Pope re-appoints pro-LGBT Fr. James Martin as adviser to Vatican communications department* [Online] Available at: www.lifesitenews.com [Accessed on: 9 January 2024]

[1933]Knuffke, L [2022] *Pro-LGBT cardinal claims he's opposed to changing Church teaching on the sinfulness of homosexual acts* [Online] Available at: www.lifesitenews.com [Accessed on: 9 January 2024]

[1934]Wimmer, AC [2022] *'Taken out of context': Pontifical Academy defends Archbishop Paglia's abortion law remarks* [Online] Available at: www.catholicnewsagency.com [Accessed on: 9 January 2024]

[1935]Lamb, C [2022] *Stubborn opposition to Vatican II 'not Catholic' says cardinal* [Online] Available at: www.thetablet.co.uk [Accessed on: 9 January 2024]

[1936]Haynes, M & Wailzer, A [2022] *Two women attempt to concelebrate Mass at Catholic church in Switzerland* [Online] Available at: www.lifesitenews.com [Accessed on: 10 January 2024]

liturgical abuses, concluding — despite the Youtube video of the homily and simulated concelebration — that the evidence showed,

> that no serious liturgical violation, the judgment of which would be reserved for the Dicastery for the Doctrine of the Faith, took place during this celebration. Therefore, no criminal proceedings are necessary according to canon law.[1937]

Marc Frings, the secretary general of the German bishop-backed Central Committee of German Catholics [ZdK] has issued a statement of support of Monika Schmid simulating priestly functions during the celebration of the Mass.[1938]

The militant pro-homosexuality Fr. James Martin S.J., criticised Bishop Donald DeGrood of the Diocese of Sioux Falls for issuing pastoral guidelines that upheld the Church's doctrine on homosexuality and banning the use of the term 'LGBT'. Bishop Donald DeGrood's pastoral guidelines stated, among other things:

> Students may not advocate, celebrate, or express same-sex attraction in such a way as to cause confusion or distraction in the context of Catholic school classes, activities, or events.

Fr. James Martin S.J., consultor to the Vatican's Secretariat for Communication, posted his criticism on social media:

> First, people should be able to, and encouraged to, 'celebrate' who they are and, more importantly, how God made them, including LGBTQ people. This is an essential part of a healthy spirituality for anyone. 'I praise you, for I am fearfully and wonderfully made.' (Ps 139). This is crucial for young people, and especially for LGBTQ youth, who feel, thanks to statements like the one above, ignored, rejected, condemned, marginalized and completely unwelcome in their own church.... Imagine being an LGBTQ student (or the parent of an LGBTQ youth) and reading that statement. Would you feel welcomed? Valued? Loved? And how people are treated by their church influences, for better or worse, how they understand themselves in God's eyes.... Of course some people will say, 'We have to call out the sin!' But where is the sin in a young person who is in no sexual relationship, and is far too young to even contemplate marriage, to say, even publicly, 'God made me this way and I am good'? Second, communities have the right to name themselves. And usage changes as communities adopt new names. To use outdated and offensive terms like 'same-sex attraction' is the opposite of the 'respect' that the *Catechism* calls for. At the very least, 'respect' means calling.... the members of a community by the name that they choose, not those that others want to impose on them. To persist in using outmoded terms is disrespectful. Besides, the Vatican, the Synod of Bishops, and various cardinals and bishops, have been using 'LGBT' for some time....[1939]

1st September

During an interview with the Canadian Catholic pro-life *LifeSiteNews* militant pro-homosexuality Cardinal Leonardo Ulrich Steiner, O.F.M., expressed his support for homosexual civil unions and disputed that homosexual sex acts were not sinful for non-Christian homosexual persons. Cardinal Steiner, elevated to the sacred College of Cardinals in 2020 by Pope Francis, said about homosexual civil unions:

> Many of them live together until the end of their lives without security. They do not have assistance from health services. This is very serious. I have seen people going toward the end (of their lives) without money. Thus, you can see that Pope Francis has spoken many times about this. This is not about a fundamentally moral question. This is about a life. This is a question about a son of God.

[1937] *Switzerland: A Simple Warning Issued to Monika Schmid* [2022][Online] Available at: www.fsspx. news [Accessed on: 10 January 2024]
[1938] Wailzer, A [2022] *Catholic lay group in Germany expresses support for woman who tried concelebrating Mass* [Online] Available at: www.lifesitenews.com [Accessed on: 10 January 2024]
[1939] Bingham, J [2022] *Pro-LGBT Jesuit James Martin attacks bishop for defending Church teaching on sexuality, gender* [Online] Available at: www.lifesitenews.com [Accessed on: 10 January 2024]

When challenged on his acceptance of doctrine regarding the intrinsic evil and grave depravity of homosexual sex acts, Cardinal Steiner responded 'How do we say if it is a sin if they do not live the Christian faith?'[1940]

3rd September

Though considered sovereign entity under international law, Pope Francis dissolved the leadership and constitution of the Sovereign Order of the Knights of Malta establishing a new Sovereign Council and Constitutional Charter. Reuters reported

> Under the previous constitution, the top Knights and the Grand Master were required to have noble lineage.... The new constitution eliminates the nobility rule as well as the tradition of Grand Masters being elected for life.... Future Grand Masters will be elected for 10-year terms, renewable only once, and will have to step down at age 85.[1941]

8th September

During an interview with the German newspaper *Die Zeit* militant pro-homosexuality Bishop Helmut Dieser of Aachen, Germany, said Homosexuality is 'willed by God' and contraception 'strengthens the protection of life'. Bishop Dieser, the head of the Forum for Sexuality and Partnership for *Der Synodale Weg* said:

> What we find in creation is good. Homosexuality is not a blunder from God, but willed by God in the same measure as the creation itself: He saw that it was good, it says in the creation story [....] Yes, my view has changed. [...] It is a sin when I do violence to another person, when I humiliate him, when I use him, when I am hypocritical, when love is not love, when I am unfaithful, unloving, indifferent. That is sin. But when it comes to love, to this variety of love, which is then an erotic form, when the body becomes an expression of this love and the language of this love, then I think: Love cannot be sin.

When asked if the Church should change her prohibition on the use of contraception, Bishop Dieser replied,

> Why must the Church reject artificial contraceptives? Is it necessary? I think: No. If we recognise — with the Second Vatican Council — that parents themselves decide in responsibility before God how many children they have, then I consider the choice of means to be of secondary importance.... would welcome a movement to reevaluate this. It is precisely by recommending contraception that we strengthen the protection of life.[1942]

8th-10th September

During the fourth Assembly of the German *Der Synodale Weg* [The Synodal Way] a large majority of the bishops, priests and laity voted to approve the text *Magisterial reassessment of Homosexuality*, that demanded changes to doctrine on homosexuality:

> Same-sex sexuality — also realised in sexual acts — is thus not a sin that separates from God, and it is not to be judged as intrinsically evil [....] In the course of this reassessment of homosexuality, among other things, the passages 2357-2359 and 2396 (homosexuality and chastity) of the *Universal Catechism* should be revised. Likewise, the corresponding passages in the *Catechism Compendium* (2005; no. 492) should be amended. In the Compendium, 'homosexual acts' need to be removed from the list of 'principal sins against chastity.'[1943]

[1940]Knuffke, L [2022] *New cardinal doubles down on dissent from Church teaching on homosexual civil unions* [Online] Available at: www.lifesitenews.com [Accessed on: 10 January 2024]
[1941]Pullella, P [2022] *Pope dissolves Knights of Malta leadership, issues new constitution* [Online] Available at: www.reuters.com [Accessed on: 10 January 2024]
[1942]Wailzer, A [2022] *German bishop: Homosexuality is 'willed by God,' contraception 'strengthens the protection of life'* [Online] Available at: www.lifesitenews.com [Accessed on: 10 January 2024]
[1943]Wailzer, A [2022] *German Synodal Way approves text calling homosexual acts 'not sinful' and 'not intrinsically evil'* [Online] Available at: www.lifesitenews.com [Accessed on: 10 January 2024]

A large majority of bishops, priests and laity also voted to accept the text *Blessing ceremonies for couples who love each other* that permitted the 'blessing' of homosexual bondings. It calls on bishops to

> officially allow blessing ceremonies in their dioceses for couples who love each other but to whom sacramental marriage is not accessible or who do not see themselves at a point of entering into a sacramental marriage. This also applies to same-sex couples on the basis of a re-evaluation of homosexuality as a norm variant of human sexuality.[1944]

A large majority of participants also voted to accept the text *Women in Services and Positions in the Church* that called for the 'ordination' of women deacons. Almost 82% of the bishops present voted in favour of the document.[1945]

15th September

Pope Francis attended the *VII Congress of Leaders of World and Traditional Religions* held in Kazakhstan. The Supreme Pontiff signed a declaration with other leaders affirming that 'the pluralism and differences in religion…are expressions of the wisdom of God's will in creation'. The Kazakhstan Declaration repeated almost word for word the Abu Dhabi Declaration which Pope Francis and the Grand Imam of Al-Azhar, Ahmed el-Tayeb, signed in February 2019. The Kazakhstan Declaration stated:

> We note that pluralism in terms of differences in skin colour, gender, race, language and culture are expressions of the wisdom of God in creation. Religious diversity is permitted by God and, therefore, any coercion to a particular religion and religious doctrine is unacceptable.[1946]

In his address to the Congress Pope Francis, without once mentioning our Lord Jesus Christ, returned to his criticism of converting non-Christians to the Faith which he condemned as 'proselytism and indoctrination':

> Each person has the right to render public testimony to his or her own creed, proposing it without ever imposing it. This is the correct method of preaching, as opposed to proselytism and indoctrination, from which all are called to step back.…On the other hand, to work for a society marked by the respectful coexistence of religious, ethnic and cultural differences is the best way to enhance the distinctive features of each, to bring people together while respecting their diversity, and to promote their loftiest aspirations without compromising their vitality.[1947]

Bishop Athanasius Schneider, the auxiliary of Astana, Kazakhstan, criticised Pope Francis' address to the Congress, re-affirming Catholic doctrine:

> [Catholicism is] the only one true religion which God commanded to all people to believe. We're not one of the many religions; we're the only one true religion which God commanded to all people to believe. There is no other way to salvation. [The Congress risked promoting] a supermarket of religions — everyone is there and you can choose what you want. But Jesus Christ is not in the supermarket of religions. He is the only one [true God]…there is only one true religion, which is the Catholic Church, founded by God himself, but commanded to all man, to all religions, to believe and accept his son Jesus Christ, the only Saviour.'[1948]

[1944]Coppen, L [2022] *German synodal way backs same-sex blessings* [Online] Available at: ww.pillarcatholic.com [Accessed on: 10 January 2024]

[1945]Wailzer, A [2022] *Over 80% of German bishops present approve Synodal Way text calling for women's ordination* [Online] Available at: www.lifesitenews.com [Accessed on: 10 January 2024]

[1946]Haynes, M [2022] *Pope Francis signs document saying 'differences in religion' are part of 'God's will in creation'* [Online] Available at: www.lifesitenews.com [Accessed on: 10 January 2024]

[1947]Pope Francis [2022] *Address to the VII Congress of Leaders of World and Traditional Religions* [Online] Available at: www.vatican.va [Accessed on: 10 January 2024]

[1948]Haynes, M [2022] *Bp.Schneider rebukes Pope Francis' remarks at ecumenical meeting: Catholicism is 'the one true religion'* [Online] Available at: www.lifesitenews.com [Accessed on: 10 January 2024]

19th September

Bishop Fintan Gavin of the Diocese of Cork & Ross, appointed by Pope Francis in 2019, ordered the Dominicans to cease celebrating Mass in the Dominican Rite at St. Mary's Dominican Priory and Pope's Quay, almost 800 years after the Order arrived in Cork city.[1949]

Archbishop Timothy Costelloe of Perth issued severe restrictions on the traditional Latin Mass in his archdiocese, limiting its celebration to just two churches: St. Anne's at Belmont and a church at Kemlscott. Priests wanting to celebrate the Latin Mass were required to sign a written declaration declaring that the Novus Ordo Mass is the 'unique expression of the *lex orandi* of the Roman Rite,' accepting the legitimacy and validity of Vatican II[1950] and the 'legitimacy of the concelebration of the Eucharist'. Fr. Michael Rowe, the much loved Rector of St Anne's Church, was unable to sign the declaration, for reasons of conscience, explaining

> I have serious problems with some of the…propositions which simply contain factual errors or attempt to assert things that I simply do not believe are true. I cannot in good conscience sign such a document with the above propositions because I do not believe they reflect the truth of Catholic doctrine and dogma as passed down in the Church throughout history. Just because the Holy Father and the Archbishop of Perth believe these statements to be true that does not necessarily of itself make them true, such statements have to be carefully considered in the light of continuity of Catholic tradition. Rather than reflecting the truth of Catholic doctrine and dogma as passed down in the Church throughout history, my concern with these statements is that they represent a rupturing from such truth and tradition.[1951]

On the 11th December 2023 Archbishop Costelloe deposed Fr. Michael Rowe as the rector of St. Anne's because he would not sign the declaration.[1952]

20th September

The Belgian Flemish bishops issued the pastoral instruction *Being Pastorally Close to Homosexual Persons — For a Welcoming Church that Excludes No One* providing clergy with liturgical guidance how to 'bless' a homosexual bonding. The Belgian Flemish bishops justified their radical move by claiming a mandate in Pope Francis' *Amoris Laetitia*. Cardinal Eijk of Utrecht protested the Flemish bishops illegitimate act:

> The statement of the Flemish bishops, in which they allow the blessing of same-sex couples and even provide a liturgical model for it, meets with inherent ethical objections, radically contradicts a recent ruling by the Congregation for the Doctrine of the Faith, and carries the risk that it may lead Catholics to views on the morality of same-sex relationships that are contrary to Church teaching. Catholics who accept the Church's teaching, including on sexual morality, therefore fervently hope that the Flemish bishops will soon be asked by ecclesiastically competent circles to withdraw their statement and that the latter will comply.[1953]

Cardinal Gerhard Müller, the former prefect of the CDF, denounced the Belgian Flemish bishops decision to 'bless' homosexual bondings:

> It's nothing more than heresy against Christian marriage. It's an absolute heresy and schism. No bishop or pope has authority to bless something which is against the will

[1949]Jackson, T [2022] *'Shameful': Irish laity denounce bishop's suppression of ancient Dominican Rite Mass* [Online] Available at: www.lifesitenews.com [Accessed on: 10 January 2024]

[1950]Haynes, M [2022] *Australian archbishop issues crushing restrictions on Latin Mass, undermining thriving parish* [Online] Available at: www.lifesitenews.com [Accessed on: 10 January 2024]

[1951]*Fr. Rowe's Open Letter on his removal by Archbishop Costello of Perth, AU* [2023] [Online: Available at: www.remnantnewspaper.com [Accessed on: 11 January 2024]

[1952]Haynes, M [2022] *Australian archbishop ousts rector of thriving Latin Mass church after years-long conflict* [Online] Available at: www.lifesitenews.com [Accessed on: 10 January 2024]

[1953]Eijk, WJ [2022] *Cardinal Eijk: stop Flemish bishops from blessing gay couples* [Online] Available at: www.wdailycompass.com[Accessed on: 10 January 2024]

of our Creator and our Redeemer. Rome must speak. Now is the time to cry out the truth from the rooftops.... We cannot make a compromise with LGBT lunacy. There's no possible compromise. That's absolutely wrong and absolutely false and absolutely dangerous for the people.[1954]

21st September

During the Wednesday papal audience Pope Francis met with 110 members of the militant Italian Catholic LGBT group *La Tenda di Gionata* [Jonathan's tent], comprising of homosexual Christians, their parents and the pastoral workers who accompany them, priests, nuns and consecrated persons. A lesbian 'couple' handed Pope Francis a number of letters from parents of homosexual children, with one of the lesbians saying, 'meeting the Pope is a confirmation of the journey of faith that will lead us to civil union.'[1955]

22nd September

During his address to the US *Catholic Partnership Summit*, Cardinal Mario Grech told participants that the 2013 Synod on Synodality could introduce radical changes to doctrine on marriage and sexuality. Cardinal Grech was elevated to the Sacred College of Cardinals by Pope Francis in 2020 and the Secretary General of the Synod of Bishops. Referring to 'complicated issues' such as divorced and remarried people receiving Holy Communion and the blessing of same-sex couples, Cardinal Grech said,

> These are not to be understood simply in terms of doctrine, but in terms of God's ongoing encounter with human beings. What has the church to fear if these two groups within the faithful are given the opportunity to express their intimate sense of spiritual realities, which they experience. Might this be an opportunity for the church to listen to the Holy Spirit speaking through them also?[1956]

Cardinal Gerhard Müller, the former prefect of the CDF, later criticised Cardinal Grech's comments:

> Here is a hermeneutic of the old cultural Protestantism and of Modernism, that the individual experience has the same level as objective Revelation of God. And God is only a wall to you, [onto] which you can project your proper ideas, and to make a certain populism in the Church; and surely everybody outside of the Church who want to destroy the Catholic Church, and the fundaments, they are very glad about these declarations. But it is obvious that is absolutely against the Catholic doctrine. We have Revelation of God in Jesus Christ. And it is definitely closed and finished in Jesus Christ.... This is absolutely clear: that Jesus has spoken about the indissolubility of matrimony.... How is it possible that Cardinal Grech is more intelligent than Jesus Christ?[1957]

24th September

The social media accounts for the Vatican's Synod on Synodality posted artwork promoting female 'priests' and homosexual ideology. Some of the images juxtaposed the words 'Catholic identity' with 'LGBTQ+ identity' and 'intolerance' with 'dialogue.' A young women was featured wearing a chasuble and stole with a church in the background.[1958]

[1954]Wolfe, R [2022] *Cardinal Müller: Belgian bishops' homosexual 'blessings' are 'heresy and schism'* [Online] Available at: www.lifesitenews.com [Accessed on: 11 January 2024]

[1955]Haynes, M [2022] *Pope Francis welcomes dissident LGBT activists, lesbian partners in latest scandalous audience* [Online] Available at: www.lifesitenews.com [Accessed on: 10 January 2024]

[1956]Lavenburg, J [2022] *Vatican's synod chief tells U.S. Church leaders to 'listen to others'* [Online] Available at: www.cruxnow.com [Accessed on: 11 January 2024]

[1957]Wolfe, R [2022] *Cardinal Müller says Pope Francis' Synod is a 'hostile takeover of the Church' in explosive interview* [Online] Available at: www.lifesitenews.com [Accessed on: 11 January 2024]

[1958]Haynes, M [2022] *'Manifestly heretical': Catholics slam Vatican Synod for posting pro-LGBT 'art' on social media* [Online] Available at: www.lifesitenews.com [Accessed on: 10 January 2024]

27th September

Bishop Francesco Antonio Soddu of the Diocese of Terni, Italy, appointed by Pope Francis in 2021, attended the inauguration ceremony for a new entrance to the Masonic Lodge of the Grand Orient of Italy in Terni.[1959]

29th September

During his interview with the German Catholic weekly *Die Tagespost*, Swiss Cardinal Kurt Koch, Prefect of the Dicastery for Promoting Christian Unity, compared *Der Synodale Weg* with Protestantism during the Nazi period. Expressing the criticism that the Synodal Way accepted new sources of revelation — such as sociology and psychology — Cardinal Kurt Koch said:

> For this phenomenon has already occurred during the National Socialist dictatorship, when the so-called 'German Christians' saw God's new revelation in blood and soil and in the rise of Hitler. The Confessing Church protested against this with its Barmen Theological Declaration in 1934, the first thesis of which reads, 'We reject the false doctrine as if the church could and must recognise as the source of preaching, apart from and in addition to this one Word of God, other events and powers, figures and truths as God's Revelation.'[1960]

Pro-homosexuality Bishop Bätzing, appointed by Pope Francis and president of the German bishops' conference, demanded that Cardinal Kurt Koch apologise, saying he had 'disqualified himself from the theological debate' about the Synodal Path, and that 'If a public apology does not happen immediately, I will file an official complaint with the Holy Father.' Cardinal Koch responded,

> I am responding promptly, but I cannot retract my essential point, simply because I have in no way compared the Synodal Way to a Nazi ideology, nor will I ever do so.... I simply assumed that we can still learn from history today, even from a very difficult period. As the vehement reaction of Bishop Bätzing and others show, I have to realise in retrospect that I failed in this attempt. And I also have to realise that memories of phenomena in the National Socialist period are obviously taboo in Germany.

Bishop Bätzing immediately rejected the cardinal's explanation saying, 'Cardinal Koch, in essence, does not apologise for the indefensible statements, but — on the contrary — aggravates them.'[1961] Cardinal Koch and Bishop Bätzing held a private meeting in Rome on the 4th October 2022, after which Matthias Kopp, the spokesman for the German Bishops' Conference, issued a statement, explaining that Cardinal Koch assured Bätzing that

> he in no way meant the synodal path of the church in Germany or the synodal assembly when he compared the theological debates on the synodal path and the events surrounding the so-called 'German Christians' during the Nazi era. Cardinal Koch expressly emphasises that he has absolutely no intention of accusing the Synodal members of the terrible ideology of the 1930s. Cardinal Koch apologises to anyone who feels offended by the comparison he made.[1962]

On the 1st October Cardinal Koch announced that he cancelled celebrating Mass and delivering a lecture in the German city of Gmünd due to hate mail, including violent threats made against him.[1963]

[1959]Knuffke, L [2022] *Italian bishop attends inauguration ceremony for new Masonic temple* [Online] Available at: www.lifesitenews.com [Accessed on: 11 January 2024]

[1960]Hickson, M [2022] *Head of German bishops angered after cardinal compares Synodal Path to Protestantism during Nazi era* [Online] Available at: www.lifesitenews.com [Accessed on: 11 January 2024]

[1961]*German bishops outraged by Cardinal Koch's Nazi comparison, demand apology* [2022] [Online] Available at: www.cruxnow.com [Accessed on: 11 January 2024]

[1962]Allen, EA [2022] *Cardinal Koch, top German bishop meet in Rome amid fracas over Nazi comparison* [Online] Available at: www.cruxnow.com [Accessed on: 11 January 2024]

[1963]Wailzer, A [2022] *Swiss cardinal threatened for comparing Synodal Way with Protestantism in Nazi era, cancels event in Germany* [Online] Available at: www.lifesitenews.com [Accessed on: 11 January 2024]

30th September

The Holy See press office announced that Pope Francis had appointed militant pro-homosexuality Cardinal José Tolentino de Mendonça to be the Prefect of the Dicastery for Culture and Education. Fr. José Tolentino de Mendonça was appointed by Pope Francis in 2019 the titular Archbishop of Suava, the Archivist of the Vatican Secret Archive, the Librarian of the Vatican Library and elevated to the Sacred College of Cardinals.

4th October

The Pontifical Academies of Sciences and Social Sciences, along with Simon Stiell, the executive secretary of the U.N. Climate Change Secretariat, held a conference on climate change in the Vatican. High ranking officials including Cardinal Pietro Parolin, Secretary of State, publicly affirmed the Holy See's commitment to the Paris Climate Agreement despite inclusion of a eugenics pro-abortion agenda.[1964]

The New Zealand Catholic Bishops Conference launched guidelines for Catholic schools entitled *Aroha and Diversity in Catholics Schools* to promote a homosexualist agenda among Catholic students:

> Individuals and groups within the Catholic Church have a range of voice, attitudes, and experiences regarding LGBTQIA+ issues. Our Catholic community has always been diverse, with faith-filled people living lives which incorporate a range of sexual orientation, expression, and loving family life. They are part of the Church.

While upholding the doctrine that sacramental marriage is only for male husbands and female wives, the New Zealand bishops dissented from Church teaching by promoting homosexual bondings:

> This does not mean that other couples cannot commit to wonderful, loving, and enduring relationships, it simply means that such relationships are not 'Sacramental marriage' within the Catholic Church as they cannot be open to the possibility of new life without external intervention.[1965]

6th October

During an interview on EWTN's *The World Over* with Raymond Arroyo, Cardinal Gerhard Müller, the former prefect of the CDF, warned that Pope Francis' Synod on Synodality was a 'hostile takeover' of the Church that threatened the 'end' of Catholicism:

> This is a system of self-revelation and is the occupation of the Catholic Church...the hostile takeover of the Church of Jesus Christ, which is a column of the Revealed Truth. This has nothing to do with Jesus Christ, with the Triune God, and they think doctrine is only like a program of a political party who can change it according to their voters...if they will succeed, but that will be the end of the Catholic Church. It's like the old heresies of Arianism, when Arius thought according to his ideas what God can do and what God cannot do. The human intellect wants to decide what is true and what is wrong....They want to abuse this process for shifting the Catholic Church and not only in another direction, but in the destruction of the Catholic Church. [Synod leaders are] dreaming of another church [that] has nothing to do with the Catholic faith and is absolutely against it, They want to abuse this process for shifting the Catholic Church and not only in another direction, but in the destruction of the Catholic Church. Nobody can make an absolute shift and to substitute the revealed doctrine of the Church, but they have these strange ideas, such as that doctrine is only a theory of some theologian. The

[1964]Haynes, M [2022] *Vatican reaffirms commitment to Paris Climate Agreement despite inclusion of pro-abortion agenda* [Online] Available at: www.lifesitenews.com [Accessed on: 10 January 2024]
[1965]*Aroha and Diversity in Catholics Schools* [2022] [Online] Available at: www.catholic.org.nz [Accessed on: 11 January 2024]

doctrine of the Apostles is a reflection and manifestation of the Revelation of the Word of God. We have to listen to the Word of God, but in the authority of the Holy Bible, of the Apostolic Tradition, and of the Magisterium, and all the councils said before that is not possible to substitute the Revelation given once and forever in Jesus Christ by another revelation.[1966]

10th October

During his homily marking the 60th anniversary of the opening of the Second Vatican Council Pope Francis yet again criticised Tradition and those faithful Catholics who upheld Tradition:

> Yet let us be careful: both the 'progressivism' that lines up behind the world and the 'traditionalism' – or 'looking backwards' – that longs for a bygone world are not evidence of love, but of infidelity. They are forms of a Pelagian selfishness that puts our own tastes and plans above the love that pleases God, the simple, humble and faithful love that Jesus asked of Peter [....] Brothers and sisters, let us return to the Council, which rediscovered the living river of Tradition without remaining mired in traditions [....] Let us not give in to his enticements or to the temptation of polarisation. How often, in the wake of the Council, did Christians prefer to choose sides in the Church, not realising that they were breaking their Mother's heart! How many times did they prefer to cheer on their own party rather than being servants of all? To be progressive or conservative rather than being brothers and sisters? To be on the 'right' or 'left', rather than with Jesus? To present themselves as 'guardians of the truth' or 'pioneers of innovation' rather than seeing themselves as humble and grateful children of Holy Mother Church.[1967]

12th October

The US Catholic newspaper *National Catholic Register* published an opinion piece by Cardinal George Pell, in which he criticised the German *Der Synodale Weg*:

> The synodal process has begun disastrously in Germany, and matters will become worse unless we soon have effective papal corrections on, for instance, Christian sexual morality, women priests, etc. We find no precedents in Catholic history for the active participation of ex-Catholics and anti-Catholics in such bodies [....] Some faithful German Catholics are already talking, not of the synodal way but the suicidal way. We must work and pray they are wrong, that no such disaster occurs anywhere in the Church in the modern world.

Professor Roberto Dell'Oro, an Ordinary Member of the 'reformed' Pontifical Academy for Life, delivered an address criticising the Supreme Court's Dobbs decision overturning of the US abortion ruling Roe Vs. Wade. Professor Roberto Dell'Oro expressed strong support for universal access to abortion:

> In the potential conflict between a woman's claim to autonomy and a state's right to determine the future of her pregnancy, the *Dobbs* decision sides with the latter over the former, rejecting any space of 'personal liberty' for women, even in cases of rape or incest. To impose a choice on women over matters that belong to their most intimate sphere threatens to compromise their integrity, bodily and otherwise, as persons.... [Dobbs] undermines basic requirements of tolerance toward the pluralism of moral perspectives within society. In matters of personal life, a democracy differs from a totalitarian regime because it maximises, rather than restricts, a space of personal freedom for all citizens, including women.

Furthermore, in an interview with *Catholic News Agency* on October 19, Professor Roberto Dell'Oro criticised the Pontifical Academy of Life under its founder, Pope

---

[1966]Wolfe, R [2022] *Cardinal Müller says Pope Francis' Synod is a 'hostile takeover of the Church' in explosive interview* [Online] Available at: www.lifesitenews.com [Accessed on: 11 January 2024]
[1967]Pope Francis [2022] *Homily at Mass for the 60th anniversary of the beginning of the Second Vatican Ecumenical Council* [Online] Available at: www.vatican.va [Accessed on: 11 January 2024]

St. John Paul II, declaring it was 'more of a space of an engagement in the pro-life movement in ways that were very much defined a priori by the boundaries of Catholic doctrine.'[1968]

13th October

During an interview with the Catholic multimedia portal of the Archdiocese of Cologne, *domradio.de*, Archbishop Ludwig Schick of Bamberg criticised Catholics who rejected other religions:

> Whoever is a Christian must stand up for freedom, for unity, for worldwide solidarity and worldwide charity, otherwise he does not deserve the name Christian. For example, I see right-wing extremist tendencies among certain pro-life activists. When it comes to interreligious dialogue, there too are right-wing extremist tendencies that fundamentally reject other religions because they insist solely on their perceived Catholic position.

He described Catholics who hold to the teaching that the Catholic faith is the one true religion as having 'right-wing extremist tendencies.'[1969]

15th October

The 'reformed' Pontifical Academy for Life, led by the pro-homosexuality Archbishop Paglia, announced Pope Francis' appointment of the atheist, pro-abortion economist Mariana Mazzucato as an ordinary member.[1970] Pope Francis also appointed pro-contraception Father Humberto Miguel Yanez, S.J. as full member of the Pontifical Academy for Life.[1971]

Pope Francis later defended his appointment of an atheist, pro-abortion economist to the Pontifical Academy for Life:

> And now I have put Marianna Mazzuccato in the Pontifical Academy for Life. She is a great economist from the United States, I put her there to give a little more humanity to it.[1972]

Dr. José María Simón Castellví, president emeritus of the International Federation of Catholic Medical Associations, published an article extremely critical of Pope Francis' latest appointments of the Pontifical Academy for Life. In the article titled 'Academy for Life: I can't remain silent anymore!', Dr. Castellví warned that the latest appointments are 'just the opposite of what John Paul II wanted.' The appointments go against 'what is reasonable for the good of the pilgrim Church on this earth. And worthy pro-life scientists were left out.'[1973]

16th October

During his Angelus address Pope Francis announced his decision to divide the Synod on Synodality into two sessions, one in October 2023 and the other in October 2024.[1974]

[1968]Knuffke, L [2022] *Pontifical Academy for Life member rejects Dobbs decision as undemocratic and totalitarian, says abortion gives women 'moral agency'* [Online] Available at: www.lifesitenews.com [Accessed on: 11 January 2024]

[1969]Wailzer, A [2022] *German bishop says Catholics who reject other religions have 'right-wing extremist tendencies'* [Online] Available at: www.lifesitenews.com [Accessed on: 12 January 2024]

[1970]Bingham, J [2022] *Pope appoints pro-abortion World Economic Forum speaker to Pontifical Academy for Life* [Online] Available at: www.lifesitenews.com [Accessed on: 11 January 2024]

[1971]Knuffke, L [2022] *Pope Francis makes pro-contraception Jesuit priest a full member of the Pontifical Academy for Life* [Online] Available at: www.lifesitenews.com [Accessed on: 11 January 2024]

[1972]*Pope Francis: 'Three world wars in one century: be pacifists!'* [2022] [Online] Available at: www. vaticannews.va [Accessed on: 12 January 2024]

[1973]*Catholic doctor criticizes Pontifical Academy for Life's appointing of abortion advocates* [2022] [Online] Available at: www.catholicnewsagency.com [Accessed on: 11 January 2024]

[1974]Wailzer, A [2022] *Pope Francis announces he will extend Synod on Synodality through 2024* [Online] Available at: www.lifesitenews.com [Accessed on: 11 January 2024]

17th October

During an interview with Spanish news outlet Vida Nueva, pro-homosexuality Cardinal Jean-Claude Hollerich, the relator general of the Synod on Synodality appointed by Pope Francis, expressed unqualified praise of Vatican II, asserting that the Church must adapt to the world:

> If we did not have that point of reform that was the Second Vatican Council, the Church today would be a small sect, unknown to most people. I am convinced that the Second Vatican Council saved the Church. Without that assembly would have been reduced to a group that performs beautiful rites, but nobody knows anything about. Today we must adapt to the changes in mental frameworks.

Cardinal Hollerich went on to criticise faithful Catholics who upheld Tradition, identifying them as offering the greatest resistance to Vatican II:

> The strongest come from the traditionalists, who curiously are also a postmodern phenomenon. They choose only one point of reference in history, without looking before and after…forgetting how the growth of tradition develops. It's a bit like what happens with Netflix series: they tell you a part of the story, but invented, not real. That's why it's no coincidence that traditionalist movements attract young people from France and the United States.[1975]

18th October

The Italian daily newspaper Corriere della Sera reported that the Vatican had renewed its secret agreement for the appointment of bishops with the Chinese Communist party. The provisional agreement was extended for another two years until 22nd October 2024. Since the signing of the agreement in 2018 faithful Catholics have reported that the communist persecution of the underground Church had intensified.[1976]

22nd October

During an interview with the German Catholic website kath.net, Cardinal Gerhard Müller, the former prefect of the CDF, stated the faithful do not owe obedience to an 'obviously heretical bishop.' To Maike Hickson's question, 'Will faithful Catholics no longer be able to go to every Mass and every bishop, but have to look for those clergy who will still teach them the true faith and will not lead them to compromise with the world?' Cardinal Müller answered,

> one does not have to obey an obviously heretical bishop just for reasons of formal fidelity. Blind obedience such as this would be cadaveric obedience, which not only contradicts reason but also faith. Objections are justified when related strictly to the revealed truth, but that termination of visible communion with the competent bishop cannot be based on differences of opinion … worldly or personal questions. If Rome fails to correct bishops for anti-faith teaching and anti-Church behaviour, there are plenty of other high dignitaries [in the Church] who will not bow their knees to the Baal of public opinion (the media cartels) or political power (the pagan Roman emperors, the atheistic dictators of yesterday and today).[1977]

24th October

During an interview with the Vatican's daily newspaper L'Osservatore Romano, pro-homosexuality Cardinal Jean-Claude Hollerich, the relator general of the Synod on Synodality, called for a paradigm shift in the Church's attitude to homosexuality:

[1975]Haynes, M [2022] Pro-LGBT cardinal claims the Church would be a 'small sect' without Vatican II [Online] Available at: www.lifesitenews.com [Accessed on: 11 January 2024]
[1976]Hall, K [2022] Vatican has reportedly renewed its secretive deal with Communist China for a second time [Online] Available at: www.lifesitenews.com [Accessed on: 11 January 2024]
[1977]Hall, K [2022] Cardinal Müller says obedience is not owed to an 'obviously heretical bishop' [Online] Available at: www.lifesitenews.com [Accessed on: 11 January 2024]

> [A] deeper change of cultural paradigm is needed, and a conversion of the spirit....We are called to announce good news, not a set of rules or prohibitions. No one excluded: even remarried divorcees, even homosexuals, everyone...the Kingdom of God is not an exclusive club but opens its doors to everyone, without discrimination. Sometimes there is discussion in the Church about the accessibility of these groups to the Kingdom of God, and this creates a perception of exclusion in a part of God's people. They feel excluded, and this is not right! This is not about theological subtleties or ethical dissertations: this is simply about affirming that Christ's message is for everyone!

Cardinal Hollerich admitted that he supports the argument that homosexuality is a 'fruit of creation,' adding that 'at every step of the creation God is pleased with his work.'[1978]

25th October

Pope Francis participated in an interfaith prayer meeting entitled 'The Cry for Peace,' joining leaders from various religions, including Islam, Judaism, Hinduism, Buddhism, Sikhism. While the Supreme Pontiff attended a Christian prayer service inside the Colosseum, Muslim, Sikh, Hindu, Buddhist, Shinto and Tenrikyo leaders simultaneously held their own prayer services. By so doing Pope Francis reduced Christianity to being just one religion among all other world religions.[1979]

27th October

The Vatican released the working Document for the Continental Stage of the Synod on Synodality, entitled 'Enlarge the space of your tent', presented by Pope Francis appointees pro-homosexuality Cardinal Jean-Claude Hollerich, relator general of the Synod, and Cardinal Mario Grech, general secretary of the Synod of Bishops. The document emphasised the Church being radically inclusive, welcoming those living in sin without any reference to repentance and amendment of life:

> Among those who ask for a more meaningful dialogue and a more welcoming space we also find those who, for various reasons, feel a tension between belonging to the Church and their own loving relationships, such as: remarried divorcees, single parents, people living in a polygamous marriage, LGBTQ people, etc. Reports show how this demand for welcome challenges many local Churches: 'People ask that the Church be a refuge for the wounded and broken, not an institution for the perfect. They want the Church to meet people wherever they are, to walk with them rather than judge them, and to build real relationships through caring and authenticity, not a purpose of superiority' (EC USA).

The Vatican document also called for the 'ordination' of women deacons, and the possibility of the 'ordination' of women to the priesthood:

> After careful listening, many reports ask that the Church continue its discernment in relation to a range of specific questions: the active role of women in the governing structures of Church bodies, the possibility for women with adequate training to preach in parish settings, and a female diaconate. Much greater diversity of opinion was expressed on the subject of priestly ordination for women, which some reports call for, while others consider a closed issue.[1980]

During the press conference pro-homosexuality Cardinal Grech defended the Synod on Synodality website displaying artwork promoting women priests and homosexuality, contrary to the Catholic faith:

[1978]Haynes, M [2022] *Top Synod cardinal calls for 'change of cultural paradigm' on homosexuality in latest scandalous remarks* [Online] Available at: www.lifesitenews.com [Accessed on: 11 January 2024]
[1979]Haynes, M [2022] *Pope Francis joins ecumenical leaders in Rome to promote peace in the 'spirit' of 1986 Assisi meeting* [Online] Available at: www.lifesitenews.com [Accessed on: 11 January 2024]
[1980]*Working Document for the Continental Stage* [2022] [Online] Available at: www.synod.va [Accessed on: 12 January 2024]

> We are listening to everybody and if you go through the document – we are not only talking about images but contents – listening to everybody without excluding anybody. [The synod has a] responsibility to take note of all voices – at this particular moment – of the people of God. Otherwise, you could also criticise us that we are not a listening Church! Our duty at this moment is to be a channel, to make the voices of the people of God, that arrived through the episcopal conferences. So we exclude nothing, we take note of everything and we submit that then to the pastors who have the responsibility to guide the people of God.[1981]

Pro-homosexuality Bishop Georg Bätzing, appointed by Pope Francis and head of the German Bishops' Conference, welcomed the Vatican document as affirming the German *Der Synodale Weg* regarding changing doctrine on homosexuality and the ordination of women to the diaconate and presbyterate.[1982]

1st November

Bishop Ray Browne of Kerry, appointed by Pope Francis in 2013, issued a statement apologising for any offence caused by one of his priests, Fr. Sean Sheehy, upholding the Church's teaching on homosexuality and abortion during a homily:

> I am aware of the deep upset and hurt caused by the contents of the homilies in question delivered over the weekend. I apologise to all who were offended. The views expressed do not represent the Christian position. The homily at a regular weekend parish Mass is not appropriate for such issues to be spoken of in such terms. I regret that this has occurred while a parish pilgrimage to the Holy Land is taking place.[1983]

During his homily on the 29th October at St. Mary's Church, Listowel, Kerry, Fr. Sean Sheehy condemned contraception, abortion, homosexuality, and transgenderism:

> What is so sad today is you rarely hear about sin, but it's rampant. We see it for example in the legislation of our governments, we see it in the promotion of abortion. We see it in the example of this lunatic approach of transgenderism. We see it, for example, in the promotion of sex between two men and two women. That is sinful. That is mortal sin, and people don't seem to realise it, but it's a fact.… You have a responsibility to call people to an awareness of the fact that sin is destructive, sin is detrimental, and sin will lead us to hell.

During his 2nd November interview on the *Radio Kerry* show *The Hard Shoulder*, Fr. Sheehy announced that Bishop Ray Browne had suspended his facilities to celebrate the Mass, responding, 'I couldn't care less really, because I know myself that what I said cannot be disproven by any honest-to-God Catholic, Christian or Catholic teaching.' He went on to criticise Bishop Browne for 'sacrificing' and 'muzzling the truth' to 'appease people because they don't want to face the reality that they need to face before they die. He [Bp. Browne] should have said to the people, "Fr. Sheehy was only preaching the truth; that's it. He's only preaching the gospel. He's only preaching the catechism; that's it."'[1984]

8th November

Cardinal Pietro Parolin, Pope Francis' Secretary of State, delivered an address at the 27th meeting of the United Nations Climate Change Conference of the Parties (COP). Cardinal Parolin expressed the Holy See's commitment to the Paris Agreement, which includes a eugenics, pro-abortion agenda:

[1981]Haynes, M [2022] *Leading synod cardinal defends promotion of LGBT images as part of being a 'listening Church'* [Online] Available at: www.lifesitenews.com [Accessed on: 12 January 2024]

[1982]Wailzer, A [2022] *Head of German bishops' conference says Vatican synod document is 'encouragement' for Synodal Way* [Online] Available at: www.lifesitenews.com [Accessed on: 11 January 2024]

[1983]Browne, R [2022] *Statement issued on behalf of the diocese of Kerry regarding the offending homilies* [Online] Available at: www.dioceseofkerry.ie [Accessed on: 12 January 2024]

[1984]Gomes, J [2022] *Cancelled Priest Rips LGBTQ-appeasing bishop* [Online] Available at: www.churchmilitant.com [Accessed on: 12 January 2024]

By acceding to the Convention and the Paris Agreement, the Holy See is even more committed to moving forward on this journey together, for the common good of humanity and especially on behalf of our youth, who are looking to us to care for present and future generations.[1985]

During an interview with the German news outlet *Deutsche Welle*, pro-homosexuality Bishop Helmut Dieser of the diocese of Aachen, the head of the Forum for Sexuality and Partnership for *Der Synodale Weg*, declared that homosexual 'attraction' and 'lovemaking' are not an 'aberration':

> [The] current state of Church teaching does not do justice to certain realities in the area of human sexuality…too simplified. This applies, for example, to the question of homosexuality. We cannot give homosexual people the answer that their feelings are unnatural and that they must therefore live celibate lives. As a Church, we have to answer these questions in a new way…homosexuality is not a mishap, not a disease, not an expression of a deficit, nor, by the way, a consequence of original sin. The world is colourful and creation is diverse. And then I may also accept a diversity in the area of sexuality that is willed by God and does not violate the Creator's will…same-sex attraction and lovemaking is not an aberration, but a variant of human sexuality.[1986]

10th November

During an interview with the heterodox UK Catholic journal *The Tablet* Archbishop Vincenzo Paglia indicated that Pope Francis was considering overturning the Church's doctrine prohibiting contraception. The pro-homosexuality Archbishop Paglia was appointed by Pope Francis in 2016 president of the 'reformed' Pontifical Academy of Life and Grand Chancellor of the John Paul II Pontifical Theological Institute for Marriage and Family Sciences. Archbishop Paglia said:

> Obviously, this question would need to be put to the Holy Father, more than to me. I believe that the day will come when Pope Francis or the next Pope [will do so]. But what can I say? Certainly, we have to address it…. We see this in what Jesus said to the Apostles before he left them. He said, 'I have other things to say to you, but you would not understand them. Then the Spirit will come.' This is also the progress of the Church.

Archbishop Paglia criticised those faithful Catholics who opposed the appointment of pro-abortion, pro-euthanasia members to the 'reformed' Pontifical Academy for Life:

> I say to those who oppose discussing these issues: I think there is a deep problem of faithfulness to the Spirit. And that is to say, that it is a pathology, it is a sick faith. And faith in the formula and not in the Spirit. I would say it runs the risk of blocking the Spirit.[1987]

10th November

Pope Francis again granted a private audience to the pro-homosexuality Fr. James Martin S.J., during which they discussed, according to Martin, 'the joys and hopes, the griefs and anxieties, of LGBTQ Catholics.' This was the third such meeting between the two since 2019.[1988]

11th November

During his address to the Vatican's Dicastery for Communications Pope Francis singled out pro-homosexuality Fr. James Martin S.J., for praise as a communicator of human values:

[1985]Haynes, M [2022] Cdl. *Parolin urges global leaders to advance goals of pro-abortion Paris Climate Agreement* [Online] Available at: www.lifesitenews.com [Accessed on: 12 January 2024]

[1986]Wailzer, A [2022] *German bishop: Homosexual 'attraction' and 'lovemaking' not an 'aberration'* [Online] Available at: www.lifesitenews.com [Accessed on: 12 January 2024]

[1987]Lamb, C [2022] *How could the Catholic Church develop its teaching on artificial contraception?* [Online] Available at: www.thetablet.co.uk [Accessed on; 12 January 2024]

[1988]Wimmer, AC [2022] *Pope Francis Meets with Father James Martin at Vatican* [Online] Available at: www.ncregister.com [Accessed on; 12 January 2024]

Then communication of values. We cannot descend to communication without values. We have to communicate with our values. This does not mean that we have to pray a novena to a saint every day. Christian values, values that are behind, values that teach about going forward. The person who is in it for human values. For example, I see James Martin here. 'Oh yes, this one works....' Yes, but he wrote a book called *Learning to Pray*. Read it because it teaches you to pray. A man who has values, a communicator who also knows how to teach you the way to communicate with God. This is being a communicator. To go, to walk, to risk, with values, convinced that I am giving my life with my values, Christian values and human values.[1989]

13th November

Bishop Franz-Josef Bode discussed his intention with journalists to advocate for the ordination of women with Pope Francis during the German bishops' ad limina meeting. Bishop Franz-Josef Bode was the co-head of the German Bishops' Conference. Asked what he would do if he were Pope, Bishop Bode replied 'I would see to it that there were women deacons. And prepare the priesthood of women.'[1990]

15th November

The official news website of the Catholic Church in Germany, *katholisch.de*, published an interview with priest-psychologist Hermann Backhaus who advocated celibate priests masturbating with pornography:

> With regard to celibate people, the consumption of explicit sexual depictions can have a relieving effect – this cannot be denied.... Almost everyone has sexual needs, but as priests and religious we are used to not noticing them, or at least not talking about them. This is a great danger.... But we are in the process in the Church of breaking down this behaviour and recognising it: Priests and religious are normal people with sexual desires. We have to deal with that.[1991]

18th November

During an interview with the German Catholic news site *kath.net*. Cardinal Gerhard Müller, the former prefect of the CDF, said a pope would lose his office if he becomes a heretic by clearly contradicting revelation and dogma on the reservation of ordination to men or introducing same sex marriage:

> It is therefore erroneous to think that a council or a pope could annul an earlier dogma or stipulate, for example, that the nature of the sacrament of Holy Orders does not include the requirement of the male sex of its recipient.... In an extreme case, a pope could become a heretic as a private person and thus automatically lose his office if the contradiction to the revelation and the dogmatic teaching of the Church is evident.

Cardinal Müller continued by making a number of thinly veiled criticisms of Pope Francis:

> Every pope must distinguish precisely between his task and himself as a private person, and must not impose his preferences on other Christians.... A pope or bishop or any other ecclesiastical superior must also not abuse the trust that is readily placed in him in a fraternal atmosphere in order to provide his incompetent or corrupt friends with ecclesiastical sinecures.

Cardinal Müller also criticised *Der Synodale Weg* for conforming to the current ideological and political zeitgeist like the German Christians did with Nazism:

[1989] Pope Francis [2022] *Address to the Employees and Participants in the Plenary Assembly of the Dicastery for Communications* [Online] Available at: www.vatican.va [Accessed on; 12 January 2024]

[1990] Wailzer, A [2022] *German bishop sees visit with Pope Francis as avenue to push agenda for women's ordinations* [Online] Available at: www.lifesitenews.com [Accessed on: 12 January 2024]

[1991] Wailzer, A [2022] *German priest touts 'relieving effect' of pornography for celibate clergy in interview on Church website* [Online] Available at: www.lifesitenews.com [Accessed on: 12 January 2024]

The baptismal creed has been replaced by the idol of pagan LGBT ideology. [Instead of] carrying the flag of victory of the Risen Christ as a guide to humanity, the protagonists of the German Synod raise the rainbow flag, which is a public rejection of the Christian image of man. They have replaced the Apostles' Creed with the creed to the idols of a neo-pagan religion.[1992]

In an exchange with the Catholic Canadian pro-life *LifeSiteNews*, pro-homosexuality Bishop John Arnold of the Diocese of Salford, England, admitted that it didn't make sense to him to have a homily about celibacy at an LGBT Mass:

I don't think that there's a need for an LGBT Mass simply to be about a homily on celibacy: that doesn't make sense to me at all. [LGBT Masses were centred] on being together in prayer, asking 'who am I, what is my mission, who am I called to be?', and we take that gently and reject nobody.[1993]

During an interview with *La Croix International*, the unofficial daily of the French episcopate, Monsignor Philippe Bordeyne, the president of the 'reformed' John Paul II Institute for Studies on Marriage and the Family discussed the 'blessing' of homosexual bondings. Appointed by Pope Francis in 2021, Monsignor Philippe Bordeyne denied that a 'blessing' gave any endorsement of an activity or lifestyle, as 'its role is not to validate a practice', rather a blessing is simply 'a prayer addressed to God, to praise God, to ask God for help and protection. It concerns people, and possibly also objects in their relationship to people…to bless, however, is to manifest the good that God 'says' about people and that God wants for them…No one can be deprived of God's blessing…the fact that homosexuals ask the Church to bless them invites us to listen to them, to enter into the complexity of their story and their situation.'[1994]

19th November

Pro-homosexuality Bishop Georg Bätzing, the president of the German Bishops' Conference, reported that at the conclusion of the German bishops *ad limina* he felt encouraged about the *Der Synodale Weg* after meeting Pope Francis, 'The Pope is a clever Jesuit. He let us wrestle among ourselves as brothers.' Bishop Georg Bätzing added that, 'we are Catholic and we will remain Catholic, we want to be Catholic differently.'[1995]

22nd November

The German bishops' news outlet, *katholisch.de*, reported that the bishops conference had voted to adopt new Church employment legislation, which allowed employees to live openly as divorced and civilly 're-married' or in homosexual relationships. The new 'Basic Order of Ecclesiastical Service' state that employees' private lives, 'in particular relationships and intimacy, are not subject to legal assessment.' Church employees, including Catholics, would therefore no longer face termination for living in a 'second marriage' or a homosexual relationship.[1996]

24th November

In his address to the International Theological Commission Pope Francis again criticised Tradition and those faithful Catholic who upheld Tradition, accusing such a focus as 'backwardism':

[1992]Wailzer, A [2022] *Cdl. Müller compares Synodal Way to pro-Nazi German Christians in the 1930s* [Online] Available at: www.lifesitenews.com [Accessed on: 12 January 2024]

[1993]Haynes, M [2022] *English bishop defends 'LGBT Masses': 'Being together' trumps preaching the virtue of chastity* [Online] Available at: www.lifesitenews.com [Accessed on: 12 January 2024]

[1994]Haynes, M [2022] *Head of John Paul II Institute: Same-sex couples shouldn't be 'deprived of God's blessing* [Online] Available at: www.lifesitenews.com [Accessed on: 12 January 2024]

[1995]Haynes, M [2022] *German Synodal Way proceeds after bishops 'encouraged' by meeting with Pope Francis* [Online] Available at: www.lifesitenews.com [Accessed on: 12 January 2024]

[1996]Wailzer, A [2022] *German bishops adopt new labor law allowing Church employees to live in same-sex relationships* [Online] Available at: www.lifesitenews.com [Accessed on: 12 January 2024]

Tradition – I want to emphasise this – makes us move in this direction – from the ground upwards, vertically. Today there is a great danger, that it will go in another direction – 'backwardism'. Going backward. 'It has always been done this way': it is better to go backward, which is safer, rather than going forward with tradition. This horizontal dimension, we have seen, has caused some movements, ecclesial movements, to remain fixed in time, in a backward direction…'backwardism' leads you to say that 'it has always been done this way, it is better to continue like this', and it does not enable you to grow. On this issue, you theologians, think a little about how to help.[1997]

25th November

The German bishops' official news site, *katholisch.de*, reported that the pro-homosexuality Bishop Georg Bätzing, president of the German bishops conference, declaring that he will not accept the Vatican saying 'No' about the 'ordination' of women. Bishop Bätzing said:

…even if Rome sees this point as settled, it is still an urgent question that has been asked and is therefore on the table. Access to the ecclesiastical office must be opened up, or it is hard to imagine the future of the Church in our country. We must vigorously defend our German causes.[1998]

28th November

Speaking to journalists at the conclusions of the Belgian bishops *ad limina* visit to the Vatican Cardinal Jozef De Kesel reported that they had been very warmly received by Pope Francis, despite their approval of the 'blessing' of homosexual bondings:

The atmosphere was informal. I had prepared a speech, but it was put aside. It was a moving meeting for us. Despite his age, 86, he is present in a very clear way. That atmosphere was noticeable everywhere. The reception was invariably warm.… I could say freely what I wanted, in an atmosphere of fraternity and respect. Also about pastoral care for homosexuals, for example. We could explain that we want to help those people. We talked about homosexual couples, we talked about *viri probati*, we talked about the possibility of women's diaconate.[1999]

24th November

Vatican News, the official news portal of the Vatican Holy See, posted a report suggesting that the Chinese Communist Party may not be guilty of persecuting Christians and members of other religious groups. Reporting on the trial of Cardinal Zen by the Chinese Communists, Vatican New stated,

The Cardinal, who is usually active on social media, remained silent through the trial, only asking his followers to pray for him. In the past, Cardinal Zen has also criticised the Chinese Communist Party for allegedly persecuting religious communities.[2000]

During an interview with *Schweizer Radio und Fernsehen*, pro-homosexuality Bishop Joseph Bonnemain of the Diocese of Chur announced that he had abolished the office of exorcist in his diocese:

For many questions, we do not need to look for extraordinary causes, rather we are all human beings who have strengths and weaknesses in ourselves, who are confronted with difficult family, social, and professional situations. And there are normal solutions

[1997]Pope Francis [2022] *Audience with members of the International Theological Commission* [Online] Available at: www.press.vatican.va [Accessed on: 12 January 2024]
[1998]Wailzer, A [2022] *Head of German bishops' conference says he will not accept Vatican's 'No' on women priests* [Online] Available at: www.lifesitenews.com [Accessed on: 12 January 2024]
[1999]Haynes, M [2022] *Belgian bishops pushing same-sex 'blessings' praise 'impressive' meeting with Pope Francis* [Online] Available at: www.lifesitenews.com [Accessed on: 12 January 2024]
[2000]Knuffke, L [2022] *Vatican suggests Communist China does not persecute Christians* [Online] Available at: www.lifesitenews.com [Accessed on: 12 January 2024]

for this, i.e. medical, psychological, psychotherapeutic, and one does not need to want to find secret causes.... I've never been confronted with a person where I've had to say there's a major exorcism required. Most people have emotional, psychological burdens and need support, prayer, blessings, appropriate church services but not necessarily a major exorcism.[2001]

30th November

The Italian newspaper *Domani* published a letter, in response to Pope Francis' Synod on Synodality, signed by fifty Italian priests declaring their homosexuality. The priests criticised the teachings on the Church writing that silence appears as the only way of survival' for homosexual clergy because they 'cannot speak openly about [their] homosexual orientation.... The Church is not a context in which to find immediate acceptance, especially for us.[2002]

4th December

The popular Italian Catholic news website *MessainLatino.it* reported that Pope Francis had intervened in the canonical punishment of Fr. Marko Ivan Rupnik S.J., and lifted his excommunication. Fr. Rupnik is one of Pope Francis' favourite artists who designed the Year of Mercy logo, was the director of Rome's Aletti Center, and a consultant for the Pontifical Council for Culture and the Pontifical Council for New Evangelisation. His artwork is ubiquitous in Vatican publishing.

In 2020 Fr. Rupnik had been convicted of absolving in confession a woman with whom he had engaged in sex, and consequently, violating canon 977, incurring an automatic excommunication, or a *latae sententiae* excommunication, according to Canon 1378 §1. This was confirmed by the canonical tribunal. According to high level sources Pope Francis intervened within 'a few hours' to overturn the excommunication:

> A few hours after the notification of the sentence, however, due to pressure from Fr. Rupnik the Holy Father lifted the excommunication, in contrast with the decisions of the court. The Jesuits themselves, who had a statement on the matter ready, were stopped.

Furthermore, due to 'gruesome' allegations against Fr. Rupnik of psychological and sexual abuse stretching back over thirty years, the Jesuits' attorney general planned to conduct a trial of Fr. Rupnik. This was also stopped by Pope Francis' intervention.

Weeks after the tribunal 'unanimously' declared that Fr. Rupnik had absolved an accomplice in confession, the priest was invited by Pope Francis deliver a Lenten homily to the Papal household in 2020.[2003]

On the 3rd December 2022, the Jesuits issued a press statement confirming that Fr. Rupnik was forbidden from offering confession, leading the *Spiritual Exercises*, or engaging in any 'public activities' without his local superior's permission. Despite this, Fr. Rupnik had preached at various clergy retreats and was scheduled to lead the four-day *Spiritual Exercises* at the Pontifical Sanctuary of the Holy House of Loreto.[2004]

On the 14th December 2022 Fr. Arturo Sosa, the Jesuit superior general, confirmed that Fr. Rupnik had been temporarily excommunicated, but gave no details of Pope Francis' involvement.[2005]

[2001]Wailzer, A [2022] *Swiss bishop abolishes office of exorcist, says there's no need to find 'secret causes' of problems* [Online] Available at: www.lifesitenews.com [Accessed on: 12 January 2024]

[2002]Hall, K [2022] *50 Italian priests declare their homosexuality in scandalous open letter* [Online] Available at: www.lifesitenews.com [Accessed on: 15 January 2024]

[2003]Haynes, M [2022] *Disgraced Jesuit gave homily to Papal household weeks after investigators found he absolved sexual 'accomplice'* [Online] Available at: www.lifesitenews.com [Accessed on: 15 January 2024]

[2004]Haynes, M [2022] *Pope reportedly intervened to lift excommunication of sexually active, abusive Jesuit priest* [Online] Available at: www.lifesitenews.com [Accessed on: 15 January 2024]

[2005]Winfield, N [2022] *Jesuits admit artist excommunicated before new abuse claims* [Online] Available at: www.apnews.com [Accessed on: 15 January 2024]

A former nun who was sexually abused by Fr. Rupnik testified that his sexually abuse was integral to his art and his theology:

> It was a real abuse of conscience. His sexual obsession was not extemporaneous but deeply connected to his conception of art and his theological thinking. Father Marko at first slowly and gently infiltrated my psychological and spiritual world by appealing to my uncertainties and frailties while using my relationship with God to push me to have sexual experiences with him.[2006]

In a 2023 interview with *Associated Press* Pope Francis denied any involvement in the Rupnik case, 'other than to intervene procedurally to keep the second set of accusations from the nine women with the same tribunal that had heard the first.' About the allegations against Rupnik Pope Francis said, 'For me, it was a surprise, really. This, a person, an artist of this level — for me was a big surprise, and a wound.'[2007] The Italian Catholic website *Messa in Latino* – which led the coverage of the Rupnik case – responded to Francis' interview, suggesting that he was 'lying diplomatically' in order to save face in the matter.

8th December

During his key note speech at the International Catholic Jurists Forum, Monsignor Livio Melina accused the 'reformed' Pontifical Academy for Life of undermining Catholic sexual morality. Monsignor Melina is the former head of the John Paul II Institute on Marriage and the Family. Criticising the Pontifical Academy for Life's book, *Theological Ethics of Life. Scripture, Tradition, Practical Challenges*, Monsignor Livio Melina said:

> The document of the Pontifical Academy for Life proposes, along these lines, a re-reading of the moral norms taught by the Magisterium in the encyclical *Humanae Vitae* and in the instruction *Donum vitae*, concerning contraception and medically assisted procreation, on the basis of which the discernment of conscience could lead to going beyond the letter of the prohibition, thus accepting that the conjugal sexual act can be intentionally separated from the openness to procreation and that the desired procreation can be obtained from the technical act of doctors and not from the conjugal act. As can be seen, we are not dealing here only with an interpretation that shapes the meaning of the moral norm, but with a real questioning of the entirety of sexual morality and the morality of life, which the Catholic Church has taught so far. When the moral precepts that protect the self-offering meaning of sexuality and human generation are contradicted, in reality we are not only going beyond the letter of a particular norm, but we are going against the spirit and meaning of the very law that God has written in our heart and revealed to us in the history of salvation.[2008]

12th December

The Catalan Catholic blog *Germinans Germinabit* reported that several seminarians had contacted them to testify that Pope Francis had told them that priests must grant the absolution of sins even when there is no purpose of amendment. The Supreme Pontiff told the seminarians that they must:

> forgive everything even if we see that there is no intention to repent, we must forgive all. We can never deny absolution, because we become a vehicle for an evil, unjust, and moralistic judgment.

[2006]Haynes, M [2022] *Former nun details years of 'satanic' sex abuse by Jesuit priest Fr. Rupnik* [Online] Available at: www.lifesitenews.com [Accessed on: 12 January 2024]

[2007]Winfield, N [2023] *Pope opens up on sex abuse cases, says church must do more* [Online] Available at: www.apnews.com [Accessed on: 16 January 2024]

[2008]Haynes, M [2022] *Prominent Vatican theologian: Pontifical Academy for Life is undermining Catholic sexual morality* [Online] Available at: www.lifesitenews.com [Accessed on: 15 January 2024]

According to the UK Catholic news magazine the *Catholic Herald*, Francis also used obscene expletives during a rant against 'f***ing careerists who f*** up the lives of others'. The Pope also criticised 'those who climb to show their a**'.[2009]

13th December

Archbishop Christophe Pierre, the Apostolic Nuncio to the United States, sent a letter to US bishops to inform them that America's most prominent pro-life campaigner, Fr. Frank Pavone had been laicised. Archbishop Christophe Pierre was appointed by Pope Francis in 2016. Without providing any evidence, Archbishop Pierre stated that Fr. Pavone had been dismissed from the clerical state for 'blasphemous communications on social media' and 'persistent disobedience of the lawful instructions of his diocesan bishop'. The apostolic nuncio added that there was 'no possibility of appeal.' In response, Fr. Pavone said that he had not been notified about the Vatican's judgment.[2010]

16th December

During an interview with the German bishops' news outlet, *katholisch.de*, pro-homosexuality Bishop Franz-Josef Overbeck of Essen demanded that the Church accept homosexual bondings as families. Asked if the Catholic Church needs to 'widen its understanding of the family,' Bishop Overbeck replied, 'It is high time that she does that.' Asked if homosexual 'couples' could be good parents, Bishop Overbeck replied:

> Why shouldn't they be? It is not a matter of moralising at this point, but of developing perspectives together for good pastoral care of all family models with all the people living in them.[2011]

22nd December

During his annual Christmas address to the Roman Curia Pope Francis criticised those who sought to live by the virtue of purity in the Church of committing the heresy of Catharism:

> Mercy means accepting the fact that others also have their limits. Here too, it is fair to accept that individuals and institutions, precisely because they are human, are also limited. A Church that is pure and for the pure is only a return to the heresy of Catharism. Were that the case, the Gospel and the Bible as a whole would not have told us of limitations and shortcomings of many of those whom today we acknowledge as saints.

The Supreme Pontiff also criticised the idea of the perennial Magisterium, describing it as attempting to imprison the message of Christ:

> The contrary of conversion is 'immobility', the secret belief that we have nothing else to learn from the Gospel. This is the error of trying to crystallise the message of Jesus in a single, perennially valid form. Instead, its form must be capable of constantly changing, so that its substance can remain constantly the same. True heresy consists not only in preaching another gospel (cf. Gal 1:9), as Saint Paul told us, but also in ceasing to translate its message into today's languages and ways of thinking, which is precisely what the Apostle of the Gentiles did. To preserve means to keep alive and not to imprison the message of Christ.[2012]

[2009]Mangiaracina, E [2023] *Pope Francis reportedly flouts Church teaching, says 'forgive all' sins even with 'no intention to repent'* [Online] Available at: www.lifesitenews.com; Caldwell, S [2023] *Pope curses 'delinquent' priests who withhold absolution* [Online] Available at: www.catholicherald.co.uk [Accessed on: 16 January 2024]

[2010]Mullen, S & Bukuras, J [2023] *Vatican dismisses Father Frank Pavone from priesthood* [Online] Available at: www.catholicnewsagency.com [Accessed at: 30 January 2024]

[2011]Wailzer, A [2022] *German bishop demands Church 'widen its understanding of the family' to include homosexual unions* [Online] Available at: www.lifesitenews.com [Accessed on: 15 January 2024]

[2012]Pope Francis [2022] *Address to the Roman Curia for the Exchange of Christmas Greetings* [Online] Available at: www.vatican.va [Accessed on: 15 January 2024]

30th December

The twitter account of the 'reformed' Pontifical Academy for Life retweeted a Wall Street Journal article excited about the possibility of Catholic teaching on contraception being changed. The article's speculation was fuelled by the Pontifical Academy for Life's pro-contraception book *Theological Ethics of Life*.[2013]

2023

3rd January

The official website of the German bishops *katholisch.de* reported that a Benedictine priest was punished by his abbot for a Christmas homily criticising gender ideology and *Der Synodale Weg*. Abbot Mauritius Choriol O.S.B. of Tholey Abbey suspended Fr. Joachim Wernersbach O.S.B. from performing pastoral activities and commissioned 'an ecclesiastical investigation with an analysis of the sermon text and intercession prayers'. Among other things Fr. Wernersbach preached:

> You hear about gender and transgender, transhumanism and reproductive health, wokeness and LGBTQ, diversity and identity. Of multiple genders and gender reassignment, plus this devastating new understanding of revelation from the Synodal Way. My dear friends, even the terms are absolutely disturbing. They all have one thing in common: they lack beauty, they lack coherence, and they lack naturalness. They are not aligned, not in harmony with the inconceivably beautiful Divine Order. A great dissonance has befallen our country. Christ came into the world to resolve this dissonance. He does not want us to end up in an absurd world, in a world that no longer wants to know anything about God.

Abbot Choriol responded to Fr. Wernersbach upholding the traditional family and criticising abortion, gender ideology, and *Der Synodale Weg* by stating that Tholey Abbey:

> …expressly reject the image of man drawn by him in it and the statements made there about the history of creation. We regret the anger, suffering, but also consternation caused by it. The evaluations made by our confrere lack pastoral empathy and not only contradict the reality of society, but in many ways discriminate against large segments of society, for instance when it comes to the view of women, to the understanding of family, and regarding queer human beings and the LGBT community…[they made their critique] regardless of valid Catholic doctrine.[2014]

4th January

The Italian news outlet *Left* reported that Pope Francis allegedly ignored letters from nuns Fr. Marko Rupnik S.J., sexually and psychologically abused: 'Pope Francis received 4 letters from as many former sisters…. Pope Francis never answered this and the other 3 letters.'[2015]

9th January

During his annual address to the diplomatic corps of ambassadors accredited to the Holy See Pope Francis again contradicted the Church's doctrine on the death penalty by stating that it was always 'inadmissible':

> I appeal, then, for an end to the death penalty, which is always inadmissible since it attacks the inviolability and the dignity of the person, in the legislation of all the

---

[2013]Wailzer, A [2022] *Pontifical Academy for Life retweets article on changing Church's contraception ban* [Online] Available at: www.lifesitenews.com [Accessed on: 15 January 2024]

[2014]Wailzer, A [2023] *German priest punished by superiors for preaching against gender ideology, Synodal Way* [Online] Available at: www.lifesitenews.com [Accessed on: 16 January 2024]

[2015]Haynes, M [2023] *Pope Francis ignored letters from nuns allegedly abused by Fr. Rupnik: report* [Online] Available at: www.lifesitenews.com [Accessed on: 16 January 2024]

countries of the world. We cannot overlook the fact that, up until his or her very last moment, a person can repent and change.[2016]

11th January

The UK magazine *The Spectator* published an article by Cardinal George Pell, former Prefect of the Secretariat for the Economy, in which he called Pope Francis' Synod on Synodality a 'toxic nightmare':

> The Catholic Synod of Bishops is now busy constructing what they think of as 'God's dream' of synodality. Unfortunately, this divine dream has developed into a toxic nightmare despite the bishops' professed good intentions.

Referring to the Synod Secretariat's working document for the continental phase of the synod, Cardinal Pell wrote:

> What is one to make of this potpourri, this outpouring of New Age good will? It is not a summary of Catholic faith or New Testament teaching. It is incomplete, hostile in significant ways to the apostolic tradition and nowhere acknowledges the New Testament as the Word of God, normative for all teaching on faith and morals. The Old Testament is ignored, patriarchy rejected and the Mosaic Law, including the Ten Commandments, is not acknowledged.[2017]

Following Cardinal Pell's death on the 10th January, the veteran Vatican journalist Sandro Magister reported that the cardinal was the author of the 2022 'Demos' memo sent to all cardinals. The 'Demos' memo severely criticised Pope Francis and highlighted key issues the next pope would need to address. Cardinal Pell wrote:

> Commentators of every school, if for different reasons, with the possible exception of Father Spadaro, S.J., agree that this pontificate is a disaster in many or most respects; a catastrophe…the next pope must understand that the secret of Christian and Catholic vitality comes from fidelity to the teachings of Christ and Catholic practices. It does not come from adapting to the world or from money.[2018]

12th January

Following the death of Pope Benedict XVI on the 31st December 2022, his former aide and secretary Archbishop Georg Gänswein published a book revealing the late pope's criticisms of Pope Francis. In his book *Nothing but the Truth: My Life with Benedict XVI*, Archbishop Gänswein revealed that Pope Benedict XVI considered Pope Francis' restrictions of the Latin Mass 'a mistake' and his disparaging of Latin contrary to Vatican II: 'Benedict remembered well how the Council had instead insisted that "the use of the Latin language, except for particular rights, be preserved in the Latin rites"'. Archbishop Gänswein also revealed that Pope Benedict XVI was 'surprised' that Pope Francis refused to answer the *dubia* submitted by four cardinals about *Amoris Laetitia*, 'Benedict was only humanly surprised at the absence of any hint of a reply from the pontiff, despite the fact that Francis normally showed himself willing to meet and talk to anyone.'[2019]

13th January

The Spanish language news outlet *Mundo Negro* published an interview with Pope Francis, during which he expressed a lack of interest or concern in the drastic decline of vocations in Western countries:

[2016]Pope Francis [2023] *Address to members of the Diplomatic Corps accredited to the Holy See* [Online] Available at: www.vatican.va [Accessed on: 16 January 2024]

[2017]Pell, George [2023] *The Catholic Church must free itself from this 'toxic nightmare'* [Online] Available at: www.spectator.co.uk [Accessed on: 16 January 2023]

[2018]Haynes, M [2023] *Cdl. Pell wrote memo sent to cardinals on 'catastrophe' of Pope Francis: Vatican reporter* [Online] Available at: www.lifesitenews.com [Accessed on: 15 January 2024]

[2019]Haynes, M [2023] *Pope Benedict thought Pope Francis' restriction of the Latin Mass was a 'mistake': Abp. Gänswein reveals; Abp. Gänswein: Benedict XVI was 'surprised' Pope Francis ignored the dubia* [Online] Available at: www.lifesitenews.com [Accessed on: 16 January 2024]

Five places: Belgium, Holland, Spain, Ireland and Quebec filled the world with missionaries. Today, these five places have no vocations. It is a mystery: and in less than 100 years. How do we explain this to each other? I see no explanation.... I am not concerned in the sense that we are merging, it is a sign of the times that indicates worldliness, that indicates a level of development that puts values elsewhere. This signals crises, there are crises, and crises must be experienced and overcome.[2020]

During an interview with US Catholic news website *The Pillar* Archbishop Charles Chaput, O.F.M. Cap., the emeritus archbishop of Philadelphia, warned that the Synod on Synodality was in danger of being 'manipulated':

About the process, I think it's imprudent and prone to manipulation, and manipulation always involves dishonesty. The claim that Vatican II somehow implied the need for synodality as a permanent feature of Church life is simply false. The council never came close to suggesting that. Moreover, I was a delegate to the 2018 synod, and the way 'synodality' was smuggled onto the agenda was manipulative and offensive. It had nothing at all to do with the synod's theme of young people and the faith. Synodality risks becoming a kind of Vatican III Lite; a rolling council on a much more controllable, malleable scale. That wouldn't serve the needs of the Church or her people.... I'd be very wary of the idea that synodality can somehow take the place of an ecumenical council in the life of the Church. There's no tradition of bishops delegating their personal responsibility for the universal Church to a smaller number of bishops, so any such development would need to be very carefully examined and discussed before any attempt at implementation. That's not the current spirit or reality of what's happening.[2021]

23rd January

Pro-homosexuality Cardinal Jean-Claude Hollerich S.J., the relator general of the Synod, announced at a press conference that Pope Francis had appointed pro-homosexuality Fr. Timothy Radcliffe O.P., to lead a three-day retreat preceding the Synod on Synodality.[2022] In the past Fr. Radcliffe had talked about the Eucharistic nature of homosexual sex acts:

How does all this bear on the question of gay sexuality? We cannot begin with the question of whether it is permitted or forbidden! We must ask what it means, and how far it is Eucharistic. Certainly it can be generous, vulnerable, tender, mutual and non-violent. So in many ways I think it can be expressive of Christ's self-gift.... We can also see how homosexuality can be expressive of mutual fidelity, a covenantal relationship in which two people bind themselves to each other for ever.[2023]

The pro-homosexuality Fr. James Martin S.J., recipient of many signs of favour from Pope Francis, posted on twitter that a homosexual politician's bonding with another homosexual man was a 'marriage':

Like it or not, Pete Buttigieg is legally married. You may disagree with same-sex marriage (or not). But @SecretaryPete is married in the eyes of the state, and his church, as much as anyone else is. To claim otherwise is to ignore reality.

Bishop Joseph Strickland of Tyler, Texas, admonished Fr. James Martin by posting in reply:

[2020]Haynes, M [2023] *Pope Francis condemns 'serious sin' of 'proselytism' but has 'no explanation' for vocations crisis* [Online] Available at: www.lifesitenews.com [Accessed on: 16 January 2024]
[2021]*Chaput: 'Speaking the truth is polarizing'* [2023] [Online] Available at: www.pillarcatholic.com [Accessed on: 16 January 2024]
[2022]Haynes, M [2023] *Pope invites notorious pro-LGBT priest to lead key Synod retreat for bishops* [Online] Available at: www.lifesitenews.com [Accessed on: 16 January 2024]
[2023]*A paper laying out the theology of marriage as currently articulated through the Canons and Liturgy of the Scottish Episcopal Church, and exploring whether there is a case for change based on scripture, tradition and reason* [2015] Available at: www.scotland.anglican.org [Accessed on: 16 January 2024]

Marriage is between 1 man & 1 woman, committed for life & open to children. Attempts to redefine marriage fail to change this reality. If an element of the above definition is altered then no marriage exists no matter what words are used. Living a fiction is unhealthy.[2024]

24th January

America Magazine, the heterodox US Jesuit journal, published an essay by pro-homosexuality Cardinal Robert McElroy of San Diego calling for 'radical inclusion', including homosexuals in mortal sin be given Communion and women be 'ordained' deacons. Cardinal McElroy was elevated to the Sacred College of Cardinals by Pope Francis in 2022. Basing his argument on a misunderstanding of the doctrine of the hierarchy of truth McElroy argued:

The effect of the tradition that all sexual acts outside of marriage constitute objectively grave sin has been to focus the Christian moral life disproportionately upon sexual activity. The heart of Christian discipleship is a relationship with God the Father, Son and Spirit rooted in the life, death and resurrection of Jesus Christ. The church has a hierarchy of truths that flow from this fundamental kerygma. Sexual activity, while profound, does not lie at the heart of this hierarchy. Yet in pastoral practice we have placed it at the very center of our structures of exclusion from the Eucharist. This should change.

Cardinal McElroy went as far as calling those who upheld the Church's doctrine on homosexuality as possessing a 'demonic animus':

It is a demonic mystery of the human soul why so many men and women have a profound and visceral animus toward members of the L.G.B.T. communities. The church's primary witness in the face of this bigotry must be one of embrace rather than distance or condemnation. The distinction between orientation and activity cannot be the principal focus for such a pastoral embrace because it inevitably suggests dividing the L.G.B.T. community into those who refrain from sexual activity and those who do not. Rather, the dignity of every person as a child of God struggling in this world, and the loving outreach of God, must be the heart, soul, face and substance of the church's stance and pastoral action.

Cardinal McElroy also argued that individual conscience must be able to override the truths of Divine Revelation, 'While Catholic teaching must play a critical role in the decision making of believers, it is conscience that has the privileged place.'

Cardinal EcElroy also asserted that women must be admitted to the sacrament of Holy Orders:

The church should move toward admitting women to the diaconate [so that women can] provide critically important ministries, talents and perspectives.... The call for the admission of women to priestly orders as an act of justice and a service to the church was voiced in virtually every region of our world church.[2025]

A number of US prelates criticised Cardinal McElroy's arguments, including Archbishop Joseph F. Naumann of Archdiocese of Kansas City in Kansas. Archbishop Naumann accused Cardinal McElroy of teaching grave errors:

Cardinal McElroy appears to believe that the church for 2,000 years has exaggerated the importance of her sexual moral teaching, and that radical inclusion supersedes doctrinal fidelity, especially in the area of the church's moral teaching regarding human sexuality. In my opinion, this is a most serious and dangerous error. Our understanding of sexual

---

[2024]Knuffke, L [2023] *Fr. James Martin defends Pete Buttigieg's same-sex 'marriage' as legal, legitimate* [Online] Available at: www.lifesitenews.com [Accessed on: 16 January 2024]
[2025]Wolfe, R [2023] *US cardinal demands homosexuals in mortal sin be given Communion, women be 'ordained' deacons* [Online] Available at: www.lifesitenews.com [Accessed on: 16 January 2024]

morals significantly impacts marriage and family life. The importance of marriage and family to society, culture, the nation and the church cannot be overestimated.[2026]

Bishop Thomas Paprocki of the Diocese of Springfield criticised Cardinal McElroy for seeming 'to be calling for the Church to devalue the gravity of sexual sin'[2027] Bishop Paprocki went on to accuse Cardinal McElroy of teaching heresy, for which he may have excommunicated himself:

> Thus a cardinal of the Catholic Church, like any other Catholic who denies settled Catholic teaching, embraces heresy, the result of which is automatic excommunication from the Catholic Church.[2028]

25th January

During an interview with the US news outlet *Associated Press* Pope Francis criticised bishops who supported laws that criminalised homosexuality:

> Being homosexual is not a crime but it's a sin. Bishops in particular need to undergo a process of change to recognise the dignity of everyone. These bishops have to have a process of conversion, tenderness, please, as God has for each one of us. Being homosexual is not a crime. It's not a crime. Yes, but it's a sin. Fine, but first let's distinguish between a sin and a crime. It's also a sin to lack charity with one another. We are all children of God, and God loves us as we are and for the strength that each of us fights for our dignity.[2029]

27th January

In his book length interview, *In buona fede*, Cardinal Gerhard Müller, the former prefect of the CDF, revealed that Pope Francis had hamstrung the CDF in order to prevent Italians priests convicted of sex abuse from being laicised. Regarding the infamous case of serial child abuser Fr. Inzoli Cardinal Müller said:

> Unfortunately, however, there was a curia cardinal who went knocking at Santa Marta, asking for clemency. Faced with this interventionism, the Pope was convinced and chose to modify the sentence by adjusting the punishment for Inzoli, stipulating that he remain a priest but with a ban on wearing the priestly habit or clergyman in public and without presenting himself to communities as consecrated…just one example, but I recall that there were several cardinals who reacted and showed strong opposition in the face of judgments reducing clerics guilty of abuse to the lay state. [Such cardinals]…lobbied to overturn the decisions on the grounds of excessive guarantees, saying that depriving a priest of priestly status is tantamount to condemning him to death. And since the death penalty has been removed from the Catechism it would have been an incongruity to execute it in other circumstances. So it happened that for clerics of Polish or American or foreign nationality who were condemned by the tribunal of the Congregation for the Doctrine of the Faith, the reduction of the clerical state was quickly carried out, while for Italian priests it was always such a struggle to enforce the sentence because influential friends were moving behind the scenes, knocking at Santa Marta going to the Pope to ask him to intercede. And they almost always succeeded in the end.[2030]

31st January

Radical pro-abortion Catholic President Joe Biden claimed that Pope Francis did not support the United States Conference of Catholic Bishops' call for a halt to taxpayer

---

[2026]Naumann, J [2023] *Did Jesus' teaching seek to alienate – or liberate?* [Online] Available at: www.theleaven.org [Accessed on: 18 January 2024]

[2027]Paprocki, T [2023] *A better way forward: A response to Cardinal Robert McElroy* [Online] Available at: www.catholicworldreport.com [Accessed on: 18 January 2024]

[2028]Paprocki, T [2023] *Imagining a Heretical Cardinal* [Online] Available at: www.firstthings.com [Accessed on: 18 January 2024]

[2029]Haynes, M [2023] *Pope Francis says Church must fight anti-sodomy laws and bishops who support them need conversion* [Online] Available at: www.lifesitenews.com [Accessed on: 16 January 2024]

[2030]Haynes, M [2023] *Cdl. Müller says Pope Francis revoked penalties on abusive priests at the request of cardinals* [Online] Available at: www.lifesitenews.com [Accessed on: 16 January 2024]

funded abortions. In response to an journalist stating 'Catholic bishops are demanding that federal tax dollars not fund abortions' Biden responded, 'No, they are not all doing that. Nor is the Pope doing that.'

In response to Biden's scandalous claim about Pope Francis' position about abortion, Bishop Strickland of Tyler tweeted an appeal to the Vatican, 'I implore the Vatican press office to emphatically clarify that Pope Francis rightly calls abortion murder. It is time to denounce Biden's fake Catholicism.' No clarification was forthcoming from the Vatican or Pope Francis. However, Archbishop Broglio, as president of the US bishops' conference, refuted Biden's claim that the US bishops 'were not demanding that the cessation of federal tax dollars funding abortions'.[2031]

6th February

Dr. Peter Kwasniewski, the liturgist and theologian, reported that Cardinal Arthur Roche, the Prefect of the Vatican's Congregation for Divine Worship appointed by Pope Francis in 2021, was taking behind-the-scenes steps to further restrict the traditional Latin Mass. Contravening canon law, Cardinal Roche rebuked a bishop for invoking canon 87 in order to grant a dispensation from *Traditionis Custodes* in order to allow the continuation of the traditional Latin Mass in a parish church. Canon 87 states:

> A diocesan bishop, whenever he judges that it contributes to their spiritual good, is able to dispense the faithful from universal and particular disciplinary laws issued for his territory or his subjects by the supreme authority of the Church. (Can. 87 §1.)

Without warrant, Cardinal Roche wrote to the bishop claiming that he 'did not have the authority to grant such a dispensation', because such a dispensation was 'reserved to the Holy See.' Cardinal Roche claimed that the entirety of Pope Francis' *Traditionis Custodes* was reserved to the Holy See, stripping bishops of their power to dispense from the document:

> Not only did the Holy Father issue *Traditionis Custodes* he approved the *Responsa ad dubia*, so there can be no doubt about his wishes in this regard given that it is stated in such a clear way in both documents.

Referring to the work of canon lawyers, Dr. Kwasniewski argued that Roche violated Canon Law:

> …the Responses to the Dubia were not approved *in forma specifica*, which is what would have been necessary to reserve the dispensation to the Holy See. Nevertheless, Card. Roche is proceeding as if the Responses had been so approved, and therefore that his dicastery alone can grant the dispensations.[2032]

Cardinal Roche remedied this canonical oversight on the 21st February 2023 by issuing a rescript that declared that certain dispensations were no longer under the prerogative of the local bishop, but rather are 'reserved in a special way to the Apostolic See'.[2033]

9th February

During an interview with the US Catholic newspaper *National Catholic Register*, Archbishop André-Joseph Léonard warned that the Faith was under threat from false conceptions of pastoral care and the Synod of Synodality. Archbishop André-Joseph Léonard is the archbishop emeritus of Brussels-Mechelen and former primate of

[2031]Wailzer, A & Haynes, M [2023] *Bp. Strickland urges Vatican to refute Biden's claim that Pope doesn't oppose taxpayer-funded abortions*; Haynes, M [2023] *USCCB president responds to Biden: Catholic bishops 'will work as one body' to end abortion* [Online] Available at: www.lifesitenews.com [Accessed on: 17 January 2024]

[2032]Haynes, M [2023] *Cdl. Roche's attempt to further restrict Latin Mass violates Church law: canon lawyers* [Online] Available at: www.lifesitenews.com [Accessed on: 16 January 2024]

[2033]Haynes, M [2023] *Pope Francis issues new document limiting the powers of bishops to allow the Latin Mass in their diocese* [Online] Available at: www.lifesitenews.com [Accessed on: 18 January 2024]

Belgium. When asked, *Do you think that the teachings of the Church about these topics are really threatened at the present time?* Archbishop Léonard replied:

> Yes, this threat exists! It is already present in a pastoral care that deviates from essential points of the Catholic faith, such as male priesthood, representing the (male!) Spouse of the Church, Christ, the high value of priestly celibacy in the West, and the complementarity of man and woman in marriage. Alas, I fear that many of the requests expressed in the 'Synod on Synodality' — what an abstruse wording! — will seek to undermine or relativize these vital realities.[2034]

14th February

The pro-homosexuality Bishop Helmut Dieser of Aachen allowed the Facebook of his archdiocese to post an invitation to homosexual bondings to receive a 'blessing' on St. Valentine's Day', including a photograph of two men caught in the act of kissing with the caption 'Love is everything.'[2035]

21st February

Fr. Johan Verschueren, delegate of Jesuit Superior Fr. General Arturo Sosa, issued a statement imposing further restrictions on Fr. Marko Rupnik S.J., Pope Francis' favourite artist. The statement disclosed that the Jesuit Referral Team for Complaint Cases had compiled a 150-page dossier of reported instances of spiritually, psychologically or sexually abuse committed by Rupnik between 1985 to 2018. The investigators reported that they had been unable to interview Fr. Rupnik because he had declined to cooperate. Fr. Verschueren announced that he would instigate an 'internal procedure' that could lead to disciplinary action and, in the meantime, the existing restrictions on Rupnik were tightened to include a ban on any public artistic actions, 'especially towards religious facilities (such as churches, institutions, oratories and chapels, exercise or spirituality houses).'[2036]

Fr. Rupnik defied the restrictions placed on him when he concelebrated at Sunday morning Mass on March 5 in the Basilica of Santa Prassede, Rome.[2037]

2nd March

The Jesuit heterodox magazine, *America*, published a follow up essay to his earlier controversial essay (24/01/2023) from pro-homosexuality Cardinal McElroy. Doubling down on his advocacy of 'radical inclusion', involving those unrepentant of mortal sin receiving Holy Communion, Cardinal McElroy argued:

> Everyone commits profound sins of omission or commission. At such moments we should seek the grace of the sacrament of penance. But such failures should not be the basis for categorical ongoing exclusion from the Eucharist…. Pastoral theology and accompaniment involve inviting all striving disciples to the eucharistic banquet in this world and the next, including divorced and remarried or sexually active members of the L.G.B.T. communities [….] To bar disciples from that grace blocks one of the principal pathways Christ has given to them to reform their lives and accept the Gospel ever more fully. For all of these reasons, I proposed that divorced and remarried or L.G.B.T. Catholics who are ardently seeking the grace of God in their lives should not be categorically barred from the Eucharist.

Cardinal McElroy went on to ridicule moral doctrine teaching that sexual sins are grave matter:

[2034]Tadié, S [2023] *Belgian Archbishop: The Fundamental Teachings of the Church Are Currently Under Threat* [Online] Available at: www.ncregister.com [Accessed on: 18 January 2024]
[2035]Haynes, M [2023] *German diocese offers same-sex blessings on St. Valentine's Day* [Online] Available at: www.lifesitenews.com [Accessed on: 18 January 2024]
[2036]Haynes, M [2023] *Jesuits place further restrictions on disgraced Fr. Rupnik following new abuse allegations* [Online] Available at: www.lifesitenews.com [Accessed on: 18 January 2024]
[2037]Haynes, M [2023] *Fr. Rupnik concelebrates Mass in Roman basilica despite ban on public ministry* [Online] Available at: www.lifesitenews.com [Accessed on: 18 January 2024]

The moral tradition that all sexual sins are grave matter springs from an abstract, deductivist and truncated notion of the Christian moral life that yields a definition of sin jarringly inconsistent with the larger universe of Catholic moral teaching. This is because it proceeds from the intellect alone.[2038]

Responding to Cardinal McElroy's latest heretical essay, Bishop Paprocki of Springfield said

…the suggestion being put forth here that we shouldn't pay attention to that whole question about repentance before receiving Holy Communion if you are conscious of grave sin, that's really rejecting something that has been part of the Church's teaching for the last 2,000 years going all the way back to St. Paul…. If you know in your heart that you reject Church teaching you basically put yourself outside of the Church [….] I think we're in a very difficult moment in the Church right now, because we do have things that are being put out there that are, frankly, just contrary to Church teaching and the life of the Church as it has been lived for almost 2,000 years now, and that's why I think it's important for bishops to speak out and for theologians and others in the Church to speak out about what is the teaching of the Church, what is the correct understanding of the Church, and not to be suggesting that somehow this is all up for grabs and can be overturned by a synodal process.[2039]

4th March

In an interview with Joe McClane on the US digital radio station, *The Station of the Cross*, Bishop Athanasius Schneider of Astana, Kazakhstan, said heretical bishops know Pope Francis won't punish them. In response to Cardinal McElroy's heresy Bishop Schneider said:

It is very sad, this cardinal and other bishops who publicly speak heresy *de facto*, are unpunished…they do so knowing they will not be punished, because Pope Francis… never punished such heretical bishops [….] Bishop McElroy was promoted even [when] it was publicly known his statements against the integrity of faith, and he was in some way rewarded for this.[2040]

10th March

During an interview with Argentinian news outlet *infobae* Pope Francis appeared to encourage homosexuals and divorced and 'civilly re-married' to receive Holy Communion without repenting of their sin. In response to the question, *leaving aside the choice or sexual preference, a person who has complied with the rest of what the Church mandates, would he be able to receive Communion?*, Pope Francis said:

The big answer was given by Jesus: everybody. Everybody. Everyone inside. When the exquisite ones did not want to go to the banquet: go there to the crossroads and call everyone. Good, bad, old, young, young men, young boys: everybody. Everybody. And each one resolves his positions before the Lord with the strength he has. This is a church of sinners. I don't know where the church of saints is, here we are all sinners. And who am I to judge a person if he has good will? If he belongs to the devil's gang, well, let's defend him a little bit. I think we have to go to the essence of the Gospel: Jesus calls everyone and each one resolves his relationship with God as he can or as he wants. Sometimes we want to and sometimes we cannot, but the Lord always waits.[2041]

[2038]Wolfe, R [2023] *Cdl. McElroy doubles down on heresy, pushes Communion for 'sexually active' homosexuals, adulterers* [Online] Available at: www.lifesitenews.com [Accessed on: 18 January 2024]

[2039]Wolfe, R [2023] *Bp. Paprocki, Abp. Naumann fire back at Cdl. McElroy for attacking Catholic moral teaching* [Online] Available at: www.lifesitenews.com [Accessed on: 18 January 2024]

[2040]Haynes, M [2023] *Bp. Schneider: Bishops who push 'heresy' know Pope Francis won't punish them* [Online] Available at: www.lifesitenews.com [Accessed on: 18 January 2024]

[2041]Haynes, M [2023] *Pope Francis pushes more confusion on the reception of Holy Communion in new interview* [Online] Available at: www.lifesitenews.com [Accessed on: 18 January 2024]

Participants of the German *Der Synodale Weg* voted overwhelmingly in favour of the document *Blessings for Couples Who Love Each Other*, including the blessing of homosexual bondings. Among the bishops of the German Bishops Conference, the text was approved by 38 to 9, with 11 abstaining. Those participants in favour of same-sex blessing emphasised the fact that Pope Francis had taken no action against the Belgian bishops for their promotion of same-sex 'blessings'. With the text approved, the German bishops conference committed to prepare a handbook containing the formula for such blessing.[2042]

The next day, participants voted overwhelmingly in favour of the document *Dealing with Gender Diversity* that allowed changing one's listed sex on a baptismal certificate and paved the way for 'transgender' priests:

> Access to holy orders and pastoral vocations must also be examined in each individual case for intersex and transsexual baptised and confirmed persons who sense a vocation for themselves and must not be excluded across the board.

Of the 58 German bishops, only seven voted against the text, while 13 abstained.[2043]

In response to *Der Synodale Weg* approving the blessing of homosexual bondings Cardinal Burke, the former Prefect of the Supreme Tribunal of the Apostolic Signatura, said:

> A synod exists to ponder the teaching of the Faith, sound doctrine, the discipline of the Church, to see how it can be more effectively proclaimed and examined in a particular period of time, not to invent some new teaching. If this is what's going to go on at the Synod, then this poison, this defection from Catholic teaching and practice, will affect the whole Church. It's an impossible situation. This has to stop.... Whether it's a departure, heretical teaching and denial of one of the doctrines of the faith – or apostasy in the sense of simply walking away from Christ and from His teaching in the Church to embrace some other form of religion – these are crimes. These are sins against Christ Himself.

Cardinal Müller, the former Prefect of the CDF, responded:

> …it is absolutely blasphemic to make a blessing about those forms of life which is according to the biblical and ecclesial doctrine a sin, because all forms of sexuality outside of a valid matrimony is a sin and cannot be blessed. They think the traditional doctrine of the Church is wrong, is belonging to the Middle Ages, and they are more intelligent than the Word of God, like the Gnostics in the second century when Irenaeus of Lyons said they want to be more intelligent than God, our Creator and our Redeemer. And we must absolutely resist this strange and wrong doctrine.[2044]

11th March

During an interview with the Argentinian news site *Perfil* Pope Francis stated that Hell is not a 'place' but 'a posture towards life'. The Supreme Pontiff made this declaration in response to the question, *What is your own interpretation of Hell and paradise, and what happens to people who go to Hell, and what happens to those who go to paradise?*:

> Hell is not a place. If one goes to attend the Last Judgment, and sees the faces of those who go to Hell, one gets scared. If you read Dante, you get scared. But these are media representations. Hell is a state, it is a state of the heart, of the soul, of a posture towards life, towards values, towards the family, towards everything. There are people who live in Hell because they seek it, there are others who do not, who are suffering. And who goes to Hell, to that Hell, to that state? They are already living from here.

[2042]Haynes, M [2023] *German bishops approve same-sex 'blessings' by 38 to 9 vote in contravention of Church teaching* [Online] Available at: www.lifesitenews.com [Accessed on: 18 January 2024]
[2043]Wolfe, R [2023] *German bishops declare that 'transsexual' persons should not be 'excluded' from priesthood in 38-7 vote* [Online] Available at: www.lifesitenews.com [Accessed on: 18 January 2024]
[2044]Summers,J [2023] *'Sins against Christ': Cdls. Burke, Müller slam German bishops' approval of same-sex 'blessings'* [Online] Available at: www.lifesitenews.com [Accessed on: 19 January 2024]

Pope Francis went on to imply that no one is in Hell:

> If you ask me how many people are in Hell, I answer you with a famous sculpture of the cathedral of Vézelay…[which] has Judas hanging and the devil pulling him down, and on the other side they have the Good Shepherd, Jesus who grabs Judas and puts him on his shoulders with an ironic smile. What does that mean? That salvation is stronger than damnation. This pilaster is a catechesis that should make us think. God's mercy is always at our side, and what God wants is always to be with his people, with his children, and not for them to leave him.[2045]

14th March

During the monthly online meeting held by the Confraternity of Our Lady of Fatima Bishop Athanasius Schneider of Astana, Kazakhstan, warned that complying with Pope Francis' restrictions on the traditional Latin Mass was 'false obedience':

> The order of a Pope which evidently is damaging the spiritual good of the church – we cannot obey. It would be a false obedience to cooperate with something which is evidently damaging the spiritual good of souls and of the entire church.[2046]

19th March

During an interview with BBC Radio 4 Cardinal Roche, the Prefect of the Congregation for Divine Worship appointed by Pope Francis in 2022, stated that the traditional Latin Mass needs to be restricted because the 'theology of the Church has changed':

> The theology of the Church has changed. Whereas before the priest represented, at a distance, all the people – they were channeled through this person who alone was celebrating the Mass. Now, though it is not only the priest who celebrates the liturgy but also those who are baptised with him, and that is an enormous statement to make.[2047]

24th March

Cardinal Miguel Ángel Ayuso Guixot, elevated to the Sacred College of Cardinals by Pope Francis in 2019, issued a 'congratulatory message' to Muslims at the start of Ramadan. The message failed to mention our Lord Jesus Christ, and instead claimed Ramadan was important to Christians.[2048]

During an interview with the left-wing Spanish magazine *Vida Nueva* the pro-homosexuality Cardinal Robert McElroy rejected the accusation made by brother bishops that he was a heretic:

> It hurts me to be labeled a heretic. Such language further harms the Church by degrading the dialogue we must have these days on the fundamental issues we face.[2049]

27th March

During an interview with the Croatian news outlet *Glas Koncila*, the pro-homosexuality Cardinal Jean-Claude Hollerich, S.J., declared that Pope Francis could overturn Pope St. John Paul II's summation of sacred Scripture and Tradition that women are excluded from the presbyterate. Contradicting the Congregation for the Doctrine of the Faith's declaration that Pope St. John Paul II's *Ordinatio Sacerdotalis* was infallible because it is

---

[2045]Haynes, M [2023] *Pope Francis denies that Hell is 'a place,' says it is 'a posture towards life'* [Online] Available at: www.lifesitenews.com [Accessed on: 19 January 2024]

[2046]Haynes, M [2023] *Bishop Schneider: Complying with Latin Mass restrictions is 'false obedience'* [Online] Available at: www.lifesitenews.com [Accessed on: 19 January 2024]

[2047]Haynes, M [2023] *Cdl. Roche says Latin Mass needs to be restricted because the 'theology of the Church has changed'* [Online] Available at: www.lifesitenews.com [Accessed on: 18 January 2024]

[2048]Haynes, M [2023] *Vatican's 'congratulatory message' to Muslims calls Ramadan 'important' for Christians* [Online] Available at: www.lifesitenews.com [Accessed on: 19 January 2024]

[2049]Wolfe, R [2023] *Cdl. McElroy lashes out at EWTN and critics, pushes women deacons in new interview* [Online] Available at: www.lifesitenews.com [Accessed on: 19 January 2024]

part of the Deposit of Faith, Cardinal Hollerich agreed that Pope Francis could 'decide against' the document, 'with time, yes', stating it was not 'infallible teaching':

> there might be some space to expand the teaching – to see which of the arguments of Pope John Paul II could be developed. But for the moment, if Pope Francis tells me it is not an option, it is not an option.[2050]

29th March

The Vatican's daily newspaper *L'Osservatore Romano* published another article questioning whether Judas Iscariot was in Hell, one of Pope Francis' favorite themes. In his article 'Our brother Judas' Fr. Simone Caleffi wrote:

> What could be more despairing than not accepting to be forgiven, and thus loved, by the person dearest? Yet, who can be certain of Judas' eternal perdition? What could possibly have gone through his heart at the end, what final thought, what cry? One thing is certain: Jesus, who is Mercy infinitely, offered his life for every man, and therefore also for the most unfortunate, desperate and guilty of his friends.

Fr. Caleffi even referred to Judas' kiss of betrayal in the Garden of Gethsemane (Mt 26:49) as a kiss of friendship, 'The kiss on the face was a sign of friendship, unlike the one on the hands, and was meant to indicate nothing more than a disciple's respect for his master.'[2051]

2nd April

Cardinal Raymond Burke, the former prefect of the Apostolic Signatura, issued a letter addressed to the faithful priests in Germany warning that German bishops were betraying the Apostolic Faith through the *Der Synodale Weg*:

> I can only imagine your profound sadness at the positions taken by the Assembly, including the great majority of the Bishops, which are directly opposed to what the Church has always and everywhere taught and practiced. I share your sadness and experience the temptation to discouragement, which you, no doubt, also experience [....] At times such as these, when even those who are Bishops betray the Apostolic Tradition, faithful Bishops, priests, consecrated persons, and lay faithful will necessarily suffer greatly precisely because of their fidelity.[2052]

4th April

The Chinese Communist Party again broke the secret Vatican-CCP agreement by installing another bishop without the participation of the Holy See. The Council of Chinese Bishops, a body not recognised by the Holy See and linked to the Communist Party, announced the installation of Mgr. Shen Bin as the illegitimate bishop of Shanghai. Mgr. Shen is the head of the Council of Chinese Bishops.[2053]

On 8th May 2023, Joseph Shen Bin, the illegitimate bishop Shanghai, welcomed three communist officials to investigate the diocese he had usurped. Joseph Shen Bin briefed the communists on efforts to implement the Communist Party's sinicization policy. The sinicization policy imposes strict rules ensuring conformity to the core values of 'socialism, autonomy, and supporting the leadership of the party, across ethnic and religious communities in China.'[2054]

[2050]Haynes, M [2023] *Cdl. Hollerich falsely claims Pope can reverse teaching against women priests 'with time'* [Online] Available at: www.lifesitenews.com [Accessed on: 19 January 2024]

[2051]Haynes, M [2023] *Vatican's official newspaper again questions Catholic teaching on Judas in Hell* [Online] Available at: www.lifesitenews.com [Accessed on: 19 January 2024]

[2052]Burke, R [2023] *Message to the Faithful Priests of the Church in Germany* [Online] Available at: www.cardinalburke.com [Accessed on: 24 January 2024]

[2053]*Shen Bin new bishop of Shanghai: 'unilateral' appointment, Vatican agreement broken* [2023] [Online] Available at: www.asianews.it [Accessed on: 19 January 2024]

[2054]*Chinese officials stress sinicization during Shanghai church visit* [2023] [Online] Available at: www.ucanews.com [Accessed on: 20 January 2024]

On the 15th July 2023, the Holy See Press Office announced that Pope Francis had appointed Bishop Joseph Shen Bin as Bishop of Shanghai, signalling 'to China and to the world that the secretive Vatican-China deal does indeed surrender the Vatican's authority and power to appoint bishops to the Communist authorities in Beijing.'[2055]

Bishop Michael Mulvey of Diocese of Corpus Christi, Texas, banned the celebration of the traditional Mass at St. John the Baptist Church, Corpus Christi. Thereby ending the only Mass celebrated in Corpus Christi diocese, offered since 1985 under an indult granted to the former Bishop Gracida by Pope John Paul II. Bishop Michael Mulvey claimed that he had no choice, due to the resignation of Fr. Rodolfo Vasquez, however it later emerged that Fr. Vasquez had resigned only after being told by Bishop Mulvey that the TLM would be discontinued.[2056]

18th April

A group of Anglican clergy from the Anglican Diocese of Fulham, England, were granted permission by Vatican authorities to celebrate a liturgy in the Basilica of St. John Lateran, the 'Mother of all the Churches of Rome and of the world'. The celebrant was a divorced and remarried member of the Freemasons.[2057]

19th April

During a television panel on the end of life pro-homosexuality Archbishop Paglia, president of the 'reformed' Pontifical Academy of Life, spoke in favour of assisted suicide:

> In the time when death is approaching I believe that the main response is that of accompaniment. And the first step to accompaniment is to listen to the questions, often very uncomfortable, that arise at this most delicate stage. [The question of assisted suicide] is a question with many implications, in which several factors play regarding guilt, shame, pain, control, helplessness. The interplay of projections between the sick person and the caregiver is very intricate: distinguishing between 'he suffers too much' and 'I suffer too much to see him like this' is not at all easy, just as it is very demanding to take seriously the demand for a relationship that helps to live with the radical loneliness of dying.

> In this context, it is not to be ruled out that in our society a legal mediation is feasible that would allow assistance to suicide under the conditions specified by Constitutional Court Sentence 242/2019: the person must be kept alive by life-support treatments and affected by an irreversible pathology, source of physical or psychological suffering that she considers intolerable, but fully capable of making free and conscious decisions. Personally, I would not practice suicide assistance, but I understand that legal mediation may be the greatest common good concretely possible under the conditions we find ourselves in.[2058]

Archbishop Paglia also used the occasion to undermine the teaching and moral authority of the Church: 'First of all, I would like to clarify that the Catholic Church is not that it has a ready-made, prepackaged package of truths, as if it were a dispenser of truth pills.'

21st April

Pro-homosexuality Fr. James Martin S.J., recipient of many signs of favour from Pope Francis, recommended that Christians 'shouldn't do everything' the Bible 'commands'.

[2055]Haynes, M [2023] *Pope Francis bows to Communist China and confirms bishop appointed by Beijing* [Online] Available at: Available at: www.lifesitenews.com [Accessed on: 24 January 2024]

[2056]Mershon, B [2023] *Corpus Christi bishop's reason for suspending Latin Mass '100% not true': parishioners* [Online] Available at: www.lifesitenews.com [Accessed on: 19 January 2024]

[2057]Haynes, M [2023] *Freemason Anglican bishop celebrates 'Mass' in papal basilica with Protestant clergy* [Online] Available at: www.lifesitenews.com [Accessed on: 19 January 2024]

[2058]Haynes, M [2023] *Abp. Paglia defends assisted suicide as 'greatest common good possible' for dying people* [Online] Available at: www.lifesitenews.com [Accessed on: 19 January 2024]

Regarding Bible verses that express Divine Revelation concerning God's condemnation of homosexuality, Fr. James Martin said:

> …see them in their historical context and remember that even devout Christians shouldn't do everything that [the] Old Testament commands. Likewise for the Epistles in the New Testament.[2059]

26th April

During a press conference Cardinal Grech and Cardinal Hollerich announced that lay men and women selected by Pope Francis would have 25 percent of the voting rights at the Synod on Synodality. Though contravening the hierarchical nature of the Church instituted by Christ, the Secretariat for the Synod argued that the 'episcopal specificity of the Synodal Assembly is not affected, but even confirmed.' This innovation required changes to Pope Francis' 2018 Apostolic Constitution *Episcopalis Communio*, which stipulates the governance and workings of the Synod of Bishops.[2060]

28th April

Archbishop William Nolan of Glasgow, appointed by Pope Francis in 2022, instructed Fr. Mark Morris that the traditional Latin Mass at his parish of the Immaculate Heart of Mary, Balornock, must end by Sunday 30th April. The Immaculate Heart of Mary parish had become the 'thriving hub of traditional Catholic life in Scotland' with 200 people attending every weekend for the traditional Mass.[2061]

29th April

During a meeting with Jesuits in Hungary Pope Francis again expressed his criticism of the faithful who uphold the Tradition of the Church, disparaging it as 'backwardness' and misrepresenting St. Paul and St. Vincent of Lérins' theology of Tradition:

> There is unbelievable restorationism, what I call *'indietrismo'* (backwardness), as the Letter to the Hebrews (10:39) says: 'But we do not belong to those who shrink back.' The flow of history and grace goes from the roots upward like the sap of a tree that bears fruit. But without this flow you remain a mummy. Going backwards does not preserve life, ever. You must change, as St. Vincent of Lérins wrote in his *Commonitory* when he remarked that even the dogma of the Christian religion progresses, consolidating over the years, developing with time, deepening with age. But this is a change from the bottom up. The danger today is *indietrismo*, the reaction against the modern. It is a nostalgic disease. This is why I decided that now the permission to celebrate according to the *Roman Missal* of 1962 is mandatory for all newly consecrated priests. After all the necessary consultations, I decided this because I saw that the good pastoral measures put in place by John Paul II and Benedict XVI were being used in an ideological way, to go backward. It was necessary to stop this *indietrismo*, which was not in the pastoral vision of my predecessors.[2062]

2nd May

Dr. Josef Seifert, renowned Catholic philosopher and friend of Pope St. John Paul II, issued an open letter to the cardinals warning that Pope Francis was destroying the foundations of faith and morals:

> Pope Francis – I say this with a bleeding heart – is not the 'guarantor of the faith', but is constantly increasingly destroying the foundations of faith and morals with this and

[2059]Haynes, M [2023] *Fr. James Martin on homosexuality: 'Christians shouldn't do everything' the Bible 'commands'* [Online] Available at: www.lifesitenews.com [Accessed on: 19 January 2024]

[2060]Haynes, M [2023] *Pope Francis to personally select lay men, women to form up to 25% of Synodal vote* [Online] Available at: www.lifesitenews.com [Accessed on: 19 January 2024]

[2061]Haynes, M [2023] *Scottish bishop cancels thriving Latin Mass community in Archdiocese of Glasgow* [Online] Available at: www.lifesitenews.com [Accessed on: 19 January 2024]

[2062]Spadaro, A [2023] *This is God's Style': Pope Francis' conversation with Hungarian Jesuits* [Online] Available at: www.laciviltacattolica.com [Accessed on: 20 January 2024]

many other statements and pronouncements. As far as I know, there has never been a Pope in the history of the Church who has asserted similar monstrosities? How should I answer a dear and deeply believing Lutheran friend, for whose conversion I have been praying for years, when he writes to me that with this Abu Dhabi Declaration the Catholic Church has left the soil of Christianity?

Singling out Pope Francis' Abu Dhabi Declaration for criticism Dr. Seifert warned that it expressed apostasy from the Faith:

> Wouldn't it be a heresy and a terrible confusion to claim that God – just as he willed the difference of the two sexes – i.e. with his positive will – also directly willed the difference of religions and thus all idolatry and heresies? Yes, isn't the Abu Dhabi Declaration far worse than heresy, namely apostasy? How can God, with His positive creative will, have wanted religions that reject Jesus' divinity, deny the Most Holy Trinity, reject baptism and all sacraments and the priesthood? Or how could He even have wanted polytheism or the cult of the idol Baal or Pachamama? Doesn't this totally contradict the message of the prophet Elijah and all other prophets and the words of Jesus?[2063]

3rd May

Charles Martig, the editor-in-chief of the Swiss Catholic bishops' official website, *Kath. ch*, called on the apostolic nuncio to Switzerland and Liechtenstein, to investigate Bishop Vitus Huonder, the former ordinary of the diocese of Chur, for publicity criticising Pope Francis. During a homily Bishop Huonder described Pope Francis' reign as a 'pontificate of rupture' that 'breaks with tradition.'[2064]

5th May

A number of bishops and priests across Europe participated in pro-homosexuality events as part of the 'International Day Against Homophobia and Transphobia', that marked the start of a month of activities promoting homosexuality. The culmination of the pro-homosexuality month was a meeting between Pope Francis and Mosaiko, a group of 'LGBT+ Christians' based in Rome. Mosaiko announced that the purpose of the meeting with the Supreme Pontiff 'will be a way for the group to celebrate this event, symbolically presenting itself to the Church of Jesus.'[2065]

12th May

Bishop Joseph Strickland of Tyler, Texas, posted a tweet accusing Pope Francis of undermining the Faith: '…it is time for me to say that I reject his program of undermining the Deposit of Faith. Follow Jesus.'[2066]

During an interview with the SSPX's international news outlet Father Davide Pagliarani, the Superior General of the Society of St. Pius X [SSPX] warned the Synod on Synodality aims to turn the Church upside down:

> In concrete terms, it is a determined desire to turn the Church upside-down. The teaching-Church no longer sees itself as the custodian of a Revelation coming from God, and of which it is the guardian, but as a group of bishops associated with the Pope, who listen to the faithful, and in particular to all the peripheries, i.e. with particular attention paid to anything that the most alienated souls might suggest. It is a Church where the shepherds become the sheep and the sheep become the shepherds. The underlying idea is that God does not reveal Himself through the traditional channels of Holy Scripture

---

[2063] *Seifert: Francis' Monstrosities Destroy Faith And Morals* [2023] [Online] Available at: www.gloria. tv [Accessed on: 20 January 2024]

[2064] Wailzer, A [2023] *Swiss bishops' website op-ed urges Vatican to investigate retired prelate critical of Pope Francis* [Online] Available at: www.lifesitenews.com [Accessed on: 16 January 2024]

[2065] Haynes, M [2023] *Catholic bishops, parishes across Europe hosting pro-LGBT prayer vigils for greater 'inclusion'* [Online] Available at: www.lifesitenews.com [Accessed on: 19 January 2024]

[2066] Haynes, M [2023] *Bp. Strickland: SSPX 'not in schism,' Pope Francis is 'undermining the deposit of faith'* [Online] Available at: www.lifesitenews.com [Accessed on: 20 January 2024]

and Tradition, which are safeguarded by the hierarchy, but through the 'experience of the people of God'.[2067]

During an interview with the Italian Jesuit journal *La Civiltà Cattolica* Bishop Stephen Chow, S.J., of Hong Kong, appointed by Pope Francis in 2021, welcomed the Communist Party's sinicization policy, requiring the Church to conform to the policy of the Chinese Communist Party:

> According to one of the government officials whom we met during the trip, sinicization is similar to our concept of inculturation. So, I think that it is better not to jump to a conclusion regarding sinicization for now. It should be more helpful to hold further dialogue on the topic.[2068]

17th May

During an interview with the official website of the German bishops, *katholisch-de* pro-homosexuality Bishop Johan Bonny of the Diocese of Antwerp claimed Pope Francis supported the Belgian bishops' promotion of the 'blessing' of homosexual bondings:

> From my conversations I know what my relationship with Pope Francis looks like – we speak *'cum petro et sub petro'* – ['with and under Peter']. But not the whole Vatican is *'cum petro et sub petro'*…. Regarding obedience to the Pope: None of us wants to disobey the Pope. That would be the last thing I want. That's why I had a conversation with the Pope twice. These were personal conversations. I will not say publicly what and how he said something, but I know that I and we are not going against the Pope. This is very important for me and for the other bishops in Flanders.[2069]

30th May

In conversation with EWTN's Vatican journalist Edward Pentin, Dr. Joseph Siefert, eminent Catholic philosopher and friend of Pope St. John Paul II, warned that there was a terrible danger of the complete collapse of the Church:

> [due to the] frightening silence of the majority of cardinals and bishops on this unique crisis from the top of the Church down during a whole decade…. [I have] hope that the omnipotent God, who is the truth, will awaken the fire of love for truth and for the Church in the hearts of all cardinals and bishops, and will bestow the gift of holy courage on many of them, as he has done already on some cardinals and bishops. I am not at all optimistic but truly hopeful that the cardinals and bishops will no longer watch passively the downfall of the Church which only divine intervention can prevent. God wants to use all of us, but especially chooses cardinals and bishops, just as He chose St Paul to spread the Church, and St Athanasius to save it from Arianism and destruction.

In response to the question, *What would the consequences be if they don't?* Seifert replied,

> I see a terrible danger of a complete collapse of the Catholic Church in many countries, and indeed of its total destruction in some areas of the world…but this is not possible because the truth itself has told us that the gates of hell will not ever prevail against the Church.[2070]

2nd June

Militant pro-homosexuality Fr. James Martin S.J., posted an article on his *Outreach* website claiming that celebrating active homosexuality during Pride month was

[2067]*Interview with the Superior General of the Priestly Society of Saint Pius X* [2023] [Online] Available at: www.fsspx.news [Accessed on: 20 January 2023]

[2068]Spadaro, A [2023] *A Bridge to Walk: An interview with Msgr. Stephen Chow, Bishop of Hong Kong* [Online] Available at: www.laciviltacattolica.com [Accessed on: 20 January 2024]

[2069]Schlegelmilch, R [2023] *Bishop on reforms: Rome should listen better and criticize less* [Online] Available at: www-katholisch-de [Accessed on: 20 January 2024]

[2070]Pentin, E [2023] *Professor Seifert: Catholic Church in 'terrible danger of complete collapse in many countries' unless cardinals and bishops speak up* [Online] Available at: www.edwardpentin.co.uk [Accessed on: 20 January 2024]

compatible with devotion to the Sacred Heart of Jesus.[2071] Bishop Strickland of Tyler protested on twitter,

> This blasphemy must stop, God loves every person even the most sinful, but saying sinful acts are compatible with the Sacred Heart of Jesus Christ contradicts Christ's call to go & sin no more.[2072]

14th June

The militant US Catholic homosexualist group *Outreach*, founded by the pro-homosexuality Fr. James Martin S.J., announced that Fr. Martin has received another sign of favour and approval from Pope Francis. The hand written letter from the Supreme Pontiff thanked Fr. Martin for 'all the good you are doing.'[2073]

Fr. Johan Verschueren S.J., delegate of Jesuit Superior Fr. General Arturo Sosa, issued a statement announcing that the serial sex abuser of nuns Fr. Marko Rupnik had been expelled from the Jesuits due to his 'stubborn refusal to observe the vow of obedience.' However, Fr. Rupnik remained a priest with faculties.[2074]

18th June

Pro-homosexuality Cardinal Blase Cupich, elevated to the Sacred College of Cardinals by Pope Francis in 2016, celebrated Mass to mark the 35th anniversary of the militant Catholic pro-homosexuality group, the Archdiocesan Gay and Lesbian Outreach. Founded by the notorious Cardinal Bernardin, the group openly rejects the Church's doctrine on homosexuality.[2075]

Speaking at Fr. James Martin's pro-homosexuality *Outreach* conference the homosexual Juan-Carlos Cruz revealed Pope Francis' reaction to the 2021 Vatican ban on 'blessings' homosexual bondings. Juan-Carlos Cruz was appointed to the Pontifical Commission for the Protection of Minors by Pope Francis in 2021. Juan-Carlos Cruz recounted,

> I saw his pain when – and I cannot say too much because he had really deep and profound conversations – but I wrote an article in a Chilean newspaper when that letter from the Congregation for the Doctrine of the Faith came out two years ago, saying you can't bless, you know, it's a sin to bless marriages, whatever. He was hurt with that because – and this is my view, I'm not a Vatican insider, in fact I'm scared of them – but I could see how hurt he was when people were horrified by it of course and he told me 'Look, I didn't sign it.' Such a statement doesn't explicate him as he ultimately is the pope, but in his defense, you'll have to trust me that the people that wrote that letter are no longer in the CDF. And that's really good, but we need to do much, much more.[2076]

20th June

Pro-homosexuality Cardinal Grech, Secretary General of the General Secretariat of the Synod of Bishops, and pro-homosexuality Cardinal Hollerich, the Relator General of the Synod on Synodality, presented the *Instrumentum Laboris* for the October 2023 Synod on Synodality. The working document for the synod highlighted the 'need' to 'welcome…

[2071]Martin, J [2023] *June: Celebrating the Sacred Heart and celebrating Pride* [Online] Available at: www.outreach.faith [Accessed on: 22 January 204]

[2072]Knuffke, L [2023] *Bishop Strickland denounces Fr. James Martin for juxtaposing Sacred Heart and 'pride' month* [Online] Available at: www.lifesitenews.com [Accessed on: 22 January 2024]

[2073]*Pope Francis sends greetings to this year's Outreach conference for LGBTQ Catholics* [2023] [Online] Available at: www.outreach.faith [Accessed on: 22 January 2024]

[2074]Haynes, M [2023] *Jesuits expel alleged serial abuser Fr. Rupnik, but he remains a priest* [Online] Available at: www.lifesitenews.com [Accessed on: 20 January 2024]

[2075]Knuffke, L [2023] *Cdl. Cupich to celebrate Mass for pro-LGBT group that dissents from Church teaching* [Online] Available at: www.lifesitenews.com [Accessed on: 22 January 2024]

[2076]Haynes, M [2023] *Pope Francis fired Vatican officials who issued ban on same-sex 'blessings': homosexual papal confidant* [Online] Available at: www.lifesitenews.com [Accessed on: 20 January 2024]

remarried divorcees, people in polygamous marriages, LGBTQ+ people' and called for married priests and more female governance, including possibility of female deacons:

> How can we create spaces where those who feel hurt by the Church and unwelcomed by the community feel recognised, received, free to ask questions and not judged? In the light of the Post-Synodal Apostolic Exhortation *Amoris Laetitia*, what concrete steps are needed to welcome those who feel excluded from the Church because of their status or sexuality (for example, remarried divorcees, people in polygamous marriages, LGBTQ+ people, etc.)? […] Most of the Continental Assemblies and the syntheses of several Episcopal Conferences call for the question of women's inclusion in the diaconate to be considered. Is it possible to envisage this, and in what way?[2077]

23rd June

Pro-homosexuality Cardinals Robert McElroy of San Diego and Joseph Tobin of Newark, USA, attempted to stall US Bishops' instruction banning 'transgender' mutilation or chemical castration in Catholic hospitals. Cardinal McElroy claiming the instruction did not address 'the existential question of those who are suffering from dysphoria' and Cardinal Tobin called consultations with 'transgender' persons to be part of the revision process of the directive.[2078]

To mark the 50th anniversary of the inauguration of the Vatican Museums' collection of modern and contemporary art Pope Francis welcomed around 200 artists from around the world. The Supreme Pontiff warmly greeted smiling and giving a big 'thumbs up' to Andres Serrano, notorious for his blasphemous image of a crucifix immersed in urine. The work entitled 'Immersion,' was a photograph of a small, plastic crucifix completely immersed in a liquid which Serrano attested was his own urine. His 1985 'Pieta' featured his wife holding 'a large limp fish' mocking the classic portrayal of the Virgin Mary holding the dead Christ at the foot of the cross.

Pope Francis compared the gathering of artists to biblical prophets:

> Like the biblical prophets, you confront things that at times are uncomfortable; you criticise today's false myths and new idols, its empty talk, the ploys of consumerism, the schemes of power. This is an intriguing aspect of the psychology of artists: the ability to press forward and beyond, in a tension between reality and dream [….] As visionaries, men and women of discernment, critical consciences, I consider you allies in so many things that are dear to me, like the defence of human life, social justice, concern for the poor, care for our common home, universal human fraternity. The humanness of humanity is dear to me, the human dimension of humanity. Because that is also the great passion of God. One of the things that draws art closer to faith is the fact that both tend to be troubling. Neither art nor faith can leave things simply as they are: they change, transform, move and convert them. Art can never serve as an anesthetic; it brings peace, yet far from deadening consciences, it keeps them alert. Often, as artists, you attempt to plumb the depths of the human condition, its dark abysses. We are not all light, and you remind us of this. At the same time, there is a need to let the light of hope shine in that darkness, in the midst of our selfishness and indifference. Help us to glimpse the light, the beauty that saves.[2079]

24th June

Bishop Joseph Strickland of Tyler, Texas, was subjected to an Apostolic Visitation from the Vatican's Dicastery for Bishops, undertaken by two retired US bishops, Bishop Gerald Frederick Kicanus and auxiliary Bishop Dennis Joseph Sullivan.[2080] Bishop

---

[2077]*Instrumentum Laboris: For the First Session (October 2023)* [2023][Online] Available at: www.synod.va [Accessed on: 23 January 2024]

[2078]Knuffke, L [2023] *Pro-LGBT Cdls. McElroy, Tobin challenge formalization of US bishops' decree against trans surgeries* [Online] Available at: www.lifesitenews.com [Accessed on: 22 January 2024]

[2079]Haynes, M [2023] *Pope Francis warmly greets infamous 'artist' who created image of crucifix in urine* [Online] Available at: www.lifesitenews.com [Accessed on: 20 January 2024]

[2080]*Bishop Strickland gets 'visit' from Rome* [2023] [Online] Available at: www.churchmilitant.com [Accessed on: 22 January 2024]

Strickland later commented during an interview with Terry Barber of the US radio station *Virgin Most Powerful Radio*:

> No, it's not something that I would volunteer for, to go through an apostolic visitation. Because it kind of puts a shadow over the diocese, [and] a lot of people are convinced that there's something really wrong. But I think that I went through this because I've been bold enough and love the Lord enough and His Church to simply keep preaching the truth. I know they won't stop you and they won't stop me. And we do it with love, and charity and clarity, and with humility, always ready to be corrected. But when we're speaking of the truth of Jesus Christ, there is no correction. The world can try and shout us down, but it won't work.[2081]

On the 22nd August 2023 Bishop Strickland issued a pastoral letter warning of the dangers posed by Pope Francis' Synod on Synodality, encouraging the faithful to resist any changes to the Faith:

> The Church exists not to redefine matters of faith, but to safeguard the Deposit of Faith as it has been handed down to us from Our Lord Himself through the apos-tles and the saints and martyrs…. hold fast to these truths and be wary of any attempts to present an alternative to the Gospel of Jesus Christ, or to push for a faith that speaks of dia-logue and brotherhood, while attempting to remove the fatherhood of God. Regrettably, it may be that some will label as schismatics those who disagree with the changes being pro-posed. Be assured, however, that no one who remains firmly upon the plumb line of our Catholic faith is a schismatic. We must remain unabashedly and truly Catholic, regardless of what may be brought forth. We must be aware also that it is not leaving the Church to stand firm against these proposed changes.[2082]

On the 5th September Bishop Strickland issued a pastoral letter rejecting the possibility of the ordination of women because the sacrament of Holy Orders is reserved to men who 'act as instruments of Christ *in persona Christi Capitis*, [in the person of Christ as the Head]…. Because sacramentally ordained deacons share in the apostolic ministry with priests and bishops, the Church has decreed that they must also be men, as were the apostles Jesus chose.'[2083]

On the 9th September 2023, Pope Francis met with Archbishop Robert Prevost, O.S.A., head of the Dicastery for Bishops, and Archbishop Christophe Pierre, apostolic nuncio to the United States to discuss the Apostolic Visitation of Bishop Strickland. A senior official close to the Dicastery for Bishops told *The Pillar*, 'The situation of Bishop Strickland is the agenda and the expectation is that the Holy Father will be requesting his resignation — that will certainly be the recommendation put to him.'[2084]

On the 12th September 2023, Bishop Strickland issued a pastoral letter re-affirming doctrine that unrepentant adulterers and homosexuals cannot receive Holy Communion due to being in a state of mortal sin:

> We must be clear, however, that the Church cannot offer a person Holy Communion if that person is actively engaging in a same-sex relationship, or if a person is not living as the sex that God formed them to be at their conception and birth [….] Additionally, I want to state clearly that the Church has never and will never condone the reception of the Eucharist by a Catholic who persists in any adulterous union.[2085]

[2081]Mangiaracina, E [2023] *Bishop Strickland speaks out on apostolic visitation: 'I've got nothing to hide'* [Online] Available at: www.lifesitenews.com [Accessed on: 22 January 2024]
[2082]Haynes, M [2023] *Bishop Strickland: Catholics are not 'schismatic' for rejecting changes that contradict Church teaching* [Online] Available at: www.lifesitenews.com [Accessed on: 20 January 2024]
[2083]*Bishop Strickland defends Catholic teaching condemning female 'deacons' in new pastoral letter* [Online] Available at: www.lifesitenews.com [Accessed on: 22 January 202
[2084]*Pope Francis meets to discuss Strickland resignation* [2023] [Online] Available at: www.pillarcatholic.com [Accessed on: 22 January 2024]
[2085]*Bishop Strickland reaffirms that unrepentant homosexuals, adulterers cannot receive Communion* [Online] Available at: www.lifesitenews.com [Accessed on: 22 January 2024]

On the 13th September 2023, during the 'Defending Our Faith Catholic Conference' in Tyler, Texas, Bishop Strickland said that 'guarding the deposit of faith' remained a fundamental duty for people in every sphere of life to be constantly vigilant and help preserve the Catholic faith.[2086]

On the 15th September 2023, Catholic radio host Joe McClane revealed he'd received an email from Bishop Strickland stating the 'he would not just walk away from his diocese but if the Pope removed him he would be obedient.'[2087]

On the 20th September, Bishop Strickland issued a pastoral letter reassuring the faithful of Tyler that he would not resign:

> I have said publicly that I cannot resign as Bishop of Tyler because that would be me abandoning the flock that I was given charge of by Pope Benedict XVI. I have also said that I will respect the authority of Pope Francis if he removes me from office as Bishop of Tyler. I love Jesus Christ and the Catholic Church which He established. My only desire is to speak His Truth and live God's Will to the best of my ability.[2088]

On the 21st September, Cardinal Gerhard Müller, the former prefect of the Congregation for the Doctrine of the Faith, issued a statement in support of Bishop Strickland:

> It is terrible what is being done to Bishop Strickland, an abuse of office against the divine right of the episcopate. If I could advise Bishop Strickland, he should definitely not resign, because then they [Vatican authorities] can wash their hands of it.[2089]

On the 10th October 2023, Bishop Strickland issued a pastoral letter refuting errors of relativism and universalism gaining currency under Pope Francis' pontificate:

> …the temptation exists to presume upon the mercy of God, assuming that surely a loving and merciful God will overlook our disobedience and failures even if we do not seek forgiveness because He is infinitely merciful. This line of thinking sometimes progresses to our assuming that salvation will ultimately be offered to all people simply because God is infinitely merciful, and therefore all men will be saved. This is the error of universalism. This error could lead one to ask, 'What then is the point of conversion of heart to Jesus Christ? Why bother following Christ at all?' This is extremely dangerous, as it prevents us from seeing the need for true and authentic repentance. It is a deadly indifference that imperils our immortal souls and puts us at eternal risk of separation from God. 'For the wages of sin is death, but the gift of God is eternal life in Christ Jesus our Lord.' (Rom 6:23).[2090]

On the 9th November 2023, Pope Francis, via the papal nuncio Cardinal Cristophe Pierre, requested that Bishop Strickland resign. His Lordship declined this request.

On the 11th November 2023, the Vatican announced that Pope Francis had personally deposed Bishop Strickland from the Diocese of Tyler, Texas.[2091] During his interview with *LifeSiteNews* Editor-in-Chief John-Henry Westen, Bishop Strickland responded to the question why had he been removed from his position:

> The only answer I have to that is because forces in the Church right now don't want the truth of the gospel. They want it changed. They want it ignored. They want to be rid of the truth that is gloriously not going to go away. The truth that is Jesus Christ,

[2086]Mangiaracina, E [2023] *Bishop Strickland: We must be constantly vigilant in guarding the deposit of faith* [Online] Available at: www.lifesitenews.com [Accessed on: 22 January 2024]

[2087]*Bishop Strickland says he will not resign, but will comply if removed by Pope Francis* [Online] Available at: www.lifesitenews.com [Accessed on: 22 January 2024]

[2088]Strickland, J [2023] *Bishop's Blog / A brief update from Bishop Strickland* [Online] Available at: www.bishopstrickland.com[Accessed on: 22 January 2024]

[2089]Haynes, M [2023] *Cardinal Müller defends Bishop Strickland: 'He should definitely not resign'* [Online] Available at: www.lifesitenews.com [Accessed on: 20 January 2024]

[2090]*Bishop Strickland refutes the error that 'all men will be saved,' emphasizes conversion in new letter* [2023][Online] Available at: www.lifesitenews.com [Accessed on: 22 January 2024]

[2091]Haynes, M [2023] *Pope Francis personally removes America's Bishop Joseph Strickland* [Online] Available at: www.lifesitenews.com [Accessed on: 20 January 2024]

His mystical body, which is the Church, all the wonders that the martyrs died for and the saints lived for through almost 2000 years since Christ died and rose [....] There are people in the Church, rather than glorying in the truth of Christ, they want to delete significant portions of Sacred Scripture and say, 'Oh, we got that wrong,' or : 'we're just going to ignore it'.... I really can't look to any reason except [that] I threatened some of the powers that be with the truth of the gospel. That will not change. That cannot change. It's perennial, it's everlasting. It's glorious. And if you want it to change, then I'm a problem.[2092]

On the 12th November, Terry Barber of *Virgin Most Powerful Radio* related Bishop Strickland's account of being confronted by Cardinal Christophe Pierre, appointed apostolic nuncio to the United States by Pope Francis in 2016. According to Terry Barber,

Bishop Strickland communicated to me that...Pierre confronted [him] and said, 'Look, the Holy Father is watching you. You need to stop talking about the deposit of faith. There is no deposit of faith.' Well, you can imagine how shocking that is to hear a nuncio say there's no deposit of faith, because if you don't believe in the deposit of faith, you're not Catholic. That's not just my opinion. That's the Church teaching.[2093]

26th June

It was announced that the annual *Summorum Pontificum* pilgrimage to Rome had been denied permission to celebrate the traditional Latin Mass in St. Peter's Basilica by Cardinal Gambetti, the archpriest of Saint Peter's Basilica. Cardinal Gambetti was elevated to the Sacred College of Cardinals by Pope Francis in 2020.[2094] The *Summorum Pontificum* pilgrimage had celebrated the traditional Latin Mass in St. Peter's Basilica for the past eleven years.

1st July

The Holy See Press Office announced that Pope Francis had appointed Archbishop Victor Manuel Fernández of La Plata to be the next Prefect of the Congregation for the Doctrine of the Faith. In 2009 the CDF blocked Fr. Fernández's appointment by Cardinal Jorge Bergoglio to be rector of the Pontifical Catholic University of Argentina due to concerns about his heterodox theology. His appointment was delayed until 2011 after answering objections from the CDF. Fr. Fernández had been a protege of Cardinal Jorge Bergoglio since at least 2007, appointing him Archbishop of La Plata two months into his pontificate.[2095] Archbishop Fernández was the ghost writer of Pope Francis' *Evangelii Gaudium, Laudato Sí,* and *Amoris Laetitia.*[2096]

On the 7th July, Cardinal Gerhard Müller, the former Prefect for the Doctrine of the Faith, confirmed that the CDF had a file containing theological concerns about Archbishop Victor Manuel Fernández. Regarding Fr. Fernández's application to be the rector of the Pontifical Catholic University of Argentina Cardinal Müller said:

The CDF is always involved in giving the last word. The Congregation for Catholic Education must therefore ask for the *nihil obstat* from the CDF, in giving the official yes, so the Church can be absolutely sure there isn't anything problematic with such an appointment.... it was possible that Father Fernández had sent the CDF a letter

[2092]Wailzer, A [2023] *Bishop Strickland: I was removed because forces in the Church want to change the teaching of Jesus* [Online] Available at: www.lifesitenews.com [Accessed on: 16 January 2024]
[2093]Mangiaracina, E [2023] *Terry Barber reveals US nuncio Cardinal Pierre told Bishop Strickland 'there is no deposit of faith'* [Online] Available at: www.lifesitenews.com [Accessed on: 22 January 2024]
[2094]Haynes, M [2023] *Vatican denies Summorum Pontificum pilgrimage permission to say Latin Mass in St. Peter's* [Online] Available at: www.lifesitenews.com [Accessed on: 22 January 2024]
[2095]Haynes, M [2023] *Pope appoints longtime ally and ghostwriter of Amoris Laetitia as new Vatican doctrine chief* [Online] Available at: www.lifesitenews.com [Accessed on: 23 January 2024]
[2096]Magister, S [2013] *"Amoris Laetitia" Has a Ghostwriter. His Name Is Víctor Manuel Fernández* [Online] Available at: www.chiesa.espresso.repubblica.it [Accessed on: 23 January 2024]

pledging to do better adding that this is always the tactic for these things, to destroy any doubts.'[2097]

The European Catholic news site *Gloria News* reported that Archbishop Victor Fernández wrote a theological article in 2006 arguing for the use of artificial contraception in some circumstances. During his tenure as vice-dean of the Faculty of Theology at the Catholic University of Argentina, Fr. Fernández wrote an article for the *Revista Teología* (April 2006), the quarterly of the Faculty of Theology, arguing for the use of condoms by a 'believing wife' when an 'unbelieving husband' wants sexual intercourse during her fertile period. He even asserted that it was against the primacy of charity not to use condoms in these circumstances:

> But there is also the case of sexual abstinence that contradicts the Christian hierarchy of values crowned by charity. We cannot close our eyes, for example, to the difficulty that arises for a woman when she perceives that family stability is put at risk by subjecting the non-practicing husband to periods of continence. In such a case, an inflexible refusal to use condoms at all would make compliance with an external norm take precedence over the grave obligation to care for loving communion and conjugal stability which charity more directly demands.[2098]

Following news of Archbishop Fernández's appointment, controversy ensued over a book he published in 1995 entitled, *Heal Me with Your Mouth: The Art of kissing*. The book, which he described as a 'catechesis for teenagers' included erotic poetry written by Fr. Fernández, including the lines, 'How was God so cruel as to give you that mouth.... There is no one who resists me, witch, hide it....That's why you don't ask that it happens to my mouth. Kill me already with your next kiss, bleed me to death, she-wolf. Give me back my peace without mercy.'

During an interview with Spanish-language outlet *Religión Digital* published on 17th September 2023, Cardinal Fernández, the prefect of the CDF, boasted,

> I have several other texts from years ago that could be considered much more 'dangerous' from the theological point of view and yet they have not even seen them. Maybe I am wrong to mention it, but it is the truth.[2099]

In January 2024 further controversy was caused by the discovery of another book published by Cardinal Fernández in 1998 entitled *La Pasión Mística* [*Mystical Passion: Spirituality and Sensuality*]. He admitted that he had gone to great lengths to suppress the book.[2100] The focus of the book is male and female orgasm as an experience of pleasure separated from marriage and procreation. Having provided a detailed description of male and female sex organs, Fr. Fernández identified the orgasm of the 'couple' with divinity:

> If God can be present at that level of our existence, He can also be present when two human beings love each other and reach orgasm; and that orgasm, experienced in the presence of God, can also be a sublime act of adoration of God.[2101]

Furthermore, Fr. Fernández contradicts doctrine on homosexuality by writing approvingly of homosexual sex acts:

[2097]Pentin, E [2023] *Cardinal Müller Confirms Vatican Doctrinal Office Had File Warning About Archbishop Fernández* [Online] Available at: www.ncregister.com [Accessed on: 23 January 2024]

[2098]*Condoms Are "Charity" for Francis' Destroyer of Faith* [2023] [Online] Available at: www.gloria.tv [Accessed on: 23 January 2024]; Haynes, M [2023] *Archbishop Fernández previously argued in favor of condom use, contradicting Catholic doctrine* [Online] Available at: www.lifesitenews.com [Accessed on: 23 January 2024]

[2099]Haynes, M [2023] *Archbishop Fernández says 'several' of his texts are 'more dangerous' than erotic book on kissing* [Online] Available at: www.lifesitenews.com [Accessed on: 23 January 2024]

[2100]Allen, E [2023] *25 year-old book by Vatican doctrinal czar surfaces on God and orgasms* [Online] Available at: www.cruxnow.com [Accessed on: 25 January 2024]

[2101]Scrosati, L [2024] *Orgasm like paradise, Fernández's porn-theology* [Online] Available at: www. newdailycompass.com [Accessed on: 25 January 2024]

… [This] does not mean, for example, that a homosexual will necessarily stop being homosexual. Let us remember that God's grace can coexist with weaknesses and even with sins, when there is a very strong conditioning. In those cases, the person can do things that are objectively sinful, without being guilty, and without losing the grace of God or the experience of his love.[2102]

On the 12th January 2024, during an interview with the *EFE* news agency, Cardinal Fernández admitted that Pope Francis knew of the book before appointing him the Prefect of the CDF:

I had told the pope, when he proposed this position [DDF chief] to me for the second time, that this could happen, but he was already clear about it and also knew about this book. It so happens that on one occasion many years ago they had already accused me about that book and I was not sanctioned in Rome for it. They have already exhaustively investigated me.[2103]

3rd July

The French heterodox Catholic news outlet *La Croix* reported that the Dicastery for Communications decided to continue use of the artwork of alleged serial abuser Fr. Marko Rupnik. The Dicastery for Communications oversees the Vatican's Press Office and the Vatican News website.

In the last few days, a meeting attended by some of the dicastery's top officials concluded that there was nothing to prevent the continued use of Rupnik's mosaics. They said the work should stand on its own merits and be dissociated from the personal life of the artist.[2104]

The Dicastery for Communications came to this decision despite a survivor of Fr. Marko Rupnik's alleged sexual and spiritual abuse testified that his art was inextricably connected to his abuse:

It was a real abuse of conscience. His sexual obsession was not extemporaneous but deeply connected to his conception of art and his theological thinking. Father Marko at first slowly and gently infiltrated my psychological and spiritual world by appealing to my uncertainties and frailties while using my relationship with God to push me to have sexual experiences with him.[2105]

4th July

During an interview with the Spanish-news outlet *InfoVaticana* Archbishop Victor Manuel Fernández spoke of his openness to the 'blessing' of homosexual bondings:

…if a blessing is given in such a way that it does not cause that confusion, it will have to be analysed and confirmed. As you will see, there is a point where we leave a properly theological discussion and move on to a question that is rather prudential or disciplinary.[2106]

Archbishop Hector Aguer, Archbishop Emeritus of La Plata in Argentina, published a letter criticising the *Instrumentum Laboris* for the October 2023 Synod on Synodality. Archbishop Aguer warned that Pope Francis' Synod was trying to create a 'new progressive Church' that resembles Protestantism:

[2102]Flanders, T [2024] *More Erotic Musings from Vatican Head of Doctrine* [Online] Available at: www.onepeterfive.com [Accessed on: 25 January 2024]
[2103]Silva, WS [2024] *Cardinal Fernández says Pope Francis knew about his book 'Mystical Passion'* [Online] Available at: www.catholicnewsagency.com [Accessed on: 25 January 2024]
[2104]Besmond de Senneville, L [2023] *The Vatican, St. Irenaeus and Marko Rupnik* [Online] Available at: www.international.la-croix.com [Accessed on: 23 January 2024]
[2105]Haynes, M [2023] *Vatican to continue promoting Rupnik's images despite link to his alleged sex abuse* [Online] Available at: www.lifesitenews.com [Accessed on: 23 January 2024]
[2106]Haynes, M [2023] *Archbishop Fernández hints at openness to same-sex 'blessings' if they don't 'feed confusion'* [Online] Available at: www.lifesitenews.com [Accessed on: 22 January 2024]

Although it may seem curious to observe, the Catholic Church is belatedly beginning to follow the path opened by the Protestant Reformation, at a time when Protestantism has long since been swallowed up by the world. This is the moment to quote what a Danish Lutheran who was a great Christian philosopher, Soren Kierkegaard, wrote in his *Diary* in 1848: 'Just now, when there is talk of reorganising the Church, it is clear how little Christianity there is in it' (IX A 264). On the same page he speaks of 'the unfortunate illusion of "Christianity", which replaces being Christian with being human.' It is this unfortunate illusion that now deceives the Catholic Church. The synodal program, like that of the German Synod, designs another Church, heterogeneous with respect to the great and unanimous Tradition.[2107]

7th July

The Vatican press office and the Synod press office released the list of participants for the Synod of Synodality. The list of participants included those personally appointed by Pope Francis, notable for the number of pro-homosexuality clerics chosen as voting members of the synod: Cardinals McElroy of San Diego, Cupich of Chicago, and Gregory of Washington, D.C. Cardinal Josef de Kesel, Emeritus of Mechelen-Brussel, Cardinal Jean–Claude Hollerich S.J. and Fr. James Martin S.J.[2108]

15th July

During an interview with the veteran Italian journalist Aldo Maria Valli, Archbishop Viganò criticised Pope Francis' recent appointments to senior Vatican positions. Archbishop Viganò warned that Pope Francis motivation behind such appointments was to,

> create the premises for a schism, which he denies and deplores in words, but which he has been preparing for some time…to separate, in one way or another, the good part of the faithful and clerics from the official Church; and to achieve this, to ensure that they distance themselves from the modernist Sanhedrin, he [Pope Francis] has placed in key positions in the Roman Curia those characters who guarantee the worst possible management of the dicasteries entrusted to them, with the worst possible result and the greatest damage to the ecclesial body.[2109]

23rd July

During his homily at 125th anniversary celebration of a parish church in Koblenz, pro-homosexuality Bishop Georg Bätzing, the head of the German Bishops' conference, said that he wanted to 'found the Church differently':

> New ideas are needed about how we can found the Church differently, how we can appeal to people in new ways for the fundamental acts of worship, preaching, and selfless service.… The old structure is no longer suitable for the future. All this does not mean the end of the Church, I am sure of that, but it does mean the end of a certain institutional form of church that was formative for just 100 years, but of which we have the impression that it has always been like this and should actually remain like this.[2110]

25th July

Vatican News, the official news outlet of the Vatican, released the text of a podcast featuring Pope Francis in discussion with a 22-year-old gender-confused Italian woman

---

[2107]*"What an aggressive, paradoxical imitation of Christ!": Archbishop Hector Aguer* [2023] [Online] Available at: www.rorate-caeli.blogspot.com [Accessed on: 23 January 2024]

[2108]Haynes, M [2023] *Pope Francis picks notorious pro-LGBT clerics to participate in October Synod on Synodality* [Online] Available at: www.lifesitenews.com [Accessed on: 23 January 2024]

[2109]Haynes, M [2023] *Archbishop Viganò: Pope Francis wants to create a 'schism' by excommunicating Latin Mass devotees* [Online] Available at: www.lifesitenews.com [Accessed on: 22 January 2024]

[2110]Wailzer, A [2023] *Pro-LGBT head of German bishops' conference says he wants to 'found the Church differently'* [Online] Available at: www.lifesitenews.com [Accessed on: 16 January 2024]

who calls herself 'Giona'. The Supreme Pontiff's response to the woman who presents herself as a 'man' was welcomed by LGBT groups as affirming gender ideology:

> Giona, I have listened to your story and about your path, and you know already know that which I'll tell you now. The Lord always walks with us. Always. The Lord is not disgusted with any of us. Even when we are sinners, He helps us. The Lord is not disgusted by our realities, He loves us as we are. And this is the crazy love of God.... God loves us as we are, God caresses us always. God is father, mother, brother, everyone for us. And to understand this is difficult, but He loves us as we are. Don't give up.... Go forward.[2111]

27th July

The militant pro-homosexuality Fr. James Martin S.J. announced via twitter that he had been chosen to address young Catholics at World Youth Day at Lisbon. This was just the latest sign of Fr. Martin being in favour with Pope Francis and the Vatican.[2112]

28th July

The US traditionalist blog *Rorate Caeli* posted an open letter from Archbishop Hector Aguer, Archbishop Emeritus of La Plata criticising Pope Francis and Cardinal Fernández, the Prefect of the Congregation for the Doctrine of the Faith. Archbishop Aguer characterised Pope Francis' mandate to Cardinal Fernández as follows:

> ...there is absolute freedom for all the inventions and machinations; you just have to beware of the 'backwardists' who stubbornly follow the ecclesial Tradition. To those with good understanding, this explains the meaning of the current pontifical ideology, according to which the papal monarchy persecutes and liquidates those who do not keep up with the doctrinal relativism professed by the Latin American (Argentinian, we should say) officialdom.[2113]

1st August

During an interview with the UK heterodox Catholic journal, *The Tablet*, pro-homosexuality Archbishop Malcolm McMahon, O.P., of the Archdiocese of Liverpool, expressed support for married priests, female deacons, and radical inclusion of homosexual bondings. Archbishop McMahon expressed a laissez-faire attitude to the sexual behaviour of homosexual persons:

> Well, what they do amongst themselves for all people is very much down to the couple isn't it. I mean, the Church points the way to Jesus Christ and during my own ministry as a priest and a bishop, I've never spoken on this topic at all.

Regarding the ordination of women deacons Archbishop McMahon expressed an idiosyncratic theology of the diaconate strikingly at variance with the post-conciliar understanding of the ordained ministry of deacons:

> Now women serve the church in many, many ways, so that's what I think there are many Catholics including the Holy father who want to get to the bottom of this question. Because the deacon, when you take his ministerial functions down to basics, can actually do no more than a lay person.

Deacon Nick Donnelly challenged Archbishop McMahon's 'erroneous and impoverished caricature of the diaconate':

[2111]Haynes, M [2023] *Vatican podcast featuring Pope Francis claims young people are characterized by 'sexual fluidity'*[Online] Available at: www.lifesitenews.com [Accessed on: 22 January 2024]

[2112]Haynes, M [2023] *Father James Martin to address participants of 2023 World Youth Day* [Online] Available at: www.lifesitenews.com [Accessed on: 22 January 2024]

[2113]*Archbp. Hector Aguer: The position of Francis and Fernandez is "absolutely contrary to the historical depth of the ecclesial care of the Faith"* [2023] [Online] Available at: www.rorate-caeli.blogspot.com [Accessed on: 23 January 2024]

He [McMahon] appears unaware of the fact that due to receiving the sacrament of Holy Orders, the deacon has competences not possessed by the laity — proclaiming the Gospel and delivering the homily; giving benediction with the Blessed Sacrament; being an ordinary minister of Holy Communion, and Baptism; assisting at the Sacrament of Matrimony by receiving the consent of the spouses in the name of the Church and giving the blessing of the Church (CCC 1630). The deacon possesses competences for these ministries — which he shares with priests and bishops — because he has received the sacramental character that configures him to Christ, the Servant (CCC 1570). Through the *laying on of hands* by the bishop during the rite of ordination, the deacon sacramentally and ministerially participates in the triple munera of Christ *in the mode of diakonia* [service] — teaching, sanctifying and administration, assisting his bishop and priests' leadership. (Congregation for Education [1998] *Basic Norms for the Formation of Permanent Deacons*,9).[2114]

4th August

During an interview with the Spanish-language news outlet *Vida Nueva*, Pope Francis launched yet another attack against faithful Catholics who uphold Tradition:

Behind this traditionalism, we have discovered moral problems and serious vices, double lives. We all know of bishops who, needing priests, have made use of people they had thrown out of other seminaries for immorality. I do not like rigidity because it is a bad symptom of interior life. The pastor cannot afford to be rigid. The pastor has to be ready for whatever comes…'rigidity' among young priests, who are good people who want to serve the Lord, comes from fearfulness at a time of insecurity that we are experiencing. That fear does not let them walk. We must remove this fear and help them. We need normal seminarians, with their problems, who play soccer, and who don't go to the neighbourhoods to dogmatise.… I don't like rigidity because it is a bad symptom of the inner life. [The pope also warned about people] who live trapped in a theology manual, unable to get into trouble and make theology move forward.[2115]

9th August

Cardinal Raymond Burke, the former prefect of the Apostolic Signature, posted on his website his analysis of the state of canon law during the pontificate of Pope Francis:

Today, we are sadly witnessing a return to the turmoil of the post-Conciliar period. In the past few years, law and even doctrine itself have been repeatedly called into question as a deterrent to the effective pastoral care of the faithful. Much of the turmoil is associated with a certain populist rhetoric about the Church, including her discipline. New canonical legislation has also been promulgated which is clearly outside of the canonical tradition and, in a confused manner, calls into question that tradition as it has faithfully served the truth of the faith with love. I refer, for example, to legislative acts touching upon the delicate process of the declaration of nullity of marriage which, in turn, touches upon the very foundation of our life in the Church and in society: marriage and the family [….]

Over the past few years, certain words, for example, 'pastoral,' 'mercy,' 'listening,' 'discernment,' 'accompaniment,' and 'integration' have been applied to the Church in a kind of magical way, that is, without clear definition but as the slogans of an ideology replacing what is irreplaceable for us: the constant doctrine and discipline of the Church. Some of the words, like 'pastoral,' 'mercy,' 'listening,' and 'discernment' have a place in the doctrinal and disciplinary tradition of the Church, but they are now being used with a new meaning and without reference to the Tradition. For instance,

[2114]Haynes, M [2023] *English archbishop supports female deacons, married priests, greater same-sex 'inclusion'* [Online] Available at: www.lifesitenews.com [Accessed on: 22 January 2024]
[2115]Haynes, M [2023] *Pope Francis says new council unnecessary as Vatican II 'has not yet been implemented'* [Online] Available at: www.lifesitenews.com [Accessed on: 22 January 2024]; Liedl, J [2023] *Pope Francis Confirms Vatican Envoy's Visit to China in Wide-Ranging Interview* [Online] Available at: www.ncregister.com [Accessed on: 22 January 2024]

pastoral care is now regularly contrasted with concern for the doctrine, which must be its foundation. The concern for doctrine and discipline is characterised as pharisaical, as wishing to respond coldly or even violently to the faithful who find themselves in an irregular situation morally and canonically. In this errant view, mercy is opposed to justice, listening is opposed to teaching, and discernment is opposed to judgment.[2116]

The persecution of the Chinese Catholic underground Church intensified as a consequence of the Vatican-Chinese Communist Party secret agreement. The underground priest Fr. Yang Xiaoming was found guilty of fraud by a communist court for refusing to join official bodies like the Chinese Catholic Patriotic Association [CCPA]. Fr. Yang Xiaoming was ordained by underground Bishop Peter Shao Zhuming of Wenzhou, who likewise was arrested several times for refusing to join the CCPA. Fr. Xiaoming was charged, tried and found guilty of 'conducting religious activities by deception or obtaining money by deception, under the guise of a religious cleric.' He was given an administrative sentence that included an 'order to cease his (priestly) activities' and a fine.[2117]

Steve Mosher, an expert in Chinese politics, commented,

> It goes without saying that Xi Jinping intends to crush the Underground Church and is using the Sino-Vatican Agreement for this purpose. But it is also clear that by preventing the faith from being passed on to the next generation he intends the same fate for Catholicism in general.[2118]

15th August

The Australian militant Catholic pro-homosexuality group, *Acceptance*, announced that they had received a hand-written note from Pope Francis congratulating them on their 50th anniversary.[2119]

18th August

The Holy See Press Office announced that Pope Francis had approved a new Vatican institute, the *Fray Bartolomé de las Casas Institute for Research and Promotion of Social Rights*. Pope Francis also approved his longtime friend and fellow Argentinian former supreme court judge Eugenio Raúl Zaffaroni as a member of the new Vatican-based institute, despite his long-standing record of promoting abortion and homosexuality. Eugenio Raúl Zaffaroni was also a proponent of Pachamama centred eco-spirituality which he expressed in his book *Pachamama and the Human Being*. To add to the controversy, in 2011 the Argentinian news outlet, *Perfil*, published an investigative report that revealed that apartments Zaffaroni owned in Buenos Aires were being used for a lucrative prostitution business. Though Zaffaroni denied being involved, Zaffaroni's attorney Ricardo Montivero testified in court that he had been managing the prostitution business.[2120]

20th August

The Italian secular and left-wing paper *il Fatto Quotidiano* published a commentary by Fr. Antonio Spadaro S.J., editor of *La Civiltà Cattolica* and confidant of Pope Francis, that disparaged our Lord Jesus Christ as being theologically 'rigid'. Commenting on our Lord's encounter with the Canaanite women (Mt 15:21-28):

[2116]Burke, R [2023] *Discipline and Doctrine: Law in the Service of Truth and Love* [Online] Available at: www.cardinalburke.com [Accessed on: 24 January 2024]

[2117]*Priest convicted of 'fraud' for refusing to register with the Patriotic Association* [Online] Available at: www.asianews.it [Accessed on: 25 January 2024]

[2118]Knuffke, L [2023] *Communist China charges underground Catholic priest with 'fraud' for refusing to join state-run church* [Online] Available at: www.lifesitenews.com [Accessed on: 22 January 2024]

[2119]*Pope Francis congratulates Acceptance on its 50th Anniversary* [2023] [Online] Available at: www. acceptanceperth.com [Accessed on: 24 January 2024]

[2120]Gomes, J [2023] *Pope Picks Brothel-Scandal Judge for Vatican Body* [Online] Available at: www. churchmilitant.com [Accessed on: 24 January 2024]

Jesus remains indifferent. His disciples approach him and plead with him in amazement. The woman was moving those who also misjudged her! Her cries had broken the barrier of rancour. But Jesus did not care. [His] silence was followed by Jesus' stymied and callous reply, 'I was not sent except to the lost sheep of the house of Israel.' The Master's harshness is unshakable. Now even Jesus plays the theologian: the mission received from God is limited to the children of Israel. So, no dice. Mercy is not for her. It is excluded. There is no question about it. [Christ] responds mockingly and disrespectfully to the poor woman…a fall in tone, in style, in humanity. Jesus appears as if he was blinded by nationalism and theological rigour. [The woman needed to] upset Jesus' rigidity in order to 'convert' him to himself…. Jesus, too, appears healed, and finally shows himself free, from the rigidity from the dominant theological, political and cultural elements of his time.[2121]

Archbishop Viganò condemned Fr. Spadaro's disparagement of our Lord as the 'dregs of the worst Modernism' typical of the followers of Pope Francis:

it matters little to them if in order to defend their errors they have to trample on the Son of God, offending and blaspheming Him as not even the worst heresiarchs of the past had dared to do.[2122]

Over three weeks later, Pope Francis elevated Fr. Spadaro to be the Under-Secretary of the Congregation for Culture and Education, led by the pro-homosexuality Cardinal José Tolentino de Mendonça.[2123]

21st August

Pro-homosexuality Archbishop Heiner Koch of the Archdiocese of Berlin sent a letter to all priests and deacons officially allowing them to 'bless' homosexual bondings, if they judged it appropriate. Koch was appointed Archbishop of Berlin by Pope Francis in 2015. Archbishop Koch claimed *Der Synodale Weg* and Pope Francis' *Amoris Laetitia* justified his decision. He also predicted that the CDF would soon change its position on such 'blessings' based on statements made by Cardinal Fernández.[2124]

24th August

Bishop Edward Rice of the Diocese of Springfield-Cape Girardeau, USA, banned his priests from celebrating Mass *ad orientem*.[2125]

28th August

During the Requiem Mass for Cardinal Geraldo Majella Agnelo, Archbishop Geremias Steinmetz of the Archdiocese of Londrina in Brazil gave Holy Communion to the Muslim Sheik Ahmad Saleh Mahairi. Archbishop Geremias Steinmetz was appointed the ordinary of Londrina by Pope Francis in 2017. Archbishop Steinmetz issued a statement justifying his sacrilege against the Blessed Sacrament, citing the Vatican II declaration *Nostra Aetate* and Pope Francis' *Desiderio Desideravi* in justification of the act. Steinmetz wrote,

No one had earned a place at the Last Supper. Rather, they were invited, attracted, by the burning desire of Jesus himself to eat that Passover with them, whose lamb

---

[2121]Haynes, M [2023] *Senior Jesuit priest and close friend of Pope Francis accuses Jesus of being 'stymied and callous'* [Online] Available at: www.lifesitenews.com [Accessed on: 22 January 2024]

[2122]*Viganò blasts Vatican's Secretariat for Communications for misrepresenting Jesus as 'a sick person, a prisoner of the rigidity'* [2023] [Online] Available at: www.remnantnewspaper.com [Accessed on: 24 January 2024]

[2123]Haynes, M [2023] *Pope Francis appoints Jesuit who attacked Jesus as 'callous' to prominent Vatican post* [Online] Available at: www.lifesitenews.com [Accessed on: 22 January 2024]

[2124]Wailzer, A [2023] *Archbishop of Berlin allows 'blessings' of same-sex unions, citing Pope Francis and Abp. Fernandez* [Online] Available at: www.lifesitenews.com [Accessed on: 16 January 2024]

[2125]Haynes, M [2023] *Another American bishop forbids priests from celebrating Mass ad orientem* [Online] Available at: www.lifesitenews.com [Accessed on: 22 January 2024]

is himself [....] The Eucharistic celebration teaches us the noble exercise of charity, nourishes meekness, leads us to fraternity and respect for all.[2126]

3rd September

During his apostolic journey to Mongolia Pope Francis met with leaders of non-Christian religions which he praised for being the continuation of 'ancient schools of wisdom.' Quoting from a Buddhist text, the Supreme Pontiff encouraged the leaders of non-Christian religions to promote their pagan beliefs and assumed an equivalence between our Lord Jesus Christ and the founders of non-Christian religions:

> May it be so for us, as committed followers of our respective spiritual masters and faithful stewards of their teachings, ever ready to offer the beauty of those teachings to those whom we daily encounter as friends and companions on our journey.[2127]

4th September

During his inflight press conference returning from his Apostolic Journey to Mongolia, Pope Francis criticised the faithful concerned about the Synod on Synodality:

> …a few months ago, I telephoned a Carmelite, and said to the Prioress: 'How are the nuns doing, Mother Superior?' She was a non-Italian Carmelite, and she finally replied: 'Your Holiness, we are concerned about the Synod.' I said jokingly, 'Now what's going on? Do you want to send a sister to the Synod?' 'No, we are afraid you are going to change doctrine.' And this is what she was saying, she had this idea.… But if you go to the basis of these ideas, you will find ideologies. In the Church, whenever people want to attack the path of communion, it is always an ideological attack. And they accuse the Church of this or that, but they never make a true accusation: that it is made up of sinners. They never speak of sinners. They defend a 'doctrine', a doctrine like distilled water that has no taste and is not the true Catholic doctrine, which is in the Creed. And very often, true Catholic doctrine scandalizes people. How scandalous is the idea that God became flesh, that God became Man, that Our Lady kept her virginity? This scandalizes. Catholic doctrine sometimes scandalizes. Ideologies are all distillations, they never scandalize.

Referring to the secret Vatican-Chinese Communist Party deal Pope Francis described the relationship as 'very respectful' despite the communists appointing the bishop of Shanghai without consultation with the Holy See and forbidding Chinese Catholics from travelling to Mongolia to meet the Supreme Pontiff.[2128]

5th September

HarperCollins published militant pro-homosexuality Fr. James Martin's new book *Come Forth: The Promise of Jesus's Greater Miracle*. Pope Francis appointed Fr. Martin a voting member of the Synod on Synodality. In the book Fr. Martin made the blasphemous comparison between our Lord Jesus Christ commanding Lazarus to 'come out' of the tomb with the homosexual term 'coming out':

> So 'come out' is probably a more accurate translation of the Greek in John's Gospel than 'come forth,' which has a kind of 'directional' sense to it [....] 'Coming out' means to accept, embrace and love who you are, especially your sexuality and the way that God made you, and to reveal or share that part of yourself with others. Coming out is often a critical step for LGBTQ people, who are sometimes told, either overtly or covertly, that they should not accept or love themselves. Or that they are a mistake, less valuable than

---

[2126]Haynes, M [2023] *Archbishop defends giving Holy Communion to Muslim leader, citing Pope Francis and Vatican II* [Online] Available at: www.lifesitenews.com [Accessed on: 22 January 2024]

[2127]Pope Francis [2023] *Viaggio Apostolico di Sua Santità Francesco in Mongolia (31 agosto – 4 settembre 2023) – Incontro Ecumenico e Interreligioso presso l'Hun Theatre, 03.09.2023* [Online] Available at: www.press.vatican.va [Accessed on: 24 January 2024]

[2128]Pope Francis [2023] *Inflight press conference* [Online] Available at: www.press.vatican.va [Accessed on: 24 January 2024]

straight people or less worthy of love and affection. Or, worst of all, that God doesn't love them [....] For all these reasons, when I hear the words 'Lazarus, come out!' which Jesus utters to his friend, locked inside his cold tomb, I think of the invitation for all of us to leave behind in our 'tombs' whatever keeps us bound, unfree, dead. And, just as often, I think of LGBTQ people and their own invitation to 'come out' into the sunlight of God's love.[2129]

11th September

During an interview with EWTN's Vatican correspondent Edward Pentin, pro-homosexuality Cardinal designate Fernández asserted that only Pope Francis has the charism to 'safeguard' the Faith which no one else possesses and no one can judge the 'doctrine' of Pope Francis:

> When we speak of obedience to the magisterium, this is understood in at least two senses, which are inseparable and equally important. One is the more static sense, of a 'deposit of faith,' which we must guard and preserve unscathed. But on the other hand, there is a particular charism for this safeguarding, a unique charism, which the Lord has given only to Peter and his successors. In this case, we are not talking about a deposit, but about a living and active gift, which is at work in the person of the Holy Father. I do not have this charism, nor do you, nor does Cardinal Burke. Today only Pope Francis has it. Now, if you tell me that some bishops have a special gift of the Holy Spirit to judge the doctrine of the Holy Father, we will enter into a vicious circle (where anyone can claim to have the true doctrine) and that would be heresy and schism. Remember that heretics always think they know the true doctrine of the Church. Unfortunately, today, not only do some progressives fall into this error but also, paradoxically, do some traditionalist groups.[2130]

13th September

During an interview with Christopher P. Wendt on the Confraternity of Our Lady of Fatima forum Bishop Athanasius Schneider of Astana, Kazakhstan, insisted Catholics cannot obey heretical teaching from the Synod on Synodality:

> We cannot obey here because these would be against the Divine revelation, against Divine commandment, and in this case, we have to follow God clearly [in] the constant teaching of the Church [....] I think we have to profess publicly the Catholic Truth, those Truths which are evidently undermined by the Synod agenda which we know now in the working document where there are a lot of things which are ambiguous and others which contradict the Catholic faith. Priests and lay people should publicly profess again and again the constant traditional teaching of the Church concretely regarding the hierarchical structure [....] The sixth commandment − not to commit adultery or other impure acts − is a Divine Law, and we have to proclaim this again against these cunning expressions within the document of the Synod. Welcoming LGBT people and including them and so on is basically a justification of the sin of homosexuality itself.[2131]

18th September

During an interview with the German Catholic newspaper *Die Tagespost* Archbishop Stanisław Gądecki of the Archdiocese of Poznań, Poland, expressed concern that the Synod on Synodality promoted moral relativism and globalist ideology. Archbishop Gądecki observed that the *Instrumentum Laboris* used terms like 'inclusion, as defined by the U.N., [which] refers exclusively to the inclusion of non-binary people in society and the recognition of human nature as non-binary':

[2129]Martin, James [2023] *Father James Martin: Jesus's greatest miracle and LGBTQ people* [Online] Available at: www.outreach.faith [Accessed on: 24 January 2024]

[2130]Pentin, E [2023] *Exclusive: Archbishop Fernandez Warns Against Bishops Who Think They Can Judge 'Doctrine of the Holy Father'* [Online] Available at: www.ncregister.com [Accessed on: 24 January 2024]

[2131]Bennett, P [2023] *Bishop Schneider: Catholics 'cannot obey' if the Synod on Synodality issues false teaching* [Online] Available at: www.lifesitenews.com [Accessed on: 25 January 2024]

In a sense, it [the term 'inclusion'] replaces the notion of sin and conversion in the IL text and is thus part of the ideology of moral relativism. This raises the question: is it appropriate for the Church – in search of a new language for communicating with people today – to adopt terms from the political language of the U.N., behind which there is often an ideology.[2132]

21st September

Archbishop Mario Delpini of Milan issued pastoral guidelines that appeared to normalise homosexuality as equivalent to God-given sexuality between men and women. Archbishop Mario Delpini was appointed by Pope Francis in 2017. Archbishop Delpini wrote,

> Particularly delicate attention given modern-day sensibilities must be devoted to accompanying and understanding the experience of love and the different nuances of attraction, both to people of different genders and to people of the same gender. The hasty label of 'homosexual', 'heterosexual' deadens the relational dynamic and tends to reduce it to a 'sexual practice'.[2133]

28th September

During an interview with the US Catholic news outlet *Catholic News Agency* Cardinal-elect Stephen Chow S.J., of Hong Kong, said evangelisation was not about converting others to the Catholic Faith. Bishop Chow was appointed by Pope Francis in 2021. Cardinal-elect Stephen Chow said,

> I think it is important that we say that Pope Francis made a distinction. Evangelisation is really to help people to understand the love of God — and the love of God without the agenda of turning them into Catholics — because that shouldn't be the focus, as that focus would be very restrictive. Evangelisation should help them to come to understand our God means love, means goodwill and a better life. Evangelisation should be really coming to know God, who is love.[2134]

During an interview with the Belgian daily news *La Libre Belgique* pro-homosexuality Bishop Johan Bonny of Antwerp, Belgium, expressed support for the killing of the sick and vulnerable through euthanasia:

> So the Church could adopt different positions on the question of euthanasia? Does this mean that, in the eyes of the Church, the value of life varies according to the regions of the world? Philosophy has taught me never to be satisfied with generic black and white answers. All questions deserve answers adapted to a situation: a moral judgment must always be pronounced according to the concrete situation, the culture, the circumstances, the context. I regret that, from the Vatican, the Congregation for the Doctrine of the Faith affirms that euthanasia is always an intrinsic evil, whatever the circumstance. It is too simple an answer that leaves no room for discernment. We will always oppose the desire of some to end a life too prematurely, but we must recognise that a request for euthanasia by a 40-year-old is not equivalent to that of a 90-year-old facing an incurable disease. We need to learn to better define concepts and distinguish situations [....] It is worth remembering that you cannot kill, and I am against all murders. But what is killing, what is murder? What do you say to someone who kills an enemy in the name of self-defense? What do you say to someone who has been affected by an incurable disease for years and who has decided to request euthanasia after talking to his family, his doctor, his loved ones? [....] Reference must always be made to the Bible, but nothing is more difficult than interpreting and applying it to a

[2132]Wailzer, A [2023] *Head of Polish bishops' conference criticizes Synod for using ideological 'language of the UN'* [Online] Available at: www.lifesitenews.com [Accessed on: 26 January 2024]

[2133]Knuffke, L [2023] *Archbishop of Milan promotes homosexuality in new pastoral letter days before Synod begins* [Online] Available at: www.lifesitenews.com [Accessed on: 22 January 2024]

[2134]Mares, C [2023] *New Hong Kong cardinal: Sharing 'love of God,' not conversions, goal of Church in China* [Online] Available at: www.catholicnewsagency.com [Accessed on: 24 January 2024]

particular situation without falling into fundamentalism. God relies on our intelligence to fully understand His word.[2135]

1st October

During his address to the synod participants at the pre-synod retreat pro-homosexual Fr. Timothy Radcliffe, O.P., criticised the Catholic Church for being 'too Western, too Latin, too colonial':

> For some it is defined by its ancient traditions and devotions, its inherited structures and language, the Church we have grown up with and love. It gives us a clear Christian identity. For others, the present Church does not seem to be a safe home. It is experienced as exclusive, marginalising many people, women, the divorced and remarried. For some it is too Western, too Eurocentric.

Referring to homosexuals and polygamists, and making no mention of the need for repentance and chastity, Fr. Radcliffe said, 'The IL [*Instrumentum Laboris*] mentions also gay people and people in polygamous marriages. They long for a renewed Church in which they will feel fully at home, recognised, affirmed and safe.'[2136]

During his third retreat address on the 4th October Fr. Radcliffe upended our Lord's teaching, 'How narrow is the gate, and strait is the way that leadeth to life: and few there are that find it' (Mt 7:14). Fr. Radcliffe told the participants:

> Of course not *every* hope or opinion is legitimate. But orthodoxy is spacious and heresy is narrow. The Lord leads his sheep out of the small enclosure of the sheepfold into the wide-open pastures of our faith.[2137]

2nd October

On the eve of the Synod on Synodality five cardinals announced that they had submitted two sets of *dubia* to Pope Francis regarding their concerns about the synod. The cardinals were: Walter Cardinal Brandmüller; Raymond Leo Cardinal Burke; Juan Cardinal Sandoval Íñiguez; Robert Cardinal Sarah and Joseph Cardinal Zen Ze-kiun. In a 'Notification to Christ's Faithful (can. 212 § 3)' the cardinals explained their reasons for submitting the two dubia to the Supreme Pontiff:

> …in view of various declarations of highly-placed Prelates, pertaining to the celebration of the next Synod of Bishops, that are openly contrary to the constant doctrine and discipline of the Church, and that have generated and continue to generate great confusion and the falling into error among the faithful and other persons of good will, have manifested our deepest concern to the Roman Pontiff [….] Given the gravity of the matter of the *dubia*, especially in view of the imminent session of the Synod of Bishops, we judge it our duty to inform you, the faithful (can. 212 § 3), so that you may not be subject to confusion, error, and discouragement but rather may pray for the universal Church and, in particular, the Roman Pontiff, that the Gospel may be taught ever more clearly and followed ever more faithfully.

On the 10th July, the cardinals submitted their first *dubia* to Pope Francis, containing five *dubium*:

1. *Dubium* about the claim that we should reinterpret Divine Revelation according to the cultural and anthropological changes in vogue.
2. *Dubium* about the claim that the widespread practice of the blessing of same-sex unions would be in accord with Revelation and the Magisterium (*CCC* 2357).

[2135]Knuffke, L [2023] *Belgian bishop dissents from Catholic teaching with support for euthanasia* [Online] Available at: www.lifesitenews.com [Accessed on: 25 January 2024]

[2136]Radcliffe, T [2023] *Synod Retreat Meditation: 'At home in God and God at home in us'* [Online] Available at: www.vaticannews.va [Accessed on: 26 January 2024]

[2137]Radcliffe, T [2023] *Synod Retreat Meditation: 'Friendship'* [Online] Available at: www.vaticannews.va [Accessed on: 26 January 2024]

3. *Dubium* about the assertion that synodality is a 'constitutive element of the Church' (Apostolic Constitution *Episcopalis Communio* 6), so that the Church would, by its very nature, be synodal.
4. *Dubium* about pastors' and theologians' support for the theory that 'the theology of the Church has changed' and therefore that priestly ordination can be conferred on women.
5. *Dubium* about the statement 'forgiveness is a human right' and the Holy Father's insistence on the duty to absolve everyone and always, so that repentance would not be a necessary condition for sacramental absolution.

The cardinals received answers to the *dubia* the next day, that bore the Pope's signature, but according to reports from those close to the cardinals, was judged as displaying 'the writing style of his trusted theologian, the Argentine Victor Manuel Fernández'. Pope Francis chided the five cardinals for displaying fear through their concerns:

> I tell you that it is not very good to be afraid of these question marks and questions. The Lord Jesus, who promised Peter and his successors indefectible assistance in the task of caring for the holy people of God, will help us, also thanks to this Synod, to keep ourselves always more in constant dialogue with the men and women of our time and in total fidelity to the Holy Gospel.

Regarding the second *dubium* on the blessing of homosexual bondings Pope Francis' response did not uphold the Church's prohibition, but instead opened the door for such blessings through the exercise of 'pastoral prudence':

> Pastoral prudence must therefore properly discern whether there are forms of blessing, requested by one or more people, that do not convey a misconception of marriage. Because, when a blessing is requested, it is a request for help from God, a plea to be able to live better, a trust in a Father who can help us to live better.

Regarding the fourth *dubium* on the ordination of women, Pope Francis' response stated that the issue was open to further study despite Pope St. John Paul II's definitive rejection of the possibility in his apostolic letter *Ordinatio Sacerdotalis*:

> On the other hand, to be rigorous, we should recognise that a clear and authoritative doctrine on the exact nature of a 'definitive statement' has not yet been fully developed. It is not a dogmatic definition and yet it must be complied with by all. No one can publicly contradict it and nevertheless it can be the object of study, as in the case of the validity of ordinations in the Anglican Communion.[2138]

On the 21st August, the five cardinals sent Pope Francis a *New Formulation of the* Dubia, expressing their dissatisfaction and alarm at the Supreme Pontiff's responses. First, they clarified that their concerns were not motivated by fear, as he had judged:

> …it is not out of fear of dialogue with the people of our time, nor of the questions they could ask us about the Gospel of Christ [….] With the same sincerity with which You have answered us, we must add that Your answers have not resolved the doubts we had raised, but have, if anything, deepened them. We therefore feel obliged to re-propose, reformulating them, these questions to Your Holiness, who as the successor of Peter is charged by the Lord to confirm Your brethren in the faith. This is all the more urgent in view of the upcoming Synod, which many want to use to deny Catholic doctrine on the very issues which our *dubia* concern.

Due to Pope Francis' vague and imprecise responses the cardinals required the traditional 'yes' or 'no' response.

Regarding Pope Francis' response to the second *dubium* on the blessing of homosexual bondings the cardinals' new *dubium* stated:

[2138]Pope Francis [2023] *Response to 10th July 2023 dubium* [Online] Available at: www.cardinalburke.com [Accessed on: 26 January 2023]

…we are concerned that the blessing of same-sex couples might create confusion in any case, not only in that it might make them seem analogous to marriage, but also in that homosexual acts would be presented practically as a good, or at least as the possible good that God asks of people in their journey toward Him. So let us rephrase our *dubium*: Is it possible that in some circumstances a pastor could bless unions between homosexual persons, thus suggesting that homosexual behaviour as such would not be contrary to God's law and the person's journey toward God? Linked to this *dubium* is the need to raise another: does the teaching upheld by the universal ordinary magisterium, that every sexual act outside of marriage, and in particular homosexual acts, constitutes an objectively grave sin against God's law, regardless of the circumstances in which it takes place and the intention with which it is carried out, continue to be valid?

Regarding Pope Francis' response to the fourth *dubium* on the ordination of women, the cardinals' new *dubia* stated:

We are concerned that some may interpret this statement to mean that the matter has not yet been decided in a definitive manner. In fact, St. John Paul II affirms in *Ordinatio Sacerdotalis* that this doctrine has been taught infallibly by the ordinary and universal magisterium, and therefore that it belongs to the deposit of faith. This was the response of the Congregation for the Doctrine of the Faith to a *dubium* raised about the apostolic letter, and this response was approved by John Paul II himself. We therefore must reformulate our dubium: could the Church in the future have the faculty to confer priestly ordination on women, thus contradicting that the exclusive reservation of this sacrament to baptised males belongs to the very substance of the Sacrament of Orders, which the Church cannot change?[2139]

3rd October

Cardinal-elect Fernández rebuked the cardinals for submitting the new *dubia* to Pope Francis, 'as if the Pope were their slave for errands.'[2140] Cardinal Fernández ignored the cardinals request to the pope for further clarification in response to their *New Formulation of the* Dubia.[2141]

The Congregation for the Doctrine of the Faith released responses to a *dubium* submitted by Czech Cardinal Dominik Duka regarding 'the administration of the Eucharist to divorced couples living in a new union.' The response was signed by both Pope Francis and Cardinal-elect Fernández, stating,

Amoris Laetitia opens the possibility of accessing the sacraments of reconciliation and the Eucharist when, in a particular case, there are limitations that attenuate responsibility and culpability (guilt).

The second *dubium* submitted by Cardinal Duka asked, 'Can Pope Francis' response to the question from the pastoral section of the diocese of Buenos Aires, given that the text was published in the *Acta Apostolicae Sedis*, be considered an affirmation of the ordinary magisterium of the Church?' (The pastoral section of the diocese of Buenos Aires allowed divorced and civilly remarried, with a pre-existing marriage remaining valid, receive the Sacrament of Reconciliation and the Blessed Sacrament after a period of 'accompaniment' by a priest.) Pope Francis and Cardinal-elect Fernández replied,

As indicated in the rescript accompanying the two documents on the *Acta Apostolicae Sedis*, these are published *"velut magisterium authenticum,"* that is, as authentic magisterium (teaching).[2142]

[2139]*On the Eve of the Synod, Five Cardinals Release New Set of Dubia to Pope Francis: 'We Are Concerned'* [2023] [Online] Available: www.tfp.org [Accessed on: 26 January 2024]

[2140]Liedl, J [2023] *Pope Francis responds critically to pre-synod dubia* [Online] Available at: www.thetablet.co.uk [Accessed on: 26 January 2024]

[2141]Cascioli, R [2023] *Vatican claim Pope replied to Dubia is a sensational mystification* [Online] Available at: www.newdailycompass.com

[2142]*Here's the full text of the Vatican's response to dubia on divorced and remarried Catholics* [2023] [Online] Available at: www.catholicnewsagency.com [Accessed on: 26 January 2024]

A number of high profile figures in the Church spoke of their concerns on the eve of the Synod on Synodality at the conference in Rome under the title, The Synodal Babel organised by *La Nuova Bussola Quotidiana*. The speakers included: Cardinal Raymond Burke, the canon lawyer Fr. Gerald Murray and the philosopher Professor Stefano Fontana. Among other things, Cardinal Burke said,

> We are told that the Church we profess, in communion with our ancestors in the faith since the time of the Apostles, to be one, holy, catholic and apostolic, must now be defined by synodality, a term that has no history in Church doctrine and for which there is no reasonable definition. It is obviously an artificial construction, more like a human construction than the Church built on the rock that is Christ. The *Instrumentum laboris* of the upcoming session of the Synod of Bishops certainly contains statements that depart strikingly and gravely from the perennial teaching of the Church'.[2143]

Fr. Gerald Murray, the prominent canon lawyer warned that the Synod on Synodality threatened to bring immense harm to the Church:

> The Synodal Assembly has the potential to cause immense harm to the life and mission of the Church. It is our duty in obedience to God's revelation and in charity for souls to resist steadfastly any attempts to change the teaching of the Church that may emerge from this Synodal Assembly [....]

Fr. Murray also criticised the *Instrumentum laboris* for promoting the idea of creating 'spaces' for people who have rejected Church doctrine, such as 'remarried divorcees, people in polygamous marriages, LGBTQ+ people'. Fr. Murray said:

> The trendy conceit of 'creating spaces' for people who reject various teachings of the Church gives the impression that they are not 'safe' whenever they are reminded that their behaviour is immoral according to God's law. Is being hurt by the truth a problem? Is not such pain a purifying moment, a grace from God, who challenges us to examine ourselves according to the demands of his law, and not according to our own often mistaken choices? People who reject the Church's teaching may claim to be unwelcomed by fellow believers. It is not they who are rejected, but rather it is their immoral behaviour that is rightly stigmatised.[2144]

The philosopher Professor Stefano Fontana observed how the Synod on Synodality aimed to change doctrine through praxis:

> The change of doctrine through the new synodality is not left to doctrine, but to praxis. It is praxis that decides what is done. The bishops of the Buenos Aires region *did*, and this really counted, in the sense of establishing what is to be done. What is done coincides with what must be done, from the point of view of history (and praxis) being and having to be are the same thing.[2145]

4th October

The General Secretariat for the Synod of Bishops informed the press about the rules governing the Synod on Synodality:

> [E]ach of the Participants is bound to confidentiality and privacy both with regard to their own interventions, as well as in regard to the interventions of other Participants. This duty remains in effect even after the Synod Assembly has ended.... [This to] guarantee the freedom of expression of each and all regarding their thoughts and to ensure the serenity of common discernment, which is the main task entrusted to the Assembly.[2146]

[2143]Haynes, M [2023] *Cardinal Burke responds to dubia criticism, warns Synod aims to change Church's structure* [Online] Available at: www.lifesitenews.com [Accessed on: 26 January 2024]

[2144]Murray, G [2023] *The sheep in place of the shepherds, the Synod subverts the Church* [Online] Available at: www.newdailycompass.com [Accessed on: 26 January 2024]

[2145]Fontana, S [2023] *Modernist Synod aims to make Church liberal democracy* [Online] Available at: www.newdailycompass.com [Accessed on: 26 January 2024]

[2146]Haynes, M [2023] *Synod on Synodality members ordered to observe perpetual secrecy about discussions* [Online] Available at: www.lifesitenews.com [Accessed on: 26 January 2024]

9th October

During his address at the start of the second week of the Synod on Synodality pro-homosexuality Cardinal Jean-Claude Hollerich S.J., the relator general, exhorted participants to accept the idea of 'radical inclusion.' Such a concept involves the inclusion of those engaging in mortal sin without Christ's requirement of repentance and conversion. Cardinal Hollerich said:

> …in deep communion with His Father through the Holy Spirit, Jesus extended this communion to all the sinners. Are we ready to do the same? Are we ready to do this with groups which might irritate us because their way of being might seem to threaten our identity? Todos… tutti… If we act like Jesus, we will testify to God's love for the world. Failing to do so will make us look like an identitarian club.

Pro-homosexuality Fr. Timothy Radcliffe O.P. continued the theme of 'radical inclusion':

> So many people feel excluded or marginalized in our Church because we have slapped abstract labels on them: divorced and remarried, gay people, polygamous people, refugees, Africans, Jesuits! A friend said to me the other day: 'I hate labels. I hate people being put in boxes. I cannot abide these conservatives.' But if you really meet someone, you may become angry, but hatred cannot be sustained in a truly personal encounter. If you glimpse their humanity, you will see the one who creates them and sustains them in being, whose name is 'I AM.'[2147]

The Catholic Information Agency of the Polish Bishops' Conference, *eKai*, released Archbishop Gądecki of Poznań's letter to Pope Francis expressing grave concern about the German *Der Synodale Weg*. Archbishop Gądecki was president of the Polish Bishops' Conference. Archbishop Gądecki wrote,

> The authors seem so ashamed of the way the German bishops reacted to reports of sexual abuse by clergy that they decide to make a moral and legal revolution in the universal Church. However, it seems that this would not be an evangelical revolution, but rather one inspired by left-liberal ideologies.

Furthermore, Archbishop Gądecki expressed concern that the Synod on Synodality would 'be manipulated in any way and used to authorise German theses that openly contradict the teaching of the Catholic Church.'[2148]

On the 27th November, the Polish newspaper *Rzeczpospolita* published an open letter from pro-homosexuality Bishop Georg Bätzing of Limburg to Archbishop Gądecki in response to his letter to Pope Francis. Bishop Bätzing was appointed by Pope Francis 2016 the Head of the German bishops' Conference. Bishop Bätzing wrote,

> It was with some dismay and great disappointment that I took note of the letter you sent to the Holy Father on October 9, 2023, which has now been published. We have spoken to each other several times in the four weeks during the Synod. It is – allow me to say this openly – massively un-synodal and unbrotherly behaviour if you do not say a word to me about the letter in these conversations. Instead of a conversation, you have chosen [to write] a letter to Pope Francis in which you complain about the Synodal Path of the Catholic Church in Germany with great vehemence and with imprecise and misleading statements [....] In your presentation, you attach great importance to the juxtaposition of your own Catholicity and the contradiction to Catholic doctrine that you accuse the Catholic Church in Germany of. I wonder, however, according to which ecclesiastical law the president of the bishops' conference of a particular church is entitled to judge the catholicity of another particular church and its episcopate. Let me therefore tell you clearly that I consider your letter to be a massive overstepping of your authority [....] I would like to emphasise that the numerous thematic and conceptual similarities

---

[2147]Haynes, M [2023] *Synod leaders claim 'tensions' and 'real encounter' are part of the conference process* [Online] Available at: www.lifesitenews.com [Accessed on: 26 January 2024]
[2148]Coppen, L [2023] *Bätzing v. Gądecki: What's behind the clash?* [Online] Available at: www.pillarcatholic.com [Accessed on: 30 January 2024]

between the synodal path of the Catholic Church in Germany and the World Synod do not stem from the fact that the German bishops have infiltrated, indoctrinated or even corrupted the world episcopate or the World Synod. Such ideas simply belong to the realm of abstruse conspiracy theories.[2149]

10th October

During a synod press conference pro-homosexuality Cardinal Joseph Tobin of Newark expressed his hope for the radical inclusion of homosexual persons, with no mention of repentance, amendment of life or chastity. Cardinal Tobin recalled his invitation to homosexuals to come to his cathedral in 2017:

> the real beauty of our Catholic Church is clear when the doors are open and welcoming, and it's my hope that this synod will help us do that in an even more significant way.[2150]

14th October

Pro-homosexuality Cardinal Fernández, prefect of the CDF, posted on his Facebook page a short reflection entitled 'Abuse, Clericalism and Synodality' in which he equated admonishing those in mortal sin with sexual abuse. Cardinal Fernández wrote,

> All people in authority are prone to abuse. I mean abuse of any kind (sexual, authority, conscience manipulation, etc.). For a long time it was taken for granted that the authority gave access to a kind of possession that enabled people to use for their own purposes and to impose their own desires. This has happened on every level much more than we knew: from priests abusing religious women to men abusing their domestic workers. But there was also a verbal violence that led too quickly to harshly judge others without any fear of hurting them and destroying their self-esteem. It was called: 'adulterers', 'sodomites', 'illegitimate children', 'degenerates', 'sinners', etc.[2151]

During an interview with Diane Montagna, a journalist in Rome accredited to the Holy See, Cardinal Zen criticised the Synod on Synodality for its divergence from revelation:

> The animators of the Synod seem to reduce the Word of God to the feeling of the people — by which they mean all the baptised, even those who left the Church long ago — and refer to the magisterium, not of the past twenty centuries, not of the many recent popes, but only of the reigning pontiff.[2152]

17th October

Argentina's national news agency, *Télam*, released its interview with Pope Francis, in which the Supreme Pontiff spoke of his determination to the change the Church:

> Since the Second Vatican Council, John XXIII had a very clear perception: the Church has to change. Paul VI agreed, just like the succeeding Popes. It's not just changing ways, it's about a change of growth, in favour of the dignity of people. That's theological progression, of moral theology and all the ecclesiastical sciences, even in the interpretation of Scriptures that have progressed according to the feelings of the Church. Always in harmony. Rupture is not good. We either progress through development or things don't turn out right. Rupture leaves you out of the sap of development. I like the image of a tree and its roots. The roots receive the humidity of the soil and take it upward, through the trunk. When you separate yourself from that, you end up dry, without traditions. Tradition in the good sense of the word. We all have traditions, a

[2149]Wailzer, A [2023] *Head of German bishops' conference accuses Polish counterpart of 'un-synodal' behavior* [Online] Available at: www.lifesitenews.com [Accessed on: 26 January 2024]

[2150]Haynes, M [2023] *Cardinal Tobin says he hopes Synod leads to 'significant' developments in 'welcoming' of 'LGBTQ+ people'* [Online] Available at: www.lifesitenews.com [Accessed on: 26 January 2024]

[2151]Fernández, V [2023] *Abuse, Clericalism and Synodality* [Online] Available at: www.facebook.com/victormanuel.fernandez.378 [Accessed on: 27 January 2024]

[2152]Montagna, D [2023] *'Confused and confusing': Cardinal Zen talks to the Herald about his ongoing Synod concerns* [Online] Available at: www.catholicherald.co.uk [Accessed on: 27 January 2024]

family, we were all born within the culture of a country, a political culture. We all have a tradition for which to take responsibility [....] Progress is necessary and the Church has to incorporate these novelties with a serious conversation from a human point of view. The Greek thinker Publius Terentius Afer says 'Nothing human is alien to me'. The Church holds what's human in its hand. God became a man, not a philosophical theory. Humanity is something consecrated by God. That is, everything human must be assumed and progress must be human, in harmony with humanity.[2153]

The militant US Catholic homosexual group, *New Ways Ministry*, announced that Pope Francis held a 50 minute private audience with pro-abortion, pro-homosexuality Sister Jeannine Gramick, S.L., and staff members of *New Ways Ministry*. In 2010 Cardinal Francis George, O.M.I, archbishop of Chicago and president of the United States Conference of Catholic Bishops, declared that *New Ways Ministry's*

> ...claim to be Catholic only confuses the faithful regarding the authentic teaching and ministry of the Church with respect to persons with a homosexual inclination. Accordingly, I wish to make it clear that, like other groups that claim to be Catholic but deny central aspects of Church teaching, New Ways Ministry has no approval or recognition from the Catholic Church and that they cannot speak on behalf of the Catholic faithful in the United States.[2154]

Sr. Jeannine Gramick, S.L., had been 'permanently prohibited from any pastoral work involving homosexual persons'[2155] by the CDF in 1999, with the approval of Pope St. John Paul II. A prohibition that Sr. Gramick steadfastly defied.

Regarding the private audience with Pope Francis, homosexual Francis DeBernardo, Executive Director of *New Ways Ministry*, said:

> This meeting was an affirmation not only of Sister Jeannine and New Ways Ministry but of the thousands upon thousands of LGBTQ+ people, parishes, schools, pastoral ministers, and religious communities who have been tirelessly working for equality, and who often experienced the great disapproval and ostracization that New Ways Ministry had experienced. Meeting with Pope Francis is a great encouragement for Sister Jeannine and New Ways Ministry to continue our work in the Catholic Church.[2156]

The US Diocese of Lexington's website posted Pope Francis's hand-written note thanking a militant pro-homosexuality activist for his work in the diocese. Militant pro-homosexuality Rt. Rev. John Stowe , O.F.M. Conv., is the Bishop of Lexington appointed by Pope Francis in 2015. The recipient of Pope Francis' note was Stan 'J.R.' Zerkowski the leader of the Diocese of Lexington's Diocesan LGBTQ Outreach Commission, Fortunate Families and LGBTQ Ministry Historic St. Paul. Mr. Zerkowski saw the note as 'an affirmation from the pope about LGBTQ ministry.'[2157]

19th October

During an interview with Michael Haynes of *LifeSiteNews* pro-homosexuality Cardinal Fernández talked of his openness to blessing homosexual 'couples':

> But perhaps also [they] need blessings, not only one isolated person, but two persons who are asking for a blessing because they want to be faithful to God, they want to be better, they want to grow in their Christian life. The blessing is not a sacrament. And

[2153]Llorente, B [2023] *Pope Francis: 'War is the great enemy of the universal dialogue that we need'* [Online] Available at: www.telam.com.ar [Accessed on: 26 January 2024]

[2154]George, F [2010] *USCCB President Clarifies Status of New Ways Ministry* [Online] Available at: www.usccb.org [Accessed on: 26 January 2024]

[2155]Ratzinger, J [1999] *Notification regarding Sr. Jeannine Gramick SSND and Father Robert Nugent SDS* [Online] Available at: www.vatican.va [Accessed on: 26 January 2024]

[2156]Shine, R [2023] *Pope Francis Receives Sr. Jeannine Gramick at Vatican* [Online] Available at: www.newwaysministry.org [Accessed on: 26 January 2024]

[2157]Mangiaracina, E [2023] *Pope Francis thanks LGBT activist for his 'ministry' in handwritten letter* [Online] Available at: www.lifesitenews.com [Accessed on: 27 January 2024]

we mustn't ask the same conditions [for] a simple blessing that we ask for a sacrament. Blessing is a sign of the '*opera pastorale*' [pastoral work], to every people in every situation, and we [need to] know nothing [about] the people with how is his Christian life, the morals and other things [in order] to give the blessing.[2158]

20th October

During an interview with the US Catholic news outlet *Catholic News Agency* Archbishop Anthony Fisher of Sydney reflected on the Synod on Synodality based on his participation. Archbishop Fisher said,

> [If some synod proposal] is radically at odds with the Gospel and the apostolic tradition, that's not of the Holy Spirit because we cannot have Christ and the Holy Spirit at war with each other.... [there has been] a long discussion about the ordination of women.... I don't think that's revealing anything that people didn't know already. And there's a lot of tension and emotion around an issue like that.[2159]

25th October

The Diocese of Koper, Slovenia, confirmed that Fr. Marko Rupnik had been incardinated as a diocesan priest. The diocese announced that Fr. Rupnik enjoyed 'all the rights and duties of diocesan priests', despite being excommunicated by the CDF in 2020 for absolving one of his sexual accomplices — allegedly overturned by Pope Francis — and expelled from the Jesuits in 2023.[2160]

During the Wednesday audience Pope Francis met with the leaders of homosexual groups that publicly contradict Church doctrine on homosexuality. The Supreme Pontiff spoke to the co-chairs of the 'Global Network of Rainbow Catholics', an international coalition of dissenting, pro-homosexuality, self-professed Catholic groups. According to the group leaders Pope Francis encouraged them to move forward with their campaigning with the words 'Go ahead!'[2161]

26th October

LifeSiteNews published an essay by Bishop Marian Eleganti, Emeritus Auxiliary Bishop of Chur, Switzerland, warning that the Synod on Synodality was promoting 'creeping schism'. Bishop Eleganti wrote:

> In my opinion, however, this is nothing other than a creeping schism, which is being veiled, anointed, and legitimised, no, promoted with the new 'synodality.' It will prove more and more to be such a schism as soon as the frustration of the reformers begins to boil over if, even in 2024, the reforms do not go far enough for them and once again prove to be merely words. They will then have had enough of words, words, words, and will follow them up with actions, which they are already doing now.

Bishop Eleganti also observed that Synodalization and Protestantization were synonyms:

> For the emphasis on authority and action by virtue of baptism and the new egalitarian 'synodality' associated with it repeat Reformation axioms and lead to nothing other than an Anglicanization of the Roman Catholic Church. Its sacerdotal modus operandi through the binding and empowering special ministerial priesthood is laicised and desacralised despite warnings even from Protestants that we should not make the same mistakes as the reformers.[2162]

[2158]Haynes, M [2023] *Cardinal Fernández says blessings are for 'every' person in 'every situation'* [Online] Available at: www.lifesitenews.com [Accessed on: 27 January 2024]

[2159]Mares, C [2023] *Archbishop: If a Synod Proposal is at Odds With the Gospel, 'That's Not of the Holy Spirit'* [Online] Available at: www.ncregister.com [Accessed on: 27 January 2024]

[2160]Haynes, M [2023] *Disgraced Fr. Marko Rupnik incardinated into Slovenian diocese despite history of abuse* [Online] Available at: www.lifesitenews.com [Accessed on: 26 January 2024]

[2161]*'Go ahead!': Pope Francis encourages Catholic LGBT+ leaders to move forward* [2023] [Online] Available at: www.facebook.com/gnrcatholics/ [Accessed on: 27 January 2024]

[2162]Eleganti, M [2023] *Swiss bishop warns Synod on Synodality is leading to 'creeping schism,' 'Protestantization'* [Online] Available at: www.lifesitenews.com [Accessed on: 27 January 2024]

27th October

The US journal *First Things* published an essay by Cardinal Gerhard Müller, the former prefect of the CDF, in which he warned that 'To teach contrary to the apostolic faith would automatically deprive the pope of his office.' Cardinal Müller was a participant at the Synod on Synodality. Cardinal Müller wrote,

> A Synod of Bishops should deliberate on how to meet the challenges of faith in today's world so that Christ is brought to the attention of today's people as the light of their lives. By contrast, some activists, especially those embarked on the German 'synodal way,' consider the upcoming Synod on Synodality as a kind of congress of the faithful that is authorised to give the Church of God a new constitution and new doctrines agreeable to the spirit of the age. Rest assured that even if a majority of the delegates were to 'decide' on the 'blessing' (blasphemous and contrary to Scripture itself) of homosexual couples, or the ordination of women as deacons or priests, even the authority of the pope would not be sufficient to introduce or condone such heretical teachings, or any other teachings that contradict the Word of God in Sacred Scripture, Apostolic Tradition, and the dogma of the Church. Christ commissioned Peter to strengthen his brethren in their faith in him, the Son of God, not to introduce doctrines and practices contrary to revelation. To teach contrary to the apostolic faith would automatically deprive the pope of his office. We must all pray and work courageously to spare the Church such an ordeal.[2163]

During an interview with Vatican journalist Edward Pentin for the US National Catholic Register, Cardinal Müller warned that the Synod on Synodality was being used to prepare Catholics to accept homosexuality and women's ordination. Cardinal Müller said,

> Some speakers also speak of openness and define what tradition is, [saying] that it 'is not static; it's dynamic.' But in the end, all of these so-called synodal reflections are aimed at preparing us to accept homosexuality. Only this: What wasn't spoken about was Jesus Christ [or] divine Revelation, the grace of human persons created according to the image and likeness of God, and of God as the goal of our human existence. All is being turned around so that now we must be open to homosexuality and the ordination of women. If you analyse it, all is about converting us to these two themes [....] They don't say openly what they mean. They cannot say openly, 'We want to contradict the Word of God.' But they are introducing a new hermeneutic with which they want to reconcile the Word of God with these ideologies — anti-Christian ideologies. But we cannot reconcile Christ and the Antichrist. This homosexual, 'LGBT' ideology is, at its centre, an anti-Christian ideology. It's the spirit of the Antichrist speaking through them. It is absolutely against creation. And their trick is to mix pastoral care for these persons with this anti-Christian ideology.[2164]

28th October

The *Synthesis Report* of the 16th Ordinary General Assembly of the Synod of Bishops, otherwise known as the Synod on Synodality, was released. During the press conference pro-homosexuality Cardinal Hollerich commented on the large votes in favour controversial issues such as women deacons:

> It was clear to me that some topics would have resistance. I am full of wonder that so many people have voted in favour. That means that the resistance [was] not so great as people have thought before. So yes, I am happy with that result [....] To have this freedom and openness will change the Church and I'm sure the Church will find answers, but perhaps not the exact answer this group or that group wants to have, but answers [with which] most people could feel well and listened to.

[2163]Müller, G [2023] *The Church is not a democracy* [Online] Available at: www.firstthings.com [Accessed on: 29 January 2024]

[2164]Pentin, E [2023] *Cardinal Müller Says Synod on Synodality Is Being Used by Some to Prepare the Church to Accept False Teaching* [Online] Available at: www.ncregister.com [Accessed on: 29 January 2024]

Pro-homosexuality Cardinal Grech re-emphasised the 'radical inclusion' agenda:

> This is the approach of Jesus, to create spaces for everyone so that no one feels excluded. Today there was a tremendous joy that you could see with your own eyes.[2165]

On homosexuality the *Synthesis Report* implicitly criticised Divine Revelation as inadequate to deal with the modern experience of sexual orientations:

> Some topics, such as those related to gender identity or sexual orientation [...] are also controversial in the Church because they raise new questions[....] Sometimes existing anthropological categories are not sufficient to grasp the complexity of what emerges from experience or from science, and therefore this calls for further investigation. We must take the necessary time for this reflection and devote the best of our energies to it, and not fall into simplistic judgments that hurt people or damage the body of the Church. (15:g) [Vote: passed by 307–39]

On the 'radical inclusion' agenda promoted by pro-homosexuality participants as the justification to change doctrine on homosexuality, the *Synthesis Report* stated:

> In different ways, people who feel marginalized or excluded from the Church because of their marriage status, identity or sexuality also ask to be heard and accompanied. There was a deep sense of love, mercy and compassion felt in the Assembly for those who are or feel hurt or neglected by the Church, who want a place to call 'home' where they can feel safe, be heard and respected, without fear of feeling judged. Listening is a prerequisite for walking together in search of God's will. The Assembly reiterates that Christians must always show respect for the dignity of every person. (16:h) [Vote: passed by 326–20]

On the ordination of women deacons the *Synthesis Report* kept the discussion open for future decisions:

> Theological and pastoral research on the access of women to the diaconate should be continued, benefiting from consideration of the results of the commissions specially established by the Holy Father, and from the theological, historical and exegetical research already undertaken. If possible, the results of this research should be presented to the next Session of the Assembly. (9:n) [Vote: passed by 279–67]

The wording of the *Synthesis Report* lent heavily in favour of the ordination of women deacons:

> Different positions have been expressed regarding women's access to the diaconal ministry. For some, this step would be unacceptable because they consider it a discontinuity with Tradition. For others, however, opening access for women to the diaconate would restore the practice of the Early Church. Others still, discern it as an appropriate and necessary response to the signs of the times, faithful to the Tradition, and one that would find an echo in the hearts of many who seek new energy and vitality in the Church. Some express concern that the request speaks of a worrying anthropological confusion, which, if granted, would marry the Church to the spirit of the age. (9:j) [Vote: passed by 277–69]

The *Synthesis Report* also advanced the discussion of greater 'Eucharistic hospitality', allowing non-Catholics to receive the Blessed Sacrament, even though they are not in communion with the Catholic Church and reject fundamental doctrines of the Catholic Faith:

> We need to examine the issue of Eucharistic hospitality (*Communicatio in sacris*) from theological, canonical and pastoral perspectives in light of the link between sacramental and ecclesial communion. This issue is of particular importance to inter-church couples.

[2165]Brockhaus, H [2023] *Cardinal Hollerich: The openness of the Synod on Synodality 'will change the Church'* [Online] Available at: www.catholicnewsagency.com [Accessed on: 29 January 2024]

It raises the need for a broader reflection on inter-church marriages. (7:i) [Vote: passed by 321 – 23][2166]

30th October

Catholic laymen and women held a press conference in Rome to express their concerns regarding the Synod on Synodality. The laity included *LifeSiteNews'* co-founder and editor-in-chief John-Henry Westen, *The Remnant* newspaper's Michael Matt, Ugandan MP Lucy Akello, Kenyan Alice Muchiri, French journalist Jeanne Smits, child advocate attorney Liz Yore, and British barrister (trial attorney) James Bogle. John-Henry Westen said,

> During this whole Synod on Synodality Pope Francis has made his own personal teaching contrary to the faith more explicit than ever before. Right from the outset he scandalised the faithful by selecting bishops who oppose the teaching of the faith on the family as the leadership of the synod.

Michael Matt observed,

> So, those who are breathing a sigh of relief on their YouTube channels this morning, I'm sorry. But you have no idea what you're talking about. The plan is to use the synodal process to convert the Catholic world over the next 12 months to accept massive change. Why? Because overcoming 2000 years of Bible-based Catholic moral theology is going to take time.

Lucy Akello said,

> I traveled all the way to Rome today to be counted and perhaps become a missionary to the Western world, for you have forgotten that you brought the Gospel to Africa, and we are only defending what you brought to us and what resonates with our values and practices.

Alice Muchiri said,

> It is such a confusing moment to imagine that the same institutions that brought Christianity with all its beauty to Africa and the rest of the world might be used in the same way to spread false teachings in the guise of acceptance, inclusivity, and other such terms. The same institutions that condemn polygamy amongst Africans are now condoning an abomination.

Jeanne Smits observed that the Synod on Synodality had

> inoculated … the idea that the Church's teachings can change and adapt to the world, making the Christian life a lot easier as it forgets the reality of the straight and narrow path.

Liz Yore protested that Pope Francis was running

> a protection racket for predators.…This Synod on Synodality, in both the *Instrumentum laboris* and Saturday's statement, speaks interminably of listening and dialoguing with the world. Nevertheless, this papacy has repeatedly insulted and ignored clerical abuse victims.

James Bogle observed,

> [We] are witnessing a direct infiltration of the Church by an alien spirt and at the highest levels. Although the Church can never be defeated, evil can cause immense confusion amongst the faithful and a loss of souls and that is what we are witnessing in our time.[2167]

[2166]16th Ordinary General Assembly of the Synod of Bishops [2023] *First Session (4-29 October 2023) Synthesis Report: A Synodal Church in Mission* [Online] Available at: www.synod.va; Haynes, M [2023] *Synod on Synodality report pushes female deacons and lay governance but avoids giving firm answers* [Online] Available at: www.lifesitenews.com [Accessed on: 29 October 2024]
[2167]*Pope Francis 'scandalised the faithful' from the outset of the Synod* [2023] [Online] Available at: www.lifesitenews.com [Accessed on: 29 January 2024]

31st October

During an interview with the militant US Catholic pro-homosexuality website, *Outreach*, pro-abortion, pro-homosexuality Sr. Jeannine Gramick assessed the progress of Pope Francis' pro-homosexuality agenda. Though Sr. Gramick had been censured by the CDF, she was the recipient of many signs of Pope Francis' favour. About the Synod on Synodality Sr. Gramick concluded,

> Pope Francis is laying the groundwork for change in sexuality [....] That's what Pope Francis is trying to do, to get people comfortable in sharing their experience. It may take several years or maybe a decade, I don't know, but in God's due time, I am confident that the sexual teaching of the church will change.[2168]

Addressing *LifeSiteNews'* Rome Life Forum in Rome, Italy, Cardinal Müller, Prefect Emeritus of the CDF, shared his observations about the state of the Church under Pope Francis. Cardinal Müller said:

> A Church that no longer believes in Jesus the Christ is no longer the Church of Jesus Christ. Bishops who betray their divine mission in order to avoid being accused of proselytism or of being rigourists for defending Christian morality have forgotten the meaning and reason of their existence. That relativism in doctrine does not make Christianity fit for the present [....] the Holy Spirit does not update the supposedly dead Tradition for the present through self-appointed prophetesses, as the Montanists thought in the 3rd century. The *sensus fidelium* is also not the voice of the people demanding to be heard by their shepherds or the breath of the Holy Spirit, which the pope then interprets in his own sense [....] The advice to the Church to modernise her true teaching of the Gospel with the help of a relativistic philosophy brings only illusory results. One must not fall for the following suggestion: If you want to reach the people of today and be loved by all, then, like Pilate, leave aside the truth, then you will spare yourself persecution, suffering, cross and death! In worldly terms, the power of politics, media and banks are safe, while the truth challenges contradiction and promises suffering with Christ, the crucified Saviour of the world. Jesus could have easily saved Himself with the message of the unconditionally loving heavenly Father who does not demand repentance and conversion.[2169]

US Catholic child attorney Liz Yore, who also spoke at the Rome Life Forum, accused Pope Francis of having a 'blind spot for predators who are his friends and famous':

> Typically and disturbingly, Francis continues to deal with [abuse victims], as he always does, by imposing his Sankt Gallen Mafia *omerta* of silence, yet he deploys his Synodal PR machine to churn out hypocritical talking points in hopes of anaesthetising our memory about his own catastrophic record on clergy sex abuse. In Francis's world, mercy trumps justice, and despite his endless chatter about the preference for the poor, celebrity transcends integrity. This pattern is shockingly obvious, as he has a blind spot for predators who are his friends and famous [....] While Francis clearly hears the cry of Mother Earth, he is deaf to the cries of clergy abuse victims. While the purported rising of the oceans tug at his heart, his stone cold, heartless dismissiveness, of abused consecrated nuns is chilling.[2170]

1st November

Pope Francis issued the apostolic letter, in the form of a motu proprio, *Ad Theologiam promovendam* [To promote theology]. The Supreme Pontiff opened his motu proprio with criticism of the apostolic orientation of the theological enterprise:

[2168]Di Corpo, R [2023] *Q&A: Sister Jeannine Gramick on Pope Francis, the Synod report and where the church is going* [Online] Available at: www.outreach.faith [Accessed on: 29 January 2024]
[2169]Müller, G [2023] *Cardinal Müller: Bishops must preach 'Christ crucified,' not cozy up to political elites* [Online] Available at: www.lifesitenews.com [Accessed on: 30 January 2024]
[2170]Summers, J [2023] *Liz Yore: Pope Francis extends 'mercy' to clerical sex abusers but not victims* [Online] Available at: www.lifesitenews.com [Accessed on: 30 January 2024]

Promoting theology in the future cannot be limited to abstractly re-proposing formulas and schemes of the past. Called to prophetically interpret the present and to discern new itineraries for the future, in the light of Revelation, theology will have to confront profound cultural transformations, aware that: 'What we are living through is not simply an age of change, but a change of epoch' (Address to the Roman Curia, 21 December 2019). (Art.1)'.

Pope Francis exhorted theologians to engage in a 'paradigm shift' by seeing the Catholic Faith as just one source in a multiplicity of sources that form the context of people's lives:

Theological reflection is therefore called to a turning point, to a paradigm shift, to a 'courageous cultural revolution' (Encyclical Letter *Laudato Si'*, 114) that commits it, first of all, to be a fundamentally contextual theology, capable of reading and interpreting the Gospel in the conditions in which men and women live daily, in different geographical, social and cultural environments, and having as its archetype the Incarnation of the eternal Logos, its entering into the culture, worldview, and religious tradition of a people. From here, theology cannot but develop into a culture of dialogue and encounter between different traditions and different knowledge, between different Christian denominations and different religions, openly confronting all, believers and non-believers alike. The need for dialogue is in fact intrinsic to the human being and to the whole of creation, and it is the particular task of theology to discover 'the Trinitarian imprint that makes the cosmos in which we live "a web of relationships" in which "it is proper to every living being to tend towards another thing"'. (Apostolic Constitution *Veritatis gaudium*, Proem, 4a) (Art.4).

Ad Theologiam promovendam made human experience the privileged starting point of theological reflection, not Divine Revelation, exhorting the theologian to discover among people's experiences the 'many images of God' that do not correspond 'to the Christian face of God' (Art.8).[2171]

Fr. Thomas Weinandy, O.F.M. Cap., a former member of the Vatican's International Theological Commission, commented:

The problem is, as is often the case with Francis, there is no mention that theology must be founded upon the traditional interpretation of scripture, the living theological and magisterial tradition, the infallible teaching of the Councils, and be faithful to Catholic doctrine and moral teaching. Only if all of these are taken into account can theology address contemporary culture, develop in a proper manner, be pastoral, be faithful to the *sensus fidelium* [sense of the faithful], and be evangelistic.[2172]

2nd November

Bishop Karl-Heinz Wiesemann of the Diocese of Speyer, Germany, issued a letter to the clergy and staff of his diocese instructing them to 'bless' homosexual bondings, adulterous relationships and those living in sin. Claiming a mandate from *Der Synodale Weg* approval of such 'blessings, and Pope Francis' declaration 'Who am I to judge?' Bishop Wiesemann wrote,

Both with regard to believers whose marriages have broken down and who have remarried, and especially with regard to same-sex oriented people, it is urgently time, especially against the background of a long history of deep wounds, to find a different pastoral attitude inspired by the Gospel, as many of you have been practicing for a long time.

Bishop Wiesemann also advocated the overturning of doctrine on homosexuality:

[2171]Pope Francis [2023] *Ad theologiam promovendam* [Online] Available at: www.vatican.va [Accessed on: 1 February 2024. Trans by DeepL]

[2172]'*Ad theologiam promovendam*': *A brief guide for busy readers* [2023] [Online: Available at: www. pillarcatholic.com] [Accessed on: 1 February 2024]

That is why I have advocated for a reassessment of homosexuality in church teaching and also for the possibility of blessings for same-sex couples. I stand by that. I hope that this pressing issue of our time can also be given a good further development on the path of the World Synod.[2173]

During an interview with the Italian Catholic news outlet, *Daily Compass*, Cardinal Müller, Prefect Emeritus of the CDF, criticised the homosexual agenda of the Synod on Synodality. In answer to the question *You have already stated that in the end this Synod only wanted to promote the LGBT agenda and the female diaconate. What gave this impression?* Cardinal Müller responded,

Because much was said about this and very little about the essential themes of the faith, that is, the Incarnation, salvation, redemption, justification, sin, grace, human nature, the ultimate goal of man, the Trinitarian and Eucharistic dimension of the Church, vocations, education. These are the real challenges, as is the spread of great violence, of those who justify it in the name of God, like the Muslim fundamentalists. Of this nothing, instead so many speeches on homosexuality, and all one-sided [....] Why weren't people invited who were practicing homosexuals and then rediscovered their heterosexuality, and who have written books about their experiences, such as Daniel Mattson (author of *Why I Don't Call Myself Gay. How I Reclaimed My Sexual Reality and Found Peace*, Cantagalli 2018, ed.)? There was Father James Martin, he was only there to spread propaganda. He never spoke of grace and salvation for these people, only that 'the Church must accept, the Church must..., must..., must...' But how can the Bride of Christ be the object of our invectives? It is not the Church that needs to change, it is we who need to be converted.[2174]

3rd November

During his interview with the heterodox US Jesuit journal, *America*, Cardinal Christophe Pierre, the Apostolic Nuncio to the United States, criticised traditional young Catholics. Cardinal Christophe Pierre was elevated to the Sacred College of Cardinals by Pope Francis in 2023. Cardinal Pierre said,

We are in the church at a change of epoch. People don't understand it. And this may be the reason why most of the young priests today dream about wearing the cassock and celebrating Mass in the traditional way. In some ways, they are lost in a society which has no security, and all of us when we feel lost look for some security. But which kind of security? Is the liturgy [only] something you like? Is it a refuge? Is the church a refuge? If you look at it as a refuge, you isolate yourselves. The church is missionary. It's not a reserve of people who feel well together. It is not the church that will protect me. It's not the habit.[2175]

6th November

Pope Francis met with 7,000 children in the Paul VI Audience Hall for an encounter on the theme 'Let's Learn from Boys and Girls' organised by the Dicastery for Culture and Education. Focusing on so-called climate change, Pope Francis encouraged the children to chant, 'Nature is our future'.[2176]

8th November

The Congregation for the Doctrine of the Faith issued responses to *dubia* submitted by Bishop José Negri of the Diocese of Santo Amaro, Brazil, regarding transgender

[2173]Knuffke, L [2023] *German bishop asks priests to 'bless' homosexual unions, citing Pope Francis and Synodal Way* [Online] Available at: www.lifesitenews.com [Accessed on: 29 January 2024]

[2174]Cascioli, R [2023] *Müller: 'The Synod, a step towards Protestantisation'* [Online] Available at: www.newdailycompass.com [Accessed on: 30 January 2024]

[2175]Kokx, S [2023] *US Apostolic Nuncio receives blowback for slamming the cassock, Traditional Latin Mass* [Online] Available at: www.lifesitenews.com [Accessed on: 30 January 2024]

[2176]Haynes, M [2023] *Pope Francis asks thousands of children to chant 'nature is our future' at Vatican event* [Online] Available at: www.lifesitenews.com [Accessed on: 30 January 2024]

individuals and homosexual bondings. The CDF response was signed by pro-homosexuality Cardinal Fernández and approved and signed by Pope Francis. In response to the question, *Can a transgender person be baptised*? Cardinal Fernández responded in the affirmative, that the Church would recognise such an individual's rejection of their God-given sexuality:

> A transgender person — even after undergoing hormone treatment and sex-reassignment surgery — can receive Baptism under the same conditions as other believers, if there are no situations in which there is a risk of generating public scandal or disorientation among the faithful. In the case of children or adolescents with problems of a transgender nature, if they are well-prepared and have the right disposition, they also can receive Baptism.

In response to the question, *Can a transgender person serve as a godparent*? Cardinal Fernández responded in the affirmative, implicitly accepting that a man presenting himself as a woman can be called a 'godmother' and a woman presenting herself as a man can be called a 'godfather'.

To the question, *Can a transgender person serve as a witness to a matrimony*? Cardinal Fernández responded in the affirmative, implicitly accepting that a man presenting himself as a woman can be a 'bridesmaid' or 'matron of honour', and a woman presenting herself as a man can be a 'best man'.[2177]

On the 21st November, Cardinal Gerhard Müller criticised Cardinal Fernández's ecclesial affirmation of transgenderism, saying,

> It is confusing and harmful for the Magisterium to rely on the terminology of a nihilistic and atheistic anthropology by seeming to grant its false content the status of legitimate theological opinion in the Church.[2178]

9th November

During an interview with *LifeSiteNews* journalists Maike Hickson and Andreas Wailzer Cardinal Gerhard Müller, Prefect Emeritus of the CDF, admitted that some statements by Pope Francis could be understood as material heresy. Cardinal Müller admitted that while the Supreme Pontiff had not committed formal heresy,

> …some of Pope Francis' statements are formulated in such a way that they could be reasonably understood as material heresy, independent of their unclear subjective meaning [....] At the synod, where many expect or fear that the homosexual 'blessings' will now be introduced, to write a public letter to these [LGBT] organisation's on this occasion, to receive them, to be photographed with them… that is a very clear message. It's a heresy of practice. Why didn't he receive a father, a mother, and their five children at this time? There are no photos of that.

Regarding whether a pope could neither officially introduce the 'blessing' of homosexual couples nor the ordination of women, Cardinal Müller replied,

> Well, if that were to happen, it would be invalid because the 'blessing' [of sin] would be blasphemy. Those who would carry it out or approve of it would be gravely culpable. The Pope cannot introduce the diaconate of women in the sense of the sacrament of holy orders because the Pope cannot introduce new sacraments or new conditions. One can change the rite of the sacraments, the external rite. One can say: 'Pray the Gloria, perhaps at the end or at the beginning,' but he cannot change the substance of the sacraments, and the question of the minister and the recipient of the sacraments is part of the substance. The diaconate, insofar as it designates a level within the one sacrament of holy orders, cannot be [changed] by the Pope. [This] goes beyond his

---

[2177]Haynes, M [2023] *Pope Francis says 'trans' people can be godparents, homosexual 'parents' can have children baptized* [Online] Available at: www.lifesitenews.com [Accessed on: 26 January 2024]
[2178]Haynes, M [2023] *Cardinal Müller: Pope Francis allowing 'trans' people to be godparents is 'confusing and harmful'* [Online] Available at: www.lifesitenews.com [Accessed on: 26 January 2024]

authority. That is why John Paul II did not say 'I forbid this,' but 'the Church has no authority'. The diaconate is nevertheless linked to this priestly level of ordination, that it is one sacrament. The Council of Trent says it is *unum ex septem sacramentis ecclesiae* [one of the seven sacraments of the Church]; it is one sacrament.'[2179]

19th November

Pope Francis invited a group of men who present themselves as women to take part in the Vatican-hosted lunch for the poor. The group make monthly visits from Torvaianica, Italy, to Pope Francis' Wednesday general audiences, where they are given VIP seats. Many of the men presenting themselves as women work as prostitutes.[2180]

20th November

During a meeting with the Heads of Dicasteries of the Roman Curia Pope Francis was reported to have declared that faithful Cardinal Raymond Burke his 'enemy'. Pope Francis allegedly said, 'Cardinal Burke is my enemy, so I am taking away his flat and salary.' Riccardo Cascioli commented, 'The cardinal has not yet received a formal notice, but considering precedents, it is unlikely to be just a threat, which nonetheless would be very serious.'[2181]

6th December

During his address to students at the Catholic University of America pro-homosexuality Cardinal Wilton Gregory expressed his hostility towards Tradition, in particular the traditional Latin Mass. Archbishop Wilton Gregory was elevated to the Sacred College of Cardinals by Pope Francis in 2020. Cardinal Gregory said,

> You know, when Pope Paul VI instituted the new ritual tradition, he made an exception for older priests, and don't forget, he was one of the first in Rome to celebrate the new Mass, the Pope himself, that he made an exception. He said – and I don't remember exactly the age – some of the older priests who, you know, it would have been just too much for them, they had celebrated the Mass, the Tridentine Mass, for sixty years, he made an exception for them. But it was his desire, his intent, to say when that generation goes, then everyone will be in the new Mass. Tradition dies a slow death, sometimes a bloody death.[2182]

7th December

The Catholic news agency of the German bishops, *Katholische Nachrichtenagentur*, reported that Bishop Heinrich Timmerevers of the Diocese of Dresden-Meissen called for Catholic schools to accept the LGBTQ+ agenda. Bishop Timmerevers was appointed Bishop of Dresden-Meissen in 2016 and was the chairman of the Commission for Education and Schools for the German bishops' conference. Bishop Timmerevers told his fellow bishops,

> In the future, Church-run schools should be able to be recognised by the fact that they give room to deal with the topic of sexuality...spaces of recognition for people of all sexual identities.[2183]

[2179]Hickson, M & Wailzer, A [2023] *Cardinal Müller: Some statements by Pope Francis could be understood as material heresy* [Online] Available at: www.lifesitenews.com [Accessed on: 26 January 2024]

[2180]Winfield, N & Thomas, T [2023] *For this group of trans women, the pope and his message of inclusivity are a welcome change* [Online] Available at: apnews.com [Accessed on: 30 January 204]

[2181]Cascioli, R [2023] *The Pope: 'Away with Cardinal Burke's house and salary'* [Online] Available at: www.newdailycompass.com [Accessed on: 30 January 2024]

[2182]Maria, R [2023] *Cardinal Wilton Gregory suggests the Latin Mass will die 'a slow ... bloody death'* [Online] Available at: www.lifesitenews.com [Accessed on: 26 January 2024]

[2183]Wailzer, A [2023] *German bishop says Catholic schools should be 'spaces of recognition for all sexual identities'* [Online] Available at: www.lifesitenews.com [Accessed on: 26 January 2024]

9th December

During his address to the online conference, 'Is the Pope Catholic?' Archbishop Carlo Viganò concluded about the state of the pontificate of Pope Francis, 'We are ... far beyond heresy'. Archbishop Carlo Viganò was the former apostolic nuncio to the USA, 2011 to 2016. Archbishop Viganò said,

> We have all sorts of hair-splitting about the distinctions between formal and material heresy, none of which do the least thing to impede Bergoglio's destructive action. We cannot behave as if we were resolving a question of a point of Canon Law. No. The Lord is being outraged, the Church is being humiliated, and souls are being lost because a usurper remains on the Throne. What we cannot do, because we do not have the authority, is to officially declare that Jorge Mario Bergoglio is not Pope. The terrible *impasse* in which we find ourselves makes any human solution impossible.[2184]

11th December

Archbishop Timothy Costelloe of Perth issued an open letter announcing that he had removed Fr. Michael Rowe from his role as rector of the thriving Latin Mass community of St. Anne's church, Belmont, Perth, Australia. Archbishop Costelloe claimed that he had deposed Fr. Rowe for his failure to formally request permission to celebrate 'the Mass using the Roman Missal promulgated by Saint John XXIII in 1962.' Fr. Rowe disputed Archbishop Costelloe's version of events, writing:

> The Archbishop clearly stated in his most recent letter to me on 22 December 2023, that even if I had signed the historically and factually inaccurate declaration requesting permission to say the Latin Mass decree, he still would have removed me as Rector and Spiritual Leader of the Perth Traditional Latin Mass Community. The inference from this is that the Latin Mass is being severely restricted and with no leader appointed, who else will ensure continuity and operation of St Anne's?[2185]

In his pastoral letter of the 4th December 2023 Archbishop Costelloe had explained that his actions against the celebration of the Latin Mass were about conformity to Pope Francis:

> I am conscious that some of the decisions I must now make, and the consequences of them, will upset and anger some people. I can only appeal to everyone to put aside their personal preferences and work together to ensure that our communion with the Holy Father, made concrete through our communion with the local bishop, is realised in practice as well as in words.[2186]

On the 13th January 2024 the Australian Bishops Conference announced that Pope Francis had appointed Archbishop Timothy Costelloe as a consultor of the General Secretariat of the Synod of Bishops. The appointment was in conjunction with Archbishop Costelloe's appointments as a Member of the Preparatory Commission, and as one of the nine President Delegates to the Synod.[2187]

12th December

Pro-homosexuality Cardinal Fernández, prefect of the Congregation for the Doctrine of the Faith, issued a note, counter signed by Pope Francis, overturning the traditional ban on storing cremated remains at home or scattering them. Cardinal Fernández was

---

[2184]Kokx, S [2023] *Archbishop Viganò: 'False prophet' Bergoglio is guilty of 'all-out apostasy'* [Online] Available at: www.lifesitenews.com [Accessed on: 31 January 2024]

[2185]Rowe, M [2023] *Statement on the Incident at St Anne's Church, Belmont on 2nd December 2023* [Online] Available at: drive.google.com/file/d/1GTFMv6aAEE-WU9jGuusBgNrvMmpFDrCz/view [Accessed on: 31 January 2024]

[2186]Costelloe, T [2023] *Open Letter to the faithful who worship at the Church of St Anne, Belmont, Western Australia* [Online] Available at: www.perthcatholic.org.au [Accessed on: 31 January 2024]

[2187]*New Synod of Bishops role for Archbishop Costelloe* [2024] [Online] Available at: www.mediablog.catholic.org.au [Accessed on: 31 January 2024]

responding to dubia submitted by Cardinal Matteo Zuppi, archbishop of Bologna and president of the Italian Episcopal Conference. Cardinal Zuppi asked if there could be a designated 'sacred place' for the 'commingled accumulation and preservation of the ashes of the baptized' and if family members can be permitted to keep a portion of the deceased ashes 'in a place that is significant for the history of the deceased.' Cardinal Fernández responded in the affirmative to both, overturning the CDF's 2016 prohibitions issued by Cardinal Gerhard Müller in the decree *Ad Resurgendum Cum Christo*.[2188]

18th December

Pro-homosexuality Cardinal Victor Manuel Fernández, Prefect of the Congregation for the Doctrine of the Faith, promulgated the declaration *Fiducia Supplicans* — signed by Pope Francis — allowing the blessing of homosexual bondings, divorced and civilly remarried couples, and cohabiting couples:

> …this Dicastery has considered several questions of both a formal and an informal nature about the possibility of blessing same-sex couples and — in light of Pope Francis' fatherly and pastoral approach — of offering new clarifications on the Responsum ad dubium that the Congregation for the Doctrine of the Faith published on 22 February 2021.

While insisting that the 'blessing' was not intended as a 'legitimation of their status' Cardinal Fernández stated that as a 'blessing' of 'couples of the same sex' it was intended to 'enrich' all that was 'true, good, and humanly valid in their lives and their relationships':

> Within the horizon outlined here appears the possibility of blessings for couples in irregular situations and for couples of the same sex, the form of which should not be fixed ritually by ecclesial authorities to avoid producing confusion with the blessing proper to the Sacrament of Marriage. In such cases, a blessing may be imparted that not only has an ascending value but also involves the invocation of a blessing that descends from God upon those who — recognising themselves to be destitute and in need of his help — do not claim a legitimation of their own status, but who beg that all that is true, good, and humanly valid in their lives and their relationships be enriched, healed, and elevated by the presence of the Holy Spirit. (31)

The text of *Fiducia Supplicans* makes it clear that the 'blessing' is intended to facilitate the 'relationship' of same-sex couples, making no mention of the obligation of chastity and repentance for mortally sinful sexual acts:

> …the ordained minister could ask for them to have peace, health, a spirit of patience, dialogue, and mutual assistance — but also God's light and strength to be able to fulfil his will completely. (38)

While stipulating that the blessing of 'same-sex couples' must not be associated with the accoutrements of marriage or in association with the performance of a 'civil union', *Fiducia Supplicans* does allow for the 'blessing' of homosexual bondings in public and group settings of a religious nature,

> 'Such a blessing may instead find its place in other contexts, such as a visit to a shrine, a meeting with a priest, a prayer recited in a group, or during a pilgrimage.'(40)

When stipulating that the 'non-ritualized blessings' must be spontaneous, simple gestures, Cardinal Fernández included criticism of liturgical ritual:

> In this sense, it is essential to grasp the Holy Father's concern that these non-ritualised blessings never cease being simple gestures that provide an effective means of increasing trust in God on the part of the people who ask for them, careful that they

[2188]Gomes, J [2023] *Pope's Doctrine Czar stirs up controversy on Cremation* [Online] Available at: www.churchmilitant.com [Accessed on: 31 January 2024]

should not become a liturgical or semi-liturgical act, similar to a sacrament. Indeed, such a ritualisation would constitute a serious impoverishment because it would subject a gesture of great value in popular piety to excessive control, depriving ministers of freedom and spontaneity in their pastoral accompaniment of people's lives. (36)[2189]

On the 21st January 2024, Vatican journalist Diane Montagna discovered a disparity between the English translation of *Fiducia Supplicans* and the original Italian version as well as the other translations. Diane Montagna wrote,

The English translation of n. 38 uses the noun 'individuals.' The Italian original uses the demonstrative pronoun '*costoro*,' meaning 'for them.' All other translations except English use a pronoun meaning 'for them'.[2190]

The militant pro-homosexuality priest Fr. James Martin, S.J., immediately welcomed *Fiducia Supplicans* on behalf of same-sex couples, expressed in marital terms:

This is a major step forward in the church's ministry to LGBTQ people and recognises the desire for same-sex couples for God's presence and help in their committed and loving relationships. It is also a marked shift from the conclusion 'God does not and cannot bless sin' from just two years ago. The declaration opens the door to non-liturgical blessings for same-sex couples, something that had been previously off limits for bishops, priests and deacons. Along with many priests, I will now be delighted to bless my friends in same-sex unions.[2191]

In his comments to Michael Haynes of the Canadian Catholic news outlet *LifeSiteNews*, Cardinal Fernández made it explicitly clear that it was not the 'blessing' of individual homosexual persons, but the 'blessing' of homosexual persons 'together'. 'But perhaps also [they] need blessings, not only one isolated person, but two persons who are asking for a blessing....'[2192]

Bishop Strickland, emeritus of Tyler, Texas, immediately exhorted all bishops to reject *Fiducia Supplicans*:

[I encourage] my brother bishops that we all join with a voice of strength and joy in the Lord in these last days of Advent and say 'no' to this latest document. We really simply need to be a united voice saying, 'no,' we will not respond to this. We will not incorporate this into the life of the Church because we simply must say 'no'. And it needs to be a united voice.[2193]

Pro-homosexuality Bishop Georg Bätzing of Limburg, head of the German bishops' conference, welcomed *Fiducia Supplicans* for allowing the blessing of a 'diversity of lifestyles':

I very much welcome this document and am grateful for the pastoral perspective it takes. *Fiducia supplicans* explains that it is possible and permitted in principle for the ordained minister to respond to the wishes of couples who ask for a blessing for their partnership, even if they do not live according to the norms of the Church in every respect. This means that a blessing can be given to couples who are unable to marry in the Church due to divorce, for example, and to same-sex couples. The practice of the Church knows many forms of blessings. It is good that this treasure is now elevated for the diversity of lifestyles.

[2189]Dicastery for the Doctrine of the Faith [2023] *Declaration Fiducia Supplicans: On the Pastoral Meaning of Blessings* [Online] Available at: www.vatican.va [Accessed on: 31 January 2024]

[2190]Wailzer, A [2024] *Fiducia Supplicans' English version refers to homosexual 'individuals' in contrast to other translations* [Online] Available at: www.lifesitenews.com [Accessed on: 12 February 2024]

[2191]Martin, James [2023] *Twitter account Dec 18 2023* [Online] Available at: www.twitter.com/ JamesMartinSJ [Accessed on: 31 January 2024]

[2192]Haynes, M [2023] *Pope Francis publishes norms for clergy to 'bless' homosexual couples* [Online] Available at: www.lifesitenews.com [Accessed on: 31 January 2024]

[2193]Kokx, S [2023] *Bishop Strickland urges bishops to say 'no' to Francis' 'blessings' of homosexual couples* [Online] Available at: www.lifesitenews.com [Accessed on: 31 January 2024]

Pro-homosexuality Bishop Heinrich Timmerevers of Dresden also welcomed *Fiducia Supplicans*:

> Blessing – in short, thanking and asking – is no longer conditioned by whether someone meets all moral ideals equally.[2194]

During an interview with the Austrian public TV Station *ORF* Archbishop Franz Lackner, Head of the Austrian Bishops' Conference, said priests cannot say 'no' to blessing homosexual couples anymore. Bishop Franz Lackner was appointed Archbishop of Salzburg, Austria, by Pope Francis in 2013. Archbishop Lackner said,

> I believe that the Church recognises that a relationship between two [people] of the same sex is not entirely without truth: there is love, there is fidelity, there is also hardship shared and lived in faithfulness. This should also be acknowledged.... Basically, you [priests] can no longer say no.

On the 20th December 2023 a spokesman for Archbishop Lackner walked back mandating priests to bless homosexual bondings:'No personal obligation can be derived from a general openness [to bless same-sex couples] for each individual case.'[2195]

Pro-homosexuality Bishop Josef Marketz of the diocese of Gurk-Klagenfurt, Austria, appointed bishop by Pope Francis in 2019, welcomed *Fiducia Supplicans* characterising it as taking a

> loving view of people's situation as well as their longing and desire for [a] blessing, so that their life together can succeed well or even better under the loving gaze of God.... [it has] always been very clear that same-sex couples must not be regarded as second-class Christians.[2196]

Pro-homosexuality Archbishop Cardinal Blase Cupich Chicago issued a statement praising *Fiducia Supplicans* as a 'step forward' for the Church:

> As such, the Declaration is a step forward, and in keeping not only with Pope Francis's desire to accompany people pastorally but Jesus's desire to be present to all people who desire grace and support.[2197]

Archbishop Mark O'Toole of Cardiff and Menevia issued a statement 'warmly welcoming' *Fiducia Supplicans* and encouraging his clergy to 'bless' homosexual bondings and other sinful relationships:

> I warmly welcome the desire and intention of the Holy Father to encourage and challenge us to be close to all people irrespective of their personal circumstances. The Declaration *Fiducia Supplicans*, issued yesterday by the Dicastery for the Doctrine of the Faith, is another example of this. At the heart of the Declaration is a call for those of us who are pastors to take a sensitive pastoral approach in being available and willing to draw close to people whatever their situation.[2198]

19th December

Militant pro-homosexuality Fr. James Martin, S.J., announced on twitter that he had performed his first 'blessing' of a homosexual bonding:

[2194]Wailzer, A [2023] *Heterodox German bishops laud new Vatican document on gay 'blessings' as a 'real Christmas present'* [Online] Available at: www.lifesitenews.com [Accessed on: 31 January 2024]
[2195]Wailzer, A [2023] *Austrian archbishop changes tune on mandatory 'blessings' for homosexual couples* [Online] Available at: www.lifesitenews.com [Accessed on: 31 January 2024]
[2196]Wailzer, A [2023] *Head of Austrian Bishops' Conference says priests cannot say 'no' to blessing homosexual couples anymore* [Online] Available at: www.lifesitenews.com [Accessed on: 31 January 2024]
[2197]Cupich, B [2023] *Statement of Cardinal Blase J. Cupich, archbishop of Chicago, on Declaration, Fiducia Supplicans* [Online] Available at: www.lifesitenews.com [Accessed on: 1 February 2024]
[2198]O'Toole, M [2023] *Statement of Archbishop Mark O'Toole on Fiducia supplicans* [Online] Available at: www.rcadc.org [Accessed on: 1 February 2024]

Dear friends: I was honoured to bless my friends Jason and Damien this morning in our Jesuit residence, according to the new guidelines laid out by the Vatican for same sex couples. But before this, I've been blessed by their friendship and support. It was really nice to be able to do that publicly.

Fr. James Martin also posted a photograph of the two homosexual individuals holding hands during the 'blessing'.[2199]

In response to the promulgation of *Fiducia Supplicans* the Episcopal Conference of Malawi issued a directive forbidding the blessing of homosexual bondings. The directive stated, '…to avoid creating confusion among the faithful we direct that for pastoral reasons, blessings of any kind and for same sex unions of any kind, are not permitted in Malawi.'[2200]

Archbishop Tomash Peta of Saint Mary in Astana, Kazakhstan, together with Auxiliary Bishop Athanasius Schneider, issued a statement forbidding the blessing of homosexual bondings or other sinful relationships. The Astana statement accused *Fiducia Supplicans* of perpetrating a 'great deception':

> The fact that the document does not give permission for the 'marriage' of same-sex couples should not blind pastors and faithful to the great deception and the evil that resides in the very permission to bless couples in irregular situations and same-sex couples. Such a blessing directly and seriously contradicts Divine Revelation and the uninterrupted, bimillennial doctrine and practice of the Catholic Church. To bless couples in an irregular situation and same-sex couples is a serious abuse of the most Holy Name of God, since this name is invoked upon an objectively sinful union of adultery or of homosexual activity.

The archbishop and bishop directly admonished Pope Francis for issuing *Fiducia Supplicans*:

> With sincere brotherly love, and with due respect, we address Pope Francis, who – by allowing the blessing of couples in an irregular situation and same-sex couples – 'does not walk uprightly according to the truth of the Gospel' (see Gal. 2:14), to borrow the words with which Saint Paul the Apostle publicly admonished the first Pope in Antioch. Therefore, in the spirit of episcopal collegiality, we ask Pope Francis to revoke the permission to bless couples in an irregular situation and same-sex couples, so that the Catholic Church may shine clearly as the 'pillar and ground of the truth' (1 Tim 3:15) for all those who sincerely seek to know the will of God and, by fulfilling it, to attain eternal life.[2201]

The Society of Saint Pius X (SSPX) issued a statement regarding *Fiducia Supplicans*, denouncing it as a 'scandalous text'. The SSPX stated,

> The scandal lies in the fact that, even if the DDF is careful to avoid any resemblance to marriage, the result produced on the faithful, in the newspapers and to those who are not Catholics, is one of affirmation: 'The Church authorises the blessing of same-sex couples,' without any other distinctions that the dicastery attempts to set down. Yet, it is impossible that the Curia did not anticipate this result: the DDF is therefore entirely responsible for the scandal, which according to its definition consists in an occasion to fall, that is, to sin. It is absolutely evident that in the thinking of a number of people, part of the faithful or not, this announcement is one manner of saying that the Church accepts — with nothing to add — these situations [….] But in the blessing of a 'couple,' the very object of the blessing is this illegitimate union that Catholic

---

[2199]Knuffke, L [2023] *Father James Martin blesses homosexual 'couple' at Jesuit residence in New York City* [Online] Available at: www.lifesitenews.com [Accessed on:1 February 2024]
[2200]Mangiaracina, E [2023] *Malawi bishops forbid 'blessings' of homosexual unions amid confusion over Vatican document* [Online] Available at: www.lifesitenews.com [Accessed on: 1 February 2024]
[2201]Montagna, D [2023] *Archbishop prohibits priests from 'performing any form of blessing' of same-sex couples in response to new Vatican declaration* [Online] Available at: www.catholicherald.co.uk [Accessed on: 1 February 2024]

doctrine condemns. And to say, in paragraph no. 40, that in this blessing 'there is no intention to legitimise anything,' is at best a vain wish, at worst a perjury. For in the eyes of those who are blessed just as those around them, it's a legitimisation [....] In conclusion, this Declaration, which leads the revolutionary text of *Amoris Laetitia* to its final consequences — which some had already anticipated —, introduces a seed of deep division and will do incalculable harm in the Church. We can only hope that reactions to it quickly give the authors an understanding of this.[2202]

Father Davide Pagliarani, the Superior General of the SSPX, also issued a statement warning that *Fiducia Supplicans* would 'accelerate the loss of souls' because promoting the belief that such an inherently sinful union 'could have any positive value is the worst kind of deception, and the most serious lack of charity towards these lost souls.'[2203]

The Swiss Bishops Conference issued a statement welcoming the promulgation of *Fiducia Supplicans*. The Swiss bishops stated,

> The decision [by the Vatican] is in line with the Swiss bishops' desire for an open Church that takes people in different relationship situations seriously, respects and accompanies them. [*Fiducia Supplicans*] explicitly permits the blessing of same-sex couples for the first time and states that the Church has expanded and enriched its understanding of blessings. In particular, the pastoral ideals of Pope Francis were decisive for this [....] The declaration '*Fiducia Supplicans*' shows that the Church offers a place for all people. The bishops are aware that such a Church requires tolerance and mutual respect. The discussions in the Holy Spirit that took place this year as part of the synod on synodality opened up a wide space for this.[2204]

During an interview with the heterodox Catholic newspaper, *La Croix*, Archbishop Hervé Giraud of Sens-Auxerre, France, welcomed *Fiducia Supplicans* expressing great willingness to bless homosexual bondings. Archbishop Giraud was appointed by Pope Francis in 2015. Archbishop Giraud said,

> I myself could give a blessing to a same-sex couple, because I believe it's based on a beautiful idea of blessing, according to the Gospel and the style of Christ [....] Pope Francis is trying to move away from the simple 'permit-prohibit' to place people under God's gaze in order to lead them back to safer paths. Blessing opens these safer paths. Until now, the debate in the Church has been between those who say you can bless the person but not the couple, and their opponents. With this note, the pope goes further: he asks that we take into account people's situation, to encourage them to live better Christian lives. Some will welcome it as a first step, while others — who were calling for the blessing of civil unions, for example — will feel that it doesn't go far enough. Behind these small steps lies the Church's concern for communion, because some lay people and clerics are opposed to any change on the subject, so we need to go very slowly and do a lot of teaching on the meaning of what's at stake: God wants to take us from where we are to lead us to him.[2205]

The Flemish newspaper *Het Nieuwsblad* reported the response of Geert De Kerpel, spokesman for the Flemish bishops,

> This is a very big breakthrough because it comes from the highest body of the Church and because it also explicitly says that same-sex couples can therefore have the blessing. Since the Flemish bishops took the position that they were in favour of that, it was

[2202]*Rome: The DDF Authorizes the Blessing of Same-Sex or Unmarried Couples* [2023] [Online] Available at: www.fsspx.news [Accessed on: 1 February 2024]
[2203]Mangiaracina, E [2023] *SSPX superior general: Vatican approval of same-sex blessings 'accelerates the loss of souls'* [Online] Available at: www.lifesitenews.com [Accessed on: 1 February 2024]
[2204]Wailzer, A [2023] *Swiss bishops welcome Pope Francis' approval of 'blessings' for homosexual couples* [Online] Available at: www.lifesitenews.com [Accessed on:1 February 2024]
[2205]de Neuville, H [2023] *Senior French bishop says he will bless homosexuals couples* [Online] Available at: www.international.la-croix.com; Coppen, L [2023] *'Fiducia supplicans': Who's saying what?* [Online] Available at: www.pillarcatholic.com [Accessed on: 1 February 2024]

already possible here in Flanders. It is a great help that the Vatican now confirms that position. And for the whole world Church, it is an important step forward.[2206]

The Episcopal Conference of Malawi issued a clarification regarding *Fiducia Supplicans* that prohibited the 'blessing' of homosexual bondings, no matter how they presented themselves:

> to avoid creating confusion among the faithful, we direct that for pastoral reasons, blessings of any kind and for same-sex unions of any kind, are not permitted in Malawi.

20th December

The Zambia Conference of Catholic Bishops issued a pastoral statement declaring that *Fiducia Supplicans* would not be implemented in the country:

> [*Fiducia Supplicans*] has raised several questions, confusions and anxieties among the faithful and the people of good will, as it has now become an issue of allowing blessing of same-sex marriages [....] the Conference reaffirms the traditional teaching of the Church that declares 'homosexual acts to be intrinsically disordered and contrary to natural law.' Hence, 'under no circumstance can they be approved.' In order to avoid any pastoral confusion and ambiguity as well as not to break the law of our country which forbids same-sex unions and activities, and while listening to our cultural heritage which does not accept same-sex relationships, the Conference guides that the Declaration from the Dicastery for the Doctrine of the Faith of Dec 18th 2023 concerning the blessing of same-sex couples be taken as for further reflection and not for implementation in Zambia.[2207]

During an interview with the Conference of Roman Catholic Bishops of Ukraine's website Bishop Vitaliy Kryvytskyi of Kyiv–Zhytomyr said that the bishops and priests of Ukraine would not bless homosexual bondings or any other sinful relationships:

> I myself and any other priest will give a blessing, not to a couple, but to a specific person who has embarked on the path of conversion. If a person comes to us who has a problem and is looking for a solution in accordance with the will of God, then he or she will certainly receive a blessing, but not as a couple living in concubinage [....] 'If you look at it from this point of view, it is clear that we are not talking about blessing couples living in a non-sacramental relationship and even more so when it comes to same-sex couples.[2208]

During an interview with the German Catholic news outlet *katholisch.de* Birgit Mock, the vice president of the Central Committee of German Catholics (ZDK) confirmed that in response to *Fiducia Supplicans* the German bishops planned to work on a handout for 'blessing ceremonies' to give to priests:

> We will proceed with the handout as planned. In Germany, we already have a lot of practical experience with acts of blessing. We will collect these and make them available, because we also want to contribute to pastors being able to make a qualified offer, so that they don't have to find everything themselves. We want to make prayer texts that are suitable for this easily accessible. Pope Francis also speaks of suitable prayers and sensitising pastoral workers to opportunities for acts of blessing.[2209]

The Kenyan Conference of Catholic Bishops issued a statement about *Fiducia Supplicans* that stressed homosexual bondings were not accepted in their culture, while stressing individuals could receive a blessing:

[2206]Coppen, L [2023] *'Fiducia supplicans': Who's saying what?* [Online] Available at: www.pillarcatholic.com [Accessed on: 1 February 2024]

[2207]Knuffke, L [2023] *Zambia bishops latest to forbid 'blessings' of homosexual couples* [Online] Available at: www.lifesitenews.com [Accessed on: 1 February 2024]

[2208]Brodskyi, I [2023] *Ukrainian Roman bishops criticize 'blessings' for homosexual couples, insist they will not do them* [Online] Available at: www.lifesitenews.com [Accessed on: 1 February 2024]

[2209]Knuffke, L [2023] *German church plans formal 'ceremonies' for blessing same-sex couples* [Online] Available at: www.lifesitenews.com [Accessed on:1 February 2024]

> In our African context, while recognising the confusion existing in the more developed countries, of new unchristian models of 'conjugal union' and 'styles of life,' we are very clear on what a family and marriage is. The social situation of same-sex marriages does not find acceptance in our culture.[2210]

The *Nigeria Catholic Network* published the Catholic Bishops' Conference of Nigeria issued a statement repudiating the possibility of 'blessing' homosexual bondings:

> In conclusion, the Catholic Bishops Conference of Nigeria assures the entire People of God that the teaching of the Catholic Church on marriage remains the same. There is, therefore, no possibility in the Church of blessing same-sex unions and activities. That would go against God's law, the teachings of the Church, the laws of our nation and the cultural sensibilities of our people. The CBCN thanks all the Priests for their accompaniment of married couples, asking them to continue in all they do to sustain the sacrament of holy matrimony and never to do anything that would detract from the sacredness of this sacrament.[2211]

The Togo news portal *Togo Top News* published the Episcopal Conference of Togo's statement in response to *Fiducia Supplicans*, 'the bishops of Togo direct that priests refrain from blessing homosexual couples.[2212]

Bishop François Beyrouti, head of the Melkite Catholic Diocese of Newton, which encompasses all of the United States, released guidelines concerning *Fiducia Supplicans* to Melkite clergymen. Emphasising God's institution of marriage in Genesis 1:27–28, Bishop Beyrouti insisted that any requests for 'blessings' of sinful relationship must be submitted to him in writing:

> if there is a request to attend or do a blessing or ceremony either inside or outside a church it can only be done with my prior written permission. Disregard for this prescription will result in canonical penalties.[2213]

The official news website of the Vatican, *Vatican News*, published an article by Prof. Rocco Buttiglione defending *Fiducia Supplicans*. Prof. Buttiglione was a friend of both Pope St. John Paul II and Pope Benedict XVI, whose reputation was impaired in some Catholic circles with his defence of Pope Francis' *Amoris Laetitia*.[2214] Regarding *Fiducia Supplicans* Prof. Buttiglione wrote:

> The starting point of the reality the Declaration has in mind is that of a couple in an 'irregular' situation asking for a blessing. To avoid any misunderstanding, let us imagine that they ask not a priest but their parents. Would you give this blessing? I would give it. I would not bless the irregular sexual relationship. Still, I would bless the care they have for one another, the support they give each other in life, the comfort during times of grief, and the companionship in the face of difficulties. Love is never wrong; sexual relations, on the other hand, sometimes are. In the life of this couple, the good and the bad are so closely intertwined that it is not possible to separate them with a clean break.[2215]

21st December

The British Confraternity of Catholic Clergy, representing over 500 British priests and deacons, issued a statement rejecting same-sex blessings as 'inadmissible':

[2210]Isenjia, S [2023] *Catholic Bishops in Kenya Defend Fiducia Supplicans, Say Not Endorsing Same-sex Marriages* [Online] Available at: www.aciafrica.org [Accessed on: 2 February 2024]
[2211]The Catholic Bishops' Conference of Nigeria [2023] *Concerning Fiducia Supplicans: A Declaration by the Dicastery for the Propagation of the Faith on the Pastoral Meaning of Blessings in the Church* [Online] Available at: www.nigeriacatholicnetwork.com [Accessed on: 3 February 2024]
[2212]Coppen, L [2023] Op cit [Accessed on: 3 February 2024]
[2213]Coppen, L [2023] Op cit [Accessed on: 8 February 2024]
[2214]Spinello, R [2016] On Rocco Buttiglione's Defense of *Amoris Laetitia* [Online] Available at: www.crisismagazine.com [Accessed on: 12 February 2024]
[2215]Buttiglione, R [2024] *Blessings: A pastoral development anchored in tradition* [Online] Available at: www.vaticannews.va [Accessed on: 12 February 2024]

…we see no situation in which such a blessing of a couple could be properly and adequately distinguished from some level of approval. Thus, it would inevitably lead to scandal – to the individuals concerned – to those involved directly or indirectly in the blessing – or to the minister himself. Furthermore, we fear that the practice of these blessings would confuse the faithful over the actual theology of marriage and human sexuality. Indeed, from the comments in the media over the past few days, and from concerns passed on to us by the faithful, we can already see such misunderstandings. We believe that genuine charity always follows true doctrine and that such blessings would work against the legitimate care a priest owes to his flock. With honest parresia and from our own experience as pastors we conclude that such blessings are pastorally and practically inadmissible.[2216]

Pro-homosexuality Cardinal Nichols of Westminster issued a statement to priests welcoming *Fiducia Supplicans* and allowing them to act on it:

The Declaration makes it clear that such prayer and blessings may include all people, whatever their circumstance, who wish to approach God for grace and mercy. This includes those whose pattern and partnerships in life are outside the clear and consistent norms of Church teaching – those in irregular marriages and those in same-sex partnerships and civil partnerships.[2217]

Cardinal Gerhard Müller, the former prefect of the CDF, issued a rebuttal of *Fiducia Supplicans* published by multiple outlets, stating 'Blessing a reality that is contrary to creation is not only impossible, it is blasphemy':

The difficulty of blessing a union or couple is especially evident in the case of homosexuality. For in the Bible, a blessing has to do with the order that God has created and that He has declared to be good. This order is based on the sexual difference of male and female, called to be one flesh. Blessing a reality that is contrary to creation is not only impossible, it is blasphemy. Once again, it is not a question of blessing persons who 'live in a union that cannot be compared in any way to marriage' (*FS*, n. 30), but of blessing the very union that cannot be compared to marriage. It is precisely for this purpose that a new kind of blessing is created (*FS* 7, 12) [....] In light of this, can a faithful Catholic accept the teaching of FS? Given the unity of deeds and words in the Christian faith, one can only accept that it is good to bless these unions, even in a pastoral way, if one believes that such unions are not objectively contrary to the law of God. It follows that as long as Pope Francis continues to affirm that homosexual unions are always contrary to God's law, he is implicitly affirming that such blessings cannot be given. The teaching of FS is therefore self-contradictory and thus requires further clarification. The Church cannot celebrate one thing and teach another because, as St. Ignatius of Antioch wrote, Christ was the Teacher 'who spoke and it was done' (Ephesians 15:1), and one cannot separate his flesh from his word.[2218]

The Polish Bishops' Conference issued a statement via the Catholic website *wiara.pl* insisting that contrary to *Fiducia Supplicans* people who were in same-sex relationships 'cannot receive a blessing':

Since practicing sexual acts outside marriage, that is, outside the indissoluble union of a man and a woman open to the transmission of life, is always an offence against the will and wisdom of God expressed in the sixth commandment.… people who are in such a relationship cannot receive a blessing. This applies in particular to people in same-sex relationships.[2219]

[2216]British Confraternity of Catholic Clergy [2023] *Fiducia Supplicans Response* [Online] Available at: www.confraternityccb.org.uk [Accessed on: 1 February 2024]
[2217]Nichols, V [2023] *Letter to priests* [Online] Available at: www.twitter.com/holysmoke [Accessed on:1 February 2024]
[2218]Wailzer, A [2023] *Cardinal Müller tells Pope Francis: Blessing homosexual couples is 'impossible' and 'blasphemy'* [Online] Available at: www.lifesitenews.com [Accessed on:1 February 2024]
[2219]Mangiaracina, E [2023] *Polish bishops: People in same-sex relationships 'cannot receive a blessing'* [Online] Available at: www.lifesitenews.com [Accessed on: 1 February 2024]

Bishop Robert Mutsaerts, the auxiliary bishop of the Diocese of 's-Hertogenbosch, Netherlands, issued a statement accusing *Fiducia Supplicans* of 'diabolical ambiguity':

> …nowhere in the declaration is there a call to repentance, there is no reference to truth. It does not contain a call for LGTBQ couples to live in abstinence in accordance with God's plan in which sexuality is reserved for a man/woman relationship. It is a repetitive refrain in this pontificate: the lack of clarity, the sowing of confusion. The pope who says not to change the doctrine of the Church, but at the same time creates opportunities for the practice to the contrary. You cannot maintain doctrine and provide for other criteria [….] Every blessing is meant for sinners. But not for those who believe that this is not the case with them. But then why ask for blessing at all. By definition, blessing is for sinners who recognise their shortcomings and need God's help to improve. The Declaration offers the possibility of receiving blessing, but does not speak a word about a corrective and the priest is asked to give his blessing on a disordered state that continues. This is not pastoral, nor is it merciful, but rather unloving. The priest's job is to point out their situation, his job is to bring people closer to God, not to guide them further toward the abyss. Because that is what you are doing. I will give my blessing to anyone who asks for it. But under no circumstances will I give my blessing to a sinful situation. And that has nothing to do with discrimination. The same goes for a male/female relationship where adultery is involved. Holy Father, please, be clear! You are not helping anyone with this! No one at all.[2220]

The National Episcopal Conference of Cameroon issued a strong repudiation of *Fiducia Supplicans*, stating that they 'formally forbid all blessings of "homosexual couples" in the Church of Cameroon'. The bishops also accused *Fiducia Supplicans* of 'hypocrisy':

> Literally, 'To bless is to speak well of'. And to 'speak well of' in order to gain grace through the gesture of blessing a 'homosexual couple' would be tantamount to encouraging a choice and a practice of life that cannot be recognised as being objectively ordered to the revealed designs of God. What is more, differentiating between liturgical and non-liturgical contexts in order to apply the blessing to same sex 'couples' is hypocritical. The act of blessing, whether performed in a liturgical assembly or in private, remains a blessing. We therefore declare non-compliant any form of blessing, public or private, that tends to recognise 'same-sex couples' as a state of life.[2221]

During an interview with Rod Dreher posted on Youtube Metropolitan Hilarion of Budapest and Hungary expressed his shock at Pope Francis issuing *Fiducia Supplicans*:

> My initial impression [of Fiducia Supplicans] was a kind of a shock because… we always cite the Roman Catholic Church as a beacon of traditional Christianity. This is indeed a big change. And I personally think that it is a very unfortunate change because, as you said, it is a trap. It is a loophole. And it gives the opportunity to those priests who want to bless homosexual couples to do this [….] It will mislead those who receive this blessing, and it will also mislead those who become, willingly or unwillingly, witnesses of such a blessing because everyone will believe that now the Church blesses homosexual couples. While these blessings will be misleading to the people, they will also be dangerous for the spiritual integrity of those people who receive these blessings because they will be made to believe that the Church approves of this lifestyle, of this type of sexual orientation, and not only orientation, but the sexual behaviour. And I can predict that very soon it will become a big business, a big industry in the Catholic Church because it will be on demand. Such priests will be very popular in certain circles, and they will practice these blessings, so to speak, with the permission from the Vatican [….] I think, realistically speaking, we should not hope for any reunion between the Catholics and the Orthodox. We can modestly hope for some sort of better

[2220]Mutsaerts, R [2023] *Again that diabolical ambiguity* [Online] Available at: www.lifesitenews.com [Accessed on: 1 February 2024]
[2221]National Episcopal Conference of Cameroon [2023] *Declaration of the Bishops of Cameroon on Homosexuality and the Blessing of "Homosexual Couples"* [Online] Available at: acrobat.adobe.com/id/urn:aaid:sc:VA6C2:9202418f-75dd-4834-a01d-8bad0d784078 [Accessed on: 1 February 2024]

understanding, better mutual understanding. But of course, such steps, they certainly are not going to bring us any closer. On the contrary, they will create new dividing lines, new problems, and it will be more difficult to engage in a fruitful dialog after such statements have been made.[2222]

In conversation with the US Catholic journal, *Our Sunday Visitor*, Archbishop Eamon Martin, the Primate of All Ireland, said that he welcomed *Fiducia Supplicans* allowing the blessing homosexual bondings:

> This particular declaration makes somebody like me or any priest a little bit more comfortable that they can do this without feeling, 'Am I contradicting the teaching of the Church?' So there is clarity here which I think will help pastors on the ground.[2223]

The website of the Episcopal Conference of Rwanda published their statement rejecting the 'blessing' of homosexual bondings making it clear it was a matter of God's law and not just African culture:

> the teachings of the Church on Christian marriage have not changed. For this reason, the Church cannot bless same-sex relationships because it would contradict God's law and our culture.[2224]

Bishop Robert Barron of Winona-Rochester, and chairman of the U.S. bishops' committee on laity, marriage, family life, and youth, welcomed *Fiducia Supplicans*. Fr. Barron was appointed bishop by Pope Francis in 2015 and praised Fr. James Martin S.J., as 'a winsome guide to all those who want to deepen their friendship with the Lord.'[2225] Bishop Barron emphasised that *Fiducia Supplicans* invited sinners to encounter the forgiveness of God, but he made no mention of the requirement of repentance and amendment of life:

> *Fiducia supplicans* is very much congruent with Pope Francis's long-held conviction that those who do not live up to the full demand of the Church's moral teaching are nevertheless loved and cherished by God and invited to accept the Lord's offer of forgiveness.[2226]

22nd December

The US religious journal *First Things* published an article by the Archbishop Emeritus of Philadelphia, Charles J. Chaput, in which he severely criticised *Fiducia Supplicans* and Pope Francis. He described the document as

> a double-minded exercise in simultaneously affirming and undercutting Catholic teaching on the nature of blessings and their application to 'irregular' relationships [....] while the document does not in fact change Church teaching on marriage, it does seem to change Church teaching on the sinfulness of same-sex activity. Marriage isn't the point of *Fiducia Supplicans*. Its point is the moral nature of same-sex unions, and this is a crucial distinction.

Concerning Pope Francis, Archbishop Chaput wrote:

> Popes, bishops, priests, and deacons are called by their vocations to be prophets as well as pastors. Pope Francis often seems to separate these roles while Jesus himself always embodied both in his ministry. His words to the woman caught in adultery were not simply 'Your sins are forgiven' but also 'Go and sin no more' [....] Complaints about

[2222]Wailzer, A [2023] *Russian Orthodox metropolitan says 'dangerous' Fiducia Supplicans damages ecumenical relations* [Online] Available at: www.lifesitenews.com [Accessed on: 2 February 2024]
[2223]*'Beware Of Reading Too Much Too Quickly' Into Same-Sex Blessings Document, Say Global Bishops* [2023] [Online] Available at: www.osvnews.com [Accessed on: 2 February 2024]
[2224]Coppen, L [2023] Op cit [Accessed on: 3 February 2024]
[2225]Sammons, E [2020] *The Troubling Kinship of Bishop Barron and Father Martin* [Online] Available at: www.crisismagazine.com [Accessed on: 8 February 2024]
[2226]Barron, R [2023] *Bishop Barron Says New Vatican Document Affirms Church's Timeless Teaching on Marriage* [Online] Available at: www.usccb.org [Accessed on: 8 February 2024]

'rigid ideological positions' are now the Holy See's default response to any reasoned reservations about, or honest criticism of, its actions. Every pope has personal likes, dislikes, and aggravations. That's the nature of human clay. As I've said elsewhere, and often, Pope Francis has important pastoral strengths that need our prayerful support. But his public complaining diminishes the dignity of the Petrine office and the man who inhabits it. It also disregards the collegial respect due brother bishops who question the Vatican's current course. And again, it is not of God. Characterising fidelity to Catholic belief and practice as 'fearfully sticking to rules' — the words belong to PBS, but the intent is clearly the pope's — is irresponsible and false. The faithful deserve better than such treatment. It's also worth noting that heading down 'unexplored paths and new roads' can easily lead into the desert rather than Bethlehem. Over the past decade ambiguity on certain matters of Catholic doctrine and practice has become a pattern for the current pontificate. The pope's criticism of American Catholics has too often been unjust and uninformed. Much of the German Church is effectively in schism, yet Rome first unwisely tolerated Germany's 'synodal path,' and then reacted too slowly to preclude the negative results.[2227]

His Beatitude Sviatoslav Shevchuk, the Patriarch of the Ukrainian Greek Catholic Church (UGCC), issued a Communiqué regarding the reception of *Fiducia Supplicans* stating that it had 'no legal status' in the UGCC and would not be implemented:

> The above-mentioned Declaration interprets the pastoral meaning of blessings in the Latin Church, not in the Eastern Catholic Churches. It does not address questions of Catholic faith or morals, nor does it refer to any prescriptions of the *Code of Canons for the Eastern Churches,* nor does it mention Eastern Christians. Thus, on the basis of Canon 1492 of the *CCEO,* this Declaration applies exclusively to the Latin Church and has no legal force for the faithful of the Ukrainian Greek Catholic Church [....] According to the traditions of the Byzantine rite, the concept of 'blessing' means approval, permission, or even a spiritual directive for a certain type of action, prayer or ascetic practice, including certain types of fasting and prayer. Obviously, the blessing of a priest always has an Evangelical and Catechetical dimension, and therefore can in no way contradict the teaching of the Catholic Church about the family as a faithful, indissoluble, and fruitful union of love between a man and a woman, which Our Lord Jesus Christ raised to the dignity of the Holy Sacrament of Matrimony. Pastoral prudence urges us to avoid ambiguous gestures, expressions and concepts that would distort or misrepresent God's word and the teaching of the Church. (Art. 1& 4).[2228]

The Conference of Catholic Bishops of Burundi issued a statement making it clear that no priest could bless homosexual bondings because homosexuality was 'contrary to the cultural values of our Burundian society':

> In fact, God hates sin, but loves the sinner. However, His love and mercy are never in contradiction with the truth; they always seek to lift man up so that he converts and renounces evil. No priest can bless public sinners who make no gesture of repentance to renounce their sins.[2229]

The Haitian media outlet *Haiti-Référence* published the statement from the Episcopal Conference of Haiti concerning *Fiducia Supplicans*:

> Priests have no right to bless homosexual couples who request some kind of religious recognition of their union. The Church cannot dispose of God's plans for marriage.[2230]

[2227]Chaput, C [2023] *The Cost of Making a Mess* [Online] Available at: www.firstthings.com [Accessed on: 1 February 2024]
[2228]Shevchuk, S [2023] *Communiqué regarding the reception in the UGCC of the Declaration of the Dicastery of the Doctrine of the Faith "Fiducia supplicans" on the pastoral meaning of blessings* [Online] www.onepeterfive.com [Accessed on: 1 February 2024]
[2229]Coppen, L [2023] *'Fiducia supplicans': Who's saying what?* [Online] Available at: www. pillarcatholic.com [Accessed on: 1 February 2024]
[2230]*Ibid* [Accessed on: 2 February 2024]

A group of militant pro-homosexuality Flemish bishop released a statement welcoming *Fiducia Supplicans* and attacking critics of the declaration as 'extreme right':

> Within the faithful LGBTI+ world, the recent statement by the Dicastery for the Doctrine of the Faith, *Fiducia Supplicans* is seen as a huge step toward the recognition of faithful and lasting homosexual relationships. You are fully accepted as an LGBTI+ person and can even now additionally have your relationship blessed [....] Here and there via social media we read dissenting voices. Some attempt to sow confusion through a highly selective and legalistic reading of selected Bible fragments. Others, however, not so numerous, do sometimes sound rude and loud. These loud callers are remarkably often associated with groups that preach a far-right ideology of hatred and violence. Such calls can only be condemned in the sharpest terms. Even in the name of free speech, there are limits.[2231]

23rd December

The Episcopal Conference of the Democratic Republic of the Congo issued a statement declaring that they rejected any possibility of blessing homosexual bondings:

> Taking into consideration the recognised right of the faithful to receive from sacred pastors the help that comes from the spiritual goods of the Church, especially the Word of God, the sacraments and the sacramentals (cf. can. 213, can. 1170), we say NO to any form of blessing of same-sex couples.[2232]

Archbishop Philip Anyolo of Nairobi, Kenya, issued a pastoral letter stating that priests were prohibited from 'blessing' homosexual bondings and all sinful relationships: 'all clergy residing and ministering in the Archdiocese of Nairobi are prohibited from blessing irregular relationships, unions, or same-sex couples.'[2233]

The Spanish Episcopal Conference's radio station, *COPE*, broadcast an interview with Cardinal Juan José Omella in which he attempted to justify *Fiducia Supplicans.* Archbishop Omella was elevated to the Sacred College of Cardinals by Pope Francis in 2017 and is president of the Spanish Episcopal Conference. Cardinal Omella said the declaration would require

> a change of mentality for Europe, because it is difficult for us to understand this way of asking God for things that was not done before. It is a spontaneous blessing that is also done in Latin America and that has reached Europe thanks to immigrants. If we understand it along these lines, we will understand the text published by the Congregation for the Doctrine of the Faith.[2234]

The Confraternity of Catholic Clergy (USA) released a statement warning of the dangers contained in *Fiducia Supplicans*:

> Sinful behaviour and disordered inclinations can never be blessed or condoned. Even the appearance of endorsement of any moral evil must be avoided at all cost lest one infer that the one giving the 'blessing' is also a formal cooperator in evil, which is always forbidden [....] Admonishing sinners is still a work of mercy and obscuring their moral vision is not; even if it is called a 'blessing.'[2235]

24th December

The Angolan media outlet *Observador* reported that the Episcopal Conference of Angola and São Tomé had announced that they would not implement *Fiducia Supplicans*:

[2231]*Belgian bishops publish enthusiastic statement in support of blessing homosexual 'couples'* [2024] [Online] Available at: www.lifesitenews.com [Accessed on: 8 February 2024]
[2232]Coppen, L [2023] Op cit [Accessed on: 2 February 2024]
[2233]Coppen, L [2023] Op cit [Accessed on: 2 February 2024]
[2234]Coppen, L [2023] Op cit [Accessed on: 3 February 2024]
[2235]*Statement of the Confraternity of Catholic Clergy (USA) Regarding the Recent Declaration Fiducia Supplicans* [2023] [Online] Available at: www.catholicclergy.net [Accessed on: 8 February 2024]

Regarding informal blessings for 'irregular couples' (homosexuals), although it is a sacrament different from the liturgical blessing, we consider that, in our cultural and ecclesial context, it would create enormous scandal and confusion among the faithful, so we have determined that it should not be carried out in Angola and São Tomé.[2236]

During an interview with the Brazilian radio station *Rádio Gaúcha* Archbishop Jaime Spengler, president of the Episcopal Conference of Brazil, welcomed *Fiducia Supplicans*. Bishop Spengler was appointed Archbishop of Porto Alegre by Pope Francis in 2013. Archbishop Spengler said,

I ask a very simple question, which guides me and also guides my actions: are they people? If they are people, they deserve our respect too. And when they come to us asking for a blessing, I imagine that they are also looking for a word of comfort, of hope and perhaps even the desire to cope with their own situation. We can't deny that![2237]

During an interview with the Spanish-language daily newspaper *El País* Cardinal Daniel Sturla of Montevideo questioned the authority of *Fiducia Supplicans*. Archbishop Sturla was elevated to the Sacred College of Cardinals by Pope Francis in 2015. Lamenting that it was issued at Christmas, Cardinal Sturla said,

You can't bless a couple that is not married. You cannot bless unions that the Church itself says are not in accordance with God's plan [....] What happens is that the same document says that there cannot be a ritual, that it cannot be done publicly either.... It creates a confusing situation. When you bless people, you don't ask what their situation is. And it is always done and to whomever. We will continue with the current practice until it becomes clear. The document has generated division. In the Churches of Africa they have said that in their countries, no [it will not take place] [....] In the Church there is a kind of hierarchy of documents. This is not a pronouncement of the pope that has a dogmatic value. Two years ago a document of the Holy See said the opposite. We have to wait a bit and let the situation take its proper course.[2238]

25th December

During an interview with the Italian newspaper *Corriere della Sera* pro-homosexuality Cardinal Matteo Zuppi of Bologna enthusiastically welcomed *Fiducia Supplicans*. Cardinal Zuppi was elevated to the Sacred College of Cardinals in 2020. Cardinal Zuppi said:

The Church is not made of angels, of the pure. My predecessor [as Archbishop of Bologna], Cardinal Caffarra, was a holy man, strict, concerned that people would not understand the message clearly, and so he wanted the pope to say how it is done, point out the rules [....] The world is not black and white and requires listening, discernment, acceptance. Someone may think: this way you lose the truth. In contrast, no, this is how you rediscover it: by living, by encountering, by talking about Jesus. And you discover that Christianity has deeper roots than you think.[2239]

The Nigerian media outlet *Arise News* published the Christmas message of Archbishop Ignatius Kaigama of Abuja, Nigeria, in which he sought to reassure the faithful over the scandal caused by *Fiducia Supplicans*. Archbishop Kaigama wrote,

I urge you to hold on to your faith with great tenacity. Let no arguments or controversies distract or confuse you, especially in the light of the document about the blessing of those of 'same sex' orientation [....] There is no doubt that the declaration allowing pastoral blessing for same sex 'couples' has discomforted many Catholics all over the world including other Christians and even non-Christians who look up to the Catholic Church for clear directions with regard to certain moral principles. The Catholic Church

[2236]Coppen, L [2023] *Op cit* [Accessed on: 1 February 2024]
[2237]*Ibid* [Accessed on: 1 February 2024]
[2238]*Ibid* [Accessed on: 8 February 2024]
[2239]Coppen, L [2023] *Op cit* [Accessed on: 2 February 2024]

as always, has been consistent on her stand about abortion, war, homosexuality, etc. [....] The Church, in its history of over two thousand years, has passed through very turbulent periods and survived them by the ever-present power of the Holy Spirit, so too shall this controversy pass away leaving the Church much stronger and cohesive. The Church will not succumb to the dictatorship of modern secularism, as long as you and I remain rooted in our faith, gazing with serene admiration and optimism at the One we call Lord, Master and Saviour.[2240]

27th December

Bishop Raimo Goyarrola of Helsinki issued a statement expressing concern that 'blessing' a 'couple' would be seen as blessing the sinful relationship:

> The declaration discusses how to bless a couple living in an irregular situation or with a partner of the same sex without giving a blessing to the union itself. However, what makes two people a couple is a specific kind of relationship, union, or status between them (whether by law or at the emotional level). As a consequence, it may be difficult to distinguish the blessing of a couple from blessing the union which forms the couple.[2241]

The Hungarian Catholic online portal *Magyar Kurír* published the Hungarian Bishops' Conference statement on *Fiducia Supplicans* making it clear that clergy could not bless 'couples', but can bless individuals:

> Considering the pastoral situation of our country, the bishops' conference formulates as a guideline for pastors that we can bless all people individually, regardless of their gender identity and sexual orientation, but we should always avoid giving a common blessing to couples who live together in a purely conjugal relationship, in a non-ecclesially valid marriage or in a same-sex relationship.[2242]

The Ivory Coast news portal *Abidjan.net* published the Episcopal Conference of the Ivory Coast's statement about *Fiducia Supplicans*:

> We your archbishops and bishops, your spiritual guides of the Catholic Church in Ivory Coast, reaffirm our attachment to the values of the family, of the sacrament of marriage between a man and a woman, as God willed it from the beginning. We therefore ask ordained ministers to refrain from blessing same-sex couples and couples in an irregular situation.[2243]

Bishop Paul Kariuki Njiru of the Diocese of Wote, Kenya, issued a pastoral letter exhorting his clergy and religious to totally reject *Fiducia Supplicans*:

> ...only a repentant sinner who has a firm intention to no longer sin again can receive blessings. Therefore, to bless couples in an irregular situation or the same-sex couples who are not ready for conversion directly and seriously contradicts the Scripture Teachings and Sound Magisterium. Worse more still, in this 21st Century, it will only support the propagandist of the globalist and ungodly gender ideology. In conclusion, the Declaration of the Dicastery for the Doctrine of the Faith '*FIDUCIA SUPPLICANS*' should be rejected in totality and we faithfully uphold the Gospel teachings and Catholic traditional teachings on Marriage and sexuality.[2244]

28th December

The Episcopal Conference of Mozambique rejected *Fiducia Supplicans*, prohibiting the 'blessing' of homosexual bondings and all sinful relationships:

[2240]*Archbishop Kaigama: Same-Sex Union 'Blessing' By Vatican Test Case For Catholic Church* [2023] [Online] Available at: www.arise.tv [Accessed on: 3 February 2024]
[2241]Goyarrola, R [2023] *Statement on the Declaration Fiducia Supplicans of the Dicastery of the Doctrine of the Faith* [Online] Available at: www.fides.katolinen.fi [Accessed on: 2 February 2024]
[2242]Coppen, L [2023] Op cit [2 February 2024]
[2243]Coppen, L [2023] Op cit [2 February 2024]
[2244]*Kenyan bishop prohibits blessings of same-sex 'couples'* [2024] [Online] Available at: www. lifesitenews.com [Accessed on: 8 February 2024]

However, in the minds of many of the faithful and in common language, the term blessing is understood to mean legitimising what is being blessed.... For this reason, the Episcopal Conference of Mozambique (CEM) urges all ordained ministers to show closeness and accompaniment to those living in irregular unions. We, the bishops, have decided that irregular unions and same-sex unions should not be blessed in Mozambique.[2245]

29th December

During an interview with the progressive US Catholic news site, *Crux*, pro-homosexuality Cardinal Oswald Gracias of Bombay, and a longtime member of Pope Francis' Council of Cardinals, welcomed *Fiducia Supplicans* as 'natural to India'. He admitted that the document was consonant with his own attitude to 'blessing' homosexual bondings:

> In the past I have said this and I want to say it again, they are part of our family, they need our pastoral care. I have met them when they have come to me sometimes privately in my office. Jesus never refused a blessing...that's the idea.[2246]

30th December

The Episcopal Conference of Argentina's website posted a statement from Bishop Oscar Ojea, the president of the Argentine bishops' conference, welcoming *Fiducia Supplicans* and criticising those who objected to it:

> A brutal experience of abandonment by the Church that has done so much harm to us and that has alienated so many brothers and sisters. Living in an irregular situation or carrying out a homosexual union does not obscure many aspects of the lives of people who seek to be enlightened with a blessing and upon receiving it, this becomes the greatest possible good for these brothers since it leads to conversion. Surely those bishops and ministers who have disagreed with this declaration have not lived this experience of blessing in the context of popular piety or have not been able to have this prior dialogue where the need for God's mercy is experienced in one's own life.[2247]

31st December

The Benin media outlet *Benin Web TV* issued a statement from the Episcopal Conference of Benin declaring that *Fiducia Supplicans* would not be implemented: 'We ask ordained ministers incardinated in or passing through Benin to refrain from any form of blessing to same-sex couples and couples in an irregular situation.[2248]

The German priestly group *Communio veritatis* issue a statement on their website rejecting *Fiducia Supplicans* with the title, 'Sin cannot be blessed'. The faithful priests state:

> The euphemism 'couples in irregular situations' refers to sexual unions outside of marriage valid before God. As a grave sin, such acts constitute a serious act against the Sixth Commandment and profoundly defile the human being [....] There can be no contradiction between doctrine and pastoral care in the Catholic faith. Real mercy is always linked to the truth. It does not hypocritically confirm people in their guilty situation, but tries to lead them to repentance for the sake of eternal salvation – from the death of sin to the life of grace. Sin cannot be blessed – that would be a misuse of God's most holy name. We will therefore never perform blasphemous blessings that are in blatant contradiction to the order of creation and divine revelation.[2249]

[2245]Coppen, L [2023] Op cit [2 February 2024]

[2246]Carvalho, N [2023] *Cardinal says Vatican doc on same-sex blessings a 'natural' for India* [Online] Available at: www.cruxnow.com [Accessed on: 2 February 2024]

[2247]Coppen, L [2023] Op cit [Accessed on: 1 February 2024]

[2248]Coppen, L [2023]Op cit [Accessed on: 1 February 2024]

[2249]*Sin cannot be blessed* [2023] [Online] Available at: www.communioveritatis.de [Accessed on: 8 February 2024]

2024

2nd January

The website of the Territorial Prelature of Moyobamba, Peru, published the pastoral message of Bishop Rafael Alfonso Escudero López-Brea in which he instructed his priests not to bless homosexual bondings or any other sinful relationships. Bishop López-Brea wrote that *Fiducia Supplicans*

> …damages the communion of the Church, since such blessings directly and seriously contradict Divine Revelation and the uninterrupted doctrine and practice of the Catholic Church, including the recent magisterium of Pope Francis, which is why there are no citations in the entire declaration that rely on the previous magisterium [….] On the day of my episcopal ordination, I solemnly swore to 'preserve the deposit of faith in purity and integrity, according to the Tradition always and everywhere observed in the Church since the time of the Apostles.' Therefore, I admonish the priests of the Prelature of Moyobamba not to perform any form of blessing of couples in an irregular situation or same-sex couples.[2250]

The website of the Diocese of Motherwell, Scotland, published Bishop Joseph Toal's New Year's Message in which he welcomed *Fiducia Supplicans* and recommended it to his clergy. Bishop Toal was appointed Bishop of Motherwell by Pope Francis in 2014. Bishop Toal wrote, making no mention of the requirement of chastity and repentance of sinful sexual acts:

> The value of the document is that it permits a broadening and enrichment of the classical understanding of blessings, based on the pastoral vision of Pope Francis [….] As Bishop, I welcome the initiative taken, and the possibilities it offers, and pray that it will assist the clergy in caring for those who seek our pastoral care and support, so that they experience the desired blessing from the Lord, who loves us so much that he took on our nature in order to save us all.[2251]

The US Catholic journal *Crisis Magazine* published an article from Professor Regis Martin calling on Pope Francis to resign in response to *Fiducia Supplicans*. Professor Martin is the Professor of Theology and Faculty Associate at the Franciscan University of Steubenville. Professor Martin wrote:

> Your Holiness, with all due respect, there are two things you must do, and two more you might do. The first two are fairly easy. Get rid of Fernandez; then dump the Declaration. As for the remaining two, these are optional, but I'd strongly recommend both. Resign the Office that has become so tortuous to occupy; then go off to the nearest monastery for a life of prayer and penance [….] However far Pope Francis may wish to extend the reach of his vaunted 'pastoral vision,' it can never encompass the blessing of sin. Either adultery and sodomy are wrong, and those who engage in such practices are committing serious sin and in need of repentance; or there is nothing wrong or untoward about either, and no priest should stand in the way of those who come forward to have their unions blest. That way lies madness. And the Church, which has always stood for sanity, may have to ask the Pope to step down in order to make things sane again.[2252]

Bishop Rafael Lopez-Brea of Mayobamba, Peru, issued a pastoral letter to clergy and religious rejecting *Fiducia Supplicans*. Bishop Lopez-Brea wrote:

> This document harms the communion of the Church, as such blessings directly and seriously contradict Divine revelation and the uninterrupted doctrine and practice of the Catholic Church, … [the blessing irregular couples and same-sex couples is] a grave

[2250] Coppen, L [2023/24]Op cit [Accessed on: 3 February 2024]

[2251] Toal, J [2024] *Letter from Bishop Toal to the Faithful* [Online] Available at: www.rcdom.org.uk [Accessed on: 3 February 2024]

[2252] Martin, R [2024] *My Advice? Step Down* [Online] Available at: www.crisismagazine.com [Accessed on: 8 February 2024]

abuse of the Most Holy Name of God, which is invoked upon an objectively sinful union of fornication, adultery, or even worse, homosexual activity. [He pointed out that the *Catechism of the Catholic Church* teaches that] homosexual acts are disordered and, above all, contrary to the natural law (*CCC* 2357) [....] God never blesses sin. God does not contradict Himself. God does not lie to us. God, who always loves the sinner unconditionally, for this reason, seeks that he repent, convert, and live. God desires good for all of us [....] To bless a couple is to bless the union that exists between them. There is no logical, real way to separate one thing from another. Why else would they ask for a blessing together and not two separately? [....] Dear priests and lay faithful, let us not minimise the destructive and short-sighted consequences resulting from this effort made by some hierarchs of the Church to legitimise such blessings, in some cases with good intentions and in others, as many have been saying, with the intention of destroying the Sacred Deposit of the Church's Tradition. On the day of my episcopal ordination, I solemnly swore 'to preserve the deposit of faith in purity and integrity, in accordance with Tradition always and everywhere observed in the Church since the time of the Apostles'. For this reason, I admonish the priests of the Prelature of Moyobamba not to carry out any form of blessing of couples in an irregular situation or of same-sex couples.[2253]

3rd January

Despite Pope Francis' secretive Vatican-Chinese communist deal, Chinese security forces arrested Bishop Peter Shao Zhumin of Wenzhou. Bishop Shao is not recognised by the Chinese communist government due to his refusal to join the state-controlled Patriotic Association. The communists have appointed a member of the Chinese Catholic Patriotic Association, Father Ma Xianshi as head of Bishop Shao's diocese. According to sources, Bishop Shao

> was ordered to take clothes for spring, summer, autumn, and winter. This suggests that his situation is not promising and that he will probably be held for a long time. The faithful are worried because they don't even know where he will be detained.[2254]

4th January

Pro-homosexuality Cardinal Victor Fernández, prefect of the Congregation for the Doctrine of the Faith, issued a press release concerning the reception of *Fiducia Supplicans*. Despite many episcopal conferences citing doctrine as one of the reasons for rejecting his declaration Cardinal Fernández bizarrely claimed that the widespread dispute had nothing to do with doctrine:

> What is expressed by these Episcopal Conferences cannot be interpreted as doctrinal opposition, because the document is clear and definitive about marriage and sexuality [....] Evidently, there is no room to distance ourselves doctrinally from Declaration or to consider it heretical, contrary to the Tradition of the Church or blasphemous.

Obviously responding to the widespread rejection of *Fiducia Supplicans* in Africa and elsewhere, Cardinal Fernández ruled out the possibility that bishops could totally reject his declaration:

> Prudence and attention to the ecclesial context and to the local culture could allow for different methods of application, but not a total or definitive denial of this path that is proposed to priests.

Clearly stung by the accusations of promoting heresy, Cardinal Fernández insisted,

---

[2253]Cummings McLean, D [2024] *Peruvian bishop bans same-sex 'blessings,' says Fiducia Supplicans 'harms the communion of the Church'* [Online] Available at: www.lifesitenews.com [Accessed on: 8 February 2024]

[2254]*Bishop Shao of Wenzhou arrested again* [2024] [Online] Available at: www.asianews.it [Accessed on: 8 February 2024]

> We will all have to become accustomed to accepting the fact that, if a priest gives this type of simple blessings, he is not a heretic, he is not ratifying anything nor is he denying Catholic doctrine.[2255]

On the 5th January, Cardinal Gerhard Müller, the former prefect of the CDF, issued a statement via various news outlets in response to Cardinal Fernández's defence of *Fiducia Supplicans*. Cardinal Müller wrote:

> The worldwide negative reaction from large parts of the world's episcopate and from leading lay people to the 'Recommendation for Action' issued by the Dicastery for the Doctrine of the Faith on the private blessing of people in sinful partner relationships should give those responsible in Rome food for thought [....] The Gnostic opinion that a small ruling elite has special access to the Holy Spirit or that mythologically the Holy Spirit speaks through the 'healthy people of the intellectually uncorrupted common people' (the 'popular spirit' of the Romantics) has nothing to do with the Catholic faith.[2256]

On the 6th January, *LifeSiteNews* published an interview with Archbishop Carlo Maria Viganò concerning Cardinal Fernández's defence of *Fiducia Supplicans*. Archbishop Viganò said:

> From the way this scandalous affair unfolded – even to the point of not convening the plenary session of the Dicastery to discuss the content of the document – we can understand what I have already announced for some time, namely that Bergoglio wants to cause a schism in the Church and push pastors and faithful to leave, or in any case to find themselves in a situation of voluntary or imposed ostracisation in which their resistance is effectively canceled or ignored. This is what constitutes the mark of the 'pontificate' of the Argentine Jesuit, and he himself stated it in 2016: '*I could go down in history as the one who divided the Church*' [....] To think that he did it without considering the reactions that it would arouse is therefore naive, because Tucho's aim was precisely to create division in the Church. His angry reaction confirms that synodality – like all Bergoglian pastoral fiction – is only the hypocritical screen behind which hides the tyrannical authoritarianism of a sect of corrupt heretics who make the anti-human demands of the globalist elite their own, trampling on the teaching of Christ.[2257]

6th January

The Vatican journalist Sandro Magister published on his website *diakonos.be* Cardinal Robert Sarah's statement regarding *Fiducia Supplicans*. Cardinal Sarah is the former prefect of the Congregation for Sacred Worship and the Discipline of the Sacraments, 2014 to 2021. Cardinal Sarah condemned Cardinal Fernández's declaration as 'heresy that gravely undermines the Church':

> Every successor of the apostles must dare to take seriously the words of Jesus: 'Let your word be yes if it is yes, no if it is no. Whatever is added comes from the Evil One. Anything added comes from the Evil One' (Mt 5:35). *The Catechism of the Catholic Church* gives us an example of such clear, sharp and courageous words. Anything else would inevitably be truncated, ambiguous and misleading. We hear so much rhetoric these days that is so subtle and roundabout that it ends up falling under the curse pronounced by Jesus: 'Everything else comes from the Evil One'. We invent new meanings for words, we contradict and falsify Scripture while claiming to be faithful to it. We end up no longer serving the truth.[2258]

[2255]Fernández, V [2024] *Press release concerning the reception of Fiducia Supplicans* [Online] Available at: www.vatican.va [Accessed on: 8 February 2024]

[2256]Haynes, M [2023] *Cardinal Müller: Global rejection of Fiducia Supplicans should give Vatican 'food for thought* [Online] Available at: www.lifesitenews.com [Accessed on: 8 February 2024]

[2257]Haynes, M [2023] *Archbishop Viganò: Cdl Fernández's defense of Fiducia Supplicans shows his 'manifest heresy'* [Online] Available at: www.lifesitenews.com [Accessed on: 8 February 2024]

[2258]Magister, S [2024] « Fiducia supplicans ». Le cardinal Sarah : « On s'oppose à une hérésie qui mine gravement l'Église » [Online] Available at: www.diakonos.be [Accessed on 9 February 2024 DeepL trans]

7th January

During an interview with the *Times of Malta* pro-homosexuality Archbishop Charles Scicluna expressed his desire for the end of clerical celibacy. Archbishop Scicluna is an Adjunct Secretary of the Congregation for the Doctrine of the Faith. Archbishop Scicluna said,

> This is probably the first time I'm saying it publicly and it will sound heretical to some people. If it were up to me, I would revise the requirement that priests have to be celibate. We've lost many great priests because they chose marriage. Why should I lose a priest to marriage? It was optional for the first millennium of the Church's existence and it should become optional again.[2259]

8th January

The traditionalist Argentinian Catholic blog, *Caminante Wanderer*, posted a report of its discovery of a 1998 book by pro-homosexuality Cardinal Victor Manuel Fernández entitled, *La Pasión Mística, espiritualidad y sensualidad* [Mystical Passion: Spirituality and Sensuality]. The book included chapters such as *Male and female orgasms, The Road to Orgasm, and GOD in the Couple's Orgasm*. Apart from drawing an obscene and blasphemous equivalence between the experience of sexual orgasm and mystical prayer, Cardinal Fernández downplays the immorality of homosexual sex acts:

> But this does not necessarily mean that this joyful experience of divine love, if I achieve it, will free me from all my psychological weaknesses. It does not mean, for example, that a homosexual will necessarily stop being homosexual. Let us remember that God's grace can coexist with weaknesses and even with sins, when there is a very strong conditioning. In those cases, the person can do things that are objectively sinful, without being guilty, and without losing the grace of God or the experience of his love.[2260]

In response, Archbishop Viganò, the former apostolic nuncio to the USA, called for the Swiss Guard to arrest Pope Francis and Cardinal Fernández and expel them from the Vatican:

> The blasphemous sewer regurgitations of Tucho's repulsive pamphlet show such a level of perversion and alienation to the Faith as to demand the expulsion *manu militari* of the Argentinean and his accomplices. The Swiss Guards have sworn to defend the See of Peter, not the one who is systematically demolishing it. Let them therefore be faithful to their oath and arrest these heretical perverts![2261]

On the 12th January, the online Spanish-language newspaper *Religión Digital* published an interview with Cardinal Fernández during which he admitted that Pope Francis knew about his book on orgasms, which Fernández misleadingly compared with the work of St. Hildegard of Bingen and Pope St. John Paul II:

> When the pope offered me this seat for the second time, I told him this would occur, but he was already clear about that and knew the book as well. It happens that in one instance years ago I was already accused because of this book, and I wasn't sanctioned by Rome for it. And they investigated me long and wide [....] This book calls for attention because of research on male and female orgasm, which I had done in a group of married couples. But something similar had been done by people greater and wiser

[2259] Zammit, M [2024] *Priests should have option to marry – Archbishop Charles Scicluna* [Online] Available at: www.timesofmalta.com [Accessed on: 8 January 2024]
[2260] Kwasniewski, P [2024] *Mysticism, Sex, and Justification for Sin: A Rediscovered 1998 Publication by Victor Manuel Fernández – Full text of chapters 7-9* [Online] Available at: www.rorate-caeli.blogspot.com [Accessed on: 8 February 2024]
[2261] Cummings McLean, D [2024] *Archbishop Viganò: Swiss guards should arrest Bergoglio and Fernandez, expel them from the Vatican* [Online] Available at: www.lifesitenews.com [Accessed on: 8 February 2024]

than me: Saint John Paul II and the holy abbess and Doctor of the Church Hildegard of Bingen.[2262]

Professor Emeritus Hubert Windisch of the University of Freiburg, Germany, issued a statement published by *LifeSiteNews* condemning *Fiducia Supplicans*. Professor Windisch wrote:

> …this letter represents an unprecedented increase in Vatican depravity. It is a break with Sacred Scripture and the Tradition of the Church and pushes the Catholic Church into free fall. I would, therefore, like to comment briefly on *Fiducia Supplicans*. Some statements I have read try to sanitise this ambiguous document with tricks. This does not work. This declaration is both harmful and disgraceful. It is disgraceful because it is brimming with theological, liturgical, and pastoral errors. There are not only irregular situations of a homosexual nature. Anyone who soberly perceives societal reality regarding sexuality must be shocked. And what does a blessing mean, then? *Benedicere*? Approve? Without going into details, one can sense the sophistical (Jesuitical?) attitude throughout the entire letter, which was already finely packaged in *Amoris Laetitia*, namely how a yes becomes a no and a no becomes a yes, in complete contrast to the Lord's word in Mt 5:37. It is the expression of a Church that submits to the world and its plausibilities, which demonstrates how self-assertion is achieved through self-abandonment.[2263]

The Spanish Catholic news outlet *Religión Digital* published a conversation with Cardinal José Cobo of Madrid in which he expressed his full support for *Fiducia Supplicans*. Archbishop Cobo was elevated to the Sacred College of Cardinals by Pope Francis in 2023. Cardinal Cobo said,

> In Madrid we are going to fully apply the Pope's doctrine, and that is why we are going to apply '*Fiducia Supplicans*' with the intensity that the document deserves and asks for, and whoever does not agree, I invite you to read it.

Cardinal Cobo also criticised a group of 150 Spanish priests who had signed a petition criticising *Fiducia Supplicans*, some of whom had been forced to remove their names by Cardinal Cobo and other ordinaries. Cardinal Cobo said that his priests who were involved

> have been seriously admonished, they have been asked if they have anything against the Pope, and they have been reminded of their oath of fidelity to the Holy Father.…a priest cannot be part of a civil, public forum in which the Pope is insulted.…I think they are more driven by ideology and respond more to pressure groups that are not Catholic. They don't realise in whose hands they are in.[2264]

9th January

The US Catholic pro-homosexuality website, *Outreach*, published an article co-authored by two pro-homosexuality participants at the Synod on Synodality claiming a false equivalence between homosexuality and heterosexuality. Fr. James Martin, S.J., and Fr. Agbonkhianmeghe Orobator, S.J., wrote,

> Both heterosexual and homosexual people embody the truth of their dignity as *imago Dei* in their sexuality [….] We may quarrel over how to interpret Scripture or how to understand the church's teaching on human sexuality, but we cannot deny the reality of same-sex relationships as integral to the meaning of the church as the People of

[2262]Cummings McLean, D [2024] *Cdl. Fernández says Pope Francis knew about his orgasms book before making him doctrine chief* [Online] Available at: www.lifesitenews.com [Accessed on: 8 February 2024]

[2263]Wailzer, A [2024] *German theologian: Fiducia Supplicans breaks with Scripture, pushes Church into 'free fall'* [Online] Available at: www.lifesitenews.com [Accessed on: 2 February 2024]

[2264]Haynes, M [2024] *Spanish cardinal vows to 'fully apply' Fiducia Supplicans, cracks down on priestly opposition* [Online] Available at: www.lifesitenews.com [Accessed on: 9 February 2024]

God [....] In other words, for the church to reflect on matters concerning sexuality and identity means to listen to gay, lesbian, bisexual and transgender people themselves. This means not only listening to what they feel about various church teachings, but listening to their lives....[2265]

10th January

The website of the Byzantine Catholic Eparchy of Parma, which covers part of mid-west America, published a statement from Bishop Robert Pipta regarding *Fiducia Supplicans*. Bishop Pipta was appointed by Pope Francis in 2023. Bishop Pipta made it clear that the Church cannot bless 'romantic relationships between people of the same sex':

> Important to note is that, in our society, the word 'couple' has come to be understood as two people who have entered a relationship that is either one of dating, engagement, or marriage. According to Church teaching, two people of the same sex cannot be in any of these types of relationships. There can never be a Church blessing for these. It also must be added that there are relationships between one man and one woman that, likewise, cannot be blessed unless the priest has confidence that the relationship will grow into a valid marriage recognised by the Church.[2266]

Pope Francis received a Marxist-Christian dialogue group at the Vatican during which he encouraged them, failing to mention the Church's consistent condemnation of Marxism. The Supreme Pontiff said,

> Never lose the ability to dream! Today, in a world divided by war and polarisation, we run the risk of losing the ability to dream. We Argentines say, '*no te arrugues*', meaning 'don't back off'. This is my invitation to you as well: Don't back off, don't give up, and don't stop dreaming of a better world. For it is in imagination, the ability to dream, that intelligence, intuition, experience and historical memory come together to make us be creative, take chances and run risks. How many times over the years have great dreams of freedom and equality, dignity and fraternity, reflecting God's own dream, produced breakthroughs and progress. With this in mind, I would like to commend to you three attitudes that I consider helpful for your efforts: the courage to break the mould, concern for the less fortunate and support for the rule of law.[2267]

11th January

Cardinal Fridolin Ambongo of Kinshasa, the president of the Episcopal Conferences of Africa and Madagascar, issued a statement declaring that none of the bishops will offer blessings to homosexual 'couples'. Archbishop Ambongo was elevated to the Sacred College of Cardinals by Pope Francis in 2019 and is a member of the Council of Nine advisors. Cardinal Ambongo presented a synthesis of all the African episcopal conference's opposition to the 'blessing' of homosexual bondings, entitled, 'No Blessing for Homosexual Couples in the African Churches'. The report had 'received the agreement' of Pope Francis and Cardinal Fernández.

The African bishops gave primacy to the Word of God, over cultural reasons, to support their prohibition of the blessing of same-sex 'couples':

> To support this position, a large majority of the interventions of the African Bishops are based above all on the Word of God. They cite passages which condemn homosexuality, notably Lv 18:22-23 where homosexuality is explicitly prohibited and considered an abomination. This legislative text testifies to these practices in the setting of Israel, as well as other practices that God prohibits, such as infanticide (cf. the sacrifice of Isaac).

[2265]Martin, J & Orobator, A [2024] *How to address questions of 'identity and sexuality' raised by the Synod* [Online] Available at: www.outreach.faith [Accessed on: 9 February 2024]
[2266]Pipta, R [2024] *An Abundance of Blessings: A Teaching from Bishop Robert Pipta* [Online] Available at: www.parma.org [Accessed on: 9 February 2024]
[2267]Pope Francis [2024] *Greetings to Members of the DIALOP Association* [Online] Available at: www.vatican.va [Accessed on: 12 February 2024]

One Episcopal Conference added the scandal of the homosexuals of Sodom (cf. Gen 19, 4-11). In the narration of the text, homosexuality is so abominable that it will lead to the destruction of the city. In the New Testament, Saint Paul, in the Letter to the Romans, also condemns what he calls unnatural relationships (cf. Rom 1:26-33) or shameful morals (cf. 1 Cor 6:9-10).

The synthesis report cited cultural reasons for the ban only as secondary to doctrinal reasons:

In addition to these biblical reasons, the cultural context in Africa, deeply rooted in the values of the natural law regarding marriage and family, further complicates the acceptance of unions of persons of the same sex, as they are seen as contradictory to cultural norms and intrinsically corrupt [....] we, the African Bishops, do not consider it appropriate for Africa to bless homosexual unions or same-sex couples because, in our context, this would cause confusion and would be in direct contradiction to the cultural ethos of African communities. The language of *Fiducia Supplicans* remains too subtle for simple people to understand.[2268]

On the 18th January, the French lay Catholic blog *Le Salon Beige* published an interview with Cardinal Ambongo that explained the involvement of Pope Francis and Cardinal Ambongo in the composition of the synthesis report:

I reached an agreement with him [Pope Francis] because I told him that the solution to this issue is no longer to send us documents with theological or philosophical definitions of blessings. The people are not interested in that. What is of interest now is a communication that reassures the people in Africa, that calms the spirits of the faithful. And he, as a pastor, was touched by this situation. With the prefect [Cardinal Fernández], myself in front of the computer, a secretary writing, we prepared a document. And we prepared the document in dialogue and agreement with Pope Francis, so that at every moment we called him to ask him questions, to see if he agreed with that formulation, etc. I signed the document as president of SECAM on behalf of the entire Catholic Church in Africa. And the prefect of the dicastery signed it, not the document that was made public, but the document that we keep in the archives. The document is titled 'No to the blessing of homosexual couples in the Catholic Churches.'

Cardinal Fernández confirmed that he had signed the synthesis report:

I signed it in Rome. This is to express our position today in Africa and we do it in a spirit of communion, of synodality with Pope Francis, and with the prefect of the Dicastery for the Doctrine of the Faith: In Africa there is no place to bless homosexual couples. Not at all.[2269]

The Italian newspaper *Il Messaggero* reported that Cardinal Mauro Gambetti announced that homosexual bondings were welcome to receive a 'blessing' at St. Peter's Basilica. Archbishop Gambetti was elevated to the Sacred College of Cardinals by Pope Francis in 2021 and appointed the Archpriest of St. Peter's Basilica and Vicar General of His Holiness for Vatican City. In response to *Fiducia Supplicans* Cardinal Gambetti said that clergy would undertake such 'blessings'

To show the world the maternal face of the Church and along the lines of what [Pope Francis] has asked for....[the clergy of the basilica] will move straight along the furrow that has been cut. The underlying theme is the Church's closeness to people in whatever situation they find themselves in.[2270]

[2268] Ambongo, F [2024] *No Blessing for Homosexual Couples in the African Churches'* [Online] Available at: www.lifesitenews.com [Accessed on: 10 February 2024]
[2269] Silva, WS [2024] *Cardinal explains how African rejection of Fiducia Supplicans was handled* [Online] Available at: www.catholicworldreport.com [Accessed on: 10 February 2024]
[2270] Cummings McClean, D [2024] *Vatican official says St. Peter's Basilica will bless homosexual 'couples'* [Online] Available at: www.lifesitenews.com [Accessed on: 12 February 2024]

14th January

During his appearance on the radical left-wing Italian television talk show *Che tempo che fa* Pope Francis criticised opponents of *Fiducia Supplicans*, accusing them of ignorance and bad motivations:

> Sometimes decisions are not accepted, but in most cases when decisions are not accepted, it is because they are not understood. The danger is that if I don't like something and I put it (the opposition) in my heart, I become a resistance and jump to ugly conclusions. This is what happened with these latest decisions on blessings for all. The Lord blesses everyone. But then people have to enter into a dialogue with the blessing of the Lord and see the path that the Lord proposes. We (the Church) have to take them by the hand and lead them along that path and not condemn them from the start.[2271]

15th January

The Polish Catholic news outlet, *PCh24TV – Polonia Christiana*, broadcast Bishop Athanasius Schneider of Astana's response to *Fiducia Supplicans*. Bishop Athanasius Schneider robustly criticised the Declaration:

> Of course, the document itself and some clergy and bishops behind it try to justify these gestures by claiming that we are not blessing the union itself, but a couple of people. This is merely a play on words that cannot convince anyone. Such explanations contradict elementary logic and we simply cannot be fooled by such word games. It is not worthy of an ecclesiastical document, it is not worthy of bishops and cardinals to deceive people and fool the whole world by saying that 'the Church has not changed its doctrine, but a priest can give a kind of blessing in such a situation'. Another deception, falsehood and fraud is to claim that it is not a liturgical blessing, but only a non-liturgical, spontaneous blessing. You can call it what you like, but it is a blessing, and therefore we should firmly say that we will never accept such deception, such lies, such undermining of God's revelation of the truth of our Catholic faith, which proclaims that homosexual acts are intrinsically evil in all circumstances, and that homosexual couples or homosexual relationships are in themselves a grave offence; a truth which expresses the message that simply being in a homosexual relationship is contrary to the divine order of creation and therefore constitutes a great evil.[2272]

The Bishops' Conference of the North Region of Africa (CERNA) issued a communique from Cardinal Cristóbal López Romero welcoming *Fiducia Supplicans*. Fr. López Romero was appointed Archbishop of Rabat, Morocco, by Pope Francis in 2017 and elevated to the Sacred College of Cardinals in 2019. The communique stated, 'When people in an irregular situation come together to ask for a blessing, it may be given provided this does not cause confusion for them or for others.'[2273]

17th January

The Vatican press office issued Pope Francis' message to Prof. Klaus Schwab, the president of the globalist, eugenicist *World Economic Forum*. The Supreme Pontiff stated:

> It is my hope, then, that the participants in this year's Forum will be mindful of the moral responsibility that each of us has in the fight against poverty, the attainment of an integral development for all our brothers and sisters, and the quest for a peaceful coexistence among peoples.[2274]

[2271]Pullella, P [2024] *Pope defends same-sex blessings declaration, says it is misunderstood* [Online] Available at: www.reuters.com [Accessed on: 12 February 2024]
[2272]Schneider, A [2024] *Biskup Athanasius Schneider do Polaków: Kochajcie Kościół, módlcie się szczególnie za Franciszka* [Online] Available at: www.pch24.pl [Accessed on: 12 February 2024 Trans. DeepL]
[2273]Haynes, M [2024] *Northern African bishops' conference endorses blessings for homosexual 'couples'* [Online] Available at: www.lifesitenews.com [Accessed on: 12 February 2024]
[2274]Pope Francis [2024] *Messaggio del Santo Padre al Presidente Esecutivo del 'World Economic Forum',* 17.01.2024 [Online] Available at: www.press.vatican.va [Accessed on: 12 February 2024]

The John Paul II Academy for Human Life and the Family issued a statement calling for the dismissal of Cardinal Fernández due to his publication of two erotic books that contravened the moral doctrine of the Church. The John Paul II Academy was founded in 2017 by former members of the Pontifical Academy for Life removed by Pope Francis. The Academy stated:

> The sensual-mystical literature for which the cardinal has a particular propensity is one of the worst evils of our time to the extent that under the pretext of spirituality, it, in reality, does nothing but justify the worst excesses of the sexual revolution that is deeply corrupting our society and leading our youth to the abyss [....] These scandalous episodes show that Cardinal Victor Manuel Fernández does not have the necessary minimum qualities required to fulfil the role of defender of the faith. For this reason, this Academy formally asks the Holy Father to dismiss him and appoint in his place a competent theologian faithful to the moral teachings of the Church.[2275]

21st January

Cardinal Joseph Zen, Archbishop Emeritus of Hong Kong, published his criticism of *Fiducia Supplicans* on his personal website:

> The Statement repeatedly emphasises the need to avoid confusion, but the blessings encouraged by the Statement do in fact create confusion.... [Fernández's comments that] sexual behaviour in same-sex relationships has its goodness, that it can progress and grow... is an absolute subjective error. According to objective truth, that behaviour is a grave sin and can never be good. If the Prefect of the Congregation for the Doctrine of the Faith is [...] committing a heresy by claiming a serious sin as 'good,' then shouldn't the Prefect resign or be dismissed? [....] The 'statement' seems to say that they came as a 'pair' and went back as a 'pair' after the blessing; doesn't that mean that they can, at least for the time being, continue to live in the 'wrong,' i.e., sinful, way?[2276]

25th January

Pope Francis granted the schismatic Anglican Archbishop of Canterbury, Justin Welby, permission to celebrate an 'Anglican Eucharist' at the high altar in the Catholic Basilica of St. Bartholomew, Rome. Later the same day, during an ecumenical Vespers at the Papal Basilica of St. Paul's Outside the Walls, Pope Francis and Archbishop Welby jointly 'commissioned' pairs of Catholic and Anglican bishops as if they possessed equivalent orders. This action implicitly contradicted Pope Leo XIII's apostolic letter *Apostolicae curae* that declared all Anglican ordinations to be 'absolutely null and utterly void'.[2277]

During his interview with Raymond Arroyo on the EWTN show *The World Over* Cardinal Gerhard Müller, the former prefect of the Congregation for the Doctrine of the Faith, stated that *Fiducia Supplicans* was a failed document. Cardinal Müller said,

> now the African churches, Catholic churches, are the leaders in this way of the correction of a failed document. And I think we cannot really devise [that] the Africans are only saying that [because] of their culture.... this aspect is better than our decadence culture in the West. [It is] a very important moment in Church history that now the Africans are entering the place and taking over the leadership in the Catholic Church, and it is a very good thing they are doing. [*Fiducia Supplicans*] must be rewritten in the clear, Catholic theological understanding. I think this whole document is a failed project. Jesus gave us the [instruction] how to introduce these people: by saying the Gospel to them to

[2275]The John Paul II Academy for Human Life and the Family [2024] *The Academy Calls for Pope Francis to Dismiss Cardinal Víctor Manuel Fernández* [Online] Available at: www.jahlf.org [Accessed on: 12 January 2024]
[2276]Haynes, M [2024] *Cardinal Zen warns of 'error' in Fiducia Supplicans, calls for Cdl. Fernández to resign* [Online] Available at: www.lifesitenews.com [Accessed on: 12 February 2024]
[2277]Haynes, M [2024] *Archbishop of Canterbury leads 'Anglican Eucharist' in Catholic basilica with Pope's approval* [Online] Available at: www.lifesitenews.com [Accessed on: 12 February 2024]

lead them [in] the way of Jesus Christ and to repentance of sins and to listen to the Gospel and to come to the Holy Sacraments. Jesus gave for us His life and the cross of Jesus Christ and His resurrection, these are the ways for our salvation and not only a good will to everybody like the Freemasons are speaking of the fraternity of everybody without obligation, without a conversion, without changing your life and [without] the imitation of Jesus Christ.[2278]

26th January

During his address to the plenary assembly of the Congregation for the Doctrine of the Faith Pope Francis downplayed the gravely sinful nature of homosexual sex acts during his comments on the 'blessing' of homosexual bondings and other sinful relationships as permitted by *Fiducia Supplicans*. The Supreme Pontiff described the divine prohibition of such acts in terms of seeking 'moral perfection', and ignored the obvious fact that the 'couple' is the 'union':

> I would like briefly to underline two things: the first is that these blessings, outside of any liturgical context and form, do not demand moral perfection in order to be received; the second, that when a couple approaches spontaneously to ask for a blessing, one does not bless the union, but simply the people who have requested it. The union is not blessed, but the people. Of course, one must take into account the context, the sensibilities, and the place in which one lives, as well as the most appropriate way to give the blessing.[2279]

29th January

During an interview with the Italian newspaper *La Stampa*, Pope Francis misrepresented the nature of the African bishops' opposition to *Fiducia Supplicans* as being primarily cultural, not doctrinal:

> those who vehemently protest [*Fiducia Supplicans*] belong to small ideological groups. [The Church in Africa] is a special case, since for them, homosexuality is something 'ugly' from a cultural point of view; they do not tolerate it. I trust that gradually everyone will be reassured about the spirit of the declaration, [which] aims to include, not divide. It invites us to welcome and then entrust people, and to trust in God.[2280]

1st February

During his interview with Raymond Arroyo on the EWTN show *The World Over* Cardinal Zen, the Emeritus Bishop of Hong Kong, condemned *Fiducia Supplicans* and Cardinal Fernández's January 4th defense of his declaration as heresy:

> [saying that] a homosexual couple, they are living in that continuous occasion of grievous sin and then they [Vatican officials] say this is something good which may grow, which may mature. But this is nothing good, it is a serious sin, so that's a heresy when you call a sin as something good. That's really terrible [....] now it's obvious; everybody can see clearly what was the agenda. They say 'no we don't have an agenda.' Actually they put this LGBT at the bottom of the whole list.... they moved the whole Church solemnly using a synod, just to have a chance to let people to accept an impossible thing.[2281]

The Conference of Catholic Bishops in Belarus issued a statement declaring that they did not intend to implement *Fiducia Supplicans* 'blessing' of homosexual bondings and other sinful sexual relationships:

[2278]Wailzer, A [2024] *Cardinal Müller calls Fiducia Supplicans a 'failed document' that needs to be 're-written'* [Online] Available at: www.lifesitenews.com [Accessed on: 12 February 2024]
[2279]Pope Francis [2024] *Address to Participants in the Plenary Session of the Congregation for the Doctrine of the Faith* [Online] Available at: www.vatican.va [Accessed on: 12 February 2024]
[2280]*Pope on Holy Land war: Without two states, true peace remains distant* [2024] [Online] Available at: www.vaticannews.va [Accessed on: 12 January 2024]
[2281]Haynes, M [2024] *Cardinal Zen on homosexual 'unions': Calling 'a sin as something good' is 'heresy'* [Online] Available at: www.lifesitenews.com [Accessed on: 12 February 2024]

The Catholic Church in Belarus does not intend to put into practice the possibility of blessing couples living in an irregular union and same-sex couples proposed by the Declaration [....] It is always necessary to avoid giving the blessing specifically to couples who live in a so-called 'civil marriage,' as well as to those who live in a canonically invalid marriage or same-sex couples. Such a blessing may be perceived by other believers as consent to sin.[2282]

2nd February

Ninety clergy, scholars and journalists issued a filial appeal asking cardinals and bishops to forbid the implementation of *Fiducia Supplicans* in their jurisdictions and to request that Pope Francis withdraws his declaration. The filial appeal was published simultaneously in multiple languages on websites such as *LifeSiteNews* (English), *Infovatikana.com* (Spanish), *Katholisches.info* (German), Sandro Magister (Italian and French), *Crisis Magazine*, *InfoCatólica*, and Edward Pentin. Among the signatories were numerous personalities, such as Fr. Gerald Murray, Fr. Robert Sirico, Fr. Glen Tattersall, Deacon Nick Donnelly, Professor Claudio Pierantoni, Dr. Peter Kwasniewski, Prof. John Lamont, Prof. Roberto de Mattei, Prof. Anna Silvas, Dr. Gerard van den Aardweg, and Prof. John and Anna Rist, Philip Lawler, his wife Leila, Eric Sammons, and John-Henry Westen. The Filial Appeal stated:

> The document [*Fiducia Supplicans*] effectively attempts to introduce a separation between doctrine and liturgy on the one hand, and pastoral practice on the other. But this is impossible: in fact, pastoral care, like all action, always presupposes *a theory* and, therefore, if pastoral care performs something that does not correspond to the doctrine, what is actually being proposed is *a different doctrine* [....] the concrete sign that is given with such blessing, in front of the whole world, is that 'irregular couples,' extramarital and homosexual alike, according to the Catholic Church, would now be acceptable to God, precisely in the type of union that specifically configures them as couples. Nor does it make sense to separate 'couple' from 'union,' as card. Fernández has tried to do, since a couple is a couple because of the union that gives existence to it [....] The fact is that a priest is imparting a blessing on two people who present themselves as a couple, in the sexual sense, and precisely a couple defined by its objectively sinful relationship. Therefore — regardless of the intentions and interpretations of the document, or the explanations the priest may try to give — this action will be the visible and tangible sign of a different doctrine, which contradicts traditional doctrine [....] This situation fully justifies the decided rejection of so many episcopal conferences, so many prelates, so many scholars, and so many ordinary lay people. In this context, it is definitely not justifiable, especially for a cardinal or a bishop, to remain silent, since the scandal that has already occurred is serious and public, and if it is not stopped, it is bound to be more and more amplified. The threat does not become smaller but more serious, since the error comes from the Roman See, and is destined to scandalize all the faithful, and above all the little ones, the simple faithful who have no way of orienting and defending themselves in this confusion: 'Whoever offends one of these little ones who believe in me, it would be better for him if a donkey's millstone were hung around his neck and he were drowned in the depths of the sea' (Mt 18,6).[2283]

5th February

Pope Francis invited a pioneer of the ordination of women in the Church of England to address his advisory council of nine cardinals on the role of women in the Church. Rev. Dr. Jo Bailey Wells, 'bishop' of the Church of England was joined by Sr. Linda Pocher and Giuliva Di Berardino.

[2282]*Belarusian bishops refuse to bless same-sex couples as it 'may be perceived… as consent to sin'* [2024] [Online] Available at: www.lifesitenews.com [Accessed on: 12 February 2024]

[2283]Hickson, M [2024] *Priests, scholars ask Church leaders to request the Pope withdraw Fiducia Supplicans* [Online] Available at: www.lifesitenews.com [Accessed on: 12 February 2024]

On the 8th February, the Spanish news agency *Europa Press* reported Sr. Pocher's reflections on the meeting with Pope Francis and the Council of Nine that she organised, confirming that the ordination of women to the diaconate was discussed:

> We already know that the Pope is very much in favour of the female diaconate, but it is still something we are trying to understand how to put into practice [....] [Pope Francis] is changing the way of thinking and living the difference between the ordained ministry and the baptismal priesthood, extending to all the baptized some rights that until recently belonged to bishops, priests or religious [....] I thought it would be interesting to confront the experience of the Anglican Church in this regard...what kind of process they followed to arrive at the decision to ordain women and to tell how this has changed life in their Church [Anglican Church]. So what she [Jo Bailey Wells] did was to relate an experience, which we then discussed with the cardinals and the Pope.[2284]

In response to Pope Francis' invitation to a women Anglican 'bishop' to address the Council of Nine, Archbishop Carlo Viganò commented on his twitter account,

> Bergoglio intends to fundamentally change the concept of Holy Orders, placing alongside the Priesthood (reserved for men) forms of 'non-ordained' ministry for women, with a view to their sacramental ordination.... why did Bergoglio invite an Anglican 'bishopess,' i.e., a heretical, schismatic, invalidly ordained woman, to the Council of Cardinals meeting to speak about 'gender equality and the role of women in the Church'?[2285]

8th February

During an interview with the weekly Italian journal *Credere* Pope Francis discussed his willingness to 'bless' homosexual bondings:

> I do not bless a 'homosexual marriage,' I bless two people who love each other and I also ask them to pray for me. No one is shocked if I give a blessing to an entrepreneur who maybe exploits people, and that is a very serious sin. Whereas they are scandalised if I give it to a homosexual.... This is hypocrisy! The heart of the document is welcome.

In the same interview Pope Francis described his attitude to those in sinful sexual relationships in the sacrament of confession:

> Always in confessions, when these situations arrive, homosexual people, remarried people, I always pray and bless. The blessing should not be denied to anyone. Everyone, everyone, everyone. Be careful. I'm talking about people: those who are capable of receiving Baptism. The most serious sins are those that disguise themselves with a more 'angelic appearance'.[2286]

During an interview with the Spanish news agency *Europa Press*, Sr. Linda Pocher stated that Pope Francis was 'very much in favour of the female diaconate.' Her declaration followed her invitation to address Pope Francis and his C9 group of cardinals on the role of women in the Church. Sr. Pocher is a professor of Christology and Mariology at the Pontifical Faculty of Educational Sciences Auxilium in Rome. Confirming that the faux ordination of women to the diaconate was discussed during her meeting with the Supreme Pontiff Sr. Pocher said

---

[2284]Haynes, M [2024] *Pope Francis 'is very much in favour of the female diaconate,' claims nun invited to address Vatican cardinals* [Online] Available at: www.lifesitenews.com [Accessed on: 12 February 2024]

[2285]Mangiaracina, E [2024] *Abp. Viganò: Pope Francis' invitation of Anglican 'bishopess' signals his intention to 'ordain' women* [Online] Available at: www.lifesitenews.com [Accessed on: 12 February 2024]

[2286]Haynes, M [2024] *Pope Francis: 'I bless two people who love each other' not homosexual 'marriage'* [Online] Available at: www.lifesitenews.com [Accessed on: 12 February 2024]

[Pope Francis] is changing the way of thinking and living the difference between the ordained ministry and the baptismal priesthood, extending to all the baptized some rights that until recently belonged to bishops, priests or religious.

Sr. Pocher also explained her reasoning for extending an invitation to Jo Bailey Wells, an Anglican woman 'bishop', to address the meeting with Pope Francis:

I thought it would be interesting to confront the experience of the Anglican Church in this regard…what kind of process they followed to arrive at the decision to ordain women and to tell how this has changed life in their Church [Anglican Church]. So what she did was to relate an experience, which we then discussed with the cardinals and the Pope.[2287]

Prominent US canon lawyer Fr. Gerald Murray responded to the report that Pope Francis is 'very much in favour of the female diaconate':

The reason it's not permitted is because the Church has never done it. There is no history of female deacons receiving the Sacrament of Holy Orders ever in the life of the Church. I think, for me, that's part of the propaganda effort to say simply, 'The pope is going to do this'. If this [female deacons] were done, this would mark a serious moment of heresy in the life of the Church because you would have the pope authorising something that is impossible to happen: women being given the sacrament of Holy Orders. And if that happened, the Church would be splitting apart because you'd have some bishops do it and others wouldn't. And then, if you're in a diocese in which a woman was 'ordained' a deacon, could that deacon go across the boundary to the next diocese and function as a deacon? She wouldn't even be recognised as a deacon. So this is very serious, and I really regret these basically political statements asserting things that are not known or not proven.[2288]

9th February

Bishop Liam Cary of the Diocese of Baker, Oregon, issued a statement in response to *Fiducia Supplicans* requesting that his priests not bless couples engaged in adultery, fornication or sodomy. Bishop Cary first alluded to the confusion caused by *Fiducia Supplicans*:

Despite the Cardinal's concern not to sow division, within weeks of Fiducia's release dramatically opposed responses erupted in fifty countries. Bishops in Flanders and Germany welcomed the Declaration as a 'help to move forward' on their previously chosen path toward formal blessings of same-sex couples. Photos and videos of pre-planned same-sex ceremonies filled computer screens around the globe with images of priests giving blessings Fiducia prohibited. Mass media quickly spread the news worldwide: the Catholic Church has changed her mind; she now approves of same-sex unions [....] Cardinal Ambongo promptly brought their concerns to Rome for detailed discussions with Pope Francis and Cardinal Fernandez. With the pope's approval, the two cardinals carefully worked out and signed a statement 'on behalf of the entire Catholic Church in Africa.' It stated the bishops' belief that 'the extra-liturgical blessings proposed in ... Fiducia Supplicans cannot be carried out in Africa without exposing themselves to scandals.

Referencing the concession given from Pope Francis to the African bishops not to bless sinful relationships, Bishop Cary prohibited his priests from celebrating such blessings:

I do not believe they can be carried out scandal-free in the Diocese of Baker either. Here as in Africa, if a cohabiting heterosexual couple or a same sex couple were to ask a priest to bless them, they would be seeking an official sign of approval for behaviour that the Church teaches is sinful in God's sight. If the priest complies with their request,

[2287]Haynes, M [2024] *Pope Francis 'is very much in favor of the female diaconate,' claims nun invited to address Vatican cardinals* [Online] Available at: www.lifesitenews.com [Accessed on: 6 March 2024]
[2288]Wailzer, A [2024] *Fr. Murray tells Raymond Arroyo 'women deacons' would be 'serious moment of heresy'* [Online] Available at: www.lifesitenews.com [Accessed on: 7 March 2024]

the subtle distinctions of *Fiducia Supplicans* will not keep bystanders from concluding that the Church the priest represents no longer believes as she always did before, but is now endorsing the unions of unmarried couples. That is not a message that I as bishop wish priests to be sending in the Diocese of Baker. Therefore, in accord with Cardinal Fernandez's above-noted cautions about creating confusion and the statement of the African bishops, I ask priests of Baker not to bless known cohabiting couples, of the same sex or both sexes. Individual men and women.[2289]

14th February

Bishop Joe S. Vásquez of Austin, Texas, issued a letter announcing the suppression of the Traditional Latin Mass at St. Mary's cathedral, which had been celebrated there since 2007 and attracted over 200 parishioners. The suppression had been mandated by the Vatican, as explained by Bishop Vásquez:

> As required by the rescript of the Holy Father issued in February of last year, I submitted the case of the celebrations according to the 1962 missal at the Cathedral parish to the Vatican Dicastery for Divine Worship to receive the guidance and direction of the Holy See. Following the guidance of the Holy See, the dispensation for celebrations according to the 1962 missal at the Cathedral will come to an end on March 19, the feast of St. Joseph.[2290]

15th February

A funeral service was held in St. Patrick's Cathedral, New York City, for a man who presented himself as the woman 'Cecilia Gentili', a transgender activist, former prostitute and atheist. The funeral service was the occasion of desecration and sacrilege against the Catholic faith, including a eulogy that referred to 'Cecilia Gentili' as 'this whore. This great whore. St. Cecilia, Mother of all Whores!' Furthermore, Mass cards and a picture near the altar showed a haloed Gentili surrounded by the Spanish words for 'transvestite,' 'whore,' 'blessed' and 'mother' above the text of Psalm 23. Also, a participant changed the lyrics during the 'Ave Maria' and sang 'Ave Cecilia' while dancing through the aisles. The celebrant, Fr. Edward Dougherty, a Maryknoll priest, appeared to join in with the riotous behaviour, praising the crowd for being so well dressed. He also referred to Gentili as 'our sister Cecilia.'

The pro-homosexuality Fr. James Martin, S.J., highly favoured by Pope Francis, praised holding the funeral in St. Patrick's cathedral:

> To celebrate the funeral Mass of a transgender woman at St. Patrick's is a powerful reminder, during Lent, that L.G.B.T.Q. people are as much a part of the church as anyone else. 'I wonder if it would have happened a generation ago.'[2291]

Even though Fr. James Martin, S.J., a resident of New York City, knew of the funeral of the infamous transgender militant, the cathedral staff claimed to have had no prior knowledge:

> …it only knew that family and friends were requesting a funeral Mass for a Catholic, and had no idea our welcome and prayer would be degraded in such a sacrilegious and deceptive way. At the Cardinal's directive, we have offered an appropriate Mass of Reparation.[2292]

On the 19th February, *LifeSiteNews* published an open letter from clergymen and scholars to the bishops calling on them to stop the implementation of *Fiducia Supplicans* in the

[2289]Cary, L [2024] *To Bless or Not to Bless: On the Vatican Declaration Fiducia Supplicans* [Online] Available at: www.dioceseofbaker.org [Accessed on: 8 March 2024]

[2290]Mangiaracina, E [2024] *Austin bishop affirms Vatican instructed diocese to end Latin Mass at cathedral* [Online] Available at: www.lifesitenews.com [Accessed on: 7 March 2024]

[2291]Stack, L [2024] *Mourning a Transgender Activist at a Cathedral That Once Drew Protests* [Online] Available at: www.nytimes.com [Accessed on: 7 March 2024]

[2292]Wailzer, A [2024] *Over 10,000 urge Cardinal Dolan to exorcise St. Patrick's Cathedral after sacrilegious 'trans' funeral* [Online] Available at: www.lifesitenews.com [Accessed on: 7 March 2024]

light of the desecration of St. Patrick's cathedral by LGBT militants. The signatories of the open letter were Donna Bethell, JD, Dr. Gavin Ashenden (former Anglican bishop and chaplain to the Queen, now a Catholic convert), Deacon Nick Donnelly, Dr. Jules Gomes, Dr. Peter Kwasniewski, Dr. Janet Smith, Elizabeth Yore, Esq., *LifeSite* editor-in-chief John-Henry Westen and *LifeSite's* Maike Hickson. The letter stated:

> Pope Francis' secular and political stance promoting the gender ideology by allowing the blessing of homosexual couples by Catholic priests has empowered transgender activists who seized the moment and the setting at St. Patrick's Cathedral to advance their agenda in one of the most iconic Catholic cathedrals in America. Their radical political movement was on full display in a shocking parody of a 'Catholic funeral' for a transgender activist. From start to finish, the service derided the Catholic faith, blasphemed its hallowed space, and ridiculed a holy and beloved female saint, Saint Cecilia, one of the most famous virgin martyrs of the early church. The hour-long service was fraught with crass and impudent antics, loud catcalls, and boisterous cheers. There was not one moment of prayerful devotion or piety. Despite ongoing outbursts, the congregation was never admonished by the officiating priest, Rev. Edward Dougherty, who seemingly encouraged the loud eruptions. At the beginning of the service, Dougherty complimented the attendees by stating 'Except for Easter Sunday, St. Patrick's hasn't seen such a well turned out crowd.' The congregation burst out in prolonged uproarious hoots and yells in response [....] This, Your Eminences and Your Excellencies, is what will be coming into your parishes if you do not act now and stop the document *Fiducia Supplicans* and its implementation. It will start with a priest coming together with a homosexual couple in a church for a blessing. People will gather to witness the event. There will be numerous occasions for political activists to abuse that moment to further blaspheme God and to mock the Catholic faith. This funeral at St. Patrick's Cathedral was a wake-up call. It was only the beginning.[2293]

Maike Hickson of *LifeSite* News also reported that Cardinal Timothy Dolan of the Archdiocese of New York had told Wendy Stone Long that he considered Fr. Edward Dougherty, the celebrant at 'Cecilia Gentili''s funeral service 'a hero' because 'he stopped the (funeral) Mass.' When Mrs. Stone Long objected that Fr. Dougherty had not stopped the blasphemous service, Dolan said, 'Then it went on without him.'[2294]

16th February

The Grand Orient of Italy announced that it was holding a seminar with senior Italian prelates at the Catholic Ambrosianum Cultural Foundation on the theme, 'The Catholic Church and Freemasonry.' The Grand Master Stefano Bisi of the Grand Orient of Italy was joined by pro-homosexuality Cardinal Francesco Coccopalmerio, Archbishop Mario Enrico Delpini of Milan and Bishop Antonio Staglianò, president of the Vatican's Pontifical Academy of Theology. This dialogue ignored the Church's consistent opposition to freemasonry, with 8 popes over the past 200 years issuing 20 legal interdicts condemning Freemasonry.[2295]

On the 17th February, the Italian newspaper *Il Messaggero* reported extracts of Cardinal Coccopalmerio's address to the Freemasons:

> From what I could understand, but I am little expert in this matter, I think there is an evolution in mutual understanding of relations between Catholics and Masons. Fifty years ago, there was less understanding, but things have moved on, and I hope these encounters don't stop there. I wonder if we cannot think of a permanent table, even at the level of authorities, so that we can better confront each other.'[2296]

[2293]Hickson, M [2024] *Faithful Catholics urge bishops to stop Fiducia Supplicans in light of St. Patrick's Cathedral scandal* [Online] Available at: www.lifesitenews.com [Accessed on: 7 March 2024]

[2294]Hickson, M [2024] *Cardinal Dolan praises priest who presided at 'trans' funeral in New York cathedral* [Online] Available at: www.lifesitenews.com [Accessed on: 7 March 2024]

[2295]Gomes, J [2024] *Italian Prelates Participate in Freemasonry Seminar* [Online] Available at: www.churchmilitant.com [Accessed on: 7 March 2024]

[2296]Haynes, M [2024] *Vatican cardinal calls for 'permanent' Catholic-Freemason dialogue at 'historic' joint event* [Online] Available at: www.lifesitenews.com [Accessed on: 7 March 2024]

The US religious journal *First Things* published an essay by Cardinal Gerhard Müller, the former prefect of the CDF, criticising *Fiducia Supplicans* for leading to heresy. Cardinal Müller wrote:

> Now, to bless two people together who are together precisely because of the homosexual relationship that unites them is no different than to bless the union. No matter how much one repeats that one is *not* blessing the union, that is exactly what one is doing by the very objectivity of the rite being performed [...] to bless these persons as same-sex couples is to approve their unions, even if they are not equated with marriage. This is therefore a doctrine contrary to the teaching of the Catholic Church, since its acceptance, even if not directly heretical, logically leads to heresy [....] In conclusion, as long as the DDF does not correct *Fiducia Supplicans* by clarifying that blessings cannot be given to the couple, but only to each person individually, the DDF is approving statements that are contrary to at least the second paragraph of the Profession of Faith — that is, it is approving statements that are contrary to the teaching of the Catholic Church, which, without being heretical in themselves, lead to heresy. This means that these pastoral blessings for irregular unions cannot be accepted by the Catholic faithful, and especially by those who, in assuming an ecclesiastical office, have taken the Profession of Faith and the Oath of Fidelity, which calls first of all for the preservation of the deposit of faith in its entirety.[2297]

During his address to the annual Archdiocese of Los Angeles, Religious Education Congress pro-homosexuality Cardinal Robert W. McElroy of San Diego spoke of his hopes for the 'ordination' of women 'deacons'. Cardinal McElroy claimed that during the Synod on Synodality there was the 'sense that the time has come for a "paradigm shift" with regard to the inclusion of women in the Church [that included] perhaps ending the transitional diaconate, meaning ordination as a deacon as the final step before priesthood.... [which] could make it easier to have women deacons'.[2298]

17th February

The Holy See Press Office announced that Pope Francis had appointed as consultors to the Synod on Synodality three women who advocate for the 'ordination' of female deacons and priests. Sr. Birgit Weiler, Tricia C. Bruce and Maria Clara Lucchetti Bingemer were appointed as part of a team of theologians for the second session of the Synod on Synodality to be held in October 2024. Sister Weiler is reported as saying, 'it must be possible for women who feel called to it to be admitted to the priesthood.' About the 'ordination' of women deacons she said, 'It could actually come very soon. There are no theological hurdles if one understands the diaconate as an independent office in the Church through which Christ is made present in the Church in His service to people's lives. When it comes to women's priesthood, I fear that it will take a little longer. But it is imperative that the Church recognises the urgency of this issue.' Tricia C. Bruce, authored a pro-deaconess report titled 'Called to Contribute: Findings from an In-depth Interview Study of US Catholic Women and the Diaconate.' Bruce argues that ordination of women to the diaconate is possible because of Pope Benedict XVI's 2009 changes to canon law established a distinction between deacons and the ordained priesthood. Maria Clara Lucchetti Bingemer has proposed that a woman is the proper matter for the sacrament of Holy Orders and can act as an 'alter Christus' and 'in persona Christi.' Bingemer argued in favour of ordaining women to the priesthood in her book *Transforming the Church and Society from a Feminist Perspective*, because of 'their eucharistic vocation expressed through their bodies.'[2299]

[2297]Müller, G [2024] *Does Fiducia Supplicans Affirm Heresy?* [Online] Available at: www.firstthings. com [Accessed on: 7 March 2024]

[2298]Haynes, M [2024] *Cardinal McElroy: Synod could end link between diaconate and priesthood to allow 'female deacons'* [Online] Available at: www.lifesitenews.com [Accessed on: 6 March 2024]

[2299]Gomes, J [2024] *Francis Appoints 'Women Clergy' Advocates to Synod* [Online] Available at: www. churchmilitant.com [Accessed on: 11 March 2024]

19th February

During an interview with the Luxembourg daily newspaper *L'Essentiel* pro-homosexuality Cardinal Jean-Claude Hollerich, recipient of many signs of favour by Pope Francis, spoke of his support for *Fiducia Supplicans* and the ending of priestly celibacy. Cardinal Hollerich said,

> I'm absolutely on the same line as the Pope. Would we refuse to bless a homosexual couple because they are 'sinners' and bless an entrepreneur who is going to invest against humanity? That's hypocritical. The Pope considers himself a 'sinner' and so do I. The Pope doesn't like condemning the sins of others without looking at his own. He adds: 'Why are we only interested in morality below the belt?' [....] Many bishops are questioning the marriage of priests.... Some people have a hard time being single. Giving them the choice would make it possible to have a few more people ready for the priesthood. In Europe, that 'few' can make all the difference.[2300]

Uruguay's gossip magazine, *Revista Gente*, published coverage of the 'wedding' between two men afflicted with the homosexual inclination. The men claimed to have become 'the first same-sex couple in the world to receive a Catholic blessing.' Two days after the men were civilly 'married', Fr. Francisco Gordalina gave the blessing in the presence of 400 guests. Fr. Francisco Gordalina said that the two men were 'children of God who … have asked for a blessing for you from God our Father' and that 'it is with pleasure that we are present in the name of the Church to ask to bless you. [This blessing] is a way that the Church wants to show you that God is with you, and we know very well that you are also with God because we have talked in intimacy with our bishop and we have seen your faith.'

On the 22nd March Bishop Milton Troccoli of the Diocese of Maldonado-Punta del Este-Minas issued a statement:

> …seeing the repercussions that the blessing of C. Perciavalle and J. Castilhos has had on some people in the ecclesial community, I consider it important to share with you the path taken in relation to this. After the first announcements in the media about a 'religious celebration' of marriage in a Church and a clarifying statement from the Diocese, a meeting was held – at their request – to discuss personally and clarify situations. [After a] thoughtful conversation they requested to receive the blessing, a possibility raised by (*Fiducia Supplicans*) for couples in an 'irregular situation.' [We] consulted the Apostolic Nunciature in Uruguay about how to proceed in this situation, which was expected to have media characteristics. We were informed that the blessing had to be given, given that there was a document signed by the Pope, and that we should proceed accordingly. We then informed those interested that the blessing would be given and they were reminded that it would not be in a church, that it was a blessing to the people and not to the union, (it was not a 'church marriage'), and that for the same reason it would be discreet, without the presence of guests; which was a simple blessing. I understand that the media coverage of the situation may have hurt the sensitivity of some and may have confused others [but] *Fiducia Supplicans* seeks to reach out pastorally to those who find themselves in 'irregular situations.' And it does not do so for ideological or propaganda reasons, but rather seeking that the charity of Christ reaches everyone. The novelty of the document and its pastoral implications mobilises us all. This invites us to a deep reflection about how to continue looking for ways to evangelise. It is a great challenge, which requires prayer, discernment, and reflection.[2301]

20th February

LifeSiteNews published an essay by Fr. Joachim Heimerl in which he warned that Pope Francis' rejection of the Latin Mass represents the Supreme Pontiff's 'rejection of Church

[2300]Holzer, T [2024] «*Certains prêtres vivent mal leur célibat*» [Online] Available at: www.lessentiel. lu [Accessed on: 8 March 2024. Translated with DeepL.com]

[2301]Wailzer, A [2024] *Vatican-approved 'blessing' ceremony for 'married' homosexuals sparks outrage in Uruguay* [Online] Available at: www.lifesitenews.com; *Uruguayan Bishop Forced to Release Clarification after Gay Catholic 'Marriage' Confusion* [Online] Available at: www.catholicvote.org [Accessed on: 8 March 2024]

tradition as a whole'. Fr. Joachim Heimerl wrote:

> Things have now come to a head under Francis. For him, Church unity is no longer the
> top priority. He is primarily concerned with implementing his 'reforms,' and only from
> this point of view can his attitude toward the traditional Mass be understood: Francis
> is concerned with the rejection of Church tradition as a whole. After all, a pope who
> allows adultery and homosexual relationships to be 'blessed' can no longer refer to the
> Church of Christ and the teachings of the Apostles, including when he wants to appoint
> 'deaconesses' in the near future. His pontificate marks a historical rupture, which is also
> a rupture with the 'old Mass.'[2302]

The Moscow Patriarchate's website, *www.mospat.ru*, published the Orthodox Church's
response to *Fiducia Supplicans*. The response was formulated during a plenary session
of the Synodal Biblical-Theological Commission of the Russian Orthodox Church at
the request of Russian Orthodox Patriarch Kirill. The Biblical-Theological Commission
concluded:

> The participants in the meeting shared their views on theology behind the Declaration
> *Fiducia Supplicans*, pointing out that it is the first ever document in the history of the
> Catholic Church which gives form to the blessing of 'same-sex unions'. The Commission
> members were unanimous that this innovation manifests a sharp deviation from the
> Christian moral teaching.[2303]

22nd February

In response to Pope Francis' request that Bishops' Conferences respond to the synthesis
report issued at the end of the Synod on Synodality's first session issued in October
2023, the Belgian bishops called for 'women deacons' and the end of priestly celibacy.
The Belgian bishops asserted that in response to society's demand for 'gender equality'
and 'the importance of equal opportunities for men and women' the Church must 're-
read' her Tradition, opening up 'pastoral responsibilities' and 'a recognised ecclesial
(ministry)':

> The question arises as to whether women can also be admitted to the ordained ministry
> of the diaconate [requiring] the green light for bishops' conferences or continental
> episcopal assemblies to take certain measures. Assigning increasing pastoral
> responsibility to women and the ordination of women to the diaconate should not
> be universally obligatory or forbidden [....] We ask that every bishops' conference
> or continental episcopal assembly may take certain measures in view of the priestly
> ordination of *'viri probati.'* The priestly ordination of *'viri probati'* should not be
> universally obligatory or forbidden.[2304]

23rd February

During a Q&A at theological symposium held at the Catholic University of East Africa
in Nairobi, Cardinal Robert Sarah admitted that he was 'very proud' that the African
bishops had 'completely' rejected *Fiducia Supplicans* and its instruction to 'bless' couples
engaging in fornication, adultery or sodomy. Cardinal Sarah is the former prefect of
the Sacred Congregation for Divine Worship and the Discipline of the Sacraments. His
Eminence said:

> I think *Fiducia Supplicans* has a response from the African Bishops – very clear. And
> not only the African bishops but many in Europe, in Kazakhstan, in Poland, refused,
> because the document has no scriptural basis, no theological basis. I was very proud to

---

[2302]Heimerl, J [2024] *Austrian priest: Pope Francis' fight against the Latin Mass is 'a fight against the
Church'* [Online] Available at: www.lifesitenews.com [Accessed on: 8 March 2024]
[2303]*Fiducia Supplicans: The Russian Orthodox Church Condemns the Text* [2024] [Online] Available at:
www.fsspx.news [Accessed on: 11 March 2024]
[2304]Knuffke, L [2024] *Belgian bishops renew push for 'women deacons,' married priests ahead of fall Synod
session* [Online] Available at: www.lifesitenews.com [Accessed on: 8 March 2024]

hear the African bishops rejecting completely this text. And many other bishops even in Brazil refused, so I think it seemed to me impossible to accept.[2305]

Pro-homosexuality Cardinal Vincent Nichols of Westminster sent an email to Fr. Michael Cullinan to inform him of the cancellation of the celebration of the 'Traditional Triduum' at St. Mary Moorfields, London. Cardinal Nichols' cancellation signified that for the first time since the 1990s the traditional Easter Triduum would not be celebrated in the Archdiocese of Westminster. Cardinal Nichols wrote:

> I appreciate your desire to help the group that gathers for the Triduum and the stable group at Spanish Place. But, for the sake of the wider provision, I have to decline your suggestion that the Spanish Place stable group could transfer to St. Mary Moorfields for the Triduum. I realise that this will disappoint some people, but I have to keep the wider picture in view.[2306]

26th February

Bishop José Ignacio Munilla of the Diocese of Orihuela-Alicante, Spain, posted on X (formerly Twitter) calling on the Vatican to withdraw *Fiducia Supplicans* due to 'chaos' it created. Bishop Munilla wrote, 'In the face of so much chaos, we have enough signs to conclude that the solution is to rectify; that is, to withdraw *Fiducia Supplicans*.'[2307]

27th February

Vatican News, the official news portal of the Vatican, published an article by Andrea Tornielli, *Vatican News*' editorial director, attempting to justify *Fiducia Supplicans*' innovation of 'non-liturgical blessings' Tornielli misrepresented the 2000 CDF document 'Instruction on Prayers for Healing', written by Cardinal Joseph Ratzinger and approved by Pope St. John Paul II in an attempt to justify the *Fiducia Supplicans* 'non-liturgical blessing':

> Some of the critics who have questioned the recent Declaration consider only the broad sense permissible and therefore do not accept the distinction between 'ritual' and 'liturgical' prayers or blessings, and 'pastoral' and 'spontaneous' prayers or blessings [....] In the final part of the instruction, dedicated to disciplinary norms, there is an article (2) which states: 'Prayers for healing are considered to be liturgical if they are part of the liturgical books approved by the Church's competent authority; otherwise, they are non-liturgical.' Therefore, it is established that there are prayers for healing that are liturgical or ritual and others that are not but are still legitimately admitted.[2308]

Tornielli's claim that the Declaration on Prayers for Healing sets the precedent for 'non-ritual blessing' was challenged by theologians. A Dominican told *LifeSiteNews*,

> The article argues that since there can be liturgical and non-liturgical prayers, so there can be liturgical and non-liturgical blessings. As it stands, it is obviously a fallacy; you might as well argue that therefore there can be non-liturgical altars. One difference between a prayer and a blessing is that a blessing is always in some way an act of authority, and so in that sense is always done in the name of Christ the *Leitourgos*/ Minister of the sanctuary (Heb 8:2). So in that sense all blessings are liturgical. The real objection to *Fiducia Supplicans* lies elsewhere, namely in the scandal that is inevitably given by such blessings, however they are characterised. Tornielli's statement that '*Fiducia Supplicans* repeatedly clarifies that imparting a pastoral or spontaneous blessing

[2305]Knuffke, L [2024] *Cardinal Sarah: 'Very proud' of African bishops for rejecting Pope Francis' homosexual 'blessings'* [Online] Available at: www.lifesitenews.com [Accessed on: 8 March 2024]

[2306]Pentin, E [2024] *Cardinal Nichols Prohibits Traditional Easter Triduum Services* [Online] Available at: www.ncregister.com [Accessed on: 8 March 2024]

[2307]Wailzer, A [2024] *Spanish bishop calls on Vatican to withdraw Fiducia Supplicans due to 'chaos' it created* [Online] Available at: www.lifesitenews.com [Accessed on: 11 March 2024]

[2308]Tornielli, A [2024] *Fiducia Supplicans: Non-liturgical blessings, and Pope Benedict's distinction* [Online] Available at: www.vaticannews.va [Accessed on: 11 March 2024]

... to an "irregular" couple that approaches a priest or a deacon does not imply and cannot represent in any way an approval of the union between the two' is a gratuitous assertion and obviously false. FS may say this, but it cannot clarify that this is the case, since it obviously isn't the case![2309]

On the 4th March, the US Catholic newspaper *National Catholic Register* published an essay by former Vatican theologian Monsignor Nicola Bux challenging *Vatican News'* defence of the 'orthodoxy' of *Fiducia Supplicans*. Monsignor But wrote:

> The aim of the article was to assert that distinguishing between rituals inserted into liturgical books and pastoral or spontaneous prayers is the same criterion now being used to admit the possibility of blessing irregular couples. The article juxtaposes the recent Declaration with some passages from the Vatican instruction *Ardens Felicitatis*, promulgated by Cardinal Joseph Ratzinger and the Congregation for the Doctrine of the Faith on Sept. 14, 2000. That document concerned prayers and how they can obtain healing from God, and it arose from the need to bring order to the confusion of those years about prayer gatherings and the charism of healing. However, the comparison that the Vatican News article makes between these two documents is completely wrong. Firstly, it's important to point out that prayer is an insistent request, as the word itself indicates, while a blessing is a formula of approval (*bene dicere*) from above, that is, from God. In the 2000 Instruction, it explains that the goal of prayers for healing is to invoke deliverance from bodily and spiritual evil, and it stresses that no prayer can be made to God to confirm the state of sin into which one had fallen [....] A blessing is not compatible with a state of sin: One cannot bless that which breaks, consumes, destroys. To which sacrament, therefore, is the blessing of an irregular couple ordered? It is not true that blessing promotes and justifies nothing, because it implicitly promotes 'disordered acts' and a pseudo union [....] there is no such thing as a blessing that is not liturgical, when it is made by an ordained minister, who exercises the *munus sanctificandi* with and in the sacred liturgy, on behalf of the Church. The *Vatican News* article, therefore, is misleading and constitutes a shameless falsification, perhaps with the intent to please the court.[2310]

29th February

The Italian Catholic news website *Daily Compass* published a document written by a member of the Sacred College of Cardinals under the name 'Demos II' outlining the grave problems inherent in Pope Francis' pontificate and outlining the challenges for the next pontificate. By writing under the name 'Demos II' the anonymous cardinal was honouring 'Demos I' who had penned an earlier critique and was later revealed to be Cardinal George Pell. Demos II wrote the following about the weaknesses and failings of Pope Francis' pontificate:

> Its shortcomings are equally obvious: an autocratic, at times seemingly vindictive, style of governance; a carelessness in matters of law; an intolerance for even respectful disagreement; and – most seriously – a pattern of ambiguity in matters of faith and morals causing confusion among the faithful. Confusion breeds division and conflict. It undermines confidence in the Word of God. It weakens evangelical witness. And the result today is a Church more fractured than at any time in her recent history.

> The task of the next pontificate must therefore be one of recovery and reestablishment of truths that have been slowly obscured or lost among many Christians. These include but are not limited to such basics as the following: (a) no one is saved except through, and *only* through, Jesus Christ, as he himself made clear; (b) God is merciful but also just, and is intimately concerned with every human life, He forgives but He also holds us accountable, He is both Saviour and Judge; (c) man is God's creature, not a self-

---

[2309]Haynes, M [2024] *Theologians reject Vatican News' use of Ratzinger, John Paul II to defend Fiducia Supplicans* [Online] Available at: www.lifesitenews.com [Accessed on: 11 March 2024]
[2310]Bux, N [2024] *'Non-Liturgical' Blessings Do Not Exist* [Online] Available at: www.ncregister.com [Accessed on: 11 March 2024]

invention, a creature not merely of emotion and appetites but also of intellect, free will, and an eternal destiny; (d) unchanging objective truths about the world and human nature exist and are knowable through Divine Revelation and the exercise of reason; (e) God's Word, recorded in Scripture, is reliable and has permanent force; (f) sin is real and its effects are lethal; and (g) his Church has both the authority and the duty to 'make disciples of all nations.' The failure to joyfully embrace that work of missionary, salvific love has consequences. As Paul wrote in I Corinthians 9:16, 'woe to me if I do not preach the Gospel' [....]

Ambiguity is neither evangelical nor welcoming. Rather, it breeds doubt and feeds schismatic impulses. The Church is a community not just of Word and sacrament, but also of creed. What we believe helps to define and sustain us. Thus, doctrinal issues are not burdens imposed by unfeeling 'doctors of the law.' Nor are they cerebral sideshows to the Christian life. On the contrary, they're vital to living a Christian life authentically, because they deal with applications of the truth, and the truth demands clarity, not ambivalent nuance. From the start, the current pontificate has resisted the evangelical force and intellectual clarity of its immediate predecessors. The dismantling and repurposing of Rome's John Paul II Institute for Studies on Marriage and Family and the marginalising of texts like *Veritatis Splendor* suggest an elevation of 'compassion' and emotion at the expense of reason, justice, and truth. For a creedal community, this is both unhealthy and profoundly dangerous.[2311]

During an interview with the Spanish Catholic news site, *Info Vaticana*, Bishop Mutsaerts, auxiliary of 's-Hertogenbosch, Holland, stated that *Fiducia Supplicans* was the most opposed papal declaration in the history of the Church. Bishop Mutsaerts stated:

The *Fiducia Supplicans* is also problematic. Can a priest bless sinners? Obviously yes. Can he bless sin? Obviously not. It is at this point where *FS* misses the point. *FS* says that homosexual unions can be blessed. This is a doctrine contrary to the teachings of the Catholic Church. *FS* generated a lot of controversy. It doesn't help that Cardinal Fernández makes an artificial distinction between 'couple' and 'union' in response to criticism. A priest can bless the 'couple', but not the 'union', which makes no sense. At the end of the day it is a couple because there is union. What also doesn't help is Pope Francis' claim that priests in prisons can also bless major criminals. Yes, they can, but we do not bless their activities. I can bless thieves, but not their activities. I can bless homosexuals, but not their union. I do not rule out that Pope Francis takes new steps in the direction he has taken. But we also know that where there is no continuity there is a break with tradition. We haven't seen that before in 2,000 years. That there is a break with Tradition may be evident by the resistance. In 2000 years, we have never seen so many people – not even an entire continent – oppose a Roman Declaration.[2312]

1st March

Russia's Catholic bishops and members of the Russian Orthodox Church's Biblical-Theological commission (CCER) issued a statement sharply criticising *Fiducia Supplicans*. The CCER statement emphatically warned,

In order to avoid temptation and confusion, CCER draws attention to the fact that the blessing of any kind of couples who persist in unregulated relationships (cohabiting, co-marital, same-sex) is unacceptable.[2313]

7th March

The Coptic Orthodox Church issued a statement following a plenary session of its Holy Synod criticising *Fiducia Supplicans* and suspending theological dialogue with the Catholic Church. The Statement declared:

[2311]Demos II [2024] *A profile of the next Pope, writes Cardinal* [Online] Available at: www.newdailycompass.com [Accessed on: 8 March 2024]

[2312]Arias, J [2024] *Bishop Mutsaerts: 'In 2000 Years, We Have Never Seen So Many People Oppose A Roman Declaration'* [Online] Available at: www.complicitclergy.com [Accessed on: 11 March 2024]

[2313]Pentin, E [2024] *Orthodox and Catholic Prelates in Russia Sharply Criticize 'Fiducia Supplicans'* [Available at: www.ncregister.com [Accessed on: 11 February 2024]

After consultation with the sister churches of the Eastern Orthodox family, it was decided to suspend the theological dialogue with the Catholic Church, re-evaluate the results that the dialogue has achieved since its beginning twenty years ago, and establish new standards and mechanisms for the dialogue to proceed [….] The Coptic Orthodox Church affirms its firm position of rejecting all forms of homosexual relationships, because they violate the Holy Bible and the law by which God created man male and female, and it considers that any blessing, whatever its type, for such relationships is a blessing for sin, and this is unacceptable.[2314]

12th March

On the second anniversary of his irregular removal as Bishop of Arecibo, Monsignor Daniel Fernández warned fellow bishops that if they failed to reject *Fiducia Supplicans* they risked incurring the curse of God, quoting Malachi 2:1-9:

> With deep sadness and immense pain, I am aware of the scandal and great suffering that many brothers and sisters are experiencing. The Declaration *Fiducia Supplicans*, including the Note to help clarify its reception, contributes to a situation of doubt, ambiguity, and confusion in the Church. It is contradictory, not only with the Church's perennial pastoral practice but also in its attempt to maintain that these 'couples' can be blessed without blessing the very thing that constitutes them as a 'couple,' which is their union or relationship. Two years ago, the then-Congregation for the Doctrine of the Faith clearly explained that sin cannot be blessed. During Lent, we recall that Jesus gave His life on the Cross to overcome sin, not to bless it, to save the sinner with His mercy and bring about their conversion. Even if it is interpreted differently through argumentative acrobatics, the recent Declaration does not refer to individual persons but to 'couples' in a state of sin. In this way, it seeks to permit a 'pastoral' action that contradicts Catholic doctrine. [*trans*].[2315]

The German bishops' news outlet *katholish.de* posted an interview with the openly homosexual provincial superior of the German Franciscans, Friar Markus Fuhrmann, during which he argued for the reversal of the Church's doctrine regarding homosexuality. In response to the statement, '*There are still voices saying that homosexuality is a sin…*' the provincial superior of the German Franciscans responded, ignoring Scripture and Traditions condemnation of homosexual sex acts:

> Yes, there are still people who say that homosexuality is a sin, a disease, or a developmental flaw. They usually justify this with natural law or the order of creation, claiming they can define what is 'natural' or 'in accordance with creation.' I would counter: Such derogatory and discriminatory statements neither do justice to the lived reality and experiences of queer people nor align with the current state of human scientific, sexual-ethical, and exegetical discussions. Nobody chooses their sexual orientation or gender identity. Many people are gifted by God with heterosexuality, and some people are homosexual or bisexual, trans or non-binary — they are queerly gifted. This shows the wonderful diversity of God's creation.[2316]

13th March

Cardinal Timothy Dolan of New York posted a video on the social media platform X during which he equated Easter with the Islamic season of Ramadan and the Jewish Passover:

[2314]*Coptic Orthodox Church Synod Rejects Same-Sex Relations, Suspends Dialogue with Catholics* [2024] [Online] Available at: www.ocpsociety.org [Accessed on: 11 March 2024]

[2315]*Mons. Daniel Fernández, obispo cesado por el Papa hace dos años, se pronuncia sobre Fiducia supplicans: «Contradice la doctrina católica»* [2024] [Online] Available at: infovaticana.com [Accessed on: 6 May 2025]

[2316]*Franziskanerprovinzial: Keiner muss sich im Kloster outen* [2024] [Online] Available at: katholisch. de [Accessed on: 6 May 2025]

Does it dawn on you that Lent and Ramadan and Passover always occur close to each other? They all always happen within two or three weeks apart, and you wonder why. The why is because they all take place in the spring, and the spring is the time of rebirth. Spring is the time of triumph of light and life, and that, of course, is what Good Friday and Easter Sunday is about, that's what Passover is about, that's what Ramadan is about; the renewal of God's life within us that we actually share in God's constantly reinvigorating power in the world, as we see in nature during spring. So, Ramadan, Passover, Holy Week, and Easter, it's all sort of a supernatural springtime.[2317]

Archbishop William Lori of Baltimore announced that the Vatican indult allowing a diocesan traditional Latin Mass in his archdiocese would expire in August and that, therefore, the sole Latin Mass would be offered by the Priestly Fraternity of St. Peter. Archbishop Lori wrote:

After much careful and prayerful consideration, I have discerned that for the pastoral good of all the faithful of the Archdiocese of Baltimore, the celebration of the liturgical rites and pastoral care according to the Missal of 1962 within the Archdiocese of Baltimore on or after Aug 1, 2024 will be entrusted solely to the Priestly Fraternity of St. Peter (FSSP) at the National Shrine of St. Alphonsus Liguori in Baltimore.[2318]

14th March

During a press conference on the Synod on Synodality, pro-homosexuality Cardinal Hollerich, the Relator General of the Synod on Synodality, praised *Fiducia Supplicans* for permitting the 'blessing' of adulterous unions and homosexual pairings:

I find it very beautiful because it means God loves everyone including those in irregular situations. It's truly a pastoral document, it isn't a doctrinal document. I think what the CDF with the authority of the Pope have already decided is not something we should go back and discuss in the Synod.[2319]

Fr. Daniel Klimek posted his *YouTube* interview with Bishop Athanasius Schneider, the auxiliary bishop of Astana, Kazakhstan, during which His Lordship condemned the promulgation of *Fiducia Supplicans* because it 'promotes sin' and therefore is an 'abuse of the magisterial power'. Bishop Schneider warned that Pope Francis was

abusing his powers to undermine the Catholic Faith. This is against his task, against the nature of the papacy and I have so much compassion for him really as my brother who must one day answer this before the Judgement of God. It is really serious and therefore I have compassion with his soul and pray and admonish him that he may repent.

Commenting on the rejection of Fiducia Supplicans by the majority of African bishops, many other bishops around the world, and the Russian Orthodox Church, Bishop Schneider observed:

This is an evident sign that this document is inacceptable (sic) in itself to everyone who still uses his reason, who still has common sense. It's simply against common sense. It is evidently a blessing of sin. It is a very cunning form, it is vested in, closed in a very cunning sophist form, and bishops and other Church leaders who use their reason, they will say 'no you cannot fool us, you cannot take us for idiots — this is a blessing for sin'. You can say what you want, you make mental acrobatics, it is stated blessing of homosexual couples… saying that you're blessing the couple but not the relationship is a deception and an insult to our reason. And we will not accept such a huge insult to our reason, a huge lie and cunning. It is so unworthy for bishops of the Catholic Church

---

[2317]Wailzer, A [2024] *Cardinal Dolan equates Easter with Ramadan, Passover, says all are about 'triumph of light and life'* [Online] Available at: www.lifesitenews.com [Accessed on: 6 May 2025]
[2318]Mangiaracina, E [2024] *Baltimore archbishop says Latin Mass will be suppressed at all parishes, FSSP Mass will continue* [Online] Available at: www.lifesitenews.com [Accessed on: 9 May 2025]
[2319]Haynes, M [2024] *Cardinal Hollerich says he thinks Pope Francis' text on homosexual 'blessings' is 'very beautiful'* [Online] Available at: www.lifesitenews.com [Accessed on: 5 May 2025]

to do such a document that is promoting sin and sin against nature, sodomy, and other adultery.[2320]

17th March

KTO, the French-language Catholic television channel, broadcast an interview with Cardinal Fridolin Ambongo, appointed archbishop of Kinshasa in 2018 by Pope Francis. Cardinal Ambongo criticised *Fiducia Supplicans* as a from of 'western imperialism':

> Personally, I think that what surprised and shocked us the most was the way in which the text was published. I believe that if we had consulted beforehand, if we had analysed *Fiducia Supplicans* in the spirit of synodality, perhaps we could have presented it in a different form and with a different tone, taking into account the sensitivies of others.[2321]

26th March

Cardinal Gerhard Müller, former Prefect of the CDF, criticised *Fiducia Supplicans* as a 'propaganda trick' not a genuine act of pastoral care towards homosexual persons:

> Behind *Fiducia Supplicans* there is nothing to do with the pastoral [care] for these persons of so-called same-sex attraction, but it is only a propaganda trick to show 'we are not against this worldwide movement of LGBT and we must make a certain concession that we will not be so attacked by them as a counterpart.'[2322]

His Eminence also criticised the Synod of Synodality for seeking to change the nature of the Church into a worldly health organisation:

> This is a reduction of the Church not to be the instrument and the sign, the sacrament for the deep communion of us with God in love, and to be the instrument for the unity of the mankind in Jesus Christ: they want to change the Church to another worldly health organisation like an NGO. That is absolutely wrong, and therefore neither the Synod of Synodality nor this Synodal Path, can [be permitted to] have this agenda, this program for changing the essence of the Church in an inner-worldly helped organisation.[2323]

21st March

Corriere del Ticino, the Italian-language Swiss daily newspaper, published comments in favour of woman deacons made by Cardinal Mario Grech, the Secretary General of the Synod of Bishops appointed by Pope Francis in 2020. Cardinal Grech said,

> The female diaconate and a different space for women in the Church are a natural deepening of the Lord's will, they express and demonstrate the dynamism inherent in the history of the Church.[2324]

22nd March

The Holy See Press Office issued a joint statement from the German Bishops' Conference and the Holy See about their discussions regarding cooperation between the heterodox *Der Synodale Weg* and Pope Francis Synod on Synodality. *Der Synodale Weg* had voted to implement changes to the Church's doctrine on sexual ethics to accept homosexual sex acts, masturbation, contraception, as well as the blessing of homosexual pairings and the 'ordination' of woman. The statement announced:

[2320]Klimek, D [2024] *Interview w/Bishop Schneider: 'Peter is sleeping while Judas is awake'* [Online] Available at: www.youtube.com [Accessed on: 5 May 2025]

[2321]Kokx, S [2024] *Top African cardinal: Pope's homosexual blessings document was seen as 'Western imperialism'* [Online] Available at: www.lifesitenews.com [Accessed on: 6 May 2025]

[2322]Haynes, M [2024] *EXCLUSIVE: Cardinal Müller calls Pope Francis' homosexual 'blessings' an attack on marriage* [Online] Available at: www.lifesitenews.com [Accessed on: 5 May 2025]

[2323]Haynes, M [2024] *EXCLUSIVE: Cardinal Müller slams synodal 'ideology' trying to turn the Church into an 'NGO'* [Online] Available at: www.lifesitenews.com [Accessed on: 5 May 2025]

[2324]Haynes, M [2024] *Top Synod cardinal says 'female deacons' are a 'natural deepening of the Lord's will'* [Online] Available at: www.lifesitenews.com [Accessed on: 6 May 2025]

Today's meeting, which lasted the entire day, was characterized by a positive and constructive atmosphere. Some of the open theological questions raised in the documents of the Synodal Path of the Catholic Church in Germany were discussed. As in the synthesis report of the World Synod in October 2023, differences and points of agreement were identified. A regular exchange between representatives of the German Bishops' Conference and the Holy See regarding the further work of the Synodal Path and the Synodal Committee was agreed upon. [Trans].[2325]

In an interview with the Austrian news outlet *kath.net*, Cardinal Gerhard Müller, former Prefect of the CDF, criticised the very notion of negotiations between the German bishops and the Holy See:

The absurdity of German bishops, as successors of the apostles, coming to Rome to the successor of St. Peter to negotiate faith and morals as if the Church's teachings were an offer to be sold to the highest bidder in the supermarket of ideologies is unfathomable. Instead of this disgraceful showdown at the negotiating table between worldly potentates, those involved should remember that the Church is not their property, but the flock of God, in which they are appointed by Christ in the Holy Spirit as shepherds (Acts 20:28) and teachers of the Word of God and not of man-made doctrines of salvation.[2326]

Archbishop Carlo Maria Viganò, the former papal nuncio to the USA, posted on the social media platform X a strongly worded rebuke of Bishop Powers of Diocese of Superior for allowing the desecration of his cathedral by a pagan ritual. Bishop Powers was appointed by Pope Francis in 2015. Concerning the pagan blessing at the cathedral's altar, Archbishop Viganò wrote,

The shamanic ceremony at the beginning of the function constitutes a sacrilegious act that desecrates the Cathedral of the diocese of Superior (WI) on the very day on which the Holy Chrism is consecrated. This makes Bishop Powers, present at the rite, responsible for a very serious sacrilege and for the scandal caused to those present. This is not a Successor of the Apostles, but a servant of Freemasonry. The way he celebrates Mass reveals his total alienation from the Divine Mysteries. A squalid official of the ecumenical religion, a dutiful executor of Santa Marta's wishes. [Pope Francis' place of residence].

Deacon Nick Donnelly likewise remarked on X, 'The heresy of Bergoglianism in six words: Latin Mass banned; Pagan rituals encouraged.'[2327]

28th March

For the first time, Pope Francis washed the feet of 12 women during the Maundy Thursday Mandatum ceremony, continuing the break with Tradition that only men's feet are washed because they represent the 12 male apostles. Pope Francis altered the Church's liturgy in 2016 to allow the washing of women's feet. Bishop Schneider commented:

This Holy Mass celebrates the commemoration of the institution of the sacraments of the Eucharist and the Priesthood. Therefore, the foot washing of women along with the men not only distracts from the main focus on Eucharist and on Priesthood, but generates confusion regarding the historical symbolism of the 'twelve' and of the apostles being of male sex. The universal tradition of the Church never allowed the foot washing during the Holy Mass, but instead outside of Mass, in a special ceremony. By the way: the public washing and usually also kissing of the feet of women on the part

---

[2325]*Comunicato congiunto della Santa Sede e della Conferenza Episcopale Tedesca, 22.03.2024* [Online] Available at: press.vatican.va [Accessed on: 6 May 2025]
[2326]Wailzer, A [2024] *Cardinal Müller slams 'disgraceful' Vatican meeting with German bishops to 'negotiate faith and morals'* [Online] Available at: www.lifesitenews.com [Accessed on: 6 May 2025]
[2327]Kokx, S [2024] *'Servant of Freemasonry': Viganò rebukes bishop who approved pagan ritual before Mass at cathedral* [Online] Available at: www.lifesitenews.com [Accessed on: 6 May 2025]

of a man, in our case, of a priest or a bishop, is considered by every person of common sense in all cultures as being improper and even indecent. Thanks be to God no priest or bishop is obliged to wash publicly the feet of women on Holy Thursday, for there is no binding norm for it, and the foot washing itself is only facultative.[2328]

3rd April

The Spanish publisher *Editorial Planeta* released the book length interview of *Pope Francis, Papa Francisco. El sucesor: Mis recuerdos de Benedicto XVI* [Pope Francis. The Successor: My Memories of Benedict XVI]. In his interview Pope Francis condemned Archbishop Georg Gänswein, the former private secretary of Pope Benedict XVI, for publishing his book *Nothing but the Truth* (12th January 2023) which contained criticisms of Pope Francis, saying Gänswein lacked 'nobility and humanity.'

Peter Seewald, the biographer of Pope Benedict XVI, disputed Pope Francis' claim in the interview that there existed a 'cordial relationship between himself and Pope Benedict XVI:

> From the very beginning, Bergoglio wanted to break away from the continuity of the popes, to challenge the traditional, to shake things up or simply to cause 'chaos,' as he says in the new book by Javier Martinez-Brocal. He describes traditional forms as a 'nostalgic illness.' He demonstratively showed who is the master of the house by abolishing Benedict's liberalised approach to the Old Mass. The Pope Emeritus found out about this from the newspaper. So much for the allegedly 'cordial relationship' between the two.

Also during the interview Pope Francis criticised orthodox Cardinal Robert Sarah, the former prefect for the Sacred Congregation for Divine Worship and the Discipline of the Sacraments:

> Maybe I made a mistake in naming (Cardinal Sarah) prefect of the now-Dicastery for Divine Worship. From there he was manipulated by separatist groups, but he is a good man. At times I have the impression that working in the Roman Curia made him a little bitter.[2329]

Bishop Ivo Muser of the Italian diocese of Bozen-Brixen announced that the Vatican's Dicastery for Culture and Education had reversed its block on the appointment of the pro-LGBT Fr. Martin Lintner as dean of theology at Brixen's influential Philosophical-Theological College. In 2023 the Vatican refused to make the approval 'due to Prof. Lintner's publications on issues of Catholic sexual morality.' Fr. Martin Lintner advocates for the abandonment of Catholic doctrine regarding homosexuality and homosexual sex acts, writing, 'The unconditional condemnation of a homosexual relationship as sinful is obviously not the last word of the Church on this issue.'[2330]

8th April

Pro-homosexuality Cardinal Victor Manuel Fernández, the prefect for the Dicastery for the Doctrine of the Faith, issued the Declaration *Dignitas Infinita*, on human dignity, signed by Pope Francis. As well as bizarrely ascribing the divine attribute of infinity to mortal, contingent man, *Dignitas Infinita* made the novel and erroneous claim that,

> Every human person possesses an infinite dignity, inalienably grounded in his or her very being, which prevails in and beyond every circumstance, state, or situation the person may ever encounter. (Para 1).

[2328]Haynes, M [2024] *Pope Francis washes feet of 12 women, continuing 2016 'innovation' in Holy Thursday liturgy* [Online] Available at: www.lifesitenews.com [Accessed on: 5 May 2025]
[2329]Wailzer, A [2024] *Pope Francis slams Archbishop Gänswein for 'lack of nobility and humanity' over Benedict XVI book; Benedict XVI biographer pushes back on Pope Francis' claim they had a 'cordial relationship'; Pope Francis says appointing Cardinal Sarah to Roman Curia may have been 'a mistake'* [Online] Available at: www.lifesitenews.com [Accessed on: 8 May 2025]
[2330]Haynes, M [2024] *Vatican backtracks, approves pro-homosexual priest as theology dean at Italian college* [Online] Available at: www.lifesitenews.com [Accessed on: 9 May 2025]

The declaration employed the erroneous idea that man possesses an 'infinite dignity' to propose an inviolable ontological dignity separate and distinct from three other types of violable, contingent dignities — moral dignity, social dignity, and existential dignity. Ignoring the doctrine of original sin and fallen man's concupiscent nature, Pope Francis proposed that man possesses an inviolable, infinite dignity that transcends moral circumstances, thereby relativising the gravity of sin, a consistent theme of his pontificate.[2331]

During the press conference for the launch of *Dignitas Infinita* Cardinal Fernández issued a call for the doctrinal description of homosexual sex acts as 'intrinsically disordered' to be changed,

> [the phrase in question is a] strong expression that should be explained, it would be good if we could find an expression that is even clearer. What we wish to say is that the beauty of the encounter between man and woman which is the greatest difference, is the most beautiful. The fact that they can meet, be together, and that from this encounter new life can be born, this is something which cannot be compared with anything else. So before this, homosexual acts have this characteristic that they cannot in any way match this great beauty. This expression may also be conveyed in other words that may be more appropriate to convey this mystery.[2332]

The Declaration *Dignitas Infinita* also re-iterated Pope Francis' rejection of the use of the death penalty, in contradiction to Sacred Scripture and Tradition:

> Here, one should also mention the death penalty, for this also violates the inalienable dignity of every person, regardless of the circumstances. In this regard, we must recognise that 'the firm rejection of the death penalty shows to what extent it is possible to recognise the inalienable dignity of every human being and to accept that he or she has a place in this universe. If I do not deny that dignity to the worst of criminals, I will not deny it to anyone. I will give everyone the possibility of sharing this planet with me, despite all our differences.' (*DI* 34).

Bishop Marian Eleganti, emeritus auxiliary bishop of Chur, Switzerland, criticised Pope Francis and Cardinal Fernández for contradicting divine revelation:

> Pope Francis and his protégé and ghostwriter, Cardinal Fernández, are moving away from tradition with their position and are taking on great Catholic scholars who have thought differently in this regard and have justified the traditional doctrine of just war and the death penalty with criteria based on justice in a rational way bound by the theology of revelation.[2333]

9th April

Cardinal Robert Sarah, the former prefect for the Congregation for Divine Worship and the Discipline of the Sacraments, delivered an address to the bishops of Cameroon, praising them for rejecting the pro-homosexuality declaration, *Fiducia Supplicans*:

> Dear brother Bishops of Cameroon, in your courageous and prophetic declaration of December 21st regarding homosexuality and the blessing of 'homosexual couples,' by recalling Catholic doctrine on this matter, you have greatly and deeply served the unity of the Church! You have performed a work of pastoral charity by proclaiming the truth.

Cardinal Sarah went on to challenge the narrative spread by Pope Francis[2334] and Cardinal Fridolin Ambongo[2335] that the African bishops rejected *Fiducia Supplicans*

[2331]Dicastery for the Doctrine of the Faith [2024] Declaration *Dignitas Infinita,* para 1 [Online] Available at: www.press.vatican.va [Accessed on: 16 April 2024]

[2332]Haynes, M [2024] *Cardinal Fernández calls for change to Catholic condemnation of homosexuality as 'intrinsically disordered'* [Online] Available at: www.lifesitenews.com [Accessed on: 8 May 2025]

[2333]Eleganti, M [2024] *Bishop Eleganti: Pope Francis' Dignitas Infinita contradicts Church doctrine on the death penalty, war* [Online] Available at: www.lifesitenews.com [Accessed on: 14 May 2025]

[2334]*Pope says Africans are 'special case' when it comes to LGBT blessings* [2024] [Online] Available at: www.reuters.com [Accessed on: 9 May 202]

because the African people were 'too simple' and 'not ready' for such sophisticated teaching:

> Some in the West have tried to suggest that you acted in the name of an African cultural particularism. This is false and ridiculous to attribute such motives to you! Some have claimed, in a logic of intellectual neo-colonialism, that Africans are 'not yet' ready to bless homosexual couples for cultural reasons—as if the West were ahead of a supposedly backward Africa. No! You spoke on behalf of the entire Church: 'in the name of the truth of the Gospel and for the sake of human dignity and the salvation of all humanity in Jesus Christ.' You spoke in the name of the one Lord, the one faith of the Church. Since when has the truth of the faith, the teaching of the Gospel, been subject to particular cultures? This vision of a faith adapted to cultures reveals the extent to which relativism divides and corrupts the unity of the Church. [*trans*].

Cardinal Sarah also warned his brother African bishops of the dangers posed by the upcoming Synod on Synodality in October 2024:

> Dear brother Bishops, this is a point of great vigilance to keep in mind for the upcoming session of the Synod. We know that some, even if they claim otherwise, will defend a reform agenda there. Among these is the destructive idea that the truth of the faith should be received differently depending on places, cultures, and peoples. This idea is merely a disguise for the dictatorship of relativism, so strongly denounced by Benedict XVI. It aims to allow deviations from doctrine and morality in certain places under the pretext of cultural adaptation. They would like to permit female deacons in Germany, married priests in Belgium, and confusion between the ordained priesthood and the baptismal priesthood in the Amazon. Some recently appointed theological experts do not hide their agendas. And so, with false kindness, they will say to you: 'Rest assured, in Africa, we will not impose such innovations on you. You are not culturally ready.' [*trans*].[2336]

13th April

Bishop Ludger Schepers of Essen, Germany, 'commissioned' thirteen women during Mass as 'deacons in the spirit', following a three-year 'female deacons' training program with the 'Women's Diaconate Network.' During his homily, which he delivered jointly with Sister Edith-Maria Magar, Bishop Schepers called for the recognition of women as deacons, emphasising 'that women are also called. Women rightly felt discriminated against in the Church and excluded with their calling.'[2337]

23rd April

During his address to the New York Men's Leadership Forum Cardinal Burke, the former prefect of the Supreme Tribunal of the Apostolic Signatura, condemned the practice of giving Holy Communion to pro-abortion politicians, as facilitated by Pope Francis and a number of US bishops:

> This is what is referred to as scandal. The fact that politicians, and I don't need to mention any names, it's too evident, who claim to be devout Catholics and who publicly promote an abomination like procured abortion or this transgender agenda or whatever else it may be, and they approach for Communion and are given Holy Communion – (it) scandalizes people. It gives the impression that the Church has changed its teaching with regard to these crimes, these previous sins, and it leads people to be very lax in their own conscience. You can imagine if somebody who is a pro-abortionist is receiving Holy Communion freely, are people going to be inclined to examine their consciences

[2335]*African Church 'in communion with Pope' but no blessing of same-sex couples* [2024] [Online] Available at: www.vaticannews.va [Accessed on: 9 May 202]
[2336]Magister, S [2024] *Au prochain Synode, ce sera l'Afrique qui fera barrage aux novateurs. Et le cardinal Sarah dicte la ligne directrice* [Online] Available at: www.diakonos.be [Accessed on: 9 May 202]
[2337]Haynes, M [2024] *German prelate commissions 13 female 'deacons in the spirit' with support of bishops' conference head* [Online] Available at: www.lifesitenews.com [Accessed on: 9 May 2025]

as they should, before they approach to receive the Sacrament? It dulls consciences. Today we can't take anything for granted because we're dealing with six or seven decades of poor catechesis. Many Catholics today, not through their own fault, don't know their own faith. Some express surprise that the Church has a teaching with regard the reception of Holy Communion.[2338]

24th April

Joseph Strickland, Emeritus Bishop of Tyler, Texas, posted a statement on the social media platform X, regretting not being 'strong enough' when in 2018 he addressed the United States Conference of Catholic Bishops concerning the Theodore McCarrick homosexual predation scandal. Bishop Strickland went on to question the integrity and fidelity of his fellow bishops:

> When I spoke to the bishops in that hotel ballroom in Baltimore I had no idea how many of those shepherds disagreed with me. Those who agreed that we can't allow priests or any one else to be welcomed to Catholic events as they deny Catholic teaching chose to remain silent and leave their flocks abandoned and confused. Too many of the bishops who share the mandate to guard the deposit of faith act as if they do not believe basic teachings of the Church and actively seek to change and undermine scripture and the Catechism.

Bishop Strickland went on to enumerate the betrayals of the faithful at the hands of the Vatican and the bishops:

> The litany of the gospel of wolves that has flowed out of the Vatican and gone unchecked over these 5+ years, has left many souls to wander in darkness and succumb to lies that destroy faith. To name a few…who demanded a real accounting of the McCarrick scandal and discipline for those who allowed his attacks on the faith? Who spoke up when the pachamama idol was paraded in St Peter's basilica? Who resisted when fear of a disease allowed churches to be closed and the sacraments to be denied? Who demanded that our God given free will must be respected when mandates were issued by too many leaders? Who protested a synod on synodality that promoted an openness to blessing sin? Who has said no to the ongoing attack on the liturgy? Who has protested when faithful priests, bold enough to speak the truth, bold enough to care more about the salvation of souls than keeping their position, have been cancelled or silenced?[2339]

Members of the Australian Catholic Medical Association published a research paper criticising the errors in the Pontifical Academy for Life's book *Etica Teologica Della Vita* [Theological Ethics of Life] (2023). The group of medical experts, bioethicists, and theologians set out the ways in which sections of *Etica Teologica Della Vita* 'contain statements which deviate from and contradict accepted Catholic teaching on contraception and ART [assisted reproductive technologies].' The Catholic experts observe that a 'thorough up-to-date knowledge and understanding of suitable current alternatives to contraception and ART (e.g. in-vitro fertilisation, IVF) which are safe, effective, readily accessible and consistent with Catholic ethics appears to be lacking.'[2340]

1st May

Pro-homosexuality Sister Jeannine Gramick, SL, recipient of many public signs of favour from Pope Francis, published the Supreme Pontiff's confusing clarification to her concerns about *Dignitas Infinita's* criticism of gender ideology. Sister Jeannine

[2338]Haynes, M [2024] *Cardinal Burke condemns 'persecution' of Latin Mass, 'scandal' of Communion for pro-abortion politicians* [Online] Available at: www.lifesitenews.com [Accessed on: 9 May 2025]
[2339]Strickland, J [2024] *Post on X, 1:35 PM · Apr 24, 2024, from Texas, USA* [Online] Available at: x.com//BishStrickland [Accessed on: 9 May 2025]
[2340]Wailzer, A [2024] *Catholic experts slam book by Pope Francis' Pontifical Academy for Life as 'misleading,' unscientific* [Online] Available at: www.lifesitenews.com [Accessed on: 15 May 2025]

Gramick had been censured in 1999 by the CDF for her ministry to homosexual persons for disseminating 'ambiguities and errors' that caused confusion among Catholics and harmed the Church. Pope Francis wrote to Sr. Gramick:

> Gender ideology is something other than homosexual or transsexual people. Gender ideology makes everyone equal without respect for personal history. I understand the concern about that paragraph in Dignitas Infinita, but it refers not to transgender people but to gender ideology, which nullifies differences. Transgender people must be accepted and integrated into society.[2341]

2nd May

A group of catholic academics and laity issued a statement accusing Pope Francis of causing 'an unprecedented crisis in the Catholic Church', stating 'the members of the hierarchy of the Church have a duty to act in order to prevent Francis from causing further harm.' The statement concluded:

> We therefore call for Pope Francis to resign the papal office, and to repent and do penance for his actions. If he does not do this, we request that the cardinals and bishops of the Catholic Church ask Pope Francis to resign the office of pope.

Signatories of the call for the resignation of Pope Francis included: Dr. Peter A. Kwasniewski, Dr. John R.T. Lamont, Dr. John Rist, John-Henry Westen, Elizabeth F. Yore & Dr. John Zmirak.[2342]

8th May

The German newspaper *Rheinische Post* published an interview with Bishop Ludger Schepers, an auxiliary bishop for the Diocese of Essen. During the interview Bishop Ludger Schepers criticised Catholic teaching for 'assuming there is only man and only woman' and demanded changes to the Church's doctrine on sexuality:

> No one can say exactly what is entirely male and what is entirely female. However, Church teaching still assumes that there is only man and only woman, in the language of the Old Testament: only male and only female […] Something has to change in the Catholic Church as a whole when it comes to sexual morality. And that also means, of course, that the Catechism must say different things than it does now. On the one hand, it talks about irregular relationships, but on the other, it says that people should not be discriminated against. That would be a first step if people would at least adhere to the principle of not discriminating against people.[2343]

12th May

The Global Times, owned by the *People's Daily*, the official newspaper of the Central Committee of the Communist Party of China, published an interview with Cardinal Pietro Parolin, Pope Francis' Secretary of State. During his interview Cardinal Parolin alluded to the secret deal between the Vatican and the Chinese communist government,

> The prospect opens up that two ancient, great and sophisticated international entities – like China and the Apostolic See – may become ever more aware of a common responsibility for the grave problems of our time.

Cardinal Parolin went on to praise the Chinese communist party's imposition of 'sinicization' on the Catholic Church in China:

[2341]Gramick, J [2024] *Pope Provides Sr. Jeannine a Clarification of 'Dignitas Infinita'* [Online] www. newwaysministry.org [Accessed on: 14 May 2025]
[2342]*Prominent Catholics urge bishops, cardinals to declare Francis has 'lost the papal office' if he refuses to resign* [2024][Online] [Online] Available at: www.lifesitenews.com [Accessed on: 14 May 2025]
[2343]Wailzer, A [2024] *German bishop attacks Church teaching on there being only two sexes* [Online] Available at: www.lifesitenews.com [Accessed on: 14 May 2025]

Inculturation is an essential condition for a sound proclamation of the Gospel which, in order to bear fruit, requires, on the one hand, safeguarding its authentic purity and integrity and, on the other, presenting it according to the particular experience of each people and culture. These two terms, 'inculturation' and 'sinicization,' refer to each other without confusion and without opposition. For the future, it will certainly be important to deepen this theme, especially the relationship between 'inculturation' and 'sinicization,' keeping in mind how the Chinese leadership has been able to reiterate their willingness not to undermine the nature and the doctrine of each religion.[2344]

Dr. George Weigel, Distinguished Senior Fellow at the Ethics and Public Policy Center, Washington, challenged Cardinal Parolin's conflation of 'sinicization' with inculturation:

What inculturation is not is what is happening in China today. Under the iron rule of the dictator Xi Jinping, the religious policy of the People's Republic of China is 'Sinicization.' The gullible or duplicitous regard this as simply another form of inculturation. 'Sinicization' is anything but that: It's the perverse inversion of inculturation, rightly understood. Catholic faith in China must be conformed to 'Xi Jinping Thought' [...]A true inculturation of the Gospel in China would call China and the despotic regime that currently controls it to conversion.[2345]

17th May

During his interview with the Swiss Catholic outlet *kath.ch*, Cardinal Jean-Claude Hollerich again claimed that Catholic doctrine on male-only priesthood 'can be changed'. Cardinal Hollerich was elevated to the Sacred College of Cardinals in 2019 by Pope Francis and appointed the Relator General of the Synod on Synodality. In response to the question, *Do you think Pope Francis will introduce the ordination of women?* Cardinal Hollerich replied:

This is very hard to say. The Pope is sometimes good for surprises. But generally, I'd rather say no. Shortly before the Synod, there was a 'dubia' from a few cardinals. They asked whether John Paul II's rejection of women's priesthood is binding for the Church. Francis answered very wisely: It is binding, but not forever. And he also said that theology must continue to discuss it. [*trans*][2346]

Cardinal Fernández, the prefect for the Congregation for the Doctrine of the Faith, issued new norms for determining the authenticity of alleged visions, including Marian apparitions, with the approval of Pope Francis. Entitled *For Proceeding in the Discernment of Alleged Supernatural Phenomena*, new norms marked a radical departure from previous procedures by a priori ruling out the possibility of whether or not an alleged vision was of supernatural origin:

To prevent any further delays in the resolution of a specific case involving an event of alleged supernatural origin, the Dicastery recently proposed to the Holy Father the idea of concluding the discernment process not with a declaration of '*de supernaturalitate*' but with a '*Nihil obstat*,' which would allow the Bishop to draw pastoral benefit from the spiritual phenomenon. The idea of concluding with a declaration of 'Nihil obstat' was reached after assessing the various spiritual and pastoral fruits of the event and finding no substantial negative elements in it. The Holy Father considered this proposal to be a 'right solution.'[2347]

[2344]*'No opposition between sinicization and inculturation' Parolin tells China media* [Online] Available at: www.catholicworldreport.com [Accessed on: 23 May 2025]

[2345]Weigel, G [2024] *'Sinicization' Is Not Inculturation* [Online] Available at: www.ncregister.com [Accessed on: 23 May 2025]

[2346]Straub, J [2024] *Kardinal Hollerich: «Bin dafür, dass Frauen sich in Kirche voll gleichberechtigt fühlen»* [Online] Available at: www.kath.ch [Accessed on: 14 May 2025]

[2347]*For Proceeding in the Discernment of Alleged Supernatural Phenomena* [2024] [Online] Available at: press.vatican.va [Accessed on: 21 May 2025]

The new procedures also diminished the authority of bishops in determining the nature of supernatural phenomena, centralising decision-making powers with the Dicastery for the Doctrine of the Faith:

> …the new Norms also indicate that, in some instances, the Dicastery may intervene *motu proprio* (II, Art. 26). Once a clear determination is made, the new Norms specify that 'the Dicastery, in any case, reserves the right to intervene again depending on the development of the phenomenon in question' (II, Art. 22, § 3) and request the Bishop to continue 'to watch over the phenomenon' (II, Art. 24) for the good of the faithful.

The theologian and Mariologist Dr. Mark Miravalle commented:

> Now, that's a rather significant historical shift. It's basically saying that, at this point, no bishop could make a declaration. So, as we note, [for] Fatima, a local bishop made the declaration. At Lourdes, the local bishop made the declaration […] Now the DDF is saying that only after their approval can a local bishop come up with a *nihil obstat*. In fact, they prohibit a statement on authenticity, specifically, but only *nihil obstat*. And that's the most generous of the six new categories that a bishop can do after the DDF approved. So it's a very significant historic shift indeed. The bishop submits a report to the DDF. The DDF has now a type of sub-commission, let's say six or eight or 10 members of the DDF, and they are now really making the ultimate discernment of any reported phenomena from the five continents. It's a fair question to say, well, is it really good that a smaller group of theologians has more discernment, power, and authority than groups of bishops?[2348]

18th May

During his address to inmates from Verona's Montorio prison Pope Francis again expressed religious indifferentism:

> God is one: our cultures have taught us to call Him by one name, by another, and to find Him in different ways, but He is the same Father of all of us. He is one. And all religions, all cultures, look to the one God in different ways.[2349]

The Supreme Pontiff concluded by saying,

> Now I would like to give you the blessing, but I will give it in silence, so everyone receives it from God in the way they believe. A minute of silence, and I give my blessing to all of you.[2350]

19th May

CBS, the US TV and radio network, broadcast Pope Francis' interview with Norah O'Donnell during which he criticised 'conservative' bishops in response to being asked about those who opposed him:

> A Conservative is one who clings to something and does not want to see beyond that. It is a suicidal attitude because one thing is to take Tradition into account and to consider situations from the past, but quite another is to be closed up inside a dogmatic box.[2351]

25th May

During Pope Francis' inaugural World Children's Day a male drag artist performed for young children. Carmine De Rosa stated that he was officially invited:

[2348]Western, JH [2024] *Downplaying Fatima? Vatican's HUGE shift on Marian apparitions* [Online] Available at: www.lifesitenews.com [Accessed on: 21 May 2025]
[2349]Pope Francis [2024] *Visita Pastorale del Santo Padre Francesco a Verona – Incontro con i Detenuti, 18.05.2024* [Online] press.vatican.va [Accessed on: 14 May 2025]
[2350]Wolfe, R [2024] *Pope Francis gives prisoners silent blessing 'so everyone receives it from God in the way they believe'* [Online] Available at: www.lifesitenews.com [Accessed on: 14 May 2025]
[2351]Haynes, M [2024] *Pope Francis says 'conservative' bishops have 'suicidal attitude' during 60 Minutes interview* [Online] Available at: www.lifesitenews.com [Accessed on: 14 May 2025]

I would like to point out, reading the comments, that I was WANTED at this event FOR THE TYPE OF SHOW I CARRY ON STAGE and for professionalism...But I simply defend MY ART.

Archbishop Carlo Maria Viganó, former papal nuncio to the US, posted on the social media platform X his outrage at the Vatican's inclusion of Carmine De Rosa's drag act:

It is now clear that Bergoglio is one of the main activists of the hellish LGBTQ + agenda. There are no more words to express the scandal and disgust, in the complicit and cowardly silence of the Episcopate. 'Whoever scandalises even one of these little ones who believe in me, it would be better for him if a millstone turned into a donkey's wheel were hung around his neck, and he were cast into the depths of the sea.' (Mt 18:6).[2352]

Furthermore, famous Italian comedian Roberto Benigni told young children at the Vatican's World Children's Day, in the presence of Pope Francis, that there was no purgatory or Hell:

But you, don't be afraid, because there is no such thing as hell, purgatory. There is only heaven, the one you are in now, the realm of childhood, of youth, buzzing with dreams.[2353]

2nd June

The Italian newspaper *Il Messaggero* published Pope Francis' letter to Lorenzo Michele Noè Caruso, an ex-seminarian who expressed distress that the Supreme Pontiff referred to homosexuals in seminaries as 'faggots', claiming that he had been removed from seminary for identifying as a homosexual. Pope Francis wrote:

I was struck by an expression of yours: 'toxic and elective clericalism': and it is true! Do you know that clericalism is a plague? It's an ugly 'worldliness' and, as a great theologian said, 'worldliness is the worst that can happen to the Church, even worse than the era of concubinary popes [...] Jesus calls everyone, everyone. Some people think of the Church as a customs office, and that is bad. The Church must be open to everyone [...] Brother, go ahead with your vocation.[2354]

In response to Pope Francis encouraging a homosexual person to become a priest, Archbishop Carlo Maria Viganó posted on his X social media account:

Bergoglio's goal is to normalise sodomy and all sexual perversion (both among the laity and among the Clergy), destroy the Priesthood itself, and promote the synodal transition from the Mass to celebrations without a priest. His obsessive denunciations of clericalism embody his worst flaws. They make manifest his aversion to the heart of our Faith, for where there is no priest, there is no Mass, and without the Mass the infinite Graces of Christ's Sacrifice are lacking. It is no accident that Bergoglio no longer celebrates Mass.[2355]

3rd June

Vatican News, the news service of the Holy See, published Pope Francis' preface to pro-homosexuality Fr. James Martin, S.J.'s book '*Come Forth: The Promise of Jesus's Greatest Miracle*'. In his book Fr. Martin uses Our Lord's miracle of raising Lazarus from the dead as a blasphemous metaphor to encourage homosexuals to 'come out' and live the homosexual lifestyle. In a passage of his preface it appears that Pope Francis suggests

[2352]Haynes, M [2024] *Male drag 'artist' dances for kids at Vatican's World Children's Day* [Online] Available at: www.lifesitenews.com [Accessed on: 15 May 2025]

[2353]Knuffke, L [2024] *Comedian Roberto Benigni tells children there is no hell or purgatory at Vatican World Children's Day* [Online] Available at: www.lifesitenews.com [Accessed on: 15 May 2025]

[2354]Brockhaus, H [2024] *'Go ahead with your vocation' : Pope Francis Tells Gay Man Rejected from Seminary* [Online] Available at: www.aciafrica.org [Accessed on: 15 May 2025]

[2355]Viganó, C [2024] *X post, 4:30 PM · Jun 4, 2024* [Online] Available at: x.com/carlomvigano [Accessed on: 15 May 2025]

people can be 'friends' with Jesus Christ while being 'dead' in their sins, without any mention of the necessity of repentance and firm amendment of life:

> All of us, then, are Lazarus. Rooting himself firmly in the Ignatian tradition, Father Martin brings us directly into the story of this friend of Jesus. We're His friends, too — 'dead' as we sometimes are on account of our sins, our failings and infidelities, the despondency that discourages us and crushes our spirits. Jesus is hardly afraid to get close to us — even when we 'reek' like a dead body that's been buried for three days. No, Jesus isn't afraid of our death, or our sin. He waits just outside the closed door of our hearts, that door that only opens from within, that we lock with a double bolt whenever we think God could never forgive us. But as we read James Martin's detailed analysis, we can practically feel the profound meaning of what Jesus does when He finds Himself before a dead man who is really dead, whose body gives off a nasty odour — a metaphor of the moral rot that sin produces in our souls. Jesus isn't scared of coming close to sinners — to any sinner, even the most brazen and undaunted. He has one single preoccupation: that no one goes missing, that none are deprived of the possibility of feeling the loving embrace of His Father.[2356]

5th June

Pope Francis again welcomed pro-homosexuality Sister Genevieve Jeanningros and a group of homosexual and opposite gender pretending persons to his Wednesday audience. As usual, the group defiantly rejecting Church doctrine were given seats of honour at Pope Francis' audience.[2357]

12th June

Pro-homosexuality Fr. James Martin S.J., announced on his X social media account that Pope Francis had again granted him a private audience. Notorious for his promotion of homosexuality in the Church, Fr. James Martin was granted three lengthy private audiences by Pope Francis during his pontificate, who also appointed him Consultor to the Vatican's Secretariat for Communications (2017) and a member of the Synod on Synodality (2023/2024). Fr. Martin claimed he had the Supreme Pontiff's permission to share the following from their 2024 meeting:

> I was honored to meet with Pope Francis for an hour-long conversation today at Casa Santa Marta. With his permission to share this, the Holy Father said he has known many good, holy and celibate seminarians and priests with homosexual tendencies. Once again, he confirmed my ministry with LGBTQ people and showed his openness and love for the LGBTQ community. It was also a great joy to receive his blessing on the 25th anniversary of my ordination to the priesthood.[2358]

13th June

The pro-homosexuality advocacy group *Outreach*, founded by pro-homosexuality Fr. James Martin S.J., published an op-ed blaspheming the Most Sacred Heart of Jesus. Robert Bordone, a member of the Boston Paulist Center's LGBTQIA Ministry Team, argued that there was a connection between June's devotion to the Sacred Heart and the homosexual agenda expressed by the political slogan, 'Gay Pride'. Bordone wrote:

> The image of Jesus's burning heart of love was seen as a reminder that God is with us and dearly loves each of us with great and unremitting passion. And that's why the connection of the Sacred Heart to Pride seems so connected to me. At its core, the Pride flag signals to all that love is love. It is a message of universal inclusion and

---

[2356]Pope Francis [2024] *Pope: Jesus didn't just talk about eternal life, He gave it to us* [Online] Available at: www.vaticannews.va [Accessed on: 15 May 2025]

[2357]*Pope Francis again welcomes group of 'transgender' males, homosexuals at Vatican audience.* [2024] [Online] Available at: www.lifesitenews.com [Accessed on: 15 May 2025]

[2358]Martin, J [2024] *Post on X 5:39 PM · Jun 12, 2024* [Online] Available at: x.com/JamesMartinSJ [Accessed on: 15 May 2025]

belonging, a message so central to the mission of the church and to communicating God's love for all people. This message of universal welcome and love is expressed by Pope Francis's constant exhortation, 'Todos, todos, todos!' […] Devotion to the Sacred Heart is a reminder and invitation to know and feel the love of God in our life. The Pride flag is a secular version of that message, a physical sign hoping to remind us and demonstrate the depth and legitimacy of a love that is fully inclusive and welcoming, that embraces and accepts you for who you are, no matter how you identify. For those who understand and profess belief in the Sacred Heart, perhaps you might consider flying both the Sacred Heart and the Pride flag in your home this June.[2359]

Cardinal Kurt Koch, prefect of the Dicastery for the Promotion of Christian Unity, published, with the approval of Pope Francis, the document *The Bishop of Rome. Primacy and synodality in ecumenical dialogues and responses to the encyclical Ut unum sint*. The document received input from Orthodox and Protestant theologians, as well as the Roman Curia and the Synod of Bishops. The document calls for the 're-interpretation' of Vatican I's dogmatic constitution *Pastor Aeternus* that formally defined the primacy and infallibility of the pope:

> A first proposal is a Catholic 're-reception', 're-interpretation', 'official interpretation,' 'updated commentary' or even 'rewording' of the teachings of Vatican I. Indeed, some dialogues observe that these teachings were deeply conditioned by their historical context, and suggest that the Catholic Church should look for new expressions and vocabulary faithful to the original intention but integrated into a *communio* ecclesiology and adapted to the current cultural and ecumenical context. (178)[2360]

Bishop Marian Eleganti, Emeritus Auxiliary Bishop of Chur, criticised this attempted 'relativisation' of the dogmas of Petrine primacy and infallibility by summarising the document's approach as follows:

> Forget the dogmatisation of the primacy of Roman jurisdiction at Vatican I and return to the Reformation period, to the first millennium or even to the apostolic era! Relativize those key dogmatic statements of an ecumenical council of the Latin West as one of its cultural peculiarities, which in its entire jurisdictional intensification applies only to the Latin Church! Give up this divisive yoke that the Roman pope cannot impose on all Christians ex sese (of his own accord) instead of *ex consensu* (based on the consent of a majority).[2361]

14th June

During his address at the Catholic University of America Cardinal Robert Sarah denounced the infiltration of practical atheism into the Church evidenced in the rejection of traditional Catholic morality, traditional Catholic doctrine, and the traditional form of the Catholic liturgy. Cardinal Sarah is the former prefect of the Sacred Congregation for Divine Worship and the Discipline of the Sacraments. Cardinal Sarah said:

> None of the proponents of this paradigm shift within the Church reject God outright but they treat Revelation as secondary, or at least on equal footing with experience and modern science. This is how practical atheism works. It does not deny God but functions as if God is not central. We see this approach not only in moral theology but also in liturgy. Sacred traditions that have served the Church well for hundreds of years are now portrayed as dangerous. So much focus on the horizontal pushes out the vertical, as if God is an experience rather than an ontological reality.[2362]

[2359]Bordone, R [2024] *The connection between Pride and the Sacred Heart of Jesus* [Online] Available at: www.outreach.faith [Accessed on: 15 May 2025]

[2360]Dicastery for the Promotion of Christian Unity [2024] *The Bishop of Rome. Primacy and synodality in ecumenical dialogues and responses to the encyclical Ut unum sint* [Online] Available at: www.christianunity.va [Accessed on: 16 May 2025]

[2361]Eleganti, M [2024] *Bishop Eleganti: Papal primacy must not be defined by ecumenical 'negotiations' with non-Catholics* [Online] Available at: www.lifesitenews.com [Accessed on: 16 May 2025]

[2362]Sarah, R [2024] *The Catholic Church's Enduring Answer To The Practical Atheism Of Our Age* [Online] Available at: napa-institute.org [Accessed on: 16 May 2025]

17th June

Crisis Magazine, the US Catholic journal, published an analysis of the grave errors contained in *Fiducia Supplicans* written by Bishop Athanasius Schneider, auxiliary of Astana, Kazakhstan. Among other things, Bishop Schneider observed:

> All this serves as a significant support for 'LGBTQ' groups and lobbies and their 'gay pride,' and elevates practicing homosexuals to the level of an acceptable 'community' within the Church. This 'blessing' also reinforces 'LGBTQ communities' in the false conviction that their sinful lifestyle is good, thus discouraging them from repenting. Above all, it helps them to justify their militant efforts to obtain the 'right' to marry, adopt children, and normalise homosexual activity. In this manner, entire societies, and even some Church communities, will become *de facto* promotors of the 'LGBTQ' ideology [...] Secular powers, 'LGBTQ' lobbies, and anti-Church agendas are ultimately the driving force behind the issuance of this Declaration, whose aim is to sow the seed of deep doubt in the heart of the Church. And they will surely exert significant pressure to compel Catholics to accept and promote it. They will falsely invoke the obligation to obey Church teaching, and those priests and faithful who criticise *Fiducia Supplicans,* and refuse to implement it, will be accused of being unfaithful to the Pope.[2363]

18th June

The traditionalist Italian blog *Messa in Latino* published an interview with Professor Andrea Grillo, reported to be the 'mastermind' behind *Traditionis Custodes'* restrictions of the Latin Mass. Andrea Grillo is a professor of Sacramental Theology at the Pontifical Athenaeum Sant'Anselmo in Rome and of Liturgy at the Abbey of Santa Giustina, Padua. To explain Prof. Grillo's influence, *Messa in Latino* stated, 'In the view of many in the Roman Curia, for Pope Francis, Prof. Grillo is on liturgy what Fr James Martin, S.J., is on homosexuality.' Prof. Grillo condemned Catholics who attend the Traditional Latin Mass as being unfaithful to the Church and referred to annual Chartres traditionalist pilgrims as a 'sect.' According to Prof. Grillo:

> Those you call 'traditionalists faithful to Rome' are actually people who, for various reasons, are at odds with Rome, and not in a relationship of fidelity. The point of contention does not simply concern a 'ritual form' but a way of understanding relations inside and outside the Church. It all begins with the misunderstanding generated (in good faith, but through a completely wrong judgement) by the Motu Proprio *Summorum Pontificum,* which had introduced a 'ritual parallelism' (between the *Novus Ordo* and *Vetus Ordo*) that has neither a systematic nor practical foundation: it is not theologically sound and generates greater divisions than those that were present previously. The idea of 'fidelity to Rome' must be challenged: to be faithful to Rome, one must acquire a 'ritual language' according to what Rome has communally established. One is not faithful if one has one foot in two shoes. Having demonstrated this contradiction, the merit of *Traditionis Custodes* is that it re-establishes the one *'lex orandi'* in force for the entire Catholic Church. If someone tells me he is faithful at the same time to the *Novus Ordo* and *Vetus Ordo,* I reply that he has not understood the meaning of tradition, within which there is a legitimate and insuperable progress that is irreversible.

> [*Regarding the participation of 18,000 mainly young people at the annual traditionalist Chartres pilgrimage*]. What are 18,000 people compared to the great multitude of the Catholic Church? Little more than a sect that experiences infidelity as salvation, and is often linked to moral and political positions, and very concerning customs. It isn't by changing words that things get better. Tradition and traditionalism cannot be equated. Traditionalism is not 'one among many movements' (even though it may have characteristics that are partly similar to some of the more fundamentalist movements that were inappropriately favoured over the last 40 years), but a form of 'denial of

[2363]Schneider, A [2024] *The Problem of Blessing Same-Sex Couples and Its Consequences for the Doctrine and Life of the Catholic Church* [Online] Available at: crisismagazine.com [Accessed on: 15 May 2025]

the Second Vatican Council' that cannot but be clearly obstructed within the ecclesial experience. The Church is not a 'club of notaries or lawyer' who cultivate their aesthetic passions or plan to instrumentalise the Church as 'the most famous museum'.[2364]

In response to Professor Andrea Grillo's interview with *Messa in Latino*, liturgical scholar Dom Alcuin Reid responded:

> Professor Grillo has been smugly confident in his assumption that those whom Pope Benedict XVI noted 'have discovered this liturgical form [the usus antiquior], felt its attraction, and found in it a form of encounter with the Mystery of the Most Holy Eucharist, particularly suited to them' are in fact, as he asserts in his interview, backward-looking people who do not understand the meaning of tradition and who form 'little more than a sect that experiences infidelity as salvation and is often linked to moral and political positions [presumably he means bad ones] and very concerning customs' and 'who cultivate nostalgia for the past'. Included in this damning slur are the 18,000+ Chartres pilgrims ('the future of the Church in France' according to one French diocesan bishop), the faithful and heroic Catholic families who dare to have children and raise them with the traditional liturgical forms, the seminaries, monasteries and religious houses where the usus antiquior is the living, beating heart, and of course any academic who dares to defend its ongoing value.[2365]

ZENIT, the international Catholic news site, published the letter from the Dicastery for Divine Worship and the Discipline of the Sacraments in response to the Archbishop of Melbourne's request to continue to have the Traditional Latin Mass offered at St. Patrick's Cathedral, Melbourne. Bishop Vittorio Francesco Viola, Secretary of the Dicastery, refused to grant a dispensation:

> While we recognise that Mass according to the *Missale Romanum* of 1962 has been celebrated in the Cathedral Church for some time, we are, nonetheless, constrained to deny this request. It is now opportune that the direction established by the Holy Father be followed with care in this particular case...it does not seem appropriate for the antecedent liturgy to be celebrated in the place that should serve as an example for the liturgical life of the entire diocese. The Cathedral is the first place where the celebration of the liturgy must use the current liturgical books, which form the unique expression of the lex orandi of the Roman Rite [...] One possible solution for the faithful who attend this Mass at the Cathedral Church, and a further step in travelling on the path indicated by the Holy Father, would be for Mass to be celebrated for them, in Latin, according to the Missale Romanum editio typica tertia (2008) at the same altar where Mass according to the 1962 Missale Romanum is currently celebrated. This would be a concrete sign of a desire on their part to fully embrace the unique *lex orandi* of the Roman Rite and an opportunity for you as chief liturgist of the diocese, along with the parish clergy, to ensure a thorough going catechesis and formation on the spiritual depth and richness of the renewed Missal.[2366]

20th June

Archbishop Carlo Maria Viganó, former papal nuncio to the US, announced on his X social media account, and his website *exsurgedomine*, that he faced canonical trial for 'schism'. The Dicastery for the Doctrine of the Faith accused him of 'schism' owing to a 'denial of the legitimacy of Pope Francis, rupture of communion with Him, and rejection of the Second Vatican Council.' Archbishop Viganó received the summons to appear at his extrajudicial penal trial on the 20th June at the Palace of the Holy Office

[2364]*Interview with Andrea Grillo on the Traditional Liturgy: The Church isn't a 'high-society club' or 'sect that experiences infidelity as salvation'* [2024] Available at: blog.messainlatino.it [Accessed on: 16 May 2025]

[2365]Reid, A [2024] *EXCLUSIVE: Dom Alcuin Reid's Response to Prof. Grillo's Interview* [[Online] Available at: rorate-caeli.blogspot.com [Accessed on: 16 May 2025]

[2366]*Archbishop of Melbourne asks for permission for traditional mass in cathedral: Vatican answers «no» and these are the reasons why* [2024] [Online] Available at: zenit.org [Accessed on: 16 May 2025]

from Monsignor John Kennedy of the dicastery's Disciplinary Section. Kennedy was later made a titular archbishop by Pope Francis in 2024. Archbishop Viganó responded:

> I regard the accusations against me as an honor. I believe that the very wording of the charges confirms the theses that I have repeatedly defended in my various addresses. It is no coincidence that the accusation against me concerns the questioning of the legitimacy of Jorge Mario Bergoglio and the rejection of Vatican II: the Council represents the ideological, theological, moral, and liturgical cancer of which the Bergoglian 'synodal church' is the necessary metastasis [...] In the face of the Dicastery's accusations, I claim, as Successor of the Apostles, to be in full communion with the Roman Catholic Apostolic Church, with the Magisterium of the Roman Pontiffs, and with the uninterrupted doctrinal, moral, and liturgical Tradition which they have faithfully preserved [...]
>
> I repudiate the neomodernist errors inherent in the Second Vatican Council and in the so-called 'post-conciliar magisterium,' in particular in matters of collegiality, ecumenism, religious freedom, the secularity of the State, and the liturgy. I repudiate, reject, and condemn the scandals, errors, and heresies of Jorge Mario Bergoglio, who manifests an absolutely tyrannical management of power, exercised against the purpose that legitimises Authority in the Church: an authority that is vicarious of that of Christ, and as such must obey Him alone. This separation of the Papacy from its legitimising principle, which is Christ the High Priest, transforms the ministerium into a self-referential tyranny.[2367]

21st June

In his address to the annual US Catholic Media Conference, Dr. Paolo Ruffini, prefect of the Vatican's Dicastery for Communication, downplayed the seriousness of the allegations of sexual abuse of nuns committed by the disgraced Jesuit Fr. Marko Rupnik. In response to journalists questioning the Dicastery for Communication continuing to use Fr. Rupnik's art Dr. Ruffini replied:

> Do you think that if I pull away a photo of art from my website, our website, I would be more close to victims? Do you think so? Removing, deleting, destroying art does not ever mean a good choice. This is not a Christian response. We're not talking about abuse of minors.[2368]

24th June

Father Jean-Raphaël Dubrule, superior of the traditionalist religious community the Missionaries of Divine Mercy, issued a communiqué explaining the reasons why the ordinations of its five seminarians to the diaconate had been blocked by the Vatican. The Missionaries of Divine Mercy were linked to the Diocese of Toulon-Fréjus, France. Father Jean-Raphaël Dubrule explained:

> Five seminarians of the Community of the Missionaries of Divine Mercy have been waiting for their ordination to the diaconate and then to the priesthood for over two years in the case of one of them, and one year for the other four. Their wait is no longer linked to the situation in the diocese of Fréjus-Toulon, where ordinations have resumed, but to the celebration according to the traditional ritual, as provided for in the community's statutes. After many discussions with the competent Roman authorities, led by Bishop Touvet, whom I warmly thank for his very strong support for our community, it appears that the situation is blocked not only because of the ritual of ordination, but also because with regard to the possibility for these future priests to be able to celebrate in the old rite. The Roman authorities are not providing any assurances regarding this possibility, and it is therefore possible that candidates may be ordained

[2367]Viganó, C [2024] *ATTENDITE A FALSIS PROPHETIS: Announcement regarding the start of the extrajudicial criminal trial for schism (Art. 2 SST; can. 1364 CIC)* [Online] Available at: exsurgedomine. it [Accessed on: 15 May 2025]

[2368]Kokx, S [2024] *Vatican communications head slammed for downplaying Rupnik case: 'We're not talking about abuse of minors'* [Online] Available at: www.lifesitenews.com [Accessed on: 16 May 2025]

without having the right to go on to celebrate according to the old rite. This would prevent them from exercising their ministry within the community and in accordance with its statutes.[2369]

2nd July

The Australian, the daily Australian newspaper, published an interview with Libero Milone, the former auditor general of the Vatican, in which he revealed that the death of Cardinal George Pell remains 'shrouded in mystery'. Cardinal George Pell was the Prefect of the Vatican's Secretariat for the Economy (2014–2019). Libero Milone told *The Australian* newspaper, 'At his funeral, at his coffin, I promised him that we would bring the truth to light.' Milone also revealed that Cardinal Pell's body had been 'left in post-autopsy disarray and not properly dressed, sparking further concerns about his last hours.' Edward Pentin, the EWTN Vatican journalist, reported on his X social media account:

> *The Australian* added that it had asked the Salvator Mundi hospital in Rome where Cardinal Pell had died after undergoing a routine hip operation 'to comment on claims by senior sources that internal CCTV cameras were not working on and around January 10 last year and that no medical doctor was on duty the evening the Cardinal died. At the time of publication, the hospital has not responded.' Some months ago, I sent and resent a list of six questions to the same hospital asking its health director, Dr. Luigi Macchitella, for clarification regarding the circumstances around Cardinal Pell's death but he also did not respond. Salvator Mundi is a private hospital half owned by @ UPMC (University of Pittsburgh Medical Center).[2370]

Following Libero Milone's comments to *The Australian* Andrew Bolt, a prominent journalist with Sky News Live, broadcast further information about the state of Cardinal Pell's body:

> Now, for a year I've kept a secret about the death last year of Cardinal George Pell. The secret is the final insult to a great and innocent man. Now, I promised not to reveal what I know to spare Pell's grieving family. But one line in the Australian newspaper today, and a call I made to George Pell's brother after that, leaves me free to say what I did learn, or at least most of it […] But I do know the state of his body after the Vatican sent it to Australia for burial. Now, a Pell confidant, who was at the opening of the coffin, found Pell's body being treated with gross disrespect. Perhaps it was just incompetence, but some of Pell's closest associates have told me they suspect that some in the Vatican had not forgiven Pell for exposing corruption […] A Sydney undertaker had to clean the body. Pell's nose had also been broken. Pell was also shoeless, said David Pell, his brother. In fact, I'd been told he wasn't only shoeless, all his clothes had simply been just thrown into the coffin […] the Vatican should now be deeply, deeply ashamed to have treated his body so shabbily. Now, Pell once told me he didn't feel safe in the Vatican as he chased the thieves. He hid documents in London and Sydney. What was done to him after his death makes me suspect he was right.[2371]

The Times, the UK daily newspaper, published an open letter urging the Vatican not to restrict the traditional Mass signed by leading figures in British society, including Catholics, Protestants, non-Christians, and atheists. Compared to the famous so called 'Agatha Christie' letter to Pope Paul VI, signatories included: Lord Alton of Liverpool, soprano Sophie Bevan, pianist Sir Stephen Hough, composer Sir James MacMillan, prominent historian Tom Holland, Michael Gove, former cabinet minister and current

[2369]Smits, J [2024] *Rome blocks ordinations of seminarians in French community that offers Latin Mass, superior says* [Online] Available at: www.lifesitenews.com [Accessed on: 16 May 2025]

[2370]Pentin, E [2024] *Post on X 6:07 PM · Jul 2, 2024* [Online] Available at: x.com/EdwardPentin [Accessed on: 17 May 2025]

[2371]Bolt, A [2024] *'Final insult': Andrew Bolt slams Vatican's treatment of Cardinal Pell's body* [Online] Available at: www.youtube.com [Accessed on: 17 May 2025]

member of His Majesty's Most Honourable Privy Council, and Sir Nicholas Coleridge CBE, former chairman of the prestigious Victoria and Albert Museum and provost of Eton College, Lord Stirrup KG, highly decorated Marshall of the Royal Air Force and former Chief of the Defence Staff. The letter stated:

> Recently there have been worrying reports from Rome that the Latin Mass is to be banished from nearly every Catholic church. This is a painful and confusing prospect, especially for the growing number of young Catholics whose faith has been nurtured by it [...] Not everyone appreciates its value and that is fine, but to destroy it seems an unnecessary and insensitive act in a world where history can all too easily slip away forgotten. The old rite's ability to encourage silence and contemplation is a treasure not easily replicated, and, when gone, impossible to reconstruct.[2372]

The Pontifical Academy for Life published the booklet *Piccolo lessico del fine vita* [Compact Lexicon of the End of Life], a glossary of terms pertaining to the subject end-of-life. The booklet was sent to every bishop in Italy. Its advice regarding Advance Treatment Provisions stipulating the patient's choices regarding end-of-life care was criticised for emphasising 'subjective criteria over objective medical standards for life, condoning practices tantamount to assisted suicide.' The Advance Treatment Provisions form proposed by the Pontifical Academy for Life advocated that the registrant may have the freedom to refuse life-saving treatments such as 'blood transfusions, antibiotics... invasive and non-invasive mechanical ventilation, tracheostomy, haemodialysis and [even] cardio-pulmonary resuscitation' (p. 79), and even refusing assisted nutrition and hydration (pp. 54 and 79). Tommaso Scandroglio, an associate professor in Moral Philosophy at the European University of Rome, commented:

> [The Pontifical Academy for Life] is aware that according to medical casuistry and, above all, scientific literature, life-saving treatments most often do not constitute futile treatment. Here, then, is recourse to the second criterion mentioned earlier, the subjective criterion, which is the decisive criterion for opening the door to euthanasia: if the patient believes that a certain treatment is disproportionate, then it certainly constitutes futile treatment, beyond the scientific evidence [...] Of course it is a duty to listen to the patient to see whether certain treatments are bearable and how effective they are, but the final word rests with the criterion of objective beneficence of the treatments, not with the subjective criterion of the patient's absolute opinion.[2373]

5th July

The Dicastery for the Doctrine of the Faith announced that it had judged Archbishop Carlo Maria Viganò, former papal nuncio to the US, to be guilty of 'schism' and therefore automatically excommunicated:

> His public statements manifesting his refusal to recognise and submit to the Supreme Pontiff, his rejection of communion with the members of the Church subject to him, and of the legitimacy and magisterial authority of the Second Vatican Council are well known. At the conclusion of the penal process, the Most Reverend Carlo Maria Viganò was found guilty of the reserved delict of schism. The Dicastery declared the latae sententiae excommunication in accordance with canon 1364 § 1 CIC. The lifting of the censure in these cases is reserved to the Apostolic See. This decision was communicated to the Most Reverend Viganò on 5 July 2024.[2374]

[2372]Haynes, M [2024] *Leading British figures pen defense of Latin Mass to echo Agatha Christie's famous petition* [Online] Available at: www.lifesitenews.com; Payne, D [2024] *British lords, celebrities call on Vatican to preserve 'treasure' of Latin Mass* [Online] Available at: www.catholicworldreport.com; [Accessed on: 17 May 2025]

[2373]Scandroglio, T [2024] *Vatican: PAV's latest publication condones euthanasia and assisted suicide* [Online] Available at: newdailycompass.com [Accessed on: 21 May 2025]

[2374]Haynes, M [2024] *Vatican says Archbishop Viganò 'guilty' of schism and excommunicated* [Online] Available at: www.lifesitenews.com [Accessed on: 16 May 2025]

In response to his excommunication Archbishop Carlo Maria Viganò responded on his X social media account,

> What is imputed to me as guilt for my conviction is now on record, confirming the Catholic Faith that I fully profess. To my Brothers I say: 'If you remain silent, the stones will cry out' (Lk 19:40).[2375]

7th July

il Resto del Carlino, the daily newspaper of Bologna, Italy, reported that Don Giuseppe Cavoli had been given permission by Bishop Andreozzi of Fano-Fossombrone-Cagli-Pergola to 'bless' two homosexual activists following their civil union. Andrea Andreozzi was appointed bishop by Pope Francis in 2023. Don Giuseppe Cavoli had been appointed diocesan commissioner of 'pastoral care of Lgbtqia+' by Bishop Andreozzi.[2376]

9th July

The General Secretariat of the Synod released, with the approval of Pope Francis, the *Instrumentum Laboris* for the second session of the Synod on Synodality to be held in October 2024, entitled *How to be a missionary synodal Church*. Among the proposed innovations were the following: 'There is also a call for adequately trained lay men and women to contribute to preaching the Word of God, including during the celebration of the Eucharist.' (18); using the phrase 'on the margins' as a reference to LGBT, the text stated, 'A need emerges in all continents concerning people who, for different reasons, are or feel excluded or on the margins of the ecclesial community or who struggle to find full recognition of their dignity and gifts within it. This lack of welcome leaves them feeling rejected, hinders their journey of faith and encounter with the Lord, and deprives the Church of their contribution to mission'. (33).

During the Synod on Synodality press conference launching the *Instrumentum Laboris*, pro-homosexuality Cardinal Mario Grech, Secretary General of the Synod of Bishops, announced that Pope Francis had commissioned the Dicastery for the Doctrine of the Faith to study the issue of the 'female diaconate', drawing on the October 2023 Synthesis Report and the Vatican's 2016 and 2020 commissions on 'female deacons.'[2377]

14th July

Bishop Ramón Bejarano, an auxiliary bishop of San Diego, presided at an pro-homosexuality Mass at St. John the Evangelist church, notorious for its 'LGBT ministry'. Fr. Ramón Bejarano was appointed bishop by Pope Francis in 2020. Bishop Bejarano is a supporter of the heterodox *New Ways Ministry* despite it being condemned by Archbishop James Hickey of Washington (1984); the Congregation for the Doctrine of the Faith (1999) and Cardinal Francis George (2010) for advocacy of positions contrary to Catholic teaching on homosexuality and homosexual sex acts, and causing confusion among the faithful. Bishop Bejarano apologised to the active homosexuals in the congregation for the Church's approach to homosexuality:

> Last year I went to a workshop organised by New Ways Ministry. It was not until I heard the stories of those present, that I realised the pain, the sorrow, the stigma and trauma that we have caused to others because we don't accept them, because we tell them that they do not belong, because we judge them. Jesus will never inflict that kind of pain or trauma to people. I apologise for the pain and distress that I and the Church have

[2375]Viganò, C [2024] *Post on X 5:04 PM · Jul 5, 2024* [Online] Available at: x.com/CarloMVigano [Accessed on: 16 May 2025]

[2376]Haynes, M [2024] *Italian priest to 'bless' homosexual activist 'couple' after civil union ceremony* [Online] Available at: www.lifesitenews.com [Accessed on: 17 May 2025]

[2377]Haynes, M [2024] *Vatican confirms third study group is looking at issue of 'female diaconate'* [Online] Available at: www.lifesitenews.com [Accessed on: 16 May 2025]

caused to many of you. I apologise for the stigmatisation and trauma we have caused to others, because we have told them that they are not valued and that they are not worthy of the love of God. There are many others out there who feel rejected and unvalued.[2378]

16th July

The National Catholic Register, the US Catholic newspaper, published an article by Cardinal Dominik Duka, archbishop emeritus of Prague. Drawing on his experience of being imprisoned by the Czechoslovakia communist regime between 1981 to 1982 Cardinal Duka criticised the Vatican's 'silence' about Chinese communist's persecution of Catholics in China:

> Just as silence and complicity with the communist regime damaged my country and made it easier for the government to imprison dissidents, the Church's silence in the face of human rights abuses by Communist China harms Catholic life in China [...] Vatican diplomacy must regain and raise its voice to join them in defending the human person and in defending the Gospel. The time of courage has come once again.[2379]

Allianz Gleichwürdig Katholisc, the heterodox Swiss Catholic lay organisation, published a list of parishes that offered 'blessings' for homosexual couples and couples living in adulterous relationships under the following statement:

> Blessing is a gift. No one has the right to deny this gift. In Switzerland, it is already established practice in many places for pastoral caregivers to bless unmarried, remarried, and queer couples.It is not always immediately apparent whether a parish and its staff are open to all couples and 'queer-friendly.' For couples seeking a blessing, this can create a barrier to reaching out. To make this easier, the AGK maintains a list of Catholic pastoral caregivers or parishes that offer blessings to all who desire them: respectfully, carefully, and personally.[2380]

The AGK provided parishes with a 'Blessing for All' badge that could be displayed on their websites or physically as a sticker.[2381]

17th July

Pope Francis' *Letter on the Role of Literature in Formation* used the non-Christian dating notation 'B.C.E [Before Common Era] instead of the Catholic style of 'Before Christ', signifying an acceptance of the secular campaign to de-Christianise history:

> This verse contains two quotations: one indirect, from the poet Epimenides (sixth century B.C.E.), and the other direct, from the Phaenomena of the poet Aratus of Soli (third century B.C.E.), who wrote of the constellations and the signs of good and bad weather. (12).[2382]

26th July

The Congregation for Divine Worship and the Discipline of the Sacraments released full details of its activities in 2022, revealing that it only granted permission to 57 parishes to offer the traditional Mass in the world since the promulgation of *Traditionis Custodes*.[2383]

[2378]Shine, R [2024] *In San Diego, Bishop Apologizes to LGBTQ+ Community During Pride Mass* [Online] Available at: www.newwaysministry.org [Accessed on: 23 May 2025]
[2379]Duka, D [2024] *Vatican Diplomats Must Find Courage Again to Defend the Gospel* [Online] Available at: www.ncregister.com [Accessed on: 17 May 2025]
[2380]*Segen für Alle* [2024] [Online] Available at: www.gleichwuerdig.ch [Accessed on: 17 May 2025]
[2381]Wailzer, A [2024] *Heterodox Swiss Catholic lay group publishes list of parishes offering 'blessings' to homosexual 'couples'* [Online] Available at: www.lifesitenews.com [Accessed on: 17 May 2025]
[2382]Pope Francis [2024] *Letter on the Role of Literature in Formation* [Online] Available at: www.vatican.va [Accessed on: 17 May 2025]
[2383]Haynes, M [2024] *Vatican allowed fewer than 60 parish churches worldwide to offer Latin Mass in 2022* [Online] Available at: www.lifesitenews.com [Accessed on: 17 May 2025]

1st August

The militant US Catholic homosexual group *Outreach*, founded by pro-homosexuality Fr. James Martin S.J., published on its website a photograph of a handwritten note of support from Pope Francis. The note contained the following message:

> I am glad that Cardinal Gregory will celebrate the Mass; I will be spiritually with him and with all of you, united in prayer. Thank you for praying for me. I do the same for you. May Jesus bless you and the Holy Virgin care for you. Fraternally, Francis.[2384]

During the celebration of the Mass Cardinal Wilton Gregory of Washington praised the homosexual activists who openly defy the Church's doctrine on homosexuality:

> In many respects you are engaging in an act of synodality – the vision and invitation proposed by Pope Francis that sincerely and openly speaking and listening to one another under the light and guidance of the Holy Spirit is the way that the Church grows in perfection […] Your assembly is dedicated to the pursuit of our becoming a more inclusive family of faith.[2385]

2nd August

Katholisch.de, the news outlet of the German bishops, published an interview with Fr. Maurizio Chiodi during which he again rejected the Church's doctrine on homosexuality. Fr. Chiodi was appointed a member of the 'reformed' Pontifical Academy for Life by Pope Francis in 2017 and was appointed a member of the Vatican study group on 'Theological criteria and synodal methodologies for shared discernment of controversial doctrinal, pastoral, and ethical issues.' Fr. Chiodi said:

> I believe that we must today reconsider the traditional – and for our time incomprehensible – ethical reflections on homosexuality. If in the past we spoke of homosexuality as 'contra naturam,' we must now ask: What does 'natura' mean? This Latin word has many – very different – meanings, particularly the meaning of universality, and we must acknowledge that universality is necessary for moral knowledge. But we cannot think of universality (the good and the law) without singularity (the conscience), which, in the sense of cultural anthropology, always belongs to a specific culture. Morality cannot be reduced to a reason that is not deeply committed to the experience and lived life of an individual conscience with its specific culture.

> I believe that sexual difference is constitutive for human existence, as it is the origin of our life: we all know that we descend as children from a mother and a father. A homosexual person does not deny this. However, they do not experience this difference as attractive for themselves. This sexual orientation is not a matter of their choice. We must ask: What is the possible good for such a person? The question for a homosexual person is how to live their sexuality by acknowledging their vocation to relationships capable of closeness, care, community, and fidelity to the other, while seeking the good that is concretely possible for them. [*Trans*].[2386]

14th August

Kath.ch, the Swiss Catholic news outlet, published an interview with Bishop Marian Eleganti, the emeritus auxiliary bishop of Chur, in which he voiced criticisms of the Synod on Synodality. In response to the question, '*Do you think the synodal process could lead to a division in the Church?*' Bishop Eleganti responded:

> Yes, if the frustration of repeatedly failing to advance one's own agenda becomes great enough. Although Pope Francis has made synodality his banner, he has a very

[2384]*Pope Francis 'united in prayer' with Outreach LGBTQ Catholic conference* [2024][Online] Available at: www.outreach.faith [Accessed on: 17 May 2025]

[2385]Gregory, W [2024] *Text of Cardinal Gregory's homily at Outreach Conference 2024 Mass* [Online] Available at: www.cathstan.org [Accessed on: 17 May 2025]

[2386]Trifunovic, M [2024] *Moraltheologe: Traditionelle Überlegungen zu Homosexualität überdenken* [Online] Available at: www.katholisch.de [Accessed on: 17 May 2025]

authoritarian leadership style. He intervenes in the synodal process and steers it, for example, by withdrawing important issues from the plenary assembly and delegating them to commissions that work autonomously. He also put a vote, which was rejected by the majority at the second Family Synod, back on the agenda [...] Some will wonder what synodality exactly means to him. Apparently, synodality has limits. Many see a contradiction in the Pope's actions. [*trans*][2387]

Pope Francis held a private audience with pro-homosexuality activists from Uganda during which he encouraged them to 'keep fighting for their rights'. The background to the private audience was Uganda's parliament passing the 2023 Anti-Homosexuality Act, which prohibited 'any form of sexual relations between persons of the same sex' and prohibited 'the promotion or recognition of sexual relations between persons of the same sex; and for related matters.'[2388]

15th August

Vatican News, the news outlet of the Holy See, published an article on the Assumption of the Blessed Virgin Mary that contained artwork produced by Fr. Marko Rupnik, despite the credible allegations that he sexually and spiritually abused nuns. Fr. Rupnik was accused of abusing at least 20 nuns, with some sources reporting allegations involving up to 41 women in the Loyola Community he co-founded in Slovenia. The Vatican's persistent use of Rupnik's art, despite the controversy it caused, was challenged as taunting 'the victims of rapist Marko Rupnik'.[2389]

23rd August

During ongoing synodal discussions, organised by the Pan-African Catholic Theology and Pastoral Network (PACTPAN) Archbishop Andrew Nkea Fuanya of Cameroon's Bamenda archdiocese criticised the Synod on Synodality. Archbishop Nkea said, regarding homosexuality and the 'ordination' of women:

> When we went to the Synod, it was clear that Africa had to take responsibility for its own destiny. We knew we had to make our voice heard in the first phase of the Synod. In presenting our points at the Synod, therefore, we did not want to be seen as presenting points of Africa because of the culture from which we came. Our stand had nothing to do with culture; it was about fidelity to the truth; fidelity to what Christ taught. It was about fidelity to what the Apostles handed down to generations [...] Theologians here, you must tell us whether the African brain is inferior when it comes to reflecting on African culture and civilisation. Africa was not defending a cultural idea. Africa was defending the teaching that the Church has had for 2,000 years. We are going back to the second session with the same vehement rejection of that document [*Fiducia Supplicans*]. We therefore do not buy the idea that people tell us that we are arguing from culture. And that we come from a culture that is still developing, and that is why we do not understand certain things.[2390]

27th August

Libreria Editrice Vaticana, the Vatican publishing house, released '*A Christian on Death Row: My Commitment to Those Condemned,*' by Dale Recinella, including a preface by Pope Francis. The Supreme Pontiff renewed his commitment to the universal abolition of the death penalty, quoting his own changes to the Catechism of the Catholic Church, in direct contradiction to sacred Scripture and Tradition:

[2387]Straub, J [2024] *Weihbischof Eleganti: «Papst Franziskus greift in synodalen Prozess ein»* [Online] Available at: www.kath.ch [Accessed on: 17 May 2025]

[2388]Haynes, M [2024] *Pope Francis urges Ugandan LGBT activist to 'keep fighting for your rights'* [Online] Available at: www.lifesitenews.com [Accessed on: 17 May 2025]

[2389]Mangiaracina, E [2024] *'This is sick': Vatican uses Rupnik image to celebrate the Feast of the Assumption* [Online] Available at: www.lifesitenews.com [Accessed on: 21 May 2025]

[2390]Chimtom, N [2024] *Archbishop says Africa's opposition to LGBTQ+ rights not 'cultural' but Biblical* [Online] Available at: cruxnow.com [Accessed on: 17 May 2025]

Yes, as I have repeatedly emphasised, the death penalty is in no way a solution to the violence that can strike innocent people. Capital executions, far from bringing justice, fuel a sense of revenge that becomes a dangerous poison for the body of our civil societies. States should focus on allowing prisoners the opportunity to truly change their lives, rather than investing money and resources in their execution, as if they were human beings no longer worthy of living and to be disposed of [...] the Jubilee should commit all believers to collectively call for the abolition of the death penalty, a practice that, as the Catechism of the Catholic Church states, 'is inadmissible because it is an attack on the inviolability and dignity of the person!' (n. 2267).[2391]

28th August

Pro-homosexuality Bishop John Iffert of Covington, Kentucky, celebrated Mass for the militant pro-homosexual group, 'Fortunate Families'. John Iffert was appointed bishop by Pope Francis in 2021.[2392]

4th September

During his Apostolic Journey to Indonesia Pope Francis addressed an interfaith gathering of young people involved in the *Scholas Occurrentes* movement. Dispensing with a trinitarian blessing and the Sign of the Cross, the Supreme Pontiff re-iterated his gravely erroneous religious indifferentism:

Here, you are from diverse religions, but we have only one god, he is only one. And in union, in silence, we shall pray to the lord and I shall give a blessing for all, a blessing valid for all religions. May God bless each of you. May he bless all your desires. May he bless your families. May he bless you present (here). May he bless your future. Amen.[2393]

13th September

During his Apostolic Journey to Singapore, Pope Francis addressed an inter-religious meeting of young people, re-iterating his gravely erroneous religious indifferentism. The Supreme Pontiff declared:

If we start to fight amongst ourselves and say 'my religion is more important than yours, my religion is true, yours is not,' where will that lead us? Where? It's okay to discuss [between religions]. Every religion is a way to arrive at God. There are different languages to arrive at God, but God is God for all. And how is God God for all? We are all sons and daughters of God. But my god is more important than your god, is that true? There is only one God and each of us has a language to arrive at God. Sikh, Muslim, Hindu, Christian, they are different paths.[2394]

In response, Bishop Marian Eleganti, emeritus auxiliary bishop of Chur, Switzerland, wrote:

Pope Francis says that there is only one God, the Creator, and that we are therefore already brothers and children of God by nature as His creatures. Is that true? Where is Jesus Christ in this relationship, without Whom, according to His Own words, we do not have the Father (the Creator)? Where is the talk of Jesus Christ as the only door to the Father? Where is the mention that Jesus Christ has given us the power to become children of God? That we are not without Him. Where is the mention of the fact that we pray in His Spirit, which He has given us: 'Abba, Father'? Pope Francis conceals all of this and also avoids the Sign of the Cross during the blessing so as not to alienate

---

[2391]Pope Francis [2024] *Pope: Death penalty never brings justice, but is a poison for society* [Online] Available at: www.vaticannews.va [Accessed on: 17 May 2025]

[2392]Kokx, S [2024] *Francis-appointed bishop to offer pro-LGBT Mass for heterodox group advised by Bishop Stowe* [Online] Available at: www.lifesitenews.com [Accessed on: 17 May 2025]

[2393]Haynes, M [2024] *Pope Francis skips Sign of the Cross to impart blessing 'valid for all religions'* [Online] Available at: www.lifesitenews.com [Accessed on: 21 May 2025]

[2394]Haynes, M [2024] *Pope Francis: 'Every religion is a way to arrive at God'* [Online] Available at: www.lifesitenews.com [Accessed on: 21 May 2025]

anyone's feelings or stimulate a debate in the sense of a critique of religion and a missionary impulse to confront Jesus' absolute claims. Today, we understand tolerance as the renunciation of convictions and truth claims.[2395]

Also Bishop Athanasius Schneider, auxiliary bishop of Astana, Kazakhstan, made the following criticisms to Raymond Arroyo on EWTN's *World Over Live* show:

> Such an affirmation of Pope Francis is clearly against the divine revelation, it contradicts directly the first Commandment of God which is ever valid – 'You shall not have other gods beside me' – this is so clear, and such a statement contradicts the entire Gospel. Jesus Christ said, 'No one comes to the Father except through me.' He is the only way to God, there are no other ways or paths. So in this statement sadly, regrettably Pope Francis plainly contradicts the first Commandment of God and the entire Gospel [...] God permitted that the first pope, Simon Peter, he renounced [and] denied Christ three times, and he was appointed the vicar of Christ and nevertheless he denied Christ three times. So God permitted it that it could also happen in the future, that a successor of Simon Peter would speak some words which are contrary to the divine truth.[2396]

The Rt. Rev. Charles Chaput, Archbishop Emeritus of Philadelphia, wrote in the US journal *First Things*:

> To suggest, even loosely, that Catholics walk a more or less similar path to God as other religions drains martyrdom of its meaning. Why give up your life for Christ when other paths may get us to the same God. Such a sacrifice would be senseless. But the witness of the martyrs is as important today as ever. We live in an age when the dominant religion is increasingly the worship of the self. We need the martyrs – and each of us as a confessor of Jesus Christ – to remind an unbelieving world that the path to a genuinely rich life is to give oneself fully to another, to the other [...] That all religions have equal weight is an extraordinarily flawed idea for the Successor of Peter to appear to support. Simply put: Not all religions seek the same God, and some religions are both wrong and potentially dangerous, materially and spiritually.[2397]

During the inflight press conference returning from the Apostolic Journey to Singapore, Pope Francis expressed his satisfaction with the secret Vatican-China deal. The Supreme Pontiff renewed his commitment to the deal despite the increase in persecution of Chinese Catholics and the Chinese Communist Party reneging on the deal through the unilateral appointment of bishops:

> I am pleased with the dialogue with China. The results are good. Even for the appointment of bishops, things are progressing with goodwill. I have spoken with the Secretariat of State, and I am happy with how things are going. As for China, I see China as an aspiration, meaning I would like to visit China. It's a great country, and I admire and respect China. It's a country with an ancient culture. China's capacity for dialogue to understand each other goes beyond the different systems of government it has had. I believe China is a promise and a hope for the Church. Collaboration is possible, and certainly regarding conflicts. Cardinal Zuppi is working in this area, and he has contacts with China.[2398]

18th September

Following his general audience, Pope Francis met with a group of four men from the United States presenting themselves as women organised by the trans activist priest

[2395]Eleganti, M [2024] *Bishop Eleganti: Pope Francis' comments on other religions conceal Jesus and contradict the Gospel* [Online] Available at: www.lifesitenews.com [Accessed on: 21 May 2025]

[2396]Schneider, A [2024] The World Over September 26, 2024 | *New book: Flee From Heresy: Bishop Athanasius Schneider* [Online] Available at: www.youtube.com [Accessed on: 21 May 2025]

[2397]Chaput, C [2024] *The Pope and Other Religions* [Online] Available at: firstthings.com [Accessed on: 21 May 2025]

[2398]Pope Francis [2024] *Press Conference During the Return Flight from Singapore* [Online] Available at: www.vatican.va [Accessed on: 22 May 2025]

Don Andrea Conocchia and trans activist Sr. Geneviève Jeanningros. The meeting was initiated following the 2024 meeting of Fr. James Martin, S.J.'s pro-homosexuality group Outreach. Emily Mangiaracina of *LifeSite News* commented,

> it appears that Francis is not encouraging the men, who are currently living as 'women,' to repent of their transgender lifestyles, return to the practice of the Catholic faith, and accept biological reality.[2399]

The Vatican's press office released the names of Pope Francis' personal appointments to the second Synod on Synodality, including controversial pro-homosexuality clergy such as Cardinals Francesco Coccopalmerio, Cardinals Blase Cupich, Jozef De Kesel, Wilton Gregory, Robert McElroy and Father James Martin, S.J.[2400]

19th September

L'Osservatore Romano, the newspaper of the Holy See, published an article by the militant pro-homosexuality Father Timothy Radcliffe, O.P. Following Pope Benedict XVI excluding Fr. Radcliffe from speaking at the general assembly of Caritas International in 2011 for his controversial views on homosexuality, Pope Francis rehabilitated him through a number of appointments: Consultor to the Pontifical Council for Justice and Peace (2015); Spiritual Adviser and Preacher for the Synod on Synodality (2023–2024) and elevation to the Sacred College of Cardinals in 2024. In his *L'Osservatore Romano* article Father Radcliffe advocated the right of homosexuals to express their disordered desires that contravene God's design for sex and marriage:

> I am convinced of the fundamental wisdom of the Church's teaching, but I still do not fully understand how it should be lived by young gay Catholics who accept their sexuality and rightly desire to express their affection. This cannot happen only through the denial of desire. For St. Thomas Aquinas, our passions are the driving force of our return to God. Our desires are given by God. Desires need to be educated, purified and freed from an illusory fantasy, but in all desires there is a desire for what is good and for God. The commandments are not given to deny our desires, but to direct them toward their true end.[2401]

The Congregation [Dicastery] for the Doctrine of the Faith issued the document '*The Queen of Peace': Note About the Spiritual Experience Connected with Medjugorje*. Following the novel norms set out in its document *For Proceeding in the Discernment of Alleged Supernatural Phenomena* (19th May 2024), Cardinal Fernandez refused to rule if the Medjugorje apparitions and messages are of 'supernatural origin', instead only issuing a *Nihil obstat*:

> Through the *Nihil obstat* about a spiritual event, the faithful 'are authorised to give it their adherence in a prudent manner' (Norms, art. 22, §1; cf. Benedict XVI, Verbum Domini, par. 14). While this does not imply a declaration of the supernatural character of the phenomenon in question (cf. Norms, art. 22, §2) — and recalling that the faithful are not obliged to believe in it — the Nihil obstat indicates that the faithful can receive a positive encouragement for their Christian life through this spiritual proposal, and it authorises public acts of devotion. Such a determination is possible insofar as many positive fruits have been noted in the midst of a spiritual experience, while negative and dangerous effects have not spread among the People of God. Evaluating the abundant and widespread fruits, which are so beautiful and positive, does not imply that the alleged supernatural events are declared authentic. Instead, it only highlights that the Holy Spirit is acting fruitfully for the good of the faithful 'in the midst' of this spiritual

---

[2399]Mangiaracina, E [2024] *Pope Francis meets with four 'transgender' men who attended Fr. James Martin's LGBT conference* [Online] Available at: www.lifesitenews.com [Accessed on: 22 May 2025]
[2400]*Pope Francis personally invites pro-LGBT Fr James Martin, Cardinal Cupich to October Synod* [2024] [Online] Available at: www.lifesitenews.com [Accessed on: 22 May 2025]
[2401]Mangiaracina, E [2024] *Francis-appointed Synod adviser appears to defend homosexual 'desire' in Vatican newspaper* [Online] Available at: www.lifesitenews.com [Accessed on: 22 May 2025]

phenomenon of Medjugorje. For this reason, all are invited to appreciate and share the pastoral value of this spiritual proposal (cf. Norms, par. 17). Moreover, the positive assessment that most of the messages of Medjugorje are edifying does not imply a declaration that they have a direct supernatural origin. Consequently, when referring to 'messages' from Our Lady, one should always bear in mind that they are 'alleged messages.' (38).[2402]

23rd September

Pope Francis appointed 28 new consultors to the Vatican's Dicastery for the Doctrine of the Faith, including the pro-homosexuality, anti-Humane Vitae moral theologian Father Maurizio Chiodi. This was the latest sign of Pope Francis' approval of Father Maurizio Chiodi, having appointed him a member of the 'reformed' Pontifical Academy for Life in 2017; appointed him to teach at the 'reformed' Pontifical John Paul II Institute in Rome in 2019 and in July 2024 Chiodi was appointed a member of the Synod on Synodality Study Group dealing with controversial moral issues such as homosexuality and adulterous second marriages.[2403]

24th September

Pope Francis delivered a message to participants of the International Prayer Meeting for Peace held in Paris, organised by the Sant'Egidio Community. During his address, the Supreme Pontiff again expressed his gravely erroneous religious indifferentism:

> It is against this backdrop that the title of this Paris Meeting – 'Imagine Peace' – is most eloquent. We need to keep meeting, to weave bonds of fraternity and to allow ourselves to be guided by the divine inspiration present in every faith, in order to join in 'imagining peace' among all peoples.[2404]

1st October

Pope Francis presided at a 'penitential vigil' on the eve of the second Synod on Synodality in St. Peter's Basilica, that replaced the traditional understanding of sin with a novel list, including 'Sin against creation, against indigenous populations, against migrants'; 'Sin of using doctrine as stones to be hurled', and 'Sin against synodality/ lack of listening, communion, and participation of all.'[2405]

Cardinal Gerhard Müller, the former prefect of the Congregation for the Doctrine of the Faith, criticised the synodal 'penitential vigil' for disguising as Christianity a checklist of woke and gender ideology:

> The presented catalog of alleged sins against the doctrine of the church, which is misused as a missile, or against synodality, whatever one may understand by that, reads like a checklist of woke and gender ideology, somewhat laboriously disguised as Christianity, apart from a few misdeeds that scream to high heaven [...] There is also no sin against a kind of synodality that is used as a tool for brainwashing to discredit so-called conservatives as outdated and covert Pharisees and to pass off progressive ideologies, which led to the decline of the churches in the West in the 1970s, as the fulfilment of the reforms of Vatican II, allegedly hindered by John Paul II and Benedict

[2402]Dicastery for the Doctrine of the Faith [2024] *'The Queen of Peace': Note About the Spiritual Experience Connected with Medjugorje* [Online] Available at: press.vatican.va [Accessed on: 23 May 2025]
[2403]Brockhaus, H [2024] *Pope Francis names consultants to Vatican doctrine office, including controversial theologian* [Online] Available at: www.catholicnewsagency.com; *These Are the Members of the Synod on Synodality Study Groups* [Online] Available at: www.ncregister.com [Accessed on: 22 May 2025]
[2404]Pope Francis [2024] *Message of the Holy Father Francis to the participants of the International Meeting of Prayer for Peace organised by the Community of Sant'Egidio (Paris, September 22-24, 2024)* [Online] Available at: press.vatican.va [Accessed on: 21 May 2024]
[2405]Haynes, M [2024] *Synod on Synodality to include ceremony 'confessing' sins against 'migrants,' 'synodality'* [Online] Available at: www.lifesitenews.com [Accessed on: 21 May 2025]

XVI [...] Overall, the grand agitators of the synodal paths and rampant synodalism are more concerned with securing influential positions and pushing through their un-Catholic ideologies than with renewing faith in Christ in the hearts of people. The collapse of ecclesiastical institutions in formerly entirely Christian countries (empty seminaries, dying religious communities, broken marriages and families, mass exodus from the Church—several million Catholics in Germany) does not shake them to their core. They stubbornly pursue their agenda, which leads to the destruction of Christian anthropology, until the last one turns off the light and the Church's coffers are empty. [*Trans*].[2406]

Bishop Athanasius Schneider, auxiliary bishop of Astana, Kazakhstan, criticised the synodal 'penitential vigil' for being 'a tool to promote a new agenda in the Synod to establish new doctrines which are contrary to divine revelation, or undermine divine revelation.' Regarding the synodal 'sin' of 'using doctrine as stones to be hurled' Bishop Schneider insisted:

...such new invented doctrines in this so called synodality, these are the true stones which they throw to the faithful, because they are distortions and these are harming the faithful and putting in danger their eternal salvation. A true doctrine is not against charity: to transmit doctrine is one of the highest expressions of charity towards a neighbour, to bring them to the right of truth and the light of truth only gives us true happiness. Such confused new synodal doctrines and methods bring us ambiguity, uncertainty, and this no one will give his life for something which is ambiguous. We will only give our life for what is true, for what is solid as a rock, which is Christ – He is the rock, he is the truth and only for Him. With's God's grace, every Christian must be ready to give his life.[2407]

2nd October

The study group established by Pope Francis to make proposals concerning controversial moral issues, such as homosexuality, adultery and contraception, reported to the Synod on Synodality. The group proposed the adoption of a 'new paradigm' in morality that focused on the discernment of individual experience and minimised the moral absolutes established by Divine Revelation:

Ethically speaking, it is not a matter of applying pre-packaged objective truth to the different subjective situations, as if they were mere particular cases of an immutable and universal law. The criteria of discernment arise from listening to the [living] self-gift of Revelation in Jesus in the today of the Spirit [...] It is not a matter of proclaiming and applying abstract doctrinal principles, but of vitally inhabiting the experience of faith in its personal and social relevance so that we will be open to the ever new promptings of the Holy Spirit [...] Only a vital, fruitful, and reciprocal tension between doctrine and practice embodies the living Tradition and is able to counteract the temptation to rely on the barren scleroticism of verbal pronouncements.[2408]

6th October

During his Angelus Address Pope Francis announced that he intended to elevate 21 men to the Sacred College of Cardinals including Fr. Timothy Radcliffe O.P., notorious for his many pro-homosexuality statements. During his 2013 testimony to the Church of England's commission on human sexuality Timothy Radcliffe made his strongest statement affirming homosexual sex acts:

[2406]Müller, G [2024] *Kard. Müller: Es gibt keine Sünde gegen die Lehre der Kirche, die angeblich als Waffe gebraucht wird* [Online] Available at: www.kath.net [Accessed on: 23 May 2025]
[2407]Schneider, A [2024] *The World Over September 26, 2024 | New book: Flee From Heresy: Bishop Athanasius Schneider* [Online] Available at: www.youtube.com [Accessed on: 21 May 2025]
[2408]*Presentation of the Reports of the 10 Working Groups Established by Pope Francis. Group 9: Synodal Theological and Methodological Criteria for Shared Discernment of Controversial Doctrinal, Pastoral, and Ethical Issues (SR 15)* [2024] [Online] Available at: www.synod.va [Accessed on: 27 May 2025]

How does all of this bear on the question of gay sexuality? We cannot begin with the question of whether it is permitted or forbidden! We must ask what it means, and how far it is Eucharistic. Certainly it can be generous, vulnerable, tender, mutual and non-violent. So in many ways, I would think that it can be expressive of Christ's self-gift. We can also see how it can be expressive of mutual fidelity, a covenantal relationship in which two people bind themselves to each other for ever. (Para 266).[2409]

7th October

During a Synod on Synodality press conference in the Vatican, Sister Mary Theresa Barron, OLA, president of the International Union of Superiors General spoke in support of the 'ordination' of women to the diaconate and priesthood. Sister Barron told reporters:

We tend to look at it from the question of 'can women be ordained in the church today' and I think we have to look at the question very much from the spirit. Is the spirit calling women, because some women do sense a call to priesthood or diaconate? I think we have to look broader than just a can we/can we not from a theological or canonical point of view, but in terms of the spirit calling to ministry today and in terms of the needs of mission today, are those calls there and can we continue the discussion.[2410]

12th October

Pope Francis held a private audience with members of the heterodox militant pro-homosexuality group *New Ways Ministry*. A self-described Catholic group, *New Ways Ministry* was condemned by Archbishop James Hickey of Washington (1984); the Congregation for the Doctrine of the Faith (1999) and Cardinal Francis George (2010) for advocacy of positions contrary to Catholic teaching on homosexuality and homosexual sex acts, and causing confusion among the faithful. Following the private audience it was reported that Pope Francis committed to consider 'openness to transgender people' as a criteria for appointing new U.S. bishops. Deacon Raymond Dever, a member of New Ways Ministry told *The Times* newspaper of London:

Francis mentioned that situations experienced by transgender people will be more on his mind. He said that when he appoints new bishops in the US he will consider their openness to transgender people as a criteria.[2411]

L'Osservatore Romano, the newspaper of the Holy See, published an article written by pro-homosexuality Cardinal-designate Timothy Radcliffe O.P., attacking the integrity of African bishops for rejecting *Fiducia Supplicans'* advocacy of 'gay blessings'. Radcliffe accused the African bishop of rejecting *Fiducia Supplicans* not because it contradicted doctrine on homosexuality but due to the influence of Russian, Arab-state and American money, without providing any evidence:

Another concern raised by Fiducia supplicans is that there appears to have been no consultation – even with bishops or other Vatican offices – before its release; not exactly, perhaps, a good example of synodality. African bishops are under intense pressure from Evangelicals, with American money; from Russian Orthodox, with Russian money; and from Muslims, with money from the rich Gulf countries. There should have been a discussion with them before, not after, the statement was released. Whatever we think about the statement, when we face tensions, and to overcome them, we all need to think and engage with one another on a deep level.[2412]

[2409]The House of Bishops [2024] Working Group on human sexuality. London: Church House Publishing, p.77
[2410]Cambria, A [2024] *Liberal nun tells Synod reporters some women 'feel the call' to the priesthood* [Online] Available at: www.lifesitenews.com [Accessed on: 23 May 2025]
[2411]Haynes, M [2024] *Pope Francis said he will consider 'openness' to 'transgender people' when naming new US bishops: report* [Online] Available at: www.lifesitenews.com [Accessed on: 21 May 2025]
[2412]*Cardinal-designate Radcliffe links African bishops' opposition to homosexuality to pressure from evangelicals, Moscow, and Muslims* [2024] [Online] Available at: www.catholicculture.org [Accessed on: 24 May 2025]

Bizarrely, Cardinal Fridolin Ambongo, president of the African bishops' conference, told Michael Haynes, *LifeSiteNews* senior Vatican correspondent, that Father Timothy Radcliffe denied writing the article, despite the article remaining on *L'Osservatore Romano*'s website, and being clearly ascribed to Fr. Radcliffe. (The article remained on *L'Osservatore Romano*'s website under Fr. Radcliffe's name in May 2025).[2413]

Agência Ecclesia, the Catholic Church's News Agency in Portugal, posted an interview with Cardinal Leonardo Steiner of Manaus, in the Amazon. During the interview Cardinal Steiner, an advocate of the 'ordination' of women deacons, described his para-liturgy for women that appeared to involve simulating rites associated with the sacrament of Holy Orders:

> In our reality, women exercise the deacon's ministries. The vast majority of our small communities are coordinated by women. The role of women in the church of the Amazon is fundamental. When I send someone, for example to baptise, I lay hands on them, but I don't lay hands on someone as an ordination. I lay hands as the apostles did as a sign of receiving a ministry and that this person will celebrate a sacrament.[2414]

17th October

Vatican News, the news outlet of the Holy See, reported on the address made by Bishop Joseph Yang Yongqiang of Hangzhou, China at the Synod on Synodality. Bishop Joseph Yang Yongqiang's transfer from the Diocese of Zhoucon to the Diocese of Hangzhou was granted in June 2024. He is a member of the Communist controlled Chinese Catholic Patriotic Association which the Vatican does not recognise as legitimate. During his address Bishop Joseph Yang praised 'the sinicization of Catholicism':

> We follow the evangelical spirit of 'becoming all things to all people'. We effectively adapt to society, serve it, adhere to the direction of the sinicization of Catholicism, and preach the Good News.[2415]

Dr. George Weigel, Distinguished Senior Fellow at the Ethics and Public Policy Center, Washington, described 'sinicization' as the communist iron grip control of the Church

> 'Sinicization' is… a call to the kowtow, to obsequious acquiescence to the regime's program of social control, which is essentially a refinement of what George Orwell described in the dystopian novel 1984 – although the dystopia is now promoted as a utopia of abundance, married to a restoration of national honor and dignity through domination of the world […] Catholic faith in China must be conformed to 'Xi Jinping Thought;' it must not temper, much less correct, the official state ideology. Catholic practice in China must advance the hegemonic goals of the Chinese communist regime; if Catholic witness challenges those goals, or the way in which those goals are advanced through massive human rights violations internally and aggression internationally, the result is persecution, often via the corrupt legal system of which my friend Jimmy Lai is a prominent victim.[2416]

Cardinal Zen, emeritus bishop of Hong Kong, published an article on his website *oldyosef.hkcatholic.com*, in which he expressed his concerns that the Synod on Synodality aimed to overthrow the Church's hierarchy for 'a democratic system' and change the Church's doctrine on sexual ethics:

> From the start of this Synod, the two cardinals leading the assembly and the prefect of the Dicastery for the Doctrine of the Faith, appointed by the Pope, have not emphasised

---

[2413]Haynes, M [2024] *Cardinal says Fr. Radcliffe did not write article linking same-sex 'blessings' rejection to foreign money* [Online] Available at: www.lifesitenews.com [Accessed on: 24 May 2025]

[2414]Haynes, M [2024] *Amazon cardinal 'lays hands' to confer 'ministry' on women going to 'celebrate a sacrament'* [Online] Available at: www.lifesitenews.com [Accessed on: 21 May 2025]

[2415]Tornielli, A [2024] *Chinese Bishops at Synod assembly: 'We are in communion'* [Online] Available at: www.vaticannews.va [Accessed on: 23 May 2025]

[2416]Weigel, G [2024] *'Sinicization' Is Not Inculturation* [Online] Available at: www.ncregister.com [Accessed on: 23 May 2025]

preserving the faith but instead focused on change, particularly changes to the Church's operational structure and ethical teachings, especially regarding the ethics of sexuality, including same-sex relationships [...] It is evident that the purpose of this Synod is to overturn the Church's hierarchical structure and promote a democratic system [...] If those advocating for this change cannot achieve it universally within the Church, will they push for diversity among local Churches? Could individual Bishops' Conferences gain independent authority over matters of doctrine? This is a terrifying prospect. If such an idea succeeds, we will no longer be Catholic. (The Anglican Communion in London approved same-sex marriage, and their members now represent less than 20% of the global Anglican community. Should we not take heed?). [Trans].[2417]

21st October

Sandro Magister, veteran Vatican journalist, published an essay by Cardinal Walter Brandmüller, former president of the Pontifical Committee for Historical Sciences, on the website, *www.diakonos.be*. Cardinal Brandmüller warned that national bishops conferences pose a threat to the ecclesial nature and unity of the Church instituted by Christ:

> the creation of a national body forces the loosening, if not the dissolution, of the 'communio' of the universal Church, which then finds expression in special national regulations. This is experienced in the most evident manner in the liturgy; one need only think of the introduction of the national languages. [...] In the same way, as has happened recently, a grave attack on the unity of faith within the Church is constituted by the contradictory interpretations that various episcopal conferences have given to the apostolic exhortation of Pope Francis *Amoris Laetitia* of March 19, 2016. [...][2418]

22nd October

The Vatican Press Office released a bulletin announcing that the Vatican and Chinese Communist government had renewed the secret bilateral deal for another four years, despite Cardinal Zen, emeritus bishop of Hong Kong condemning it as a 'betrayal' and the Chinese government reneging on the deal by unilaterally appointing bishops. The bulletin stated:

> In light of the consensus reached for an effective application of the Provisional Agreement regarding the Appointment of Bishops, after appropriate consultation and assessment, the Holy See and the People's Republic of China have agreed to extend further its validity for four years from the present date. The Vatican Party remains dedicated to furthering the respectful and constructive dialogue with the Chinese Party, in view of the further development of bilateral relations for the benefit of the Catholic Church in China and the Chinese people as a whole.[2419]

26th October

The Vatican Press Office released the Final Document of the Synod on Synodality which included controversial proposals concerning the curtailment of papal and episcopal authority by synodal consultation, changes to the liturgy, openness to considering the 'ordination' of women deacons and openness to the 'perspectives' of other religions:

> *Papal and episcopal authority*
>
> In a synodal Church, the authority of the Bishop, of the Episcopal College and of the Bishop of Rome in regard to decision-taking is inviolable as it is grounded in the hierarchical

---

[2417]Zen, J [2024] 我們要祈禱，願主教會議順利結束 [Online] Available at: oldyosef.hkcatholic.com [Accessed on: 24 May 2025]

[2418]Brandmüller, W [2024] *The Synod and the Real Church. Apart from the Choir, the Voice of a Renowned Historian and Cardinal* [Online] Available at: www.diakonos.be [Accessed on 24 May 2025]

[2419]*Communiqué on the extension of the Provisional Agreement between the Holy See and the People's Republic of China regarding the appointment of bishops, 22.10.2024* [2024] [Online] Available at: press. vatican.va [Accessed on: 23 May 2025]

structure of the Church established by Christ; it both serves unity and legitimate diversity (cf. LG 13). Such an exercise of authority, however, is not without limits: it may not ignore a direction which emerges through proper discernment within a consultative process, especially if this is done by participatory bodies. It is not appropriate to set the consultative and deliberative elements involved in reaching a decision in opposition to each other: in the Church, the deliberative element is undertaken with the help of all and never without those whose pastoral governance allows them to take a decision by virtue of their office. For this reason, the recurring formula in the Code of Canon Law, 'merely consultative' vote (*tantum consultivum*) should be reviewed to eliminate the possibility of ambiguity. It seems appropriate to carry out a revision of Canon Law from a synodal perspective, clarifying the distinction and relation between consultation and deliberation and shedding light on the responsibilities of those who play different roles in the decision-making process. (92).

Synodal liturgy

Deepening the link between liturgy and synodality will help all Christian communities, in the diversity of their cultures and traditions, to adopt celebratory styles that make visible the face of a synodal Church. To this end, we call for the establishment of a specific Study Group which would be entrusted with reflection on how to make liturgical celebrations more an expression of synodality. (27).

Women 'deacons'

There is no reason or impediment that should prevent women from carrying out leadership roles in the Church: what comes from the Holy Spirit cannot be stopped. Additionally, the question of women's access to diaconal ministry remains open. This discernment needs to continue. (60).

Openness to religious diversity

The plurality of religions and cultures, the diversity of spiritual and theological traditions, the variety of the gifts of the Spirit and of the tasks of the community, as well as the diversity of age, sex and social affiliation within the Church, are an invitation to each person to recognise their particular situatedness, resist the temptation of being at the centre, and open oneself to the acceptance of other perspectives. (42).[2420]

31st October

EWTN's The World Over broadcast an interview with Cardinal Raymond Burke, the former prefect of the Supreme Tribunal of the Apostolic Signatura, during which he expressed concerns about the Final Document of the Synod on Synodality. Cardinal Burke told Raymond Arroyo:

No one has been able to define what the meaning of synodality is – this has become kind of a place holder for advancing all kind of ideas about the Church, about the sacred liturgy. [Rejecting the idea that the synod] is an essential mark of the Church. The Church's hierarchical communion has taught, and the Second Vatican Council is clear from Our Lord's own example informing the Church in the very beginning of its public ministry, while there is a role for consultation according to the ancient synods, this is not an essential mark of the Church. This is extremely troublesome and dangerous and it needs to be corrected.[2421]

2nd November

Bishop Marian Eleganti, Emeritus auxiliary bishop of Chur, Switzerland, posted on his website, *www.marian-eleganti.ch*, his criticisms of the Synod on Synodality:

[2420]Francis, XVI Ordinary General Assembly of the Synod of Bishops [2024] *For a Synodal Church: Communion, Participation, Mission: Final Document* [Online] Available at: www.synod.va [Accessed on: 27 May 2025]

[2421]Haynes, M [2024] *Cardinal Burke: Synodality is not a 'mark of the Church,' final proposals are 'dangerous'* [Online] Available at: www.lifesitenews.com [Accessed on: 21 May 2025]

The Pope is sovereign anyway, can intervene anywhere, and cannot be judged by anyone. He's done so extensively thus far. From the ship, it's clear that he and his allies have steered the synodal process behind the scenes. That's why his role in the new synodality will need to be 'rethought,' they say. *Fiducia Supplicans* was, in any case, a (synodal) misstep, as it lacked a synodal mandate. Cardinal Fernández rushed ahead after the penultimate synod, and Francis backed him. As we see, the hierarchy behaves quite freely toward the synodal process. In the end, those who draft and present the texts or 'moderate' the process—to avoid saying 'steer'—are decisive. The appeal to the Holy Spirit feels strained. They, and above all the Pope, decide what comes out as binding in the end. The broad preliminary consultations change nothing about that.[2422]

5th November

Pope Francis made a much publicised 'private' visit to the home of the militant abortion and euthanasia Italian politician Emma Bonino. Previously the Supreme Pontiff had praised Emma Bonino as one of Italy's 'forgotten greats' (February 2026), despite her involvement in 10,000 illegal abortion, some in her own apartment and her role in spearheading the legalisation of abortion in Italy.[2423]

During *LifeSiteNews'* US election coverage Bishop Joseph Strickland, emeritus bishop of Tyler, Texas, expressed his rejection of the Synod on Synodality:

> There are threats on the horizon. This Synod on Synodality, I reject, because it's not Catholic. Many voices have already said this is not the Catholic Church. We're in a time when Judas Iscariot is raising his ugly head. We're in dangerous territory for this nation, but more importantly, and more critically, I believe, for the Catholic faith. The Catholic faith, the Catholic Church, will not collapse. Christ has promised it will prevail against the gates of hell until the end of the age…if it comes to opposing a priest or bishop or someone from the Vatican that is proclaiming a false message, we have to be strong enough disciples of Jesus Christ to say, 'No. We live the truth that is Christ. He's truth incarnate.'[2424]

6th November

Religión Digital, the Spanish-language portal for religious information, published an interview with Cardinal Cristóbal Romero of the Archdiocese of Rabat, Morocco. Fr. Cristóbal Romero was appointed bishop by Pope Francis in 2017 and elevated to the Sacred College of Cardinals in 2019. Cardinal Romero expressed strong support for the Final Document of the Synod on Synodality, arguing that it was morally binding on everyone in the Church:

> Synodality is a process of discernment so that decision-making is consensual to the maximum. And when a decision is made, even those who disagreed are morally obligated to support something that has been decided after a process in which we have all been able to participate and express opinions and even pray together to ask for the enlightenment of the Holy Spirit. In the end, it is the pope, the bishop, the parish priest who, after having listened to everyone, and not capriciously, makes a decision and everyone goes that way. Democracy is little, we want more: we want fraternity, joint work, search for the common good.[2425]

The Archdiocese of Mechelen-Brussels, Belgium, issued a memo to clergy in the vicariate of Brabant Walloon, proposing naming Rebecca Alsberge, an episcopal delegate, alongside the pope and the local bishop in the Eucharistic Prayer:

[2422]Eleganti, M [2024] *Der Grosse Durchbruch ist es nicht: Ein Kommentar zum Abschluss der Synode über Synodalitä* [Online] Available at: www.marian-eleganti.ch [Accessed on: 28 May 2025]

[2423]Haynes, M [2024] *Pope Francis makes personal visit to notorious abortionist Emma Bonino* [Online] Available at: www.lifesitenews.com [Accessed on: 27 May 2025]

[2424]Kokx, S [2024] *Bishop Strickland slams Synod on Synodality: 'I reject' it, 'it's not Catholic'* [Online] Available at: www.lifesitenews.com [Accessed on: 28 May 2025]

[2425]Haynes, M [2024] *Leading African cardinal claims Catholics are 'morally obligated to support' Synod decisions* [Online] Available at: www.lifesitenews.com [Accessed on: 28 May 2025]

For Eucharistic Prayer I, it proposed the wording 'we present them in union with your servant, our Pope N., our Bishop N., our episcopal delegate N., and all those who faithfully keep the Catholic faith received from the Apostles.'[2426]

9th November

Cardinal Zen, the emeritus bishop of Hong Kong, published on his website, *oldyosef. hkcatholic.com*, his criticisms of the Synod on Synodality. Cardinal Zen expressed wide-ranging criticism of Pope Francis' manipulation of synods to change the Church's doctrine and discipline:

> From the 'Synods' held under Pope Francis, we can see that he wants to change the Church's doctrines or disciplines each time rather than discuss how to safeguard these doctrines and disciplines. He used the Synod on the Family (2004-2005) to try to let the divorced and remarried Catholics receive Holy Communion. He wanted to use the Synod of Amazon to introduce 'the ordination of highly respected married laymen (*viri probati*) as priests'. And for the Synod this time, from the two leading figures he appointed and the documents issued by the secretariat, we can see that he has some broader goals: to change the hierarchical system of the Church (replace with a democratic group of baptized people); to establish female deacons (opening way for female priests); to abolish priestly celibacy; and to change the traditional doctrine on 'sexual' ethics (beginning with the blessings the homosexual couples). To achieve these ends, the Synod meetings were held with the procedure in which sharing was emphasised while discussion was limited. Bishops, along with the non-bishops surrounding a table, were led by the nose by the so-called 'facilitators.' Everything in the assembly was kept strictly confidential, that we, the People of God, had no way to learn about the progress of the assembly, though the 'leaders' said they gave much importance to sharing and participating.[2427]

22nd November

The US journal *First Things* published an article by Cardinal Gerhard Müller, the former prefect of the Congregation for the Doctrine of the Faith, criticising the Synod on Synodality under the title, 'The Seven Sins Against the Holy Spirit: A Synodal Tragedy.' Cardinal Müller wrote:

> The direct communication between the Holy Spirit and Synod participants is invoked to justify arbitrary doctrinal concessions ('marriage for all'; lay officials at the helm of ecclesiastical 'power'; the ordination of female deacons as a trophy in the fight for women's rights) as the result of a higher insight, which can overcome any objections from established Catholic doctrine. But anyone who, by appealing to personal and collective inspiration from the Holy Spirit, seeks to reconcile the teaching of the Church with an ideology hostile to revelation and with the tyranny of relativism is guilty in various ways of a 'sin against the Holy Spirit' (Matt. 12:31; Mark 3:29; Luke 12:10). The most current sin of the seven sins against the Holy Spirit is when the supernatural origin and character of Christianity is denied in order to subordinate the Church of the Triune God to the goals and purposes of a worldly salvation project, be it eco-socialist climate neutrality or Agenda 2030 of the 'globalist elite.'[2428]

25th November

Pope Francis promulgated a formal 'Note' expressing his decision that the Synod on Synodality's Final Document must be accepted as part of the Magisterium of the Church:

[2426]Coppen, L [2024] *Lay 'episcopal delegate' added to Eucharistic Prayer in Belgian province* [Online] Available at: www.pillarcatholic.com [Accessed on: 28 May 2025]

[2427]Zen, J [2024] *Did the Synod on "Synodality" End Smoothly?* [Online] Available at: oldyosef. hkcatholic.com [Accessed on: 28 May 2025]

[2428]Müller, G [2024] *The Seven Sins Against the Holy Spirit: A Synodal Tragedy* [Online] Available at: firstthings.com [Accessed on: 27 May 2025]

The Final Document participates in the ordinary Magisterium of the Successor of Peter (cf. EC 18 § 1; CCC 892) and as such I ask that it be accepted. It represents a form of exercising the authentic teaching of the Bishop of Rome that has novel features but in fact corresponds to what I had occasion to point out on October 17, 2015, when I stated that synodality is the proper interpretive framework for understanding hierarchical ministry. [Trans].[2429]

6th December

Il Messaggero, the Italian newspaper, reported that Pope Francis approved an official homosexual themed pilgrimage during the 2025 Jubilee Year, with the approval of Cardinal Zuppi of Bologna and the Jesuit Superior General Fr. Sosa, 'the historic Baroque church of the Gesù has become the promoter of welcoming LGBT+ pilgrims, their parents, workers and all those who gravitate to these rainbow associations.' The homosexual themed pilgrimage to the Holy Door would be organised by *Tenda di Gionata* [Jonathan's Tent] one of Italy's most prominent LGBT 'Catholic organisations.[2430]

LifeSiteNews, the Canadian Catholic news outlet, published an essay by Fr. Joachim Heimerl of the Archdiocese of Vienna, warning that the 'synodal' church was under the control of 'old homosexual men':

> …the homosexuals stranded in the priesthood and especially in the episcopate are now vehemently pushing behind the scenes of the Vatican for the Church to open up to the new course. To put it bluntly: the Church has fallen into the hands of older homosexual men. It is only against this backdrop that it is understandable that the Pope made possible the egregious *Fiducia supplicans* and at the same time encountered so conspicuously little opposition: Very few people cared about the 'blessing' of sin and apostasy from God; most of them obviously identified with it long ago and deliberately instigated the document under the leadership of Cardinal Victor Manuel Fernández […] They have understood – as if by a miracle – that homosexuality is 'willed' by God and is by no means a sin, contrary to revelation and the 2000-year-old teachings of the Church. An astonishing change, don't you think? Or is it not more likely that all these prelates were just seizing the opportunity to finally justify their predisposition and 'approve' it with the help of the Pope? Who else could promote 'gay heresy' if not those most reverend gentlemen who are themselves 'gay' and who are only driven by it and not by the 'Holy Spirit'?[2431]

12th December

Panorama, the Italian media outlet, published an interview with an anonymous Vatican employee, a member of the Vatican's labour union, who complained about Pope Francis's strong preference for those who were in favour of the homosexual and leftist political agenda:

> The spies, however, are always at work: we are no longer serene. If you ask for a raise you risk excommunication, if you ask for overtime you get dirty looks. Woe to you if you ask for an explanation as to why they gave an outside consultancy. Working in the Vatican today is not worthwhile either for the salary or, much less, for the profession. Career moves blocked except if you are friends with one of the two lobbies that matter. The first is the extensive and very powerful gay lobby; the second is the 'Santa Marta club' that belts out the Pope…you have to speak Spanish because Latin is the language of tradition that has to be abolished. You have to be green, pro-migrant and especially

[2429]Pope Francis [2024] *Nota di accompagnamento del Documento finale della XVI Assemblea Generale Ordinaria del Sinodo dei Vescovi del Santo Padre Francesco, 25.11.2024* [Online] Available at: press.vatican.va [Accessed on: 27 May 2025]
[2430]Haynes, M [2024] *Pope Francis approves LGBT 'pilgrimage' for 2025 Jubilee: report; Vatican quietly returns LGBT Jubilee 'pilgrimage' to official calendar* [Online] Available at: www.lifesitenews.com [Accessed on: 29 May 2025]
[2431]Heimerl, J [2024] *Fr. Heimerl: Francis' 'synodal church' is controlled by old homosexual men* [Online] Available at: www.lifesitenews.com [Accessed on: 29 May 2025]

pro-Palestinian. To them Venezuelan Nicolás Maduro is a saint and Donald Trump the devil. And you have to watch out for Bergoglio's sudden changes in mood and opinion. Maybe then the salary increases. The result is that today they are struggling to find qualified staff. To save money, they have asked for overtime from nuns and priests: they don't pay them…[Trans].[2432]

2025

5th January

Il Giornale, the daily newspaper of Milan, published a report that Cardinal Domenico Battaglia of Naples allowed a militant homosexual activist, Cristiano Cimmino, address the congregation at the '*Te Deum Mass*' at the Naples cathedral on the 31st December. Fr. Domenico Battaglia was appointed bishop by Pope Francis in 2016, archbishop of Naples in 2021 and elevated to the Sacred College of Cardinals in 2024. *Il Giornale* reported:

> The opportunity given to a representative of the LGBT cultural association during the celebration presided over by the newly appointed Cardinal Domenico 'Mimmo' Battaglia filled the Neapolitan rainbow community with pride. The Lgbt Channel Tv portal noted that 'for the first time, an LGBTQIA+ voice (...) found space in such a solemn context.' For activists, 'what happened (...) was not just a celebration. It was a historic step.' [Trans].[2433]

6th January

The Holy See Press Office announced that Pope Francis had appointed militant pro-homosexuality Cardinal Robert McElroy to lead the Archdiocese of Washington, D.C. Bishop McElroy was elevated to the Sacred College of Cardinals by Pope Francis in 2022. Cardinal McElroy had issued calls to admit the divorced and 'remarried,' and people actively engaged in homosexual lifestyles, to receive Holy Communion.[2434]

Catholics protested against the installation of Cardinal Robert McElroy as the new archbishop of Washington, D.C., including Rachel Mastrogiacomo, a survivor of ritual sexual abuse, protesting Bishop McElroy's alleged cover-up of her abuse by Fr. Jacob Bertrand, formerly incardinated in the Diocese of San Diego, where McElroy was previously bishop.[2435]

Outreach, the US 'Catholic' homosexual website founded by militant pro-homosexuality Fr. James Martin S.J., published an article by pro-homosexuality Cardinal Blase Cupich of Chicago. Cardinal Cupich had been singled out to receive many signs of favour by Pope Francis. Making the assumption that Catholics don't understand active homosexuals Cardinal Cupich wrote:

> …we should listen to them rather than presume that we know how they understand church teaching, or that we know how they view carrying out the responsibilities of their office. This approach of putting aside our preconceptions and really listening also applies to how church leaders ought to consider people in a variety of life situations. This includes not only LGBTQ Catholics, but also people who are married or single, those in so-called irregular situations, those who are living with physical and psychological disabilities and others. Many LGBTQ people also learn and know what sacrificial love is, as they take on the role of parenting children who otherwise would not have a

[2432]Cambi, C [2024] *Vaticano, la Via Crucis dell'impiegato* [Online] Available at: www.panorama.it [Accessed on: 29 May 2025]

[2433]Spuntoni, N [2025] *Il Te Deum arcobaleno del cardinale di Napoli* [Online] Available at: www. ilgiornale.it [Accessed on: 29 May 2025]

[2434]McLoone, D & Haynes, M [2025] *Pope Francis names pro-LGBT Cardinal McElroy to Washington Archdiocese* [Online] Available at: www.lifesitenews.com [Accessed on: 29 May 2025]

[2435]*Catholics protest installation of Cardinal McElroy as archbishop of Washington, DC* [2025] [Online] Available at: www.lifesitenews.com [Accessed on: 29 May 2025]

home. This also happens when LGBTQ people put the social Gospel into practice by volunteering for good causes and by dealing compassionately with others, as so many of them already know what it means to feel excluded.[2436]

14th January

The Italian publisher *Mondadori* and the English publisher *Penguin Books Ltd* launched Pope Francis' autobiography, *Speranza* [Hope]. In his autobiography the Supreme Pontiff re-iterated his criticisms of traditional Catholics and his affirmation of homosexual persons:

Criticisms of traditional Catholics

From a sociological point of view, it is interesting to consider the phenomenon of traditionalism, this 'backwardism' that regularly returns each century, this reference to a supposed perfect age that each time is another age. It has now been ruled that the possibility of celebrating Mass in Latin, following the missal prior to the Second Vatican Council, must be expressly authorised by the Dicastery for Divine Worship, who will allow it only in special cases, for the reason that it is unhealthy for the liturgy to become ideology […] This rigidity is often accompanied by elegant and costly tailoring, lace, fancy trimmings, rochets. Not a taste for tradition but clerical ostentation, which then is none other than an ecclesiastic version of individualism. Not a return to the sacred but to quite the opposite, to sectarian worldliness. These ways of dressing up sometimes conceal mental imbalance, emotional deviation, behavioural difficulties, a personal problem that may be exploited.[2437]

Affirmation of homosexual persons

God the Father loves them with the same unconditional love, He loves them as they are, and He accompanies them in the same way that He does with all of us, being close by, merciful, and tender.[2438]

22nd January

Daily Compass, the Italian Catholic news outlet, published an address delivered by Cardinal Robert Sarah, the emeritus prefect of the Congregation for Divine Worship, concerning 'a diabolical project against the Latin Mass'. Cardinal Sarah said:

…the plan to definitively abolish the traditional Tridentine Mass, a rite that dates back to St Gregory the Great, a liturgy that is 1,600 years old, a Mass celebrated by so many saints: St Padre Pio, St Philip Neri, St John Mary Vianney: the Curé of Ars, St Francis de Sales, St Josemaria Escrivá, etc. And all the way back to Pope Gregory the Great (590-604) and even to Pope Damasus (366-384). This project, if it is true, seems to me to be an insult to the history of the Church and to Sacred Tradition, a diabolical project that seeks to break with the Church of Christ, the Apostles and the Saints. Pope Benedict XVI reminds us that 'the First Vatican Council did not define the Pope as an absolute monarch but, on the contrary, as the guarantor of obedience to the word handed down: his authority is linked to the tradition of the faith: this is also true in the area of the liturgy. It is not 'made' by a bureaucratic apparatus. Even the Pope can only be a humble servant of its proper development and of its constant integrity and identity… The Pope's authority is not unlimited; it is at the service of Sacred Tradition'.[2439]

[2436]Cupich, B [2025] *Cardinal Cupich: Put aside preconceptions and listen to LGBTQ people* [Online] Available at: outreach.faith[Accessed on: 29 May 2025]

[2437]Haynes, M [2025] *Pope Francis accuses young Catholic priests who like the Latin Mass of 'mental imbalance'* [Online] Available at: www.lifesitenews.com [Accessed on: 29 May 2025]

[2438]Haynes, M [2025] *Pope Francis says God loves homosexuals 'as they are' in new memoir* [Online] Available at: www.lifesitenews.com [Accessed on: 29 May 2025]

[2439]Sarah, R [2025] *Cardinal Robert Sarah: 'A diabolical project against the Latin Mass'* [Online] Available at: newdailycompass.com [Accessed on: 29 May 2025]

26th February

Renewal Ministries, a US charismatic group, posted a video by its founder Dr. Ralph Martin in which he expressed concerns about the presence of 'heretical' cardinals in a future Conclave to elect the next pope. Referencing Bishop Thomas Paprocki of Springfield, Illinois, 2023 article *'Imagining a Heretical Cardinal'* Dr. Martin highlighted the dangers of the participation of heretical cardinals, such as Cardinals McElroy and Hollerich, in the next papal conclave:

> ...once you depart from the faith in a serious way like they have, like departing from believing the Word of God, the Catholic Church has taught for 2,000 years, you may have automatically excommunicated yourself. And then he raises the question: how could we have the next conclave that elects the next pope be participated in by Cardinals who don't believe the faith? And he says, 'I hope that Pope Francis would never let that happen.' Well, not only has nothing happened — to ask Cardinal McElroy to change his views or to retract them — but he just recently has been appointed to be the new Archbishop of Washington D.C., which, I must say, is really scandalous [...] So, anyway, we're in a pretty serious state right now. You know, there will be another papal election coming sometime and, you know, Bishop Paprocki was hoping that Pope Francis would do something about Cardinal McElroy so he wouldn't be an elector in the next conclave, but he hasn't. And not only has he not corrected him anyway, but he's elevated him to one of the most important sees in the world: Washington D.C.[2440]

1st March

Vatican News, the Holy See's news outlet, published an article equating the Muslim observance of Ramadan with the Christian preparation for Holy Week during Lent, omitting any mention of Our Lord Jesus Christ:

> Ramadan and Lent are moments for Muslims and Christians to engage in deep reflection on shared themes. For both, it is a period of fasting and contemplation, where the faithful are called to reflect on their existence, their relationship with Creation, and with the Creator.[2441]

7th March

The Catholic Herald, a UK Catholic weekly newspaper, published an interview with Cardinal Arthur Roche, the Prefect of the Dicastery [Congregation] for Divine Worship and the Discipline of the Sacraments. Responsible for the severe restriction of the traditional Latin Mass around the world following the promulgation of *Traditionis Custodes* Cardinal Roche gave his views on the Latin Mass. In response to the question, *'what advice would you give to those who want to remain faithful members of the Church and love the Latin Mass but find themselves restricted in attending?* Cardinal Roche responded:

> Of course, it is good that people want to be part of the Church, and there is no reason why they cannot. There is nothing wrong with attending the Mass celebrated with the 1962 missal. That has been accepted since the time of Pope St John Paul II, Pope Benedict and now Pope Francis. What Pope Francis said in *Traditionis Custodes* is that it is not the norm. For very good reasons, the Church, through conciliar legislation, decided to move away from what had become an overly elaborate form of celebrating the Mass [...] One of the things that has been very interesting to me is observing this situation worldwide. The numbers devoted to the Traditional Latin Mass are, in reality, quite small, but some of the groups are quite clamorous. They are more noticeable because they make their voices heard [...] I often hear people say, 'Cardinal Roche is against the Latin Mass.' Well, if they only knew that most days I celebrate Mass in Latin because

---

[2440]*Heresy in High Places?* [Ralph Martin] [2025] [Online] Available at: www.youtube.com [Accessed on: 29 May 2025]

[2441]Sabatinelli, F [2025] *Il Ramadan, tempo di preghiera e riconciliazione per il bene del Creato* [Online] Available at: www.vaticannews.va [Accessed on: 29 May 2025]

it is the common language for all of us here. It is the *Novus Ordo* Mass in Latin. I was trained as an altar boy until the age of 20, serving the Tridentine Form.[2442]

AsiaNews, the news agency of the Pontifical Institute for Foreign Missions, reported that the Public Security Bureau, the Chinese communist security agency, arrested Bishop Peter Shao Zhumin, the underground bishop of Wenzhou (Zhejiang) after he refused to pay a 200,000 yuan fine for celebrating Mass on 27 December before 200 people. *AsiaNews* reported:

> The authorities claim that the religious service was 'illegal' and a 'serious crime' in violation of Article 71 of the Religious Affairs Regulations. For this reason, they imposed a fine of 200,000 yuan (US$ 26,500), which Bishop Shao challenged, insisting that the Church's activities do not violate the law. As a result, the prelate was arrested for his own 'safety', the Public Security Bureau (PSB) claimed. His whereabouts are unknown and it is unclear how long he will be held. Among his flock, people are concerned about his safety and health [...] Over the past few years, every Sunday, plainclothes agents have also entered underground churches in Wenzhou, to stop children and teenagers from attending. More recently, the PSB has changed methods, delegating surveillance to neighbourhood authorities. Officials are deployed to watch churches from 7 am until noon, not only to prevent children and teenagers from entering, but also to prevent priests from celebrating Mass. Bishop Shao has refused to join Catholic bodies controlled by the Communist Party of China and for this reason he is not recognised by the authorities [...] For his refusal to join the Chinese Catholic Patriotic Association, the authorities consider the episcopal see to be vacant and back Fr Ma Xianshi, a 'patriotic' priest, as the leader of the local Catholic community.[2443]

15th March

Vatican News, the Holy See's news service, reported that Pope Francis had approved the convocation of post-synodal Ecclesial Assembly in 2028 as part of a three year process to implement the Final Document of the Synod on Synodality and the work of the ten Study Groups established in March 2024 to examine issues that emerged during the first session of the Synod on Synodality in 2023. The implementation process would include the celebration of a 'Jubilee of Synodal Teams and Participatory Bodies' scheduled for October 24-26 2025. Cardinal Mario Grech, the Secretary General of the Synod's General Secretariat, explained that this was 'an important event' that placed 'the commitment to an increasingly synodal Church within the horizon of the hope that does not disappoint, the central theme of the ongoing Holy Year.'[2444]

Vatican News, the Holy See's news service, also published an interview with Cardinal Mario Grech, the Secretary General of the Synod's General Secretariat, in which he explained the role of the Ecclesial Assembly:

> The meetings planned for 2027 and early 2028 will naturally lead toward the Ecclesial Assembly of October 2028. This final Assembly will then be able to offer the Holy Father valuable insights—fruits of a real ecclesial experience—to aid his discernment as the Successor of Peter, with perspectives to propose to the entire Church. Implementation and evaluation must proceed together, intertwining in a dynamic and shared process— this is precisely the culture of accountability evoked in the Final Document.[2445]

[2442]Edwards, T [2025] *Cardinal Arthur Roche – 'If they only knew that most days I celebrate Mass in Latin'* [Online] Available at: thecatholicherald.com [Accessed on: 29 May 2025]

[2443]*Bishop Shao arrested over 'illegal' Jubilee opening Mass* [2025][Online] Available at: www.asianews. it [Accessed on: 29 May 2025]

[2444]Piro, I [2025] *Pope approves convocation of post-synodal Ecclesial Assembly in 2028* [Online] Available at: www.vaticannews.va [Accessed on: 29 May 2025]

[2445]Tornielli, A [2025] *Cardinal Grech: A new path to help the Church walk in a synodal style* [Online] Available at: www.vaticannews.va [Accessed on: 29 May 2025]

The Catholic Thing, the online US website, published an article by Fr. Gerald E. Murray, J.C.D., the US canon lawyer and broadcaster, warning that the 'ecclesial assembly' was an anti-Catholic innovation that every bishop must oppose:

> So, the Ecclesial Assembly will not be 'substantially' an assembly of bishops. It will be substantially an assembly of non-bishops, which means that most participants will be lay people. The Ecclesial Assembly will more or less mirror the demographics of the Ecclesia (Church) in which the clergy, let alone the bishops, make up a tiny fraction of the number of baptized Catholics [...] The Ecclesial Assembly will be hailed by a relative few as a long overdue embrace of progress, de-clericalising the Church, and allowing the prophetic voice of the supposedly heretofore silenced laity to be heard and heeded. It will be hailed as Vatican III. If this assembly meets according to the form set forth by Cardinal Grech, it will be a destructive moment for the Church. The hierarchy alone was given charge by Christ 'to teach, govern, and sanctify' the flock of Christ in His name and by His authority. The bishops under and with the pope are the sole shepherds by the express design of Our Lord. Their authority is not subject to the majority vote of any assembly of laity. The bishops of the Church must oppose this manifestly anti-Catholic innovation that would turn the Church into something akin to a Protestant body.[2446]

21st April

The Holy See Press Office announced the death of Pope Francis at 7.35 am,[2447] his funeral taking place on Saturday, 26th in St. Peter's Square, with his body buried in the Basilica of Santa Maria Maggiore.[2448] A group of men presenting themselves as women joined others in forming an official 'honour guard' to bid farewell to the body of Pope Francis on the steps of Santa Maria Maggiore.[2449]

6th May

Pope Francis' Fisherman's Ring and Seal were broken in the presence of the College of Cardinals during their last General Congregation.[2450]

[2446]Murray, G [2025] *Processes, Accompaniment, Implementation: Synodality Forever!* [Online] Available at: www.thecatholicthing.org [Accessed on: 29 May 2025]

[2447]Haynes, M [2025] *OBITUARY: Pope Francis has died aged 88* [Online] Available at: www.lifesitenews.com [Accessed on: 29 May 2025]

[2448]Haynes, M [2025] *Pope Francis' funeral is held at the Vatican* [Online] Available at: www.lifesitenews.com [Accessed on: 29 May 2025]

[2449]*Transgender People Are Part of Pope Francis' Funeral Rites Today* [2025] [Online] Available at: www.newwaysministry.org [Accessed on: 29 May 2025]

[2450]Brockhaus, H [2025] *Cardinals witness destruction of Pope Francis' ring, seal* [Online] Available at: www.catholicnewsagency.com [Accessed on: 29 May 2025]

Roll of Honour

The following have paid a high price for publicly questioning the erroneous teachings of Pope Francis:

Alessandro Gnocchi and Mario Palmaro were sacked from Catholic broadcaster Radio Maria Italy for publishing an article critical of some of the teachings of Pope Francis (October 2013)

Professor Roberto de Mattei was sacked from Radio Maria Italy for publishing an article critical of some of the teachings of Pope Francis (February 2014)

Henk Rijkers, the editor of the Catholic weekly, *Katholiek Nieuwsblad*, was sacked on Christmas eve for questioning Pope Francis' *Amoris Laetitia* (December 2016)

Professor Josef Seifert was sacked by Archbishop Javier Martínez Fernández of Granada from the Dietrich von Hildebrand Chair at the International Academy of Philosophy for publishing essays critiquing *Amoris Laetitia* (September 2017)

Fr. Thomas Weinandy OFM, Cap., was asked to resign his position as advisor to the US bishops' conference (USCCB) Committee on Doctrine for publishing a letter addressed to Pope Francis questioning aspects of *Amoris Laetitia*, and other matters (November 2017)

Henry Sire was expelled from the Sovereign Order of Malta for publishing the book, *The Dictator Pope*, which was highly critical of Pope Francis' pontificate (November 2018)

Fr. Jesusmary Missigbètò was expelled from Opus Dei for criticising Pope Francis for his support of homosexual pairings. A later decree from the Congregation for Bishops, signed by Pope Francis and Cardinal Ouellet, suspended his priestly faculties (July 2022)

Bishop Joseph Strickland, deposed as the Ordinary of the Diocese of Tyler, Texas, for challenging the errors of Pope Francis (November 2023)

Archbishop Carlo Maria Viganò, excommunicated for challenging the grave errors and scandalous actions of Pope Francis (July 2024)

Sources: The Errors in the Light of Scripture, Tradition, and the Magisterium

Anthropology

Pope Francis: 2013 to 2025

A. *Individuals possess an infinite dignity due to two reasons: firstly, being the recipients of the infinite love of God, and secondly, being created in the image and likeness of God. As such, individuals possess an inviolable ontological dignity that can never be annulled by any circumstance in which the person may find themselves or any evil that they commit, no matter how wicked.*

Apostolic Exhortation *Evangelii Gaudium*, 178. (24th November 2013)
To believe in a Father who loves all men and women with an infinite love means realising that 'he thereby confers upon them an infinite dignity.' [John Paul II, Message to the Handicapped, Angelus (16 November 1980)][2451]

Encyclical *Laudato si'*, 65. (24th May 2015)
The Bible teaches that every man and woman is created out of love and made in God's image and likeness (cf. Gen 1:26). This shows us the immense dignity of each person, 'who is not just something, but someone. He is capable of self-knowledge, of self-possession and of freely giving himself and entering into communion with other persons'. Saint John Paul II stated that the special love of the Creator for each human being 'confers upon him or her an infinite dignity'. [John Paul II, Message to the Handicapped, Angelus. 16 November 1980][2452]

Pope Francis' words to homosexual British comedian Stephen K Amos. BBC Two documentary *Pilgrimage: The Road To Rome*. (19th April 2019)
Giving more importance to the adjective [gay] rather than the noun [man], this is not good. We are all human beings and have dignity. It does not matter who you are, or how you live your life – you do not lose your dignity.[2453]

Encyclical *Fratelli Tutti*, 85. (3rd October 2020)
Faith has untold power to inspire and sustain our respect for others, for believers come to know that God loves every man and woman with infinite love and 'thereby confers infinite dignity' [John Paul II, Message to the Handicapped, Angelus (16 November 1980)] upon all humanity.[2454]

The Presentation of the Declaration *Dignitas Infinita*. (8th April 2024)
This dignity of every human being can be understood as 'infinite' (dignitas infinita), as Pope St. John Paul II affirmed in a meeting for people living with various

---

[2451]Pope Francis [2013] Apostolic exhortation *Evangelii Gaudium*, para 178 [Online] Available at: www.vatican.va [Accessed on: 16 April 2024]

[2452]Pope Francis [2015] Encyclical *Laudato si'*, para 65 [Online] Available at: www.vatican.va [Accessed on: 22 April 2024]

[2453]Dodd, L [2019] *Pope condemns 'heartless' discrimination against gay people* [Online] Available at: www.thetablet.co.uk [Accessed on: 22 April 2024]

[2454]Pope Francis [2020] Encyclical *Fratelli Tutti*, para 85 [Online] Available at: www.vatican.va [Accessed on: 22 April 2024]

limitations or disabilities. He said this to show how human dignity transcends all outward appearances and specific aspects of people's lives. [John Paul II, Message to the Handicapped, Angelus.16 November 1980][2455]

Declaration *Dignitas Infinita*, 1,3,7, 8, 11,16, 22 (8th April 2024)
Every human person possesses an infinite dignity, inalienably grounded in his or her very being, which prevails in and beyond every circumstance, state, or situation the person may ever encounter. This principle, which is fully recognisable even by reason alone, underlies the primacy of the human person and the protection of human rights. In the light of Revelation, the Church resolutely reiterates and confirms the ontological dignity of the human person, created in the image and likeness of God and redeemed in Jesus Christ. From this truth, the Church draws the reasons for her commitment to the weak and those less endowed with power, always insisting on 'the primacy of the human person and the defense of his or her dignity beyond every circumstance.'[2456]

From the start of his pontificate, Pope Francis has invited the Church to 'believe in a Father who loves all men and women with an infinite love, realising that 'he thereby confers upon them an infinite dignity.' [Francis, Apostolic Exhortation *Evangelii Gaudium* (24 November 2013), no. 178; cf. John Paul II, Message to the Handicapped, Angelus (16 November 1980)][2457]

This brings us to recognise the possibility of a fourfold distinction of the concept of dignity: ontological dignity, moral dignity, social dignity, and existential dignity. The most important among these is the ontological dignity that belongs to the person as such simply because he or she exists and is willed, created, and loved by God. Ontological dignity is indelible and remains valid beyond any circumstances in which the person may find themselves. When we speak of moral dignity, we refer to how people exercise their freedom. While people are endowed with conscience, they can always act against it. However, were they to do so, they would behave in a way that is 'not dignified' with respect to their nature as creatures who are loved by God and called to love others. Yet, this possibility always exists for human freedom, and history illustrates how individuals — when exercising their freedom against the law of love revealed by the Gospel — can commit inestimably profound acts of evil against others. Those who act this way seem to have lost any trace of humanity and dignity. This is where the present distinction can help us discern between the moral dignity that de facto can be 'lost' and the ontological dignity that can never be annulled. And it is precisely because of this latter point that we must work with all our might so that all those who have done evil may repent and convert.[2458]

There are still two other possible aspects of dignity to consider: social and existential. When we speak of social dignity, we refer to the quality of a person's living conditions. For example, in cases of extreme poverty, where individuals do not even have what is minimally necessary to live according to their ontological dignity, it is said that those poor people are living in an 'undignified' manner. This expression does not imply a judgment on those individuals but highlights how the situation in which they are forced to live contradicts their inalienable dignity. The last meaning is that of existential dignity, which is the type of dignity implied in the ever-increasing discussion about a 'dignified' life and one that is 'not dignified.' For instance, while some people may appear to lack nothing essential for life, for various reasons, they may still struggle to live with peace, joy, and hope. In other situations, the presence of serious illnesses, violent family environments, pathological addictions, and other hardships may drive people to experience their life conditions as 'undignified' vis-à-vis their perception of

[2455]Dicastery for the Doctrine of the Faith [2024] Presentation of the Declaration *Dignitas Infinita* [Online] Available at: www.press.vatican.va [Accessed on: 16 April 2024]
[2456]Dicastery for the Doctrine of the Faith [2024] Declaration *Dignitas Infinita* [Online] Available at: www.press.vatican.va [Accessed on: 16 April 2024]
[2457]*Op cit.*, para 6.
[2458]*Ibid.*, para 7.

that ontological dignity that can never be obscured. These distinctions remind us of the inalienable value of the ontological dignity that is rooted in the very being of the human person in all circumstances.[2459]

Biblical Revelation teaches that all human beings possess inherent dignity because they are created in the image and likeness of God: 'God said, "Let us make man in our image, after our likeness" [....] So God created man in his own image, in the image of God he created him; male and female he created them' (Gen 1:26-27). With this, humanity has a specific quality that means it is not reducible to purely material elements. Moreover, the 'image' does not define the soul or its intellectual abilities but the dignity of man and woman. In their relationship of equality and mutual love, both the man and the woman represent God in the world and are also called to cherish and nurture the world. Because of this, to be created in the image of God means to possess a sacred value that transcends every distinction of a sexual, social, political, cultural, and religious nature. Our dignity is bestowed upon us by God; it is neither claimed nor deserved. Every human being is loved and willed by God and, thus, has an inviolable dignity.[2460]

…the Second Vatican Council speaks of the 'sublime dignity of the human person, who stands above all things and whose rights and duties are universal and inviolable'. (*GS* 26). As the opening line of the conciliar Declaration *Dignitatis Humanae* recalls, 'contemporary man is becoming increasingly conscious of the dignity of the human person; more and more people are demanding that men should exercise fully their own judgment and a responsible freedom in their actions and should not be subject to the pressure of coercion but be inspired by a sense of duty.' (*DH* 1). Such freedom of thought and conscience, both individual and communal, is based on the recognition of human dignity 'as known through the revealed Word of God and by reason itself.' (*DH* 2). The Church's Magisterium progressively developed an ever-greater understanding of the meaning of human dignity, along with its demands and consequences, until it arrived at the recognition that the dignity of every human being prevails beyond all circumstances.[2461]

Every individual possesses an inalienable and intrinsic dignity from the beginning of his or her existence as an irrevocable gift. However, the choice to express that dignity and manifest it to the full or to obscure it depends on each person's free and responsible decision. Some Church Fathers, such as St. Irenaeus and St. John Damascene, distinguished between the 'image' and 'likeness' mentioned in Genesis (cf. 1:26). This allowed for a dynamic perspective on human dignity that understands that the image of God is entrusted to human freedom so that — under the guidance and action of the Spirit — the person's likeness to God may grow and each person may attain their highest dignity. All people are called to manifest the ontological scope of their dignity on an existential and moral level as they, by their freedom, orient themselves toward the true good in response to God's love. Thus, as one who is created in the image of God, the human person never loses his or her dignity and never ceases to be called to embrace the good freely. At the same time, to the extent that the person responds to the good, the individual's dignity can manifest itself freely, dynamically, and progressively; with that, it can also grow and mature. Consequently, each person must also strive to live up to the full measure of their dignity. In light of this, one can understand how sin can wound and obscure human dignity, as it is an act contrary to that dignity; yet, sin can never cancel the fact that the human being is created in the image and likeness of God. In this way, faith plays a decisive role in helping reason perceive human dignity and in accepting, consolidating, and clarifying its essential features.[2462]

[2459]*Ibid.*, para 8.

[2460]*Ibid.*, para 11.

[2461]*Ibid.*, para 16.

[2462]*Ibid.*, para 22.

Sacred Scripture

Revelation 1:8; 4:8

I am Alpha and Omega, the beginning and the end, saith the Lord God, who is, and who was, and who is to come, the Almighty.

Holy, holy, holy, Lord God Almighty, who was, and who is, and who is to come.

Isaiah 40:28

Knowest thou not, or hast thou not heard? the Lord is the everlasting God, who hath created the ends of the earth: he shall not faint, nor labour, neither is there any searching out of his wisdom

Psalm 89:2

Before the mountains were made, or the earth and the world was formed; from eternity and to eternity thou art God.

Psalm 144:3

Great is the Lord, and greatly to be praised: and of his greatness there is no end.

Psalm 146:5

Great is our Lord, and great is his power: and of his wisdom there is no number.

Romans 1:24-25; 7:17-20

Wherefore God gave them up to the desires of their heart, unto uncleanness, to dishonour their own bodies among themselves. Who changed the truth of God into a lie; and worshipped and served the creature rather than the Creator, who is blessed for ever. Amen.

Now then it is no more I that do it, but sin that dwelleth in me. For I know that there dwelleth not in me, that is to say, in my flesh, that which is good. For to will, is present with me; but to accomplish that which is good, I find not. For the good which I will, I do not; but the evil which I will not, that I do. Now if I do that which I will not, it is no more I that do it, but sin that dwelleth in me.

Ephesians 2:1-5

And you, when you were dead in your offences, and sins, Wherein in time past you walked according to the course of this world, according to the prince of the power of this air, of the spirit that now worketh on the children of unbelief: In which also we all conversed in time past, in the desires of our flesh, fulfilling the will of the flesh and of our thoughts, and were by nature children of wrath, even as the rest: But God, (who is rich in mercy,) for his exceeding charity wherewith he loved us, Even when we were dead in sins, hath quickened us together in Christ, (by whose grace you are saved).

James 1:14-15

But every man is tempted by his own concupiscence, being drawn away and allured. Then when concupiscence hath conceived, it bringeth forth sin. But sin, when it is completed, begetteth death.

I John 2:16-17

For all that is in the world, is the concupiscence of the flesh, and the concupiscence of the eyes, and the pride of life, which is not of the Father, but is of the world. And the world passeth away, and the concupiscence thereof.

Genesis 3: 16-19

To the woman also he said: I will multiply thy sorrows, and thy conceptions: in sorrow shalt thou bring forth children, and thou shalt be under thy husband's power, and he shall have dominion over thee. And to Adam he said: Because thou hast hearkened to the voice of thy wife, and hast eaten of the tree, whereof I commanded thee that thou shouldst not eat, cursed is the earth in thy work; with labour and toil shalt thou eat thereof all the days of thy life. Thorns and thistles shall it bring forth to thee; and thou shalt eat the herbs of the earth. In the sweat of thy face shalt thou eat bread till thou return to the earth, out of which thou wast taken: for dust thou art, and into dust thou shalt return.

Genesis 6:5-7
And God seeing that the wickedness of men was great on the earth, and that all the thought of their heart was bent upon evil at all times, It repented him that he had made man on the earth. And being touched inwardly with sorrow of heart, He said: I will destroy man, whom I have created, from the face of the earth, from man even to beasts, from the creeping thing even to the fowls of the air, for it repenteth me that I have made them.

Genesis 8:21
…for the imagination and thought of man's heart are prone to evil from his youth.

Proverbs 6: 16-19
Six things there are, which the Lord hateth, and the seventh his soul detesteth: Haughty eyes, a lying tongue, hands that shed innocent blood, A heart that deviseth wicked plots, feet that are swift to run into mischief, A deceitful witness that uttereth lies, and him that soweth discord among brethren.

Psalm 5: 6-7
Neither shall the wicked dwell near thee: nor shall the unjust abide before thy eyes. Thou hatest all the workers of iniquity: Thou wilt destroy all that speak a lie. The bloody and the deceitful man the Lord will abhor.

Psalm 10: 6-7
The Lord trieth the just and the wicked: but he that loveth iniquity hateth his own soul. He shall rain snares upon sinners: fire and brimstone and storms of winds shall be the portion of their cup.

Psalm 50: 7
For behold I was conceived in iniquities; and in sins did my mother conceive me.

Wisdom 4:12
For the bewitching of vanity obscureth good things, and the wandering of concupiscence overturneth the innocent mind.

Sacred Tradition

St. Irenaeus: c. 130 to c. 202

Against Heresies, Bk. IV, Chap. 4; Bk V, Chaps. 6 & 16
Wherefore also he shall be justly condemned, because, having been created a rational being, he lost the true rationality, and living irrationally, opposed the righteousness of God, giving himself over to every earthly spirit, and serving all lusts; as says the prophet, 'Man, being in honour, did not understand: he was assimilated to senseless beasts, and made like to them.'

But when the spirit here blended with the soul is united to [God's] handiwork, the man is rendered spiritual and perfect because of the outpouring of the Spirit, and this is he who was made in the image and likeness of God. But if the Spirit be wanting to the soul, he who is such is indeed of an animal nature, and being left carnal, shall be an imperfect being, possessing indeed the image [of God] in his formation (*in plasmate*), but not receiving the similitude through the Spirit; and thus is this being imperfect.

And then, again, this Word was manifested when the Word of God was made man, assimilating Himself to man, and man to Himself, so that by means of his resemblance to the Son, man might become precious to the Father. For in times long past, it was said that man was created after the image of God, but it was not [actually] shown; for the Word was as yet invisible, after whose image man was created, Wherefore also he did easily lose the similitude. When, however, the Word of God became flesh, He confirmed both these: for He both showed forth the image truly, since He became Himself what was His image; and He re-established the similitude after a sure manner, by assimilating man to the invisible Father through means of the visible Word.[2463]

Origen: 185 to 253

De Principiis, Bk. III, Chap. 6

'And God said, Let Us make man in Our own image, and after Our likeness;' and then he adds the words: 'So God created man in His own image: in the image of God created He him; male and female created He them, and He blessed them.' Now the expression, 'In the image of God created He him,' without any mention of the word likeness, conveys no other meaning than this, that man received the dignity of God's image at his first creation; but that the perfection of his likeness has been reserved for the consummation — namely, that he might acquire it for himself by the exercise of his own diligence in the imitation of God, the possibility of attaining to perfection being granted him at the beginning through the dignity of the divine image, and the perfect realisation of the divine likeness being reached in the end by the fulfilment of the (necessary) works. Now, that such is the case, the Apostle John points out more clearly and unmistakably, when he makes this declaration: 'Little children, we do not yet know what we shall be; but if a revelation be made to us from the Saviour, you will say, without any doubt, we shall be like Him.' By which expression he points out with the utmost certainty, that not only was the end of all things to be hoped for, which he says was still unknown to him, but also the likeness to God, which will be conferred in proportion to the completeness of our deserts. The Lord Himself, in the Gospel, not only declares that these same results are future, but that they are to be brought about by His own intercession, He Himself deigning to obtain them from the Father for His disciples, saying, 'Father, I will that where I am, these also may be with Me; and as You and I are one, they also may be one in Us.' In which the divine likeness itself already appears to advance, if we may so express ourselves, and from being merely similar, to become the same, because undoubtedly in the consummation or end God is 'all and in all.' And with reference to this, it is made a question by some whether the nature of bodily matter, although cleansed and purified, and rendered altogether spiritual, does not seem either to offer an obstruction towards attaining the dignity of the (divine) likeness, or to the property of unity, because neither can a corporeal nature appear capable of any resemblance to a divine nature which is certainly incorporeal; nor can it be truly and deservedly designated one with it, especially since we are taught by the truths of our religion that that which alone is one, viz., the Son with the Father, must be referred to a peculiarity of the (divine) nature.[2464]

St. Augustine: 354 to 430

Commentary on Psalm 144

There is no limit to his greatness, and we are bidden to praise him whom we cannot comprehend. If we could comprehend him, there would be a limit to his greatness; but because his greatness is without limit, we can comprehend something of God, but never the whole. Since this is so, since we are weak and fall far short of his grandeur, let us look to what he has made, so that we may be strengthened by his goodness.[2465]

Commentary on Psalm 146

His understanding cannot be reckoned! Think of it, brothers and sisters: Could we possibly count grains of sand? We could not, but God can. He to whom the number of hairs on

---

[2463]St. Irenaeus. *Against Heresies.* Bk. IV, Chap. 4, Bk. V, Chaps. 6 & 16 [Online] Available at: www. newadvent.org [Accessed on: 22 April 2024]

[2464]Origen. *De Principiis,* Bk. III, Chap. 6 [Online] Available at: www.newadvent.org [Accessed on: 19 April 2024]

[2465]The Works of Saint Augustine: A Translation for the 21st Century. *Expositions of the Psalms. 121-150.* New York: New City Press,1990 p. 383

our heads is known has also counted the sand. Any infinite thing this world embraces, though innumerable to human beings, is not innumerable to God [....] *And so, his understanding cannot be reckoned.* Let human voices fall silent and human thought be still. Let them not stretch towards what is incomprehensible as though they could comprehend, but only as seeking to participate in it. For we shall indeed participate. We shall not ourselves be that reality which we attempt to grasp, nor shall we grasp it totally, but we shall be participants in it.[2466]

The Enchiridion on Faith, Hope and Love, Chap. 45
However, even in that one sin, which 'by one man entered into the world, and so passed upon all men,' and on account of which infants are baptized, a number of distinct sins may be observed, if it be analysed as it were into its separate elements. For there is in it pride, because man chose to be under his own dominion, rather than under the dominion of God; and blasphemy, because he did not believe God; and murder, for he brought death upon himself; and spiritual fornication, for the purity of the human soul was corrupted by the seducing blandishments of the serpent; and theft, for man turned to his own use the food he had been forbidden to touch; and avarice, for he had a craving for more than should have been sufficient for him; and whatever other sin can be discovered on careful reflection to be involved in this one admitted sin.[2467]

On the Trinity, Bk. VII, Chap. 4; Bk. XII, Chap. 3; Bk. XIV, Chap. 5 & 16
But because that image of God was not made altogether equal to Him, as being not born of Him, but created by Him; in order to signify this, he is in such way the image as that he is 'after the image,' that is, he is not made equal by parity, but approaches to Him by a sort of likeness. For approach to God is not by intervals of place, but by likeness, and withdrawal from Him is by unlikeness. For there are some who draw this distinction, that they will have the Son to be the image, but man not to be the image, but 'after the image.' But the apostle refutes them, saying, 'For a man indeed ought not to cover his head, forasmuch as he is the image and glory of God.' He did not say after the image, but the image. And this image, since it is elsewhere spoken of as after the image, is not as if it were said relatively to the Son, who is the image equal to the Father; otherwise he would not say *after our image.* For how *our*, when the Son is the image of the Father alone? But man is said to be 'after the image,' on account, as we have said, of the inequality of the likeness; and therefore after our image, that man might be the image of the Trinity; not equal to the Trinity as the Son is equal to the Father, but approaching to it, as has been said, by a certain likeness; just as nearness may in a sense be signified in things distant from each other, not in respect of place, but of a sort of imitation. For it is also said, 'Be transformed by the renewing of your mind;' to whom he likewise says, 'Be therefore imitators of God as dear children.' For it is said to the new man, 'which is renewed to the knowledge of God, after the image of Him that created him.'
For just as a snake does not walk with open strides but wriggles along by the tiny little movements of its scales, so the careless glide little by little along the slippery path of failure, and beginning from a distorted appetite for being like God they end up by becoming like beasts. So it is that stripped naked of their first robe they earned the skin garments of mortality. For man's true honor is God's image and likeness in him, but it can only be preserved when facing him from whom its impression is received. And so the less love he has for what is his very own the more closely can he cling to God. But out of greed to experience his own power he tumbled down at a nod from himself into himself as though down to the middle level. And then, while he wants to be like God under nobody, he is thrust down as a punishment from his own half-way level to the bottom, to the things in which the beasts find their pleasure. And thus, since his honor consists in being like God and his disgrace in being like an animal, *man*

[2466]*Op. cit.* p. 430
[2467]*St. Augustine. The Enchiridion on Faith, Hope and Love,* Chap. 45 [Online] Available at: www. newadvent.org [Accessed on: 14 May 2024]

established in honor did not understand; he was matched with senseless cattle and became like them (Ps 49:12).[2468]

Those who do, on being reminded, turn to the Lord from the deformity which had conformed them by worldly lusts to this world are reformed by him; they listen to the apostle saying, *Do not conform to this world, but be reformed in the newness of your minds* (Rom 12:2). And thus the image begins to be reformed by him who formed it in the first place. It cannot reform itself in the way it was able to deform itself. As he says elsewhere, Be renewed in the spirit of your minds, and put on the new man who was created according to God in justice and the holiness of truth (Eph 4:23). 'Created according to God' means the same as 'to the image of God' in another text. But by sinning man lost justice and the holiness of truth, and thus the image became deformed and discoloured; he gets those qualities back again when he is reformed and renovated.[2469]

But those who, by being reminded, are turned to the Lord from that deformity whereby they were through worldly lusts conformed to this world, are formed anew from the world, when they hearken to the apostle, saying, 'Be not conformed to this world, but be formed again in the renewing of your mind;' that that image may begin to be formed again by Him by whom it had been formed at first. For that image cannot form itself again, as it could deform itself. He says again elsewhere: 'Be renewed in the spirit of your mind; and put ye on the new man, which after God is created in righteousness and true holiness.' That which is meant by 'created after God,' is expressed in another place by 'after the image of God.' But it lost righteousness and true holiness by sinning, through which that image became defaced and tarnished; and this it recovers when it is formed again and renewed.[2470]

On Marriage and Concupiscence, Bk. I, Chap. 28
Carnal concupiscence is remitted, indeed, in baptism; not so that it is put out of existence, but so that it is not to be imputed for sin. Although its guilt is now taken away, it still remains until our entire infirmity be healed by the advancing renewal of our inner man, day by day, when at last our outward man shall be clothed with incorruption.[2471]

St. Thomas Aquinas: 1225 to 1274
De Rationibus Fidei, Chap. 7
But no mere man has the infinite dignity required to satisfy justly an offence against God. Therefore there had to be a man of infinite dignity who would undergo the penalty for all so as to satisfy fully for the sins of the whole world. Therefore the only-begotten Word of God, true God and Son of God, assumed a human nature and willed to suffer death in it so as to purify the whole human race indebted by sin. Thus Peter says (I Pet 3:18): 'Christ himself died once and for all for sins, the upright for the sake of the guilty.'[2472]

Summa Theologiae, Prima Pars. Q 93. Art. 1
But equality does not belong to the essence of an image; for as Augustine says (QQ. 83, qu. 74): 'Where there is an image there is not necessarily equality,' as we see in a person's image reflected in a glass. Yet this is of the essence of a perfect image; for in a perfect image nothing is wanting that is to be found in that of which it is a copy. Now it is manifest that in man there is some likeness to God, copied from God as from an exemplar; yet this likeness is not one of equality, for such an exemplar infinitely excels

---

[2468]The Works of Saint Augustine: A Translation for the 21st Century: *The Trinity*. New York: New City Press, 1990 p.231, p.331
[2469]*Op. cit.*, p.388
[2470]St. Augustine. *On the Trinity* [Online] Available at: www.newadvent.org [Accessed on: 20 April 2024]
[2471]St. Augustine. *On Marriage and Concupiscence*, Bk. I, Chap. 28 [Online] [Online] Available at: www.newadvent.org [Accessed on: 14 May 2024]
[2472]St. Thomas Aquinas. *De Rationibus Fidei*, Chap. 7 [Online] Available at: www.isidore.co [Accessed on: 22 April 2024]

its copy. Therefore there is in man a likeness to God; not, indeed, a perfect likeness, but imperfect. And Scripture implies the same when it says that man was made 'to' God's likeness; for the preposition 'to' signifies a certain approach, as of something at a distance.[2473]

Summa Theologiae, Secunda Secundæ Pars. Q 64. Art. 2
By sinning man departs from the order of reason, and consequently falls away from the dignity of his manhood, in so far as he is naturally free, and exists for himself, and he falls into the slavish state of the beasts.[2474]

Summa Theologiae, Tertia Pars. Q 1. Art. 2
Satisfaction may be said to be sufficient in two ways — first, perfectly, inasmuch as it is condign, being adequate to make good the fault committed, and in this way the satisfaction of a mere man cannot be sufficient for sin, both because the whole of human nature has been corrupted by sin, whereas the goodness of any person or persons could not be made up adequately for the harm done to the whole of the nature; and also because a sin committed against God has a kind of infinity from the infinity of the Divine majesty, because the greater the person we offend, the more grievous the offence. Hence for condign satisfaction it was necessary that the act of the one satisfying should have an infinite efficiency, as being of God and man. Secondly, man's satisfaction may be termed sufficient, imperfectly — i.e. in the acceptation of him who is content with it, even though it is not condign, and in this way the satisfaction of a mere man is sufficient. And forasmuch as every imperfect presupposes some perfect thing, by which it is sustained, hence it is that satisfaction of every mere man has its efficiency from the satisfaction of Christ.[2475]

Summa Theologiae, Tertia Pars. Q 89. Art. 3
By sin, mans loses a twofold dignity, one in respect of God, the other in respect of the Church. In respect of God he again loses a twofold dignity. one is his principal dignity, whereby he was counted among the children of God, and this he recovers by Penance, which is signified (Lk 15) in the prodigal son, for when he repented, his father commanded that the first garment should be restored to him, together with a ring and shoes. The other is his secondary dignity, viz. innocence, of which, as we read in the same chapter, the elder son boasted saying (Lk 15:29): 'Behold, for so many years do I serve thee, and I have never transgressed thy commandments': and this dignity the penitent cannot recover. Nevertheless he recovers something greater sometimes; because as Gregory says (Hom. de centum Ovibus [34 in Evang.]), 'those who acknowledge themselves to have strayed away from God, make up for their past losses, by subsequent gains: so that there is more joy in heaven on their account, even as in battle, the commanding officer thinks more of the soldier who, after running away, returns and bravely attacks the foe, than of one who has never turned his back, but has done nothing brave.'[2476]

The Magisterium of the Church

Infinity is an attribute of God, and as such cannot be applied to man. The creaturely, finite dignity of man being made in the image and likeness of God was stained and deformed by the sin of our first parents, Adam and Eve. Original sin, with the loss of sanctifying grace, disfigured and distorted fallen man at an ontological level to such a degree that we are 'by nature

---

[2473]St. Thomas Aquinas. *Summa Theologiae. Prima Pars.* Q 93 Art. 1 [Online] Available at: www.newadvent.org [Accessed on: 22 April 2024]

[2474]St. Thomas Aquinas. *Summa theologiae, Secunda Secundæ Pars.* Q 64. Art. 2 [Online] Available at: www.newadvent.org [Accessed on: 22 April 2024]

[2475]St. Thomas Aquinas. *Summa Theologiae, Tertia Pars.* Q 1. Art. 2 [Online] Available at: www.newadvent.org [Accessed on: 22 April 2024]

[2476]St. Thomas Aquinas. *Summa Theologiae. Tertia Pars.* Q 89. Art. 3 [Online] Available at: www.newadvent.org [Accessed on: 22 April 2024]

children of wrath' (Eph 2:3). Even when liberated from the dominion of the devil by faith and baptism, restored by Jesus Christ, the true image of God, man bears the ontological wound of concupiscence, that leaves him attracted to sin and evil.

Council of Florence (Seventeenth Ecumenical, 1431 to 1447)

Bull of Union with the Copts and the Ethiopians Cantate Domino (4th February 1442)
She firmly believes, professes and teaches that never was anyone conceived by a man and a woman liberated from the devil's dominion except by faith in our Lord Jesus Christ, the Mediator between God and man [cf. I Tim 2:5], who without sin was conceived, born, and died. He alone by his death overthrew the enemy of the human race, cancelling our sins, and unlocked the entrance to the heavenly kingdom, which the first man by his own sin, together with all his posterity, had lost.[2477]

Council of Trent (Nineteenth Ecumenical, 1545 to 1563)

Decree Concerning Original Sin. (17th June 1546)
If anyone does not profess that Adam, the first man, by transgressing God's commandment in paradise, at once lost the holiness and justice in which he had been constituted; and that, through the offence of this sin, he drew upon himself the wrath and indignation of God and consequently death with which God had threatened him and, together with death, captivity in the power of him who henceforth 'has the power of death' [Heb 2:14], that is, the devil; and that 'the whole Adam, body and soul, was changed for the worse through the offence of his sin', let him be anathema. (1)

'If anyone asserts that Adam's sin harmed only him, and not his descendants and that the holiness and justice received from God that he lost was lost only for him and not for us also; or that, stained by the sin of disobedience, he transmitted to all mankind 'only death' and the sufferings 'of the body but not sin as well, which is death to the soul', let him be anathema. 'For he contradicts the words of the apostle: "Sin came into the world through one man and death through sin, and so death spread to all men as all sinned in him"'. [Rom 5:12] (2)[2478]

Decree Concerning Justification. (6th January 1547)
First the holy council declares that for a correct and clear understanding of the doctrine of justification it is necessary that each one admits and confesses that all men, having lost innocence through the sin of Adam [cf. Rom 5:12; I Cor 15:22], 'became unclean' [Is 64:6] and, according to the apostle were 'by nature children of wrath' [Eph 2:3], as the council taught in its decree on original sin. So completely were they the slaves of sin [cf. Rom 6:20] and under the power of the devil and of death that not only the Gentiles by means of the power of nature but even the Jews by means of the letter of the law of Moses were unable to liberate themselves and to rise from that state, even though their free will, weakened and distorted as it was, was in no way extinct.[2479]

First Vatican Council (Twentieth Ecumenical, 1869 to 1870)

Dogmatic Constitution, Dei Filius, Chap. 1. (24th April 1870)
The holy, catholic, apostolic Roman Church believes and confesses there is one God, true and living, Creator and Lord of heaven and earth, almighty, eternal, immense, incomprehensible, infinite in his intellect and will and in all perfection. As he is one, unique, and spiritual substance, entirely simple and unchangeable, we must proclaim him distinct from the world in existence and essence, all blissful in himself and from himself, ineffably exalted above all things that exist or can be conceived besides him.[2480]

[2477]Denzinger, H [2010] *Op. cit.*, p.346-347 *Dz* 1347
[2478]*Ibid.*, p.372 *Dz* 1511-1512
[2479]*Ibid.*, p. 374-375 *Dz* 1521
[2480]*Ibid.*, p. 601 *Dz* 3001

Second Vatican Council (Twenty-First Ecumenical, 1962 to 1965)

Pastoral Constitution, *Gaudium et Spes,* 13, 22. (7th December 1965)
Although he was made by God in a state of holiness, from the very onset of his history man abused his liberty, at the urging of the Evil One. Man set himself against God and sought to attain his goal apart from God. Although they knew God, they did not glorify Him as God, but their senseless minds were darkened and they served the creature rather than the Creator. What divine revelation makes known to us agrees with experience. Examining his heart, man finds that he has inclinations toward evil too, and is engulfed by manifold ills which cannot come from his good Creator. Often refusing to acknowledge God as his beginning, man has disrupted also his proper relationship to his own ultimate goal as well as his whole relationship toward himself and others and all created things. Therefore man is split within himself. As a result, all of human life, whether individual or collective, shows itself to be a dramatic struggle between good and evil, between light and darkness. Indeed, man finds that by himself he is incapable of battling the assaults of evil successfully, so that everyone feels as though he is bound by chains. But the Lord Himself came to free and strengthen man, renewing him inwardly and casting out that 'prince of this world' (Jn 12:31) who held him in the bondage of sin. For sin has diminished man, blocking his path to fulfilment. The call to grandeur and the depths of misery, both of which are a part of human experience, find their ultimate and simultaneous explanation in the light of this revelation.

He Who is 'the image of the invisible God' (Col 1:15), is Himself the perfect man. To the sons of Adam He restores the divine likeness which had been disfigured from the first sin onward. Since human nature as He assumed it was not annulled, by that very fact it has been raised up to a divine dignity in our respect too. For by His incarnation the Son of God has united Himself in some fashion with every man. He worked with human hands, He thought with a human mind, acted by human choice and loved with a human heart. Born of the Virgin Mary, He has truly been made one of us, like us in all things except sin.[2481]

Pope Benedict XVI: 2005 to 2013

Compendium of the Catechism of the Catholic Church. (28th June 2005)

75. What was the first human sin?
When tempted by the devil, the first man and woman allowed trust in their Creator to die in their hearts. In their disobedience they wished to become 'like God' but without God and not in accordance with God (Gen 3:5). Thus, Adam and Eve immediately lost for themselves and for all their descendants the original grace of holiness and justice.

76. What is original sin?
Original sin, in which all human beings are born, is the state of deprivation of original holiness and justice. It is a sin 'contracted' by us not 'committed'; it is a state of birth and not a personal act. Because of the original unity of all human beings, it is transmitted to the descendants of Adam 'not by imitation, but by propagation'. This transmission remains a mystery which we cannot fully understand.

77. What other consequences derive from original sin?
In consequence of original sin human nature, without being totally corrupted, is wounded in its natural powers. It is subject to ignorance, to suffering, and to the dominion of death and is inclined toward sin. This inclination is called concupiscence.[2482]

[2481]Second Vatican Council [1965] Pastoral Constitution, *Gaudium et Spes,* paras 13; 22 [Online] Available at: www.vatican.va [Accessed on: 24 April 2024]
[2482]*Compendium of the Catechism of the Catholic Church* [2005] [Online] Available at: www.vatican.va [Accessed on: 25 April 2024]

Homily on the Solemnity of the Immaculate Conception of the Blessed Virgin Mary. (8th December 2005)

Dear brothers and sisters, if we sincerely reflect about ourselves and our history, we have to say that with this narrative is described not only the history of the beginning but the history of all times, and that we all carry within us a drop of the poison of that way of thinking, illustrated by the images in the Book of Genesis. We call this drop of poison 'original sin'. Precisely on the Feast of the Immaculate Conception, we have a lurking suspicion that a person who does not sin must really be basically boring and that something is missing from his life: the dramatic dimension of being autonomous; that the freedom to say no, to descend into the shadows of sin and to want to do things on one's own is part of being truly human; that only then can we make the most of all the vastness and depth of our being men and women, of being truly ourselves; that we should put this freedom to the test, even in opposition to God, in order to become, in reality, fully ourselves.

In a word, we think that evil is basically good, we think that we need it, at least a little, in order to experience the fullness of being. We think that Mephistopheles — the tempter — is right when he says he is the power 'that always wants evil and always does good' (J.W. von Goethe, *Faust* I, 3). We think that a little bargaining with evil, keeping for oneself a little freedom against God, is basically a good thing, perhaps even necessary. If we look, however, at the world that surrounds us we can see that this is not so; in other words, that evil is always poisonous, does not uplift human beings but degrades and humiliates them. It does not make them any the greater, purer or wealthier, but harms and belittles them.[2483]

General Audience Address. (3rd December 2008)

However, as people of today we must ask ourselves: what is this original sin? What does St Paul teach, what does the Church teach? Is this doctrine still sustainable today? Many think that in light of the history of evolution, there is no longer room for the doctrine of a first sin that then would have permeated the whole of human history. And, as a result, the matter of Redemption and of the Redeemer would also lose its foundation. Therefore, does original sin exist or not? In order to respond, we must distinguish between two aspects of the doctrine on original sin. There exists an empirical aspect, that is, a reality that is concrete, visible, I would say tangible to all. And an aspect of mystery concerning the ontological foundation of this event. The empirical fact is that a contradiction exists in our being. On the one hand every person knows that he must do good and intimately wants to do it. Yet at the same time he also feels the other impulse to do the contrary, to follow the path of selfishness and violence, to do only what pleases him, while also knowing that in this way he is acting against the good, against God and against his neighbour. In his Letter to the Romans St. Paul expressed this contradiction in our being in this way: 'I can will what is right, but I cannot do it. For I do not do the good I want, but I do the evil I do not want' (7: 18-19). This inner contradiction of our being is not a theory. Each one of us experiences it every day. And above all we always see around us the prevalence of this second will. It is enough to think of the daily news of injustice, violence, falsehood and lust. We see it every day. It is a fact.

As a consequence of this evil power in our souls, a murky river developed in history which poisons the geography of human history. Blaise Pascal, the great French thinker, spoke of a 'second nature', which superimposes our original, good nature. This 'second nature' makes evil appear normal to man. Hence even the common expression 'he's human' has a double meaning. 'He's human', can mean: this man is good, he really acts as one should act. But 'he's human', can also imply falsity: evil is normal, it is human. Evil seems to have become our second nature. This contradiction of the human being, of our history, must evoke, and still evokes today, the desire for redemption. And, in

---

[2483]Pope Benedict XVI [2008] *Homily on the Solemnity of the Immaculate Conception of the Blessed Virgin Mary* [Online] Available at: www.vatican.va [Accessed on: 25 April 2024]

reality, the desire for the world to be changed and the promise that a world of justice, peace and good will be created exists everywhere. In politics, for example, everyone speaks of this need to change the world, to create a more just world. And this is precisely an expression of the longing for liberation from the contradiction we experience within us.[2484]

Message for the 33rd Meeting for Friendship Among Peoples. (19th-25th August 2012)
Speaking of man and of his desire for the infinite means first of all recognising his constitutive relationship with the Creator. Man is a creature of God. Today this word — creature — seems almost to have gone out of fashion. People prefer to think of the human being as a being complete in himself and the absolute master of his own destiny. Viewing man as a creature seems 'reductive', because it involves an essential reference to something else or rather, Someone else — who cannot be managed by man — who comes into it to define his identity in an essential way; a relational identity, whose first given is his original and ontological dependence on the One who wanted and created us. Yet this dependence, from which modern and contemporary men and women seek to free themselves, not only does not conceal or diminish but rather reveals clearly the greatness and supreme dignity of the human being, called to life to enter into a relationship with Life itself, with God.

To say: 'By nature, man is relation to the infinite' thus means saying that every person has been created so that he or she may enter into dialogue with God, with the Infinite. At the beginning of the world's history Adam and Eve were the result of an act of love by God, made in his image and likeness, and their life and relationship with the Creator coincided: 'God created man in his own image; in the image of God he created him; male and female he created them' (Gen 1:27). Moreover original sin is ultimately rooted precisely in our first parents' evasion from this constitutive relationship, in their desire to put themselves in God's place, in their belief that they could do without him. Even after their sin, however, human beings are left with this all-consuming desire for this dialogue, almost as if the Creator himself had branded their soul and their flesh with it.[2485]

General Audience Address. (6th February 2013)
I would like to highlight a final teaching in the accounts of the Creation; sin begets sin and all the sins of history are interconnected. This aspect impels us to speak of what is called 'original sin'. What is the meaning of this reality that is not easy to understand? I would just like to suggest a few points. First of all we must consider that no human being is closed in on himself, no one can live solely for himself and by himself; we receive life from the other and not only at the moment of our birth but every day. Being human is a relationship: I am myself only in the 'you' and through the 'you', in the relationship of love with the 'you' of God and the 'you' of others. Well, sin is the distortion or destruction of the relationship with God, this is its essence: it ruins the relationship with God, the fundamental relationship, by putting ourselves in God's place.

The Catechism of the Catholic Church states that with the first sin man 'chose himself over and against God, against the requirements of his creaturely status and therefore against his own good' (n. 398). Once the fundamental relationship is spoilt, the other relational poles are also jeopardised or destroyed: sin ruins relationships, thus it ruins everything, because we are relational. Now, if the relationship structure is disordered from the outset, every human being comes into a world marked by this relational distortion, comes into a world disturbed by sin, by which he or she is marked personally; the initial sin tarnishes and wounds human nature (cf. *Catechism of the Catholic Church,*

[2484]Pope Benedict XVI [2008] *General Audience Address* [Online] Available at: www.vatican.va [Accessed on: 25 April 2024]
[2485]Pope Benedict XVI [2012] *Message for the 33rd Meeting for Friendship Among Peoples* [Online] Available at: www.vatican.va [Accessed on: 25 April 2024]

404-406). And by himself, on his own, man is unable to extricate himself from this situation, on his own he cannot redeem himself; only the Creator himself can right relationships.[2486]

Pope St. John Paul II: 1978 to 2005

General Audience Address. (28th May 1980)
A Fundamental Disquiet in All Human Existence. We are reading again the first chapters of Genesis, to understand how — with original sin — the 'man of lust' took the place of the 'man of original innocence.' The words of Genesis 3:10, 'I was afraid, because I was naked, and I hid myself,' provide evidence of the first experience of man's shame with regard to his Creator — a shame that could also be called 'cosmic'. However, this 'cosmic shame' — if it is possible to perceive its features in man's total situation after original sin — makes way in the biblical text for another form of shame. It is the shame produced in humanity itself. It is caused by the deep disorder in that reality on account of which man, in the mystery of creation, was God's image. He was God's image both in his personal 'ego' and in the interpersonal relationship, through the original communion of persons, constituted by the man and the woman together. That shame, the cause of which is in humanity itself, is at once immanent and relative. It is manifested in the dimension of human interiority and at the same time refers to the 'other' […] a certain constitutive break within the human person is revealed, which is almost a rupture of man's original spiritual and somatic unity. He realises for the first time that his body has ceased drawing upon the power of the spirit, which raised him to the level of the image of God. His original shame bears within it the signs of a specific humiliation mediated by the body. It conceals the germ of that contradiction, which will accompany historical man in his whole earthly path, as St. Paul writes: 'For I delight in the law of God, in my inmost self, but I see in my members another law at war with the law of my mind' (Rom 7:22-23).

In this way, that shame is immanent. It contains such a cognitive acuteness as to create a fundamental disquiet in all human existence. This is not only in face of the prospect of death, but also before that on which the value and dignity of the person in his ethical significance depends. In this sense the original shame of the body ('I am naked') is already fear ('I was afraid'), and announces the uneasiness of conscience connected with lust. The body is not subordinated to the spirit as in the state of original innocence. It bears within it a constant centre of resistance to the spirit. It threatens, in a way, the unity of the person, that is, of the moral nature, which is firmly rooted in the constitution of the person. Lust, especially the lust of the body, is a specific threat to the structure of self-control and self-mastery, through which the human person is formed. It also constitutes a specific challenge for it. In any case, the man of lust does not control his own body in the same way, with equal simplicity and naturalness, as the man of original innocence did. The structure of self-mastery, essential for the person, is shaken to the very foundations in him. He again identifies himself with it in that he is continually ready to win it. Interior imbalance.[2487]

Angelus during Apostolic Journey to Germany. (16th November 1980)
Together with all of you, we will soon praise God and thank Him for the great gift of His love. This love is the foundation of your hope and your courage to live. God has shown us with Jesus Christ in an unsurpassable way how He loves each man and thereby gives him infinite dignity [….] For us Christians it matters little whether someone is sick or healthy; what ultimately matters is this: Are you ready to realise with conscience

[2486]Pope Benedict XVI [2013] General Audience Address [Online] Available at: www.vatican.va [Accessed on: 25 April 2024]
[2487]Pope St. John Paul II [2005] The Redemption of the Body and Sacramentality of Marriage *(Theology of the Body): From the Weekly Audiences of His Holiness, September 5, 1979 — November 28, 1984)* [Online] Available at: www.stmarys-waco.org [Accessed on: 29 April 2024]

and faith the dignity conferred by God in all your life situations and in your behaviour as a true Christian, or do you want to lose [gamble away] this dignity of yours in a superficial and irresponsible life, in sin and guilt before God?[2488]

Encyclical *Dominum et Vivificantem, 36.* (18th May 1986)

According to the witness concerning the beginning which we find in the Scriptures and in Tradition, after the first (and also more complete) description in the Book of Genesis, sin in its original form is understood as 'disobedience,' and this means simply and directly transgression of a prohibition laid down by God. But in the light of the whole context it is also obvious that the ultimate roots of this disobedience are to be sought in the whole real situation of man. Having been called into existence, the human being-man and woman-is a creature. The 'image of God,' consisting in rationality and freedom, expresses the greatness and dignity of the human subject, who is a person. But this personal subject is also always a creature: in his existence and essence he depends on the Creator. According to the Book of Genesis, 'the tree of the knowledge of good and evil' was to express and constantly remind man of the 'limit' impassable for a created being. God's prohibition is to be understood in this sense: the Creator forbids man and woman to eat of the fruit of the tree of the knowledge of good and evil. The words of the enticement, that is to say the temptation, as formulated in the sacred text, are an inducement to transgress this prohibition-that is to say, to go beyond that 'limit': 'When you eat of it your eyes will be opened, and you will be like God ["like gods"], knowing good and evil.'

'Disobedience' means precisely going beyond that limit, which remains impassable to the will and the freedom of man as a created being. For God the Creator is the one definitive source of the moral order in the world created by him. Man cannot decide by himself what is good and what is evil-cannot 'know good and evil, like God.' In the created world God indeed remains the first and sovereign source for deciding about good and evil, through the intimate truth of being, which is the reflection of the Word, the eternal Son, consubstantial with the Father. To man, created to the image of God, the Holy Spirit gives the gift of conscience, so that in this conscience the image may faithfully reflect its model, which is both Wisdom and eternal Law, the source of the moral order in man and in the world. 'Disobedience' as the original dimension of sin, means the rejection of this source, through man's claim to become an independent and exclusive source for deciding about good and evil.[2489]

General Audience Address. (10th September 1986)

Original Sin Causes a Fundamental Change in Mankind.... the fact that really matters is of a moral nature and is imprinted in the very roots of the human spirit. It gives rise to a fundamental change in the human condition. Man is driven forth from the state of original justice and finds himself in a state of sinfulness (*status naturae lapsae*). Sin exists in this state, which is also marked by an inclination to sin. From that moment, the whole history of humanity will be burdened by this state. In fact the first human being (man and woman) received sanctifying grace from God not only for himself, but as founder of the human family, for all his descendants. Therefore through sin which set man in conflict with God, he forfeited grace (he fell into disgrace) even in regard to the inheritance for his descendants. According to the Church's teaching based on revelation, the essence of original sin as the heritage of our progenitors consists in this privation of grace added to nature [....]

It is not difficult to discern in this text the essential problems of human life hidden under an apparently simple form. To eat or not to eat the fruit of a certain tree may itself

---

[2488]Pope St. John Paul II [1980] Angelus [Online] Available at: www.vatican.va [Accessed on: 25 April 2024]

[2489]Pope St. John Paul II [1986] Encyclical *Dominum et Vivificantem*, para 36 [Online] Available at: www.vatican.va [Accessed on: 29 April 2024]

seem irrelevant. However, the tree 'of the knowledge of good and evil' denotes the first principle of human life to which a fundamental problem is linked. The tempter knows this very well, for he says: 'When you eat of it...you will be like God, knowing good and evil.' The tree therefore signifies the insurmountable limit for man and for any creature, however perfect. The creature is always merely a creature, and not God. Certainly he cannot claim to be 'like God,' to 'know good and evil' like God. God alone is the source of all being, God alone is absolute Truth and Goodness, according to which good and evil are measured and from which they receive their distinction. God alone is the eternal legislator, from whom every law in the created world derives, and in particular the law of human nature (*lex naturae*). As a rational creature, man knows this law and should let himself be guided by it in his own conduct. He himself cannot pretend to establish the moral law, to decide himself what is good and what is bad, independently of the Creator, even against the Creator. Neither man nor any other creature can set himself in the place of God, claiming for himself the mastery of the moral order. This is contrary to creation's own ontological constitution which is reflected in the psychological-ethical sphere by the fundamental imperatives of conscience and therefore human conduct.

In the Genesis account, in the guise of an apparently irrelevant plot, we find man's fundamental problem linked to his very condition as a creature. Man as a rational being should let himself be guided by the 'First Truth,' which is moreover the truth of his very existence. Man cannot claim to substitute himself for this truth or to place himself on a par with it. If this principle is called into question, the foundation of the 'justice' of the creature in regard to the Creator is shaken to the roots of human action. The tempter, 'the father of lies,' calls in question the state of original justice by insinuating doubt on the truth of the relationship with God. In yielding to the tempter, man commits a personal sin and causes the state of original sin in human nature [....]

According to Genesis 3, the words which the first man heard beside the 'tree of the knowledge of good and evil' contain all the assault of evil that can arise in the free will of the creature in regard to him who, as Creator, is the source of all being and of all good — he who, being absolutely disinterested and authentically paternal love, is in his very essence the will to give! This gift of love meets with objection, contradiction and rejection. The creature who wishes to be 'like God' concretely realises the attitude expressed so well by St. Augustine: 'love of self to the point of contempt of God' (cf. *De Civitate Dei*, XIV, 28; PL 41, 436). This is perhaps the most penetrating explanation possible of the concept of that sin at the beginning of history, which occurred through man's yielding to the devil's suggestion — *contemptus Dei*, rejection of God, contempt of God, hatred of everything connected with God or that comes from God.[2490]

Catechism of the Catholic Church, 398-400, 405. (1992)

Man's first sin [....] In that sin man *preferred* himself to God and by that very act scorned him. He chose himself over and against God, against the requirements of his creaturely status and therefore against his own good. Constituted in a state of holiness, man was destined to be fully 'divinised' by God in glory. Seduced by the devil, he wanted to 'be like God', but 'without God, before God, and not in accordance with God'.

Scripture portrays the tragic consequences of this first disobedience. Adam and Eve immediately lose the grace of original holiness. They become afraid of the God of whom they have conceived a distorted image — that of a God jealous of his prerogatives.

The harmony in which they had found themselves, thanks to original justice, is now destroyed: the control of the soul's spiritual faculties over the body is shattered; the union of man and woman becomes subject to tensions, their relations henceforth marked by lust and domination. Harmony with creation is broken: visible creation has become alien and hostile to man. Because of man, creation is now subject 'to its bondage to decay'. Finally, the consequence explicitly foretold for this disobedience

---

[2490]Pope St. John Paul II [1986] General Audience — Original Sin Causes a Fundamental Change in Mankind [Online] Available at: www.web.archive.org [Accessed on: 25th April 2024]

will come true: man will 'return to the ground', for out of it he was taken. *Death makes its entrance into human history.*

Although it is proper to each individual, original sin does not have the character of a personal fault in any of Adam's descendants. It is a deprivation of original holiness and justice, but human nature has not been totally corrupted: it is wounded in the natural powers proper to it, subject to ignorance, suffering and the dominion of death, and inclined to sin — an inclination to evil that is called 'concupiscence'. Baptism, by imparting the life of Christ's grace, erases original sin and turns a man back towards God, but the consequences for nature, weakened and inclined to evil, persist in man and summon him to spiritual battle.[2491]

Encyclical *Veritatis Splendor, 1. (6th August 1993)*

As a result of that mysterious original sin, committed at the prompting of Satan, the one who is 'a liar and the father of lies' (Jn 8:44), man is constantly tempted to turn his gaze away from the living and true God in order to direct it towards idols (cf. I Thes 1:9), exchanging 'the truth about God for a lie' (Rom 1:25). Man's capacity to know the truth is also darkened, and his will to submit to it is weakened. Thus, giving himself over to relativism and scepticism (cf. Jn 18:38), he goes off in search of an illusory freedom apart from truth itself.[2492]

Encyclical *Evangelium Vitae, 7, 36. (25th March 1995)*

The Gospel of life, proclaimed in the beginning when man was created in the image of God for a destiny of full and perfect life (cf. Gen 2:7; Wis 9:2-3), is contradicted by the painful experience of death which enters the world and casts its shadow of meaninglessness over man's entire existence. Death came into the world as a result of the devil's envy (cf. Gen 3:1,4-5) and the sin of our first parents (cf. Gen 2:17, 3:17-19). And death entered it in a violent way, through the killing of Abel by his brother Cain: 'And when they were in the field, Cain rose up against his brother Abel, and killed him' (Gen 4:8).

Unfortunately, God's marvellous plan was marred by the appearance of sin in history. Through sin, man rebels against his Creator and ends up by worshipping creatures: 'They exchanged the truth about God for a lie and worshipped and served the creature rather than the Creator' (Rom 1:25). As a result man not only deforms the image of God in his own person, but is tempted to offences against it in others as well, replacing relationships of communion by attitudes of distrust, indifference, hostility and even murderous hatred. When God is not acknowledged as God, the profound meaning of man is betrayed and communion between people is compromised.

In the life of man, God's image shines forth anew and is again revealed in all its fullness at the coming of the Son of God in human flesh. 'Christ is the image of the invisible God' (Col 1:15), he 'reflects the glory of God and bears the very stamp of his nature' (Heb 1:3). He is the perfect image of the Father [....] All who commit themselves to following Christ are given the fullness of life: the divine image is restored, renewed and brought to perfection in them. God's plan for human beings is this, that they should 'be conformed to the image of his Son' (Rom 8:29). Only thus, in the splendour of this image, can man be freed from the slavery of idolatry, rebuild lost fellowship and rediscover his true identity.[2493]

[2491]*Catechism of the Catholic Church* [1992] [Online] Available at: scborromeo2.org [Accessed on: 29 April 2024]

[2492]Pope St. John Paul II [1993] Encyclical *Veritatis Splendor*, para 1 [Online] Available at: www.vatican.va [Accessed on: 29 April 2024]

[2493]Pope St. John Paul II [1995] Encyclical *Evangelium Vitae*, para 7, 36 [Online] Available at: www.vatican.va [Accessed on: 29 April 2024]

Pope St. Paul VI: 1963 to 1978

Encyclical *Ecclesiam Suam, 39, 41. (6th August 1964)*

They [the baptised] have indeed been called to a new kind of life, but they have lost nothing of their own humanity except the unhappy state of original sin. Rather, the humanity in them is now capable of bearing the fairest flowers of perfection and the most precious and holiest of fruits [....] For without reference to Christ's teaching handed on by the Church, it is not possible for man to pass judgment on himself and his own nature, his former state of perfection and the ruinous consequences of original sin, his capacity for good and his need for help in desiring and achieving what is good, the importance and purpose of this present life, the good that he seeks or already possesses, how best to acquire perfection and holiness, and how to attain to the highest degree of perfection and completeness.[2494]

Apostolic Constitution *Indulgentiarum Doctrina, 2. (1st January 1967)*

Every sin in fact causes a perturbation in the universal order established by God in His ineffable wisdom and infinite charity, and the destruction of immense values with respect to the sinner himself and to the human community. Christians throughout history have always regarded sin not only as a transgression of divine law but also — though not always in a direct and evident way — as contempt for or disregard of the friendship between God and man, just as they have regarded it as a real and unfathomable offence against God and indeed an ungrateful rejection of the love of God shown us through Jesus Christ, who called his disciples friends and not servants.[2495]

Apostolic Letter *Solemni hac Liturgia, 16-18. (30th June 1968)*

Original Offence. We believe that in Adam all have sinned, which means that the original offence committed by him caused human nature, common to all men, to fall to a state in which it bears the consequences of that offence, and which is not the state in which it was at first in our first parents — established as they were in holiness and justice, and in which man knew neither evil nor death. It is human nature so fallen, stripped of the grace that clothed it, injured in its own natural powers and subjected to the dominion of death, that is transmitted to all men, and it is in this sense that every man is born in sin. We therefore hold, with the Council of Trent, that original sin is transmitted with human nature, 'not by imitation, but by propagation' and that it is thus 'proper to everyone.' Reborn of the Holy Spirit. We believe that our Lord Jesus Christ, by the sacrifice of the cross redeemed us from original sin and all the personal sins committed by each one of us, so that, in accordance with the word of the apostle, 'where sin abounded, grace did more abound.' Baptism. We believe in one Baptism instituted by our Lord Jesus Christ for the remission of sins. Baptism should be administered even to little children who have not yet been able to be guilty of any personal sin, in order that, though born deprived of supernatural grace, they may be reborn 'of water and the Holy Spirit' to the divine life in Christ Jesus.[2496]

General Audience Address. (15th November 1972)

Man's fatal tempter. There are many things we do know, however, about this diabolical world, things that touch on our lives and on the whole history of mankind. The devil is at the origin of mankind's first misfortune — he was the wily, fatal tempter involved in the first sin, the original sin. That fall of Adam gave the devil a certain dominion over man, from which only Christ's Redemption can free us. It is a history that is still

---

[2494]Pope St. Paul VI [1964] Encyclical *Ecclesiam Suam*, paras 39 & 41 [Online] Available at: www.vatican.va [Accessed on: 29 April 2024]

[2495]Pope St. Paul VI [1967] Apostolic Constitution *Indulgentiarum Doctrina*, para 2 [Online] Available at: www.vatican.va [Accessed on: 29 April 2024]

[2496]Pope St. Paul VI [1968] Apostolic Letter *Solemni hac Liturgia*, paras 16-18 [Online] Available at: www.vatican.va [Accessed on: 29 April 2024]

going on: let us recall the exorcisms at Baptism, and the frequent references in Sacred Scripture and in the liturgy to the aggressive and oppressive 'power of darkness.' The devil is the number one enemy, the preeminent tempter [....] He undermines man's moral equilibrium with his sophistry. He is the malign, clever seducer who knows how to make his way into us through the senses, the imagination and the libido, through utopian logic, or through disordered social contacts in the give and take of our activities, so that he can bring about in us deviations that are all the more harmful because they seem to conform to our physical or mental makeup, or to our profound, instinctive aspirations.[2497]

Pope Ven. Pius XII: 1939 to 1958

Encyclical *Mystici Corporis, 12. (29th June 1943)*

But after the unhappy fall of Adam, the whole human race, infected by the hereditary stain, lost their participation in the divine nature, and we were all 'children of wrath.' But the all-merciful God 'so loved the world as to give his only-begotten Son'; and the Word of the Eternal Father with the same divine love assumed human nature from the race of Adam — but an innocent and spotless nature — so that He, as the new Adam, might be the source whence the grace of the Holy Spirit should flow unto all the children of the first parent. Through the sin of the first man they had been excluded from adoption as children of God; through the Word incarnate, made brothers according to the flesh of the only-begotten Son of God, they receive also the power to become the sons of God. As He hung upon the Cross, Christ Jesus not only appeased the justice of the Eternal Father which had been violated, but He also won for us, His brethren, an ineffable flow of graces. it was possible for Him of Himself to impart these graces to mankind directly; but He willed to do so only through a visible Church made up of men, so that through her all might cooperate with Him in dispensing the graces of Redemption. As the Word of God willed to make use of our nature, when in excruciating agony He would redeem mankind, so in the same way throughout the centuries He makes use of the Church that the work begun might endure.[2498]

Encyclical *Mediator Dei, 1. (20th November 1947)*

Sin had disturbed the right relationship between man and his Creator; the Son of God would restore it. The children of Adam were wretched heirs to the infection of original sin; He would bring them back to their heavenly Father, the primal source and final destiny of all things.[2499]

Encyclical *Humani Generis, 2. (12th August 1950)*

The truths that have to do with God and the relations between God and men, completely surpass the sensible order and demand self-surrender and self-abnegation in order to be put into practice and to influence practical life. Now the human intellect, in gaining the knowledge of such truths is hampered both by the activity of the senses and the imagination, and by evil passions arising from original sin. Hence men easily persuade themselves in such matters that what they do not wish to believe is false or at least doubtful.[2500]

[2497]Pope St. Paul VI [1972] Confronting The Devil's Power [Available at: www.papalencyclicals. net [Accessed on: 29 April 2024]

[2498]Pope Ven. Pius XII [1943] Encyclical *Mystici Corporis*, para 12 [Available at: www. papalencyclicals.net [Accessed on: 29 April 2024]

[2499]Pope Ven. Pius XII [1947] Encyclical *Mediator Dei*, para 1 [Online] Available at: www.vatican. va [Accessed on: 29 April 2024]

[2500]Ven. Pope Pius XII [1950] Encyclical *Humani Generis*, para 2 [Online] Available at: www. vatican.va [Accessed on: 29 April 2024]

An Address to the Fifth International Congress on Psychotherapy and Clinical Psychology, 11. (13th April 1953)

Original sin did not take away from man the possibility or the obligation of directing his own actions himself through his soul. It cannot be alleged that the psychic troubles and disorders which disturb the normal functioning of the psychic being represent what usually happens. The moral struggle to remain on the right path does not prove that it is impossible to follow that path, nor does it authorise any drawing back.[2501]

Pope Pius XI: 1922 to 1939

Encyclical *Miserentissimus Redemptor, 8.* (8th May 1928)

Moreover this duty of expiation is laid upon the whole race of men since, as we are taught by the Christian faith, after Adam's miserable fall, infected by hereditary stain, subject to concupiscences and most wretchedly depraved, it would have been thrust down into eternal destruction. This indeed is denied by the wise men of this age of ours, who following the ancient error of Pelagius, ascribe to human nature a certain native virtue by which of its own force it can go onward to higher things; but the Apostle rejects these false opinions of human pride, admonishing us that we 'were by nature children of wrath' (Eph ii, 3). And indeed, even from the beginning, men in a manner acknowledged this common debt of expiation and, led by a certain natural instinct, they endeavoured to appease God by public sacrifices.[2502]

Encyclical *Divini Illius Magistri, 58, 60.* (31st December 1929)

In fact it must never be forgotten that the subject of Christian education is man whole and entire, soul united to body in unity of nature, with all his faculties natural and supernatural, such as right reason and revelation show him to be; man, therefore, fallen from his original estate, but redeemed by Christ and restored to the supernatural condition of adopted son of God, though without the preternatural privileges of bodily immortality or perfect control of appetite. There remain therefore, in human nature the effects of original sin, the chief of which are weakness of will and disorderly inclinations [....] Every method of education founded, wholly or in part, on the denial or forgetfulness of original sin and of grace, and relying on the sole powers of human nature, is unsound.[2503]

Encyclical *Mit brennender Sorge, 25.* (14 March 1937)

'Original sin' is the hereditary but impersonal fault of Adam's descendants, who have sinned in him (Rom. v. 12). It is the loss of grace, and therefore of eternal life, together with a propensity to evil, which everybody must, with the assistance of grace, penance, resistance and moral effort, repress and conquer. The passion and death of the Son of God has redeemed the world from the hereditary curse of sin and death. Faith in these truths, which in your country are today the butt of the cheap derision of Christ's enemies, belongs to the inalienable treasury of Christian revelation.[2504]

Pope St. Pius X: 1903 to 1914

Encyclical *Ad Diem illum Laetissimum, 5.* (2nd February 1904)

What truly is the point of departure of the enemies of religion for the sowing of the great and serious errors by which the faith of so many is shaken? They begin by denying that

---

[2501]Ven. Pope Pius XII [1953] An Address to the Fifth International Congress on Psychotherapy and Clinical Psychology, para 11 [Available at: www.papalencyclicals.net [Accessed on: 29 April 2024]

[2502]Pope Pius XI [1928] Encyclical *Miserentissimus Redemptor*, para 8 [Online] Available at: www.vatican.va [Accessed on: 30 April 2024]

[2503]Pope Pius XI [1929] Encyclical *Divini illius Magistri*, paras 58,60 [Online] Available at: www.vatican.va [Accessed on: 30 April 2024]

[2504]Pope Pius XI [1937] Encyclical *Mit brennender Sorge*, para 25 [Online] Available at: www.vatican.va [Accessed on: 29 April 2024]

man has fallen by sin and been cast down from his former position. Hence they regard as mere fables original sin and the evils that were its consequence. Humanity vitiated in its source vitiated in its turn the whole race of man; and thus was evil introduced amongst men and the necessity for a Redeemer involved. All this rejected it is easy to understand that no place is left for Christ, for the Church, for grace or for anything that is above and beyond nature; in one word the whole edifice of faith is shaken from top to bottom.[2505]

Encyclical *Acerbo Nimis, 3.* (15th April 1905)

For the will of man retains but little of that divinely implanted love of virtue and righteousness by which it was, as it were, attracted strongly toward the real and not merely apparent good. Disordered by the stain of the first sin, and almost forgetful of God, its Author, it improperly turns every affection to a love of vanity and deceit. This erring will, blinded by its own evil desires, has need therefore of a guide to lead it back to the paths of justice whence it has so unfortunately strayed. The intellect itself is this guide, which need not be sought elsewhere, but is provided by nature itself. It is a guide, though, that, if it lack its companion light, the knowledge of divine things, will be only an instance of the blind leading the blind so that both will fall into the pit. The holy king David, praising God for the light of truth with which He had illumined the intellect, exclaimed: 'The light of Thy countenance, O Lord, is signed upon us.' Then he described the effect of this light by adding: 'Thou hast given gladness in my heart,' gladness, that is, which enlarges our heart so that it runs in the way of God's Commandments.[2506]

Catechism of St. Pius X. (1908)
Man

Q. Why do we say that man was created to the image and likeness of God?

A. We say that man was created to the image and likeness of God because the human soul is spiritual and rational, free in its operations, capable of knowing and loving God and of enjoying Him for ever — perfections which reflect a ray of the infinite greatness of the Lord in us.

Q. In what state did God place our first parents, Adam and Eve?

A. God placed our first parents, Adam and Eve, in the state of innocence and grace; but they soon fell away by sin.

Q. Besides innocence and sanctifying grace did God confer any other gifts on our first parents?

A. Besides innocence and sanctifying grace, God conferred on our first parents other gifts, which, along with sanctifying . grace, they were to transmit to their descendants; these were: (1) Integrity, that is, the perfect subjection of sense and reason; (2) Immortality; (3) Immunity from all pain and sorrow; (4) A knowledge in keeping with their state.

Q. What was the nature of Adam's sin?

A. Adam's sin was a sin of pride and of grave disobedience.

Q. What chastisement was meted out to the sin of Adam and Eve?

A. Adam and Eve lost the grace of God and the right they had to Heaven; they were driven out of the earthly Paradise, subjected to many miseries of soul and body, and condemned to death.

Q. If Adam and Eve had not sinned, would they have been exempt from death?

A. If Adam and Eve had not sinned and if they had remained faithful to God, they would, after a happy and tranquil sojourn here on earth, and without dying, have

---

[2505]Pope St. Pius X [1904] Encyclical *Ad Diem illum Laetissimum*, para 5 [Online] Available at: www.vatican.va [Accessed on: 30 April 2024]

[2506]Pope St. Pius X [1905] Encyclical *Acerbo Nimis*, para 3 [Online] Available at: www.vatican.va [Accessed on: 30 April 2024]

been transferred by God into Heaven, to enjoy a life of unending glory [....]

Q. How is it possible for original sin to be transmitted to all men?

A. Original sin is transmitted to all men because God, having conferred sanctifying grace and other supernatural gifts on the human race in Adam, on the condition that Adam should not disobey Him; and Adam having disobeyed, as head and father of the human race, rendered human nature rebellious against God. And hence, human nature is transmitted to all the descendants of Adam in a state of rebellion against God, and deprived of divine grace and other gifts [....]

The Main Kinds of Sin

Q. What is original sin?

A. Original sin is the sin in which we are all born, and which we contracted by the disobedience of our first parent, Adam.

Q. What evil effects has the sin of Adam brought upon us?

A. The evil effects of the sin of Adam are: The privation of grace, the loss of Paradise, together with ignorance, inclination to evil, death, and all our other miseries.[2507]

Pope Leo XIII: 1878 to 1903

Encyclical *Humanum Genus*, 1, 20. (20 April 1884)

The race of man, after its miserable fall from God, the Creator and the Giver of heavenly gifts, 'through the envy of the devil,' separated into two diverse and opposite parts, of which the one steadfastly contends for truth and virtue, the other of those things which are contrary to virtue and to truth. The one is the kingdom of God on earth, namely, the true Church of Jesus Christ; and those who desire from their heart to be united with it, so as to gain salvation, must of necessity serve God and His only-begotten Son with their whole mind and with an entire will. The other is the kingdom of Satan, in whose possession and control are all whosoever follow the fatal example of their leader and of our first parents, those who refuse to obey the divine and eternal law, and who have many aims of their own in contempt of God, and many aims also against God.

Moreover, human nature was stained by original sin, and is therefore more disposed to vice than to virtue. For a virtuous life it is absolutely necessary to restrain the disorderly movements of the soul, and to make the passions obedient to reason. In this conflict human things must very often be despised, and the greatest labours and hardships must be undergone, in order that reason may always hold its sway. But the naturalists and Freemasons, having no faith in those things which we have learned by the revelation of God, deny that our first parents sinned, and consequently think that free will is not at all weakened and inclined to evil. On the contrary, exaggerating rather the power and the excellence of nature, and placing therein alone the principle and rule of justice, they cannot even imagine that there is any need at all of a constant struggle and a perfect steadfastness to overcome the violence and rule of our passions.[2508]

Encyclical *Divinum illud Munus, 8-9.* (9th May 1897)

Human nature is by necessity the servant of God: 'The creature is a servant; we are the servants of God by nature' (St. Cyr. Alex., *Thesaur.* 1. v., c. 5). On account, however, of original sin, our whole nature had fallen into such guilt and dishonour that we had become enemies to God. 'We were by nature the children of wrath' (Eph ii., 3). There was no power which could raise us and deliver us from this ruin and eternal destruction. But God, the Creator of mankind and infinitely merciful, did this through His only begotten Son, by whose benefit it was brought about that man was restored so that rank and dignity whence he had fallen, and was adorned with still more abundant graces. No one can express the greatness of this work of divine grace in the souls of men.

[2507]*Catechism of St. Pius X* [1908] [Online] Available at: www.ewtn.com [Accessed on: 30 April 2024]

[2508]Pope Leo XIII [1884] Encyclical *Humanum Genus*, paras 1, 20 [Online] Available at: www. vatican.va [Accessed on: 30 April 2024]

Wherefore, both in Holy Scripture and in the writings of the fathers, men are styled regenerated, new creatures, partakers of the Divine Nature, children of God, god-like, and similar epithets [....] The beginnings of this regeneration and renovation of man are by Baptism. In this sacrament, when the unclean spirit has been expelled from the soul, the Holy Ghost enters in and makes it like to Himself. 'That which is born of the Spirit, is spirit' (Jn iii., 6). The same Spirit gives Himself more abundantly in Confirmation, strengthening and confirming Christian life; from which proceeded the victory of the martyrs and the triumph of the virgins over temptations and corruptions.[2509]

Pope Bl. Pius IX: 1846 to 1878

Encyclical *Ineffabilis Deus*, 1. (8th December 1854)

God Ineffable — whose ways are mercy and truth, whose will is omnipotence itself, and whose wisdom 'reaches from end to end mightily, and orders all things sweetly' — having foreseen from all eternity the lamentable wretchedness of the entire human race which would result from the sin of Adam, decreed, by a plan hidden from the centuries, to complete the first work of his goodness by a mystery yet more wondrously sublime through the Incarnation of the Word. This he decreed in order that man who, contrary to the plan of Divine Mercy had been led into sin by the cunning malice of Satan, should not perish; and in order that what had been lost in the first Adam would be gloriously restored in the Second Adam.[2510]

Pope Gregory XVI: 1831 to 1846

Encyclical *Mirari Vos*, 14. (15th August 1832)

When all restraints are removed by which men are kept on the narrow path of truth, their nature, which is already inclined to evil, propels them to ruin. Then truly 'the bottomless pit' is open from which John saw smoke ascending which obscured the sun, and out of which locusts flew forth to devastate the earth.[2511]

Pope Leo IV: 847 to 855

Synod of Quiercy, chaps. 1, 2. (May 853)

The omnipotent God created man upright without sin, and with free will, and he placed <man>, whom he wished to remain in the holiness of justice, in paradise. Man, using his free will badly, sinned and fell and became the 'mass of perdition' of the entire human race. The just and good God, however, chose from this same mass of perdition according to his foreknowledge those whom through grace he predestined to life [Rom 8:9ff.; Eph 1:11], and he predestined for these eternal life; the others, whom by the judgment of justice he left in the 'mass of perdition', however, he knew would perish; but he did not predestine that they would perish; because he is just, however, he predestined eternal punishment for them. And on account of this we speak of only one predestination of God, which pertains either to the gift of grace or to the retribution of justice.

The freedom of will that we lost in the first man, we have received back through Christ our Lord; and we have free will for good, preceded and aided by grace, and we have free will for evil, abandoned by grace. But we have free will because it has been liberated by grace and healed from corruption by grace.[2512]

[2509]Pope Leo XIII [1897] Encyclical *Divinum illud Munus*, paras 8-9 [Online] Available at: www.vatican.va [Accessed on: 30 April 2024]

[2510]Pope Bl. Pius IX [1854] Encyclical *Ineffabilis Deus*, para 1 [Online] Available at: www.papalencyclicals [Accessed on:1 May 2024]

[2511]Pope Gregory XVI [1832] Encyclical *Mirari Vos*, para14 [Online] Available at: www.papalencyclicals [Accessed on:1 May 2024]

[2512]Denzinger, H [2010] *Op. cit.*, p. 213 *Dz* 621, *Dz* 622

Pope Boniface II: 530 to 532

Letter Per folium nostrum to Bishop Caesarius of Arles, 2. (25th January 531)

So We marvel very much that those who believe the contrary are oppressed by the remains of an ancient error even to the point that they believe that we come to Christ, not by the favour of God, but by that of nature and say that the good of that very nature, which is known to have been perverted by Adam's sin, is the author of our faith rather than Christ; and do not perceive that they contradict the statement of the Master, who said: 'No one comes to me, except it be given to him by my Father' [Jn 6:44]....[2513]

Pope Felix III: 526 to 530

Second Synod of Orange, Canons 1, 8, 13, 21. (3rd July 529)

If anyone says that through the offence of Adam's sin the whole person, body and soul, was not 'changed for the worse' but believes that only the body was subjected to corruption while the freedom of the soul remained unharmed, such a one is misled by the error of Pelagius and goes against Scripture, which says: 'The soul that sins shall die' [Ez 18:20]. And: 'Do you not know that if you yield to anyone as obedient slaves, you are slaves of the one whom you obey?' [Rom 6:16]' and again: 'Whatever overcomes one, to that he is enslaved' [II Pet 2:19].

...[free will] is wounded in all those who are born from the transgression of the first man...free will has been weakened in all by the sin of the first man....

Freedom of will weakened in the first man cannot be repaired except through the grace of baptism; once it has been lost, it cannot be restored except by him by whom it could be given. Thus Truth itself says: 'If the Son makes you free, you will be free indeed.' [Jn 8:36]

Nature and grace. Just as the apostle most truly says to those who, wishing to be justified in the law, have fallen even from grace: 'If justice is from the law, then Christ died in vain' [Gal 2:21]; so it is most truly said to those who think that grace, which the faith of Christ commends and obtains, is nature: If justice is through nature 'then Christ died in vain'. For the law was already here and it did not justify; nature, too, was already present, and it did not justify. Therefore, Christ did not die in vain, that the law also might be fulfilled through him who said: 'I have come not to destroy the law, but to fulfil [it]' [Mt 5:17], and in order that nature ruined by Adam might be repaired by him who said he came : 'to seek and to save that which had been lost' [Lk 19:10].

Conclusions Drawn up by Bishop Caesarius of Arles

Thus, according to the texts of Holy Scripture and the explanations of the early Fathers quoted above, we must with God's help preach and believe the following: free will has been so distorted and weakened by the sin of the first man that thereafter no one could love God as was required or believe in God or perform for the sake of God what is good, unless the grace of the divine mercy first attained him. Therefore, we believe that that excellent faith, so highly proclaimed to their praise by St. Paul [Heb 11], which was given to the just Abel, to Noah, to Abraham, Isaac, and Jacob, and to the vast multitude of saints of old, was offered through the grace of God, and not through the natural goodness that had been first given to Adam.[2514]

Pope Simplicus: 468 to 483

Synod of Arles' Formula of Submission of the Priest Lucidus (473)

I uphold the grace of God in order that I may always unite the striving of man and the impulse of grace, and I declare that the freedom of the human will is not destroyed but weakened and enfeebled and that he who is saved is [still] in danger; and he who has perished could have been saved.[2515]

[2513] *Ibid.*, p.141-142 Dz 400
[2214] *Ibid.*, p.134-139 Dz 371, Dz 378, Dz 383, Dz 391, Dz 396
[2515] *Ibid.*, p.119 Dz 339

Pope Celestine I: 422 to 432

The Indiculus, 1

In the transgression of Adam, all men lost their natural capacity and their innocence, and no one can rise from the depths of that collapse through free will unless the grace of the merciful God lifts him up, as Pope Innocent of blessed memory proclaims and says in his letter to the Synod of Carthage: 'For long ago that man, a victim of his free will in making quite rash use of his goods, fell into the depths of transgression and sank and found no means by which he might be able to rise from there; and, deceived forever by his own freedom, he would have lain under the crushing weight of this collapse if the subsequent coming of Christ had not lifted him up again by virtue of the grace of him who, through the purification of the new rebirth, has washed away every past fault in his baptismal bath.'[2516]

[2516]*Ibid.*, p.88-89 *Dz* 239

Christology

Pope Francis: 2013 to 2025

B. *Jesus of Nazareth's sufferings are the proof of proofs that at the Incarnation He ceased to be God, and instead became an exceptionally virtuous man; remaining only a man until His death on the cross.*

Eugenio Scalfari's interview with Pope Francis. *La Repubblica.* (7th July 2017)
The Pope knows that Jesus really became incarnate, he became a man until he was crucified. The 'Resurrectio' is in fact the proof that a God who became man only after his death becomes God again.[2517]

Eugenio Scalfari's interview with Pope Francis. *La Repubblica.* (8th October 2019)
[*Though Communications prefect Paolo Ruffini stated that Eugenio Scalfari's quotation of Pope Francis cannot be considered a faithful account, Pope Francis did not repudiate, contradict or demand a retraction from Eugenio Scalfari*][2518]
    Whoever has had, as I have several times, the luck of meeting him and speaking to him with the utmost cultural confidence, knows that Pope Francis conceives Christ as Jesus of Nazareth, man, not God incarnate. Once incarnated, Jesus ceases to be a god and becomes a man until his death on the cross.
    Jesus of Nazareth, once he became a man, though a man of exceptional virtues, was not a God at all.[2519]
    The proof that confirms this reality and creates a Church completely different from the others is proved by some episodes that deserve to be remembered. The first is what happens in the Garden of Gethsemane where Jesus goes after the Last Supper. The apostles who are a few meters from him hear him pray to God with words that were at one time reported by Simon Peter: 'Lord' — said Jesus —'if you can remove this bitter chalice from me, please do it, but if you can't or you don't want to, I will drink it all the way.' He was arrested by Pilate's guards as soon as he left the garden. Another episode, also well known, occurs when Jesus is already crucified and once again repeats himself and is listened to by the apostles and by the women who are kneeling at the foot of the cross: 'Lord, you have forsaken me.'
    When I happened to discuss these sentences, Pope Francis said to me: 'These are the "proof-of-proofs" that Jesus of Nazareth, once he became a man, though a man of exceptional virtues, was not a god at all.'[2520]

Sacred Scripture

Matthew 1:23
Behold a virgin shall be with child, and bring forth a son, and they shall call his name Emmanuel, which being interpreted is, God with us.

Matthew 14:33
And they that were in the boat came and adored him, saying: Indeed thou art the Son of God.

Matthew 16:16
Simon Peter answered and said: Thou art Christ, the Son of the living God.

[2517]Scalfari, E [7 July 2017] *Scalfari intervista Francesco: 'Il mio grido al G20 sui migranti'* [Online] Available at: www.repubblica.it [Accessed on: 17 September 2022]
[2518]Roberts, J. [10 October 2019] *Scalfari claims Pope does not believe Jesus 'the man' was divine* [Online] Available at: www.thetablet.co.uk [Accessed 20 June 2022]
[2519]Skojek, S [9 October 2019] *Scalfari, Friend of Francis, Claims Pope Believes Jesus Was 'Not a God At All'* [Online] Available at: onepeterfive.wpengine.com [Accessed on: 17 September 2022]
[2520]*Francis to Favorite Journalist: 'Jesus was not at all a God.'* [Online] Available at: rorate-caeli. blogspot.com [Accessed on: 21 September 2022]

Matthew 28:9
And behold Jesus met them, saying: All hail. But they came up and took hold of his feet, and adored him.

Matthew 28:19
Going therefore, teach ye all nations; baptizing them in the name of the Father, and of the Son, and of the Holy Ghost.

Mark 2:5-12
And when Jesus had seen their faith, he saith to the sick of the palsy: Son, thy sins are forgiven thee. And there were some of the scribes sitting there, and thinking in their hearts: Why doth this man speak thus? he blasphemeth. Who can forgive sins, but God only? Which Jesus presently knowing in his spirit, that they so thought within themselves, saith to them: Why think you these things in your hearts? Which is easier, to say to the sick of the palsy: Thy sins are forgiven thee; or to say: Arise, take up thy bed, and walk? But that you may know that the Son of man hath power on earth to forgive sins, (he saith to the sick of the palsy,) I say to thee: Arise, take up thy bed, and go into thy house. And immediately he arose; and taking up his bed, went his way in the sight of all; so that all wondered and glorified God, saying: We never saw the like.

John 1:14
And the Word was made flesh, and dwelt among us, (and we saw his glory, the glory as it were of the only begotten of the Father,) full of grace and truth.

John 1:18
No man hath seen God at any time: the only begotten Son who is in the bosom of the Father, he hath declared him.

John 5:18
Hereupon therefore the Jews sought the more to kill him, because he did not only break the sabbath, but also said God was his Father, making himself equal to God.

John 8:58
Jesus said to them: Amen, amen I say to you, before Abraham was made, I am.

John 10:30-33
I and the Father are one. The Jews then took up stones to stone him. Jesus answered them: Many good works I have shewed you from my Father; for which of those works do you stone me? The Jews answered him: For a good work we stone thee not, but for blasphemy; and because that thou, being a man, makest thyself God.

John 17:21
That they all may be one, as thou, Father, in me, and I in thee; that they also may be one in us; that the world may believe that thou hast sent me.

John 20:28
Thomas answered, and said to him: My Lord, and my God.

Sacred Tradition

St. Ignatius of Antioch: c. 50 to c 98/117

Epistle to the Ephesians, Chap. 18
For our God, Jesus Christ, was, according to the appointment of God, conceived in the womb by Mary, of the seed of David, but by the Holy Ghost.[2521]

[2521]St. Ignatius of Antioch. *Epistle to the Ephesians*, Chap. 18. [Online] Available at: www.newadvent. org [Accessed on: 22 June 2022]

St. Athanasius: c. 296 to 373

On the Incarnation of the Word, Chap 18, 19

Therefore, even to begin with, when He was descending to us, He fashioned His body for Himself from a Virgin, thus to afford to all no small proof of His Godhead, in that He Who formed this is also Maker of everything else as well. For who, seeing a body proceeding forth from a Virgin alone without man, can fail to infer that He Who appears in it is Maker and Lord of other bodies also? Or who, seeing the substance of water changed and transformed into wine, fails to perceive that He Who did this is Lord and Creator of the substance of all waters? For to this end He went upon the sea also as its Master, and walked as on dry land, to afford evidence to them that saw it of His lordship over all things. And in feeding so vast a multitude on little, and of His own self yielding abundance where none was, so that from five loaves five thousand had enough, and left so much again over, did He show Himself to be any other than the very Lord Whose Providence is over all things? [...]

For who that saw His power over evil spirits, or who that saw the evil spirits confess that He was their Lord, will hold his mind any longer in doubt whether this be the Son and Wisdom and Power of God? For He made even the creation break silence: in that even at His death, marvellous to relate, or rather at His actual trophy over death — the Cross I mean — all creation was confessing that He that was made manifest and suffered in the body was not man merely, but the Son of God and Saviour of all. For the sun hid His face, and the earth quaked and the mountains were rent: all men were awed. Now these things showed that Christ on the Cross was God, while all creation was His slave, and was witnessing by its fear to its Master's presence. Thus, then, God the Word showed Himself to men by His works.[2522]

St. Hilary of Poitiers: 315 to 368

On the Trinity, Bk. X, Chap. 19, 22

Being, then, Man with this body, Jesus Christ is both the Son of God and Son of Man, Who emptied Himself of the form of God, and received the form of a servant. There is not one Son of Man and another Son of God; nor one in the form of God, and another born perfect man in the form of a servant: so that, as by the nature determined for us by God, the Author of our being, man is born with body and soul, so likewise Jesus Christ, by His own power, is God and Man with flesh and soul, possessing in Himself whole and perfect manhood, and whole and perfect Godhead. [...]

He was born also not to be at one time two separate beings, but that it might be made plain, that He Who was God before He was Man, now that He has taken humanity, is God and Man. How could Jesus Christ, the Son of God, have been born of Mary, except by the Word becoming flesh: that is by the Son of God, though in the form of God, taking the form of a slave? When He Who was in the form of God took the form of a slave, two contraries were brought together. Thus it was just as true, that He received the form of a slave, as that He remained in the form of God. The use of the one word 'form' to describe both natures compels us to recognise that He truly possessed both. He is in the form of a servant, Who is also in the form of God. And though He is the latter by His eternal nature, and the former in accordance with the divine Plan of Grace, the word has its true significance equally in both cases, because He is both: as truly in the form of God as in the form of Man. Just as to take the form of a servant is none other than to be born a man, so to be in the form of God is none other than to be God: and we confess Him as one and the same Person, not by loss of the Godhead, but by assumption of the manhood: in the form of God through His divine nature, in the form of man from His conception by the Holy Ghost, being found in fashion as a man.[2523]

[2522]St. Athanasius. *On the Incarnation of the Word,* Chap. 18, 19. [Online] Available at: www.newadvent.org [Accessed on: 22 June 2022]

[2523]St. Hilary of Poitiers. *On the Trinity,* Bk. X, Chap. 19 [Online] Available at: www.newadvent.org [Accessed on: 22 June 2022]

St. John Chrysostom: c. 347 to 407

Homily 6 on Philippians 2:5-8
Tell me now, what means, 'He took the form of a servant'? It means, He became man. Wherefore 'being in the form of God,' He was God. For one 'form' and another 'form' is named; if the one be true, the other is also. 'The form of a servant' means, Man by nature, wherefore 'the form of God' means, God by nature. And he not only bears record of this, but of His equality too, as John also does, that he is no way inferior to the Father, for he says, 'He thought it not a thing to seize, to be equal with God.' [...]

I said that the 'form of a servant' was a true form, and nothing less. Therefore 'the form of God' also is perfect, and no less. Why says he not, 'being made in the form of God,' but 'being in the form of God'? This is the same as the saying, 'I am that I am.' Exodus 3:14 'Form' implies unchangeableness, so far as it is form. It is not possible that things of one substance should have the form of another, as no man has the form of an angel, neither has a beast the form of a man. How then should the Son?[2524]

Homily 7 on Philippians 2:5-11
For lest when you hear that He emptied Himself, you should think that some change, and degeneracy, and loss is here; he says, while He remained what He was, He took that which He was not, and being made flesh He remained God, in that He was the Word.

What then means, Being made in the likeness of men? He had many things belonging to us, and many He had not; for instance, He was not born of wedlock. He did no sin. These things had He which no man has. He was not what he seemed only, but He was God also; He seemed to be a man, but He was not like the mass of men. For He was like them in flesh. He means then, that He was not a mere man. Wherefore he says, 'in the likeness of men.' For we indeed are soul and body, but He was God, and soul and body, wherefore he says, 'in the likeness.'[2525]

St. Augustine: 354 to 430

Tractates on the Gospel of John, 23
'He emptied Himself, taking upon Him the form of a servant;' Philippians 2:6 not, therefore, by losing the form of God. He became man who was God, by receiving what He was not, not by losing what He was: so God became man.[2526]

St. Thomas Aquinas: 1225 to 1274

Summa Theologiae. Tertia Pars. q1, a1
As Augustine replies (Ep. ad Volusian. 137): 'The Christian doctrine nowhere holds that God was so joined to human flesh as either to desert or lose, or to transfer and as it were, contract within this frail body, the care of governing the universe. This is the thought of men unable to see anything but corporeal things . . . God is great not in mass, but in might. Hence the greatness of His might feels no straits in narrow surroundings. Nor, if the passing word of a man is heard at once by many, and wholly by each, is it incredible that the abiding Word of God should be everywhere at once?' Hence nothing unfitting arises from God becoming incarnate.[2527]

The Magisterium of the Church

Our Lord Jesus Christ became truly man while remaining truly God. He is inseparably true God and true man. He is truly the Son of God who, without ceasing to be God and Lord, became a man. The true understanding of kenosis is that the Son of God 'emptied' Himself of divine glory, pushed to the point of death on the Cross. The false understanding of kenosis makes the mistake of imagining that the divinity was taken away from the Word in Christ.

[2524]St. John Chrysostom. *Homily 6 on Philippians* [Online] Available at: www.newadvent.org [Accessed on: 28 September 2022]

[2525]St. John Chrysostom. *Homily 7 on Philippians* [Online] Available at: www.newadvent.org [Accessed on: 22 June 2022]

[2526]St. Augustine. *Tractate* 23 (John 5:19-40) [Online] Available at: www.newadvent.org [Accessed on: 22 June 2022]

[2527]St. Thomas Aquinas. *Summa Theologiae*. Tertia Pars. q1, a1 [Online] Available at: www.newadvent.org [Accessed on: 22 June 2022]

Council of Nicaea (First Ecumenical, 325)

I believe in one God, the Father almighty, maker of heaven and earth, of all things visible and invisible. And in one Lord Jesus Christ, the Only Begotten Son of God, born of the Father before all ages. God from God, Light from Light, true God from true God, begotten, not made, consubstantial with the Father; through him all things were made. For us men and for our salvation he came down from heaven, and by the Holy Spirit was incarnate of the Virgin Mary, and became man. For our sake he was crucified under Pontius Pilate, he suffered death and was buried...

Council of Chalcedon (Fourth Ecumenical, 451)

The Chalcedonian Creed

So, following the saintly fathers, we all with one voice teach the confession of one and the same Son, our Lord Jesus Christ: the same perfect in divinity and perfect in humanity, the same truly God and truly man, of a rational soul and a body; consubstantial with the Father as regards his divinity, and the same consubstantial with us as regards his humanity; like us in all respects except for sin; begotten before the ages from the Father as regards his divinity, and in the last days the same for us and for our salvation from Mary, the virgin God-bearer as regards his humanity; one and the same Christ, Son, Lord, only-begotten, acknowledged in two natures which undergo no confusion, no change, no division, no separation; at no point was the difference between the natures taken away through the union, but rather the property of both natures is preserved and comes together into a single person and a single subsistent being; he is not parted or divided into two persons, but is one and the same only-begotten Son, God, Word, Lord Jesus Christ, just as the prophets taught from the beginning about him, and as the Lord Jesus Christ himself instructed us, and as the creed of the fathers handed it down to us.[2528]

Third Council of Constantinople (Sixth Ecumenical, 680 to 681)

...begotten before the ages from the Father as regards his divinity, and in the last days the same for us and for our salvation from the holy Spirit and the virgin Mary, who is properly and truly called mother of God, as regards his humanity; one and the same Christ, Son, Lord, only-begotten, acknowledged in two natures which undergo no confusion, no change, no separation, no division; at no point was the difference between the natures taken away through the union, but rather the property of both natures is preserved and comes together into a single subsistent being [*in unam personam et in unam subsistentiam concurrente*]; he is not parted or divided into two persons, but is one and the same only-begotten Son, Word of God, lord Jesus Christ, just as the prophets taught from the beginning about him, and as Jesus the Christ himself instructed us, and as the creed of the holy fathers handed it down to us. [...]

For just as his flesh is said to be and is flesh of the Word of God, so too the natural will of his flesh is said to and does belong to the Word of God, just as he says himself: I have come down from heaven, not to do my own will, but the will of the Father who sent me, calling his own will that of his flesh, since his flesh too became his own. For in the same way that his all holy and blameless animate flesh was not destroyed in being made divine but remained in its own limit and category, so his human will as well was not destroyed by being made divine, but rather was preserved, according to the theologian Gregory, who says: 'For his willing, when he is considered as saviour, is not in opposition to God, being made divine in its entirety.' And we hold there to be two natural principles of action in the same Jesus Christ our lord and true God, which undergo no division, no change, no partition, no confusion, that is, a divine principle of action and a human principle of action, according to the godly-speaking Leo, who says

---

[2528]Tanner, N. [1990] *Decrees of the Ecumenical Councils*: Volume 1 [Online] Available at: www.papalencyclicals.net [Accessed: 21 June 2022]

most clearly: 'For each form does in a communion with the other that activity which it possesses as its own, the Word working that which is the Word's and the body accomplishing the things that are the body's'.

For of course we will not grant the existence of only a single natural principle of action of both God and creature, lest we raise what is made to the level of divine being, or indeed reduce what is most specifically proper to the divine nature to a level befitting creatures for we acknowledge that the miracles and the sufferings are of one and the same according to one or the other of the two natures out of which he is and in which he has his being, as the admirable Cyril said. Therefore, protecting on all sides the 'no confusion' and 'no division', we announce the whole in these brief words: Believing our lord Jesus Christ, even after his incarnation, to be one of the holy Trinity and our true God, we say that he has two natures shining forth in his one subsistence in which he demonstrated the miracles and the sufferings throughout his entire providential dwelling here, not in appearance but in truth, the difference of the natures being made known in the same one subsistence in that each nature wills and performs the things that are proper to it in a communion with the other; then in accord with this reasoning we hold that two natural wills and principles of action meet in correspondence for the salvation of the human race.[2529]

Council of Vienne (Fifteenth Ecumenical, 1311 to 1312)

Constitution Fidei Catholicae.
Adhering firmly to the foundation of the catholic faith, other than which, as the Apostle testifies, n o o ne c an l ay, w e o penly p rofess w ith h oly m other c hurch t hat t he only begotten Son of God, subsisting eternally together with the Father in everything in which God the Father exists, assumed in time in the womb of a virgin the parts of our nature united together, from which he himself true God became true man: namely the human, passible body and the intellectual or rational soul truly of itself and essentially informing the body. And that in this assumed nature the Word of God willed for the salvation of all not only to be nailed to the cross and to die on it...[2530]

Second Vatican Council (Twenty-First Ecumenical, 1962 to 1965)

Pastoral Constitution Gaudium et Spes, 41. (7th December 1965)
For by His incarnation the Son of God has united Himself in some fashion with every man. He worked with human hands, He thought with a human mind, acted by human choice and loved with a human heart. Born of the Virgin Mary, He has truly been made one of us, like us in all things except sin.[2531]

Pope Benedict XVI: 2005 to 2013

General Audience Address. (1st June 2005)

Canticle cf. Letter to the Philippians (2: 6-11). ...He certainly possesses the divine nature with all its prerogatives. But this transcendent reality is not interpreted or lived out under the banner of power, greatness and dominion. Christ does not use his equality with God, his glorious dignity or his power as an instrument of triumph, a sign of remoteness or an expression of incontestable supremacy (cf. v. 6). On the contrary, he strips or 'empties himself', immersing himself without reserve in our weak and wretched human condition. In Christ the divine 'form' (*morphé*) is concealed beneath

---

[2529]Third Council of Constantinople: 680-681 A. D. [Online] Available at: www.papalencyclicals. net [Accessed: 21 June 2022]
[2530]Council of Vienne 1311-1312 A.D. [Online] Available at: www.papalencyclicals.net [Accessed: 21 June 2022]
[2531]Second Vatican Council [1965] *Pastoral Constitution Gaudium et Spes,* para 41 [Online] Available at: www.vatican.va [Accessed on: 28 September 2022]

the human 'form' (*morphé*), that is, beneath our reality marked by suffering, poverty, limitation and death (cf. v. 7).

Consequently, it was not a mere disguise or a change in appearance such as people believed the deities of the Greco-Roman culture could assume. The form Christ took was divine reality in an authentically human experience. God does not appear only as a man, but he makes himself man and truly becomes one of us, he truly becomes the 'God-with-us' who is not satisfied with looking down kindly upon us from the throne of his glory, but plunges in person into human history, becoming 'flesh' or, in other words, a fragile reality, conditioned by time and space (cf. Jn 1: 14).[2532]

Compendium of the Catechism of the Catholic Church. (28th June 2005)

86. What does the word 'Incarnation' mean?

The Church calls the mystery of the wonderful union of the divine and human natures in the one divine Person of the Word the 'Incarnation'. To bring about our salvation the Son of God was made 'flesh' (Jn 1:14) and became truly man. Faith in the Incarnation is a distinctive sign of the Christian faith.

87. In what way is Jesus Christ true God and true man?

Jesus is inseparably true God and true man in the unity of his divine Person. As the Son of God, who is 'begotten, not made, consubstantial with the Father,' he was made true man, our brother, without ceasing to be God, our Lord.

89. How does the Church set forth the Mystery of the Incarnation?

The Church confesses that Jesus Christ is true God and true man, with two natures, a divine nature and a human nature, not confused with each other but united in the Person of the Word. Therefore, in the humanity of Jesus all things — his miracles, his suffering, and his death — must be attributed to his divine Person which acts by means of his assumed human nature.[2533]

General Audience Address. (26th October 2005)

Canticle Phil 2:6-11. ...Let us now turn to the meditation on our hymn that has been interwoven with great wisdom by St. Gregory of Nazianzus. In a poem in honour of Christ, the great fourth-century Doctor of the Church declares that Jesus Christ 'does not empty himself of any part that makes up his divine nature, and not-withstanding this he saves me like a healer who bends over festering wounds.... He was of the line of David, but was the Creator of Adam; he was made of flesh, but was also a stranger to it; he was generated by a mother, but by a virgin mother; he was limited, but also immense; he was born in a stable, but a star led the Magi to him, who brought him gifts and bowed down and knelt before him. As a mortal man he battled with the devil, but, invincible as he was, he overcame the tempter with a three-fold strategy.... He was victim, but also High Priest; he was sacrificed, but was God; he offered his blood to God and in this way he purified the entire world. A cross raised him up from the earth, but sin remained nailed to it.... He descended to the dead, but came back from the netherworld redeeming many who were dead. The first event is typical of human misery, but the second is part of the richness of the incorporeal being..., that earthly form the immortal Son takes upon himself because he loves us' (*Carmina Arcana*, 2: Collana di Testi Patristici, LVIII, Rome, 1986, pp. 236-238).[2534]

[2532]Pope Benedict XVI [1 June 2005] *General Audience Address* [Online] Available at: www.vatican.va [Accessed on: 28 September 2022]

[2533]*Compendium of the Catechism of the Catholic Church* [2005] [Online] Available at: www.vatican.va [Accessed on: 28 September 2022]

[2534]Pope Benedict XVI [26 October 2005] *General Audience Address* [Online] Available at: www.vatican.va [Accessed on: 28 September 2022]

Encyclical *Spe Salvi, 39. (30th November 2007)*

...God — Truth and Love in person — desired to suffer for us and with us. Bernard of Clairvaux coined the marvellous expression: *Impassibilis est Deus, sed non incompassibilis* (*Sermones in Cant.*, Sermo 26, 5) — God cannot suffer, but he can suffer with. Man is worth so much to God that he himself became man in order to suffer with man in an utterly real way — in flesh and blood — as is revealed to us in the account of Jesus's Passion.[2535]

Angelus Address. (18th September 2011)

...the Letter to the Philippians contains a hymn to Christ which presents a complete synthesis of his mystery: incarnation, kenosis, that is, self-emptying to the point of death on the cross, and glorification.[2536]

General Audience Address. (9th January 2013)

In these days the term the 'Incarnation' of God has rung out several times in our churches, expressing the reality we celebrate at Holy Christmas: the Son of God was made man, as we say in the Creed. But what does this word, so central to the Christian faith, mean? Incarnation derives from the Latin *incarnatio*. St. Ignatius of Antioch — at the end of the first century — and, especially, St. Irenaeus used this term in reflecting on the Prologue to the Gospel according to St. John, in particular in the sentence 'the Word became flesh' (Jn 1:14). Here the word 'flesh', according to the Hebrew usage, indicates man in his whole self, the whole man, but in particular in the dimension of his transience and his temporality, his poverty and his contingency. This was in order to tell us that the salvation brought by God, who became man in Jesus of Nazareth, affects man in his material reality and in whatever situation he may be. God assumed the human condition to heal it from all that separates it from him, to enable us to call him, in his Only-Begotten Son, by the name of 'Abba, Father', and truly to be children of God.[2537]

General Audience Address. (16th January 2013)

In Jesus of Nazareth God really visited his people, he visited humanity in a manner that surpassed every expectation: he sent his Only-Begotten Son: God himself became man. Jesus does not tell us something about God, he does not merely speak of the Father but is the Revelation of God, because he is God and thus reveals the face of God. In the Prologue to his Gospel St. John wrote: 'no one has ever seen God; the only Son, who is in the bosom of the Father, he has made him known' (Jn 1:18).[2538]

Pope St. John Paul II: 1978 to 2005

Apostolic Letter *Salvifici Doloris, 23. (11th February 1984)*
Those who share in Christ's sufferings have before their eyes the Paschal Mystery of the Cross and Resurrection, in which Christ descends, in a first phase, to the ultimate limits of human weakness and impotence: indeed, he dies nailed to the Cross. But if at the same time in this weakness there is accomplished his lifting up, confirmed by the power of the Resurrection, then this means that the weaknesses of all human sufferings are capable of being infused with the same power of God manifested in Christ's Cross. In such a concept, to suffer means to become particularly susceptible, particularly open to the working of the salvific powers of God, offered to humanity in Christ. In

---

[2535]Pope Benedict XVI [26 October 2005] Encyclical *Spe Salvi*, para 31 [Online] Available at: www.vatican.va [Accessed on: 28 September 2022]

[2536]Pope Benedict XVI [18 September 2011] *Angelus Address* [Online] Available at: www.vatican.va [Accessed on: 28 September 2022]

[2537]Pope Benedict XVI [9 January 2013] *General Audience Address* [Online] Available at: www.vatican.va [Accessed on: 28 September 2022]

[2538]Pope Benedict XVI [16 January 2013] *General Audience Address* [Online] Available at: www.vatican.va [Accessed on: 28 September 2022]

him God has confirmed his desire to act especially through suffering, which is man's weakness and emptying of self, and he wishes to make his power known precisely in this weakness and emptying of self.[2539]

Catechism of the Catholic Church, 461, 464, 469, 470. (8th September 1997)

THE INCARNATION

Taking up St. John's expression, 'The Word became flesh', the Church calls 'Incarnation' the fact that the Son of God assumed a human nature in order to accomplish our salvation in it. [...]

TRUE GOD AND TRUE MAN

The unique and altogether singular event of the Incarnation of the Son of God does not mean that Jesus Christ is part God and part man, nor does it imply that he is the result of a confused mixture of the divine and the human. He became truly man while remaining truly God. Jesus Christ is true God and true man. [...]

The Church thus confesses that Jesus is inseparably true God and true man. He is truly the Son of God who, without ceasing to be God and Lord, became a man and our brother [...]

HOW IS THE SON OF GOD MAN?

Because 'human nature was assumed, not absorbed', in the mysterious union of the Incarnation, the Church was led over the course of centuries to confess the full reality of Christ's human soul, with its operations of intellect and will, and of his human body. In parallel fashion, she had to recall on each occasion that Christ's human nature belongs, as his own, to the divine person of the Son of God, who assumed it. Everything that Christ is and does in this nature derives from 'one of the Trinity'. The Son of God therefore communicates to his humanity his own personal mode of existence in the Trinity. In his soul as in his body, Christ thus expresses humanly the divine ways of the Trinity....[2540]

Encyclical *Fides et Ratio, 93. (14th September 1998)*

The very heart of theological enquiry will thus be the contemplation of the mystery of the Triune God. The approach to this mystery begins with reflection upon the mystery of the Incarnation of the Son of God: his coming as man, his going to his Passion and Death, a mystery issuing into his glorious Resurrection and Ascension to the right hand of the Father, whence he would send the Spirit of truth to bring his Church to birth and give her growth. From this vantage-point, the prime commitment of theology is seen to be the understanding of God's kenosis, a grand and mysterious truth for the human mind, which finds it inconceivable that suffering and death can express a love which gives itself and seeks nothing in return....[2541]

Apostolic letter *Novo Millennio Ineunte, 22. (6th January 2001)*

'The Word became flesh' (Jn 1:14). This striking formulation by John of the mystery of Christ is confirmed by the entire New Testament. The Apostle Paul takes this same approach when he affirms that the Son of God was born 'of the race of David, according to the flesh' (cf. Rom 1:3; cf. 9:5). If today, because of the rationalism found in so much of contemporary culture, it is above all faith in the divinity of Christ that has become problematic, in other historical and cultural contexts there was a tendency to diminish and do away with the historical concreteness of Jesus' humanity. But for the Church's

---

[2539]Pope St. John Paul II [1984] *Apostolic Letter Salvifici Doloris*, para 23 [Online] Available at: www. vatican.va [Accessed on: 28 September 2022]

[2540]*Catechism of the Catholic Church* [1997] paras 461, 464, 469, 470 [Online] Available at: scborromeo2. org Accessed on: 28 September 2022]

[2541]Pope St. John Paul II [1998] Encyclical *Fides et Ratio*, para 93 [Online] Available at: www.vatican. va [Accessed on: 28 September 2022]

faith it is essential and indispensable to affirm that the Word truly 'became flesh' and took on every aspect of humanity, except sin (cf. Heb 4:15). From this perspective, the incarnation is truly a kenosis — a 'self-emptying' — on the part of the Son of God of that glory which is his from all eternity (Phil 2:6-8; cf. I Pet 3:18).

On the other hand, this abasement of the Son of God is not an end in itself; it tends rather towards the full glorification of Christ, even in his humanity: 'Therefore God has highly exalted him and bestowed on him the name which is above every name, that at the name of Jesus every knee should bow, in heaven and on earth and under the earth, and every tongue confess that Jesus Christ is Lord, to the glory of God the Father' (Phil 2:9-11).[2542]

General Audience Address. (19th November 2003)

Canticle of the first Sunday of Vespers, Philippians 2: 6-11. The Canticle unfolds in a double vertical trajectory: a first movement is one of descent followed by ascension. Indeed, on one hand, there is the humiliating descent of the Son of God when, in the Incarnation, he becomes man out of love for humankind. He plummets into the *kenosis*, the 'emptying' of his divine glory, pushed to the point of death on the Cross, the punishment of slaves who were least among men, thus making him a true brother of suffering humanity, sinful and rejected.

On the other hand, there is the triumphant ascension which takes place on Easter Day, when the Father reinstates Christ in the divine splendour and he is celebrated as Lord by the entire cosmos and by all men and women now redeemed. We are placed before a magnificent re-reading of Christ's mystery, primarily the Paschal one. St. Paul, along with proclaiming the Resurrection (cf. I Cor 15: 3-5), defines Christ's Paschal mystery as the 'exaltation', 'raising up', 'glorification'.

Therefore, from the bright horizon of divine transcendence, the Son of God crossed the infinite distance between Creator and creature. He did not grasp on, as if to a prey, to his 'equality with God', which was due to him by nature and not from usurpation. He did not want to claim jealously this prerogative as a treasure, nor use it for his own interests. Rather, Christ 'emptied', 'humbled' himself and appeared poor, weak, destined for the shameful death of crucifixion; it is precisely from this extreme humiliation that the great movement of ascension takes off, described in the second part of the Pauline hymn (cf. Phil 2, 9-11).[2543]

General Audience Address. (4th August 2004)

The Canticle starts from the divinity of Jesus Christ. Indeed, the divine 'nature' and condition are his — in Greek, *morphé* — that is, the essential transcendent reality of God (cf. v. 6). Yet he does not consider his supreme and glorious identity as a proud privilege of which to boast nor as a sign of power and mere superiority.

Our hymn clearly moves downwards, that is, towards humanity. It is on this path of 'emptying' himself, or as it were, stripping himself of that glory to take on the morphé, in other words, the reality and condition of a servant, that the Word takes on in order to enter the horizon of human history. Indeed, he assumes the 'likeness' of human beings (cf. v. 7) and even goes so far as to accept the sign of limitation and finality which death is. It is an extreme humiliation, for he even accepted death on the cross, which the society in his time held to be the vilest form (v. 8).

Christ chose to lower himself from glory to death on a cross; this is the first movement of the Canticle to which, in order to reveal its other nuances, we will have occasion to return.[2544]

[2542]Pope St, John Paul II [2001] Apostolic Letter *Novo Millennio Ineunte*, para 22 [Online] Available at: www.vatican.va [Accessed on: 28 September 2022]

[2543]Pope St. John Paul II [19th November 2003] *General Audience Address* [Online] Available at: www.vatican.va [Accessed on: 28 September 2022]

[2544]Pope St. John Paul II [4th August 2004] *General Audience Address* [Online] Available at: www. vatican.va [Accessed on: 28 September 2022]

Pope St. Paul VI: 1963 to 1978

Motu Proprio, *Solemni Hac Liturgia*, 11. (30th June 1968)

The Son. We believe in our Lord Jesus Christ, who is the Son of God. He is the Eternal Word, born of the Father before time began, and one in substance with the Father, *homoousios to Patri*, and through Him all things were made. He was incarnate of the Virgin Mary by the power of the Holy Spirit, and was made man: equal therefore to the Father according to His divinity, and inferior to the Father according to His humanity; and Himself one, not by some impossible confusion of His natures, but by the unity of His person.[2545]

Homily Delivered at Manila, Philippines. (29th November 1970)

Jesus Christ is the beginning and the end, the Alpha and the Omega; he is the king of the new world; he is the secret of history; he is the key to our destiny. He is the mediator, the bridge, between heaven and earth. He is more perfectly than anyone else the Son of Man, because he is the Son of God, eternal and infinite.[2546]

Pope St. John XXIII: 1958 to 1963

Encyclical *Aeterna Dei Sapientia*, on commemorating the Fifteenth Centennial of the death of Pope St. Leo I, 13-15.

On the Incarnation: *His Letter to Flavian.* Most noteworthy, perhaps, is his timely and authoritative intervention in the controversy as to whether there was in Jesus Christ a human nature in addition to the divine nature. His efforts were responsible for the magnificent triumph of the true doctrine concerning the incarnation of the Word of God. This fact alone would assure him his place in history.

Our principal evidence for it is his *Epistle to Flavian*, Bishop of Constantinople, in which he expounds the dogma of the Incarnation with remarkable clarity and precision, showing how it accords with the teaching of the Prophets, the Gospel, the apostolic writings, and the Creed. Let Us quote a significant passage from this Epistle: 'Without detriment, therefore, to the properties of either of the two natures and substances which are joined in the one person, majesty took on humility; strength, weakness; eternity, mortality; and, in order to pay off the debt which attached to our condition, inviolable nature was united with passible nature, so that, as suited the cure of our ills, one and the same Mediator between God and men, the Man Jesus Christ, could die with the one nature and not die with the other. Thus true God was born in the whole and perfect nature of true man; complete in what was His own, complete in what was ours.[2547]

Pope Ven. Pius XII: 1939 to 1958

Encyclical *Mystici Corporis Christi*, 12. (29th June 1943)

…the all-merciful God 'so loved the world as to give His only-begotten Son,'(Jn 3:16) and the Word of the Eternal Father with the same divine love assumed human nature from the race of Adam — but as an innocent and spotless nature — so that He, as the new Adam, might be the source whence the grace of the Holy Spirit should flow unto all the children of the first parent. Through the sin of the first man they had been excluded from adoption as children of God; through the Word incarnate, made brothers according to the flesh of the only-begotten Son of God, they receive also the power to become the sons of God.[2548]

[2545]Pope St. Paul VI [1968] Motu Proprio, *Solemni Hac Liturgia*, para 11 [Online] Available at: www.vatican.va [Accessed on: 28 September 2022]

[2546]Pope St. Paul VI [1970] *Homily Delivered at Manila, Philippines* [Online] Available at: www.vatican.va [Accessed on: 28 September 2022]

[2547]Pope St. John XXIII [1961] Encyclical *Aeterna Dei Sapientia*, para 13-15 [Online] Available at: www.vatican.va [Accessed on: 28 September 2022]

[2548]Ven. Pope Pius XII [1943] Encyclical *Mystici Corporis Christi*, para 12 [Online] Available at: www.vatican.va [Accessed on: 28 September 2022]

Encyclical *Sempiternus Rex Christus, 29, 31. (8th September 1951)*

There is another enemy of the faith of Chalcedon, widely diffused outside the fold of the Catholic religion. This is an opinion for which a rashly and falsely understood sentence of St. Paul's Epistle to the Philippians (ii, 7), supplies a basis and a shape. This is called the kenotic doctrine, and according to it, they imagine that the divinity was taken away from the Word in Christ. It is a wicked invention, equally to be condemned with the Docetism opposed to it. It reduces the whole mystery of the Incarnation and Redemption to empty the bloodless imaginations. 'With the entire and perfect nature of man' - thus grandly St. Leo the Great – 'He Who was true God was born, complete in his own nature, complete in ours' (*Ep.* xxviii, 3. PL. liv, 763. Cf. *Serm.* xxiii, 2. PL. lvi, 201). [...]

These emphasise the state and condition of Christ's human nature to such an extent as to make it seem something existing in its own right (*subjectum quoddam sui juris*), and not as subsisting in the Word itself. But the council of Chalcedon in full accord with that of Ephesus, clearly asserts that both natures are united in 'One Person and subsistence', and rules out the placing of two individuals in Christ, as if some one man, completely autonomous in himself, had been taken up and placed by the side of the Word. St. Leo not only adheres to this opinion (i.e. that of Chalcedon), but he also indicates the source whence he derives his sound doctrine. 'Whatever', he says, 'we have written has manifestly clearly been taken from the doctrine of the Apostles and of the Gospels' (*Ep.* clii. PL. liv, 1123).[2549]

Encyclical *Haurietis Aquas, 42-43. (15th May 1956)*

However, even though the Word of God took to Himself a true and perfect human nature, and made and fashioned for Himself a heart of flesh, which, no less than ours could suffer and be pierced, unless this fact is considered in the light of the hypostatic and substantial union and in the light of its complement, the fact of man' s redemption, it can be a stumbling block and foolishness to some, just as Jesus Christ, nailed to the Cross, actually was to the Jewish race and to the Gentiles.

The official teachings of the Catholic faith, in complete agreement with Scripture, assure us that the only begotten Son of God took a human nature capable of suffering and death especially because He desired, as He hung from the Cross, to offer a bloody sacrifice in order to complete the work of man's salvation.[2550]

Pope Pius XI: 1922 to 1939

Encyclical *Quas Primas, 13. (11th December 1925)*

The foundation of this power and dignity of Our Lord is rightly indicated by Cyril of Alexandria. 'Christ,' he says, 'has dominion over all creatures, a dominion not seized by violence nor usurped, but his by essence and by nature.' His kingship is founded upon the ineffable hypostatic union. From this it follows not only that Christ is to be adored by angels and men, but that to him as man angels and men are subject, and must recognize his empire; by reason of the hypostatic union Christ has power over all creatures.[2551]

Encyclical *Lux Veritatis, on the Council of Ephesus, 28-29. (25th December 1925)*

For when Nestorius, as We have said, obstinately contended that the Divine Word was not united to the human nature in Christ substantially and hypostatically, but by a certain accidental and moral bond, the Fathers of Ephesus, in condemning Nestorius,

[2549]Ven. Pope Pius XII [1951] Encyclical *Sempiternus Rex Christus*, para 29,31 [Online] Available at: www.vatican.va [Accessed on: 28 September 2022]
[2550]Ven. Pope Pius XII [1956] Encyclical *Haurietis Aquas*, para 42-43 [Online] Available at: www.vatican.va [Accessed on: 28 September 2022]
[2551]Pope Pius XI [1952] Encyclical *Quas Primas*, para 13 [Online] Available at: www.vatican.va [Accessed on: 28 September 2022]

openly professed the right doctrine concerning the Incarnation, which must be firmly held by all. And indeed, Cyril in the letters and chapters already addressed to Nestorius beforehand, and inserted in the acts of this Ecumenical Synod, in wonderful agreement with the Roman Church, maintained these things in eloquent and reiterated words: 'In no wise, therefore, is it lawful to divide the one Lord Jesus Christ into two Sons.... For the Scripture does not say that the Word associated the person of a man with Himself, but that He was made flesh. But when it is said that the Word was made flesh, that means nothing else but that He partook of flesh and blood, even as we do; wherefore, He made our body His own, and came forth man, born of a woman, at the same time without laying aside His Godhead, or His birth from the Father; for in assuming flesh He still remained what He was.' (*Mansi*, l.c. IV. 891.)

For we are taught, by Holy Scripture and by Divine Tradition, that the Word of God the Father did not join Himself to a certain man already subsisting in Himself, but that Christ the Word of God is one and the same, enjoying eternity in the bosom of the Father, and made man in time. For, indeed, that the Godhead and Manhood in Jesus Christ, the Redeemer of mankind, are bound together by that wondrous union which is justly and deservedly called hypostatic, is luminously evident from the fact that in the Sacred Scriptures the same one Christ is not only called God and man, but it is also clearly declared that He works as God and also as man, and again that He dies as man and as God He arises from the dead. That is to say, He who is conceived in the Virgin's womb by the operation of the Holy Ghost, who is born, who lies in a manger, who calls Himself the son of man, who suffers and dies, fastened to the cross, is the very same who, in a solemn and marvellous manner, is called by the Eternal Father 'my beloved Son' (Mt 3:17; 17:5; II Peter 1:17), who pardons sins by His divine authority (Mt 9:2-6; Lk 5:20-24; 7:48; and elsewhere), and likewise by His own power recalls the sick to health (Mt 7:3; Mk 1 and 41; Lk 5:13; Jn 9; and elsewhere). As all these things show clearly that in Christ there are natures by which both divine and human works are performed, so do they bear witness no less clearly that the one Christ is at once both God and man because of that unity of person from which He is called '*Theanthropos*' (God-Man).[2552]

Pope St. Pius X: 1903 to 1914

Encyclical *Ad Diem Illum Laetissimum, 5. (2nd February 1904)*

...that she would conceive and bring forth the Son of God and if she did receive in her breast Him who is by nature Truth itself in order that 'He, generated in a new order and with a new nativity, though invisible in Himself, might become visible in our flesh' (St. Leo the Great, *Ser.* 2, De Nativ. Dom.): the Son of God made man...[2553]

Encyclical *Pascendi Dominici Gregis, 2. (8th day September 1907)*

We allude, Venerable Brethren, to many who belong to the Catholic laity, nay, and this is far more lamentable, to the ranks of the priesthood itself, who, feigning a love for the Church, lacking the firm protection of philosophy and theology, nay more, thoroughly imbued with the poisonous doctrines taught by the enemies of the Church, and lost to all sense of modesty, vaunt themselves as reformers of the Church; and, forming more boldly into line of attack, assail all that is most sacred in the work of Christ, not sparing even the person of the Divine Redeemer, whom, with sacrilegious daring, they reduce to a simple, mere man.[2554]

[2552]Pope Pius XI [1925] Encyclical *Lux Veritatis*, para 28-29 [Online] Available at: www.papalencyclicals.net [Accessed on: 29 September 2022]
[2553]Pope St. Pius X [1904] Encyclical *Ad Diem Illum Laetissimum*, para 5 [Online] Available at: www.vatican.va [Accessed on: 28 September 2022]
[2554]Pope St. Pius X [1907] Encyclical *Pascendi Dominici Gregis*, para 2 [Online] Available at: www.vatican.va [Accessed on: 28 September 2022]

Catechism of Pope St. Pius X. (1908)

The Third Article of the Creed

4 Q. In becoming man did the Son of God cease to be God?

A. No, the Son of God became man without ceasing to be God.

5 Q. Jesus Christ, then, is God and man at the same time?

A. Yes, the incarnate Son of God, that is, Jesus Christ, is both God and man, perfect God and perfect man.

6 Q. Are there, then, two natures in Jesus Christ?

A. Yes, in Jesus Christ, who is both God and man, there are two natures, the divine and the human.[2555]

Pope Leo XIII: 1878 to 1903

Encyclical *Tametsi Futura Prospicientibus, 3. (1st November 1900)*

The human race, exiled and disinherited, had for ages been daily hurrying into ruin, involved in the terrible and numberless ills brought about by the sin of our first parents, nor was there any human hope of salvation, when Christ Our Lord came down as the Saviour from Heaven. At the very beginning of the world, God had promised Him as the conqueror of 'the Serpent,' hence, succeeding ages had eagerly looked forward to His coming. The Prophets had long and clearly declared that all hope was in Him. The varying fortunes, the achievements, customs, laws, ceremonies and sacrifices of the Chosen People had distinctly and lucidly foreshadowed the truth, that the salvation of mankind was to be accomplished in Him who should be the Priest, Victim, Liberator, Prince of Peace, Teacher of all Nations, Founder of an Eternal Kingdom. By all these titles, images and prophecies, differing in kind though like in meaning, He alone was designated who 'for His exceeding charity wherewith He loved us,' gave Himself up for our salvation. And so, when the fullness of time came in God's Divine Providence, the only-begotten Son of God became man, and on behalf of mankind made most abundant satisfaction in His Blood to the outraged majesty of His Father and by this infinite price He redeemed man for His own.[2556]

Pope Bl. Pius IX: 1846 to 1878

Apostolic Constitution *Ineffabilis Deus. (8th December 1854)*

From the very beginning, and before time began, the eternal Father chose and prepared for his only-begotten Son a Mother in whom the Son of God would become incarnate and from whom, in the blessed fullness of time, he would be born into this world.[2557]

Pope Benedict XIV: 1740 to 1758

Constitution *Nuper ad Nos. (16th March 1743)*

The Council of Chalcedon, fourth in order, and I profess that which was defined against Eutyches and Dioscorus, both of pernicious memory, that the one and the same Son of God, our Lord Jesus Christ, was perfect in divinity and perfect in humanity, true God and true man, consisting of rational soul and body, consubstantial with the Father in regard to his divinity and consubstantial with us in regard to his humanity, in all things similar to us, without sin; that before time he was generated from the Father according to divinity, but that in these latter days the same One, for us and for our

---

[2555]*Catechism of Pope St. Pius X* [1908] [Online] Available at: www.ewtn.com [Accessed on: 29 September 2022]

[2556]Pope Leo XIII [1900] Encyclical *Tametsi Futura Prospicientibus*, para 3 [Online] Available at: www.vatican.va [Accessed on: 28 September 2022]

[2557]Pope Bl. Pius IX [1854] Apostolic Constitution *Ineffabilis Deus* [Online] Available at: www.papalencyclicals.net [Accessed on: 29 September 2022]

salvation, was begotten of the Virgin Mary, Mother of God, according to humanity, and that the one same Christ, Son, Lord, Only-Begotten, must be recognised in the two natures without confusion, without change, without division, without separation, never removing the difference of the natures because of their union and preserving the characteristic property of each nature joined in one Person and substance; that this same Lord is not separated and divided into two persons, but is one and the same Son and only begotten of God, the Word, the Lord Jesus Christ; likewise that the divinity of our same Lord Jesus Christ, according to which he is consubstantial with the Father and the Holy Spirit, is impassible and immortal....[2558]

Pope St. Pius V: 1566 to 1572

The Roman Catechism: The Catechism of the Council of Trent. (1556)

First Part of this Article: 'Who was Conceived,'... The Word, which is a Person of the Divine Nature, assumed human nature in such a manner that there should be one and the same Person in both the divine and human natures. Hence this admirable union preserved the actions and properties of both natures; and as Pope St. Leo the Great said: The lowliness of the inferior nature was not consumed in the glory of the superior, nor did the assumption of the inferior lessen the glory of the superior. [...]

In The Incarnation Some Things Were Natural, Others Supernatural. In this mystery we perceive that some things were done which transcend the order of nature, some by the power of nature. Thus, in believing that the body of Christ was formed from the most pure blood of His Virgin Mother we acknowledge the operation of human nature, this being a law common to the formation of all human bodies, that they should be formed from the blood of the mother.

But what surpasses the order of nature and human comprehension is, that as soon as the Blessed Virgin assented to the announcement of the Angel in these words, Behold the handmaid of the Lord; be it done unto me according to thy word, the most sacred body of Christ was immediately formed, and to it was united a rational soul enjoying the use of reason; and thus in the same instant of time He was perfect God and perfect man. That this was the astonishing and admirable work of the Holy Ghost cannot be doubted; for according to the order of nature the rational soul is united to the body only after a certain lapse of time.

Again — and this should overwhelm us with astonishment — as soon as the soul of Christ was united to His body, the Divinity became united to both; and thus at the same time His body was formed and animated, and the Divinity united to body and soul.

Hence, at the same instant He was perfect God and perfect man, and the most Holy Virgin, having at the same moment conceived God and man, is truly and properly called Mother of God and man. This the Angel signified to her when he said: Behold thou shalt conceive in thy womb, and shalt bring forth a son; and thou shalt call his name Jesus. He shall be great, and shall be called the Son of the Most High. The event verified the prophecy of Isaias: Behold a virgin shall conceive, and bear a son. Elizabeth also declared the same truth when, being filled with the Holy Ghost, she understood the Conception of the Son of God, and said: Whence is this to me, that the mother of my Lord should come to me? [...]

How To Profit By The Mystery Of The Incarnation. These truths comprise the substance of what appears to demand explanation regarding the admirable mystery of the Conception. To reap from them abundant fruit for salvation the faithful should particularly recall, and frequently reflect, that it is God who assumed human flesh; that the manner in which He became man exceeds our comprehension, not to say our powers of expression; and finally, that He vouchsafed to become man in order that we men might be born again as children of God. When to these subjects they shall have given mature consideration, let them, in the humility of faith, believe and adore all the mysteries

---

[2558]Denzinger, H [2010] *Op. cit.,* p.511-512, *Dz* 2529

contained in this Article, and not indulge a curious inquisitiveness by investigating and scrutinising them — an attempt scarcely ever unattended with danger.

'*Suffered*"'. It cannot be a matter of doubt that His soul, as to its inferior part, was sensible of these torments; for as He really assumed human nature, it is a necessary consequence that He really, and in His soul, experienced a most acute sense of pain. Hence these words of the Saviour: My soul is sorrowful even unto death. Although human nature was united to the Divine Person, He felt the bitterness of His Passion as acutely as if no such union had existed, because in the one Person of Jesus Christ were preserved the properties of both natures, human and divine; and therefore what was passible and mortal remained passible and mortal; while what was impassible and immortal, that is, His Divine Nature, continued impassible and immortal.[2559]

Pope Leo III: 795 to 816

Profession of Faith, Synod of Friuli. *(796 or 797)*

From this ineffable Trinity only the Person of the Word, that is, the Son…came down from heaven, from which he never departed. He became incarnate by the Holy Spirit and became true man from the ever-virgin Mary, and remains true God.[2560]

Pope Benedict II: 684 to 685

Fourteenth Synod of Toledo (14th to 20th November 684)

…the indivisible properties of the two natures in the one Person of Christ, Son of God, remain indivisible and inseparable as well as without confusion or change, the one of the divinity, the other of humanity, the one in which he was generated from God the Father, the other in which he was born from the Virgin Mary. Both of these births, therefore, are complete; both are perfect; he, not having anything less of the divinity and taking nothing imperfect from humanity, is not divided by the two natures, nor is he twofold in his Person, but, as complete God and complete man apart from any sin, he is one Christ in the singularity of Person.

Existing thus one in the two natures, he is resplendent with signs of divinity and subject to the sufferings of humanity. Indeed, he was not generated as one from the Father and another from the Mother, though he was born differently from the Father and the Mother; nevertheless, he is not divided in the twofold forms of nature, but he is one and the same Son of God and Son of man; he himself lives although he dies and dies although he lives; he is himself incapable of suffering although he suffers; he does not yield to suffering; he is neither subject to it in divinity nor does he remove himself from humanity; from the nature of divinity he has the inability to die; from the substance of humanity, he has the wish not to die and yet the ability to die. On the basis of one, he has immortality; on the basis of the other, he is subject to the conditions of mortals; in the eternal will of divinity, he has assumed what pertains to men; in the human will assumed, he has made it subject to God. Therefore, he says to the Father: 'Father, not my will but yours be done' (Lk 22:42). thus clearly showing that the one is the will of God by which the man has been assumed, and the other that of man in which God must be obeyed.[2561]

Pope Agatho: 678 to 681

Synod of Rome: Synodal Letter *Omnium Bonorum Spes to the Emperors. (27th March 680)*

…we also acknowledge after the subsistent [hypostatic] union, one and the same only begotten Son, God the Word, our Lord Jesus Christ, neither the one in the other nor

---

[2559]*The Roman Catechism: The Catechism of the Council of Trent* [1556] [Online] Available at: www.saintsbooks.net [Accessed on: 29 September 2022]

[2560]Denzinger, H [2010] *Op. cit.,* p.212, *Dz* 619

[2561]*Ibid.,* p.196-197, *Dz* 564

the one and the other, but the very same in two natures, that is, in the divinity and in the humanity: because neither has the Word been changed into the nature of the flesh, nor has the flesh been transformed into the nature of the Word; for each remains what by nature it was; indeed, we discern in contemplation alone a difference in the united natures in that from which it is composed without confusion, separation, and change: for one from both and both through one, because there is simultaneously present both the majesty of the Deity and the humility of the flesh, each nature, even after the union, preserving without defect its own property, and each form operating in communion with the other what it has as its own; the Word operating what it is of the Word, and the flesh accomplishing what is of the flesh; the one shines forth in miracles, the other succumbs to injuries.[2562]

Pope Martin I: 649 to 655

Lateran Synod, Session 5, *Profession of Faith, Canons. (31st October 649)*

Can. 9. If anyone does not, following the holy Fathers, confess properly and truly that the natural properties of the divinity of Christ and of his humanity are fully preserved in him, unimpaired and undiminished, by which is truly confirmed the fact that the same is perfect God and perfect man by nature, let him be condemned.[2563]

Pope Honorius I: 625 to 638

Letter *Scripta Dilectissimi Filii, to Sergius of Constantinople. (634)*

…confess that each of the two natures, joined by a unity of nature in the one Christ, operates and acts in common with the other, that is, the divine performs what is[2564] of God, and the human accomplishes what is of the flesh; teaching that, without division and without confusion or alteration, the nature of God is transferred into man and the human is transferred into God, but confessing the complete differences of the natures…

Pope Pelagius I: 556 to 561

Letter *Humani Generis to King Childebert I. (3rd February 557)*

I believe and profess that from this holy and most blessed and consubstantial Trinity one Person, that is, the Son of God, descended from heaven on behalf of the salvation of the human race in these latter days, without relinquishing the throne of God the Father and the governance of the world; and when the Holy Spirit came upon the blessed Virgin Mary and the power of the most high overshadowed her, this same Word and Son of God lovingly entered into the womb of the same holy Virgin Mary and from her flesh united to himself flesh animated by a rational soul and intellect; it was not that first there was created the flesh and then the Son of God came (into her), but, as it is written, 'Wisdom building a house for herself' (Prov 9:1), immediately the flesh in the womb of the Virgin (was made) the flesh of the Word of God; and accordingly the Word and the Son of God became man without any change or transformation of the nature of the Word and the nature of the flesh, one in both natures, namely, divine and human, and (thus) Christ Jesus came forth as true God and true man…[2565]

Pope Vigilius: 537 to 555

Letter *Dum in Sanctae to All the People of God. (5th February 552)*

Uniting flesh to himself in an unconfused, undivided, unchangeable, and substantial manner, God the Word, our Emmanuel, for whom (the world) waited, since he was announced by the law and the prophets, came among us. 'Therefore, the Word became

---

[2562]*Ibid.*, p.190-191, *Dz* 584
[2563]*Ibid.*, p.176, *Dz* 509
[2564]*Ibid.*, p.168-169, *Dz* 488
[2565]*Ibid.*, p.154, *Dz* 441

flesh and dwelt among us' (Jn 1:14), wholly existing in his own nature, wholly in ours, taking from the maternal womb his flesh, together with a rational and intellectual soul...[2566]

Pope John II: 533 to 535

Letter *Olim Quidem to the Senators of Constantinople. (March 534)*

...the Roman Church maintains and reveres, namely, that Christ our Lord, as we have often said, is one of the Holy Trinity, to be understood as (composed) of two natures, perfect in divinity and humanity, not in the sense that the flesh existed first and was afterwards united to the Word, but that it received the origins of its being in God the Word himself. For since the flesh of the Word received its origin from his Mother's body, without detriment to the true and proper character of both his natures, that is, the human and divine, we profess the Catholic doctrine of the Son of God, our Lord, Jesus Christ, having ruled out any subsequent change or confusion (of his natures).[2567]

Pope Hormisdas: 514 to 523

Letter *Inter ea quae to Emperor Justinian, Chap. 12. (26th March 521)*

...the Son of God is himself God and man, the same (Person) is strength and weakness, lowliness and majesty, the one who redeems and the one sold, hung on the Cross and besting the kingdom of heaven, so much in our weakness that he could be killed and so much in his innate power that he could not be destroyed by death.[2568]

Pope St. Leo the Great: c. 440 to 461

Letter *Licet per Nostros to Julianus of Cos, Chap. 2. (13th June 449)*

...for the flesh did not lessen what belongs to His Godhead, nor the Godhead destroy what belongs to His flesh. For He is at once both eternal from His Father and temporal from His mother, inviolable in His strength, passible in our weakness: in the Triune Godhead, of one and the same substance with the Father and the Holy Spirit, but in taking Manhood on Himself, not of one substance but of one and the same person [so that He was at once rich in poverty, almighty in submission, impassible in punishment, immortal in death]. For the Word was not in any part of It turned either into flesh or into soul, seeing that the absolute and unchangeable nature of the Godhead is ever entire in its Essence, receiving no loss nor increase, and so beatifying the nature that It had assumed that that nature remained for ever glorified in the person of the Glorifier. [But why should it seem unsuitable or impossible that the Word and flesh and soul should be one Jesus Christ, and that the Son of God and the Son of Man should be one, if flesh and soul which are of different natures make one person even without the Incarnation of the Word: since it is much easier for the power of the Godhead to produce this union of Himself and man than for the weakness of manhood by itself to effect it in its own substance.] Therefore neither was the Word changed into flesh nor flesh into the Word: but both remains in one and one is in both, not divided by the diversity and not confounded by intermixture: He is not one by His Father and another by His mother, but the same, in one way by His Father before every beginning, and in another by His mother at the end of the ages: so that He was 'mediator between God and men, the man Christ Jesus' (I Timothy 2:5), in whom dwelt 'the fullness of the Godhead bodily (Colossians 2:9):' because it was the assumed (nature) not the Assuming (nature) which was raised, because God 'exalted Him and gave Him the Name which is above every name: that in the name of Jesus every knee should bow, of things in heaven and things on earth and things under the earth, and that every tongue should confess that Jesus Christ the Lord is in the glory of God the Father' (Philippians 2:9-11).[2569]

[2566] *Ibid.*, p.145, *Dz* 413

[2567] *Ibid.*, p.143, *Dz* 402

[2568] *Ibid.*, p. 133, Dz 369

[2569] Pope St. Leo the Great [449] Letter *Licet per Nostros* to Julianus of Cos, Chap. 2 [Online] Available at: www.newadvent.org [Accessed on: 28 September 2022]

Ecclesiology

Pope Francis: 2013 to 2025

C. *It is wrong to be obsessed with guarding a monolithic body of doctrine, to insist on imposing doctrines or to use completely orthodox language. Doctrinal formulations can be alien to the authentic Gospel of Jesus Christ. Instead of having closed ideas, we should be open to the God of Surprises. These self-styled keepers of the truth, who insist on rigidly upholding doctrine, are narcissistic, authoritarian elitists who are frightened of change and are hiding their own imbalance. Their transmission of doctrine hurls stones at others and bores the young.*

Homily for Pentecost Sunday, 1. (19 May 2013)

Let us ask ourselves today: Are we open to 'God's surprises'? Or are we closed and fearful before the newness of the Holy Spirit? Do we have the courage to strike out along the new paths which God's newness sets before us, or do we resist, barricaded in transient structures which have lost their capacity for openness to what is new? We would do well to ask ourselves these questions all through the day.[2570]

Apostolic Exhortation *Evangelii Gaudium*, 35, 40, 41, 94, 95, 165. (24th November 2013)

Pastoral ministry in a missionary style is not obsessed with the disjointed transmission of a multitude of doctrines to be insistently imposed.[...]

Differing currents of thought in philosophy, theology and pastoral practice, if open to being reconciled by the Spirit in respect and love, can enable the Church to grow, since all of them help to express more clearly the immense riches of God's word. For those who long for a monolithic body of doctrine guarded by all and leaving no room for nuance, this might appear as undesirable and leading to confusion. But in fact such variety serves to bring out and develop different facets of the inexhaustible riches of the Gospel. [...]

There are times when the faithful, in listening to completely orthodox language, take away something alien to the authentic Gospel of Jesus Christ, because that language is alien to their own way of speaking to and understanding one another. With the holy intent of communicating the truth about God and humanity, we sometimes give them a false god or a human ideal which is not really Christian. In this way, we hold fast to a formulation while failing to convey its substance. This is the greatest danger. [...]

The other is the self-absorbed promethean neopelagianism of those who ultimately trust only in their own powers and feel superior to others because they observe certain rules or remain intransigently faithful to a particular Catholic style from the past. A supposed soundness of doctrine or discipline leads instead to a narcissistic and authoritarian elitism, whereby instead of evangelising, one analyses and classifies others, and instead of opening the door to grace, one exhausts his or her energies in inspecting and verifying. [...]

In some people we see an ostentatious preoccupation for the liturgy, for doctrine and for the Church's prestige, but without any concern that the Gospel have a real impact on God's faithful people and the concrete needs of the present time. In this way, the life of the Church turns into a museum piece or something which is the property of a select few.[...]

The centrality of the kerygma calls for stressing those elements which are most needed today: it has to express God's saving love which precedes any moral and religious obligation on our part; it should not impose the truth but appeal to freedom; it should be marked by joy, encouragement, liveliness and a harmonious balance which

---

[2570]Pope Francis. [2013] *Homily at Holy Mass with the Ecclesial Movements on Pentecost Sunday*, para 1 [Online] Available at: www.vatican.va [Accessed on: 28 September 2022]

will not reduce preaching to a few doctrines which are at times more philosophical than evangelical.[2571]

Morning Meditation in the Chapel of the Domus Sanctae Marthae. (13th October 2014)

The Pope then moved on to his final instruction, to reflect on this theme, to ask oneself about these aspects: 'Am I attached to my things, to my ideas, closed? Or am I open to the God of surprises?'. And also: 'Am I a stationary person or a person on a journey?'[2572]

Address for the conclusion of the Third Extraordinary General Assembly of the Synod of Bishops. (18th October 2014)

One, a temptation to hostile inflexibility, that is, wanting to close oneself within the written word, (the letter) and not allowing oneself to be surprised by God, by the God of surprises, (the spirit); within the law, within the certitude of what we know and not of what we still need to learn and to achieve. From the time of Christ, it is the temptation of the zealous, of the scrupulous, of the solicitous and of the so-called – today –'traditionalists' and also of the intellectuals.[2573]

Address for the conclusion of the Fourteenth Ordinary General Assembly of the Synod of Bishops. (24th October 2015)

It was about bearing witness to everyone that, for the Church, the Gospel continues to be a vital source of eternal newness, against all those who would 'indoctrinate' it in dead stones to be hurled at others. It was also about laying closed hearts, which bare the closed hearts which frequently hide even behind the Church's teachings or good intentions, in order to sit in the chair of Moses and judge, sometimes with superiority and superficiality, difficult cases and wounded families.[2574]

Apostolic Exhortation *Amoris Laetitia, 59, 134. (19th March 2016)*

Our teaching on marriage and the family cannot fail to be inspired and transformed by this message of love and tenderness; otherwise, it becomes nothing more than the defence of a dry and lifeless doctrine.

More and more! Marital love is not defended primarily by presenting indissolubility as a duty, or by repeating doctrine, but by helping it to grow ever stronger under the impulse of grace.[2575]

Morning Meditation in the Chapel of the Domus Sanctae Marthae. (9th June 2016)

It is not Catholic (to say) 'or this or nothing:' This is not Catholic, this is heretical. Jesus always knows how to accompany us, he gives us the ideal, he accompanies us towards the ideal, He frees us from the chains of the laws' rigidity and tells us: 'But do that up to the point that you are capable.' And he understands us very well. He is our Lord and this is what he teaches us.[2576]

[2571]C Pope Francis [2013] Apostolic Exhortation *Evangelii Gaudium*, paras 35, 40, 41, 94, 95, 165 [Online] Available at: www.vatican.va. [Accessed on: 23 June 2022]

[2572]Pope Francis [13 October 2014] *Morning Meditation in the Chapel of the Domus Sanctae Marthae* [Online] Available at: www.vatican.va. [Accessed on: 23 June 2022]

[2573]Pope Francis [2014] Address for the conclusion of the Third Extraordinary General Assembly of the Synod of Bishops. [Online] Available at: www.vatican.va. [Accessed on: 23 June 2022]

[2574]Pope Francis [2015] *Conclusion to the Synod of Bishops.* [Online] Available at: www.vatican.va. [Accessed on: 23 June 2022]

[2575]Pope Francis [2016] Apostolic Exhortation *Amoris Llaetitia*, paras 59, 134. [Online] Available at: www.vatican.va. [Accessed on: 23 June 2022]

[2576]Pope Francis [9th June 2016] *Morning Meditation in the Chapel of the Domus Sanctae Marthae* [Online] Available at: www.vatican.va. [Accessed on: 23 June 2022]

Morning Meditation in the Chapel of the Domus Sanctae Marthae. (8 May 2017)

'…this God, our Father, who always surprises us: the God of surprises'. This is 'because he is a living God, a God who abides in us, a God who moves our heart, a God who is in the Church and walks with us; and he always surprises us on this path'. Thus, 'just as he had the creativity to create the world, so he has the creativity to create new things every day', the Pope continued. He is the God who surprises'.[2577]

Apostolic Exhortation *Christus Vivit, 212. (25th March 2019)*

In some places, it happens that young people are helped to have a powerful experience of God, an encounter with Jesus that touched their hearts. But the only follow-up to this is a series of 'formation' meetings featuring talks about doctrinal and moral issues, the evils of today's world, the Church, her social doctrine, chastity, marriage, birth control and so on. As a result, many young people get bored, they lose the fire of their encounter with Christ and the joy of following him; many give up and others become downcast or negative. Rather than being too concerned with communicating a great deal of doctrine, let us first try to awaken and consolidate the great experiences that sustain the Christian life.[2578]

Christmas Address to the Curia. (21st December 2019)

…there is a need to be wary of the temptation to rigidity. A rigidity born of the fear of change, which ends up erecting fences and obstacles on the terrain of the common good, turning it into a minefield of incomprehension and hatred. Let us always remember that behind every form of rigidity lies some kind of imbalance. Rigidity and imbalance feed one another in a vicious circle. And today this temptation to rigidity has become very real.[2579]

Encyclical *Fratelli Tutti, 4. (3rd October 2020)*

Francis did not wage a war of words aimed at imposing doctrines; he simply spread the love of God. As believers, we are convinced that human nature, as the source of ethical principles, was created by God, and that ultimately it is he who gives those principles their solid foundation. This does not result in an ethical rigidity nor does it lead to the imposition of any one moral system, since fundamental and universally valid moral principles can be embodied in different practical rules. Thus, room for dialogue will always exist.

General Audience Address. (23rd June 2021)

Indeed, today too there is no shortage of preachers who, especially through the new means of communication, can disturb communities. They present themselves not primarily to announce the Gospel of God who loves man in Jesus, Crucified and Risen, but to insist, as true 'keepers of the truth' — so they call themselves — on the best way to be Christians. And they strongly affirm that the true Christianity is the one they adhere to, often identified with certain forms of the past, and that the solution to the crises of today is to go back so as not to lose the genuineness of the faith. Today too, as then, there is a temptation to close oneself up in some of the certainties acquired in past traditions. But how can we recognize these people? For example, one of the features of this way of proceeding is inflexibility. Faced with the preaching of the Gospel that

[2577]Pope Francis [8 May 2017] *Morning Meditation in the Chapel of the Domus Sanctae Marthae.* [Online] Available at: www.vatican.va. [Accessed on: 23 June 2022]
[2578]Pope Francis [2019] Apostolic Exhortation *Christus Vivit*, para 212 [Online] Available at: www.vatican.va. [Accessed on: 23 June 2022]
[2579]Pope Francis [2019] *Christmas Address to the Curia* [Online] Available at: www.vatican.va. [Accessed on: 23 June 2022]

makes us free, that makes us joyful, these people are rigid. Always the rigidity: you must do this, you must do that.... Inflexibility is typical of these people.[2580]

Address to representatives from the Diocese of Rome. (18th September 2021)

As happens also today, there is a rigid way of considering the circumstances, which mortifies the *makrothymía* of God, namely, that patience of the gaze that is nourished by profound and wide and long visions; God sees far, God is not in a hurry. Rigidity is another perversion that is a sin against God's patience; it's a sin against the sovereignty of God. This happens also today.[2581]

Homily at the Mass for the opening of the Synodal Path. (10th October 2021)

Let us not soundproof our hearts; let us not remain barricaded in our certainties. So often our certainties can make us closed.[2582]

Sacred Scripture

Matthew 28:18-20
And Jesus coming, spoke to them, saying: All power is given to me in heaven and in earth. Going therefore, teach ye all nations; baptizing them in the name of the Father, and of the Son, and of the Holy Ghost. Teaching them to observe all things whatsoever I have commanded you: and behold I am with you all days, even to the consummation of the world.

Luke 6:47-49
Every one that cometh to me, and heareth my words, and doth them, I will shew you to whom he is like. He is like to a man building a house, who digged deep, and laid the foundation upon a rock. And when a flood came, the stream beat vehemently upon that house, and it could not shake it; for it was founded on a rock. But he that heareth, and doth not, is like to a man building his house upon the earth without a foundation: against which the stream beat vehemently, and immediately it fell, and the ruin of that house was great.

Romans 16:17
Now I beseech you, brethren, to mark them who make dissensions and offences contrary to the doctrine which you have learned, and avoid them.

II Corinthians 11:3-4
But I fear lest, as the serpent seduced Eve by his subtilty, so your minds should be corrupted, and fall from the simplicity that is in Christ. For if he that cometh preacheth another Christ, whom we have not preached; or if you receive another Spirit, whom you have not received; or another gospel which you have not received; you might well bear with him.

Ephesians 4:14
That henceforth we be no more children tossed to and fro, and carried about with every wind of doctrine by the wickedness of men, by cunning craftiness, by which they lie in wait to deceive.

Galatians 1:8
But though we, or an angel from heaven, preach a gospel to you besides that which we have preached to you, let him be anathema.

[2580] Pope Francis [2021] *General Audience Address* [Online] Available at: www.vatican.va. [Accessed on: 23 June 2022]

[2581] Pope Francis [2021] *Address to the faithful of Rome* [Online] Available at: www.exaudi.org [Accessed on: 23 June 2022]

[2582] Pope Francis [2021] *Homily at Mass for the Opening of the Synodal Path* [Online] Available at: www.vatican.va. [Accessed on: 23 June 2022]

Colossians 2:7-8
Rooted and built up in him, and confirmed in the faith, as also you have learned, abounding in him in thanksgiving. Beware lest any man cheat you by philosophy, and vain deceit; according to the tradition of men according to the elements of the world, and not according to Christ.

II Thessalonians 2:15
Therefore, brethren, stand fast; and hold the traditions which you have learned, whether by word, or by our epistle.

Titus 1:9
Embracing that faithful word which is according to doctrine, that he may be able to exhort in sound doctrine, and to convince the gainsayers.

Titus 2:1
But speak thou the things that become sound doctrine.

I Timothy 1:9-11
Knowing this, that the law is not made for the just man, but for the unjust and disobedient, for the ungodly, and for sinners, for the wicked and defiled, for murderers of fathers, and murderers of mothers, for manslayers, For fornicators, for them who defile themselves with mankind, for menstealers, for liars, for perjured persons, and whatever other thing is contrary to sound doctrine, Which is according to the gospel of the glory of the blessed God, which hath been committed to my trust.

I Timothy 4:1-2
Now the Spirit manifestly saith, that in the last times some shall depart from the faith, giving heed to spirits of error, and doctrines of devils, Speaking lies in hypocrisy, and having their conscience seared.

I Timothy 4:6
These things proposing to the brethren, thou shalt be a good minister of Christ Jesus, nourished up in the words of faith, and of the good doctrine which thou hast attained unto.

I Timothy 4:16
Take heed to thyself and to doctrine: be earnest in them. For in doing this thou shalt both save thyself and them that hear thee.

I Timothy 6:3-5
If any man teach otherwise, and consent not to the sound words of our Lord Jesus Christ, and to that doctrine which is according to godliness, He is proud, knowing nothing, but sick about questions and strifes of words; from which arise envies, contentions, blasphemies, evil suspicions, Conflicts of men corrupted in mind, and who are destitute of the truth, supposing gain to be godliness.

I Timothy 6:20
O Timothy, keep that which is committed to thy trust, avoiding the profane novelties of words, and oppositions of knowledge falsely so called.

II Timothy 1:13-14
Hold the form of sound words, which thou hast heard of me in faith, and in the love which is in Christ Jesus. Keep the good thing committed to thy trust by the Holy Ghost, who dwelleth in us.

II Timothy 4:3
For there shall be a time, when they will not endure sound doctrine; but, according to their own desires, they will heap to themselves teachers, having itching ears.

Hebrews 13:8-9
Jesus Christ, yesterday, and to day; and the same for ever. Be not led away with various and strange doctrines.

Jude 1:3
Dearly beloved, taking all care to write unto you concerning your common salvation, I was under a necessity to write unto you: to beseech you to contend earnestly for the faith once delivered to the saints.

II Peter 2:1-3
But there were also false prophets among the people, even as there shall be among you lying teachers, who shall bring in sects of perdition, and deny the Lord who bought them: bringing upon themselves swift destruction. And many shall follow their riotousness, through whom the way of truth shall be evil spoken of. And through covetousness shall they with feigned words make merchandise of you. Whose judgment now of a long time lingereth not, and their perdition slumbereth not.

II John 1:9-10
Whosoever revolteth, and continueth not in the doctrine of Christ, hath not God. He that continueth in the doctrine, the same hath both the Father and the Son. If any man come to you, and bring not this doctrine, receive him not into the house nor say to him, God speed you.

Sacred Tradition

St. Irenaeus: c. 130 AD to c. 202
Against the Heresies. Bk. III, Chap. 3; Bk. I, Chap. 10
The blessed apostles, then, having founded and built up the Church [...] In this order, and by this succession, the ecclesiastical tradition from the apostles, and the preaching of the truth, have come down to us. And this is most abundant proof that there is one and the same vivifying faith, which has been preserved in the Church from the apostles until now, and handed down in truth.

As I have already observed, the Church, having received this preaching and this faith, although scattered throughout the whole world, yet, as if occupying but one house, carefully preserves it. She also believes these points [of doctrine] just as if she had but one soul, and one and the same heart, and she proclaims them, and teaches them, and hands them down, with perfect harmony, as if she possessed only one mouth. For, although the languages of the world are dissimilar, yet the import of the tradition is one and the same. For the Churches which have been planted in Germany do not believe or hand down anything different, nor do those in Spain, nor those in Gaul, nor those in the East, nor those in Egypt, nor those in Libya, nor those which have been established in the central regions of the world. But as the sun, that creature of God, is one and the same throughout the whole world, so also the preaching of the truth shines every-where, and enlightens all men that are willing to come to a knowledge of the truth. Nor will any one of the rulers in the Churches, however highly gifted he may be in point of eloquence, teach doctrines different from these (for no one is greater than the Master); nor, on the other hand, will he who is deficient in power of expression inflict injury on the tradition. For the faith being ever one and the same, neither does one who is able at great length to discourse regarding it, make any addition to it, nor does one, who can say but little diminish it.[2583]

Tertullian: c. 160 to 225
Prescription against Heretics, Chap. 21
From this, therefore, do we draw up our rule. Since the Lord Jesus Christ sent the apostles to preach, (our rule is) that no others ought to be received as preachers than those whom Christ appointed [...] If, then, these things are so, it is in the same degree manifest that all doctrine which agrees with the apostolic churches — those moulds and original sources of the faith must be reckoned for truth, as undoubtedly containing that

---

[2583] St. Irenaeus of Lyons. *Against the Heresies*, Bk. I Chap. 10; Bk 3, Chap. 3 [Online] Available at: www.newadvent.org [Accessed on: 27 June 2022]

which the (said) churches received from the apostles, the apostles from Christ, Christ from God. Whereas all doctrine must be prejudged as false which savours of contrariety to the truth of the churches and apostles of Christ and God. It remains, then, that we demonstrate whether this doctrine of ours, of which we have now given the rule, has its origin in the tradition of the apostles, and whether all other doctrines do not ipso facto proceed from falsehood. We hold communion with the apostolic churches because our doctrine is in no respect different from theirs. This is our witness of truth.[2584]

Eusebius of Caesarea: c. 260 to c. 340

Ecclesiastical History. Bk. III, Chap. 36
And as he [St. Ignatius of Antioch] made the journey through Asia under the strictest military surveillance, he fortified the parishes in the various cities where he stopped by oral homilies and exhortations, and warned them above all to be especially on their guard against the heresies that were then beginning to prevail, and exhorted them to hold fast to the tradition of the apostles. Moreover, he thought it necessary to attest that tradition in writing, and to give it a fixed form for the sake of greater security.[2585]

St. Gregory of Nazianzus: 329 to 390

Oratio 40, Chap. 41
Above all guard for me this great deposit of faith for which I live and fight, which I want to take with me as a companion, and which makes me bear all evils and despise all pleasures.[2586]

St. Augustine: 354 to 430

The City of God, Bk. XVI, Chap. 2
For while the hot restlessness of heretics stirs questions about many articles of the Catholic faith, the necessity of defending them forces us both to investigate them more accurately, to understand them more clearly, and to proclaim them more earnestly; and the question mooted by an adversary becomes the occasion of instruction.[2587]

Of Faith and the Creed, Chap. 1
And it must be our aim, by pious and careful watchfulness, to provide against the possibility of the said faith sustaining any injury in us, on any side, through the fraudulent artifices [or, cunning fraud] of the heretics.[2588]

St. John Chrysostom: c. 347 to 407

Homily XXXII on St. Paul's Epistle to the Romans, 16:17-18
For this is, if anything the subversion of the Church, the being in divisions. This is the devil's weapon, this turns all things upside-down. For so long as the body is joined into one, he has no power to get an entrance, but it is from division that the offence comes. And whence is division? From opinions contrary to the teaching of the Apostles. And whence come opinions of this sort? From men's being slaves to the belly, and the other passions. For 'such,' he says, 'serve not the Lord, but their own belly.' And so there would be no offence, there would be no division, unless some opinion were thought of contrary to the doctrine of the Apostles. And this he here points out by saying, 'contrary to the doctrine.' And he does not say which we have taught, but 'which you

---

[2584]Tertullian. *Prescription against Heretics*, Chap. 21 [Online] Available at: www.newadvent.org [Accessed on: 27 June 2022]
[2585]Eusebius of Caesarea. *Ecclesiastical History.* Bk. III, Chap. 36 [Online] Available at: www. newadvent.org [Accessed on: 27 June 2022]
[2586]St. Gregory of Nazianzus. *Oratio* 40, Chap. 41 quoted in the *Catechism of the Catholic Church*, para 256 [Online] Available at: http://www.scborromeo.org [Accessed on: 29 September 2022]
[2587]St. Augustine. *The City of God*, Bk. XVI, Chap. 2 [Online] Available at: www.newadvent.org [Accessed on: 27 June 2022]
[2588]St. Augustine. *Of Faith and the Creed*, Chap. 1 [Online] Available at: www.newadvent.org [Accessed on: 27 June 2022]

have learned,' so anticipating them, and showing that they were persuaded of and had heard them and received them. And what are we to do to those who make mischief in this way? He does not say have a meeting and come to blows, but 'avoid them.' For if it was from ignorance or error that they did this, one ought to set them right. But if they sin willingly, spring away from them.[2589]

Theodoret of Cyrus: c. 393 to c. 457

Letter to Florentius the Patrician, 89
So have I learned not only from the apostles and prophets but also from the interpreters of their writings, Ignatius, Eustathius, Athanasius, Basil, Gregory, John, and the rest of the lights of the world; and before these from the holy Fathers in council at Nicæa, whose confession of the faith I preserve in its integrity, like an ancestral inheritance, styling corrupt and enemies of the truth all who dare to transgress its decrees.[2590]

St. Vincent of Lerins: ? to 450

Commonitory, Chap. 28.
Therefore, as soon as the corruption of each mischievous error begins to break forth, and to defend itself by filching certain passages of Scripture, and expounding them fraudulently and deceitfully, immediately, the opinions of the ancients in the interpretation of the Canon are to be collected, whereby the novelty, and consequently the profaneness, whatever it may be, that arises, may both without any doubt be exposed, and without any tergiversation be condemned. But the opinions of those Fathers only are to be used for comparison, who living and teaching, holily, wisely, and with constancy, in the Catholic faith and communion, were counted worthy either to die in the faith of Christ, or to suffer death happily for Christ. Whom yet we are to believe in this condition, that that only is to be accounted indubitable, certain, established, which either all, or the more part, have supported and confirmed manifestly, frequently, persistently, in one and the same sense, forming, as it were, a consentient council of doctors, all receiving, holding, handing on the same doctrine. But whatsoever a teacher holds, other than all, or contrary to all, be he holy and learned, be he a bishop, be he a Confessor, be he a martyr, let that be regarded as a private fancy of his own, and be separated from the authority of common, public, general persuasion, lest, after the sacrilegious custom of heretics and schismatics, rejecting the ancient truth of the universal Creed, we follow, at the utmost peril of our eternal salvation, the newly devised error of one man.[2591]

The Magisterium of the Church

We must guard with care the faith that we have received from the Church, this deposit of great price. One of our primary duties is to safeguard the deposit of faith entrusted to the Church by Our Lord because Christian doctrine is the doctrine which Jesus Christ our Lord taught us to show us the way of salvation. It is necessary to learn the doctrine taught by Jesus Christ, and those who fail to do so are guilty of a grave breach of duty. We can be certain that the doctrine which we receive from the Holy Catholic Church is true, because Jesus Christ, the divine Author of this doctrine, committed it through His Apostles to the Church, which He founded and made the infallible teacher of all men, promising her His divine assistance until the end of time.

Second Council of Nicaea (Seventh Ecumenical, 787)

The one who granted us the light of recognising him, the one who redeemed us from the darkness of idolatrous insanity, Christ our God, when he took for his bride his

---

[2589]St. John Chrysostom. *Homily XXXII on St. Paul's Epistle to the Romans*, 16:17-18. [Online] Available at: www.newadvent.org [Accessed on: 27 June 2022]
[2590]Theodoret of Cyrus. *Letter to Florentius the Patrician*, 89 [Online] Available at: www.newadvent. org [Accessed on: 27 June 2022]
[2591]St. Vincent of Lerins. *Commonitory*, Chap. 28 [Online] Available at: www.newadvent.org [Accessed on: 27 June 2022]

holy catholic church, having no blemish or wrinkle, promised he would guard her and assured his holy disciples saying, *I am with you every day until the consummation of this age*. This promise however he made not only to them but also to us, who thanks to them have come to believe in his name. To this gracious offer some people paid no attention, being hoodwinked by the treacherous foe they abandoned the true line of reasoning, and setting themselves against the tradition of the catholic church they faltered in their grasp of the truth. As the proverbial saying puts it, they turned askew the axles of their farm carts and gathered no harvest in their hands. Indeed they had the effrontery to criticise the beauty pleasing to God established in the holy monuments; they were priests in name, but not in reality. They were those of whom God calls out by prophecy, *Many pastors have destroyed my vine, they have defiled my portion*. For they followed unholy men and trusting to their own frenzies they calumniated the holy church, which Christ our God has espoused to himself, and they failed to distinguish the holy from the profane....[2592]

Fourth Council of Constantinople (Eighth Ecumenical, 869 to 870)

Canon 1. (28th February 870)
If we wish to proceed without offence along the true and royal road of divine justice, we must keep the declarations and teachings of the holy fathers as if they were so many lamps which are always alight and illuminating our steps which are directed towards God. Therefore, considering and esteeming these as a second word of God, in accordance with the great and most wise Denis, let us sing most willingly along with the divinely inspired David, *The commandment of the Lord is bright, enlightening the eyes, and, Your word is a lamp to my feet and a light to my paths*; and with the author of Proverbs we say, *Your commandment is a lamp and your law a light, and like Isaiah we cry to the lord God with loud voice, because your commands are a light for the earth*. For the exhortations and warnings of the divine canons are rightly likened to light inasmuch as the better is distinguished from the worse and what is advantageous and useful is distinguished from what is not helpful but harmful.

Therefore we declare that we are preserving and maintaining the canons which have been entrusted to the holy, catholic and apostolic church by the holy and renowned apostles, and by universal as well as local councils of orthodox [bishops], and even by any inspired father or teacher of the church. Consequently, we rule our own life and conduct by these canons and we decree that all those who have the rank of priests and all those who are described by the name of Christian are, by ecclesiastical law, included under the penalties and condemnations as well as, on the other hand, the absolutions and acquittals which have been imposed and defined by them. For Paul, the great apostle, openly urges us to preserve the traditions which we have received, either by word or by letter, of the saints who were famous in times past.[2593]

First Vatican Council (Twentieth Ecumenical, 1869 to 1870)

Dogmatic Constitution, *Dei Filius Chap. 3, 1, 8; Chap. 4, 13-14. (24th April 1870)*
Since human beings are totally dependent on God as their creator and lord, and created reason is completely subject to uncreated truth, we are obliged to yield to God the revealer full submission of intellect and will by faith.

Wherefore, by divine and catholic faith all those things are to be believed which are contained in the word of God as found in scripture and tradition, and which are proposed by the Church as matters to be believed as divinely revealed, whether by her solemn judgment or in her ordinary and universal magisterium.

For the doctrine of the faith which God has revealed is put forward not as some philosophical discovery capable of being perfected by human intelligence, but as a

---

[2592]Tanner, N. [1990] *Decrees of the Ecumenical Councils*: Volume 1 [Online] Available at: www.papalencyclicals.net [Accessed: 24 June 2022]
[2593]*Ibid.*

divine deposit committed to the spouse of Christ to be faithfully protected and infallibly promulgated. Hence, too, that meaning of the sacred dogmas is ever to be maintained which has once been declared by holy mother church, and there must never be any abandonment of this sense under the pretext or in the name of a more profound understanding. May understanding, knowledge and wisdom increase as ages and centuries roll along, and greatly and vigorously flourish, in each and all, in the individual and the whole church: but this only in its own proper kind, that is to say, in the same doctrine, the same sense, and the same understanding.

If anyone says that it is possible that at some time, given the advancement of knowledge, a sense may be assigned to the dogmas propounded by the church which is different from that which the Church has understood and understands: let him be anathema. (*On Faith and Reason*, Canon 3).[2594]

Dogmatic Constitution, *Pastor Aeternus, 6-7. (18th July 1870)*

For the Holy Spirit was promised to the successors of Peter not so that they might, by his revelation, make known some new doctrine, but that, by his assistance, they might religiously guard and faithfully expound the revelation or deposit of faith transmitted by the apostles. Indeed, their apostolic teaching was embraced by all the venerable fathers and reverenced and followed by all the holy orthodox doctors, for they knew very well that this See of St. Peter always remains unblemished by any error, in accordance with the divine promise of our Lord and Saviour to the prince of his disciples: 'I have prayed for you that your faith may not fail; and when you have turned again, strengthen your brethren.'

This gift of truth and never-failing faith was therefore divinely conferred on Peter and his successors in this See so that they might discharge their exalted office for the salvation of all, and so that the whole flock of Christ might be kept away by them from the poisonous food of error and be nourished with the sustenance of heavenly doctrine. Thus the tendency to schism is removed and the whole Church is preserved in unity, and, resting on its foundation, can stand firm against the gates of hell.[2595]

Second Vatican Council (Twenty-First Ecumenical, 1962 to 1965)

Dogmatic Constitution *on the Church, Lumen Gentium, 25. (21st November 1964)*

Among the principal duties of bishops the preaching of the Gospel occupies an eminent place. For bishops are preachers of the faith, who lead new disciples to Christ, and they are authentic teachers, that is, teachers endowed with the authority of Christ, who preach to the people committed to them the faith they must believe and put into practice, and by the light of the Holy Spirit illustrate that faith. They bring forth from the treasury of Revelation new things and old,(Mt 13:52) making it bear fruit and vigilantly warding off any errors that threaten their flock.(II Tim 4:1-4) Bishops, teaching in communion with the Roman Pontiff, are to be respected by all as witnesses to divine and Catholic truth. In matters of faith and morals, the bishops speak in the name of Christ and the faithful are to accept their teaching and adhere to it with a religious assent. This religious submission of mind and will must be shown in a special way to the authentic magisterium of the Roman Pontiff, even when he is not speaking ex cathedra; that is, it must be shown in such a way that his supreme magisterium is acknowledged with reverence, the judgments made by him are sincerely adhered to, according to his manifest mind and will. His mind and will in the matter may be known either from the character of the documents, from his frequent repetition of the same doctrine, or from his manner of speaking.

[2594]*Decrees of the First Vatican Council*. Dogmatic Constitution *Dei Filius*, Chap. 4 [Online] Available at: www.papalencyclicals.net [Accessed: 24 June 2022]
[2595]Vatican I's Dogmatic Constitution, *Pastor Aeternus, on the Church of Christ*, Chap. 4, para 6 [Online] Available at: www.ewtn.com [Accessed: 24 June 2022]

Although the individual bishops do not enjoy the prerogative of infallibility, they nevertheless proclaim Christ's doctrine infallibly whenever, even though dispersed through the world, but still maintaining the bond of communion among themselves and with the successor of Peter, and authentically teaching matters of faith and morals, they are in agreement on one position as definitively to be held. This is even more clearly verified when, gathered together in an ecumenical council, they are teachers and judges of faith and morals for the universal Church, whose definitions must be adhered to with the submission of faith.[2596]

Dogmatic Constitution *on Divine Revelation, Dei Verbum, 5, 8, 10, 21. (18th November 1965)*

'The obedience of faith' (Rom 16:26; see 1:5; II Cor 10:5-6) 'is to be given to God who reveals, an obedience by which man commits his whole self freely to God, offering the full submission of intellect and will to God who reveals,' and freely assenting to the truth revealed by Him. To make this act of faith, the grace of God and the interior help of the Holy Spirit must precede and assist, moving the heart and turning it to God, opening the eyes of the mind and giving 'joy and ease to everyone in assenting to the truth and believing it.' To bring about an ever deeper understanding of revelation the same Holy Spirit constantly brings faith to completion by His gifts.

Therefore the Apostles, handing on what they themselves had received, warn the faithful to hold fast to the traditions which they have learned either by word of mouth or by letter (see II Thess 2:15), and to fight in defense of the faith handed on once and for all (see Jude 1:3). Now what was handed on by the Apostles includes everything which contributes toward the holiness of life and increase in faith of the peoples of God; and so the Church, in her teaching, life and worship, perpetuates and hands on to all generations all that she herself is, all that she believes.

Sacred tradition and Sacred Scripture form one sacred deposit of the word of God, committed to the Church. Holding fast to this deposit the entire holy people united with their shepherds remain always steadfast in the teaching of the Apostles...

The Church has always venerated the divine Scriptures just as she venerates the body of the Lord, since, especially in the sacred liturgy, she unceasingly receives and offers to the faithful the bread of life from the table both of God's word and of Christ's body. She has always maintained them, and continues to do so, together with sacred tradition, as the supreme rule of faith, since, as inspired by God and committed once and for all to writing, they impart the word of God Himself without change, and make the voice of the Holy Spirit resound in the words of the prophets and Apostles.[2597]

Pope Benedict XVI: 2005 to 2013

Compendium of the Catechism of the Catholic Church. (28th June 2005)

15. To whom is the deposit of faith entrusted?
The Apostles entrusted the deposit of faith to the whole of the Church. Thanks to its supernatural sense of faith the people of God as a whole, assisted by the Holy Spirit and guided by the Magisterium of the Church, never ceases to welcome, to penetrate more deeply and to live more fully from the gift of divine revelation.[2598]

General Audience Address. (5th April 2006)

The Apostles and their successors are therefore the custodians and authoritative witnesses of the deposit of truth consigned to the Church, and are likewise the ministers

---

[2596]Second Vatican Council [1964] Dogmatic Constitution on the Church, *Lumen Gentium*, Chap. III, para 25 [Online] Available at: www.vatican.va. [Accessed: 24 June 2022]
[2597]Second Vatican Council [1965] Dogmatic Constitution on Divine Revelation, *Dei Verbum*, Chap. II, para 8 [Online] Available at: www.vatican.va. [Accessed: 24 June 2022]
[2598]Pope Benedict XVI [2005] *Compendium of the Catechism of the Catholic Church.* Online] Available at: www.vatican.va [Accessed on: 18 August 2022]

of charity. These are two aspects that go together. They must always be mindful of the inseparable nature of this twofold service which in fact is only one: truth and love, revealed and given by the Lord Jesus. In this regard, their service is first and foremost a service of love: and the charity they live and foster is inseparable from the truth they preserve and pass on. Truth and love are the two faces of the same gift that comes from God and, thanks to the apostolic ministry, is safeguarded in the Church and handed down to us, to our present time![2599]

Message for the Twenty-Sixth World Youth Day, 2-3. (6th August 2010)

In order to highlight the importance of faith in the lives of believers, I would like to reflect with you on each of the three terms used by Saint Paul in the expression: 'Planted and built up in Jesus Christ, firm in the faith' (cf. Col 2:7). We can distinguish three images: 'planted' calls to mind a tree and the roots that feed it; 'built up' refers to the construction of a house; 'firm' indicates growth in physical or moral strength. These images are very eloquent. […]

Just as the roots of a tree keep it firmly planted in the soil, so the foundations of a house give it long-lasting stability. Through faith, we have been built up in Jesus Christ (cf. Col 2:7), even as a house is built on its foundations. […]

You are 'planted and built up in Jesus Christ, firm in the faith' (cf. Col 2:7). The Letter from which these words are taken was written by Saint Paul in order to respond to a specific need of the Christians in the city of Colossae. That community was threatened by the influence of certain cultural trends that were turning the faithful away from the Gospel. Our own cultural context, dear young people, is not unlike that of the ancient Colossians.[2600]

Apostolic Exhortation, *Verbum Domini, 30. (30th September 2010)*

Saint Jerome recalls that we can never read Scripture simply on our own. We come up against too many closed doors and we slip too easily into error…An authentic interpretation of the Bible must always be in harmony with the faith of the Catholic Church. He thus wrote to a priest: 'Remain firmly attached to the traditional doctrine that you have been taught, so that you may exhort according to sound doctrine and confound those who contradict it'.[2601]

Motu Proprio, *Porta Fidei, 9. (11th October 2011)*

Not without reason, Christians in the early centuries were required to learn the creed from memory. It served them as a daily prayer not to forget the commitment they had undertaken in baptism. With words rich in meaning, Saint Augustine speaks of this in a homily on the *redditio symboli*, the handing over of the creed: 'the symbol of the holy mystery that you have all received together and that today you have recited one by one, are the words on which the faith of Mother Church is firmly built above the stable foundation that is Christ the Lord. You have received it and recited it, but in your minds and hearts you must keep it ever present, you must repeat it in your beds, recall it in the public squares and not forget it during meals: even when your body is asleep, you must watch over it with your hearts.'[2602]

[2599]Pope Benedict XVI [2006] General Audience Address [Online] Available at: www.vatican.va [Accessed on: 28th June 2022]

[2600]Pope Benedict XVI [2010] *Message for the Twenty-Sixth World Youth Day*, paras 2-3 [Online] Available at: www.vatican.va [Accessed on: 28th June 2022]

[2601]Pope Benedict XVI [2010] Apostolic Exhortation *Verbum Domini*, para 30 [Online] Available at: www.vatican.va [Accessed on: 28th June 2022]

[2602]Pope Benedict XVI [2011] Motu Proprio, *Porta Fidei*, para 9 [Online] Available at: www.vatican.va [Accessed on: 30 September 2022]

Address to participants in the plenary meeting of the Congregation for the Doctrine of the Faith. (27th January 2012)

I would like to mention one last matter: the moral problem, which is a new challenge to the ecumenical process. In the dialogue we cannot ignore the great moral questions regarding human life, the family, sexuality, bioethics, freedom, justice and peace. It will be important to speak about these topics with one voice, drawing from the foundations in Scripture and in the living Tradition of the Church. This Tradition helps us to decipher the language of the Creator in his creation. In defending the fundamental values of the Church's great Tradition, we defend the human being, we defend creation.[2603]

Homily at Mass for the opening of the Year of Faith. (11th October 2012)

The Council Fathers wished to present the faith in a meaningful way; and if they opened themselves trustingly to dialogue with the modern world it is because they were certain of their faith, of the solid rock on which they stood. In the years following, however, many embraced uncritically the dominant mentality, placing in doubt the very foundations of the deposit of faith, which they sadly no longer felt able to accept as truths.[2604]

Pope St. John Paul II: 1978 to 2005

Homily (24th May 1979)

The words of Jesus became a treasure for the Church to guard and to proclaim, to meditate on and to rive. And at the same time, the Holy Spirit implanted in the Church an apostolic charism, in order to keep this revelation intact. Through his words Jesus was to live on in his Church: I am with you always. And so the whole ecclesial community became conscious of the need for fidelity to the instructions of Jesus, to the deposit of faith. This solicitude was to pass from generation to generation – down to our own day.[2605]

Revised Code of Canon Law. (1983)

A person must believe with divine and Catholic faith all those things contained in the word of God, written or handed on, that is, in the one deposit of faith entrusted to the Church, and at the same time proposed as divinely revealed either by the solemn magisterium of the Church or by its ordinary and universal magisterium which is manifested by the common adherence of the Christian faithful under the leadership of the sacred magisterium; therefore all are bound to avoid any doctrines whatsoever contrary to them. (Can. 750 §1)

Each and every thing which is proposed definitively by the magisterium of the Church concerning the doctrine of faith and morals, that is, each and every thing which is required to safeguard reverently and to expound faithfully the same deposit of faith, is also to be firmly embraced and retained; therefore, one who rejects those propositions which are to be held definitively is opposed to the doctrine of the Catholic Church. (Can. 750 §2).[2606]

Congregation for the Doctrine of the Faith. Instruction Donum Veritatis, 6, 10, 11,16, 21, 41. (24th May 1990)

Among the vocations awakened in this way by the Spirit in the Church is that of the theologian. His role is to pursue in a particular way an ever deeper understanding of the

[2603]Pope Benedict XVI [2012] *Address to participants in the plenary meeting of the Congregation for the Doctrine of the Faith* [Online] Available at: www.vatican.va [Accessed on: 30 September 2022]

[2604]Pope Benedict XVI [2012] *Homily at Mass for the opening of the Year of Faith* [Online] Available at: www.vatican.va [Accessed on: 30 September 2022]

[2605]Pope St. John Paul II [1979] *Homily on the Ascension of our Lord* [Online] Available at: www. vatican.va [Accessed on: 30 September 2022]

[2606]*Code of Canon Law,* [1983] [Online] Available at: www.vatican.va [Accessed on: 6 September 2022]

Word of God found in the inspired Scriptures and handed on by the living Tradition of the Church. He does this in communion with the Magisterium which has been charged with the responsibility of preserving the deposit of faith. [...]

Here it is important to emphasise that when theology employs the elements and conceptual tools of philosophy or other disciplines, discernment is needed. The ultimate normative principle for such discernment is revealed doctrine which itself must furnish the criteria for the evaluation of these elements and conceptual tools and not vice versa. Never forgetting that he is also a member of the People of God, the theologian must foster respect far them and be committed to offering them a teaching which in no way does harm to the doctrine of the faith. [...]

By its nature, the task of religiously guarding and loyally expounding the deposit of divine Revelation (in all its integrity and purity), implies that the Magisterium can make a pronouncement 'in a definitive way' on propositions which, even if not contained among the truths of faith, are nonetheless intimately connected with them, in such a way, that the definitive character of such affirmations derives in the final analysis from revelation itself. [...]

The living Magisterium of the Church and theology, while having different gifts and functions, ultimately have the same goal: preserving the People of God in the truth which sets free and thereby making them 'a light to the nations'. This service to the ecclesial community brings the theologian and the Magisterium into a reciprocal relationship. The latter authentically teaches the doctrine of the Apostles. And, benefiting from the work of theologians, it refutes objections to and distortions of the faith and promotes, with the authority received from Jesus Christ, new and deeper comprehension, clarification, and application of revealed doctrine. [...]

By virtue of the divine mandate given to it in the Church, the Magisterium has the mission to set forth the Gospel's teaching, guard its integrity, and thereby protect the Faith of the People of God. In order to fulfil this duty, it can at times be led to take serious measures as, for example, when it withdraws from a theologian, who departs from the doctrine of the faith, the canonical mission or the teaching mandate it had given him, or declares that some writings do not conform to this doctrine. When it acts in such ways, the Magisterium seeks to be faithful to its mission of defending the right of the People of God to receive the message of the Church in its purity and integrity and not be disturbed by a particular dangerous opinion. [...]

In this way, all can become ever better servants of the Word and of the People of God, so that the People of God, persevering in the doctrine of truth and freedom heard from the beginning, may abide also in the Son and the Father and obtain eternal life, the fulfilment of the Promise (cf. I Jn 2:24-25).[2607]

Apostolic Constitution, *Fidei Depositum, Introduction. (11th October 1992)*

Guarding the deposit of faith is the mission which the Lord has entrusted to his Church and which she fulfils in every age. [...]

The principal task entrusted to the Council by Pope John XXIII was to guard and present better the precious deposit of Christian doctrine in order to make it more accessible to the Christian faithful and to all people of good will. For this reason the Council was not first of all to condemn the errors of the time, but above all to strive calmly to show the strength and beauty of the doctrine of the faith.[2608]

Catechism of the Catholic Church (1992)

The heritage of faith entrusted to the whole of the Church. The apostles entrusted the 'Sacred deposit' of the faith (the *depositum fidei*), (I Tim 6:20; II Tim 1:12-14) contained in Sacred Scripture and Tradition, to the whole of the Church. 'By adhering to [this heritage] the entire holy people, united to its pastors, remains always faithful to the

---

[2607]Congregation for the Doctrine of the Faith [1990] Instruction *Donum Veritatis*, paras 6, 10, 11,16, 21, 41 [Online] Available at: www.vatican.va [Accessed on: 30 September 2022]

[2608]Pope St. John Paul II [1992] Apostolic Constitution *Fidei Depositum*, Introduction [Online] Available at: www.vatican.va [Accessed on: 30 September 2022]

teaching of the apostles, to the brotherhood, to the breaking of bread and the prayers. So, in maintaining, practicing and professing the faith that has been handed on, there should be a remarkable harmony between the bishops and the faithful.' (84)

'We guard with care the faith that we have received from the Church, for without ceasing, under the action of God's Spirit, this deposit of great price, as if in an excellent vessel, is constantly being renewed and causes the very vessel that contains it to be renewed.' (St. Irenaeus, *Adv. Haeres.* 3, 24, 1) (175)[2609]

Encyclical *Veritatis Splendor, 4, 5, 113, 116. (6th August 1993)*

Today, however, it seems necessary to reflect on the whole of the Church's moral teaching, with the precise goal of recalling certain fundamental truths of Catholic doctrine which, in the present circumstances, risk being distorted or denied. In fact, a new situation has come about within the Christian community itself, which has experienced the spread of numerous doubts and objections of a human and psychological, social and cultural, religious and even properly theological nature, with regard to the Church's moral teachings. It is no longer a matter of limited and occasional dissent, but of an overall and systematic calling into question of traditional moral doctrine, on the basis of certain anthropological and ethical presuppositions. At the root of these presuppositions is the more or less obvious influence of currents of thought which end by detaching human freedom from its essential and constitutive relationship to truth. Thus the traditional doctrine regarding the natural law, and the universality and the permanent validity of its precepts, is rejected; certain of the Church's moral teachings are found simply unacceptable; and the Magisterium itself is considered capable of intervening in matters of morality only in order to 'exhort consciences' and to 'propose values', in the light of which each individual will independently make his or her decisions and life choices.

In particular, note should be taken of the lack of harmony between the traditional response of the Church and certain theological positions, encountered even in Seminaries and in Faculties of Theology, with regard to questions of the greatest importance for the Church and for the life of faith of Christians, as well as for the life of society itself. In particular, the question is asked: do the commandments of God, which are written on the human heart and are part of the Covenant, really have the capacity to clarify the daily decisions of individuals and entire societies? Is it possible to obey God and thus love God and neighbour, without respecting these commandments in all circumstances? Also, an opinion is frequently heard which questions the intrinsic and unbreakable bond between faith and morality, as if membership in the Church and her internal unity were to be decided on the basis of faith alone, while in the sphere of morality a pluralism of opinions and of kinds of behaviour could be tolerated, these being left to the judgment of the individual subjective conscience or to the diversity of social and cultural contexts. [...]

I address myself to you, Venerable Brothers in the Episcopate, who share with me the responsibility of safeguarding 'sound teaching' (II Tim 4:3), with the intention of clearly setting forth certain aspects of doctrine which are of crucial importance in facing what is certainly a genuine crisis, since the difficulties which it engenders have most serious implications for the moral life of the faithful and for communion in the Church, as well as for a just and fraternal social life. [...]

While exchanges and conflicts of opinion may constitute normal expressions of public life in a representative democracy, moral teaching certainly cannot depend simply upon respect for a process: indeed, it is in no way established by following the rules and deliberative procedures typical of a democracy. Dissent, in the form of carefully orchestrated protests and polemics carried on in the media, is opposed to ecclesial communion and to a correct understanding of the hierarchical constitution of the People of God. Opposition to the teaching of the Church's Pastors cannot be seen

---

[2609]*Catechism of the Catholic Church.* [1992] [Online] Available at: http://www.scborromeo.org [Accessed on 4 July 2022]

as a legitimate expression either of Christian freedom or of the diversity of the Spirit's gifts. When this happens, the Church's Pastors have the duty to act in conformity with their apostolic mission, insisting that the right of the faithful to receive Catholic doctrine in its purity and integrity must always be respected. 'Never forgetting that he too is a member of the People of God, the theologian must be respectful of them, and be committed to offering them a teaching which in no way does harm to the doctrine of the faith'.

We have the duty, as Bishops, to be vigilant that the word of God is faithfully taught. My Brothers in the Episcopate, it is part of our pastoral ministry to see to it that this moral teaching is faithfully handed down and to have recourse to appropriate measures to ensure that the faithful are guarded from every doctrine and theory contrary to it. In carrying out this task we are all assisted by theologians; even so, theological opinions constitute neither the rule nor the norm of our teaching. Its authority is derived, by the assistance of the Holy Spirit and in communion cum Petro et sub Petro, from our fidelity to the Catholic faith which comes from the Apostles. As Bishops, we have the grave obligation to be personally vigilant that the 'sound doctrine' (I Tim 1:10) of faith and morals is taught in our Dioceses.[2610]

Motu Proprio, *Ad Tuendam Fidem, 1-4. (18th May 1998)*

To protect the faith of the Catholic Church against errors arising from certain members of the Christian faithful, especially from among those dedicated to the various disciplines of sacred theology, we, whose principal duty is to confirm the brethren in the faith (Lk 22:32), consider it absolutely necessary to add to the existing texts of the *Code of Canon Law* and the *Code of Canons of the Eastern Churches*, new norms which expressly impose the obligation of upholding truths proposed in a definitive way by the Magisterium of the Church, and which also establish related canonical sanctions.

From the first centuries to the present day, the Church has professed the truths of her faith in Christ and the mystery of his redemption. These truths were subsequently gathered into the Symbols of the faith, today known and proclaimed in common by the faithful in the solemn and festive celebration of Mass as the Apostles' Creed or the Nicene-Constantinopolitan Creed.

This same Nicene-Constantinopolitan Creed is contained in the Profession of faith developed by the Congregation for the Doctrine of the Faith, which must be made by specific members of the faithful when they receive an office, that is directly or indirectly related to deeper investigation into the truths of faith and morals, or is united to a particular power in the governance of the Church. [...]

The first paragraph states: 'With firm faith, I also believe everything contained in the word of God, whether written or handed down in Tradition, which the Church either by a solemn judgment or by the ordinary and universal Magisterium sets forth to be believed as divinely revealed'...

The third paragraph states: 'Moreover I adhere with submission of will and intellect to the teachings which either the Roman Pontiff or the College of Bishops enunciate when they exercise their authentic Magisterium, even if they do not intend to proclaim these teachings by a definitive act'....

The second paragraph, however, which states 'I also firmly accept and hold each and everything definitively proposed by the Church regarding teaching on faith and morals,' has no corresponding canon in the Codes of the Catholic Church. This second paragraph of the Profession of faith is of utmost importance since it refers to truths that are necessarily connected to divine revelation. These truths, in the investigation of Catholic doctrine, illustrate the Divine Spirit's particular inspiration for the Church's deeper understanding of a truth concerning faith and morals, with which they are connected either for historical reasons or by a logical relationship.

[2610]Pope St. John Paul II [1993] Encyclical *Veritatis Splendor*, paras 4, 5, 113, 116 [Online] Available at: www.vatican.va [Accessed on: 30 September 2022]

Moved therefore by this need, and after careful deliberation, we have decided to overcome this lacuna in the universal law in the following way:

A) Canon 750 of the *Code of Canon Law* will now consist of two paragraphs; the first will present the text of the existing canon; the second will contain a new text. Thus, canon 750, in its complete form, will read:

Canon 750 – § 1. Those things are to be believed by divine and catholic faith which are contained in the word of God as it has been written or handed down by tradition, that is, in the single deposit of faith entrusted to the Church, and which are at the same time proposed as divinely revealed either by the solemn Magisterium of the Church, or by its ordinary and universal Magisterium, which in fact is manifested by the common adherence of Christ's faithful under the guidance of the sacred Magisterium. All are therefore bound to avoid any contrary doctrines.

§ 2. Furthermore, each and everything set forth definitively by the Magisterium of the Church regarding teaching on faith and morals must be firmly accepted and held; namely, those things required for the holy keeping and faithful exposition of the deposit of faith; therefore, anyone who rejects propositions which are to be held definitively sets himself against the teaching of the Catholic Church.

Canon 1371, n. 1 of the *Code of Canon Law*, consequently, will receive an appropriate reference to canon 750 § 2, so that it will now read:

Canon 1371 – The following are to be punished with a just penalty:

1° a person who, apart from the case mentioned in canon 1364 § 1, teaches a doctrine condemned by the Roman Pontiff, or by an Ecumenical Council, or obstinately rejects the teachings mentioned in canon 750 § 2 or in canon 752 and, when warned by the Apostolic See or by the Ordinary, does not retract;

2° a person who in any other way does not obey the lawful command or prohibition of the Apostolic See or the Ordinary or Superior and, after being warned, persists in disobedience.[2611]

Congregation for the Doctrine of the Faith. Doctrinal Commentary on concluding formula of 'Professio fidei', 12. (29th June 1998)

In every profession of faith, the Church verifies different stages she has reached on her path toward the definitive meeting with the Lord. No content is abrogated with the passage of time; instead, all of it becomes an irreplaceable inheritance through which the faith of all time, of all believers, and lived out in every place, contemplates the constant action of the Spirit of the risen Christ, the Spirit who accompanies and gives life to his Church and leads her into the fullness of the truth.[2612]

Encyclical *Fides et Ratio*, 55. (14th September 1998)

The 'supreme rule of her faith' derives from the unity which the Spirit has created between Sacred Tradition, Sacred Scripture and the Magisterium of the Church in a reciprocity which means that none of the three can survive without the others.[2613]

Pope St. Paul VI: 1963 to 1978

Encyclical *Ecclesiam Suam*, 26, 64. (6th August 1964)

The Church itself is being engulfed and shaken by this tidal wave of change, for however much men may be committed to the Church, they are deeply affected by the climate of the world. They run the risk of becoming confused, bewildered and alarmed, and this

---

[2611]Pope St. John Paul II [1998] Motu Proprio, *Ad Tuendam Fidem*, paras 1-4 [Online] Available at: www.vatican.va [Accessed on: 30 September 2022]
[2612]Congregation for the *Doctrine of the Faith [1998] Doctrinal Commentary on concluding formula of 'Professio fidei', para 12* [Online] Available at: www.ewtn.com [Accessed on: 30 September 2022]
[2613]Pope St. John Paul II [1998] Encyclical *Fides et Ratio*, para 55 [Online] Available at: www.vatican.va [Accessed on: 28th June 2022]

is a state of affairs which strikes at the very roots of the Church. It drives many people to adopt the most outlandish views. They imagine that the Church should abdicate its proper role, and adopt an entirely new and unprecedented mode of existence. Modernism might be cited as an example. This is an error which is still making its appearance under various new guises, wholly inconsistent with any genuine religious expression. It is surely an attempt on the part of secular philosophies and secular trends to vitiate the true teaching and discipline of the Church of Christ.

An effective remedy is needed if all these dangers, which are prevalent in many quarters, are to be obviated, and We believe that such a remedy is to be found in an increased self-awareness on the part of the Church. The Church must get a clearer idea of what it really is in the mind of Jesus Christ as recorded and preserved in Sacred Scripture and in Apostolic Tradition, and interpreted and explained by the tradition of the Church under the inspiration and guidance of the Holy Spirit.

Merely to remain true to the faith is not enough. Certainly we must preserve and defend the treasure of truth and grace that we have inherited through Christian tradition. As St. Paul said, 'keep that which is committed to thy trust.' (I Tim 6:20). But neither the preservation nor the defense of the faith exhausts the duty of the Church in regard to the gifts it has been given. The very nature of the gifts which Christ has given the Church demands that they be extended to others and shared with others.[2614]

Encyclical *Mysterium Fidei, 10. (3rd September 1965)*

For We can see that some of those who are dealing with this Most Holy Mystery in speech and writing are disseminating opinions on Masses celebrated in private or on the dogma of transubstantiation that are disturbing the minds of the faithful and causing them no small measure of confusion about matters of faith, just as if it were all right for someone to take doctrine that has already been defined by the Church and consign it to oblivion or else interpret it in such a way as to weaken the genuine meaning of the words or the recognized force of the concepts involved.[2615]

Address during the last General Meeting of the Second Vatican Council. (7th December 1965)

This council hands over to posterity not only the image of the Church but also the patrimony of her doctrine and of her commandments, the 'deposit' received from Christ and meditated upon through centuries, lived and expressed now and clarified in so many of its parts, settled and arranged in its integrity. The deposit, that is, which lives on by the divine power of truth and of grace which constitutes it, and is, therefore, able to vivify anyone who receives it and nourishes with it his own human existence.[2616]

Motu Proprio, *Solemni Hac Liturgia, 1,4. (30th June 1968)*

With this solemn liturgy we end the celebration of the nineteenth centenary of the martyrdom of the holy apostles Peter and Paul, and thus close the Year of Faith. We dedicated it to the commemoration of the holy apostles in order that we might give witness to our steadfast will to be faithful to the deposit of the faith (I Tim 6:20) which they transmitted to us, and that we might strengthen our desire to live by it in the historical circumstances in which the Church finds herself in her pilgrimage in the midst of the world. […]

In making this profession, we are aware of the disquiet which agitates certain modern quarters with regard to the faith. They do not escape the influence of a world being profoundly changed, in which so many certainties are being disputed or dis-

[2614]Pope St. Paul VI [1964] Encyclical *Ecclesiam Suam,* para 26 [Online] Available at: www.vatican.va [Accessed on: 28th June 2022]
[2615]Pope St. Paul VI [1965] Encyclical *Mysterium Fidei,* para 10 [Online] Available at: www.vatican.va [Accessed on: 28th June 2022]
[2616]Pope St. Paul VI [1965] *Address during the last General Meeting of the Second Vatican Council* [Online] Available at: www.vatican.va [Accessed on: 28th June 2022]

cussed. We see even Catholics allowing themselves to be seized by a kind of passion for change and novelty. The Church, most assuredly, has always the duty to carry on the effort to study more deeply and to present, in a manner ever better adapted to successive generations, the unfathomable mysteries of God, rich for all in fruits of salvation. But at the same time the greatest care must be taken, while fulfilling the indispensable duty of research, to do no injury to the teachings of Christian doctrine. For that would be to give rise, as is unfortunately seen in these days, to disturbance and perplexity in many faithful souls.[2617]

Congregation for the Doctrine of the Faith. Declaration for safeguarding the belief in the mysteries of the Incarnation and of the Most Holy Trinity against some recent errors, 6-7. (21st February 1972)

This certainty does not prevent the Church in her awareness of the progress of human thought from considering that it is her duty to take steps to have the aforesaid mysteries continually examined by contemplation and by theological examination and to have them more fully expounded in up to date terminology. But while the necessary duty of investigation is being pursued, diligent care must be taken that these profound mysteries do not be interpreted in a meaning other than that in which "the Church has understood and understands them".

The unimpaired truth of these mysteries is of the greatest moment for the whole Revelation of Christ, because they pertain to its very core, in such a way indeed that if they are undermined, the rest of the treasure of Revelation is falsified. The truth of these same mysteries is of no less concern to the Christian way of life both because nothing so effectively manifests the charity of God, to which the whole of Christian life should be a response, as does the Incarnation of the Son of God, our Redeemer (I Jn 4, 9 f.), and also because 'through Christ, the Word made flesh, men have access to the Father in the Holy Spirit and are made partakers of the divine nature'. […]

This function of the Bishops belongs to the office divinely committed to them 'of keeping pure and whole'… 'the deposit of faith' in common with the Successor of Peter and 'of proclaiming the Gospel without ceasing'; and by reason of this same office they are bound not to permit that ministers of the word of God, deviating from the way of sound doctrine, should pass it on corrupted or incomplete. The people, committed as they are to the care of the Bishops who 'have to render account to God" for them, enjoy "the sacred and inalienable right of receiving the word of God, the whole word of God, into which the Church does not cease to penetrate ever more profoundly'.[2618]

Pope St. John XXIII: 1958 to 1963

Encyclical *Paenitentiam Agere, 15. (1st July 1962)*

Certainly, Venerable Brethren, when one views the faith which distinguishes the Church, the sacraments which nourish and perfect her, the universal laws and precepts which govern her, the unfailing glory that is hers by reason of the heroic virtue and constancy of so many of her elect, there can be no doubt that the Bride of Christ, so dear to her divine Redeemer, has always kept herself holy and unsullied.[2619]

Address on the occasion of the solemn opening of the Second Vatican Council. (11th October 1962)

The greatest concern of the Ecumenical Council is this: that the sacred deposit of Christian doctrine should be guarded and taught more efficaciously. That doctrine

---

[2617]Pope St. Paul VI [1968] Motu Proprio, *Solemni Hac Liturgia*, paras 1,4 [Online] Available at: www.vatican.va [Accessed on: 28th June 2022]

[2618]Congregation for the Doctrine of the Faith [1972] *Declaration for safeguarding the belief in the mysteries of the Incarnation and of the Most Holy Trinity against some recent errors*, paras 6-7 [Online] Available at: www.vatican.va [Accessed on: 28th June 2022]

[2619]Pope St. John XXIII [1962] Encyclical *Paenitentiam Agere*, para 15 [Online] Available at: www. vatican.va [Accessed on: 28th June 2022]

embraces the whole of man, composed as he is of body and soul. And, since he is a pilgrim on this earth, it commands him to tend always toward heaven.[2620]

Pope Ven. Pius XII: 1939 to 1958

Encyclical *Summi Pontificatus, 31. (20th October 1939)*

Many perhaps, while abandoning the teaching of Christ, were not fully conscious of being led astray by a mirage of glittering phrases, which proclaimed such estrangement as an escape from the slavery in which they were before held; nor did they then foresee the bitter consequences of bartering the truth that sets free, for error which enslaves. They did not realise that, in renouncing the infinitely wise and paternal laws of God, and the unifying and elevating doctrines of Christ's love, they were resigning themselves to the whim of a poor, fickle human wisdom; they spoke of progress, when they were going back; of being raised, when they grovelled; of arriving at man's estate, when they stooped to servility. They did not perceive the inability of all human effort to replace the law of Christ by anything equal to it; 'they became vain in their thoughts' (Rom 1:21).[2621]

Encyclical *Mystici Corporis Christi, 20. (29th June 1943)*

Through Holy Orders men are set aside and consecrated to God, to offer the Sacrifice of the Eucharistic Victim, to nourish the flock of the faithful with the Bread of Angels and the food of doctrine, to guide them in the way of God's commandments and counsels and to strengthen them with all other supernatural helps.[2622]

Encyclical *Humani Generis, 18, 21. (12th August 1950)*

And although this sacred Office of Teacher in matters of faith and morals must be the proximate and universal criterion of truth for all theologians, since to it has been entrusted by Christ Our Lord the whole deposit of faith — Sacred Scripture and divine Tradition — to be preserved, guarded and interpreted, still the duty that is incumbent on the faithful to flee also those errors which more or less approach heresy, and accordingly 'to keep also the constitutions and decrees by which such evil opinions are proscribed and forbidden by the Holy See,' is sometimes as little known as if it did not exist.

Besides, each source of divinely revealed doctrine contains so many rich treasures of truth, that they can really never be exhausted. Hence it is that theology through the study of its sacred sources remains ever fresh; on the other hand, speculation which neglects a deeper search into the deposit of faith, proves sterile, as we know from experience.[2623]

Apostolic Constitution *Munificentissimus Deus, 12. (1st November 1950)*

Certainly this teaching authority of the Church, not by any merely human effort but under the protection of the Spirit of Truth, (Jn 14:26) and therefore absolutely without error, carries out the commission entrusted to it, that of preserving the revealed truths pure and entire throughout every age, in such a way that it presents them undefiled, adding nothing to them and taking nothing away from them. For, as the Vatican Council teaches, 'the Holy Spirit was not promised to the successors of Peter in such a way that, by his revelation, they might manifest new doctrine, but so that, by his assistance, they

---

[2620]Pope St. John XXIII [1962] *Address on the occasion of the solemn opening of the Second Vatican Council* [Online] Available at: vatican2voice.org [Accessed on: 30 September 2022]

[2621]Pope Ven. Pius XII [1939] Encyclical *Summi Pontificatus*, para 31 [Online] Available at: www.vatican.va [Accessed on: 28th June 2022]

[2622]Pope Ven. Pius XII [1943] Encyclical *Mystici Corporis Christi*, para 20 [Online] Available at: www.vatican.va [Accessed on: 28th June 2022]

[2623]Pope Ven. Pius XII [1950] Encyclical *Humani Generis*, paras 18, 21 [Online] Available at: www.vatican.va [Accessed on: 28th June 2022]

might guard as sacred and might faithfully propose the revelation delivered through the apostles, or the deposit of faith.'[2624]

Pope Pius XI: 1922 to 1939

Encyclical *Mortalium Animos, 8. (6th January 1928)*

But the Only-begotten Son of God, when He commanded His representatives to teach all nations, obliged all men to give credence to whatever was made known to them by 'witnesses preordained by God,' (Acts 10:41) and also confirmed His command with this sanction: 'He that believeth and is baptized shall be saved; but he that believeth not shall be condemned.' (Mk 16:16). These two commands of Christ, which must be fulfilled, the one, namely, to teach, and the other to believe, cannot even be understood, unless the Church proposes a complete and easily understood teaching, and is immune when it thus teaches from all danger of erring. In this matter, those also turn aside from the right path, who think that the deposit of truth such laborious trouble, and with such lengthy study and discussion, that a man's life would hardly suffice to find and take possession of it; as if the most merciful God had spoken through the prophets and His Only-begotten Son merely in order that a few, and those stricken in years, should learn what He had revealed through them, and not that He might inculcate a doctrine of faith and morals, by which man should be guided through the whole course of his moral life.[2625]

Encyclical *Divini Illius Magistri, 15-17. (31st December 1929)*

And first of all education belongs preeminently to the Church, by reason of a double title in the supernatural order, conferred exclusively upon her by God Himself; absolutely superior therefore to any other title in the natural order.

The first title is founded upon the express mission and supreme authority to teach, given her by her divine Founder: 'All power is given to me in heaven and in earth. Going therefore teach ye all nations, baptizing them in the name of the Father, and of the Son, and of the Holy Ghost, teaching them to observe all things whatsoever I have commanded you, and behold I am with you all days, even to the consummation of the world.' (Mt 28:18-20). Upon this magisterial office Christ conferred infallibility, together with the command to teach His doctrine. Hence the Church 'was set by her divine Author as the pillar and ground of truth, in order to teach the divine Faith to men, and keep whole and inviolate the deposit confided to her; to direct and fashion men, in all their actions individually and socially, to purity of morals and integrity of life, in accordance with revealed doctrine.'

The second title is the supernatural motherhood, in virtue of which the Church, spotless spouse of Christ, generates, nurtures and educates souls in the divine life of grace, with her Sacraments and her doctrine.[2626]

Pope Benedict XV: 1914 to 1922

Encyclical *Ad Beatissimi Apostolorum, 24, 25. (1st November 1914)*

Such is the nature of Catholicism that it does not admit of more or less, but must be held as a whole or as a whole rejected: 'This is the Catholic faith, which unless a man believe faithfully and firmly; he cannot be saved' (Athanasian Creed). [...]

Besides, the Church demands from those who have devoted themselves to furthering her interests, something very different from the dwelling upon profitless questions; she demands that they should devote the whole of their energy to preserve the faith

[2624]Pope Ven. Pius XII [1950] Apostolic Constitution *Munificentissimus Deus*, 12 [Online] Available at: www.vatican.va [Accessed on: 28th June 2022]
[2625]Pope Pius XI [1928] Encyclical *Mortalium Animos*, para 8 [Online] Available at: www.vatican.va [Accessed on: 28th June 2022]
[2626]Pope Pius XI [1929] Encyclical *Divini Illius Magistri*, paras 15-17 [Online] Available at: www.vatican.va [Accessed on: 28th June 2022]

intact and unsullied by any breath of error, and follow most closely him whom Christ has appointed to be the guardian and interpreter of the truth. There are to be found today, and in no small numbers, men, of whom the Apostle says that: 'having itching ears, they will not endure sound doctrine: but according to their own desires they will heap up to themselves teachers, and will indeed turn away their hearing from the truth, but will be turned unto fables' (II Tim 4:34). Infatuated and carried away by a lofty idea of the human intellect, by which God's good gift has certainly made incredible progress in the study of nature, confident in their own judgment, and contemptuous of the authority of the Church, they have reached such a degree of rashness as not to hesitate to measure by the standard of their own mind even the hidden things of God and all that God has revealed to men. Hence arose the monstrous errors of 'Modernism,' which Our Predecessor rightly declared to be 'the synthesis of all heresies,' and solemnly condemned. We hereby renew that condemnation in all its fulness, Venerable Brethren, and as the plague is not yet entirely stamped out, but lurks here and there in hidden places, We exhort all to be carefully here and there in hidden places, We exhort all to be carefully on their guard against any contagion of the evil, to which we may apply the words Job used in other circumstances: 'It is a fire that devoureth even to destruction, and rooteth up all things that spring' (Job xxxi. 12). Nor do We merely desire that Catholics should shrink from the errors of Modernism, but also from the tendencies or what is called the spirit of Modernism. Those who are infected by that spirit develop a keen dislike for all that savours of antiquity and become eager searchers after novelties in everything: in the way in which they carry out religious functions, in the ruling of Catholic institutions, and even in private exercises of piety. Therefore it is Our will that the law of our forefathers should still be held sacred: 'Let there be no innovation; keep to what has been handed down.' In matters of faith that must be inviolably adhered to as the law; it may however also serve as a guide even in matters subject to change, but even in such cases the rule would hold: 'Old things, but in a new way.'[2627]

Pope St. Pius X: 1903 to 1914

Encyclical *Acerbo Nimis, 27. (15th April 1905)*

And now, Venerable Brethren, permit Us to close this letter by addressing to you these words of Moses: 'If any man be on the Lord's side, let him join with me.' We pray and entreat you to reflect on the great loss of souls due solely to ignorance of divine things. You have doubtless accomplished many useful and most praiseworthy works in your respective dioceses for the good of the flock entrusted to your care, but before all else, and with all possible zeal and diligence and care, see to it and urge on others that the knowledge of Christian doctrine pervades and imbues fully and deeply the minds of all.[2628]

Encyclical *Pascendi Dominici Gregis, 1, 13, 42. (8th September 1907)*

The office divinely committed to Us of feeding the Lord's flock has especially this duty assigned to it by Christ, namely, to guard with the greatest vigilance the deposit of the faith delivered to the saints, rejecting the profane novelties of words and oppositions of knowledge falsely so called. There has never been a time when this watchfulness of the supreme pastor was not necessary to the Catholic body; for, owing to the efforts of the enemy of the human race, there have never been lacking 'men speaking perverse things' (Acts 20:30), 'vain talkers and seducers' (Titus 1:10), 'erring and driving into error' (II Tim 3:13).

Blind that they are, and leaders of the blind, inflated with a boastful science, they have reached that pitch of folly where they pervert the eternal concept of truth and the

---

[2627]Pope Benedict XV [1914] Encyclical *Ad Beatissimi Apostolorum*, paras 24,25 [Online] Available at: www.vatican.va [Accessed on: 28th June 2022]

[2628]Pope St. Pius X [1905] Encyclical *Acerbo Nimis*, para 27 [Online] Available at: www.vatican.va [Accessed on: 28th June 2022]

true nature of the religious sentiment; with that new system of theirs they are seen to be under the sway of a blind and unchecked passion for novelty, thinking not at all of finding some solid foundation of truth, but despising the holy and apostolic traditions, they embrace other vain, futile, uncertain doctrines, condemned by the Church, on which, in the height of their vanity, they think they can rest and maintain truth itself.

They [Modernists] exercise all their ingenuity in diminishing the force and falsifying the character of tradition, so as to rob it of all its weight. But for Catholics the second Council of Nicea will always have the force of law, where it condemns those who dare, after the impious fashion of heretics, to deride the ecclesiastical traditions, to invent novelties of some kind . . . or endeavour by malice or craft to overthrow any one of the legitimate traditions of the Catholic Church; and Catholics will hold for law, also, the profession of the fourth Council of Constantinople: We therefore profess to conserve and guard the rules bequeathed to the Holy Catholic and Apostolic Church by the Holy and most illustrious Apostles, by the orthodox Councils, both general and local, and by every one of those divine interpreters the Fathers and Doctors of the Church. Wherefore the Roman Pontiffs, Pius IV. and Pius IX., ordered the insertion in the profession of faith of the following declaration: I most firmly admit and embrace the apostolic and ecclesiastical traditions and other observances and constitutions of the Church. The Modernists pass the same judgment on the most holy Fathers of the Church as they pass on tradition; decreeing, with amazing effrontery that, while personally most worthy of all veneration, they were entirely ignorant of history and criticism, for which they are only excusable on account of the time in which they lived.

Finally, the Modernists try in every way to diminish and weaken the authority of the ecclesiastical magisterium itself by sacrilegiously falsifying its origin, character, and rights, and by freely repeating the calumnies of its adversaries. To all the band of Modernists may be applied those words which Our Predecessor wrote with such pain: To bring contempt and odium on the mystic Spouse of Christ, who is the true light, the children of darkness have been wont to cast in her face before the world a stupid calumny, and perverting the meaning and force of things and words, to depict her as the friend of darkness and ignorance, and the enemy of light, science, and progress (Motu-proprio, *Ut Mysticum*, 14 March, 1891). This being so, Venerable Brethren, no wonder the Modernists vent all their gall and hatred on Catholics who sturdily fight the battles of the Church. But of all the insults they heap on them those of ignorance and obstinacy are the favourites. When an adversary rises up against them with an erudition and force that render him redoubtable, they try to make a conspiracy of silence around him to nullify the effects of his attack, while in flagrant contrast with this policy towards Catholics, they load with constant praise the writers who range themselves on their side, hailing their works, excluding novelty in every page, with choruses of applause; for them the scholarship of a writer is in direct proportion to the recklessness of his attacks on antiquity, and of his efforts to undermine tradition and the ecclesiastical magisterium; when one of their number falls under the condemnations of the Church the rest of them, to the horror of good Catholics, gather round him, heap public praise upon him, venerate him almost as a martyr to truth. The young, excited and confused by all this glamour of praise and abuse, some of them afraid of being branded as ignorant, others ambitious to be considered learned, and both classes goaded internally by curiosity and pride, often surrender and give themselves up to Modernism.[2629]

The Oath Against Modernism. (1 September 1910)

. . . I sincerely hold that the doctrine of faith was handed down to us from the apostles through the orthodox Fathers in exactly the same meaning and always in the same purport. Therefore, I entirely reject the heretical' misrepresentation that dogmas evolve and change from one meaning to another different from the one which the Church held

---

[2629]Pope St. Pius X [1907] Encyclical *Pascendi Dominici Gregis*, para 42 [Online] Available at: www. vatican.va [Accessed on: 28th June 2022]

previously. I also condemn every error according to which, in place of the divine deposit which has been given to the spouse of Christ to be carefully guarded by her, there is put a philosophical figment or product of a human conscience that has gradually been developed by human effort and will continue to develop indefinitely.[2630]

Catechism of St. Pius X. (1908)

Preliminary Lessons

Q. What is Christian Doctrine?

A. Christian doctrine is the doctrine which Jesus Christ our Lord taught us to show us the way of salvation.

Q. Is it necessary to learn the doctrine taught by Jesus Christ?

A. It certainly is necessary to learn the doctrine taught by Jesus Christ, and those who fail to do so are guilty of a grave breach of duty.

Q. Are parents and guardians bound to send their children and those dependent on them to catechism?

A. Parents and guardians are bound to see that their children And dependents learn Christian Doctrine, and they are guilty before God if they neglect this duty.

Q. From whom are we to receive and learn Christian Doctrine?

A. We are to receive and learn Christian Doctrine from the Holy Catholic Church.

Q. How are we certain that the Christian Doctrine which we receive from the Holy Catholic Church is really true?

A. We are certain that the doctrine which we receive from the Holy Catholic Church is true, because Jesus Christ, the divine Author of this doctrine, committed it through His Apostles to the Church, which He founded and made the infallible teacher of all men, promising her His divine assistance until the end of time.

Q. Are there other proofs of the truth of Christian Doctrine?

A. The truth of Christian Doctrine is also shown by the eminent sanctity of numbers who have professed it and who still profess it, by the heroic fortitude of the martyrs, by its marvellous and rapid propagation in the world, and by its perfect preservation throughout so many centuries of ceaseless and varied struggles.[2631]

Pope Leo XIII: 1878 to 1903

Encyclical *Inscrutabili Dei Consilio, 13. (21st April 1878)*

In the next place, in order that the union of hearts between their chief Pastor and the whole Catholic flock may daily be strengthened, We here call upon you, venerable brothers, with particular earnestness, and strongly urge you to kindle, with priestly zeal and pastoral care, the fire of the love of religion among the faithful entrusted to you, that their attachment to this chair of truth and justice may become closer and firmer, that they may welcome all its teachings with thorough assent of mind and will, wholly rejecting such opinion, even when most widely received, as they know to be contrary to the Church's doctrine. In this matter, the Roman Pontiffs, Our predecessors, and the last of all, Pius IX, of sacred memory, especially in the General Council of the Vatican, have not neglected, so often as there was need, to condemn widespreading errors and to smite them with the apostolic condemnation. This they did, keeping before their eyes the words of St. Paul: 'Beware lest any man cheat you by philosophy and vain deceit, according to the tradition of men, according to the elements of the

---

[2630]Pope St. Pius X [1910] *The Oath Against Modernism* [Online] Available at: www.ewtn.com [Accessed on: 30 September 2022]

[2631]*Catechism of St. Pius X* [1908] [Online] Available at: www.ewtn.com [Accessed on: 28 August 2022]

world and not according to Christ.' (Col 2:8). All such censures, We, following in the steps of Our predecessors, do confirm and renew from this apostolic seat of truth, whilst We earnestly ask of the Father of lights (James 1:17) that all the faithful, brought to thorough agreement in the like feeling and the same belief, may think and speak even as Ourselves. It is your duty, venerable brothers, sedulously to strive that the seed of heavenly doctrine be sown broadcast in the field of God, and that the teachings of the Catholic faith may be implanted early in the souls of the faithful, may strike deep root in them, and be kept free from the ruinous blight of error. The more the enemies of religion exert themselves to offer the uninformed, especially the young, such instruction as darkens the mind and corrupts morals, the more actively should we endeavour that not only a suitable and solid method of education may flourish but above all that this education be wholly in harmony with the Catholic faith....[2632]

Encyclical *Aeterni Patris, 1, 27. (4th August 1879)*

The only-begotten Son of the Eternal Father, who came on earth to bring salvation and the light of divine wisdom to men, conferred a great and wonderful blessing on the world when, about to ascend again into heaven, He commanded the Apostles to go and teach all nations and left the Church which He had founded to be the common and supreme teacher of the peoples. For men whom the truth had set free were to be preserved by the truth; nor would the fruits of heavenly doctrines by which salvation comes to men have long remained had not the Lord Christ appointed an unfailing teaching authority to train the minds to faith. And the Church built upon the promises of its own divine Author, whose charity it imitated, so faithfully followed out His commands that its constant aim and chief wish was this: to teach religion and contend forever against errors. [...]

Many are the reasons why We are so desirous of this. In the first place, then, since in the tempest that is on us the Christian faith is being constantly assailed by the machinations and craft of a certain false wisdom, all youths, but especially those who are the growing hope of the Church, should be nourished on the strong and robust food of doctrine, that so, mighty in strength and armed at all points, they may become habituated to advance the cause of religion with force and judgment, 'being ready always, according to the apostolic counsel, to satisfy every one that asketh you a reason of that hope which is in you,' and that 'they may be able to exhort in sound doctrine and to convince the gainsayers.' Many of those who, with minds alienated from the faith, hate Catholic institutions, claim reason as their sole mistress and guide. Now, We think that, apart from the supernatural help of God, nothing is better calculated to heal those minds and to bring them into favour with the Catholic faith than the solid doctrine of the Fathers and the Scholastics, who so clearly and forcibly demonstrate the firm foundations of the faith, its divine origin, its certain truth, the arguments that sustain it, the benefits it has conferred on the human race, and its perfect accord with reason, in a manner to satisfy completely minds open to persuasion, however unwilling and repugnant.[2633]

Encyclical *Satis Cognitum, 9. (29th June 1896)*

Every Revealed Truth, without Exception, Must be Accepted. The Church, founded on these principles and mindful of her office, has done nothing with greater zeal and endeavour than she has displayed in guarding the integrity of the faith. Hence she regarded as rebels and expelled from the ranks of her children all who held beliefs on any point of doctrine different from her own. The Arians, the Montanists, the Novatians, the Quartodecimans, the Eutychians, did not certainly reject all Catholic doctrine: they abandoned only a tertian portion of it. Still who does not know that they

---

[2632]Pope Leo XIII [1878] Encyclical *Inscrutabili Dei Consilio*, para 13 [Online] Available at: www.vatican.va [Accessed on: 28th June 2022]

[2633]Pope Leo XIII [1879] Encyclical *Aeterni Patris*, paras 1, 27 [Online] Available at: www.vatican.va [Accessed on: 28th June 2022]

were declared heretics and banished from the bosom of the Church? In like manner were condemned all authors of heretical tenets who followed them in subsequent ages. "There can be nothing more dangerous than those heretics who admit nearly the whole cycle of doctrine, and yet by one word, as with a drop of poison, infect the real and simple faith taught by our Lord and handed down by Apostolic tradition" (Auctor Tract. *De Fide Orthodoxa contra Arianos*).

The practice of the Church has always been the same, as is shown by the unanimous teaching of the Fathers, who were wont to hold as outside Catholic communion, and alien to the Church, whoever would recede in the least degree from any point of doctrine proposed by her authoritative Magisterium. Epiphanius, Augustine, Theodoret, drew up a long list of the heresies of their times. St. Augustine notes that other heresies may spring up, to a single one of which, should any one give his assent, he is by the very fact cut off from Catholic unity. 'No one who merely disbelieves in all (these heresies) can for that reason regard himself as a Catholic or call himself one. For there may be or may arise some other heresies, which are not set out in this work of ours, and, if any one holds to one single one of these he is not a Catholic' (S. Augustinus, *De Haeresibus*, n. 88).

The need of this divinely instituted means for the preservation of unity, about which we speak is urged by St. Paul in his epistle to the Ephesians. In this he first admonishes them to preserve with every care concord of minds: 'Solicitous to keep the unity of the Spirit in the bond of peace' (Eph 4:3, et seq.). And as souls cannot be perfectly united in charity unless minds agree in faith, he wishes all to hold the same faith: 'One Lord, one faith,' and this so perfectly one as to prevent all danger of error: 'that henceforth we be no more children, tossed to and fro, and carried about with every wind of doctrine by the wickedness of men, by cunning craftiness, by which they lie in wait to deceive' (Eph 4:14): and this he teaches is to be observed, not for a time only-'but until we all meet in the unity of faith...unto the measure of the age of the fulness of Christ'. But, in what has Christ placed the primary principle, and the means of preserving this unity? In that-'He gave some Apostles-and other some pastors and doctors, for the perfecting of the saints, for the work of the ministry, for the edifying of the body of Christ' (11-12).

Wherefore, from the very earliest times the fathers and doctors of the Church have been accustomed to follow and, with one accord to defend this rule. Origen writes: 'As often as the heretics allege the possession of the canonical scriptures, to which all Christians give unanimous assent, they seem to say: "Behold the word of truth is in the houses." But we should believe them not and abandon not the primary and ecclesiastical tradition. We should believe not otherwise than has been handed down by the tradition of the Church of God' (*Vetus Interpretatio Commentariorum in Matt.* n. 46). Irenaeus too says: 'The doctrine of the Apostles is the true faith...which is known to us through the Episcopal succession...which has reached even unto our age by the very fact that the Scriptures have been zealously guarded and fully interpreted' (*Contra Haereses*, lib. iv., cap. 33, n. 8). And Tertullian: 'It is therefore clear that all doctrine which agrees with that of the Apostolic churches — the matrices and original centres of the faith, must be looked upon as the truth, holding without hesitation that the Church received it from the Apostles, the Apostles from Christ and Christ from God....We are in communion with the Apostolic churches, and by the very fact that they agree amongst themselves we have a testimony of the truth' (*De Praescrip.*, cap. xxxi). And so Hilary: 'Christ teaching from the ship signifies that those who are outside the Church can never grasp the divine teaching; for the ship typifies the Church where the word of life is deposited and preached. Those who are outside are like sterile and worthless sand: they cannot comprehend' (*Comment. in Matt.* xiii., n. I). Rufinus praises Gregory of Nazianzum and Basil because 'they studied the text of Holy Scripture alone, and took the interpretation of its meaning not from their own inner consciousness, but from the writings and on the authority of the ancients, who in their turn, as it is clear, took their rule for understanding the meaning from the Apostolic succession' (*Hist. Eccl.*, lib. ii., cap. 9).

Wherefore, as appears from what has been said, Christ instituted in the Church a living, authoritative and permanent Magisterium, which by His own power He strengthened, by the Spirit of truth He taught, and by miracles confirmed. He willed and ordered, under the gravest penalties, that its teachings should be received as if they were His own. As often, therefore, as it is declared on the authority of this teaching that this or that is contained in the deposit of divine revelation, it must be believed by every one as true. If it could in any way be false, an evident contradiction follows; for then God Himself would be the author of error in man. 'Lord, if we be in error, we are being deceived by Thee' (Richardus de S. Victore, *De Trin.*, lib. i., cap. 2). In this wise, all cause for doubting being removed, can it be lawful for anyone to reject any one of those truths without by the very fact falling into heresy?-without separating himself from the Church?-without repudiating in one sweeping act the whole of Christian teaching? For such is the nature of faith that nothing can be more absurd than to accept some things and reject others. Faith, as the Church teaches, is 'that supernatural virtue by which, through the help of God and through the assistance of His grace, we believe what he has revealed to be true, not on account of the intrinsic truth perceived by the natural light of reason, but because of the authority of God Himself, the Revealer, who can neither deceive nor be deceived' (Conc. Vat., Sess. iii., cap. 3). If then it be certain that anything is revealed by God, and this is not believed, then nothing whatever is believed by divine Faith: for what the Apostle St. James judges to be the effect of a moral delinquency, the same is to be said of an erroneous opinion in the matter of faith. 'Whosoever shall offend in one point, is become guilty of all' (James 2:10). Nay, it applies with greater force to an erroneous opinion. For it can be said with less truth that every law is violated by one who commits a single sin, since it may be that he only virtually despises the majesty of God the Legislator. But he who dissents even in one point from divinely revealed truth absolutely rejects all faith, since he thereby refuses to honour God as the supreme truth and the formal motive of faith. 'In many things they are with me, in a few things not with me; but in those few things in which they are not with me the many things in which they are will not profit them' (S. Augustinus in *Psal.* liv., n. 19). And this indeed most deservedly; for they, who take from Christian doctrine what they please, lean on their own judgments, not on faith; and not 'bringing into captivity every understanding unto the obedience of Christ' (II Cor 10: 5), they more truly obey themselves than God. 'You, who believe what you like, believe yourselves rather than the gospel' (S. Augustinus, lib. xvii., *Contra Faustum Manichaeum*, cap. 3). […]

It is then undoubtedly the office of the church to guard Christian doctrine and to propagate it in its integrity and purity. But this is not all: the object for which the Church has been instituted is not wholly attained by the performance of this duty. For, since Jesus Christ delivered Himself up for the salvation of the human race, and to this end directed all His teaching and commands, so He ordered the Church to strive, by the truth of its doctrine, to sanctify and to save mankind.[2633]

Letter written to Cardinal James Gibbons, Archbishop of Baltimore, Testem Benevolentiae Nostrae. (22nd January 1899)

The underlying principle of these new opinions is that, in order to more easily attract those who differ from her, the Church should shape her teachings more in accord with the spirit of the age and relax some of her ancient severity and make some concessions to new opinions. Many think that these concessions should be made not only in regard to ways of living, but even in regard to doctrines which belong to the deposit of the faith. They contend that it would be opportune, in order to gain those who differ from us, to omit certain points of her teaching which are of lesser importance, and to tone down the meaning which the Church has always attached to them. It does not need many words, beloved son, to prove the falsity of these ideas if the nature and origin

[2634]Pope Leo XIII [1896] Encyclical *Satis Cognitum*, para 9 [Online] Available at: www.vatican.va [Accessed on: 28th June 2022]

of the doctrine which the Church proposes are recalled to mind. The Vatican Council says concerning this point: 'For the doctrine of faith which God has revealed has not been proposed, like a philosophical invention to be perfected by human ingenuity, but has been delivered as a divine deposit to the Spouse of Christ to be faithfully kept and infallibly declared. Hence that meaning of the sacred dogmas is perpetually to be retained which our Holy Mother, the Church, has once declared, nor is that meaning ever to be departed from under the pretense or pretext of a deeper comprehension of them' (*Constitutio de Fide Catholica*, Chapter IV).

We cannot consider as altogether blameless the silence which purposely leads to the omission or neglect of some of the principles of Christian doctrine, for all the principles come from the same Author and Master, 'the Only Begotten Son, Who is in the bosom of the Father' (Jn 1:I8). They are adapted to all times and all nations, as is clearly seen from the words of our Lord to His apostles: 'Going, therefore, teach all nations; teaching them to observe all things whatsoever I have commanded you, and behold, I am with you all days, even to the end of the world' (Mt 28:19). Concerning this point the Vatican Council says: 'All those things are to be believed with divine and catholic faith which are contained in the Word of God, written or handed down, and which the Church, either by a solemn judgment or by her ordinary and universal magisterium, proposes for belief as having been divinely revealed.' (*Const. de Fide*, Chapter III).

Let it be far from anyone's mind to suppress for any reason any doctrine that has been handed down. Such a policy would tend rather to separate Catholics from the Church than to bring in those who differ. There is nothing closer to our heart than to have those who are separated from the fold of Christ return to it, but in no other way than the way pointed out by Christ.

The rule of life laid down for Catholics is not of such a nature that it cannot accommodate itself to the exigencies of various times and places. (VOL. XXIV-13.) The Church has, guided by her Divine Master, a kind and merciful spirit, for which reason from the very beginning she has been what St. Paul said of himself: 'I became all things to all men that I might save all.'

History proves clearly that the Apostolic See, to which has been entrusted the mission not only of teaching but of governing the whole Church, has continued "in one and the same doctrine, one and the same sense, and one and the same judgment" (*Const. de Fide*, Chapter IV).[2635]

Pope Bl. Pius IX: 1846 to 1878
Encyclical *Qui Pluribus, 4, 8. (9th November 1846)*

Each of you has noticed, venerable brothers, that a very bitter and fearsome war against the whole Catholic commonwealth is being stirred up by men bound together in a lawless alliance. These men do not preserve sound doctrine, but turn their hearing from the truth. They eagerly attempt to produce from their darkness all sorts of prodigious beliefs, and then to magnify them with all their strength, and to publish them and spread them among ordinary people. We shudder indeed and suffer bitter pain when We reflect on all their outlandish errors and their many harmful methods, plots and contrivances. These men use these means to spread their hatred for truth and light. They are experienced and skillful in deceit, which they use to set in motion their plans to quench peoples' zeal for piety, justice and virtue, to corrupt morals, to cast all divine and human laws into confusion, and to weaken and even possibly overthrow the Catholic religion and civil society. For you know, venerable brothers, that these bitter enemies of the Christian name, are carried wretchedly along by some blind momentum of their mad impiety; they go so far in their rash imagining as to teach without blushing,

---

[2635]Pope Leo XIII [1899] *Letter written to Cardinal James Gibbons, Archbishop of Baltimore, Testem Benevolentiae Nostrae* [Online] Available at: www.papalencyclicals [Accessed on: 30th September2022]

openly and publicly, daring and unheard-of doctrines, thereby uttering blasphemies against God. [...]

But how many wonderful and shining proofs are ready at hand to convince the human reason in the clearest way that the religion of Christ is divine and that 'the whole principle of our doctrines has taken root from the Lord of the heavens above'; therefore nothing exists more definite, more settled or more holy than our faith, which rests on the strongest foundations.[2636]

Encyclical *Quanta Cura, 1, 6. (8th December 1864)*

With how great care and pastoral vigilance the Roman Pontiffs, our predecessors, fulfilling the duty and office committed to them by the Lord Christ Himself in the person of most Blessed Peter, Prince of the Apostles, of feeding the lambs and the sheep, have never ceased sedulously to nourish the Lord's whole flock with words of faith and with salutary doctrine, and to guard it from poisoned pastures, is thoroughly known to all, and especially to you, Venerable Brethren. And truly the same, Our Predecessors, asserters of justice, being especially anxious for the salvation of souls, had nothing ever more at heart than by their most wise Letters and Constitutions to unveil and condemn all those heresies and errors which, being adverse to our Divine Faith, to the doctrine of the Catholic Church, to purity of morals, and to the eternal salvation of men, have frequently excited violent tempests, and have miserably afflicted both Church and State. For which cause the same Our Predecessors, have, with Apostolic fortitude, constantly resisted the nefarious enterprises of wicked men, who, like raging waves of the sea foaming out their own confusion, and promising liberty whereas they are the slaves of corruption, have striven by their deceptive opinions and most pernicious writings to raze the foundations of the Catholic religion and of civil society, to remove from among men all virtue and justice, to deprave persons, and especially inexperienced youth, to lead it into the snares of error, and at length to tear it from the bosom of the Catholic Church. [...]

Amidst, therefore, such great perversity of depraved opinions, we, well remembering our Apostolic Office, and very greatly solicitous for our most holy Religion, for sound doctrine and the salvation of souls which is entrusted to us by God, and (solicitous also) for the welfare of human society itself, have thought it right again to raise up our Apostolic voice. Therefore, by our Apostolic authority, we reprobate, proscribe, and condemn all the singular and evil opinions and doctrines severally mentioned in this letter, and will and command that they be thoroughly held by all children of the Catholic Church as reprobated, proscribed and condemned.[2637]

Encyclical *Gravibus Ecclesiae, 3. (24th December 1874)*

The many evils which afflict the Church include the following: attempts to separate souls from their faith in Christ, corruption of sound doctrine and the spreading of impiety, widespread scandals, the spreading corruption of morals, and the overturning of divine and human rights which could lead to the collapse of undistorted thinking.[2638]

Pope Gregory XVI: 1831 to 1846

Encyclical *Quo Graviora, 13. (4th October 1833)*

It is your duty to protect the holy deposit of faith and sacred doctrine. It is your duty to drive every profane reform far away from the Church and to exert yourselves with your whole heart against those who try to infringe on the rights of this Holy See.

[2636]Pope Bl. Pius IX [1846] Encyclical *Qui Pluribus*, paras 4, 8 [Online] Available at: www. papalencyclicals [Accessed on: 28th June 2022]
[2637]Pope Bl. Pius IX [1864] Encyclical *Quanta Cura*, para 1 [Online] Available at: www. papalencyclicals [Accessed on: 28th June 2022]
[2638]Pope Bl. Pius IX [1874] Encyclical *Gravibus Ecclesiae*, para 3 [Online] Available at: www. papalencyclicals [Accessed on: 28th June 2022]

Therefore, draw the sword of the spirit, which is the word of God. Preach as the apostle Paul impresses upon you in the person of Timothy his disciple. Stand firm in good times and in bad. Denounce, beseech, rebuke in all patience and teaching. Nothing should deter you from throwing yourselves into every conflict for the glory of God, for the protection of the Church, and for the salvation of the souls entrusted to your care. Meditate on Him who endured a similar opposition from sinners.[2639]

Pope Pius VIII: 1829 to 1830

Encyclical *Traditi Humilitati, 3, 7. (24th May 1829)*

Although God may console Us with you, We are nonetheless sad. This is due to the numberless errors and the teachings of perverse doctrines which, no longer secretly and clandestinely but openly and vigorously, attack the Catholic faith. You know how evil men have raised the standard of revolt against religion through philosophy (of which they proclaim themselves doctors) and through empty fallacies devised according to natural reason. [...]

We want you to know of another secret society organised not so long ago for the corruption of young people who are taught in the gymnasia and the lycea. Its cunning purpose is to engage evil teachers to lead the students along the paths of Baal by teaching them un-Christian doctrines. The perpetrators know well that the students' minds and morals are molded by the precepts of the teachers. Its influence is already so persuasive that all fear of religion has been lost, all discipline of morals has been abandoned, the sanctity of pure doctrine has been contested, and the rights of the sacred and of the civil powers have been trampled upon. Nor are they ashamed of any disgraceful crime or error.[2640]

Pope Pius VII: 1800 to 1823

Encyclical *Diu Satis, 11. (15th May 1800)*

Therefore it is Our duty to help men and nations who are in distress, and to eliminate all present and threatening evils. For 'Christ has given pastors and teachers for the perfecting of the saints, for the work of the ministry, for the building up of Christ's Body, until we all come together to the unity of faith and knowledge of God's son.' (Eph 4.12). If ever anything deters, prevents, or delays any one of us from performing this task, what a disgraceful sin he will commit! Therefore, omit no watchfulness, diligence, care, and effort, in order to 'guard the deposit' of Christ's teaching whose destruction has been planned, as you know, by a great conspiracy.[2641]

Pope Clement XIV: 1769 to 1774

Encyclical *Cum Summi, 4. (12th December 1769)*

By His own laws and institutions He founded and re-enforced this holy city which is His Church. To it he entrusted, as it were, the deposit of faith in Him to be preserved piously and without contamination. He wished it to be the bulwark of His teaching and truth against which the gates of hell would never prevail. We, therefore, the overseers and guardians of this holy city, must preserve the magnificent heritage of Our laws and faith which has been passed down intact to Us; We must transmit it pure and sound to our successors. If We direct all our actions to this norm found in sacred scripture and moreover cling to the footsteps of our ancestors, We will be best equipped to avoid

---

[2639]Pope Gregory XVI [1833] Encyclical *Quo Graviora*, 13 [Online] Available at: www. papalencyclicals [Accessed on: 28th June 2022]

[2640]Pope Pius VIII [1829] Encyclical *Traditi Humilitati*, paras 3, 7 [Online] Available at: www. papalencyclicals [Accessed on: 28th June 2022]

[2641]Pope Pius VII [1800] Encyclical *Diu Satis*, para 11 [Online] Available at: www.papalencyclicals [Accessed on: 28th June 2022]

whatever could weaken and destroy the faith of the Christian people and loosen in any way the unity of the Church.[2642]

Pope Clement XIII: 1758 to 1769

Encyclical *Christianae Reipublicae, 2. (25th November 1766)*

It is principally your duty to stand as a wall so that no foundation can be laid other than the one that is already laid. Watch over the most holy deposit of faith to whose protection you committed yourselves on oath at your solemn consecration. Reveal to the faithful the wolves which are demolishing the Lord's vineyard. They should be warned not to allow themselves to be ensnared by the splendid writing of certain authors in order to halt the diffusion of error by cunning and wicked men. In a word, they should detest books which contain elements shocking to the reader; which are contrary to faith, religion, and good morals; and which lack an atmosphere of Christian virtue.[2643]

Pope Pius IV: 1559 to 1565

Bull *Iniunctum Nobis. (13th November 1564)*

I unhesitatingly accept and profess also all other things transmitted, defined, and declared by the sacred canons and the ecumenical councils, especially by the most holy Council of Trent [and by the ecumenical Vatican Council, mostly as regards the primacy of the Roman pontiff and his infallible teaching authority]. At the same time, all contrary propositions and whatever heresies have been condemned, rejected, and anathematised by the Church, I too condemn, reject, and anathematise.

This true Catholic faith, outside of which no one can be saved, which of my own accord I now profess and truly hold, I, N., do promise, vow, and swear that, with the help of God, I shall most faithfully keep and confess entire and inviolate, to my last breath, and that I shall take care, as far as it lies in my power, that it be held, taught, and preached by those under me or those over whom I have charge by virtue of my office. So help me God and these his holy Gospels.[2644]

Pope Leo X: 1513 to 1521

Bull *Exsurge Domine. (15th June 1520)*

Let all this holy Church of God, I say, arise, and with the blessed apostles intercede with almighty God to purge the errors of His sheep, to banish all heresies from the lands of the faithful, and be pleased to maintain the peace and unity of His holy Church.

For we can scarcely express, from distress and grief of mind, what has reached our ears for some time by the report of reliable men and general rumour; alas, we have even seen with our eyes and read the many diverse errors. Some of these have already been condemned by councils and the constitutions of our predecessors, and expressly contain even the heresy of the Greeks and Bohemians. Other errors are either heretical, false, scandalous, or offensive to pious ears, as seductive of simple minds, originating with false exponents of the faith who in their proud curiosity yearn for the world's glory, and contrary to the Apostle's teaching, wish to be wiser than they should be. Their talkativeness, unsupported by the authority of the Scriptures, as Jerome says, would not win credence unless they appeared to support their perverse doctrine even with divine testimonies however badly interpreted. From their sight fear of God has now passed. [...]

[2642]Pope Clement XIV [1769] Encyclical *Cum Summi*, para 4 [Online] Available at: www. papalencyclicals.net [Accessed on: 29 September 2022]

[2643]Pope Clement XIII [1766] Encyclical *Christianae Reipublicae*, para 2 [Online] Available at: www. papalencyclicals [Accessed on: 28th June 2022]

[2644]Denzinger, H [2010] *Op. cit.*, p.437, *Dz* 1869-1870

We have found that these errors or theses are not Catholic, as mentioned above, and are not to be taught, as such; but rather are against the doctrine and tradition of the Catholic Church, and against the true interpretation of the sacred Scriptures received from the Church. Now Augustine maintained that her authority had to be accepted so completely that he stated he would not have believed the Gospel unless the authority of the Catholic Church had vouched for it. For, according to these errors, or any one or several of them, it clearly follows that the Church which is guided by the Holy Spirit is in error and has always erred. This is against what Christ at his ascension promised to his disciples (as is read in the holy Gospel of Matthew): 'I will be with you to the consummation of the world'; it is against the determinations of the holy Fathers, or the express ordinances and canons of the councils and the supreme pontiffs. Failure to comply with these canons, according to the testimony of Cyprian, will be the fuel and cause of all heresy and schism.[2645]

[2645]Pope Leo X [1520] Encyclical *Exsurge Domine* [Online] Available at: www.papalencyclicals [Accessed on: 28th June 2022]

Eschatology (1) — Denial of the Necessity of Faith

Pope Francis: 2013 to 2025

D. *An atheist who does good, such as loving others at least as much as himself or getting his children baptised, will be welcomed by the Father after death.*

Eugenio Scalfari's interview with Pope Francis. La Repubblica. *(15th March 2015)*

[Pope Francis did not repudiate, contradict or demand a retraction of Eugenio Scalfari's account of their interview]

Death is a celebration and should be faced as such by those with faith in the Father who awaits them in highest heaven. Yet, what about those with no faith? The answer is that if one has loved others at least as much as himself, (possibly a little more than self) the Father will welcome him. Faith is of help but that is not the element of the one who judges — it's life itself. Sin and repentance are part of life [and include]: remorse, a sense of guilt, a desire for redemption and the abandonment of egoism.[2646]

Pastoral visit to the Roman parish of San Paolo della Croce in Corviale. (15th April 2018)

I asked Emanuele permission to say the question in public and he said yes. This is why I will say to you: 'A short time ago my father died. He was an atheist, but he had all four children baptized. He was a good man. Is Daddy in Heaven?' How nice for a son to say of his father: 'He was good'. What beautiful witness that man bore to his children, because his children will be able to say: 'He was a good man'. It is a beautiful testimony of the son who inherited the strength of his father and, also, had the courage to cry in front of us all. If that man was able to make children like that, it's true, he was a good man. He was a good man. That man did not have the gift of faith, he was not a believer, but he had his children baptized. He had a good heart. And he [Emanuele] has the doubt that his father, not having been a believer, may not be in Heaven. It is God Who says who goes to Heaven. But how is the heart of God, faced with such a father? How is it? How does it seem to you?... The heart of a father! God has a father's heart. And before a non-believer father, who was able to baptize his children and give that goodness to his children, do you think that God would be able to leave him far away? Do you think this? Out loudly, bravely...
  Everyone: No!
  Pope Francis: Does God abandon His children?
  Everyone: No!
  Pope Francis: Does God abandon His children when they are good?
  Everyone: No!
  Pope Francis: So, Emanuele, this is the answer. God was certainly proud of your father, because it is easier to be a believer and baptize your children, than to baptize them while not a believer. Certainly this pleased God greatly. Speak with your father, pray to your father.[2647]

Sacred Scripture

Matthew 10:32-33

Every one therefore that shall confess me before men, I will also confess him before my Father who is in heaven. But he that shall deny me before men, I will also deny him before my Father who is in heaven.

John 3:36

He that believeth in the Son, hath life everlasting; but he that believeth not the Son, shall not see life; but the wrath of God abideth on him.

[2646]Scalfari, E [15 March 2015] *What Pope Francis may say to Europe's Nonbelievers* [Online] rorate-caeli.blogspot.com [Accessed on: 30 September 2022]
[2647]Pope Francis [2018] *Pastoral visit to the Roman parish of San Paolo della Croce in Corviale.* [Online] Available at: press.vatican.va [Accessed on: 29 June 2022]

Romans 1:20-21

For the invisible things of him, from the creation of the world, are clearly seen, being understood by the things that are made; his eternal power also, and divinity: so that they are inexcusable. Because that, when they knew God, they have not glorified him as God, or given thanks; but became vain in their thoughts, and their foolish heart was darkened.

I Timothy 4:1

Now the Spirit manifestly saith, that in the last times some shall depart from the faith, giving heed to spirits of error, and doctrines of devils.

Colossians 2:8

Beware lest any man cheat you by philosophy, and vain deceit; according to the tradition of men according to the elements of the world, and not according to Christ.

Apocalypse 21:8

But the fearful, and unbelieving, and the abominable, and murderers, and whoremongers, and sorcerers, and idolaters, and all liars, they shall have their portion in the pool burning with fire and brimstone, which is the second death.

Psalm 13:1

The fool hath said in his heart: There is no God. They are corrupt, and are become abominable in their ways: there is none that doth good, no not one.

Ezra 8:22

The hand of our God is upon all them that seek him in goodness: and his power and strength, and wrath upon all them that forsake him.

Sacred Tradition

St. Irenaeus: c. 130 AD to c. 202

Against the Heresies. Bk. III, Chap. 22
And thus also it was that the knot of Eve's disobedience was loosed by the obedience of Mary. For what the virgin Eve had bound fast through unbelief, this did the virgin Mary set free through faith.[2648]

St. Augustine: 354 to 430

Commentary on Psalm 13
The ignorant person has said in his heart, There is no God. Ignorant indeed, for not even profane and abominable philosophers, who hold perverse and false opinions about him, have dared to say, 'There is no God.' This, therefore, is the reason why the phrase, *has said in his heart*, is used, because no one dares to say this out loud, even if he has dared to think it. *They are corrupt and have become detestable in their desires*, that is, in loving this world, and not loving God. These are the desires which corrupt the soul, and blind it so completely that the ignorant can go so far as to say in their hearts, *There is no God.* When such people are not content to acknowledge God, he gives them over to their own depraved way of thinking.[2649]

Tractate 14 (John 3:29-36)

He, then, that will not believe the Son, on the same 'the wrath of God abides.' What wrath of God? That of which the apostle says, 'We also were by nature the children of wrath, even as the rest.' (Eph 2:3). All are therefore children of wrath, because coming

---

[2648]St. Irenaeus. *Against Heresies*, Bk. III, Chap. 22, para 4 [Online] Available at: www.newadvent. org [Accessed on; 30 June 2022]
[2649]The Works of Saint Augustine: A Translation for the 21st Century [1990] *Expositions of the Psalms*. 1-32. New York: New City Press, p.175

of the curse of death. Believe on Christ, for you made mortal, that you may receive Him, the immortal; and when you shall have received His immortality, you shall no longer be mortal. He lived, you were dead; He died that you should live. He has brought us the grace of God, and has taken away the wrath of God. God has conquered death, lest death should conquer man.[2650]

City of God. Book XIV, Chap. 28
Accordingly, two cities have been formed by two loves: the earthly by the love of self, even to the contempt of God; the heavenly by the love of God, even to the contempt of self. The former, in a word, glories in itself, the latter in the Lord. For the one seeks glory from men; but the greatest glory of the other is God, the witness of conscience. The one lifts up its head in its own glory; the other says to its God, 'You are my glory, and the lifter up of mine head.'[2651]

St. John Chrysostom: c. 347 to 407

Homily *31 on the Gospel of John, 3:36*
And after that, knowing that great is the force of punishment, and that the many are not so much led by the promise of good things as by the threat of the terrible, he concludes his discourse with these words; 'He that believes in the Son has everlasting life; but he that believes not the Son shall not see life; but the wrath of God abides on him.' Here again he refers the account of punishment to the Father, for he says not 'the wrath of the Son,' (yet He is the Judge,) but sets over them the Father, desiring so the more to terrify them.[2652]

St. Thomas Aquinas: 1225 to 1274

Summa Theologiae. Secunda Secundæ Pars. Q 10. Art 3.
…unbelief is the greatest of sins. Every sin consists formally in aversion from God… Hence the more a sin severs man from God, the graver it is. Now man is more than ever separated from God by unbelief, because he has not even true knowledge of God: and by false knowledge of God, man does not approach Him, but is severed from Him. Nor is it possible for one who has a false opinion of God, to know Him in any way at all, because the object of his opinion is not God. Therefore it is clear that the sin of unbelief is greater than any sin that occurs in the perversion of morals.[2653]

St. John Henry Newman: 1801 to 1890

Sermons Preached on Various Occasions (1857)
…our Lord praised easiness of belief, and condemned hardness of belief. To be easy in believing is nothing more or less than to have been ready to inquire; to be hard of belief is nothing else but to have been loth and reluctant to inquire. Those whose faith He praised had no stronger evidence than those whose unbelief He condemned; but they had used their eyes, used their reason, exerted their minds, and persevered in inquiry till they found; while the others, whose unbelief He condemned, had heard indeed, but had let the divine seed lie by the roadside, or in the rocky soil, or among the thorns which choked it.[2654]

[2650]St. Augustine. *Tractate* 14, John 3:29-36, para 6 [Online] Available at: www.newadvent.org [Accessed on: 30 June 2022]
[2651]St. Augustine. *City of God.* Bk. XIV, Chap. 28 [Online] Available at: www.newadvent.org [Accessed on: 30 June 2022]
[2652]St. John Chrysostom. *Homily 31 on the Gospel of John,* John 3:35-36, para 1 [Online] Available at: www.newadvent.org [Accessed on; 30 June 2022]
[2653]St. Thomas Aquinas. *Summa Theologiae.* Secunda Secundæ Pars. Q 10. Art 3 [Online] Available at: www.newadvent.org [Accessed on: 30 June 2022]
[2654]St. John Henry Newman [1857] *Sermons Preached on Various Occasions.* Sermon 5 [Online] Available at: www.newmanreader.org [Accessed on: 30 June 2022]

The Magisterium of the Church

By refusing to believe in Christ, atheists exclude themselves from His salvation, putting themselves in danger of that definitive exclusion from God's love called Hell.

Council of Trent (Nineteenth Ecumenical, 1545 to 1563)

Decree on Justification, *Chap. XV. (13th January 1547)*
In opposition also to the subtle wits of certain men, who, by pleasing speeches and good words, seduce the hearts of the innocent, it is to be maintained, that the received grace of Justification is lost, not only by infidelity whereby even faith itself is lost, but also by any other mortal sin whatever, though faith be not lost; thus defending the doctrine of the divine law, which excludes from the kingdom of God not only the unbelieving....[2655]

First Vatican Council (Twentieth Ecumenical, 1869 to 1870)

Dogmatic Constitution, *Dei Filius, Canons 1-2; 5 (24th April 1870)*
If anyone denies the one true God, Creator and Lord of things visible and invisible, let him be anathema.

If anyone is not ashamed to assert that nothing exist besides matter, let him be anathema.

If anyone refuses to confess that the world and all things contained in it, the spiritual as well as the material, were in their whole substance produced by God out of nothing [...] let him be anathema.[2656]

Second Vatican Council (Twenty-First Ecumenical, 1962 to 1965)

Pastoral Constitution *Gaudium et Spes, 19; 21 (7th December 1965)*
Undeniably, those who wilfully shut out God from their hearts and try to dodge religious questions are not following the dictates of their consciences, and hence are not free of blame [...] In her loyal devotion to God and men, the Church has already repudiated and cannot cease repudiating, sorrowfully but as firmly as possible, those poisonous doctrines and actions which contradict reason and the common experience of humanity, and dethrone man from his native excellence [...] While rejecting atheism, root and branch...[2657]

Pope Benedict XVI: 2005 to 2013

Letter from Cardinal Francis Arinze, Prefect of the Sacred Congregation for Divine Worship and the Discipline of the Sacraments on the Translation of Pro Multis. (17th October 2006)
The expression 'for many,' while remaining open to the inclusion of each human person, is reflective also of the fact that this salvation is not brought about in some mechanistic way, without one's own willing or participation; rather, the believer is invited to accept in faith the gift that is being offered and to receive the supernatural life that is given to those who participate in this mystery, living it out in their lives as well so as to be numbered among the 'many' to whom the text refers.[2658]

Homily (25th March 2007)
Jesus came to tell us that he wants us all in Paradise and that hell, about which little is said in our time, exists and is eternal for those who close their hearts to his love.[2659]

[2655]Council of Trent [1547] *Decree on Justification*, Chap. 15 [Online] Available at: www.thecounciloftrent.com [Accessed on: 29 June 2022]

[2656]Denzinger, H [2010] Op. cit., p. 607, Dz 3021, 3022, 3025

[2657]Second Vatican Council [1965] Pastoral Constitution *Gaudium et Spes*, paras 19,21 [Online] Available at: www.vatican.va [Accessed on: 29 June 2022]

[2658]*Letter from Cardinal Francis Arinze, Prefect of the Sacred Congregation for Divine Worship and the Discipline of the Sacraments on the Translation of Pro Multis* [17th October 2006] [Online] Available at: www.usccb.org [Accessed on: 30 September 2022]

[2659]Pope Benedict XVI [2007] *Homily* [Online] Available at: www.vatican.va [Accessed on: 29 June 2022]

Pope St. John Paul II: 1978 to 2005

Encyclical *Dominum et Vivificantem*, 38. (18th May 1986)

For in spite of all the witness of creation and of the salvific economy inherent in it, the spirit of darkness is capable of showing God as an enemy of his own creature, and in the first place as an enemy of man, as a source of danger and threat to man. In this way Satan manages to sow in man's soul the seed of opposition to the one who 'from the beginning' would be considered as man's enemy — and not as Father. Man is challenged to become the adversary of God! The analysis of sin in its original dimension indicates that, through the influence of the 'father of lies,' throughout the history of humanity there will be a constant pressure on man to reject God, even to the point of hating him: 'Love of self to the point of contempt for God,' as St. Augustine puts it.[2660]

Summary of Catechesis on Original Sin. General Audiences. (8th September to 8th October 1986)

[The fallen angels] were the first who had claimed the power 'to know good and evil like God' and they had chosen themselves over God. And man, by yielding to the suggestion of the tempter, became the slave and accomplice of the rebellious spirits! This is perhaps the most penetrating explanation possible of the concept of that sin at the beginning of history which occurred through man's yielding to the devil's suggestion: *contemptus Dei*, the rejection of God, contempt of God, hatred of everything connected with God or that comes from God.[2661]

Catechism of the Catholic Church (8th September 1997)

Since it rejects or denies the existence of God, atheism is a sin against the virtue of religion. The imputability of this offence can be significantly diminished in virtue of the intentions and the circumstance… (2125)

We cannot be united with God unless we freely choose to love him. But we cannot love God if we sin gravely against him, against our neighbour or against ourselves…To die in mortal sin without repenting and accepting God's merciful love means remaining separated from him for ever by our own free choice. This state of definitive self-exclusion from communion with God and the blessed is called 'hell.' (1033)

Jesus often speaks of 'Gehenna' of 'the unquenchable fire' reserved for those who to the end of their lives refuse to believe and be converted, where both soul and body can be lost…(1034)

The affirmations of Sacred Scripture and the teachings of the Church on the subject of hell are a call to the responsibility incumbent upon man to make use of his freedom in view of his eternal destiny. They are at the same time an urgent call to conversion: 'Enter by the narrow gate; for the gate is wide and the way is easy, that leads to destruction, and those who enter by it are many. For the gate is narrow and the way is hard, that leads to life, and those who find it are few.' (Mt 7:13-14) (1036)[2662]

General Audience. (28th July 1999)

God is the infinitely good and merciful Father. But man, called to respond to him freely, can unfortunately choose to reject his love and forgiveness once and for all, thus separating himself for ever from joyful communion with him. It is precisely this tragic situation that Christian doctrine explains when it speaks of eternal damnation or hell. It is not a punishment imposed externally by God but a development of premises already set by people in this life. The very dimension of unhappiness which this obscure

---

[2660]Pope St. John Paul II [1986] Encyclical *Dominum et Vivificantem*, para 38 [Online] Available at: www.vatican.va [Accessed on: 30 June 2022]
[2661]Pope St. John Paul II [1986] *Summary of Catechesis on Original Sin. General Audiences.* [Online] Available at: www.ewtn.com [Accessed on: 1 July 2022]
[2662]*Catechism of the Catholic Church* [1992] [Online] Available at: http://www.scborromeo.org [Accessed on 4 July 2022]

condition brings can in a certain way be sensed in the light of some of the terrible experiences we have suffered which, as is commonly said, make life 'hell'.[2663]

Pope St. Paul VI: 1963 to 1978

Encyclical *Ecclesiam Suam, 99-100. (6th August 1964)*
Atheism a Growing Evil. Sad to say, this vast circle comprises very many people who profess no religion at all. Many, too, subscribe to atheism in one of its many different forms. They parade their godlessness openly, asserting its claims in education and politics, in the foolish and fatal belief that they are emancipating mankind from false and outworn notions about life and the world and substituting a view that is scientific and up-to-date.

This is the most serious problem of our time. We are firmly convinced that the basic propositions of atheism are utterly false and irreconcilable with the underlying principles of thought. They strike at the genuine and effective foundation for man's acceptance of a rational order in the universe, and introduce into human life a futile kind of dogmatism which far from solving life's difficulties, only degrades it and saddens it. Any social system based on these principles is doomed to utter destruction. Atheism, therefore, is not a liberating force, but a catastrophic one, for it seeks to quench the light of the living God. We shall therefore resist this growing evil with all our strength, spurred on by our great zeal for safeguarding the truth, inspired by our social duty of loyally professing Christ and His gospel, and driven on by a burning, unquenchable love, which makes man's good our constant concern. We shall resist in the invincible hope that modern man may recognize the religious ideals which the Catholic faith sets before him and feel himself drawn to seek a form of civilisation which will never fail him but will lead on to the natural and supernatural perfection of the human spirit. May the grace of God enable him to possess his temporal goods in peace and honor and to live in the assurance of acquiring those that are eternal.[2664]

Address to the 31st General Congregation of the Society of Jesus. (7th May 1965)

We gladly take this opportunity to lay serious stress, however briefly, on a matter of grave importance: We mean the fearful danger of atheism threatening human society. Needless to say it does not always show itself in the same manner but advances and spreads under many forms. Of these, the anti-God movement is clearly to be reckoned the most pernicious: not content with a thoroughgoing denial of God's existence, this violent movement against God attacks theism, aiming at the extirpation of the sense of religion and all that is good and holy. There is also philosophical atheism that denies God's existence or maintains that God is unknowable, hedonistic atheism, atheism that rejects all religious worship or honor, reckoning it superstitious, profitless and irksome to reverence and serve the Creator of us all or to obey His law. Their adherents live without Christ, having no hope of the promise, and without God in this world. This is the atheism spreading today, openly or covertly, frequently masquerading as cultural, scientific or social progress.[2665]

Pope Ven. Pius XII: 1939 to 1958

Encyclical *Anni Sacri, 3-4. (12th March 1950)*
That which seems to Us not only the greatest evil but the root of all evil is this: often the lie is substituted for the truth, and is then used as an instrument of dispute. On the part of not a few religion is passed by as a thing of no importance, and elsewhere absolutely

---

[2663]Pope St. John Paul II [28 July 1999] *General Audience Address* [Online] Available at: www. vatican.va [Accessed on: 30 June 2022]
[2664]Pope St. Paul VI [1964] Encyclical *Ecclesiam Suam,* paras 99 -100 [Online] Available at: www. vatican.va [Accessed on: 30 June 2022]
[2665]Pope St. Paul VI [1965] *Address to the 31st General Congregation of the Society of Jesus* [Online] Available at: whosoeverdesires.wordpress.com [Accessed on: 30 June 2022]

prohibited in family and social life as a remnant of ancient superstitions; public and private atheism is exalted in such a way that God and His law are being abolished, and morals no longer have any foundation. The Press also too often vulgarly reviles religious feeling, while it does not hesitate to spread the most shameful obscenities, agitating and with incalculable harm leading into vice tender childhood and betrayed youth. By means of false promises a people is deceived and provoked to hatred, rivalry and rebellion, especially when the hereditary faith, the only relief in this earthly exile, is successfully torn from its heart.[2666]

Pope Pius XI: 1922 to 1939

Encyclical *Ad Salutem, 27. (30th April 1930)*

Everyone probably is acquainted with the matchless word *De Civitate Dei*, in which with surpassing skill he [St. Augustine] traces God's guiding and ruling hand in the march of human history... In the successive steps that marked the growth of human society, his keen vision discerns and discriminates two cities, which 'two loves' had founded, 'namely, the earthly City, built by love of self even to contempt of God, the heavenly city, by love of God even to contempt of self.' Babylon is one, Jerusalem the other. The two 'are intermingled and hold a mingled course from the beginning of the human race to the end of time.' But the issue of both is not one and the same, since at long last the citizens of Jerusalem will reign with God forever, while the subjects of Babylon in company with demons will eternally expiate their crimes.[2667]

Encyclical *Caritate Christi Compulsi, 10. (3rd May 1932)*

But when We behold so much impiety, so much trampling under foot of the most holy institutions, such great destruction of immortal souls, and lastly such great contempt of the Divine Majesty, We cannot refrain, Venerable Brethren, from pouring out the most bitter sorrow by which We are oppressed, and from lifting up Our voice with all the strength of the apostolic heart, in defense of the outraged rights of God, and of the holy desires of the human soul in its absolute need of God; and We do this the more readily because these hostile hosts, raging with diabolical spirit, are not content with declamation, but are striving with all their strength to give effect to their nefarious plans as speedily as possible. Woe to the race of men if God, being treated with such contempt by the natures He has made, should leave an open course to these floods of devastation, and should use them as scourges to punish the world withal![2668]

Encyclical *Divini Redemptoris, 39-40; 72. (19th March 1937)*

We cherish the firm hope that the fanaticism with which the sons of darkness work day and night at their materialistic and atheistic propaganda will at least serve the holy purpose of stimulating the sons of light to a like and even greater zeal for the honor of the Divine Majesty. What then must be done, what remedies must be employed to defend Christ and Christian civilisation from this pernicious enemy?

But in this battle joined by the powers of darkness against the very idea of Divinity, it is Our fond hope that, besides the host which glories in the name of Christ, all those — and they comprise the overwhelming majority of mankind, — who still believe in God and pay Him homage may take a decisive part. We therefore renew the invitation extended to them five years ago in Our Encyclical Caritate Christi, invoking their loyal and hearty collaboration 'in order to ward off from mankind the great danger that threatens all alike.' Since, as We then said, 'belief in God is the unshakable foundation

---

[2666]Pope Ven. Pius XII [1950] Encyclical *Anni Sacri*, paras 3-4 [Online] Available at: www.vatican. va [Accessed on: 30 June 2022]

[2667]Pope Pius XI [1930] Encyclical *Ad Salutem*, para 27 [Online] Available at: www.papalencyclicals. net/ [Accessed on: 1 July 2022]

[2668]Pope Pius XI [1932] Encyclical *Caritate Christi Compulsi*, para 10 [Online] Available at: www. vatican.va [Accessed on: 30 June 2022]

of all social order and of all responsibility on earth, it follows that all those who do not want anarchy and terrorism ought to take energetic steps to prevent the enemies of religion from attaining the goal they have so brazenly proclaimed to the world.'[2669]

Pope St. Pius X: 1903 to 1914

Encyclical *Acerbo Nimis, 5. (15th April 1905)*
But We do maintain that the will cannot be upright nor the conduct good when the mind is shrouded in the darkness of crass ignorance. A man who walks with open eyes may, indeed, turn aside from the right path, but a blind man is in much more imminent danger of wandering away. Furthermore, there is always some hope for a reform of perverse conduct so long as the light of faith is not entirely extinguished; but if lack of faith is added to depraved morality because of ignorance, the evil hardly admits of remedy, and the road to ruin lies open.[2670]

Pope Leo XIII: 1878 to 1903

Encyclical *Humanum Genus, 1-2. (20th April, 1884)*
The race of man, after its miserable fall from God, the Creator and the Giver of heavenly gifts, 'through the envy of the devil,' separated into two diverse and opposite parts, of which the one steadfastly contends for truth and virtue, the other of those things which are contrary to virtue and to truth. The one is the kingdom of God on earth, namely, the true Church of Jesus Christ; and those who desire from their heart to be united with it, so as to gain salvation, must of necessity serve God and His only-begotten Son with their whole mind and with an entire will. The other is the kingdom of Satan, in whose possession and control are all whosoever follow the fatal example of their leader and of our first parents, those who refuse to obey the divine and eternal law, and who have many aims of their own in contempt of God, and many aims also against God.

This twofold kingdom St. Augustine keenly discerned and described after the manner of two cities, contrary in their laws because striving for contrary objects; and with a subtle brevity he expressed the efficient cause of each in these words: 'Two loves formed two cities: the love of self, reaching even to contempt of God, an earthly city; and the love of God, reaching to contempt of self, a heavenly one.' At every period of time each has been in conflict with the other, with a variety and multiplicity of weapons and of warfare, although not always with equal ardour and assault.[2671]

Encyclical *Libertas, 36-37. (20th June1888)*

To deny the existence of this authority in God, or to refuse to submit to it, means to act, not as a free man, but as one who treasonably abuses his liberty; and in such a disposition of mind the chief and deadly vice of liberalism essentially consists. The form, however, of the sin is manifold; for in more ways and degrees than one can the will depart from the obedience which is due to God or to those who share the divine power.

For, to reject the supreme authority to God, and to cast off all obedience to Him in public matters, or even in private and domestic affairs, is the greatest perversion of liberty and the worst kind of liberalism; and what We have said must be understood to apply to this alone in its fullest sense.[2672]

[2669]Pope Pius XI [1937] Encyclical *Divini Redemptoris*, para 72 [Online] Available at: www.vatican. va [Accessed on: 30 June 2022]
[2670]Pope St. Pius X [1905] Encyclical *Acerbo Nimis*, para 5 [Online] Available at: www.vatican.va [Accessed on: 30 June 2022]
[2671]Pope Leo XIII [1884] Encyclical *Humanum Genus*, para 1-2 [Online] Available at: www.vatican. va [Accessed on: 1 July 2022]
[2672]Pope Leo XIII [1888]. Encyclical *Libertas*, para 36-37 [Online] Available at: www.papalencyclicals. net/ [Accessed on: 1 July 2022]

Pope Bl. Pius IX: 1846 to 1878

Encyclical *Quanto Conficiamur Moerore, 7-8. (10th August 1863)*

…it is again necessary to mention and censure a very grave error entrapping some Catholics who believe that it is possible to arrive at eternal salvation although living in error and alienated from the true faith and Catholic unity. Such belief is certainly opposed to Catholic teaching. There are, of course, those who are struggling with invincible ignorance about our most holy religion. Sincerely observing the natural law and its precepts inscribed by God on all hearts and ready to obey God, they live honest lives and are able to attain eternal life by the efficacious virtue of divine light and grace. Because God knows, searches and clearly understands the minds, hearts, thoughts, and nature of all, his supreme kindness and clemency do not permit anyone at all who is not guilty of deliberate sin to suffer eternal punishments.

Also well known is the Catholic teaching that no one can be saved outside the Catholic Church. Eternal salvation cannot be obtained by those who oppose the authority and statements of the same Church and are stubbornly separated from the unity of the Church and also from the successor of Peter, the Roman Pontiff, to whom 'the custody of the vineyard has been committed by the Savior.' The words of Christ are clear enough: "If he refuses to listen even to the Church, let him be to you a Gentile and a tax collector' (Mt 15:17); 'He who hears you hears me, and he who rejects you, rejects me, and he who rejects me, rejects him who sent me" (Lk 10:16); 'He who does not believe will be condemned '(Mk 16:16); 'He who does not believe is already condemned' (Jn 3:18); 'He who is not with me is against me, and he who does not gather with me scatters.' (Lk 11:23). The Apostle Paul says that such persons are 'perverted and self-condemned' (Ti 3:11); the Prince of the Apostles calls them 'false teachers . . . who will secretly bring in destructive heresies, even denying the Master. . . bringing upon themselves swift destruction.' (II Pet 2:1).[2673]

Encyclical *Maximae Quidem, 2 (18th August 1864)*

The bishops are also bound to explain and to show to both the highest princes and the government the deplorable evils and damage which affect the people and the princes themselves. This is the result of the present-day contempt of religion and of the spirit of unbelief rising from the darkness under the fallacious appearance of social progress; this, of course, harms the Christian and the civil government. Everywhere it daily grows stronger; it perverts and corrupts the minds and souls of men.[2674]

Pope Gregory XVI: 1831 to 1846

Encyclical *Probe Nostis, 1. (18th September 1840)*

…holy religion is being attacked by the pollution of errors of every kind and by the unbridled rashness of renegades. At the same time heretics and unbelievers attempt by cleverness and deceit to pervert the hearts and minds of the faithful. You are aware, in shore, that practically no effort has been left untried in the attempt to overthrow the unshakeable building of the holy city. In particular, We are obliged, alas! to see the wicked enemies of truth spread everywhere unpunished. They harass religion with ridicule, the Church with insults, and Catholics with arrogance and calumny. They even enter cities and towns, establish schools of error and impiety, and publish their poisonous teachings which are adapted to secret deceit by misusing the natural sciences and recent discoveries.[2675]

[2673]Pope Bl. Pius IX [1863] Encyclical *Quanto Conficiamur Moerore*, para 7-8 [Online] Available at: www.papalencyclicals.net/ [Accessed on: 1 July 2022]

[2674]Pope Bl. Pius IX [1864] Encyclical *Maximae Quidem*, para 2 [Online] Available at: www. papalencyclicals.net/ [Accessed on: 1 July 2022]

[2675]Pope Gregory XVI [1840] Encyclical *Probe Nostis*, 1 [Online] Available at: www.papalencyclicals. net/ [Accessed on: 1 July 2022]

Encyclical *Mirari Vos, 14. (15th August 1832)*

This shameful font of indifferentism gives rise to that absurd and erroneous proposition which claims that liberty of conscience must be maintained for everyone. It spreads ruin in sacred and civil affairs, though some repeat over and over again with the greatest impudence that some advantage accrues to religion from it. 'But the death of the soul is worse than freedom of error,' as Augustine was wont to say. When all restraints are removed by which men are kept on the narrow path of truth, their nature, which is already inclined to evil, propels them to ruin. Then truly 'the bottomless pit' is open from which John saw smoke ascending which obscured the sun, and out of which locusts flew forth to devastate the earth. Thence comes transformation of minds, corruption of youths, contempt of sacred things and holy laws — in other words, a pestilence more deadly to the state than any other. Experience shows, even from earliest times, that cities renowned for wealth, dominion, and glory perished as a result of this single evil, namely immoderate freedom of opinion, license of free speech, and desire for novelty.[2676]

[2676]Pope Gregory XVI [1832] Encyclical *Mirari Vos*, para 14 [Online] Available at: www.papalencyclicals.net/ [Accessed on: 1 July 2022]

Eschatology (2) — Annihilationism

Pope Francis: 2013 to 2025

E. *Souls that die in a state of unrepented sin are not punished but are annihilated at the moment of death. There is no hell.*

Eugenio Scalfari's interview with Pope Francis. La Repubblica. (15th March 2015)

[Pope Francis did not repudiate, contradict or demand a retraction of Eugenio Scalfari's account of their interview]

If egoism overpowers and suffocates his love for others, it darkens the divine spark within him and he is self-condemned.
What happens to that lifeless soul? Will it be punished? How?
Francis' answer is very clear: there is no punishment, but the annihilation of that soul. All the others will participate in the bliss of living in the presence of the Father. The annihilated souls will not be part of that banquet; with the death of the body their journey is ended ....[2677]

Eugenio Scalfari's interview with Pope Francis. La Repubblica. (29th March 2018)

[Though the Vatican stated Scalfari's account is 'not a faithful transcription of the Holy Father's words', Pope Francis did not repudiate, contradict or demand a retraction of Eugenio Scalfari's account of their interview.]

[Scalfari:] Your Holiness, in our previous meeting you told me that our species will disappear in a certain moment and that God, still out of his creative force, will create new species. You have never spoken to me about the souls who died in sin and will go to hell to suffer it for eternity. You have however spoken to me of good souls, admitted to the contemplation of God. But what about bad souls? Where are they punished?

[Francis:] 'They are not punished, those who repent obtain the forgiveness of God and enter the rank of souls who contemplate him, but those who do not repent and cannot therefore be forgiven disappear. There is no hell, there is the disappearance of sinful souls.'[2678]

Sacred Scripture

Matthew 5: 29-30

And if thy right eye scandalize thee, pluck it out and cast it from thee. For it is expedient for thee that one of thy members should perish, rather than that thy whole body be cast into hell. And if thy right hand scandalize thee, cut it off, and cast it from thee: for it is expedient for thee that one of thy members should perish, rather than that thy whole body go into hell.

Matthew 13:49-50

So shall it be at the end of the world. The angels shall go out, and shall separate the wicked from among the just. And shall cast them into the furnace of fire: there shall be weeping and gnashing of teeth.

Matthew 25:41;46

Then he shall say to them also that shall be on his left hand: Depart from me, you cursed, into everlasting fire which was prepared for the devil and his angels.... And these shall go into everlasting punishment: but the just, into life everlasting.

Mark 9:46-47

...cast into the hell of fire: Where their worm dieth not, and the fire is not extinguished.

[2677]Scalfari, E. [15 March 2015] *What Pope Francis may say to Europe's Nonbelievers* [Online] rorate-caeli.blogspot.com [Accessed on: 2 July 2022]

[2678]New Catholic [29th March 2018] *'There is no Hell'* — *new Francis revelation to atheist journalist just in time for Good Friday* [Online] rorate-caeli.blogspot.com [Accessed on: 2 July 2022]

Luke 16: 22-25

And it came to pass, that the beggar died, and was carried by the angels into Abraham's bosom. And the rich man also died: and he was buried in hell. And lifting up his eyes when he was in torments, he saw Abraham afar off, and Lazarus in his bosom: And he cried, and said: Father Abraham, have mercy on me, and send Lazarus, that he may dip the tip of his finger in water, to cool my tongue: for I am tormented in this flame. And Abraham said to him: Son, remember that thou didst receive good things in thy lifetime, and likewise Lazarus evil things, but now he is comforted; and thou art tormented.

Romans 2:8-9

But to them that are contentious, and who obey not the truth, but give credit to iniquity, wrath and indignation. Tribulation and anguish upon every soul of man that worketh evil.

Romans 13:2

Therefore he that resisteth the power, resisteth the ordinance of God. And they that resist, purchase to themselves damnation.

II Thessalonians 1:9

Who shall suffer eternal punishment in destruction, from the face of the Lord, and from the glory of his power.

Apocalypse 20:15

...and they were judged every one according to their works. And hell and death were cast into the pool of fire. This is the second death. And whosoever was not found written in the book of life, was cast into the pool of fire.

Apocalypse 21:8

But the fearful, and unbelieving, and the abominable, and murderers, and whoremongers, and sorcerers, and idolaters, and all liars, they shall have their portion in the pool burning with fire and brimstone....

Daniel 12:2

Many of those who sleep in the dust of the earth shall awake, some to everlasting life, and some to shame and everlasting contempt. (NRSVCE)

Isaiah 66:24

...see the carcasses of the men that have transgressed against me: their worm shall not die, and their fire shall not be quenched.

Judith 16:20-21

....for the Lord almighty will take revenge on them, in the day of judgment he will visit them. For he will give fire, and worms into their flesh, that they may burn, and may feel for ever.

Sacred Tradition
Pope St. Clement: 35 to 99

The Second Epistle, Chap. 6.
For if we do the will of Christ, we shall find rest; otherwise, nothing shall deliver us from eternal punishment, if we disobey His commandments.[2679]

[2679]Pope St. Clement. *The Second Epistle of Clement*, Chap. 6 [Online] Available at: http://www.earlychristianwritings.com [Accessed on: 4 July 2022]

St. Ignatius of Antioch: c. 50 to c. 98/117

The Epistle to the Ephesians, Chap. 16.
...one who corrupts by wicked doctrine the faith of God, for which Jesus Christ was crucified! Such an one becoming defiled [in this way], shall go away into everlasting fire, and so shall every one that hearkens unto him.[2680]

St. Polycarp: 69 to 155

The Martyrdom of St. Polycarp, Chap 11
Thou threatenest me with fire which burneth for an hour, and after a little is extinguished, but art ignorant of the fire of the coming judgment and of eternal punishment, reserved for the ungodly.[2681]

St. Irenaeus: c. 130 AD to c. 202

Against Heresies, Bk. IV, Chap. 28
...the punishment of those who do not believe the Word of God, and despise His advent, and are turned away backwards, is increased; being not merely temporal, but rendered also eternal. For to whomsoever the Lord shall say, 'Depart from me, you cursed, into everlasting fire,' (Mt 25:41) these shall be damned for ever...[2682]

St. Justin Martyr: 100 to 165

Dialogue with Trypho, Chap 5
But I do not say, indeed, that all souls die; for that would truly be a piece of good fortune to the evil. What then? The souls of the pious remain in a better place, while those of the unjust and the wicked are in a worse, waiting for the time of judgement.[2683]

Tertullian: c.160 to 225

A Treatise on the Soul, Chap. 22
The soul, then, we define to be sprung from the breath of God, immortal....[2684]

St. Cyprian of Carthage: c. 246

To Demetrian, Chap. 24.
An ever burning Gehenna and a devouring punishment of lively flames will consume the condemned, and there will be no means whereby the torments can at any time have respite and end. Souls with their bodies will be reserved in infinite tortures for suffering.[2685]

St. Athanasius: c. 296 to 373

Against the Heathen, Part 2
But that the soul is made immortal is a further point in the Church's teaching which you must know [...] shall it not all the more, when separated from the body at the time appointed by God Who coupled them together, have its knowledge of immortality more clear? [...] its life continue after the death of the body, and live without ceasing by reason of God Who made it thus by His own Word, our Lord Jesus Christ. For this is the reason why the soul thinks of and bears in mind things immortal and eternal, namely,

[2680] St. Ignatius of Antioch. *The Epistle to the Ephesians*, Chap. 16 [Online] Available at: www.newadvent.org [Accessed on: 30 June 2022]
[2681] St. Polycarp. *Martyrdoms of the Church Fathers* — Saint Polycarp, Chap. 11 [Online] Available at: www.logoslibrary.org [Accessed on: 4 July 2022]
[2682] St. Irenaeus. *Against Heresies*, Bk. IV, Chap. 28 [Online] Available at: www.newadvent.org [Accessed on: 30 June 2022]
[2683] Willis, J [2002] *The Teachings of the Church Fathers.* San Francisco: Ignatius Press, p. 222
[2684] Tertullian. *A Treatise on the Soul*, Chap. 22 [Online] Available at: www.newadvent.org [Accessed on: 4 July 2022]
[2685] St. Cyprian. *To Demetrian*, Chap. 24. [Online] Available at: www.ewtn.com [Accessed on: 4 July 2022]

because it is itself immortal. And just as, the body being mortal, its senses also have mortal things as their objects, so, since the soul contemplates and beholds immortal things, it follows that it is immortal and lives forever. For ideas and thoughts about immortality never desert the soul, but abide in it, and are as it were the fuel in it which ensures its immortality.[2686]

St. Cyril of Jerusalem: c. 313 to 386

Catechetical Lecture 4, 18.

…learn further what you yourself art: that as man you are of a two-fold nature, consisting of soul and body; and that, as was said a short time ago, the same God is the Creator both of soul and body. Know also that you have a soul self-governed, the noblest work of God, made after the image of its Creator: immortal because of God that gives it immortality; a living being, rational, imperishable, because of Him that bestowed these gifts: having free power to do what it wills.[2687]

St. Gregory of Nyssa: c. 335 to c. 395

On the Soul and the Resurrection

…the Divine utterances seemed to me like mere commands compelling us to believe that the soul lasts for ever…[2688]

St. Augustine: 354 to 430

City of God, Bk. XXI, Chap. 9.

But they who make no doubt that in that future punishment both body and soul shall suffer, affirm that the body shall be burned with fire, while the soul shall be, as it were, gnawed by a worm of anguish. Though this view is more reasonable — for it is absurd to suppose that either body or soul will escape pain in the future punishment — yet, for my own part, I find it easier to understand both as referring to the body than to suppose that neither does; and I think that Scripture is silent regarding the spiritual pain of the damned, because, though not expressed, it is necessarily understood that in a body thus tormented the soul also is tortured with a fruitless repentance.[2689]

City of God, Bk. XXI, Chap. 21.

…they who desire to be rid of eternal punishment ought to abstain from arguing against God, and rather, while yet there is opportunity, obey the divine commands. Then what a fond fancy is it to suppose that eternal punishment means long continued punishment, while eternal life means life without end, since Christ in the very same passage spoke of both in similar terms in one and the same sentence, 'These shall go away into eternal punishment, but the righteous into life eternal!' (Mt 25:46) If both destinies are 'eternal,' then we must either understand both as long-continued but at last terminating, or both as endless. For they are correlative — on the one hand, punishment eternal, on the other hand, life eternal. And to say in one and the same sense, life eternal shall be endless, punishment eternal shall come to an end, is the height of absurdity. Wherefore, as the eternal life of the saints shall be endless, so too the eternal punishment of those who are doomed to it shall have no end.[2690]

[2686]St. Athanasius. *Against the Heathen,* Part 2 [Online] Available at: www.newadvent.org [Accessed on: 4 July 2022]

[2687]St. Cyril of Jerusalem. *Catechetical Lecture* 4, para 18 [Online] Available at: www.newadvent.org [Accessed on: 4 July 2022]

[2688]St. Gregory of Nyssa. *On the Soul and the Resurrection* [Online] Available at: www.newadvent.org [Accessed on: 4 July 2022]

[2689]St. Augustine. *City of God,* Bk. XXI, Chap. 9 [Online] Available at: www.newadvent.org [Accessed on: 4 July 2022]

[2690]*Ibid.,* Bk. XXI, Chap. 21

The Magisterium of the Church

Each soul is individually created by God in His image and likeness at the moment of conception with an immortal, imperishable nature that is destined for either eternal beatitude in heaven or eternal punishment in hell.

Fourth Lateran Council (Twelfth Ecumenical, 1215)

All of them will rise with their own bodies, which they now wear, so as to receive according to their deserts, whether these be good or bad; for the latter perpetual punishment with the devil, for the former eternal glory with Christ.[2691]

Second Council of Lyons (Fourteenth Ecumenical, 1274)

Fourth Session, The Profession of Faith *of Emperor Michael to Pope Gregory X*
As for the souls of those who die in mortal sin or with original sin only, they go down immediately to hell, to be punished, with different punishments.[2692]

Council of Florence (Seventeenth Ecumenical, 1431 to 1449)

Sixth Session. (6th July 1439)
But the souls of those who depart this life in actual mortal sin, or in original sin alone, go down straightaway to hell to be punished, but with unequal pains.[2693]

Fifth Lateran Council (Eighteenth Ecumenical, 1512 to 1517)

Eighth Session. (19th December 1513)
Consequently, since in our days (which we endure with sorrow) the sower of cockle, the ancient enemy of the human race, has dared to scatter and multiply in the Lord's field some extremely pernicious errors, which have always been rejected by the faithful, especially on the nature of the rational soul, with the claim that it is mortal, or only one among all human beings, and since some, playing the philosopher without due care, assert that this proposition is true at least according to philosophy, it is our desire to apply suitable remedies against this infection and, with the approval of the sacred council, we condemn and reject all those who insist that the intellectual soul is mortal, or that it is only one among all human beings, and those who suggest doubts on this topic. For the soul not only truly exists of itself and essentially as the form of the human body, as is said in the canon of our predecessor of happy memory, pope Clement V, promulgated in the general council of Vienne, but it is also immortal. and further, for the enormous number of bodies into which it is infused individually, it can and ought to be and is multiplied. This is clearly established from the gospel when the Lord says, They cannot kill the soul; and in another place, Whoever hates his life in this world, will keep it for eternal life and when he promises eternal rewards and eternal punishments to those who will be judged according to the merits of their life; otherwise, the incarnation and other mysteries of Christ would be of no benefit to us, nor would resurrection be something to look forward to, and the saints and the just would be (as the Apostle says) the most miserable of all people.[2694]

Second Vatican Council (Twenty-First Ecumenical, 1962 to 1965)

Dogmatic Constitution, *Lumen Gentium, 48. (21st November 1964)*
…at the end of the world 'they who have done good shall come forth unto resurrection of life; but those who have done evil unto resurrection of judgment' (Jn 5:29; Mt 25:46).[2695]

[2691]Fourth Lateran Council: 1215. [Online] Available at: www.papalencyclicals.net/ [Accessed on: 2 July 2022]
[2692]Denzinger, H [2010] p. 283, Dz 858
[2693]Tanner, N [1990] *Council of Basel-Ferrara-Florence,* 1431-49 A.D.[Online] Available at: www.papalencyclicals.net [Accessed on: 1 October 2022]
[2694]Tanner, N [1990] *Fifth Lateran Council 1512-17 A.D.* [Online] Available at: www.papalencyclicals.net [Accessed on: 1 October 2022]
[2695]Second Vatican Council [1964] Dogmatic Constitution, *Lumen Gentium,* para 48 [Online] Available at: www.vatican.va [Accessed on: 2 July 2022]

Pope Benedict XVI: 2005 to 2013

Compendium of the Catechism of the Catholic Church. (28th June 2005)
212. In what does hell consist?
Hell consists in the eternal damnation of those who die in mortal sin through their own free choice. The principal suffering of hell is eternal separation from God in whom alone we can have the life and happiness for which we were created and for which we long. Christ proclaimed this reality with the words, 'Depart from me, you cursed, into the eternal fire' (Mt 25:41).[2696]

Encyclical *Spe Salvi, 44-45. (30th November 2007)*

In the parable of the rich man and Lazarus (cf. Lk 16:19-31), Jesus admonishes us through the image of a soul destroyed by arrogance and opulence, who has created an impassable chasm between himself and the poor man; the chasm of being trapped within material pleasures; the chasm of forgetting the other, of incapacity to love, which then becomes a burning and unquenchable thirst. We must note that in this parable Jesus is not referring to the final destiny after the Last Judgement, but is taking up a notion found, *inter alia*, in early Judaism, namely that of an intermediate state between death and resurrection, a state in which the final sentence is yet to be pronounced.

This early Jewish idea of an intermediate state includes the view that these souls are not simply in a sort of temporary custody but, as the parable of the rich man illustrates, are already being punished or are experiencing a provisional form of bliss.[2697]

Address at Meeting with the Parish Priests and the Clergy of the Diocese of Rome.

(7th February 2008)
…perhaps those who have destroyed themselves in this way, who are for ever unredeemable, who no longer possess any elements on which God's love can rest, who no longer have a minimal capacity for loving, may not be so numerous. This would be Hell.[2698]

Homily during visit to the Roman Parish of St. Felicity & her Children, Martyrs. (25th March 2007)

Jesus came to tell us that he wants us all in Paradise and that hell, about which little is said in our time, exists and is eternal for those who close their hearts to his love.[2699]

Pope St. John Paul II: 1978 to 2005

Letter of the Congregation for the Doctrine of the Faith to All Bishops Recentiores Episcoporum Synodi, 7. (17th May 1979)
In fidelity to the New Testament and tradition, the Church believes in the happiness of the just who will one day be with Christ. She believes that there will be eternal punishment for the sinner, who will deprived of the sight of God, and that this punishment will have repercussion on the whole being of the sinner.[2700]

Apostolic Exhortation *Familiaris Consortio, 11. (22nd November 1981)*

As an incarnate spirit, that is a soul which expresses itself in a body and a body informed by an immortal spirit, man is called to love in his unified totality.[2701]

[2696]Pope Benedict XVI [2005] *Compendium of the Catechism of the Catholic Church.* [Online] Available at: www.vatican.va [Accessed on: 1 October 2022]
[2697]Pope Benedict XVI [2007] Encyclical *Spe Salvi*, paras 44-45 [Online] Available at: www.vatican.va [Accessed on: 4 July 2022]
[2698]Pope Benedict XVI [2008] *Address at Meeting with the Parish Priests and the Clergy of the Diocese of Rome* [Online] Available at: www.vatican.va [Accessed on: 4 July 2022]
[2699]Pope Benedict XVI [2007] *Homily during visit to the Roman Parish of St. Felicity & her Children, Martyrs* [Online] Available at: www.vatican.va [Accessed on: 4 July 2022]
[2700]Denzinger, H [2010] p. 1027-1028, *Dz* 4657
[2701]Pope St. John Paul II [1981] Apostolic Exhortation *Familiaris Consortio*, para 11 [Online] Available at: www.vatican.va [Accessed on: 4 July 2022]

Encyclical *Veritatis Splendor, 48. (6th August 1993)*

The spiritual and immortal soul is the principle of unity of the human being, whereby it exists as a whole — *corpore et anima unus* — as a person.[2702]

Catechism of the Catholic Church. (1992)

The Church teaches that every spiritual soul is created immediately by God — it is not 'produced' by the parents — and also that it is immortal: it does not perish when it separates from the body at death, and it will be reunited with the body at the final Resurrection. (366).

The teaching of the Church affirms the existence of hell and its eternity. Immediately after death the souls of those who die in a state of mortal sin descend into hell, where they suffer the punishments of hell, 'eternal fire.' The chief punishment of hell is eternal separation from God, in whom alone man can possess the life and happiness for which he was created and for which he longs. (1035).[2703]

Encyclical *Evangelium Vitae, 43. (25th March 1995)*

In procreation therefore, through the communication of life from parents to child, God's own image and likeness is transmitted, thanks to the creation of the immortal soul.[2704]

General Audience Address, 1; 2; 3. (28th July 1999)

God is the infinitely good and merciful Father. But man, called to respond to him freely, can unfortunately choose to reject his love and forgiveness once and for all, thus separating himself for ever from joyful communion with him. It is precisely this tragic situation that Christian doctrine explains when it speaks of eternal damnation or hell. It is not a punishment imposed externally by God but a development of premises already set by people in this life. The very dimension of unhappiness which this obscure condition brings can in a certain way be sensed in the light of some of the terrible experiences we have suffered which, as is commonly said, make life 'hell'.

In a theological sense however, hell is something else: it is the ultimate consequence of sin itself, which turns against the person who committed it. It is the state of those who definitively reject the Father's mercy, even at the last moment of their life. […]

Redemption nevertheless remains an offer of salvation which it is up to people to accept freely. This is why they will all be judged 'by what they [have done]' (Rev 20:13). By using images, the New Testament presents the place destined for evildoers as a fiery furnace, where people will 'weep and gnash their teeth' (Mt 13:42; cf. 25:30, 41), or like Gehenna with its 'unquenchable fire' (Mk 9:43). All this is narrated in the parable of the rich man, which explains that hell is a place of eternal suffering, with no possibility of return, nor of the alleviation of pain (cf. Lk 16:19-31).

'Eternal damnation', therefore, is not attributed to God's initiative because in his merciful love he can only desire the salvation of the beings he created. In reality, it is the creature who closes himself to his love. Damnation consists precisely in definitive separation from God, freely chosen by the human person and confirmed with death that seals his choice for ever. God's judgement ratifies this state.[2705]

Pope St. Paul VI: 1963 to 1978

Apostolic Constitution, *Indulgentiarum Doctrina, Chap.1, 2. (1st January 1967)*

It is a divinely revealed truth that sins bring punishments inflicted by God's sanctity and justice. These must be expiated either on this earth through the sorrows, miseries

---

[2702]Pope St. John Paul II [1993] Encyclical *Veritatis Splendor*, para 48 [Online] Available at: www.vatican.va [Accessed on: 4 July 2022]

[2703]*Catechism of the Catholic Church* [1992] [Online] Available at: http://www.scborromeo.org [Accessed on 4 July 2022]

[2704]Pope St. John Paul II [1995] Encyclical *Evangelium Vitae*, para 43 [Online] Available at: www.vatican.va [Accessed on: 1 October 2022]

[2705]Pope St. John Paul II [1999] *General Audience Address*, paras 1-2, 3 [Online] Available at: www.vatican.va [Accessed on: 1 October 2022]

and calamities of this life and above all through death, (Gen 3:16-19) or else in the life beyond through fire and torments or 'purifying' punishments. (Cf. Mt 25:41-42; see also Mk 9:42-43; Jn 5:28-29; Rom 2:9; Gal 6:6-8.) Therefore it has always been the conviction of the faithful that the paths of evil are fraught with many stumbling blocks and bring adversities, bitterness and harm to those who follow them.[2706]

Motu Proprio, *Solemni Hac Liturgia, 8. (30th June 1968)*

We believe in one only God, Father, Son and Holy Spirit, creator of things visible such as this world in which our transient life passes, of things invisible such as the pure spirits which are also called angels, and creator in each man of his spiritual and immortal soul.[2707]

Pope St. John XXIII: 1958 to 1963

Encyclical *Sacerdotii Nostri Primordia, 92. (1st August 1959)*
But the sufferings of souls who have remained attached to their sins in hell did not add to the strength and vigour of his own sorrow and words as much as did the anguish he felt at the fact that divine love had been carelessly neglected or violated by some offence. This stubbornness in sin and ungrateful disregard for God's great goodness made rivers of tears flow from his eyes. 'My friend' — he said — 'I am weeping because you are not.'[2708]

Pope Ven. Pius XII: 1939 to 1958

Encyclical *Summi Pontificatus, 38 (20th October 1939)*
…in the unity of nature which in every man is equally composed of material body and spiritual, immortal soul.…[2709]

Encyclical *Mystici Corporis Christi, 61. (29th June 1943)*

And thus — to return to Our theme — as the Son of the Eternal Father came down from heaven for the salvation of us all, He likewise established the body of the Church and enriched it with the divine Spirit to ensure that immortal souls should attain eternal happiness.…[2710]

Encyclical *Mediator Dei, 73. (20th November 1947)*

Certainly, no one was better fitted to make satisfaction to Almighty God for all the sins of men than was Christ. Therefore, He desired to be immolated upon the cross 'as a propitiation for our sins, not for ours only but also for those of the whole world' (I Jn 2:2) and likewise He daily offers Himself upon our altars for our redemption, that we may be rescued from eternal damnation and admitted into the company of the elect.[2711]

Pope Pius XI: 1922 to 1939

Encyclical *Divini Redemptoris, 27. (19th March 1937)*
Man has a spiritual and immortal soul. He is a person, marvellously endowed by his Creator with gifts of body and mind. He is a true 'microcosm,' as the ancients said, a

---

[2706]Pope St. Paul VI [1968] Apostolic Constitution, *Indulgentiarum Doctrina,* Chap. 1-2 [Online] Available at: www.vatican.va [Accessed on: 1 October 2022]
[2707]Pope St. Paul VI [1968] Motu Proprio, *Solemni Hac Liturgia,* para 8 [Online] Available at: www. vatican.va [Accessed on: 1 October 2022]
[2708]Pope St. John XXIII [1959] Encyclical *Sacerdotii Nostri Primordia,* para 92 [Online] Available at: www.vatican.va [Accessed on: 1 October 2022]
[2709]Pope Ven. Pius XII [1939] Encyclical *Summi Pontificatus,* para 38 [Online] Available at: www. vatican.va [Accessed on: 1 October 2022]
[2710]Pope Ven. Pius XII [1943] Encyclical *Mystici Corporis Christi,* para 61 [Online] Available at: www.vatican.va [Accessed on: 1 October 2022]
[2711]Pope Ven. Pius XII [1947] Encyclical *Mediator Dei,* para 73 [Online] Available at: www.vatican. va [Accessed on: 1 October 2022]

world in miniature, with a value far surpassing that of the vast inanimate cosmos. God alone is his last end, in this life and the next.[2712]

Pope Benedict XV: 1914 to 1922

Encyclical *Ad Beatissimi Apostolorum, 10. (1st November 1914)*
From which principle the Apostle of the Gentiles infers that he who contumaciously resists the legitimate exercise of human authority, resists God and is preparing for himself eternal punishment: 'Therefore he that resisteth the power, resisteth the ordinance of God, and they that resist, purchase to themselves damnation' (Rom 13:2).[2713]

Encyclical *Humani Generis Redemptionem, 19. (15th June 1917)*

Therefore all Christ's doctrines and commands, even the sterner ones, were so proclaimed by St. Paul that he did not restrict, gloss over or tone down what Christ taught regarding humility, self-denial, chastity, contempt of the world, obedience, forgiveness of enemies, and the like, nor was he afraid to tell his hearers that they had to make a choice between the service of God and the service of Belial, for they could not serve both, that when they leave this world, a dread judgment awaits them; that they cannot bargain with God; they may hope for life everlasting if they keep His entire law, but if they neglect their duty and indulge their passions, they will have nothing to expect but eternal fire.[2714]

Encyclical *In Praeclara Summorum, on Dante, 4. (30th April 1921)*

Therefore the divine poet depicted the triple life of souls as he imagined it in a such way as to illuminate with the light of the true doctrine of the faith the condemnation of the impious, the purgation of the good spirits and the eternal happiness of the blessed before the final judgment.[2715]

Pope St. Pius X: 1903 to 1914

Encyclical *Averbo Nimis, 2. (15th April 1905)*
And so Our Predecessor, Benedict XIV, had just cause to write: 'We declare that a great number of those who are condemned to eternal punishment suffer that everlasting calamity because of ignorance of those mysteries of faith which must be known and believed in order to be numbered among the elect.' (*Instit.*, 27:18).[2716]

Encyclical *Pieni l'Animo, 8. (28th July 1906)*
Let the subject of their sermons be that which the Divine Savior indicated when He said: 'Preach the gospel' (Mk 16:15.). . . 'teaching them to observe all that I commanded you.' (Mt 28:20) Or, according to the Council of Trent, 'announcing to them the vices they should avoid and the virtues they should follow in order to escape eternal punishment and attain heavenly glory.'(Sess. V, c. 2, *De Reform.*)[2717]

[2712]Pope Pius XI [1937] Encyclical *Divini Redemptoris*, para 27 [Online] Available at: www.vatican.va [Accessed on: 1 October 2022]
[2713]Pope Benedict XV [1914] Encyclical *Ad Beatissimi Apostolorum*, para 10 [Online] Available at: www.vatican.va [Accessed on: 1 October 2022]
[2714]Pope Benedict XV [1917] Encyclical *Humani Generis Redemptionem*, para 19 [Online] Available at: www.vatican.va [Accessed on: 1 October 2022]
[2715]Pope Benedict XV [1921] Encyclical *In Praeclara Summorum*, para 4 [Online] Available at: www.vatican.va [Accessed on: 1 October 2022]
[2716]Pope St. Pius X [1905] Encyclical *Averbo Nimis*, para 2 [Online] Available at: www.vatican.va [Accessed on: 1 October 2022]
[2717]Pope St. Pius X [1906] Encyclical *Pieni l'Animo*, para 8 [Online] Available at: www.vatican.va [Accessed on: 1 October 2022]

Catechism of Pope St. Pius X. (1908)

The Twelfth Article of the Creed

1 Q. What are we taught by the Last Article: Life Everlasting?

A. The Last Article of the Creed teaches us that, after the present life there is another life, eternally happy for the elect in heaven, or eternally miserable for the damned in hell.

On Angels

21 Q. Why do they [demons] tempt us?

A. The demons tempt us because of the envy they bear us, which makes them desire our eternal damnation....

The Seventh Petition of the Our Father

39 Q. What do we ask in the Seventh Petition: But deliver us from evil?

A. In the Seventh Petition: But deliver us from evil, we ask God to free us from evils, past, present, and future, and particularly from the greatest of all evils which is sin, and from eternal damnation, which is its penalty.

The Dispositions necessary to Receive Holy Communion worthily

37 Q. Does he who goes to Communion in mortal sin receive Jesus Christ?

A. He who goes to Communion in mortal sin receives Jesus Christ but not His grace; moreover, he commits a sacrilege and renders himself deserving of sentence of damnation.[2718]

Pope Leo XIII: 1878 to 1903

Encyclical *Libertas, 4. (20th June 1888)*

As the Catholic Church declares in the strongest terms the simplicity, spirituality, and immortality of the soul, so with unequalled constancy and publicity she ever also asserts its freedom.[2719]

Pope Bl. Pius IX: 1846 to 1878

Encyclical *Qui Pluribus, para 26. (9th November 1846)*

They should explain precisely the particular duties of individuals, frighten them from vice, and inspire them with a love of piety. In this way the faithful will avoid all vices and pursue virtues, and so, will be able to escape eternal punishment and gain heavenly glory.[2720]

Encyclical *Quanto Conficiamur Moerore, 7. (10th August 1863)*

Because God knows, searches and clearly understands the minds, hearts, thoughts, and nature of all, his supreme kindness and clemency do not permit anyone at all who is not guilty of deliberate sin to suffer eternal punishments.[2721]

Pope Leo XII: 1823 to 1829

Encyclical *Charitate Christi, 3. (25th December 1825)*

Implant in the minds of the people a salutary fear; dwell on the severity of the impending divine judgment and the agony of the punishments prepared for those who die in sin.[2722]

[2718]Pope St. Pius X [1908] *Catechism of Pope St. Pius X* [Online] Available at: www.ewtn.com [Accessed on: 7 July 2022]

[2719]Pope Leo XIII [1888] Encyclical *Libertas*, para 4 [Online] Available at: www.vatican.va [Accessed on: 1 October 2022]

[2720]Pope Bl. Pius IX [1846] Encyclical *Qui Pluribus*, para 26 [Online] Available at: www.papalencyclicals.net [Accessed on: 4 July 2022]

[2721]Pope Bl. Pius IX [1863] Encyclical *Quanto Conficiamur Moerore*, para 7 [Online] Available at: www.papalencyclicals.net [Accessed on: 4 July 2022]

[2722]Pope Leo XII [1825] Encyclical *Charitate Christi*, para 3 [Online] Available at: www.papalencyclicals.net [Accessed on: 4 July 2022]

Pope St. Pius V: 1566 to 1572

The Roman Catechism: The Catechism of the Council of Trent. (1556)

Article V: 'He descended into Hell, the third day He rose again from the dead.'

…that most loathsome and dark prison in which the souls of the damned are tormented with the unclean spirits in eternal and inextinguishable fire. This place is called Gehenna, the bottomless pit, and is hell strictly so called.[2723]

Pope Clement VI: 1342 to 1352

Letter *Super Quibusdam, to the Mekhithar, Catholicos of the Armenians. (29th September 1351)*

The souls of those departing in mortal sin descend into hell.[2724]

Pope Benedict XII: 1334 to 1342

Constitution *Benedictus Dei. (29th January 1336)*

Moreover we define that according to the general disposition of God, the souls of those who die in actual mortal sin go down into hell immediately after death and there suffer the pain of hell. Nevertheless, on the day of judgment all men will appear with their bodies 'before the judgment seat of Christ' to give an account of their personal deeds, 'so that each one may receive good or evil, according to what he has done in the body' (II Cor 5:10).[2725]

Pope John XXII: 1316 to 1334

Letter *Nequaquam Sine Dolore to the Armenians. (21st November 1321)*

The souls, however, of those who die in mortal sin or with original sin only descend immediately into hell; to be punished, with different pains in different places.[2726]

Pope Leo IV: 847 to 855

Synod of Valence, Can. 2. (8th January 855)

…that the wicked have known that through their own malice they would do evil deeds and that through his justice they would be condemned with eternal punishment….[2727]

Pope Pelagius I: 556 to 561

Letter *Humani Generis to King Childebert I. (3rd February 557)*

…the wicked, however, remaining by their own choice as 'vessels of wrath fit for destruction' [Rom 9:22], who either did not know the way of the Lord or, knowing it, abandoned it when seduced by various transgressions, he will hand over by a most just judgement to the punishment of the eternal and inextinguishable fire, so that they may burn without end.[2728]

[2723]Pope St. Pius V [1556] *The Roman Catechism: The Catechism of the Council of Trent* [Online] Available at: http://www.clerus.org [Accessed on: 1 October 2022]

[2724]Denzinger, H [2010] p. 312, *Dz* 1075

[2725]Pope Benedict XII [1336] *Constitution Benedictus Dei* [Online] Available at: www.papalencyclicals. net [Accessed on: 1 October 2022]

[2726]Denzinger, H [2010] *Op. cit.,* p. 294, Dz 926

[2727]*Ibid.,* p.215, *Dz* 626

[2728]*Ibid,* p. 155, *Dz* 443

Evangelisation

Pope Francis: 2013 to 2025

F. *It is wrong to convince others, especially non-Catholic Christians, to convert to the Catholic Faith. All such efforts to convince others of the truth of Christianity in order to bring about their conversion are to be condemned as proselytism. The last thing one should do is seek to convince a Jew or Muslim to convert to Christianity. Christians living in non-Christian countries should not engage in arguments, disputes or seek to impose doctrines in order to convince others to convert, but instead they should seek to help them become more fully themselves as non-Christians.*

Message for the Feast of Saint Cajetan. (7th August 2013)
Am I going to go out to convince someone to become a Catholic? No, no, no! You are going to meet with him, he is your brother! That's enough![2729]

Address at meeting with priests, religious, seminarians and pastoral workers during apostolic visitation to Georgia and Azerbaijan. (1st October 2016)
But what should I do with a friend, neighbour, an Orthodox person? Be open, be a friend. 'But should I make efforts to convert him or her?' There is a very grave sin against ecumenism: proselytism. We should never proselytise the Orthodox![2730]

Dialogue with students of the Pilo Albertelli State High School, Rome. (20th December 2019)
It didn't occur to me and it doesn't have to be like saying to a boy or a girl: 'You are Jewish, you are Muslim: come, be converted!' [...]The first is all. In front of an unbeliever the last thing I have to do is try to convince him. Never. The last thing I have to do is speak.[2731]

Address to the Christians of Morocco. (31st March 2019)
...trying to convert people to one's own belief 'always leads to an impasse,'[2732]

Conversation with Jesuits in Mozambique. (5th September 2019)
Today I felt a certain bitterness after a meeting with young people. A woman approached me with a young man and a young woman. I was told they were part of a slightly fundamentalist movement. She said to me in perfect Spanish: 'Your Holiness, I am from South Africa. This boy was a Hindu and converted to Catholicism. This girl was Anglican and converted to Catholicism.' But she told me in a triumphant way, as though she was showing off a hunting trophy. I felt uncomfortable and said to her, 'Madam, evangelization yes, proselytism no.'

What I mean is that evangelization is free! Proselytism, on the other hand, makes you lose your freedom. Proselytism is incapable of creating a religious path in freedom. It always sees people being subjugated in one way or another. In evangelization the protagonist is God, in proselytism it is the I.

Of course, there are many forms of proselytism. The one practiced by soccer teams, acquiring fans, is all right, obviously! And then it is clear that there are those forms of proselytism for commerce and business, for political parties. Proselytism is widespread, we know that. But it doesn't have to be the case with us. We must evangelize, which is very different from proselytizing.

[2729]Pope Francis [2013] *Message for the Feast of St. Cajetan* [Online] Available at: www.vatican.va [Accessed on: 3rd October 2022]
[2730]Pope Francis [2016] *Address at meeting with priests, religious, seminarians and pastoral workers during apostolic visitation to Georgia and Azerbaijan* [Online] Available at: www.vatican.va [Accessed on: 5 July 2022]
[2731]Prestigiacomo, A [2019] *Pope Francis Tells Students How Not To Convert Unbelievers.* [Online] Available at: www.dailywire.com [Accessed on: 5 July 2022]
[2732]Agence France-Presse [2019] *Pope Francis urges Moroccan Christians against converting others* [Online] Available at: www.telegraph.co.uk [Accessed on: 5 July 2022]

St. Francis of Assisi told his friars: 'Go out to the world, evangelize. And, if necessary, use words, too.' Evangelization is essentially witness. Proselytizing is convincing, but it is all about membership and takes your freedom away.[2733]

Encyclical *Fratelli Tutti, 3-4. (3rd October 2020)*
[*Pope Francis misrepresents St. Francis of Assisi's approach to the evangelisation of 'Saracens and other nonbelievers' through a partial quotation of the Early Rule that omits the importance St. Francis gave to proclaiming to Muslims the doctrine of the Most Holy Trinity, Jesus as the Redeemer and Savior, and the necessity of Baptism*][2734]

Unconcerned for the hardships and dangers involved, Francis went to meet the Sultan with the same attitude that he instilled in his disciples: if they found themselves 'among the Saracens and other nonbelievers', without renouncing their own identity they were not to 'engage in arguments or disputes, but to be subject to every human creature for God's sake'. (*Early Rule*, Chap. 16, 6). In the context of the times, this was an extraordinary recommendation. We are impressed that some eight hundred years ago Saint Francis urged that all forms of hostility or conflict be avoided and that a humble and fraternal 'subjection' be shown to those who did not share his faith. Francis did not wage a war of words aimed at imposing doctrines; he simply spread the love of God. In this way, he became a father to all and inspired the vision of a fraternal society. Indeed, 'only the man who approaches others, not to draw them into his own life, but to help them become ever more fully themselves, can truly be called a father'.[2735]

Sacred Scripture

Matthew 28:18-20
But Jesus came near and spoke to them; All authority in heaven and on earth, he said, has been given to me, you, therefore, must go out, making disciples of all nations, and baptizing them in the name of the Father, and of the Son, and of the Holy Ghost, teaching them to observe all the commandments which I have given you.

Matthew 12: 30
He that is not with me, is against me: and he that gathereth not with me, scattereth.

Luke 14:23
And the Lord said to the servant: Go out into the highways and hedges, and compel them to come in, that my house may be filled.

Acts of the Apostles 2:37-38; 40-41
Now when they had heard these things, they had compunction in their heart, and said to Peter, and to the rest of the apostles: What shall we do, men and brethren? But Peter said to them: Do penance, and be baptized every one of you in the name of Jesus Christ,

---

[2733]Spadaro, A. [2019] '*The Sovereignty of the People of God': The Pontiff meets the Jesuits of Mozambique and Madagascar* [Online] Available at www.laciviltacattolica.com [Accessed on: 5 July 2022]

[2734] As for the brothers who go, they can live spiritually among [the Saracens and non believers] in two ways. One way is not to engage in arguments or disputes, but to be subject to every human creature for God's sake (I Pet 2:13) and to acknowledge that they are Christians. Another way is to proclaim the word of God when they see that it pleases the Lord, so that they believe in the all-powerful God — Father, and Son, and Holy Spirit — the Creator of all, in the Son Who is the Redeemer and Savior, and that they be baptised and become Christians; *because whoever has not been born again of water and the Holy Spirit cannot enter into the kingdom of God* (cf. Jn 3:5). They can say to [the Saracens] and to others these and other things which will have pleased the Lord, for the Lord says in the Gospel: *Everyone who acknowledges me before men I will also acknowledge before my Father Who is in heaven* (Mt 10:32). And: *Whoever is ashamed of me and my words, the Son of Man will also be ashamed of him when He comes in His majesty and that of the Father and the angels* (Lk 9:26)'. *Francis and Clare: The Complete Works* [1982] The Classics of Western Spirituality. New York: Paulist Press, p. 121-122

[2735]Pope Francis [2020] Encyclical *Fratelli Tutti*, para 3-4 [Online] Available at: www.vatican.va [Accessed on: 5 July 2022]

for the remission of your sins: and you shall receive the gift of the Holy Ghost.…And with very many other words did he testify and exhort them, saying: Save yourselves from this perverse generation. They therefore that received his word, were baptized; and there were added in that day about three thousand souls.

Acts of the Apostles 17:2-3
And Paul, according to his custom, went in unto them; and for three sabbath days he reasoned with them out of the scriptures: Declaring and insinuating that the Christ was to suffer, and to rise again from the dead; and that this is Jesus Christ, whom I preach to you.

Acts of the Apostles 18:4
And he reasoned in the synagogue every sabbath, bringing in the name of the Lord Jesus; and he persuaded the Jews and the Greeks.

Acts of the Apostles 19:8
And entering into the synagogue, he spoke boldly for the space of three months, disputing and exhorting concerning the kingdom of God.

Acts of the Apostles 26:27-29
Believest thou the prophets, O king Agrippa? I know that thou believest. And Agrippa said to Paul: In a little thou persuadest me to become a Christian. And Paul said: I would to God, that both in a little and in much, not only thou, but also all that hear me, this day, should become such as I also am, except these bands.

Romans 10:14-17
How then shall they call on him, in whom they have not believed? Or how shall they believe him, of whom they have not heard? And how shall they hear, without a preacher? And how shall they preach unless they be sent as it is written: How beautiful are the feet of them that preach the gospel of peace, of them that bring glad tidings of good things! But all do not obey the gospel. For Isaias saith: Lord, who hath believed our report? Faith then cometh by hearing; and hearing by the word of Christ.

II Corinthians 4:2
But we renounce the hidden things of dishonesty, not walking in craftiness, nor adulterating the word of God; but by manifestation of the truth commending ourselves to every man's conscience, in the sight of God.

II Corinthians 5:11
Knowing therefore the fear of the Lord, we use persuasion to men.

II Corinthians 10:4-5
For the weapons of our warfare are not carnal, but mighty to God unto the pulling down of fortifications, destroying counsels, And every height that exalteth itself against the knowledge of God, and bringing into captivity every understanding unto the obedience of Christ.

II Timothy 4:17
But the Lord stood by me, and strengthened me, that by me the preaching may be accomplished, and that all the Gentiles may hear.…

I Peter 3:15
But sanctify the Lord Christ in your hearts, being ready always to satisfy every one that asketh you a reason of that hope which is in you.

Sacred Tradition

St. John Chrysostom: c. 347 to 407

Homily 3 on First Corinthians, 8.
[On the Apostles] And observe; the fisherman, the tentmaker, the publican, the ignorant, the unlettered, coming from the far distant country of Palestine, and having beaten

off their own ground the philosophers, the masters of oratory, the skilful debaters, alone prevailed against them in a short space of time; in the midst of many perils; the opposition of peoples and kings, the striving of nature herself, length of time, the vehement resistance of inveterate custom, demons in arms, the devil in battle array and stirring up all, kings, rulers, peoples, nations, cities, barbarians, Greeks, philosophers, orators, sophists, historians, laws, tribunals, various kinds of punishments, deaths innumerable and of all sorts. But nevertheless all these were confuted and gave way when the fisherman spoke; just like the light dust which cannot bear the rush of violent winds. Now what I say is, let us learn thus to dispute with the Greeks; that we be not like beasts and cattle, but prepared concerning 'the hope which is in us.' (I Pet 3:15). And let us pause for a while to work out this topic, no unimportant one; and let us say to them, How did the weak overcome the strong; the twelve, the world? Not by using the same armour, but in nakedness contending with men in arms.[2736]

Homily 7 on the Acts of the Apostles, 2:37-47
For see here; he [St. Peter] gently reminds them of the outrages they have committed, adding no comment; he declares the gift of God, he goes on to speak of the grace which bore testimony to the event, and so draws out his discourse to a still greater length. So they stood in awe of the gentleness of Peter, in that he, speaking to men who had crucified his Master, and breathed murder against himself and his companions, discoursed to them in the character of an affectionate father and teacher. Not merely were they persuaded; they even condemned themselves, they came to a sense of their past behavior. For he gave no room for their anger to be roused, and darken their judgment, but by means of humility he dispersed, as it were, the mist and darkness of their indignation, and then pointed out to them the daring outrage they had committed. [...]
    Such was the conduct of Peter. He did not accuse them harshly; on the contrary, he almost endeavoured to plead for them, as far as was possible. And this was the very reason that he penetrated into their souls.[2737]

St. Augustine: 354 to 430

Tractate 92 (John 15:26-27)
For when on the day of Pentecost the Holy Spirit fell upon an assembly of one hundred and twenty men, among whom were all the apostles; and when they, filled therewith were speaking in the language of every nation; a goodly number of those who had hated, amazed at the magnitude of the miracle (especially when they perceived in Peter's address so great and divine a testimony borne in behalf of Christ, as that He, who was slain by them and accounted among the dead, was proved to have risen again, and to be now alive), were pricked in their hearts and converted....[2738]

Sermon 77, 4
From the same people also came those who were cut to the heart as Peter was speaking, urging on them the meaning of the passion, resurrection and divinity of Christ; the occasion being when he had received the Holy Spirit, and when all those upon whom the Holy Spirit came were speaking in the languages of all nations. Well, those who were listening were Jewish people, and they asked for his advice about being saved....They were converted from among the Jewish people; they were converted and baptised.[2739]

[2736]St. John Chrysostom. *Homily 3 on First Corinthians*, para 8 [Online] Available at: www. newadvent.org [Accessed on: 6 July 2022]
[2737]St. John Chrysostom. *Homily 7 on the Acts of the Apostles*, 2:37-47 [Online] Available at: www. newadvent.org [Accessed on: 3 October 2022]
[2738]St. Augustine. *Tractate 92*, John 15:26-27, para 1 [Online] Available at: www.newadvent.org [Accessed on: 6 July 2022]
[2739]The Works of Saint Augustine [1991] *Sermons, III*, Sermon 77, para 4 New York: New City Press, p. 319

Pope St Gregory the Great: 590 to 604

Pastoral Rule, *Bk Three, Chap 34*

For hence it is that it is said to Jeremiah when sent to preach, *See, I have this day set you over the nations and over the kingdoms, to pluck out, and to pull down, and to destroy, and to scatter, and to build, and to plant* (Jer 1:10). Because, unless he first destroyed wrong things, he could not profitably build right things; unless he plucked out of the hearts of his hearers the thorns of vain love, he would certainly plant to no purpose the words of holy preaching. Hence it is that Peter first overthrows, that he may afterwards build up, when he in no wise admonished the Jews as to what they were now to do, but reproved them for what they had done, saying, *Jesus of Nazareth, a man approved of God among you by powers and wonders and signs, which God did by Him in the midst of you, as you yourselves know; Him, being delivered by the determinate counsel and foreknowledge of God, you have by the hands of wicked men crucified and slain; whom God has raised up, having loosed the pains of hell* (Acts 2:22-24); in order, to wit, that having been thrown down by a recognition of their cruelty, they might hear the building up of holy preaching by so much the more profitably as they anxiously sought it. Whence also they immediately replied, *What then shall we do, men and brethren?* And it is presently said to them, *Repent and be baptized, every one of you* (ibid., 37, 38). Which words of building up they would surely have despised, had they not first wholesomely become aware of the ruin of their throwing down.[2740]

The Magisterium of the Church

All Catholics have received the solemn mandate of Christ to proclaim the saving truth from the apostles and must carry it out to the very ends of the earth; observing the Pauline imperative, "Woe to me, if I do not preach the Gospel" (I Cor 9:16). The Church must never forget the billions of souls who live in the darkness of unbelief, and strive through the proclamation of the doctrines of the Catholic Faith to snatch them from the slavery of error and of idols. It is not proselytism to seek to convince others to convert because every person has the right to hear the "Good News" of the God who reveals and gives himself in Christ.

First Vatican Council (Twentieth Ecumenical, 1869 to 1870)

Dogmatic Constitution, *Pastor Aeternus, on the Church of Christ, para 1.*

The eternal shepherd and guardian of our souls in order to render permanent the saving work of redemption, determined to build a church in which, as in the house of the living God, all the faithful should be linked by the bond of one faith and charity.[2741]

Second Vatican Council (Twenty-First Ecumenical, 1962 to 1965)

Constitution on the Sacred Liturgy *Sacrosanctum Concilium, 6, 9. (4th December 1963)*

Just as Christ was sent by the Father, so also He sent the apostles, filled with the Holy Spirit. This He did that, by preaching the gospel to every creature (Mk 16:15) they might proclaim that the Son of God, by His death and resurrection, had freed us from the power of Satan (Acts 26:18) and from death, and brought us into the kingdom of His Father.

Before men can come to the liturgy they must be called to faith and to conversion: 'How then are they to call upon him in whom they have not yet believed? But how are they to believe him whom they have not heard? And how are they to hear if no one preaches? And how are men to preach unless they be sent?' (Rom 10:14-15).

Therefore the Church announces the good tidings of salvation to those who do not believe, so that all men may know the true God and Jesus Christ whom He has sent, and may be converted from their ways, doing penance (Jn 17:3; Lk 24:27; Acts 2:38).[2742]

[2740]Pope St. Gregory the Great. [590] *Pastoral Rule*, Bk. 3, Chap. 34 [Online] Available at: www.newadvent.org [Accessed on: 6 July 2022]

[2741]First Vatican Council [1870] Dogmatic Constitution, *Pastor Aeternus, on the Church of Christ*, para 1. [Online] www.papalencyclicals.net [Accessed on: 5 July 2022]

[2742]Second Vatican Council [1963] Constitution on the Sacred Liturgy *Sacrosanctum Concilium*, paras 6, 9 [Online] Available at: www.vatican.va [Accessed on: 5 July 2022]

Dogmatic Constitution *Lumen Gentium, 3, 9, 13, 17. (21st November 1964)*
All men are called to this union with Christ, who is the light of the world, from whom we go forth, through whom we live, and toward whom our whole life strains. [...]

While it transcends all limits of time and confines of race, the Church is destined to extend to all regions of the earth and so enters into the history of mankind. [...]

All men are called to belong to the new people of God. Wherefore this people, while remaining one and only one, is to be spread throughout the whole world and must exist in all ages, so that the decree of God's will may be fulfilled.

As the Son was sent by the Father (Jn 20:21), so He too sent the Apostles, saying: 'Go, therefore, make disciples of all nations, baptizing them in the name of the Father and of the Son and of the Holy Spirit, teaching them to observe all things whatsoever I have commanded you. And behold I am with you all days even to the consummation of the world' (Mt 28:19-20). The Church has received this solemn mandate of Christ to proclaim the saving truth from the apostles and must carry it out to the very ends of the earth (Acts 1:8). Wherefore she makes the words of the Apostle her own: 'Woe to me, if I do not preach the Gospel' (I Cor 9:16), and continues unceasingly to send heralds of the Gospel until such time as the infant churches are fully established and can themselves continue the work of evangelising. For the Church is compelled by the Holy Spirit to do her part that God's plan may be fully realized, whereby He has constituted Christ as the source of salvation for the whole world. By the proclamation of the Gospel she prepares her hearers to receive and profess the faith. She gives them the dispositions necessary for baptism, snatches them from the slavery of error and of idols and incorporates them in Christ so that through charity they may grow up into full maturity in Christ. Through her work, whatever good is in the minds and hearts of men, whatever good lies latent in the religious practices and cultures of diverse peoples, is not only saved from destruction but is also cleansed, raised up and perfected unto the glory of God, the confusion of the devil and the happiness of man. The obligation of spreading the faith is imposed on every disciple of Christ, according to his state.[2743]

Pastoral Constitution *Gaudium et Spes, 1, 32. (7th December 1965)*
United in Christ, they are led by the Holy Spirit in their journey to the Kingdom of their Father and they have welcomed the news of salvation which is meant for every man.

He commanded His Apostles to preach to all peoples the Gospel's message that the human race was to become the Family of God, in which the fullness of the Law would be love.[2744]

Decree *Ad Gentes, 13, 15, 30, 39, 40. (7th December 1965)*
Wherever God opens a door of speech for proclaiming the mystery of Christ (cf. Col 4:3), there is announced to all men (cf. Mk 16:15; I Cor 9:15; Rom 10:14) with confidence and constancy (cf. Acts 4:13, 29, 31; 9:27, 28; 13:46; 14:3; 19:8; 26:26; 28:31; I Thess 2:2; II Cor 3:12; 7:4; Phil 1:20; Eph 3:12; 6:19, 20) the living God, and He Whom He has sent for the salvation of all, Jesus Christ (cf. I Thess 1:9-10; I Cor 1:18-21; Gal 1:31; Acts 14:15-17, 17:22-31), in order that non-Christians, when the Holy Spirit opens their heart (cf. Acts 16:14), may believe and be freely converted to the Lord, that they may cleave sincerely to Him Who, being the 'way, the truth, and the life' (Jn 14:6), fulfils all their spiritual expectations, and even infinitely surpasses them. [...]

The Church strictly forbids forcing anyone to embrace the Faith, or alluring or enticing people by worrisome wiles. By the same token, she also strongly insists on this right, that no one be frightened away from the Faith by unjust vexations on the part of others. [...]

[2743]Second Vatican Council [1964] Dogmatic Constitution, *Lumen Gentium*, paras 3, 9, 13, 17 [Online] Available at: www.vatican.va [Accessed on: 5 July 2022]

[2744]Second Vatican Council [1965] Pastoral Constitution *Gaudium et Spes*, paras 1, 32 [Online] Available at: www.vatican.va [Accessed on: 3 October 2022]

But it is not enough that the Christian people be present and be organised in a given nation, nor is it enough to carry out an apostolate by way of example. They are organised for this purpose, they are present for this, to announce Christ to their non-Christian fellow citizens by word and example, and to aid them toward the full reception of Christ. [...]

A fair proportion of personnel and funds should be assigned to the evangelization of non-Christians. [...]

They shall therefore plan their pastoral care in such a way that it will serve to spread the Gospel among non-Christians. [...]

Professors in seminaries and universities will teach young people the true state of the world and of the Church, so that the necessity of a more intense evangelization of non-Christians will become clear to them and will nurture their zeal. [...]

God who opens the minds of non-Christians to hear the Gospel (cf. Acts 16:14), and God who fructifies the word of salvation in their hearts (cf. I Cor 3:7).[2745]

Decree *Unitatis Redintegratio, 4. (21st November 1964)*
However, it is evident that, when individuals [non Catholic Christians] wish for full Catholic communion, their preparation and reconciliation is an undertaking which of its nature is distinct from ecumenical action. But there is no opposition between the two, since both proceed from the marvelous ways of God. Catholics, in their ecumenical work, must assuredly be concerned for their separated brethren, praying for them, keeping them informed about the Church, making the first approaches toward them.[2746]

Pope Benedict XVI: 2005 to 2013

Homily during visit to the Roman Basilica of St. Paul-Outside-the-Walls. (25th April 2005)
The Church is by nature missionary; her urgent duty is to evangelize. The Second Vatican Council dedicated to missionary activity the Decree entitled, precisely, *Ad Gentes*. It recalls that 'the Apostles... following the footsteps of Christ', "preached the word of truth and begot churches" (St. Augustine, *Enarr. in Ps.* 44, 23: PL 36, 508; CChr. 30, 510), and that it is the duty of their successors to carry on this work so that "the word of God may run and be glorified" (II Thess 3:1) and the Kingdom of God proclaimed and renewed throughout the whole world' (*Ad Gentes*, n.1).[2747]

Compendium of the Catechism of the Catholic Church. (28th June 2005)

172. Why must the Church proclaim the Gospel to the whole world?
The Church must do so because Christ has given the command: 'Go therefore and make disciples of all nations, baptizing them in the name of the Father and of the Son and of the Holy Spirit' (Mt 28:19). This missionary mandate of the Lord has its origin in the eternal love of God who has sent his Son and the Holy Spirit because 'he desires all men to be saved and to come to the knowledge of the truth' (I Tim 2:4).

173. In what sense is the Church missionary?
The Church, guided by the Holy Spirit, continues the mission of Christ himself in the course of history. Christians must, therefore, proclaim to everyone the Good News borne by Christ; and, following his path, they must be ready for self-sacrifice, even unto martyrdom.[2748]

[2745]Second Vatican Council [1965] Decree, *Ad Gentes*, paras 13, 30 [Online] Available at: www.vatican.va [Accessed on: 3 October 2022]
[2746]Second Vatican Council [1964] Decree, *Unitatis Redintegratio*, para 4 [Online] Available at: www.vatican.va [Accessed on: 3 October 2022]
[2747]Pope Benedict XVI [2005] *Homily during visit to the Roman Basilica of St. Paul-Outside-the-Walls* [Online] Available at: www.vatican.va [Accessed on: 3 October 2022]
[2748]*Compendium of the Catechism of the Catholic Church* [2005] [Online] Available at: www.vatican.va [Accessed on: 3 October 2022]

Address to the participants of the International Conference on the occasion of the 40th anniversary of the Conciliar Decree Ad Gentes. (11th March 2006)
The Church has acquired an ever clearer awareness of her innate missionary vocation, recognising it as a constitutive element of her very nature.

Out of obedience to the command of Christ, who sent his disciples to proclaim the Gospel to all the nations (cf. Mt 28:18-20), the Christian community in our time too feels sent to the men and women of the third millennium in order to acquaint them with the truth of the Gospel message and thereby give them access to the path of salvation.

And this, as I said, is not an option but the vocation proper to the People of God, a duty incumbent upon it by the command of the Lord Jesus Christ himself (cf. *Evangelii Nuntiandi*, n. 5).

Actually, the proclamation of and witness to the Gospel are the first service that Christians can render to every person and to the entire human race, called as they are to communicate to all God's love, which was fully manifested in Jesus Christ, the one Redeemer of the world. [...]

From the outset, the Christian People has been clearly aware of the importance of sharing the riches of this love with those who do not yet know Christ through constant missionary activity.

The need to reaffirm this commitment has been felt even more forcefully in recent years, because in the modern epoch, as my beloved Predecessor John Paul II observed, the missio ad gentes has sometimes seemed to be slowing down because of difficulties due to changes in humanity's anthropological, cultural, social and religious contexts.[2749]

Congregation for the Doctrine of the Faith. Doctrinal Note on Some Aspects of Evangelisation, 3, 7, 10, 12. (3d December 2007)
There is today, however, a growing confusion which leads many to leave the missionary command of the Lord unheard and ineffective (cf. Mt 28:19). Often it is maintained that any attempt to convince others on religious matters is a limitation of their freedom. From this perspective, it would only be legitimate to present one's own ideas and to invite people to act according to their consciences, without aiming at their conversion to Christ and to the Catholic faith. It is enough, so they say, to help people to become more human or more faithful to their own religion; it is enough to build communities which strive for justice, freedom, peace and solidarity. Furthermore, some maintain that Christ should not be proclaimed to those who do not know him, nor should joining the Church be promoted, since it would also be possible to be saved without explicit knowledge of Christ and without formal incorporation in the Church. [...]

Although non-Christians can be saved through the grace which God bestows in 'ways known to him', the Church cannot fail to recognize that such persons are lacking a tremendous benefit in this world: to know the true face of God and the friendship of Jesus Christ, God-with-us. Indeed 'there is nothing more beautiful than to be surprised by the Gospel, by the encounter with Christ. There is nothing more beautiful than to know him and to speak to others of our friendship with him'. The revelation of the fundamental truths about God, about the human person and the world, is a great good for every human person, while living in darkness without the truths about ultimate questions is an evil and is often at the root of suffering and slavery which can at times be grievous. This is why Saint Paul does not hesitate to describe conversion to the Christian faith as liberation 'from the power of darkness' and entrance into 'the kingdom of his beloved Son in whom we have redemption and the forgiveness of our sins' (Col 1:13-14). Therefore, fully belonging to Christ, who is the Truth, and entering the Church do not lessen human freedom, but rather exalt it and direct it towards its fulfilment, in a love that is freely given and which overflows with care for the good of all people. It is an inestimable benefit to live within the universal embrace of the friends of God which flows from communion in the life-giving flesh of his Son, to receive from

---

[2749]Pope Benedict XVI [2006] *Address to the participants of the International Conference on the occasion of the 40th anniversary of the Conciliar Decree Ad Gentes* [Online] Available at: www.vatican.va [Accessed on: 7 July 2022]

him the certainty of forgiveness of sins and to live in the love that is born of faith. The Church wants everyone to share in these goods so that they may possess the fullness of truth and the fullness of the means of salvation, in order 'to enter into the freedom of the glory of the children of God' (Rom 8:21).

However, the Church's 'missionary proclamation is endangered today by relativistic theories which seek to justify religious pluralism, not only *de facto* but also *de iure* (or in principle)'. For a long time, the reason for evangelization has not been clear to many among the Catholic faithful. It is even stated that the claim to have received the gift of the fullness of God's revelation masks an attitude of intolerance and a danger to peace.

Those who make such claims are overlooking the fact that the fullness of the gift of truth, which God makes by revealing himself to man, respects the freedom which he himself created as an indelible mark of human nature: a freedom which is not indifference, but which is rather directed towards truth. This kind of respect is a requirement of the Catholic faith itself and of the love of Christ; it is a constitutive element of evangelization and, therefore, a good which is to be promoted inseparably with the commitment to making the fullness of salvation, which God offers to the human race in the Church, known and freely embraced.

Respect for religious freedom and its promotion 'must not in any way make us indifferent towards truth and goodness. Indeed, love impels the followers of Christ to proclaim to all the truth which saves'.

…it needs also to be recalled that if a non-Catholic Christian, for reasons of conscience and having been convinced of Catholic truth, asks to enter into the full communion of the Catholic Church, this is to be respected as the work of the Holy Spirit and as an expression of freedom of conscience and of religion. In such a case, it would not be a question of proselytism in the negative sense that has been attributed to this term. As explicitly recognized in the Decree on Ecumenism of the Second Vatican Council, 'it is evident that the work of preparing and reconciling those individuals who desire full Catholic communion is of its nature distinct from ecumenical action, but there is no opposition between the two, since both proceed from the marvelous ways of God'. Therefore, the work of ecumenism does not remove the right or take away the responsibility of proclaiming in fullness the Catholic faith to other Christians, who freely wish to receive it.[2750]

Message for the 82nd World Mission Sunday. (11th May 2008)
It is therefore an urgent duty for everyone to proclaim Christ and his saving message. St. Paul said, 'Woe to me if I do not preach it [the Gospel]!' (I Cor 9:16). […] It is important to reaffirm that even in the presence of growing difficulties, Christ's command to evangelize all peoples continues to be a priority.[2751]

Message for the 83rd World Mission Sunday. (29th June 2009)
'The nations will walk in its light' (Rev 21:24). The goal of the Church's mission is to illumine all peoples with the light of the Gospel as they journey through history towards God, so that in Him they may reach their full potential and fulfilment. We should have a longing and a passion to illumine all peoples with the light of Christ that shines on the face of the Church, so that all may be gathered into the one human family, under God's loving fatherhood. […]

The mission of the Church, therefore, is to call all peoples to the salvation accomplished by God through his incarnate Son. It is therefore necessary to renew our commitment to proclaiming the Gospel which is a leaven of freedom and progress, brotherhood, unity and peace (cf. *Ad Gentes*, 8). I would 'confirm once more that the task of evangelising all people constitutes the essential mission of the Church' (*Evangelii*

[2750]Congregation for the Doctrine of the Faith [2007] *Doctrinal Note on Some Aspects of Evangelisation*, paras 3,7,10,12 [Online] Available at: www.vatican.va [Accessed on: 7 July 2022]

[2751]Pope Benedict [2008] *Message for the 82nd World Mission Sunday* [Online] Available at: www.vatican.va [Accessed on: 7 July 2022]

Nuntiandi, 14), a duty and a mission which the widespread and profound changes in present-day society render ever more urgent. At stake is the eternal salvation of persons, the goal and the fulfilment of human history and the universe.[2752]

Message for the 85th World Mission Sunday. (6th January 2011)
On the occasion of the Great Jubilee of the Year 2000, at the beginning of a new millennium of the Christian era Venerable John Paul II forcefully reaffirmed the need to renew the commitment to bear the proclamation of the Gospel to everyone, sharing 'the enthusiasm of the very first Christians' (*Novo Millennio Ineunte*, n. 58). It is the most precious service that the Church can render to humanity and to all individuals who are seeking the profound reasons to live their life to the full.

The proclamation of the Gospel is intended for all peoples. The Church is 'by her very nature missionary since, according to the plan of the Father, she has her origin in the mission of the Son and the Holy Spirit' (Decree on the Church's Missionary Activity *Ad Gentes*, n. 2). [...]

This is 'the grace and vocation proper to the Church, her deepest identity. She exists in order to evangelize '(Paul VI, Apostolic Exhortation *Evangelii Nuntiandi*, n. 14). Consequently she can never be closed in on herself. She is rooted in specific places in order to go beyond them. Her action, in adherence to Christ's word and under the influence of his grace and his charity, is fully and currently present to all people and all peoples, to lead them to faith in Christ, (cf. *Ad Gentes*, n. 5).

This task has lost none of its urgency. Indeed 'The mission of Christ the Redeemer, which is entrusted to the Church, is still very far from completion... an overall view of the human race shows that this mission is still only beginning and that we must commit ourselves wholeheartedly to its service' (John Paul II, Encyclical *Redemptoris Missio*, n. 1). We cannot reconcile ourselves to the thought that after 2,000 years there are still people who do not know Christ and have never heard his Message of salvation.[2753]

Motu Proprio *Porta Fidei, 7. (11th October 2011)*
'*Caritas Christi urget nos*' (II Cor 5:14): it is the love of Christ that fills our hearts and impels us to evangelize. Today as in the past, he sends us through the highways of the world to proclaim his Gospel to all the peoples of the earth (cf. Mt 28:19). Through his love, Jesus Christ attracts to himself the people of every generation: in every age he convokes the Church, entrusting her with the proclamation of the Gospel by a mandate that is ever new.[2754]

Apostolic Exhortation *Ecclesia in Medio Oriente, 88. (14th September 2012)*
As heir to the apostolic outreach which brought the Good News to distant lands, each of the Catholic Churches present in the Middle East is also called to renew its missionary spirit by training and sending forth men and women proud of their faith in Christ crucified and risen, and able to proclaim the Gospel courageously both in the region and throughout the diaspora, and even in other countries around the world. The Year of Faith, which is linked to the new evangelization, if lived with intense conviction, will provide an excellent incentive for Churches of the region to evangelize themselves and to consolidate their witness to Christ. To make known the Son of God who died and rose again, the sole Saviour of mankind, is an essential duty of the Church and a grave responsibility for all the baptized. 'God desires everyone to be saved and to come to the knowledge of the truth' (cf. I Tim 2:4).[2755]

[2752]Pope Benedict XVI [2009] *Message for the 83rd World Mission Sunday* [Online] Available at: www.vatican.va [Accessed on: 3 October 2022]

[2753]Pope Benedict XVI [2011] *Message for the 85th World Mission Sunday* [Online] Available at: www. vatican.va [Accessed on: 3 October 2022]

[2754]Pope Benedict XVI [2011] Motu Proprio *Porta Fidei*, para 7 [Online] Available at: www.vatican. va [Accessed on: 3 October 2022]

[2755]Pope Benedict XVI [2012] Apostolic Exhortation *Ecclesia in Medio Oriente*, para 88 [Online] Available at: www.vatican.va [Accessed on: 3 October 2022]

Pope St. John Paul II: 1978 to 2005

Address to the Members and Staff of the Secretariat for Non-Christians, 3, 4. (28th April 1987)
Your assembly must thus reaffirm the commitment of the Catholic Church both to dialogue and to the proclamation of the Gospel. There can be no question of choosing one and ignoring or rejecting the other. Even in situations where the proclamation of our faith is difficult, we must have the courage to speak of God who is the foundation of that faith, the reason for our hope, and the source of our love. It is also true that in those circumstances in which the proclamation of the Gospel bears much fruit we must not forget that dialogue with others is a Christian work desired by God. Moreover, the proclamation of the Gospel has to take due notice of the religious and cultural background of those to whom it is addressed. [...]

Just as interreligious dialogue is one element in the mission of the Church, the proclamation of God's saving work in our Lord Jesus Christ is another. Christ's followers must carry out his mandate to make disciples of all nations, to baptize and to teach the observance of the commandments (Cf. Mt 28:19-20). As Saints Peter and John told the Sanhedrin: 'We cannot but speak of what we have seen and heard' (Acts 4:20). Likewise with St. Paul we must be aware of the consequences of neglecting to proclaim the Gospel (Cf. I Cor 9:16). The Second Vatican Council reminds us that Jesus Christ announces the universal love of our Heavenly Father, reveals his saving deeds, and embodies his new and eternal Covenant with humanity. Hence, the Council states that 'the Church painstakingly fosters her missionary work' (*Lumen Gentium* 16).

Address to the Bishops of Ethiopia on the occasion of their 'Ad Limina' visit, 4. (15th May 1987)
It is your particular responsibility, my Brothers, to adopt those means most appropriate for proclaiming the Gospel message in a multi-religious society. The Church has a deep respect for non-Christian religions because 'they are the living expression of the soul of vast groups of people' (*Evangelii Nuntiandi* 53). Since the plan of salvation encompasses all those who acknowledge the Creator, there exists between Christian and non-Christians a profound basis for understanding and peaceful coexistence. In relation to non-Christian religions, the Church affirms her commitment not only to dialogue but also to the proclamation of the Gospel. 'Neither respect and esteem for these religions nor the complexity of the questions raised is an invitation to the Church to withhold from these non-Christians the proclamation of Jesus Christ' (Cf. Paul VI *Evangelii Nuntiandi*, 61). The Lord clearly exhorts his followers to make disciples of all nations, to baptize and to teach the observance of the commandments (Cf. Mt 28:19-20).[2756]

Encyclical *Redemptoris Missio, 2, 3, 11, 46. (7th December 1990)*
Missionary activity specifically directed 'to the nations' (*ad gentes*) appears to be waning, and this tendency is certainly not in line with the directives of the Council and of subsequent statements of the Magisterium. Difficulties both internal and external have weakened the Church's missionary thrust toward non-Christians, a fact which must arouse concern among all who believe in Christ. For in the Church's history, missionary drive has always been a sign of vitality, just as its lessening is a sign of a crisis of faith. [...]

Peoples everywhere, open the doors to Christ! His Gospel in no way detracts from man's freedom, from the respect that is owed to every culture and to whatever is good in each religion. By accepting Christ, you open yourselves to the definitive Word of God, to the One in whom God has made himself fully known and has shown us the path to himself. The number of those who do not know Christ and do not belong to the Church is constantly on the increase. Indeed, since the end of the Council it has almost doubled. When we consider this immense portion of humanity which is loved by the Father and for whom he sent his Son, the urgency of the Church's mission is obvious. [...]

[2756]Pope St. John Paul II [1987] *Address to the Bishops of Ethiopia on the occasion of their 'Ad Limina' visit*, para 4 [Online] Available at: www.vatican.va [Accessed on: 7 July 2022]

The temptation today is to reduce Christianity to merely human wisdom, a pseudo-science of well-being. In our heavily secularized world a 'gradual secularization of salvation' has taken place, so that people strive for the good of man, but man who is truncated, reduced to his merely horizontal dimension. We know, however, that Jesus came to bring integral salvation, one which embraces the whole person and all mankind, and opens up the wondrous prospect of divine filiation. Why mission? Because to us, as to St. Paul, 'this grace was given, to preach to the Gentiles the unsearchable riches of Christ' (Eph 3:8). Newness of life in him is the 'Good News' for men and women of every age: all are called to it and destined for it. Indeed, all people are searching for it, albeit at times in a confused way, and have a right to know the value of this gift and to approach it freely. The Church, and every individual Christian within her, may not keep hidden or monopolise this newness and richness which has been received from God's bounty in order to be communicated to all mankind. [...]

The number of those who do not know Christ and do not belong to the Church is constantly on the increase. Indeed, since the end of the Council it has almost doubled. When we consider this immense portion of humanity which is loved by the Father and for whom he sent his Son, the urgency of the Church's mission is obvious.

The proclamation of the Word of God has Christian conversion as its aim: a complete and sincere adherence to Christ and his Gospel through faith. Conversion is a gift of God, a work of the Blessed Trinity. It is the Spirit who opens people's hearts so that they can believe in Christ and 'confess him' (cf. I Cor 12:3); of those who draw near to him through faith Jesus says: 'No one can come to me unless the Father who sent me draws him' (Jn 6:44).

From the outset, conversion is expressed in faith which is total and radical, and which neither limits nor hinders God's gift. At the same time, it gives rise to a dynamic and lifelong process which demands a continual turning away from 'life according to the flesh' to 'life according to the Spirit' (cf. Rom 8:3-13). Conversion means accepting, by a personal decision, the saving sovereignty of Christ and becoming his disciple.

The Church calls all people to this conversion, following the example of John the Baptist, who prepared the way for Christ by 'preaching a baptism of repentance for the forgiveness of sins' (Mk 1:4), as well as the example of Christ himself, who 'after John was arrested,...came into Galilee preaching the Gospel of God and saying: "The time is fulfilled, and the kingdom of God is at hand; repent and believe in the Gospel"' (Mk 1:14-15).

Nowadays the call to conversion which missionaries address to non-Christians is put into question or passed over in silence. It is seen as an act of 'proselytizing'; it is claimed that it is enough to help people to become more human or more faithful to their own religion, that it is enough to build communities capable of working for justice, freedom, peace and solidarity. What is overlooked is that every person has the right to hear the 'Good News' of the God who reveals and gives himself in Christ, so that each one can live out in its fullness his or her proper calling. This lofty reality is expressed in the words of Jesus to the Samaritan woman: 'If you knew the gift of God,' and in the unconscious but ardent desire of the woman: 'Sir, give me this water, that I may not thirst' (Jn 4:10, 15).[2757]

Address to the Federation of Asian Bishops' Conferences, 11. (15th January 1995)
In these years of preparation for the Great Jubilee of the Year 2000, your particular Churches are fully committed to giving a fresh impulse to the evangelization of Asia. Just as in the first millennium the Cross was planted on the soil of Europe, and in the second on that of the Americas and Africa, we can pray that in the Third Christian Millennium a great harvest of faith will be reaped in this vast and vital Continent. If the Church in Asia is to fulfil its providential destiny, evangelization as the joyful, patient

---

[2757]Pope St. John Paul II [1990] Encyclical *Redemptoris Missio*, 46 [Online] Available at: www.vatican.va [Accessed on: 7 July 2022]

and progressive preaching of the saving Death and Resurrection of Jesus Christ must be your absolute priority.[2758]

Apostolic Exhortation *Ecclesia in Africa, 47. (14th September 1995)*
The Synod recognized the urgency of proclaiming the Good News to the millions of people in Africa who are not yet evangelised. The Church certainly respects and esteems the non-Christian religions professed by very many Africans, for these religions are the living expression of the soul of vast groups of people. However, 'neither respect and esteem for these religions nor the complexity of the questions raised is an invitation to the Church to withhold from these non-Christians the proclamation of Jesus Christ. On the contrary the Church holds that these multitudes have the right to know the riches of the mystery of Christ (cf. Eph 3:8) — riches in which we believe that the whole of humanity can find, in unsuspected fullness, everything that it is gropingly searching for concerning God, man and his destiny, life and death, and truth'.[2759]

Apostolic Exhortation *Ecclesia in Asia, 20. (6th November 1999)*
Deeply aware of the complexity of so many different situations in Asia, and 'speaking the truth in love' (Eph 4:15), the Church proclaims the Good News with loving respect and esteem for her listeners. Proclamation which respects the rights of consciences does not violate freedom, since faith always demands a free response on the part of the individual. Respect, however, does not eliminate the need for the explicit proclamation of the Gospel in its fullness. Especially in the context of the rich array of cultures and religions in Asia it must be pointed out that 'neither respect and esteem for these religions nor the complexity of the questions raised are an invitation to the Church to withhold from these non-Christians the proclamation of Jesus Christ'.[2760]

Pope St. Paul VI: 1963 to 1978

Encyclical *Evangelii Nuntiandi, 53, 88. (8th December 1975)*
We wish to point out, above all today, that neither respect and esteem for these religions nor the complexity of the questions raised is an invitation to the Church to withhold from these non-Christians the proclamation of Jesus Christ. On the contrary the Church holds that these multitudes have the right to know the riches of the mystery of Christ (Eph 3:8) - riches in which we believe that the whole of humanity can find, in unsuspected fullness, everything that it is gropingly searching for concerning God, man and his destiny, life and death, and truth. Even in the face of natural religious expressions most worthy of esteem, the Church finds support in the fact that the religion of Jesus, which she proclaims through evangelization, objectively places man in relation with the plan of God, with His living presence and with His action; she thus causes an encounter with the mystery of divine paternity that bends over towards humanity. In other words, our religion effectively establishes with God an authentic and living relationship which the other religions do not succeed in doing, even though they have, as it were, their arms stretched out towards heaven. […]

It would certainly be an error to impose something on the consciences of our brethren. But to propose to their consciences the truth of the Gospel and salvation in Jesus Christ, with complete clarity and with a total respect for the free options which it presents — 'without coercion, or dishonourable or unworthy pressure' — far from being an attack on religious liberty is fully to respect that liberty, which is offered the choice of a way that even non-believers consider noble and uplifting. Is it then a crime against others' freedom to proclaim with joy a Good News which one has come to know through

---

[2758]Pope St. John Paul II [1995] *Address to the Federation of Asian Bishops' Conferences*, para 11 [Online] Available at: globalnation.inquirer.net [Accessed on: 3 October 2022]
[2759]Pope St. John Paul II [1995] Apostolic Exhortation *Ecclesia in Africa*, 47 [Online] Available at: www.vatican.va [Accessed on: 3 October 2022]
[2760]Pope St. John Paul II [1999] Apostolic Exhortation *Ecclesia in Asia*, para 20 [Online] Available at: www.vatican.va [Accessed on: 3 October 2022]

the Lord's mercy? And why should only falsehood and error, debasement and pornography have the right to be put before people and often unfortunately imposed on them by the destructive propaganda of the mass media, by the tolerance of legislation, the timidity of the good and the impudence of the wicked? The respectful presentation of Christ and His kingdom is more than the evangeliser's right; it is his duty. It is likewise the right of his fellow men to receive from him the proclamation of the Good News of salvation. God can accomplish this salvation in whomsoever He wishes by ways which He alone knows. And yet, if His Son came, it was precisely in order to reveal to us, by His word and by His life, the ordinary paths of salvation. And He has commanded us to transmit this revelation to others with His own authority. It would be useful if every Christian and every evangeliser were to pray about the following thought: men can gain salvation also in other ways, by God's mercy, even though we do not preach the Gospel to them; but as for us, can we gain salvation if through negligence or fear or shame- what St. Paul called 'blushing for the Gospel' (Rom 1:16) - or as a result of false ideas we fail to preach it? For that would be to betray the call of God, who wishes the seed to bear fruit through the voice of the ministers of the Gospel; and it will depend on us whether this grows into trees and produces its full fruit.[2761]

Pope St. John XXIII: 1958 to 1963

Encyclical *Princeps Pastorum*, 1, 3, 6. *(28th November 1959)*
On the day when 'the Prince of the Shepherds' (I Pet 5:4) entrusted to Us His lambs and sheep, (Jn 21:15-17) God's flock, which dwells all over the earth, We responded to the sweet invitation of His love with a sense of Our unworthiness but with trust in His all-powerful assistance. And the magnitude, the beauty, and the importance of the Catholic Missions have been constantly on Our mind. For this reason, We have never ceased to devote to them Our greatest solicitude and attention. And at the close of the first year marking the anniversary of Our reception of the triple Tiara, in the sermon which We delivered on that solemn occasion We mentioned as among the happiest events of Our Pontificate the day, October 10th, on which over four hundred missionaries gathered in the most holy Vatican Basilica to receive from Our hands the crucifix, image of Jesus Christ Crucified, before leaving for distant parts of the world to illumine them with the light of Christianity. [...]

Also at the time Our predecessor Pius XII by word and example incited Us to give Our warmest support to missionary activities and projects. Just before the College of Cardinals was convened for the Conclave during which, by divine inspiration, he was chosen as the successor of St. Peter, he spoke the following words in Our presence: 'We cannot expect anything greater or more beneficial from the new Vicar of Christ than these two most important things: that he will strive with all his might to propagate the doctrine of the Gospel among all men, and that he will bring peoples together in a spirit of true peace and strengthen them therein.' [...]

When We turn Our mind and Our heart to the supernatural blessings of the Church that are to be shared with those people whose souls have not yet been suffused with the light of the Gospel, there appear before Our eyes either regions of the world where bountiful crops grow, thrive, and ripen, or regions where the labours of the toilers in God's vineyard are very arduous, or regions where the enemies of God and Jesus Christ are harassing and threatening to destroy Christian communities by violence and persecutions, and are striving to smother and crush the seed of God's word. (Mt 13:19) We are everywhere confronted by appeals to Us to ensure the eternal salvation of souls in the best way We can, and a cry seems to reach Our ears: 'Help us!' (Acts 16:9) Innumerable regions have already been made fruitful by the sweat and blood of messengers of the Gospel 'from every nation under heaven,' (Acts 2:5) and native apostles, with the help of divine grace, are blossoming like new buds and are bringing forth saving fruits.

[2761]Pope St. Paul VI [1975] Encyclical *Evangelii Nuntiandi*, paras 53, 88 [Online] Available at: www.vatican.va [Accessed on: 7 July 2022]

We desire to reach those regions with Our words of praise and encouragement, and with Our affection. We also wish to give them Our instructions and admonitions, which are prompted by firm hope based on the infallible promise of Our Divine Master, that is contained in these words: 'Behold, I am with you all days, even unto the consummation of the world.' (Mt 28:20) 'Take courage, I have overcome the world' (Jn 16:33).[2762]

Pope Ven. Pius XII: 1939 to 1958

Encyclical *Mystici Corporis Christi, 3. (29th June 1943).*
We do not deny, rather from a heart filled with gratitude to God We admit, that even in our turbulent times there are many who, though outside the fold of Jesus Christ, look to the Church as the only haven of salvation; but We are also aware that the Church of God not only is despised and hated maliciously by those who shut their eyes to the light of Christian wisdom and miserably return to the teachings, customs and practices of ancient paganism....[2763]

Encyclical *Evangelii Praecones, 16-17, 20. (2nd June 1951)*
Now what We have touched upon above, must be particularly borne in mind, namely, that what still remains to be accomplished in this field calls for an enormous effort and innumerable labourers. Let us remember that our brethren 'who sat in darkness and shadow' (Ps 106:10) form an immense multitude that can be reckoned at about 1,000,000,000. Hence it appears that the ineffable sigh of the most loving Heart of Christ is echoing still: 'And other sheep I have that are not of this fold: them also I must bring. And they shall hear my voice: and there shall be one fold and one shepherd.'

There are some shepherds, as you know, Venerable Brethren, who strive to lead away the sheep from this one fold and haven of salvation; you likewise know that this danger is daily growing greater. When We consider before God the immense number of men without the truth of the Gospel, and duly reckon the grave danger that faces many from the prevalence of atheistic materialism or from a certain so-called Christian creed which is infected by the tenets and errors of communism, We feel the deepest concern and solicitude that nothing be left undone to promote the work of the apostolate throughout the world. We make Our own the exhortation of the Prophet saying: 'Cry, cease not, lift up thy voice like a trumpet.'

We pray God especially for those missionaries who labor in the interior of Latin America, since We are aware of the dangerous pitfalls to which they are exposed from the open and covert attacks of heretical teaching. [...]

First of all it is to be observed that the person who had been called by God to evangelize distant non-Christian lands, has received a very great and sublime vocation. He consecrates his life to God in order to spread His Kingdom to the farthest ends of the earth.[2764]

Encyclical *Fidei Donum, 4-5, 19-20. (21st April 1957)*
As We direct our thoughts, on the one hand, to the countless multitudes of Our sons who have a share in the blessings of divine faith, especially in countries that have long since become Christian, and on the other hand as We consider the far more numerous throngs of those who are still waiting for the day of salvation to be announced to them, We are filled with a great desire to exhort you again and again, Venerable Brethren, to support with zealous interest the most holy cause of bringing the Church of God to all the world. May it come to pass that Our admonitions will arouse a keener interest in the missionary apostolate among your priests and through them set the hearts of the faithful on fire!

[2762]Pope St. John XXIII [1959] Encyclical *Princeps Pastorum*, paras 1,3,6 [Online] Available at: www.vatican.va [Accessed on: 7 July 2022]
[2763]Pope Ven. Pius XII [1943] Encyclical *Mystici Corporis Christi*, paras 3 [Online] Available at: www.vatican.va [Accessed on: 7 July 2022]
[2764]Pope Ven. Pius XII [1951] Encyclical *Evangelii Praecones*, paras 16-17, 20 [Online] Available at: www.vatican.va [Accessed on: 7 July 2022]

This sort of consideration, a very serious one indeed, has been advanced more than once by Our Predecessors, and We Ourselves, as you well know, have been most earnest in touching upon it. It should inspire all Catholics with apostolic zeal, as their awareness of having received the faith demands. Let them direct this zeal toward those regions of Europe in which the Christian religion has been cast off, or to the boundless spaces of South America; in both of these continents there are great difficulties to be overcome, as We know well. Let them give financial assistance to the Catholics of Oceania and to the missions in Asia; such assistance is of the utmost importance, especially in those countries where the battles of the Lord are being fought so fiercely. Let them likewise perform the duties of fraternal charity in behalf of those countless Christians who are very dear to Us and are the glory of the Church, since they have earned the evangelical beatitude proper to those 'who suffer persecution for justice' sake.' (Mt 5:10). Let them grieve for the lamentable state of innumerable souls, especially of those young people who because of the atheistic propaganda of our times are growing up in the wretched condition of complete ignorance of religion and, in some cases, of active hatred of God. [...]

Now that those who hate God are zealously bringing their insidious attacks to bear upon this great continent, other serious difficulties have arisen to hinder the spread of the Gospel in certain districts of Africa. Of course, you know the religious tenets of those people who, although they are quick to profess that they worship God, nevertheless are easily attracting and enticing the minds of many into another path which is not that of Jesus Christ, the Savior of all nations. Our heart, which is that of the common Father of all, is open to every man of good will; but We, who are the representative on earth of Him, Who is the Way, the Truth, and the Life, cannot contemplate such a situation without great sorrow.

This situation has come about from a number of causes, which are in general the outcome of rather recent historical events, and it has further been influenced to some extent by the conduct of certain nations that glory in the fact that the light of Christianity illuminates their annals. There is every reason, therefore, why We should be subject to no small anxiety with regard to the fortunes of Catholicism in Africa. There is every reason too why all the Church's children should clearly realise their serious obligation to give more effective assistance to the missionaries. This they must do at the opportune moment in order that the message of saving truth may be brought to what is called 'darkest' Africa, where some 85,000,000 people still sit in the darkness of idolatry.[2765]

Pope Pius XI: 1922 to 1939

Encyclical *Rerum Ecclesiae, 2, 3, 4, 23. (28th February 1926)*
It is a well-known fact that Our Predecessors fulfilled at all times the Divine Commission wherewith they were charged of teaching and baptizing all nations, that the priests sent by them (many of whom the Church publicly venerates because of the holiness of their lives or because they so courageously suffered martyrdom) zealously strove with varying results to enlighten by the Faith first Europe, and, later on, even unknown lands, and this almost immediately after their discovery. [...]

As for Ourselves, Venerable Brothers, you well know that, from the beginning of Our Pontificate, We determined to leave nothing undone which might, by means of apostolic preachers, extend farther and farther the light of the Gospel and make easy for heathen nations the way unto salvation. [...]

For Our part, so long as Divine Providence shall preserve Our life, this duty of Our Apostolic office will always be a special obligation to us, for when We ponder over the fact that the pagans number, even in our day, almost a billion, 'We have no rest in our spirit' (II Cor 7:5) and seem to hear sounding in Our ears the words, 'Cry, cease not, lift up thy voice like a trumpet.' (Isa 58:1). [...]

[2765]Pope Ven. XII [1957] Encyclical *Fidei Donum*, para 20 [Online] Available at: www.vatican.va [Accessed on: 7 July 2022]

Moreover, since the words of Christ 'the harvest indeed is great, but the labourers are few' (Mt 9:35; Lk 10:2) are true, even in the present condition of affairs, Europe from whence most of the missionaries have come is itself in need of priests, and this at a time when, with the help of God, it is most important that our separated brethren be led back to the unity of the Church and that non-Catholics be convinced of and delivered from their errors.[2766]

Encyclical *Rite Expiatis, 37. (13th April 1926)*
St. Francis, 'a man who was truly Catholic and apostolic,' in the same admirable fashion that he had attended to the reformation of the faithful, so likewise set about personally and commanded his disciples to occupy themselves before everything else with the conversion of the heathen to the Faith and Law of Christ. Nor need We dwell at length on a subject so well known to all. Moved by an ardent desire to spread the Gospel and even to undergo martyrdom, he did not hesitate to go to Egypt and there bravely to appear in the very presence of the Sultan. In the annals of the Church, too, are not the names of those numerous apostles of the Gospel who, from the beginning, that is to say, in the springtime of the Order of Minors, found martyrdom in Syria and Morocco recorded in words of highest praise? With the passing of time this apostolate had been developed with much zeal and often with great shedding of blood by the numerous Franciscan brotherhood, for many lands inhabited by the heathen have been entrusted to their care through the express commands of the Roman Pontiffs.[2767]

Pope Benedict XV: 1914 to 1922

Apostolic Letter *Maximum Illud, 1, 6-7. (30th November 1919)*
Before He returned to His Father, Our Lord Jesus Christ addressed to His disciples the words: 'Go into the whole world and preach the Gospel to all creation' (Mk 16:15). With these words He committed to them a duty, a momentous and a holy charge, that was not to lapse with the death of the Apostles but would bind their successors, one after another, until the end of the world – as long, that is, as there remained on this earth men whom the truth might set free. Entrusted with this mandate, 'they went forth and preached everywhere' (Mk 16:20) the word of God, so that 'through all the earth their voice resounds, and to the ends of the world, their message' (Ps 18:5). From that time on, as the centuries have passed, the Church has never forgotten that command God gave her, and never yet has she ceased to dispatch to every corner of the world her couriers of the doctrine He entrusted to her, and her ministers of the eternal salvation that was delivered through Christ to the human race. [...]

Anyone who studies the facts of this great saga cannot help being profoundly impressed by them: by all the stupendous hardships our missionaries have undergone in extending the Faith, the magnificent devotion they have shown, and the overwhelming examples of intrepid endurance they have afforded us. And to anyone who weighs these facts the realisation must come as a shock that right now, there still remain in the world immense multitudes of people who dwell in darkness and in the shadow of death. According to a recent estimate, the number of non-believers in the world approximates one billion souls. The misfortune of this vast number of souls is for Us a source of great sorrow. From the days when We first took up the responsibilities of this apostolic office We have yearned to share with them the divine blessings of the Redemption.[2768]

[2766]Pope Pius XI [1926] Encyclical *Rerum Ecclesiae*, para 23 [Online] Available at: www.vatican.va [Accessed on: 7 July 2022]
[2767]Pope Pius XI [1926] Encyclical *Rite Expiatis*, para 37 [Online] Available at: www.vatican.va [Accessed on: 7 July 2022]
[2768]Pope Benedict XV [1919] Apostolic Letter *Maximum Illud*, paras 1,6-7 [Online] Available at: www.vatican.va [Accessed on: 7 July 2022]

Pope St. Pius X: 1903 to 1914

Encyclical *E Supremi, 9. (4th October 1903)*
Now the way to reach Christ is not hard to find: it is the Church. Rightly does Chrysostom inculcate: 'The Church is thy hope, the Church is thy salvation, the Church is thy refuge.' (*Hom. de capto Euthropio*, n. 6.) It was for this that Christ founded it, gaining it at the price of His blood, and made it the depositary of His doctrine and His laws, bestowing upon it at the same time an inexhaustible treasury of graces for the sanctification and salvation of men. You see, then, Venerable Brethren, the duty that has been imposed alike upon Us and upon you of bringing back to the discipline of the Church human society, now estranged from the wisdom of Christ; the Church will then subject it to Christ, and Christ to God. If We, through the goodness of God Himself, bring this task to a happy issue, We shall be rejoiced to see evil giving place to good, and hear, for our gladness, 'a loud voice from heaven saying: Now is come salvation, and strength, and the kingdom of our God and the power of his Christ.' (Apoc. 12:10.) But if our desire to obtain this is to be fulfilled, we must use every means and exert all our energy to bring about the utter disappearance of the enormous and detestable wickedness, so characteristic of our time — the substitution of man for God; this done, it remains to restore to their ancient place of honor the most holy laws and counsels of the gospel; to proclaim aloud the truths taught by the Church, and her teachings on the sanctity of marriage, on the education and discipline of youth, on the possession and use of property, the duties that men owe to those who rule the State; and lastly to restore equilibrium between the different classes of society according to Christian precept and custom. This is what We, in submitting Ourselves to the manifestations of the Divine will, purpose to aim at during Our Pontificate, and We will use all our industry to attain it. It is for you, Venerable Brethren, to second Our efforts by your holiness, knowledge and experience and above all by your zeal for the glory of God, with no other aim than that Christ may be formed in all.[2769]

Catechism of Pope St. Pius X. (1908)
Those Outside the Communion of Saints
12 Q. Who are infidels?
A. Infidels are those who have not been baptised and do not believe in Jesus Christ, because they either believe in and worship false gods as idolaters do, or though admitting one true God, they do not believe in the Messiah, neither as already come in the Person of Jesus Christ, nor as to come; for instance, Mohammedans and the like.[2770]

Pope Leo XIII: 1878 to 1903

Encyclical *Immortale Dei, 8. (1st November 1885)*
For the only-begotten Son of God established on earth a society which is called the Church, and to it He handed over the exalted and divine office which He had received from His Father, to be continued through the ages to come. 'As the Father hath sent Me, I also send you. Behold I am with you all days, even to the consummation of the world.' (Mt 28:20) Consequently, as Jesus Christ came into the world that men 'might have life and have it more abundantly,' (Jn 10:10) so also has the Church for its aim and end the eternal salvation of souls, and hence it is so constituted as to open wide its arms to all mankind, unhampered by any limit of either time or place. 'Preach ye the Gospel to every creature.'(Mk 16:15).[2771]

Encyclical *Catholicae Ecclesiae, 3. (20th November 1890)*
Besides protecting freedom, another more serious apostolic concern orders Us to spread the teaching of the Gospel in Africa. This teaching should bathe those inhabitants living

---

[2769]Pope St. Pius X [1903] Encyclical *E Supremi*, para 9 [Online] Available at: www.vatican.va [Accessed on: 3 October 2022]
[2770]Pope St. Pius X [1908] *Catechism of Pope St. Pius X.* Those Outside the Communion of Saints 12 Q. Who are infidels? [Online] Available at: www.ewtn.com [Accessed on: 7 July 2022]
[2771]Pope Leo XIII [1885] Encyclical *Immortale Dei*, para 8. [Online] Available at: www.vatican.va [Accessed on: 7 July 2022]

in darkness and blind superstition with the light of divine truth, by which they can become co-heirs with Us of the kingdom of God. We are the more concerned about this because those who have received this light have also shaken off the yoke of human slavery. Wherever Christian customs and laws are in force, wherever religion establishes that men serve justice and honor human dignity, wherever the spirit of brotherly love taught by Christ spreads itself, there neither slavery nor savage barbarism can exist. Rather, mildness of character and civilised Christian liberty flourish there. Many apostolic men, like standard-bearing soldiers of Christ, go to the African interior to shed their sweat, even life itself for the welfare of their brothers. But 'the harvest indeed is great; the labourers are few.'[2772]

Encyclical *Ad Extremas, 1-2. (24th June 1893)*
We reflect upon those immense regions of the Indies where for many centuries men of the Gospel have expended their labor. Our thoughts turn first of all to the blessed Apostle Thomas who is rightly called the founder of preaching the Gospel to the Hindus. Then, there is Francis Xavier, who long afterwards dedicated himself zealously to the same praiseworthy calling. Through his extraordinary perseverance, he converted hundreds of thousands of Hindus from the myths and vile superstitions of the Brahmans to the true religion. In the footsteps of this holy man followed numerous priests, secular and religious, who with the authority and permission of the Holy See strove untiringly to preserve and promote the Christian mysteries and institutions introduced by Thomas and renewed by Xavier. To this day, they are continuing these noble efforts; nevertheless, in the vast reaches of the earth, many are still deprived of the truth, miserably imprisoned in the darkness of superstition! How very great a field, especially in the north, lies yet uncultivated to receive the seed of the Gospel!

Pondering these needs, We place our trust in Our Savior who alone knows the exact circumstance and time to bestow his light; he is wont to direct the mind and hearts of men by divine inspiration. But, assuredly, We ought to exert every possible effort to convert such a great part of the world. We have been searching for possible ways of better organising and expanding Christianity in the East Indies, we have decided upon certain measures to help achieve Our goal.[2773]

Pope Gregory XVI: 1831 to 1846

Encyclical *Probe Nostis, 6. (18th September 1840)*
We are thankful for the success of apostolic missions in America, the Indies, and other faithless lands. The indefatigable zeal of many apostolic men has led them abroad into those places. Relying not on wealth nor on any army, they are protected by the shield of faith alone. They fearlessly fight the Lord's battles against heresy and unbelief by private and public speech and writings. They are inspired with a burning love and undeterred by rough roads and heavy toil. They search out those who sit in darkness and the shadow of death to summon them to the light and life of the Catholic Religion. So, fearless in the face of every danger, they bravely enter the woods and caves of savages, gradually pacify them by Christian kindness, and prepare them for true faith and real virtue. At length they snatch them from the devil's rule, by the bath of regeneration and promote them to the freedom of God's adopted sons.[2774]

Pope Alexander VI: 1492 to 1503

Bull *Inter Caetera. (4th May1493)*
We have indeed learned that you, who for a long time had intended to seek out and discover certain islands and mainlands remote and unknown and not hitherto

---

[2772]Pope Leo XIII [1890] Encyclical *Catholicae Ecclesiae*, para 3 [Online] Available at: www.vatican. va [Accessed on: 7 July 2022]

[2773]Pope Leo XIII [1893] Encyclical *Ad Extremas*, para 1 [Online] Available at: www.vatican.va [Accessed on: 7 July 2022]

[2774]Pope Gregory XV [1840] Encyclical *Probe Nostis*, para 6 [Online] Available at: www. papalencyclicals.net [Accessed on: 7 July 2022]

discovered by others, to the end that you might bring to the worship of our Redeemer and the profession of the Catholic faith their residents and inhabitants....

Moreover, as your aforesaid envoys are of opinion, these very peoples living in the said islands and countries believe in one God, the Creator in heaven, and seem sufficiently disposed to embrace the Catholic faith and be trained in good morals....

Wherefore, as becomes Catholic kings and princes, after earnest consideration of all matters, especially of the rise and spread of the Catholic faith, as was the fashion of your ancestors, kings of renowned memory, you have purposed with the favor of divine clemency to bring under your sway the said mainlands and islands with their residents and inhabitants and to bring them to the Catholic faith. Hence, heartily commending in the Lord this your holy and praiseworthy purpose, and desirous that it be duly accomplished, and that the name of our Savior be carried into those regions, we exhort you very earnestly in the Lord and by your reception of holy baptism, whereby you are bound to our apostolic commands, and by the bowels of the mercy of our Lord Jesus Christ, enjoin strictly, that inasmuch as with eager zeal for the true faith you design to equip and despatch this expedition, you purpose also, as is your duty, to lead the peoples dwelling in those islands and countries to embrace the Christian religion; nor at any time let dangers or hardships deter you therefrom, with the stout hope and trust in your hearts that Almighty God will further your undertakings.[2775]

[2775]Pope Alexander VI [1493] Bull *Inter Caetera* [Online] Available at: www.papalencyclicals.net [Accessed on: 3 October 2022]

Hamartiology (1) — 'Boasting about One's Sins'

Pope Francis: 2013 to 2025

G. *Our sins are the privileged place of encounter with Christ, and as such we can 'boast of our sins' (misquoting II Cor 12:9).*

Conversation with the Union of Superiors General of Men. (29th November 2013)
Life is complicated. It consists of grace and sin. He who does not sin is not human. We all make mistakes and we need to recognise our weakness.[2776]

Morning meditation in the Chapel of the Domus Sanctae Marthae. (4th September 2014)
Rather 'he boasted of only two things, and these things that Paul boasted of are precisely the place where the Word of God can come and be strong'. Indeed, he said of himself: 'I boast only of my sins'. These were 'scandalous words'....[2777]

Morning meditation in the Chapel of the Domus Sanctae Marthae. (18th September 2014)
In this regard the Pope repeated an expression especially dear to him: 'the privileged place for the encounter with Christ is our sins'. Pope Francis commented that to the untrained ear this 'would almost seem heresy, but even St. Paul said it' in the Second Letter to the Corinthians (12:9), when he affirmed boasting of 'only two things: of his sins and of the Risen Christ who saved him'.[2778]

Address to Participants in the Plenary Assembly of the Catholic Biblical Federation. (19th June 2015)
At the end he has this beautiful phrase, 'to boast', after I boast of this, of so many journeys, of countless beatings, of a stoning... all of this.... 'But if I must boast' — today he said in that passage —'I will boast of the things that show my weakness'(cf. II Cor 11:30). In another passage — you biblicists know it — he says: 'I will boast of my sins' (cf. II Cor 12:9).[2779]

Sacred Scripture

II Corinthians 12:9
And he said to me: My grace is sufficient for thee: for power is made perfect in infirmity. Gladly therefore will I glory in my infirmities, that the power of Christ may dwell in me.

John 12:40
He hath blinded their eyes, and hardened their heart, that they should not see with their eyes, nor understand with their heart, and be converted, and I should heal them.

Romans 1:18; 9:18
For the wrath of God is revealed from heaven against all ungodliness and injustice of those men that detain the truth of God in injustice....
   Therefore he hath mercy on whom he will; and whom he will, he hardeneth.

II Thessalonians 2:10-11
Therefore God shall send them the operation of error, to believe lying: That all may be judged who have not believed the truth, but have consented to iniquity.

I John 3:8-9; 5:16-17
He that committeth sin is of the devil: for the devil sinneth from the beginning. For this purpose, the Son of God appeared, that he might destroy the works of the devil.

[2776]*Francis calls on religious men to 'wake up the world'* [3 January 2014] [Online] Available at: www.lastampa.it [Accessed on: 7 July 2022]
[2777]Pope Francis [4th September 2014] *Morning meditation in the Chapel of the Domus Sanctae Marthae* [Online] Available at: www.vatican.va [Accessed on: 7 July 2022]
[2778]Pope Francis [18 September 2014] *Morning meditation in the Chapel of the Domus* [Online] Available at: www.vatican.va [Accessed on: 7 July 2022]
[2779]Pope Francis [2015] *Address to Participants in the Plenary Assembly of the Catholic Biblical Federation* [Online] Available at: www.vatican.va [Accessed on: 7 July 2022]

Whosoever is born of God, committeth not sin: for his seed abideth in him, and he can not sin, because he is born of God.

He that knoweth his brother to sin a sin which is not to death, let him ask, and life shall be given to him, who sinneth not to death. There is a sin unto death: for that I say not that any man ask. All iniquity is sin. And there is a sin unto death.

Hebrews 10: 26-31
For if we sin wilfully after having the knowledge of the truth, there is now left no sacrifice for sins, but a certain dreadful expectation of judgment, and the rage of a fire which shall consume the adversaries. A man making void the law of Moses, dieth without any mercy under two or three witnesses: How much more, do you think he deserveth worse punishments, who hath trodden under foot the Son of God, and hath esteemed the blood of the testament unclean, by which he was sanctified, and hath offered an affront to the Spirit of grace? For we know him that hath said: Vengeance belongeth to me, and I will repay. And again: The Lord shall judge his people. It is a fearful thing to fall into the hands of the living God.

II Peter 2:18-22
For, speaking proud words of vanity, they allure by the desires of fleshly riotousness, those who for a little while escape, such as converse in error: Promising them liberty, whereas they themselves are the slaves of corruption. For by whom a man is overcome, of the same also he is the slave. For if, flying from the pollutions of the world, through the knowledge of our Lord and Saviour Jesus Christ, they be again entangled in them and overcome: their latter state is become unto them worse than the former. For it had been better for them not to have known the way of justice, than after they have known it, to turn back from that holy commandment which was delivered to them. For, that of the true proverb has happened to them: The dog is returned to his vomit: and, The sow that was washed, to her wallowing in the mire.

Ezekiel 18:24
But if the just man turn himself away from his justice, and do iniquity according to all the abominations which the wicked man useth to work, shall he live? all his justices which he hath done, shall not be remembered: in the prevarication, by which he hath prevaricated, and in his sin, which he hath committed, in them he shall die.

Isaiah 6:10; 59:2-3
Blind the heart of this people, and make their ears heavy, and shut their eyes: lest they see with their eyes, and hear with their ears, and understand with their heart, and be converted and I heal them.

But your iniquities have divided between you and your God, and your sins have hid his face from you that he should not hear. For your hands are defiled with blood, and your fingers with iniquity: your lips have spoken lies, and your tongue uttereth iniquity.

Proverbs 6:16-19
Six things there are, which the Lord hateth, and the seventh his soul detesteth: Haughty eyes, a lying tongue, hands that shed innocent blood, A heart that deviseth wicked plots, feet that are swift to run into mischief, A deceitful witness that uttereth lies, and him that soweth discord among brethren.

Psalm 5: 6-7
Neither shall the wicked dwell near thee: nor shall the unjust abide before thy eyes. Thou hatest all the workers of iniquity: thou wilt destroy all that speak a lie. The bloody and the deceitful man the Lord will abhor.

Nahum 1:2
The Lord is a jealous God, and a revenger: the Lord is a revenger, and hath wrath: the Lord taketh vengeance on his adversaries, and he is angry with his enemies.

Zephaniah 1:15-17
That day is a day of wrath, a day of tribulation and distress, a day of calamity and misery, a day of darkness and obscurity, a day of clouds and whirlwinds, A day of the trumpet and alarm against the fenced cities, and against the high bulwarks. And I will distress men, and they shall walk like blind men, because they have sinned against the Lord: and their blood shall be poured out as earth, and their bodies as dung.

Sacred Tradition

Lactantius: c. 250 to c. 325

On the Anger of God. Chaps. 18, 21
What need is there, they say, of anger, since faults can be corrected without this affection? But there is no one who can calmly see any one committing an offence.... We, undoubtedly, when an offence is committed by our household at home, whether we see or perceive it, must be indignant; for the very sight of a sin is unbecoming. For he who is altogether unmoved either approves of faults, which is more disgraceful and unjust, or avoids the trouble of reproving them, which a tranquil spirit and a quiet mind despises and refuses, unless anger shall have aroused and incited it. But when any one is moved, and yet through unseasonable leniency grants pardon more frequently than is necessary, or at all times, he evidently both destroys the life of those whose audacity he is fostering for greater crimes, and furnishes himself with a perpetual source of annoyances. Therefore the restraining of one's anger in the case of sins is faulty.

But because I had said that the anger of God is not for a time only, as is the case with man, who becomes inflamed with an immediate excitement, and on account of his frailty is unable easily to govern himself, we ought to understand that because God is eternal, His anger also remains to eternity; but, on the other hand, that because He is endued with the greatest excellence, He controls His anger, and is not ruled by it, but that He regulates it according to His will. And it is plain that this is not opposed to that which has just been said. For if His anger had been altogether immortal, there would be no place after a fault for satisfaction or kind feeling, though He Himself commands men to be reconciled before the setting of the sun. But the divine anger remains for ever against those who ever sin. Therefore God is appeased not by incense or a victim, not by costly offerings, which things are all corruptible, but by a reformation of the morals: and he who ceases to sin renders the anger of God mortal. For this reason He does not immediately punish every one who is guilty, that man may have the opportunity of coming to a right mind, and correcting himself.[2780]

St. Cyprian: c. 210 to 258

Epistle 54, para 13
'They received not the love of the truth, that they might be saved. And for this cause God shall send them strong delusion, that they should believe a lie: that they all might be judged who believed not the truth, but had pleasure in unrighteousness.' (II Thess 2:10-11) The highest degree of happiness is, not to sin; the second, to acknowledge our sins. In the former, innocence flows pure and unstained to preserve us; in the latter, there comes a medicine to heal us. Both of these they have lost by offending God, both because the grace is lost which is received from the sanctification of baptism, and repentance comes not to their help, whereby the sin is healed. Think you, brother, that their wickednesses against God are trifling, their sins small and moderate — since by their means the majesty of an angry God is not besought, since the anger and the fire and the day of the Lord is not feared — since, when Antichrist is at hand the faith of the militant people is disarmed by the taking away of the power of Christ and His fear? Let the laity see to it how they may amend this.[2781]

[2780]Lactantius. *On the Anger of God*, Chap. 21 [Online] Available at: www.newadvent.org [Accessed on: 12 July 2022]
[2781]St. Cyprian. *Epistle* 54, para 13 [Online] Available at: www.newadvent.org [Accessed on: 12 July 2022]

On the Lapsed, para 33

Unrighteously pleasing themselves, and mad with the alienation of a hardened mind, they despise the Lord's precepts, neglect the medicine for their wound, and will not repent. Thoughtless before their sin was acknowledged, after their sin they are obstinate; neither steadfast before, nor suppliant afterwards: when they ought to have stood fast, they fell; when they ought to fall and prostrate themselves to God, they think they stand fast. They have taken peace for themselves of their own accord when nobody granted it; seduced by false promises, and linked with apostates and unbelievers, they take hold of error instead of truth: they regard a communion as valid with those who are not communicants; they believe men against God, although they have not believed God against men.[2782]

St. Augustine: 354 to 430

Sermon 47

By sinning, of course, you make an enemy of God.[2783]

Sermon 109

If you sin, your adversary is God's word. For example, perhaps you enjoy getting drunk; it says to you, 'Don't.' You enjoy watching the games and vain pastimes; its says to you, 'Don't.' You enjoy committing adultery; God's word says to you, 'Don't.' In whatever kinds of sin you want to do by your own will, its says to you, 'Don't.' It's the adversary of your will, until it can become the author of your salvation. Oh what a good adversary, what a useful adversary! It's an adversary to us, just as long as we are so to ourselves. As long as you are your own enemy, you also have God's word as your enemy; be a friend to yourself, and you agree with it. *You shall not commit murder*; listen and you've agreed. *You shall not commit theft*; listen, and you've agreed. *You shall not commit adultery*; listen and you've agreed. *You shall not bear false witness*; listen, and you've agreed. You shall not covet your neighbour's goods (Ex 20:13-17); listen, and you've agreed.

In all these matters you've agreed with your adversary, and what have you lost for yourself? Not only have you lost nothing, you've even found yourself, whom you had lost. The road is this life; if we have reached agreement with him, if we have given him our consent, then when the road reaches its end, we won't have to fear either judge, officer, or prison.[2784]

Sermon 113A

Notice what the scripture said: The sinner has provoked the Lord; in the greatness of his wrath he will not search out (Ps 10:4). What does it mean, in the greatness of his wrath he will not search out? Because he is very angry he will not search out, that is, he will leave them to perish. So if it means he is very angry when he doesn't search out, it means he is very merciful when he puts us through our paces. And he puts us through our paces when he scourges us, when he fixes our hearts on himself. So let us stick it out, this saving medicine of his, and don't let us run away from his scourge. That's what he's teaching us with, that's what he's warning us with, that's how he's building us up.[2785]

Sermon 142

Does he only love, or only hate, or does he hate and love? Indeed, he both loves and hates. He hates what is yours, he loves you. What does it mean to say, he hates yours, he loves you? He hates what you have made, he loves what God has made. What is yours,

[2782] St. Cyprian. *On the Lapsed,* para 33 [Online] Available at: www.newadvent.org [Accessed on: 12 July 2022]

[2783] The Works of Saint Augustine: A Translation for the 21st Century [1990] *Sermons II (20-50) on the Old Testament.* New York: New City Press, p.303

[2784] The Works of Saint Augustine: A Translation for the 21st Century [1990] *Sermons III/4 (94A-147A) on the New Testament.* New York: New City Press, p.133-134

[2785] *Ibid.,* p.181-182

after all, other than sins? And who are you, other than what God has made? You neglect what you have been made, you cherish what you have made; you love your own works outside you, you neglect within you the work of God.[2786]

A Treatise on the Spirit and the Letter, Chap. 52.
If, therefore, they are the slaves of sin, why do they boast of free will? For by what a man is overcome, to the same is he delivered as a slave. But if they have been freed, why do they vaunt themselves as if it were by their own doing, and boast, as if they had not received? Or are they free in such sort that they do not choose to have Him for their Lord who says to them: 'Without me ye can do nothing;' (Jn 15:5) and 'If the Son shall make you free, ye shall be free indeed?' (Jn 8:36).[2787]

St. Thomas Aquinas: 1225 to 1274

Summa Theologiae. Prima Secundæ Pars. Q 79. Art 3; Art 4
On the other hand, God, of His own accord, withholds His grace from those in whom He finds an obstacle: so that the cause of grace being withheld is not only the man who raises an obstacle to grace; but God, Who, of His own accord, withholds His grace. In this way, God is the cause of spiritual blindness, deafness of ear, and hardness of heart.

Blindness is a kind of preamble to sin. Now sin has a twofold relation—to one thing directly, viz. to the sinner's damnation—to another, by reason of God's mercy or providence, viz. that the sinner may be healed, in so far as God permits some to fall into sin, that by acknowledging their sin, they may be humbled and converted, as Augustine states (*De Nat. et Grat.* xxii). Therefore blindness, of its very nature, is directed to the damnation of those who are blinded; for which reason it is accounted an effect of reprobation. But, through God's mercy, temporary blindness is directed medicinally to the spiritual welfare of those who are blinded. This mercy, however, is not vouchsafed to all those who are blinded, but only to the predestinated, to whom 'all things work together unto good' (Rom 8:28). Therefore as regards some, blindness is directed to their healing; but as regards others, to their damnation; as Augustine says (*De Quaest. Evang.* iii).[2788]

The Magisterium of the Church

Our sins should inspire us with the deepest horror and sorrow because they incur the wrath and enmity of God that is only removed through our response to the grace of repentance. Our sins deeply offend God, and make us His enemies.

Council of Trent (Nineteenth Ecumenical, 1545 to 1563)

Decree on Justification, Chap. 1, 15. (13th January 1547)
…it is necessary that each one recognise and confess, that, whereas all men had lost their innocence in the prevarication of Adam-having become unclean, and, as the apostle says, by nature children of wrath, as (this Synod) has set forth in the decree on original sin,-they were so far the servants of sin, and under the power of the devil and of death…

That, by every mortal sin, grace is lost, but not faith. In opposition also to the subtle wits of certain men, who, by pleasing speeches and good words, seduce the hearts of the innocent, it is to be maintained, that the received grace of Justification is lost, not only by infidelity whereby even faith itself is lost, but also by any other mortal sin whatever, though faith be not lost; thus defending the doctrine of the divine law, which excludes from the kingdom of God not only the unbelieving, but the faithful also (who are) fornicators, adulterers, effeminate, liers with mankind, thieves, covetous, drunk-

---

[2786]*Ibid.,* p.415
[2787]St. Augustine. *On the Spirit and the Letter,* Chap. 52. [Online] Available at: www.newadvent.org [Accessed on: 12 July 2022]
[2788]St. Thomas Aquinas. *Summa Theologiae.* First Part of the Second Part. Q. 79, A. 3 [Online] Available at: www.newadvent.org [Accessed on: 9 July 2022]

ards, railers, extortioners, and all others who commit deadly sins; from which, with the help of divine grace, they can refrain, and on account of which they are separated from the grace of Christ.

CANON XXVII. If any one saith, that there is no mortal sin but that of infidelity; or, that grace once received is not lost by any other sin, however grievous and enormous, save by that of infidelity; let him be anathema.[2789]

Decree on the Sacrament of Penance, Chaps. 5, 8 (25th November 1551)
...all mortal sins, even those of thought, render men 'children of wrath' (Eph 2:3), and enemies of God....

And it beseems the divine clemency, that sins be not in such wise pardoned us without any satisfaction, as that, taking occasion therefrom, thinking sins less grievous, we, offering as it were an insult and an outrage to the Holy Ghost (Heb 10:29), should fall into more grievous sins, treasuring up wrath against the day of wrath (cf. Rom 2:5; Jas 5:3). For, doubtless, these satisfactory punishments greatly recall from sin, and check as it were with a bridle, and make penitents more cautious and watchful for the future; they are also remedies for the remains of sin, and, by acts of the opposite virtues, they remove the habits acquired by evil living.[2790]

Second Vatican Council (Twenty-First Ecumenical, 1962 to 1965)

Dogmatic Constitution *Lumen Gentium, 16. (21st November 1964)*
But often men, deceived by the Evil One, have become vain in their reasonings and have exchanged the truth of God for a lie, serving the creature rather than the Creator (Rom 1:21, 25). Or some there are who, living and dying in this world without God, are exposed to final despair.[2791]

Pastoral Constitution *Gaudium et Spes, 13,16. (7th December 1965)*
Although he was made by God in a state of holiness, from the very onset of his history man abused his liberty, at the urging of the Evil One. Man set himself against God and sought to attain his goal apart from God. Although they knew God, they did not glorify Him as God, but their senseless minds were darkened and they served the creature rather than the Creator (Rom 1:21-25). What divine revelation makes known to us agrees with experience. Examining his heart, man finds that he has inclinations toward evil too, and is engulfed by manifold ills which cannot come from his good Creator. Often refusing to acknowledge God as his beginning, man has disrupted also his proper relationship to his own ultimate goal as well as his whole relationship toward himself and others and all created things.

Therefore man is split within himself. As a result, all of human life, whether individual or collective, shows itself to be a dramatic struggle between good and evil, between light and darkness. Indeed, man finds that by himself he is incapable of battling the assaults of evil successfully, so that everyone feels as though he is bound by chains. But the Lord Himself came to free and strengthen man, renewing him inwardly and casting out that 'prince of this world' (John 12:31) who held him in the bondage of sin (Jn 8:34). For sin has diminished man, blocking his path to fulfilment.

Conscience frequently errs from invincible ignorance without losing its dignity. The same cannot be said for a man who cares but little for truth and goodness, or for a conscience which by degrees grows practically sightless as a result of habitual sin.[2792]

[2789]The Council of Trent. [1547] *Decree on Justification,* Chap. 1, 15 [Online] Available at: www.thecounciloftrent.com [Accessed on: 8 July 2022]
[2790]The Council of Trent. [1551] *Decree on the Sacrament of Penance,* Chap 5 [Online] Available at: www.thecounciloftrent.com [Accessed on: 8 July 2022]
[2791]Second Vatican Council [1964] Dogmatic Constitution, *Lumen Gentium,* para 16 [Online] Available at: www.vatican.va [Accessed on: 5 July 2022]
[2792]Second Vatican Council [1965] Pastoral Constitution *Gaudium et Spes,* Part 1, Chap. 1, para 13 [Online] Available at: www.vatican.va [Accessed on: 9 July 2022]

Pope Benedict XVI: 2005 to 2013

Angelus Address. (15th February 2009)
It is possible to see leprosy as a symbol of sin, which is the true impurity of heart that can distance us from God. It is not in fact the physical disease of leprosy that separates us from God as the ancient norms supposed but sin, spiritual and moral evil....The sins that we commit distance us from God and, if we do not humbly confess them, trusting in divine mercy, they will finally bring about the death of the soul.[2793]

Homily for Mass of the Lord's Supper. (5th April 2012)
This pride is the real essence of sin. We think we are free and truly ourselves only if we follow our own will. God appears as the opposite of our freedom. We need to be free of him – so we think – and only then will we be free. This is the fundamental rebellion present throughout history and the fundamental lie which perverts life. When human beings set themselves against God, they set themselves against the truth of their own being and consequently do not become free, but alienated from themselves.[2794]

Pope St. John Paul II: 1978 to 2005

Encyclical *Reconciliatio et Paenitentia, 31. (2nd December1984)*
God is always the one who is principally offended by sin — 'Tibi soli peccavi!'"[2795]

Encyclical *Dominum et Vivificantem, 39. (18th May 1986)*
For from the beginning the Spirit 'is invoked' in order to 'convince the world concerning sin.' He is invoked in a definitive way through the Cross of Christ. Convincing concerning sin means showing the evil that sin contains, and this is equivalent to revealing the mystery of iniquity. It is not possible to grasp the evil of sin in all its sad reality without 'searching the depths of God.' From the very beginning, the obscure mystery of sin has appeared in the world against the background of a reference to the Creator of human freedom. Sin has appeared as an act of the will of the creature-man contrary to the will of God, to the salvific will of God; indeed, sin has appeared in opposition to the truth, on the basis of the lie which has now been definitively 'judged': the lie that has placed in a state of accusation, a state of permanent suspicion, creative and salvific love itself. Man has followed the 'father of lies,' setting himself up in opposition to the Father of life and the Spirit of truth.

The Church, taking her inspiration from Revelation, believes and professes that sin is an offence against God. What corresponds, in the inscrutable intimacy of the Father, the Word and the Holy Spirit, to this 'offence,' this rejection of the Spirit who is love and gift? The concept of God as the necessarily most perfect being certainly excludes from God any pain deriving from deficiencies or wounds; but in the 'depths of God' there is a Father's love that, faced with man's sin, in the language of the Bible reacts so deeply as to say: 'I am sorry that I have made him.' (Gen 6:7). 'The Lord saw that the wickedness of man was great in the earth.... And the Lord was sorry that he had made man on the earth.... The Lord said: 'I am sorry that I have made them.' (Gen 6:5-7).[2796]

Catechism of the Catholic Church. (1992)
Man, tempted by the devil, let his trust in his Creator die in his heart and, abusing his freedom, disobeyed God's command. This is what man's first sin consisted of. (Gen 3:1-11; Rom 5:19). All subsequent sin would be disobedience toward God and lack of trust in his goodness. (397)

[2793]Pope Benedict XVI [2009] *Angelus Address* [Online] Available at: www.vatican.va [Accessed on: 3 October 2022]

[2794]Pope Benedict XVI [2012] *Homily for Mass of the Lord's Supper* [Online] Available at: www.vatican.va [Accessed on: 3 October 2022]

[2795]Pope St. John Paul II [1984] Post Synodal Apostolic Exhortation *Reconciliatio et Paenitentia,* para 31 [Online] Available at: www.vatican.va [Accessed on: 3 October 2022]

[2796]Pope St. John Paul II [1986] Encyclical *Dominum et Vivificantem,* para 39 [Online] Available at: www.vatican.va [Accessed on: 12 July 2022]

Sin is before all else an offence against God, a rupture of communion with him. At the same time it damages communion with the Church. (1440)

Sin is an offence against God: 'Against you, you alone, have I sinned, and done that which is evil in your sight.' (Ps 51:4). Sin sets itself against God's love for us and turns our hearts away from it. Like the first sin, it is disobedience, a revolt against God through the will to become 'like gods, '(Gen 3:5) knowing and determining good and evil. Sin is thus 'love of oneself even to contempt of God.' In this proud self-exaltation, sin is diametrically opposed to the obedience of Jesus, which achieves our salvation (Phil 2:6-9). (1850)[2797]

General Audience Address, 3. (25th August 1999)
While he offends God and harms himself, the sinner also becomes responsible for the bad example and negative influences linked to his behaviour. Even when the sin is interior, it still causes a worsening of the human condition and diminishes that contribution which every person is called to make to the spiritual progress of the human community.[2798]

General Audience Address, 2. (19th May 2004)
The sinner felt God's hand weighing upon him, aware as he was that God is not indifferent to the evil committed by his creature, since he is the guardian of justice and truth.[2799]

Pope St. Paul VI: 1963 to 1978

Apostolic Constitution, *Paenitemini, Chap. 1. (17th February 1966)*
In the Old Testament the religious sense of penitence is revealed with even greater richness. Even though man generally has recourse to it in the aftermath of sin to placate the wrath of God. (I Sam. 7:6; I Kings 21:20-21, 27; Jer. 3:3, 7, 9; Jn 1:2; 3:4-5).[2800]

Apostolic Constitution, *Indulgentiarum Doctrina, 2. (1st January 1967)*
It is a divinely revealed truth that sins bring punishments inflicted by God's sanctity and justice. These must be expiated either on this earth through the sorrows, miseries and calamities of this life and above all through death (Gen 3:16-19; also cf. Lk 19:41-44; Rom 2:9 and I Cor 11:30.), or else in the life beyond through fire and torments or 'purifying' punishments (Mt 25:41-42; see also Mk 9:42-43; Jn 5:28-29; Rom 2:9; Gal 6:6-8). Therefore it has always been the conviction of the faithful that the paths of evil are fraught with many stumbling blocks and bring adversities, bitterness and harm to those who follow them.[2801]

Pope St. John XXIII: 1958 to 1963

Encyclical *Paenitentiam Agere, 14. (1st July 1962)*
This being so, well may those sinners who have stained the white robe of their sacred baptism fear the just punishments of God. Their remedy is 'to wash their robes in the blood of the Lamb' (Apoc 7:14) — to restore themselves to their former splendor in the sacrament of Penance — and to school themselves in the practice of Christian virtue. Hence the Apostle Paul's severe warning: 'A man making void the law of Moses dies without any mercy on the word of two or three witnesses; how much worse punishments do you think he deserves, who has trodden under foot the Son of God,

---

[2797]*Catechism of the Catholic Church* [1992] [Online] Available at: scborromeo2.org [Accessed on: 12 July 2022]
[2798]Pope St. John Paul II [1999] *General Audience Address*, para 3 [Online] Available at: www. vatican.va [Accessed on: 12 July 2022]
[2799]Pope St. John Paul II [2004] *General Audience Address*, para 2 [Online] Available at: www. vatican.va [Accessed on: 12 July 2022]
[2800]Pope St. Paul VI [1966] Apostolic Constitution *Paenitemini*, Chap. 1 [Online] Available at: www. vatican.va [Accessed on: 3 October 2022]
[2801]Pope St. Paul VI [1967] Apostolic Constitution *Indulgentiarum Doctrina*, para 2 [Online] Available at: www.vatican.va [Accessed on: 3 October 2022]

and has regarded as unclean the blood of the covenant through which he was sanctified, and has insulted the Spirit of grace?... It is a fearful thing to fall into the hands of the living God' (Heb 10:28-29; 31).[2802]

Pope Ven. Pius XII: 1939 to 1958

Allocution to the pastors of Rome and preachers of the Holy Season of Lent: on the precepts of the Decalogue. (22nd February 1944)
Do not faith and theology teach every sin is an offence of God and that it intends to offend Him, because the intention which is included in a grievous fault, goes against God's will, as this is expressed in His commandment that one violates? When a man says 'yes' to the forbidden fruit, he says 'no' to God who forbids it. When he prefers himself and his own will to the divine law, he estranges himself from God and the divine will. In this consists aversion from God and the inner nature of grave sin.[2803]

Radio Message to Participants in the National Catechetical Congress of the United States in Boston. (26th October 1946)
If men believing in God, to echo St. Paul again, if men believing in God do not glorify Him as God and give thanks; if their faith is kept in a hidden closet of their private chamber, while immodesty, malice, avarice and all manner of wickedness are given full use of the drawing-room and public resorts, is it surprising that God should give them up in the lustful desires of their heart to uncleanness, so that women have changed the natural use for that which is against nature, men become full of envy and murder, contention, hateful to God, irreverent, proud, haughty, disobedient to parents, without affection, without fidelity, without mercy? (Rom 1:18-32). […]

To know Jesus crucified is to know God's horror of sin; its guilt could be washed away only in the precious blood of God's only begotten Son become man.

Perhaps the greatest sin in the world today is that men have begun to lose the sense of sin. Smother that, deaden it — it can hardly be wholly cut out from the heart of man — let it not be awakened by any glimpse of the God-man dying on Golgotha's cross to pay the penalty of sin, and what is there to hold back the hordes of God's enemy from over-running the selfishness, the pride, the sensuality and unlawful ambitions of sinful man?[2804]

Prayer to Our Lady
O Conqueress of Evil and Death, inspire in us a deep horror of sin, which makes the soul detestable to God and a slave of hell![2805]

Pope Pius XI: 1922 to 1939

Encyclical *Miserentissimus Redemptor, 13; 17-18. (8th May 1928)*
And the minds of the pious meditate on all these things the more truly, because the sins of men and their crimes committed in every age were the cause why Christ was delivered up to death, and now also they would of themselves bring death to Christ, joined with the same griefs and sorrows, since each several sin in its own way is held to renew the passion of Our Lord: 'Crucifying again to themselves the Son of God, and making him a mockery' (Heb 6:6).

But all these evils as it were culminate in the cowardice and the sloth of those who, after the manner of the sleeping and fleeing disciples, wavering in their faith, miserably forsake Christ when He is oppressed by anguish or surrounded by the satellites of

---

[2802]Pope St. John XXIII [1962] Encyclical *Paenitentiam Agere*, para 14 [Online] Available at: www.vatican.va [Accessed on: 3 October 2022]
[2803]Letter, Fr. de [1947] *Horror of Sin (Horror Peccati)* [Online] Available at: fsspx.asia [Accessed on: 12 July 2022]
[2804]Pope Ven. Pius XII [1946] *Radio Message to Participants in the National Catechetical Congress of the United States in Boston.* [Online] Available at: www.vatican.va [Accessed on: 12 July 2022]
[2805]Pope Ven. Pius XII. *Bend Tenderly Over Our Wounds* [Online] Available at: udayton.edu [Accessed on: 12 July 2022]

Satan, and in the perfidy of those others who following the example of the traitor Judas, either partake of the holy table rashly and sacrilegiously, or go over to the camp of the enemy. And thus, even against our will, the thought rises in the mind that now those days draw near of which Our Lord prophesied: 'And because iniquity hath abounded, the charity of many shall grow cold' (Mt 24:12). [...]

For indeed if any one will lovingly dwell on those things of which we have been speaking, and will have them deeply fixed in his mind, it cannot be but he will shrink with horror from all sin as from the greatest evil, and more than this he will yield himself wholly to the will of God, and will strive to repair the injured honor of the Divine Majesty, as well by constantly praying, as by voluntary mortifications, by patiently bearing the afflictions that befall him, and lastly by spending his whole life in this exercise of expiation.[2806]

Pope St. Pius X: 1903 to 1914

Encyclical *Ad Diem Illum Laetissimum, 19. (2nd February 1904)*
If then God has such a horror of sin as to have willed to keep free the future Mother of His Son not only from stains which are voluntarily contracted but, by a special favor and in prevision of the merits of Jesus Christ, from that other stain of which the sad sign is transmitted to all us sons of Adam by a sort of hapless heritage: who can doubt that it is a duty for everyone who seeks by his homage to gain the heart of Mary to correct his vicious and depraved habits and to subdue the passions which incite him to evil?[2807]

Catechism of Pope St. Pius X. (1908)
The Fourth Article of the Creed
13 Q. Why, then, did Jesus suffer so much?
A. Jesus Christ suffered so much in order to satisfy divine justice all the more abundantly; to display His love for us still more; and to inspire us with the deepest horror of sin.

Sorrow
49 Q. Why must sorrow be supreme?
A. Sorrow must be supreme because we must look upon and hate sin as the greatest of all evils, being as it is an offence against God.

50 Q. To have sorrow for sin, is it necessary to weep, as we sometimes do, in consequence of the misfortunes of this life?
A. It is not necessary to shed tears of sorrow for our sins; it is enough if in our heart we make more of having offended God than of any other misfortune whatsoever.[2808]

Pope Leo XIII: 1878 to 1903

Encyclical *Rerum Novarum, 20. (15th May, 1891)*
To defraud any one of wages that are his due is a great crime which cries to the avenging anger of Heaven.[2809]

Encyclical *Divinum Illud Munus, 8. (9th May 1897)*
On account, however, of original sin, our whole nature had fallen into such guilt and dishonour that we had become enemies to God. 'We were by nature the children of wrath' (Eph 2:3). There was no power which could raise us and deliver us from this ruin and eternal destruction.[2810]

[2806] Pope Pius XI [1928] Encyclical *Miserentissimus Redemptor*, para 18 Online] Available at: www. vatican.va [Accessed on: 12 July 2022]
[2807] Pope St. Pius X [1904] Encyclical *Ad Diem Illum Laetissimum*, para 19 [Online] Available at: www.papalencyclicals.net [Accessed on: 3 October 2022]
[2808] *Catechism of St. Pius X* [1908] The Fourth Article of the Creed [Online] Available at: www.ewtn. com [Accessed on: 12 July 2022]
[2809] Pope Leo XIII [1891] Encyclical *Rerum Novarum*, para 20 [Online] Available at: www.vatican.va [Accessed on: 3 October 2022]
[2810] Pope Leo XIII [1897] Encyclical *Divinum Illud Munus*, para 8 [Online] Available at: www. vatican.va [Accessed on: 3 October 2022]

Pope Bl. Pius IX: 1846 to 1878

Encyclical *Ubi Primum, 5. (2nd February 1849)*
…the punishments of God's anger which afflict the world because of the sins of men.[2811]

Encyclical *Ineffabilis Deus. (8th December, 1854)*
…all the snares of the poisonous serpent, the incorruptible wood that the worm of sin had never corrupted…[2812]

[2811]Pope Bl. Pius IX [1849] Encyclical *Ubi Primum*, para 5 [Online] Available at: www.papalencyclicals.net [Accessed on: 12 July 2022]
[2812]Pope Bl. Pius IX [1854] Encyclical *Ineffabilis Deus* [Online] Available at: www.papalencyclicals.net [Accessed on: 12 July 2022]

Hamartiology (2) — Situation Ethics

Pope Francis: 2013 to 2025

H. *A person can commit a sexual act ordinarily seen as being a mortal sin, with full knowledge of the commandment transgressed or with difficulty in understanding its value, and due to circumstances remain in a state of sanctifying grace. Sexual sins are the least serious sins because the flesh is weak, compared to 'angelical' sins of pride, arrogance, seeking dominion over others.*

Post Synodal Apostolic Exhortation *Amoris Laetitia, 301-302 (19th March 2016)*
Hence it is can no longer simply be said that all those in any 'irregular' situation are living in a state of mortal sin and are deprived of sanctifying grace. More is involved here than mere ignorance of the rule. A subject may know full well the rule, yet have great difficulty in understanding 'its inherent values',[2813] or be in a c oncrete situation which does not allow him or her to act differently and decide otherwise without further sin. As the Synod Fathers put it, 'factors may exist which limit the ability to make a decision'. […]

I consider very fitting what many Synod Fathers wanted to affirm: 'Under certain circumstances people find it very difficult to act differently. Therefore, while upholding a general rule, it is necessary to recognize that responsibility with respect to certain actions or decisions is not the same in all cases. Pastoral discernment, while taking into account a person's properly formed conscience, must take responsibility for these situations. Even the consequences of actions taken are not necessarily the same in all cases'.[2814]

Interview with Dominique Wolton in A Future of Faith: The Path of Change in Politics and Society. (7th August 2018)
It is because some prefer to talk about morality, in their homilies or from the chairs of theology. There is a great danger for preachers, and it is that of condemning only the morality that is — pardon me — 'below the belt.' But other sins that are more serious, hatred, envy, pride, vanity, killing another, taking a life… these are rarely mentioned. […]

Sins of the flesh are the lightest sins. Because the flesh is weak. The most dangerous sins are those of the spirit. I am talking about angelism: pride, vanity are sins of angelism. Priests have the temptation — not all, but many — of focusing on the sins of sexuality, what I call morality below the belt. But the more serious sins are elsewhere.

No, but there are good priests…. I know a cardinal who is a good example. He confided to me, speaking of these things, that as soon as someone goes to him to talk about those sins below the belt, he immediately says: 'I understand, let's move on.' He stops him, as if to say: 'I understand, but let's see if you have something more important. Do you pray? Are you seeking the Lord? Do you read the Gospel? He makes him understand that there are mistakes that are much more important than that. Yes, it is a sin, but… He says to him: 'I understand': And he moves on. On the opposite end there are some who when they receive the confession of a sin of this kind, ask: 'How did you do it, and when did you do it, and how many times?' And they make a 'film' in their head. But these are in need of a psychiatrist.[2815]

Conversations with Mozambican and Malagasy Jesuit brothers. (5th September 2019)
One dimension of clericalism is the exclusive moral fixation on the sixth commandment. Once a Jesuit, a great Jesuit, told me to be careful in giving absolution, because the most serious sins are those that are more angelical: pride, arrogance, dominion… And the least serious are those that are less angelical, such as greed and lust. We focus on sex

---

[2813]St. John Paul II, Apostolic Exhortation *Familiaris Consortio* (1981) 121.
[2814]Pope Francis [2016] Post Synodal Apostolic Exhortation *Amoris Laetitia*, para 301 [Online] Available at: www.vatican.va [Accessed on: 13 July 2022]
[2815]Magister, S [21 January 2019] *Memo For the Summit On Abuse. For Francis, the Sins "Below the Belt" Are "the Lightest"* [Online] Available at: magister.blogautore.espresso.repubblica.it [Accessed on: 13 July 2022]

and then we do not give weight to social injustice, slander, gossip and lies. The Church today needs a profound conversion in this area. On the other hand, great shepherds give people a lot of freedom. The good shepherd knows how to lead his flock without enslaving it to rules that deaden people.[2816]

Sacred Scripture

Matthew 5:27-30; 18:7-9
You have heard that it was said to them of old: Thou shalt not commit adultery. But I say to you, that whosoever shall look on a woman to lust after her, hath already committed adultery with her in his heart. And if thy right eye scandalise thee, pluck it out and cast it from thee. For it is expedient for thee that one of thy members should perish, rather than that thy whole body be cast into hell. And if thy right hand scandalise thee, cut it off, and cast it from thee: for it is expedient for thee that one of thy members should perish, rather than that thy whole body go into hell.

Woe to the world because of scandals. For it must needs be that scandals come: but nevertheless woe to that man by whom the scandal cometh. And if thy hand, or thy foot scandalise thee, cut it off, and cast it from thee. It is better for thee to go into life maimed or lame, than having two hands or two feet, to be cast into everlasting fire. And if thy eye scandalise thee, pluck it out, and cast it from thee. It is better for thee having one eye to enter into life, than having two eyes to be cast into hell fire.

Mark 9:41-47; 10: 6-9
And whosoever shall scandalise one of these little ones that believe in me; it were better for him that a millstone were hanged about his neck, and he were cast into the sea. And if thy hand scandalise thee, cut it off: it is better for thee to enter into life, maimed, than having two hands to go into hell, into unquenchable fire: Where their worm dieth not, and the fire is not extinguished. And if thy foot scandalise thee, cut it off. It is better for thee to enter lame into life everlasting, than having two feet, to be cast into the hell of unquenchable fire: Where their worm dieth not, and the fire is not extinguished. And if thy eye scandalise thee, pluck it out. It is better for thee with one eye to enter into the kingdom of God, than having two eyes to be cast into the hell of fire: Where their worm dieth not, and the fire is not extinguished.

But from the beginning of the creation, God made them male and female. For this cause a man shall leave his father and mother; and shall cleave to his wife. And they two shall be in one flesh. Therefore now they are not two, but one flesh. What therefore God hath joined together, let no man put asunder.

Romans 1:20-21; 26-32; 6:11-13
For the invisible things of him, from the creation of the world, are clearly seen, being understood by the things that are made; his eternal power also, and divinity: so that they are inexcusable. Because that, when they knew God, they have not glorified him as God, or given thanks; but became vain in their thoughts, and their foolish heart was darkened.

For their women have changed the natural use into that use which is against nature. And, in like manner, the men also, leaving the natural use of the women, have burned in their lusts one towards another, men with men working that which is filthy, and receiving in themselves the recompense which was due to their error. And as they liked not to have God in their knowledge, God delivered them up to a reprobate sense, to do those things which are not convenient; Being filled with all iniquity, malice, fornication, avarice, wickedness, full of envy, murder, contention, deceit, malignity, whisperers, detractors, hateful to God, contumelious, proud, haughty, inventors of evil things, disobedient to parents, Foolish, dissolute, without affection, without fidelity, without mercy. Who, having known the justice of God, did not understand that they who do such things, are worthy of death; and not only they that do them, but they also that consent to them that do them.

[2816]Spadaro, A [September 2019] *Pope's meeting with Jesuits in Mozambique and Madagascar* [Online] Available at: www.vaticannews.va/ [Accessed on: 13 July 2022]

So do you also reckon, that you are dead to sin, but alive unto God, in Christ Jesus our Lord. Let not sin therefore reign in your mortal body, so as to obey the lusts thereof. Neither yield ye your members as instruments of iniquity unto sin; but present yourselves to God, as those that are alive from the dead, and your members as instruments of justice unto God.

I Corinthians 6:9-10; 16-19
Know you not that the unjust shall not possess the kingdom of God? Do not err: neither fornicators, nor idolaters, nor adulterers, nor the effeminate.

Know you not that your bodies are the members of Christ? Shall I then take the members of Christ, and make them the members of an harlot? God forbid. Or know you not, that he who is joined to a harlot, is made one body? For they shall be, saith he, two in one flesh. But he who is joined to the Lord, is one spirit. Fly fornication. Every sin that a man doth, is without the body; but he that committeth fornication, sinneth against his own body. Or know you not, that your members are the temple of the Holy Ghost, who is in you, whom you have from God; and you are not your own?

Colossians 3:5-6
Mortify therefore your members which are upon the earth; fornication, uncleanness, lust, evil concupiscence, and covetousness, which is the service of idols. For which things the wrath of God cometh upon the children of unbelief.

Jude 1:7
As Sodom and Gomorrha, and the neighbouring cities, in like manner, having given themselves to fornication, and going after other flesh, were made an example, suffering the punishment of eternal fire.

Genesis 2:23-24; 9:7
And Adam said: This now is bone of my bones, and flesh of my flesh; she shall be called woman, because she was taken out of man. Wherefore a man shall leave father and mother, and shall cleave to his wife: and they shall be two in one flesh.

But increase you and multiply, and go upon the earth, and fill it.

Leviticus 18:22; 20:10; 20:13
Thou shalt not lie with mankind as with womankind, because it is an abomination.

If any man commit adultery with the wife of another, and defile his neighbour's wife, let them be put to death, both the adulterer and the adulteress.

If any one lie with a man as with a woman, both have committed an abomination, let them be put to death: their blood be upon them.

Proverbs 6:32
But he that is an adulterer, for the folly of his heart shall destroy his own soul.

Exodus 20:13
Thou shalt not commit adultery.

Jeremiah 31:33
…I will give my law in their bowels, and I will write it in their heart.

Sacred Tradition

St. Justin Martyr: 100 to 165

The First Apology, Chap. 15
For not only he who in act commits adultery is rejected by Him, but also he who desires to commit adultery: since not only our works, but also our thoughts, are open before God.[2817]

[2817]St. Justin Martyr. *The First Apology*, Chap 15 [Online] Available at: www.newadvent.org [Accessed on: 16 July 2022]

St. Irenaeus: c. 130 to c. 202

Against Heresies, Bk. IV, Chap. 27
As then the unrighteous, the idolaters, and fornicators perished, so also is it now: for both the Lord declares, that such person are sent into eternal fire.[2818]

Athenagoras: 133 to 190

A Plea for the Christians, Chap 32
Those, then, who are forbidden to look at anything more than that for which God formed the eyes, which were intended to be a light to us, and to whom a wanton look is adultery, the eyes being made for other purposes, and who are to be called to account for their very thoughts, how can any one doubt that such persons practice self-control? For our account lies not with human laws, which a bad man can evade (at the outset I proved to you, sovereign lords, that our doctrine is from the teaching of God), but we have a law which makes the measure of rectitude to consist in dealing with our neighbour as ourselves.[2819]

Tertullian: c. 155 to c. 220

De Corona, Chap. 6.
'Does not even Nature teach you?' — as when to the Romans, affirming that the heathen do by nature those things which the law requires, he suggests both natural law and a law-revealing nature. Yes, and also in the first chapter of the epistle he authenticates nature, when he asserts that males and females changed among themselves the natural use of the creature into that which is unnatural by way of penal retribution for their error.[2820]

Origen: c 184 to c 253

Commentary on the Gospel of Matthew, Bk. XIV, Chap. 10
But observe here that every great sin is a loss of the talents of the master of the house, and such sins are committed by fornicators, adulterers, abusers of themselves with men, effeminate, idolaters, murderers. Perhaps then the one who is brought to the king owing many talents has committed no small sin but all that are great and heinous.[2821]

St. Jerome: c 340-2 to 420

Against Jovinianus, Bk. II, Chap. 30
Some offences are light, some heavy. It is one thing to owe ten thousand talents, another to owe a farthing. We shall have to give account of the idle word no less than of adultery; but it is not the same thing to be put to the blush, and to be put upon the rack, to grow red in the face and to ensure lasting torment.[2822]

St. Augustine: 354 to 430

Sermon 32 on the New Testament, para 13.
Let no one say in his heart, 'God cares not for sins of the flesh.' 'Do you not know,' says the Apostle, 'that you are the temple of God, and the Spirit of God dwells in you? If any man defile the temple of God, him will God destroy.' 'Let no man deceive himself.' But perhaps a man will say, 'My soul is the temple of God, not my body,' and will add this testimony also, 'All flesh is as grass, and all the glory of man as the flower of

---

[2818]St. Irenaeus. *Against Heresies*, Bk. IV, Chap. 27 [Online] Available at: www.newadvent.org [Accessed on: 16 July 2022]

[2819]Athenagoras. *A Plea for the Christians*, Chap 32 [Online] www.newadvent.org [Accessed on: 16 July 2022]

[2820]Tertullian. *De Corona*, Chap 6. [Online] www.newadvent.org [Accessed on: 16 July 2022]

[2821]Origen. *Commentary on the Gospel of Matthew*, Bk. XIV, Chap. 10 [Online] www.newadvent.org [Accessed on: 4 October 2022]

[2822]St. Jerome. *Against Jovinianus*, Bk. II, Chap. 30 [Online] www.newadvent.org [Accessed on: 4 October 2022]

grass.' Unhappy interpretation! conceit meet for punishment! The flesh is called grass, because it dies; but take heed that that which dies for a time, rise not again with guilt. Would you ascertain a plain judgment on this point also? 'Do you not know,' says the same Apostle, 'that your body is the temple of the Holy Ghost which is in you, which you have of God?' Do not then any longer disregard sins of the body; seeing that your 'bodies are the temples of the Holy Ghost which is in you, which you have of God.' If you disregarded a sin of the body, will you disregard a sin which you commit against a temple? Your very body is a temple of the Spirit of God within you. Now take heed what you do with the temple of God. If you were to choose to commit adultery in the Church within these walls, what wickedness could be greater? But now you are yourself the temple of God. In your going out, in your coming in, as you abide in your house, as you rise up, in all you are a temple. Take heed then what you do, take heed that you offend not the Indweller of the temple, lest He forsake you, and you fall into ruins. 'Do you not know,' he says, 'that your bodies' (and this the Apostle spoke touching fornication, that they might not think lightly of sins of the body) 'are the temples of the Holy Ghost which is in you, which you have of God, and you are not your own?' For 'you have been bought with a great price.' If you think so lightly of your own body, have some consideration for your price.[2823]

St. Thomas Aquinas: 1225 to 1274

Summa Theologiae. Prima Secundæ Partis. Q 91. Art 2
…it is evident that all things partake somewhat of the eternal law, in so far as, namely, from its being imprinted on them, they derive their respective inclinations to their proper acts and ends. Now among all others, the rational creature is subject to Divine providence in the most excellent way, in so far as it partakes of a share of providence, by being provident both for itself and for others. Wherefore it has a share of the Eternal Reason, whereby it has a natural inclination to its proper act and end: and this participation of the eternal law in the rational creature is called the natural law.[2824]

Collationes in Decem Praeceptis, Prologue, 1.
The first is the law of nature, and that is nothing other than the light of the intellect planted in us by God, by which we know what should be done and what should be avoided. God gave this light and this law in creation. But many believe that they are excused by ignorance if they do not observe this law. Against them the Prophet says in Psalm 4:6: 'Many say: who will show us good things?' — as if they do not know what they should do. But he replies (v. 7): 'The light of your face, Lord, is stamped on us' — that is, the light of the intellect, through which we know what should be done. For no one is ignorant that what he would not like to be done to himself he should not do to others, and similar norms. Yet, though God gave man this law of nature in creation, the devil has sown in man another law on top of it, that of concupiscence. For in the first man, to the extent that the soul was subject to God, keeping the divine precepts, his flesh was also subject in all things to the soul or reason. But after the devil by his suggestion drew man away from he observance of the divine commands, his flesh likewise became disobedient to reason. The result is that, although man may wish good according to reason, nevertheless by concupiscence he tends to the contrary. That is what the Apostle says (Rom 7:23): 'But I see another law in my members, fighting the law of my mind.' Thus frequently he law of concupiscence corrupts the law of nature and the order of reason. And therefore the Apostle adds (ibid.):'...captivating me in the law of sin, which is in my members.'[2825]

[2823]St. Augustine. *Sermon 32 on the New Testament*, para 13. [Online] Available at: www.newadvent. org [Accessed on: 16 July 2022]
[2824]St. Thomas Aquinas. *Summa Theologiae.* Prima Secundæ Partis. Q 91. Art 2. Online] Available at: www.newadvent.org [Accessed on: 16 July 2022]
[2825]St. Thomas Aquinas. *Collationes in Decem Praeceptis*, Prologue, para 1. [Online] Available at: https://isidore.co [Accessed on: 16 July 2022]

Summa Theologiae. Prima Secundæ Partis. Q 77. Art 8

Mortal sin, as stated above (I-II:72:5), consists in turning away from our last end which is God, which aversion pertains to the deliberating reason, whose function it is also to direct towards the end. Therefore that which is contrary to the last end can happen not to be a mortal sin, only when the deliberating reason is unable to come to the rescue, which is the case in sudden movements. Now when anyone proceeds from passion to a sinful act, or to a deliberate consent, this does not happen suddenly: and so the deliberating reason can come to the rescue here, since it can drive the passion away, or at least prevent it from having its effect, as stated above: wherefore if it does not come to the rescue, there is a mortal sin; and it is thus, as we see, that many murders and adulteries are committed through passion.[2826]

The Magisterium of the Church

God does not ask the impossible, and His commands are not impossible for the just to observe. Therefore, there is no justification for disobeying the Sixth and Ninth Commandments. To commit a sexual act knowing it is against God's commandments is a mortal sin, that if unrepented, deprives the sinner of sanctifying grace, resulting in exclusion from the kingdom of God and the eternal punishment of Hell. Sexual sins are grave and abominable in the sight of God and man. Instead of being a Temple of the Holy Spirit, the sinner is lowered to the condition of the brute.

First Council of Lyons (Thirteenth Ecumenical, 1245)

Moreover concerning fornication that an unmarried man commits with an unmarried woman, there must not be any doubt at all that it is a mortal sin, since the apostle declares that fornicators like adulterers are cast out from the kingdom of God (cf. I Cor 6:9).

But if anyone dies in mortal sin without repentance, beyond any doubt, he will be tortured forever by the flames of everlasting hell.[2827]

Second Council of Lyons (Fourteenth Ecumenical, 1274)

As for the souls of those who die in mortal sin or with original sin only, they go down immediately to hell, to be punished, however, with different punishments.[2828]

Council of Florence (Seventeenth Ecumenical, 1431 to 1449)

Session Six. (6th July 1439)

But the souls of those who depart this life in actual mortal sin, or in original sin alone, go down straightaway to hell to be punished, but with unequal pains.[2829]

Council of Trent (Nineteenth Ecumenical, 1545 to 1563)

On Justification, First Decree, Chap. XV. (13th January 1547)

That, by every mortal sin, grace is lost, but not faith.

In opposition also to the subtle wits of certain men, who, by pleasing speeches and good words, seduce the hearts of the innocent, (Rom 16:18) it is to be maintained, that the received grace of Justification is lost, not only by infidelity whereby even faith itself is lost, but also by any other mortal sin whatever, though faith be not lost; thus defending the doctrine of the divine law, which excludes from the kingdom of God not only the unbelieving, but the faithful also (who are) fornicators, adulterers, effeminate, liars with mankind, thieves, covetous, drunkards, railers, extortioners, (I Cor 6:9, 10) and all others who commit deadly sins; from which, with the help of divine grace, they can refrain, and on account of which they are separated from the grace of Christ.

[2826]St. Thomas Aquinas. *Summa Theologiae.* Prima Secundæ Partis. Q 77. Art 8 [Online] Available at: www.newadvent.org [Accessed on: 4 October 2022]

[2827]Denzinger, H [2010] *Op. cit.,* p. 277, *Dz* 835; p.278, *Dz* 839

[2828]*Ibid.,* p.283, *Dz* 858

[2829]Council of Florence [1439] *Session Six* [Online] Available at: www.ewtn.com [Accessed on: 4 October 2022]

CANON XXVII. If any one saith, that there is no mortal sin but that of infidelity; or, that grace once received is not lost by any other sin, however grievous and enormous, save by that of infidelity; let him be anathema.[2830]

Doctrine on the Sacrament of Penance, Chap. V. (25th November 1551)
…all mortal sins, even those of thought, make of men 'children of wrath' (Eph 2:3) and enemies of God, there is need to seek God's pardon equally for them all through an open and humble confession.[2831]

First Vatican Council (Twentieth Ecumenical, 1869 to 1870)

Dogmatic Constitution, *Dei Filius, Chap. 2. (24th April 1870)*
The same Holy Mother Church holds and teaches that God, the beginning and end of all things, may be known with certainty from the things that were created through the natural light of human reason, 'ever since the creation of the world his invisible nature…has been clearly perceived in the things that have been made (Rom 1:20). […]

It is to be ascribed to this Divine Revelation, that such truths among things Divine that of themselves are not beyond human reason can, even in the present condition of mankind, be known by everyone with facility, with firm assurance, and with no admixture of error.[2832]

Second Vatican Council (Twenty-First Ecumenical, 1962 to 1965)

Pastoral Constitution *Gaudium et Spes, 14, 16 (7th December 1965)*
[Man] is obliged to regard his body as good and honourable since God has created it and will raise it up on the last day. Nevertheless, wounded by sin, man experiences rebellious stirrings in his body. But the very dignity of man postulates that man glorify God in his body and forbid it to serve the evil inclinations of his heart.

Now, man is not wrong when he regards himself as superior to bodily concerns, and as more than a speck of nature or a nameless constituent of the city of man. For by his interior qualities he outstrips the whole sum of mere things. He plunges into the depths of reality whenever he enters into his own heart; God, Who probes the heart, awaits him there; there he discerns his proper destiny beneath the eyes of God. Thus, when he recognises in himself a spiritual and immortal soul, he is not being mocked by a fantasy born only of physical or social influences, but is rather laying hold of the proper truth of the matter.

In the depths of his conscience, man detects a law which he does not impose upon himself, but which holds him to obedience. Always summoning him to love good and avoid evil, the voice of conscience when necessary speaks to his heart: do this, shun that. For man has in his heart a law written by God; to obey it is the very dignity of man; according to it he will be judged. Conscience is the most secret core and sanctuary of a man. There he is alone with God, Whose voice echoes in his depths. In a wonderful manner conscience reveals that law which is fulfilled by love of God and neighbour.[2833]

Declaration *Dignitatis Humanae, 3. (7th December 1965)*
Further light is shed on the subject if one considers that the highest norm of human life is the divine law-eternal, objective and universal-whereby God orders, directs and governs the entire universe and all the ways of the human community by a plan conceived in wisdom and love. Man has been made by God to participate in this law, with the result that, under the gentle disposition of divine Providence, he can come to perceive ever more fully the truth that is unchanging. Wherefore every man has the

---

[2830]Council of Trent [1547] *Decree on Justification*, Chap. 15. [Online] www.thecounciloftrent.com [Accessed on: 18 July 2022]

[2831]Denzinger, H [2010] *Op. cit.*, p. 403, *Dz* 1680

[2832]*Ibid.*, p. 1870, *Dz* 3005

[2833]Second Vatican Council [1965] Pastoral Constitution *Gaudium et Spes*, paras 14, 16. [Online] Available at: www.vatican.va [Accessed on: 14 July 2022]

duty, and therefore the right, to seek the truth in matters religious in order that he may with prudence form for himself right and true judgments of conscience, under use of all suitable means.[2834]

Pope Benedict XVI: 2005 to 2013

Compendium of the Catechism of the Catholic Church. (28th June 2005)
395. When does one commit a mortal sin?
One commits a mortal sin when there are simultaneously present: grave matter, full knowledge, and deliberate consent. This sin destroys charity in us, deprives us of sanctifying grace, and, if unrepented, leads us to the eternal death of hell. It can be forgiven in the ordinary way by means of the sacraments of Baptism and of Penance or Reconciliation.

492. What are the principal sins against chastity?
Grave sins against chastity differ according to their object: adultery, masturbation, fornication, pornography, prostitution, rape, and homosexual acts. These sins are expressions of the vice of lust. These kinds of acts committed against the physical and moral integrity of minors become even more grave.[2835]

Address to the Bishops of the United States of America from Region VIII on their 'Ad Limina' visit. (9th March 2012)
…we cannot overlook the serious pastoral problem presented by the widespread practice of cohabitation, often by couples who seem unaware that it is gravely sinful, not to mention damaging to the stability of society.[2836]

Message for the 33rd Meeting for Friendship Among People. (19th-25th August 2012)
The Apostle to the Gentiles speaks of an 'evil' slavery: the slavery of sin, of the law, of the passions of the flesh.[2837]

Pope St. John Paul II: 1978 to 2005

General Audience Address. (7th January 1981)
When he speaks of the necessity of putting to death the deeds of the body with the help of the Spirit, Paul expresses precisely what Christ spoke about in the Sermon on the Mount, appealing to the human heart and exhorting it to control desires, even those expressed in a man's look at a woman for the purpose of satisfying the lust of the flesh. This mastery, or as Paul writes, 'putting to death the works of the body with the help of the Spirit,' is an indispensable condition of life according to the Spirit, that is, of the life which is an antithesis of the death spoken about in the same context. Life according to the flesh has death as its fruit. That is, it involves as its effect the 'death' of the spirit.

So the term 'death' does not mean only the death of the body, but also sin, which moral theology will call 'mortal.' In Romans and Galatians, the Apostle continually widens the horizon of 'sin-death,' both toward the beginning of human history, and toward its end. Therefore, after listing the multiform works of the flesh, he affirms that 'those who do such things shall not inherit the kingdom of God' (Gal 5:21). Elsewhere he will write with similar firmness: 'Be sure of this, that no fornicator or impure man, or one who is covetous (that is, an idolater), has any inheritance in the kingdom of God' (Eph 5:5). In this case, too, the works that exclude inheritance in the kingdom of Christ and of God — that is, the works of the flesh — are listed as an example and with general

---

[2834]Second Vatican Council [1965] Declaration *Dignitatis Humanae*, para 3. [Online] Available at: www.vatican.va [Accessed on: 14 July 2022]
[2835]*Compendium of the Catechism of the Catholic Church* [2005] [Online] Available at: www.vatican.va [Accessed on: 3 October 2022]
[2836]Pope Benedict XVI [2012] *Address to the Bishops of the United States of America from Region VIII on their 'Ad Limina' visit* [Online] Available at: www.vatican.va [Accessed on: 4 October 2022]
[2837]Pope Benedict XVI [2012] *Message for the 33rd Meeting for Friendship Among People* [Online] Available at: www.vatican.va [Accessed on: 4 October 2022]

value, although sins against purity in the specific sense are at the top of the list here (cf. Eph 5:3-7).[2838]

Post Synodal Apostolic Exhortation *Reconciliatio et Paenitentia, 17. (2nd December 1984)*
With the whole tradition of the church, we call mortal sin the act by which man freely and consciously rejects God, his law, the covenant of love that God offers, preferring to turn in on himself or to some created and finite reality, something contrary to the divine will (*conversio ad creaturam*). This can occur in a direct and formal way in the sins of idolatry, apostasy and atheism; or in an equivalent way as in every act of disobedience to God's commandments in a grave matter. Man perceives that this disobedience to God destroys the bond that unites him with his life principle: It is a mortal sin, that is, an act which gravely offends God and ends in turning against man himself with a dark and powerful force of destruction.

For mortal sin exists also when a person knowingly and willingly, for whatever reason, chooses something gravely disordered. In fact, such a choice already includes contempt for the divine law, a rejection of God's love for humanity and the whole of creation; the person turns away from God and loses charity. Thus the fundamental orientation can be radically changed by individual acts. Clearly there can occur situations which are very complex and obscure from a psychological viewpoint and which have an influence on the sinner's subjective culpability. But from a consideration of the psychological sphere one cannot proceed to the construction of a theological category, which is what the 'fundamental option' precisely is, understanding it in such a way that it objectively changes or casts doubt upon the traditional concept of mortal sin.[2839]

Catechism of the Catholic Church. (1992)
Mortal sin destroys charity in the heart of man by a grave violation of God's law; it turns man away from God, who is his ultimate end and his beatitude, by preferring an inferior good to him. (1855)

Mortal sin requires full knowledge and complete consent. It presupposes knowledge of the sinful character of the act, of its opposition to God's law. It also implies a consent sufficiently deliberate to be a personal choice. Feigned ignorance and hardness of heart do not diminish, but rather increase, the voluntary character of a sin. (1859)

Lust is disordered desire for or inordinate enjoyment of sexual pleasure. Sexual pleasure is morally disordered when sought for itself, isolated from its procreative and unitive purposes. (2351)

The 'divine and natural' law shows man the way to follow so as to practice the good and attain his end. The natural law states the first and essential precepts which govern the moral life. It hinges upon the desire for God and submission to him, who is the source and judge of all that is good, as well as upon the sense that the other is one's equal. Its principal precepts are expressed in the Decalogue. This law is called 'natural,' not in reference to the nature of irrational beings, but because reason which decrees it properly belongs to human nature (1955)

The natural law, present in the heart of each man and established by reason, is universal in its precepts and its authority extends to all men. It expresses the dignity of the person and determines the basis for his fundamental rights and duties (1956)

The precepts of natural law are not perceived by everyone clearly and immediately. In the present situation sinful man needs grace and revelation so moral and religious truths may be known 'by everyone with facility, with firm certainty and with no admixture of error.' The natural law provides revealed law and grace with a foundation prepared by God and in accordance with the work of the Spirit (1960).[2840]

[2838]Pope St. John Paul II [7th January 1981] *Opposition Between the Flesh and the Spirit* [Online] Available at: www.ewtn.com/ [Accessed on: 18 July 2022]

[2839]Pope St. John Paul II [1984] Post Synodal Apostolic Exhortation *Reconciliatio et Paenitentia*, para 17 [Online] Available at: www.vatican.va [Accessed on: 18 July 2022]

[2840]*Catechism of the Catholic Church* [1992] [Online] Available at: scborromeo2.org [Accessed on: 12 July 2022]

Encyclical *Veritatis Splendor, 12, 49, 51, 60, 68.* (6 August 1993)
Only God can answer the question about the good, because he is the Good. But God has already given an answer to this question: he did so by creating man and ordering him with wisdom and love to his final end, through the law which is inscribed in his heart (cf. Rom 2:15), the 'natural law'. The latter 'is nothing other than the light of understanding infused in us by God, whereby we understand what must be done and what must be avoided. God gave this light and this law to man at creation'.

A doctrine which dissociates the moral act from the bodily dimensions of its exercise is contrary to the teaching of Scripture and Tradition. Such a doctrine revives, in new forms, certain ancient errors which have always been opposed by the Church, inasmuch as they reduce the human person to a 'spiritual' and purely formal freedom. This reduction misunderstands the moral meaning of the body and of kinds of behaviour involving it (cf. I Cor 6:19). Saint Paul declares that 'the immoral, idolaters, adulterers, sexual perverts, thieves, the greedy, drunkards, revilers, robbers' are excluded from the Kingdom of God (cf. I Cor 6:9). This condemnation — repeated by the Council of Trent — lists as 'mortal sins' or 'immoral practices' certain specific kinds of behaviour the wilful acceptance of which prevents believers from sharing in the inheritance promised to them. In fact, body and soul are inseparable: in the person, in the willing agent and in the deliberate act, they stand or fall together.

But inasmuch as the natural law expresses the dignity of the human person and lays the foundation for his fundamental rights and duties, it is universal in its precepts and its authority extends to all mankind. This universality does not ignore the individuality of human beings, nor is it opposed to the absolute uniqueness of each person. On the contrary, it embraces at its root each of the person's free acts, which are meant to bear witness to the universality of the true good.

The judgment of conscience does not establish the law; rather it bears witness to the authority of the natural law and of the practical reason with reference to the supreme good, whose attractiveness the human person perceives and whose commandments he accepts. 'Conscience is not an independent and exclusive capacity to decide what is good and what is evil. Rather there is profoundly imprinted upon it a principle of obedience vis-à-vis the objective norm which establishes and conditions the correspondence of its decisions with the commands and prohibitions which are at the basis of human behaviour'.

With every freely committed mortal sin, he offends God as the giver of the law and as a result becomes guilty with regard to the entire law (cf. Jas 2:8-11); even if he perseveres in faith, he loses 'sanctifying grace', 'charity' and 'eternal happiness'. As the Council of Trent teaches, 'the grace of justification once received is lost not only by apostasy, by which faith itself is lost, but also by any other mortal sin'.[2841]

Pope St. Paul VI: 1963 to 1978

Encyclical *Humanae Vitae, 17.* (25th July 1968)
Not much experience is needed to be fully aware of human weakness and to understand that human beings — and especially the young, who are so exposed to temptation — need incentives to keep the moral law, and it is an evil thing to make it easy for them to break that law. Another effect that gives cause for alarm is that a man who grows accustomed to the use of contraceptive methods may forget the reverence due to a woman, and, disregarding her physical and emotional equilibrium, reduce her to being a mere instrument for the satisfaction of his own desires, no longer considering her as his partner whom he should surround with care and affection.[2842]

[2841]Pope St. John Paul II [1993] Encyclical *Veritatis Splendor*, paras 12, 49, 51, 60, 68 [Online] Available at: www.vatican.va [Accessed on: 18 July 2022]
[2842]Pope St. Paul VI [1968] Encyclical *Humanae Vitae*, para 17 [Online] Available at: www.vatican.va [Accessed on: 18 July 2022]

Sacred Congregation for the Doctrine of the Faith, Persona Humana, X. (29th December 1975)
The observance of the moral law in the field of sexuality and the practice of chastity
have been considerably endangered, especially among less fervent Christians, by the
current tendency to minimise as far as possible, when not denying outright, the reality
of grave sin, at least in people's actual lives. [...]

Now according to these authors, a change of the fundamental option towards God
less easily comes about in the field of sexual activity, where a person generally does
not transgress the moral order in a fully deliberate and responsible manner but rather
under the influence of passion, weakness, immaturity, sometimes even through the
illusion of thus showing love for someone else. To these causes there is often added the
pressure of the social environment.

In reality, it is precisely the fundamental option which in the last resort defines a
person's moral disposition. But it can be completely changed by particular acts, especially when, as often happens, these have been prepared for by previous more superficial acts. Whatever the case, it is wrong to say that particular acts are not enough to
constitute mortal sin.

According to the Church's teaching, mortal sin, which is opposed to God, does not
consist only in formal and direct resistance to the commandment of charity. It is equally
to be found in this opposition to authentic love which is included in every deliberate
transgression, in serious matter, of each of the moral laws.[...]

A person therefore sins mortally not only when his action comes from direct contempt for love of God and neighbour, but also when he consciously and freely, for
whatever reason, chooses something which is seriously disordered. For in this choice,
as has been said above, there is already included contempt for the Divine commandment: the person turns himself away from God and loses charity. Now according to
Christian tradition and the Church's teaching, and as right reason also recognises, the
moral order of sexuality involves such high values of human life that every direct violation of this order is objectively serious.

It is true that in sins of the sexual order, in view of their kind and their causes, it
more easily happens that free consent is not fully given; this is a fact which calls for
caution in all judgment as to the subject's responsibility. In this matter it is particularly
opportune to recall the following words of Scripture: 'Man looks at appearances but
God looks at the heart.' (Sam 16:7). However, although prudence is recommended in
judging the subjective seriousness of a particular sinful act, it in no way follows that one
can hold the view that in the sexual field mortal sins are not committed.[2843]

Pope Ven. Pius XII: 1939 to 1958

Allocution to Midwives. (29th October 1951)
Nevertheless, here also, husband and wife must know how to keep themselves within
the limits of a just moderation. As with the pleasure of food and drink so with the sexual
they must not abandon themselves without restraint to the impulses of the senses. The
right rule is this: the use of the natural procreative disposition is morally lawful in
matrimony only, in the service of and in accordance with the ends of marriage itself.
Hence it follows that only in marriage with the observing of this rule is the desire and
fruition of this pleasure and of this satisfaction lawful. For the pleasure is subordinate
to the law of the action whence it derives, and not vice versa — the action to the law of
pleasure. And this law, so very reasonable, concerns not only the substance but also the
circumstances of the action, so that, even when the substance of the act remains morally
safe, it is possible to sin in the way it is performed.

The transgression of this law is as old as original sin. But in our times there is the
risk that one may lose sight of the fundamental principle itself. At present, in fact, it is
usual to support in words and in writing (and this by Catholics in certain circles) the

---

[2843]Sacred Congregation for the Doctrine of the Faith [1975] *Persona Humana,* para 10 [Online]
Available at: www.vatican.va [Accessed on: 18 July 2022]

necessary autonomy, the proper end, and the proper value of sexuality and of its real-isation, independently of the purpose of procreating a new life. There is a tendency to subject to a new examination and to a new norm the very order established by God and not to admit any other restraint to the way of satisfying the instinct than by considering the essence of the instinctive act. In addition there would be substituted a license to serve blindly and without restraint the whims and instincts of nature in the place of the moral obligations to dominate passions; and this sooner or later cannot but turn out to be a danger to morals, conscience and human dignity.[2844]

Radio Message on the Occasion of 'Family Day', 6-8. (23rd March 1952)
In the law of the Creator, engraved on the heart of each one (cf. Rom 2:14-16), and in revelation; that is, in the entirety of the truths and precepts taught by the divine Master. Both the law written in the heart, that is, the natural law, as well as the truths and precepts of supernatural revelation, which Jesus the Redeemer entrusted, as the moral treasure of humanity, into the hands of His Church, so that she may preach them to all creatures, explaining them and transmitting them, intact and free of all contamination and error, from generation to generation.

Against this doctrine, uncontested for long ages, there now arise difficulties and objections that must be clarified. As for dogmatic doctrine, so also for the Catholic moral order, one might would want to institute a radical revision in order to deduce a new judgement of it.

The first step, or to say it better, the first blow against the edifice of Christian moral norms would be that of separating them – as is intended – from the constrictive and oppressive vigilance of the authority of the Church, so that, freed from the sophistical subtleties of the casuistic method, morality is restored to its original form and returned to simply the intelligence and determination of the individual conscience. [...]

In leaving every ethical criterion to the individual conscience, it jealously closes in on itself and, having been made the absolute arbiter of its own determinations, far from making the way easier for it [conscience], the way, it would divert it from the highroad, which is Christ.[2845]

Encyclical *Sacra Virginitas, 53.* (25th March 1954)
Hence we must watch particularly over the movements of our passions and of our senses, and so control them by voluntary discipline in our lives and by bodily mortification that we render them obedient to right reason and God's law: 'And they that are Christ's have crucified their flesh, with its vices and concupiscences.'(Gal 5:24) The Apostle of the Gentiles says this about himself: 'But I chastise my body, and bring it into subjection: lest perhaps, when I have preached to others, I myself should become a castaway.'(I Cor 9:27). All holy men and women have most carefully guarded the movements of their senses and their passions, and at times have very harshly crushed them, in keeping with the teaching of the Divine Master: 'But I say to you, that whosoever shall look on a woman to lust after her, hath already committed adultery with her in his heart. And if thy right eye scandalise thee, pluck it out and cast it from thee. For it is expedient for thee that one of thy members should perish, rather than that thy whole body be cast into hell.' (Mt 5: 28-29). It is abundantly clear that with this warning Our Savior demands of us above all that we never consent to any sin, even internally, and that we steadfastly remove far from us anything that can even slightly tarnish the beautiful virtue of purity. In this matter no diligence, no severity can be considered exaggerated. If ill health or other reasons do not allow one heavier corporal austerities, yet they never free one from vigilance and internal self-control.[2846]

[2844]Pope Ven. Pius XII [1951] *Allocution to Midwives* [Online] Available at: www.ewtn.com [Accessed on: 4 October 2022]

[2845]Pope Ven. Pius XII [1952] *Radio Message on the Occasion of 'Family Day'*, para 6-8 [Online] Available at: www.catholicculture.org [Accessed on 18 July 2022]

[2846]Pope Ven. Pius XII [1954] Encyclical *Sacra Virginitas*, para 53 [Online] Available at: www. catholicculture.org [Accessed on 4 October 2022]

Sacred Congregation of the Holy Office. Instruction Contra Doctrinam. (2nd February 1956)
Contrary to the moral doctrine and its application that is traditional in the Catholic
Church, there has begun to be spread abroad in many regions, even among Catholics,
an ethical system that generally goes by the name of a certain 'Situation Ethics,' and
which, they claim, does not rest upon the principles of objective ethics (which ultimately
is rooted in 'Being' itself), rather, it is not merely subject to the same limit as objective
ethics, but transcends it.

The authors who follow this system hold that the decisive and ultimate norm of
conduct is not the objective right order, determined by the law of nature and known
with certainty from that law, but a certain intimate judgment and light of the mind of
each individual, by means of which, in the concrete situation in which he is placed, he
learns what he ought to do.

And so, according to them, this ultimate decision a man makes is not, as the objective ethics handed down by authors of great weight teaches, the application of the
objective law to a particular case, which at the same time takes into account and weighs
according to the rules of prudence the particular circumstances of the 'situation', but
that immediate, internal light and judgment. Ultimately, at least in many matters, this
judgment is not measured, must not and cannot be measured, as regards its objective
rectitude and truth, by any objective norm situated outside man and independent of his
subjective persuasion but is entirely self-sufficient. [...]

Having accepted these principles and put them into practice, they assert and teach
that men are preserved or easily liberated from many otherwise insoluble ethical conflicts when each one judges in his own conscience, not primarily according to objective
laws, but by means of that internal, individual light based on personal intuition, what
he must do in a concrete situation.[2847]

Pope Pius XI: 1922 to 1939

Encyclical *Casti Connubii, 61-62, 97-99, 107.* (31st December 1930)
No difficulty can arise that justifies the putting aside of the law of God which forbids
all acts intrinsically evil. There is no possible circumstance in which husband and wife
cannot, strengthened by the grace of God, fulfil faithfully their duties and preserve
in wedlock their chastity unspotted. This truth of Christian Faith is expressed by the
teaching of the Council of Trent. 'Let no one be so rash as to assert that which the
Fathers of the Council have placed under anathema, namely, that there are precepts
of God impossible for the just to observe. God does not ask the impossible, but by His
commands, instructs you to do what you are able, to pray for what you are not able that
He may help you.'

This same doctrine was again solemnly repeated and confirmed by the Church in
the condemnation of the Jansenist heresy which dared to utter this blasphemy against
the goodness of God: 'Some precepts of God are, when one considers the powers which
man possesses, impossible of fulfilment even to the just who wish to keep the law and
strive to do so; grace is lacking whereby these laws could be fulfilled.'

Wherefore, since the chief obstacle to this study is the power of unbridled lust,
which indeed is the most potent cause of sinning against the sacred laws of matrimony,
and since man cannot hold in check his passions, unless he first subject himself to God,
this must be his primary endeavour, in accordance with the plan divinely ordained.
For it is a sacred ordinance that whoever shall have first subjected himself to God will,
by the aid of divine grace, be glad to subject to himself his own passions and concupiscence; while he who is a rebel against God will, to his sorrow, experience within himself
the violent rebellion of his worst passions.

And how wisely this has been decreed St. Augustine thus shows: 'This indeed is fitting, that the lower be subject to the higher, so that he who would have subject to himself whatever is below him, should himself submit to whatever is above him. Acknowledge order, seek peace. Be thou subject to God, and thy flesh subject to thee. What more

---

[2847]Sacred Congregation of the Holy Office. [1956] Instruction *Contra Doctrinam* [Online] Available
at: www.catholicculture.org [Accessed on 18 July 2022]

fitting! What more fair! Thou art subject to the higher and the lower is subject to thee. Do thou serve Him who made thee, so that that which was made for thee may serve thee. For we do not commend this order, namely, "The flesh to thee and thou to God," but "Thou to God, and the flesh to thee." If, however, thou despisest the subjection of thyself to God, thou shalt never bring about the subjection of the flesh to thyself. If thou dost not obey the Lord, thou shalt be tormented by thy servant.' This right ordering on the part of God's wisdom is mentioned by the holy Doctor of the Gentiles, inspired by the Holy Ghost, for in speaking of those ancient philosophers who refused to adore and reverence Him whom they knew to be the Creator of the universe, he says: 'Wherefore God gave them up to the desires of their heart, unto uncleanness, to dishonour their own bodies among themselves'; and again: 'For this same God delivered them up to shameful affections' (Rom I: 24, 26). And St. James says: 'God resisteth the proud and giveth grace to the humble' (James 4:6), without which grace, as the same Doctor of the Gentiles reminds us, man cannot subdue the rebellion of his flesh (Rom 7,8).

Consequently, as the onslaughts of these uncontrolled passions cannot in any way be lessened, unless the spirit first shows a humble compliance of duty and reverence towards its Maker....

Thus will it come to pass that the faithful will wholeheartedly thank God that they are bound together by His command and led by gentle compulsion to fly as far as possible from every kind of idolatry of the flesh and from the base slavery of the passions. They will, in a great measure, turn and be turned away from these abominable opinions which to the dishonour of man's dignity are now spread about in speech and in writing and collected under the title of 'perfect marriage' and which indeed would make that perfect marriage nothing better than 'depraved marriage,' as it has been rightly and truly called.[2848]

Pope Benedict XV: 1914 to 1922

Encyclical *Sacra Propediem, 18. (6th January 1921)*
Now there are two passions today dominant in the profound lawlessness of morals — an unlimited desire of riches and an insatiable thirst for pleasures. It is this which marks with a shameful stigma our epoch....[2849]

Pope St. Pius X: 1903 to 1914

Catechism of Pope St. Pius X. (1908)
The Sixth and Ninth Commandment
1 Q. What does the Sixth Commandment, Thou shalt not commit adultery, forbid?
A. The Sixth Commandment, Thou shalt not commit adultery, forbids every act, every look and every word contrary to chastity; it also forbids infidelity in marriage.

2 Q. What does the Ninth Commandment forbid?
A. The Ninth Commandment expressly forbids every desire contrary to that fidelity which husband and wife vowed to observe when contracting marriage; and it also forbids every guilty thought or desire of anything that is prohibited by the Sixth Commandment.

3 Q. Is impurity a great sin?
A. It is a most grave and abominable sin in the sight of God and man; it lowers man to the condition of the brute; it drags him into many other sins and vices; and it provokes the most terrible chastisements both in this world and in the next.

4 Q. Is every thought that comes into the mind against purity a sin?
A. The thoughts that come into the mind against purity are not of themselves sins, but rather temptations and incentives to sin.

[2848]Pope Pius XI [1930] Encyclical *Casti Connubii*, paras 61-62, 97-99, 107 [Online] Available at: www.vatican.va [Accessed on: 4 October 2022]
[2849]Pope Benedict XV [1921] Encyclical *Sacra Propediem*, para 18 [Online] Available at: www.vatican.va [Accessed on: 4 October 2022]

5 Q. When is a bad thought a sin?
A. Bad thoughts, even though resulting in no bad deed, are sins when we culpably entertain them, or consent to them, or expose ourselves to the proximate danger of consenting to them.

6 Q. What do the Sixth and Ninth Commandments command?
A. The Sixth Commandment commands us to be chaste and modest in act, in look, in behaviour, and in speech. The Ninth Commandment commands us in addition to this to be chaste and pure interiorly, that is, in mind and in heart.[2850]

The Main Kinds of Sins
7 Q. What is mortal sin?
A. Mortal sin is a transgression of the divine Law by which we seriously fail in our duties towards God, towards our neighbour, or towards ourselves.

8 Q. Why is it called mortal?
A. It is called mortal because it brings death on the soul by making it lose sanctifying grace which is the life of the soul, just as the soul itself is the life of the body.

9 Q. What injury does mortal sin do the soul?
A. (1) Mortal sin deprives the soul of grace and of the friendship of God; (2) It makes it lose Heaven; (3) It deprives it of merits already acquired, and renders it incapable of acquiring new merits; (4) It makes it the slave of the devil; (5) It makes it deserve hell as well as the chastisements of this life.

10 Q. Besides grave matter, what is required to constitute a mortal sin?
A. To constitute a mortal sin, besides grave matter there is also required full consciousness of the gravity of the matter, along with the deliberate will to commit the sin.

The Vices and other Very Grievous Sins
1 Q. What is a vice?
A. A vice is an evil disposition of the mind to shirk good and do evil, arising from the frequent repetition of evil acts.

2 Q. What difference is there between a sin and a vice?
A. Between sin and vice there is this difference that sin is a passing act, whereas vice is a bad habit, contracted by continually falling into some sin.

3 Q. Which are the vices called capital?
A. The vices called capital are seven: Pride, Covetousness, Lust, Anger, Gluttony, Envy and Sloth.

Pope Leo XIII: 1878 to 1903

Encyclical *Libertas*, 7- 8. (20th June 1888)
In man's free will, therefore, or in the moral necessity of our voluntary acts being in accordance with reason, lies the very root of the necessity of law. Nothing more foolish can be uttered or conceived than the notion that, because man is free by nature, he is therefore exempt from law. Were this the case, it would follow that to become free we must be deprived of reason; whereas the truth is that we are bound to submit to law precisely because we are free by our very nature. For, law is the guide of man's actions; it turns him toward good by its rewards, and deters him from evil by its punishments.

Foremost in this office comes the natural law, which is written and engraved in the mind of every man; and this is nothing but our reason, commanding us to do right and forbidding sin. Nevertheless, all prescriptions of human reason can have force of law only inasmuch as they are the voice and the interpreters of some higher power on which our reason and liberty necessarily depend. For, since the force of law consists in the imposing of obligations and the granting of rights, authority is the one and

---

[2850]*Catechism of St. Pius X* [1908] The Sixth and Ninth Commandment [Online] Available at: www. ewtn.com [Accessed on: 12 July 2022]

only foundation of all law — the power, that is, of fixing duties and defining rights, as also of assigning the necessary sanctions of reward and chastisement to each and all of its commands. But all this, clearly, cannot be found in man, if, as his own supreme legislator, he is to be the rule of his own actions. It follows, therefore, that the law of nature is the same thing as the eternal law, implanted in rational creatures, and inclining them to their right action and end; and can be nothing else but the eternal reason of God, the Creator and Ruler of all the world. To this rule of action and restraint of evil God has vouchsafed to give special and most suitable aids for strengthening and ordering the human will. The first and most excellent of these is the power of His divine grace, whereby the mind can be enlightened and the will wholesomely invigorated and moved to the constant pursuit of moral good, so that the use of our inborn liberty becomes at once less difficult and less dangerous. Not that the divine assistance hinders in any way the free movement of our will; just the contrary, for grace works inwardly in man and in harmony with his natural inclinations, since it flows from the very Creator of his mind and will, by whom all things are moved in conformity with their nature. As the Angelic Doctor points out, it is because divine grace comes from the Author of nature that it is so admirably adapted to be the safeguard of all natures, and to maintain the character, efficiency, and operations of each.[2851]

Encyclical *Arcanum Divinae Sapientiae, 16, 27. (10th February 1880)*
Yet, owing to the efforts of the archenemy of mankind, there are persons who, thanklessly casting away so many other blessings of redemption, despise also or utterly ignore the restoration of marriage to its original perfection. It is a reproach to some of the ancients that they showed themselves the enemies of marriage in many ways; but in our own age, much more pernicious is the sin of those who would fain pervert utterly the nature of marriage, perfect though it is, and complete in all its details and parts. The chief reason why they act in this way is because very many, imbued with the maxims of a false philosophy and corrupted in morals, judge nothing so unbearable as submission and obedience; and strive with all their might to bring about that not only individual men, but families, also-indeed, human society itself-may in haughty pride despise the sovereignty of God.

When the Christian religion is rejected and repudiated, marriage sinks of necessity into the slavery of man's vicious nature and vile passions, and finds but little protection in the help of natural goodness. A very torrent of evil has flowed from this source, not only into private families, but also into States. For, the salutary fear of God being removed, and there being no longer that refreshment in toil which is nowhere more abounding than in the Christian religion, it very often happens, as indeed is natural, that the mutual services and duties of marriage seem almost unbearable; and thus very many yearn for the loosening of the tie which they believe to be woven by human law and of their own will, whenever incompatibility of temper, or quarrels, or the violation of the marriage vow, or mutual consent, or other reasons induce them to think that it would be well to be set free. Then, if they are hindered by law from carrying out this shameless desire, they contend that the laws are iniquitous, inhuman, and at variance with the rights of free citizens; adding that every effort should be made to repeal such enactments, and to introduce a more humane code sanctioning divorce.[2852]

Pope Benedict XII: 1334 to 1342

Constitution *Benedictus Deus (29th January 1336)*
Moreover, we define that according to the general disposition of God, the souls of those who die in actual mortal sin go down into hell immediately after death and there suffer the pain of hell.[2853]

[2851]Pope Leo XIII [1888] Encyclical *Libertas, paras 7-8* [Online] Available at: www.vatican.va [Accessed on: 4 October 2022]
[2852]Pope Leo XIII [1880] Encyclical *Arcanum Divinae Sapientiae*, paras 16, 27 [Online] Available at: www.vatican.va [Accessed on: 4 October 2022]
[2853]Denzinger, H [2010] *Op. cit.*, p.303, *Dz* 1002

Liturgy

Pope Francis: 2013 to 2025

I. *The celebration of the Traditional Latin Mass, according to the Missale Romanum of 1962, is causing disagreements and division and is injuring the unity of the Church. Therefore, the only celebration of the Mass in vernacular languages, according to the liturgical books of Pope St. Paul VI and Pope St. John Paul II, is universally permitted. Only this is the unique expression of the lex orandi of the Roman Rite. The only understanding of Tradition that is allowed is one that accepts changes inspired by the Holy Spirit that break with Tradition. Accordingly, all norms, instructions, permissions and customs of previous popes are abrogated. Henceforth, the celebration of the Mass in Latin by Latin rite priests is only to be allowed as an exception, and treated under provisions for bi-ritualism. However, this will be tightly controlled, and perennial norms disallowed. For example, listening to sacred Scripture in Latin, which people don't understand, is banned because it's like laughing at the Word of God.*

Apostolic Letter issued Motu Proprio *Traditionis Custodes*. (16th July 2021)
Art. 1. The liturgical books promulgated by St. Paul VI and St. John Paul II, in conformity with the decrees of Vatican Council II, are the unique expression of the *lex orandi* of the Roman Rite.
    Art. 8. Previous norms, instructions, permissions, and customs that do not conform to the provisions of the present Motu Proprio are abrogated.
    Everything that I have declared in this Apostolic Letter in the form of Motu Proprio, I order to be observed in all its parts, anything else to the contrary notwithstanding, even if worthy of particular mention, and I establish that it be promulgated by way of publication in *L'Osservatore Romano*, entering immediately in force and, subsequently, that it be published in the official Commentary of the Holy See, *Acta Apostolicae Sedis*.[2854]

Letter to the Bishops of the Whole World, that Accompanies the Apostolic Letter Motu Proprio Data Traditionis Custodes. (16th July 2021)
….I take the firm decision to abrogate all the norms, instructions, permissions and customs that precede the present Motu Proprio, and declare that the liturgical books promulgated by the saintly Pontiffs Paul VI and John Paul II, in conformity with the decrees of Vatican Council II, constitute the unique expression of the *lex orandi* of the Roman Rite. I take comfort in this decision from the fact that, after the Council of Trent, St. Pius V also abrogated all the rites that could not claim a proven antiquity, establishing for the whole Latin Church a single *Missale Romanum*. For four centuries this *Missale Romanum*, promulgated by St. Pius V was thus the principal expression of the *lex orandi* of the Roman Rite, and functioned to maintain the unity of the Church. Without denying the dignity and grandeur of this Rite, the Bishops gathered in ecumenical council asked that it be reformed; their intention was that 'the faithful would not assist as strangers and silent spectators in the mystery of faith, but, with a full understanding of the rites and prayers, would participate in the sacred action consciously, piously, and actively'. St. Paul VI, recalling that the work of adaptation of the *Roman Missal* had already been initiated by Pius XII, declared that the revision of the *Roman Missal*, carried out in the light of ancient liturgical sources, had the goal of permitting the Church to raise up, in the variety of languages, 'a single and identical prayer,' that expressed her unity. This unity I intend to re-establish throughout the Church of the Roman Rite. […]
    The responses reveal a situation that preoccupies and saddens me, and persuades me of the need to intervene. Regrettably, the pastoral objective of my Predecessors, who had intended 'to do everything possible to ensure that all those who truly possessed the desire for unity would find it possible to remain in this unity or to rediscover it anew', has often been seriously disregarded. An opportunity offered by St. John Paul II and, with even greater magnanimity, by Benedict XVI, intended to recover the unity of an

---

[2854]Pope Francis [2021] Motu Proprio *Traditionis Custodes*, arts.1, 8 [Online] Available at: www.vatican.va [Accessed on: 19 July 2022]

ecclesial body with diverse liturgical sensibilities, was exploited to widen the gaps, reinforce the divergences, and encourage disagreements that injure the Church, block her path, and expose her to the peril of division. […]

But I am nonetheless saddened that the instrumental use of *Missale Romanum* of 1962 is often characterized by a rejection not only of the liturgical reform, but of the Vatican Council II itself, claiming, with unfounded and unsustainable assertions, that it betrayed the Tradition and the 'true Church'. […]

A final reason for my decision is this: ever more plain in the words and attitudes of many is the close connection between the choice of celebrations according to the liturgical books prior to Vatican Council II and the rejection of the Church and her institutions in the name of what is called the 'true Church.' One is dealing here with comportment that contradicts communion and nurtures the divisive tendency −'I belong to Paul; I belong instead to Apollo; I belong to Cephas; I belong to Christ' − against which the Apostle Paul so vigorously reacted. In defense of the unity of the Body of Christ, I am constrained to revoke the faculty granted by my Predecessors. The distorted use that has been made of this faculty is contrary to the intentions that led to granting the freedom to celebrate the Mass with the *Missale Romanum* of 1962.

In the Motu Proprio I have desired to affirm that it is up to the Bishop, as moderator, promoter, and guardian of the liturgical life of the Church of which he is the principle of unity, to regulate the liturgical celebrations. It is up to you to authorize in your Churches, as local Ordinaries, the use of the *Missale Romanum* of 1962, applying the norms of the present Motu Proprio. It is up to you to proceed in such a way as to return to a unitary form of celebration, and to determine case by case the reality of the groups which celebrate with this *Missale Romanum*.[2855]

Interview with Carlos Herrera on Radio COPE. (1st Sept 2021)
And the result was that pastoral care that must be taken, with some good limits. For example, that the proclamation of the Word be in a language that everyone understands; otherwise it would be like laughing at the Word of God. Little things. But yes, the limit is very clear. After this Motu Proprio, a priest who wants to celebrate that is not in the same condition as before − that it was for nostalgia, for desire, &c. − and so he has to ask permission from Rome. A kind of permission for bi-ritualism, which is given only by Rome. [Like] a priest who celebrates in the Eastern Rite and the Latin Rite, he is bi-ritual but with the permission of Rome.[2856]

Conversations with Jesuits during his Apostolic Journey to Bratislava. (12th September 2021)
Now I hope that with the decision to stop the automatism of the ancient rite we can return to the true intentions of Benedict XVI and John Paul II. My decision is the result of a consultation with all the bishops of the world made last year. From now on those who want to celebrate with the *vetus ordo* must ask permission from as is done with biritualism. But there are young people who after a month of ordination go to the bishop to ask for it. This is a phenomenon that indicates that we are going backward.

A cardinal told me that two newly ordained priests came to him asking him for permission to study Latin so as to celebrate well. With a sense of humour he replied: 'But there are many Hispanics in the diocese! Study Spanish to be able to preach. Then, when you have studied Spanish, come back to me and I'll tell you how many Vietnamese there are in the diocese, and I'll ask you to study Vietnamese. Then, when you have learned Vietnamese, I will give you permission to study Latin.' So he made them 'land,' he made them return to earth. I go ahead, not because I want to start a revolution. I do what I feel I must do. It takes a lot of patience, prayer and a lot of charity.[2857]

[2855]Pope Francis [2021] *Letter to the Bishops of the whole world, that accompanies the Apostolic Letter Motu Proprio data Traditionis Custodes* [Online] Available at: www.vatican.va [Accessed on: 19 July 2022]
[2856]Pope Francis [2021] *Interview with Carlos Herrera on Radio COPE.* [Online] Available at: www.vaticannews.va [Accessed on: 19 July 2022]
[2857]Spadaro, A. [20 October 2021] *'Freedom Scares Us': Pope Francis' conversation with Slovak Jesuits.* [Online] Available at: www.laciviltacattolica.com [Accessed on: 20 July 2022]

General Audience Address. (27th October 2021)
Today, there are many who still seek religious security rather than the living and true God, focusing on rituals and precepts instead of embracing God's love with their whole being. And this is the temptation of the new fundamentalists, isn't it? Of those who seem to be afraid to make progress, and who regress because they feel more secure.[2858]

Apostolic Letter, Desiderio Desideravi, 61. (29th June 2022)
We are called continually to rediscover the richness of the general principles exposed in the first numbers of *Sacrosanctum Concilium*, grasping the intimate bond between this first of the Council's constitutions and all the others. For this reason we cannot go back to that ritual form which the Council fathers, cum Petro et sub Petro, felt the need to reform, approving, under the guidance of the Holy Spirit and following their conscience as pastors, the principles from which was born the reform. The holy pontiffs St. Paul VI and St. John Paul II, approving the reformed liturgical books *ex decreto Sacrosancti Œcumenici Concilii Vaticani II*, have guaranteed the fidelity of the reform of the Council. For this reason I wrote *Traditionis Custodes*, so that the Church may lift up, in the variety of so many languages, one and the same prayer capable of expressing her unity.

As I have already written, I intend that this unity be re-established in the whole Church of the Roman Rite.[2859]

Sacred Scripture

Matthew 13:52
He said unto them: Therefore every scribe instructed in the kingdom of heaven, is like to a man that is a householder, who bringeth forth out of his treasure new things and old.

Luke 2:42
And when he was twelve years old, they going up into Jerusalem, according to the custom of the feast.

I Corinthians 11:2
Now I praise you, brethren, that in all things you are mindful of me: and keep my ordinances as I have delivered them to you.

I Corinthians 11:23
For I have received of the Lord that which also I delivered unto you, that the Lord Jesus, the same night in which he was betrayed, took bread....

I Corinthians 15:1
Now I make known unto you, brethren, the gospel which I preached to you, which also you have received, and wherein you stand....

Ephesians 2:20
Built upon the foundation of the apostles and prophets, Jesus Christ himself being the chief corner stone.

I Thessalonians 5:21
But prove all things; hold fast that which is good.

II Thessalonians 2:14
Therefore, brethren, stand fast; and hold the traditions which you have learned, whether by word, or by our epistle.

II Thessalonians 3:6
And we charge you, brethren, in the name of our Lord Jesus Christ, that you withdraw

---

[2858]Pope Francis [7th October 2021] *General Audience Address* [Online] Available at: www.vatican. va [Accessed on: 19 July 2022]
[2859]Pope Francis [2022] Apostolic Letter, *Desiderio Desideravi*, para 61 [Online] Available at: www. vatican.va [Accessed on: 19 July 2022]

yourselves from every brother walking disorderly, and not according to the tradition which they have received of us.

II Timothy 2:2
And the things which thou hast heard of me by many witnesses, the same commend to faithful men, who shall be fit to teach others also.

Deuteronomy 4:9-10
Keep thyself therefore, and thy soul carefully. Forget not the words that thy eyes have seen, and let them not go out of thy heart all the days of thy life. Thou shalt teach them to thy sons and to thy grandsons, from the day in which thou didst stand before the Lord thy God in Horeb, when the Lord spoke to me, saying: Call together the people unto me, that they may hear my words, and may learn to fear me all the time that they live on the earth, and may teach their children.

Deuteronomy 6:4-9
Hear, O Israel, the Lord our God is one Lord. Thou shalt love the Lord thy God with thy whole heart, and with thy whole soul, and with thy whole strength. And these words which I command thee this day, shall be in thy heart: And thou shalt tell them to thy children, and thou shalt meditate upon them sitting·in thy house, and walking on thy journey, sleeping and rising. And thou shalt bind them as a sign on thy hand, and they shall be and shall move between thy eyes. And thou shalt write them in the entry, and on the doors of thy house.

Sacred Tradition

St. Irenaeus: c. 130 to c. 202

Against Heresies. Bk. IV, Chap. 33.
True knowledge is [that which consists in] the doctrine of the apostles, and the ancient constitution of the Church throughout all the world, and the distinctive manifestation of the body of Christ according to the successions of the bishops, by which they have handed down that Church which exists in every place, and has come even unto us, being guarded and preserved without any forging of Scriptures, by a very complete system of doctrine, and neither receiving addition nor [suffering] curtailment [in the truths which she believes]; and [it consists in] reading [the word of God] without falsification, and a lawful and diligent exposition in harmony with the Scriptures, both without danger and without blasphemy....[2860]

Tertullian: c. 160 to 225

The Prescription Against Heretics, Chap. 19.
For wherever it shall be manifest that the true Christian rule and faith shall be, there will likewise be the true Scriptures and expositions thereof, and all the Christian traditions.[2861]

St. Athanasius: c. 296 to 373

Festal Letters 2
Again we write, again keeping to the apostolic traditions, we remind each other when we come together for prayer; and keeping the feast in common, with one mouth we truly give thanks to the Lord. Thus giving thanks unto Him, and being followers of the saints, 'we shall make our praise in the Lord all the day,' as the Psalmist says. So, when we rightly keep the feast, we shall be counted worthy of that joy which is in heaven.[2862]

[2860]St. Irenaeus. *Against Heresies.* Bk. IV, Chap. 33 [Online] Available at: www.newadvent.org [Accessed on: 22 July 2022]

[2861]Tertullian. *The Prescription Against Heretics,* Chap. 19 [Online] Available at: www.newadvent.org [Accessed on: 22 July 2022]

[2862]St. Athanasius. *Festal Letters* 2, para 6 [Online] Available at: www.newadvent.org [Accessed on: 22 July 2022]

St. Basil of Caesarea: 330 to 379

On the Holy Spirit, Chap. 27.

Of the beliefs and practices whether generally accepted or publicly enjoined which are preserved in the Church some we possess derived from written teaching; others we have received delivered to us 'in a mystery' by the tradition of the apostles; and both of these in relation to true religion have the same force. And these no one will gainsay — no one, at all events, who is even moderately versed in the institutions of the Church. For were we to attempt to reject such customs as have no written authority, on the ground that the importance they possess is small, we should unintentionally injure the Gospel in its very vitals; or, rather, should make our public definition a mere phrase and nothing more. For instance, to take the first and most general example, who is thence who has taught us in writing to sign with the sign of the cross those who have trusted in the name of our Lord Jesus Christ? What writing has taught us to turn to the East at the prayer? Which of the saints has left us in writing the words of the invocation at the displaying of the bread of the Eucharist and the cup of blessing? For we are not, as is well known, content with what the apostle or the Gospel has recorded, but both in preface and conclusion we add other words as being of great importance to the validity of the ministry, and these we derive from unwritten teaching.

Moreover we bless the water of baptism and the oil of the chrism, and besides this the catechumen who is being baptized. On what written authority do we do this? Is not our authority silent and mystical tradition? Nay, by what written word is the anointing of oil itself taught? And whence comes the custom of baptizing thrice? And as to the other customs of baptism from what Scripture do we derive the renunciation of Satan and his angels? Does not this come from that unpublished and secret teaching which our fathers guarded in a silence out of the reach of curious meddling and inquisitive investigation? Well had they learned the lesson that the awful dignity of the mysteries is best preserved by silence. What the uninitiated are not even allowed to look at was hardly likely to be publicly paraded about in written documents. What was the meaning of the mighty Moses in not making all the parts of the tabernacle open to every one? The profane he stationed without the sacred barriers; the first courts he conceded to the purer; the Levites alone he judged worthy of being servants of the Deity; sacrifices and burnt offerings and the rest of the priestly functions he allotted to the priests; one chosen out of all he admitted to the shrine, and even this one not always but on only one day in the year, and of this one day a time was fixed for his entry so that he might gaze on the Holy of Holies amazed at the strangeness and novelty of the sight. Moses was wise enough to know that contempt stretches to the trite and to the obvious, while a keen interest is naturally associated with the unusual and the unfamiliar. In the same manner the Apostles and Fathers who laid down laws for the Church from the beginning thus guarded the awful dignity of the mysteries in secrecy and silence, for what is bruited abroad random among the common folk is no mystery at all. This is the reason for our tradition of unwritten precepts and practices, that the knowledge of our dogmas may not become neglected and contemned by the multitude through familiarity.[2863]

St. Vincent of Lerins: ? to 450

Commonitory, Chap. 2

Moreover, in the Catholic Church itself, all possible care must be taken, that we hold that faith which has been believed everywhere, always, by all. For that is truly and in the strictest sense 'Catholic', which, as the name itself and the reason of the thing declare, comprehends all universally. This rule we shall observe if we follow universality, antiquity, consent. We shall follow universality if we confess that one faith to be true, which the whole Church throughout the world confesses; antiquity, if we in no wise depart from those interpretations which it is manifest were notoriously held by our

---

[2863]St. Basil of Caesarea. *On the Holy Spirit,* Chap. 27 [Online] Available at: www.newadvent.org [Accessed on: 22 July 2022]

holy ancestors and fathers; consent, in like manner, if in antiquity itself we adhere to the consentient definitions and determinations of all, or at the least of almost all priests and doctors.

What then will a Catholic Christian do, if a small portion of the Church have cut itself off from the communion of the universal faith? What, surely, but prefer the soundness of the whole body to the unsoundness of a pestilent and corrupt member? What, if some novel contagion seek to infect not merely an insignificant portion of the Church, but the whole? Then it will be his care to cleave to antiquity, which at this day cannot possibly be seduced by any fraud of novelty.[2864]

The Magisterium of the Church

The Traditional Latin Mass has been universally received from apostolic and unbroken Tradition. Therefore, what earlier generations held as sacred, remains sacred and great, and it cannot be all of a sudden entirely forbidden or even considered harmful. It has never been abrogated and must be honoured for its venerable and ancient usage. The language proper to the Roman Church is Latin, which has been esteemed 'a treasure of incomparable worth' by the Roman Pontiffs. In particular, Gregorian chant is especially suited to the Roman liturgy and should be given pride of place in liturgical services.

Council of Trent (Nineteenth Ecumenical, 1545 to 1563)

Decree Concerning The Canonical Scriptures (8th April 1546)
If anyone does not accept as sacred and canonical the aforesaid books in their entirety and with all their parts, as they have been accustomed to be read in the Catholic Church and as they are contained in the old Latin Vulgate Edition, and knowingly and deliberately rejects the aforesaid traditions, let him be anathema.

Decree Concerning The Edition And Use Of The Sacred Books (8th April 1546)
Moreover, the same holy council considering that not a little advantage will accrue to the Church of God if it be made known which of all the Latin editions of the sacred books now in circulation is to be regarded as authentic, ordains and declares that the old Latin Vulgate Edition, which, in use for so many hundred years, has been approved by the Church, be in public lectures, disputations, sermons and expositions held as authentic, and that no one dare or presume under any pretext whatsoever to reject it.[2865]

Doctrine Concerning the Sacrifice of the Mass, Chaps. 4, 5, 8, Canons 6, 7, 9. (17th September 1562)
And since it is becoming that holy things be administered in a holy manner, and of all things this sacrifice is the most holy, the Catholic Church, to the end that it might be worthily and reverently offered and received, instituted many centuries ago the holy canon, which is so free from error that it contains nothing that does not in the highest degree savour of a certain holiness and piety and raise up to God the minds of those who offer. For it consists partly of the very words of the Lord, partly of the traditions of the Apostles, and also of pious regulations of holy pontiffs.

The Solemn Ceremonies of the Sacrifice of the Mass. And since the nature of man is such that he cannot without external means be raised easily to meditation on divine things, holy mother Church has instituted certain rites, namely, that some things in the mass be pronounced in a low tone and others in a louder tone. She has likewise, in accordance with apostolic discipline and tradition, made use of ceremonies, such as mystical blessings, lights, incense, vestments, and many other things of this kind, whereby both the majesty of so great a sacrifice might be emphasised and the minds of

---

[2864]St. Vincent of Lerins. *Commonitory*, Chap. 2, para 6 [Online] Available at: www.newadvent.org [Accessed on: 22 July 2022]
[2865]Council of Trent [1546] *Decree Concerning the Canonical Scriptures & Decree Concerning the Edition and Use of the Sacred Books* [Online] Available at: www.ewtn.com [Accessed on: 20 July 2022]

the faithful excited by those visible signs of religion and piety to the contemplation of those most sublime things which are hidden in this sacrifice.

Though the Mass contains much instruction for the faithful, it has, nevertheless, not been deemed advisable by the Fathers that it should be celebrated everywhere in the vernacular tongue. Wherefore, the ancient rite of each Church, approved by the holy Roman Church, the mother and mistress of all churches, being everywhere retained, that the sheep of Christ may not suffer hunger, or 'the little ones ask for bread and there is none to break it unto them,' (Lam 4:4) the holy council commands pastors and all who have the '*cura animarum*' that they, either themselves or through others, explain frequently during the celebration of the mass some of the things read during the mass, and that among other things they explain some mystery of this most holy sacrifice, especially on Sundays and festival days.

Canon 6. If anyone says that the canon of the Mass contains errors and is therefore to be abrogated, let him be anathema.

Canon 7. If anyone says that the ceremonies, vestments, and outward signs which the Catholic Church uses in the celebration of masses, are incentives to impiety rather than stimulants to piety, let him be anathema.

Canon 9. If anyone says that the rite of the Roman Church, according to which a part of the canon and the words of consecration are pronounced in a low tone, is to be condemned; or that the Mass ought to be celebrated in the vernacular tongue only; or that water ought not to be mixed with the wine that is to be offered in the chalice because it is contrary to the institution of Christ, let him be anathema.[2866]

First Vatican Council (Twentieth Ecumenical, 1869 to 1870)

Dogmatic Constitution, *Dei Filius, Chap. 2 (24th April 1870)*
The complete books of the old and the new Testament with all their parts, as they are listed in the decree of the said Council and as they are found in the old Latin Vulgate edition, are to be received as sacred and canonical.[2867]

Second Vatican Council (Twenty-First Ecumenical, 1962 to 1965)

Constitution on the Sacred Liturgy *Sacrosanctum Concilium, 36 §1, 54, 101§1, 116* (4th December 1963)
Particular law remaining in force, the use of the Latin language is to be preserved in the Latin rites.

Nevertheless steps should be taken so that the faithful may also be able to say or to sing together in Latin those parts of the Ordinary of the Mass which pertain to them.

In accordance with the centuries-old tradition of the Latin rite, the Latin language is to be retained by clerics in the divine office. But in individual cases the ordinary has the power of granting the use of a vernacular translation to those clerics for whom the use of Latin constitutes a grave obstacle to their praying the office properly.

The Church acknowledges Gregorian chant as specially suited to the Roman liturgy: therefore, other things being equal, it should be given pride of place in liturgical services.[2868]

Decree on Priestly Training, *Optatam Totius, 13. (28th October 1965)*
Before beginning specifically ecclesiastical subjects, seminarians should be equipped with that humanistic and scientific training which young men in their own countries are wont to have as a foundation for higher studies. Moreover they are to acquire a knowledge of Latin which will enable them to understand and make use of the sources

---

[2866]Council of Trent [1562] *Doctrine Concerning the Sacrifice of the Mass* [Online] Available at: www.ewtn.com [Accessed on: 20 July 2022]
[2867]First Vatican Council [1870] *Dogmatic Constitution, Dei Filius,* Chap. 2 [Online] Available at: www.ewtn.com [Accessed on: 20 July 2022]
[2868]Second Vatican Council [1963] Constitution on the Sacred Liturgy *Sacrosanctum Concilium,* 36 §1, 54, 101§1, 116 [Online] Available at: www.vatican.va [Accessed on: 19 July 2022]

of so many sciences and of the documents of the Church. The study of the liturgical language proper to each rite should be considered necessary; a suitable knowledge of the languages of the Bible and of Tradition should be greatly encouraged.[2869]

Pope Benedict XVI: 2005 to 2013

Motu Proprio, *Summorum Pontificum. (7th July 2007)*
As from time immemorial, so too in the future, it is necessary to maintain the principle that 'each particular Church must be in accord with the universal Church not only regarding the doctrine of the faith and sacramental signs, but also as to the usages universally received from apostolic and unbroken tradition. These are to be observed not only so that errors may be avoided, but also that the faith may be handed on in its integrity, since the Church's rule of prayer (*lex orandi*) corresponds to her rule of faith (*lex credendi*).'

Eminent among the Popes who showed such proper concern was St. Gregory the Great, who sought to hand on to the new peoples of Europe both the Catholic faith and the treasures of worship and culture amassed by the Romans in preceding centuries. He ordered that the form of the sacred liturgy, both of the sacrifice of the Mass and the Divine Office, as celebrated in Rome, should be defined and preserved. He greatly encouraged those monks and nuns who, following the Rule of St. Benedict, everywhere proclaimed the Gospel and illustrated by their lives the salutary provision of the Rule that 'nothing is to be preferred to the work of God.' In this way the sacred liturgy, celebrated according to the Roman usage, enriched the faith and piety, as well as the culture, of numerous peoples. It is well known that in every century of the Christian era the Church's Latin liturgy in its various forms has inspired countless saints in their spiritual life, confirmed many peoples in the virtue of religion and enriched their devotion.

In the course of the centuries, many other Roman Pontiffs took particular care that the sacred liturgy should accomplish this task more effectively. Outstanding among them was St. Pius V, who in response to the desire expressed by the Council of Trent, renewed with great pastoral zeal the Church's entire worship, saw to the publication of liturgical books corrected and 'restored in accordance with the norm of the Fathers,' and provided them for the use of the Latin Church.

Among the liturgical books of the Roman rite, a particular place belongs to the *Roman Missal*, which developed in the city of Rome and over the centuries gradually took on forms very similar to the form which it had in more recent generations. [...]

Art 1. *The Roman Missal* promulgated by Pope Paul VI is the ordinary expression of the *lex orandi* (rule of prayer) of the Catholic Church of the Latin rite. *The Roman Missal* promulgated by St. Pius V and revised by Bl. John XXIII is nonetheless to be considered an extraordinary expression of the same *lex orandi* of the Church and duly honoured for its venerable and ancient usage. These two expressions of the Church's *lex orandi* will in no way lead to a division in the Church's *lex credendi* (rule of faith); for they are two usages of the one Roman rite.

It is therefore permitted to celebrate the Sacrifice of the Mass following the typical edition of the *Roman Missal*, which was promulgated by Bl. John XXIII in 1962 and never abrogated, as an extraordinary form of the Church's Liturgy.[2870]

Letter to the Bishops on the Occasion of the Publication of the Apostolic Letter 'Motu Proprio Data' Summorum Pontificum. (7th July 2007)
There is no contradiction between the two editions of the *Roman Missal*. In the history of the liturgy there is growth and progress, but no rupture. What earlier generations held as sacred, remains sacred and great for us too, and it cannot be all of a sudden entirely forbidden or even considered harmful. It behooves all of us to preserve the

---

[2869]Second Vatican Council [1965] Decree on Priestly Training, *Optatam Totius*, para 13. [Online] Available at: www.vatican.va [Accessed on: 19 July 2022]
[2870]Pope Benedict XVI [2007] *Summorum Pontificum*, art.1 [Online] Available at: www.vatican.va [Accessed on: 19 July 2022]

riches which have developed in the Church's faith and prayer, and to give them their proper place.[2871]

Address to Members of the Vatican Chapter. (8th October 2007)
I appreciated, Your Excellency, the fact that as Archpriest you referred to the uninterrupted presence of clergy praying in the Vatican Basilica since the time of St. Gregory the Great. It has been a continuous, deliberately discreet but faithful and persevering presence. [...] It is more necessary than elsewhere that a permanent community of prayer should exist here, by Peter's tomb, in this sacred place visited every day by thousands of pilgrims and tourists from all over the world, which can guarantee continuity with tradition....[2872]

Letter to the Grand Chancellor of the Pontifical Institute of Sacred Music celebrating its 100th anniversary. (13th May 2011)
The Pontiffs Paul VI and John Paul II in particular wished to reaffirm the aim of sacred music in the light of the conciliar Constitution *Sacrosanctum Concilium*: in other words: 'the glory of God and the sanctification of the faithful' (n. 112), as well as the fundamental criteria of tradition; I limit myself to recalling: the sense of prayer, of dignity and of beauty; full adherence to the texts and to the liturgical gestures; the involvement of the assembly, hence a legitimate adaptation to the local culture while preserving at the same time the universality of the language; the primacy of Gregorian chant as a supreme model of sacred music and the wise use of other modes of expression that are part of the Church's historical and liturgical patrimony, especially, but not only polyphony; the importance of the *schola cantorum*, particularly in cathedral churches. Today too these are important criteria which should be taken into careful consideration.[2873]

Motu Proprio, *Latina Lingua*, 1-2. (10th November 2012)
The Latin language has always been held in very high esteem by the Catholic Church and by the Roman Pontiffs. They have assiduously encouraged the knowledge and dissemination of Latin, adopting it as the Church's language, capable of passing on the Gospel message throughout the world. This is authoritatively stated by the Apostolic Constitution *Veterum Sapientia* of my Predecessor, Bl. John XXIII.

Indeed the Church has spoken and prayed in the languages of all peoples since Pentecost. Nevertheless, the Christian communities of the early centuries made frequent use of Greek and Latin, languages of universal communication in the world in which they lived and through which the newness of Christ's word encountered the heritage of the Roman-Hellenistic culture.

After the fall of the Roman Empire of the West, the Church of Rome not only continued to use Latin but, in a certain way, made herself its custodian and champion in both the theological and liturgical sectors as well as in formation and in the transmission of knowledge.

In our time too, knowledge of the Latin language and culture is proving to be more necessary than ever for the study of the sources, which, among others, numerous ecclesiastical disciplines draw from, such as, for example, theology, liturgy, patristics and canon law, as the Second Vatican Ecumenical Council teaches.

In addition, precisely in order to highlight the Church's universal character, the liturgical books of the Roman Rite, the most important documents of the Papal Mag-

---

[2871]Pope Benedict XVI [2007] *Letter to the Bishops on the occasion of the publication of the Apostolic Letter 'Motu Proprio Data' Summorum Pontificum* [Online] Available at: www.vatican.va [Accessed on: 23 July 2022]
[2872]Pope Benedict XVI [2007] *Address to members of the Vatican Chapter*. [Online] Available at: www. vatican.va [Accessed on: 23 July 2022]
[2873]Pope Benedict XVI [2011] *Letter to the Grand Chancellor of the Pontifical Institute of Sacred Music celebrating its 100th anniversary* [Online] Available at: www.vatican.va [Accessed on: 4 October 2022]

isterium and the most solemn official Acts of the Roman Pontiffs are written in this language in their authentic form.[2874]

Pope St. John Paul II: 1978 to 2005

Address to participants in the Certamen Vaticanum. *(27th November 1978)*
We highly praise this '*Certamen Vaticanum*' which in the past was established with the approval and assistance of Pius XII, since it encourages the study of Latin so that one may deepen one's knowledge of it and promote its use.

There is no one who is ignorant of the fact that this age is less favourable to the study of Latin, when men today are more interested in science and technology and consider the vernacular to be more expressive. Nevertheless we do not wish to ignore the important documents of our predecessors who time and again emphasised the importance of Latin even in this age, especially in so far as the Church is concerned. For Latin is in a way a universal language cutting across national boundaries and as such the Apostolic See still constantly makes use of it in letters and acts addressed to the whole Catholic family.[2875]

Code of Canon Law. (1983)
The program of priestly formation is to provide that students not only are carefully taught their native language but also understand Latin well and have a suitable understanding of those foreign languages which seem necessary or useful for their formation or for the exercise of pastoral ministry. (Can. 249)

The eucharistic celebration is to be carried out in the Latin language or in another language provided that the liturgical texts have been legitimately approved. (Can. 928).[2876]

Motu Proprio *Ecclesia Dei, 5, 6.c (2nd July 1988)*
To all those Catholic faithful who feel attached to some previous liturgical and disciplinary forms of the Latin tradition I wish to manifest my will to facilitate their ecclesial communion by means of the necessary measures to guarantee respect for their rightful aspirations. In this matter I ask for the support of the bishops and of all those engaged in the pastoral ministry in the Church.

…moreover, respect must everywhere be shown for the feelings of all those who are attached to the Latin liturgical tradition, by a wide and generous application of the directives already issued some time ago by the Apostolic See for the use of the Roman Missal according to the typical edition of 1962.[2877]

Address to the Professors and Students of The Pontifical Institute of Sacred Music. (19th January 2001
You, teachers and students, are asked to make the most of your artistic gifts, maintaining and furthering the study and practice of music and song in the forms and with the instruments privileged by the Second Vatican Council: Gregorian chant, sacred polyphony and the organ. Only in this way will liturgical music worthily fulfil its function during the celebration of the sacraments and, especially, of Holy Mass.[2878]

Encyclical *Ecclesia de Eucharistia, 49. (17th April 2003)*
The designs of altars and tabernacles within Church interiors were often not simply motivated by artistic inspiration but also by a clear understanding of the mystery. The

---

[2874]Pope Benedict XVI [2012] Motu Proprio, *Latina Lingua*, paras 1-2 [Online] Available at: www.vatican.va [Accessed on: 4 October 2022]
[2875]Pope St. John Paul II [1978] *Address to participants in the Certamen Vaticanum* [Online] Available at: www.vatican.va [Accessed on: 4 October 2022]
[2876]*Code of Canon Law* [1983] [Online] Available at: www.vatican.va [Accessed on: 6 September 2022]
[2877]Pope St. John Paul II [1988] Motu Proprio *Ecclesia Dei*, paras 5, 6.c [Online] Available at: www.vatican.va [Accessed on: 23 July 2022]
[2878]Pope St. John Paul II [2001] *Address to the Professors and Students of The Pontifical Institute of Sacred Music* [Online] Available at: https://adoremus.org [Accessed on: 24 September 2023]

same could be said for sacred music, if we but think of the inspired Gregorian melodies and the many, often great, composers who sought to do justice to the liturgical texts of the Mass.[2879]

Chirograph for the centenary of the Motu Proprio, Tra le Sollecitudini, 7. (22nd November 2003)

Among the musical expressions that correspond best with the qualities demanded by the notion of sacred music, especially liturgical music, Gregorian chant has a special place. The Second Vatican Council recognized that 'being specially suited to the Roman Liturgy' it should be given, other things being equal, pride of place in liturgical services sung in Latin. St. Pius X pointed out that the Church had 'inherited it from the Fathers of the Church', that she has 'jealously guarded [it] for centuries in her liturgical codices' and still 'proposes it to the faithful' 'as her own, considering it 'the supreme model of sacred music'. Thus, Gregorian chant continues also today to be an element of unity in the Roman Liturgy.[2880]

Sacred Congregation for Divine Worship and the Discipline of the Sacraments, Redemptionis Sacramentum, 112. (25th March 2004)

Mass is celebrated either in Latin or in another language, provided that liturgical texts are used which have been approved according to the norm of law. Except in the case of celebrations of the Mass that are scheduled by the ecclesiastical authorities to take place in the language of the people, Priests are always and everywhere permitted to celebrate Mass in Latin.[2881]

Pope St. Paul VI: 1963 to 1978

Apostolic Letter, Sacrificium Laudis — To the supreme moderators of clerical religious institutes obliged to the choral recitation of the divine office. (15h August 1966)

Yet, from letters which some of you have sent, and from many other sources, We learn that discordant practices have been introduced into the sacred liturgy by your communities or provinces (We speak of those only that belong to the Latin Rite.) For while some are very faithful to the Latin language, others wish to use the vernacular within the choral office. Others, in various places, wish to exchange that chant which is called 'Gregorian', for newly-minted melodies. Indeed, some even insist that Latin should be wholly suppressed.

We must acknowledge that We have been somewhat disturbed and saddened by these requests. One may well wonder what the origin is of this new way of thinking and this sudden dislike for the past; one may well wonder why these things have been fostered. [...]

What is in question here is not only the retention within the choral office of the Latin language, though it is of course right that this should be eagerly guarded and should certainly not be lightly esteemed. For this language is, within the Latin Church, an abundant well-spring of Christian civilisation and a very rich treasure-trove of devotion. But it is also the seemliness, the beauty and the native strength of these prayers and canticles which is at stake: the choral office itself, 'the lovely voice of the Church in song' (Cf. St. Augustine's *Confessions*, Bk. IX, 6). Your founders and teachers, the holy ones who are as it were so many lights within your religious families, have transmitted this to you. The traditions of the elders, your glory throughout long ages, must not be belittled. Indeed, your manner of celebrating the choral office has been one of the chief

---

[2879]Pope St. John Paul II [2003] Encyclical *Ecclesia de Eucharistia*, para 49 [Online] Available at: www.vatican.va [Accessed on: 4 October 2022]

[2880]Pope St. John Paul II [2003] *Chirograph for the centenary of the Motu Proprio, Tra le Sollecitudini*, para 7 [Online] Available at: www.vatican.va [Accessed on: 4 October 2022]

[2881]Sacred Congregation for Divine Worship and the Discipline of the Sacraments [2004] *Redemptionis Sacramentum*, para 112. [Online] Available at: www.vatican.va [Accessed on: 23 July 2022]

reasons why these families of yours have lasted so long, and happily increased. It is thus most surprising that under the influence of a sudden agitation, some now think that it should be given up.

In present conditions, what words or melodies could replace the forms of Catholic devotion which you have used until now? You should reflect and carefully consider whether things would not be worse, should this fine inheritance be discarded. It is to be feared that the choral office would turn into a mere bland recitation, suffering from poverty and begetting weariness, as you yourselves would perhaps be the first to experience. One can also wonder whether men would come in such numbers to your churches in quest of the sacred prayer, if its ancient and native tongue, joined to a chant full of grave beauty, resounded no more within your walls. We therefore ask all those to whom it pertains, to ponder what they wish to give up, and not to let that spring run dry from which, until the present, they have themselves drunk deep.

Of course, the Latin language presents some difficulties, and perhaps not inconsiderable ones, for the new recruits to your holy ranks. But such difficulties, as you know, should not be reckoned insuperable. This is especially true for you, who can more easily give yourselves to study, being more set apart from the business and bother of the world. Moreover, those prayers, with their antiquity, their excellence, their noble majesty, will continue to draw to you young men and women, called to the inheritance of our Lord. On the other hand, that choir from which is removed this language of wondrous spiritual power, transcending the boundaries of the nations, and from which is removed this melody proceeding from the inmost sanctuary of the soul, where faith dwells and charity burns — We speak of Gregorian chant — such a choir will be like to a snuffed candle, which gives light no more, no more attracts the eyes and minds of men.[2882]

Pope St. John XXIII: 1958 to 1963

Apostolic Constitution *Veterum Sapientia*. (22nd February 1962)
A primary place
But amid this variety of languages a primary place must surely be given to that language which had its origins in Latium, and later proved so admirable a means for the spreading of Christianity throughout the West.

And since in God's special Providence this language united so many nations together under the authority of the Roman Empire — and that for so many centuries — it also became the rightful language of the Apostolic See. Preserved for posterity, it proved to be a bond of unity for the Christian peoples of Europe.

The nature of Latin
Of its very nature Latin is most suitable for promoting every form of culture among peoples. It gives rise to no jealousies. It does not favor any one nation, but presents itself with equal impartiality to all and is equally acceptable to all.

Nor must we overlook the characteristic nobility of Latin formal structure. Its 'concise, varied and harmonious style, full of majesty and dignity' makes for singular clarity and impressiveness of expression. [...]

Preservation of Latin by the Holy See
Thus the 'knowledge and use of this language,' so intimately bound up with the Church's life, 'is important not so much on cultural or literary grounds, as for religious reasons.' These are the words of Our Predecessor Pius XI, who conducted a scientific inquiry into this whole subject, and indicated three qualities of the Latin language which harmonise to a remarkable degree with the Church's nature. 'For the Church, precisely because it embraces all nations and is destined to endure to the end of time … of its very nature requires a language which is universal, immutable, and non-vernacular.' [...]

[2842]Pope St. Paul VI [1966] Apostolic Letter, *Sacrificium Laudis* [Online] Available at: lms.org.uk [Accessed on: 23 July 2022]

Immutable

Furthermore, the Church's language must be not only universal but also immutable. Modern languages are liable to change, and no single one of them is superior to the others in authority. Thus if the truths of the Catholic Church were entrusted to an unspecified number of them, the meaning of these truths, varied as they are, would not be manifested to everyone with sufficient clarity and precision. There would, moreover, be no language which could serve as a common and constant norm by which to gauge the exact meaning of other renderings.

But Latin is indeed such a language. It is set and unchanging. it has long since ceased to be affected by those alterations in the meaning of words which are the normal result of daily, popular use. Certain Latin words, it is true, acquired new meanings as Christian teaching developed and needed to be explained and defended, but these new meanings have long since become accepted and firmly established.

Non-vernacular

Finally, the Catholic Church has a dignity far surpassing that of every merely human society, for it was founded by Christ the Lord. It is altogether fitting, therefore, that the language it uses should be noble, majestic, and non-vernacular.

In addition, the Latin language 'can be called truly catholic.' It has been consecrated through constant use by the Apostolic See, the mother and teacher of all Churches, and must be esteemed 'a treasure … of incomparable worth.' It is a general passport to the proper understanding of the Christian writers of antiquity and the documents of the Church's teaching. It is also a most effective bond, binding the Church of today with that of the past and of the future in wonderful continuity.

Responsibility for enforcement

1. Bishops and superiors-general of religious orders shall take pains to ensure that in their seminaries and in their schools where adolescents are trained for the priesthood, all shall studiously observe the Apostolic See's decision in this matter and obey these Our prescriptions most carefully.
2. In the exercise of their paternal care they shall be on their guard lest anyone under their jurisdiction, eager for revolutionary changes, writes against the use of Latin in the teaching of the higher sacred studies or in the Liturgy, or through prejudice makes light of the Holy See's will in this regard or interprets it falsely.[2883]

Pope Ven. Pius XII: 1939 to 1958

Encyclical *Mediator Dei*, 60. *(20th November 1947)*

The use of the Latin language, customary in a considerable portion of the Church, is a manifest and beautiful sign of unity, as well as an effective antidote for any corruption of doctrinal truth.[2884]

Encyclical *Musicae Sacrae*, 44-45. *(25th December 1955)*

It is the duty of all those to whom Christ the Lord has entrusted the task of guarding and dispensing the Church's riches to preserve this precious treasure of Gregorian chant diligently and to impart it generously to the Christian people. Hence what Our predecessors, St. Pius X, who is rightly called the renewer of Gregorian chant, and Pius XI have wisely ordained and taught, We also, in view of the outstanding qualities which genuine Gregorian chant possesses, will and prescribe that this be done. In the performance of the sacred liturgical rites this same Gregorian chant should be most widely used and great care should be taken that it should be performed properly, worthily and reverently. And if, because of recently instituted feast days, new Gregorian

---

[2883]Pope St. John XIII [1962] *Veterum Sapientia* [Online] Available at: www.papalencyclicals.net [Accessed on: 23 July 2022]

[2884]Pope Ven. Pius XII [1947] Encyclical *Mediator Dei*, para 60. [Online] Available at: www.vatican. va [Accessed on: 23 July 2022]

melodies must be composed, this should be done by true masters of the art. It should be done in such a way that these new compositions obey the laws proper to genuine Gregorian chant and are in worthy harmony with the older melodies in their virtue and purity.

If these prescriptions are really observed in their entirety, the requirements of the other property of sacred music — that property by virtue of which it should be an example of true art — will be duly satisfied. And if in Catholic churches throughout the entire world Gregorian chant sounds forth without corruption or diminution, the chant itself, like the sacred Roman liturgy, will have a characteristic of universality, so that the faithful, wherever they may be, will hear music that is familiar to them and a part of their own home. In this way they may experience, with much spiritual consolation, the wonderful unity of the Church. This is one of the most important reasons why the Church so greatly desires that the Gregorian chant traditionally associated with the Latin words of the sacred liturgy be used.[2885]

Address to the International Congress on Pastoral Liturgy. (24th September 1956)
Latin in the Liturgy. Yet it would be superfluous to call once more to mind that the Church has grave motives for firmly insisting that in the Latin rite the priest celebrating Mass has an absolute obligation to use Latin, and also, when Gregorian chant accompanies the Holy Sacrifice, that this be done in the Church's tongue.[2886]

Sacred Congregation of Seminaries and Universities, Letter on the Proper Study of Latin. (27th October 1957)
Latin is not merely another foreign language to be equated as a required subject or as an elective on the same level with French, German, Spanish, or Russian. Latin has been a great unifying element in Western civilisation and has been, since the fourth century AD, the official and liturgical language of the Western Church. The matter may be put as simply as this: as long as Latin remains the official and liturgical language of the Church, and, especially, of the Liturgy, Latin must have an essential place in Catholic education in general and should be studied by every Catholic capable of learning it, if he wishes to be regarded as a truly educated Catholic in the strict sense of the term.[2887]

Pope Pius XI: 1922 to 1939

Apostolic Letter *Officiorum Omnium. (1st August 1922)*
But if, in any layman who is indeed imbued with literature, ignorance of the Latin language, which we can truly call the 'catholic' language, indicates a certain sluggishness in his love towards the Church, how much more fitting it is that each and every cleric should be adequately practised and skilled in that language! It is certainly their task to defend Latinity with all the more steadfastness, since they are aware that it was with all the more violence that it was attacked by the adversaries of catholic wisdom who in the 16th century shattered the accord Europe had in the single doctrine of the Faith.[2888]

Apostolic Constitution *Divini Cultus. (20th December 1928)*
These public prayers, called at first 'the work of God' and later 'the divine office' or the daily 'debt' which man owes to God, used to be offered both day and night in the presence of a great concourse of the faithful. From the earliest times the simple chants which graced the sacred prayers and the Liturgy gave a wonderful impulse to the piety of the people. History tells us how in the ancient basilicas, where bishop, clergy and

[2885]Pope Ven. Pius XII [1955] Encyclical *Musicae Sacrae*, paras 44-45 [Online] Available at: www.vatican.va [Accessed on: 23 July 2022]
[2886]Pope Ven. Pius XII [1956] *Address to the International Congress on Pastoral Liturgy.* [Online] Available at: archive.ccwatershed.org [Accessed on: 23 July 2022]
[2887]The Sacred Congregation of Seminaries and Universities [1958] *Letter on the Proper Study of Latin.* [Online] Available at: greek-latin.catholic.edu [Accessed on : 23 July 2022]
[2888]Pope Pius XI [1922] Apostolic Letter *Officiorum Omnium.* [Online] Available at: lms.org.uk [Accessed on: 22 July 2022]

people alternately sang the divine praises, the liturgical chant played no small part in converting many barbarians to Christianity and civilisation. It was in the churches that heretics came to understand more fully the meaning of the communion of saints; thus the Emperor Valens, an Arian, being present at Mass celebrated by St. Basil, was overcome by an extraordinary seizure and fainted. At Milan, Saint Ambrose was accused by heretics of attracting the crowds by means of liturgical chants. It was due to these that St. Augustine made up his mind to become a Christian. It was in the churches, finally, where practically the whole city formed a great joint choir, that the workers, builders, artists, sculptors and writers gained from the Liturgy that deep knowledge of theology which is now so apparent in the monuments of the Middle Ages.

No wonder, then, that the Roman Pontiffs have been so solicitous to safeguard and protect the Liturgy. They have used the same care in making laws for the regulation of the Liturgy, in preserving it from adulteration, as they have in giving accurate expression to the dogmas of the faith. This is the reason why the Fathers made both spoken and written commentary upon the Liturgy or 'the law of worship'; for this reason the Council of Trent ordained that the Liturgy should be expounded and explained to the faithful.

In our times too, the chief object of Pope Pius X, in the Motu Proprio [*Tra le Solleci-tudini*] which he issued twenty-five years ago, making certain prescriptions concerning Gregorian Chant and sacred music, was to arouse and foster a Christian spirit in the faithful, by wisely excluding all that might ill befit the sacredness and majesty of our churches. The faithful come to church in order to derive piety from its chief source, by taking an active part in the venerated mysteries and the public solemn prayers of the Church. [...]

In order that the faithful may more actively participate in divine worship, let them be made once more to sing the Gregorian Chant, so far as it belongs to them to take part in it. It is most important that when the faithful assist at the sacred ceremonies, or when pious sodalities take part with the clergy in a procession, they should not be merely detached and silent spectators, but, filled with a deep sense of the beauty of the Liturgy, they should sing alternately with the clergy or the choir, as it is prescribed. If this is done, then it will no longer happen that the people either make no answer at all to the public prayers — whether in the language of the Liturgy or in the vernacular — or at best utter the responses in a low and subdued manner.[2889]

Pope St. Pius X: 1903 to 1914

Motu Proprio *Tra le Sollecitudini, 3, 7. (22nd November 1903)*
Sacred music should consequently possess, in the highest degree, the qualities proper to the liturgy, and in particular sanctity and goodness of form, which will spontaneously produce the final quality of universality.

It must be holy, and must, therefore, exclude all profanity not only in itself, but in the manner in which it is presented by those who execute it.

It must be true art, for otherwise it will be impossible for it to exercise on the minds of those who listen to it that efficacy which the Church aims at obtaining in admitting into her liturgy the art of musical sounds.

But it must, at the same time, be universal....These qualities are to be found, in the highest degree, in Gregorian Chant, which is, consequently the Chant proper to the Roman Church, the only chant she has inherited from the ancient fathers, which she has jealously guarded for centuries in her liturgical codices, which she directly proposes to the faithful as her own, which she prescribes exclusively for some parts of the liturgy, and which the most recent studies have so happily restored to their integrity and purity.

On these grounds Gregorian Chant has always been regarded as the supreme model for sacred music, so that it is fully legitimate to lay down the following rule: the more

---

[2889]Pope Pius XI [1928] *Divini Cultus.* [Online] Available at: adoremus.org [Accessed on: 23 July 2022]

closely a composition for church approaches in its movement, inspiration and savour the Gregorian form, the more sacred and liturgical it becomes; and the more out of harmony it is with that supreme model, the less worthy it is of the temple.

The ancient traditional Gregorian Chant must, therefore, in a large measure be restored to the functions of public worship, and the fact must be accepted by all that an ecclesiastical function loses none of its solemnity when accompanied by this music alone.

Special efforts are to be made to restore the use of the Gregorian Chant by the people, so that the faithful may again take a more active part in the ecclesiastical offices, as was the case in ancient times. [...]

The language proper to the Roman Church is Latin. Hence it is forbidden to sing anything whatever in the vernacular in solemn liturgical functions — much more to sing in the vernacular the variable or common parts of the Mass and Office.[2890]

Pope Leo XIII: 1878 to 1903

Encyclical *Depuis le Jour*, 12. *(8th September 1899)*
But if the methods of pedagogy in vogue in the State establishments have been for several years past progressively reducing the study of Latin and suppressing the exercises in prose and poetry which our fathers justly considered should hold a large place in college classes, the junior seminaries must put themselves on their guard against these innovations, inspired by utilitarian motives and working to the detriment of the solid formation of the mind. To the ancient methods so often justified by their results we would freely apply the words of St. Paul to his disciple Timothy, and with the apostles we would say to you, Venerable Brothers, 'Guard the deposit' (I Tim 6:20) with jealous care. If it should be destined — which God forbid! — one day to disappear from the other public schools, let your junior seminaries and free colleges keep it with an intelligent and patriotic solicitude. Doing so, you will be imitating the priests of Jerusalem, who, saving the sacred fire of the temple from the barbarian invader, so hid it as to be able to find it again and restore it to its splendor when the evil day should have passed (II Macc 1:19-22).[2891]

Pope St. Pius V: 1566 to 1572

The Bull *Quo Primum Tempore. (14 July 1570)*
From the very first, upon Our elevation to the chief Apostleship, We gladly turned our mind and energies and directed all our thoughts to those matters which concerned the preservation of a pure liturgy, and We strove with God's help, by every means in our power, to accomplish this purpose. [...]

Furthermore, by these presents [this law], in virtue of Our Apostolic authority, We grant and concede in perpetuity that, for the chanting or reading of the Mass in any church whatsoever, this Missal is hereafter to be followed absolutely, without any scruple of conscience or fear of incurring any penalty, judgment, or censure, and may freely and lawfully be used. Nor are superiors, administrators, canons, chaplains, and other secular priests, or religious, of whatever title designated, obliged to celebrate the Mass otherwise than as enjoined by Us. We likewise declare and ordain that no one whosoever is forced or coerced to alter this Missal, and that this present document cannot be revoked or modified, but remain always valid and retain its full force - notwithstanding the previous constitutions and decrees of the Holy See, as well as any general or special constitutions or edicts of provincial or synodal councils, and notwithstanding the practice and custom of the aforesaid churches, established by long and immemorial prescription - except, however, if more than two hundred years' standing.[2892]

[2890]Pope St. Pius X [1903] Motu Proprio *Tra le Sollecitudini*, para 7 [Online] Available at: adoremus. org [Accessed on: 23 July 2022]

[2891]Pope Leo XIII [1899] Encyclical *Depuis le Jour*, para 12 [Online] Available at: www.vatican.va [Accessed on: 23 July 2022]

[2892]Pope St. Pius V [1570] *The Bull Quo Primum Tempore* [Online] Available at: lms.org.uk [Accessed on: 19 July 2022]

Mariology (1) — The Blessed Virgin Mary Lost Faith in God's Promises

Pope Francis: 2013 to 2025

J. *At the foot of the Cross, witnessing the suffering of her Son, Mary recalled the promises of the Annunciation and accused the Archangel Gabriel of being a liar and a deceiver.*

Morning Meditation in the Chapel of the Domus Sanctae Marthae. (December 20, 2013)

The Gospel tells us nothing: whether She said a word or not…She was silent, but in Her heart, how many things did she tell the Lord! 'You, that day – this is what we read – told me that He would be great; You told me that you would give Him the Throne of David, His father, that He would reign forever and now I see him there!' Our Lady was human! And perhaps she had the urge to say: 'Lies! I was deceived!' John Paul II said this, speaking about Our Lady in that moment. But She, with silence, covered the mystery that She did not understand and with this silence she left this mystery so that it could grow and flourish in hope.[2893]

Meeting with a Group of Gravely Ill Children and their Families. Chapel of the Domus Sanctae Marthae. (29 May 2015)

There is also a question, whose explanation one does not learn in a catechesis. It is a question I frequently ask myself and many of you, many people ask: 'Why do children suffer?' And there are no answers. This too is a mystery. I just look to God and ask: 'But why?' And looking at the Cross: 'Why is your Son there? Why?' It is the mystery of the Cross.

I often think of Our Lady, when they handed down to her the dead body of her Son, covered with wounds, spat on, bloodied and soiled. And what did Our Lady do? 'Did she carry him away?' No, she embraced him, she caressed him. Our Lady, too, did not understand. Because she, in that moment, remembered what the Angel had said to her: 'He will be King, he will be great, he will be a prophet…'; and inside, surely, with that wounded body lying in her arms, that body that suffered so before dying, inside surely she wanted to say to the Angel: 'Liar! I was deceived.' She, too, had no answers.[2894]

Sacred Scripture

Luke 1:28; 38
And the angel being come in, said unto her: Hail, full of grace, the Lord is with thee: blessed art thou among women.

And Mary said: Behold the handmaid of the Lord; be it done to me according to thy word.

Genesis 3:15
I will put enmities between thee and the woman, and thy seed and her seed: she shall crush thy head, and thou shalt lie in wait for her heel.

Sacred Tradition

St. Ephraem: c. 306 to 373

Carmina Nisibena
Thou, Lord, and thy mother, you alone are perfect holy; for in thee, Lord, there is no stain, nor is there any blemish in thy mother.[2895]

[2893]Pope Francis [21 December 2013] *Silence Reveals the Mystery of God's Plan*. [Online] Available at: aleteia.org [Accessed on: 24 July 2022]
[2894]Pope Francis [2015] *Meeting with a Group of Gravely Ill Children and their Families. Chapel of the Domus Sanctae Marthae*. [Online] Available at: www.vatican.va [Accessed on: 24 July 2022]
[2895]Scheeben, M [1946] *Mariology*. Vol.2. Jackson: Ex Fontibus Company LLC, p. 64.

St. Ambrose: c. 340 to 397

Commentary on Psalm 118, Sermon 22.
…[Mary] is a virgin not only uncorrupted, but a virgin untouched by all stain of sin.[2896]

De Institutione Virginis 49
His mother stood before the Cross, and, while the men fled, she remained undaunted. Consider whether the Mother of Jesus, who did not lose her courage, could ever lose her virginal purity. With eyes full of pity, she looked upon her Son's wounds, by which, as she knew, would come the redemption of the world. She, who did not fear her Son's killers, assisted at his generous martyrdom.[2897]

Expositio in Lucam 10
For her part, Mary did not fail to live up to her station as the Mother of Christ. When the apostles fled, she stood before the Cross and gazed tenderly on the wounds of her Son, because she was waiting, not for her Son's death, but for the salvation of the world.[2898]

St. Augustine: 354 to 430

On Nature and Grace, Chap. 36
We must except the holy Virgin Mary, concerning whom I wish to raise no question when it touches the subject of sins, out of honour to the Lord; for from Him we know what abundance of grace for overcoming sin in every particular was conferred upon her who had the merit to conceive and bear Him who undoubtedly had no sin.[2899]

St. Cyril of Alexandria c. 376 to 444

On the Gospel According to John, Bk. XII
We hail you, O Mary Mother of God, venerable treasure of the entire world, inextinguishable lamp, crown of virginity, sceptre of orthodoxy, imperishable lamp, container of Him Who cannot be contained, Mother and Virgin, through whom it is said in the holy Gospels: 'Blessed is He Who comes in the name of the Lord'(Mt 21:9).

Hail, you who held the Uncontainable One in your holy and virginal womb! Through you, the Holy Trinity is glorified; the precious Cross is celebrated and adored throughout the world; heaven exults, the angels and archangels rejoice, the demons are put to flight, the tempter falls from heaven, the fallen creation is brought back to Paradise, all creatures trapped in idolatry come to know of the truth.[2900]

St. Bernard of Clairvaux: c. 1090 to 1153

Letter XLV, to the Canons of Lyons, On the Conception of the Blessed Virgin Mary
I am of the opinion that a more abundant blessing of sanctification descended on her, which not only sanctified her birth, but also kept her immune from sin, a blessing bestowed on no other living woman. It was very becoming that, by a privilege of singular holiness, the Queen of virgins should have led a life without sin, in order that she, whilst she brought forth the destroyer of sin and death might obtain the gift of life and justice.[2901]

St. Louis de Montfort: 1673 to 1716

True Devotion to the Blessed Virgin 18
Even at his death she had to be present so that he might be united with her in one sacrifice and be immolated with her consent to the eternal Father, just as formerly Isaac

---

[2896]*Ibid.*, p.64.

[2897]Gambero, L [1999] *Mary and the Fathers of the Church.* San Francisco: Ignatius Press, p 202-203

[2898]Ibid.

[2899]St. Augustine. *On Nature and Grace*, Chap. 36 [Online] Available at: www.newadvent.org [Accessed on: 26 July 2022]

[2900]St. Cyril of Alexandria. *On the Gospel According to John*, Bk. XII [Online] Available at: www. tertullian.org [Accessed on: 24 July 2022]

[2901]Quoted in Scheeben, M [1946] Op. cit., p.128

was offered in sacrifice by Abraham when he accepted the will of God. It was Mary who nursed him, fed him, cared for him, reared him, and sacrificed him for us.[2902]

St. Alphonsus Liguori CSsR: 1696 to 1787

The Glories of Mary (1750)
...she gave him to us a thousand times at the foot of the cross during the three hours she watched him die. Every moment of those three hours, as her heart overflowed with sorrow and with love for us, she constantly offered the sacrifice of her son's life for us. So much so that Saint Anselm and Saint Antoninus maintain that, if there had been no executioners, she herself would have crucified him to obey the will of the Father who wished his Son to die for our salvation. If Abraham showed a similar courage in his willingness to sacrifice his son with his own hands, we must believe that Mary would have fulfilled God's will with even greater courage, since she is more holy and more obedient than Abraham.[2903]

Moreover, says Saint Antonius, while other martyrs suffered by sacrificing their own lives, the Blessed Virgin suffered by sacrificing her son's life, a life dearer than her own.[2904]

'Everybody who saw Mary standing there silently and uttering no complaint amid such suffering,' says Simon of Cassia, 'was filled with astonishment.' But while Mary's lips were silent, her heart was not, for she was incessantly offering the life of her son for our salvation.[2905]

The Magisterium of the Church

The Blessed Virgin Mary faithfully cooperated in the redemption, according to God's plan, united to Jesus on the Cross, sharing in His suffering, consenting to His immolation

Council of Trent (Nineteenth Ecumenical, 1545 to 1563)

Decree on Justification, Canon 23. (13th January 1547)
If anyone says that a man once justified can sin no more, nor lose grace, and that therefore he that falls and sins was never truly justified; or on the contrary, that he can during his whole life avoid all sins, even those that are venial, except by a special privilege from God, as the Church holds in regard to the Blessed Virgin, let him be anathema.[2906]

Second Vatican Council (Twenty-First Ecumenical, 1962 to 1965)

Dogmatic Constitution *Lumen Gentium, 58, 61. (21st November 1964)*
...the Blessed Virgin advanced in her pilgrimage of faith, and faithfully persevered in her union with her Son unto the cross, where she stood, in keeping with the divine plan (cf. Jn 19:25), grieving exceedingly with her only begotten Son, uniting herself with a maternal heart with His sacrifice, and lovingly consenting to the immolation of this Victim which she herself had brought forth.

She presented Him to the Father in the temple, and was united with Him by compassion as He died on the Cross. In this singular way she cooperated by her obedience, faith, hope and burning charity in the work of the Saviour in giving back supernatural life to souls.[2907]

[2902]St. Louis de Montfort [1843] *True Devotion to the Blessed Virgin*, 18. [Online] Available at: www.montfort.org.uk [Accessed on: 26 July 2022]

[2903]St. Alphonsus Liguori [1750] *The Glories of Mary*. Liguori Publications, p.17

[2904]*Ibid.*, p.286

[2905]*Ibid.*, p.316

[2906]Council of Trent [1547] *Decree on Justification*, Canon 23 [Online] Available at: www.ewtn.com [Accessed on: 25 July 2022]

[2907]Second Vatican Council [1964] Dogmatic Constitution, *Lumen Gentium*, para 58, 61. [Online] Available at: www.vatican.va [Accessed on: 25 July 2022]

Pope Benedict XVI: 2005 to 2013

Homily on the occasion of the fortieth anniversary of the closure of the Second Vatican Council. (8th December 2005)

...the image of the Virgin who listens and lives in the Word of God, who cherishes in her heart the words that God addresses to her and, piecing them together like a mosaic, learns to understand them (cf. Lk 2:19, 51). It refers us to the great Believer who, full of faith, put herself in God's hands, abandoning herself to his will; it refers us to the humble Mother who, when the Son's mission so required, became part of it, and at the same time, to the courageous woman who stood beneath the Cross while the disciples fled.[2908]

Angelus Address. 7 September 2006

The Evangelist recounts: Mary was standing by the Cross (cf. Jn 19:25-27). Her sorrow is united with that of her Son. It is a sorrow full of faith and love. The Virgin on Calvary participates in the saving power of the suffering of Christ, joining her 'fiat', her 'yes', to that of her Son.[2909]

Post-synodal Apostolic Exhortation Sacramentum Caritatis, 33. (22nd February 2007)

From the Annunciation to the Cross, Mary is the one who received the Word, made flesh within her and then silenced in death. It is she, lastly, who took into her arms the lifeless body of the one who truly loved his own 'to the end' (Jn 13:1).[2910]

Encyclical Spe Salvi, par 50. (30th November 2007)

Notwithstanding the great joy that marked the beginning of Jesus's ministry, in the synagogue of Nazareth you must already have experienced the truth of the saying about the 'sign of contradiction' (cf. Lk 4:28ff). In this way you saw the growing power of hostility and rejection which built up around Jesus until the hour of the Cross, when you had to look upon the Saviour of the world, the heir of David, the Son of God dying like a failure, exposed to mockery, between criminals. Then you received the word of Jesus: 'Woman, behold, your Son!' (Jn 19:26). From the Cross you received a new mission. From the Cross you became a mother in a new way: the mother of all those who believe in your Son Jesus and wish to follow him.

The sword of sorrow pierced your heart. Did hope die? Did the world remain definitively without light, and life without purpose? At that moment, deep down, you probably listened again to the word spoken by the angel in answer to your fear at the time of the Annunciation: 'Do not be afraid, Mary!' (Lk 1:30). How many times had the Lord, your Son, said the same thing to his disciples: do not be afraid! In your heart, you heard this word again during the night of Golgotha. Before the hour of his betrayal he had said to his disciples: 'Be of good cheer, I have overcome the world' (Jn 16:33). 'Let not your hearts be troubled, neither let them be afraid' (Jn 14:27). 'Do not be afraid, Mary!' In that hour at Nazareth the angel had also said to you: 'Of his kingdom there will be no end' (Lk 1:33). Could it have ended before it began? No, at the foot of the Cross, on the strength of Jesus's own word, you became the mother of believers. In this faith, which even in the darkness of Holy Saturday bore the certitude of hope, you made your way towards Easter morning. The joy of the Resurrection touched your heart and united you in a new way to the disciples, destined to become the family of Jesus through faith.[2911]

[2908]Pope Benedict XVI [2005] *Homily on the occasion of the fortieth anniversary of the closure of the Second Vatican Council* [Online] Available at: www.vatican.va [Accessed on: 4th October 2022]

[2909]Pope Benedict XVI [2006] *Angelus Address* [Online] Available at: www.vatican.va [Accessed on: 4th October 2022]

[2910]Pope Benedict XVI [2007] Post-synodal Apostolic Exhortation *Sacramentum Caritatis*, para 33 [Online] Available at: www.vatican.va [Accessed on: 4th October 2022]

[2911]Pope Benedict XVI [2007] Encyclical *Spe Salvi*, para 50 [Online] Available at: www.vatican.va [Accessed on: 27 July 2022]

Message for the sixteenth Word Day of the Sick. (11th January 2008)
Mary is a model of total self-abandonment to God's will: she received in her heart the
eternal Word and she conceived it in her virginal womb; she trusted in God and, with
her soul pierced by a sword (cf. Lk 2:35), she did not hesitate to share the Passion of
her Son, renewing on Calvary at the foot of the Cross her 'yes' of the Annunciation.[2912]

*Prayer to Our Lady of Sheshan on the occasion of the World Day of Prayer for the Church in
China. (24th May 2008)*
When you obediently said 'yes' in the house of Nazareth, you allowed God's eternal
Son to take flesh in your virginal womb and thus to begin in history the work of our
redemption. You willingly and generously cooperated in that work, allowing the sword
of pain to pierce your soul, until the supreme hour of the Cross, when you kept watch
on Calvary, standing beside your Son, who died that we might live.[2913]

*Homily on the occasion of the one hundred & fiftieth anniversary of the apparitions of the Blessed
Virgin Mary at Lourdes. (15th September 2008)*
As St. Bernard declares, the Mother of Christ entered into the Passion of her Son
through her compassion (cf. Homily for Sunday in the Octave of the Assumption). At
the foot of the Cross, the prophecy of Simeon is fulfilled: her mother's heart is pierced
through (cf. Lk 2:35) by the torment inflicted on the Innocent One born of her flesh. Just
as Jesus cried (cf. Jn 11:35), so too Mary certainly cried over the tortured body of her
Son. Her self-restraint, however, prevents us from plumbing the depths of her grief; the
full extent of her suffering is merely suggested by the traditional symbol of the seven
swords.[2914]

*Address to German pilgrims following Angelus message, Fifth Sunday of Lent. (29th March
2009)*
In these days of preparation for Easter, we want to look to Mary, who accompanied
her Son on the way of suffering to his death on the cross. Her 'yes' to God's plan of
salvation, that she spoke at the Annunciation of the Angel, redeemed her under the
cross. Thus Mary is totally integrated in the redemption work of Christ.[2915]

Pope St. John Paul II: 1978 to 2005

Apostolic Exhortation *Redemptionis Donum, 17. (25th March 1984)*
How poor she was on Bethlehem night and how poor on Calvary! How obedient she
was at the moment of the Annunciation, and then — at the foot of the cross — obedient
even to the point of assenting to the death of her Son, who became obedient 'unto
death'! How dedicated she was in all her earthly life to the cause of the kingdom of
heaven through most chaste love.[2916]

Encyclical *Redemptoris Mater, 17-18. (25th March 1987)*
'Blessed is she who believed.' This blessing reaches its full meaning when Mary stands
beneath the Cross of her Son (cf. Jn 19:25). The Council says that this happened 'not
without a divine plan': by 'suffering deeply with her only-begotten Son and joining
herself with her maternal spirit to his sacrifice, lovingly consenting to the immolation
of the victim to whom she had given birth,' in this way Mary 'faithfully preserved her

[2912]Pope Benedict XVI [2008] *Message for the 16th Word Day of the Sick* [Online] Available at: www.
vatican.va [Accessed on: 4th October 2022]
[2913]Pope Benedict XVI [2008] *Prayer to Our Lady of Sheshan on the occasion of the World Day of Prayer
for the Church in China* [Online] Available at: www.vatican.va [Accessed on: 4 October 2022]
[2914]Pope Benedict XVI [2008] *Homily on the occasion of the 150th anniversary of the apparitions of the
Blessed Virgin Mary at Lourdes* [Online] Available at: www.vatican.va [Accessed on: 4 October
2022]
[2915]Clarke, K [2009] *Divinely Given 'Into Our Reality': Mary's Maternal Mediation According to Pope
Benedict XVI* [Online] Available at: www.academia.edu [Accessed on: 4 October 2022]
[2916]Pope St. John Paul [1984] Apostolic Exhortation *Redemptionis Donum*, para 17 [Online] Available
at: www.vatican.va [Accessed on: 27 July 2022]

union with her Son even to the Cross.' (*LG* 58). It is a union through faith — the same faith with which she had received the angel's revelation at the Annunciation. At that moment she had also heard the words: 'He will be great...and the Lord God will give to him the throne of his father David, and he will reign over the house of Jacob for ever; and of his kingdom there will be no end' (Lk 1:32-33).

And now, standing at the foot of the Cross, Mary is the witness, humanly speaking, of the complete negation of these words. On that wood of the Cross her Son hangs in agony as one condemned. 'He was despised and rejected by men; a man of sorrows...he was despised, and we esteemed him not': as one destroyed (cf. Isa 53:3-5). How great, how heroic then is the obedience of faith shown by Mary in the face of God's 'unsearchable judgments'! How completely she 'abandons herself to God without reserve, offering the full assent of the intellect and the will' to him whose 'ways are inscrutable' (cf. Rom 11:33)! And how powerful too is the action of grace in her soul, how all-pervading is the influence of the Holy Spirit and of his light and power!

Through this faith Mary is perfectly united with Christ in his self-emptying....At the foot of the Cross Mary shares through faith in the shocking mystery of this self-emptying. This is perhaps the deepest 'kenosis' of faith in human history. Through faith the Mother shares in the death of her Son, in his redeeming death; but in contrast with the faith of the disciples who fled, hers was far more enlightened. On Golgotha, Jesus through the Cross definitively confirmed that he was the 'sign of contradiction' foretold by Simeon. At the same time, there were also fulfilled on Golgotha the words which Simeon had addressed to Mary: 'and a sword will pierce through your own soul also.' (cf. Lk 2:35)[2917]

Letter to Priests for Holy Thursday, 2. (31rd March 1988)
We must not forget this suffering of his Mother, in whom were fulfilled Simeon's words in the Temple at Jerusalem: 'A sword will pierce through your own soul also' (Lk 2:35). They were spoken directly to Mary forty days after Jesus' birth. On Golgotha, beneath the cross, these words were completely fulfilled. When on the cross Mary's Son revealed himself fully as the 'sign of contradiction,' it was then that this immolation and mortal agony also reached her maternal heart.

Behold the agony of the heart of the Mother who suffered together with him, 'consenting to the immolation of this victim which she herself had brought forth.' Here we reach the high point of Mary's presence in the mystery of Christ and of the Church on earth.[2918]

Encyclical Evangelium Vitae, 103. (25th March 1995)
'Standing by the cross of Jesus' (Jn 19:25), Mary shares in the gift which the Son makes of himself: she offers Jesus, gives him over, and begets him to the end for our sake. The 'yes' spoken on the day of the Annunciation reaches full maturity on the day of the Cross, when the time comes for Mary to receive and beget as her children all those who become disciples, pouring out upon them the saving love of her Son: 'When Jesus saw his mother, and the disciple whom he loved standing near, he said to his mother, "Woman, behold, your son!"' (Jn 19:26).[2919]

General Audience on the Blessed Virgin Mary. (25 October 1995)
Mary is united to Christ in the whole work of Redemption, sharing, according to God's plan, in the Cross and suffering for our salvation. She remained united to the Son 'in every deed, attitude and wish' (cf. *Life of Mary*, Bol. 196, f. 122 v.). Mary's association with Jesus' saving work came about through her Mother's love, a love inspired by

---

[2917]Pope St. John Paul II [1987] Encyclical *Redemptoris Mater*, para 17-18 [Online] Available at: www.vatican.va [Accessed on: 27 July 2022]

[2918]Pope St. John Paul II [1988] *Letter to Priests for Holy Thursday*, para 2 [Online] Available at: www.vatican.va [Accessed on: 27 July 2022]

[2919]Pope St. John Paul II [1995] Encyclical *Evangelium Vitae*, para 103 [Online] Available at: www.vatican.va [Accessed on: 27 July 2022]

grace, which conferred a higher power on it: love freed of passion proves to be the most compassionate (cf. ibid., Bol. 196, f. 123 v.)....A disciple and friend of St. Bernard, Arnold of Chartres, shed light particularly on Mary's offering in the sacrifice of Calvary. He distinguished in the Cross 'two altars: one in Mary's heart, the other in Christ's body. Christ sacrificed his flesh, Mary her soul'. Mary sacrificed herself spiritually in deep communion with Christ, and implored the world's salvation: 'What the mother asks, the Son approves and the Father grants' (cf. *De Septem Verbis Domini in Cruce*, 3: PL 189, 1694).[2920]

Catechism of the Catholic Church. (8th September 1997)
Mary gave her consent in faith at the Annunciation and maintained it without hesitation at the foot of the Cross. (2674).

Espousing the divine will for salvation wholeheartedly, without a single sin to restrain her, she gave herself entirely to the person and to the work of her Son; she did so in order to serve the mystery of redemption with him and dependent on him, by God's grace (494).[2921]

Encyclical *Ecclesia de Eucharistia, 56. (17 Apri 2003)*
Mary, throughout her life at Christ's side and not only on Calvary, made her own the sacrificial dimension of the Eucharist. When she brought the child Jesus to the Temple in Jerusalem 'to present him to the Lord' (Lk 2:22), she heard the aged Simeon announce that the child would be a 'sign of contradiction' and that a sword would also pierce her own heart (cf. Lk 2:34-35). The tragedy of her Son's crucifixion was thus foretold, and in some sense Mary's Stabat Mater at the foot of the Cross was foreshadowed. In her daily preparation for Calvary, Mary experienced a kind of 'anticipated Eucharist' – one might say a 'spiritual communion' – of desire and of oblation, which would culminate in her union with her Son in his passion....[2922]

Pope St. Paul VI: 1963 to 1978

Apostolic Exhortation *Signum Magnum. (13th May 1967)*
We, therefore, associating ourselves with the Evangelists, with the Fathers and the Doctors of the Church, recalled in the Dogmatic Constitution '*Lumen Gentium*' (Chap. VIII), full of admiration, contemplate Mary, firm in her faith, ready in her obedience, simple in humility, exulting in praising the Lord, ardent in charity, strong and constant in the fulfilment of her mission to the point of sacrificing herself, in full communion of sentiments with her Son who immolated Himself on the Cross to give men a new life.[2923]

Apostolic Exhortation *Marialis Cultus. (2nd February 1974)*
They called her the 'Temple of the Holy Spirit', an expression that emphasises the sacred character of the Virgin, now the permanent dwelling of the Spirit of God. Delving deeply into the doctrine of the Paraclete, they saw that from Him as from a spring there flowed forth the fullness of grace (cf. Lk 1:28) and the abundance of gifts that adorned her. Thus they attributed to the Spirit the faith, hope and charity that animated the Virgin's heart, the strength that sustained her acceptance of the will of God, and the vigour that upheld her in her suffering at the foot of the cross.[2924]

[2920]Pope St. John Paul II [1995] *Mary Was United to Jesus on the Cross* [Online] Available at: www. ewtn.com [Accessed on: 27 July 2022]
[2921]*Catechism of the Catholic Church* [1992] [Online] Available at: scborromeo2.org [Accessed on: 12 July 2022]
[2922]Pope St. John Paul II [2003] Encyclical *Ecclesia de Eucharistia*, para 56 [Online] Available at: www.vatican.va [Accessed on: 4 October 2022]
[2923]Pope St. Paul VI [1967] Apostolic Exhortation *Signum Magnum* [Online] Available at: www. vatican.va [Accessed on: 4 October 2022]
[2924]Pope St. Paul VI [1974] Apostolic Exhortation *Marialis Cultus* [Online] Available at: www. vatican.va [Accessed on: 4 October 2022]

Letter of Pope St. Paul VI to Cardinal Léon Josef Suenens on the Occasion of the International Marian Congress. (13th May 1975)
It was the Holy Spirit who strengthened the soul of the Mother of Jesus as she stood beneath the cross, and inspired her once again, as he had at the Annunciation, to consent to the will of the heavenly Father who wanted her to be associated as a mother with the sacrifice her Son was offering for mankind's redemption.[2925]

Pope Ven. Pius XII: 1939 to 1958

Encyclical *Mystici Corporis Christi, 110. (29th June 1943)*
It was she, the second Eve, who, free from all sin, original or personal, and always more intimately united with her Son, offered Him on Golgotha to the Eternal Father for all the children of Adam, sin-stained by his unhappy fall, and her mother's rights and her mother's love were included in the holocaust. Thus she who, according to the flesh, was the mother of our Head, through the added title of pain and glory became, according to the Spirit, the mother of all His members.[2926]

Apostolic Constitution *Munificentissimus Deus, 5. (1st November 1950)*
Now God has willed that the Blessed Virgin Mary should be exempted from this general rule. She, by an entirely unique privilege, completely overcame sin by her Immaculate Conception, and as a result she was not subject to the law of remaining in the corruption of the grave, and she did not have to wait until the end of time for the redemption of her body.[2927]

Encyclical *Fulgens Corona, 13, 24. (8th September 1953)*
And again, if we consider the matter with attention, and especially if we consider the burning and sweet love which Almighty God without doubt had, and has, for the mother of His only begotten Son, for what reason can we even think that she was, even for the briefest moment of time, subject to sin and destitute of divine grace. Almighty God could certainly, by virtue of the merits of the Redeemer, bestow on her this singular privilege; that therefore He did not do so, we cannot even suppose. It was fitting that Jesus Christ should have such a mother as would be worthy of Him as far as possible; and she would not have been worthy, if, contaminated by the hereditary stain even for the first moment only of her conception, she had been subject to the abominable power of Satan.

And it seems to Us that the Blessed Virgin, who throughout the whole course of her life — both in joys, which affected her deeply, as in distress and atrocious suffering, through which she is Queen of Martyrs — never departed from the precepts and example of her own Divine Son, it seems to us, We say, that she repeats to each of us those words, with which she addressed the servers at the wedding feast of Cana, pointing as it were to Jesus Christ: 'Whatsoever He shall say to you, do ye' (Jn 2:5).[2928]

Encyclical *Ad Caeli Reginam, 38. (11th October 1954)*
If Mary, in taking an active part in the work of salvation, was, by God's design, associated with Jesus Christ, the source of salvation itself, in a manner comparable to that in which Eve was associated with Adam, the source of death, so that it may be stated that the work of our salvation was accomplished by a kind of 'recapitulation,' in which a virgin was instrumental in the salvation of the human race, just as a virgin

---

[2925]Pope St. Paul VI [1975] *Letter of Pope Paul VI to Cardinal Léon Josef Suenens on the Occasion of the International Marian Congress.* [Online] Available at: www.piercedhearts.org [Accessed on: 27 July 2022]

[2926]Pope Ven. Pius XII [1943] Encyclical *Mystici Corporis Christi*, para 110 [Online] Available at: www.vatican.va [Accessed on: 27 July 2022]

[2927]Pope Ven. Pius XII [1950] Apostolic Constitution *Munificentissimus Deus*, para 5 [Online] Available at: www.vatican.va [Accessed on: 27 July 2022]

[2928]Pope Ven. Pius XII [1953] Encyclical *Fulgens Corona*, paras 13, 24 [Online] Available at: www.vatican.va [Accessed on: 4 October 2022]

had been closely associated with its death; if, moreover, it can likewise be stated that this glorious Lady had been chosen Mother of Christ 'in order that she might become a partner in the redemption of the human race'.[2929]

Pope Pius XI: 1922 to 1939

Encyclical *Miserentissimus Redemptor, 21. (8th May 1928)*
And now lastly may the most benign Virgin Mother of God smile on this purpose and on these desires of ours; for since she brought forth for us Jesus our Redeemer, and nourished Him, and offered Him as a victim by the Cross, by her mystic union with Christ and His very special grace she likewise became and is piously called a reparatress.[2930]

Pope Benedict XV: 1914 to 1922

Epistle *Admodum Probatur. (20th June 1917)*
With her suffering and dying Son she suffered and almost died, so did she surrender her mother's rights over her Son for the salvation of human beings, and to appease the justice of God, so far as pertained to her, she immolated her Son, so that it can be rightly said, that she together with Christ has redeemed the human race.[2931]

Pope St. Pius X: 1903 to 1914

Encyclical *Ad Diem Illum Laetissimum, 12. (2nd February 1904)*
When the supreme hour of the Son came, beside the Cross of Jesus there stood Mary His Mother, not merely occupied in contemplating the cruel spectacle, but rejoicing that her Only Son was offered for the salvation of mankind, and so entirely participating in His Passion, that if it had been possible she would have gladly borne all the torments that her Son bore (S. Bonav. 1. Sent d. 48, ad Litt. dub. 4).[2932]

Pope Leo XIII: 1878 to 1903

Encyclical *Iucunda Semper Expectatione, 3. (8th September1884)*
In the Garden of Gethsemane, where Jesus is in an agony; in the judgment-hall, where He is scourged, crowned with thorns, condemned to death, not there do we find Mary. But she knew beforehand all these agonies; she knew and saw them. When she professed herself the handmaid of the Lord for the mother's office, and when, at the foot of the altar, she offered up her whole self with her Child Jesus — then and thereafter she took her part in the laborious expiation made by her Son for the sins of the world. It is certain, therefore, that she suffered in the very depths of her soul with His most bitter sufferings and with His torments. Moreover, it was before the eyes of Mary that was to be finished the Divine Sacrifice for which she had borne and brought up the Victim. As we contemplate Him in the last and most piteous of those Mysteries, there stood by the Cross of Jesus His Mother, who, in a miracle of charity, so that she might receive us as her sons, offered generously to Divine Justice her own Son, and died in her heart with Him, stabbed with the sword of sorrow.[2933]

Pope Bl. Pius IX: 1846 to 1878

Apostolic Constitution *Ineffabilis Deus. (8 December 1854)*
…far above all the angels and all the saints so wondrously did God endow her with the abundance of all heavenly gifts poured from the treasury of his divinity that this mother,

---

[2929]Pope Ven. Pius XII [1954] Encyclical *Ad Caeli Reginam*, para 38 [Online] Available at: www.vatican.va [Accessed on: 4 October 2022]
[2930]Pope Pius XI [1928] Encyclical *Miserentissimus Redemptor*, para 21 [Online] Available at: www.vatican.va [Accessed on: 27 July 2022]
[2931]Pope Benedict XV [1917] Epistle *Admodum Probatur* [Online] www.ewtn.com [Accessed on: 27 July 2022]
[2932]Pope St. Pius X [1904] Encyclical *Ad Diem Illum Laetissimum*, para 12 [Online] Available at: www.vatican.va [Accessed on: 27 July 2022]
[2933]Pope Leo XIII [1884] Encyclical *Iucunda Semper Expectatione*, para 3 [Online] Available at: www.vatican.va [Accessed on: 27 July 2022]

ever absolutely free of all stain of sin, all fair and perfect, would possess that fullness of holy innocence and sanctity than which, under God, one cannot even imagine anything greater, and which, outside of God, no mind can succeed in comprehending fully.

These ecclesiastical writers in quoting the words by which at the beginning of the world God announced his merciful remedies prepared for the regeneration of mankind — words by which he crushed the audacity of the deceitful serpent and wondrously raised up the hope of our race, saying, 'I will put enmities between you and the woman, between your seed and her seed' — taught that by this divine prophecy the merciful Redeemer of mankind, Jesus Christ, the only begotten Son of God, was clearly foretold: That his most Blessed Mother, the Virgin Mary, was prophetically indicated; and, at the same time, the very enmity of both against the evil one was significantly expressed. Hence, just as Christ, the Mediator between God and man, assumed human nature, blotted the handwriting of the decree that stood against us, and fastened it triumphantly to the cross, so the most holy Virgin, united with him by a most intimate and indissoluble bond, was, with him and through him, eternally at enmity with the evil serpent, and most completely triumphed over him, and thus crushed his head with her immaculate foot.[2934]

[2934]Pope Bl. Pius IX [1854] Apostolic Constitution *Ineffabilis Deus*. [Online] www.papalencyclicals. net [Accessed on: 27 July 2022]

Mariology (2) — Denial of Mary as Coredemptrix & Other Marian Titles

Pope Francis: 2013 to 2025

K. *Mary is merely disciple and Mother, and does not require any functional titles such as Coredemptrix.*

Homily for the Feast of Our Lady of Guadalupe. (12th December 2019)
Being faithful to her Master, who is her Son, the only Redeemer, she never wanted to take anything away from her Son. She never presented herself as a Coredemptrix. No. disciple....When they come to us with the story according to which we should declare this, or that other dogma, let's not get lost in foolishness. Mary is woman, she is Our Lady, Mary is the Mother of her Son and of the Holy Mother hierarchical Church.[2935]

Morning Meditation in the Chapel of the Domus Sanctae Marthae. (3rd April 2020) Honour Our Lady and say: 'This is my Mother', because she is a Mother. And this is the title she received from Jesus, right there, at the moment of the Cross (see Jn 19:26-27). Your children, you are Mother. He did not make her prime minister or give her 'functional' titles. Only 'Mother'. And then, the Acts of the Apostles show her in prayer with the apostles as Mother (see Acts 1:14). Our Lady did not want to take away any title from Jesus; she received the gift of being His Mother and the duty to accompany us as Mother, to be our Mother. She did not ask for herself to be a quasi-redeemer or a co-redeemer: no. There is only one Redeemer and this title cannot be duplicated. She is merely disciple and Mother.[2936]

General Audience Address. (24th March 2021)
Christ is the Mediator, Christ is the bridge that we cross to turn to the Father (see *Catechism of the Catholic Church*, 2674). He is the only Redeemer: there are no co-redeemers with Christ. He is the only one. He is the Mediator par excellence. He is the Mediator. Each prayer we raise to God is through Christ, with Christ and in Christ and it is fulfilled thanks to his intercession. The Holy Spirit extends Christ's mediation through every time and every place: there is no other name by which we can be saved: Jesus Christ, the only Mediator between God and humanity (see Acts 4:12) [...]

...the Madonna who 'covers', like a Mother, to whom Jesus entrusted us, all of us; but as a Mother, not as a goddess, not as co-redeemer: as Mother. It is true that Christian piety has always given her beautiful titles, as a child gives his or her mamma: how many beautiful things children say about their mamma whom they love so much! How many beautiful things. But we need to be careful: the things the Church, the Saints, say about her, beautiful things, about Mary, subtract nothing from Christ's sole Redemp-tion. He is the only Redeemer. They are expressions of love like a child for his or her mamma – some are exaggerated. But love, as we know, always makes us exaggerate things, but out of love.[2937]

Sacred Scripture

Luke 1:28; 38; 2:34-35
Hail, full of grace, the Lord is with thee: blessed art thou among women.

And Mary said: Behold the handmaid of the Lord; be it done to me according to thy word.

And Simeon blessed them, and said to Mary his mother: Behold this child is set for the fall, and for the resurrection of many in Israel, and for a sign which shall be contra-dicted; And thy own soul a sword shall pierce, that, out of many hearts, thoughts may be revealed.

[2935]Miravalle, M [2019] *Pope Francis' Guadalupe Homily and Mary 'Co-Redemptrix'* [Online] Available at: www.ncregister.com [Accessed on: 28 July 2022]

[2936]Pope Francis [3rd April 2020] *Morning Meditation in the Chapel of the Domus Sanctae Marthae.* [Online] Available at: www.vatican.va [Accessed on: 28 July 2022]

[2937]Pope Francis [24th March 2021] *General Audience Address.* [Online] Available at: www.vatican.va [Accessed on: 28 July 2022]

John 19:25-27

Now there stood by the cross of Jesus, his mother, and his mother's sister, Mary of Cleophas, and Mary Magdalen. When Jesus therefore had seen his mother and the disciple standing whom he loved, he saith to his mother: Woman, behold thy son. After that, he saith to the disciple: Behold thy mother. And from that hour, the disciple took her to his own.

Genesis 3:15

I will put enmities between thee and the woman, and thy seed and her seed: she shall crush thy head, and thou shalt lie in wait for her heel.

Isaiah 7:10-14

And the Lord spoke again to Achaz, saying: Ask thee a sign of the Lord thy God, either unto the depth of hell, or unto the height above. And Achaz said: I will not ask, and I will not tempt the Lord. And he said: Hear ye therefore, O house of David: Is it a small thing for you to be grievous to men, that you are grievous to my God also? Therefore the Lord himself shall give you a sign. Behold a virgin shall conceive, and bear a son, and his name shall be called Emmanuel.

Micah 5:1-2

Now shalt thou be laid waste, O daughter of the robber: they have laid siege against us, with a rod shall they strike the cheek of the judge of Israel. And thou, Bethlehem Ephrata, art a little one among the thousands of Juda: out of thee shall he come forth unto me that is to be the ruler in Israel: and his going forth is from the beginning, from the days of eternity.

Zephaniah 3:14-17

Give praise, O daughter of Sion: shout, O Israel: be glad, and rejoice with all thy heart, O daughter of Jerusalem. The Lord hath taken away thy judgment, he hath turned away thy enemies: the king of Israel, the Lord, is in the midst of thee, thou shalt fear evil no more. In that day it shall be said to Jerusalem: Fear not: to Sion: Let not thy hands be weakened. he Lord thy God in the midst of thee is mighty, he will save: he will rejoice over thee with gladness, he will be silent in his love, he will be joyful over thee in praise.

Ecclesiasticus 24:3-4; 12-13

And in the midst of her own people she shall be exalted, and shall be admired in the holy assembly. And in the multitude of the elect she shall have praise, and among the blessed she shall be blessed....Then the creator of all things commanded, and said to me: and he that made me, rested in my tabernacle, And he said to me: Let thy dwelling be in Jacob, and thy inheritance in Israel, and take root in my elect.

Proverbs 8:22-23

The Lord possessed me in the beginning of his ways, before he made any thing from the beginning. I was set up from eternity, and of old before the earth was made.

Sacred Tradition

St. Ignatius of Antioch: c. 50 to c. 98/117

Epistle to the Ephesians, Chap. 19

Now the virginity of Mary was hidden from the prince of this world, as was also her offspring, and the death of the Lord; three mysteries of renown, which were wrought in silence by God.[2938]

[2938]St. Ignatius of Antioch. *Epistle to the Ephesians*, Chap. 19 [Online] Available at: www.newadvent. org [Accessed on: 4 August 2022]

St. Irenaeus: c. 130 to c. 202

Against Heresies Bk. III, Chap. 22, para 4
...so also did Mary, having a man betrothed [to her], and being nevertheless a virgin, by yielding obedience, became the cause of salvation, both to herself and the whole human race.[2939]

St. Ephrem the Syrian: c. 306 to 373

Oratio *IV, Ad Deiparam*
After the Mediator, you [Mary] are the Mediatrix of the whole world.[2940]

St. Modestus of Jerusalem: ? to 630

Through Mary, we 'are redeemed from the tyranny of the devil'.[2941]

St. Andrew of Crete: c. 650 to c. 740

The Great Canon of Repentance
And as you are gracious, compassionate, and tender-hearted, be ever present with me in this life as my Mediatrix and helper, to repel the assaults of my adversaries and to guide me to salvation....[2942]

St. John Damascene: 675 to 749

Second Homily on the Dormition
For our sake she became Mediatrix of all blessings; in her God became man, and man became God.[2943]

St. Bonaventure: 1221 to 1274

Collatio de donis Spiritus Sancti 6, n.16
She paid the price [of redemption] as a woman brave and loving — namely when Christ suffered on the cross to pay that price in order to purge and wash and redeem us, the Blessed Virgin was present, accepting and agreeing with the divine will.[2944]

St. Thomas Aquinas: 1225 to 1274

Commentary on the Hail Mary, 2
It is necessary that whosoever desires to obtain favors with God, should approach this mediatrix, approach her with a most devout heart because, since she is the Queen of Mercy, possessing everything in the kingdom of God's justice, she cannot refuse your petition.[2945]

St. Catherine of Siena: 1347 to 1380

Oratio XI, delivered in Rome. (25th March 1379)
O Mary...bearer of the light...Mary, Germinatrix of the fruit, Mary, Redemptrix of the human race because, by providing your flesh in the Word you redeemed the world. Christ redeemed with His Passion and you with your sorrow of body and mind.[2946]

[2939]St. Irenaeus. *Against Heresies* Bk. III, Chap. 22, para 4 [Online] Available at: www.newadvent. org [Accessed on: 4 August 2022]
[2940]Quoted in Miravalle, M [2017] *Introduction to Mary: The Heart of Marian Doctrine and Devotion.* CreateSpace Independent Publishing Platform p.104
[2941]Quoted in Miravalle, M. [2002] M*ary Coredemptrix: A Response to 7 Common Objections in Mary at the Foot of the Cross*, Vol. II. New Bedford: Franciscans of the Immaculate, p.154
[2942]St. Andrew of Crete. *The Great Canon of Repentance.* [Online] Available at: smg.org.au [Accessed on: 4 August 2022]
[2943]St. John Damascene. *A Little Treatise on Mary.* [Online] Available at: http://catholictradition. org [Accessed on: 4 August 2022]
[2944]Quoted in Miravalle, M. [2002] *Op. cit.,* p. 168
[2945]Mezard, P [1940] *Saint Thomas Aquinas: Meditations, For Every Day.* Columbus. Ohio: College Book Co. p. 416
[2946]*Ibid.,* p.100

St. John Eudes: 1601 to 1680

The Priest: His Dignity and Obligation
Why did He confer upon her so much wisdom, goodness, meekness and such great power in heaven, in hell and on earth? It was simply that she might be worthy to cooperate with her Divine Son in man's redemption. All the Fathers of the Church say clearly that she is co-redemptrix with Christ in the work of our salvation.[2947]

St. Louis de Montfort: 1673 to 1716

True Devotion to the Blessed Virgin, 28, 55
For God has made her queen of heaven and earth, leader of his armies, keeper of his treasures, dispenser of his graces, worker of his wonders, restorer of the human race, mediatrix on behalf of men, destroyer of his enemies, and faithful associate in his great works and triumphs.

In all circumstances they will have recourse to her as their advocate and mediatrix with Jesus Christ. They will see clearly that she is the safest, easiest, shortest and most perfect way of approaching Jesus and will surrender themselves to her, body and soul, without reserve in order to belong entirely to Jesus.[2948]

The Magisterium of the Church

The Blessed Virgin Mary is rightly honoured with various titles by the Church such as Mediatrix, Coredemptrix, and others, recognising her cooperation, in a wholly singular way, in her Son's redemption of mankind.

The Council of Ephesus (Third Ecumenical, 431)

From the Epistle of St. Cyril of Alexandria to Nestorius, *read and approved in action*
For it was no ordinary man who was first born of the Holy Virgin and upon whom the Word afterwards descended; but being united from the womb itself He is said to have undergone flesh birth, claiming as His own the birth of His own flesh. Thus [the holy Fathers] did not hesitate to speak of the holy Virgin as the Mother of God.

The Anathemas of the Chapter of Cyril
Can. 1. If anyone does not confess that God is truly Emmanuel, and that on this account the Holy Virgin is the Mother of God (for according to the flesh she gave birth to the Word of God become flesh by birth), let him be anathema.[2949]

Second Council of Constantinople (Fifth Ecumenical, 551)

Anathemas Concerning the Three Chapters
Can. 2. If anyone does not confess that there are two generations of the Word of God, the one from the Father before the ages, without time and incorporeally, the other in the last days, when the same came down from heaven, and was incarnate of the holy and glorious Mother of God and ever Virgin Mary, and was born of her, let such a one be anathema.[2950]

Second Council of Nicaea (Seventh Ecumenical, 787)

Definition of the Sacred Images and Tradition
…our undefiled lady, or holy Mother of God…[2951]

[2947]St. John Eudes [1947] *The Priest: His Dignity and Obligation.* New York: PJ Kennedy & Son, p. 135
[2948]St. Louis de Montfort. *True Devotion to the Blessed Virgin,* paras 28, 55 [Online] Available at: www.montfort.org.uk [Accessed on: 7 October 2022]
[2949]The Council of Ephesus [431] *The Anathemas of the Chapter of Cyril, Can.* 1 [Online] Available at: http://patristica.net [Accessed on: 28 July 2022]
[2950]Second Council of Constantinople [551] *Anathemas Concerning the Three Chapters,* Can. 2. [Online] Available at: patristica.net [Accessed on: 28 July 2022]
[2951]Second Council of Nicaea [787] *Definition of the Sacred Images and Tradition.* [Online] Available at: patristica.net [Accessed on: 28 July 2022]

Council of Trent (Nineteenth Ecumenical, 1545 to 1563)

Decree On Original Sin. (17th June 1546).
…the blessed and immaculate Virgin Mary mother of God….[2952]

Second Vatican Council (Twenty-First Ecumenical, 1962 to 1965)

Dogmatic Constitution *Lumen Gentium, 61- 62. (21st November 1964)*
She presented Him to the Father in the temple, and was united with Him by compassion as He died on the Cross. In this singular way she cooperated by her obedience, faith, hope and burning charity in the work of the Saviour in giving back supernatural life to souls. Wherefore she is our mother in the order of grace. […]

   Taken up to heaven she did not lay aside this salvific duty, but by her constant intercession continued to bring us the gifts of eternal salvation. By her maternal charity, she cares for the brethren of her Son, who still journey on earth surrounded by dangers and cultics, until they are led into the happiness of their true home. Therefore the Blessed Virgin is invoked by the Church under the titles of Advocate, Auxiliatrix, Adjutrix, and Mediatrix. This, however, is to be so understood that it neither takes away from nor adds anything to the dignity and efficaciousness of Christ the one Mediator.[2953]

Pope St. John Paul II: 1978 to 2005

General Audience Address. (8th September 1982)
Mary, though conceived and born without the taint of sin, participated in a marvelous way in the sufferings of her divine Son, in order to be Coredemptrix of humanity.[2954]

Angelus Message. (4th November 1984)
To Our Lady — the Coredemptrix — St. Charles [Borromeo] turned with singularly revealing accents. Commenting on the loss of the twelve-year-old Jesus in the Temple, he reconstructed the interior dialogue that could have run between the Mother and the Son, and he added, 'You will endure much greater sorrows, O blessed Mother, and you will continue to live; but life will be for you a thousand times more bitter than death. You will see your innocent Son handed over into the hands of sinners…. You will see him brutally crucified between thieves; you will see his holy side pierced by the cruel thrust of a lance; finally, you will see the blood that you gave him spilling. And nevertheless you will not be able to die!'[2955]

Homily at the Shrine of Our Lady de la Alborada in Guayaquil, Ecuador. (31st January 1985)
The Gospels do not tell us of an appearance of the risen Christ to Mary. Nevertheless, as she was in a special way close to the Cross of her Son, she also had to have a privileged experience of his Resurrection. In fact, Mary's role as Coredemptrix did not cease with the glorification of her Son.[2956]

Homily for Palm Sunday. (31st March 1985)
Mary accompanied her divine Son in the most discreet concealment pondering everything in the depths of her heart. On Calvary, at the foot of the Cross, in the vastness and in the depth of her maternal sacrifice, she had John, the youngest Apostle, beside her…May Mary our Protectress, the Coredemptrix, to whom we offer our prayer with great outpouring, make our desire generously correspond to the desire of the Redeemer.[2957]

[2952]Council of Trent. [1546] *Decree on Original Sin.* [Online] Available at: patristica.net [Accessed on: 28 July 2022]
[2953]Second Vatican Council [1964] Dogmatic Constitution, *Lumen Gentium,* paras 61-62 [Online] Available at: www.vatican.va [Accessed on: 28 July 2022]
[2954]*Mary at the Foot of the Cross: Acts of the International Symposium on Marian Coredemption.* New Bedford, Franciscans of the Immaculate, 2001. p.158
[2955]*Ibid.*
[2956]*Ibid.,* p.159
[2957]*Ibid.,* p.160

Homily on the occasion of the sixth centenary of the canonisation of St. Bridget of Sweden. (6th October 1991)

St. Bridget looked to Mary as her model and support in the various moments of her life. She spoke energetically about the divine privilege of Mary's Immaculate Conception. She contemplated her astonishing mission as Mother of the Saviour. She invoked her as the Immaculate Conception, Our Lady of Sorrows, and Coredemptrix, exalting Mary's singular role in the history of salvation and the life of the Christian people.[2958]

Encyclical Redemptoris Mater, 21, 41. *(25th March 1987)*

Mary places herself between her Son and mankind in the reality of their wants, needs and sufferings. She puts herself 'in the middle,' that is to say she acts as a mediatrix not as an outsider, but in her position as mother. She knows that as such she can point out to her Son the needs of mankind, and in fact, she 'has the right' to do so. Her mediation is thus in the nature of intercession: Mary 'intercedes' for mankind.

...she also has that specifically maternal role of mediatrix of mercy at his final coming, when all those who belong to Christ 'shall be made alive,' when 'the last enemy to be destroyed is death' (I Cor. 15:26).[2959]

General Audience Address. (13th December 1995)

During the Council sessions, many Fathers wished further to enrich Marian doctrine with other statements on Mary's role in the work of salvation. The particular context in which Vatican II's Mariological debate took place did not allow these wishes, although substantial and widespread, to be accepted....The hesitation of some Fathers regarding the title of Mediatrix did not prevent the Council from using this title once, and from stating in other terms Mary's mediating role from her consent to the Angel's message to her motherhood in the order of grace (cf. *Lumen Gentium* 62). Furthermore, the Council asserts her co-operation 'in a wholly singular way' in the work of restoring supernatural life to souls (*ibid.*, 61).[2960]

General Audience Address. (24th September 1997)

'Therefore the Blessed Virgin is invoked in the Church under the titles of Advocate, Helper, Benefactress and Mediatrix.' (*Lumen Gentium* 62). These titles, suggested by the faith of the Christian people, help us better to understand the nature of the Mother of the Lord's intervention in the life of the Church and of the individual believer.

The title 'Advocate' goes back to St. Irenaeus. With regard to Eve's disobedience and Mary's obedience, he says that at the moment of the Annunciation 'the Virgin Mary became the Advocate' of Eve (*Haer.* 5, 19, 1; PG 7, 1175-1176). In fact, with her 'yes' she defended our first mother and freed her from the consequences of her disobedience, becoming the cause of salvation for her and the whole human race.

Mary exercises her role as 'Advocate' by co-operating both with the Spirit the Para-clete and with the One who interceded on the Cross for his persecutors (cf. Lk 23:34), whom John calls our 'advocate with the Father' (I Jn 2:1). As a mother, she defends her children and protects them from the harm caused by their own sins.

Christians call upon Mary as 'Helper', recognising her motherly love which sees her children's needs and is ready to come to their aid, especially when their eternal salvation is at stake.

The conviction that Mary is close to those who are suffering or in situations of serious danger has prompted the faithful to invoke her as 'Benefactress'. The same trusting certainty is expressed in the most ancient Marian prayer with the words: 'We fly to thy patronage, O holy Mother of God; despise not our petitions in our necessities but deliver us always from all dangers, O glorious and blessed Virgin' (from the *Roman Breviary*).

[2958]*Ibid.*, p.160

[2959]Pope St. John Paul II [1987] Encyclical *Redemptoris Mater*, paras 21, 41 [Online] Available at: www.vatican.va [Accessed on: 7 October 2022]

[2960]Burton Calkins, A. [1997] *Pope John Paul II's Teaching on Marian Coredemption* [Online: Available at: www.christendom-awake.org [Accessed on: 7 October 2022]

As maternal Mediatrix, Mary presents our desires and petitions to Christ, and transmits the divine gifts to us, interceding continually on our behalf.[2961]

General Audience Address. (1 October 1997)
Among the titles attributed to Mary in the Church's devotion, chapter eight of *Lumen Gentium* recalls that of 'Mediatrix'. Although some Council Fathers did not fully agree with this choice of title (cf. *Acta Synodalia* III, 8, 163-164), it was nevertheless inserted into the Dogmatic Constitution on the Church as confirmation of the value of the truth it expresses. Care was therefore taken not to associate it with any particular theology of mediation, but merely to list it among Mary's other recognized titles.

Moreover the conciliar text had already described the meaning of the title 'Mediatrix' when it said that Mary 'by her manifold intercession continues to bring us the gifts of eternal salvation' (*Lumen Gentium* 62). [...]

With regard to the objections made by some of the Council Fathers concerning the term 'Mediatrix', the Council itself provided an answer by saying that Mary is 'a mother to us in the order of grace' (*Lumen Gentium* 61). We recall that Mary's mediation is essentially defined by her divine motherhood. Recognition of her role as mediatrix is moreover implicit in the expression 'our Mother', which presents the doctrine of Marian mediation by putting the accent on her motherhood. Lastly, the title 'Mother in the order of grace' explains that the Blessed Virgin co-operates with Christ in humanity's spiritual rebirth.[2962]

Pope Ven. Pius XII: 1939 to 1958

Encyclical Mystici Corporis Christi, 110. (29th June 1943)
It was she, the second Eve, who, free from all sin, original or personal, and always more intimately united with her Son, offered Him on Golgotha to the Eternal Father for all the children of Adam, sin-stained by his unhappy fall, and her mother's rights and her mother's love were included in the holocaust.[2963]

Apostolic Constitution Munificentissimus Deus, 39-40
We must remember especially that, since the second century, the Virgin Mary has been designated by the holy Fathers as the new Eve, who, although subject to the new Adam, is most intimately associated with him in that struggle against the infernal foe which, as foretold in the protoevangelium, would finally result in that most complete victory over the sin and death which are always mentioned together in the writings of the Apostle of the Gentiles. [...]

Hence the revered Mother of God, from all eternity joined in a hidden way with Jesus Christ in one and the same decree of predestination, immaculate in her conception, a most perfect virgin in her divine motherhood, the noble associate of the divine Redeemer who has won a complete triumph over sin and its consequences....[2964]

Pope Pius XI: 1922 to 1939

Encyclical Caritate Christi Compulsi, 31. (3rd May 1932)
Let them pray to Him, interposing likewise the powerful patronage of the Blessed Virgin Mary, Mediatrix of all graces, for themselves and for their families, for their country, for the Church.[2965]

[2961]Pope St. John Paul II [1997] *General Audience Address* [Online] Available at: www.vatican.va [Accessed on: 10 August 2022]
[2962]Pope St. John Paul II [1 October 1997] *General Audience Address* [Online] Available at: www.vatican.va [Accessed on: 10 August 2022]
[2963]Pope Ven. Pius XII [1943] Encyclical *Mystici Corporis Christi*, para 110 [Online] Available at: www.vatican.va [Accessed on: 7 October 2022]
[2964]Pope Ven. Pius XII [1950] Apostolic Constitution *Munificentissimus Deus*, paras 39-40 [Online] Available at: www.vatican.va [Accessed on: 7 October 2022]
[2965]Pope Pius XI [1932] Encyclical *Caritate Christi Compulsi*, para 31 [Online] Available at: www.vatican.va [Accessed on: 7 October 2022]

Papal Allocution to the pilgrims of Vicenza, Italy. (30th November 1933)
By necessity, the Redeemer could not but associate his Mother in his work. For this reason we invoke her under the title of Coredemptrix. She gave us the Saviour, she accompanied Him in the work of Redemption as far as the Cross itself, sharing with Him the sorrows of the agony and of the death in which Jesus consummated the Redemption of mankind.[2966]

Papal Allocution to pilgrims from Spain (25th March 1934)
These young pilgrims must follow the thoughts and wishes of Mary most holy, who is our mother and Coredemptrix. They too must make every effort to be Coredeemers and apostles.[2967]

Radio Message to Lourdes (28th April 1935)
O Mother of love and mercy, when your sweet Son was consummating the Redemption of the human race on the altar of the cross, you stood next to Him, suffering with Him as a Coredemptrix....Day by day preserve and increase in us, we beg you, the precious fruit of His redemption and your compassion as His Mother.[2968]

Pope Benedict XV: 1914 to 1922

Encyclical Inter Sodalicia. (22nd March 1918)
… the fact that she was with Him crucified and dying, was in accord with the divine plan. For with her suffering and dying Son, Mary endured suffering and almost death. She gave up her Mother's rights over her Son to procure the salvation of mankind, and to appease the divine justice, she, as much as she could, immolated her Son, so that one can truly affirm that together with Christ she has redeemed the human race. But if for this reason, every kind of grace we receive from the treasury of the redemption is ministered as it were through the hands of the same Sorrowful Virgin, everyone can see that a holy death should be expected from her, since it is precisely by this gift that the work of the Redemption is effectively and permanently completed in each one.... further, there is a most constant belief among the faithful, proved by long experience, that as many as employ the same Virgin as Patron, will not at all perish forever.[2969]

Encyclical Fausto Appetente Die, 11. (29th June 1921)
[St. Dominic] knew, on the one hand, Mary's authority with her Son to be such that whatever graces he confers on men she has their distribution and apportionment. On the other hand, he knew that she is of a nature so kind and merciful that, seeing that it is her custom to succor the miserable of her own accord, it is impossible she should refuse the petitions of those who pray to her. Accordingly the Church, which is wont to salute her 'the Mother of Grace and the Mother of Mercy,' has so found her always, but especially in answer to the Rosary.[2970]

Pope St. Pius X: 1903 to 1914

Encyclical Ad Diem Illum Laetissimum, 12, 13. (2nd February 1904)
And from this community of will and suffering between Christ and Mary she merited

---

[2966] *Popes of the Marian Age and Mary Co-redemptrix* [Online] Available at: www.motherofallpeoples. com] [Accessed on: 7 October 2022]; Schug, J & Miravalle, M. *Mary, Coredemptrix: The Significance of Her Title in the Magisterium of The Church* [Online] Available at: www.christendom-awake.org [Accessed on: 7 October 2022]

[2967] *L'Osservatore Romano* [March 25th, 1934] cited in *Mary at the Foot of the Cross: Acts of the International Symposium on Marian Coredemption*. New Bedford: Franciscans of the Immaculate, 2000. p. 45

[2968] *L'Osservatore Romano* [April 29-30, 1935] cited in Schug, J and .S

[2969] Most, W. *Teaching of the Popes and Vatican II on Mary as Mediatrix of (All) Graces* [Online] www. ewtn.com [Accessed on: 7 October 2022]

[2970] Pope Benedict XV [1921] Encyclical *Fausto Appetente Die*, para 11 [Online] Available at: www. vatican.va [Accessed on: 7 October 2022]

to become most worthily the Reparatrix of the lost world and Dispensatrix of all the gifts that Our Savior purchased for us by His Death and by His Blood.[2971]

It cannot, of course, be denied that the dispensation of these treasures is the particular and peculiar right of Jesus Christ, for they are the exclusive fruit of His Death, who by His nature is the mediator between God and man. Nevertheless, by this companionship in sorrow and suffering already mentioned between the Mother and the Son, it has been allowed to the august Virgin to be the most powerful mediatrix and advocate [conciliatrix] of the whole world with her Divine Son (Pius IX. *Ineffabilis*).[2972]

Congregation for Rites (13th May 1908)
Through this decree…may devotion to the merciful Coredemptrix increase.[2973]

Holy Office. Prayer for reparation addressed to the Blessed Virgin Mary. Indulgences (January 1914)
…I praised thine exalted privilege of being truly Mother of God, Ever Virgin, conceived without stain of sin, Coredemptrix of the human race.[2974]

Pope Leo XIII: 1878 to 1903

Encyclical Supremi Apostolatus Officio, 1. (1st September 1883)
We deem that there could be no surer and more efficacious means to this end than by religion and piety to obtain the favour of the great Virgin Mary, the Mother of God, the guardian of our peace and the minister [*administra*] to us of heavenly grace.…[2975]

Encyclical Octobri Mense Adventante, 4. (22nd September 1891)
With equal truth may it be also affirmed that, by the will of God, Mary is the intermediary through whom is distributed unto us this immense treasure of mercies gathered by God, for mercy and truth were created by Jesus Christ. (Jn 1:17). Thus as no man goeth to the Father but by the Son, so no man goeth to Christ but by His Mother.[2976]

Encyclical Adiutricem Populi, 8. (5th September 1895)
How rightly, too, has every nation and every liturgy without exception acclaimed her great renown, which has grown greater with the voice of each succeeding century. Among her many other titles we find her hailed as 'our Lady, our Mediatrix,' 'the Reparatrix of the whole world,' 'the Dispenser of all heavenly gifts.'[2977]

Encyclical Fidentem Piumque Animum. (20th September 1896)
Undoubtedly the name and attributes of the absolute Mediator belong to no other than to Christ, for being one person, and yet both man and God, He restored the human race to the favour of the Heavenly Father: One Mediator of God and men, the man Christ Jesus, who gave Himself a redemption for all (I Tim. 2:5, 6). And yet, as the Angelic Doctor teaches, there is no reason why certain others should not be called in a certain way mediators between God and man, that is to say, in so far as they cooperate by predisposing and ministering in the union of man with God (*Summa*, p. III, q. xxvi., articles 1, 2). Such are the angels and saints, the prophets and priests of both Testaments; but especially has the Blessed Virgin a claim to the glory of this title.

[2971]Pope St. Pius X [1904] Encyclical *Ad Diem Illum Laetissimum*, 12-13 [Online] Available at: www. vatican.va [Accessed on: 10 August 2022]
[2972]*Ibid.*
[2973]*Acta Apostolicae Sedis*, 41 [1908] quoted in Jones, J [2000] T*he Assumption of the Blessed Virgin Mary in Her Role as the Coredemptrix in Mary at the Foot of the Cross: Acts of the International Symposium on Marian Coredemption*. New Bedford: Franciscans of the Immaculate, p.43
[2974]Holy Office [Jan 1914] *Sacred Penitentiary Apostolic*, Dec 4, 1934 cited in *Ibid.* p.43
[2975]Pope Leo XIII [1883] Encyclical *Supremi Apostolatus Officio*, 1. [Online] Available at: www. vatican.va [Accessed on: 10 August 2022]
[2976]Pope Leo XIII [1891] Encyclical *Octobri Mense Adventante*, 4 [Online] Available at: www.vatican. va [Accessed on: 10 August 2022]
[2977]Pope Leo XIII [1895] Encyclical *Adiutricem Populi*, para 8 Online] Available at: www.vatican.va [Accessed on: 10 August 2022]

For no single individual can even be imagined who has ever contributed or ever will contribute so much towards reconciling man with God. She offered to mankind, hastening to eternal ruin, a Saviour, at that moment when she received the announcement of the mystery of peace brought to this earth by the Angel, with that admirable act of consent in the name of the whole human race (*Summa*, p. III, q. xxx., art. 1). She it is from whom is born Jesus; she is therefore truly His mother, and for this reason a worthy and acceptable 'Mediatrix to the Mediator.'[2978]

Pope Bl. Pope Pius IX: 1846 to 1878

Apostolic Constitution *Ineffabilis Deus. (8th December 1854)*
Accordingly, the Fathers have never ceased to call the Mother of God the lily among thorns, the land entirely intact, the Virgin undefiled, immaculate, ever blessed, and free from all contagion of sin, she from whom was formed the new Adam, the flawless, brightest, and most beautiful paradise of innocence, immortality and delights planted by God himself and protected against all the snares of the poisonous serpent, the incorruptible wood that the worm of sin had never corrupted, the fountain ever clear and sealed with the power of the Holy Spirit, the most holy temple, the treasure of immortality, the one and only daughter of life — not of death — the plant not of anger but of grace, through the singular providence of God growing ever green contrary to the common law, coming as it does from a corrupted and tainted root.

As if these splendid eulogies and tributes were not sufficient, the Fathers proclaimed with particular and definite statements that when one treats of sin, the holy Virgin Mary is not even to be mentioned; for to her more grace was given than was necessary to conquer sin completely. They also declared that the most glorious Virgin was Reparatrix of the first parents, the giver of life to posterity; that she was chosen before the ages, prepared for himself by the Most High, foretold by God when he said to the serpent, 'I will put enmities between you and the woman,' unmistakable evidence that she was crushed the poisonous head of the serpent.

All our hope do we repose in the most Blessed Virgin — in the all fair and immaculate one who has crushed the poisonous head of the most cruel serpent and brought salvation to the world: in her who is the glory of the prophets and apostles, the honor of the martyrs, the crown and joy of all the saints; in her who is the safest refuge and the most trustworthy helper of all who are in danger; in her who, with her only-begotten Son, is the most powerful Mediatrix and Conciliatrix in the whole world.[2979]

[2978]Pope Bl. Pius IX [1854] Apostolic Constitution *Ineffabilis Deus*. [Online] Available at: www.papalencyclicals.net [Accessed on: 10 August 2022]

[2979]Pope Bl. Pius IX [1854] Apostolic Constitution *Ineffabilis Deus*. [Online] Available at: www.papalencyclicals.net [Accessed on: 10 August 2022]

Morality (1) — Antinomianism

Pope Francis: 2013 to 2025

L. *There are situations in which it may be too difficult, or not possible, to obey such commandments, laws and rules. The Church's rules and precepts are historically conditioned, and some are no longer useful to shape or direct people's lives.*

To strictly obey the letter of commandments, laws and rules can be an expression of pelagian egotism and self-righteousness, contrary to the promptings of the Holy Spirit. Seeking to obey all the commandments, laws and rules, and not risking stepping outside them, leads to a mummified, museum piece Christian discipleship, and intransigent judges of others.

A Big Heart Open to God: An interview with Pope Francis. (30th September 2013)
The dogmatic and moral teachings of the church are not all equivalent. The church's pastoral ministry cannot be obsessed with the transmission of a disjointed multitude of doctrines to be imposed insistently.[2980]

Apostolic Exhortation Evangelii Gaudium, 43, 49, 94. (24th November 2013)
At the same time, the Church has rules or precepts which may have been quite effective in their time, but no longer have the same usefulness for directing and shaping people's lives. St. Thomas Aquinas pointed out that the precepts which Christ and the apostles gave to the people of God 'are very few'. Citing St. Augustine, he noted that the precepts subsequently enjoined by the Church should be insisted upon with moderation 'so as not to burden the lives of the faithful' and make our religion a form of servitude, whereas 'God's mercy has willed that we should be free'. This warning, issued many centuries ago, is most timely today. It ought to be one of the criteria to be taken into account in considering a reform of the Church and her preaching which would enable it to reach everyone.

More than by fear of going astray, my hope is that we will be moved by the fear of remaining shut up within structures which give us a false sense of security, within rules which make us harsh judges, within habits which make us feel safe, while at our door people are starving and Jesus does not tire of saying to us: 'Give them something to eat' (Mk 6:37).

The other is the self-absorbed promethean neopelagianism of those who ultimately trust only in their own powers and feel superior to others because they observe certain rules or remain intransigently faithful to a particular Catholic style from the past.[2981]

Address at Conclusion of the Synod of Bishops. (24th October 2015)
The Synod experience also made us better realise that the true defenders of doctrine are not those who uphold its letter, but its spirit; not ideas but people; not formulae but the gratuitousness of God's love and forgiveness. Their hearts, closed to God's truth, clutch only at the truth of the Law, taking it by 'the letter'. The path that Jesus teaches us [is] totally opposite to that of the doctors of law. And it's [the] path from love and justice that leads to God. Instead, the other path, of being attached only to the laws, to the letter of the laws, leads to closure, leads to egoism [self-righteousness].The path that leads from love to knowledge and discernment, to total fulfilment, leads to holiness, salvation and the encounter with Jesus.[2982]

Post Synodal Apostolic Exhortation Amoris Laetitia, 301, 304. (19th March 2016) Hence it is can no longer simply be said that all those in any 'irregular' situation are living in a state of mortal sin and are deprived of sanctifying grace. More is involved

---

[2980]Spadaro, A [2013] *A Big Heart Open to God: An Interview with Pope Francis* [Online] Available at: www.americamagazine.org [Accessed on: 7 October 2022]
[2981]Pope Francis [2013] Apostolic Exhortation *Evangelii Gaudium*, para 43. [Online] Available at: www.vatican.va [Accessed on: 12 August 2022]
[2982]Echeverria, E [2015] *Is the Gospel Opposed to the Law?* [Online] Available at: www.thecatholicthing. org [Accessed on: 12 August 2022]

here than mere ignorance of the rule. A subject may know full well the rule, yet have great difficulty in understanding 'its inherent values', or be in a concrete situation which does not allow him or her to act differently and decide otherwise without further sin. As the Synod Fathers put it, 'factors may exist which limit the ability to make a decision'.

It is reductive simply to consider whether or not an individual's actions correspond to a general law or rule, because that is not enough to discern and ensure full fidelity to God in the concrete life of a human being. I earnestly ask that we always recall a teaching of St. Thomas Aquinas and learn to incorporate it in our pastoral discernment: 'Although there is necessity in the general principles, the more we descend to matters of detail, the more frequently we encounter defects.... In matters of action, truth or practical rectitude is not the same for all, as to matters of detail, but only as to the general principles; and where there is the same rectitude in matters of detail, it is not equally known to all.... The principle will be found to fail, according as we descend further into detail'. It is true that general rules set forth a good which can never be disregarded or neglected, but in their formulation they cannot provide absolutely for all particular situations.[2983]

Morning Meditation in the Chapel of the Domus Sanctae Marthae. (27th January 2017)
...you follow 'all the commandments, yes, it's true; but this paralyses you, it makes you forget many graces you have received; it takes away your memory; it takes away your hope because it doesn't allow you to go'. Thus, 'the present of a Christian is like that of a person going along the road when an unexpected rain comes, and his or her garment is not very good and the fabric shrinks: shrunken souls'. This very image shows the sin of 'pusillanimity: the sin against memory, courage, patience and hope'.[2984]

Apostolic Exhortation *Gaudete et Exsultate, 49, 58, 59, 61, 134, 173. (19 March 2018)*
Those who yield to this pelagian or semi-pelagian mindset, even though they speak warmly of God's grace, 'ultimately trust only in their own powers and feel superior to others because they observe certain rules or remain intransigently faithful to a particular Catholic style'.[2985] When some of them tell the weak that all things can be accomplished with God's grace, deep down they tend to give the idea that all things are possible by the human will, as if it were something pure, perfect, all-powerful, to which grace is then added. They fail to realise that 'not everyone can do everything', and that in this life human weaknesses are not healed completely and once for all by grace. In every case, as St. Augustine taught, God commands you to do what you can and to ask for what you cannot and indeed to pray to him humbly: 'Grant what you command, and command what you will'.

Not infrequently, contrary to the promptings of the Spirit, the life of the Church can become a museum piece or the possession of a select few. This can occur when some groups of Christians give excessive importance to certain rules, customs or ways of acting. The Gospel then tends to be reduced and constricted, deprived of its simplicity, allure and savour.

Once we believe that everything depends on human effort as channelled by ecclesial rules and structures, we unconsciously complicate the Gospel and become enslaved to a blueprint that leaves few openings for the working of grace. St. Thomas Aquinas reminded us that the precepts added to the Gospel by the Church should be imposed with moderation 'lest the conduct of the faithful become burdensome', for then our religion would become a form of servitude.

In other words, amid the thicket of precepts and prescriptions, Jesus clears a way to seeing two faces, that of the Father and that of our brother. He does not give us two

[2983]Pope Francis [2016] Apostolic Exhortation *Amoris Laetitia*, para 301. [Online] Available at: www.vatican.va [Accessed on: 12 August 2022]
[2984]Pope Francis [27 January 2017] *Morning Meditation in the Chapel of the Domus Sanctae Marthae* [Online] Available at: www.vatican.va [Accessed on: 7 October 2022]
[2985]Pope Francis [2013] Apostolic Exhortation *Evangelii Gaudium, op. cit.,* para 94

more formulas or two more commands. He gives us two faces, or better yet, one alone: the face of God reflected in so many other faces.

Like the prophet Jonah, we are constantly tempted to flee to a safe haven. It can have many names: individualism, spiritualism, living in a little world, addiction, intransigence, the rejection of new ideas and approaches, dogmatism, nostalgia, pessimism, hiding behind rules and regulations.

It is not a matter of applying rules or repeating what was done in the past, since the same solutions are not valid in all circumstances and what was useful in one context may not prove so in another.[2986]

General Audience Address. (28th November 2018)
In this way we can better understand why the Lord Jesus did not come to abolish the law but to fulfil it, to develop it, and as the law according to the flesh was a series of prescriptions and prohibitions, according to the Spirit this same law becomes life (cf. Jn 6:63; Eph 2:15), because it is no longer a rule but the very flesh of Christ, who loves us, seeks us, forgives us, consoles us and in his Body recreates the communion with the Father, lost through the disobedience of sin. And thus, the literal negative, the negative expression used in the Commandments − 'you shall not steal', 'you shall not insult', 'you shall not kill' − that 'not' is transformed into a positive approach: to love, to make room in my heart for others, all desires that sow positivity. And this is the fullness of the law that Jesus came to bring us.[2987]

Homily for World Day of the Poor. (15th November 2020)
Those measured Christians who never step outside the rules, never, because they are afraid of risk. And these, allow me the image, these who take care of themselves so that they never risk, these begin in life a process of mummification of the soul, and end up with mummies. This is not enough, it is not enough to observe the rules; fidelity to Jesus is not only not making mistakes, it is negative.[2988]

General Audience Address. (18th August 2021)
Once one has come to faith, the Law exhausts its propaedeutic value and must give way to another authority. What does this mean? That after the Law we can say, 'We believe in Jesus Christ and do what we want'? No! The Commandments exist, but they do not justify us. What justifies is Jesus Christ. The Commandments must be observed, but they do not give us justice; there is the gratuitousness of Jesus Christ, the encounter with Jesus Christ that freely justifies us. The merit of faith is receiving Jesus. The only merit: opening the heart. So what do we do with the Commandments? We must observe them, but as an aid to the encounter with Jesus Christ.

This teaching on the value of the law is very important, and deserves to be considered carefully so as not to fall into misunderstandings and take false steps. It will do us good to ask ourselves whether we still live in the period in which we need the Law, or if instead we are fully aware of having received the grace of becoming children of God so as to live in love. How do I live? In the fear that if I do not do this, I will go to hell? Or do I live with that hope too, with that joy of the gratuitousness of salvation in Jesus Christ? It is a good question. And also a second one: do I scorn the Commandments? No. I observe them, but not as absolutes, because I know that it is Jesus Christ who justifies me.[2989]

[2986]Pope Francis [2018] Apostolic Exhortation *Gaudete et Exsultate*, 49 [Online] Available at: www. vatican.va [Accessed on: 12 August 2022]

[2987]Pope Francis [28 November 2018] *General Audience Address* [Online] Available at: www.vatican. va [Accessed on: 12 August 2022]

[2988]Gledhill, R [16 November 2020] *Pope tells Christians to break 'rules'* [Online] Available at: www. thetablet.co.uk [Accessed on: 7 October 2022]

[2989]Pope Francis [18 August 2021] *General Audience Address.* [Online] Available at: www.vatican.va [Accessed on: 12 August 2022]

General Audience Address. (20th October 2021)

Reborn in Christ, we have passed from a religiosity made up of precepts – we have moved on from a religiosity made up of precepts — to a living faith, which has its centre in communion with God and with our brothers and sisters, that is, in love. We have passed from the slavery of fear and sin to the freedom of God's children. Here, again, is the word freedom. ...[2990]

Sacred Scripture

Matthew 11:29-30; 19:17

Take up my yoke upon you, and learn of me, because I am meek, and humble of heart: and you shall find rest to your souls. For my yoke is sweet and my burden light.

But if thou wilt enter into life, keep the commandments.

John 14:15

If you love me, keep my commandments.

John 15:10

If you keep my commandments, you shall abide in my love; as I also have kept my Father's commandments, and do abide in his love.

I John 5:3

For this is the charity of God, that we keep his commandments: and his commandments are not heavy.

I John 2: 3-5

And by this we know that we have known him, if we keep his commandments. He who saith that he knoweth him, and keepeth not his commandments, is a liar, and the truth is not in him. But he that keepeth his word, in him in very deed the charity of God is perfected; and by this we know that we are in him.

II John 1:6

And this is charity, that we walk according to his commandments. For this is the commandment, that, as you have heard from the beginning, you should walk in the same.

Deuteronomy 6:4-9

Hear, O Israel, the Lord our God is one Lord. Thou shalt love the Lord thy God with thy whole heart, and with thy whole soul, and with thy whole strength. And these words which I command thee this day, shall be in thy heart: And thou shalt tell them to thy children, and thou shalt meditate upon them sitting in thy house, and walking on thy journey, sleeping and rising. And thou shalt bind them as a sign on thy hand, and they shall be and shall move between thy eyes. And thou shalt write them in the entry, and on the doors of thy house.

Deuteronomy 30: 10-17

Yet so if thou hear the voice of the Lord thy God, and keep his precepts and ceremonies, which are written in this law: and return to the Lord thy God with all thy heart, and with all thy soul. This commandment, that I command thee this day is not above thee, nor far off from thee: Nor is it in heaven, that thou shouldst say: Which of us can go up to heaven to bring it unto us, and we may hear and fulfil it in work? Nor is it beyond the sea: that thou mayst excuse thyself, and say: Which of us can cross the sea, and bring it unto us: that we may hear, and do that which is commanded? But the word is very nigh unto thee, in thy mouth and in thy heart, that thou mayst do it. Consider that I have set before thee this day life and good, and on the other hand death and evil: That thou mayst love the Lord thy God, and walk in his ways, and keep his commandments and

---

[2990]Pope Francis [20th October 2021] *General Audience Address*. [Online] Available at: www.vatican.va [Accessed on: 12 August 2022]

ceremonies and judgments, and thou mayst live, and he may multiply thee, and bless thee in the land, which thou shalt go in to possess. But if thy heart be turned away, so that thou wilt not hear, and being deceived with error thou adore strange gods, and serve them:

Jeremiah 31:33
But this shall be the covenant that I will make with the house of Israel, after those days, saith the Lord: I will give my law in their bowels, and I will write it in their heart: and I will be their God, and they shall be my people.

Ecclesiasticus 15:21-22
He hath commanded no man to do wickedly, and he hath given no man license to sin: For he desireth not a multitude of faithless and unprofitable children.

Sacred Tradition
St. Cyprian of Carthage: c. 200 to 258

Treatise 1
But how can a man say that he believes in Christ, who does not do what Christ commanded him to do? Or whence shall he attain to the reward of faith, who will not keep the faith of the commandment? He must of necessity waver and wander, and, caught away by a spirit of error, like dust which is shaken by the wind, be blown about; and he will make no advance in his walk towards salvation, because he does not keep the truth of the way of salvation.[2991]

Epistle 24. To Moyses and Maximus and the Rest of the Confessors
You prompt the keeping of these precepts; you observe the divine and heavenly commands. This is to be a confessor of the Lord; this is to be a martyr of Christ – to keep the firmness of one's profession inviolate among all evils, and secure. For to wish to become a martyr for the Lord, and to try to overthrow the Lord's precepts; to use against Him the condescension that He has granted you – to become, as it were, a rebel with arms that you have received from Him – this is to wish to confess Christ, and to deny Christ's Gospel.[2992]

St. John Chrysostom: c. 347 to 407

Homily 38 on Matthew
And if you are still afraid and tremblest at hearing of the yoke and the burden, the fear comes not of the nature of the thing, but of your remissness; since if you are prepared, and in earnest, all will be easy to you and light. Since for this cause Christ also, to signify that we too must needs labor ourselves, did not mention the gracious things only, and then hold His peace, nor the painful things only, but set down both. Thus He both spoke of 'a yoke,' and called it 'easy' both named a burden, and added that it was 'light' that you should neither flee from them as toilsome, nor despise them as over easy.[2993]

St. Jerome: c. 340-2 to 420

Against Jovinianus, Bk. II, Chap. 2
In vain do we make our boast in him whose commandments we keep not. To him that knows what is good, and does it not, it is sin.[2994]

[2991]St. Cyprian of Carthage. *Treatise* 1, On the Unity of the Church, para 2. [Online] Available at: www.newadvent.org [Accessed on: 16 August 2022]
[2992]St. Cyprian of Carthage. *Epistle* 24, To Moyses and Maximus and the Rest of the Confessors, para 2. [Online] Available at: www.newadvent.org [Accessed on: 16 August 2022]
[2993]St. John Chrysostom. *Homily 38 on Matthew* [Online] Available at: www.newadvent.org [Accessed on: 7 October 2022]
[2994]St. Jerome. *Against Jovinianus*, Bk. II, Chap. 2. [Online] Available at: www.newadvent.org [Accessed on: 16 August 2022]

St. Augustine: 354 to 430

A Treatise on Nature and Grace, Chaps. 43, 83

God does not command what is impossible, but when He commands, He commands, He warns you to do what you can and to ask His aid for what is beyond your powers, and He gives His help to make that possible for you.

But 'the precepts of the law are very good,' if we use them lawfully (I Tim 1:8). Indeed, by the very fact (of which we have the firmest conviction) 'that the just and good God could not possibly have enjoined impossibilities,' we are admonished both what to do in easy paths and what to ask for when they are difficult. Now all things are easy for love to effect, to which (and which alone) 'Christ's burden is light' (Mt 11:30) or rather, it is itself alone the burden which is light. Accordingly it is said, 'And His commandments are not grievous;' (I John 5:3) so that whoever finds them grievous must regard the inspired statement about their 'not being grievous' as having been capable of only this meaning, that there may be a state of heart to which they are not burdensome, and he must pray for that disposition which he at present wants, so as to be able to fulfil all that is commanded him. [...] No man, therefore, who 'returns to the Lord his God,' as he is there commanded, 'with all his heart and with all his soul,' (Deut 30:2) will find God's commandment 'grievous.' How, indeed, can it be grievous, when it is the precept of love? Either, therefore, a man has not love, and then it is grievous; or he has love, and then it is not grievous. But he possesses love if he does what is there enjoined on Israel, by returning to the Lord his God with all his heart and with all his soul.[2995]

On Merit and the Forgiveness of Sins, and the Baptism of Infants. Bk. II, Chap. 7

I cannot doubt that God has laid no impossible command on man; and that, by God's aid and help, nothing is impossible, by which is wrought what He commands. In this way may a man, if he pleases, be without sin by the assistance of God.[2996]

St. Thomas Aquinas: 1225 to 1274

Summa Theologiae. Ia-IIae, q. 19, a.4

It is therefore evident that the goodness of the human will depends on the eternal law much more than on human reason: and when human reason fails we must have recourse to the Eternal Reason.[2997]

The Magisterium of the Church

We are bound to observe the Commandments, because we are all bound to live according to the will of God who created us, and because a serious transgression against even one of them is enough to merit hell. We are able to observe God's Commandments, because God never commands anything that is impossible, and because He gives grace to observe them to those who ask it as they should. We are also bound to observe the precepts of the Church, which are nothing but practical specifications of rules of the Gospels. Obeying all of God's Commandments is necessary because they are intrinsic to our nature and commanded by God.

Council of Vienne (Fifteenth Ecumenical, 1311 to 1312)

Errors of the Beghards and the Beguines on the State of Perfection

Thirdly, that those who have reached the said degree of perfection and spirit of liberty, are not subject to human obedience nor obliged to any commandments of the Church, for, as they say, where the spirit of the Lord is, there is freedom.[2998]

[2995]St. Augustine. *On Nature and Grace,* Chap. 29 [Online] Available at: www.newadvent.org [Accessed on: 16 August 2022]

[2996]St. Augustine. *On Merit and the Forgiveness of Sins, and the Baptism of Infants.* Bk. II, Chap. 7. [Online] Available at: www.newadvent.org [Accessed on: 16 August 2022]

[2997]St. Thomas Aquinas. *Summa Theologiae.* Ia-IIae, q. 19, a.4 [Online] Available at: www.newadvent. org [Accessed on: 16 August 2022]

[2998]Council of Vienne 1311-1312 A.D. [Online] Available at: www.papalencyclicals.net [Accessed on: 13 August 2022]

Council of Trent (Nineteenth Ecumenical, 1545 to 1563)

Decree on Justification, *Chap. XI, Can. 18, 20, 21 (13th January 1547)*
But no one, however much justified, should consider himself exempt from the observance of the commandments; no one should use that rash statement, once forbidden by the Fathers under anathema, that the observance of the commandments of God is impossible for one that is justified.

For God does not command impossibilities, but by commanding admonishes thee to do what thou canst and to pray for what thou canst not, and aids thee that thou mayest be able. (St. Augustine)

His commandments are not heavy, (I Jn 5:3) and his yoke is sweet and burden light (Mt 11:30).

For they who are the sons of God love Christ, but they who love Him, keep His commandments, as He Himself testifies; (Jn 14:23) which, indeed, with the divine help they can do. [...] For God does not forsake those who have been once justified by His grace, unless He be first forsaken by them.

If anyone says that the commandments of God are, even for one that is justified and constituted in grace, impossible to observe, let him be anathema.

If anyone says that a man who is justified and however perfect is not bound to observe the commandments of God and the Church, but only to believe, as if the Gospel were a bare and absolute promise of eternal life without the condition of observing the commandments, let him be anathema.

If anyone says that Christ Jesus was given by God to men as a redeemer in whom to trust, and not also as a legislator whom to obey, let him be anathema.[2999]

Second Vatican Council (Twenty-First Ecumenical, 1962 to 1965)

Dogmatic Constitution *Lumen Gentium, 48. (21st November 1964)*
...all men may attain to salvation by faith, baptism and the fulfilment of the commandments.[3000]

Pastoral Constitution *Gaudium et Spes, 41. (7th December 1965)*
For we are tempted to think that our personal rights are fully ensured only when we are exempt from every requirement of divine law. But this way lies not the maintenance of the dignity of the human person, but its annihilation.[3001]

Declaration *Dignitatis Humanae, 3. (7th December 1965)*
...the highest norm of human life is the divine law-eternal, objective and universal-whereby God orders, directs and governs the entire universe and all the ways of the human community by a plan conceived in wisdom and love. Man has been made by God to participate in this law, with the result that, under the gentle disposition of divine Providence, he can come to perceive ever more fully the truth that is unchanging.[3002]

Pope Benedict XVI: 2005 to 2013

Compendium of the Catechism of the Catholic Church. (28th June 2005)

416. In what does the natural moral law consist?
The natural law which is inscribed by the Creator on the heart of every person consists in a participation in the wisdom and the goodness of God. It expresses that original moral sense which enables one to discern by reason the good and the bad. It is universal

---

[2999]Council of Trent [1547] *Decree Concerning Justification*, Chap. 11. [Online] Available at: www.ewtn.com [Accessed on: 13 August 2022]
[3000]Second Vatican Council [1964] Dogmatic Constitution, *Lumen Gentium*, para 48 [Online] Available at: www.vatican.va [Accessed on: 7 October 2022]
[3001]Second Vatican Council [1965] Pastoral Constitution *Gaudium et Spes*, para 41 [Online] Available at: www.vatican.va [Accessed on: 3 October 2022]
[3002]Second Vatican Council [1965] Declaration, *Dignitatis Humanae*, para 3 [Online] Available at: www.vatican.va [Accessed on: 7 October 2022]

and immutable and determines the basis of the duties and fundamental rights of the person as well as those of the human community and civil law.

438. What importance does the Church give to the Decalogue?
The Church, in fidelity to Scripture and to the example of Christ, acknowledges the primordial importance and significance of the Decalogue. Christians are obliged to keep it.

439. Why does the Decalogue constitute an organic unity?
The Ten Commandments form an organic and indivisible whole because each commandment refers to the other commandments and to the entire Decalogue. To break one commandment, therefore, is to violate the entire law.

441. Is it possible to keep the Decalogue?
Yes, because Christ without whom we can do nothing enables us to keep it with the gift of his Spirit and his grace.[3003]

Encyclical Deus Caritas Est, *14, 18. (25th December 2005)*
…the 'commandment' of love is only possible because it is more than a requirement. Love can be "commanded" because it has first been given. […]

Love of God and love of neighbour are thus inseparable, they form a single commandment. But both live from the love of God who has loved us first. No longer is it a question, then, of a 'commandment' imposed from without and calling for the impossible, but rather of a freely-bestowed experience of love from within, a love which by its very nature must then be shared with others.[3004]

Address to Members of the Pontifical Biblical Commission. (27th April 2006)
The advocates of this 'secular morality' say that man as a rational being not only can but must decide freely on the value of his behaviour. This erroneous conviction is based on the presumed conflict between human freedom and every form of law. In fact, the Creator, because we are creatures, has inscribed his 'natural law', a reflection of his creative idea, in our hearts, in our very being, as a compass and inner guide for our life.

For this very reason, Sacred Scripture, Tradition and the Magisterium of the Church tell us that the vocation and complete fulfilment of the human being are not attained by rejecting God's law, but by abiding by the new law that consists in the grace of the Holy Spirit. Together with the Word of God and the teaching of the Church, it is expressed in 'faith working through love' (Gal 5: 6).

And it is precisely in this acceptance of the love that comes from God (*Deus Caritas Est*), that the freedom of man finds its loftiest realisation. There is no contradiction between God's law and human freedom: God's law correctly interpreted neither attenuates nor, even less, eliminates man's freedom. On the contrary, it guarantees and fosters this freedom because, as the *Catechism of the Catholic Church* reminds us, 'freedom... attains its perfection when directed toward God, our beatitude' (n. 1731).[3005]

Homily at Mass in Piłsudski Square, Poland. (26th May 2006)
Yet living one's personal faith as a love-relationship with Christ also means being ready to renounce everything that constitutes a denial of his love. That is why Jesus said to the Apostles: 'If you love me, you will keep my commandments.' But what are Christ's commandments? When the Lord Jesus was teaching the crowds, he did not fail to confirm the law which the Creator had inscribed on men's hearts and had then formulated on the tablets of the Decalogue. 'Think not that I have come to abolish the law and the prophets; I have come not to abolish them but to fulfil them. For truly, I

[3003]Pope Benedict XVI [2005] *Compendium of the Catechism of the Catholic Church.* [Online] Available at: www.vatican.va [Accessed on: 18 August 2022]
[3004]Pope Benedict XVI [2005] Encyclical *Deus Caritas Est,* paras 14, 18 [Online] Available at: www. vatican.va [Accessed on: 7 October 2022]
[3005]Pope Benedict XVI [2006] *Divine Law Does Not Eliminate Human Freedom* [Online] Available at: www.catholicculture.org [Accessed on: 7 October 2022]

say to you, till heaven and earth pass away, not an iota, not a dot, will pass from the law until all is accomplished' (Mt 5:17-18). But Jesus showed us with a new clarity the unifying centre of the divine laws revealed on Sinai, namely love of God and love of neighbour: 'To love [God] with all the heart, and with all the understanding, and with all the strength, and to love one's neighbour as oneself, is much more than all whole burnt offerings and sacrifices' (Mk 12:33). Indeed, in his life and in his Paschal Mystery Jesus brought the entire law to completion. Uniting himself with us through the gift of the Holy Spirit, he carries with us and in us the 'yoke' of the law, which thereby becomes a 'light burden' (Mt 11:30).[3006]

Message on the Occasion of the Twenty-Fifth World Youth Day, 6. (28th March 2010)
The Commandments, the Way to Authentic Love. The Commandments are essential points of reference if we are to live in love, to distinguish clearly between good and evil, and to build a life plan that is solid and enduring. Jesus is asking you too whether you know the Commandments, whether you are trying to form your conscience according to God's law, and putting the Commandments into practice. [...]

Jesus reminded the rich young man that obedience to the Ten Commandments is necessary in order to 'inherit eternal life'. The Commandments are essential points of reference if we are to live in love, to distinguish clearly between good and evil, and to build a life plan that is solid and enduring. Jesus is asking you too whether you know the Commandments, whether you are trying to form your conscience according to God's law, and putting the Commandments into practice.

God gives us the Commandments because he wants to teach us true freedom. He wants to build a Kingdom of love, justice and peace together with us. When we listen to the Commandments and put them into practice, it does not mean that we become estranged from ourselves, but that we find the way to freedom and authentic love. The commandments do not place limits on happiness, but rather show us how to find it. At the beginning of the conversation with the rich young man, Jesus reminds him that the law which God gives is itself good, because 'God is good'.[3007]

Pope St. John Paul II: 1978 to 2005

Catechism of the Catholic Church. (1992)
The natural law is immutable and permanent throughout the variations of history; it subsists under the flux of ideas and customs and supports their progress. The rules that express it remain substantially valid. Even when it is rejected in its very principles, it cannot be destroyed or removed from the heart of man. It always rises again in the life of individuals and societies. (1958)

The Council of Trent teaches that the Ten Commandments are obligatory for Christians and that the justified man is still bound to keep them; the Second Vatican Council confirms: 'The bishops, successors of the apostles, receive from the Lord . . . the mission of teaching all peoples, and of preaching the Gospel to every creature, so that all men may attain salvation through faith, Baptism and the observance of the Commandments.' (LG 24). (2068)

Since they express man's fundamental duties towards God and towards his neighbour, the Ten Commandments reveal, in their primordial content, grave obligations. They are fundamentally immutable, and they oblige always and everywhere. No one can dispense from them. The Ten Commandments are engraved by God in the human heart. (2072)

What God commands he makes possible by his grace. (2082)[3008]

[3006]Pope Benedict XVI [2006] *Homily at Mass in Piłsudski Square, Poland* [Online] Available at: www.vatican.va [Accessed on: 7 October 2022]
[3007]Pope Benedict XVI [2010] *Message on the Occasion of the Twenty-Fifth World Youth Day*, para 6 [Online] Available at: www.vatican.va [Accessed on: 7 October 2022]
[3008]*Catechism of the Catholic Church* [1992] [Online] Available at: scborromeo2.org [Accessed on: 12 July 2022]

Encyclical *Veritatis Splendor, 12, 26, 67, 102. (6th August 1993)*
'If you wish to enter into life, keep the commandments' (Mt 19:17). In this way, a close connection is made between eternal life and obedience to God's commandments: God's commandments show man the path of life and they lead to it. From the very lips of Jesus, the new Moses, man is once again given the commandments of the Decalogue. Jesus himself definitively confirms them and proposes them to us as the way and condition of salvation.

No damage must be done to the harmony between faith and life: the unity of the Church is damaged not only by Christians who reject or distort the truths of faith but also by those who disregard the moral obligations to which they are called by the Gospel (cf. I Cor 5:9-13). The Apostles decisively rejected any separation between the commitment of the heart and the actions which express or prove it (cf. I Jn 2:3-6). And ever since Apostolic times the Church's Pastors have unambiguously condemned the behaviour of those who fostered division by their teaching or by their actions.

But the negative moral precepts, those prohibiting certain concrete actions or kinds of behaviour as intrinsically evil, do not allow for any legitimate exception. They do not leave room, in any morally acceptable way, for the 'creativity' of any contrary determination whatsoever. Once the moral species of an action prohibited by a universal rule is concretely recognized, the only morally good act is that of obeying the moral law and of refraining from the action which it forbids.

Grace and obedience to God's law. Even in the most difficult situations man must respect the norm of morality so that he can be obedient to God's holy commandment and consistent with his own dignity as a person. Certainly, maintaining a harmony between freedom and truth occasionally demands uncommon sacrifices, and must be won at a high price: it can even involve martyrdom. But, as universal and daily experience demonstrates, man is tempted to break that harmony: 'I do not do what I want, but I do the very thing I hate... I do not do the good I want, but the evil I do not want' (Rom 7:15, 19).

What is the ultimate source of this inner division of man? His history of sin begins when he no longer acknowledges the Lord as his Creator and himself wishes to be the one who determines, with complete independence, what is good and what is evil. 'You will be like God, knowing good and evil' (Gen 3:5): this was the first temptation, and it is echoed in all the other temptations to which man is more easily inclined to yield as a result of the original Fall.

But temptations can be overcome, sins can be avoided, because together with the commandments the Lord gives us the possibility of keeping them: 'His eyes are on those who fear him, and he knows every deed of man. He has not commanded any one to be ungodly, and he has not given any one permission to sin' (Sir 15:19-20). Keeping God's law in particular situations can be difficult, extremely difficult, but it is never impossible. This is the constant teaching of the Church's tradition....[3009]

Homily at Celebration of the Word at Mount Sinai, 3,4. (26th February 2000)
The Ten Commandments are not an arbitrary imposition of a tyrannical Lord. They were written in stone; but before that, they were written on the human heart as the universal moral law, valid in every time and place. Today as always, the Ten Words of the Law provide the only true basis for the lives of individuals, societies and nations. Today as always, they are the only future of the human family. They save man from the destructive force of egoism, hatred and falsehood.

The Ten Commandments are the law of freedom: not the freedom to follow our blind passions, but the freedom to love, to choose what is good in every situation, even when to do so is a burden. It is not an impersonal law that we obey; what is required

---

[3009]Pope St. John Paul II [1993] Encyclical *Veritatis Splendor*, paras 12, 26, 67, 102 [Online] Available at: www.vatican.va [Accessed on: 18 August 2022]

is loving surrender to the Father through Christ Jesus in the Holy Spirit (cf. Rom 6:14; Gal 5:18).[3010]

Pope St. Paul VI: 1963 to 1978

Apostolic Constitution, *Indulgentiarum Doctrina, 2. (1st January 1967)*
Christians throughout history have always regarded sin not only as a transgression of divine law but also — though not always in a direct and evident way — as contempt for or disregard of the friendship between God and man, just as they have regarded it as a real and unfathomable offence against God and indeed an ungrateful rejection of the love of God shown us through Jesus Christ, who called his disciples friends and not servants.[3011]

Encyclical *Humanae Vitae, 20. (25th July 1968)*
The teaching of the Church regarding the proper regulation of birth is a promulgation of the law of God Himself. And yet there is no doubt that to many it will appear not merely difficult but even impossible to observe. Now it is true that like all good things which are outstanding for their nobility and for the benefits which they confer on men, so this law demands from individual men and women, from families and from human society, a resolute purpose and great endurance. Indeed it cannot be observed unless God comes to their help with the grace by which the goodwill of men is sustained and strengthened. But to those who consider this matter diligently it will indeed be evident that this endurance enhances man's dignity and confers benefits on human society.[3012]

Pope St. John XXIII: 1958 to 1963

Encyclical *Pacem in Terris, 38. (11th April 1963)*
God and the Moral Order. But such an order — universal, absolute and immutable in its principles — finds its source in the true, personal and transcendent God. He is the first truth, the sovereign good, and as such the deepest source from which human society, if it is to be properly constituted, creative, and worthy of man's dignity, draws its genuine vitality. This is what St. Thomas means when he says: 'Human reason is the standard which measures the degree of goodness of the human will, and as such it derives from the eternal law, which is divine reason. . . . Hence it is clear that the goodness of the human will depends much more on the eternal law than on human reason.' (*Summa*. Ia-IIae, q. 19, a.4).[3013]

Pope Ven. Pope Pius XII: 1939 to 1958

Encyclical *Summi Pontificatus, 7. (20th October 1939)*
Who among 'the Soldiers of Christ' — ecclesiastic or layman — does not feel himself incited and spurred on to a greater vigilance, to a more determined resistance, by the sight of the ever-increasing host of Christ's enemies; as he perceives the spokesmen of these tendencies deny or in practice neglect the vivifying truths and the values inherent in belief in God and in Christ; as he perceives them wantonly break the Tables of God's Commandments to substitute other tables and other standards stripped of the ethical content of the Revelation on Sinai, standards in which the spirit of the Sermon on the Mount and of the Cross has no place?[3014]

[3010]Pope St. John Paul II [2000] *Homily at Celebration of the Word at Mount Sinai*, paras 3, 4. [Online] Available at: www.vatican.va [Accessed on: 18 August 2022]
[3011]Pope St. Paul VI [1967] *Apostolic Constitution, Indulgentiarum Doctrina*, para 2 [Online] Available at: www.vatican.va [Accessed on: 7 October 2022]
[3012]Pope St. Paul VI [1968] Encyclical *Humanae Vitae*, para 20 [Online] Available at: www.vatican.va [Accessed on: 7 October 2022]
[3013]Pope St. John XXIII [1963] Encyclical *Pacem in Terris*, para 38 [Online] Available at: www.vatican.va [Accessed on: 7 October 2022]
[3014]Pope Ven. Pius XII [1939] Encyclical *Summi Pontificatus*, para 7 [Online] Available at: www.vatican.va [Accessed on: 7 October 2022]

Encyclical *Mystici Corporis Christi, 92. (23rd June 1943)*
As her children, it is our duty, not only to make a return to her for her maternal goodness to us, but also to respect the authority which she has received from Christ in virtue of which she brings into captivity our understanding unto the obedience of Christ (II Cor 10:5). Thus we are commanded to obey her laws and her moral precepts, even if at times they are difficult to our fallen nature; to bring our rebellious body into subjection through voluntary mortification; and at times we are warned to abstain even from harmless pleasures.[3015]

Vegliare con Sollecitudine — Address to the Italian Association of Catholic Midwives. (29th October 1951)
…we have the doctrine of the Council of Trent which, in the chapter on the necessary and possible observance of the Commandments, referring to a passage in the works of Augustine, teaches: 'God does not command what is impossible, but when He commands, He commands, He warns you to do what you can and to ask His aid for what is beyond your powers, and He gives His help to make that possible for you' (Conc. Trid., sess. 6, ch. xi, Denzinger n. 804 – St. August. *De Natura et Gratia*, ch. 43, no. 50; Migne *PL* vol. 44, col. 271.).

Do not be disturbed when, in the practice of your profession and in your apostolate, you hear this clamour about impossibility. Do not let it cloud your internal judgment, nor affect your exterior conduct. Never lend yourselves to anything whatsoever which is opposed to the law of God and your Christian conscience. To judge men and women of today incapable of continuous heroism is to do them wrong. In these days, for many reasons – perhaps through dire necessity, or even at times under pressure of injustice – heroism is being practiced to a degree and extent that in times past would have been thought impossible. Why then, if circumstances demand it, should this heroism stop at the limits prescribed by passion and the inclinations of nature? It is obvious that he who does not want to master himself, will not be able to do so; and he who thinks he can master himself, relying solely on his own powers and not sincerely and perseveringly seeking divine aid, will be miserably deceived.[3016]

La Famiglia — Radio Message on the Occasion of 'Family Day', 4, 11. (23rd March 1952)
The divine Savior has brought to man, ignorant and weak, his truth and his grace: truth to indicate for him the path that leads to his end; grace to confer upon him the strength to be able to reach it. To follow this path means, in practice, accepting the will and the commandments of Christ and conforming one's life to them, that is, the individual acts, internal and external, which the free human will chooses and settles upon.

He spoke of the 'narrow gate' and the 'narrow road' that leads to life (cf. Mt 7:13-14), and added: 'Strive to enter through the narrow gate: for many, I tell you, will try to enter and will not be able' (Lk 13:24). He has established the observance of the commandments as the touchstone and the distinctive sign of love for Himself, Christ (Jn 14:21-24).[3017]

Soyez les bienvenues — discourse to the World Federation of Catholic Young Women, 4, 8, 9-10. (18th April 1952)
'Situation Ethics'– Its Distinctive Sign. The distinctive mark of this morality is that it is not based in effect on universal moral laws, such as, for example, the Ten Commandments, but on the real and concrete conditions or circumstances in which men must act, and according to which the conscience of the individual must judge and choose. Such a state of things is unique, and is applicable only once for every human action. That is why the

---

[3015]Pope Ven. Pius XII [1943] Encyclical *Mystici Corporis Christi*, para 92 [Online] Available at: www.vatican.va [Accessed on: 7 October 2022]

[3016]Pope Ven. Pius XII. *Pius XII's Condemnation of Situation Ethics: 'Accusations of rigidity first attack the adorable person of Christ'* [Online] Available at: rorate-caeli.blogspot.com [Accessed on: 17 August 2022]

[3017]*Ibid.*

decision of conscience, as the advocates of this ethic assert, cannot be commanded by ideas, principles and universal laws. [...]

Stated thus expressly, the new ethic is so foreign to the faith and to Catholic principles that even a child, if he knows his catechism, will be aware of it and will feel it. It is not difficult to recognize how this new moral system derives from existentialism which either prescinds from God or simply denies Him, and, in any case, leaves man to himself. It is possible that present-day conditions may have led men to attempt to transplant this 'new morality' into Catholic soil, in order to make the hardships of Christian life more bearable for the faithful. In fact, millions of them are being called upon today, and in an extraordinary degree, to practice firmness, patience, constancy, and the spirit of sacrifice, if they wish to preserve their faith intact. For they suffer the blows of fate, or are placed in surroundings which put within their reach everything which their passionate heart yearns for or desires. Such an attempt can never succeed.

It will be asked, how the moral law, which is universal, can be sufficient, and even have binding force, in an individual case, which, in the concrete, is always unique and 'happens only once.' It can be sufficient and binding, and it actually is because precisely by reason of its universality, the moral law includes necessarily and 'intentionally' all particular cases in which its meaning is verified. In very many cases it does so with such convincing logic that even the conscience of the simple faithful sees immediately, and with full certitude, the decision to be taken.

This is especially true of the negative obligations of the moral law, namely those which oblige us not to do something, or to set something else aside. Yet it is not true only of these obligations. The fundamental obligations of the moral law are based on the essence and the nature of man, and on his essential relationships, and thus they have force wherever we find man. The fundamental obligations of the Christian law, in the degree in which they are superior to those of the natural law, are based on the essence of the supernatural order established by the Divine Redeemer. From the essential relationships between man and God, between man and man, between husband and wife, between parents and children; from the essential community relationships found in the family, in the Church, and in the State, it follows, among other things, that hatred of God, blasphemy, idolatry, abandoning the true faith, denial of the faith, perjury, murder, bearing false witness, calumny, adultery and fornication, the abuse of marriage, the solitary sin, stealing and robbery, taking away the necessities of life, depriving workers of their just wage (Jas 5:4), monopolising vital foodstuffs and unjustifiably increasing prices, fraudulent bankruptcy, unjust manoeuvring in speculation – all this is gravely forbidden by the divine Lawmaker. No examination is necessary. No matter what the situation of the individual may be, there is no other course open to him but to obey.[3018]

Pope Pius XI: 1922 to 1939

Encyclical *Quas Primas, 14. (11th December 1925)*
Let Us explain briefly the nature and meaning of this lordship of Christ. It consists, We need scarcely say, in a threefold power which is essential to lordship. This is sufficiently clear from the scriptural testimony already adduced concerning the universal dominion of our Redeemer, and moreover it is a dogma of faith that Jesus Christ was given to man, not only as our Redeemer, but also as a law-giver, to whom obedience is due. Not only do the gospels tell us that he made laws, but they present him to us in the act of making them. Those who keep them show their love for their Divine Master, and he promises that they shall remain in his love. (Jn 14:15; 15:10). He claimed judicial power as received from his Father, when the Jews accused him of breaking the Sabbath by the miraculous cure of a sick man. 'For neither doth the Father judge any man; but hath given all judgment to the Son.' (Jn 5:22). In this power is included the right

---

[3018]Pope Ven. Pius XII [1952] *Soyez les bienvenues – discourse to the World Federation of Catholic Young Women*, paras 9-10 [Online] Available at: www.catholicculture.org [Accessed on: 17 August 2022]

of rewarding and punishing all men living, for this right is inseparable from that of judging. Executive power, too, belongs to Christ, for all must obey his commands; none may escape them, nor the sanctions he has imposed.[3019]

Encyclical *Mit brennender sorge, 10,12,18, 29. (14th March 1937)*
This God, this Sovereign Master, has issued commandments whose value is independent of time and space, country and race. As God's sun shines on every human face so His law knows neither privilege nor exception. Rulers and subjects, crowned and uncrowned, rich and poor are equally subject to His word. From the fullness of the Creators' right there naturally arises the fullness of His right to be obeyed by individuals and communities, whoever they are. This obedience permeates all branches of activity in which moral values claim harmony with the law of God, and pervades all integration of the ever-changing laws of man into the immutable laws of God.

It is part of their [bishops] sacred obligations to do whatever is in their power to enforce respect for, and obedience to, the commandments of God, as these are the necessary foundation of all private life and public morality.

His command to hear the Church (Mt 18:15), to welcome in the words and commands of the Church His own words and His own commands (Luke 10:16), is addressed to all men, of all times and of all countries.

The conscientious observation of the ten commandments of God and the precepts of the Church (which are nothing but practical specifications of rules of the Gospels) is for every one an unrivalled school of personal discipline, moral education and formation of character, a school that is exacting, but not to excess. A merciful God, who as Legislator, says — Thou must! — also gives by His grace the power to will and to do. [...] To hand over the moral law to man's subjective opinion, which changes with the times, instead of anchoring it in the holy will of the eternal God and His commandments, is to open wide every door to the forces of destruction. The resulting dereliction of the eternal principles of an objective morality, which educates conscience and ennobles every department and organization of life, is a sin against the destiny of a nation, a sin whose bitter fruit will poison future generations.[3020]

Encyclical *Ingravescentibus Malis, 4. (29th September 1937)*
In fact, because the supreme and eternal authority of God, which commands and forbids, is despised and completely repudiated by men, the result is that the consciousness of Christian duty is weakened, and that faith becomes tepid in souls or entirely lost, and this afterward affects and ruins the very basis of human society.[3021]

Pope Benedict XV: 1914 to 1922

Encyclical *Ad Beatissimi Apostolorum, 5. (1st November 1914)*
For ever since the precepts and practices of Christian wisdom ceased to be observed in the ruling of states, it followed that, as they contained the peace and stability of institutions, the very foundations of states necessarily began to be shaken. Such, moreover, has been the change in the ideas and the morals of men, that unless God comes soon to our help, the end of civilisation would seem to be at hand.[3022]

[3019]Pope Pius XI [1925] Encyclical *Quas Primas*, para 14 [Online] Available at: www.vatican.va [Accessed on: 16 August 2022]

[3020]Pope Pius XI [1937] Encyclical *Mit Brennender Sorge*, para 10, 12, 18, 29 [Online] Available at: www.vatican.va [Accessed on: 16 August 2022]

[3021]Pope Pius XI [1937] Encyclical *Ingravescentibus Malis*, para 4 [Online] Available at: www. vatican.va [Accessed on: 7 October 2022]

[3022]Pope Benedict XV [1914] Encyclical *Ad Beatissimi Apostolorum*, para 5 [Online] Available at: www.vatican.va [Accessed on: 7 October 2022]

Pope St. Pius X: 1903 to 1914

Catechism of St. Pius X. (1908)
On the Commandments of God and of the Church
3 Q. Why are the Commandments of God so named?
A. The Commandments of God are so named because God Himself has stamped them on the soul of every man; promulgated them, engraved on two tables of stone, on Mount Sinai, in the Old Law; and Jesus Christ has confirmed them in the New Law.

6 Q. Are we bound to observe the Commandments?
A. Yes, we are bound to observe the Commandments, because we are all bound to live according to the will of God who created us, and because a serious transgression against even one of them is enough to merit hell.

7 Q. Are we able to observe the Commandments?
A. Yes, without doubt we are able to observe God's Commandments, because God never commands anything that is impossible, and because He gives grace to observe them to those who ask it as they should.[3023]

The Precepts of the Church
The Precepts of the Church in General
1 Q. Besides the Commandments of God what else must we observe?
A. Besides the Commandments of God we must also observe the Precepts of the Church.

2 Q. Are we obliged to obey the Church?
A. Undoubtedly we are obliged to obey the Church, because Jesus Christ Himself commands us to do so, and because the Precepts of the Church help us to observe the Commandments of God.

3 Q. When does the obligation to observe the Precepts of the Church begin to bind?
A. As a rule the obligation to observe the Precepts of the Church begins to bind us as soon as we come to the age of reason.

4 Q. Is it a sin to transgress a Precept of the Church?
A. Knowingly to transgress a Precept of the Church in grave matter is a mortal sin.

5 Q. Who can dispense from a Precept of the Church?
A. Only the Pope, or one who has received from him the power to do so, can dispense from a Precept of the Church.

Encyclical *Communium Rerum*, 56. *(21st April 1909)*
And would to God that these poor wanderers on whose lips one so often hears the fair words of sincerity, conscience, religious experience, the faith that is felt and lived, and so on, learned their lessons from Anselm, understood his holy teachings, imitated his glorious example, and, above all, took deeply to heart those words of his: 'First the heart is to be purified by faith, and first the eyes are to be illuminated by the observance of the precepts of the Lord . . . and first with humble obedience to the testimonies of God we must become small to learn wisdom . . . and not only when faith and obedience to the commandments are removed is the mind hindered from ascending to the intelligence of higher truths, but often enough the intelligence that has been given is taken away and faith is overthrown, when right conscience is neglected' (*De Fide Trinitatis*, Chap. 2).[3024]

Pope Leo XIII: 1878 to 1903

Encyclical *Libertas*, 8. *(20th June 1888)*
Foremost in this office comes the natural law, which is written and engraved in the mind of every man; and this is nothing but our reason, commanding us to do right and forbidding sin. Nevertheless, all prescriptions of human reason can have force of

---

[3023]Pope St. Pius X [1908] *Catechism of St. Pius X*, On the Commandments of God and of the Church. [Online] Available at: www.ewtn.com [Accessed on: 17 August 2022]
[3024]Pope St. Pius X [1909] Encyclical *Communium Rerum*, para 56. [Online] Available at: www. vatican.va [Accessed on: 17 August 2022]

law only inasmuch as they are the voice and the interpreters of some higher power on which our reason and liberty necessarily depend. For, since the force of law consists in the imposing of obligations and the granting of rights, authority is the one and only foundation of all law — the power, that is, of fixing duties and defining rights, as also of assigning the necessary sanctions of reward and chastisement to each and all of its commands. But all this, clearly, cannot be found in man, if, as his own supreme legislator, he is to be the rule of his own actions. It follows, therefore, that the law of nature is the same thing as the eternal law, implanted in rational creatures, and inclining them to their right action and end; and can be nothing else but the eternal reason of God, the Creator and Ruler of all the world. To this rule of action and restraint of evil God has vouchsafed to give special and most suitable aids for strengthening and ordering the human will. The first and most excellent of these is the power of His divine grace, whereby the mind can be enlightened and the will wholesomely invigorated and moved to the constant pursuit of moral good, so that the use of our inborn liberty becomes at once less difficult and less dangerous. Not that the divine assistance hinders in any way the free movement of our will; just the contrary, for grace works inwardly in man and in harmony with his natural inclinations, since it flows from the very Creator of his mind and will, by whom all things are moved in conformity with their nature. As the Angelic Doctor points out, it is because divine grace comes from the Author of nature that it is so admirably adapted to be the safeguard of all natures, and to maintain the character, efficiency, and operations of each.[3025]

Pope Bl. Pius IX: 1846 to 1878

Encyclical *Neminem Vestrum*, 7. (2 February 1854)
Let the faithful be instructed more each day in the salutary teaching of the Catholic faith and in its holy precepts, and let them be strengthened by the gifts of grace so that, avoiding evil and doing good, they may grow in the wisdom of God. They will thus progress more quickly on the paths of the Lord and enter the way which leads to life. Thus moral decency, integrity of life and virtue, religion, and piety will grow each day, flourishing and dominating in the souls of all.[3026]

Encyclical *Qui Pluribus*, 21. (9th November 1846)
Therefore, never stop preaching the Gospel, so that the Christian people may grow in the knowledge of God by being daily better versed in the most holy precepts of the Christian law; as a result, they may turn from evil, do good, and walk in the ways of the Lord.[3027]

Pope Clement XI: 1700 to 1721

Constitution Unigenitus *Dei Filius*, 71. (8th september 1713)
Jansenistic Errors of Pasquier Quesnel
For the preservation of himself man can dispense himself from the law which God established for his use (Mk 2:28).[3028]

Pope Innocent X: 1644 to 1655

Constitution *Cum Occasione*, 1. (31st May 1653)
Errors of Cornelius Jansen on Grace
Some of God's commandments cannot be observed by just men with the strength they have in the present state, even if they wish and strive to observe them; nor do they have the grace that would make their observance possible.[3029]

[3025]Pope Leo XIII [1888] Encyclical *Libertas*, para 8 [Online] Available at: www.vatican.va [Accessed on: 16 August 2022]
[3026]Pope Bl. Pius IX [1854] Encyclical *Neminem Vestrum*, para 7 [Online] Available at: www.papalencyclicals.net [Accessed on: 17 August 2022]
[3027]Pope Bl. Pius IX [1846] Encyclical *Qui Pluribus*, para 21 [Online] Available at: www.papalencyclicals.net [Accessed on: 17 August 2022]
[3028]Denzinger, H [2010] *Op. cit.*, p.503, Dz 2471
[3029]Heinrich Denzinger [2010] *Op. cit.*, p.455-456, Dz 2001

Morality (2) – Death Penalty

Pope Francis: 2013 to 2025

M. *The death penalty is a sin and is always inadmissible because it is an offence against the inviolability of life and the dignity of the person. Criminals have an inviolable, God-given right to life and not even a murderer loses his personal dignity. The death penalty is contrary to the Gospel because human life never ceases to be sacred in the eyes of its Creator, who is the only true judge.*

Address to the Delegates of the International Association of Penal Law. (23rd October 2014)
It is impossible to imagine that States today fail to employ a means other than capital punishment to protect the lives of other people from the unjust aggressor. St. John Paul II condemned the death penalty (cf. Encyclical Letter *Evangelium Vitae*, n. 56), as does the *Catechism of the Catholic Church* (n. 2267).

It can be established, however, that States take life not only through the death penalty and through war, but also when, in order to justify their crimes, public officials take refuge in the shadow of State prerogatives. So-called extra-judicial or extra-legal executions are homicides deliberately committed by certain States and by their agents, often passed off as clashes with criminals or presented as the unintended consequences of the reasonable, necessary and proportionate use of force in applying the law. In this way, although among the 60 Countries that sanction the death penalty, 35 have not applied it in the last 10 years, the death penalty is applied illegally and in varying degrees throughout the planet.

The same extra-judicial executions are performed in a systematic way not only by States in the international community, but also by entities not recognised as such, and they are genuine crimes.

There are many well known arguments against the death penalty. The Church has duly highlighted several, such as the possibility of judicial error and the use made of such punishment by totalitarian and dictatorial regimes who use it as a means of suppressing political dissidence or of persecuting religious and cultural minorities, all victims who, in their respective legislation are termed 'delinquents'. All Christians and men of good will are thus called today to fight not only for the abolition of the death penalty, whether legal or illegal, and in all its forms, but also in order to improve prison conditions, with respect for the human dignity of the people deprived of their freedom. And I link this to life imprisonment. Recently the life sentence was taken out of the Vatican's Criminal Code. A life sentence is just a death penalty in disguise.[3030]

Letter to the President of the International Commission against the Death Penalty. (20th March 2015)
Today capital punishment is unacceptable, however serious the condemned's crime may have been. It is an offence to the inviolability of life and to the dignity of the human person which contradicts God's plan for man and for society and his merciful justice, and it fails to conform to any just purpose of punishment. It does not render justice to the victims, but rather foments revenge.

For a constitutional state the death penalty represents a failure, because it obliges the State to kill in the name of justice. Dostoyevsky wrote: 'To kill a murderer is a punishment incomparably worse than the crime itself. Murder by legal sentence is immeasurably more terrible than murder by a criminal'. Justice is never reached by killing a human being.

The death penalty loses all legitimacy due to the defective selectivity of the criminal justice system and in the face of the possibility of judicial error. Human justice is imperfect, and the failure to recognise its fallibility can transform it into a source of injustice. With the application of capital punishment, the person sentenced is denied the possi-

---

[3030]Pope Francis [2014] *Address to the Delegates of the International Association of Penal Law* [Online] Available at: www.vatican.va [Accessed on: 21 May 2024]

bility to make amends or to repent of the harm done; the possibility of confession, with which man expresses his inner conversion; and of contrition, the means of repentance and atonement, in order to reach the encounter with the merciful and healing love of God.

Furthermore, capital punishment is a frequent practice to which totalitarian regimes and fanatical groups resort, for the extermination of political dissidents, minorities, and every individual labelled as 'dangerous' or who might be perceived as a threat to their power or to the attainment of their objectives. As in the first centuries and also in the current one, the Church suffers from the application of this penalty to her new martyrs.

The death penalty is contrary to the meaning of *humanitas* and to divine mercy, which must be models for human justice. It entails cruel, inhumane and degrading treatment, as is the anguish before the moment of execution and the terrible suspense between the issuing of the sentence and the execution of the penalty, a form of 'torture' which, in the name of correct procedure, tends to last many years, and which often-times leads to illness and insanity on death row.[3031]

Address to the Joint Session of the United States Congress. (24th September 2015)
Let us treat others with the same passion and compassion with which we want to be treated. Let us seek for others the same possibilities which we seek for ourselves. Let us help others to grow, as we would like to be helped ourselves. In a word, if we want security, let us give security; if we want life, let us give life; if we want opportunities, let us provide opportunities. The yardstick we use for others will be the yardstick which time will use for us. The Golden Rule also reminds us of our responsibility to protect and defend human life at every stage of its development.

This conviction has led me, from the beginning of my ministry, to advocate at different levels for the global abolition of the death penalty. I am convinced that this way is the best, since every life is sacred, every human person is endowed with an inalienable dignity, and society can only benefit from the rehabilitation of those convicted of crimes. Recently my brother bishops here in the United States renewed their call for the abolition of the death penalty. Not only do I support them, but I also offer encouragement to all those who are convinced that a just and necessary punishment must never exclude the dimension of hope and the goal of rehabilitation.[3032]

Angelus Address. (21st February 2016)
Dear brothers and sisters, tomorrow in Rome begins an international conference entitled 'For a World Without the Death Penalty,' sponsored by the Sant'Egidio Community. I hope that this conference might give new strength to efforts to abolish the death penalty. A spreading opposition to the death penalty, even as an instrument of legitimate social defence, has developed in public opinion, and this is a sign of hope. In fact, modern societies have the ability to effectively control crime without definitively taking away a criminal's chance to redeem himself. The issue lies in the context of a perspective on a criminal justice system that is ever more conformed to the dignity of man and God's design for man and for society. And also a criminal justice system open to the hope of reintegration in society. The commandment 'thou shall not kill' has absolute value and pertains to the innocent as well as the guilty.

The Extraordinary Jubilee of Mercy is a propitious occasion to promote in the world a growing maturity for ways to respect life and the dignity of each person. Because even a criminal has the inviolable right to life, a gift of God. I appeal to the consciences of leaders, that they come to an international consensus aimed at abolishing the death penalty. And to those among them who are Catholic, may they carry out an act of

---

[3031]Pope Francis [2015] *Letter to the President of the International Commission against the Death Penalty* [Online] Available at: www.vatican.va [Accessed on: 21 May 2024]
[3032]Pope Francis [2015] *Address to the Joint Session of the United States Congress* [Online] Available at: www.vatican.va [Accessed on: 21 May 2024]

courage, giving an example that the death penalty not be applied in this Holy Year of Mercy.[3033]

Video Message to the 6th World Congress Against the Death Penalty. (21st-23rd June 2016)
One sign of hope is that public opinion is manifesting a growing opposition to the death penalty, even as a means of legitimate social defense. Indeed, nowadays the death penalty is unacceptable, however grave the crime of the convicted person. It is an offence to the inviolability of life and to the dignity of the human person; it likewise contradicts God's plan for individuals and society, and his merciful justice. Nor is it consonant with any just purpose of punishment. It does not render justice to victims, but instead fosters vengeance. The commandment 'Thou shalt not kill' has absolute value and applies both to the innocent and to the guilty. The Extraordinary Jubilee of Mercy is an auspicious occasion for promoting worldwide ever more evolved forms of respect for the life and dignity of each person. It must not be forgotten that the inviolable and God-given right to life also belongs to the criminal.[3034]

Address to Participants in the Meeting Promoted by the Pontifical Council for Promoting the New Evangelisation. (11th October 2017)
Along these same lines, I would like now to bring up a subject that ought to find in the *Catechism of the Catholic Church* a more adequate and coherent treatment in the light of these expressed aims. I am speaking of the death penalty. This issue cannot be reduced to a mere résumé of traditional teaching without taking into account not only the doctrine as it has developed in the teaching of recent Popes, but also the change in the awareness of the Christian people which rejects an attitude of complacency before a punishment deeply injurious of human dignity. It must be clearly stated that the death penalty is an inhumane measure that, regardless of how it is carried out, abases human dignity. It is per se contrary to the Gospel, because it entails the wilful suppression of a human life that never ceases to be sacred in the eyes of its Creator and of which – ultimately – only God is the true judge and guarantor. No man, 'not even a murderer, loses his personal dignity' (Letter to the President of the International Commission against the Death Penalty, 20 March 2015), because God is a Father who always awaits the return of his children who, knowing that they have made mistakes, ask for forgiveness and begin a new life. No one ought to be deprived not only of life, but also of the chance for a moral and existential redemption that in turn can benefit the community.

In past centuries, when means of defence were scarce and society had yet to develop and mature as it has, recourse to the death penalty appeared to be the logical consequence of the correct application of justice. Sadly, even in the Papal States recourse was had to this extreme and inhumane remedy that ignored the primacy of mercy over justice. Let us take responsibility for the past and recognise that the imposition of the death penalty was dictated by a mentality more legalistic than Christian. Concern for preserving power and material wealth led to an over-estimation of the value of the law and prevented a deeper understanding of the Gospel. Nowadays, however, were we to remain neutral before the new demands of upholding personal dignity, we would be even more guilty.

Here we are not in any way contradicting past teaching, for the defence of the dignity of human life from the first moment of conception to natural death has been taught by the Church consistently and authoritatively. Yet the harmonious development of doctrine demands that we cease to defend arguments that now appear clearly contrary to the new understanding of Christian truth. Indeed, as St. Vincent of Lérins pointed out, 'Some may say: Shall there be no progress of religion in Christ's Church? Certainly;

[3033]Pope Francis [2015] *Angelus Address, 21st February 2016* [Online] Available at: www.vatican.va [Accessed on: 21 May 2024]
[3034]Pope Francis [2016] *Video Message to the 6th World Congress Against the Death Penalty* [Online] Available at: www.vatican.va [Accessed on: 21 May 2024]

all possible progress. For who is there, so envious of men, so full of hatred to God, who would seek to forbid it?' (*Commonitorium*, 23.1; PL 50). It is necessary, therefore, to reaffirm that no matter how serious the crime that has been committed, the death penalty is inadmissible because it is an attack on the inviolability and the dignity of the person.[3035]

New revision of number 2267 of the Catechism of the Catholic Church on the death penalty – Rescriptum 'ex Audientia SS.mi'. (2nd August 2018)

Recourse to the death penalty on the part of legitimate authority, following a fair trial, was long considered an appropriate response to the gravity of certain crimes and an acceptable, albeit extreme, means of safeguarding the common good. Today, however, there is an increasing awareness that the dignity of the person is not lost even after the commission of very serious crimes. In addition, a new understanding has emerged of the significance of penal sanctions imposed by the state. Lastly, more effective systems of detention have been developed, which ensure the due protection of citizens but, at the same time, do not definitively deprive the guilty of the possibility of redemption. Consequently, the Church teaches, in the light of the Gospel, that 'the death penalty is inadmissible because it is an attack on the inviolability and dignity of the person', and she works with determination for its abolition worldwide. (CCC 2267).[3036]

Letter to the Bishops regarding the new revision of number 2267 of the Catechism of the Catholic Church on the death penalty, 2, 3, 8, 9. (2nd August 2018)

It is in the same light that one should understand the attitude towards the death penalty that is expressed ever more widely in the teaching of pastors and in the sensibility of the people of God. If, in fact, the political and social situation of the past made the death penalty an acceptable means for the protection of the common good, today the increasing understanding that the dignity of a person is not lost even after committing the most serious crimes, the deepened understanding of the significance of penal sanctions applied by the State, and the development of more efficacious detention systems that guarantee the due protection of citizens have given rise to a new awareness that recognises the inadmissibility of the death penalty and, therefore, calling for its abolition [....] The new text, following the footsteps of the teaching of John Paul II in *Evangelium Vitæ*, affirms that ending the life of a criminal as punishment for a crime is inadmissible because it attacks the dignity of the person, a dignity that is not lost even after having committed the most serious crimes. This conclusion is reached taking into account the new understanding of penal sanctions applied by the modern State, which should be oriented above all to the rehabilitation and social reintegration of the criminal. Finally, given that modern society possesses more efficient detention systems, the death penalty becomes unnecessary as protection for the life of innocent people.

All of this shows that the new formulation of number 2267 of the *Catechism* expresses an authentic development of doctrine that is not in contradiction with the prior teachings of the Magisterium. These teachings, in fact, can be explained in the light of the primary responsibility of the public authority to protect the common good in a social context in which the penal sanctions were understood differently, and had developed in an environment in which it was more difficult to guarantee that the criminal could not repeat his crime. The new revision affirms that the understanding of the inadmissibility of the death penalty grew 'in the light of the Gospel.' The Gospel, in fact, helps to understand better the order of creation that the Son of God assumed, purified, and

---

[3035]Pope Francis [2017] *Address to Participants in the Meeting Promoted by the Pontifical Council for Promoting the New Evangelisation* [Online] Available at: www.vatican.va [Accessed on: 21 May 2024]

[3036]Congregation for the Doctrine of the Faith [2018] *New revision of number 2267 of the Catechism of the Catholic Church on the death penalty – Rescriptum 'ex Audentia SS.mi'* [Online] www.press.vatican.va [Accessed on: 16 May 2024]

brought to fulfilment. It also invites us to the mercy and patience of the Lord that gives to each person the time to convert oneself.[3037]

Audience with the Delegation of the International Commission against the Death Penalty. (17th December 2018)

The certainty that every life is sacred and that human dignity must be safeguarded without exception has led me, from the beginning of my ministry, to work at different levels for the universal abolition of the death penalty.

This was reflected recently in the new wording of no. 2267 of the *Catechism of the Catholic Church*, which now expresses the progress of the doctrine of the most recent Pontiffs as well as the change in the conscience of the Christian people, which rejects a penalty that seriously harms human dignity (cf. Address on the occasion of the 25th anniversary of the *Catechism of the Catholic Church*, 11 October 2017). It is a penalty contrary to the Gospel as it implies suppressing a life that is always sacred in the eyes of the Creator, and of which only God is the true judge and guarantor (see Letter to the President of the International Commission against the Death Penalty, 20 March 2015).

In past centuries, when the instruments available to us for the protection of society were lacking and the current level of development of human rights had not yet been achieved, recourse to the death penalty was sometimes presented as a logical and just consequence. Even in the Papal State, this inhuman form of punishment was resorted to, ignoring the primacy of mercy over justice.

That is why the new wording of the *Catechism* also implies taking responsibility for the past and recognising that the acceptance of this form of punishment was a consequence of a mentality of the time, more legalistic than Christian, that secularised the value of laws lacking in humanity and mercy. The Church cannot remain in a neutral position in the face of the current demands for the reaffirmation of personal dignity. The reform of the text of the *Catechism* in the point dedicated to the death penalty does not imply any contradiction with the teaching of the past, because the Church has always defended the dignity of human life. However, the harmonious development of the doctrine imposes the need to reflect in the *Catechism* that, notwithstanding the gravity of the crime committed, the Church teaches, in the light of the Gospel, that the death penalty is always inadmissible because it counters the inviolability and the dignity of the person.[3038]

Encyclical Fratelli Tutti, 263, 265-270. (3rd October 2020)

There is yet another way to eliminate others, one aimed not at countries but at individuals. It is the death penalty. St. John Paul II stated clearly and firmly that the death penalty is inadequate from a moral standpoint and no longer necessary from that of penal justice. There can be no stepping back from this position. Today we state clearly that 'the death penalty is inadmissible'[3039] and the Church is firmly committed to calling for its abolition worldwide [....]

From the earliest centuries of the Church, some were clearly opposed to capital punishment. Lactantius, for example, held that 'there ought to be no exception at all; that it is always unlawful to put a man to death'.[3040] Pope Nicholas I urged that efforts be made 'to free from the punishment of death not only each of the innocent, but all the guilty as well'.[3041] During the trial of the murderers of two priests, St. Augustine asked

---

[3037]Congregation for the Doctrine of the Faith [2018] *Letter to the Bishops regarding the new revision of number 2267 of the Catechism of the Catholic Church on the death penalty* [Online] Available at: www. press.vatican.va [Accessed on: 16 May 2024]

[3038]Pope Francis [2018] *Audience with the Delegation of the International Commission against the Death Penalty* [Online] Available at: www.vatican.va [Accessed on: 21 May 2024]

[3039]Address on the Twenty-fifth Anniversary of the Promulgation of the *Catechism of the Catholic Church* (11 October 2017): AAS 109 (2017), 1196.

[3040]*Divinae Institutiones* Bk. VI, 20, 17: PL 6, 708.

[3041]*Epistola* 97 (Responsa ad consulta Bulgarorum), 25: PL 119, 991.

the judge not to take the life of the assassins with this argument: 'We do not object to your depriving these wicked men of the freedom to commit further crimes. Our desire is rather that justice be satisfied without the taking of their lives or the maiming of their bodies in any part. And, at the same time, that by the coercive measures provided by the law, they be turned from their irrational fury to the calmness of men of sound mind, and from their evil deeds to some useful employment. This too is considered a condemnation, but who does not see that, when savage violence is restrained and remedies meant to produce repentance are provided, it should be considered a benefit rather than a mere punitive measure.... Do not let the atrocity of their sins feed a desire for vengeance, but desire instead to heal the wounds which those deeds have inflicted on their souls'.[3042]

Fear and resentment can easily lead to viewing punishment in a vindictive and even cruel way, rather than as part of a process of healing and reintegration into society. Nowadays, 'in some political sectors and certain media, public and private violence and revenge are incited, not only against those responsible for committing crimes, but also against those suspected, whether proven or not, of breaking the law.... There is at times a tendency to deliberately fabricate enemies: stereotyped figures who represent all the characteristics that society perceives or interprets as threatening. The mechanisms that form these images are the same that allowed the spread of racist ideas in their time'.[3043] This has made all the more dangerous the growing practice in some countries of resorting to preventive custody, imprisonment without trial and especially the death penalty.

Here I would stress that 'it is impossible to imagine that states today have no other means than capital punishment to protect the lives of other people from the unjust aggressor'. Particularly serious in this regard are so-called extrajudicial or extralegal executions, which are 'homicides deliberately committed by certain states and by their agents, often passed off as clashes with criminals or presented as the unintended consequences of the reasonable, necessary and proportionate use of force in applying the law'.[3044]

'The arguments against the death penalty are numerous and well-known. The Church has rightly called attention to several of these, such as the possibility of judicial error and the use made of such punishment by totalitarian and dictatorial regimes as a means of suppressing political dissidence or persecuting religious and cultural minorities, all victims whom the legislation of those regimes consider "delinquents". All Christians and people of good will are today called to work not only for the abolition of the death penalty, legal or illegal, in all its forms, but also to work for the improvement of prison conditions, out of respect for the human dignity of persons deprived of their freedom. I would link this to life imprisonment.... A life sentence is a secret death penalty'.[3045]

Let us keep in mind that 'not even a murderer loses his personal dignity, and God himself pledges to guarantee this'.[3046] The firm rejection of the death penalty shows to what extent it is possible to recognise the inalienable dignity of every human being and to accept that he or she has a place in this universe. If I do not deny that dignity to the worst of criminals, I will not deny it to anyone. I will give everyone the possibility of sharing this planet with me, despite all our differences.

I ask Christians who remain hesitant on this point, and those tempted to yield to violence in any form, to keep in mind the words of the book of Isaiah: 'They shall beat their swords into plowshares' (2:4). For us, this prophecy took flesh in Christ Jesus who, seeing a disciple tempted to violence, said firmly: 'Put your sword back into its place;

[3042]*Epistola ad Marcellinum* 133, 1.2: PL 33, 509.

[3043]Address to Delegates of the International Association of Penal Law (23 October 2014): *AAS* 106 (2014), 840-841.

[3044]*Ibid.*, 842.

[3045]*Ibid.*

[3046]St. John Paul II, Encyclical *Evangelium Vitae* (25 March 1995), 9: *AAS* 87 (1995), 411.

for all who take the sword will perish by the sword' (Mt 26:52). These words echoed the ancient warning: 'I will require a reckoning for human life. Whoever sheds the blood of a man, by man shall his blood be shed' (Gen 9:5-6). Jesus' reaction, which sprang from his heart, bridges the gap of the centuries and reaches the present as an enduring appeal.[3047]

Pope Francis' Prayer Intention for September 2022 — For the Abolition of the Death Penalty. (31st August 2022)

Each day, there is a growing 'NO' to the death penalty around the world. For the Church, this is a sign of hope. From a legal point of view, it is not necessary. Society can effectively repress crime without definitively depriving the offenders of the possibility of redeeming themselves. Always, in every legal sentence, there must be a window of hope. Capital punishment offers no justice to victims, but rather encourages revenge. And it prevents any possibility of undoing a possible miscarriage of justice. Additionally, the death penalty is morally inadmissible, for it destroys the most important gift we have received: life. Let us not forget that, up to the very last moment, a person can convert and change. And in the light of the Gospel, the death penalty is unacceptable. The commandment, 'Thou shalt not kill,' refers to both the innocent and the guilty. I, therefore, call on all people of goodwill to mobilise for the abolition of the death penalty throughout the world. Let us pray that the death penalty, which attacks the dignity of the human person, may be legally abolished in every country.[3048]

Question-and-Answer Session with Jesuits during Apostolic Journey for World Youth Day, Portugal. (5th August 2023)

Let us get to specifics. Today it is a sin to possess atomic bombs; the death penalty is a sin. You cannot employ it, but it was not so before. As for slavery, some pontiffs before me tolerated it, but things are different today. So you change, you change, but with the criteria just mentioned. I like to use the 'upward' image, that is, *ut annis consolidetur, dilatetur tempore, sublimetur aetate* [consolidated by years, enlarged by time and refined by age]. Always on this path, starting from the root with sap that flows up and up, and that is why change is necessary. Vincent of Lérins makes the comparison between human biological development and the transmission from one age to another of the *depositum fidei*, which grows and is consolidated with the passage of time. Here, our understanding of the human person changes with time, and our consciousness also deepens. The other sciences and their evolution also help the Church in this growth in understanding. The view of Church doctrine as monolithic is erroneous.[3049]

Declaration *Dignitas Infinita, 34. (8th April 2024)*

…one should also mention the death penalty, for this also violates the inalienable dignity of every person, regardless of the circumstances. In this regard, we must recognise that 'the firm rejection of the death penalty shows to what extent it is possible to recognise the inalienable dignity of every human being and to accept that he or she has a place in this universe. If I do not deny that dignity to the worst of criminals, I will not deny it to anyone. I will give everyone the possibility of sharing this planet with me, despite all our differences.'[3050]

[3047]Pope Francis [2017] Encyclical *Fratelli Tutti*, paras 263, 265-270 [Online] Available at: www.vatican.va [Accessed on: 21 May 2024]

[3048]Pope Francis [2022] *For the abolition of the death penalty — September 2022* [Available at: www.youtube.com [Accessed on: 21 May 2024]

[3049]Spadaro, A [2023] '*The Water Has Been Agitated*' [Online] Available at: www.laciviltacattolica.com [Accessed on: 21 May 2024]

[3050]Dicastery for the Doctrine of the Faith [2024] Declaration *Dignitas Infinita* [Online] Available at: www.press.vatican.va [Accessed on: 16 May 2024]

Sacred Scripture

Matthew 15:3-4
Why do you also transgress the commandment of God for your tradition? For God said: Honour thy father and mother: And: He that shall curse father or mother, let him die the death.

Matthew 22:7
But when the king had heard of it, he was angry, and sending his armies, he destroyed those murderers, and burnt their city.

Luke 19:27
But as for those my enemies, who would not have me reign over them, bring them hither, and kill them before me.

John 19:10-11
Pilate therefore saith to him: Speakest thou not to me? knowest thou not that I have power to crucify thee, and I have power to release thee? Jesus answered: Thou shouldst not have any power against me, unless it were given thee from above.

Acts of the Apostles 25:12
For if I have injured them, or have committed any thing worthy of death, I refuse not to die.

Apocalypse 21:8
But the fearful, and unbelieving, and the abominable, and murderers, and whoremongers, and sorcerers, and idolaters, and all liars, they shall have their portion in the pool burning with fire and brimstone, which is the second death.

Romans 13:3-5
For princes are not a terror to the good work, but to the evil. Wilt thou then not be afraid of the power? Do that which is good: and thou shalt have praise from the same. For he is God's minister to thee, for good. But if thou do that which is evil, fear: for he beareth not the sword in vain. For he is God's minister: an avenger to execute wrath upon him that doth evil. Wherefore be subject of necessity, not only for wrath, but also for conscience' sake.

Hebrews 10:28
A man making void the law of Moses, dieth without any mercy under two or three witnesses....

Genesis 6:5-7
And God seeing that the wickedness of men was great on the earth, and that all the thought of their heart was bent upon evil at all times, It repented him that he had made man on the earth. And being touched inwardly with sorrow of heart, He said: I will destroy man, whom I have created, from the face of the earth, from man even to beasts, from the creeping thing even to the fowls of the air, for it repenteth me that I have made them.

Genesis 19: 20, 24-25
And the Lord said: The cry of Sodom and Gomorrha is multiplied, and their sin is become exceedingly grievous. I will go down and see whether they have done according to the cry that is come to me: or whether it be not so, that I may know [....] And the Lord rained upon Sodom and Gomorrha brimstone and fire from the Lord out of heaven. And he destroyed these cities, and all the country about, all the inhabitants of the cities, and all things that spring from the earth.

Genesis 9:6
Whosoever shall shed man's blood, his blood shall be shed: for man was made to the image of God.

Exodus 21:12; 14-17
He that striketh a man with a will to kill him, shall be put to death.

He that shall steal a man, and sell him, being convicted of guilt, shall be put to death. He that curseth his father, or mother, shall die the death. If a man kill his neighbour on set purpose and by lying in wait for him: thou shalt take him away from my altar, that he may die. He that striketh his father or mother, shall be put to death.

Deuteronomy 17: 2-7
When there shall be found among you within any of thy gates, which the Lord thy God shall give thee, man or woman that do evil in the sight of the Lord thy God, and transgress his covenant, So as to go and serve strange gods, and adore them, the sun and the moon. and all the host of heaven, which I have not commanded: And this is told thee, and hearing it thou hast inquired diligently, and found it to be true, and that the abomination is committed in Israel: Thou shalt bring forth the man or the woman, who have committed that most wicked thing, to the gates of thy city, and they shall be stoned. By the mouth of two or three witnesses shall he die that is to be slain. Let no man be put to death, when only one beareth witness against him. The hands of the witnesses shall be first upon him to kill him, and afterwards the hands of the rest of the people: that thou mayst take away the evil out of the midst of thee.

Deuteronomy 21:18-23
If a man have a stubborn and unruly son, who will not hear the commandments of his father or mother, and being corrected, slighteth obedience: They shall take him and bring him to the ancients of his city, and to the gate of judgment, And shall say to them: This our son is rebellious and stubborn, he slighteth hearing our admonitions, he giveth himself to revelling, and to debauchery and banquetings: The people of the city shall stone him: and he shall die, that you may take away the evil out of the midst of you, and all Israel hearing it may be afraid. When a man hath committed a crime for which he is to be punished with death, and being condemned to die is hanged on a gibbet: His body shall not remain upon the tree, but shall be buried the same day: for he is accursed of God that hangeth on a tree: and thou shalt not defile thy land, which the Lord thy God shall give thee in possession.

Leviticus 20: 7-16, 26
Sanctify yourselves, and be ye holy because I am the Lord your God. Keep my precepts, and do them. I am the Lord that sanctify you. He that curseth his father, or mother, dying let him die: he hath cursed his father, and mother, let his blood be upon him. If any man commit adultery with the wife of another, and defile his neighbour's wife, let them be put to death, both the adulterer and the adulteress. If a man lie with his stepmother, and discover the nakedness of his father, let them both be put to death: their blood be upon them. If any man lie with his daughter in law, let both die, because they have done a heinous crime: their blood be upon them. If any one lie with a man as with a woman, both have committed an abomination, let them be put to death: their blood be upon them. If any man after marrying the daughter, marry her mother, he hath done a heinous crime: he shall be burnt alive with them: neither shall so great an abomination remain in the midst of you. He that shall copulate with any beast or cattle, dying let him die, the beast also ye shall kill. The woman that shall lie under any beast, shall be killed together with the same: their blood be upon them [....] You shall be holy unto me, because I the Lord am holy, and I have separated you from other people, that you should be mine.

Leviticus 24:11-17
And when he had blasphemed the name, and had cursed it, he was brought to Moses: (now his mother was called Salumith, the daughter of Dabri, of the tribe of Dan:) And they put him into prison, till they might know what the Lord would command. And the Lord spoke to Moses, Saying: Bring forth the blasphemer without the camp, and let them that heard him, put their hands upon his head, and let all the people stone

him. And thou shalt speak to the children of Israel: the man that curseth his God, shall bear his sin: And he that blasphemeth the name of the Lord, dying let him die: all the multitude shall stone him, whether he be a native or a stranger. He that blasphemeth the name of the Lord, dying let him die. He that striketh and killeth a man, dying let him die.

Sacred Tradition

St. Irenaeus: c. 130 to c. 202

Against Heresies, Bk. IV, Chap. 36, Para 6
This is the Father of our Lord, by whose providence all things consist, and all are administered by His command; and He confers His free gifts upon those who should [receive them]; but the most righteous Retributor metes out [punishment] according to their deserts, most deservedly, to the ungrateful and to those that are insensible of His kindness; and therefore does He say, 'He sent His armies, and destroyed those murderers, and burned up their city.' [Mt 22:7] [....] Wherefore also the Apostle Paul says in the Epistle to the Romans, 'For there is no power but of God; the powers that be are ordained of God. Whosoever resisteth the power, resisteth the ordinance of God; and they that resist shall receive unto themselves condemnation. For rulers are not for a terror to a good work, but to an evil. Wilt thou then not be afraid of the power? Do that which is good, and thou shalt have praise of the same; for he is the minister of God to thee for good. But if thou do that which is evil, be afraid; for he beareth not the sword in vain: for he is the minister of God, the avenger for wrath upon him that doeth evil. Wherefore ye must needs be subject, not only for wrath, but also for conscience sake. For this cause pay ye tribute also; for they are God's ministers, attending continually upon this very thing.' [Rm 13:1-7].[3051]

Origen: c. 184 to c. 253

Commentary on the Gospel of Matthew, Bk. XI, Chap. 9
Jesus, however, does not accuse them with reference to a tradition of the Jewish elders, but with regard to two most imperative commandments of God, the one of which was the fifth in the decalogue, being as follows: 'Honour your father and your mother, that it may be well with you, and that your days may be long on the land which the Lord your God gives you;' Exodus 20:12 and the other was written thus in Leviticus, 'If a man speak evil of his father or his mother, let him die the death; he has spoken evil of his father or mother, he shall be guilty.' Leviticus 20:9.[3052]

St. Cyprian of Carthage: c. 200 to 258

Epistle 72, 19
…Christ Himself lays down in the Gospel, and says, 'He that curseth father or mother, let him die the death'…[he] bids that those who curse their parents after the flesh should be punished and slain.…[3053]

St. Augustine: 354 to 430

Contra Faustum, Bk. XVI, Chap. 24; Bk. XXII, Chap. 14
For when the Jews blamed His disciples for eating with unwashen hands, in which they transgressed not a commandment of God, but the traditions of the elders, Christ said, 'Why do ye also transgress the commandment of God, that ye may observe your traditions?' He then quotes a commandment of God, which we know to have been given by Moses. 'For God said,' He adds, 'Honor thy father and mother, and he that

[3051]St. Irenaeus. *Against Heresies*, Bk. IV, Chap. 36, Para 6 [Online] Available at: www.newadvent.org [Accessed on: 23 May 2024]

[3052]Origen. *Commentary on the Gospel of Matthew*, Bk. XI, Chap. 9 [Online] Available at: www.newadvent.org [Accessed on: 23 May 2024]

[3053]St. Cyprian of Carthage. *Epistle* 72, To Jubaianus, Concerning the Baptism of Heretics, para 19 [Available at] www.newadvent.org [Accessed on: 23 May 2024]

curseth father or mother shall die the death…From this several things maybe learned: that Christ did not turn away the Jews from their God; that He not only did not Himself break God's commandments, but found fault with those who did so; and that it was God Himself who gave these commandments by Moses.

…not wishing to have Christ for a king, which is the sin of which Christ says, 'Those that would not have me to reign over them, bring hither and slay before me;'… Faustus blames God in the Old Testament for slaughtering thousands of human beings for slight offences, as Faustus calls them, or for nothing [….] Faustus finds fault with God's threatening to come with the sword, and to spare neither the righteous nor the wicked.[3054]

The City of God, Bk. I, Chap. 21

…there are some exceptions made by the divine authority to its own law, that men may not be put to death. These exceptions are of two kinds, being justified either by a general law, or by a special commission granted for a time to some individual. And in this latter case, he to whom authority is delegated, and who is but the sword in the hand of him who uses it, is not himself responsible for the death he deals. And, accordingly, they who have waged war in obedience to the divine command, or in conformity with His laws, have represented in their persons the public justice or the wisdom of government, and in this capacity have put to death wicked men; such persons have by no means violated the commandment, 'You shall not kill.' […] With the exception, then, of these two classes of cases, which are justified either by a just law that applies generally, or by a special intimation from God Himself, the fountain of all justice, whoever kills a man, either himself or another, is implicated in the guilt of murder.[3055]

On the Sermon on the Mount, Bk. I, Chap. 20

But great and holy men, although they at the time knew excellently well that that death which separates the soul from the body is not to be dreaded, yet, in accordance with the sentiment of those who might fear it, punished some sins with death, both because the living were struck with a salutary fear, and because it was not death itself that would injure those who were being punished with death, but sin, which might be increased if they continued to live. They did not judge rashly on whom God had bestowed such a power of judging. Hence it is that Elijah inflicted death on many, both with his own hand and by calling down fire from heaven; as was done also without rashness by many other great and godlike men, in the same spirit of concern for the good of humanity.[3056]

St. John Chrysostom: c. 347 to 407

Homily 23 on Romans 13:4-7

'For he bears not the sword in vain.' You see how he has furnished him with arms, and set him on guard like a soldier, for a terror to those that commit sin. 'For he is the minister of God to execute wrath, a revenger upon him that does evil.' Now lest you should start off at hearing again of punishment, and vengeance, and a sword, he says again that it is God's law he is carrying out. For what if he does not know it himself? Yet it is God that has so shaped things (οὕτως ἐτύπωσεν). If then, whether in punishing, or in honoring, he be a Minister, in avenging virtue's cause, in driving vice away, as God wills, why be captious against him, when he is the cause of so many good doings, and paves the way for yours too? Since there are many who first practised virtue through the fear of God. For there are a duller sort, whom things to come have not such a hold upon as things present. He then who by fear and rewards gives the soul of the majority

---

[3054]St. Augustine. *Contra Faustum*, Bk. XVI, Chap. 24; Bk. XXII, Chap. 14 [Online] Available at: www.newadvent.org [Accessed on: 23 May 2024]

[3055]St. Augustine. *The City of God*, Bk. I, Chap. 21 [Online] Available at: www.newadvent.org [Accessed on: 23 May 2024]

[3056]St. Augustine. *On the Sermon on the Mount*, Bk. I, Chap. 20 [Online] Available at: www. newadvent.org [Accessed on: 23 May 2024]

a preparatory turn towards its becoming more suited for the word of doctrine, is with good reason called 'the Minister of God.'[3057]

St. Thomas Aquinas: 1225 to 1274

Summa Contra Gentiles, Bk. III, Chaps. 144 & 146

Natural equity would seem to demand that everyone be deprived of that good against which he has acted, since by this he renders himself unworthy of that good. Hence it is that, according to civil justice, he who sins against the state is altogether deprived of the society of his fellow citizens, either by being put to death, or by being condemned to exile for life [....]

As the physician in his operation aims at health, consisting in the ordered harmony of the humors, so the governor of a state in his operation aims at peace, which is the ordered harmony of the citizens. Now, the surgeon rightly and usefully cuts off the unhealthy member if it threatens the health of the body. Justly, therefore, and rightly the governor of the state slays pestilential subjects, lest the peace of the state be disturbed. Hence the Apostle says: Do you not know that a little leaven corrupts the whole lump? (I Cor 5:6). And a little further on he adds: Drive out the wicked person from among you (I Cor 5:13). Again, speaking of earthly authority, he says that he does not bear the sword in vain; he is the servant of God to execute his wrath on the wrongdoer (Rom 13:4). Again, it is said: Be subject for the Lord's sake to every human institution, whether it be to the king as supreme, or to governors as sent by him to punish those who do wrong and to praise those who do right (I Pet 2:13–14).

Hereby we refute the error of those who say that capital punishment is unlawful. They base their error on the words of Exodus 20:13, You shall not kill, which are quoted in Matthew 5:21. They also quote the saying of our Lord in reply to the servants who wished to gather the cockle from the midst of the wheat: Let both grow together until the harvest (Mt 13:30): for the cockle signifies the sons of the evil one, and the harvest is the close of the age, as stated in the same passage (Mt 13:38–39). Therefore, the wicked should not be cut off from the midst of the good by being condemned to death. They also point out that as long as he is on earth man may be converted to better ways. Therefore, he should not be put away from the world, but should be kept there that he may repent.

But these arguments are of no account. For the same law that says: You shall not kill, afterwards adds: You shall not permit wizards to live (Ex 22:18). Hence we are to understand that the prohibition is against the unjust slaying of a man. This is also evident from our Lord's words in Matt 5. For after saying: You have heard that it was said to the men of old: You shall not kill, he added: I say to you that every one who is angry with his brother shall be liable to judgment (Mt 5:22). By which he gives us to understand that it is forbidden to kill through anger, but not through zeal for righteousness. How we ought to take our Lord's words: Let both grow together until the harvest, is clear from what follows: Lest in gathering the cockle you root up the wheat along with it (Mt 13:30). Hence it is forbidden to slay the wicked when this cannot be done without danger to the good. And this is often the case when the wicked are not yet discernible from the good by notorious sins, or when it is to be feared lest the wicked draw many good men after them.

The fact that the wicked are able to amend while alive does not prevent their being justly slain, for the peril that threatens through their remaining alive is greater and more certain than the good to be expected from their amendment. Moreover, in the very hour of death they are able to repent and be converted to God. And if they be so obstinate that even in the hour of death their heart does not abandon its wickedness, it may be reckoned with sufficient probability that they will never recover from their evil ways.[3058]

[3057]St. John Chrysostom. *Homily 23 on Romans* 13:4-7 [Online] www.newadvent.org [Accessed on: 28 August 2028]

[3058]St. Thomas Aquinas. *Summa Contra Gentiles*, Bk. III, Chaps. 144 & 146 [Available at: www.aquinas.cc [Accessed on: 23 May 2024]

Summa Theologiae, Secunda Secundæ Partis, Q 64, a. 2, a.3
…we observe that if the health of the whole body demands the excision of a member, through its being decayed or infectious to the other members, it will be both praiseworthy and advantageous to have it cut away. Now every individual person is compared to the whole community, as part to whole. Therefore if a man be dangerous and infectious to the community, on account of some sin, it is praiseworthy and advantageous that he be killed in order to safeguard the common good, since 'a little leaven corrupteth the whole lump' (I Cor 5:6) [....]

…it is lawful to kill an evildoer in so far as it is directed to the welfare of the whole community, so that it belongs to him alone who has charge of the community's welfare. Thus it belongs to a physician to cut off a decayed limb, when he has been entrusted with the care of the health of the whole body. Now the care of the common good is entrusted to persons of rank having public authority: wherefore they alone, and not private individuals, can lawfully put evildoers to death.[3059]

The Magisterium of the Church

Divine revelation confirms that God gives those holding legitimate civl authority the power of 'the sword' to inflict capital punishment on the wrong-doer (Rm 13:4). By divine decree the State is the legitimate avenger of crime through applying the death penalty to punish the wicked and protect the innocent, with the emphasis on punishing the wicked. The just use of the death penalty is not murder but an act of paramount obedience to the Commandment which prohibits murder. The condemned person is deprived of life in expiation of his crime when, by his crime, he has already disposed himself of his right to live. The Church's upholding of divine revelation concerning the death penalty has a general and abiding validity, and is not historically, culturally conditioned.

First Vatican Council (Twentieth Ecumenical, 1869 to 1870)

Dogmatic Constitution, *Dei Filius, Chap. 1. (24th April 1870)*
It is to be ascribed to this divine revelation that such truths among things divine that of themselves are not beyond human reason can, even in the present condition of mankind, be known by everyone with facility, with firm c ertitude, a nd w ith n o a dmixture of error.[3060]

Second Vatican Council (Twenty-First Ecumenical, 1962 to 1965)

Dogmatic Constitution, *Dei Verbum, Chap. 1, para 6; Chap. 6, para 21. (18th November 1965)*
Through divine revelation, God chose to show forth and communicate Himself and the eternal decisions of His will regarding the salvation of men. That is to say, He chose to share with them those divine treasures which totally transcend the understanding of the human mind. As a sacred synod has affirmed, God, the beginning and end of all things, can be known with certainty from created reality by the light of human reason (see Rom. 1:20); but teaches that it is through His revelation that those religious truths which are by their nature accessible to human reason can be known by all men with ease, with solid certitude and with no trace of error, even in this present state of the human race.

The Church has always venerated the divine Scriptures just as she venerates the body of the Lord, since, especially in the sacred liturgy, she unceasingly receives and offers to the faithful the bread of life from the table both of God's word and of Christ's body. She has always maintained them, and continues to do so, together with sacred tradition, as the supreme rule of faith, since, as inspired by God and committed once and for all to writing, they impart the word of God Himself without change, and make the voice of the Holy Spirit resound in the words of the prophets and Apostles. There-

---

[3059]St. Thomas Aquinas. *Summa Theologiae, Secunda Secundæ Partis,* Q 64, a. 2, a.3 [Available at: www.newadvent.org [Accessed on: 27 May 2024]
[3060]Denzinger, H [2010] *op. cit.,* p. 602 3005

fore, like the Christian religion itself, all the preaching of the Church must be nourished and regulated by Sacred Scripture. For in the sacred books, the Father who is in heaven meets His children with great love and speaks with them; and the force and power in the word of God is so great that it stands as the support and energy of the Church, the strength of faith for her sons, the food of the soul, the pure and everlasting source of spiritual life. Consequently these words are perfectly applicable to Sacred Scripture: 'For the word of God is living and active' (Heb. 4:12) and 'it has power to build you up and give you your heritage among all those who are sanctified' (Acts 20:32; see I Thess 2:13).[3061]

Pope St. John Paul II: 1978 to 2005
Catechism of the Catholic Church. (1992)
Preserving the common good of society requires rendering the aggressor unable to inflict harm. For this reason the traditional teaching of the Church has acknowledged as well-founded the right and duty of legitimate public authority to punish malefactors by means of punishments commensurate with the gravity of the crime, not excluding, in cases of extreme gravity, the death penalty. The primary effect of *punishment* is to redress the disorder caused by the offence. (2266).

Catechism of the Catholic Church, Second Edition. (1994)
Assuming that the guilty party's identity and responsibil¬ity have been fully determined, the traditional teaching of the Church does not exclude recourse to the death penalty, if this is the only possible way of effectively defending human lives against the unjust aggressor. If, however, non-lethal means are sufficient to defend and protect people's safety from the aggressor, authority will limit itself to such means, as these are more in keeping with the concrete conditions of the common good and more in conformity with the dignity of the human person.

Today, in fact, as a consequence of the possibilities which the state has for effectively preventing crime, by rendering one who has committed an offence incapable of doing harm — without definitively taking away from him the possibility of redeeming himself — the cases in which the execution of the offender is an absolute necessity 'are very rare, if not practically non-existent.' (2267)

Congregation for the Doctrine of the Faith. Worthiness to Receive Holy Communion: General Principles, 3. (July 2004)
Not all moral issues have the same moral weight as abortion and euthanasia. For example, if a Catholic were to be at odds with the Holy Father on the application of capital punishment or on the decision to wage war, he would not for that reason be considered unworthy to present himself to receive Holy Communion. While the Church exhorts civil authorities to seek peace, not war, and to exercise discretion and mercy in imposing punishment on criminals, it may still be permissible to take up arms to repel an aggressor or to have recourse to capital punishment. There may be a legitimate diversity of opinion even among Catholics about waging war and applying the death penalty, but not however with regard to abortion and euthanasia.[3062]

Pope Ven. Pius XII: 1939 to 1958
Encyclical *Humani Generis (12th August 1950)*
…divine 'revelation' must be considered morally necessary so that those religious and moral truths that are not of their nature beyond the reach of reason in the present condition of the human race may be known by all men readily with a firm certainty and freedom from all error.[3063]

[3061]Second Vatican Council [1965] Dogmatic Constitution, *Dei Verbum*, Chap. 1, para 6, Chap. 6, para 21 [Available at: www.vatican.va [Accessed on: 29 May 2024]
[3062]Ratzinger, J [2004] Worthiness to Receive Holy Communion: General Principles [Available at: wwww.EWTN.com [Accessed on: 28 May 2024]
[3063]Denzinger, H [2010] *op. cit.*, p. 800 *Dz* 3876

Address to the First International Congress on the Histopathology of the Nervous System. (14th September 1952)
Even when it is a question of the execution of a condemned man, the State does not dispose of the individual's right to life. In this case it is reserved to the public power to deprive the condemned person of the of life in expiation of his crime when, by his crime, he has already disposed himself of his right to live.[3064]

Address to the Sixth International Congress of Penal Law. (3rd October 1953)
These reflections help to a better appreciation of another age, which some regard as outmoded, which distinguished between medicinal punishment — *poenae medicinales* — and vindicative punishment — *poenae vindicativae.* In vindicative punishment the function of expiation is to the fore; the function of protection is comprised in both types of punishment. Canon Law, as you know, still maintains the distinction, which attitude is founded on the convictions already detailed. Only it gives full meaning to the well known word of the Apostle in the Epistle to the Romans: '*Non enim sine causa gladium portat; ...vindex in iram ei qui malum agit.*' (Rom 13:4). 'It is not for nothing that he bears the Sword: he is God's minister still, to inflict punishment on the wrong-doer.' Here it is expiation which is brought out.

Finally, it is only the expiatory function which gives the key to the last judgment of the Creator Himself, Who 'renders to everyone according to his works,' as both Testaments often repeat (cf. especially Mt 16:27; Rom 2:6). The function of protection disappears completely in the afterlife. The Omnipotent and All-Knowing Creator can always prevent the repetition of a crime by the interior moral conversion of the delinquent. But the supreme Judge, in His last judgment, applies uniquely the principle of retribution. This, then, must be of great importance.[3065]

Address to the Union of Italian Catholic Jurists. (5th February 1955)
In Our discourse of 3rd October, 1953, to the Sixth International Congress of Penal Law (*Discorsi e Radio messaggi*, Vol. XV, p. 352), and also on the present occasion (*Osservatore Romano*, 6th-7th December, 1954), we called attention to the fact that many, perhaps the majority, of civil jurists reject vindictive punishment; We noted, however, that perhaps the considerations and arguments adduced as proof were being given a greater importance and force than they have in fact. We also pointed out that the Church in her theory and practice has maintained this double type of penalty (medicinal and vindictive), and that this is more in agreement with what the sources of revelation and traditional doctrine teach regarding the coercive power of legitimate human authority. It is not a sufficient reply to this assertion to say that the aforementioned sources contain only thoughts which correspond to the historic circumstances and to the culture of the time, and that a general and abiding validity cannot therefore be attributed to them. The reason is that the words of the sources and of the living teaching power do not refer to the specific content of individual juridical prescriptions or rules of action (cf. particularly Ep. to the Romans 13:4), but rather to the essential foundation itself of penal power and of its immanent finality. This in turn is as little determined by the conditions of time and culture as the nature of man and the human society decreed by nature itself. But, whatever the attitude of positive human law on this problem, it is sufficient for Our present purpose to make clear that in any total or partial remission of punishment, the vindictive penalties (no less than the medicinal) can, and even should, be taken into consideration.[3066]

[3064]Guernsey, A [2017] *Addresses of Pius XII on the Law, Purposes of Punishment, and the Death Penalty* [Available at: www.aguernz.medium.com [Accessed on: 28 May 2024]
[3065]*Op. cit.*
[3066]*Ibid.*

Pope St. Pius X: 1903 to 1914

Catechism of Pope St. Pius X. (1908)
The Fifth Commandment
Q. Are there cases in which it is lawful to kill?
A. It is lawful to kill when fighting in a just war; when carrying out by order of the Supreme Authority a sentence of death in punishment of a crime; and, finally, in cases of necessary and lawful defence of one's own life against an unjust aggressor.[3067]

Pope St. Pius V: 1566 to 1572

The Roman Catechism: The Catechism of the Council of Trent. (1556)
Baptism Does Not Exempt From Penalties Of The Civil Law. Although the remission by Baptism of the punishments due to sin cannot be questioned, we are not to infer that it exempts an offender from the punishments decreed by civil tribunals for some grave crime. Thus a person sentenced to death is not rescued by Baptism from the penalty ordained by the law. We cannot, however, too highly commend the religion and piety of those rulers who remit the sentence of the law, that the glory of God may be the more strikingly displayed in His Sacraments.

Another kind of lawful slaying belongs to the civil authorities, to whom is entrusted power of life and death, by the legal and judicious exercise of which they punish the guilty and protect the innocent. The just use of this power, far from involving the crime of murder, is an act of paramount obedience to this Commandment which prohibits murder. The end of the Commandment¬ is the preservation and security of human life. Now the punishments inflicted by the civil authority, which is the legitimate avenger of crime, naturally tend to this end, since they give security to life by repressing outrage and violence. Hence these words of David: In the morning I put to death all the wicked of the land, that I might cut off all the workers of iniquity from the city of the Lord.[3068]

Pope Innocent III: 1198 to 1216

Letter *Eius exemplo to the Archbishop of Tarragona. (18th December 1208)*
With regard to the secular power, we affirm that it can exercise a judgment of blood without mortal sin provided that in carrying out the punishment it proceeds, not out of hatred, but judiciously, not in a precipitous manner, but with caution.[3069]

Pope St. Innocent I: 401 to 417

Letter *to the Bishop of Toulouse. (20th February 405)*
About these things we read nothing definitive from the forefathers. For they had remembered that these powers [of judging a man on capital offences and in application of the death penalty] had been granted by God and that for the sake of punishing harm-doers the sword has been allowed; in this way a minister of God, an avenger, has been given. How therefore would they criticise something which they see to have been granted to the authority of God. About these matters therefore, we hold to what has been observed hitherto, lest we may seem either to overturn sound order or to go against the authority of the Lord.[3070]

[3067]*Catechism of St. Pius X* [1908] [Online] Available at: www.ewtn.com [Accessed on: 28 May 2024]
[3068]Pope St. Pius V [1556] The Roman Catechism: *The Catechism of the Council of Trent*, The Sacraments: The Sacrament of Baptism; The Fifth Commandment: Execution Of Criminals [Online] Available at: http://www.clerus.org [Accessed on: 28 May 2024]
[3069]Denzinger, H [2010] *op. cit.,* p.264 *Dz* 795
[3070]Brugger, E [2003] *Capital Punishment and Roman Catholic Moral Tradition. Notre Dame,* Indiana: University of Notre Dame Press, p.89

Morality (3) — Homosexuality

Pope Francis: 2013 to 2025

N. *The tendency to homosexuality is not a problem. God created individuals to be homosexuals and loves them as homosexuals. It does not matter how a homosexual lives their life, they 'do not lose' their 'dignity.' The Old Testament account of the sin of Sodom is not about homosexual sex acts but concerns the sin of being inhospitable and hostile towards the stranger. The archaic, historically conditioned Biblical texts on homosexuality should be interpreted with the help of modern science.*

In-flight press conference on return from World Youth Day. (29th July 2013)
When I meet a gay person, I have to distinguish between their being gay and being part of a lobby. If they accept the Lord and have goodwill, who am I to judge them? They shouldn't be marginalized. The tendency [to homosexuality] is not the problem ... they're our brothers.[3071]

Interview with Fr. Antonio Spadaro SJ. (30th September 2013)
A person once asked me, in a provocative manner, if I approved of homosexuality. I replied with another question: 'Tell me: when God looks at a gay person, does he endorse the existence of this person with love, or reject and condemn this person?'[3072]

In-flight press conference on return from Apostolic Visit to Armenia. (26th June 2016)
I think that the Church not only should apologise ... to a gay person whom it offended....[3073]

Reported comments to Juan Carlos Cruz, who is openly homosexual. (21st May 2018)
Juan Carlos, that you are gay doesn't matter. God made you like this and loves you like this and it doesn't matter to me. The pope loves you like this, you have to be happy with who you are.[3074]
[*Pope Francis did not repudiate, contradict or demand a retraction of Juan Carlos Cruz's account of their conversation*]

Pope Francis' response to Stephen K. Amos when he admits he's a 'gay' man, broadcast on the BBC2 show Pilgrimage: The Road To Rome. (20th April 2019)
We are all human beings and have dignity. It does not matter who you are or how you live your life, you do not lose your dignity.[3075]

Pontifical Biblical Commission. What is Man? An Itinerary of Biblical Anthropology. Chap. 3. The Human Family — Homosexuality. (December 2019)
(*This report published by the CDF's Pontifical Biblical Commission was requested by Pope Francis*)[3076]
    For some time now, particularly in Western culture, voices of dissent have been heard about the anthropological approach of Scripture, as it is understood and transmitted by the Church in its normative aspects; in fact, all this is judged as simply reflecting an archaic, historically-conditioned mentality. We know that many biblical statements, in the fields of cosmology, biology, and sociology, have gradually been considered out-

[3071]Allen, J [2013] *Pope on homosexuals: 'Who am I to judge?'* [Online] Available at: www.ncronline.org [Accessed on: 19 August 2022]

[3072]Spadaro, A [2013] *A Big Heart Open to God: An interview with Pope Francis* [Online] Available at: www.americamagazine.org [Accessed on: 8 October 2022]

[3073]Pullella, P [2016] *Pope says Church should ask forgiveness from gays for past treatment* [Online] Available at: www.reuters.com [Accessed on: 8 October 2022]

[3074]San Martín, I [2018] *Abuse victim says Pope Francis told him 'being gay doesn't matter'.* [Online] Available at: cruxnow.com [Accessed on: 19 August 2022]

[3075]Collins, C [2019] *Pope Francis tells gay man 'you do not lose your dignity' on BBC show.* [Online] Available at: cruxnow.com [Accessed on: 19 August 2022]

[3076]*Vatican News* [2019] *Pontifical Biblical Commission examines question: What is man?* [Online] Available at: www.vaticannews.va [Accessed on: 19 August 2022]

dated with the progressive establishment of the natural and human sciences. Similarly — some people conclude — a new and more adequate understanding of the human person calls for a radical qualification of the exclusive value of the heterosexual union, in favor of a similar acceptance of homosexuality and homosexual unions as a legitimate and worthy expression of the human being. Moreover — it is sometimes argued — the Bible says little or nothing about this type of erotic relationship, which is therefore not condemned, because it is often unduly confused with other aberrant sexual behaviours. It therefore seems necessary to examine the passages of Sacred Scripture in which the problem of homosexuality is discussed, in particular those in which it is denounced and blamed. [...]

It should be immediately noted that the Bible does not speak of an erotic inclination towards a person of the same sex, but only of homosexual acts. And it deals with these in a few texts, which differ from each other in terms of literary genre and importance. As far as the Old Testament is concerned, we have two accounts (Gen 19 and Judg 19) that improperly evoke this aspect, and then some norms in a legislative Code (Lev 18:22 and 20:13) that condemn homosexual relations.

[The city of Sodom] is blamed for a disgraceful sexual practice, called 'sodomy,' consisting in the erotic relationship with people of the same sex. This would seem to have, at first glance, clear support in the biblical account. In Genesis 19 it is said, in fact, that two 'angels' hosted for the night in the house of Lot, are besieged by the 'men of Sodom,' young and old, all the population at large, with the intention of sexually abusing these strangers. The Hebrew verb used here is 'to know,' a euphemism to indicate sexual relations, as confirmed by the proposal of Lot, who, in order to protect his guests, is willing to sacrifice his two daughters who 'have not known man.' [...]

The story, however, is not intended to present the image of an entire city dominated by irrepressible homosexual cravings; rather, it denounces the conduct of a social and political entity that does not want to welcome the foreigner with respect, and therefore claims to humiliate him, forcing him to undergo an infamous treatment of submission.

This way of reading the story of Sodom is confirmed by Wisdom (19:13–17), where the exemplary punishment of sinners (first Sodom and then Egypt) is motivated by the fact that they had shown a deep hatred towards the foreigner.

We must therefore say that the story about the city of Sodom (as well as that of Gabaa) illustrates a sin that consists in the lack of hospitality, with hostility and violence towards the stranger, a behavior judged very serious and therefore deserving to be sanctioned with the utmost severity, because the rejection of the different, of the needy and defenceless stranger, is a principle of social disintegration, having in itself a deadly violence that deserves an adequate punishment [...]

We do not find in the narrative tradition of the Bible indications concerning homosexual practices, either as behaviours to be faulted or as attitudes tolerated or welcomed. Friendship between people of the same sex (like David and Jonathan, exalted in II Sam 1:26) cannot be considered a sign in favor of the recognition of homosexuality in Israelite society. The prophetic traditions do not mention practices of this nature, neither among the people of God, nor among the pagan nations; and this silence contrasts with the attestations of Leviticus 18:3-5, 24-30 that are attributed to the Egyptians, to the Canaanites, and in general to the non-Israelites as unacceptable sexual behaviours, including homosexual rape. This indicates, as we shall see, a negative evaluation of this practice. [...]

In conclusion, our exegetical examination of the texts of the Old and of the New Testaments has brought to light elements that must be considered for an evaluation of homosexuality in its ethical implications. Certain formulations of biblical authors, as well as the disciplinary directives of Leviticus, require an intelligent interpretation that safeguards the values that the sacred text intends to promote, thus avoiding repetition to the letter that which carries with it cultural traits of that time. The contribution provided by science, together with the reflections of theologians and moralists, will be indispensable for an adequate exposition of the problem that is only sketched out in this Document. In addition, pastoral care will be required, particularly with regard to individual persons, in order to realise the service to the good that the Church has to assume in her mission for mankind.[3077]

General Audience Address, including message to parents of LGBT children. (18th September 2020)
God loves your children as they are. The Pope loves your children as they are, because they are children of God.[3078]

Comments in documentary film Francesco. *(22nd October 2020)*
Homosexual people have a right to be in a family. They are children of God and have a right to a family. Nobody should be thrown out or be made miserable over it.[3079]

In-flight press conference on return from Apostolic Visit to Slovakia. (15th September 2021)
But if they want to support a homosexual couple in life together, states have the possibility of civilly supporting them, of giving security through inheritance, health [insurance]. But the French have a law on this not only for homosexuals, but for all people who want to associate with each other [in a legally recognized relationship].[3080]

Cardinal Jean-Claude Hollerich SJ's interview with Richard Smaglick, Holy Child Jesus parish, Chicago, Illinois. (31st July 2022)
[*Pope Francis did not repudiate, contradict or demand a retraction of Cardinal Jean-Claude Hollerich's claims about his personal views on homosexuality*]
  Cardinal Hollerich SJ, the relator general of the 2023 synod, claimed that his erroneous views on homosexuality were 'in full agreement with Pope Francis'. When asked 'After the synod do you believe sodomy should be considered a grave sin?' Cardinal Hollerich responded, 'I think that first of all, I would never consider sexuality separated from love.' In response to the statement, 'The Bible has taught and the Church has taught for 2,000 years that sodomy is a sin, an abomination that cries out to heaven', Cardinal Hollerich replied, 'But the Bible also said we should stone the woman who is adulterous. The Bible has said that the sun turns around the earth. So, the Bible is … [we] have to give an interpretation to the Bible.' When challenged, 'So the fundamental scriptural teaching on sin is being changed? Cardinal Hollerich replied, 'I know that I am in full agreement with Pope Francis'.[3081]

Sacred Scripture

Matthew 10:14-15
And whosoever shall not receive you, nor hear your words: going forth out of that house or city shake off the dust from your feet. Amen I say to you, it shall be more tolerable for the land of Sodom and Gomorrha in the day of judgment, than for that city.

Luke 17: 28-30
Likewise as it came to pass, in the days of Lot: they did eat and drink, they bought and sold, they planted and built. And in the day that Lot went out of Sodom, it rained fire and brimstone from heaven, and destroyed them all. Even thus shall it be in the day when the Son of man shall be revealed.

[3077]Edward Pentin [19 December 2019] *Pontifical Biblical Commission Asks, 'What is Man?'* [Online] Available at: www.ncregister.com [Accessed on: 19 August 2022]; Diane Montagna [19 December 2019] *Vatican publishes new book reducing 'sin of Sodom' to 'lack of hospitality'* [Online] Available at: www.lifesitenews.com [Accessed on: 19 August 2022]

[3078]Lamb, C [2020] *Gay children are 'children of God', Pope tells parents.* [Online] Available: www.thetablet.co.uk [Accessed on: 19 August]

[3079]Pullella, P [21 October 2020] *Pope says same-sex couples should be covered by civil union laws* [Online] Available at: www.reuters.com [Accessed on: 19 August 2022]

[3080]Pope Francis [2021] *In-flight press conference on return from Apostolic Visit to Slovakia.* [Online] Available at: www.catholicnewsagency.com [Accessed on: 19 August 2022]

[3081]McLoone, D [2022] *Pro-LGBT cardinal claims Pope Francis is in 'full agreement' with his stance.* [Online] Available at: www.lifesitenews.com [Accessed on: 20 August 2022]

Romans 1:26-27
For this cause God delivered them up to shameful affections. For their women have changed the natural use into that use which is against nature. And, in like manner, the men also, leaving the natural use of the women, have burned in their lusts one towards another, men with men working that which is filthy, and receiving in themselves the recompense which was due to their error.

I Corinthians 6:10
Know you not that the unjust shall not possess the kingdom of God? Do not err: neither fornicators, nor idolaters, nor adulterers, Nor the effeminate, nor liers with mankind, nor thieves, nor covetous, nor drunkards, nor railers, nor extortioners, shall possess the kingdom of God.

II Peter 2:6,10
And reducing the cities of the Sodomites, and of the Gomorrhites, into ashes, condemned them to be overthrown, making them an example to those that should after act wickedly…And especially them who walk after the flesh in the lust of uncleanness, and despise government, audacious, self willed, they fear not to bring in sects, blaspheming.

Jude 1:7
As Sodom and Gomorrha, and the neighbouring cities, in like manner, having given themselves to fornication, and going after other flesh [*unnatural lust*], were made an example, suffering the punishment of eternal fire.

Genesis 13:13
And the men of Sodom were very wicked, and sinners before the face of the Lord, beyond measure.

Leviticus 18:22; 20:13
Thou shalt not lie with mankind as with womankind, because it is an abomination.
    If any one lie with a man as with a woman, both have committed an abomination, let them be put to death: their blood be upon them.

I Kings 14:24; 15:11-12
And there were also sodomites in the land: and they did according to all the abominations of the nations which the LORD cast out before the children of Israel.
    And Asa did that which was right in the eyes of the LORD, as did David his father. And he took away the sodomites out of the land, and removed all the idols that his fathers had made.

Sacred Tradition

Tertullian: c. 160 to 225

On Modesty, Chap. 4
But all the other frenzies of passions — impious both toward the bodies and toward the sexes — beyond the laws of nature, we banish not only from the threshold, but from all shelter of the Church, because they are not sins, but monstrosities.[3082]

St. John Chrysostom: c. 347 to 407

Homily 4 on Romans 1, 26-27
All these affections then were vile, but chiefly the mad lust after males; for the soul is more the sufferer in sins, and more dishonoured, than the body in diseases. But behold how here too, as in the case of the doctrines, he deprives them of excuse, by saying of the women, that '*they changed the natural use.*' For no one, he means, can say that it was by being hindered of legitimate intercourse that they came to this pass, or that it was from having no means to fulfil their desire that they were driven into this monstrous

---

[3082]Tertullian. *On Modesty*, Chap 4. [Online] www.newadvent.org [Accessed on: 24 August 2022]

insanity. For the changing implies possession. Which also when discoursing upon the doctrines he said, *'They changed the truth of God for a lie.'* And with regard to the men again, he shows the same thing by saying, *'Leaving the natural use of the woman.'* And in a like way with those, these he also puts out of all means of defending themselves by charging them not only that they had the means of gratification, and left that which they had, and went after another, but that having dishonoured that which was natural, they ran after that which was contrary to nature. But that which is contrary to nature has in it an irksomeness and displeasingness, so that they could not fairly allege even pleasure. For genuine pleasure is that which is according to nature. But when God has left one, then all things are turned upside down. And thus not only was their doctrine Satanical, but their life too was diabolical. [...]

Consider how great is that sin, to have forced hell to appear even before its time! For whereas many thought scorn of His words, by His deeds did God show them the image thereof in a certain novel way. For that rain was unwonted, for that the intercourse was contrary to nature, and it deluged the land, since lust had done so with their souls. Wherefore also the rain was the opposite of the customary rain. Now not only did it fail to stir up the womb of the earth to the production of fruits, but made it even useless for the reception of seed. For such was also the intercourse of the men, making a body of this sort more worthless than the very land of Sodom. And what is there more detestable than a man who hath pandered himself, or what more execrable? Oh, what madness! Oh, what distraction! Whence came this lust lewdly revelling and making man's nature all that enemies could? or even worse than that, by as much as the soul is better than the body. Oh, ye that were more senseless than irrational creatures, and more shameless than dogs! for in no case does such intercourse take place with them, but nature acknowledgeth her own limits. But ye have even made our race dishonored below things irrational, by such indignities inflicted upon and by each other. Whence then were these evils born? Of luxury; of not knowing God. For so soon as any have cast out the fear of Him, all that is good straightway goes to ruin.[3083]

St. Augustine: 354 to 430

The Confessions, Bk. III, Chap. 8
Therefore those offences which be contrary to nature are everywhere and at all times to be held in detestation and punished; such were those of the Sodomites, which should all nations commit, they should all be held guilty of the same crime by the divine law, which has not so made men that they should in that way abuse one another.[3084]

Sermon on the New Testament, 98
But people, who by doing what is wrong also tie themselves up in evil habits, become defenders of their own evil deeds. They get angry when they are reproved to the extent that the men of Sodom, for example, once said to the just man who was reproving them for their depraved and wicked intentions, You came here to live, not to give us laws (Gen 19:9). So habituated were they to their unspeakable vileness, that now wickedness set the standard of justice, and it was the person who forbade it rather than the one who perpetrated it that was reproved. Such people, weighed down by malignant habit, are as it were not only dead but buried. But what must I say, brothers and sisters? Not only buried, but as it was said about Lazarus, He's already stinking. That massive stone placed against the tomb, that is the hard force of habit which weighs on the soul and doesn't allow it either to rise or even breathe.[3085]

[3083]St. John Chrysostom. *Homily 4 on Romans* 1, 26-27 [Online] www.newadvent.org [Accessed on: 24 August 2022]
[3084]St. Augustine. *The Confessions,* Bk. III, Chap. 8 [Online] www.newadvent.org [Accessed on: 25 August 2022]
[3085]St. Augustine. The Works of Saint Augustine: A Translation for the 21st Century [1990] *Sermons on the New Testament, III/4* (94A-146A). New York: New City Press, p.46

Pope St. Gregory the Great: c. 540 to 604

Commentary on Moralia in Job, XIV, 23

Brimstone calls to mind the foul odours of the flesh, as Sacred Scripture itself confirms when it speaks of the rain of fire and brimstone poured by the Lord upon Sodom. He had decided to punish in it the crimes of the flesh, and the very type of punishment emphasised the shame of that crime, since brimstone exhales stench and fire burns. It was, therefore, just that the sodomites, burning with perverse desires that originated from the foul odour of flesh, should perish at the same time by fire and brimstone so that through this just chastisement they might realise the evil perpetrated under the impulse of a perverse desire.[3086]

St. Thomas Aquinas: 1225 to 1274

Summa Theologiae, Secunda Secundæ Partis. Q 154. a11

…wherever there occurs a special kind of deformity whereby the venereal act is rendered unbecoming, there is a determinate species of lust. This may occur in two ways: First, through being contrary to right reason, and this is common to all lustful vices; secondly, because, in addition, it is contrary to the natural order of the venereal act as becoming to the human race: and this is called 'the unnatural vice.' This may happen in several ways. First, by procuring pollution, without any copulation, for the sake of venereal pleasure: this pertains to the sin of 'uncleanness' which some call 'effeminacy.' Secondly, by copulation with a thing of undue species, and this is called 'bestiality.' Thirdly, by copulation with an undue sex, male with male, or female with female, as the Apostle states (Rom 1:27): and this is called the 'vice of sodomy.' Fourthly, by not observing the natural manner of copulation, either as to undue means, or as to other monstrous and bestial manners of copulation.[3087]

The Magisterium of the Church

Homosexuality is a more or less strong tendency toward an intrinsic moral evil; and thus the inclination itself must be seen as an objective disorder. Basing itself on Sacred Scripture, which presents homosexual acts as acts of grave depravity, (Gen 191-29; Rom 124-27; I Cor 6:10; I Tim 1:10), tradition has always declared that 'homosexual acts are intrinsically disordered.' (CDF, Persona Humana 8). The sin of sodomy is one of the sins that are said to cry to God for vengeance because it is a horrendous crime that degrades man to the level of beasts.

Third Lateran Council (Eleventh Ecumenical, 1179)

Canon 11

Let all who are found guilty of that unnatural vice for which the wrath of God came down upon the sons of disobedience and destroyed the five cities with fire, if they are clerics be expelled from the clergy or confined in monasteries to do penance; if they are laymen they are to incur excommunication and be completely separated from the society of the faithful.[3088]

Fourth Lateran Council (Twelfth Ecumenical, 1215)

Constitution 14

In order that the morals and conduct of clerics may be reformed for the better, let all of them strive to live in a continent and chaste way, especially those in holy orders. Let them beware of every vice involving lust, especially that on account of which the wrath of God came down from heaven upon the sons of disobedience, so that they may

---

[3086]Pope St. Gregory the Great. *Commentary on Moralia in Job*, XIV, 23. [Online] Available at: www.awrsipe.com [Accessed on: 25 August 2022]

[3087]St. Thomas Aquinas. *Summa Theologiae*, Secunda Secundæ Partis. Q 154. a11 [Online] www.newadvent.org [Accessed on: 25 August 2022]

[3088]Tanner, N [1990] Third Lateran Council – 1179 A.D. Canon 11. [Online] Available at: www.papalencyclicals.net [Accessed on: 19 August 2022]

be worthy to minister in the sight of almighty God with a pure heart and an unsullied body.[3089]

Council of Vienne (15th Ecumenical, 1311 to 1312)

Bulls and ordinances of the Roman Curia concerning the order of the Templars and the business of the Holy Land
Therefore, it was against the Lord Jesus Christ himself that they fell into the sin of impious apostasy, the abominable vice of idolatry, the deadly crime of the Sodomites, and various heresies.[3090]

Fifth Lateran Council (Eighteenth Ecumenical, 1512 to 1517)

Reform of the Curia. Session 9, Chap. 4. (5th May 1514)
In order that clerics, especially, may live in continence and chastity according to canonical legislation, we rule that offenders be severely punished as the canons lay down. If anyone, lay or cleric, has been found guilty of a charge on account of which the wrath of God comes upon the sons of disobedience, let him be punished by the penalties respectively imposed by the sacred canons or by civil law.[3091]

Second Vatican Council (Twenty-First Ecumenical, 1962 to 1965)

Pastoral Constitution *Gaudium et Spes, 48, 51. (7th December 1965)*
The intimate partnership of married life and love has been established by the Creator and qualified by His laws, and is rooted in the conjugal covenant of irrevocable personal consent. Hence by that human act whereby spouses mutually bestow and accept each other a relationship arises which by divine will and in the eyes of society too is a lasting one. For the good of the spouses and their off-springs as well as of society, the existence of the sacred bond no longer depends on human decisions alone. For, God Himself is the author of matrimony, endowed as it is with various benefits and purposes. [...]

By their very nature, the institution of matrimony itself and conjugal love are ordained for the procreation and education of children, and find in them their ultimate crown. Thus a man and a woman, who by their compact of conjugal love 'are no longer two, but one flesh' (Mt 19:ff), render mutual help and service to each other through an intimate union of their persons and of their actions. [...]

The sexual characteristics of man and the human faculty of reproduction wonderfully exceed the dispositions of lower forms of life. Hence the acts themselves which are proper to conjugal love and which are exercised in accord with genuine human dignity must be honoured with great reverence.[3092]

Pope Benedict XVI: 2005 to 2013

Compendium of the Catechism of the Catholic Church. (28th June 2005)
492. What are the principal sins against chastity?
Grave sins against chastity differ according to their object: adultery, masturbation, fornication, pornography, prostitution, rape, and homosexual acts. These sins are expressions of the vice of lust. These kinds of acts committed against the physical and moral integrity of minors become even more grave.

[3089]Tanner, N [1990] Fourth Lateran Council: 1215. Constitution 14. [Online] Available at: www.papalencyclicals.net [Accessed on: 19 August 2022]
[3090]Council of Vienne 1311-1312 A.D. [Online] Available at: www.papalencyclicals.net [Accessed on: 20 August 2022]
[3091]Tanner, N [1990] Fifth Lateran Council 1512-17 A.D. *Reform of the Curia.* [Online] Available at: www.papalencyclicals.net [Accessed on: 19 August 2022]
[3092]Second Vatican Council [1965] Pastoral Constitution *Gaudium et Spes*, paras 48, 51 [Online] Available at: www.vatican.va [Accessed on: 20 August 2022]

Congregation for Catholic Education. Instruction concerning the Criteria for the Discernment of Vocations with regard to Persons with Homosexual Tendencies in view of their Admission to the Seminary and to Holy Orders. (31st August 2005)
From the time of the Second Vatican Council until today, various Documents of the Magisterium, and especially the *Catechism of the Catholic Church,* have confirmed the teaching of the Church on homosexuality. The Catechism distinguishes between homosexual acts and homosexual tendencies.

Regarding acts, it teaches that Sacred Scripture presents them as grave sins. The Tradition has constantly considered them as intrinsically immoral and contrary to the natural law. Consequently, under no circumstance can they be approved.

Deep-seated homosexual tendencies, which are found in a number of men and women, are also objectively disordered and, for those same people, often constitute a trial. Such persons must be accepted with respect and sensitivity. Every sign of unjust discrimination in their regard should be avoided. They are called to fulfil God's will in their lives and to unite to the sacrifice of the Lord's Cross the difficulties they may encounter. (CCC 2357-2358).

In the light of such teaching, this Dicastery, in accord with the Congregation for Divine Worship and the Discipline of the Sacraments, believes it necessary to state clearly that the Church, while profoundly respecting the persons in question (CCC 2358) cannot admit to the seminary or to holy orders those who practise homosexuality, present deep-seated homosexual tendencies or support the so-called 'gay culture'.

Such persons, in fact, find themselves in a situation that gravely hinders them from relating correctly to men and women. One must in no way overlook the negative consequences that can derive from the ordination of persons with deep-seated homosexual tendencies.[3093]

General Audience Address. (18th May 2011)
The first text on which we shall reflect is in chapter 18 of the Book of Genesis. It is recounted that the evil of the inhabitants of Sodom and Gomorrah had reached the height of depravity so as to require an intervention of God, an act of justice, that would prevent the evil from destroying those cities. [...]

However, not even 10 just people were to be found in Sodom and Gomorrah so the cities were destroyed; a destruction paradoxically deemed necessary by the prayer of Abraham's intercession itself. Because that very prayer revealed the saving will of God: the Lord was prepared to forgive, he wanted to forgive but the cities were locked into a totalising and paralysing evil, without even a few innocents from whom to start in order to turn evil into good.

This the very path to salvation that Abraham too was asking for: being saved does not mean merely escaping punishment but being delivered from the evil that dwells within us. It is not punishment that must be eliminated but sin, the rejection of God and of love which already bears the punishment in itself.[3094]

Pope St. John Paul II: 1978 to 2005

Address to the Bishops of the United States of America, 6. (5th October 1979)
As 'men with the message of truth and the power of God' (II Cor 6:7), as authentic teachers of God's law and as compassionate pastors you also rightly stated: 'Homosexual activity... as distinguished from homosexual orientation, is morally wrong'. In the clarity of this truth, you exemplified the real charity of Christ; you did not betray those people who, because of homosexuality, are confronted with difficult moral problems, as would have happened if, in the name of understanding and compassion, or for any other reason, you had held out false hope to any brother or sister. Rather, by your

[3093]Congregation for Catholic Education [2005] *Instruction concerning the Criteria for the Discernment of Vocations with regard to Persons with Homosexual Tendencies in view of their Admission to the Seminary and to Holy Orders.* [Online] Available at: www.vatican.va [Accessed on: 8 October 2022]
[3094]Pope Benedict XVI [18th May 2011] *General Audience Address.* [Online] Available at: www.vatican.va [Accessed on: 28 August 2022]

witness to the truth of humanity in God's plan, you effectively manifested fraternal love, upholding the true dignity, the true human dignity, of those who look to Christ's Church for the guidance which comes from the light of God's word.[3095]

Congregation for the Doctrine of the Faith. Letter to the Bishops of Catholic Church on the Pastoral Care of Homosexual Persons, 3, 6, 7. (1st October 1986)
Explicit treatment of the problem was given in this Congregation's 'Declaration on Certain Questions Concerning Sexual Ethics' of December 29, 1975. That document stressed the duty of trying to understand the homosexual condition and noted that culpability for homosexual acts should only be judged with prudence. At the same time the Congregation took note of the distinction commonly drawn between the homosexual condition or tendency and individual homosexual actions. These were described as deprived of their essential and indispensable finality, as being "intrinsically disordered", and able in no case to be approved of (cf. n. 8, §4).

In the discussion which followed the publication of the Declaration, however, an overly benign interpretation was given to the homosexual condition itself, some going so far as to call it neutral, or even good. Although the particular inclination of the homosexual person is not a sin, it is a more or less strong tendency ordered toward an intrinsic moral evil; and thus the inclination itself must be seen as an objective disorder.

In Genesis 3, we find that this truth about persons being an image of God has been obscured by original sin. There inevitably follows a loss of awareness of the covenantal character of the union these persons had with God and with each other. The human body retains its 'spousal significance' but this is now clouded by sin. Thus, in Genesis 19:1-11, the deterioration due to sin continues in the story of the men of Sodom. There can be no doubt of the moral judgement made there against homosexual relations. In Leviticus 18:22 and 20:13, in the course of describing the conditions necessary for belonging to the Chosen People, the author excludes from the People of God those who behave in a homosexual fashion.

Against the background of this exposition of theocratic law, an eschatological perspective is developed by St. Paul when, in I Cor 6:9, he proposes the same doctrine and lists those who behave in a homosexual fashion among those who shall not enter the Kingdom of God.

In Romans 1:18-32, still building on the moral traditions of his forebears, but in the new context of the confrontation between Christianity and the pagan society of his day, Paul uses homosexual behaviour as an example of the blindness which has overcome humankind. Instead of the original harmony between Creator and creatures, the acute distortion of idolatry has led to all kinds of moral excess. Paul is at a loss to find a clearer example of this disharmony than homosexual relations. Finally, I Tim 1, in full continuity with the Biblical position, singles out those who spread wrong doctrine and in v. 10 explicitly names as sinners those who engage in homosexual acts.

A person engaging in homosexual behaviour therefore acts immorally. To chose someone of the same sex for one's sexual activity is to annul the rich symbolism and meaning, not to mention the goals, of the Creator's sexual design. Homosexual activity is not a complementary union, able to transmit life; and so it thwarts the call to a life of that form of self-giving which the Gospel says is the essence of Christian living. This does not mean that homosexual persons are not often generous and giving of themselves; but when they engage in homosexual activity they confirm within themselves a disordered sexual inclination which is essentially self-indulgent. As in every moral disorder, homosexual activity prevents one's own fulfilment and happiness by acting contrary to the creative wisdom of God.[3096]

[3095]Pope St. John Paul II [1979] *Address to the Bishops of the United States of America*, para 6. [Online] Available at: www.vatican.va [Accessed on: 28 August 2022]
[3096]Congregation for the Doctrine of the Faith. *Letter to the Bishops of Catholic Church on the Pastoral Care of Homosexual Persons*, para 3, 7 [Online] Available at: www.vatican.va [Accessed on: 28 August 2022]

Catechism of the Catholic Church. (1992)
The catechetical tradition also recalls that there are 'sins that cry to heaven': the blood of Abel, the sin of the Sodomites (Gen 18:20; 19:13), the cry of the people oppressed in Egypt, the cry of the foreigner, the widow, and the orphan, injustice to the wage earner. (1867)

Basing itself on Sacred Scripture, which presents homosexual acts as acts of grave depravity (Gen 191-29; Rom 124-27; I Cor 6:10; I Tim 1:10), tradition has always declared that 'homosexual acts are intrinsically disordered.' (CDF, *Persona Humana*, 8). They are contrary to the natural law. They close the sexual act to the gift of life. They do not proceed from a genuine affective and sexual complementarity. Under no circumstances can they be approved. (2357)

Angelus Address. (9th July 2000)
The Church cannot be silent about the truth, because she would fail in her fidelity to God the Creator and would not help to distinguish good from evil. In this regard, I wish merely to read what is said in the *Catechism of the Catholic Church*, which, after noting that homosexual acts are contrary to the natural law, then states: 'The number of men and women who have deep-seated homosexual tendencies is not negligible. This inclination, which is objectively disordered, constitutes for most of them a trial. They must be accepted with respect, compassion and sensitivity. Every sign of unjust discrimination in their regard should be avoided.'[3097]

Pope St. Paul VI: 1963 to 1978

Encyclical *Humanae Vitae, 13.* (25th July 1968)
Just as man does not have unlimited dominion over his body in general, so also, and with more particular reason, he has no such dominion over his specifically sexual faculties, for these are concerned by their very nature with the generation of life, of which God is the source.[3098]

Congregation for the Doctrine of the Faith. Declaration Persona Humana, *8. (29th December 1975)*
At the present time there are those who, basing themselves on observations in the psychological order, have begun to judge indulgently, and even to excuse completely, homosexual relations between certain people. This they do in opposition to the constant teaching of the Magisterium and to the moral sense of the Christian people.

A distinction is drawn, and it seems with some reason, between homosexuals whose tendency comes from a false education, from a lack of normal sexual development, from habit, from bad example, or from other similar causes, and is transitory or at least not incurable; and homosexuals who are definitively such because of some kind of innate instinct or a pathological constitution judged to be incurable.

In regard to this second category of subjects, some people conclude that their tendency is so natural that it justifies in their case homosexual relations within a sincere communion of life and love analogous to marriage, in so far as such homosexuals feel incapable of enduring a solitary life.

In the pastoral field, these homosexuals must certainly be treated with understanding and sustained in the hope of overcoming their personal difficulties and their inability to fit into society. Their culpability will be judged with prudence. But no pastoral method can be employed which would give moral justification to these acts on the grounds that they would be consonant with the condition of such people. For according to the objective moral order, homosexual relations are acts which lack an essential and indispensable finality. In Sacred Scripture they are condemned as a serious depravity and even presented as the sad consequence of rejecting God. This judgment of Scrip-

---

[3097]Pope St. John Paul II [9 July 2000] *Angelus.* [Online] Available at: www.vatican.va [Accessed on: 28 August 2022]
[3098]Pope St. Paul VI [1968] Encyclical *Humanae Vitae*, para 13 [Online] Available at: www.vatican.va [Accessed on: 8 October 2022]

ture does not of course permit us to conclude that all those who suffer from this anomaly are personally responsible for it, but it does attest to the fact that homosexual acts are intrinsically disordered and can in no case be approved of.[3099]

Pope St. John XXIII: 1958 to 1963

Congregation for Religious. Religiosorum Institutio, 4. (2nd February 1961)
Advancement to religious vows and ordination should be barred to those who are afflicted with evil tendencies to homosexuality or pederasty, since for them the common life and the priestly ministry would constitute serious dangers.[3100]

Pope Ven. Pius XII: 1939 to 1958

Allocution to newlyweds. (29th October 1951)
The golden rule is then, this: The use of the natural generative instinct is morally licit only in marriage, in the service of and according to the order of the ultimate reason for marriage itself.... The transgression of this norm is as ancient as original sin itself. But in our time there is a danger that people may lose sight of the fundamental principle itself.[3101]

Pope Benedict XV: 1914 to 1922

The 1917 or Pio-Benedictine Code of Canon Law. (27th May 1917)
Laity legitimately convicted of a delict against the sixth [commandment of the Decalogue] with a minor below the age of sixteen, or of debauchery, sodomy, incest, or pandering, are by that fact infamous, besides other penalties that the Ordinary decides should be inflicted. Canon 2357 § 1

If they [clergy] engage in a delict against the sixth precept of the Decalogue with a minor below the age of sixteen, or engage in adultery, debauchery, bestiality, sodomy, pandering, incest with blood-relatives or affines in the first degree, they are suspended, declared infamous, and are deprived of any office, benefice, dignity, responsibility, if they have such, whatsoever, and in more serious cases, they are to be deposed. Canon 2359 § 2[3102]

Pope St. Pius X: 1903 to 1914

Catechism of Pope St. Pius X. (1908)
The Vices and other Very Grievous Sins
8 Q. Which are the sins that are said to cry to God for vengeance?
A. The sins that are said to cry to God for vengeance are these four: (1) Wilful murder; (2) The sin of sodomy; (3) Oppression of the poor; (4) Defrauding labourers of their wages.

9 Q. Why are these sins said to cry to God for vengeance?
A. These sins are said to cry to God for vengeance because the Holy Ghost says so, and because their iniquity is so great and so manifest that it provokes God to punish them with the severest chastisements.[3103]

Pope Alexander VII: 1655 to 1667

Forty-Five Propositions Condemned in the Decree of the Holy Office, 24th September 1665 & 18th March 1666
24. Pederasty, sodomy and bestiality are sins of the same inferior species; therefore it suffices to say in confession that one has procured a pollution.[3104]

[2965]Peters, E N [2001] *The 1917 or Pio-Benedictine Code of Canon Law in English Translation with Extensive Scholarly Apparatus.* San Francisco: Ignatius Press
[2966]*Catechism of St. Pius X* [1908] [Online] Available at: www.ewtn.com [Accessed on: 28 August 2022]
[2967]Denzinger, H [2010] *Op. cit.,* p. 462, Dz 2044

Pope St. Pius V: 1566 to 1572

The Roman Catechism: The Catechism of the Council of Trent. (1556)
The Sixth Commandment: 'Thou shalt not commit adultery'
Other Sins Against Chastity Are Forbidden
But that every species of immodesty and impurity are included in this prohibition of adultery, is proved by the testimonies of St. Augustine and St. Ambrose; and that such is the meaning of the Commandment is borne out by the Old, as well as the New Testament. In the writings of Moses, besides adultery, other sins against chastity are said to have been punished. [...]

In the Gospel, too, Christ the Lord says: From the heart come forth adulteries and fornications, which defile a man. The Apostle Paul expresses his detestation of this crime frequently, and in the strongest terms: This is the will of God, your sanctification, that you should abstain from fornication; Fly fornication; Keep not company with fornicators; Fornication, and an uncleanness and covetousness, let it not so much as be named among you; 'Neither fornicators nor adulterers, nor the effeminate nor sodomites shall possess the kingdom of God'.

Means of practicing purity
Avoidance Of Idleness. We now come to the remedies which consist in action. The first is studiously to avoid idleness; for, according to Ezechiel, it was by yielding to the enervating influence of idleness that the Sodomites plunged into the most shameful crime of criminal lust.[2968]

Constitution Horrendum Illud Scelus. *(30th August 1568)*
That horrible crime, on account of which corrupt and obscene cities were destroyed by fire through divine condemnation, causes us most bitter sorrow and shocks our mind, impelling us to repress such a crime with the greatest possible zeal.

Quite opportunely the Fifth Lateran Council [1512 to 1517] issued this decree: 'Let any member of the clergy caught in that vice against nature, given that the wrath of God falls over the sons of perfidy, be removed from the clerical order or forced to do penance in a monastery' (Chap. 4, X, V, 31).

So that the contagion of such a grave offence may not advance with greater audacity by taking advantage of impunity, which is the greatest incitement to sin, and so as to more severely punish the clerics who are guilty of this nefarious crime and who are not frightened by the death of their souls, we determine that they should be handed over to the severity of the secular authority, which enforces civil law.[2969]

Pope St.Leo IX: 1049 to 1054

Cardinal St. Peter Damian. *Book of Gomorrah, Chap. 14, 16*
And it certainly is proper enough that those who trade their flesh to demons through such foul commerce against the law of nature, against the order of human reason, should receive a common place of prayer with the demonically possessed. For as human nature itself deeply resists these evils, and the lack of sexual difference is abhorrent, it is clearer than light that they never would have dared to engage in such perversities unless evil spirits had fully possessed them as 'vessels of wrath, fitted for destruction.' (Rom 9:22) But when they begin to possess them, they pour in the infernal poison of their malignity throughout the invaded heart that they fill, so that they might now eagerly desire not those things that a natural movement of the body demands, but that which only diabolic haste supplies. For when a man thrusts himself upon another man to commit impure acts, it is not from a natural carnal drive, but only the stimulus of diabolical impulse. [...]

[2968]Pope St. Pius V [1556] *The Roman Catechism: The Catechism of the Council of Trent,* The Sixth Commandment : 'Thou shalt not commit adultery' [Online] Available at: www.clerus.org [Accessed on: 1 October 2022]
[2969]Pope St. Pius V [1568] *Horrendum Illud Scelus* [Online] Available at: www.traditioninaction.org [Accessed on: 26 August 2022]

This vice eliminates men from the choir of ecclesiastical assembly and compels them to pray with those who are possessed and oppressed by the devil. It separates the soul from God, to unite it with demons. This most pestilent queen of the sodomites renders him who is submissive to the laws of her tyranny indecent to men and hateful to God. In order to sow impious wars against God, she requires a militancy of the most wretched spirit. She separates the unhappy soul from the fellowship of the angels, removing it from its nobility to place it under the yoke of her own domination. She strips her soldiers of the armaments of the virtues, and to strike them down, exposes them to the darts of every vice. In the Church she humiliates, and in the forum she condemns. She defiles in secrecy and dishonors in public. She gnaws the conscience like worms, burns the flesh like a fire, and pants with desire for pleasure. But in contrast she fears to be exposed, to come out in public, to be known by others. For whom should he not fear, who also dreads the participant in common ruin with fearful suspicion, lest the same man who sins with him become judge of the crime by confession, when he might not hesitate not only to confess his sin but also to name the one with whom he sinned? Just as one could not die by sin without the other dying, so each one offers the other the occasion of rising again, when he rises.[2970]

Pope St. Leo IX. Letter *Ad Splendidum Nitentis to St. Peter Damian. (1054)*
…lest the unrestrained license of filthy lust should spread abroad, it is necessary that it be repelled by a suitable reprimand of apostolic severity and that some attempt at more austere discipline should be made….

Those who have polluted by impurity of any of the four kinds[2971] mentioned are expelled from all grades of the immaculate Church both by the appropriate censure envisaged by the sacred canons as well as by Our judgement. But We, proceeding with much clemency and trusting in the divine mercy, will and indeed command that those who have brought forth the seed either by their own hands or among themselves or who have even shed it between the legs, but not by long habit nor with many people, if they restrain their desire and wash away their shameful deeds by worthy repentance, should be admitted to the same grades that they would not have retained forever if they had remained in their pollution; but We withdraw any hope of recovering their order from those others who have been stained either of the two sorts of impurity that you have described, whether during a long period alone or with others, or even for a short period with many people, or who, horrible to say or hear, have sinned in the back of others. If anyone shall dare to judge or complain against this Our decree of apostolic sanction, let him know that he acts in peril of his order.[2972]

Pope St. Damasus I: 366 to 384
The First Canonical Epistle of St. Basil, Archbishop of Caesarea in Cappadocia to Amphilochius, Bishop of Iconium, Canon VII.
They who have committed sodomy with men or brutes, murderers, wizards, adulterers, and idolaters, have been thought worthy of the same punishment; therefore observe the same method with these which you do with others. We ought not to make any doubt of receiving those who have repented thirty years for the uncleanness which they committed through ignorance; for their ignorance pleads their pardon, and their willingness in confessing it; therefore command them to be forthwith received, especially if they have tears to prevail on your tenderness, and have [since their lapse] led such a life as to deserve your compassion.[2973]

[2970]St. Peter Damian. *Liber Gomorrhianus*, Chap. 14. [Online] Available at: ia802308.us.archive.org [Accessed on: 26 August 2022]
[2971]St. Peter Damian distinguished four different kinds of sodomitic act: (1) solitary masturbation; (2) mutual masturbation; (3) sex between the thighs of same-sex partners; (4) anal sex (the most vile). Sundell, C [2022] Peter Damian's *Book of Gomorrah* [Online] Available at catholicinsight.com [Accessed on 20 August 2022]
[2972]Denzinger, H [1990] *Op. cit.,* p. 233-234, Dz 687-688
[2973]Peters, E N [2001] *The 1917 or Pio-Benedictine Code of Canon Law in English Translation with Extensive Scholarly Apparatus.* San Francisco: Ignatius Press

Pope St. Marcellinus, 296 to 304
Synod of Elvira, Canon 71. (c. 300-303?)
Men who sexually abuse boys shall not be given communion even at the approach of death.[2974]

[2974]Synod of Elvira. *81 Canons of the Synod of Elvira*, Canon 71. [Online] Available at: strannikjournal. wordpress.com [Accessed on: 26 August 2022]

Sacraments (1) — Divorce and the Sacraments

Pope Francis: 2013 to 2025

O. *Those who are divorced and have entered into a civil union, and cannot obtain a decree of nullity for their sacramental marriage, can receive the sacraments of confession and the Eucharist following a period of 'accompaniment' with a priest. Informing this laxism is Pope Francis' erroneous teaching that sins of the flesh are not grave sins and the Eucharist is not a prize for the perfect but the medicine of sinners.*

The Sacrament of Confession

Post synodal Apostolic Exhortation *Evangelii Gaudium, 44. (24 November 2013)*
I want to remind priests that the confessional must not be a torture chamber but rather an encounter with the Lord's mercy which spurs us on to do our best. A small step, in the midst of great human limitations, can be more pleasing to God than a life which appears outwardly in order but moves through the day without confronting great difficulties.[2975]

Pope Francis' interview with Dominique Wolton. (7th August 2018)

Sins of the flesh are the lightest sins. Because the flesh is weak. The most dangerous sins are those of the spirit. I am talking about angelism: pride, vanity are sins of angelism. Priests have the temptation — not all, but many — of focusing on the sins of sexuality, what I call morality below the belt. But the more serious sins are elsewhere. [...]

I know a cardinal who is a good example. He confided to me, speaking of these things, that as soon as someone goes to him to talk about those sins below the belt, he immediately says: 'I understand, let's move on.' He stops him, as if to say: 'I understand, but let's see if you have something more important. Do you pray? Are you seeking the Lord? Do you read the Gospel?' He makes him understand that there are mistakes that are much more important than that. Yes, it is a sin, but... He says to him: 'I understand': And he moves on. On the opposite end there are some who when they receive the confession of a sin of this kind, ask: 'How did you do it, and when did you do it, and how many times?' And they make a 'film' in their head. But these are in need of a psychiatrist.[2976]

Press conference on return from Apostolic Journey to Cyprus and Greece (6th December 2021) in response to the resignation of Archbishop Aupetit of Paris over allegations of sexual relations with a woman.

...it was a failing on his part, a failing against the sixth commandment, but not total but of little caresses and massages that he did: that was the accusation. This is sin, but one of the more grave sins, because sins of the flesh are not the gravest sin: the gravest sins are those that have more of an 'angelic' character; pride, hatred... these are the most grave.[2977]

The Sacrament of the Eucharist

Post synodal Apostolic Exhortation *Evangelii Gaudium, 47. (24 November 2013)*
The Church is called to be the house of the Father, with doors always wide open. One concrete sign of such openness is that our church doors should always be open, so that if someone, moved by the Spirit, comes there looking for God, he or she will not find a closed door. There are other doors that should not be closed either. Everyone can share in some way in the life of the Church; everyone can be part of the community, nor should

[2975]Pope Francis [2013] Post Synodal Apostolic Exhortation *Evangelii Gaudium*, para 47 [Online] Available at: www.vatican.va [Accessed on: 31 August 2022]

[2976]Magister, S [21 January 2019] *Memo For the Summit On Abuse. For Francis, the Sins 'Below the Belt' Are 'the Lightest'.* [Online] Available at: magister.blogautore.espresso.repubblica.it [Accessed on: 30 August 2022]

[2977]Pope Francis [2021] *Press conference on return from Apostolic Journey to Cyprus and Greece* [Online] Available at: www.vatican.va [Accessed on: 31 August 2022]

the doors of the sacraments be closed for simply any reason....The Eucharist, although it is the fullness of sacramental life, is not a prize for the perfect but a powerful medicine and nourishment for the weak. These convictions have pastoral consequences that we are called to consider with prudence and boldness. Frequently, we act as arbiters of grace rather than its facilitators. But the Church is not a tollhouse; it is the house of the Father, where there is a place for everyone, with all their problem (sic).[2978]

Angelus Address. (6th June 2021)
The church of the perfect and pure is a room where there isn't a place for anyone; the church with open doors that celebrates around Christ is, on the other hand, a large hall where everyone − the righteous and sinners − can enter. [...] there is another strength that stands out in the fragility of the Eucharist: the strength to love those who make mistakes. It is *on the night he is betrayed* that Jesus gives us the Bread of Life. He gives us the greatest gift while he feels the deepest abyss in his heart: the disciple who eats with Him, who dips the morsel in the same plate, is betraying Him. And betrayal is the worst suffering for one who loves. And what does Jesus do? He reacts to the evil with a greater good. He responds to Judas' 'no' with the 'yes' of mercy. He does not punish the sinner, but rather gives His life for him; He pays for him. When we receive the Eucharist, Jesus does the same with us: he knows us; he knows we are sinners; and he knows we make many mistakes, but he does not give up on joining his life to ours. He knows that we need it, because the Eucharist is not the reward of saints, no, it is *the Bread of sinners*. This is why he exhorts us: 'Do not be afraid! *Take and eat*'.[2979]

Apostolic Letter *Desiderio Desideravi, 5. (29th June 2022)*
The world still does not know it, but everyone is invited to the supper of the wedding of the Lamb (Rev 19:9). To be admitted to the feast all that is required is the wedding garment of faith which comes from the hearing of his Word (cf. Rom 10:17).[2980]

Communion for the divorced and remarried engaging in sexual relations

Post Synodal Apostolic Exhortation *Amoris Laetitia, 298 & footnote 329, 300 & footnote 336, 305 & footnote 351. (19th March 2016)*
Amoris Laetitia 298. The divorced who have entered a new union, for example, can find themselves in a variety of situations, which should not be pigeonholed or fit into overly rigid classifications leaving no room for a suitable personal and pastoral discernment. One thing is a second union consolidated over time, with new children, proven fidelity, generous self-giving, Christian commitment, a consciousness of its irregularity and of the great difficulty of going back without feeling in conscience that one would fall into new sins. The Church acknowledges situations 'where, for serious reasons, such as the children's upbringing, a man and woman cannot satisfy the obligation to separate'. There are also the cases of those who made every effort to save their first marriage and were unjustly abandoned, or of 'those who have entered into a second union for the sake of the children's upbringing, and are sometimes subjectively certain in conscience that their previous and irreparably broken marriage had never been valid'. Another thing is a new union arising from a recent divorce, with all the suffering and confusion which this entails for children and entire families, or the case of someone who has consistently failed in his obligations to the family. It must remain clear that this is not the ideal which the Gospel proposes for marriage and the family. The Synod Fathers stated that the discernment of pastors must always take place 'by adequately distinguishing', with an approach which 'carefully discerns situations'. We know that no 'easy recipes' exist.

[2978]Pope Francis [2013] Post Synodal Apostolic Exhortation *Evangelii Gaudium*, para 47 [Online] Available at: www.vatican.va [Accessed on: 31 August 2022]
[2979]Pope Francis [6th June 2021] *Angelus Address.* [Online] Available at: www.vatican.va [Accessed on: 31 August 2022]
[2980]Pope Francis [2022] Apostolic Letter *Desiderio Desideravi*, 5 [Online] Available at: www.vatican. va [Accessed on: 2nd September 2022]

Footnote 329. John Paul II, Apostolic Exhortation *Familiaris Consortio* (22 November 1981), 84: *AAS* 74 (1982), 186. In such situations, many people, knowing and accepting the possibility of living 'as brothers and sisters' which the Church offers them, point out that if certain expressions of intimacy are lacking, 'it often happens that faithfulness is endangered and the good of the children suffers' (Second Vatican Ecumenical Council, Pastoral Constitution on the Church in the Modern World, *Gaudium et Spes* 51).

Amoris Laetitia 300. If we consider the immense variety of concrete situations such as those I have mentioned, it is understandable that neither the Synod nor this Exhortation could be expected to provide a new set of general rules, canonical in nature and applicable to all cases. What is possible is simply a renewed encouragement to undertake a responsible personal and pastoral discernment of particular cases, one which would recognize that, since 'the degree of responsibility is not equal in all cases' the consequences or effects of a rule need not necessarily always be the same. (336).

Footnote 336. This is also the case with regard to sacramental discipline, since discernment can recognize that in a particular situation no grave fault exists. In such cases, what is found in another document applies: cf. *Evangelii Gaudium* (24 November 2013), 44 and 47: AAS 105 (2013), 1038-1040.

Amoris Laetitia 305. Because of forms of conditioning and mitigating factors, it is possible that in an objective situation of sin – which may not be subjectively culpable, or fully such – a person can be living in God's grace, can love and can also grow in the life of grace and charity, while receiving the Church's help to this end. Discernment must help to find possible ways of responding to God and growing in the midst of limits. By thinking that everything is black and white, we sometimes close off the way of grace and of growth, and discourage paths of sanctification which give glory to God. Let us remember that 'a small step, in the midst of great human limitations, can be more pleasing to God than a life which appears outwardly in order, but moves through the day without confronting great difficulties'. The practical pastoral care of ministers and of communities must not fail to embrace this reality.

Footnote 351. In certain cases, this can include the help of the sacraments. Hence, 'I want to remind priests that the confessional must not be a torture chamber, but rather an encounter with the Lord's mercy' (Apostolic Exhortation *Evangelii Gaudium* [24 November 2013], 44: *AAS* 105 [2013], 1038). I would also point out that the Eucharist 'is not a prize for the perfect, but a powerful medicine and nourishment for the weak' (*ibid.*, 47: 1039)[2981]

Acta Apostolicae Sedis. *Buenos Aires Pastoral Region. Basic criteria for the implementation of chapter VIII of Amoris Laetitia. October 2016.*
We will now focus on chapter VIII, since it refers to the 'guidelines of the bishop' in order to discern on the potential access to sacraments of the 'divorced who have entered a new union.' [...]

3) Pastoral accompaniment is an exercise of the '*via caritas.*' It is an invitation to follow 'the way of Jesus, the way of mercy and reinstatement' This itinerary requires the pastoral charity of the priest who receives the penitent, listens to him/her attentively and shows him/her the maternal face of the Church, while also accepting his/her righteous intention and good purpose to devote his/her whole life to the light of the Gospel and to practise charity (cf. 306). [...]

6) In more complex cases, and when a declaration of nullity has not been obtained, the above mentioned option may not, in fact, be feasible. Nonetheless, a path of discernment is still possible. If it is acknowledged that, in a concrete case, there are limitations that mitigate responsibility and culpability (cf. 301-302), especially when a person believes he/she would incur a subsequent fault by harming the children of the new union, *Amoris Laetitia* offers the possibility of having access to the sacraments of Reconciliation and Eucharist (cf. footnotes 336 and 351).

[2981]Pope Francis [2016] Post Synodal Apostolic Exhortation *Amoris Laetitia* [Online] Available at: www.vatican.va [Accessed on: 31 August 2022]

These sacraments, in turn, prepare the person to continue maturing and growing with the power of grace.[2982]

Les confidences du Pape François. Le Figaro. (1st September 2017)
There is what I did after the two synods, *Amoris Laetitia*.... It is something clear and positive, that some with too traditionalist tendencies fight by saying that it is not the true doctrine. Regarding the injured families, I say in the eighth chapter that there are four criteria: to welcome, to accompany, to discern situations and to integrate. And that's not a fixed standard. This opens a way, a path of communication. I was immediately asked, 'But can we give communion to the divorced?' I reply: 'Speak with the divorced, speak with the divorced, welcome, accompany, integrate, discern!'

Alas, we priests are accustomed to fixed norms. At fixed standards. And it is difficult for us, this 'accompanying on the way, integrating, discerning, good'. But my proposal is that. (...) What is really happening is that people can be heard saying, 'They can not receive communion', 'They can not do this': the temptation of the Church, it is there. But no, no and no! This type of prohibition is what we find in the drama of Jesus with the Pharisees. The same! The great ones of the Church are those who have a vision that goes beyond, those who understand the missionaries.[2983]

Address to Tribunal of the Roman Rota on the occasion of the inauguration of the Judicial Year. (29th January 2021)
However, how can it be explained to children that, for example, their mother, abandoned by their father and often without the intention of contracting another matrimonial bond, may receive the Eucharist with them on a Sunday, whereas their father, living with them or awaiting the declaration of nullity of marriage, cannot receive the Eucharist? On the occasion of the Extraordinary General Assembly of the Synod of Bishops in 2014 and in the Ordinary Assembly in 2015, the Synod Fathers, reflecting on the theme of the family, posed themselves these questions, thus making themselves aware that it is difficult, at times impossible, to offer answers.[2984]

Sacred Scripture

Matthew 5: 27-30
You have heard that it was said to them of old: Thou shalt not commit adultery. But I say to you, that whosoever shall look on a woman to lust after her, hath already committed adultery with her in his heart. And if thy right eye scandalize thee, pluck it out and cast it from thee. For it is expedient for thee that one of thy members should perish, rather than that thy whole body be cast into hell. And if thy right hand scandalize thee, cut it off, and cast it from thee: for it is expedient for thee that one of thy members should perish, rather than that thy whole body go into hell.

Matthew 5:31-32
And it hath been said, Whosoever shall put away his wife, let him give her a bill of divorce. But I say to you, that whosoever shall put away his wife, excepting for the cause of fornication, maketh her to commit adultery: and he that shall marry her that is put away, committeth adultery.

Matthew 19:6-7
And there came to him the Pharisees tempting him, saying: Is it lawful for a man to put away his wife for every cause? Who answering, said to them: Have ye not read, that he

---

[2982]*Pope Francis Promulgates Buenos Aires Guidelines Allowing Communion for Some Adulterers in AAS as his 'Authentic Magisterium'* [Online] Available at: rorate-caeli.blogspot.com [Accessed on: 31 August 2022]

[2983]Pope Francis [1st September 2017] *Les confidences du pape François à Dominique Wolton* [Online] Available at: www.cath.ch [Accessed on: 31 August 2022] Trans. Andrew Guernsey

[2984]Pope Francis [2021] *Address to Tribunal of the Roman Rota on the occasion of the inauguration of the Judicial Year* [Online] Available at: www.vatican.va [Accessed on: 8 October 2022]

who made man from the beginning, Made them male and female? And he said: For this
cause shall a man leave father and mother, and shall cleave to his wife, and they two
shall be in one flesh. Therefore now they are not two, but one flesh. What therefore God
hath joined together, let no man put asunder. They say to him: Why then did Moses
command to give a bill of divorce, and to put away? He saith to them: Because Moses
by reason of the hardness of your heart permitted you to put away your wives: but
from the beginning it was not so. And I say to you, that whosoever shall put away his
wife, except it be for fornication, and shall marry another, committeth adultery: and he
that shall marry her that is put away, committeth adultery.

Mark 10:2-12
And the Pharisees coming to him asked him: Is it lawful for a man to put away his wife?
tempting him. But he answering, saith to them: What did Moses command you? Who
said: Moses permitted to write a bill of divorce, and to put her away. To whom Jesus
answering, said: Because of the hardness of your heart he wrote you that precept. But
from the beginning of the creation, God made them male and female. For this cause a
man shall leave his father and mother; and shall cleave to his wife. And they two shall
be in one flesh. Therefore now they are not two, but one flesh. What therefore God hath
joined together, let no man put asunder. And in the house again his disciples asked him
concerning the same thing. And he saith to them: Whosoever shall put away his wife
and marry another, committeth adultery against her. And if the wife shall put away her
husband, and be married to another, she committeth adultery.

Luke 16:18
Every one that putteth away his wife, and marrieth another, committeth adultery: and
he that marrieth her that is put away from her husband, committeth adultery.

Romans 7:2-3
For the woman that hath an husband, whilst her husband liveth is bound to the law.
But if her husband be dead, she is loosed from the law of her husband. Therefore, whilst
her husband liveth, she shall be called an adulteress, if she be with another man: but if
her husband be dead, she is delivered from the law of her husband; so that she is not an
adulteress, if she be with another man.

I Corinthians 6:9
Know you not that the unjust shall not possess the kingdom of God? Do not err: neither
fornicators, nor idolaters, nor adulterers....

I Corinthians 7:11-13
But to them that are married, not I but the Lord commandeth, that the wife depart not
from her husband. And if she depart, that she remain unmarried, or be reconciled to
her husband. And let not the husband put away his wife. For to the rest I speak, not the
Lord. If any brother hath a wife that believeth not, and she consent to dwell with him,
let him not put her away. And if any woman hath a husband that believeth not, and he
consent to dwell with her, let her not put away her husband.

I Corinthians 11:27-30
Therefore whosoever shall eat this bread, or drink the chalice of the Lord unworthily,
shall be guilty of the body and of the blood of the Lord. But let a man prove himself:
and so let him eat of that bread, and drink of the chalice. For he that eateth and drinketh
unworthily, eateth and drinketh judgment to himself, not discerning the body of the
Lord. Therefore are there many infirm and weak among you, and many sleep.

Hebrews 13:4
Marriage honourable in all, and the bed undefiled. For fornicators and adulterers God
will judge.

Exodus 20:14
Thou shalt not commit adultery.

Deuteronomy 22:22
If a man lie with another man's wife, they shall both die, that is to say, the adulterer and the adulteress: and thou shalt take away the evil out of Israel.

Leviticus 20:10
If any man commit adultery with the wife of another, and defile his neighbour's wife, let them be put to death, both the adulterer and the adulteress.

Proverbs 6:32
But he that is an adulterer, for the folly of his heart shall destroy his own soul.

Hosea 4:2
Cursing, and lying, and killing, and theft, and adultery have overflowed, and blood hath touched blood.

Sacred Tradition — The Sacrament of Marriage

St. Justin Martyr: 100 to 165

The First Apology, Chap. 15
Concerning chastity, He uttered such sentiments as these: 'Whosoever looks upon a woman to lust after her, has committed adultery with her already in his heart before God.' And, 'If your right eye offend you, cut it out; for it is better for you to enter into the kingdom of heaven with one eye, than, having two eyes, to be cast into everlasting fire.' And, 'Whosoever shall marry her that is divorced from another husband, commits adultery.' And, 'There are some who have been made eunuchs of men, and some who were born eunuchs, and some who have made themselves eunuchs for the kingdom of heaven's sake; but all cannot receive this saying.' (Mt 19:12). So that all who, by human law, are twice married, are in the eye of our Master sinners, and those who look upon a woman to lust after her. For not only he who in act commits adultery is rejected by Him, but also he who desires to commit adultery: since not only our works, but also our thoughts, are open before God.[2985]

Tertullian: c. 160 to 225

Against Marcion, Bk. IV, Chap. 34
I maintain, then, that there was a condition in the prohibition which He now made of divorce; the case supposed being, that a man put away his wife for the express purpose of marrying another. His words are: 'Whosoever puts away his wife, and marries another, commits adultery; and whosoever marries her that is put away from her husband, also commits adultery,' (Lk 16:18) — 'put away,' that is, for the reason wherefore a woman ought not to be dismissed, that another wife may be obtained. For he who marries a woman who is unlawfully put away is as much of an adulterer as the man who marries one who is un-divorced.[2986]

Origen: c. 184 to c. 253

Commentary on the Gospel of Matthew, Bk. XIV, 24
For confessedly he who puts away his wife when she is not a fornicator, makes her an adulteress, so far as it lies with him, for if, 'when the husband is living she shall be called an adulteress if she be joined to another man;' (Rom 7:3) and when by putting her away, he gives to her the excuse of a second marriage, very plainly in this way he makes her an adulteress.[2987]

[2985]St. Justin Martyr. *The First Apology,* Chap. 15 [Online] Available at: www.newadvent.org [Accessed on: 4 September 2022]

[2986]Tertullian. *Against Marcion,* Bk. IV, Chap. 34 [Online] Available at: www.newadvent.org [Accessed on: 4 September 2022]

[2987]Origen. *Commentary on the Gospel of Matthew,* Bk. XIV, 24 [Online] Available at: www. newadvent.org [Accessed on: 8 October 2022]

St. Ambrose: c. 340 to 397

Commentary on Luke 8:5

You dismiss your wife, therefore, as if by right and without being charged with wrongdoing; and you suppose it is proper for you to do so because no human law forbids it; but divine law forbids it. Anyone who obeys men ought to stand in awe of God. Hear the law of the Lord, which even they who propose our laws must obey: 'What God has joined together let no man put asunder'.[2988]

St. Jerome: c. 340-2 to 420

To Amandus, Letter 55

…if a woman marries again while her husband is living, she is an adulteress. You must not speak to me of the violence of a ravisher, a mother's pleading, a father's bidding, the influence of relatives, the insolence and the intrigues of servants, household losses. A husband may be an adulterer or a sodomite, he may be stained with every crime and may have been left by his wife because of his sins; yet he is still her husband and, so long as he lives, she may not marry another.[2989]

St. Augustine: 354 to 430

Of the Good of Marriage, 17

But a marriage once for all entered upon in the City of our God, where, even from the first union of the two, the man and the woman, marriage bears a certain sacramental character, can no way be dissolved but by the death of one of them. For the bond of marriage remains, although a family, for the sake of which it was entered upon, do not follow through manifest barrenness; so that, when now married persons know that they shall not have children, yet it is not lawful for them to separate even for the very sake of children, and to join themselves unto others. And if they shall so do, they commit adultery with those unto whom they join themselves, but themselves remain husbands and wives.[2990]

The Sacrament of Confession

Pope St. Clement: 88 to 99

Second Letter to the Corinthians, Chap. 8-9

As long, therefore, as we are upon earth, let us practise repentance, for we are as clay in the hand of the artificer. For as the potter, if he make a vessel, and it be distorted or broken in his hands, fashions it over again; but if he have before this cast it into the furnace of fire, can no longer find any help for it: so let us also, while we are in this world, repent with our whole heart of the evil deeds we have done in the flesh, that we may be saved by the Lord, while we have yet an opportunity of repentance. For after we have gone out of the world, no further power of confessing or repenting will there belong to us. Wherefore, brethren, by doing the will of the Father, and keeping the flesh holy, and observing the commandments of the Lord, we shall obtain eternal life…. This, then, is what He means: 'Keep the flesh holy and the seal undefiled, that you may receive eternal life.'

And let no one of you say that this very flesh shall not be judged, nor rise again. Consider in what [state] you were saved, in what you received sight, if not while you were in this flesh. We must therefore preserve the flesh as the temple of God.[2991]

[2988]St. Ambrose. *Commentary on Luke* 8:5 [Online] Available at: www.churchfathers.org [Accessed on: 4 September 2022]

[2989]St. Jerome. To Amandus, *Letter* 55 [Online] Available at: www.newadvent.org [Accessed on: 4 September 2022]

[2990]St. Augustine. *Of the Good of Marriage*, para 17 [Online] Available at: www.newadvent.org [Accessed on: 4 September 2022]

[2991]Pope St. Clement. *Second Letter to the Corinthians*, Chap. 8. [Online] Available at: www. newadvent.org [Accessed on: 4 September 2022]

St. Irenaeus: c. 130 to c. 202

Against Heresies, Bk. I, Chap. 13, para 7

Such are the words and deeds [sexual sins] by which, in our own district of the Rhone, they have deluded many women, who have their consciences seared as with a hot iron. (II Tim 3:6) Some of them, indeed, make a public confession of their sins; but others of them are ashamed to do this, and in a tacit kind of way, despairing of [attaining to] the life of God, have, some of them, apostatised altogether; while others hesitate between the two courses, and incur that which is implied in the proverb, 'neither without nor within;' possessing this as the fruit from the seed of the children of knowledge.[2992]

Tertullian: c. 160 to 225

On Repentance, Chap. 8

…if you leave behind you the swine, that unclean herd — if you again seek your Father, offended though He be, saying, 'I have sinned, nor am worthy any longer to be called Yours.' Confession of sins lightens, as much as dissimulation aggravates them; for confession is counselled by (a desire to make) satisfaction, dissimulation by contumacy.[2993]

The Sacrament of the Eucharist

St. Cyprian of Carthage: c. 200 to 258

Treatise 3, On the Lapsed, Chap. 16

All these warnings being scorned and contemned — before their sin is expiated, before confession has been made of their crime, before their conscience has been purged by sacrifice and by the hand of the priest, before the offence of an angry and threatening Lord has been appeased, violence is done to His body and blood; and they sin now against their Lord more with their hand and mouth than when they denied their Lord. They think that that is peace which some with deceiving words are blazoning forth: that is not peace, but war; and he is not joined to the Church who is separated from the Gospel. Why do they call an injury a kindness? Why do they call impiety by the name of piety? Why do they hinder those who ought to weep continually and to entreat their Lord, from the sorrowing of repentance, and pretend to receive them to communion? This is the same kind of thing to the lapsed as hail to the harvests; as the stormy star to the trees; as the destruction of pestilence to the herds; as the raging tempest to shipping. They take away the consolation of eternal hope; they overturn the tree from the roots; they creep on to a deadly contagion with their pestilent words; they dash the ship on the rocks, so that it may not reach to the harbour. Such a facility does not grant peace, but takes it away; nor does it give communion, but it hinders from salvation. This is another persecution, and another temptation, by which the crafty enemy still further assaults the lapsed; attacking them by a secret corruption, that their lamentation may be hushed, that their grief may be silent, that the memory of their sin may pass away, that the groaning of their heart may be repressed, that the weeping of their eyes may be quenched; nor long and full penitence deprecate the Lord so grievously offended, although it is written, 'Remember from whence you are fallen, and repent' (Rev 2:5).[2994]

The Epistles of Cyprian. To Cornelius, Concerning Fortunatus and Felicissimus, or Against the Heretics, para 13

….it is proposed by the sacrilegious, and said, Let not the wrath of God be considered, let not the judgment of the Lord be feared, let not any knock at the Church of Christ;

[2992]St. Irenaeus. *Against Heresies,* Bk. I, Chap. 13, para 7 [Online] Available at: www.newadvent.org [Accessed on: 5 September 2022]

[2993]Tertullian. *On Repentance,* Chap. 8 [Online] Available at: www.newadvent.org [Accessed on: 5 September 2022]

[2994]St. Cyprian of Carthage. *Treatise* 3, On the Lapsed, Chap. 16 [Online] Available at: www. newadvent.org [Accessed on: 5 September 2022]

but repentance being done away with, and no confession of sin being made, the bishops being despised and trodden under foot, let peace be proclaimed by the presbyters in deceitful words; and lest the lapsed should rise up, or those placed without should return to the Church, let communion be offered to those who are not in communion?[2995]

St. John Chrysostom: c. 347 to 407

Homily 82 on Matthew

Wherefore it is needful in all respects to be vigilant, for indeed no small punishment is appointed to them that partake unworthily. Consider how indignant you are against the traitor, against them that crucified Him. Look therefore, lest you also yourself become guilty of the body and blood of Christ. They slaughtered the all-holy body, but you receive it in a filthy soul after such great benefits. For neither was it enough for Him to be made man, to be smitten and slaughtered, but He also commingles Himself with us, and not by faith only, but also in very deed makes us His body. What then ought not he to exceed in purity that has the benefit of this sacrifice, than what sunbeam should not that hand be more pure which is to sever this flesh, the mouth that is filled with spiritual fire, the tongue that is reddened by that most awful blood? Consider with what sort of honor you were honored, of what sort of table you are partaking. That which when angels behold, they tremble, and dare not so much as look up at it without awe on account of the brightness that comes thence, with this we are fed, with this we are commingled, and we are made one body and one flesh with Christ. 'Who shall declare the mighty works of the Lord, and cause all His praises to be heard?' What shepherd feeds his sheep with his own limbs? And why do I say, shepherd? There are often mothers that after the travail of birth send out their children to other women as nurses; but He endures not to do this, but Himself feeds us with His own blood, and by all means entwines us with Himself.[2996]

St. Thomas Aquinas: 1225 to 1274

Summa Theologiae. Tertia Pars. Q 80. Art 4.

On the contrary, The Apostle says (I Cor 11:29): 'He that eateth and drinketh unworthily, eateth and drinketh judgment to himself.' Now the gloss says on this passage: 'He eats and drinks unworthily who is in sin, or who handles it irreverently.' Therefore, if anyone, while in mortal sin, receives this sacrament, he purchases damnation, by sinning mortally.

I answer that, In this sacrament, as in the others, that which is a sacrament is a sign of the reality of the sacrament. Now there is a twofold reality of this sacrament, as stated above (III:73:6): one which is signified and contained, namely, Christ Himself; while the other is signified but not contained, namely, Christ's mystical body, which is the fellowship of the saints. Therefore, whoever receives this sacrament, expresses thereby that he is made one with Christ, and incorporated in His members; and this is done by living faith, which no one has who is in mortal sin. And therefore it is manifest that whoever receives this sacrament while in mortal sin, is guilty of lying to this sacrament, and consequently of sacrilege, because he profanes the sacrament: and therefore he sins mortally.[2997]

The Magisterium of the Church

Matrimony is a sacrament, instituted by our Lord Jesus Christ, which creates a holy and indissoluble union between a man and woman. The marriage bond is irrevocable and cannot

---

[2995]St. Cyprian of Carthage. *The Epistles of Cyprian. To Cornelius, Concerning Fortunatus and Felicissimus, or Against the Heretics*, para 13 [Online] Available at: www.newadvent.org [Accessed on: 9 October 2022]

[2996]St. John Chrysostom. *Homily 82 on Matthew* [Online] Available at: www.newadvent.org [Accessed on: 5 September 2022]

[2997]St. Thomas Aquinas. *Summa Theologiae.* Tertia Pars. Q 80. Art 4 [Online] Available at: www.newadvent.org [Accessed on: 5 September 2022]

be dissolved except by the death of either husband or wife. The Church does not have the power to contravene this divine command. Therefore, regarding divorced persons who have civilly remarried, the Church must insist that they are not admitted to Eucharistic Communion. To do so would scandalously contradict that union of love between Christ and the Church which is signified and effected by the Eucharist. Personal conscience cannot come to a decision about the existence or absence of a previous marriage and the value of the new union. Those who 'obstinately persist in manifest grave sin' are not to be admitted to Eucharistic communion.

Council of Trent (Nineteenth Ecumenical, 1545 to 1563)

Doctrine and Canons of The Sacrament Of Matrimony. (11th November1563)
The first parent of the human race, under the influence of the divine Spirit, pronounced the bond of matrimony perpetual and indissoluble, when he said; This now is bone of my bones, and flesh of my flesh. Wherefore a man shall leave father and mother, and shall cleave to his wife, and they shall be two in one flesh. But, that by this bond two only are united and joined together, our Lord taught more plainly, when rehearsing those last words as having been uttered by God, He said, therefore now they are not two, but one flesh; and straightway confirmed the firmness of that tie, proclaimed so long before by Adam, by these words; What therefore God hath joined together, let no man put asunder. But, the grace which might perfect that natural love, and confirm that indissoluble union, and sanctify the married, Christ Himself, the institutor and perfecter of the venerable sacraments, merited for us by His passion; as the Apostle Paul intimates, saying: Husbands love your wives, as Christ also loved the Church, and delivered himself up for it; adding shortly after, This is a great sacrament, but I speak in Christ and in the Church.

CANON V. If any one saith, that on account of heresy, or irksome cohabitation, or the affected absence of one of the parties, the bond of matrimony may be dissolved; let him be anathema.

CANON VII. If any one saith, that the Church has erred, in that she hath taught, and doth teach, in accordance with the evangelical and apostolical doctrine, that the bond of matrimony cannot be dissolved on account of the adultery of one of the married parties; and that both, or even the innocent one who gave not occasion to the adultery, cannot contract another marriage, during the life-time of the other; and, that he is guilty of adultery, who, having put away the adulteress, shall take another wife, as also she, who, having put away the adulterer, shall take another husband; let him be anathema.[2998]

Decree on the Most Holy Eucharist. (11th October 1551)
On the preparation to be given that one may worthily receive the sacred Eucharist. If it is unbeseeming for any one to approach to any of the sacred functions, unless he approach holily; assuredly, the more the holiness and divinity of this heavenly sacrament are understood by a Christian, the more diligently ought he to give heed that he approach not to receive it but with great reverence and holiness, especially as we read in the Apostle those words full of terror; He that eateth and drinketh unworthily, eateth and drinketh judgment to himself. Wherefore, he who would communicate, ought to recall to mind the precept of the Apostle; Let a man prove himself. Now ecclesiastical usage declares that necessary proof to be, that no one, conscious to himself of mortal sin, how contrite soever he may seem to himself, ought to approach to the sacred Eucharist without previous sacramental confession. This the holy Synod hath decreed is to be invariably observed by all Christians....

CANON XI. If any one saith, that faith alone is a sufficient preparation for receiving the sacrament of the most holy Eucharist; let him be anathema. And for fear lest so great a sacrament may be received unworthily, and so unto death and condemnation, this holy Synod ordains and declares, that sacramental confession, when a confessor may

[2998]Council of Trent [1563] *Doctrine on the Sacrament of Marriage* [Online] Available at: www.thecounciloftrent.com [Accessed on: 1 September 2022]

be had, is of necessity to be made beforehand, by those whose conscience is burthened with mortal sin, how contrite even soever they may think themselves. But if any one shall presume to teach, preach, or obstinately to assert, or even in public disputation to defend the contrary, he shall be thereupon excommunicated.[2999]

Second Vatican Council (Twenty-First Ecumenical, 1962 to 1965)

Pastoral Constitution *Gaudium et Spes, 48, 49, 50. (7th December 1965)*
As a mutual gift of two persons, this intimate union and the good of the children impose total fidelity on the spouses and argue for an unbreakable oneness between them. [...]

This love is uniquely expressed and perfected through the appropriate enterprise of matrimony. The actions within marriage by which the couple are united intimately and chastely are noble and worthy ones. Expressed in a manner which is truly human, these actions promote that mutual self-giving by which spouses enrich each other with a joyful and a ready will. Sealed by mutual faithfulness and hallowed above all by Christ's sacrament, this love remains steadfastly true in body and in mind, in bright days or dark. It will never be profaned by adultery or divorce. Firmly established by the Lord, the unity of marriage will radiate from the equal personal dignity of wife and husband, a dignity acknowledged by mutual and total love. The constant fulfilment of the duties of this Christian vocation demands notable virtue. For this reason, strength-ened by grace for holiness of life, the couple will painstakingly cultivate and pray for steadiness of love, large heartedness and the spirit of sacrifice. [...]

Marriage to be sure is not instituted solely for procreation; rather, its very nature as an unbreakable compact between persons, and the welfare of the children, both demand that the mutual love of the spouses be embodied in a rightly ordered manner, that it grow and ripen. Therefore, marriage persists as a whole manner and communion of life, and maintains its value and indissolubility, even when despite the often intense desire of the couple, offspring are lacking.[3000]

Pope Benedict XVI: 2005 to 2013

Compendium of the Catechism of the Catholic Church. (28th June 2005)
347. What sins are gravely opposed to the sacrament of Matrimony?
Adultery and polygamy are opposed to the sacrament of matrimony because they contradict the equal dignity of man and woman and the unity and exclusivity of married love. Other sins include the deliberate refusal of one's procreative potential which deprives conjugal love of the gift of children and divorce which goes against the indissolubility of marriage.

349. What is the attitude of the Church toward those people who are divorced and then remarried?
The Church, since she is faithful to her Lord, cannot recognize the union of people who are civilly divorced and remarried. 'Whoever divorces his wife and marries another, commits adultery against her; and if she divorces her husband and marries another, she commits adultery' (Mk 10:11-12). The Church manifests an attentive solicitude toward such people and encourages them to a life of faith, prayer, works of charity and the Christian education of their children. However, they cannot receive sacramental absolution, take Holy Communion, or exercise certain ecclesial responsibilities as long as their situation, which objectively contravenes God's law, persists.[3001]

[2999]Council of Trent [1551] *Concerning the Most Holy Sacrament of the Eucharist*, Chap. VII. [Online] Available at: www.thecounciloftrent.com [Accessed on: 2 September 2022]
[3000]Second Vatican Council [1965] Pastoral Constitution *Gaudium et Spes*, para 48, 49 [Online] Available at: www.vatican.va [Accessed on: 2 September 2022]
[3001]Pope Benedict XVI [2005] *Compendium of the Catechism of the Catholic Church*, Q. 349 [Online] Available at: www.vatican.va [Accessed on: 7 September 2022]

Apostolic Exhortation *Sacramentum Caritatis, 20, 29. (22nd February 2007)*
We know that the faithful are surrounded by a culture that tends to eliminate the sense of sin and to promote a superficial approach that overlooks the need to be in a state of grace in order to approach sacramental communion worthily (CCC 1385). The loss of a consciousness of sin always entails a certain superficiality in the understanding of God's love.

If the Eucharist expresses the irrevocable nature of God's love in Christ for his Church, we can then understand why it implies, with regard to the sacrament of Matrimony, that indissolubility to which all true love necessarily aspires. There was good reason for the pastoral attention that the Synod gave to the painful situations experienced by some of the faithful who, having celebrated the sacrament of Matrimony, then divorced and remarried. This represents a complex and troubling pastoral problem, a real scourge for contemporary society, and one which increasingly affects the Catholic community as well. The Church's pastors, out of love for the truth, are obliged to discern different situations carefully, in order to be able to offer appropriate spiritual guidance to the faithful involved. The Synod of Bishops confirmed the Church's practice, based on Sacred Scripture (cf. Mk 10:2-12), of not admitting the divorced and remarried to the sacraments, since their state and their condition of life objectively contradict the loving union of Christ and the Church signified and made present in the Eucharist. Yet the divorced and remarried continue to belong to the Church, which accompanies them with special concern and encourages them to live as fully as possible the Christian life through regular participation at Mass, albeit without receiving communion, listening to the word of God, eucharistic adoration, prayer, participation in the life of the community, honest dialogue with a priest or spiritual director, dedication to the life of charity, works of penance, and commitment to the education of their children. [...]

At the same time, pastoral care must not be understood as if it were somehow in conflict with the law. Rather, one should begin by assuming that the fundamental point of encounter between the law and pastoral care is love for the truth: truth is never something purely abstract, but 'a real part of the human and Christian journey of every member of the faithful' Finally, where the nullity of the marriage bond is not declared and objective circumstances make it impossible to cease cohabitation, the Church encourages these members of the faithful to commit themselves to living their relationship in fidelity to the demands of God's law, as friends, as brother and sister; in this way they will be able to return to the table of the Eucharist, taking care to observe the Church's established and approved practice in this regard. This path, if it is to be possible and fruitful, must be supported by pastors and by adequate ecclesial initiatives, nor can it ever involve the blessing of these relations, lest confusion arise among the faithful concerning the value of marriage.[3002]

Address to the members of the Tribunal of the Roman Rota. (28th January 2006)
Indeed, pastoral love can sometimes be contaminated by complacent attitudes towards the parties. Such attitudes can seem pastoral, but in fact they do not correspond with the good of the parties and of the Ecclesial Community itself; by avoiding confrontation with the truth that saves, they can even turn out to be counterproductive with regard to each person's saving encounter with Christ. The principle of the indissolubility of marriage forcefully reaffirmed here by John Paul II (cf. Addresses: 21 January 2000, in *ORE*, 26 January 2000, p. 1; 28 January 2002, in *ibid.*, 6 February 2002, p. 6) pertains to the integrity of the Christian mystery. Today, unfortunately, we may observe that this truth is sometimes obscured in the consciences of Christians and of people of good will. For this very reason, the service that can be offered to the faithful and to non-Christian spouses in difficulty is deceptive: it reinforces in them, if only implicitly, the tendency to forget the indissolubility of their union.[3003]

[3002]Pope Benedict XVI [2007] Post Synodal Apostolic Exhortation *Sacramentum Caritatis*, para 20 [Online] Available at: www.vatican.va [Accessed on: 7 September 2022]
[3003]Pope Benedict XVI [2006] *Address to the members of the Tribunal of the Roman Rota* [Online] Available at: www.vatican.va [Accessed on: 7 September 2022]

Address to the members of the Tribunal of the Roman Rota. (27th January 2007)
Indeed, it seems to some that the conciliar teaching on marriage, and in particular, the description of this institution as *'intima communitas vitae et amoris'* [the intimate partnership of life and love] (Pastoral Constitution on the Church in the Modern World, *Gaudium et Spes* 48), must lead to a denial of the existence of an indissoluble conjugal bond because this would be a question of an 'ideal' to which 'normal Christians' cannot be 'constrained'.

In fact, the conviction that the pastoral good of the person in an irregular marital situation requires a sort of canonical regularisation, independently of the validity or nullity of his/her marriage, independently, that is, of the 'truth' of his/her personal status, has also spread in certain ecclesiastical milieus. The process of the declaration of matrimonial nullity is actually considered as a legal means for achieving this objective, according to a logic in which the law becomes the formalisation of subjective claims. In this regard, it should first be pointed out that the Council certainly described marriage as *intima communitas vitae et amoris*, but this partnership is determined, in accordance with the tradition of the Church, by a whole set of principles of the divine law which establish its true and permanent anthropological meaning (cf. *ibid.*). [...]

The anthropological and saving truth of marriage — also in its juridical dimension — is already presented in Sacred Scripture. Jesus' response to those Pharisees who asked his opinion about the lawfulness of repudiation is well known: 'Have you not read that he who made them from the beginning made them male and female, and said, "For this reason a man shall leave his father and mother and be joined to his wife, and the two shall become one"? So they are no longer two but one. What therefore God has joined together, let no man put asunder' (Mt 19:4-6).

The citations of Genesis (1:27; 2:24) propose the matrimonial truth of the 'principle', that truth whose fullness is found in connection with Christ's union with the Church (cf. Eph 5:30-31) and was the object of such broad and deep reflections on the part of Pope John Paul II in his cycles of catechesis on human love in the divine design.

On the basis of this dual unity of the human couple, it is possible to work out an authentic juridical anthropology of marriage. In this sense, Jesus' conclusive words are especially enlightening: 'What therefore God has joined together, let no man put asunder'. Every marriage is of course the result of the free consent of the man and the woman, but in practice their freedom expresses the natural capacity inherent in their masculinity and femininity.

The union takes place by virtue of the very plan of God who created them male and female and gives them the power to unite for ever those natural and complementary dimensions of their persons.

The indissolubility of marriage does not derive from the definitive commitment of those who contract it but is intrinsic in the nature of the 'powerful bond established by the Creator' (John Paul II, Catechesis, General Audience 21 November 1979, n. 2; *ORE*, 26 November 1979, p, 1).

People who contract marriage must be definitively committed to it because marriage is such in the plan of creation and of redemption. And the essential juridical character of marriage is inherent precisely in this bond which represents for the man and for the woman a requirement of justice and love from which, for their good and for the good of all, they may not withdraw without contradicting what God himself has wrought within them.[3004]

Homily during visit to the Roman parish of St. Felicity and her children, martyrs. (25th March 2007)
Jesus sent the adulterous woman away with this recommendation: 'Go, and do not sin again'. He forgives her so that 'from now on' she will sin no more. In a similar episode,

---

[3004]Pope Benedict XVI [2007] *Address to the members of the Tribunal of the Roman Rota* [Online] Available at: www.vatican.va [Accessed on: 9 October 2022]

that of the repentant woman, a former sinner whom we come across in Luke's Gospel (cf. 7:36-50), he welcomed a woman who had repented and sent her peacefully on her way. Here, instead, the adulterous woman simply receives an unconditional pardon. In both cases — for the repentant woman sinner and for the adulterous woman — the message is the same. In one case it is stressed that there is no forgiveness without the desire for forgiveness, without opening the heart to forgiveness; here it is highlighted that only divine forgiveness and divine love received with an open and sincere heart give us the strength to resist evil and 'to sin no more', to let ourselves be struck by God's love so that it becomes our strength.[3005]

General Audience Address. (10th December 2008)
A genuine marriage will be well lived if in the constant human and emotional growth an effort is made to remain continually bound to the efficacy of the Word and to the meaning of Baptism. Christ sanctified the Church, purifying her through the washing with water, accompanied by the Word. Apart from making it visible, a participation in the Body and Blood of the Lord does no more than seal a union rendered indissoluble by grace.[3006]

Address to the Roman Rota on the Indissolubility of Marriage. (29th January 2010)
One must avoid pseudo-pastoral claims that would situate questions on a purely horizontal plane, in which what matters is to satisfy subjective requests to arrive at a declaration of nullity at any cost, so that the parties may be able to overcome, among other things, obstacles to receiving the Sacraments of Penance and the Eucharist. The supreme good of readmission to Eucharistic Communion after sacramental Reconciliation demands, instead, that due consideration be given to the authentic good of the individuals, inseparable from the truth of their canonical situation. It would be a false 'good' and a grave lack of justice and love to pave the way for them to receive the sacraments nevertheless, and would risk causing them to live in objective contradiction to the truth of their own personal condition. [...]

In this sense, existential, person-centred and relational consideration of the conjugal union can never be at the expense of indissolubility, an essential property which, in Christian marriage, obtains, with unity, a special firmness by reason of the sacrament (cf. CIC, can. 1056). Moreover, it must not be forgotten that matrimony is favoured by the law. Consequently, in case of doubt, it must be considered valid until the contrary has been proven (cf. CIC, can. 1060). Otherwise, there is a grave risk of losing any objective reference point for pronouncements on nullity, by transforming every conjugal difficulty into a symptom of failure to establish a union whose essential nucleus of justice — the indissoluble bond — is effectively denied.[3007]

Homily at the Mass for the opening of the Synod of the Bishops on the New Evangelisation. (7th October 2012)

The union of a man and a woman, their becoming 'one flesh' in charity, in fruitful and indissoluble love, is a sign that speaks of God with a force and an eloquence which in our days has become greater because unfortunately, for various reasons, marriage, in precisely the oldest regions evangelised, is going through a profound crisis. And it is not by chance. Marriage is linked to faith, but not in a general way. Marriage, as a union of faithful and indissoluble love, is based upon the grace that comes from the triune God, who in Christ loved us with a faithful love, even to the Cross. Today we ought to grasp the full truth of this statement, in contrast to the painful reality of many marriages

---

[3005]Pope Benedict XVI [2007] *Homily during visit to the Roman parish of St. Felicity and her children, martyrs* [Online] Available at: www.vatican.va [Accessed on: 9 October 2022]
[3006]Pope Benedict XVI [2008] *General Audience Address* [Online] Available at: www.vatican.va [Accessed on: 9 October 2022]
[3007]Pope Benedict XVI [2010] *Address to the Roman Rota on the Indissolubility of Marriage* [Online] Available at: www.ewtn.com [Accessed on: 9 October 2022]

which, unhappily, end badly. There is a clear link between the crisis in faith and the crisis in marriage.[3008]

Address for the inauguration of the judicial year of the Tribunal of the Roman Rota, 1. (26th January 2013)
I would like to reflect in particular on several aspects of the relationship between faith and marriage, noting that the current crisis of faith, which is affecting various parts of the world, brings with it a crisis of the conjugal society with the whole burden of suffering and hardship that this entails, also for the offspring. We can take as a starting point the linguistic root that the Latin terms *fides* and *foedus* have in common. *Foedus* is a word with which the *Code of Canon Law* designates the natural reality of matrimony as an irrevocable covenant between a man and a woman (cf. can. 1055 § 1). Mutual entrustment is in fact the indispensable basis for any pact or covenant. At the theological level, the relationship between faith and marriage acquires an even deeper meaning. Indeed, although the spousal bond is a natural reality, it has been raised by Christ to the dignity of a sacrament between the baptized.[3009]

Pope St. John Paul II: 1978 to 2005
Apostolic Exhortation Familiaris Consortio, 20, 84. *(22nd November 1981)*
…the indissolubility of marriage finds i ts u ltimate t ruth i n t he p lan t hat G od has manifested in His revelation: He wills and He communicates the indissolubility of marriage as a fruit, a sign and a requirement of the absolutely faithful love that God has for man and that the Lord Jesus has for the Church. […]

Just as the Lord Jesus is the 'faithful witness,' the 'yes' of the promises of God and thus the supreme realisation of the unconditional faithfulness with which God loves His people, so Christian couples are called to participate truly in the irrevocable indissolubility that binds Christ to the Church His bride, loved by Him to the end.

…the Church reaffirms her practice, which is based upon Sacred Scripture, of not admitting to Eucharistic Communion divorced persons who have remarried. They are unable to be admitted thereto from the fact that their state and condition of life objectively contradict that union of love between Christ and the Church which is signified and effected by the Eucharist. Besides this, there is another special pastoral reason: if these people were admitted to the Eucharist, the faithful would be led into error and confusion regarding the Church's teaching about the indissolubility of marriage.

Reconciliation in the sacrament of Penance which would open the way to the Eucharist, can only be granted to those who, repenting of having broken the sign of the Covenant and of fidelity to Christ, are sincerely ready to undertake a way of life that is no longer in contradiction to the indissolubility of marriage. This means, in practice, that when, for serious reasons, such as for example the children's upbringing, a man and a woman cannot satisfy the obligation to separate, they 'take on themselves the duty to live in complete continence, that is, by abstinence from the acts proper to married couples.'

Similarly, the respect due to the sacrament of Matrimony, to the couples themselves and their families, and also to the community of the faithful, forbids any pastor, for whatever reason or pretext even of a pastoral nature, to perform ceremonies of any kind for divorced people who remarry. Such ceremonies would give the impression of the celebration of a new sacramentally valid marriage, and would thus lead people into error concerning the indissolubility of a validly contracted marriage.

By acting in this way, the Church professes her own fidelity to Christ and to His truth. At the same time she shows motherly concern for these children of hers, espe-

---

[3008]Pope Benedict XVI [2012] *Homily at the Mass for the opening of the Synod of the Bishops on the New Evangelisation* [Online] Available at: www.vatican.va [Accessed on: 9 October 2022]
[3009]Pope Benedict XVI [2013] *Address for the inauguration of the judicial year of the Tribunal of the Roman Rota*, para 1 [Online] Available at: www.vatican.va [Accessed on: 9 October 2022]

cially those who, through no fault of their own, have been abandoned by their legitimate partner.

With firm confidence she believes that those who have rejected the Lord's command and are still living in this state will be able to obtain from God the grace of conversion and salvation, provided that they have persevered in prayer, penance and charity.[3010]

Code of Canon Law. (1983)

Those who have been excommunicated or interdicted after the imposition or declaration of the penalty and others obstinately persevering in manifest grave sin are not to be admitted to holy communion. (Can. 915)

A person who is conscious of grave sin is not to celebrate Mass or receive the body of the Lord without previous sacramental confession unless there is a grave reason and there is no opportunity to confess; in this case the person is to remember the obligation to make an act of perfect contrition which includes the resolution of confessing as soon as possible. (Can. 916)

The essential properties of marriage are unity and indissolubility, which in Christian marriage obtain a special firmness by reason of the sacrament. (Can. 1056)

Matrimonial consent is an act of the will by which a man and a woman mutually give and accept each other through an irrevocable covenant in order to establish marriage. (Can. 1057 §2)

From a valid marriage there arises between the spouses a bond which by its nature is perpetual and exclusive. Moreover, a special sacrament strengthens and, as it were, consecrates the spouses in a Christian marriage for the duties and dignity of their state. (Can. 1134)

A marriage that is *ratum et consummatum* can be dissolved by no human power and by no cause, except death. (Can. 1141)[3011]

Catechism of the Catholic Church. (1992)

The Lord addresses an invitation to us, urging us to receive him in the sacrament of the Eucharist: 'Truly, I say to you, unless you eat the flesh of the Son of man and drink his blood, you have no life in you' (Jn 6:53). (1384)

To respond to this invitation we must prepare ourselves for so great and so holy a moment. St. Paul urges us to examine our conscience: 'Whoever, therefore, eats the bread or drinks the cup of the Lord in an unworthy manner will be guilty of profaning the body and blood of the Lord. Let a man examine himself, and so eat of the bread and drink of the cup. For any one who eats and drinks without discerning the body eats and drinks judgment upon himself.' (I Cor 11:27-29). Anyone conscious of a grave sin must receive the sacrament of Reconciliation before coming to communion. (1385)

Anyone who desires to receive Christ in Eucharistic communion must be in the state of grace. Anyone aware of having sinned mortally must not receive communion without having received absolution in the sacrament of penance. (1415)[3012]

Thus the marriage bond has been established by God himself in such a way that a marriage concluded and consummated between baptized persons can never be dissolved. This bond, which results from the free human act of the spouses and their consummation of the marriage, is a reality, henceforth irrevocable, and gives rise to a covenant guaranteed by God's fidelity. The Church does not have the power to contravene this disposition of divine wisdom. (1640).

Today there are numerous Catholics in many countries who have recourse to civil divorce and contract new civil unions. In fidelity to the words of Jesus Christ – 'Who-

---

[3010]Pope St. John Paul II [1981] Apostolic Exhortation *Familiaris Consortio* [Online] Available at: www.vatican.va [Accessed on: 6 September 2022]

[3011]*Code of Canon Law* [1983] [Online] Available at: www.vatican.va [Accessed on: 6 September 2022]

[3012]Catechism of the Catholic Church [1992] [Online] Available at: scborromeo2.org [Accessed on: 12 July 2022]

ever divorces his wife and marries another, commits adultery against her; and if she divorces her husband and marries another, she commits adultery' (Mk 10:11-12) the Church maintains that a new union cannot be recognized as valid, if the first marriage was. If the divorced are remarried civilly, they find themselves in a situation that objectively contravenes God's law. Consequently, they cannot receive Eucharistic communion as long as this situation persists. For the same reason, they cannot exercise certain ecclesial responsibilities. Reconciliation through the sacrament of Penance can be granted only to those who have repented for having violated the sign of the covenant and of fidelity to Christ, and who are committed to living in complete continence. (1650).

Congregation for the Doctrine of the Faith. Letter to the bishops of the Catholic Church concerning the reception of holy communion by the divorced and remarried members of the faithful, 4, 6, 7, 8. (14th September 1994)
In fidelity to the words of Jesus Christ (Mk 10:11-12), the Church affirms that a new union cannot be recognised as valid if the preceding marriage was valid. If the divorced are remarried civilly, they find themselves in a situation that objectively contravenes God's law. Consequently, they cannot receive Holy Communion as long as this situation persists (*CCC* 1650).

This norm is not at all a punishment or a discrimination against the divorced and remarried, but rather expresses an objective situation that of itself renders impossible the reception of Holy Communion: 'They are unable to be admitted thereto from the fact that their state and condition of life objectively contradict that union of love between Christ and his Church which is signified and effected by the Eucharist. Besides this, there is another special pastoral reason: if these people were admitted to the Eucharist, the faithful would be led into error and confusion regarding the Church's teaching about the indissolubility of marriage' (*Familiaris Consortio* 84).

The faithful who persist in such a situation may receive Holy Communion only after obtaining sacramental absolution, which may be given only 'to those who, repenting of having broken the sign of the Covenant and of fidelity to Christ, are sincerely ready to undertake a way of life that is no longer in contradiction to the indissolubility of marriage. This means, in practice, that when for serious reasons, for example, for the children's upbringing, a man and a woman cannot satisfy the obligation to separate, they "take on themselves the duty to live in complete continence, that is, by abstinence from the acts proper to married couples"'. In such a case they may receive Holy Communion as long as they respect the obligation to avoid giving scandal. [...]

Members of the faithful who live together as husband and wife with persons other than their legitimate spouses may not receive Holy Communion. Should they judge it possible to do so, pastors and confessors, given the gravity of the matter and the spiritual good of these persons as well as the common good of the Church, have the serious duty to admonish them that such a judgment of conscience openly contradicts the Church's teaching (*Code of Canon Law*, 978 §2). Pastors in their teaching must also remind the faithful entrusted to their care of this doctrine. [...]

The mistaken conviction of a divorced and remarried person that he may receive Holy Communion normally presupposes that personal conscience is considered in the final analysis to be able, on the basis of one's own convictions, to come to a decision about the existence or absence of a previous marriage and the value of the new union. However, such a position is inadmissible (*Code of Canon Law*, 1085 § 2). Marriage, in fact, because it is both the image of the spousal relationship between Christ and his Church as well as the fundamental core and an important factor in the life of civil society, is essentially a public reality.

It is certainly true that a judgment about one's own dispositions for the reception of Holy Communion must be made by a properly formed moral conscience. But it is equally true that the consent that is the foundation of marriage is not simply a private decision since it creates a specifically ecclesial and social situation for the spouses, both individually and as a couple. Thus the judgment of conscience of one's own marital situation does not regard only the immediate relationship between man and God, as if one could prescind from the Church's mediation, that also includes canonical laws binding in conscience. Not to recognise this essential aspect would mean in fact to deny that marriage is a reality of the Church, that is to say, a sacrament.[3013]

Address to the members of the Tribunal of the Roman Rota, 2-3. (21st January 2000)
...the Church's 'fundamental duty' is 'to reaffirm strongly, as the Synod Fathers did, the doctrine of the indissolubility of marriage' (*Familiaris Consortio* 20), in order to dispel the shadow that seems to be cast over the value of the indissolubility of the conjugal bond by certain opinions stemming from theological and canonical research. I am referring to theories in favour of rejecting the absolute incompatibility of a ratified and consummated marriage (cf. *CIC*, can. 1061, 1) with a new marriage by one of the spouses while the other is still alive.

In fidelity to Christ, the Church must firmly stress 'the good news of the definitive nature of that conjugal love that has in Christ its foundation and strength (cf. Eph 5:25)' (*Familiaris Consortio* 20) to those in our day who think that it is difficult or even impossible to be bound to one person for their whole life, and to those who are unfortunately caught up in a culture that rejects the indissolubility of marriage and openly mocks the couple's commitment to fidelity.

In fact, 'being rooted in the personal and total self-giving of the couple, and being required by the good of the children, the indissolubility of marriage finds its ultimate truth in the plan that God has manifested in his revelation: he wills and he communicates the indissolubility of marriage as a fruit, a sign and a requirement of the absolutely faithful love that God has for man and that the Lord Jesus has for the Church' (*Familiaris Consortio* 20).

The 'good news of the definitive nature of conjugal love' is not a vague abstraction or a beautiful phrase reflecting the common desire of those who decide to marry. This message is rooted instead in the Christian newness that makes marriage a sacrament.

Christian spouses, who have received 'the gift of the sacrament', are called by the grace of God to bear witness 'to the holy will of the Lord: "What therefore God has joined together, let not man put asunder" (Mt 19:6), that is, to the inestimable value of the indissolubility... of marriage' (*Familiaris Consortio* 20). For these reasons — the *Catechism of the Catholic Church* says – 'in fidelity to the words of Christ (Mk 10:11-12)... the Church maintains that a new union cannot be recognized as valid, if the first marriage was' (1650).[3014]

Address to the members of the Tribunal of the Roman Rota, 4. (28th January 2002)
To treat indissolubility not as a natural juridical norm but as a mere ideal empties of meaning the unequivocal declaration of Jesus Christ, who absolutely refused divorce because 'from the beginning it was not so' (Mt 19:8). Marriage 'is' indissoluble: this property expresses a dimension of its objective being, it is not a mere subjective fact. Consequently, the good of indissolubility is the good of marriage itself; and the lack of understanding of its indissoluble character constitutes the lack of understanding of the essence of marriage.[3015]

Encyclical *Ecclesia de Eucharistia, 36-37. (17th April 2003)*

Invisible communion, though by its nature always growing, presupposes the life of grace, by which we become 'partakers of the divine nature' (II Pet 1:4), and the practice

---

[3013]Congregation for the Doctrine of the Faith. [1994] *Letter to the bishops of the catholic Church concerning the reception of holy communion by the divorced and remarried members of the faithful,* 4 [Online] Available at: www.vatican.va [Accessed on: 6 September 2022]
[3014]Pope St. John Paul II [2000] *Address to the members of the Tribunal of the Roman Rota,* paras 2-3 [Online] Available at: www.vatican.va [Accessed on: 6 September 2022]
[3015]Pope St. John Paul II [2002] *Address to the members of the Tribunal of the Roman Rota,* 4. [Online] Available at: www.vatican.va [Accessed on: 6 September 2022]

of the virtues of faith, hope and love. Only in this way do we have true communion with the Father, the Son and the Holy Spirit. Nor is faith sufficient; we must persevere in sanctifying grace and love, remaining within the Church 'bodily' as well as 'in our heart'; what is required, in the words of St. Paul, is 'faith working through love' (Gal 5:6).

Keeping these invisible bonds intact is a specific moral duty incumbent upon Christians who wish to participate fully in the Eucharist by receiving the body and blood of Christ. The Apostle Paul appeals to this duty when he warns: 'Let a man examine himself, and so eat of the bread and drink of the cup' (I Cor 11:28). St. John Chrysostom, with his stirring eloquence, exhorted the faithful: 'I too raise my voice, I beseech, beg and implore that no one draw near to this sacred table with a sullied and corrupt conscience. Such an act, in fact, can never be called "communion", not even were we to touch the Lord's body a thousand times over, but "condemnation", "torment" and "increase of punishment"'. (*Homiliae in Isaiam*, 6, 3).

Along these same lines, the *Catechism of the Catholic Church* rightly stipulates that 'anyone conscious of a grave sin must receive the sacrament of Reconciliation before coming to communion'. (*CCC* 1385; *CIC* 916). I therefore desire to reaffirm that in the Church there remains in force, now and in the future, the rule by which the Council of Trent gave concrete expression to the Apostle Paul's stern warning when it affirmed that, in order to receive the Eucharist in a worthy manner, 'one must first confess one's sins, when one is aware of mortal sin'.

The two sacraments of the Eucharist and Penance are very closely connected. Because the Eucharist makes present the redeeming sacrifice of the Cross, perpetuating it sacramentally, it naturally gives rise to a continuous need for conversion, for a personal response to the appeal made by St. Paul to the Christians of Corinth: 'We beseech you on behalf of Christ, be reconciled to God' (II Cor 5:20). If a Christian's conscience is burdened by serious sin, then the path of penance through the sacrament of Reconciliation becomes necessary for full participation in the Eucharistic Sacrifice.

The judgment of one's state of grace obviously belongs only to the person involved, since it is a question of examining one's conscience. However, in cases of outward conduct which is seriously, clearly and steadfastly contrary to the moral norm, the Church, in her pastoral concern for the good order of the community and out of respect for the sacrament, cannot fail to feel directly involved. *The Code of Canon Law* refers to this situation of a manifest lack of proper moral disposition when it states that those who 'obstinately persist in manifest grave sin' are not to be admitted to Eucharistic communion. (*CIC* 915).[3016]

Pope St. Paul VI: 1963 to 1978

Encyclical *Humanae Vitae*, 8, 9. (25th July 1968)
Marriage, then, is far from being the effect of chance or the result of the blind evolution of natural forces. It is in reality the wise and provident institution of God the Creator, whose purpose was to effect in man His loving design. As a consequence, husband and wife, through that mutual gift of themselves, which is specific and exclusive to them alone, develop that union of two persons in which they perfect one another, cooperating with God in the generation and rearing of new lives.

The marriage of those who have been baptized is, in addition, invested with the dignity of a sacramental sign of grace, for it represents the union of Christ and His Church. [...]

Married love is also faithful and exclusive of all other, and this until death. This is how husband and wife understood it on the day on which, fully aware of what they were doing, they freely vowed themselves to one another in marriage. Though this

---

[3016]Pope St. John Paul II [2003] *Encyclical Ecclesia de Eucharistia*, para 36 [Online] Available at: www.vatican.va [Accessed on: 6 September 2022]

fidelity of husband and wife sometimes presents difficulties, no one has the right to assert that it is impossible; it is, on the contrary, always honourable and meritorious. The example of countless married couples proves not only that fidelity is in accord with the nature of marriage, but also that it is the source of profound and enduring happiness.[3017]

Pope St. John XXIII: 1958 to 1963

Encyclical *Mater et Magistra, 193. (15th May 1961)*
We must solemnly proclaim that human life is transmitted by means of the family, and the family is based upon a marriage which is one and indissoluble and, with respect to Christians, raised to the dignity of a sacrament.[3018]

Encyclical *Pacem in Terris, 16. (11th April 1963)*
The family, founded upon marriage freely contracted, one and indissoluble, must be regarded as the natural, primary cell of human society.[3019]

Pope Ven. Pius XII: 1939 to 1958

Address to the Roman Rota. (3rd October 1941)
A ratified and consummated marriage is by divine law indissoluble, since it cannot be dissolved by any human authority (can. 1118).[3020]

Audience with newlywed couples. (22nd April 1942)
In the face of such a law of indissolubility, human passion in every age, chained and repressed in the free satisfaction of its inordinate appetites, has sought in every way to throw off its yoke. Passion sees in this law only a hard tyranny, arbitrarily weighing down conscience with an unsupportable burden, with a slavery repugnant to the sacred rights of the human person. It is true; a bond can at times constitute a burden, a slavery, like the chains which bind the prisoner. But it can also be a powerful aid and a sure guarantee, like the rope which binds the alpine climber to his companion during the ascent, or the ligaments which unite the parts of the human body, making its movements free and easy. This is clearly the case with the indissoluble bond of marriage.[3021]

Pope Pius XI: 1922 to 1939

Encyclical *Casti Connubii, 20-21, 32-34, 87, 110. (31st December 1930)*
With reason, therefore, does the Sacred Council of Trent solemnly declare: 'Christ Our Lord very clearly taught that in this bond two persons only are to be united and joined together when He said: "Therefore they are no longer two, but one flesh"'.

Nor did Christ Our Lord wish only to condemn any form of polygamy or polyandry, as they are called, whether successive or simultaneous, and every other external dishonorable act, but, in order that the sacred bonds of marriage may be guarded absolutely inviolate, He forbade also even willful thoughts and desires of such like things: 'But I say to you, that whosoever shall look on a woman to lust after her hath already committed adultery with her in his heart.' (Mt 5:28). Which words of Christ Our Lord cannot be annulled even by the consent of one of the partners of marriage for they express a law of God and of nature which no will of man can break or bend.

[3017]Pope St. Paul VI [1968] Encyclical *Humanae Vitae*, paras 8,9 [Online] Available at: www.vatican.va [Accessed on: 9 October 2022]
[3018]Pope St. John XXIII [1961] Encyclical *Mater et Magistra*, para 193 [Online] Available at: www.vatican.va [Accessed on: 9 October 2022]
[3019]Pope St. John XXIII [1963] Encyclical *Pacem in Terris*, para 16 [Online] Available at: www.vatican.va [Accessed on: 9 October 2022]
[3020]Pope Ven. Pius XII [1941] *Address to the Roman Rota* quoted by Pope St. John Paul II [2000] Address to the Roman Rota [Online] Available at: www.vatican.va [Accessed on: 9 October 2022]
[3021]Pope Ven. Pius XII [1942] *Audience with newly-wed couples.* [Online] Available at: www.marriageuniqueforareason.org [Accessed on: 6 September 2022]

In the first place Christ Himself lays stress on the indissolubility and firmness of the marriage bond when He says: 'What God hath joined together let no man put asunder,' (Mt 29:6) and: 'Everyone that putteth away his wife and marrieth another committeth adultery, and he that marrieth her that is put away from her husband committeth adultery.' (Lk 16:18).

And St. Augustine clearly places what he calls the blessing of matrimony in this indissolubility when he says: 'In the sacrament it is provided that the marriage bond should not be broken, and that a husband or wife, if separated, should not be joined to another even for the sake of offspring.'

And this inviolable stability, although not in the same perfect measure in every case, belongs to every true marriage, for the word of the Lord: 'What God hath joined together let no man put asunder,' must of necessity include all true marriages without exception, since it was spoken of the marriage of our first parents, the prototype of every future marriage. Therefore although before Christ the sublimeness and the severity of the primeval law was so tempered that Moses permitted to the chosen people of God on account of the hardness of their hearts that a bill of divorce might be given in certain circumstances, nevertheless, Christ, by virtue of His supreme legislative power, recalled this concession of greater liberty and restored the primeval law in its integrity by those words which must never be forgotten, 'What God hath joined together let no man put asunder.'

Opposed to all these reckless opinions, Venerable Brethren, stands the unalterable law of God, fully confirmed by Christ, a law that can never be deprived of its force by the decrees of men, the ideas of a people or the will of any legislator: 'What God hath joined together, let no man put asunder.' And if any man, acting contrary to this law, shall have put asunder, his action is null and void, and the consequence remains, as Christ Himself has explicitly confirmed: 'Everyone that putteth away his wife and marrieth another, committeth adultery: and he that marrieth her that is put away from her husband committeth adultery.'(Lk 16:18). Moreover, these words refer to every kind of marriage, even that which is natural and legitimate only; for, as has already been observed, that indissolubility by which the loosening of the bond is once and for all removed from the whim of the parties and from every secular power, is a property of every true marriage.

Let them constantly keep in mind, that they have been sanctified and strengthened for the duties and for the dignity of their state by a special sacrament, the efficacious power of which, although it does not impress a character, is undying. To this purpose we may ponder over the words full of real comfort of holy Cardinal Robert Bellarmine, who with other well-known theologians with devout conviction thus expresses himself: 'The sacrament of matrimony can be regarded in two ways: first, in the making, and then in its permanent state. For it is a sacrament like to that of the Eucharist, which not only when it is being conferred, but also whilst it remains, is a sacrament; for as long as the married parties are alive, so long is their union a sacrament of Christ and the Church.'[3022]

Pope St. Pius X: 1903 to 1914

Catechism of Pope St. Pius X. (1908)

The Sacrament of Matrimony

Nature of the Sacrament of Matrimony

1 Q. What is the sacrament of Matrimony?
A. Matrimony is a sacrament, instituted by our Lord Jesus Christ, which creates a holy and indissoluble union between a man and woman, and gives them grace to love one another holily and to bring up their children as Christians.

[3022]Pope Pius XI [1930] Encyclical *Casti Connubii*, para 87 [Online] Available at: www.vatican.va [Accessed on: 6 September 2022]

3 Q. Has the sacrament of Matrimony any special signification?
A. The sacrament of Matrimony signifies the indissoluble union of Jesus Christ with the Church, His Spouse, and our holy Mother.

4 Q. Why do we say that the bond of marriage is indissoluble?
A. We say that the bond of marriage is indissoluble or that it cannot be dissolved except by the death of either husband or wife, because God so ordained from the beginning and so Jesus Christ our Lord solemnly proclaimed.

5 Q. Can the contract be separated from the sacrament in Christian marriage?
A. No, in marriage among Christians the contract cannot be separated from the sacrament, because, for Christians, marriage is nothing else than the natural contract itself, raised by Jesus Christ to the dignity of a sacrament.

22 Q. Can the civil authority dissolve the bonds of Christian marriage by divorce?
A. No, the bond of Christian marriage cannot be dissolved by the civil authority, because the civil authority cannot interfere with the matter of the sacrament nor can it put asunder what God has joined together.

23 Q. What is a civil marriage?
A. It is nothing but a mere formality prescribed by the [civil] law to give and insure the civil effects of the marriage to the spouses and their children.

24 Q. Is it sufficient for a Christian to get only the civil marriage or contract?
A. For a Christian, it is not sufficient to get only the civil contract, because it is not a sacrament, and therefore not a true marriage.

25 Q. In what condition would the spouses be who would live together united only by a civil marriage?
A. Spouses who would live together united by only a civil marriage would be in an habitual state of mortal sin, and their union would always be illegitimate in the sight of God and of the Church.[3023]

Pope Leo XIII: 1878 to 1903

Encyclical *Arcanum Divinae Sapientiae, 9. (10th February 1880)*
…Christ our Lord raised marriage to the dignity of a sacrament; that to husband and wife, guarded and strengthened by the heavenly grace which His merits gained for them, He gave power to attain holiness in the married state; and that, in a wondrous way, making marriage an example of the mystical union between Himself and His Church, He not only perfected that love which is according to nature, but also made the naturally indivisible union of one man with one woman far more perfect through the bond of heavenly love. […]

In like manner from the teaching of the Apostles we learn that the unity of marriage and its perpetual indissolubility, the indispensable conditions of its very origin, must, according to the command of Christ, be holy and inviolable without exception.[3024]

Pope Bl. Pius IX: 1846 to 1878

The Syllabus of Errors, error 67. (8th December 1864)
By the law of nature, the marriage tie is not indissoluble, and in many cases divorce properly so called may be decreed by the civil authority. (*ibid.*; Allocution *Acerbissimum*, Sept. 27, 1852)[3025]

[3023]Pope St. Pius X [1908] *Catechism of Pope St. Pius X* [Online] Available at: www.ewtn.com [Accessed on: 6 September 2022]
[3024]Pope Leo XIII [1880] *Arcanum Divinae Sapientiae*, para 9 [Online] Available at: www.vatican.va [Accessed on: 9 October 2022]
[3025]Pope Bl. Pius IX [1864] *The Syllabus of Errors*, error 67 [Online] www.papalencyclicals.net [Accessed on: 6 September 2022]

Allocution *Acerbissimum* Vobiscum. *(27th September 1857)*
...no Catholic is ignorant or cannot know that matrimony is truly and properly one of the seven sacraments of the evangelical law, instituted by Christ the Lord, and that for that reason, there can be no marriage between the faithful without there being at one and the same time a sacrament, and that, therefore, any other union of man and woman among Christians, except the sacramental union, even if contracted under the power of any civil law, is nothing else than a disgraceful and death-bringing concubinage very frequently condemned by the Church, and, hence, that the sacrament can never be separated from the conjugal agreement (see n. 1773), and that it pertains absolutely to the power of the Church to discern those things which can pertain in any way to the same matrimony.[3026]

Pope Pius VII: 1800 to 1823

Brief *Etsi Fraternitatis to the Archbishop of Mainz. (8th October 1803)*
The second principle is that the sentence of lay tribunals and non-Catholic assemblies which issue sentences of nullity and attempt to dissolve marriages have no value or effect in the eyes of the Church. You ask what a parish priest must do when one of the parties, freed from his first marriage and having obtained his liberty by a sentence of a non-Catholic tribunal, wishes to wed a Catholic. You ask if the parish priest can assist at this marriage and give the nuptial blessing, as some have dared to do in your diocese, (as you tell us) you yourselves, by the wisdom that distinguishes you, should understand that such priests commit a very grave crime and betray the sacred ministry, if they approve of such marriages by their presence and ratify them with their blessing! On the other hand, it cannot be called a marriage but an adulterous union, since the impediment – the bond of the first marriage – which persists and remains unaltered – cannot be dissolved or annulled by the sentence of a non-Catholic tribunal. As long as such an impediment remains and persists every other union between the man and the woman is adulterous. Therefore, instead of sweet and persuasive words, it is preferable that the parish priest seriously exhort the person not to commit such a grave crime and sin against the law of God, a law He established from the beginning of the world, and therefore He said: 'What God hath joined together, let no man put asunder' (Mt 19:6). If the person obstinately refuses to listen to his parish priest and unites himself with a non-Catholic, thus committing an infamous adultery, and if the parish priest sees that it could be highly dangerous to religion to insist again and oppose his will to such a union, he can then bear in silence such a monstrous crime, but he can never assist at such a union, much less bless it. If the secular power orders, threatens or reproves, 'we must obey God rather than men' (Acts 5:29). The priest of God, according to the words of St. Cyprian, servant of the Gospel and defender of Christ's precepts, can be put to death but he can never be vanquished (*Letter to Cornelius Contra Haereticos*).[3027]

Pope Benedict XIV: 1740 to 1758

Constitution *Nuper ad Nos. (16th March 1743)*
Likewise, I profess that the bond of the sacrament of matrimony is indissoluble and that, although a separation of bed and board may be possible between spouses because of adultery, heresy, and some other causes, nevertheless it is not lawful for them to contract another marriage.[3028]

[3026]Pope Bl. Pius IX [1857] *Allocution Acerbissimum Vobiscum* [Online] Available at: sensusfidelium. com [Accessed on: 9 October 2022]
[3027]Pope Pius VII [1803] Brief *Etsi Fraternitatis* to the Archbishop of Mainz (Trans. Andrew Guernsey) [Online] Available at: aguernz.medium.com [Accessed on 6 September 2022]
[3028]Denzinger, H [2010] *Op. cit.*, p.513, Dz 2536

Pope Innocent III: 1198 to 1216

Letter Eius Exemplo *to the Archbishop of Tarragona. (18th December 1208)*
We do not deny that marriages can be contracted following what is said by the apostle (cf. I Cor 7); but we strictly forbid that those rightly contracted be broken.[3029]

Pope St. Marcellinus: 295 to 304

Synod of Elvira, canon 9. (300-303)
Likewise, if a believing woman has left her believing, adulterous husband and wishes to marry another, let her be forbidden to marry; if she does marry, she may not receive communion unless the husband she abandoned has previously departed this world, unless, perhaps, the exigency of illness urges the giving of it to her.[3030]

[3029]*Ibid.*, p.264, *Dz* 794
[3030]*Ibid.* p.49, *Dz* 117

Sacraments (2) — Sacramentals: Blessings

Pope Francis: 2013 to 2025

P. *God blesses everyone, so the Church should bless everyone, including couples in irregular relationships that are morally unacceptable from an objective point of view — including couples of the same sex. Ministers of blessings must embrace pastoral charity which means not imposing moral judgements on couples engaging in sexual immorality. By making a distinction between ritualised and non-ritualised blessings, ministers of blessings do not have to impose the moral requirements expected for reception of the sacraments.*

General Audience Address. (2nd December 2020)
We are more important to God than all of the sins that we can commit, because he is a father, he is a mother, he is pure love, he has blessed us forever. And he will never stop blessing us [....] We cannot just bless this God who blesses us; we must bless everyone in him, all people, bless God and bless our brothers and sisters, bless the world.[3031]

Address at Welcome Ceremony of World Youth Day. (3rd August 2023)
...in the Church, there is room for everyone. Everyone. In the Church, no one is left out or left over. There is room for everyone. Just the way we are. Everyone. Jesus says this clearly. When he sends the apostles to invite people to the banquet which a man had prepared, he tells them: 'Go out and bring in everyone', young and old, healthy and infirm, righteous and sinners. Everyone, everyone, everyone! In the Church there is room for everyone. 'Father, but I am a wretch, is there room for me?' There is room for everyone! All together now, everyone, repeat with me in your own language: Everyone, everyone, everyone. I can't hear you: again! Everyone. Everyone. Everyone. That is the Church, the Mother of all. There is room for everyone. The Lord does not point a finger, but opens his arms. It is odd: the Lord does not know how to do this (pointing), but that (opening wide). He embraces us all. He shows us Jesus on the cross, who opened his arms wide in order to be crucified and die for us.[3032]

Respuestas to the Dubia of Two Cardinals. (25th September 2023)
(d) Nevertheless, in our dealings with people, we must not lose pastoral charity, which should permeate all our decisions and attitudes. The defense of objective truth is not the only expression of this charity; it also includes kindness, patience, understanding, tenderness, and encouragement. Therefore, we cannot become judges who only deny, reject, and exclude.
(e) For this reason, pastoral prudence must adequately discern whether there are forms of blessing, requested by one or more persons, that do not convey an erroneous conception of marriage. For, when one asks for a blessing, one is expressing a petition for God's assistance, a plea to live better, and confidence in a Father who can help us live better.
(f) On the other hand, even though there are situations that are not morally acceptable from an objective point of view, the same pastoral charity requires us not to treat simply as 'sinners' those whose guilt or responsibility may be attenuated by various factors affecting subjective imputability.[3033]

Homily during Mass at Opening of the Synod on Synodality. (4th October 2023)
...the church is here for you! Tutti, tutti, tutti! (Everyone, everyone, everyone!)[3034]

[3031]Pope Francis [2020] *General Audience Address* [Online] Available at: www.vatican.va [Accessed on: 19 February 2024]
[3032]Pope Francis [2023] *Address at Welcome Ceremony of World Youth Day* [Online] Available at: www.vatican.va [Accessed on: 19 February 2024]
[3033]Pope Francis [2023] *Respuestas to the Dubia of Two Cardinals* [Online] Available at: www.vatican.va [Accessed on: 19 February 2024]
[3034]Pope Francis [2023] *Full text: Pope Francis' homily opening the Synod on Synodality* [Online] Available at: www.americamagazine.org [Accessed on: 19 February 2024]

Declaration *Fiducia Supplicans, On the Pastoral Meaning of Blessings. (18th December 2023)* This Declaration considers several questions that have come to this Dicastery in recent years. In preparing the document, the Dicastery, as is its practice, consulted experts, undertook a careful drafting process, and discussed the text in the *Congresso* of the Doctrinal Section of the Dicastery. During that time, the document was discussed with the Holy Father. Finally, the text of the Declaration was submitted to the Holy Father for his review, and he approved it with his signature.[3035]

The supplicating trust of the faithful People of God receives the gift of blessing that flows from the Heart of Christ through his Church. Pope Francis offers this timely reminder: 'The great blessing of God is Jesus Christ. He is the great gift of God, his own Son. He is a blessing for all humanity, a blessing that has saved us all. He is the Eternal Word, with whom the Father blessed us "while we were still sinners" (Rom. 5:8), as St. Paul says. He is the Word made flesh, offered for us on the cross.'[3036]

One must also avoid the risk of reducing the meaning of blessings to this point of view alone, for it would lead us to expect the same moral conditions for a simple blessing that are called for in the reception of the sacraments. Such a risk requires that we broaden this perspective further. Indeed, there is the danger that a pastoral gesture that is so beloved and widespread will be subjected to too many moral prerequisites, which, under the claim of control, could overshadow the unconditional power of God's love that forms the basis for the gesture of blessing.[3037]

Precisely in this regard, Pope Francis urged us not to 'lose pastoral charity, which should permeate all our decisions and attitudes' and to avoid being 'judges who only deny, reject, and exclude.' Let us then respond to the Holy Father's proposal by developing a broader understanding of blessings.[3038]

In his mystery of love, through Christ, God communicates to his Church the power to bless. Granted by God to human beings and bestowed by them on their neighbours, the blessing is transformed into inclusion, solidarity, and peacemaking. It is a positive message of comfort, care, and encouragement. The blessing expresses God's merciful embrace and the Church's motherhood, which invites the faithful to have the same feelings as God toward their brothers and sisters.[3039]

From the point of view of pastoral care, blessings should be evaluated as acts of devotion that 'are external to the celebration of the Holy Eucharist and of the other sacraments.' Indeed, the 'language, rhythm, course, and theological emphasis' of popular piety differ 'from those of the corresponding liturgical action.' For this reason, 'pious practices must conserve their proper style, simplicity, and language, [and] attempts to impose forms of "liturgical celebration" on them are always to be avoided.'[3040]

The Church, moreover, must shy away from resting its pastoral praxis on the fixed nature of certain doctrinal or disciplinary schemes, especially when they lead to 'a narcissistic and authoritarian elitism, whereby instead of evangelising, one analyses and classifies others, and instead of opening the door to grace, one exhausts his or her energies in inspecting and verifying.' Thus, when people ask for a blessing, an exhaustive moral analysis should not be placed as a precondition for conferring it. For, those seeking a blessing should not be required to have prior moral perfection.[3041]

In this perspective, the Holy Father's *Respuestas* aid in expanding the Congregation for the Doctrine of the Faith's 2021 pronouncement from a pastoral point of view. For, the *Respuestas* invite discernment concerning the possibility of 'forms of blessing,

---

[3035]Dicastery for the Doctrine of the Faith [2023] *Declaration Fiducia Supplicans* [Online] Available at: www.vatican.va [Accessed on: 19 February 2024]
[3036]*Op cit*, para 1.
[3037]*Ibid*, para 12.
[3038]*Ibid*, para 13.
[3039]*Ibid*, para 19.
[3040]*Ibid*, para 24.
[3041]*Ibid*, para 25.

requested by one or more persons, that do not convey an erroneous conception of marriage' and, in situations that are morally unacceptable from an objective point of view, account for the fact that 'pastoral charity requires us not to treat simply as "sinners" those whose guilt or responsibility may be attenuated by various factors affecting subjective imputability.'[3042]

So we are more important to God than all the sins we can commit because he is father, he is mother, he is pure love, he has blessed us forever. And he will never stop blessing us. It is a powerful experience to read these biblical texts of blessing in a prison or in a rehabilitation group. To make those people feel that they are still blessed, notwithstanding their serious mistakes, that their heavenly Father continues to will their good and to hope that they will ultimately open themselves to the good. Even if their closest relatives have abandoned them, because they now judge them to be irredeemable, God always sees them as his children.[3043]

There are several occasions when people spontaneously ask for a blessing, whether on pilgrimages, at shrines, or even on the street when they meet a priest. By way of example, we can refer to the Book of Blessings, which provides several rites for blessing people, including the elderly, the sick, participants in a catechetical or prayer meeting, pilgrims, those embarking on a journey, volunteer groups and associations, and more. Such blessings are meant for everyone; no one is to be excluded from them.[3044]

Within the horizon outlined here appears the possibility of blessings for couples in irregular situations and for couples of the same sex, the form of which should not be fixed ritually by ecclesial authorities to avoid producing confusion with the blessing proper to the Sacrament of Marriage. In such cases, a blessing may be imparted that not only has an ascending value but also involves the invocation of a blessing that descends from God upon those who — recognising themselves to be destitute and in need of his help — do not claim a legitimation of their own status, but who beg that all that is true, good, and humanly valid in their lives and their relationships be enriched, healed, and elevated by the presence of the Holy Spirit. These forms of blessing express a supplication that God may grant those aids that come from the impulses of his Spirit — what classical theology calls 'actual grace' — so that human relationships may mature and grow in fidelity to the Gospel, that they may be freed from their imperfections and frailties, and that they may express themselves in the ever-increasing dimension of the divine love.[3045]

In this sense, it is essential to grasp the Holy Father's concern that these non-ritualized blessings never cease being simple gestures that provide an effective means of increasing trust in God on the part of the people who ask for them, careful that they should not become a liturgical or semi-liturgical act, similar to a sacrament. Indeed, such a ritualisation would constitute a serious impoverishment because it would subject a gesture of great value in popular piety to excessive control, depriving ministers of freedom and spontaneity in their pastoral accompaniment of people's lives.[3046]

Interview on the Che Tempo Che Fa *TV program, Italy's Channel 9. (15th January 2024)*
Sometimes decisions are not accepted, but in most cases when decisions are not accepted, it is because they are not understood. The danger is that if I don't like something and I put it (the opposition) in my heart, I become a resistance and jump to ugly conclusions.... This is what happened with these latest decisions on blessings for all.... The Lord blesses everyone. But then people have to enter into a dialogue with the blessing of the Lord and see the path that the Lord proposes. We (the Church) have to take them by the hand and lead them along that path and not condemn them from the start.[3047]

[3042]*Ibid*, para 26.
[3043]*Ibid*, para 27.
[3044]*Ibid*, para 28.
[3045]*Ibid*, para 31.
[3046]*Ibid*, para 36.
[3047]Pullella, P [2024] *Pope defends same-sex blessings declaration, says it is misunderstood* [Online] Available at: www.reuters.com [Accessed on: 19 February 2024]

Interview in the Italian periodical Credere. *(8th February 2024)*
No one is scandalized if I give a blessing to an entrepreneur who perhaps exploits people: and this is a very serious sin. Whereas they are scandalized if I give it to a homosexual…. This is hypocrisy! We must all respect each other. Everyone. I don't bless a 'homosexual marriage'. I bless two people who love each other and I also ask them to pray for me. Always in confessions, when these situations arrive, homosexual people, remarried people, I always pray and bless. The blessing is not to be denied to anyone. Everyone, everyone. Mind you, I am talking about people: those who are capable of receiving baptism.[3048]

Address to Participants in the Plenary Session of the Dicastery for the Doctrine of the Faith. (26th January 2024).
I would like briefly to underline two things: the first is that these blessings, outside of any liturgical context and form, do not demand moral perfection in order to be received; the second, that when a couple approaches spontaneously to ask for a blessing, one does not bless the union, but simply the people who have requested it. The union is not blessed, but the people. Of course, one must take into account the context, the sensibilities, and the place in which one lives, as well as the most appropriate way to give the blessing.[3049]

Sacred Scripture

Matthew 13: 13-15
Therefore do I speak to them in parables: because seeing they see not, and hearing they hear not, neither do they understand. And the prophecy of Isaias is fulfilled in them, who saith: By hearing you shall hear, and shall not understand: and seeing you shall see, and shall not perceive. For the heart of this people is grown gross, and with their ears they have been dull of hearing, and their eyes they have shut: lest at any time they should see with their eyes, and hear with their ears, and understand with their heart, and be converted, and I should heal them.

John 12:40
He hath blinded their eyes, and hardened their heart, that they should not see with their eyes, nor understand with their heart, and be converted, and I should heal them.

Romans 1:18; 9:18
For the wrath of God is revealed from heaven against all ungodliness and injustice of those men that detain the truth of God in injustice…Therefore he hath mercy on whom he will; and whom he will, he hardeneth.

Romans 1:24-32
Wherefore God gave them up to the desires of their heart, unto uncleanness, to dishonour their own bodies among themselves. Who changed the truth of God into a lie; and worshipped and served the creature rather than the Creator, who is blessed for ever. Amen. For this cause God delivered them up to shameful affections. For their women have changed the natural use into that use which is against nature. And, in like manner, the men also, leaving the natural use of the women, have burned in their lusts one towards another, men with men working that which is filthy, and receiving in themselves the recompense which was due to their error. And as they liked not to have God in their knowledge, God delivered them up to a reprobate sense, to do those things which are not convenient; being filled with all iniquity, malice, fornication, avarice, wickedness, full of envy, murder, contention, deceit, malignity, whisperers, detractors, hateful to God, contumelious, proud, haughty, inventors of evil things, disobedient

---

[3048]Santucci, M [2024] *Pope Francis: To be 'scandalized' by gay couple blessings is 'hypocrisy'* [Online] Available at: www.catholicnewsagency.com [Accessed on 19 February 2024]
[3049]Pope Francis [2024] *Address to Participants in the Plenary Session of the Dicastery for the Doctrine of the Faith* [Online] Available at: www.vatican.va [Accessed on: 19 February 2024]

to parents, foolish, dissolute, without affection, without fidelity, without mercy. Who, having known the justice of God, did not understand that they who do such things, are worthy of death; and not only they that do them, but they also that consent to them that do them.

Romans 6: 19-20; 21-23
I speak an human thing, because of the infirmity of your flesh. For as you have yielded your members to serve uncleanness and iniquity, unto iniquity; so now yield your members to serve justice, unto sanctification [....] What fruit therefore had you then in those things, of which you are now ashamed? For the end of them is death. But now being made free from sin, and become servants to God, you have your fruit unto sanctification, and the end life everlasting. For the wages of sin is death. But the grace of God, life everlasting, in Christ Jesus our Lord.

Romans 8:6-8
For the wisdom of the flesh is death; but the wisdom of the spirit is life and peace. Because the wisdom of the flesh is an enemy to God; for it is not subject to the law of God, neither can it be. And they who are in the flesh, cannot please God.

I Corinthians 5: 1; 3-5; 9-13
It is absolutely heard, that there is fornication among you, and such fornication as the like is not among the heathens [....] I indeed, absent in body, but present in spirit, have already judged, as though I were present, him that hath so done, In the name of our Lord Jesus Christ, you being gathered together, and my spirit, with the power of our Lord Jesus; to deliver such a one to Satan for the destruction of the flesh, that the spirit may be saved in the day of our Lord Jesus Christ [....] I wrote to you in an epistle, not to keep company with fornicators. I mean not with the fornicators of this world, or with the covetous, or the extortioners, or the servers of idols; otherwise you must needs go out of this world. But now I have written to you, not to keep company, if any man that is named a brother, be a fornicator, or covetous, or a server of idols, or a railer, or a drunkard, or an extortioner: with such a one, not so much as to eat. For what have I to do to judge them that are without? Do not you judge them that are within? For them that are without, God will judge. Put away the evil one from among yourselves.

I Corinthians 6: 9-10;16-20
Do not err: neither fornicators, nor idolaters, nor adulterers, Nor the effeminate, nor liers with mankind, nor thieves, nor covetous, nor drunkards, nor railers, nor extortioners, shall possess the kingdom of God [....] Know you not that your bodies are the members of Christ? Shall I then take the members of Christ, and make them the members of an harlot? God forbid. Or know you not, that he who is joined to a harlot, is made one body? For they shall be, saith he, two in one flesh. But he who is joined to the Lord, is one spirit. Fly fornication. Every sin that a man doth, is without the body; but he that committeth fornication, sinneth against his own body. Or know you not, that your members are the temple of the Holy Ghost, who is in you, whom you have from God; and you are not your own? For you are bought with a great price. Glorify and bear God in your body.

II Corinthians 6: 14-15; 17
Bear not the yoke with unbelievers. For what participation hath justice with injustice? Or what fellowship hath light with darkness? And what concord hath Christ with Belial? Or what part hath the faithful with the unbeliever? [....] Wherefore, Go out from among them, and be ye separate, saith the Lord, and touch not the unclean thing....

II Thessalonians 2:10-11
And in all seduction of iniquity to them that perish; because they receive not the love of the truth, that they might be saved. Therefore God shall send them the operation of error, to believe lying: That all may be judged who have not believed the truth, but have consented to iniquity.

Ephesians 2:1-3
And you, when you were dead in your offences, and sins, Wherein in time past you walked according to the course of this world, according to the prince of the power of this air, of the spirit that now worketh on the children of unbelief: In which also we all conversed in time past, in the desires of our flesh, fulfilling the will of the flesh and of our thoughts, and were by nature children of wrath, even as the rest.

Colossians 3:5-6
Mortify therefore your members which are upon the earth; fornication, uncleanness, lust, evil concupiscence, and covetousness, which is the service of idols. For which things the wrath of God cometh upon the children of unbelief.

Galatians 5: 19-21
Now the works of the flesh are manifest, which are fornication, uncleanness, immodesty, luxury, Idolatry, witchcrafts, enmities, contentions, emulations, wraths, quarrels, dissensions, sects, envies, murders, drunkenness, revellings, and such like. Of the which I foretell you, as I have foretold to you, that they who do such things shall not obtain the kingdom of God.

Galatians 6:7-8
Be not deceived, God is not mocked. For what things a man shall sow, those also shall he reap. For he that soweth in his flesh, of the flesh also shall reap corruption.

Hebrews 13:4
Marriage honourable in all, and the bed undefiled. For fornicators and adulterers God will judge.

James 4:3-5
You ask, and receive not; because you ask amiss: that you may consume it on your concupiscences. Adulterers, know you not that the friendship of this world is the enemy of God? Whosoever therefore will be a friend of this world, becometh an enemy of God. Or do you think that the scripture saith in vain: To envy doth the spirit covet which dwelleth in you?

Revelation 21: 8
But the fearful, and unbelieving, and the abominable, and murderers, and whoremongers, and sorcerers, and idolaters, and all liars, they shall have their portion in the pool burning with fire and brimstone, which is the second death.

Deuteronomy 11:26-28; 28: 16-20
Behold I set forth in your sight this day a blessing and a curse: A blessing, if you obey the commandments of the Lord your God, which I command you this day: A curse, if you obey not the commandments of the Lord your God, but revolt from the way which now I shew you, and walk after strange gods which you know not.

But if thou wilt not hear the voice of the Lord thy God, to keep and to do all his commandments and ceremonies, which I command thee this day, all these curses shall come upon thee, and overtake thee. Cursed shalt thou be in the city, cursed in the field. Cursed shall be thy barn, and cursed thy stores. Cursed shall be the fruit of thy womb, and the fruit of thy ground, the herds of thy oxen, and the flocks of thy sheep. Cursed shalt thou be coming in, and cursed going out. The Lord shall send upon thee famine and hunger, and a rebuke upon all the works which thou shalt do: until he consume and destroy thee quickly, for thy most wicked inventions, by which thou hast forsaken me.

Isaiah 6:10; 59:2-3
Blind the heart of this people, and make their ears heavy, and shut their eyes: lest they see with their eyes, and hear with their ears, and understand with their heart, and be converted and I heal them.

But your iniquities have divided between you and your God, and your sins have hid his face from you that he should not hear. For your hands are defiled with blood, and your fingers with iniquity: your lips have spoken lies, and your tongue uttereth iniquity.

Micah 3:4
Then shall they cry to the Lord, and he will not hear them: and he will hide his face from them at that time, as they have behaved wickedly in their devices.

Psalm 5: 6-7
Neither shall the wicked dwell near thee: nor shall the unjust abide before thy eyes. Thou hatest all the workers of iniquity: thou wilt destroy all that speak a lie. The bloody and the deceitful man the Lord will abhor.

Psalm 9: 102-105
Whilst the wicked man is proud, the poor is set on fire: they are caught in the counsels which they devise. For the sinner is praised in the desires of his soul: and the unjust man is blessed. The sinner hath provoked the Lord according to the multitude of his wrath he will not seek him: God is not before his eyes: his ways are filthy at all times. Thy judgments are removed from his sight.

Psalm 49: 16-21
But to the sinner God hath said: Why dost thou declare my justices, and take my covenant in thy mouth? Seeing thou hast hated discipline: and hast cast my words behind thee. If thou didst see a thief thou didst run with him: and with adulterers thou hast been a partaker. Thy mouth hath abounded with evil, and thy tongue framed deceits. Sitting thou didst speak against thy brother, and didst lay a scandal against thy mother's son: These things hast thou done, and I was silent. Thou thoughtest unjustly that I should be like to thee: but I will reprove thee, and set before thy face.

Sacred Tradition
St. Irenaeus: c. 130 to c. 202

Against the Heresies, Bk. IV, Chap. 29
For one and the same God [that blesses others] inflicts blindness upon those who do not believe, but who set Him at naught; just as the sun, which is a creature of His, [acts with regard] to those who, by reason of any weakness of the eyes cannot behold his light; but to those who believe in Him and follow Him, He grants a fuller and greater illumination of mind [....] If, therefore, in the present time also, God, knowing the number of those who will not believe, since He foreknows all things, has given them over to unbelief, and turned away His face from men of this stamp, leaving them in the darkness which they have themselves chosen for themselves.[3050]

St. Cyprian of Carthage: c. 200 to 258

Epistle 54
'They received not the love of the truth, that they might be saved. And for this cause God shall send them strong delusion, that they should believe a lie: that they all might be judged who believed not the truth, but had pleasure in unrighteousness.' (II Thess. 2:10-12). The highest degree of happiness is, not to sin; the second, to acknowledge our sins. In the former, innocence flows pure and unstained to preserve us; in the latter, there comes a medicine to heal us. Both of these they have lost by offending God, both because the grace is lost which is received from the sanctification of baptism, and repentance comes not to their help, whereby the sin is healed. Think you, brother, that their wickednesses against God are trifling, their sins small and moderate — since by

---

[3050]St. Irenaeus of Lyons. *Against the Heresies, Bk 4, Chap 29* [Online] Available at: www.newadvent. org [Accessed on: 23 February 204]

their means the majesty of an angry God is not besought, since the anger and the fire and the day of the Lord is not feared.[3051]

Epistle 67
…since the Holy Spirit threatens such in the Psalms, saying, 'But you hate instruction, and cast my words behind you: when you saw a thief, you consented unto him, and hast been partaker with adulterers.' [Psalm 49:17-18]. He shows that they become sharers and partakers of other men's sins who are associated with the delinquents. And besides, Paul the apostle writes, and says the same thing: 'Whisperers, backbiters, haters of God, injurious, proud, boasters of themselves, inventors of evil things, who, although they knew the judgment of God, did not understand that they which commit such things are worthy of death, not only they which commit those things, but they also which consent unto those who do these things.' [Romans 1:30-32]. Since they, says he, who do such things are worthy of death, he makes manifest and proves that not only they are worthy of death, and come into punishment who do evil things, but also those who consent unto those who do such things — who, while they are mingled in unlawful communion with the evil and sinners, and the unrepenting, are polluted by the contact of the guilty, and, being joined in the fault, are thus not separated in its penalty. For which reason we not only approve, but applaud, dearly beloved brethren, the religious solicitude of your integrity and faith, and exhort you as much as we can by our letters, not to mingle in sacrilegious communion with profane and polluted priests, but maintain the sound and sincere constancy of your faith with religious fear.[3052]

St. Augustine: 354 to 430

Tractates on the Gospel of John
For God does not compel any one to sin simply because He knows already the future sins of men. For He foreknew sins that were theirs, not His own; sins that were referable to no one else, but to their own selves [….] For God thus blinds and hardens, simply by letting alone and withdrawing His aid: and God can do this by a judgment that is hidden, although not by one that is unrighteous.[3053]

Commentary on Psalm 49
Whenever you saw a thief, you would collude with him, and you threw in your lot with adulterers. This is pointed out so that the accused cannot say, 'I have not committed theft or adultery.' No? But what if you approved someone else's action? Did you not concur simply by approving? Did you not throw in your lot with the perpetrator by commending him? My brothers and sisters, this is what it means to comply with a thief or to throw in your lot with an adulterer, because even if you do not commit the sin yourself, you commend what is done and support the deed. The sinner is praised for the longings of his soul, and whoever does evil is blessed. You don't do wrong, but you praise those who do. Is that a trivial wrong? *You threw in your lot with adulterers.*[3054]

Commentary on Psalm 9
They are caught in the thoughts they think, that is, their evil thoughts become like chains to them. But why do they become chains? Because, says the psalmist, *the sinner is praised in the longings of his own soul*. The tongues of sycophants tie souls up in sins, for it is delightful to do those things in which not only is there no need to fear rebuke from

---

[3051]St. Cyprian. *Epistle 54, para 13* [Online] Available at: www.newadvent.org [Accessed on: 23 February 2024]

[3052]St. Cyprian. *Epistle 67*, para 9 [Online] Available at: www.newadvent.org [Accessed on: 22 February 2024]

[3053]St. Augustine. *Tractates on the Gospel of John*, 53, para 4,6 [Online] Available at: www.newadvent.org [Accessed on: 26 February 2024]

[3054]The Works of Saint Augustine: A Translation for the 21st Century. *Expositions of the Psalms. 33-50*. New York: New City Press,1990 p. 403

anyone, but one may even hear oneself praised. *And whoever does evil deeds is blessed.* This is how they are caught in the thoughts they think.

   The sinner has provoked the Lord. Nobody should congratulate the person who prospers in his own way, whose sins go unavenged and who has someone to praise him. This is the Lord's anger, an anger all the greater. The sinner has provoked the Lord, and deserved to suffer precisely this absence of any lashes of reproach. *The sinner has provoked the Lord, but the Lord is too angry to demand an account.* He is seething with anger all the time he does not conduct his search and seems to forget and not give heed to sins....*God is not in his sight, his ways are defiled all the time.* Whoever knows what gives joy or delight in the soul knows how great an evil it is to be abandoned by the light of truth. People consider physical blindness, which means the withdrawal of daylight, a greater evil. Just imagine, then, how great the punishment people suffer who, while their sins are a roaring success, are led to the point where God is no longer in their field of vision, and where their ways are defiled all the time, which means that their thoughts and machinations are absolutely filthy! *Your judgements are removed from before his face.* People with bad consciences may believe that God does not judge; in this way God's judgements have been removed from before their face, and though they imagine that they are suffering no punishment whatsoever, this itself is the greatest condemnation.[3055]

Contra Faustum, Bk. XXI

'For this cause God gave them up to the lusts of their own heart, to uncleanness, to dishonor their own bodies between themselves;' and immediately after, 'For this cause God gave them up unto vile affections;' and again, 'And even as they did not like to retain God in their knowledge, God gave them over to a reprobate mind.' Here we see how the true and just God blinds the minds of unbelievers. For in all these words quoted from the apostle no other God is understood than He whose Son, sent by Him, came saying, 'For judgment am I come into this world, that they which see not might see, and that they which see might be made blind.' [Jn 9:39]. Here, again, it is plain to the minds of believers how God blinds the minds of unbelievers. For among the secret things, which contain the righteous principles of God's judgment, there is a secret which determines that the minds of some shall be blinded, and the minds of some enlightened.[3056]

Nature and Grace, Chap. 24

The apostle says of them, *Though they knew God, they did not glorify him as God or give thanks. Rather, they became vain in their thoughts. And their foolish heart was darkened* (Rom 1: 21). Certainly, this darkening of their heart was punishment and penalty, and yet through this penalty, that is the blindness of their heart, which is caused by the light of wisdom abandoning them, they fell into many serious sins [....] *God handed them over to the desires of their heart, to impurity* (Rom 1:24). Observe how God punished them more severely in handing them over to the desires of their heart, to impurity. See what they do as a result of this punishment, he says, so that among themselves they treat their own bodies shamefully (Rom 1:24). And he teaches more clearly that this is the penalty of wickedness, though it is itself wickedness [....] For this reason, he says, *God handed them over to shameful passions* (Rom 1:25-26). See how many times God inflicts punishment, and from the same punishment many more serious sins Arise. *For their women exchanged natural intercourse for that which is against nature. Likewise, the men too abandoned natural relations with women and burned with desire for one another, men committing perversities upon men* (Rom 1:26-27). And to show that these are sins, though they are also penalties for sins, he added to these words, *They received in themselves the mutual recompense of*

[3055]The Works of Saint Augustine: A Translation for the 21st Century. *Expositions of the Psalms.* 1-32. New York: New City Press,1990 p. 152-153
[3056]St. Augustine. *Contra Faustum,* Bk XXI, para 2 [Online] Available at: www.newadvent.org [Accessed on: 22 February 2024]

their error, as they deserved (Rom 1:27). See how often he punishes, and punishes with the same punishment that brings forth and breeds sins.[3057]

St. John Chrysostom: c. 347 to 407

Homily 4 on Romans 1: 26-27

All these affections then were vile, but chiefly the mad lust after males; for the soul is more the sufferer in sins, and more dishonoured, than the body in diseases. But behold how here too, as in the case of the doctrines, he deprives them of excuse, by saying of the women, that *'they changed the natural use.'* For no one, he means, can say that it was by being hindered of legitimate intercourse that they came to this pass, or that it was from having no means to fulfil their desire that they were driven into this monstrous insanity. For the changing implies possession. Which also when discoursing upon the doctrines he said, *'They changed the truth of God for a lie.'* And with regard to the men again, he shows the same thing by saying, *'Leaving the natural use of the woman.'* And in a like way with those, these he also puts out of all means of defending themselves by charging them not only that they had the means of gratification, and left that which they had, and went after another, but that having dishonoured that which was natural, they ran after that which was contrary to nature. But that which is contrary to nature has in it an irksomeness and displeasingness, so that they could not fairly allege even pleasure. For genuine pleasure is that which is according to nature. But when God has left one, then all things are turned upside down. And thus not only was their doctrine Satanical, but their life too was diabolical [....]

Consider how great is that sin, to have forced hell to appear even before its time! For whereas many thought scorn of His words, by His deeds did God show them the image thereof in a certain novel way. For that rain was unwonted, for that the intercourse was contrary to nature, and it deluged the land, since lust had done so with their souls. Wherefore also the rain was the opposite of the customary rain. Now not only did it fail to stir up the womb of the earth to the production of fruits, but made it even useless for the reception of seed. For such was also the intercourse of the men, making a body of this sort more worthless than the very land of Sodom. And what is there more detestable than a man who hath pandered himself, or what more execrable? Oh, what madness! Oh, what distraction! Whence came this lust lewdly revelling and making man's nature all that enemies could? or even worse than that, by as much as the soul is better than the body. Oh, ye that were more senseless than irrational creatures, and more shameless than dogs! for in no case does such intercourse take place with them, but nature acknowledgeth her own limits. But ye have even made our race dishonored below things irrational, by such indignities inflicted upon and by each other. Whence then were these evils born? Of luxury; of not knowing God. For so soon as any have cast out the fear of Him, all that is good straightway goes to ruin.[3058]

Pope St. Gregory the Great: c. 540 to 604

Commentary on Moralia in Job, XIV, 23

Brimstone calls to mind the foul odours of the flesh, as Sacred Scripture itself confirms when it speaks of the rain of fire and brimstone poured by the Lord upon Sodom. He had decided to punish in it the crimes of the flesh, and the very type of punishment emphasised the shame of that crime, since brimstone exhales stench and fire burns. It was, therefore, just that the sodomites, burning with perverse desires that originated from the foul odour of flesh, should perish at the same time by fire and brimstone so that through this just chastisement they might realise the evil perpetrated under the impulse of a perverse desire.[3059]

[3057]The Works of Saint Augustine: A Translation for the 21st Century. *Answer to the Pelagians*, I/23 New York: New City Press,1990 p. 236-237

[3058]St. John Chrysostom. *Homily* 4 on Romans 1: 26-27 [Online] www.newadvent.org [Accessed on: 27 February 2024]

[3059]Pope St. Gregory the Great. *Commentary on Moralia in Job*, XIV, 23. [Online] Available at: http://www.awrsipe.com [Accessed on: 27 February 2024]

The Magisterium of the Church

Sodomy and adultery are such heinous crimes against the Sixth Commandment that, if unrepentented, are punished by God, who allows obstinate sinners to sink into spiritual and moral blindness. Homosexual sex acts in particular express a defiant rejection of God deserving not blessing but the very opposite — the punishment of divine wrath.

Third Lateran Council (Eleventh Ecumenical, 1179)

Canon 11

Let all who are found guilty of that unnatural vice for which the wrath of God came down upon the sons of disobedience and destroyed the five cities with fire, if they are clerics be expelled from the clergy or confined in monasteries to do penance; if they are laymen they are to incur excommunication and be completely separated from the society of the faithful.[3060]

Fourth Lateran Council (Twelfth Ecumenical, 1215)

Constitution 14

In order that the morals and conduct of clerics may be reformed for the better, let all of them strive to live in a continent and chaste way, especially those in holy orders. Let them beware of every vice involving lust, especially that on account of which the wrath of God came down from heaven upon the sons of disobedience, so that they may be worthy to minister in the sight of almighty God with a pure heart and an unsullied body.[3061]

First Council of Lyons (Thirteenth Ecumenical, 1245)

Moreover concerning fornication that an unmarried man commits with an unmarried woman, there must not be any doubt at all that it is a mortal sin, since the apostle declares that fornicators like adulterers are cast out from the kingdom of God (cf. I Cor 6:9).

But if anyone dies in mortal sin without repentance, beyond any doubt, he will be tortured forever by the flames of everlasting hell.[3062]

Council of Vienne (15th Ecumenical, 1311 to 1312)

Bulls and ordinances of the Roman Curia concerning the order of the Templars and the business of the Holy Land.

Therefore, it was against the Lord Jesus Christ himself that they fell into the sin of impious apostasy, the abominable vice of idolatry, the deadly crime of the Sodomites, and various heresies.[3063]

Fifth Lateran Council (Eighteenth Ecumenical, 1512 to 1517)

Reform of the Curia. Session 9, chap. 4, X. (5th May 1514)

In order that clerics, especially, may live in continence and chastity according to canonical legislation, we rule that offenders be severely punished as the canons lay down. If anyone, lay or cleric, has been found guilty of a charge on account of which the wrath of God comes upon the sons of disobedience, let him be punished by the penalties respectively imposed by the sacred canons or by civil law.[3064]

[3060]Tanner, N [1990] *Third Lateran Council – 1179 A.D. Canon 11.* [Online] Available at: www.papalencyclicals.net [Accessed on: 27 February 2024]

[3061]Tanner, N [1990] *Fourth Lateran Council : 1215. Constitution 14.* [Online] Available at: www.papalencyclicals.net [Accessed on: 27 February 2024]

[3062]Denzinger, H [2010] *Op. cit.,* p. 277, 835; p. 278, 839

[3063]Council of Vienne 1311-1312 A.D [Online] Available at: www.papalencyclicals.net [Accessed on: 27 February 2024]

[3064]Tanner, N [1990] *Fifth Lateran Council 1512-17 A.D. Reform of the Curia.* [Online] Available at: www.papalencyclicals.net [Accessed on: 19 August 2022]

Council of Trent (Nineteenth Ecumenical, 1545 to 1563)

Decree Concerning the Most Holy Sacrament of the Eucharist, Chap. VII. (11th October 1551)
…it is unbeseeming for any one to approach to any of the sacred functions, unless he approach holily.[3065]

Decree on Justification, Chap. V. (13th January 1547)
…while God touches the heart of man by the illumination of the Holy Ghost, neither is man himself utterly without doing anything while he receives that inspiration, forasmuch as he is also able to reject it.…[3066]

Second Vatican Council (Twenty-First Ecumenical, 1962 to 1965)

Dogmatic Constitution, *Lumen Gentium, 14, 48. (21st November 1964)*
He remains indeed in the bosom of the Church, but, as it were, only in a 'bodily' manner and not 'in his heart.' All the Church's children should remember that their exalted status is to be attributed not to their own merits but to the special grace of Christ. If they fail moreover to respond to that grace in thought, word and deed, not only shall they not be saved but they will be the more severely judged.

…at the end of the world 'they who have done good shall come forth unto resurrection of life; but those who have done evil unto resurrection of judgment' (Jn 5:29; Mt 25:46).[3067]

Pope Benedict XVI: 2005 to 2013

Compendium of the Catechism of the Catholic Church. (28th June 2005)
212. In what does hell consist?
Hell consists in the eternal damnation of those who die in mortal sin through their own free choice. The principal suffering of hell is eternal separation from God in whom alone we can have the life and happiness for which we were created and for which we long. Christ proclaimed this reality with the words, 'Depart from me, you cursed, into the eternal fire' (Mt 25:41).[3068]

492. What are the principal sins against chastity?
Grave sins against chastity differ according to their object: adultery, masturbation, fornication, pornography, prostitution, rape, and homosexual acts. These sins are expressions of the vice of lust. These kinds of acts committed against the physical and moral integrity of minors become even more grave.

Congregation for Catholic Education. Instruction Concerning the Criteria for the Discernment of Vocations with regard to Persons with Homosexual Tendencies in view of their Admission to the Seminary and to Holy Orders. (31st August 2005)
Regarding acts, it teaches that Sacred Scripture presents them [homosexual acts] as grave sins. The Tradition has constantly considered them as intrinsically immoral and contrary to the natural law. Consequently, under no circumstance can they be approved.[3069]

[3065]General Council of Trent: Thirteenth Session [1551] *Decree Concerning the Most Holy Sacrament of the Eucharist* [Online] Available at: www.papalencyclicals.net [Accessed on:26 February 2024]
[3066]General Council of Trent: Sixth Session [1547] *Decree on Justification* [Online] Available at: www.papalencyclicals.net [Accessed on: 26 February 2024]
[3067]Second Vatican Council [1965] Dogmatic Constitution on the Church, *Lumen Gentium*, para 14, 48 [Online] Available at: www.vatican.va [Accessed on: 26 February 2024]
[3068]Pope Benedict XVI [2005] *Compendium of the Catechism of the Catholic Church.* [Online] Available at: www.vatican.va [Accessed on: 1 October 2022]
[3069]Congregation for Catholic Education [2005] *Instruction concerning the Criteria for the Discernment of Vocations with regard to Persons with Homosexual Tendencies in view of their Admission to the Seminary and to Holy Orders.* [Online] Available at: www.vatican.va [Accessed on: 8 October 2022]

Angelus Address (6th November 2006)
The authentic death, which one must fear, is that of the soul, called by the Book of Revelation 'second death' (cf. 20:14-15; 21:8). In fact, he who dies in mortal sin, without repentance, locked in prideful rejection of God's love, excludes himself from the Kingdom of life.[3070]

Address at Meeting with the Parish Priests and the Clergy of the Diocese of Rome. (7th February 2008)
...perhaps those who have destroyed themselves in this way, who are for ever unredeemable, who no longer possess any elements on which God's love can rest, who no longer have a minimal capacity for loving, may not be so numerous. This would be Hell.[3071]

Homily during visit to the Roman Parish of St. Felicity & her Children, Martyrs. (25th March 2007)
Jesus came to tell us that he wants us all in Paradise and that hell, about which little is said in our time, exists and is eternal for those who close their hearts to his love.[3072]

Angelus Address. (15th February 2009)
It is possible to see leprosy as a symbol of sin, which is the true impurity of heart that can distance us from God. It is not in fact the physical disease of leprosy that separates us from God as the ancient norms supposed but sin, spiritual and moral evil....The sins that we commit distance us from God and, if we do not humbly confess them, trusting in divine mercy, they will finally bring about the death of the soul.[3073]

General Audience Address. (18th May 2011)
The first text on which we shall reflect is in chapter 18 of the Book of Genesis. It is recounted that the evil of the inhabitants of Sodom and Gomorrah had reached the height of depravity so as to require an intervention of God, an act of justice, that would prevent the evil from destroying those cities. [...]

However, not even 10 just people were to be found in Sodom and Gomorrah so the cities were destroyed; a destruction paradoxically deemed necessary by the prayer of Abraham's intercession itself. Because that very prayer revealed the saving will of God: the Lord was prepared to forgive, he wanted to forgive but the cities were locked into a totalising and paralysing evil, without even a few innocents from whom to start in order to turn evil into good.

This the very path to salvation that Abraham too was asking for: being saved does not mean merely escaping punishment but being delivered from the evil that dwells within us. It is not punishment that must be eliminated but sin, the rejection of God and of love which already bears the punishment in itself.[3074]

Homily for Mass of the Lord's Supper. (5th April 2012)
This pride is the real essence of sin. We think we are free and truly ourselves only if we follow our own will. God appears as the opposite of our freedom. We need to be free of him – so we think – and only then will we be free. This is the fundamental rebellion present throughout history and the fundamental lie which perverts life. When human

---

[3070]Pope Benedict XVI [2006] *Angelus Address* [Online] Available at: www.catholic.org [Accessed on: 28 February 2024]
[3071]Pope Benedict XVI [2008] *Address at Meeting with the Parish Priests and the Clergy of the Diocese of Rome* [Online] Available at: www.vatican.va [Accessed on: 4 July 2022]
[3072]Pope Benedict XVI [2007] *Homily during visit to the Roman Parish of St. Felicity & her Children, Martyrs* [Online] Available at: www.vatican.va [Accessed on: 4 July 2022]
[3073]Pope Benedict XVI [2009] *Angelus Address* [Online] Available at: www.vatican.va [Accessed on: 3 October 2022]
[3074]Pope Benedict XVI [18th May 2011] *General Audience Address.* [Online] Available at: www. vatican.va [Accessed on: 28 February 2024]

beings set themselves against God, they set themselves against the truth of their own being and consequently do not become free, but alienated from themselves.[3075]

Pope St. John Paul II: 1978 to 2005

Letter of the Congregation for the Doctrine of the Faith to All Bishops Recentiores Episcoporum Synodi, 7. (17th May 1979)
In fidelity to the New Testament and tradition, the Church believes in the happiness of the just who will one day be with Christ. She believes that there will be eternal punishment for the sinner, who will deprived of the sight of God, and that this punishment will have repercussion on the whole being of the sinner.[3076]

General Audience Address. (7th January 1981)
When he speaks of the necessity of putting to death the deeds of the body with the help of the Spirit, Paul expresses precisely what Christ spoke about in the Sermon on the Mount, appealing to the human heart and exhorting it to control desires, even those expressed in a man's look at a woman for the purpose of satisfying the lust of the flesh. This mastery, or as Paul writes, 'putting to death the works of the body with the help of the Spirit,' is an indispensable condition of life according to the Spirit, that is, of the life which is an antithesis of the death spoken about in the same context. Life according to the flesh has death as its fruit. That is, it involves as its effect the 'death' of the spirit.

So the term 'death' does not mean only the death of the body, but also sin, which moral theology will call 'mortal.' In Romans and Galatians, the Apostle continually widens the horizon of 'sin-death,' both toward the beginning of human history, and toward its end. Therefore, after listing the multiform works of the flesh, he affirms that 'those who do such things shall not inherit the kingdom of God' (Gal 5:21). Elsewhere he will write with similar firmness: 'Be sure of this, that no fornicator or impure man, or one who is covetous (that is, an idolater), has any inheritance in the kingdom of God' (Eph 5:5). In this case, too, the works that exclude inheritance in the kingdom of Christ and of God — that is, the works of the flesh — are listed as an example and with general value, although sins against purity in the specific sense are at the top of the list here (cf. Eph 5:3-7).[3077]

Post Synodal Apostolic Exhortation, *Reconciliatio et Paenitentia, 17.* (2nd December 1984)
With the whole tradition of the church, we call mortal sin the act by which man freely and consciously rejects God, his law, the covenant of love that God offers, preferring to turn in on himself or to some created and finite reality, something contrary to the divine will (conversio ad creaturam). This can occur in a direct and formal way in the sins of idolatry, apostasy and atheism; or in an equivalent way as in every act of disobedience to God's commandments in a grave matter. Man perceives that this disobedience to God destroys the bond that unites him with his life principle: It is a mortal sin, that is, an act which gravely offends God and ends in turning against man himself with a dark and powerful force of destruction.

For mortal sin exists also when a person knowingly and willingly, for whatever reason, chooses something gravely disordered. In fact, such a choice already includes contempt for the divine law, a rejection of God's love for humanity and the whole of creation; the person turns away from God and loses charity. Thus the fundamental orientation can be radically changed by individual acts. Clearly there can occur situations which are very complex and obscure from a psychological viewpoint and which have an influence on the sinner's subjective culpability. But from a consideration of the psychological sphere one cannot proceed to the construction of a theological category,

---

[3075]Pope Benedict XVI [2012] *Homily for Mass of the Lord's Supper* [Online] Available at: www.vatican.va [Accessed on: 28 February 2024]
[3076]Denzinger, H [2010] p. 1027-1028, 4657
[3077]Pope St. John Paul II [7th January 1981] *Opposition Between the Flesh and the Spirit* [Online] Available at: www.ewtn.com/ [Accessed on: 29 February 2024]

which is what the "fundamental option" precisely is, understanding it in such a way that it objectively changes or casts doubt upon the traditional concept of mortal sin.[3078]

Congregation for the Doctrine of the Faith. Letter to the Bishops of Catholic Church On the Pastoral Care of Homosexual Persons, 6. (1st October 1986)
In Genesis 3, we find that this truth about persons being an image of God has been obscured by original sin. There inevitably follows a loss of awareness of the covenantal character of the union these persons had with God and with each other. The human body retains its 'spousal significance' but this is now clouded by sin. Thus, in Genesis 19:1-11, the deterioration due to sin continues in the story of the men of Sodom. There can be no doubt of the moral judgement made there against homosexual relations. In Leviticus 18:22 and 20:13, in the course of describing the conditions necessary for belonging to the Chosen People, the author excludes from the People of God those who behave in a homosexual fashion [....]

In Romans 1:18-32, still building on the moral traditions of his forebears, but in the new context of the confrontation between Christianity and the pagan society of his day, Paul uses homosexual behaviour as an example of the blindness which has overcome humankind. Instead of the original harmony between Creator and creatures, the acute distortion of idolatry has led to all kinds of moral excess. Paul is at a loss to find a clearer example of this disharmony than homosexual relations. Finally, I Tim. 1, in full continuity with the Biblical position, singles out those who spread wrong doctrine and in v. 10 explicitly names as sinners those who engage in homosexual acts.[3079]

Catechism of the Catholic Church. (1992)
The teaching of the Church affirms the existence of hell and its eternity. Immediately after death the souls of those who die in a state of mortal sin descend into hell, where they suffer the punishments of hell, 'eternal fire.' The chief punishment of hell is eternal separation from God, in whom alone man can possess the life and happiness for which he was created and for which he longs. (1035)

The punishments of sin. To understand this doctrine and practice of the Church, it is necessary to understand that sin has a *double consequence.* Grave sin deprives us of communion with God and therefore makes us incapable of eternal life, the privation of which is called the 'eternal punishment' of sin. On the other hand every sin, even venial, entails an unhealthy attachment to creatures, which must be purified either here on earth, or after death in the state called Purgatory. This purification frees one from what is called the 'temporal punishment' of sin. These two punishments must not be conceived of as a kind of vengeance inflicted by God from without, but as following from the very nature of sin. A conversion which proceeds from a fervent charity can attain the complete purification of the sinner in such a way that no punishment would remain. (1472)

The catechetical tradition also recalls that there are 'sins that cry to heaven': the blood of Abel, the sin of the Sodomites, (Gen 18:20; 19:13) the cry of the people oppressed in Egypt, the cry of the foreigner, the widow, and the orphan, injustice to the wage earner. (1867)

Mortal sin is a radical possibility of human freedom, as is love itself. It results in the loss of charity and the privation of sanctifying grace, that is, of the state of grace. If it is not redeemed by repentance and God's forgiveness, it causes exclusion from Christ's kingdom and the eternal death of hell, for our freedom has the power to make choices for ever, with no turning back. (1861)

[3078]Pope St. John Paul II [1984] Post Synodal Apostolic Exhortation *Reconciliatio et Paenitentia*, para 17 [Online] Available at: www.vatican.va [Accessed on: 29 February 2024]
[3079]Congregation for the Doctrine of the Faith. *Letter to the Bishops of Catholic Church on the Pastoral Care of Homosexual Persons, para 3, 7* [Online] Available at: www.vatican.va [Accessed on: 28 February 2024]

Basing itself on Sacred Scripture, which presents homosexual acts as acts of grave depravity, (Gen 191-29; Rom 1:24-27; I Cor 6:10; I Tim 1:10), tradition has always declared that 'homosexual acts are intrinsically disordered.' (CDF, *Persona Humana* 8). They are contrary to the natural law. They close the sexual act to the gift of life. They do not proceed from a genuine affective and sexual complementarity. Under no circumstances can they be approved. (2357)

Encyclical *Veritatis Splendor, 49, 68 (6 August 1993)*

Saint Paul declares that 'the immoral, idolaters, adulterers, sexual perverts, thieves, the greedy, drunkards, revilers, robbers' are excluded from the Kingdom of God (cf. I Cor 6:9). This condemnation — repeated by the Council of Trent — lists as 'mortal sins' or 'immoral practices' certain specific kinds of behaviour the wilful acceptance of which prevents believers from sharing in the inheritance promised to them. In fact, body and soul are inseparable: in the person, in the willing agent and in the deliberate act, they stand or fall together [....] With every freely committed mortal sin, he offends God as the giver of the law and as a result becomes guilty with regard to the entire law (cf. Jas 2:8-11); even if he perseveres in faith, he loses 'sanctifying grace', 'charity' and 'eternal happiness'. As the Council of Trent teaches, 'the grace of justification once received is lost not only by apostasy, by which faith itself is lost, but also by any other mortal sin'.[3080]

General Audience Address, 1,2,3. (28th July 1999)

God is the infinitely good and merciful Father. But man, called to respond to him freely, can unfortunately choose to reject his love and forgiveness once and for all, thus separating himself for ever from joyful communion with him. It is precisely this tragic situation that Christian doctrine explains when it speaks of eternal damnation or hell. It is not a punishment imposed externally by God but a development of premises already set by people in this life. The very dimension of unhappiness which this obscure condition brings can in a certain way be sensed in the light of some of the terrible experiences we have suffered which, as is commonly said, make life 'hell'.

In a theological sense however, hell is something else: it is the ultimate consequence of sin itself, which turns against the person who committed it. It is the state of those who definitively reject the Father's mercy, even at the last moment of their life. [...]

Redemption nevertheless remains an offer of salvation which it is up to people to accept freely. This is why they will all be judged 'by what they [have done]' (Rv 20:13). By using images, the New Testament presents the place destined for evildoers as a fiery furnace, where people will 'weep and gnash their teeth' (Mt 13:42; cf. 25:30, 41), or like Gehenna with its 'unquenchable fire' (Mk 9:43). All this is narrated in the parable of the rich man, which explains that hell is a place of eternal suffering, with no possibility of return, nor of the alleviation of pain (cf. Lk 16:19-31).

'Eternal damnation', therefore, is not attributed to God's initiative because in his merciful love he can only desire the salvation of the beings he created. In reality, it is the creature who closes himself to his love. Damnation consists precisely in definitive separation from God, freely chosen by the human person and confirmed with death that seals his choice for ever. God's judgement ratifies this state.[3081]

Pope St. Paul VI: 1963 to 1978

Apostolic Constitution, *Indulgentiarum Doctrina*, Chaps.1, 2. (1st January 1967)
It is a divinely revealed truth that sins bring punishments inflicted by God's sanctity and justice. These must be expiated either on this earth through the sorrows, miseries and calamities of this life and above all through death, (Gen 3:16-19) or else in the life

---

[3080]Pope St. John Paul II [1993] *Encyclical Veritatis Splendor*, paras 12, 68 [Online] Available at: www.vatican.va [Accessed on: 29 February 2024]

[3081]Pope St. John Paul II [1999] *General Audience Address*, paras 1-2,3 [Online] Available at: www. vatican.va [Accessed on: 28 February 2024]

beyond through fire and torments or 'purifying' punishments. (Cf. Mt 25:41-42; see also Mk 9:42-43; Jn 5:28-29; Rom 2:9; Gal 6:6-8.) Therefore it has always been the conviction of the faithful that the paths of evil are fraught with many stumbling blocks and bring adversities, bitterness and harm to those who follow them.[3082]

Congregation for the Doctrine of the Faith. Declaration Persona Humana, 8, 10 (29th December 1975)
In Sacred Scripture they [homosexual sex acts] are condemned as a serious depravity and even presented as the sad consequence of rejecting God.

According to the Church's teaching, mortal sin, which is opposed to God, does not consist only in formal and direct resistance to the commandment of charity. It is equally to be found in this opposition to authentic love which is included in every deliberate transgression, in serious matter, of each of the moral laws.[...]

A person therefore sins mortally not only when his action comes from direct contempt for love of God and neighbour, but also when he consciously and freely, for whatever reason, chooses something which is seriously disordered. For in this choice, as has been said above, there is already included contempt for the Divine commandment: the person turns himself away from God and loses charity. Now according to Christian tradition and the Church's teaching, and as right reason also recognises, the moral order of sexuality involves such high values of human life that every direct violation of this order is objectively serious.

It is true that in sins of the sexual order, in view of their kind and their causes, it more easily happens that free consent is not fully given; this is a fact which calls for caution in all judgment as to the subject's responsibility. In this matter it is particularly opportune to recall the following words of Scripture: 'Man looks at appearances but God looks at the heart.' (Sam 16:7). However, although prudence is recommended in judging the subjective seriousness of a particular sinful act, it in no way follows that one can hold the view that in the sexual field mortal sins are not committed.[3083]

Pope Benedict XV: 1914 to 1922

The 1917 or Pio-Benedictine Code of Canon Law. (27th May 1917)
Laity legitimately convicted of a delict against the sixth [commandment of the Decalogue] with a minor below the age of sixteen, or of debauchery, sodomy, incest, or pandering, are by that fact infamous, besides other penalties that the Ordinary decides should be inflicted. Canon 2357 § 1

If they [clergy] engage in a delict against the sixth precept of the Decalogue with a minor below the age of sixteen, or engage in adultery, debauchery, bestiality, sodomy, pandering, incest with blood-relatives or affines in the first degree, they are suspended, declared infamous, and are deprived of any office, benefice, dignity, responsibility, if they have such, whatsoever, and in more serious cases, they are to be deposed. Canon 2359 § 2[3084]

Pope St. Pius X: 1903 to 1914

Catechism of Pope St. Pius X. (1908)
The Main Kinds of Sins
7 Q. What is mortal sin?
A. Mortal sin is a transgression of the divine Law by which we seriously fail in our duties towards God, towards our neighbour, or towards ourselves.

[3082]Pope St. Paul VI [1968] Apostolic Constitution, *Indulgentiarum Doctrine*, Chap1-2 [Online] Available at: www.vatican.va [Accessed on: 1 October 2022]
[3083]Sacred Congregation for the Doctrine of the Faith [1975] *Persona Humana, para, 8,10* [Online] Available at: www.vatican.va [Accessed on: 18 July 2022]
[3084]Peters, E N [2001] *The 1917 or Pio-Benedictine Code of Canon Law in English Translation with Extensive Scholarly Apparatus.* San Francisco: Ignatius Press

8 Q. Why is it called mortal?
A. It is called mortal because it brings death on the soul by making it lose sanctifying grace which is the life of the soul, just as the soul itself is the life of the body.

9 Q. What injury does mortal sin do the soul?
A. (1) Mortal sin deprives the soul of grace and of the friendship of God; (2) It makes it lose Heaven; (3) It deprives it of merits already acquired, and renders it incapable of acquiring new merits; (4) It makes it the slave of the devil; (5) It makes it deserve hell as well as the chastisements of this life.

10 Q. Besides grave matter, what is required to constitute a mortal sin?
A. To constitute a mortal sin, besides grave matter there is also required full consciousness of the gravity of the matter, along with the deliberate will to commit the sin.

The Vices and other Very Grievous Sins
8 Q. Which are the sins that are said to cry to God for vengeance?
A. The sins that are said to cry to God for vengeance are these four: (1) Wilful murder; (2) The sin of sodomy; (3) Oppression of the poor; (4) Defrauding labourers of their wages.

9 Q. Why are these sins said to cry to God for vengeance?
A. These sins are said to cry to God for vengeance because the Holy Ghost says so, and because their iniquity is so great and so manifest that it provokes God to punish them with the severest chastisements.[3085]

Pope St. Pius V: 1566 to 1572

The Roman Catechism: The Catechism of the Council of Trent. (1556)
The Sixth Commandment: 'Thou shalt not commit adultery'
Other Sins Against Chastity Are Forbidden
In the Gospel, too, Christ the Lord says: From the heart come forth adulteries and fornications, which defile a man. The Apostle Paul expresses his detestation of this crime frequently, and in the strongest terms: This is the will of God, your sanctification, that you should abstain from fornication; Fly fornication; Keep not company with fornicators; Fornication, and an uncleanness and covetousness, let it not so much as be named among you; 'Neither fornicators nor adulterers, nor the effeminate nor sodomites shall possess the kingdom of God'.

Means of practicing purity
Avoidance Of Idleness We now come to the remedies which consist in action. The first is studiously to avoid idleness; for, according to Ezechiel, it was by yielding to the enervating influence of idleness that the Sodomites plunged into the most shameful crime of criminal lust.[3086]

Constitution *Horrendum illud Scelus.* (30th August 1568)
That horrible crime, on account of which corrupt and obscene cities were destroyed by fire through divine condemnation, causes us most bitter sorrow and shocks our mind, impelling us to repress such a crime with the greatest possible zeal.

Quite opportunely the Fifth Lateran Council [1512-1517] issued this decree: 'Let any member of the clergy caught in that vice against nature, given that the wrath of God falls over the sons of perfidy, be removed from the clerical order or forced to do penance in a monastery' (chap. 4, X, V, 31).

[3085]*Catechism of St. Pius X* [1908] [Online] Available at: www.ewtn.com [Accessed on: 28 August 2022]
[3086]Pope St. Pius V [1556] *The Roman Catechism: The Catechism of the Council of Trent, The Sixth Commandment : 'Thou shalt not commit adultery'* [Online] Available at: http://www.clerus.org [Accessed on: 28 February 2022]

So that the contagion of such a grave offence may not advance with greater audacity by taking advantage of impunity, which is the greatest incitement to sin, and so as to more severely punish the clerics who are guilty of this nefarious crime and who are not frightened by the death of their souls, we determine that they should be handed over to the severity of the secular authority, which enforces civil law.[3087]

Pope Benedict XII: 1334 to 1342

Constitution *Benedictus Deus.* (29th January 1336)
Moreover, we define that according to the general disposition of God, the souls of those who die in actual mortal sin go down into hell immediately after death and there suffer the pain of hell.[3088]

Pope St. Leo IX: 1049 to 1054

Cardinal St. Peter Damian. Letter 31 to Pope St. Leo IX, also known as the Book of Gomorrah. Chaps. 10, 11
Who can turn a deaf ear, or, more to the point, who does not tremble through and through at the words Paul, like a mighty trumpet, blasts at such as these? 'God abandoned them to their hearts' desire and to the practices with which they dishonor their own bodies.' And almost immediately following he said, 'that is why God has abandoned them to degrading passions. For their women have turned from natural intercourse to unnatural practices, and their menfolk likewise have given up natural intercourse with women to be consumed with passion for each other, men doing shameless things with men and getting an appropriate reward for their perversion. And since they refused to see that it was rational to acknowledge God, God has abandoned them to their depraved ideas to do that which was reprehensible.' Why is it that they are so eager to reach the top in ecclesiastical rank after such a grievous fall? What should we think, and what conclusion should we draw but that God has abandoned them to their depravity? While they are slaves to sin he does not permit them to see what they need to do. Since the sun, that is, he who rises over death, has set for them, and after losing the sight furnished by their conscience, they are unable to judge the malice of the filthy acts that they perform, and to conclude that it is even worse that they desire ordination uncanonically, against the will of God. Accordingly, as is usually the case according to God's decrees, they who defile themselves with this corrupting vice are smitten with a due judgement of punishment and incur a benighting blindness [....]

Surely, they are struck with blindness, because by the just decree of God they fall into interior darkness. They are thus unable to find the door because in their separation from God by sin they do not know how to return to him. One who tries to reach God by the tortuous road of arrogance and conceit, rather than by the path of humility, will certainly fail to recognise the entrance that is obviously right before him, or even that the door is Christ, as he himself says: 'I am the door.'[3089] Those who lose Christ because of their addiction to sin, never find the gate that leads to the heavenly dwelling of the saints.[3090]

Pope St. Leo IX. Letter *Ad Splendidum Nitentis to St. Peter Damian (1054)*
...lest the unrestrained license of filthy lust should spread abroad, it is necessary that it be repelled by a suitable reprimand of apostolic severity and that some attempt at more austere discipline should be made....

Those who have polluted by impurity of any of the four kinds[3091] mentioned are

---

[3087]Pope St. Pius V [1568] *Horrendum Illud Scelus* [Online] Available at: www.traditioninaction.org [Accessed on: 26 August 2022]
[3088]Denzinger, H [2010] *Op. cit.*, p.303, 1002
[3089]John 10.9.
[3090]St. Peter Damian [1049] *The Book of Gomorrah: St. Peter Damian's Letter 31* (1049) [Online] Available at: www.stpeterdamian.com [Accessed on: 4 March 2024]
[3091]St Peter Damian distinguished four different kinds of sodomitic act: (1) solitary masturbation; (2) mutual masturbation; (3) sex between the thighs of same-sex partners; (4) anal sex (the most vile). Sund

expelled from all grades of the immaculate Church both by the appropriate censure envisaged by the sacred canons as well as by Our judgement. But We, proceeding with much clemency and trusting in the divine mercy, will and indeed command that those who have brought forth the seed either by their own hands or among themselves or who have even shed it between the legs, but not by long habit nor with many people, if they restrain their desire and wash away their shameful deeds by worthy repentance, should be admitted to the same grades that they would not have retained forever if they had remained in their pollution; but We withdraw any hope of recovering their order from those others who have been stained either of the two sorts of impurity that you have described, whether during a long period alone or with others, or even for a short period with many people, or who, horrible to say or hear, have sinned in the back [of others]. If anyone shall dare to judge or complain against this Our decree of apostolic sanction, let him know that he acts in peril of his order.[3092]

Pope St. Damasus I: 366 to 384

The First Canonical Epistle of St. Basil, Archbishop of Caesarea in Cappadocia to Amphilochius, Bishop of Iconium, Canon VII.

They who have committed sodomy with men or brutes, murderers, wizards, adulterers, and idolaters, have been thought worthy of the same punishment; therefore observe the same method with these which you do with others. We ought not to make any doubt of receiving those who have repented thirty years for the uncleanness which they committed through ignorance; for their ignorance pleads their pardon, and their willingness in confessing it; therefore command them to be forthwith received, especially if they have tears to prevail on your tenderness, and have [since their lapse] led such a life as to deserve your compassion.[3093]

[3092]Denzinger, H [1990] *Op. cit.*, p. 233-234 687-688
[3093]Peters, E N [2001] *The 1917 or Pio-Benedictine Code of Canon Law in English Translation with Extensive Scholarly Apparatus.* San Francisco: Ignatius Press

Soteriology

Pope Francis: 2013 to 2025

Q. *Non-Christians can live justified by the grace of God. The sacramental dimension of sanctifying grace works through non-Christian signs, rites, sacred expressions which are channels of the Holy Spirit. God wills the pluralism and diversity of religions.*

Message to Muslims throughout the world for the end of Ramadan. (July 10, 2013)
Turning to mutual respect in interreligious relations, especially between Christians and Muslims, we are called to respect the religion of the other, its teachings, its symbols, its values. Particular respect is due to religious leaders and to places of worship.... I send you my prayerful good wishes, that your lives may glorify the Almighty and give joy to those around you.[3094]

Post Synodal Apostolic Exhortation Evangelii Gaudium, 252, 254. (24 November 2013)
We must never forget that they [Muslims] 'profess to hold the faith of Abraham, and together with us they adore the one, merciful God, who will judge humanity on the last day'. The sacred writings of Islam have retained some Christian teachings; Jesus and Mary receive profound veneration and it is admirable to see how Muslims both young and old, men and women, make time for daily prayer and faithfully take part in religious services. Many of them also have a deep conviction that their life, in its entirety, is from God and for God. They also acknowledge the need to respond to God with an ethical commitment and with mercy towards those most in need.

Non-Christians, by God's gracious initiative, when they are faithful to their own consciences, can live 'justified by the grace of God', and thus be 'associated to the paschal mystery of Jesus Christ'. But due to the sacramental dimension of sanctifying grace, God's working in them tends to produce signs and rites, sacred expressions which in turn bring others to a communitarian experience of journeying towards God. While these lack the meaning and efficacy of the sacraments instituted by Christ, they can be channels which the Holy Spirit raises up in order to liberate non-Christians from atheistic immanentism or from purely individual religious experiences. The same Spirit everywhere brings forth various forms of practical wisdom which help people to bear suffering and to live in greater peace and harmony. As Christians, we can also benefit from these treasures built up over many centuries, which can help us better to live our own beliefs.[3095]

In-flight press conference from Istanbul to Rome. (30th November 2014)
.... when I entered the Mosque, I couldn't say: now, I'm a tourist! No, it was completely religious. And I saw that wonder! The Mufti explained things very well to me, with such meekness, and using the Quran, which speaks of Mary and John the Baptist. He explained it all to me.... At that moment I felt the need to pray. So I asked him: 'Shall we pray a little?'. To which he responded: 'Yes, yes'.[3096]

Meeting with refugees at Sacred Heart Parish, Rome. (19th January 2015)
Those who are Christians with the Bible and those who are Muslims with the Koran, with the faith you have received from your fathers, a faith that will always help you move forward. Share your faith, because there is one single God, the same God. Some have spoken in one way, others in another...but move forward. Share.[3097]

[3094]Pope Francis [2013] *Message to Muslims throughout the world for the end of Ramadan* [Online] Available at: www.vatican.va [Accessed on: 9 October 2022]
[3095]Pope Francis [2013] *Post Synodal Apostolic Exhortation Evangelii Gaudium, paras 252, 254* [Online] Available at: www.vatican.va [Accessed on: 9 October 2022]
[3096]Pope Francis [2014] *In-flight press conference from Istanbul to Rome* [Online] Available at: www.vatican.va [Accessed on: 9 October 2022]
[3097]Pope Francis [2015] *Meeting with refugees at Sacred Heart Parish, Rome* [Online] Available at: endenzingerbergoglio.com/ [Accessed on: 9 October 2022]

Introduction to the video of Pope Francis' prayer intentions for January 2016. (6th January 2016)
Many think differently, feel differently, seeking God or meeting God in different ways. In this crowd, in this range of religions, there is only one certainty that we have for all: we are all children of God.[3098]

Document on Human Fraternity for World Peace and Living Together. (4th February 2019)
The pluralism and the diversity of religions, colour, sex, race and language are willed by God in His wisdom, through which He created human beings. This divine wisdom is the source from which the right to freedom of belief and the freedom to be different derives.[3099]

General Audience. (3rd April 2019)
…why are there many religions? Along with the Muslims, we are the descendants of the same Father, Abraham: why does God allow many religions? God wanted to allow this: Scolastica [*sic*] theologians used to refer to God's *voluntas permissiva*. He wanted to allow this reality: there are many religions. Some are born from culture, but they always look to heaven; they look to God. But what God wants is fraternity among us and in a special way, this was the reason for the trip, with our brothers, Abraham's children like us, the Muslims. We must not fear differences. God allowed this. We should be afraid were we to fail to work fraternally to walk together in life.[3100]

Encyclical Fratelli Tutti, 274, 277, 281. (4th October 2020)
From our faith experience and from the wisdom accumulated over centuries, but also from lessons learned from our many weaknesses and failures, we, the believers of the different religions, know that our witness to God benefits our societies. The effort to seek God with a sincere heart, provided it is never sullied by ideological or self-serving aims, helps us recognize one another as travelling companions, truly brothers and sisters.

The Church esteems the ways in which God works in other religions, and 'rejects nothing of what is true and holy in these religions. She has a high regard for their manner of life and conduct, their precepts and doctrines which… often reflect a ray of that truth which enlightens all men and women' …Others drink from other sources. For us the wellspring of human dignity and fraternity is in the Gospel of Jesus Christ. From it, there arises, 'for Christian thought and for the action of the Church, the primacy given to relationship, to the encounter with the sacred mystery of the other, to universal communion with the entire human family, as a vocation of all'.

And God's love is the same for everyone, regardless of religion. Even if they are atheists, his love is the same. When the last day comes, and there is sufficient light to see things as they really are, we are going to find ourselves quite surprised.[3101]

Introduction to the video of his prayer intentions for January 2021
When we pray to God following Jesus, we come together as brothers and sisters with those who pray according to other cultures, other traditions and other beliefs. We are brothers and sisters who pray….The Church values God's action in other religions, without forgetting that for us Christians, the wellspring of human dignity and fraternity, is in the Gospel of Jesus Christ.[3102]

[3098]Pope Francis [2016] *Introduction to the video of Pope Francis' prayer intentions for January 2016* [Online] Available at: www.youtube.com [Accessed on: 9 September 2022]

[3099]Pope Francis & Ahmad Al-Tayyeb [2019] *Document on Human Fraternity for World Peace and Living Together.* [Online] Available at: www.vatican.va [Accessed on: 9 September 2022]

[3100]Pope Francis [2019] *General Audience – Catechesis on the Apostolic visit to Morocco.* [Online] Available at: www.vatican.va [Accessed on: 9 September 2022]

[3101]Pope Francis [2020] Encyclical *Fratelli Tutti*, para 277 [Online] Available at: www.vatican.va [Accessed on: 10 September 2022]

[3102]Pope Francis [2021] *Introduction to the video of his prayer intentions for January 2021* [Online] Available at: www.youtube.com [Accessed on: 9 October 2022]

Address to Interreligious Meeting, Iraq. (6th March 2021)
This blessed place brings us back to our origins, to the sources of God's work, to the birth of our religions. Here, where Abraham our father lived, we seem to have returned home. It was here that Abraham heard God's call; it was from here that he set out on a journey that would change history. We are the fruits of that call and that journey. God asked Abraham to raise his eyes to heaven and to count its stars (cf. Gen 15:5). In those stars, he saw the promise of his descendants; he saw us. Today we, Jews, Christians and Muslims, together with our brothers and sisters of other religions, honour our father Abraham by doing as he did: we look up to heaven and we journey on earth. […] May we – the descendants of Abraham and the representatives of different religions – sense that, above all, we have this role: to help our brothers and sisters to raise their eyes and prayers to heaven.

Final Declaration of the 7th Congress of Leaders of World and Traditional Religions, Kazakhstan, to which Pope Francis was a signatory. (15th September 2022)
We note that pluralism and differences in religion, skin colour, gender, race and language are expressions of the wisdom of God's will in creation. Thus any incident of coercion to a particular religion and religious doctrine is unacceptable. (Original Declaration, para 10).[3103]

Address to members of the Scholas Occurrentes movementApostolic Journey to Indonesia. (4th September 2024)
Here, you are from diverse religions, but we have only one god, he is only one. And in union, in silence, we shall pray to the lord and I shall give a blessing for all, a blessing valid for all religions. May God bless each of you. May he bless all your desires. May he bless your families. May he bless you present (here). May he bless your future. Amen.[3104]

Address to inter-religious meeting of young people during Apostolic Journey to Singapore (13th September 2024)
If we start to fight amongst ourselves and say 'my religion is more important than yours, my religion is true, yours is not,' where will that lead us? Where? It's okay to discuss [between religions]. Every religion is a way to arrive at God. There are different languages to arrive at God, but God is God for all. And how is God God for all? We are all sons and daughters of God. But my god is more important than your god, is that true? There is only one God and each of us has a language to arrive at God. Sikh, Muslim, Hindu, Christian, they are different paths.[3105]

Message to participants of the International Prayer Meeting for Peace held in Paris (24th September 2024)
It is against this backdrop that the title of this Paris Meeting – 'Imagine Peace' – is most eloquent. We need to keep meeting, to weave bonds of fraternity and to allow ourselves to be guided by the divine inspiration present in every faith, in order to join in 'imagining peace' among all peoples.[3106]

Sacred Scripture

Matthew 4:10; 11:27, 12:30
Then Jesus saith to him: Begone, Satan: for it is written, The Lord thy God shalt thou adore, and him only shalt thou serve.

[3103]Haynes, M [2022] *Document saying God wills 'differences in religion' was quietly changed just hours after Pope signed it* [Online] Available at: www.lifesitenews.com [Accessed on: 10 October 2022]
[3104]Haynes, M [2024] *Pope Francis skips Sign of the Cross to impart blessing 'valid for all religions'* [Online] Available at: www.lifesitenews.com [Accessed on: 21 May 2025]
[3105]Haynes, M [2024] *Pope Francis: 'Every religion is a way to arrive at God'* [Online] Available at: www.lifesitenews.com [Accessed on: 21 May 2025]
[3106]Pope Francis [2024] *Message of the Holy Father Francis to the participants of the International Meeting of Prayer for Peace organised by the Community of Sant'Egidio* (Paris, September 22-24, 2024) [Online] Available at: press.vatican.va [Accessed on: 21 May 2024]

All things are delivered to me by my Father. And no one knoweth the Son, but the Father: neither doth any one know the Father, but the Son, and he to whom it shall please the Son to reveal him.

He that is not with me, is against me: and he that gathereth not with me, scattereth.

Mark 16:16
He that believeth and is baptized, shall be saved: but he that believeth not shall be condemned.

Luke 4:8
And Jesus answering said to him: It is written: Thou shalt adore the Lord thy God, and him only shalt thou serve.

John 3:16, 6:54, 14:6, 17:2-3
For God so loved the world, as to give his only begotten Son; that whosoever believeth in him, may not perish, but may have life everlasting.

Then Jesus said to them: Amen, amen I say unto you: Except you eat the flesh of the Son of man, and drink his blood, you shall not have life in you.

Jesus saith to him: I am the way, and the truth, and the life. No man cometh to the Father, but by me.

As thou hast given him power over all flesh, that he may give eternal life to all whom thou hast given him. Now this is eternal life: That they may know thee, the only true God, and Jesus Christ, whom thou hast sent.

Acts 4:12
Neither is there salvation in any other. For there is no other name under heaven given to men, whereby we must be saved.

I Corinthians 10:20-21
But the things which the heathens sacrifice, they sacrifice to devils, and not to God. And I would not that you should be made partakers with devils.

II Corinthians 6:14-18
Bear not the yoke with unbelievers. For what participation hath justice with injustice? Or what fellowship hath light with darkness? And what concord hath Christ with Belial? Or what part hath the faithful with the unbeliever? And what agreement hath the temple of God with idols? For you are the temple of the living God; as God saith: I will dwell in them, and walk among them; and I will be their God, and they shall be my people. Wherefore, Go out from among them, and be ye separate, saith the Lord, and touch not the unclean thing: And I will receive you; and I will be a Father to you; and you shall be my sons and daughters, saith the Lord Almighty.

Deuteronomy 6: 13-15; 32:15-18
Thou shalt fear the Lord thy God, and shalt serve him only, and thou shalt swear by his name. You shall not go after the strange gods of all the nations, that are round about you: Because the Lord thy God is a jealous God in the midst of thee: lest at any time the wrath of the Lord thy God be kindled against thee, and take thee away from the face of the earth.

The beloved grew fat, and kicked: he grew fat, and thick and gross, he forsook God who made him, and departed from God his saviour. They provoked him by strange gods, and stirred him up to anger, with their abominations. They sacrificed to devils and not to God: to gods whom they knew not: that were newly come up, whom their fathers worshipped not. Thou hast forsaken the God that begot thee, and hast forgotten the Lord that created thee.

Joshua 24:23
Now therefore, said he, put away strange gods from among you, and incline your hearts to the Lord the God of Israel.

Sacred Tradition

St. Ignatius of Antioch: c. 50 to c 98/117

The Epistle of Ignatius to the Ephesians, longer version, Chap. IX
Now the way is unerring, namely, Jesus Christ. For, says He, 'I am the way and the life.'
And this way leads to the Father. For 'no man,' says He, 'cometh to the Father but by
Me.' Blessed, then, are ye who are God-bearers, spirit-bearers, temple-bearers, bearers
of holiness, adorned in all respects with the commandments of Jesus Christ, being 'a
royal priesthood, a holy nation, a peculiar people'.[3107]

St. Irenaeus: c. 130 to c. 202

Against Heresies. Bk. III, Chap. 4
For she [the Church] is the entrance to life; all others are thieves and robbers. On this
account are we bound to avoid them, but to make choice of the thing pertaining to the
Church with the utmost diligence, and to lay hold of the tradition of the truth.[3108]

Origen: c. 184 to c. 253

Homilies on Joshua
If someone of that people wishes to be saved, let him come into this house, so that he
may be able to obtain his salvation.... Let no one, then, be persuaded otherwise, nor let
anyone deceive himself: outside this house, that is, outside the Church, no one is saved
[*extra ecclesiam nemo salvatur*] For if anyone go outside, he shall be guilty of his own
death.[3109]

St. Cyprian of Carthage: c. 200 to 258

To Jubaianus, Concerning the Baptism of Heretics, epistle 72, para 21
... there is no salvation out of the Church [*salus extra ecclesiam non est*]....[3110]

Treatise 1. On the Unity of the Church, 6
Whoever is separated from the Church and is joined to an adulteress, is separated from
the promises of the Church; nor can he who forsakes the Church of Christ attain to the
rewards of Christ. He is a stranger; he is profane; he is an enemy. He can no longer have
God for his Father, who has not the Church for his mother. If any one could escape
who was outside the Ark of Noah, then he also may escape who shall be outside of the
Church. The Lord warns, saying, 'He who is not with me is against me, and he who
gathers not with me scatters.' (Mt 12:30). He who breaks the peace and the concord of
Christ, does so in opposition to Christ; he who gathers elsewhere than in the Church,
scatters the Church of Christ.[3111]

St. Athanasius: c. 296 to 373

The Athanasian Creed
Whosoever will be saved, before all things it is necessary that he hold the Catholic
Faith. Which Faith except everyone do keep whole and undefiled, without doubt he
shall perish everlastingly.[3112]

[3107]St. Ignatius of Antioch. *The Epistle of Ignatius to the Ephesians,* longer version, Chap. IX [Online]
Available at: www.earlychristianwritings.com [Accessed on: 14 September 2022]
[3108]St. Irenaeus. *Against Heresies.* Bk. III, Chap. 4 [Online] Available at: www.newadvent.org
[Accessed on: 14 September 2022]
[3109]Origen. *Extra Ecclesiam Nulla Salus (Outside the Church there is no salvation)* [Online] Available at:
www.ewtn.com [Accessed on: 15 September 2022]
[3110]St. Cyprian. *To Jubaianus, Concerning the Baptism of Heretics,* epistle 72, para 21 [Online] Available
at: www.newadvent.org [Accessed on: 14 September 2022]
[3111]St. Cyprian. *Treatise* 1, on the Unity of the Church, para 6 [Online] Available at: www.
newadvent.org [Accessed on: 14 September 2022]
[3112]St. Athanasius. *The Athanasian Creed* [Online] Available at: www.newadvent.org [Accessed on:
9 October 2022]

St. Augustine: 354 to 430

Sermons on the Old Testament, 15:3, 24:6
There are adulterous souls and there are fornicating souls. Let's see what the difference is. Fornicating souls are those which in one way or another have prostituted themselves to many false gods. Adulterous ones have, so to say, already been married to a lawful consort and do not preserve chastity of soul for that lawful consort. To put it more plainly: the pagan has a fornicating soul, the bad Christian an adulterous one. The pagan soul has no lawful husband; it is corrupted by prostituting itself with a variety of demons. And why is the bad Christian's soul adulterous? Because it neither loves chastity nor leaves its husband.

...we must be thankful that you want what God wants. That every superstition of the pagans and the Gentiles should be abolished is what God wants, God has ordered, God has foretold, God has begun to bring about, and in many parts of the world has already in great measure achieved.[3113]

Sermons on Various Subjects, 400:10
Let us be of one mind and heart, brothers and sisters, as we worship the one God, so that we may urge them to abandon their many gods, after a fashion, by our very concord, so that they may come to the peace and unity of worshipping the one God.[3114]

St. Thomas Aquinas: 1225 to 1274

Summa Theologiae. Tertia Pars. Q 73. Art 3.
...there is no entering into salvation outside the Church, just as in the time of the deluge there was none outside the Ark, which denotes the Church.[3115]

The Magisterium of the Church

The Church warns against the indifferentism that acts as if all religions are as good as each other, teaching that our Lord Jesus Christ, the unique and universal Saviour of mankind, instituted the Church as necessary for salvation.

Fourth Lateran Council (Twelfth Ecumenical, 1215)

There is indeed one universal church of the faithful, outside of which nobody at all is saved, in which Jesus Christ is both priest and sacrifice.[3116]

Council of Florence (Seventeenth Ecumenical, 1439 to 1445)

Bull *Cantate Domino. (4th February 1442)*
She firmly believes, professes, and preaches that 'none of those who are outside of the Catholic Church, not only pagans', but also Jews, heretics, and schismatics, can become sharers of eternal life, but they will go into the eternal fire 'that was prepared for the devil and his angels' (Mt 25:41) unless, before the end of their life, they are joined to her.[3117]

Second Vatican Council (Twenty-First Ecumenical, 1962 to 1965)

Dogmatic Constitution *Lumen Gentium, 14, 16. (21st November 1964)*
Basing itself upon Sacred Scripture and Tradition, it teaches that the Church, now sojourning on earth as an exile, is necessary for salvation. Christ, present to us in His Body, which is the Church, is the one Mediator and the unique way of salvation. In

---

[3113]The Works of Saint Augustine: A Translation for the 21st Century 1990] *Sermons on the Old Testament*, I (1-19). New York: New City Press, p.324.
[3114]*Ibid. Sermons on Various Subjects*, (III/10) p. 478
[3115]St. Thomas Aquinas. *Summa Theologiae*. Tertia Pars. Q 73. Art 3 [Online] [Online] Available at: www.newadvent.org [Accessed on: 15 September 2022]
[3116]Fourth Lateran Council [1215] *Confession of Faith*. [Online] Available at: www.papalencyclicals.net [Accessed on: 5 July 2022]
[3117]Denzinger, H [2010] *Op. cit.*, p.1442, Dz 1351

explicit terms He Himself affirmed the necessity of faith and baptism and thereby affirmed also the necessity of the Church, for through baptism as through a door men enter the Church. Whosoever, therefore, knowing that the Catholic Church was made necessary by Christ, would refuse to enter or to remain in it, could not be saved.

[...]

Finally, those who have not yet received the Gospel are related in various ways to the people of God...Nor is God far distant from those who in shadows and images seek the unknown God, for it is He who gives to all men life and breath and all things (Acts 17:25-28), and as Saviour wills that all men be saved. (I Tim 2:4). Those also can attain to salvation who through no fault of their own do not know the Gospel of Christ or His Church, yet sincerely seek God and moved by grace strive by their deeds to do His will as it is known to them through the dictates of conscience. Nor does Divine Providence deny the helps necessary for salvation to those who, without blame on their part, have not yet arrived at an explicit knowledge of God and with His grace strive to live a good life. Whatever good or truth is found amongst them is looked upon by the Church as a preparation for the Gospel. She knows that it is given by Him who enlightens all men so that they may finally have life. But often men, deceived by the Evil One, have become vain in their reasonings and have exchanged the truth of God for a lie, serving the creature rather than the Creator (Rom 1:21, 25). Or some there are who, living and dying in this world without God, are exposed to final despair. Wherefore to promote the glory of God and procure the salvation of all of these, and mindful of the command of the Lord, 'Preach the Gospel to every creature'(Mk 16:16.), the Church fosters the missions with care and attention.[3118]

Decree on the Mission Activity of the Church, *Ad Gentes, 3. (7th December 1965)*
This universal design of God for the salvation of the human race is carried out not only, as it were, secretly in the soul of a man, or by the attempts (even religious ones by which in diverse ways it seeks after God) if perchance it may contact Him or find Him, though He be not far from anyone of us (cf. Acts 17:27). For these attempts need to be enlightened and healed; even though, through the kindly workings of Divine Providence, they may sometimes serve as leading strings toward God, or as a preparation for the Gospel. Now God, in order to establish peace or the communion of sinful human beings with Himself, as well as to fashion them into a fraternal community, did ordain to intervene in human history in a way both new and finally sending His Son, clothed in our flesh, in order that through Him He might snatch men from the power of darkness and Satan (cf. Col 1:13; Acts 10:38) and reconcile the world to Himself in Him (cf. II Cor 5:19). Him, then, by whom He made the world, He appointed heir of all things, that in Him He might restore all (cf. Eph 1:10).

Decree on the Ministry and Life of Priests, *Presbyterorum Ordinis, 4. (7th December 1965)*
Since no one can be saved who does not first believe, (Mk 16:16) priests, as co-workers with their bishops, have the primary duty of proclaiming the Gospel of God to all.[3119]

Declaration on Religious Freedom *Dignitatis Humanae, 1. (7th December 1965)*
Religious freedom, in turn, which men demand as necessary to fulfil their duty to worship God, has to do with immunity from coercion in civil society. Therefore it leaves untouched traditional Catholic doctrine on the moral duty of men and societies toward the true religion and toward the one Church of Christ.[3120]

[3118]Second Vatican Council [1964] Dogmatic Constitution, *Lumen Gentium*, para 14, 16 [Online] Available at: www.vatican.va [Accessed on: 10 October 2022]
[3119]Second Vatican Council [1965] Decree on the Ministry and Life of Priests, *Presbyterorum Ordinis*, para 4 [Online] Available at: www.vatican.va [Accessed on: 10 October 2022]
[3120]Second Vatican Council [1965] Declaration on Religious Freedom, *Dignitatis Humanae*, para 1 [Online] Available at: www.vatican.va [Accessed on: 10 October 2022]

Pope St. John Paul II: 1978 to 2005

Encyclical *Redemptoris Missio, 36. (7th December 1990)*
But one of the most serious reasons for the lack of interest in the missionary task is a widespread indifferentism, which, sad to say, is found also among Christians. It is based on incorrect theological perspectives and is characterised by a religious relativism which leads to the belief that 'one religion is as good as another.' We can add, using the words of Pope Paul VI, that there are also certain 'excuses which would impede evangelisation. The most insidious of these excuses are certainly the ones which people claim to find support for in such and such a teaching of the Council.'[3121]

Catechism of the Catholic Church. (8th September 1997)
In their religious behavior, however, men also display the limits and errors that disfigure the image of God in them:

> Very often, deceived by the Evil One, men have become vain in their reasonings, and have exchanged the truth of God for a lie, and served the creature rather than the Creator. Or else, living and dying in this world without God, they are exposed to ultimate despair. (844)

To reunite all his children, scattered and led astray by sin, the Father willed to call the whole of humanity together into his Son's Church. The Church is the place where humanity must rediscover its unity and salvation. The Church is 'the world reconciled.' She is that bark which 'in the full sail of the Lord's cross, by the breath of the Holy Spirit, navigates safely in this world.' According to another image dear to the Church Fathers, she is prefigured by Noah's ark, which alone saves from the flood. (845)[3122]

Address to the Members, Consultors and Staff of the Congregation for the Doctrine of the Faith, 4. (28th January 2000)
In recent years a mentality has arisen in theological and ecclesial circles that tends to relativize Christ's revelation and his unique and universal mediation of salvation, as well as to diminish the need for Christ's Church as the universal sacrament of salvation. [...]
It is a mistake, then, to regard the Church as a way of salvation along with those constituted by other religions, which would be complementary to the Church, even if converging with her on the eschatological kingdom of God. Therefore we must reject a certain indifferentist mentality 'characterised by a religious relativism which leads to the belief that one religion is as good as another' (cf. *Redemptoris Missio* 36).[3123]

Congregation for the Doctrine of the Faith, Declaration Dominus Jesus, 22. (6th August 2000)
With the coming of the Saviour Jesus Christ, God has willed that the Church founded by him be the instrument for the salvation of all humanity (cf. Acts 17:30-31). This truth of faith does not lessen the sincere respect which the Church has for the religions of the world, but at the same time, it rules out, in a radical way, that mentality of indifferentism 'characterised by a religious relativism which leads to the belief that 'one religion is as good as another''. If it is true that the followers of other religions can receive divine grace, it is also certain that objectively speaking they are in a gravely deficient situation in comparison with those who, in the Church, have the fullness of the means of salvation.[3124]

[3121]Pope St. John Paul II [1990] Encyclical, *Redemptoris Missio*, para 36 [Online] Available at: www.vatican.va [Accessed on: 16 September 2022]
[3122]*Catechism of the Catholic Church* [1992] [Online] Available at: scborromeo2.org [Accessed on: 12 July 2022]
[3123]Pope St. John Paul II [2000] *Address to the Members, Consultors and Staff of the Congregation for the Doctrine of the Faith*, para 4 [Online] Available at: www.vatican.va [Accessed on: 16 September 2022]
[3124]Congregation for the Doctrine of the Faith [2000] Declaration *Dominus Jesus*, para 22 [Online] Available at: www.vatican.va [Accessed on: 10 October 2022]

Pope St Paul VI: 1963 to 1978

Apostolic Exhortation *Evangeli Nuntiandi, 5, 53. (8th December 1975)*
…the presentation of the Gospel message is not an optional contribution for the Church. It is the duty incumbent on her by the command of the Lord Jesus, so that people can believe and be saved. This message is indeed necessary. It is unique. It cannot be replaced. It does not permit either indifference, syncretism or accommodation. It is a question of people's salvation.

     …the religion of Jesus, which she proclaims through evangelisation, objectively places man in relation with the plan of God, with His living presence and with His action; she thus causes an encounter with the mystery of divine paternity that bends over towards humanity. In other words, our religion effectively establishes with God an authentic and living relationship which the other religions do not succeed in doing, even though they have, as it were, their arms stretched out towards heaven.[3125]

Pope Pius XI: 1922 to 1939

Encyclical *Mortalium Animos, 2. (6th January 1928)*
For since they hold it for certain that men destitute of all religious sense are very rarely to be found, they seem to have founded on that belief a hope that the nations, although they differ among themselves in certain religious matters, will without much difficulty come to agree as brethren in professing certain doctrines, which form as it were a common basis of the spiritual life. For which reason conventions, meetings and addresses are frequently arranged by these persons, at which a large number of listeners are present, and at which all without distinction are invited to join in the discussion, both infidels of every kind, and Christians, even those who have unhappily fallen away from Christ or who with obstinacy and pertinacity deny His divine nature and mission. Certainly such attempts can nowise be approved by Catholics, founded as they are on that false opinion which considers all religions to be more or less good and praiseworthy, since they all in different ways manifest and signify that sense which is inborn in us all, and by which we are led to God and to the obedient acknowledgment of His rule. Not only are those who hold this opinion in error and deceived, but also in distorting the idea of true religion they reject it, and little by little. turn aside to naturalism and atheism, as it is called; from which it clearly follows that one who supports those who hold these theories and attempt to realise them, is altogether abandoning the divinely revealed religion.[3126]

Pope St. Pius X: 1903 to 1914

Encyclical *Pascendi Dominici Gregis, 14. (8th September 1907)*
Here it is well to note at once that, given this doctrine of experience united with the other doctrine of symbolism, every religion, even that of paganism, must be held to be true. What is to prevent such experiences from being met within every religion? In fact that they are to be found is asserted by not a few. And with what right will Modernists deny the truth of an experience affirmed by a follower of Islam? With what right can they claim true experiences for Catholics alone? Indeed Modernists do not deny but actually admit, some confusedly, others in the most open manner, that all religions are true. That they cannot feel otherwise is clear.[3127]

Catechism of St. Pius X. (1908)

The Fourth Article of the Creed, Question 18
Q. If Jesus Christ died for the salvation of all men, why are not all men saved?

[3125]Pope St. Paul VI [1975] Apostolic Exhortation *Evangeli Nuntiandi*, paras 5, 53 [Online] Available at: www.vatican.va [Accessed on: 16 September 2022]
[3126]Pope Pius XI [1928] Encyclical *Mortalium Animos*, para 2 [Online] Available at: www.vatican.va [Accessed on: 16 September 2022]
[3127]Pope St. Pius X [1907] Encyclical *Pascendi Dominici Gregis*, para 14 [Online] Available at: www. vatican.va [Accessed on: 12 September 2022]

A. Jesus Christ died for all, but not all are saved, because not all will acknowledge Him; all do not observe His Law; all do not avail themselves of the means of salvation He has left us.

Those Outside the Communion of Saints, Question 10 -12
Q. Who are they who do not belong to the Communion of Saints?
A. Those who are damned do not belong to the Communion of Saints in the other life; and in this life those who belong neither to the body nor to the soul of the Church, that is, those who are in mortal sin, and who are outside the true Church.

Q. Who are they who are outside the true Church?
A. Outside the true Church are: Infidels, Jews, heretics, apostates, schismatics, and the excommunicated.

Q. Who are infidels?
A. Infidels are those who have not been baptised and do not believe in Jesus Christ, because they either believe in and worship false gods as idolaters do, or though admitting one true God, they do not believe in the Messiah, neither as already come in the Person of Jesus Christ, nor as to come; for instance, Mohammedans and the like.

The Ninth Article of the Creed: The Church in General, Question 27, 29
Q. Can one be saved outside the Catholic, Apostolic and Roman Church?
A. No, no one can be saved outside the Catholic, Apostolic Roman Church, just as no one could be saved from the flood outside the Ark of Noah, which was a figure of the Church.

Q. But if a man through no fault of his own is outside the Church, can he be saved?
A. If he is outside the Church through no fault of his, that is, if he is in good faith, and if he has received Baptism, or at least has the implicit desire of Baptism; and if, moreover, he sincerely seeks the truth and does God's will as best he can such a man is indeed separated from the body of the Church, but is united to the soul of the Church and consequently is on the way of salvation.[3128]

Pope Leo XIII: 1878 to 1903

Encyclical *Satis Cognitum*, 4. (29th June 1896)
But the mission of Christ is to save that which had perished: that is to say, not some nations or peoples, but the whole human race, without distinction of time or place. 'The Son of Man came that the world might be saved by Him' (Jn 3:17). 'For there is no other name under Heaven given to men whereby we must be saved' (Acts 4:12). The Church, therefore, is bound to communicate without stint to all men, and to transmit through all ages, the salvation effected by Jesus Christ, and the blessings flowing there from.[3129]

Pope Bl. Pius IX: 1846 to 1878

Encyclical *Qui Pluribus*, 15. (9th November 1846)
Also perverse is the shocking theory that it makes no difference to which religion one belongs, a theory which is greatly at variance even with reason. By means of this theory, those crafty men remove all distinction between virtue and vice, truth and error, honourable and vile action. They pretend that men can gain eternal salvation by the practice of any religion, as if there could ever be any sharing between justice and iniquity, any collaboration between light and darkness, or any agreement between Christ and Belial.[3130]

[3128]Pope St. Pius X [1908] *Catechism of St. Pius X*, The Fourth Article of the Creed, Question 18; Those Outside the Communion of Saints, Question 10 -12; The Ninth Article of the Creed: The Church in General, Question 27, 29 [Online] Available at: www.ewtn.com [Accessed on: 16 September 2022]
[3129]Pope Leo XIII [1896] Encyclical *Satis Cognitum*, para 4 [Online] Available at: www.vatican.va [Accessed on: 10 October 2022]
[3130]Pope Bl. Pius IX [1846] Encyclical *Qui Pluribus*, para 15 [Online] Available at: www. papalencyclicals.net [Accessed on: 16 September 2022]

Encyclical *Singulari Quidem, 7. (17th March 1856)*
The Church clearly declares that the only hope of salvation for mankind is placed in the Christian faith, which teaches the truth, scatters the darkness of ignorance by the splendor of its light, and works through love. This hope of salvation is placed in the Catholic Church which, in preserving the true worship, is the solid home of this faith and the temple of God. Outside of the Church, nobody can hope for life or salvation unless he is excused through ignorance beyond his control.[3131]

Allocution *Maxima Quidem. (9th June 1862)*
But since they perversely dare to derive all truths of religion from the inborn force of human reason, they assign to man a certain basic right, from which he can think and speak about religion as he likes, and give such honor and worship to God as he finds more agreeable to himself.[3132]

Encyclical *Quanto Conficiamur Moerore, 7-8. (10th August 1863)*
…it is again necessary to mention and censure a very grave error entrapping some Catholics who believe that it is possible to arrive at eternal salvation although living in error and alienated from the true faith and Catholic unity. Such belief is certainly opposed to Catholic teaching. There are, of course, those who are struggling with invincible ignorance about our most holy religion. Sincerely observing the natural law and its precepts inscribed by God on all hearts and ready to obey God, they live honest lives and are able to attain eternal life by the efficacious virtue of divine light and grace. Because God knows, searches and clearly understands the minds, hearts, thoughts, and nature of all, his supreme kindness and clemency do not permit anyone at all who is not guilty of deliberate sin to suffer eternal punishments.

    Also well known is the Catholic teaching that no one can be saved outside the Catholic Church. Eternal salvation cannot be obtained by those who oppose the authority and statements of the same Church and are stubbornly separated from the unity of the Church and also from the successor of Peter, the Roman Pontiff, to whom 'the custody of the vineyard has been committed by the Savior.' The words of Christ are clear enough: 'If he refuses to listen even to the Church, let him be to you a Gentile and a tax collector'(Mt 15:17); 'He who hears you hears me, and he who rejects you, rejects me, and he who rejects me, rejects him who sent me' (Lk 10:16); 'He who does not believe will be condemned'(Mk 16:16); 'He who does not believe is already condemned' (Jn 3:18); 'He who is not with me is against me, and he who does not gather with me scatters.' (Lk 11:23). The Apostle Paul says that such persons are 'perverted and self-condemned' (Titus 3:11); the Prince of the Apostles calls them 'false teachers . . . who will secretly bring in destructive heresies, even denying the Master. . . bringing upon themselves swift destruction.' (II Pet 2:1).[3133]

The Syllabus of Errors. (8th December 1864)
III. *Indifferentism, Latitudinarianism*
    15. Every man is free to embrace and profess that religion which, guided by the light of reason, he shall consider true. (Allocution *Maxima Quidem*, June 9, 1862; *Multiplices Inter*, June 10, 1851)
    16. Man may, in the observance of any religion whatever, find the way of eternal salvation, and arrive at eternal salvation. (Encyclical *Qui Pluribus*, Nov. 9, 1846)
    17. Good hope at least is to be entertained of the eternal salvation of all those who are not at all in the true Church of Christ. (Encyclical *Quanto Conficiamur*, Aug. 10, 1863, etc)[3134]

[3131]Pope Bl. Pius IX [1856] Encyclical *Singulari Quidem*, para 7 [Online] Available at: www.papalencyclicals.net [Accessed on: 10 October 2022]
[3132]Pope Bl. Pius IX [1846] Allocution *Maxima Quidem* [Online] Available at: thejosias.com [Accessed on: 10 October 2022]
[3133]Pope Bl. Pius IX [1863] Encyclical *Quanto Conficiamur Moerore*, para 7-8 [Online] Available at: www.papalencyclicals.net [Accessed on: 16 September 2022]
[3134]Pope Bl. Pius IX [1864] *The Syllabus Of Errors* [Online] Available at: www.papalencyclicals.net [Accessed on: 10 October 2022]

Pope Gregory XVI: 1831 to 1846

Encyclical *Mirari Vos Arbitramur, 13. (15th August 1832)*
Now We consider another abundant source of the evils with which the Church is afflicted at present: indifferentism. This perverse opinion is spread on all sides by the fraud of the wicked who claim that it is possible to obtain the eternal salvation of the soul by the profession of any kind of religion, as long as morality is maintained. Surely, in so clear a matter, you will drive this deadly error far from the people committed to your care. With the admonition of the apostle that 'there is one God, one faith, one baptism' (Eph 4:5) may those fear who contrive the notion that the safe harbor of salvation is open to persons of any religion whatever. They should consider the testimony of Christ Himself that 'those who are not with Christ are against Him,' (Lk 11:23) and that they disperse unhappily who do not gather with Him. Therefore 'without a doubt, they will perish forever, unless they hold the Catholic faith whole and inviolate.' (Athanasian Creed).[3135]

Pope Pius VIII: 1829 to 1830

Encyclical *Traditi Humilitati, 4. (24th May 1829)*
Among these heresies belongs that foul contrivance of the sophists of this age who do not admit any difference among the different professions of faith and who think that the portal of eternal salvation opens for all from any religion.[3136]

Pope Leo XII: 1823 to 1829

Encyclical *Ubi Primum, 12-14. (5th May 1824)*
A certain sect, which you surely know, has unjustly arrogated to itself the name of philosophy, and has aroused from the ashes the disorderly ranks of practically every error. Under the gentle appearance of piety and liberality this sect professes what they call tolerance or indifferentism. It preaches that not only in civil affairs, which is not Our concern here, but also in religion, God has given every individual a wide freedom to embrace and adopt without danger to his salvation whatever sect or opinion appeals to him on the basis of his private judgment. [...]

The current indifferentism has developed to the point of arguing that everyone is on the right road. This includes not only all those sects which though outside the Catholic Church verbally accept revelation as a foundation, but those groups too which spurn the idea of divine revelation and profess a pure deism or even a pure naturalism. The indifferentism of Rhetorius seemed absurd to St. Augustine, and rightly so, but it did acknowledge certain limits. But a tolerance which extends to Deism and Naturalism, which even the ancient heretics rejected, can never be approved by anyone who uses his reason. Nevertheless — alas for the times; alas for this lying philosophy! — such a tolerance is approved, defended, and praised by these pseudo-philosophers.

Certainly many remarkable authors, adherents of the true philosophy, have taken pains to attack and crush this strange view. But the matter is so self-evident that it is superfluous to give additional arguments. It is impossible for the most true God, who is Truth Itself, the best, the wisest Provider, and the Rewarder of good men, to approve all sects who profess false teachings which are often inconsistent with one another and contradictory, and to confer eternal rewards on their members. For we have a surer word of the prophet, and in writing to you We speak wisdom among the perfect; not the wisdom of this world but the wisdom of God in a mystery. By it we are taught, and by divine faith we hold one Lord, one faith, one baptism, and that no other name under heaven is given to men except the name of Jesus Christ of Nazareth in which we must be saved. This is why we profess that there is no salvation outside the Church.[3137]

[3135]Pope Gregory XVI [1832] Encyclical *Mirari Vos Arbitramur*, 13 [Online] Available at: www.papalencyclicals.net [Accessed on: 16 September 2022]
[3136]Pope Pius VIII [1829] Encyclical *Traditi Humilitati*, para 4 [Online] Available at: www.papalencyclicals.net [Accessed on: 16 September 2022]
[3137]Pope Leo XII [1824] Encyclical *Ubi Primum*, para 12-14 [Online] Available at: www.papalencyclicals.net [Accessed on: 16 September 2022]

Pope St. Pius V: 1566 to 1572

The Roman Catechism: The Catechism of the Council of Trent. (1556)

First Part of this Article: 'I Believe in the Holy Catholic Church', Those who are not members of the Church
Hence there are but three classes of persons excluded from the Church's pale: infidels, heretics and schismatics, and excommunicated persons. Infidels are outside the Church because they never belonged to, and never knew the Church, and were never made partakers of any of her Sacraments.

The First Petition of The Lord's Prayer 'Hallowed Be Thy Name'
To that Church alone and to those whom she embraces in her bosom and holds in her arms, appertains the invocation of that divine name, outside of which there is no other name under Heaven given to men whereby we must be saved. (Acts 4:12).[3138]

Pope Boniface VIII: 1294 to 1303

Bull *Unam Sanctam*. (18th November 1302)
Urged by faith, we are obliged to believe and to maintain that the Church is one, holy, catholic, and also apostolic. We believe in her firmly and we confess with simplicity that outside of her there is neither salvation nor the remission of sins, as the Spouse in the Canticles (Song of Sol 6:8) proclaims: 'One is my dove, my perfect one. She is the only one, the chosen of her who bore her,' and she represents one sole mystical body whose Head is Christ and the head of Christ is God (I Cor 11:3). In her then is one Lord, one faith, one baptism (Eph 4:5). There had been at the time of the deluge only one ark of Noah, prefiguring the one Church, which ark, having been finished to a single cubit, had only one pilot and guide, i.e., Noah, and we read that, outside of this ark, all that subsisted on the earth was destroyed.[3139]

Pope Innocent III: 1198 to 1216

Letter *Eius Exemplo to the Archbishop of Tarragona. (18 December 1208)*
We believe in our heart and confess with our tongue the one Church, not of heretics, but the holy Roman, catholic, and apostolic Church outside which we believe no one is saved.[3140]

Pope Sergius I: 687 to 701

Sixteenth Synod of Toledo (693)
The holy Catholic Church who has this faith, cleansed by the water of baptism, redeemed by the precious blood of Christ, having no wrinkle in faith and bearing no blemish of impure work (cf. Eph 5:23-27), is in fact rich in signs of eminence, brilliant in virtues, and resplendent in the gifts of the Holy Spirit. She, indeed, will reign forever with her head, Jesus Christ, our Lord, whose body, without doubt, she is; and all those now who are not at all in her or will not be in her or have departed or will depart from her…these will be punished by the sentence of everlasting damnation, and they will be burned on flaming pyres with the devil and his associates until the end of time.[3141]

[3138]Pope St. Pius V [1556] *The Roman Catechism: The Catechism of the Council of Trent*, The First Petition of The Lord's Prayer 'Hallowed Be Thy Name' [Online] Available at: www.docdroid.net [Accessed on: 16 September 2022]
[3139]Pope Boniface VIII [1302] Bull *Unam Sanctam* [Online] Available at: www.papalencyclicals.net [accessed on: 16 September 2022]
[3140]Denzinger, H [2010] *Op. cit.*, p. 263, *Dz 792*
[3141]*Ibid.*, p. 202, *Dz 575*

The Demos Memoranda

In 2022 Sandro Magister, the Vatican journalist for the Italian newspaper *L'Espresso,* published the Demos Memorandum written by an anonymous cardinal and distributed among the Sacred College of Cardinals. By way of an introduction, Sandro Magister wrote, '

> Since the beginning of Lent, 2022 the cardinals who will elect the future pope have been passing this memorandum around. Its author, who goes by the name of Demos, 'people' in Greek, is unknown, but shows himself a thorough master of the subject. It cannot be ruled out that he himself is a cardinal.[1]

In 2023, following the death of Cardinal George Pell, Sandro Magister revealed that His Eminence was the anonymous author of the Demos Memorandum, 'the text was handed over to me personally by Cardinal Pell who was very pleased that I published it, provided I did not mention the name of the author.'[2]

The Vatican today

Commentators of every school, if for different reasons, with the possible exception of Father Spadaro, SJ, agree that this pontificate is a disaster in many or most respects; a catastrophe.

1. The Successor of St. Peter is the rock on which the Church is built, a major source and cause of worldwide unity. Historically (St. Irenaeus), the Pope and the Church of Rome have a unique role in preserving the apostolic tradition, the rule of faith, in ensuring that the Churches continue to teach what Christ and the apostles taught. Previously it was: 'Roma locuta. Causa finita est.' [Rome has spoken. The matter is settled]. Today it is: 'Roma loquitur. Confusio augetur.' [Rome speaks. Confusion increases].
    (A) The German synod speaks on homosexuality, women priests, communion for the divorced. The Papacy is silent.
    (B) Cardinal Hollerich rejects the Christian teaching on sexuality. The Papacy is silent. This is doubly significant because the Cardinal is explicitly heretical; he does not use code or hints. If the Cardinal were to continue without Roman correction, this would represent another deeper breakdown of discipline, with few (any?) precedents in history. The Congregation for the Doctrine of the Faith must act and speak.
    (C) The silence is emphasised when contrasted with the active persecution of the Traditionalists and the contemplative convents.
2. The Christo-centricity of teaching is being weakened; Christ is being moved from the centre. Sometimes Rome even seems to be confused about the importance of a strict monotheism, hinting at some wider concept of divinity; not quite pantheism, but like a Hindu panentheism variant.
    (A) Pachamama is idolatrous; perhaps it was not intended as such initially.
    (B) The contemplative nuns are being persecuted and attempts are being made to change the teachings of the charismatics.
    (C) The Christo-centric legacy of St. John Paul II in faith and morals is under systematic attack. Many of the staff of the Roman Institute for the Family have been dismissed;

[1]Demos [2022] *The Cardinal Pell memo in full* [Online] www.cal-catholic.com [Accessed on: 25 March 2025]
[2]Pentin, E [2023] *Cardinal Pell and the 'Demos' Memorandum* [Online] Available at: www.ncregister.com [Accessed on: 25 March 2025]

most students have left. The Academy for Life is gravely damaged, e.g., some members recently supported assisted suicide. The Pontifical Academies have members and visiting speakers who support abortion.

3. The lack of respect for the law in the Vatican risks becoming an international scandal. These issues have been crystallised through the present Vatican trial of ten accused of financial malpractices, but the problem is older and wider.

   (A) The Pope has changed the law four times during the trial to help the prosecution.

   (B) Cardinal Becciu has not been treated justly because he was removed from his position and stripped of his cardinalatial dignities without any trial. He did not receive due process. Everyone has a right to due process.

   (C) As the Pope is head of the Vatican state and the source of all legal authority, he has used this power to intervene in legal procedures.

   (D) The Pope sometimes (often) rules by papal decrees (motu proprio) which eliminate the right to appeal of those affected.

   (E) Many staff, often priests, have been summarily dismissed from the Vatican Curia, often without good reason.

   (F) Phone tapping is regularly practised. I am not sure how often it is authorised.

   (G) In the English case against Torzi, the judge criticised the Vatican prosecutors harshly. They are either incompetent and/or were nobbled, prevented from giving the full picture.

   (H) The raid by the Vatican Gendarmeria, led by Dr. Giani in 2017 on the auditor's (Libero Milone) office on Italian territory was probably illegal and certainly intimidating and violent. It is possible that evidence against Milone was fabricated.

4. (A) The financial situation of the Vatican is grave. For the past ten years (at least), there have nearly always been financial deficits. Before COVID, these deficits ranged around €20 million annually. For the last three years, they have been around €30-35 million annually. The problems predate both Pope Francis and Pope Benedict.

   (B) The Vatican is facing a large deficit in the Pensions Fund. Around 2014 the experts from COSEA estimated the deficit would be around € 800 million in 2030. This was before COVID.

   (C) It is estimated that the Vatican has lost € 217 million on the Sloane Avenue property in London. In the 1980's, the Vatican was forced to pay out $ 230 million after the Banco Ambrosiano scandal. Through inefficiency and corruption during the past 25-30 years, the Vatican has lost at least another € 100 million, and it probably would be much higher (perhaps 150-200 million).

   (D) Despite the Holy Father's recent decision, the process of investing has not been centralised (as recommended by COSEA in 2014 and attempted by the Secretariat for the Economy in 2015-16) and remains immune to expert advice. For decades, the Vatican has dealt with disreputable financiers avoided by all respectable bankers in Italy.

   (E) The return on the 5261 Vatican properties remains scandalously low. In 2019, the return (before COVID) was nearly $ 4,500 a year. In 2020, it was € 2,900 per property.

   (F) The changing role of Pope Francis in the financial reforms (incomplete but substantial progress as far as reducing crime is concerned, much less successful, except at IOR, in terms of profitability) is a mystery and an enigma.

Initially the Holy Father strongly backed the reforms. He then prevented the centralisation of investments, opposed the reforms and most attempts to unveil corruption, and supported (then) Archbishop Becciu, at the centre of Vatican financial establishment. Then in 2020, the Pope turned on Becciu and eventually ten persons were placed on trial and charged. Over the years, few prosecutions were attempted from AIF reports of infringements.

The external auditors Price Waterhouse and Cooper were dismissed and the Auditor General Libero Milone was forced to resign on trumped up charges in 2017. They were coming too close to the corruption in the Secretariat of State.

5. The political influence of Pope Francis and the Vatican is negligible. Intellectually, Papal writings demonstrate a decline from the standard of St. John Paul II and Pope Benedict. Decisions and policies are often "politically correct", but there have been grave failures to support human rights in Venezuela, Hong Kong, mainland China, and now in the Russian invasion.

There has been no public support for the loyal Catholics in China who have been intermittently persecuted for their loyally to the Papacy for more than 70 years. No public Vatican support for the Catholic community in Ukraine, especially the Greek Catholics.

These issues should be revisited by the next Pope. The Vatican's political prestige is now at a low ebb.

6. At a different, lower level, the situation of Tridentine traditionalists (Catholic) should be regularised.

At a further and lower level, the celebration of "individual" and small group Masses in the mornings in St. Peter's Basilica should be permitted once again. At the moment, this great basilica is like a desert in the early morning.

The COVID crisis has covered up the large decline in the number of pilgrims attending Papal audiences and Masses.

The Holy Father has little support among seminarians and young priests and widespread disaffection exists in the Vatican Curia.

The Next Conclave

1. The College of Cardinals has been weakened by eccentric nominations and has not been reconvened after the rejection of Cardinal Kasper's views in the 2014 consistory. Many Cardinals are unknown to one another, adding a new dimension of unpredictability to the next conclave.
2. After Vatican II, Catholic authorities often underestimated the hostile power of secularisation, the world, flesh, and the devil, especially in the Western world and overestimated the influence and strength of the Catholic Church.
    We are weaker than 50 years ago and many factors are beyond our control, in the short term at least, e.g. the decline in the number of believers, the frequency of Mass attendance, the demise or extinction of many religious orders.
3. The Pope does not need to be the world's best evangelist, nor a political force. The successor of Peter, as head of the College of Bishops, also successors of the Apostles, has a foundational role for unity and doctrine. The new pope must understand that the secret of Christian and Catholic vitality comes from fidelity to the teachings of Christ and Catholic practices. It does not come from adapting to the world or from money.
4. The first tasks of the new pope will be to restore normality, restore doctrinal clarity in faith and morals, restore a proper respect for the law and ensure that the first criterion for the nomination of bishops is acceptance of the apostolic tradition. Theological expertise and learning are an advantage, not a hinderance for all bishops and especially archbishops.

These are necessary foundations for living and preaching the Gospel.

5. If the synodal gatherings continue around the world, they will consume much time and money, probably distracting energy from evangelisation and service rather than deepening these essential activities.

If the national or continental synods are given doctrinal authority, we will have a new danger to world-wide Church unity, whereby e.g., the German church holds doctrinal views not shared by other Churches and not compatible with the apostolic tradition.

If there was no Roman correction of such heresy, the Church would be reduced to a loose federation of local Churches, holding different views, probably closer to an Anglican or Protestant model, than an Orthodox model.

An early priority for the next pope must be to remove and prevent such a threatening development, by requiring unity in essentials and not permitting unacceptable doctrinal differences. The morality of homosexual activity will be one such flash point.

6. While the younger clergy and seminarians are almost completely orthodox, sometimes quite conservative, the new Pope will need to be aware of the substantial changes effected on the Church's leadership since 2013, perhaps especially in South and Central America. There is a new spring in the step of the Protestant liberals in the Catholic Church.

Schism is not likely to occur from the left, who often sit lightly to doctrinal issues. Schism is more likely to come from the right and is always possible when liturgical tensions are inflamed and not dampened.

Unity in the essentials. Diversity in the non-essentials. Charity on all issues.

7. Despite the dangerous decline in the West and the inherent fragility and instability in many places, serious consideration should be given to the feasibility of a visitation on the Jesuit Order. They are in a situation of catastrophic numerical decline from 36,000 members during the Council to less than 16,000 in 2017 (with probably 20-25% above 75 years of age). In some places, there is catastrophic moral decline.

The order is highly centralised, susceptible to reform or damage from the top. The Jesuit charism and contribution have been and are so important to the Church that they should not be allowed to pass away into history undisturbed or become simply an Asian-African community.

8. The disastrous decline in Catholic numbers and Protestant expansion in South America should be addressed. It was scarcely mentioned in the Amazonian Synod.
9. Obviously, a lot of work is needed on the financial reforms in the Vatican, but this should not be the most important criterion in the selection of the next Pope.

The Vatican has no substantial debts but continuing annual deficits will eventually lead to bankruptcy. Obviously, steps will be taken to remedy this, to separate the Vatican from criminal accomplices and balance revenue and expenditure. The Vatican will need to demonstrate competence and integrity to attract substantial donations to help with this problem.

Despite the improved financial procedures and greater clarity, continuing financial pressures represent a major challenge, but they are much less important than the spiritual and doctrinal threats facing the Church, especially in the First World.

– *Demos*
Original story by Sandro Magister in L'Espresso. March 15, 2022.

The Demos II Memorandum

In 2024, the Italian Catholic news outlet *La Nuova Bussola Quotidiana* [*The Daily Compass*] published a new document circulating among the cardinals authored by the anonymous Demos II. The editor explained,

> Two years after the text signed 'Demos' (later revealed to have been written by Cardinal Pell) a new anonymous document, linked to the first, defines the seven priorities of the next Conclave to repair the confusion and crisis created by this Pontificate…The text was written principally by a cardinal after he collated the suggestions of other cardinals and bishops. They have chosen to remain anonymous for the reasons explained in the letter.[3]

[3]Demos II [2024] *A profile of the next Pope, writes Cardinal* [Online] Available at: newdailycompass. com [Accessed on: 25 March 2025]

The Vatican Tomorrow

In March 2022, an anonymous text appeared – signed "Demos" and titled the 'The Vatican Today' – that raised a number of serious questions and criticisms regarding the pontificate of Pope Francis. Conditions in the Church since that text appeared have not materially changed, much less improved. Thus, the thoughts offered here are intended to build on those original reflections in light of the needs of the Vatican tomorrow.

The concluding years of a pontificate, any pontificate, are a time to assess the condition of the Church in the present, and the needs of the Church and her faithful going forward. It is clear that the strength of Pope Francis' pontificate is the added emphasis he has given to compassion toward the weak, outreach to the poor and marginalized, concern for the dignity of creation and the environmental issues that flow from it, and efforts to accompany the suffering and alienated in their burdens.

Its shortcomings are equally obvious: an autocratic, at times seemingly vindictive, style of governance; a carelessness in matters of law; an intolerance for even respectful disagreement; and – most seriously – a pattern of ambiguity in matters of faith and morals causing confusion among the faithful. Confusion breeds division and conflict. It undermines confidence in the Word of God. It weakens evangelical witness. And the result today is a Church more fractured than at any time in her recent history.

The task of the next pontificate must therefore be one of recovery and reestablishment of truths that have been slowly obscured or lost among many Christians. These include but are not limited to such basics as the following: (a) no one is saved except through, and only through, Jesus Christ, as he himself made clear; (b) God is merciful but also just, and is intimately concerned with every human life, He forgives but He also holds us accountable, He is both Saviour and Judge; (c) man is God's creature, not a self-invention, a creature not merely of emotion and appetites but also of intellect, free will, and an eternal destiny; (d) unchanging objective truths about the world and human nature exist and are knowable through Divine Revelation and the exercise of reason; (e) God's Word, recorded in Scripture, is reliable and has permanent force; (f) sin is real and its effects are lethal; and (g) his Church has both the authority and the duty to "make disciples of all nations." The failure to joyfully embrace that work of missionary, salvific love has consequences. As Paul wrote in 1 Corinthians 9:16, "woe to me if I do not preach the Gospel."

Some practical observations flow from the task and list above.

First: Real authority is damaged by authoritarian means in its exercise. The Pope is a Successor of Peter and the guarantor of Church unity. But he is not an autocrat. He cannot change Church doctrine, and he must not invent or alter the Church's discipline arbitrarily. He governs the Church collegially with his brother bishops in local dioceses. And he does so always in faithful continuity with the Word of God and Church teaching. "New paradigms" and "unexplored new paths" that deviate from either are not of God. A new Pope must restore the hermeneutic of continuity in Catholic life and reassert Vatican II's understanding of the papacy's proper role.

Second: Just as the Church is not an autocracy, neither is she a democracy. The Church belongs to Jesus Christ. She is his Church. She is Christ's Mystical Body, made up of many members. We have no authority to refashion her teachings to fit more comfortably with the world. Moreover, the Catholic sensus fidelium is not a matter of opinion surveys nor even the view of a baptized majority. It derives only from those who genuinely believe and actively practice, or at least sincerely seek to practice, the faith and teachings of the Church.

Third: Ambiguity is neither evangelical nor welcoming. Rather, it breeds doubt and feeds schismatic impulses. The Church is a community not just of Word and sacrament, but also of creed. What we believe helps to define and sustain us. Thus, doctrinal issues are not burdens imposed by unfeeling "doctors of the law." Nor are they cerebral sideshows to the Christian life. On the contrary, they're vital to living a Christian life authentically, because they deal with applications of the truth, and the truth demands clarity, not ambivalent nuance. From the start, the current pontificate has resisted the evangelical force and intellectual clarity of its immediate predecessors. The dismantling and repurposing of Rome's John Paul II Institute for Studies on Marriage and Family and the marginalising of texts like Veritatis Splendor suggest an elevation of "compassion" and emotion at the expense of reason, justice, and truth. For a creedal community, this is both unhealthy and profoundly dangerous.

Fourth: The Catholic Church, in addition to Word, sacrament, and creed, is also a community of law. Canon law orders Church life, harmonises its institutions and procedures, and guarantees the rights of believers. Among the marks of the current pontificate are its excessive reliance on the motu proprio as a tool for governance and a general carelessness and distaste for canonical detail. Again, as with ambiguity of doctrine, disregard for canon law and proper canonical procedure undermines confidence in the purity of the Church's mission.

Fifth: The Church, as John XXIII so beautifully described her, is mater et magistra, the "mother and teacher" of humanity, not its dutiful follower; the defender of man as the subject of history, not its object. She is the bride of Christ; her nature is personal, supernatural, and intimate, not merely institutional. She can never be reduced to a system of flexible ethics or sociological analysis and remodelling to fit the instincts and appetites (and sexual confusions) of an age. One of the key flaws in the current pontificate is its retreat from a convincing "theology of the body" and its lack of a compelling Christian anthropology . . . precisely at a time when attacks on human nature and identity, from transgenderism to transhumanism, are mounting.

Sixth: Global travel served a pastor like Pope John Paul II so well because of his unique personal gifts and the nature of the times. But the times and circumstances have changed. The Church in Italy and throughout Europe – the historic home of the faith – is in crisis. The Vatican itself urgently needs a renewal of its morale, a cleansing of its institutions, procedures, and personnel, and a thorough reform of its finances to prepare for a more challenging future. These are not small things. They demand the presence, direct attention, and personal engagement of any new Pope.

Seventh and finally: The College of Cardinals exists to provide senior counsel to the Pope and to elect his successor upon his death. That service requires men of clean character, strong theological formation, mature leadership experience, and personal holiness. It also requires a Pope willing to seek advice and then to listen. It's unclear to what degree this applies in the Pope Francis pontificate. The current pontificate has placed an emphasis on diversifying the college, but it has failed to bring cardinals together in regular consistories designed to foster genuine collegiality and trust among brothers. As a result, many of the voting electors in the next conclave will not really know each other, and thus may be more vulnerable to manipulation. In the future, if the college is to serve its purposes, the cardinals who inhabit it need more than a red zucchetto and a ring. Today's College of Cardinals should be proactive about getting to know each other to better understand their particular views regarding the Church, their local church situations, and their personalities – which impact their consideration of the next pope.

Readers will quite reasonably ask why this text is anonymous. The answer should be evident from the tenor of today's Roman environment: Candor is not welcome, and its consequences can be unpleasant. And yet these thoughts could continue for many more paragraphs, noting especially the current pontificate's heavy dependence on the Society of Jesus, the recent problematic work by the DDF's Cardinal Victor Manuel Fernández, and the emergence of a small oligarchy of confidants with excessive influence within the Vatican – all despite synodality's decentralising claims, among other things.

Exactly because of these matters, the cautionary reflections noted here may be useful in the months ahead. It is hoped that this contribution will help guide much needed conversations about what the Vatican should look like in the next pontificate.

Demos II

Further reading

Bishop Athanasius Schneider

Christus Vincit: Christ's Triumph Over the Darkness of the Age: In conversation with Diane Montagna. Brooklyn, New York: Angelico Press, 2019

The Springtime That Never Came: In Conversation with Pawel Lisicki. Manchester, New Hampshire: Sophia Institute Press, 2021

Marcantonio Colonna [Henry Sire]

The Dictator Pope: The Inside Story of the Francis Papacy. Washington: Regnery Publishing, 2018

Dr. Peter Kwasniewski

Holy Bread of Eternal Life: Restoring Eucharistic Reverence in an Age of Impiety. Manchester, New Hampshire: Sophia Institute Press, 2020

Ministers of Christ: Recovering the Roles of Clergy and Laity in an Age of Confusion. Manchester, New Hampshire: Crisis Publications, 2021

The Road from Hyperpapalism to Catholicism: Rethinking the Papacy in a Time of Ecclesial Disintegration. 2 volumes. Waterloo, Ontario: Arouca Press, 2022

True Obedience in the Church: A Guide to Discernment in Challenging Times. Manchester, New Hampshire: Sophia Institute Press, 2022

John Lamont & Claudio Pierantoni

Defending the Faith Against Present Heresies. Ontario: Arouca Press, 2021

Philip F. Lawler

Lost Shepherd: How Pope Francis is Misleading His Flock. Regnery Gateway: Washington, 2018

Prof. Roberto de Mattei

Love for the Papacy and Filial Resistance to the Pope in the History of the Church. Brooklyn, New York: Angelico Press, 2019

Julia Meloni

The St. Gallen Mafia: Exposing the Secret Reformist Group Within the Church. Gastonia: TAN Books, 2021

George Neumayr

The Political Pope: How Pope Francis Is Delighting the Liberal Left and Abandoning Conservatives. New York: Center Street, 2017

Edward Pentin

The Next Pope: The Leading Cardinal Candidates. Manchester, New Hampshire: Sophia Institute Press, 2020

Eric Sammons

Deadly Indifference: How the Church Lost Her Mission, and How We Can Reclaim It. Manchester, New Hampshire: Crisis Publications, 2021

www.ingramcontent.com/pod-product-compliance
Lightning Source LLC
Chambersburg PA
CBHW080412030426
42335CB00020B/2432